THE

Canadian Political System

ENVIRONMENT,
STRUCTURE,
AND
PROCESS

THIRD EDITION

THE Canadian Political System

ENVIRONMENT, STRUCTURE, AND PROCESS

THIRD EDITION

Richard J. Van Loon
Department of Public Administration
Carleton University

Michael S. Whittington
Department of Political Science
Carleton University

McGRAW-HILL RYERSON LIMITED
Toronto   Montreal   New York   St. Louis   San Francisco
Auckland   Bogotá   Guatemala   Hamburg   Johannesburg
Lisbon   London   Madrid   Mexico   New Delhi   Panama
Paris   San Juan   São Paulo   Singapore   Sydney   Tokyo

THE CANADIAN POLITICAL SYSTEM
Third Edition

ISBN   0-07-548025-5

 2 3 4 5 6 7 8 9 10   D   0 9 8 7 6 5 4 3 2

Printed and bound in Canada

CANADIAN CATALOGUING IN PUBLICATION DATA

Van Loon, Richard J., date
    The Canadian political system

Includes index.
Bibliography: p.
ISBN 0-07-548025-5

1. Canada—Politics and government. I. Whittington,
Michael S., date   II. Title.

JL15.V36 1981   320.971   C81-094143-0

CONTENTS

PREFACE

It is a major occupational hazard for writers of political science texts that their work is likely to become quickly outdated. Our risk is even higher than usual with this third edition of *The Canadian Political System*, for sometime between the writing of these words and our publication date the Supreme Court will rule upon the legality of the federal government's constitutional package and shortly thereafter the formal constitution of Canada may look quite different than it does today. In order to deal with this possibility we have appended the final version of the (Constitution Act) as it will be transmitted to Westminster when and if parliament completes the final formal stages of a joint address to the parliament of Great Britain. Moreover, wherever possible in looking at constitutional issues we have tried to take some account of the evolution of Canadian constitutionalism up to this point.

However, as this text is at great pains to point out, the formal constitution is but one part among many in the complex machinery of Canadian government. Moreover the formal constitution embodied in statute is but one part of the larger "real" constitution which encompasses all the practices of government in Canada. Thus while the changes which may be about to take place are crucial, they leave many of the workings of day-to-day government in Canada largely unchanged and hence do not affect the concerns of most of the material in this text.

While it is the travail of the textbook writer to have to deal with such uncertainties, we have had a great deal of assistance in the preparation of this material. Beyond the obvious debt to the proliferating body of scholarship on Canadian government, we have benefited from research assistance from Bob Cook and the bibliography has been worked on by several people including Vivian Hostetler and David Johnston. Many people have worked patiently at typing sections of the manuscript, particularly Julie Beaubien of the Department of Political Science at Carleton. Many of our colleagues at Carleton University—Khayyam Paltiel, George Roseme, and Jon Pammett deserve special mention—and friends within the federal and provincial governments have read and commented upon parts of the manuscript. We have also benefited from comments from users of the earlier editions of the text, both students and faculty in universities in Canada and the United States. We will greatly appreciate continuing to receive these comments. Needless to say the faults can all be attributed to those others while we alone should receive credit for the excellence of any material contained herein!

M. S. Whittington
R. J. Van Loon

1

Introduction

If it is true as one prominent Canadian public figure once stated that "the government has no place in the bedrooms of the nation," it is clear that government has surely found a place in every other room of the house. Picture for a moment a middle-aged political scientist standing in front of his bathroom mirror about to scrape the excess hair from his haggard features. "In here," he might be overheard to say with satisfaction, "the government certainly has no place."

But then he might pause and ponder his immediate surroundings. He notices that there is a little note etched on the corner of the mirror which indicates that this particular piece of glass meets a certain government standard. The label on the aerosol can containing his shaving cream warns him, "Do not puncture or incinerate." A government agency somewhere has decided that such warnings are necessary. The same label tells him that the can contains "350 mL" (however much that is!), because still another government agency has abolished fluid ounces; moreover, the government requires that the information on the label be repeated in the two official languages. As he brushes his teeth, our hero, by now on the verge of paranoia, remembers that the electricity and the water in the small room are supplied by public utilities, and that the municipality puts various chemicals in the water to protect him from typhoid, dysentery, tooth decay, and sundry other public health horrors. Trembling with the embarrassment of how public his bathroom has become, he glances out the window and notices an elderly gentleman walking his dog along the municipally owned and operated sidewalk. The dog is on a leash because a municipal by-law decrees it; and, as if to add insult to injury, the man is carrying a small shovel and a little plastic "doggie bag" because the municipality is very concerned about keeping its streets clean.

The point of this little vignette is that governments in the 1980s touch upon literally every aspect of our day-to-day existence. What is still more significant, perhaps, is that most of the examples of government's ubiquity cited in our brief fable are fairly recent in their origins. Governments are not only very prominent actors in our lives today, but trends in the past two decades indicate that government is increasing in the extent to which its decisions touch upon our daily routines. We exclaimed in an earlier edition of this text that in 1971 *all*

1

governments in Canada spent a total of $35 billion; the 1980-81 estimates show us that the federal government alone intends to spend almost $67 billion in the 1981-82 fiscal year. Even if we try to reduce the enormity of the federal budget by taking into account a decade of inflation, we would still see that the total expenditures of federal, provincial, and municipal levels of government in 1971 were about 38 percent of the gross national product, while in 1980 they had risen to 45 percent of the GNP. Indeed, government is a dominant actor in our day-to-day affairs and its presence in society and the economy is growing at a very rapid pace.

Governments in Canada today provide a myriad of services ranging from the defence of our borders to the redistribution of income. Government regulates industry, labour, and the professions; it provides the roads we drive on, the water we drink, national communications networks, public education, medical care, and low cost housing; it engages in commercial enterprises ranging from running airlines to producing synthetic rubber. The scope of government's activities range from the godlike manipulation of the national economy through fiscal, monetary and exchange rate policies,[1] to the more mundane hosting of an annual First of July "bash" on Parliament Hill. Finally, government with one hand preserves peace and order in our society, and with the other hand opens our mail, taps our phones, and decides what films (or, in Ontario, what parts of them) we will be permitted to see.

Beyond the provision of goods and services and the redistribution of material resources, governments are also important symbolic reference points to their citizens. They provide symbols such as flags, anthems, and a political apparatus with which we can identify, or against which we can vent hostility. Moreover, through their antics, posturings, and sincere concerns, our politicians provide us with psychological stimuli which may have little direct relevance to the political system, but which form a significant and often entertaining dimension to modern life.

In sum, governments are the dominant actors on the world's stage in 1981, and their activities constantly affect the economic, social, and psychological dimensions of our everyday lives. This book is about how government works at the national level in Canada. The relevance of this inquiry is clear enough, given the importance of government in the modern world. But, if that is not reason enough for such a

---

[1] See: Economic Council of Canada, *Eighth Annual Review: Design for Decision Making* (Information Canada, 1971), esp. pp. 5-16, for a brief but succinct discussion of the increased role of government.

study, the subject and the questions it poses are also inherently fascinating: What is the real meaning of our electoral process? How do our political parties work? What is the nature and importance of relations between the provinces and Ottawa? How do other Canadians think and feel about our political process? What difference does it make whether the government has a majority or not? And, most important of all, how do the needs of society become translated into the policies of government? Before attempting to answer any of these questions, it is necessary to provide some framework within which such processes can be systematically described and analyzed.

THE POLITICAL FUNCTION

All societies,[2] however primitive, possess some form of government. It is logical, therefore, to assume that there must be some common underlying function[3] (or set of functions) which is performed by such institutions. There are two simple reasons for the existence and nature of the governmental or political function: first, human beings have a multitude of basic needs and wants which must be satisfied if the species is to survive and if individuals are to attain happiness; second, the resources necessary for the satisfaction of these needs and wants must be extracted from an environment that is limited. The combination of virtually unlimited human wants and limited resources produces a situation where an individual must compete with others to maximize personal satisfaction. The function of government is to resolve the conflict which arises over who gets what resources in a given society.

The Limited Environment
Canadians are immensely lucky in terms of where they live. Although our climate is hard on people, automobiles, and brass monkeys, and although resource depletion faces Canada as well as other countries in the world, the natural resources available to Canadians

---

[2] By "society" we mean the network of social relationships that exists among individuals and is continuous through successive generations. This rather perfunctory definition is intended merely as a starting point for the reader and will be elaborated as the discussion unfolds. See: Marion J. Levy, *The Structure of Society* (Princeton University Press, Princeton, 1952), p. 113; and J. W. Vander Zanden, *Sociology* (The Ronald Press, New York, 1965), p. 153.

[3] Marion Levy defines the term as well as anybody: "A function is a condition or state of affairs resultant from the operation . . . of a structure through time. . . . A structure is a pattern, i.e., an observable uniformity of action or operation." in Roland Young, *Approaches to the Study of Politics* (Northwestern, Evanston, 1958), p. XV.

are relatively so abundant that our economic standard of living and the general quality of life is among the highest in the world. No matter how abundant our resources, however, they are still limited. No one would argue that the Canadian economy produces enough material goods to satisfy every Canadian, and, in fact, because our expectations tend to rise with our standard of living, the elimination of material scarcity may be an impossible dream. Furthermore, as we will see in the next chapter, our material well-being is offset by significant inequalities in the distribution of what is available.

But material scarcity is only one dimension of the limited environment. Even if there were no limit to the material resources of a society, there are other situations where scarcity cannot be eliminated or even significantly reduced. *Status,* for instance, is a psychological need which can be satisfied only relative to other people.[4] One's status is high because that of others is lower. It is illogical therefore to speak of eliminating scarcity in such a resource. The inequality of the allocation of psychological goods such as status can be reduced only if people can be conditioned not to need them.

Conflict and Cooperation
The result of a limited environment is that in Canada, as in all societies, people must compete with others for the resources they require to survive and to be content. This competition occurs at several levels. At one level, one may compete directly with others. In spite of some halting evidence of changing values in North America, getting a promotion or raise, finding a job in the first place, winning a scholarship and, in general, "keeping up with the Joneses" is still a central concern of life. But competition often transcends the individual level. Groups of people with interests in common are also in competition with other groups; labour unions compete with management, farmers compete with non-agricultural occupational groups, and dentists compete with denturists. Intergroup competition is a sort of bargaining game where the "prize" is the larger share of an available but limited resource.

But competition among groups in society is transcended by an even broader "intersector" conflict. In our post-industrial society, some

---

[4] Whether the need for status is biologically determined and common to other animals than humans, or whether it is a culturally determined feature of human society, is an interesting debate but is not really germane here. The point here is that Canadians do seem to have a need for status and that their political behaviour is influenced by this need. Those interested in the debate itself may wish to peruse Robert Ardrey, *The Social Contract* (Delta, New York, 1970).

would argue that traditional interpersonal and intergroup conflict has been superseded by a "balance of bigness," with big business, big labour, and big government as the main protagonists.[5] Moreover, in federal systems such as Canada's, intergovernmental conflict itself is an important dimension of the competition for scarce resources.

Finally, of course, whole societies are perpetually in conflict, not only in the international arena, where governments are the actors, but also even within the confines of a single state where, for example, national or cultural groups are the adversaries. The French-English conflict which colours so much of Canadian politics is our most obvious example of the latter, and the increasing demands of our native peoples for the settlement of land claims might also be viewed in this way.

So far conflict has been our central focus. Conflict is inherently neither good nor bad, but simply an inevitable state of affairs which occurs when people's boundless appetites are loosed on a limited environment. However, cooperation is as inevitable as conflict in society. The very fact that human beings do live in societies and not alone testifies to the fundamentally cooperative side of human nature. Cooperation is useful because one can accomplish more with others than one can do alone. Within the context of a modern industrial society this has led to highly developed systems of cooperation called organizations, which permit a high division of labour and increase the capacity of a society to reduce material scarcity. Furthermore, as pointed out earlier, many of an individual's psychological needs can be satisfied only in relation to others. While the drive to satisfy these needs results in interpersonal competition, without cooperation there would be no social resources for which to compete. In sum, while conflict often seems more interesting and more visible, the cooperative mechanisms which permit a society to come into existence in the first place are at least equally significant and form the real cornerstone of our study.[6]

---

[5] This thesis is set forth most succinctly in J. K. Galbraith's *The New Industrial State* (Houghton Mifflin, Boston, 1969), and in *Economics and the Public Purpose* (Thomas Allen & Son Ltd., New York, 1973). For a different perspective, see articles in M. D. Hancock and G. Sjoberg (eds.), *Politics in the Post-Welfare State* (Columbia University Press, New York, 1972), esp. pp. 37-55.

[6] When we come to analyze the bases of conflict and cooperation within Canadian society we will use the terms *cleavage* and *consensus*. A cleavage is a line of conflict between two groups which are in competition for the same resourcesm Hence, for example, we will often speak of French-English cleavage, class cleavage, or regional cleavage. *Consensus* is a state of agreement among a group of people over the desirability of some end. Consensus is the foundation for cooperation among individuals, within groups, and within societies.

Conflict Resolution and Resource Allocation

In any society there are a number of different *systems*[7] or sets of human relationships which perform the function of resource allocation. For example, in Canadian society the economic system, through a medium of exchange we call money and by a complex process of bargaining we call prices, does much to determine what material resources individuals and groups will possess. Resources may also be allocated by our system of beliefs and values. For example, the value our society places upon competitive sports means that an outstanding athlete receives greater rewards in terms of status and money than an outstanding clergyman or professor. While the way in which these different systems interact in the process of resource allocation will vary from society to society and from time to time, the allocative function is always performed.

Government too is a system for allocating resources, but it is unique. Unlike the other allocative systems in society it can be viewed as the master system; there are virtually no limits on what resources government can allocate. Furthermore, all persons in a given society are subject to the allocative decisions of government whether they choose to be or not. The jurisdiction of government is general rather than specific.

Government can also be viewed as the "master" allocative system in a society because it is empowered to control the functioning of the other allocative systems. For example, the family may be regarded as an allocative system. In most societies the head of the family will be permitted to distribute allowances to the children, but prohibited by laws enacted by government from killing unwanted infants. Similarly, the operation of the economic system is limited by a host of laws prohibiting such things as misleading advertising, undue restriction of competition, or unfair employment practices, and regulating matters as disparate as labour relations or the emission of pollutants into the environment. Thus, government is different from other allocative systems in a society in that its jurisdiction or sphere of control, while limited territorially by national boundaries, is comprehensive.

However, there are reasons for not taking this description of the government as the "master" system too far. Governments in Canada may be formally omnipotent, but they are constrained by the distri-

---

[7] The examination of society as a group of systems and sub-systems has a history too long to be traced in a footnote. Most recently the concept has been promoted by Talcott Parsons in most of his voluminous writings, and in political science by Gabriel Almond, David Easton, and Karl Deutsch, among others. A listing of the relevant books is to be found in the bibliography and in other footnotes in this chapter.

bution of economic power, the prevailing value system of the society, and by the values and beliefs of the decision makers themselves. For example it is inconceivable that a government in Canada could decree that all Roman Catholics be summarily executed or that all corporations be summarily nationalized. The prevailing ideology and the prevailing distribution of economic power would obviously prohibit the untrammelled exercise of governmental power in these areas. We will discuss in depth later the realistic limitations on government activity in Canada, but government, while certainly not omnipotent, is far and away the single most powerful and ubiquitous allocative system in any modern society.

Legitimacy and Authority

Another distinguishing characteristic of governments is that the decisions they make are *authoritative*.[8] In part, this means that government possesses a monopoly over the use of the collective coercive power of the society to back up its decisions. The exclusive ability to employ coercion obviously lends a great deal of authority to governmental enactments; but a system which relied only on coercion in order to make its allocations effective would be neither stable nor efficient. Too large a percentage of the available resources would be utilized in merely keeping the citizenry in line, and the slightest letup in the use of force would leave the system vulnerable to overthrow or collapse. For a governmental system to persist, it must acquire *legitimacy*. The members of the society must accept the system not merely because they have to but also because there is some agreement that it is good, or at least adequate.

A system becomes legitimate in many ways. Often it happens simply because people accept it out of habit or because it is easier to accept the existing regime than to rebel against it. But whatever the origins of a system's legitimacy, it can persist only if the values and norms the system supports through its actions are basically acceptable to the society as a whole. It must resolve conflicts and allocate resources in such a way as to gain and retain the support of most of the members of society.

Our original conception of the political function as the resolution of conflict can now be filled out somewhat in the light of what has been said about the allocative role of government, the authoritative nature of governmental decisions, and the comprehensiveness of the sphere

[8] David Easton, *A Systems Analysis of Political Life* (John Wiley & Sons, New York, 1965), ch. 1.

of control of government. A more complete statement of the political function is: *conflict resolution through the authoritative allocation of the scarce resources of a society*. "Politics" can then be defined as the process[9] by which the political function is performed; it is the way that authoritative decisions concerning the allocation of scarce resources are made and carried out in a society.

GOVERNMENT AS A SYSTEM: ENVIRONMENT AND STRUCTURE

While we have so far avoided the use of the term, we view government as a system, specifically as that system which performs the political function. Moreover, because the political function has been defined in terms of "what government does for society" our political system is an open one: it exists in and is influenced by its environment.[10] The environment of the political system includes not only the society for which it performs the allocative function, but other societies as well. On a still wider plane, the environment of the system includes non-human factors (such as topography, climate, and vegetation) which directly affect the lot of human beings. However, the important thing to remember when considering the environment of the political system is that it is composed of things that have varying relevance to politics, ranging from the virtually irrelevant, such as sunspots and quasars, to the very relevant, such as voters and the mass media.

But if we define the environment of the political system as everything other than the system itself, must we not ask where the system-environment boundary lies? Until now we have made no attempt to speak of politics or of the political system in other than functional terms; that is, we have said what the political system does without bothering about what it is. When we want to define it in structural

---

[9] Note: it is necessary to make an analytical distinction here between the concepts of function and process. *Function* is viewed as outcome, effect, or result of organizational activity. *Process* is viewed as the activity that produces outcomes, effects, or results.

[10] While open system theory has been popularized for political scientists, most notably by the works of David Easton and Gabriel Almond, it has been far more completely developed in other disciplines. See particularly: L. von Bertalanffy, "The Theory of Open Systems in Physics and Biology," *Science* 1950, vol. III, pp. 23-28; J. G. Miller, "Toward a General Theory for the Behavioral Sciences," *American Psychologist*, vol. 10, 1955, pp. 513-531; T. Parsons, *The Social System* (Free Press, New York, 1951); and more recently D. Katz, and R. L. Kahn, *The Social Psychology of Organizations* (John Wiley & Sons, New York, 1966). There are as well innumerable articles in *General Systems: The Yearbook of the Society for the Advancement of General Systems Theory*.

terms, we can state that the political system is a social structure or set of institutions that performs the political function, and because the basic unit of social structure is the *role*, it follows that the political system must be seen ultimately as a complex of interrelated roles.

A role is a pattern of behaviour that is defined by the expectations a society has of one who is occupying that position. Thus, the Prime Minister performs a set of interrelated roles which include, among other things, acting as chairman of cabinet meetings, chief advisor to the Governor General, Privy Councillor, party leader, and Member of Parliament. The way in which a Prime Minister behaves in each of these roles is determined largely by what society expects the behaviour to be. Sometimes, as in the case of the Prime Minister's more formal roles, the society has made its expectations explicit through constitutional conventions and statutes. The Prime Minister is, in this manner, constrained to behave according to the expectations implicit in the role itself, and not according to personal predispositions.

But unfortunately role theory is not as neat in practice as it seems in the abstract. In the first place, most roles are defined partly by the person playing them. It is only roles which are defined legally or constitutionally that leave little room for improvisation on the part of the incumbent. Moreover, each person occupies many roles in life, and all of these become interrelated. For example, the fact that Prime Minister Trudeau's son accompanied him on his trip to the Vatican modified both his behaviour and that of his hosts even though, strictly speaking, his role as "father" has little connection with his role as Canadian Prime Minister. The roles themselves may not be connected, but the fact that the same person occupies all of them will probably cause them to impinge on each other in many ways. Nevertheless, despite the limitations of role theory, it is still useful to refer to the political system, structurally, as a complex of interrelated political roles. What makes a role political is the fact that it directly concerns the authoritative allocation of resources.

There are also roles such as the "voter" role which are relevant to politics but which cannot be said to affect the authoritative allocation of resources directly and immediately. Such *politically relevant* roles are probably best considered as part of the environment of the political system and not part of the system itself. However, the boundary between the political and the politically relevant cannot be drawn distinctly, and the boundary between the politically relevant and the apolitical is similarly impossible to define.

While recognizing this thorny problem of boundaries, it is still possible to say that certain roles and complexes of roles which we refer to as *institutions* are definitely political, and that certain others definitely are not. By looking then at the roles and institutions of the "gray area" in terms of their relationship to roles and institutions that are either clearly political or clearly not, we will come to understand their overall significance for the political process. It does not matter whether we decide that an interest group is a part of the political system or a politically relevant part of the environment—we will come to understand the political functions of interest groups through looking at their place in the process of politics. Thus, in our discussion of interest groups, we will point out that they perform both political and nonpolitical activities. They are acting politically when their agents attempt to "lobby" cabinet ministers or bureaucrats, but they are acting apolitically when they publish a monthly newsletter devoted to new methods and techniques which may assist their members in the day-to-day performance of their jobs. The key to the subsequent analysis of the Canadian political system is that it is to be viewed in terms of processes and not in terms of structures *per se*. The structures are simply the institutional context within which the process occurs.

What follows is an overview or model of the political process which will be utilized as a framework for our detailed description of the Canadian system. This model has a purely pedagogical function. It should be used as a mental peg board on which to organize information. To use another metaphor, this chapter provides a rough map of the Canadian political process, without which the subsequent masses of information might be but an array of disjointed facts. Later chapters can be regarded as the "real world" topography which is rather imperfectly represented and oversimplified on our map.

GOVERNMENT AS A SYSTEM: AN INFORMATION FLOW MODEL

For the political system to be responsive to a changing environment, and for it to be able to effect changes in that environment, there must be a two-way flow of communication. This communication takes the form of information flow referred to as *input, output,* and *feedback.*[11] These categories of information flow are illustrated in Figure 1-1.

Input
An input is an exchange of information flowing from the environment into the political system. One basic class of input is the *demand* input. This takes the form of information indicating to the political decision makers that a certain allocation or reallocation of resources is

[11] The terminology utilized here is that of David Easton. See: *A Systems Analysis of Political Life.*

Figure 1-1

AN INFORMATION FLOW MODEL

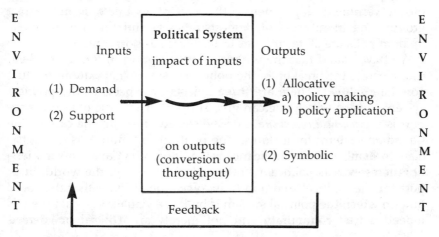

Adapted from David Easton, *A Systems Analysis of Political Life*, Chapter 1.

needed. In one sense demands can be perceived in the literal sense of the word—firmly stated requests by interested parties for allocative outputs which will be to their advantage. At the local level, the request by a developer for a re-zoning by-law would be such a demand; at the national level, a request by the Canadian Manufacturers' Association for a reduction in the level of corporate income tax would be another. Demand inputs can also be information actively sought by the political decision makers regarding the need for certain allocations. The essential characteristic is that there is an input of information which leads the political decision makers to consider making an output.

A second class of incoming communication between the system and the environment is the *support* input. A support input is information which indicates a positive orientation toward the system; such inputs function as a barometer telling the political decision makers in the system whether and to what extent the members of the society are satisfied with the system's performance. If there is an indication that the public is withdrawing its support, the political decision makers will attempt to alleviate the situation by making new allocative decisions. If the system continues to lose support, it is said to be in a situation of *stress*, which, if not relieved, can ultimately lead to its breakup.

There is often a difficulty in conceptualizing support for the system as an input, for it exists only in the form of attitudes or orientations toward the system held by persons in its environment. The Canadian political system employs a number of mechanisms to gauge the level of support. Elections, party policy conventions, field offices in various government departments, the receipt of briefs from interest groups, the monitoring of demonstrations, and the use of public opinion polls are all techniques to facilitate support inputs.

We have stated that the withdrawal of support, if left unchecked, could lead to the breakup of the political system. That statement must now be qualified. There are three objects or aspects of the political system toward which one can give support. The basic object of support is the *political community*, or the society itself. In the case of the Canadian system, for instance, the political community is the Canadian "nation" and its significance is that it permits Canadians to identify themselves as politically "other" than the rest of the world. Support for the political community involves the attitude that the social unit on which the political system is built is a viable one—that there is indeed a true community and not merely an artificial or coerced unity.

A second fundamental object of support is the *regime*. The regime is the set of structures, norms, and values which define the form of the state. It not only sets broad system goals and defines the limits of legitimate governmental activity, but it also provides the institutional mechanisms and the "rules of the game" of politics in a given country. In Canada the regime is composed of our political institutional arrangements such as federalism, parliamentary government, and cabinet responsibility. Support for the regime involves the acceptance that the values implicit in the particular form of political system are good.

Finally, the *authorities* of the system can be an object of support as well. Support for the authorities means support for the individuals occupying the positions or roles of the political system—the incumbents to whom we have been referring as the political decision makers.

For a society to be stable, it is important that support for the political community and the regime be sustained at a relatively high level. If there is a withdrawal of support for the political community, one of the results can be separation of the dissatisfied section. For example, separatist activities in the Province of Quebec reflect a lack of support for the political community of Canada by some of its members. Similarly, if there is withdrawal of support for the regime, the result can be the destruction or radical alteration of the existing system. The Communist Party of Canada, for instance, accepts the Canadian political community but rejects the liberal democratic form of the regime. This party would like to see the present regime supplanted by one similar in principle to that of the Soviet Union.

While the stability and persistence of a political system depends on the retention of support for the political community and the regime, in liberal democratic systems the regime explicitly provides institutional devices for expressing the withdrawal of support from the authorities. In fact, such systems could be said to encourage the periodic withdrawal of support for one set of authorities and their replacement by another set through elections and the party system.

Outputs

The basic form of outgoing communication from the system to the environment is the *allocative* output. This takes the form of information which produces allocations of resources in the environment. Allocative outputs, however, are of two basic types. First there are general statements known as *laws*. Laws state "who gets what, when, and how" in general terms. Second, there are outputs which apply the laws to individuals in society—statements which tell an individual how one is affected by the law and what one's rights and obligations are vis-à-vis that law. These two basic types of allocative output correspond roughly to the more traditional classification of governmental functions: the first kind of allocative output corresponds to *rule making*, the latter to *rule application*, which includes both the executive and adjudicative functions.[12]

There is a second form of output of the political system which is not allocative in any direct sense. This is an output of information which is aimed at educating, informing, or propagandizing, and which can be styled a *symbolic output*. The usual function of symbolic outputs is to communicate information about the outputs of the system to those who might be affected by them. In this sense symbolic outputs tell us about new laws which must be obeyed, about new opportunities created for us through government policies, and about the day-to-day activities of government that may be of interest to us. However, another important function of symbolic outputs is to increase support for the system without having to make any new allocative decisions. In this sense the government attempts to convince us of the "goodness" and legitimacy of the system simply by extolling its virtues to us.

Feedback

Once an allocative or symbolic decision is made there will normally be some sort of reaction to it from people in the environment. As time

---

[12] See: Chapters 6 and 7.

passes, it will become apparent whether or not the allocation has had the desired effect and the decision makers in the system can modify their future decision making accordingly. This process is known as feedback. In a primitive system this is a simple process, because direct personal contact is possible between decision makers and the environment. Indeed, in a simple system the decision maker leaves a meeting and becomes a major part of the social environment. In Canada the decision maker also has roles—such as the role in one's family—which make one a part of the environment, and there will be some limited opportunity to gain feedback in that way. However, our political system relies primarily on those parts of its institutions which operate on the "input side" of the process to gather information about the impact of its policies on society. In fact, as we will see when we look at the policy process, a major activity in which policy makers become involved is the evaluation of the impact of their decisions on the real world.

INSIDE THE SYSTEM: POLICY MAKING

While we have briefly described how the political system interacts with its environment, we have so far left untouched what is really the core concern of the political scientist: the *conversion process*,[13] whereby the decision makers in the political system decide how the system should respond to inputs. The resolution of conflicts that arise over the distribution of resources is the operational goal of the political system, and the activities which directly contribute to the attainment of that goal are the central process of politics. The part of the process which is internal to the system is *policy making*, and it forms the dominant focus of this book.

However, in selecting policy making as our central theme we must recognize that other processes of politics have great relevance as well. For the political system to pursue effectively its operational goal of conflict resolution it must persist over time. Thus, while the attainment of operational goals is the "job" government does on a day-to-day basis, there are functions related directly to the maintenance of the system which must be performed first.

Goal Attainment and System Maintenance
In one sense, the maintenance of the system is very closely related to

---

[13] In Fig. 1-1 this is described as the impact of input on outputs. It is the process of converting demands into outputs which are directed at meeting those demands. It is also sometimes referred to as "throughput."

its effectiveness in attaining operational goals, for if the "clients"[14] of the system are not satisfied with the standard of service being performed for them they will not continue to support it. In this way the legitimacy of a system is achieved at least in part through effective goal attainment. Similarly, if the system is to continue to perform its allocative function effectively, it will be necessary from time to time for the system to initiate structural changes and sometimes even to redefine goals[15] in response to environmental changes. It is the *adaptive mechanisms* of a political system that permit it to persist even when faced with large-scale social and economic changes or major shifts in the predominant value system of a population.[16]

Other aspects of the process of system maintenance, however, are linked less closely to policy making. For instance, because the political system is goal directed, the persons who occupy roles must be induced to engage in activity which is directed at the attainment of system goals. Because the goals of the system will likely not be identical to the personal goals of the occupants of system roles, the actors within the system must be made willing to put off the satisfaction of their immediate preferences in the interest of working toward the attainment of system goals. This *integrative function* is a critical dimension of system maintenance and it is achieved through a number of

[14] The term "clientele" has been developed and utilized most in the literature of administrative theory and policy analysis, although the concept is implicit in the notion of legitimacy. See: L. C. Freeman et al., "Role of Community and Clientele Leaders: Identifying Community Leaders in Decision-Making"; B. L. Bible and E. J. Brown, "Role of Community and Clientele Leaders: Coopting Clientele in Decision-Making"; and R. G. Mason, "Securing Clientele Acceptance and Cooperation"—all articles in F. J. Lyden et al. (eds.), *Policies, Decisions and Organization* (Appleton-Century-Crofts, New York, 1969), pp. 66-87, 214-228.

[15] While Roberto Michels is normally credited with origination of the concept of *goal displacement*, there is a large body of literature which has developed the concept and applied it to specific organizations. This phenomenon is discussed briefly and clearly in A. Etzioni, *Modern Organizations* (Prentice-Hall Inc., Englewood Cliffs, 1964), pp. 10-14. See also R. J. Merton, *Social Theory and Social Structure* (the Free Press of Glencoe, 1957), pp. 197 ff., and P. Selznick "An Approach to a Theory of Bureaucracy," *American Sociological Review*, vol. 8, no. 1, 1943, pp. 47-54. The redefinition of goals in the interest of the survival of the organization is elaborated in a case study of the Salvation Army by S. D. Clark. See: *Church and Sect in Canada* (University of Toronto Press, Toronto, 1948).

[16] Note here that there are some value parameters beyond which a system may not adapt without becoming a new system entirely. The maintenance of these is referred to as "pattern maintenance" and is described as protecting "the basic ordering principles of the system with regard to both the value of such patterns and the commitment of system units to them." T. Parsons, "The Political Aspect of Social Structure and Process," in D. Easton (ed.), *Varieties of Political Theory* (Prentice-Hall Inc., Englewood Cliffs, 1966), p. 105. In other words, whereas adaptation is the dynamic element in the system, pattern maintenance is the conservative element. The "raw material" of pattern maintenance can be found in the fundamental values of the members of the society, and/or the "clientele" of the system.

processes related to political recruitment, socialization, and the manipulation of material and non-material rewards, and in the bureaucracy through the process of management. All of these facets of system maintenance will be discussed in the chapters that follow.

To summarize, our aim is to look at political institutions and processes primarily in terms of their relationship to goal attainment. Because goal attainment activity within the context of the political system amounts to policy making, that will be our central concern. While it is our intention neither to ignore nor to deemphasize the processes of politics related to the maintenance of the system, these will be viewed primarily in terms of their relationship to effective policy making.

The Policy Concept

A *policy* can best be defined as a course of action that the authorities of the political system have decided should become an output. In other words a policy is the intention to produce a certain allocative output, and the process of policy making involves deciding what that output should be. However, while such a definition is simple enough on the surface it includes a number of implications that need elaboration.

In the first place, it is possible to think of policy and the process of policy making within the context of any organization, not just the political system. For example, it is quite reasonable to speak of "company policy" without implying any connection to the political system, and if the structural focus is specified, the above definition of policy is compatible with all of these usages of the term.[17] However, unless otherwise specified, the term "policy" within the context of this book will refer only to public policy or governmental policy.

The second implication of this definition of policy is that the policy process consists of decision-making activity. Because political decision making is in the end the prerogative of individual minds acting in complex organizations, in order to understand the policy process completely it would be necessary to consider social-psychological factors as well as a host of influences that arise because of the organizational context within which decisions are made. But our concern is more with the question of which people occupying which political roles have the power to make various kinds of political decisions rather than with the process whereby a human mind in the organizational setting perceives a problem, looks for alternative solutions to

---

[17] "Company policy," for instance, may be viewed as decisions by the people who occupy authority positions within a company that a certain course of action should be expressed as an organizational "output."

the problem, and then chooses one of the alternatives.[18] This is not to assert that the social-psychological and organizational imperatives are not vital, but rather that they are too complex to be discussed extensively in a basic text.

Finally, this definition of policy recognizes that there is a distinction between "policy" and "output." While the outputs of a political system are always a reflection of policy decisions taken within the system, the conversion of a policy to an output often requires formal steps which legitimize or render authoritative the internal decisions. For example, a bill passed by parliament does not become a legislative output until it has been assented to by the Governor General, proclaimed, and printed in the Canada Gazette. Because "being the government" in Canada to a large extent means having control over these formal legitimizing procedures, the conversion of government policy to outputs is a routine matter. The decision to employ those procedures is in reality the final step in the policy process; what occurs subsequently is virtually automatic and not strictly a part of policy making. Thus, while we will occasionally speak of "outputs" and "policies" as synonymous terms, and while it would be rare empirically for one to occur without the other, it must be recognized that there is an analytical distinction.

There have been many attempts to define policy in more restrictive terms than ours. For instance, policy decisions are frequently viewed as those more properly taken by politicians than by administrators or bureaucrats. In this view a distinction is made between "political" decisions, which involve "policy," and "administrative" decisions, which do not.[19] While the distinction between policy making and policy implementation or between deciding and doing may be analytically appealing, empirically the distinction very quickly breaks down. The decision to pass a piece of major legislation may be more important than the decision of a customs official to inspect or not to inspect someone's luggage, but each of these activities does involve making a governmental decision. To say that one process is policy and the other is not is to introduce an artificial distinction.

---

[18] Herbert Simon refers to these stages of decision making as "intelligence activity," "design activity," and "choice activity." See: *The Scope of Automation: For Men and Management* (Harper & Row, New York, 1965), pp. 53-54. J. G. March and H. A. Simon, *Organizations* (John Wiley & Sons Ltd., New York, 1958), chs. 6-7. We will make extensive use of organization theory when discussing the cabinet and the bureaucracy in Canada.

[19] Peter Drucker speaks of a split between the "deciders and the doers" in the political system and sees a clear delineation of these functions as a solution to some of the problems of the "age of discontinuity." Peter Drucker, *The Age of Discontinuity* (Harper & Row, New York, 1969), p. 233.

While it is artificial to attempt to classify "political" decisions as policy and administrative decisions as some lower species, it is useful to classify policy into different types. The simplest yet one of the most useful classifications is to divide outputs into those generated by the legislative process, those by the executive or administrative process and those by the judicial process. By describing legislative, executive, and adjudicative decisions by the common term "policy," we can avoid a good deal of semantic debate about what is a policy, while still being able to relate each type of output back to a particular, analytically distinct process.

These three types of process and output are themselves very closely interrelated. Both the executive and adjudicative outputs depend upon the preexistence of *laws*, with the former having the effect of implementing and the latter of interpreting them. Consequently, there is a certain primacy about legislation which has caused the lawmaking process to be viewed traditionally as the "master" allocative function of government. In conformity with this, our analysis of the Canadian political system will focus primarily on the decision-making processes which result in the formation of legislation and secondarily on the processes which result in the executive and judicial implementation of law.

Our presumption of the primacy of the legislative policy process is not intended to minimize the importance of executive or judicial processes. Because the effectiveness of the political system in meeting the demands of a diverse clientele to a large extent depends upon the details of how the vast tax revenues of the system are spent, executive decision making within the political system, particularly that related to the preparation of the budget and the expenditure of public funds, is an increasingly important dimension of policy making. Over 90 percent of the money spent by the Canadian government each year is spent on already existing programs and hence is allocated primarily through executive and administrative decisions. Similarly we see how judicial decisions not only mediate the relationship between the individual and the state, but that judicial interpretations have in fact shaped the institutional framework of the Canadian federal system. Thus judicial and administrative decision making must be viewed as important categories of policy making. Nevertheless, because each of the continuing programs was generated originally by new legislation and because the key issues of politics today still involve new policies more than the ongoing ones, our initial analytical departure point is the process whereby decisions about new legislation are taken.

The Policy Process in a Technological Age

The theory of parliamentary democracy posits an ideal system of government where legislative outputs prevail over all other outputs of the system and where the power to legislate is vested in an elected parliament. Furthermore, the executive power in a perfect parliamentary system resides with the Prime Minister and the cabinet, who are in turn responsible directly to parliament. Thus, in an ideal parliamentary democracy, ultimate power rests with the people who elect the parliament, which in turn controls the Prime Minister and the cabinet. The administrative arm of the government, the bureaucracy, is responsible directly to the cabinet and indirectly, through the budgetary process, to parliament. The bureaucracy is responsible for the implementation or application of the laws passed by parliament, and such responsibilities are totally divorced from the legislative process.

While it seems unlikely that this theoretical version of parliamentary democracy was ever a fact, it is part of the conventional wisdom that there was a "Golden Age" of parliamentary democracy when reality conformed much better to the ideal than it does today. One major factor associated with this trend away from the hypothetical ideal of parliamentary democracy is technological change, although in large part it is not technology but the social and economic consequences of technology which have altered the policy process most startlingly.

Technological advances precipitated industrialization which has been the single most important variable in determining the nature of modern societies. The movement from a pre-industrial or agricultural society produced social discontinuities which were so great that existing mechanisms of social adaptation could not cope. Industrialization, for instance, created in Canada the phenomenon of the employable unemployed. The problem of welfare within the pre-industrial system had concerned the care of those unable to find employment because of physical or mental disability, a problem which could be dealt with by agencies such as the church and local charities. With the massive unemployment that resulted from economic fluctuations in industrial society, the traditional agencies were no longer capable of carrying the burden of welfare. By default, more than anything else, government was forced to step into the field of income redistribution and social insurance in order to alleviate the intense economic hardships of depression and unemployment.

Similarly, because an industrial society is complex and very sensitive to the activities of individuals who control large amounts of capital, economic stability can be maximized only if there is a degree of control and planning of the economy. Governments were the natural structures in society to step in and regulate the economic system, with anti-combines, labour relations, fair employment practices, and other legislation. The "unseen hand" of Adam Smith did not effectively keep the economy in a state of equilibrium, and government stepped in to attempt to restore the balance.

Technology not only made industrialization possible in the first instance but, through developments in the field of economics, also made possible the intervention of government as a planner and regulator of the industrial economy: "Even in the most conservative of the industrial states, technology has steadily expanded governmental activity in the fields once left exclusively to the private entrepreneurs."[20] Technology and industrialization thus stimulated a change in the role of the political system in society. Where governments had once been very passive and negative, they assumed positive and active roles in society. Where the public attitude to the role of government had once been that the government that governed least was the best form of government, the political system was now expected as a matter of course to perform broad regulatory and redistributive functions heretofore left to economic and social mechanisms or not performed at all.

The immediate implications of this changing role of government for the political system were three. First, the number of outputs of government increased because the role of government expanded. There has been a linear increase in the amount of governmental activity which means that the number of policies considered in any given year will normally be greater than in the year before.[21]

Second, the complexity of legislation increased enormously after the turn of the century. The amount of detail required in legislation that spells out the procedures and formulae in a national pension plan, for instance, is much greater than that required in legislation to amend a criminal code, and an increasing percentage of legislation deals with subjects like pension plans and welfare schemes.

Finally, not only have governmental outputs increased in number and the amount of detail they encompass, but their content has increased in technological sophistication as well. Policies dealing with subjects such as economic planning, scientific research and taxation must of necessity be highly technical, reflecting as they do the most advanced levels of knowledge in the given field. The combination of increased volume, complexity, and technological sophistication of governmental activity has made a high level of specialization and technical expertise necessary for effective policy making. This has had important consequences for the ideal of parliamentary democracy.

In the first place, parliament, being neither specialized nor highly expert, is disqualified in practical terms from taking the central part in

---

[20] E. G. Mesthene, *Technological Change* (Harvard University Press, Cambridge, 1970), pp. 64-65, and V. C. Ferkiss, *Technological Man* (Braziller, New York, 1969), p. 177.
[21] Ferkiss, *Technological Man*, p. 178.

the policy process. In part, the lawmaking power in the Canadian political system has shifted to the cabinet, for it is this body which has acquired and retains the *de facto* authority to set goals or establish priorities for governmental action. Through party discipline and through its access to the expertise within the various government departments, the cabinet member is placed in a position of considerable advantage over the backbench MP.

In part, however, the policy function has moved out of the cabinet as well and into the hands of the thousands of experts throughout the public service. These experts are entrusted with the responsibility of tendering policy advice to the ministers. The power to advise, which sounds harmless enough, becomes a very real political power when the advice given is highly technical in nature and when the person being advised is not an expert. In Peter Drucker's terms, knowledge has become power; it is the "central capital" of modern society: "Scientists and scholars are no longer merely 'on tap' they are 'on top. . . .' They largely determine what policies can be considered seriously in such crucial areas as defence or economics."[22]

While the power to decide policy still resides with political office holders such as the Prime Minister and the cabinet, this is in many ways *positional* power. That is to say, it derives from the role an individual occupies and is only secondarily affected by the character and ability of the individual. Because rational decision making in a modern system necessitates the use of specialized and technical information which politicians do not possess, the real power that accrues to them through their positions is significantly reduced. As Jacques Ellul has pointed out:

The task of the expert is to furnish the politician with information and estimates on which he can base a decision. . . . When the expert has effectively performed his task of pointing out the necessary ways and means, there is generally only one logical and admissible solution. The politician will then find himself obliged to choose between the technician's solution, which is the only reasonable one, and other solutions which he can indeed try out at his own peril, but which are not reasonable. . . . In fact, the politician no longer has any real choice; decision follows automatically from the preparatory technical labours.[23]

Finally it is also a fact of modern government that senior bureaucrats are the central contact point between the technocrats and the politicians. Lacking the positional authority of the politician and the expertise of the technocrats, the senior public servants gain their

[22] Drucker, *The Age of Discontinuity*, p. 372.
[23] Mesthene, *Technological Change*, pp. 64-65.

power as the "managers" of expertise. They are the men and women who try to translate the technical information into terms the politician in the cabinet can understand, and through this role they have maintained a high level of power in the system as well.

While the above generalizations likely apply fairly accurately to the Canadian situation, the fact remains that cabinet ministers and the Prime Minister will not infrequently make decisions which go contrary to the advice of their technical hired hands. Whether they are inspired by sincere doubts about the validity of the advice tendered, by political opportunism, or by simple whim, our politicians still possess the positional power to make policy decisions against the advice of technicians and senior bureaucrats. However, for the most part technical advice to our political leaders does have a profound influence on their decisions.

The outcome of the shift in policy-making power from those who occupy political authority roles to those who possess technical knowledge or information is that the institutions that concentrate expertise such as bureaucratic agencies will tend to dominate the institutions, such as parliament, that do not. *Prima facie*, there is no reason why concentrations of expertise in non-governmental locales such as industry, the universities, and pressure groups could not provide important sources of policy influence to compete with the governmental bureaucracy. In some instances they do. However two factors intervene. First, "the development and the application of technology seem necessarily to require large scale and complex social concentration,"[24] which occurs most commonly in government. There are few non-governmental organizations which control sufficient resources to gather expertise and technological information on a scale that would permit them to compete effectively with the governmental bureaucracy. Those that might, the multinational corporations, are so large and diversified that they must be analyzed as "proto governments" rather than as private enterprise. This means that the relationship between multinationals and government is more akin to the relationships among sovereign states than between a sovereign government and its domestic corporations. Thus, in terms of the public policy process within Canada, the conclusion must be that power has shifted within government rather than to non-governmental institutions.[25]

Second, the number of sources of information which the harried

[24] J. Ellul, *Technological Society* (Alfred A. Knopf, Inc., New York), pp. 258-9.
[25] For an opposite point of view see M. Lamontagne, "The Influence of the Politician," *Canadian Public Administration*, vol. 11, no. 3, pp. 263-71.

formal or positional decision makers in the cabinet and its support agencies can deal with is limited. There is simply not time to consider a larger number of alternative viewpoints. The decision maker therefore "satisfices," to use Herbert Simon's now famous term, by selecting the first passable solution, and since it is the public service which for the most part screens the information flowing to ministers it is their selection of information which tends to be dominant.

Public servants can also influence governmental outputs more directly through the instrument of delegated power. It is frequently necessary, because of the complexity of the matters being dealt with by government, for legislation to leave a great deal of discretion to the public servants who implement it. The power to work out the details of a particular government program is often delegated to the administrative agency charged with the responsibility for administering it in such a way that the administrators become, in a limited way, legislators. This presents serious problems of political control. The bureaucrats, unlike the politicians, are not elected. Although parliament attempts to control this problem through its Statutory Instruments Committee, perhaps the most effective way of preventing the abuse of delegated power today is through judicial process, which provides remedies through civil action for an individual who is harmed by misuse of administrative discretion.

The foregoing paints a picture quite different from the traditional one of a supreme parliament, responsible to an informed and active electorate, making policy on the basis of a grand concept of "national interest." Nevertheless, while the policy process in the positive state does not match our classical image of parliamentary democracy, the system does seem to work after a fashion. Furthermore, it is important to emphasize that there is no blame to be assigned for this shift in power within our system. Power is moving from parliament to the cabinet and from the cabinet to the bureaucracy simply because the environment of the political system is such that experts in large information-gathering organizations are the ones most likely to find solutions to current problems. The bureaucrats and technocrats have not deliberately wrested policy-making power from the hands of those who should rightfully possess it. There has been no *coup d'état!*

THE POLICY PROCESS IN CANADA: A MODEL

The Initiation of Policies

The policy process has been defined as internal to the political system. It is the process whereby persons "inside" the system decide what should become system outputs. A distinction has already been made between policy and output, but little has been said about the "input side" of the process. The authorities do not make policy decisions on a purely random or whimsical basis (even though this sometimes appears to be the case). The policy process is triggered by information from outside the system, specifically by information about problems which can be solved by governmental action. Hence, given that the origins of public policy lie in information about environmental circumstances, the process whereby that information comes to the attention of the policy makers is the first stage in the formation of policy.

The key problem in initiating or triggering the policy process is in finding channels through which demand inputs can be brought to the attention of people occupying policy roles. Points of access occur naturally where people within the system are paying attention to what is going on outside; in order to ensure continued attentiveness, MPs and cabinet ministers are subject to periodic evaluation through the institutional device of elections. Institutions such as political parties and pressure groups have come to play a key role in rationalizing and articulating to parliament and cabinet the wants and needs of people in the environment. However, given the diversity of problems that exist in modern societies and given the overall movement of decision-making power from the political institutions to bureaucratic ones, newer, less traditional channels of access to the political system have developed at the bureaucratic level.

Many government departments have as their organizational *raison d'être* a specific clientele. For instance, the Department of Agriculture exists to serve agricultural interests and to solve agricultural problems, and the Department of Veterans' Affairs exists to serve the interest of ex-servicemen. The survival and growth of these departments depends almost entirely on their success in representing the interest of their clienteles. The more problems they can define and begin to solve, the greater will be their budgetary allocations and manpower establishment. As a result clientele-oriented departments constantly seek environmental information in an effort to anticipate the needs and problems of their clientele. Because of this bureaucratic attentiveness, important channels of access to the policy process have been created within the public service.

Today even large interest groups focus their attention on bureaucratic channels, frequently by seeking the establishment of a separate department that will serve their clientele. Close symbiotic relationships exist today between organizations such as the Canadian Legion or the Canadian Federation of Agriculture and departments such as Veterans' Affairs or Agriculture. While bureaucratic channels of access have not completely replaced the traditional ones through parliament and cabinet, they are often more effective for policy initiation. Because so many bureaucratic agencies are clientele oriented, and because they possess the expertise that makes them more effective than political institutions in ferreting out problems among their clientele, the political channels are increasingly in competition with the bureaucratic ones.

Nor is this situation confined to the federal government. There are similar points of access at the provincial level in Canada. The trends there are similar to those at the federal level: decision-making power generally has been moving from the political to the bureaucratic institutions, with the consequent increase in the importance of provincial departments as channels of policy initiation. The trend is more marked in large provinces than in smaller ones, but it exists everywhere.

The Establishment of Policy Priorities

The inflow of information from the environment is a necessary condition for policy making. If that flow of information should cease for some reason, the policy process would grind to a halt. In the modern political system, however, the central problem is not in garnering information but in coping with vast amounts of it. The problems of modern societies are so numerous and so complex that the greatest threat to the stability of the system lies in *information overload*. The first internal step in the policy process therefore involves weeding out, reducing, and ordering in importance the vast quantity of information with which the priority setters are constantly bombarded.[26]

The core institutions or the key authorities involved in the establishment of policy priorities in the Canadian system are the cabinet, the Prime Minister and federal-provincial conferences. It is the cabinet that possesses the formal authority to set the broadest directions of public policy. Because of the vast bulk of inputs, however, much of the initial reduction of policy demands and the preliminary weeding out of information must be performed elsewhere. The channels of input themselves act as "gatekeepers" in filtering policy information even before it comes to the attention of the cabinet and the Prime Minister. Pressure groups, for instance, establish priorities among the objectives of their membership in order to maximize policy influence. Not all of the needs of the entire clientele of an interest group can be met simultaneously, so the organizational leaders must decide which

---

[26] Victor Thompson speaks of "the knowledge explosion" and of "information affluence." See: *Bureaucracy and Innovation* (University of Alabama, 1969), pp. 1-6.

policy objectives are most important and which, within a given time, are achievable. Similarly, a clientele-oriented government department must limit and order the policy demands of its clientele; in doing so it reduces the number of choices facing the political decision makers.

At a point closer to the cabinet and the Prime Minister still more reduction and ordering of information occurs. The "gatekeepers" here are found among the advisory staff of the Prime Minister and cabinet, located primarily in the Prime Minister's Office (PMO), the Privy Council Office (PCO) and to a growing degree in the Ministries of State. While the Prime Minister and the cabinet can bypass the PMO and PCO and the Ministries of State in seeking information, most information flowing from the bureaucracy and interest groups is in fact filtered through these offices. By deciding which information that they receive is important enough to be passed on to their cabinet "masters," by summarizing information so as to brief the ministers, and by helping to set the agenda for cabinet and cabinet committee meetings, the people in these agencies play a significant role in determining what policy demands will even be considered by the priority setters. However, whether gleaned independently, or filtered through the various information "gatekeepers," a great many policy ideas ultimately do come to the attention of the cabinet; it is these that make up the raw material of cabinet-level priority decisions.

The initial cabinet-level decision in the process is whether to reject a policy idea outright or to consider it further. For those deemed important enough to be considered further, the cabinet must then decide which should be dealt with first and which government agency should be given the responsibility for formulating specific operational alternatives. The rejection of a policy idea outright can be considered as a negative output of the system and can have important consequences not only in terms of support for the system but also in terms of future inflow of information.

Most policy decisions at this stage will inevitably be negative ones. Although the number of demands being made on the system is potentially limitless, the resources of the system are severely limited. These resources, calculated in terms of human energy and finance, must be parsimoniously allocated to a very few policy suggestions that are deemed most "worthy." These negative priority decisions are often not noticed by the media or the public but they are important since they are effectively the same as opting for the status quo.[27]

---

[27] See: P. Bachrach and M. S. Baratz, *Power and Poverty* (Oxford University Press, New York, 1970), pp. 39-51.

While these cabinet-level choices as to what should be done and when may seem relatively simple, given the reduction and ordering that has already taken place, they may not be so. Because of the complex and technical nature of most subjects of governmental concern today, further information is usually necessary, first in order to establish general principles and standards and second, to measure the various choices against those standards. This information can be examined within a four-fold classification system.

i) The first type is *normative information*. This involves knowledge about the basic values of the system, which set the broadest parameters for governmental action. Such information will be possessed by virtually all participants in the policy process as part of their personal value systems, acquired through the process of socialization. It is this type of information that provides vague criteria such as justice, human dignity, freedom, and equality, against which people in modern Western democracies automatically measure all policies. The problem with normative information is that it sets only very broad limits on governmental activity. Thus, for example, if someone suggests that we exterminate the Jews, the basic values of Canadian policy makers will prohibit consideration of such a policy alternative. However, if someone suggests nationalizing automobile insurance, the answer is not implicit in a set of shared values but must be weighed against less fundamental criteria.

Normative information is not drawn from specialized institutions but from the shared values of virtually all Canadians and from what is often only implicit in our constitution. This means that at this level of policy determination, the political authorities in the cabinet and parliament do possess real decision-making power. This is more an apparent than a real power, however, since such fundamental decisions arise only very infrequently.

ii) *Political information* is the second type of information necessary in establishing policy priorities. This is information concerning the political feasibility or advisability of undertaking various policies. The criteria that must be employed in measuring the political advisability of a policy are shaped by the political institutions themselves. Thus, in the Canadian system, which features elections with a "universal" franchise, the criterion is simply how many votes will a policy ultimately win and lose for the current political office holders.

The main institutions tendering political advice to the cabinet are the Prime Minister's Office and the political party organization. By monitoring information flowing from political parties, pressure groups, the press and the provincial governments, the people in the PMO and party organizations keep themselves attuned to political developments across the country. The bureaucracy also pays considerable attention to political information, for senior bureaucrats are well aware that there is no point in tendering politically unrealistic advice to the cabinet and Prime Minister. Political information is very often intuitive information based on the "gut" feelings of politicians or senior officials, but in the 1960s and 1970s techniques of data gathering have begun to replace at least some of the more intuitive methods used in the past.

iii) *Technical information* is that possessed by the line departments of the public service. These technocrats are called upon to advise the politicians of the technical feasibility of various possible policy suggestions and to make estimates of cost. While technical information may be available from non-governmental sources, at the level of cabinet decisions concerning broad policy priorities, the most significant competition for the federal departments will come from the federal central agencies such as Ministries of State or the Department of Finance or from the provincial bureaucracies, through the provincial cabinets and senior bureaucrats.

iv) *Financial information* concerns the fundamental problem of funding governmental projects. When an estimate of the cost of undertaking a certain policy is provided by a line department, the financial advisors to the government in the Ministries of State, the Department of Finance, and the Treasury Board Secretariat, must provide information as to the financial feasibility of the suggested policy. In broad terms, the financial experts within the bureaucracy must advise the government of the day whether they can "afford" the suggested policy and whether implementing this policy will necessitate the increase of taxes or the cancellation of existing programs.

Having obtained political, technical, and financial information about the policy proposal under consideration, the cabinet must ultimately decide whether to act. When there is conflicting advice, the cabinet must make a choice. If the experts do not agree as to the feasibility of the policy suggestion, it is a common response for the cabinet simply not to act at all. The immediate effect here is the same as if a negative decision had been taken.

Another common response to conflicting technical information is for the cabinet to refer the matter to a specialized body for further study. Royal Commissions and task forces can often provide a vehicle through which difficult decisions can be postponed, and at the same time new technical information can be gathered.

Perhaps the most common form of conflicting advice at the level of priority setting is that which occurs between political and technical information. In private, technocrats are very quick to accuse the politicians of "playing politics" when pet projects have been rejected. What often has happened, of course, is that their technical advice has been rejected because of competing advice from the "political techno-crats." In that case, as Jacques Ellul points out, "the conflict is not be-tween politicians and technicians, but among technicians of differing categories."[28] If the advice of the various categories of experts does point in generally the same direction, the cabinet will usually follow that advice. While it is always conceivable that a Prime Minister and cabinet can assert their positional power and refuse to heed advisors, most evidence indicates that Prime Ministers and cabinets do, with a few exceptions, act according to the advice of those with superior information.

Once a number of policy ideas are adopted by the cabinet, the next step is determining which of the policies should be tackled first. This decision is normally implicit in the advice from the technical, political, and financial experts, and can be made without further information. Finally, the decision must be made as to who will formulate the spe-cific alternatives for putting the policy idea into effect. In other words, the cabinet must decide which department or agency will take the re-sponsibility for the next stage in the process, *policy formulation.*

The Formulation of Policy

Until this stage the concern has been with the broad directions of public policy rather than with the specifics. At the formulation stage of the process the object is to narrow down the number of specific choices to a few "best" ones from which the final choice can be made.

There are two analytically separate steps in the formulation of pol-icy alternatives. First, the myriad experts within the public service must design a few workable schemes; second, the politicians must choose the one that appears to be best.

Design activity[29] initially involves narrowing down the number of possible approaches to a workable few; this becomes the responsibil-ity of the more senior "generalists" in a department, likely in consul-tation with other departments and possibly with other levels of gov-ernment as well. Then, those few viable choices must be "fleshed out" through the activity of a great many technocrats often with very specialized expertise. In Galbraith's terms: "Knowledge is brought to bear on the ultimate microfraction of the task; then on that in combi-nation with some other fraction; then, on some further combination and thus on to final completion."[30]

[28] Ellul, *Technological Society,* p. 257.
[29] Simon, *The Scope of Automation.*
[30] Galbraith, *The New Industrial State,* p. 13.

In this sense, only very broad direction is given at the more senior bureaucratic and ministerial levels. The bulk of the responsibility for the ultimate detail of policy resides with the many highly specialized technocrats at lower levels of the hierarchy. The end product is produced incrementally as many individuals make small technical decisions.

Given the incremental nature of the process of policy design, the choice of the politician is seriously curtailed. Departmental proposals have been produced through a hierarchy of decisions, beginning with the most highly specialized at the middle levels and proceeding to ever more general ones at the higher levels. At each higher level of decision making, there is less choice than at the previous one, because there is proportionately less information transmitted with the proposals. By the time the politician, who is at the top of the hierarchy, comes to make the "choice" it often will be simply to accept or reject the incrementally generated and monolithic conclusion of "the department." The choice, in other words, will be determined largely through the design process itself.

Politicians sometimes appear to reject "irrationally" a detailed policy proposal that has been meticulously produced by the technocrats in a department. Normally, however, policies are significantly altered or rejected at this stage only because of new political circumstances. But while a policy must continue to meet important political criteria and while political or budgetary circumstances may temporarily stall the process, in most cases some form of output is inevitable once the formulation process has commenced.

The complicated process we have spelled out here is, in fact, a simplified version of reality; at both the priority and the formulation stages of the policy process innumerable complications can occur. The most pervasive of such complications result from the unavoidable lack of clarity in the jurisdictional boundaries between the federal and the provincial governments and among departments within those governments. As we discuss the policy process in more detail we will see that the Canadian political system has developed an array of devices to handle these complications as well as those already mentioned here.

The Refinement of Policy

At this stage in the policy process, the detailed policy proposal formulated by the bureaucracy and approved formally by the cabinet must be translated into "legalese." The technical details of the policy proposal must be put into the language of legislative outputs. This task is performed by legislative drafters in the Department of Justice, after which the draft legislation must be introduced in parliament as a bill.

The basic problem at this stage of the process is to ensure that the legislative proposal accurately reflects the aims of the priority setters and that there are no ambiguities in the bill that might lead to administrative problems in its implementation. In addition to the legal drafters, the standing committees in the House of Commons play a major role in refining the legislation before it is converted to output. As well, at this time, through discussion and through opposition probing, the government is forced to justify its policy publicly. The legislation is thus legitimized by receiving the "seal of approval" of the people's representatives.

Because of party discipline and because of the complex and technical nature of most legislation, the MP can have relatively little impact on the substance of policy at this stage. Faced with a proposal that has taken years of full-time attention on the part of perhaps a few hundred specialists of different types, the overworked MP, who is not an expert in the field in question, and who must deal with a large number of proposals per session, is unlikely to be able to make substantive criticisms that cannot be answered by the government and its advisors. There has never been a piece of government legislation defeated by the House of Commons in a majority situation, and even with a minority government, government legislation has only been defeated on rare occasions.

Members of Parliament do however have a significant negative power at this stage. It is far from unknown for a government to withdraw legislation previously approved by cabinet in the face of concerted opposition from members of its own caucus and more than one significant piece of government legislation has been withdrawn in the face of concerted opposition threats to hold up the business of the House until the government backs down. However one should not make too much of this power. While the opposition may stall government legislation temporarily because of their control over a considerable amount of time in the House of Commons, this does not happen often and while the government caucus may occasionally be obstreperous it will always in the end rally to the support of its leaders in cabinet. Furthermore, even granting that a parliament could in legal terms reject a government policy proposal, the power here is only negative; the initiative to introduce legislation still resides with the cabinet and if a majority government is really determined that a piece of legislation will pass, it will indeed pass parliament.

Limitations of the Model

Any model abstracts from reality. Accordingly, it distorts some of the features of that reality. One weakness of the policy model posited above is that it attempts to represent a complex and multidimensional process in what is admittedly a linear framework. The "stages" in the policy process are established arbitrarily. In the real world, formulation begins while priorities are being established, new policy ideas emerge in the process of formulating other ones, and governmental priorities occasionally change so drastically during the process of formulation that a policy proposal may die at an advanced stage in its development. Government and, by implication, the governmental policy process is so complex that it cannot accurately be described in such simple terms. A second major weakness of the policy model is that it fails to deal adequately with the policy process in multijurisdictional systems. That is a failing which we will attempt to rectify as we discuss the process in more detail.

But though our model oversimplifies, it does direct our attention to certain patterns which can be observed in the real world. Most of the phenomena we have described as clustering in "stages" do occur at some point in the evolution of any policy. To understand the whole panorama at once would be an impossible task. It is quite simply convenient to view logically related activities as occurring at distinct stages. We are distorting reality in order to understand it! The rest of this text is, in effect, an elaboration of this model in the direction of greater reality.

PART 1

The Cultural and Demographic Environment

2
Environment: Social and Economic Context

The summer of 1973 was a period of rapidly rising food prices in Canada and through-out the western world. The price of steak rose from $1.29 a pound a year earlier to as high as $2.49, and hamburger meat rose from 69¢ to $1.09 a pound. The price of wheat more than doubled in a short time, and the price of a loaf of bread rose by over 33 percent. In the same summer, gasoline which had been available for 40¢ a gallon at discount service stations in June rose to 55 cents in September and to over 60 cents in December. Canada—and indeed all of the western world—was caught in the initial grip of a spiralling inflation. Under circumstances such as these the cry for the government to do something grew louder as individual Canadians felt more and more pinched by the inflation.

Thus went the introductory paragraph of this chapter in the second edition of this text. It went on to point out that the economy was booming and Canada's trade picture had seldom looked better. Many companies were enjoying record levels of revenues produced by rapidly growing personal incomes.

By 1981 Canadian governments faced a very different world. The economic boom had evaporated but the inflation continued. Government revenues were no longer rising rapidly and unemployment had risen into the 8 to 9 percent range. Moreover the ideological background against which government operates had changed significantly. In 1973 there was broad agreement that government was the appropriate tool to solve most major social and economic problems and that more government was a quite acceptable prescription. The neo-conservatism which constitutes the orthodoxy of many opinion leaders at the beginning of the 1980s takes virtually the opposite point of view as its philosophical touchstone.

Consider the conflicting sets of demands on Canadian governments created by the situation in 1981. Many of the nearly one million unemployed badly need government assistance and would hardly agree that unemployment insurance reductions would be beneficial—yet many business people who face persistent problems in keeping employees feel such cutbacks to be essential. Female members of the labour force are consistently paid less then their male counterparts and that situation is unlikely to change much without considerable government intervention—yet such intervention is difficult for government in a period whenever bigger government is not in style. Inflation, economic orthodoxy tells us, cannot be cured without extremely high interest rates, restricted money supplies and reduced government spending—solutions which now appear to be more surely guaranteed to create higher unemployment and lower economic growth than to cure inflation. Yet governments are still expected to deal with unemployment and inflation. Consumers object to higher oil prices; oil companies demand them. Provincial governments of oil-producing provinces feel far differently about increased oil prices than do the governments of consuming provinces, again producing conflicting sets of demands for federal political authorities to handle.

Now consider the sources of these problems. Inflation was endemic throughout the world and frequently higher among Canada's major financial partners than in Canada. When those trading partners raised interest rates to record levels, most Canadian leaders felt Canada had little choice but to follow. After all there is nothing so readily transportable as money and it will flow to the place where it gets the highest interest. The effect on Canada's already depressed currency could have been devastating and since Canada imports such a large proportion of what it consumes, the effect on inflation would have been very severe.

Oil prices are in part determined in Canada by a complex process of federal-provincial bargaining but the real framework within which that bargaining takes place is established by the OPEC cartel over which Canadian governments have no influence. The prices of basic foods are determined by climatic conditions throughout the world. The weather in China or Russia is far more important in determining the prices Prairie farmers receive for their grain than is anything which happens in Canada, and hog prices in Canada depend largely on how many hogs U.S. Midwestern farmers raise.

Now consider the policy conundrum created for governments by forces such as these. Neo-conservatism demands decreased government spending—one million unemployed, an increased welfare load, and the need to protect steadily increasing numbers of pensioners against inflation make that nearly impossible. Inflation calls for high interest rates—which can create a recession. Hog farmers want protection from low-priced imports—consumers certainly do not. The price of oil must be raised to encourage further production—but not so much as to alienate the vast majority of voters who are consumers. What policy choices is a government to make in view of all these forces?

The cynic will suggest that in trying to please everyone the federal government will please no one, and that its raft of self-contradictory policies is bound to founder. The optimist will assert that government action does somewhat alleviate the problem and that no government is doing a better job than Canada's. We need not take either position here for our object is only to point out the difficulty of the problem: these are typical illustrations of the types of conflicting demands which can be generated by the environment of a political system and they push decision makers in contradictory directions.

Another illustration of influences from the environment can be found in the federal response to pressures from French Canada. Since Confederation, the federal public service has been basically unilingual and, particularly over the last fifty years, there have been relatively few French Canadians in the upper levels of the service. This made it difficult for French-speaking Canadians to communicate with the federal public service and was thought by federal politicians to be partially responsible for the increase in unrest in Quebec in the 1960s and 1970s. No one attributed French Canada's "quiet revolution" and the growth of its unquiet aspects solely to this cause, but the situation in Quebec did put pressure upon federal political decision makers and created a strain within the Canadian political system which could only be alleviated by structural change. One of the structural changes was that the federal government decided to make the federal public service bilingual by establishing training programs for its employees and by emphasizing bilingualism in its recruitment programs. Later it created the Official Languages Act intended to make it possible for French Canadians to deal with the federal government in French wherever there were significant concentrations of Francophones. The success of these programs in creating a truly bilingual civil service and in allaying discontent in Quebec is still in doubt and they have evoked a degree of backlash in parts of English Canada; but the programs demonstrate the type of change which may be induced within a political system through stress generated by its own social environment and the kind of reciprocal stress which may subsequently be generated in the environment.

Few of the stresses generated by the environment of a political system are simple. What pleases French-speaking Quebeckers may not please English-speaking Albertans, and what pleases farmers may not please consumers. Moreover, the more complex the environment of a political system, the more complex the demands it generates. The reconciliation of these various demands, the balancing of one against another, is at the heart of the political process. In some cases the competition can be reconciled through the economic system or other social systems, but in Canada today it is more and more often the political system which allocates the available resources among competing groups which make up the social environment.

CLEAVAGE AND CONSENSUS

Many of the conflicting demands which impinge upon a political system are generated by cleavages. The term cleavage is used rather loosely in political science, sometimes referring to differences of opinion over specific issues and other times referring to generalized splits created by differences in the environment. In this book we will use the term in the latter sense.

Specific differences over particular items will be referred to simply as issues. Thus we shall speak of a general "cleavage" between French and English Canadians, whereas a specific difference between French and English Canadians over a particular matter such as educational institutions within Quebec would be referred to as an "issue."

Cleavages created by one factor are often reinforced by another. For example, the cultural cleavage between French- and English-speaking Canadians is reinforced by the fact that most French Canadians live in one province (creating a geographical cleavage), and that that province is one of the less well developed in Canada (creating an economic cleavage). When cleavages are reinforced by a number of factors they naturally tend to become more difficult for the political system because they generate more issues which then tend to reinforce the original cleavage.

We have described politics as a process of both conflict and cooperation. The conflict arises from cleavage; from what does the cooperation arise? Consider for a moment what happens within a group of people who are in conflict with another group over some issue. A consensus, which we define as a state of agreement among a group of people over the desirability of some end, may well form within the group over the issue in question and possibly over a common stance to adopt. For instance, among residents of the Atlantic provinces there is a near-unanimous agreement that it is appropriate government policy to subsidize the costs of imported oil in order to bring its cost to the consumer in line with the price paid for oil in other Canadian provinces. This consensus is further strengthened by the fact that many issues based upon geographic and economic cleavages divide the residents of the Atlantic provinces from those in other parts of Canada.

A consensus is often specific to a particular issue. It is therefore not simply the opposite of a cleavage. There may be substantial disagreement within a group over other issues. However, the consensus created by one issue may spill over into other areas as well, simply because the people involved come to know each other or because their leaders find the coalitions so created to be useful over longer periods of time. Moreover, conflict between large groups tends to create large areas of consensus. A war against an external enemy can do wonders to unify a divided nation.

There is another type of consensus which for the political process in general is perhaps more important than that within sub-groups of a society about particular issues. It is a consensus not so much about what is to be done as about how things are to be done—the process by which outputs are produced. It is particularly important when applied to politics because of the implication that even if a group does not agree with the political decisions that have been made, it will abide by them because they have been made in keeping with the accepted rules of the game. This *procedural consensus* is closely linked to the concept of legitimacy. If there is a fairly broad agreement on the process by which decisions are made, the political system attains an important element of stability and legitimacy not present in systems which lack procedural consensus.

To sum up, where there is unity over either one item or a broad range of items or procedures, we speak of a consensus. Where there is a division over one item we speak of that division as an issue. A cleavage is a division in society caused by cultural, economic, or geographical factors which may cause differences between groups over any number of issues. It is the environment of a political system which generates cleavages, issues, and consensus. It is the major function of a political system to reduce the intensity of cleavages in such a way as to generate sufficient consensus for the political community to persist.

In the rest of this chapter and in the next we will look at the three most important types of cleavage in the environment of Canadian politics: geographical and general economic cleavages, cleavages based on stratification, and ethnic cleavages. The first type is often referred to as a vertical cleavage and the second as a horizontal cleavage. We shall ask two questions about all these types: (1) Of what does it consist? (2) What are its political consequences? Perhaps by the end of the chapter we will recognize that the Canadian political system exists in spite of immense difficulties generated by its environment and that even with all its warts and blemishes, it is quite unique among the political experiments of humanity.

GEOGRAPHIC AND ECONOMIC CLEAVAGES

Canada is unique among nations in that she shares a land border with only one other nation—a giant ten times her size. She is separated from all the rest of the world by thousands of miles of water, land, or ice. This geographic situation has led Canada to rely on trade patterns which are overwhelmingly dominated by exchanges with the United States. Thus, in 1977, 69.8 percent of Canada's exports went to the

United States and 70.3 percent of imports came from there. Our next biggest trading partner was Japan, which took less than 6 percent of Canada's exports, and the whole of the European Common Market took only a little over 6 percent.[1] Canada has had a balance of trade surplus in every year but one since 1961, but that surplus tends to be counterbalanced by the outflow of Canadian dollars as dividends and interest payments to foreign sources, particularly in the United States.[2]

Canada is the sixth largest trading nation in the Western world, ranking behind the United States, West Germany, England, Japan, and France. In terms of trade per capita, it ranks tenth. Less populous countries tend to have higher per capita figures than larger countries, so that in this respect Canada is outranked by such nations as the Netherlands, Belgium, Switzerland, and Sweden.

Canada is in a more difficult position than such countries in two important respects. First, she does not belong to any regional trading block as do other small nations similarly dependent upon trade. This gives them a form of access, which Canada lacks, to large and stable markets with relatively low or nonexistent trade barriers. Canada is thus exposed to rapidly changing world conditions in a way that they are not. In part this problem has been overcome through the negotiation of a series of special agreements with the United States; at least 15 percent of Canada's gross national product is generated by trade with the U.S. and one out of every two jobs in goods-producing industry depends upon that trade.[3] By contrast less than 2 percent of the U.S. GNP is directly dependent on trade with Canada.

Canada is principally an exporter of primary goods and an importer of secondary or manufactured goods. Thus in 1977, only 34.5 percent of Canadian exports were fully manufactured "end products" whereas 61.7 percent of imports were fully manufactured. American exports are usually about 37 percent primary goods and European Economic Community exports are usually about 33 percent primary goods.[4] Primary goods such as lumber, agricultural products, and metals are far more susceptible to international competition than are

---

[1] Statistics Canada, *Canada Year Book, 1978-79*, pp. 728-30. Canada's trade ties with the U.S. have been growing in recent years but they have also come into closer balance. In 1964 the U.S. provided 68.9 percent of Canada's imports and took only 52.7 percent of Canadian exports; in that year, Britain bought 14.8 percent of Canadian exports. By 1971 the U.S. provided 70.3 percent of Canada's imports and took 67.5 percent of her exports.

[2] *Canada Year Book, 1978-79*, pp. 758-59.

[3] Standing Senate Committee on Foreign Affairs, *Canada-United States Relations,* vol. II (Queen's Printer, Ottawa, 1978), p. 5.

[4] 1971 Canadian figures are from *Canada Year Book, 1978-79*, pp. 759-60. Comparative data is available in United Nations, *Yearbook of International Trade Statistics.*

manufactured goods, because the latter often depend upon specialized knowledge and techniques specific to one particular nation. Exports of primary goods may be suddenly and drastically affected by unpredictable factors, such as rainfall in Russia and China, or the discovery of nickel deposits in New Caledonia. For example, the effects of the Depression were worsened in Canada not only by a prolonged drought in our own wheat-growing area but by good growing conditions in some other wheat-producing areas of the world. On the other hand, primary products are becoming very scarce and the rapidly rising prices for primary goods have left the Canadian economy in a relatively strong position. Being hewers of wood and drawers of water is not necessarily all bad if one has plenty of wood and water.

In sum, Canada's global position forces her to be more heavily dependent on the United States for her trade relationships than many of her political decision makers and citizens might prefer. However, unlike the trade of such countries as Britain and Japan, much of Canada's import trade is for discretionary items. Whereas without trade Britain could scarcely produce enough food to survive, relatively few of the most basic necessities of diet or shelter need be imported into Canada. Ultimately, Canada does have some flexibility which may not be available to other nations.

Canada and the United States

The Canadian preoccupation with the United States is readily understandable in view of the foregoing trade figures. During a visit to Washington early in 1969, Pierre Trudeau suggested that sharing a continent with the United States was rather like sleeping with an elephant—he may not know you're there, but you must be sensitive to his every twitch.[5] The elephant in this case has a population ten times as large as Canada and generates twelve times the gross national product. Over 90 percent of Canadians live within 300 miles of the United States and most live in a narrow strip within 100 miles of the borders.[6] The presence of Canada is of relatively little consequence to the United States but the presence of the United States is of immense consequence to Canada.[7]

Defence and Foreign Affairs   This geographic position has significant consequences for Canada's military position. As recently as 1895 the Canadian military made substantial defence preparations against

[5] Prime Minister Trudeau in a speech to the Washington Press Club, March 25, 1969.
[6] T. R. Weir, "The People," in John Warkentin (ed.), *Canada: A Geographic Interpretation* (Methuen, Toronto, 1968), p. 138.
[7] See John H. Redekop, "Continentalism: The Key to Canadian Politics" in his *Approaches to Canadian Politics* (Prentice-Hall, Scarborough, 1978), pp. 28-57 for a more extensive description of the U.S. impact on Canada. Redekop has provided a valuable annotated bibliography on the subject, pp. 55-57. In addition to the specific sources

the U.S. Even between the two World Wars, the only defence plans drawn up by the Canadian military were for defence from an attack from the south! Fears of a direct attack have finally vanished—or at least Canadians have recognized the dubious benefits of defence against an immensely improbable military enemy which, in any case, could not be resisted.

In a more significant sense, however, Canada's proximity to the U.S. still shapes Canadian defence policy. It makes Canada strategically one target with the United States; an attacker would hardly discriminate between these two parts of North America. In the period prior to 1941, when America was not particularly active in world affairs, this was not too important. But since the end of World War II American involvement in world politics has led, among other things, to the formation of regional alliances such as NATO (the North Atlantic Treaty Organization) and NORAD (the North American Air Defence Command) in which Canada has of necessity participated. Whether the necessity was felt because of American pressure on the Canadian government or because of some real conviction on the part of Canadian politicians is not particularly important; the point is that the American presence on our doorstep would, in any case, have made abstention difficult and withdrawal impossible. Changing world circumstances and changing American commitments may be more important than anything Canada can do in determining a valid Canadian defence and foreign policy.[8]

Cultural Encroachments   Perhaps more important in the long run than the various military and foreign policy ramifications of American

cited below, the general reader should consult Janet Morchain (ed.), *Sharing a Continent* (Toronto, McGraw-Hill Ryerson, 1973); Andrew Axline et al (eds), *Continental Community* (Toronto, McClelland & Stewart, 1974); J. S. Dickey, *Canada and the American Presence* (New York, New York University Press, 1975); Ian Lumsden (ed), *Close the 49th Parallel Etc.* (Toronto, University of Toronto Press, 1970); and Joseph Nye and Robert Keohane, *Power and Interdependence* (Little, Brown, Boston, 1977).

[8] For further discussions and elaborations of Canada's role in world affairs and in particular her place in NORAD and NATO see: P. V. Lyon, *The Policy Question* (McClelland and Stewart, Toronto, 1963); J. W. Holmes, *The Better Part of Valour: Essays on Canadian Diplomacy* (Carleton Library, Toronto, 1970), and *Canada and the United States: Political and Security Issues* (Canadian Institute of International Affairs, Toronto, 1970); J. L. Granatstein, *Canadian Foreign Policy Since 1945: Middle Power or Satellite?* (Copp Clark, Toronto, 1969); Jan B. McLin, *Canada's Changing Defense Policy, 1957-63* (Copp Clark, Toronto, 1967); L. Hertzman, John Warnock, and Thomas Hockin, *Alliances and Illusions: Canada and the NATO-NORAD Question* (Hurtig, Edmonton, 1969); J. Eayrs, *The Art of the Possible: Government and Foreign Policy in Canada* (University of Toronto Press, Toronto, 1961); J. Eayrs, *Northern Approaches: Canada and the Search for Peace* (Macmillan, Toronto, 1961); P. V. Lyon and B. W. Tomlin, *Canada as An International Actor* (MacMillan, Toronto 1979); J. W. Holmes, *Canada: A Middle-Aged Power* (McClelland and Stewart, Toronto, 1976); D. C. Thomson and R. F. Swanson, *Canadian Foreign Policy: Options and Perspectives* (McGraw-Hill Ryerson, Toronto, 1971); and N. Hillmer and G. Stevenson, *Foremost Nation: Canadian Foreign Policy and a Changing World* (McClelland and Stewart, Toronto, 1977).

proximity to Canada is cultural encroachment. A number of factors facilitate the imposition of American culture on Canada and most of them derive basically from our geographical proximity.[9] American television reaches almost everyone in Canada. English-Canadian stations carry a great deal of American programming, and more important, some 55 percent of Canadians are in direct range of American television stations and some 90 percent can receive them on cable systems. In areas where both Canadian and American sources are available the latter are generally preferred. For example, Colborne, Ontario, a town of about 1,400 located some 80 miles from Toronto, receives at least two Canadian and three American television stations. In October of 1968 an extensive survey was conducted of all the town's students in grades 4, 5, 6, and 7. Eighty-two percent of the children interviewed claimed to watch the news on television sometimes or every day, and of these over 56 percent usually watched American news broadcasts.[10] In 1973 a survey in Toronto showed only 13 percent of evening viewers watching Canadian programs and in prime time only 9 percent.[11] Children and adults alike pick up cultural images from television and consequently are socialized by it.[12] This is one of the ways in which the values of American culture may be imported into Canada.[13]

Much of French Canada is also within range of American television, but fewer French Canadians watch American channels because of the language barrier. The Canadian content of the French network of the CBC is much higher than that of the English network, so the television exposure of French Canadians to foreign culture has been less than that of English Canadians. The language barrier has been instrumental in helping to preserve French-Canadian culture from the overwhelming geographical proximity of the United States.

The problems of preserving a cultural identity in English-speaking Canada are compounded when the effects of radio, magazines, and other segments of the mass media are added in. In 1969, 95 percent of all the various magazines available in Canadian retail outlets were

---

[9] For an extensive discussion see S. M. Crean, *Who's Afraid of Canadian Culture* (General Publishing, Don Mills, 1970).

[10] John Hill, "The Political Socialization of Children in a Rural Environment," (Unpublished B.A. thesis, Queen's University, 1969), p. 52.

[11] Redekop, *Approaches to Canadian Politics*, p. 47.

[12] Political socialization is the learning of the political values and behaviour patterns of a society. Canadian political socialization will be discussed at some length in Chapter 5.

[13] There is recognition of this fact at many levels in Canadian government and there are even occasional attempts to counteract the problem. For example, in 1970 the Canadian Radio Television Commission (CRTC) announced a series of steps to increase the Canadian content of radio, prime-time television, and cablevision services. This has no doubt helped, but what viewers watch cannot be dictated and English Canadian viewers still watch American television.

American imports. For decades the two American giants—*Time* and *Reader's Digest* took about 40 percent of total magazine advertising in Canada. The *Reader's Digest* had a circulation of 1,250,000 monthly and *Time* 550,000. In 1969 *Maclean's* switched to the size and format used by *Time* so that ads appearing in the giant American magazine could be switched to *Maclean's* at no additional cost.[14] But because *Maclean's* could not simply use editorial material prepared for the U.S. market, the rates for advertising in *Maclean's* remained much higher. In 1976 a Canadian content legislation brought about the demise of the Canadian edition of *Time* but most subscribers simply switched to the U.S. edition and so did the advertisers. As the Davey Committee on the mass media noted, "We spend more money buying American comic books than we do on seventeen leading Canadian-owned magazines."[15]

While the military implications of proximity to the United States are often viewed by Canadians with resignation if not applause, and while cultural domination is frequently decried, it is the economic dimension of United States-Canadian relations which often receives the most publicity. We have already indicated the closeness of trade ties between the two neighbours, but there are other crucial aspects of Canadian-United States economic relations which deserve attention.

The Foreign Investment Question Table 2-1 indicates two basic trends in the picture of foreign investment in Canada. First, the ratio of foreign investment to gross national product has been decreasing, which at first hand would appear to suggest that the situation is improving. Second, the proportion of foreign investment held by Amer-

Table 2-1

CANADIAN BALANCE OF INTERNATIONAL INDEBTEDNESS, 1926-1975 (PORTFOLIO AND DIRECT INVESTMENT)

	1926	1939	1949	1959	1969	1975
Gross liabilities (in billions of dollars)	6.4	7.4	9.3	23.8	46.9	75.6
Percent held in U.S.	55	61	69	71	74	75
Percent held in U.K.	42	35	19	14	10	8
Gross national product (in billions of dollars)	5.1	5.6	16.3	32.3	79.8	165.4
Foreign indebtedness as percent of GNP	125	132	57	74	59	46

Source: *Canada Year Book,* 1972, pp. 1177 and 1211, and *Canada Year Book,* 1978-79, pp. 871-2, adapted.

[14] Redekop, *Approaches to Canadian Politics*, p. 48.
[15] Ibid.

icans has steadily increased and that held by Britons has steadily decreased. We will examine below the ramifications of the latter point.

The first point is deceptive because the nature of foreign investment has changed significantly since 1926. The more normal form of investment before World War II was "portfolio" investment— primarily in bonds or debentures which gave the investor relatively little managerial control over the firm. Since 1945, investment has been increasingly "direct," that is in the shares of a firm, which may give the investor control over what the company actually does.[16] Moreover, in accounting for the amount of international indebtedness, Statistics Canada uses the "book value" of foreign-controlled assets—a value relecting the original cost of assets rather than their value after the inflation—whereas GNP figures reflect the full impact of inflation. Thus when uninflated book values are compared to inflated GNP figures, the magnitude of direct foreign investment appears to decrease. However, even with these caveats, the fact remains that foreign investment is not now as great as it once was.

Table 2-2 indicates the changes in the percentage of Canadian in-

Table 2-2

NON-RESIDENT CONTROL* AS A PERCENTAGE OF SELECTED CANADIAN INDUSTRIES, 1926-1976

Percentage of Total Controlled by All Non-Residents

	1926	1939	1948	1963	1969	1976
Manufacturing	35	38	43	60	60	57
Petroleum and natural gas	—	—	—	74	74	73
Mining and smelting	38	42	40	59	70	57
Railways	3	3	3	2	2	1
Other utilities	20	26	24	4	6	4
TOTAL	17	21	25	34	36	33

Percentage of Total Controlled by U.S. Residents

Manufacturing	30	32	39	46	47	43
Petroleum and natural gas	—	—	—	62	60	57
Mining and smelting	32	38	37	52	59	44
Railways	3	3	3	2	2	1
Other utilities	20	26	24	4	4	4
TOTAL	15	19	22	27	28	35

*Control is computed as percentage of total output in that sector from companies over 50 percent foreign-owned.
Source: *International Investment Position,* 1975, Statistics Canada, 1979, p. 35.

[16] See I. A. Litvak, C. J. Maule, and R. D. Robinson, *Dual Loyalty* (McGraw-Hill Ryerson, Toronto, 1971), p. 2. In 1926 there was twice as much portfolio investment as direct investment. The situation has now reversed.

dustry controlled by non-residents and by United States residents. The table indicates that the extent of foreign control over Canadian industry may have peaked in the mid to late 1960s but that it has declined very little from its peak levels.

The table also demonstrates that not all Canadian industries have fallen under foreign control. For example, at various times Canadian governments have decided that banking and finance, railways, communications, insurance, and uranium mining were too vital to be allowed to fall into the hands of foreigners.[17] But foreign control is concentrated in many of Canada's most profitable and fastest growing manufacturing and resource industries. A number of questions follow from these facts. How did ownership of Canadian industry get that way? What is wrong with foreign ownership? What have Canadian responses been? The complete story of how so much of Canadian industry came to be owned by foreigners cannot be covered in an elementary text, but a couple of explanations are of interest.[18]

Firstly, some responsibility for the situation must be laid squarely on a policy which was designed to avoid American domination. Macdonald's famous "National Policy" of the nineteenth century had three prongs: build railways, encourage immigration, and erect tariff barriers. The first two components of the policy did serve the purpose of preempting United States settlement in the Northwest and preserving that territory for Canada. The third component, designed to encourage Canadian industry, backfired. What happened was that foreign firms—first British and later American—seeing a lucrative territory for their investments, moved in behind the tariff barriers which protected them from competition. They then set up miniature replicas of their home operations but without any attempt to develop and implement new technology or to sell to wider markets. To add to the problem, most of the plants they set up were too small to be highly productive, leading to a situation where Canadian productivity has been persistently lower than that of her major trading partners. Meanwhile, other foreign entrepreneurs, who must be given credit

---

[17] Ibid., p. 7.

[18] There is an immense economics literature on the effects of foreign ownership in Canada and it cannot all be cited here. However, the key works are *The Report of the Task Force on Foreign Ownership and the Structure of Canadian Industry*: The Watkins Report (Queen's Printer, Ottawa, 1965); A. E. Safarian, *Foreign Ownerships of Canadian Industry*, (McGraw-Hill, Toronto, 1966); A. Rotstein (ed.), *The Prospect of Change* (McGraw-Hill, Toronto, 1965); Kari Levitt, *Silent Surrender* (Liveright, New York; published in Canada by Macmillan, Toronto, 1970), (Student Edition, 1971); Litvak, *Dual Loyalty; Foreign Direct Investment in Canada* (Ottawa, Queen's Printer, 1972), most widely known as the Gray Report; P. Marchak, *In Whose Interest?*; G. Teeple, *Capitalism and the National Question in Canada*; R. Laxer, *(Canada) Ltd.*

for seeing more possibilities in Canadian resource industries than did Canadians themselves, invested in primary industry and exported the primary goods to their own home bases to be made into manufactured goods, thus providing jobs for workers in other nations. It is extremely difficult for governments to foresee all the consequences of the policies they make and in this case, one consequence of Macdonalds National Policy was, ironically, exactly the opposite of what was intended.

Another argument often advanced to explain the prevalence of American ownership in the Canadian economy is that Americans have provided necessary capital which was not otherwise available. Table 2-3 indicates, however, that Canada's need for foreign investment to ensure her economic growth is largely fictional: the capital that has been used by foreign entrepreneurs to expand Canadian industry is Canadian, not foreign.

Table 2-3

USE OF FOREIGN AND DOMESTIC RESOURCES IN GROSS CAPITAL FORMATION IN CANADA, SELECTED YEARS 1950-1977

	1950	1955	1960	1965	1977
Gross capital formation (in billions of dollars)	4.5	6.6	8.7	13.7	47.6
Percent from domestic sources	84	74	74	79	87

Source: Adapted from Statistics Canada, *The Canadian Balance of International Payments and International Investment Position, 1963, 1964, 1965,* Queen's Printer, Ottawa, p. 76, and cited in I.A. Litvak et al., *Dual Loyalty,* p. 3. The 1977 figures are from *Canada Year Book, 1978-9,* p. 859 and p. 871.

At no time since records have been kept has foreign capital ever been more than 30 percent of total new investments in a given year.[19] In 1977, the last year for which figures were available, only about one-eighth of the capital used to expand Canadian industry came from foreign sources. Kari Levitt has put the case bluntly:

It is simply not true that Canada is short of capital. The expensive infrastructure required by her peculiar geography has long been put in place and paid for. . . . The brutal fact is that acquisition of control by U.S. companies over the commodity-producing sectors of the Canadian economy has largely been financed from corporate savings deriving from the sale of Canadian resources, extracted and processed by Canadian labour, or from the sale(s) of branch plant manufacturing businesses to Canadian consumers at tariff-protected prices. Thus over the period 1957 to 1964 U.S. direct

[19] Litvak, *Dual Loyalty,* pp. 21-2.

investments in manufacturing, mining, and petroleum secured 73 percent of their funds from retained earnings and depreciation reserves, a further 12 percent from Canadian banks and other intermediaries and only 15 percent in the form of new funds from the United States. Furthermore, throughout the period, payout of dividends, interest, royalties, and management fees exceeded the inflow of new capital. [20]

The question then arises—so what? What difference does it make if a considerable proportion of Canadian industry is U.S. controlled? Foreign control may be undesirable for reasons related to both economic growth and economic stability. [21] To the extent that Canada depends on the investment decisions of foreign-controlled corporations she is vulnerable to changes in her growth patterns depending on how these operations see their growth prospects elsewhere in the world. Since 1950 United States corporations have concentrated their foreign investments (some of which are financed by the earnings of Canadian subsidiaries) in Europe and in developing areas with low labour costs such as Korea, Hong Kong, or Taiwan rather than in Canada. The corporations involved can always cite good reasons but the fact remains that the economic stability of Canada and the job opportunities for her residents can be influenced by decisions made by foreign firms. If these decisions run contrary to Canadian economic needs they may destabilize the Canadian economy and Canadian governments have little real control over them.

Another factor to consider is that Canada has experienced chronic and increasing problems with her balance of payments and this severely limits the freedom of Canadian governments in managing the economy. The problem does not arise from an inability to sell goods (particularly resource-based goods) abroad; Canada normally has a surplus in its merchandise trade accounts. Rather the problem stems primarily from the need to service the Canadian debt and most particularly from the heavy flow of dividends to foreign investors. For example in 1977 a merchandise trade surplus of $2.9 billions was obliterated by interest and dividend payments of $4.3 billions. [22] Moreover, these figures probably greatly understate the case, for various accounting devices can be used to transfer funds back to foreign head offices without declaring dividends and without ever paying Canadian taxes.

With regard to individual firms, concern has been expressed that foreign ownership results in a situation whereby research and development activities are not carried out in Canada; that insufficient

[20] Levitt, *Silent Surrender*, Student Edition, pp. 63-64.
[21] Litvak, *Dual Loyalty*, pp. 21-2.
[22] *Canada Year Book, 1978-79*, pp. 570-71.

numbers of Canadians have access to management roles; that exports to third countries are usually from the home base plant; that supplies are not purchased in Canada; and, that the firms evade taxation by various subterfuges.[23] Yet, "with regard to most of these activities, researchers have found that, in fact, American affiliates perform as well, if not better, than comparable Canadian firms but worse than comparable American firms in the U.S."[24] Nonetheless, after considering all these factors, the 1972 federal study *Foreign Direct Investment in Canada* (the "Gray Report") was introduced by the statement that:

The high and growing degree of foreign and particularly U.S. control of Canadian business activity has led to a Canadian industrial structure which largely reflects the growth priorities of foreign corporations (and has) . . . led to the establishment of "truncated" firms for which many important functions are performed abroad by the parent company with the result that Canadian capacities or activities in these areas is stultified. . . . These developments have made it more difficult for the government to control the domestic national economic environment. They have also influenced the development of the social, political, and cultural environment in Canada.

Extraterritoriality   As the Gray Report indicates, the problems posed by foreign subsidiaries cannot be understood or dealt with solely in economic terms. Perhaps the major political problem created by the more than 9,000 American-owned factories in Canada is that of extraterritoriality—the application of the laws of one nation within the boundaries of another. In 1957 a Canadian trader charged that Ford Canada had refused to ship trucks to China because of fear that the parent company would be penalized under the United States Treasury's Foreign Assets Control Regulations and the United States' Trading with the Enemy Act. That case was never satisfactorily resolved, in part because the order itself was mysteriously withdrawn by the Chinese when it began to appear possible that it would be filled. In 1958 John Diefenbaker obtained assurances from President Eisenhower that, to quote Diefenbaker:

If cases arose in the future where the refusal of orders by companies operating in Canada might have an effect on Canadian economic activity, the U.S. government would consider favourably exempting the parent company in the U.S. from the application of foreign asset control regulations with respect to such orders.[25]

Yet some incidents continued and some Canadian subsidiaries shied

---

[23] Litvak, *Dual Loyalty*, p. 22.
[24] Ibid.
[25] Canada, House of Commons, *Debates* (Hansard), July 14, 1958, p. 2142 and quoted in Litvak, *Dual Loyalty*, p. 25.

away from trade with North Vietnam, North Korea, and Cuba for fear of the U.S. Trading with the Enemy Act or adverse U.S. reaction which might affect their markets.[26]

The United States regulations were changed in 1969 to permit U.S. subsidiaries to trade with China, but as some analysts point out: "This change in policy clearly confirms that these policies do have an extraterritorial reach."[27] A more recent example further confirmed that the Trading with the Enemy Act still potentially hampered the activity of Canadian firms which are subsidiaries of American ones but also seemed to indicate that the policy of the U.S. administration was not to apply the Act in most cases. In 1974, a Montreal locomotive company, MLW-Worthington Ltd., had arranged to build twenty-five locomotives for Cuba, a transaction with costs estimated at $18 million. Trouble arose, however, when the American parent company, Studebaker-Worthington, Inc., felt obliged under the Trading with the Enemy Act to seek a licence for the transaction from the American government.[28] For weeks the American government made no decision on the matter. Ultimately, after considerable controversy in the Canadian press and very substantial pressure from the Canadian government, the Canadian subsidiary's board of directors did vote to go ahead with the sale, although the American members of the board voted against it in the hope of avoiding personal prosecution by the U.S. government.[29] The chronology of this case indicates that even though the U.S. government chose not to intervene directly to block the sale to Cuba, the policy defined by the Trading with the Enemy Act could affect the behaviour of the Canadian company. There have been no recent instances of problems of this particular form of extraterritoriality but the legislation remains an annoying reminder of some aspects of Canada's lack of economic sovereignty. It also indicates that by the mid 1970s, in most foreseeable cases the Trading with the Enemy Act was "manageable" from Canada's point of view, for the U.S. would not apply it in the face of a strong Canadian stance.

There have been several other instances when other U.S. regulations have been applied to the Canadian political system through U.S.-controlled firms operating in Canada. For example, in January 1968 the U.S. introduced mandatory controls on foreign investment

[26] Litvak, *Dual Loyalty*, pp. 25-6.
[27] Ibid., p. 26.
[28] Geoffrey Stevens, "Like the Bad Old Days," *Globe and Mail*, February 27, 1974, p. 6.
[29] *Globe and Mail*, Saturday, March 9, 1974.

by U.S. companies. This resulted in an outflow of Canadian funds to the U.S., and it was not until March that Canada was able to gain some exemptions to avoid too much damage to her economy. Despite the existence of a U.S.-Canada consultative committee to discuss problems such as these, the Canadian government had no warning of the move or of similar and even more drastic moves by the U.S. in August 1971. Balance of payment difficulties in the U.S. can thus be transmitted to Canada via subsidiaries of U.S. firms.

More broadly, U.S. antitrust legislation applies to all aspects of the operations of U.S.-controlled firms. In some cases the U.S. legislation may run into Canadian government policy when the latter attempts to encourage the creation of firms of sufficient size to be internationally competitive.

Aside from these general problems and potential problems there have also been less important but equally upsetting instances of misbehaviour by individual U.S. firms in Canada, aided by the U.S. government. Two examples are particularly glaring. The first involved the purchase of the Mercantile Bank of Canada by the New York-based Rockefeller interests. Canadian officials warned the Rockefellers that the Canadian government would act retroactively to limit foreign holdings of Canadian banks if U.S. interests purchased more than 25 percent of the Mercantile. The Rockefellers went ahead with this purchase and then were able to apply sufficient economic and political pressure through the U.S. State Department to ensure that the Canadian government did not act.[30]

The second involved a Canadian decision no longer to allow businesses to deduct from their taxes expenditures on advertising in foreign-owned periodicals even if these had a Canadian supplement and were printed in Canada. The idea was to encourage the Canadian magazine industry. The publications which stood to lose most by the regulation were *Time* and *Reader's Digest*, and the owner of the former, Henry Luce, was able to apply sufficient pressure, again through the State Department in Washington, to ensure that the Canadian government did not carry out its policy for more than five years after it had stated its intentions.[31]

It should be apparent by now that foreign investment has been at best a mixed blessing for Canadians. Canadian policy makers feel inhibited, at least to some extent, in promoting economic policies aimed

[30] Peter Newman, *The Distemper of Our Times* (McClelland and Stewart, 1968), pp. 418-23, 511-518.
[31] Ibid., pp. 224-6. The legislation (an amendment to the Income Tax Act) was finally passed in 1976.

at serving Canadian political interests. Their international trade policies must constantly take account of U.S. interests, as must their taxation and monetary policies. When Canadian prime interest rates rose to over 17 percent in 1980 the sole justification provided was that increases in the U.S. rate had made the Canadian increases necessary. The promotion of east-west ties within Canada is made difficult by the prevalence of north-south economic relationships, and the provision of distinctive Canadian wage and social security policies may be made more difficult by the presence of both multinational corporations and international unions. The desire to provide more employment for Canadians in secondary industry using Canadian raw materials may be subverted, not necessarily intentionally, by the decisions of firms whose primary loyalty is to workers in another country.

Canada has attempted to counter these problems. There are laws relating to the level of foreign investment in key sectors, there is a 15 percent withholding tax on interest and dividends to foreigners, and much of the financial disclosure legislation currently on the books in Canada is aimed at foreign companies. In December 1973 the federal government passed legislation which set up a Foreign Investment Review Agency (FIRA) to advise cabinet on the acceptability of the takeover of Canadian companies or the expansion into Canada by foreign corporations. There have been several bilateral agreements with the U.S. government such as that made by Diefenbaker and Eisenhower in 1958. But, with the exception of the automobile agreements, the effects of these has been judged by some commentators to be a mixed success at best from Canada's point of view. One perspective is provided in the following quotation:

To date the bilateral consultations and arrangements between Canada and the U.S. have rarely realized Canadian objectives because the political bargaining takes place between two very unequal partners. Canada is fully able to articulate the problems to the U.S. government but it lacks the political power to negotiate mutually beneficial solutions. . . . In short, as the two economies become more closely integrated along "continentalist" (North American) lines, the threat to Canadian political sovereignty is escalated. . . . Experience to date has shown that Canada alone has little political bargaining power, vis-à-vis the U.S. in cases where the loci of decision-making power are centered in U.S. multinational corporations, and where the U.S. government has been unwilling to renounce the extraterritorial reach of its laws.[32]

However, it must be recognized that there is another analytical perspective on the situation. In *Power and Interdependence* Joseph Nye and Robert Keohane have attempted to "score" Canada-U.S. agreements in the postwar era to determine which country has most often come

[32] Litvak, *Dual Loyalty*, p. 154.

out ahead and they then compared the Canada-U.S. scores with similar results from Australia-U.S. relationships.[33] Surprisingly they found that for the majority of the decisions in question, Canada came out ahead in economic terms and that Canada did much better than Australia in relations with the U.S. It seems then that empirical reality may not always fit initial perceptions. Given Canadian tenderness on the issue of Canada-U.S. relations, the Canadian press and public may tend to make a major issue out of cases where Canadian interests are imperilled and very little of the majority of cases where Canada's interests are well served.

In any event it is quite clear that one of the most vital features of the environment of the Canadian political system is her geographic and economic ties with the United States. Canadians have reaped many benefits from this relationship, but there have been problems too. What Canadian decision makers can and cannot do is clearly conditioned by this relationship.

Canada's Internal Geographical and Economic Environment

In the years between Confederation and 1980, Canada's population has risen from 3.5 million to 24 million. Many features of the population have changed but many have remained the same. For example, in 1867, 75 percent of all Canadians lived in that part of Southern Ontario and Quebec called the St. Lawrence Lowlands; in 1980 over 60 percent still did. Within these regions, as elsewhere in Canada, there has been a general movement off the farms and into urban centres. In 1871 only 3.3 percent of Canadians lived in centres of over 100,000 population (Montreal was the only one). By 1976 there were 24 urban areas larger than Montreal had been in 1871, and 70 percent of Canadians lived in such centres.[34] By 1959-1961 only 5.1 percent of the gross domestic product (that part of the GNP consumed within the country) came from agriculture.[35] By 1976, only 4.7 percent of the Canadian labour force worked on a producing farm.[36]

In short, Canada has changed over the past century from a rural agricultural society to an urban industrialized one and is now one of the

---

[33] Little-Brown, Boston, 1977
[34] Statistics Canada, *Canada Year Book, 1978-79*, pp. 156-7.
[35] Weir, "The People," in Warkentin, *Canada: A Geographical Interpretation*, p. 154.
[36] Statistics Canada, *Canada Year Book, 1978-79*, p. 360 and C. McConnell and W. H. Pope, *Economics* (McGraw-Hill Ryerson, Toronto, 1978), p. 720.

most highly urbanized of Western societies.[37] The rapid adjustments necessary have often put strains on the political system as people moved from farms to cities faster than the urban structures of Canadian politics could move to accommodate them. Yet although Canada is an urban society with manufacturing and service industries accounting for the largest portion of its GNP, it is still in many ways a resource-based society.[38] Many of Canada's larger industrial complexes are still in the primary sector of the economy, in industries like mining or pulpwood production. In terms of numbers of workers, secondary and service industries far outrank primary industries, but Canada exports a very high proportion of its primary products and imports a relatively high proportion of its manufactured goods. Thus, the standard of living enjoyed by Canadians today is significantly dependent upon her natural resources.[39]

Canada has a climate more severe than that of most industrialized countries. This has been one reason for the concentration of her population along her southern boundary. When to a harsh climate is added a land whose largest areas are covered by marsh, rock, or permafrost, the picture emerges of a difficult environment indeed.

For the political system, a number of stresses result from the climate. Seasonal employment in outdoor and construction industries, although today a less significant factor than it was two decades ago, often adds a quarter of a million to the list of Canada's unemployed; a short prime construction season adds to the cost of large projects; low-cost transportation of bulk cargoes to and from the interior de-

---

[37] One must be careful not to underemphasize the importance of agriculture in Canada. In one way or another food and agriculture and agriculture-related service and manufacturing activities account for more than 25 percent of the country's economic activity; and agricultural exports accounted for over 20 percent of the value of the country's total exports in 1977. In 1971, more than four times as many workers were engaged in agriculture as in all other primary industries combined. See Statistics Canada, *Canada Year Book 1978-79*, pp. 453-504.

[38] In 1970-74, only 9.3 percent of Canada's domestic product came directly from primary industries whereas 24.8 percent came from manufacturing and approximately 40 percent from service industries. See: *A Time For Change*, 15th Annual Review, Economic Council of Canada, Ottawa, 1978.

[39] Canada's economic growth possibly *could* have been based on other than primary industries but it *was* based on resource industries. See J. K. Galbraith, "The Causes of Economic Growth: The Canadian Case," *Queen's Quarterly*, Summer, 1958. The argument that Canada's growth did depend on resource industries is usually called the staple products theory. The numerous works of H. A. Innis represent the most complete statement of the theory. See also M. H. Watkins, "A Staple Theory of Canada's Economic Growth," *Canadian Journal of Economics and Political Science*, May, 1963, in favour of the theory and K. Buckley, "The Role of Staple Industries in Canada's Economic Development," *The Journal of Economic History*, vol. 18, 1958 against it. There is a succinct summary of the staple products theory in L. R. Marsden and E. B. Harvey, *Fragile Federation*, McGraw-Hill Ryerson, Toronto, 1979.

pends on the St. Lawrence Seaway, a route which is closed by ice for four months of the year; and, it costs over twenty dollars a year per capita just to scrape the snow off our streets and highways.[40]

As well, the sheer physical dimensions of Canada create difficulties. Distances between the major industrial centres in the St. Lawrence Lowlands are relatively small, but in the rest of the country Canadians must maintain communication links between units of population separated by vast distances. Indeed, paradoxically, one reason for the high level of urbanization in Canada may be its vast size. The maintenance of adequate communications and services in small population centres widely separated from each other is much more costly per capita than the maintenance of similar services in centres which are close together. One way around this problem is to concentrate population in large centres which can collectively afford the costly communication links involved. Thus, small, densely populated nations can afford to be less urbanized than Canada.

From what has been said so far, we can piece together a partial picture of the internal geographical and economic environment within which the Canadian political system must operate. It functions in a highly urbanized context, serving a nation which, in order to uphold its standard of living, depends significantly on resources found far from the urban centres. The climate and the physical structure combine to make much of the land scenic, but not well suited to permanent habitation, and to make transportation and construction very expensive. Canada lives next door to a giant which acknowledges her presence and independence grudgingly and rather infrequently. We import more manufactured goods than we export, and we depend upon trade to keep us living in the style to which we are accustomed.

The consequences of all this for the political system are immense. Major transportation projects have always required government assistance; indeed, much of the politics of the first fifty years of Confederation was concerned directly with railway construction.[41] Settlement and development of our territory have depended on vast expenditures and intervention by all levels of government, for only governments have had large enough resources to be able to take on

[40] Roy I. Wolfe, "Economic Development," in Warkentin, *Canada: A Geographical Interpretation*, pp. 189-191.
[41] See Pierre Berton, *The National Dream* (McClelland and Stewart, Toronto, 1971) and *The Last Spike* (McClelland and Stewart, Toronto, 1972); W. T. Easterbrook and M. G. Aitken, *Canadian Economic History* (Macmillan, Toronto, 1965), ch. 18; and D. Creighton, *John A. Macdonald*, vol. II, *The Old Chieftain* (Macmillan, Toronto, 1955).

the risks involved. The harsh climate produces cyclical economic effects which the efforts of only very large governmental units can hope to overcome. In short, the scattering of a small population over a large area accustomed Canadians early to "big government" and prepared the way naturally for the further growth of government in the mid-twentieth century. [42]

Regional Disparity in Canada So far the focus has been on factors which are common to most of Canada. Now the discussion will turn to cleavages in the geographical and economic environment—in particular those regional differences which generate very different and often conflicting demands on the political system. Table 2-4 gives some indication of the great discrepancies in income across Canada. A person living in Ontario is likely to have an annual income 65 percent greater than a person living in Newfoundland and 46 percent greater than someone living in New Brunswick. The Atlantic provinces as a whole have levels of income only about 75 percent of the national average, while those of British Columbia, Ontario and Alberta are far above it. In previous editions we remarked upon the "stubborn resistance of these patterns to change" and noted that the relative positions of provinces had remained basically unchanged as long as records had been kept. Over the last decade, however,

Table 2-4

GEOGRAPHICAL DISTRIBUTION OF PER CAPITA INCOME IN
CANADA, 1978

Province	Percent of National Average	$ Per Capita Per Year
Newfoundland	66	5315
P.E.I.	69	5574
Nova Scotia	80	6447
New Brunswick	74	5984
Quebec	95	7268
Ontario	109	8735
Manitoba	93	7456
Saskatchewan	92	7432
Alberta	105	8407
British Columbia	109	8784
TOTALS	100	8049

Source: Statistics Canada, *National Income and Expenditure Accounts.* Figures include government transfer payments.

[42] See Creighton, op. cit., ch. 14.

changes have begun to appear. The most striking of these has been the movement of Alberta from a situation of slightly below average per capita income at the start of the 1970s to some 5 percent above that average in 1978. Moreover, there has been an overall tendency for disparities to diminish. For example, in 1970 the per capita income in Ontario was some 76 percent greater than that in Newfoundland and this discrepancy dropped by some ten percentage points by 1979. Quebec's per capita income has risen from less than 90 percent of the national average to more than 95 percent over the decade. By 1979 the disparities in government access to revenue had changed to such an extent that if revenues from land sales and leases for oil exploration were included as a standard source of government revenue, Ontario was actually eligible for federal equalization payments.

Regardless of their relative diminution, these regional economic cleavages continue to put stress on the Canadian political system. Thus, for example, there is a constant cry expressed at every federal-provincial finance ministers' conference that Canada's poorer regions should get more of Canada's goods and services, and there is a constant resistance from richer areas to any quick move in the direction of equality. With the exception of the Atlantic provinces, the poorer regions have frequently spawned protest movements—often in the form of minor political parties—and in their protests usually accuse the richer regions of exploiting the poorer. The "Barons of Bay Street," the "Robbers of St. James Street," and more recently the "Blue-eyed Sheiks" of Alberta are familiar Canadian villains.

To some extent Canadian public policies have favoured the central regions over the peripheral. For instance corporation tax collected from a firm whose head office is in Toronto is split only between the federal and Ontario governments in spite of the fact that the earnings of the corporation may come from anywhere in Canada. The effects of this are now mitigated by equalization payments from the federal government to poorer provinces and by the regional redistributive effects of massive federal transfers to individuals and the provinces. But this has not always been the case, and poorer regions claim that the head start given the richer central areas cannot be overcome by the payment of present-day equalization settlements. Too, the Maritimes and Prairies claim with considerable justification that the tariff barriers which prevailed in Canada from the mid-nineteenth to the mid-twentieth century protected industry in the central provinces but did nothing to protect the resources of the poorer areas from the fluctuations of world markets. The central provinces counter by suggesting that their own resource industries do not appear to have been badly harmed by world competition, and that their citizens also paid tariff-protected prices for manufactured products.

Part of the problem in poorer areas in Canada stems from the type of industry located there. Relative to the rest of Canada, the Atlantic provinces have a very low proportion of their production in manufacturing industries and a very high proportion in primary industries such as mining, fishing and forestry. These industries are less likely to create jobs and more likely to hide under-employment—the employment of people in jobs which do not really need to be done or the employment of people for longer periods than are necessary to do the job.[43]

However important government policies may have been in creating regional disparities, geographical factors have been much more important.[44] Differences of terrain, climate, and the distribution of mineral and forest resources by themselves create regional disparities. Of these three factors, climate is probably the least troublesome for, in spite of the overall harshness of the weather, there are fairly large areas of Canada where rainfall and mean temperatures are sufficient to grow productive crops if the soil is fertile enough.[45] Growing seasons vary greatly from region to region, but if climate were the only determinant, regional disparities would not be as great as they are.

Another of Canada's problems is that most of the country has only shallow, young soil spread thinly over rocky terrain. In the West the Cordillera rises to spectacular heights more suited to viewing than farming. Most of Manitoba, Ontario, Quebec, and the Northwest Territories and much of Saskatchewan are covered by the Canadian Shield, whose old, low hills and valleys were scoured nearly clean of soil during the last ice age. Much of the Atlantic region is covered by the rocky northern extension of the Appalachian mountains. Only on the Prairies and in the Great Lakes–St. Lawrence Lowlands is there any extensive region of fertile soil combined with a climate conducive to agriculture. The regions which do possess good climate and good soil tend to have higher population, better per capita income, and superior services, while other regions are more sparsely populated and poorer—if, indeed, anyone lives there at all!

Canada's vast size and her expanses of bare Precambrian rock have not been entirely a curse, for they have provided her with at least four crucial resources—water, forests, petroleum, and minerals. Water has enabled Canada to generate large amounts of electricity cheaply and has consequently made electrical energy one of her most plentiful

---

[43] Economic Council of Canada, *Living Together*, Ottawa, 1978, pp. 31-60.
[44] For a general description see P. B. Clibbon and L. E. Hamelin, "Landforms," in Warkentin, *Canada: A Geographical Interpretation*, pp. 57-77.
[45] See F. B. Watts, "Climate, Vegetation, Soil," in Warkentin, op. cit., pp. 77-111.

commodities. This in turn has provided the basis for industrial development she might not otherwise have had and has helped to temper the effects of the energy shortages of the 1970s. Water has also provided the basis for one of Canada's largest industries, tourism. The oil and gas reserves in the Western provinces have helped Canada avoid the brunt of the oil shortages which have afflicted most industrial nations in the seventies even if they have exacerbated regional economic disparities. Potential reserves off the east coast and in the far north may similarly protect her world position in the 1980s. Trees have made Canada the Western world's largest producer of newsprint and one of the largest producers of paper.[46] Mineral deposits have made isolated areas of the Canadian Shield and the Cordillera pockets of prosperity. However, Canada's primary resources are not evenly distributed. Significant amounts of hydroelectric power can be generated only in large watersheds, and mineralization occurs in isolated pockets in the rock. The best forest stands tend to be in provinces already better off than the others. Ontario, whose secondary industries are Canada's largest, in addition has the largest mineral production. British Columbia, with fertile interior valleys and a congenial climate, also has large deposits of minerals and the best timber stands; and Alberta, already agriculturally advanced, currently has the largest confirmed reserves of oil. With the exception of Newfoundland, the Atlantic provinces, with poor agricultural prospects, also lack the large mineral deposits, petroleum reserves, stands of timber, and hydroelectric power resources of Central and Western Canada.

Geography has contrived as well to cut sections of Canada off from one another. The Maritimes are separated from the rest of Canada by the Northern Appalachians, and the Canadian Shield cuts off Ontario and Quebec from the Prairies, which are in turn separated from British Columbia by the Cordillera. This often leads to the observation that Canada is really five distinct regions, and that Canadian nationhood has been achieved in spite of physical barriers which should have lined us up along a north-south rather than an east-west axis.[47] The difficult geographical environment has meant that the building of communication lines has had to be a cooperative venture, national in scope. The lessons learned about cooperation and about the uses to

---

[46] The manufacture of pulp and paper is Canada's leading industry in terms of employment, salaries, and wages paid and in value added by manufacture.

[47] The number of regions into which Canada should be divided for economic analysis is the subject of some debate. For example, one text has suggested that 68 regions is a more appropriate number than five. See P. Camu, E. P. Weeks, and Z. Q. Sametz, *Economic Geography of Canada* (Macmillan, Toronto, 1964).

which government can be put to overcome big obstacles may have done much to help in building Canadian attitudes toward government.

At any rate, it is clear that regional disparity is one of the most significant factors producing cleavages in the Canadian system, and that peculiar Canadian geographical problems have brought about responses by the Canadian political system which make it distinctive. Aside from the vital problems of ethnic cleavage, which we will discuss shortly, perhaps the greatest problems of Canadian federalism derive from regional cleavages caused by geographical discrepancies.

For those who must make political decisions, the difficulties posed by regional disparities are intensified by the fact that even among specialists in the field there is not unanimous agreement on what must be done to solve the problem. For example, can the Atlantic provinces best be helped by a decrease in national tariffs combined with economic aid to industries already there, or would they be better helped by encouraging new and growing industries to locate there, while letting the older ones die a natural death? Or might the problem best be attacked by encouraging greater mobility of the labour force while leaving industry alone to locate where it can grow fastest— usually in Southern Ontario or Quebec?[48]

In general, policy makers have adopted the policy of encouraging growth in certain "designated areas" which are at present depressed but in which the application of capital might be expected to produce significant growth. The Agricultural and Rural Development Act (ARDA), the Fund for Rural Economic Development, the Atlantic Development Board, the Area Development Agency, and more recently, the amalgamation of many of these plans under the Department of Regional Economic Expansion have all been variants of this approach.[49] The most important of the federal responses, however, has been the provision of transfer and equalization payments to provincial governments and transfer payments to individuals.

Finally, it should be reemphasized that in a very large and very sparsely settled territory like Canada, solutions which may be appro-

---

[48] Two articles epitomizing the different sides of this debate are W. J. Woodfine, "Canada's Atlantic Provinces: A Study in Regional Economic Retardation," *The Commerce Journal*, 1962, and T. W. Wilson, "Financial Assistance with Regional Development," in J. H. Deutsch et al. (eds.), *The Canadian Economy* (Macmillan, Toronto, 1965), pp. 402 ff.
[49] See T. N. Brewis, "Regional Development," in T. N. Brewis et al., *Canadian Economic Policy* (Macmillan, Toronto, 1965), pp. 316 ff. Equalization devices are covered much more extensively in Chapter 9.

priate elsewhere do not always fit. For example, the methods of transportation development which were successful in the United States could not be applied in Canada. Because transportation links to remote areas of low population density do not pay, most major developments in Canada have been carried out by government alone or by private enterprise with huge government subsidies. Examples include the national railways and more recently the Trans-Canada Pipeline. Later, when the links themselves create a market for their own use it may be possible to make a profit, and in that situation private business can be induced to invest capital; but for many such projects, private enterprise in Canada is shored up by huge government subsidies. Broadcasting could be suggested as another example: in the early days of radio there were not enough customers to allow a national network to pay its own way, yet a national network could obviously be useful in fostering national unity. The solution adopted was for the government to step in to create the Canadian Radio Broadcasting Commission. In fact, the Commission and its successor, the Canadian Broadcasting Corporation, have never been operated as profit-seeking enterprises because they have had to provide services to remote areas and because they have often dealt with topics with little sponsor appeal. The Canadian situation in this respect can be contrasted with the American where there are no publicly owned railways (although the U.S. government has recently moved into the operation of rail passenger services) and where public broadcasting is relatively young.

SOCIAL STRATIFICATION: CLASS CLEAVAGE IN CANADA

In addition to the *"horizontal"* cleavages we have discussed, most societies have *vertical lines of cleavage* deriving from class differences or social stratifications which cut across regional boundaries.[50] One's place in the class structure is by no means wholly tied to money or possessions.[51] In pre-industrial societies there were many criteria other than the possession of property by which a person's social posi-

---

[50] We will use the terms *class cleavage, vertical cleavage,* and *social stratification* virtually synonymously, although if one were to delve deeper into the literature it might become clear that there are subtle distinctions that can be made among these terms, depending upon who is using them.

[51] Bernard R. Blishen, "A Socio-Economic Index for Occupations in Canada," *Canadian Review of Sociology and Anthropology,* vol. 4, no. 1, February 1967.

tion could be determined, and even in North American society, money or possessions are not the only ways in which high status is reflected. For example, priests usually have almost no personal possessions and little income, yet their status is usually thought of as being higher than, for example, that of plumbers, who may make a great deal more money.

There are a number of criteria that may be used to measure a person's socioeconomic status. One scale proposed for the Canadian setting depends upon a ranking of occupations based on a combination of factors such as years of education or annual income. Another depends upon a survey of people's perceptions of other people's occupations.[52] These objective systems of measurement can be buttressed by subjective systems, in which people are asked to rate their own status. No one of these scales is perfect, and occasionally someone like the priest, who ranks fairly low on the income scale, will rank fairly high on some of the other scales. For the most part, however, the scales are highly interrelated. A person who ranks high on one is likely to rank high on others as well. For this reason it is fairly safe to use any scale, whether of occupation, education, or income, as an index of social class in Canada. Since income data are the most readily collected and the most widely available, we will base most of our discussions on the income scale. The terms "upper class," "middle class," and "lower class," however, also connote distinctions based on education and life-style as well as on income.

The Poor in Canada[53]

The question of just how unequal the distribution of income is in Canada can be answered by reference to Figure 2-1. This figure is a Lorenz curve which shows, graphically, inequalities of income.[54]

---

[52] Peter C. Pineo and John Porter, "Occupational Prestige in Canada," *Canadian Review of Sociology and Anthropology*, vol. 4, no. 1, pp. 24-40, February, 1967. With respect to stratification in general and particularly with respect to Canada, see: Dennis Forcese, *The Canadian Class Structure* (McGraw-Hill Ryerson, Toronto, 1980).

[53] The "discovery" by social scientists in the mid-1960s that the affluent society had a very large poverty component produced a deluge of literature on the subject. There were many books published on poverty in Canada in that period. For example, in addition to the sources cited elsewhere in this section, see Special Senate Committee on Poverty, *Poverty in Canada* (Ottawa, Information Canada, 1971); Ian Adams et al., *The Real Poverty Report* (M. G. Hurtig, Edmonton, 1971); T. E. Reid, *Canada's Poor* (Holt, Rinehart and Winston, Toronto, 1972).

[54] For a more detailed explanation see McConnell and Pope, *Economics*, pp. 764-786.

Figure 2-1

DISTRIBUTION OF FAMILY INCOME IN CANADA, 1974

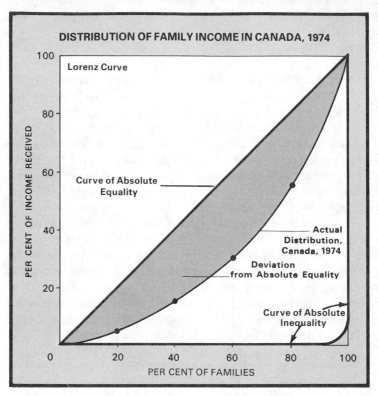

Source: Paul A. Samuelson and Anthony Scott, *Economics*, Fifth Canadian Edition, McGraw-Hill Ryerson Limited, Toronto, 1980, p. 100. Since the relative shares of income of different income classes scarcely vary over time, the curve used in 1974 is still appropriate in 1980.

If all people had equal income, then the curve, which expresses the cumulative percent of income received versus the cumulative percentage of individuals, would be a straight line with a slope of 45 degrees. In that case 50 percent of the families would have 50 percent of total income, and the lowest 1 percent of the families would have the same proportion of income as the highest 1 percent (in which case, of course, there would be no "highest" and "lowest." From this diagram and from Table 2-5 it can be seen that in 1977 the lowest 20 percent of families and unattached individuals in Canada received only 3.8 percent of all income, while the upper 20 percent received 42.0 percent. Put otherwise this means that the lowest 20 percent of the population received only about one-tenth the income of the highest 20 percent.

Table 2-5

LOW-INCOME FAMILIES
AND UNATTACHED INDIVIDUALS IN CANADA

Percentile	Percent of Total Income				Upper Limit of Quintile		
	1951	1967	1975	1977	1967	1973	1977
1 to 20	4.4	4.2	4.0	3.8	2,592	3,980	5,973
21 to 40	11.2	11.4	10.6	10.7	4,524	7,620	12,013
41 to 60	18.3	17.8	17.6	17.9	6,807	11,286	17,993
61 to 80	23.3	24.6	25.1	25.6	9,468	15,943	25,594
81 to 100	42.8	42.0	42.6	42.0	—	—	—

Source: Statistics Canada, *Income Distribution by Size in Canada*, Ottawa, Aug. 1979.

This situation is highly resistant to change. The distribution of income in Canada today is little different from what it was in 1945, although it has improved since the 1920s. Table 2-5 indicates the distribution of income in Canada in a sampling of four postwar years.[55] It can be seen that these figures have changed only slowly and sometimes for the worse over the 26-year period covered. The extreme right-hand column of the table indicates the highest income per family or individual for those in each group. Thus, for example, the highest income of families in the fourth group (having that income below which 80 percent of families fall) was $25,594. Expressed otherwise, the most affluent family in the lowest 20 percent of the population received only about $6,000 in 1977, while no family or individual in the highest 20 percent received less than $25,594.

Table 2-5 shows the picture in broad outline. More detailed figures reveal that in 1977, 11.2 percent of families (659,000 family units) and 36.6 percent of unattached individuals (842,000 people) were living below the Statistics Canada low-income cutoff—the point at which more than 62 percent of income must be spent to obtain adequate food, shelter, and clothing.[56] In sum, in 1977, some 3.2 million people in Canada were living in, at best, difficult economic circumstances. These figures vary with time and particularly with the point in the economic cycle but even by the somewhat conservative definition implied in Statistics Canada's low-income cutoff, poverty is very widespread in Canada.

---

[55] A percentile is defined as the figure below which that percentage of cases lie. Thus the 20th percentile of family income is that income below which 20 percent of the incomes in Canada lie.

[56] *Income Distributions by Size in Canada, 1977*, p. 155.

Where are the poor? Why do other Canadians not see more of them and consequently become more aware of the problem? To a large extent, poverty can be hidden in modern society. Clothing has become relatively cheaper so that the poor no longer live in rags even if they do suffer from dietary deficiencies and live in condemned and overcrowded homes. Expressways may cross over poor neighbourhoods but the eighty-kilometre per hour commuter never sees them. The poor have been and continue to be collectively inarticulate so that unless someone speaks for them or organizes them they are unheard.

The poor in Canada do not live only in depressed areas of the country. We often think of the Maritimes and Eastern Quebec as being Canada's poorest regions, and indeed the concentration of poor people is higher in those areas, but 67 percent of low-income families live in urban regions and over 32 percent live in supposedly affluent metropolitan areas. While we think of the poor as being unemployed, the heads of 45 percent of poor families were active in the labour force at least part of the year. The heads of 25 percent of low-income families worked 50 to 52 weeks in 1977 and 4 percent of all families whose head was employed full time all year were poor. While we think of the poor as tending to be elderly, the heads of 77 percent of poor families were under 65. Sixty-seven percent of poor families are headed by men although 38 percent of female-headed households are below the low-income cutoff and only 8.4 percent of male-headed households are.[57]

In Canada one of the highest incidences of poverty is found among the native peoples.[58] In 1980, over 40 percent of Indian families were living with at least two families in a dwelling unit and half of all Indian housing had inadequate sewage disposal and unsafe water supplies.[59] The death rate for Indians in the 22–44-year age group is four times the national average. Violent deaths are also four times the national average while Indians in the 15–24-year age group commit suicide at six times the rate of other Canadians. Some 50 to 60 percent of Indian deaths and illnesses are alcohol related. Seven times as many Indians per capita as whites are in penitentiaries. In spite of all this, the Indian population is the fastest growing in Canada. But fewer

---

[57] All figures in this paragraph are from Statistics Canada, *Income Distributions by Size,* 1977.

[58] Among Canadian native peoples there were 18,000 Inuit and 297,000 Indians in 1971, *Canada Year Book, 1978-79,* p. 161. The federal government estimated that there were 385,000 Indians in 1980. The Economic Council of Canada, *Fifth Annual Report,* p. 121, estimates that there were about 60,000 Métis in 1961, and a reasonable estimate for 1980 would be 100,000.

[59] 1980 data were supplied by the Federal Department of Indian and Northern Affairs.

than one-third of present reservation lands could be made capable of supporting even their present populations in reasonable fashion, and 45 percent are accessible only by water or seaplane.[60]

Undoubtedly the greatest handicap the poor face in modern society is simply low income. The problem goes deeper than that, though, for poverty creates a sub-culture within the larger Canadian culture— a sub-culture with its own norms and values. Some of these norms, such as a lack of respect for education or a lack of belief in its necessity, make it extremely difficult for the poor to escape their situation. Poverty leads as well to crime, disease, and low productivity and constitutes a vast waste of potential talent within Canadian society.[61]

The existence of such large numbers of economically deprived people in Canada obviously produces a strain on the Canadian political system. The stress is felt everywhere in the system but probably most acutely at the provincial and local levels, which are responsible under the British North America Act for welfare and for otherwise alleviating many of the problems caused by poverty. However, lack of financial resources on the part of many of the provinces and municipalities prompted Ottawa to take over the unemployment insurance scheme by constitutional amendment in 1940 and has since led the federal government into other income redistribution programs such as family allowances, old age security, and the provision of assistance to provinces for welfare programs.

The Canadian Economic Elite

So far our discussion of stratification in Canada has been far from complete. If 15–20 percent of Canadians are below the discomfort line, then some 80 percent are above it; and these constitute a heterogeneous group. On the top end of the scale is a very small group holding the top positions in industry, business, the professions, and the bureaucracy. Estimates of the size of this "elite" vary depending on the criteria used to describe it, but at most it comprises some 2 or 3 percent of the population.

Undoubtedly the key works in this area are John Porter's *The Vertical Mosaic* and Wallace Clement's *The Canadian Corporate Elite.*[62] Porter first addresses himself to the question of whether or not there is a Canadian elite and, having decided that there is, he examines its characteristics. His data indicate that the 985 occupants of the top po-

---

[60] The Economic Council of Canada, *Fifth Annual Report*, p. 122.

[61] See Ian Adams, *The Poverty Wall* (McClelland and Stewart, Toronto, 1970), and W. E. Mann (ed.), *Poverty and Social Policy in Canada* (Copp Clark, Toronto, 1970).

[62] (University of Toronto Press, Toronto, 1965) and (McClelland and Stewart, Toronto, 1975) respectively.

sitions in a number of hierarchies such as those of business, religion, education, politics, and the bureaucracy are likely to be occupied by people with similar backgrounds. These include Charter group (British or French) ethnic origin, a middle- or upper-class upbringing, and Catholic, Anglican, or United Church religious affiliations. There are also similarities in educational background in this group and there exists among them a web of social interconnections. Clement's more recent data (1973) tend to corroborate Porter's initial conclusions with the significant exception that Clement finds a much higher proportion of non-resident control than did Porter. In firms with more than $25 millions in assets, Clement finds that 62 percent of directors come from outside Canada; for the earlier period in which Porter worked the figure was only 27 percent.[63]

But if these people are potentially a "ruling class," do they actually behave as one? As the rest of this text indicates, the great complexity of the decision-making process in Canada ensures that control by any one small group is extremely difficult. Furthermore, the fact that members of the various elites may share a similar outlook on life is no guarantee that under the complex pressures which come to bear on any particular decision they will act as a uniform class. On the other hand, given that the decision makers are primarily middle and upper class in origin and that most inputs from the environment are channelled through middle-class organizations, it seems probable that the voice of lower-class citizens is, at best, muffled.[64] The result, as we will conclude after a more detailed study of this issue in later chapters is not any sort of conscious conspiracy but rather a persistent tendency for political decision makers to avoid doing anything which will seriously jeopardize the interests of the middle and upper class Canadians. In a situation of slow or non-existent growth in real incomes such as Canada has found in the later 1970s, it is likely that improvements in the situation of poorer Canadians will be slow at best.

The Swollen Middle

If the various elites make up only 2 or 3 percent of the population and those below the poverty line about 20 percent, obviously the middle

---

[63] Wallace Clement, *Continental Corporate Power* (McClelland and Stewart, Toronto, 1977).

[64] The whole question of elites and political decision making is discussed in much more detail in Chapter 14. This text is primarily informed by the liberal-pluralist perspective. For a Marxist class analysis perspective see Leo Panitch (ed.), *The Canadian State* (University of Toronto Press, 1977).

income group of the population, made up of the middle class and better-off members of the working class, constitutes a majority of the Canadian population.[65] It must not be supposed that this middle-income group is by any means homogeneous, for there are wide variations in behavioural patterns which may lead to differences in political behaviour and in the type of demands fed into the political system.

Within this middle-income group, the dividing line between the middle class and the working class depends not so much on income as on type of occupation. Many skilled tradespeople such as plumbers or electricians earn more money than many junior executives, yet the junior executive tends to emulate the life-style of corporate seniors while the tradesperson does not.[66] The differences in behaviour appear to derive mainly from family traditions, for working-class families tend to remain working class for many generations, and from job security, for the junior executive is less subject to the vagaries of the business cycle than is the tradesperson or industrial worker. Thus there is stratification and there are deep class differences *within* the "swollen middle" of Canadian society and these presumably could become deep political cleavages.

Stratification and Canadian Politics

There are, indeed, *prima facie* reasons to suggest that class-based cleavages are important to the Canadian political system for, as we will see when we discuss political participation, lower-class Canadians take little interest in the political system, have little awareness of its relevance to them, and do very little to attempt to influence it, whereas the higher up the economic hierarchy we go, the greater the amount of interest, participation, and actual influence in the political process.

On the other hand, we will soon see that class is not a vital determinant of Canadian voting behaviour or party identification. There have been attempts to establish class-based parties, but these have been less than overwhelmingly successful. The Independent Labour Party flashed briefly across Ontario politics in the 1920s and died. The Communist Party of Canada has never been anything but a token

---

[65] In 1977 the median income of all Canadian families was $20,101 and in Ontario it was $21,600. Statistics Canada, *Income Distributions by Size*, pp. 840-41.

[66] There is an extensive discussion of the impact of stratification on life-styles in Forcese, *The Canadian Class Structure*, chs. 3 and 4. See also the older but still interesting summary of different behaviour patterns in Nariman K. Dhalla, *These Canadians: A Sourcebook of Marketing and Socio-Economic Facts* (McGraw-Hill, Toronto, 1966), pp. 177-84.

presence, and even the more broadly based CCF-NDP has had trouble establishing itself as a credible threat to gain national power. In fact the CCF-NDP has tended to succeed in inverse proportion to the amount of attention it has paid to class-related issues and cleavages.

Whatever the influence of social class on the political behaviour of Canadians, the presence of inequalities of opportunity and of large disparities in the distribution of wealth has called forth many responses from the political decision makers. Thus in 1976-7 direct welfare expenditures by Canadian governments totalled 27.4 billion dollars or nearly 31 percent of all expenditures by all levels of government that year.[67] The proportion has remained approximately constant since then. In 1966-7, comparable figures were $4.96 billions or 23 percent of government expenditures. There are literally hundreds of federal, provincial, and municipal welfare programs, ranging from the Old Age Security payments, which resulted in the payment of 8.4 billion dollars in 1981-82, down to local welfare programs in the smallest municipal governments.[68] The last forty years have seen a rapid and steady growth in the size of such programs, both in absolute terms and as a proportion of GNP. If these programs have not significantly reduced income disparities, they have at least helped to ensure that fewer Canadians live in absolute poverty than was previously the case. The public expenditures on this problem suggest that our political system will respond, even if slowly, to major economic problems such as poverty. However it has also been argued that welfare policies tend to simply legitimize the existing system, with all of its inequities, rather than to reduce the inequities themselves. The poor are not starving, and are therefore quiescent, but the rich are getting richer as well. Welfare programs therefore function in some way as an inoculation against demands for more radical economic reforms that would be heard if the lot of the poor were permitted to deteriorate in absolute terms.[69]

[67] Figures from Statistics Canada, *Consolidated Expenditure Accounts*, updated annually. Expenditures include Unemployment Insurance, Family Allowances, Canada/Quebec Pension Plans, Old Age Security and Guaranteed Income Supplements, the Canada Assistance Plan, and provincial and municipal social security expenditures.

[68] Unlike their American counterpart, Canadian governments are fairly proud of their welfare programs and go to great lengths to describe them to the public. Thus, detailed information on the structure of welfare programs can be found in any bookstore selling government publications. Useful brief descriptions are available in *The Canada Year Book* or in The Canadian Tax Foundation's annual review called *The National Finances*.

[69] This argument is well put in Leo Panitch, "The Role and Nature of the Canadian State," in Panitch, *The Canadian State*, p. 8.

3

Environment: French-English Relations in Canada

For much of the period since the British conquest in 1760, the most obvious of Canada's cleavages has been that between Canadians of French origin and the rest of Canada—"English" Canada, so called. French Canadians do form a most substantial minority. In 1976 Canadians claiming French as their mother tongue constituted 25.6 percent of the Canadian population. But the rest of Canada is not an undifferentiated "majority." About 25 percent of Canadians are of neither British nor French ethnic background, and some 13.5 percent learned some language other than English or French in childhood and still understand it. Why, then, does the cleavage between French and English constantly confront Canadian politicians while the potential cleavage between the "other" Canadians and the two original groups of Canadians remains largely in the background? What are the reasons for the importance of the French-English cleavage in Canada and how does this major environmental factor affect Canada's political process?

THE CAUSES OF FRENCH-ENGLISH CLEAVAGE

Undoubtedly the main reason why the French-English cleavage is the major one in Canada and why other ethnic groups tend to fade into merely local political significance is that no single one of the other groups is very large. About 4.5 percent of the Canadian population is of German origin, and Ukrainians, Italians, Dutch, and Scandinavians each constitute between 1 and 2 percent of the total population. Thus, the French Canadians are over five times as numerous as the biggest of the other ethnic groups and each of the other groups seems to feel as close to the English Canadians as to any of the other small ethnic groups.[1]

---

[1] There are many small groups of "other" Canadians who prefer not to be assimilated but rather to maintain their distinct traditions. These may occasionally be significant in local politics, but unless they become violent, as did one fanatical sect of the Russian Doukhobors in the 1950s, they remain unnoticed in national politics. Even locally they are much less likely to be politically active (except within their own sect)

There are other factors in addition to simple numbers which tend to exacerbate the English-French cleavage in Canada. One is simply the regional concentration of Francophones. In 1971, over 80 percent of the residents of Quebec listed French as their mother tongue, while only 13 percent listed English as the language they had first learned.[2] Sixty-two percent of the population of Quebec speaks only French. Outside of the Montreal area, the proportion of the population of Quebec claiming French ancestry rises to over 90 percent, and 77 percent speak only French. In the rest of Canada, of course, the position is reversed: French is the mother tongue of only about 6.6 percent of the people, and in British Columbia the proportion is only 1.7 percent.

This geographical homogeneity of both the French and non-French groups is important, for without it, it is unlikely that French Canada would have persisted as a cultural entity. As it is, the day-to-day contacts of most French Canadians are with their ethnic confrères, and while there is the occasional requirement to use English, especially in Montreal, it is quite possible for many French-speaking Quebeckers to get along without ever speaking English or seeing an English person. What is true for Quebeckers is true in reverse for many Western Canadians; they have absolutely no need to use the French language in their home provinces.

While the coincidence of ethnic and geographic cleavage is probably the most important factor in maintaining the cultural duality of Canada, there are other important coincident cleavages. Of particular importance is the coincidence of religious and ethnic lines. In 1971, some 46 percent of the population of Canada was Roman Catholic and 50 percent Protestant—and virtually all French Canadians were Roman Catholic. Granted that there is a difference between being nominally a member of a particular denomination and being a practising member, it can still be argued that certain cultural characteristics are transmitted via religion. In any case French Canadians were, up to the recent past at least, much more likely to attend church than English Canadians. In 1965 eighty-five percent of French-speaking Roman Catholics in Canada attended church at least weekly com-

---

than the original or "charter" ethnic groups. The possible exception today is our unrecognized "charter groups" the native peoples. Canadian Indians and Inuit, while a small proportion of Canadian society, have been making very strong claims to aboriginal title to lands, basically in the far north. The native organizations are becoming very well organized, are opposed to the notion of assimilation, and are very active in lobbying government on the Land Claims issue. So far they are also basically non-violent.

[2] Statistics Canada, *Canada Year Book*, 1972, p. 1370, Table 4.

pared with 31 percent of English-speaking Protestants.[3] The influence of the Roman Catholic Church in Quebec has been directed toward the preservation of the cultural integrity of French Canada, for the Church in Quebec has viewed assimilation as a threat to its position.[4] Furthermore, the churches formed the social centres of small Quebec communities and traditionally provided the sort of gathering place which is essential to the establishment of that group cohesion which maintains cultural independence.

Although the significance of religious factors has declined continuously over the last two decades, through long periods of Canada's early history the French-English cleavage was actually overshadowed by religious differences.[5] The Irish immigrants of the 1840s transplanted much of the Orange-Roman Catholic strife from Ireland, and for some 50 years afterwards the predominant cleavage in Canada was Protestant-Catholic rather than French-English. Schools were denominational, not ethnic, as were hospitals, welfare institutions, newspapers, and many of the other institutions which connect citizens to society.

Still, nineteenth-century Canadians, no less than some of their descendents today, had a tendency to equate religious and ethnic differences. Thus, Protestants in the nineteenth and early twentieth centuries often saw a close tie between "popery" and knavery," and since the French Canadians were all papist, it followed that they must also be knaves. In 1889 the *Toronto Mail* warned:

Ontario will not be safe. . . . Our eastern gate has already been opened . . . Catholic invasion is already streaming through, . . . to detach Eastern Ontario from the British and Protestant civilization of which it now forms a part and annex it to the territory of the French race which is also the dominion of the priest.

and, added Dalton McCarthy in speaking of the Jesuit Estates Bill:

This is a British country and the sooner we take in hand our French Canadians and make them British in sentiment and teach them the English language the less trouble

---

[3] Data from a 1965 public opinion survey directed by Professor J. Meisel of Queen's University.

[4] On the role of the Church in French Canada, see Jean Charles Falardeau, "The Role and Importance of the Church in French Canada," translated from *Esprit, Paris,* août—septembre 1952, in Marcel Rioux and Yves Martin, *French Canadian Society* (McClelland and Stewart, Toronto, 1964). A more passionately separatist statement of somewhat the same ideas can be found in Marcel Rioux, *Quebec in Question* (James Lewis and Samuel, Toronto, 1971), ch. 3, p. 27 ff. and *passim.*

[5] K. D. McRae, "Consociationalism and the Canadian Political System," K. D. McRae (ed.), *Consociational Democracy: Political Accommodation in Segmented Societies* (McClelland and Stewart, Carleton Library No. 79, 1974), pp. 242 ff.

we shall have to prevent. Now is the time when the ballot box will decide this great question; and if it does not supply the remedy in this generation, bayonets will supply it in the next.[6]

Today there are cleavages other than the religious and geographic that aggravate the ethnic dimension of the French-English cleavage. The most important of these is the economic disparity that has existed between Quebec and most of the provinces west of her, between French Canadians and English Canadians in general, and between French and English within Quebec.

In 1961 the income of French-Canadian male members of the labour force was 85.8 percent of the national average, whereas that of men who were of British origin was 110 percent of the average.[7] Within Quebec, French-Canadian incomes were 92 percent of the provincial average while English Canadians received 140 percent of the provincial average.[8] Among Canadian ethnic groups in 1961, only Italians had lower income levels than French Canadians. In Quebec, per capita income in 1970 was 90 percent of the national average and only 78 percent of that of Ontario. Among French Canadians there was a larger proportion of poor families than among English Canadians, and there may also have been a larger disparity in incomes, for in 1961, 37 percent of the French-Canadian labour force received less than $3,000 per year and fully 78 percent were receiving less than $5,000, while the figures for English Canada were 31 and 70 percent.

However, since 1961, and particularly throughout the 1970s, the turnaround in these figures has been dramatic. In 1961, Anglophone Montrealers earned 51 percent more on average than did Francophone Montrealers. By 1977, the gap had closed to 15 percent. In 1961, Anglophones in the top 20 percent of the Anglophone population earned 76 percent more than Francophones in the top 20 percent of the population. This disparity was reduced to 50 percent by 1970 and to 19 percent by 1977. Less than one-half a percent of the highest 15 percent of incomes in Quebec went to Francophones in 1961. In 1977, seventy percent did.[9] The economic picture for Francophones in Quebec, then, is rapidly improving relative to their Anglophone counterparts; however, problems remain.

Unemployment figures by ethnic origin are not available but, aside from the Atlantic provinces, Quebec consistently has the highest

---

[6] Both quoted in Joseph Schull, *Laurier* (Macmillan, Toronto, 1965), p. 227.
[7] Report of the Royal Commission on Bilingualism and Biculturalism, Book III, *The Work World*, vol. 3A (Ottawa, 1969), pp. 18-19.
[8] Ibid.
[9] Figures cited in *The Financial Post*, Nov. 10, 1979, p. S18.

levels of unemployment in Canada with an average 9.1 percent rate in 1979 versus a 7.1 percent Canadian average. [10] The causes of these high unemployment figures are many, and it is not our intention to deal with them here; however, the effect has been to create fertile soil upon which further ethnic tensions may grow.

This dissatisfaction of French Quebeckers has been further fed by the fact that, both within and outside of Quebec, French Canadians have tended to hold jobs with lower status than those held by English Canadians. The "repatriation" of industry in Quebec (by which is meant the taking over of executive jobs by French Canadians) has been going on since the start of the 1960s, and the results have been outlined above, but a disproportionate percentage of "boss" jobs, from foreman to company president, are still held by English Canadians.

Quebec is, next to British Columbia, the least agricultural province in Canada, with only 4.5 percent of the labour force in agriculture versus 6.5 percent for Canada as a whole. [11] Although considerable consolidation of Quebec farms has taken place since then, in 1963, a survey by the Agricultural and Rural Development Agency showed that over half of Quebec's farm units were not properly profitable and that Quebec had the lowest farm incomes, the lowest educational levels of farmers, the largest per capita debt among farmers, and the largest farm family size in Canada.

Overall it is not at all correct to designate the Quebec economy as "backward." In fact, in the sense of being industrialized it is well advanced. Yet, although we have seen that the situation has been rapidly improving, French Canadians have not shared fully in the fruits of this industrial society, and this fact has helped deepen the French-English cleavage in Canada.

A number of conflicting theories have been advanced to explain the failure of French Canadians to share until recently in industrial rewards. Probably the most venerable, but also the least accurate, is the theory that because of their cultural background French Canadians are simply unable to operate a modern economy. This view was stated at length at the turn of the century by one Sir John Bourinet:

In commercial and financial enterprise the French Canadians cannot compete with their fellow citizens of British origin who practically control the great commercial un-

---

[10] In Quebec unemployment rates have risen from an average of 3.3 percent in the five-year period from 1946 to 1951 to 9.3 percent in 1956-60. The corresponding figures for all of Canada are 2.9 and 5.6 percent. They have fluctuated around 2 percent higher than the Canadian average through the late 1970s.

[11] Statistics Canada, *Canada Year Book, 1972,* p. 834.

dertakings and bank institutions of Lower Canada, especially in Montreal. Generally speaking, the French Canadians cannot compare with the English population as agriculturalists. . . . It must be admitted, too, that the French population has less enterprise and less disposition to adopt new machines and improved agricultural implements than the people of other provinces.

As a rule the habitant lives contentedly on very little. Give him a pipe of native tobacco, a chance for discussing politics, a gossip with his fellows at the church door after service, a visit now and then to the country town and he will be happy. It does not take much to amuse him, while he is quite satisfied that his spiritual safety is secured as long as he is within the sound of the church bells, goes regularly to confession, and observes all the fêtes d'obligation. If he or one of his family can only get a little office in the municipality or the "government," then his happiness is nearly perfect.

Like the people from whom he is descended—many of whose characteristics he has never lost since his residence of centuries on the American continent—he is greatly influenced by matters of feeling and sentiment, and the skillful master of rhetoric, etc. [12]

One wonders whether this is a description of people or of hound dogs. It is an expression, albeit an extreme one, of the point of view which saw French Canada as simply an isolated folk society, but it does not stand up to close examination. At the time the above quotation was written, Quebec was undergoing a rapid burst of industrialization, and by the end of World War I less than half the population of Quebec was rural: Quebec was ahead of Canada in this respect. [13] The annual rate of industrial growth in Quebec since then has been about equal to that of Ontario, although the gap between the two provinces has not closed appreciably.

However, if we do not accept the more extreme forms of the "cultural difference" hypothesis, we must suggest something in its place: an historical interpretation may be valuable here. [14] It is generally

---

[12] Sir John Bourinet, *Canada* (G.P. Putman and Sons, New York, 1898), pp. 438-439.

[13] Raynauld, *The Canadian Economic System*, pp. 69-71.

[14] There has been for many years a great debate about the nature of French-Canadian society after the conquest and prior to industrialization, and the consequences of this structure for present-day society in Quebec. On one side are the folk society analysts represented by Gerin, Miner, Hughes, and, in an early extreme, Bourinet, and on the other are those who saw the Quebec of the nineteenth and early twentieth centuries as being much more than simply a folk culture. The most prominent member of this school is Philip Garigue. A synthesis produced by Herbert Guindon: "The Social Evolution of Quebec Reconsidered," *Canadian Journal of Economics and Political Science*, vol. 26, Nov. 1969, pp. 533-551 sums up the argument and produces a challenging synthesis. Parts of the debate are reproduced in Rioux and Martin, *French Canadian Society*, and a summary can be found in Lorne R. Marsden and Edward Harvey, *Fragile Federation* (McGraw-Hill Ryerson, Toronto, 1979), pp. 60-70. An interpretation similar to the one given here but with a separatist slant may be found in Rioux, *Quebec in Question*.

agreed that prior to the British conquest, French Canada was a feudal society with a mercantile bourgeoisie capable of operating business and industry. The conquest destroyed the commercial structure of French-Canadian society, and the British presence, plus the impoverishment of the colony by the war, induced most of the bourgeoisie to return to France. The loss of the entrepreneurial French elite was followed initially by a movement of French workers and small businessmen back to the soil and later to employee positions in industry. The proper ambition for a bright young French Canadian was not to enter business, but rather to become a member of the clergy, a doctor or a lawyer, or failing that, a farmer or a worker. The elite left in the colony was that of the Church, and it moved naturally, together with newly arrived English-speaking businessmen, to fill whatever power gap remained. The Church took care of the spiritual and social needs of Quebec, and the English businessmen replaced the departed bourgeoisie and took care of its business needs.

Once a cycle like this had started it was extremely difficult to break. The Church and English business elites naturally moved to perpetuate themselves, and a new elite, the governmental, arose to join the other two. Each of these elites developed vast bureaucratic structures and these structures had their own "maintenance needs" which conditioned their recruiting patterns. The Church and governmental hierarchies were French-speaking, the business hierarchy English-speaking, and since recruitment into organizations is determined by the characteristics of those already there, the lack of Francophones in the private sector was exacerbated. To this was added a paucity of technically trained Francophones, for the Church, the largest of the hierarchies and the one which dominated Francophone education in the province, had no need for them, with the result that technical or commercial jobs were not defined as constituting an appropriate ambition for a young French Canadian.

For a cycle like this to be broken, one of the hierarchies (in this case the governmental) had to gain ascendancy over the others and then respond to the emerging needs of the environment. This has been happening in Quebec at an accelerated rate since 1960. The government has displaced the Church in such fields as education and in providing social welfare. One of the results has been an increasing number of technically trained French Canadians capable of handling many of the developmental needs of Quebec society. But an English-dominated business elite cannot simply turf out its many settled English technocrats and managers, so there arose a situation of under-employment of large numbers of intelligent and qualified young French Canadians who could see that the English held the jobs to which they aspired—and in their own province at that. Control of the

Quebec economy hung tantalizingly just beyond the grasp of this rising class of French Canadians. Understandably they grew impatient with "200 years of waiting" and turned in large numbers to support the separatist leanings of the Parti Québécois and its precursors. The changes in distribution of income and the increasing availability of better job opportunities may have come too late and, indeed, it may simply be creating a growing cadre of younger French Canadians able to pursue nationalist ends but with more vigour, skill, and economic power.

To conclude, then, the cultural differences between French and English Canada run very deep and would undoubtedly constitute a lasting cleavage in themselves, but it is the coincidence of the ethnic dimensions of this conflict with economic, geographical, and religious cleavages that has made it loom so important. Quebec is not Canada's poorest province, nor is she the only province in rapid transition, and all of Canada's five regions can make equal claims to unique geographic problems. It is the running together of so many lines of cleavage that has created Canada's most serious political problem.

ETHNIC CRISES IN CANADA

The chronology of French-English relations in Canada since the conquest of Quebec has been one of a series of crises of varying proportions, interspersed with periods of relative calm. Those who are the witnesses to each separate crisis tend to see it as the ultimate threat to the Canadian political community. In some ways each crisis of French-English relations is unique, but there are many features common to all of them. Thus, for example, while the FLQ crisis of 1970 was unique in its use of kidnapping, it was similar to crises of the past in other ways and a good deal less violent than some, notably the conscription crisis of 1917; and while the crisis of the 1970s and 80s is unique in the amount of emphasis placed upon separatism, earlier crises have also had separatist overtones. It is therefore important to examine briefly some of the crises which have occurred since 1867 both as a set of case studies in the way in which the Canadian political system handles crises, and in order to give the current chapters of the ongoing crisis of Confederation a proper historical perspective.[15]

---

[15] We were assisted in the preparation of this section by unpublished material prepared by Professor Richard Simeon of Queen's University. We have not here considered the first of Canada's ethnic crises, the 1837 rebellion led by Louis Joseph Papineau. For a more extensive general description of French-English relations in Canada from a more French-Canadian perspective see André Bernard, *What Does Quebec Want?* (James Lorimer & Co., Toronto, 1978).

The Riel Crisis

The period immediately following Confederation could be called a honeymoon period in ethnic relationships in Canada. Upper Canadians had achieved their goal of "representation by population" and French Canadians had a government in Quebec which they felt they could call their own. The coalition of Macdonald and Cartier seemed to be working well at the federal level, and the two ethnic groups seemed more concerned with internal than external problems. There was a brief uprising of the Métis people in Manitoba in 1870, in which an Ontario Orangeman died, but Louis Riel, the leader of the rebellion, fled to the United States and little more was heard of the incident. Riel, however, returned to Canada in 1885, and Canada's first major post-Confederation ethnic quarrel broke around him. On his return he regrouped his Métis and Indian forces and led them in a second rebellion. Troops were sent from Eastern Canada to put down the insurrection and Riel himself was captured together with several of his followers and sentenced to death for treason. He became a symbol for anti-Catholic Protestants in Ontario and even more so for anti-Protestant Catholics in Quebec, who were disturbed that the originally Catholic and French-speaking communities of Manitoba were being swamped by English-speaking settlers. Mass rallies swept both provinces. In Montreal *La Presse* screamed, "Henceforward there are no more Liberals nor Conservatives nor Castors. There are only PATRIOTS and TRAITORS." For Quebec the issue was one of the execution or pardon of a patriot; for Ontario, one of the execution or pardon of a traitor and murderer. Riel was executed, but the bitter dispute did not end with his death. Even today, he is often presented in French Canada as a hero and in English Canada if not as a traitor at least as an addled, misguided, and vaguely dishonest mystic.

The Riel controversy illustrates a number of important aspects of ethnic conflict in Canada. The first is the role played by the incumbent political leaders in dealing with the political results of cleavage. In this case the conflict had originated in large measure from various religious and ethnic organizations, and politicians of both major parties had tried to moderate it. Macdonald tried to delay Riel's execution but was forced to give in to pressure from Ontario and particularly from the Orange Lodge, that most potent of forces in early Ontario politics. The French-Canadian members of Macdonald's cabinet, while privately opposed to the execution, refused to break with Macdonald and urged calm in Quebec. Sir Wilfrid Laurier, then leader of the opposition, opposed the government's handling of the matter, but urged his countrymen to adopt a moderate approach. The higher clergy of the Catholic Church also played a moderating role, and Bishop Taché even urged French-Canadian Conservative MPs not to vote against their own party.

Another set of leaders, however, acted to foster and exacerbate the conflict. In Ontario, the Orange Lodge and other Protestant groups played an important role in condemning the French-Canadian "papists." The Ontario press also played on ethnic hostilities. For example, the *Toronto Mail* declared: "As Britons, we believe that the conquest will have to be fought over again. Lower Canada may depend on it, there will be no new treaty of 1763. The victors will not capitulate the next time."

In Quebec, on the other hand, the "out"political leaders seized this opportunity to overthrow and virtually destroy the provincial Conservative party. Playing on the same sort of ethnic hostility as that used by Ontario's Orangemen, Honoré Mercier formed the *Parti National*, which was aimed at uniting all French Canadians in all provinces in a single party. The Parti National was never successful at the federal level, but it did gain power provincially in spite of the fact that it was opposed both by the church hierarchy (though not necessarily the lower clergy) and by the incumbent political leaders.

A pattern can be discerned here which recurs frequently in Canadian politics. The incumbent leaders and some important community institutions acted to minimize intergroup conflict. Other potential leaders, currently out of power, built up the hostilities on either side. From another perspective, the "outs" were attempting to use the crisis to gain political power, while the entrenched "ins" tried to save the *status quo*.

The Manitoba Schools Crisis

The bitterness left by the Riel affair and the hostilities raised in English Canada by many of the actions of the Mercier government in Quebec inspired a general climate of distrust, especially among middle levels of the elites of both sides. It was against this background that the Manitoba schools crisis erupted. Conflicts over schools were to provide the focal point for ethnic disagreements for the next 20 years and are still important today. All the earlier ones involved attempts by provincial governments to abolish or limit French-Catholic educational rights. In 1890, Manitoba passed a law establishing a completely non-sectarian educational system; previously Catholic schools had received provincial aid.[16]

The Manitoba schools crisis placed the opponents of the legislation in an anomalous position, for most of them were French, Roman

---

[16] Similar situations arose in New Brunswick, in Alberta and Saskatchewan when they became provinces in 1905, and most ominously, in Ontario just before World War I.

Catholic, and from Quebec. To oppose Manitoba's school law was to demand that the federal government use its power to disallow provincial legislation to kill the plan. This would obviously be a case of federal interference in provincial affairs, and on principle, Quebec was opposed to this idea. Provincial politicians in Quebec squirmed uncomfortably while the church pressured the federal government to disallow the legislation. Laurier, still leader of the opposition, took his stand on the side of provincial rights. The courts finally declared the Manitoba legislation to be within provincial powers, but recommended that the federal government disallow it anyway, and the Conservative government finally did introduce a bill to invalidate the law. An election intervened and the subsequent campaign was fought largely on the school issue.

For once ethnic and religious divisions did not coincide, since the church, demanding that the legislation be killed, supported its traditional ally, the Conservative party, while Laurier, the first French Canadian to lead a national majority party, appealed to the Quebec electorate on ethnic grounds. Quebeckers could vote either for their church or for their ethnic group. They voted for their ethnic group, and Ontarians split their votes. The result was a Liberal victory. In Quebec Laurier received 54 percent of the vote and the Liberals were never to drop below 50 percent again, except in 1958.

It was pointed out earlier that conflicts may be made worse by coincident cleavage lines. Similarly they may be muted when cleavage lines do not coincide. The lack of coincidence of two major cleavages did much to reduce the bitterness of this particular issue. It was settled by negotiations between Laurier and the provincial government in 1897, with the substance of the legislation basically unchanged.

In the early part of the twentieth century, several nationalist movements appeared in French Canada. The most important of these was led by Henri Bourassa. At this time the term "nationalist" implied more power for the government of Quebec in cultural matters and more independence of Canada from the British connection. Although Bourassa stopped short of any call for the separation of Quebec from Canada, this was not necessarily true of his followers, just as it had not been true of several members of the previous nationalist movement, the Parti Nationale in the 1880s. The new movements posed a threat to Laurier, as the nationalist demands generally ran counter to the Laurier policy of moderation and compromise. The movements may have been partially a response to defeats on the questions of language and education; but, ironically, it was the defection of Bourassa and his followers from the Quebec Liberal party which led to the election of the English-Canadian-dominated and strongly pro-British Borden government in 1911. Bourassa and the other nationalists supported the Conservatives in that election campaign, and this led to a 6 percent decline in Liberal votes in Quebec. The campaign was unscrupulous on both sides and left a further residue of bitterness as Canada approached one of the greatest ethnic crises of its national life.

The Conscription Crisis of 1917 and the Ontario Schools Crisis

That crisis came during World War I. Perhaps Canada came closer to civil war then than at any other time in its history, as two issues combined to bring ethnic tensions to the boiling point. The first was yet another school crisis, brought on by a 1913 Ontario regulation limiting the use of French in Ontario schools. The second was the battle over conscription for war service.

At a time when national unity was most vital, the agitation over schools made it impossible. For Quebec, traditionally inward-looking, the educational issue was far more important than fighting a foreign war. There were frequent mass rallies and demonstrations in the province. Quebec school children and school boards contributed money to maintain the French schools in Ontario, as did many municipal governments in Quebec. A petition signed by 600,000 people asking for disallowance of the Ontario regulation was presented to the federal government. Virtually all elements of the Quebec population supported the attack on Ontario's "Regulation Seventeen." As Le Soleil, a Quebec City newspaper, put it: "The hour of mobilization of the French-Canadian race has come." This agitation had its counterpart in Ontario. The Orange Lodge demanded an end to all teaching of French in Ontario schools. English-Canadian newspapers presented the issue as a question of papist domination and as a French-Canadian conspiracy to dominate English Canada. Said one overwrought and undoubtedly unilingual Member of Parliament: "Never shall we let the French Canadians plant in Ontario the disgusting speech they use." How widespread such feelings were on either side will never be known, but it appears they were general.

It was in this already tense atmosphere that the conscription crisis arose. At first all elements of the population had enthusiastically supported Canadian participation in the war, though some nationalist leaders like Bourassa advocated only limited activity. As the war went on, however, enlistments from Quebec, which had never been high, dwindled. There were many reasons for this: the overwhelmingly English nature of the armed forces, the lack of French-speaking units and the failure to promote French Canadians, the hostility arising out of the school issue, and the contrast in outlook between Quebeckers, who had been cut off from Europe since 1759, and English Canadians, many of whom had only recently arrived from England. As Canadian casualties in Europe mounted, the need became more and more urgent for new recruits to maintain Canada's commitments. In efforts to stave off the possibility of conscription, political leaders like Laurier, and even the Church hierarchy, campaigned for French Canadians to volunteer. There was widespread resentment among English Canadians who felt that the *Québécois* were not "pulling their weight." Finally in 1917, after a visit to the troops in Europe, Borden became convinced that conscription was necessary.

In May, 1917, he announced that selective conscription would soon be introduced. The Quebec reaction included riots, attacks on progovernment newspapers, and mass demonstrations. Laurier, still playing the mediating role, warned that if the Liberals agreed to conscription, they would, in effect, be handing Quebec over to the nationalists, for the Liberals were the only political representatives of the majority in the province which was both pro-Canadian and anticonscription, and Laurier judged that anti-conscription feelings were stronger than pro-Canadian sentiment. Conscription would, he said, "create a line of cleavage within the population, the consequences of which I know too well, and for which I will not be responsible." But he also signified his continuing Canadianism by asserting that if the English-Canadian majority passed a conscription law, he would attempt to secure Quebec's compliance. All but one French-Canadian cabinet minister resigned from Borden's Conservative government, as did the Deputy Speaker and the chief government whip from Quebec. The depth of feeling was revealed in speeches by French-Canadian Members of Parliament. Said Louis-Joseph Gauthier: "My people are willing to go to the limit if you impose on them such a piece of legislation." Another MP warned that conscription might mean civil war and the end of Confederation. When the vote on conscription came, party lines were crossed and ethnic lines maintained; most English-speaking Liberals supported it, virtually all French-speaking Conservatives voted against it.

The extreme polarization of the electorate was revealed in the bitter election fight which followed passage of the bill and there was serious threat of civil strife in Quebec. English Liberals united with the Conservatives to form a Union government which ran Union candidates. The French-Canadian nationalists this time supported the Laurier Liberals in Quebec, the Laurier followers won 84 percent of the vote and 62 of the 65 seats; the Unionists won only three seats and 15 percent of the vote. Outside Quebec, the split in popular vote was not so glaring, as the Laurier Liberals gained 35 percent of the vote versus the Unionists' 65 percent, but Laurier's Liberals won only 20 seats while the Union government won 150. In terms of parliamentary seats, a united Quebec faced a united English Canada. The split which Laurier had always feared, and which he had worked all his life to avoid, was at hand.

Fortunately the war ended soon thereafter. Few people were actually drafted and the conscription crisis blew over, but the bitterness remained and served to nourish a new movement which was distinctly provincialist and sometimes separatist in outlook. In the first postwar election, in 1921, the Unionist government broke up, and the Liberals again formed the government, winning all 65 Quebec seats and 53 seats elsewhere in Canada. In the first Quebec provincial election after the war, the Conservatives were so weak that they did not even bother to run candidates in 41 of the 83 Quebec constituencies and with the sole exception of the 1958 federal election they have never since been a strong force in Quebec politics, at either the federal or the provincial level.

The Inter-War Period

During the 1920s and 1930s nationalist agitation grew in Quebec, partly as a result of the wartime hostility and partly in response to the economic factors which were discussed earlier. It gained strength under the impact of the Depression and found expression in the rise of a new Quebec provincial party, l'Union Nationale, led by Maurice Duplessis. Duplessis was elected in 1936 on a program of provincial rights and opposition to the federal government and English-owned business. With one exception in 1939 this appeal led him to victory in every election until his death in 1959.

Under his leadership conflict between the Quebec and federal governments often took the form of provincial protests against alleged federal encroachments on provincial jurisdiction, especially federal anti-Depression measures. The conflict thus became a more institutionalized one between governments, and this institutionalization was important in maintaining some restraint in French-English relations during most of the Duplessis period. With the exception of the 1944 conscription crisis, the most obvious expressions of the French-English cleavage were the arguments which broke out in federal-provincial conferences and in the "Ottawa-baiting" speeches of Duplessis.

The Conscription Crisis of 1944

Although this period could be characterized as one in which grievances for the future were stored up, the only sharp crisis in Canadian ethnic relations during the Duplessis years came during World War II and again revolved around conscription. When Canada entered the war in 1939, the Mackenzie King government was understandably afraid of a recurrence of the 1917 crisis and hence promised not to institute conscription. But, just as in World War I, the demands of total war soon outran voluntary enlistment and the Conservative opposition as well as other elements in English Canada and the military began to demand conscription again. Mackenzie King, in the hope of avoiding a full-scale crisis, sought a national referendum to permit the government to back out of its promise to French Canada. The referendum was a disaster. French Canadian groups such as *La ligue pour la défense du Canada,* supported by much of the lower clergy, campaigned for a *"non"* vote. In this they opposed the politicians and the upper hierarchy of the Catholic Church. In the eight English-speaking provinces the vote went 80 percent in favour of the referendum; in Quebec it was 72 percent against and among French Canadians in Quebec the *"non"* vote rose to 85 percent. Opposition to the war in Quebec was polarized by the campaign and statements on each side grew more bitter. *La ligue* grew stronger and became a political party, the *Bloc Populaire.*

The government avoided imposing conscription until 1944 when it finally appeared that King could no longer walk a tightrope between the English and French section of his party and the country. In the final parliamentary vote on conscription, King lost the support of 34 French-Canadian Liberals, although they continued to support him as Prime Minister. His dismissal of his pro-conscription Defence Minister, J. L. Ralston, allayed some French-Canadian suspicion, but once again, as is so often the case in government, it was simply the passage of time which saved the day for, fortunately, the war was by now near conclusion and it did not become necessary to use any of the conscripts in battle. In any event, most French-Canadian leaders appeared to realize that it was better to have limited conscription under King than full conscription under the English-dominated government which would replace him should he fall. King's political skill and the end of the war avoided a conscription crisis of anything like the magnitude of the earlier one, but again a residue of mistrust was left.

The Separatist Crisis

The immediate postwar period and the 1950s was a time of apparent calm in Quebec, and except for the occasional forays of Maurice Duplessis against the federal government, there was relatively little activity across the lines of French-English cleavage in Canada. The calm was more apparent than real, however, for the rapid urbanization and industrialization of Quebec society combined with the economic hegemony of the English population both within and outside of Quebec, were sowing the seeds for the next crisis.

That crisis which has proven to be more drawn-out and more threatening to the system than any of the earlier ones, really began with the death of Maurice Duplessis in 1959. His successors were unable to establish the tight control he had had over Quebec society. In 1960 the Liberals under the leadership of Jean Lesage defeated the *Union Nationale* using the slogan *maîtres chez nous*. It is difficult to know just how seriously most of the Lesage Liberals took their slogan. It seems likely, in retrospect, that some, such as René Lévesque, took it very seriously indeed and so did a fair number of other politically active Quebeckers, for starting with a number of pamphlets such as one called *Pourquoi je suis séparatiste* by Marcel Chaput, a disaffected scientist with the federal Defence Research Board, and carrying on with a wave of terrorism under the *Front de la Libération du Québec* (FLQ), separatism steadily gained strength in Quebec. The growth culminated when René Lévesque formally joined the cause and united the movement's various factions under the *Parti Québécois* banner.

In the period since its formation in 1968 the Parti Québécois has gained steadily in popular vote. In the 1966 Quebec election, 8 percent of Quebec voters supported one of the PQ's predecessors, the RIN *(Rassemblement pour l'indépendance nationale)*. In 1970 some 23 percent supported Lévesque's Parti Québécois and some 33 percent of the French-speaking population of the province voted for it. The PQ won seven seats in that election. Its representation in the National Assembly fell to six after the 1973 election in spite of the fact that it won 30 percent of the popular vote in that election. However, in the provincial election of November 15, 1976, the Parti Québécois took power gaining 71 of the seats in the Quebec National Assembly.[17]

It is difficult to evaluate what proportion of PQ voters were actually *séparatistes*, what proportion were supporters of Lévesque the man or of the democratic socialism the party espouses, and what percent were simply disgruntled with the Bourassa Liberals. The PQ came to power with only 41 percent of the popular vote although with an overwhelming majority of seats. Surveys taken at the time of the election indicated that only 49 percent of PQ voters supported independence in 1976.[18] The level of popular support for independence fluc-

---

[17] For a general description of the rise of the Parti Québécois, see Vera Murray, *Le Parti Québécois: de la fondation à la prise du pouvoir* (Montreal, Editions Hurtubise, HMH, 1976).

[18] Maurice Pinard and Richard Hamilton, "The Parti Québécois Comes to Power," *CJPS*, XI, 4, Dec. 1978, p. 745.

tuated around 20 percent of Quebec voters throughout the 1970s and did not change significantly after the PQ took power. On the basis of a detailed examination of public opinion surveys prior to and at the same time as the 1976 election, Maurice Pinard and Richard Hamilton conclude:

What made the difference between the PQ victory in 1976 and its previous defeats rests on factors other than independence. Very succinctly, these factors can be summarized as a set of very negative evaluations of the incumbent Liberal government as well as a set of positive evaluations of the PQ party, its leadership, and its platform on issues other than independence. The independence issue did not contribute much to the growth of the PQ in the election of 1976; actually, that option prevented a more decisive PQ victory (in terms of popular vote) by leading non-separatist voters to opt for third parties, despite their relative electoral weakness, or to opt for the Liberals, despite their political shortcomings. [19]

The PQ victory in 1976, then, can be attributed to a feeling that it could provide a "good government" alternative to what was widely viewed as a dishonest Liberal government which had mismanaged the economy and which was largely responsible for a spate of strikes which was crippling the public sector in Quebec. The Parti Québécois succeeded in maximizing its support by virtue of the strategy, adopted at its 1974 convention, of separating the election from the independence issue by declaring that after the election a referendum on the question of sovereignty association would be held.

Since support for sovereignty association did not seem to be growing, the referendum was put off for almost four years, but was finally held on May 20, 1980 after a fairly brief but intensive campaign. The wording of the referendum question itself was described as "soft." The Lévesque government did not want to scare off Quebeckers who wanted change but were not sure about how much change, so the question asked only for the right "to negotiate" sovereignty association, and promised that no action would be taken on the results of such negotiations until a further referendum was held. However, despite the cautious and conciliatory wording on the referendum ballot, the result was a rejection of the Parti Québécois proposal. Approximately 83 percent of Quebeckers turned out, and the final tally was 59.5 percent "NON" and 40.5 percent "OUI." In fact when we take into account that well over 90 percent of the non-French residents of Quebec supported the "NON" side, the result indicates that French-Canadian Québécois split almost evenly on the question as posed.

Thus while it is tempting to cite the referendum decision as a vic-

---

[19] Ibid., pp. 739-40.

tory for Canadian unity, we must be more realistic about the result. In fact there are a large number of Québécois who are dissatisfied with their place in the federal system. Even many of those who voted against the Lévesque proposition still favour fairly radical change in the structure of the federal system, and the opposition Liberal Party of Quebec, headed by Claude Ryan has espoused some fairly radical constitutional reforms short of sovereignty association. Given these circumstances, we can only guess that the decade of the 80s will bring us continuing debate on the question of French-English relations in Canada, and on reform of the federal system.

In summary, the "crisis" of the 1960s and 1970s in Quebec arose from demands for a revision of the constitution in the direction of greater provincial autonomy. The demands ran the gamut from those for the outright separation of Quebec, through recognition of a "special status" for Quebec, to relatively minor changes in the financial structure of Canadian federalism. Such differing ideas, said the Royal Commission on Bilingualism and Biculturalism, all have a common denominator: "They expressed a wide and deep dissatisfaction with the present political position and a manifest will to conduct a search for many possible roads, which almost all went in the direction of more or less radical reforms."[20]

The current situation evokes a different and less extreme kind of ethnic hostility from that of past conflicts. Inflammatory declarations such as those that accompanied the Riel, the Manitoba schools, and conscription crises are notably absent, religion is no longer such a major and explosive component of the French-non-French cleavage in Canada, and the majority of Canadians avoid the recriminations of the past in seeking redress of current grievances.

But perhaps the more peaceful face of French-Canadian nationalism as we enter the 1980s should not surprise us. The conflict here is not French vs. English, but rather a conflict between differing opinions of the direction Quebec should take in the future among French Canadians themselves. The referendum result itself, with French-speaking Québécois splitting virtually evenly suggests that the debate is between two sets of attitudes in Quebec and not between Quebec and Canada. In fact all of the referendum rhetoric propounded by the leaders of the "OUI" campaign, attempting to make the point that French Canadians should be given control over their own destiny, must have seemed puzzling to anybody outside of Can-

---

[20] *The Preliminary Report of the Royal Commission on Bilingualism and Biculturalism* (Queen's Printer, Ottawa, 1967).

ada. It does not take very sophisticated analysis to discover that given the results of the 1980 federal election French Canadians make up a majority of the governing Liberal Party, while the Prime Minister and a significant percentage of the cabinet are from the Province of Quebec. The outside observer might also be pardoned for asking whether the conduct of a referendum on separation did not already constitute as complete a measure of control over one's destiny as that available to any people in the world.

Nonetheless the events of the past decade are hardly reassuring to those who want to see the maintenance of some form of federation. The persistence of the current commitment within Quebec to some form of separation, sovereignty association, or special status, and the fact that among young politically active French Quebeckers there is a very high degree of commitment to some form of major constitutional change, leads to an obvious prediction of continuing difficulties in the rolling political compromise which holds Canada together.[21]

ANALYTICAL PERSPECTIVES ON FRENCH-ENGLISH RELATIONS

For most of the period since Confederation, the French-English division of Canadian society has been the country's single most visible cleavage. Hence it figures prominently in most analyses of politics in Canada. Different writers have brought widely differing analytical perspectives and personal values to bear on the problem. At one extreme are those analysts who have viewed the French-English cleavage as a red herring which obscures what should be the most important cleavage in Canada, that between the rich and the poor. At the other extreme are the separatist analysts who view the French-English cleavage as so predominant that until it is resolved and Quebec has achieved separate statehood, nothing can be done to redress other problems.[22]

Perhaps the most popular recent framework within which to cast French-English relations in Canada (and also the relationships

---

[21] Bernard, *What Does Quebec Want?*, p. 11 points out that there have been three other occasions in Quebec history when the concept of separation has had an airing. These were during the 1830s with the *Parti Patriote*, the 1880s with the *Parti Nationale* and the 1930s with the *Union Nationale*.

[22] The clearest example of the first type of analysis is John Porter's *The Vertical Mosaic*. Most of the separatist analysts also view the class cleavage as important but see the ethnic cleavage as logically prior. The clearest exposition of that point of view which has been translated into English is Rioux, *Quebec in Question*, but see also Sheilagh Hodgins and Henry Milner, *The Decolonization of Quebec*.

formed across other cleavage lines) is that of consociational democracy.[23] In its barest form the theory suggests that democratic politics in highly pluralist societies works best when its operating principles include at least partial segregation of the masses along either side of whatever cleavage lines are in question, together with a process of accommodation among the elites at the head of the various subsections of society.

The essential characteristic of consociational democracy is not so much any particular institutional arrangement as overarching cooperation at the elite level with the deliberate aim of concentrating disintegrative tendencies in the system.[24]

Deep, mutually reinforcing social cleavages do not form an insuperable obstacle to viable democracy. The crucial factor in the establishment and preservation of democratic stability is the quality of leadership. The politics of accommodation open up the possibility of viable democracy even when the social condition appears unpromising.[25]

In order for consociationalism to work it is not essential that subcultures be separated in a physical sense, but most consociational theorists at least imply that the work of the elites is made easier if there is considerable segregation. This will minimize tensions at the mass level and help maintain cohesion within each subculture, thus helping the elites to gain support for agreements they have made and to articulate adequately the interests of their subcultures.[26]

If we apply these ideas to the study of French-English relations in Canada some suggestions appear which have long been familiar to French-Canadian students of politics, but which often startle English Canadians. In theory, according to the assumptions of most English-speaking Canadians, if the two solitudes which are French and English Canada could be thrust together and the masses of the two groups partially integrated, then French-English tensions would dis-

[23] The framework was originally developed by A. Lijphart and other European analysts. For a brief description see A. Lijphart, "Consociational Democracy," *World Politics*, 21 (1969), 207-225, "Cultural Diversity and Theories of Political Integration," *Canadian Journal of Political Science*, 4 (1971), pp. 1-14, and "Consociation and Federation: Conceptual and Empirical Links," *CJPS*, XII, 3, Sept. 1977, pp. 499-515. For Canadian applications see S. J. R. Noel, "Consociational Democracy and Canadian Federalism," *CJPS*, 4 (1971), pp. 15-18, and *Democracy in Plural Societies: A Comparative Exploration* (New Haven, Yale University, 1977), and especially K. D. McRae, *Consociational Democracy*, and "Federation, Consociation, Corporatism—An Addendum to Arend Lijphart," *CJPS*, XII, 3, Sept. 1979, pp. 517-522.

[24] A. Lijphart, "Typologies of Democratic Systems," *Comparative Political Studies*, 1 (1968), p. 21.

[25] A. Lijphart, *The Politics of Accommodation, Pluralism and Democracy in the Netherlands* (Berkeley, 1968), p. 211. Both these quotations may be found in McRae, "The Concept of Consociationalism" in *Consociational Democracy*.

[26] McRae, "Introduction," in *Consociational Democracy*, pp. 1-28.

appear. In fact, the industrialization of Canada has partially achieved such a mixing of the two populations. It could be argued, for instance, that if hard rock miners from Chapais P.Q., and Timmins Ontario were put in the same tavern, they would very soon recognize that they have much more in common with each other than either group has with its provincial elites in Quebec City and Toronto. Yet why have inter-ethnic relations not been improving, particularly when the scene of most unrest is Montreal, where the two groups come together most closely?

Consociational analysis suggests that this worsening of relations may be caused indirectly by the very integration that was supposed to ameliorate the problem. The integration of the French and English solitudes may simply make it harder for the elites to establish the accommodations which produce inter-ethnic harmony or it may reduce the significance of culture and ethnicity to both groups, and thus destroy the basis for the hegemony of the nationalist elites. The problem may be exacerbated by the fact that the French-Canadian elite sees its traditional clientele disappearing as more French people learn English and become part of the English-Canadian industrial tradition. Paradoxically, it is at least conceivable that the nearer cultural cleavage comes to disappearing at the mass level, the more desperately French-Canadian elites, particularly those whose only power base stems from the continued preeminence of cultural as opposed to economic issues, may fight to maintain or even escalate ethnic hostility.

For current French-Canadian elites the alternatives may be painfully clear: the separation of French-Canadian culture in which case they can continue to play a predominant role, or the amelioration of French-English cultural conflict which will see the current French-Canadian elite replaced by one whose ideological *raison d'être* is economics and not ethnicity.

K. D. McRae has pointed out that there are both ideological and structural factors in the Canadian political tradition which may act to reinforce this apparently insoluble dilemma.[27] These factors are, paradoxically, the very ones which political scientists have thought held the country together. Structurally, Canada has lacked political parties which express and formulate the interests of English and French Canadians separately. In the politics of some ethnically plural European countries there are such parties and the accommodations which must be made between various ethnic groups are then made

---

[27] McRae, "Consociationalism and the Canadian Political System," in *Consociational Democracy*, pp. 238-261.

among the parties themselves—often in the process of forming a coalition to govern. In Canada some accommodations may be worked out within the parties, particularly the Liberal party, but most must be worked out on the federal-provincial stage. There the rigidities introduced by the categories of the BNA Act and particularly by ponderous governmental structures with their own maintenance needs may impede the establishment of livable accommodations.

Perhaps equally important is that despite all the "mosaic rhetoric" the dominant but unstated premise of English-Canadian political ideology is that there is no particular need to accommodate ethnic minorities other than by encouraging them to do folk dances on July 1, because it is the political destiny (and indeed duty) of minorities either to become a majority or be assimilated and disappear. This premise, reminiscent of the Durham Report, is workable only if the minority is not a large and permanent one. It is hardly likely to be appealing to French Canadians who clearly will never become a majority in Canada as a whole, and who certainly do not want to assimilate and disappear.

According to the postulates of consociational theory, the implication of this English-Canadian mind-set for French Canada is clear: to be a majority one must either separate or revert to the kind of "Quebec Reserve" politics which characterized the most tranquil periods during the years from 1867 to 1960. In that situation, French-Canadian politicians play a rather minor national role, while Quebec politics are left to them as their exclusive preserve. As long as Quebec life was controlled by the alliance of the Church and the state, this "Fortress Quebec" option was viable. However, under the impact of modernization, its viability has diminished to the point where, viewed from the perspective of many elements of the French-Canadian elite, the separatist option is the only option. English Canadians do not seem to have grasped the point that special accomodative devices are needed, and

. . . *because they (the English) have not done so, French-Canadians have reacted in the only way open to them; by an instinctive attempt to build—either by themselves or in concert with others—stable majorities of their own. As long as English Canadians remain majority minded, many French Canadians will find their most effective response in an increasingly autonomous Quebec. . . . Any genuinely pluralist society must learn to do better.*[28]

Devices like the Official Languages Act or the bilingualization of the federal public service may be steps in the right direction, although

---

[28] From McRae, *Consociational Democracy*, p. 301. Reprinted by permission of The Canadian publishers, McClelland and Stewart Limited, Toronto.

from this analytical perspective that is doubtful. Rather, what may be required if the separatist option is not to prevail is a much more fundamental restructuring of Canadian politics and a change of attitudes (on both sides) to permit the genuine accommodation of minorities in the central institutions. That a change in English-Canadian attitudes might help convince French Canadians that they have a place in Confederation is not a new point, but attitudes, as we shall see in Chapters 4 and 5 do not change very rapidly. However, the logic of the "restructuring" approach has been in part manifested by efforts such as the provision of more Francophone representation within the federal bureaucracy, proposed restructuring of the senate, and suggestions for a form of proportional representation within the House of Commons. More realistic than such symbolic and institutional "fiddling," according to this line of reasoning, might be to give Quebec constitutional jurisdiction over heretofore federal matters such as telecommunications and cable TV whereby the provincial government could really have the final say on all cultural matters within the province. However, ultimately only time and the relentless imperatives of economics will determine the fate of Quebec, and in the final analysis, the alternative may well be some form of sovereignty for Quebec and some form of association with the other parts of Canada. That this bears a remarkable similarity to our current form of federation should not be so surprising. Mankind's capacity for re-inventing the wheel is inexhaustible.

In the meantime it might also be acknowledged that John Porter and a good number of other left-leaning analysts of Canadian politics have an important point to make too: for vast numbers of Canadians, French- and English-speaking alike, the tragedy of the situation is that while English and French elites fight out the consequences of their earlier failures to develop adequate mechanisms of accommodation, the problems generated by other regional, class, and economic cleavages remain unsolved. The consequences of this real or apparent lack of attention to the problems of other regions are manifested in such phenomena as Western alienation, or increasing fractiousness on the part of Newfoundland. Moreover, in a time of extreme economic problems for all Canadians of all ethnic backgrounds, one can't help feeling that, to a considerable degree, our preoccupation with French-English relations is a luxury we simply cannot afford.

CONCLUSION

The reader may well wonder at this point whether the emphasis in these two chapters is not misplaced. Have we, perhaps, by concentrating on cleavages and neglecting the sources of consensus in Canada, painted too bleak a picture of the problems with which the political system must deal?[29]

We think not. In these chapters, our emphasis on cleavages and problems is intentional. Politics is a process of conflict resolution, and in the end much of that conflict is generated by cleavages in society. There is a very broad area of consensus in Canada concerning politics. But the things Canadians agree about do not become political issues. Our intention here has been to emphasize for our reader the many extremely difficult problems with which the political system must cope. Much of the rest of the book is concerned with the institutional and procedural manifestations of consensus which allow it to do so.

Whatever the difficulties Canadians often have with the array of cleavages which cross our society, it must be said that, viewed in the context of a world where lesser differences often lead to bloody war, the Canadian political system copes with them very well indeed.

[29] A. Cairns, "Alternative Styles in the Study of Canadian Politics," *Canadian Journal of Political Science*, VII, 1, (March, 1974), p. 115.

4
Canadian Political Culture: Values, Attitudes, and Public Opinion

The determinants of political behaviour can logically be reduced to two significant groups of variables: those which are external to the individual and those which are internal or "of the mind." Having discussed many of the former in Chapters 2 and 3, we now seek to describe the latter, the basic values and attitudes which in the aggregate compose the Canadian political culture, and to elaborate upon their consequences for the Canadian political system.

We use the term "political culture" with some reservations, for there are nearly as many definitions of the term as there are political scientists. Most would agree, however, that it is composed of the political values, attitudes, and empirical beliefs of the citizens of a political system and that it is a determinant of political action or behaviour.[1] We shall use the term in this descriptive and basically uncomplicated sense.

There are three major approaches to the study of political culture. The most obvious focus is the values and attitudes that make up that culture. It is possible to establish what these attitudes and values are simply by asking a scientifically selected sample of individuals a set of carefully designed questions which answer the basic question: "What are your values and attitudes?" Another approach is to speculate about the predominant attitudes of a political culture by observing the patterns of political behaviour which are typical of the political system. The researcher works backwards, deducing the likely attitudinal causes from the observed behavioural patterns. There are two broad styles of behavioural research commonly employed here. One utilizes the quantitative tools and "hard data" of survey research[2] and the

---

[1] See especially: Sydney Verba, "Comparative Political Culture," in Lucien Pye and Sydney Verba (eds.), *Political Culture and Political Development* (Princeton, 1965), p. 513, and Samuel C. Patterson, "The Political Cultures of American States," in N. R. Luttbeg, *Public Opinion and Public Policy* (Dorsey, Homewood, 1968), p. 276; see also: Whittington, "Political Culture: The Attitudinal Matrix of Politics," in J. Redekop (ed.), *Approaches to Canadian Politics* (Prentice-Hall, 1978), pp. 140-41.
[2] Examples of the approach to political culture in Canada are provided by R. Simeon and D. Elkins "Regional Political Cultures in Canada," *CJPS*, September 1974, and J. Wilson, "The Canadian Political Cultures," *CJPS*, September 1974.

other employs the softer and more impressionistic techniques of historical analysis.[3]

The third and the most macroscopic of the approaches to political culture is institutional in its focus. Here the presumption is that we can discover something about the long-run value preferences of a society by investigating the legal and institutional framework within which politics occurs. For example, the existence of parliamentary institutions likely reflects a fairly deep-seated commitment to the values of popular sovereignty and representative democracy in the Canadian political culture.

Finally it must be noted at this point that the above approaches to the study of political culture all focus on the need to discover the actual "stuff" of political culture—the attitudes and values that make it up. A fourth approach to political culture is to view it as the *result* of the process called political socialization. Here it is assumed that important clues to the nature of the political culture may lie in the nascent political values and attitudes of children and that certainly the process by which children acquire such attitudes and values can have a significant impact on their nature and intensity, and hence on the political culture itself.

In general, Chapters 4 and 5 are concerned with the values, attitudes, opinions, and patterns of political participation of that large part of the Canadian population which is not engaged full-time in playing political roles. We are concerned here not so much with politicians, senior bureaucrats, or the leaders of the largest interest groups as with the man on the street or the woman in the middle row of a community association meeting.[4] However, it is important to point out that most of the values and attitudes described here are shared by the players of more highly politicized roles. Indeed it is this sharing of values which does a great deal to stabilize the Canadian political system and to ensure that, in spite of the barriers which the ordinary man or woman may encounter when trying to participate in

---

[3] While Hartz, McRae, and Horowitz (cited infra) are the best known proponents of an historical approach to Canadian political culture, a recent article by Reg Whitaker breaks new ground, extending the usefulness of this approach. See: "Images of The State in Canada," in Panitch (ed.), *The Canadian State: Political Economy and Political Power* (University of Toronto Press, 1977). See also: D. Bell and L. Tepperman, *The Roots of Disunity: A Look at Canadian Political Culture* (McClelland and Stewart, Toronto, 1979).

[4] For a critical assessment of the significance of mass values for the political system see J. Shiry, "Mass Values and System Outputs," in Pammett and Whittington, (eds.), *The Foundations of Political Culture: Political Socialization in Canada* (Macmillan, Toronto, 1976), pp. 36-58.

politics, political decision makers do take account of many of the average person's attitudes. Their attitudes are very often the same.[5]

The counter to this argument comes primarily from class analysis where the elites of the political system are seen as manipulating the process of political socialization, so that the values inculcated in the masses are those that serve the interests of the dominant class. In this way the status quo is legitimized by creating false consciousness among the working class so that they accept and even positively support a status quo which is contrary to their own interests. However, whether mass and elite values are congruent because of spontaneous social forces or because the elites are manipulating the masses (or both) is not as important at this stage of our analysis as the fact of that congruence.[6]

In the first of this pair of chapters, we will attempt to describe the basic values and attitudes that make up our political culture, as well as to deal with the more specific manifestation of such values and attitudes in public opinion. In the second, we will look at the two processes, political socialization and political participation. The former is the manner in which political culture is formed and transmitted from generation to generation and the latter is the way in which political culture affects political behaviour.

POLITICAL VALUES IN CANADA

Political values underlie attitudes toward specific political objects and also set the broadest parameters of political behaviour in a society. Because they are basic they are seldom articulated; but they form the guiding principles for the operation of the political system. Hence, they are usually reflected in its institutions as well as in the behaviour of citizens and governmental officials alike.

The most basic values held by Canadians are rooted in the Western political tradition, in the Judaeo-Christian religious tradition, and in eighteenth- and nineteenth-century democratic theory modified to some extent by the traditions and events of the twentieth century. These basic values include a commitment to popular sovereignty, political equality, and majoritarianism. They form a set of unstated

---

[5] On this point see Norman R. Luttbeg, *Public Opinion and Public Policy*, Part V, pp. 245-390.
[6] See Panitch, *The Canadian State*, articles by Panitch and Whitaker for a full development of this argument. See also Zureik, "Major Issues in Political Socialization Research," in Zureik and Pike (eds.), *Socialization and Values in Canadian Society, Vol. I: Political Socialization* (McClelland and Stewart, 1975).

premises which underlie attitudes more directly related to the day-to-day workings of the political system.

Popular Sovereignty

Canadian political values are traditionally broadly described as democratic. Democracy may be viewed as a set of ultimate values, but we prefer to view it primarily as a set of operational procedures for realizing certain broad societal goals. Stated as a theoretical abstraction, the democratic aim or ultimate democratic value, is the "common good" or the common interest. Democracy as a means of realizing the common good is a system of government designed to reflect the will of the people as a whole rather than that of an individual or of a small elite. The limitations of democracy, as stated in such ethereal terms as these, follow from the fact that there is likely to be no agreement as to what the common good is. In many cases the "common good" will conflict directly with the particular short-run demands put forward by individuals and groups within the society. Therefore, democracy is perhaps best viewed as a form of government which attempts to maximize or "optimize" the common good by satisfying the needs of as many people as possible. This attempt is expressed in the principle of popular control or *popular sovereignty*.

Direct democracy, or the actual involvement of all of the members of a society in the policy process, is not possible in a large nation state. The complex and technical policies being dealt with by governments today do not encourage direct participation in government by all of the people. Indeed, the difficulty of passing even non-technical legislation in a legislature of 23 million is plainly ludicrous. Some indirect means must be found, therefore, to give effect to popular sovereignty, and the most common method of achieving this in a modern democracy is through elected representatives. Thus, in a modern democracy, the people do not govern; rather they choose their governors.

Political Equality[7]

Popular sovereignty is usually institutionalized through a system of periodic elections, which in turn presumes certain secondary values. The secondary values have been referred to collectively as the principles of political equality: every adult should have the right to vote;

---

[7] Note here that Robert Dahl views political equality as a goal of democracy and majority rule as a guiding principle for attaining it. The sociopolitical process for attaining the democratic goal he calls "polyarchy." See R. A. Dahl and C. E. Lindblom, *Politics, Economics and Welfare* (Harper and Row, New York, 1953), p. 41, chs., 10-11.

each person should have one vote; no person's vote should be weighted differently from any other person's vote; and representation should be at least roughly proportional to population.

Political equality, however, means more than "one man, one vote," for a further assumption behind democratic elections is that the voter has real alternatives from which to choose, and that one can make one's choice freely. Thus, the political freedoms, such as freedom of assembly, association, conscience, and expression are fundamental values tied up inextricably with democracy as a governmental form. The institutional guarantees of these basic freedoms are to be found in devices such as the secret ballot, and in legal documents such as the Canadian Bill of Rights and the 1981 constitutional Charter of Human Rights.

Majoritarianism
Majority rule is a key operational principle of democratic government. The term means two things. First it applies to the electoral process itself, in that the candidate who gets the largest number of votes in an election becomes the representative for the societal unit. Second, it applies when the representatives make policy decisions. In cases where there is not unanimous agreement as to what should be done, the alternative preferred by the largest number of representatives is the one implemented. However, the majoritarian principle is not absolute; there are limits placed on majority. For instance, if a majority decided to abolish one of the basic freedoms, such as freedom of association, the system would cease to be democratic. Such tampering with democratic values, even by the majority, is normally considered to be unacceptable in democratic political systems. Thus, while majority rule is a very important principle of democracy, it is seldom if ever deemed to be absolute.

A corollary of the limitation on the principle of majority rule is that the minority will accept decisions of the majority as long as the majority does not violate other democratic values such as political equality. Should a dissident minority refuse to abide by a policy decision of the majority, or should the majority take an extreme measure to suppress the legitimate rights of the minority, the political system would be in danger either of breaking up or of ceasing to be democratic.

Liberal and Non-Liberal Democracy
Many Canadians have come to identify democratic values with the somewhat more specific principles embodied in the "semi-ideology" of liberal democracy. In its most extreme incarnation, liberalism includes a commitment to individualism and to individual liberties, a closely related commitment to the principles of private property and

individual property rights, and a commitment to economic free enterprise and capitalism. These may very well be important values held by a majority of people in the Western democracies and particularly in the United States, but they are not necessary to a system of democratic politics. As Professor C. B. Macpherson has pointed out:

Democracy is not properly to be equated with our unique Western liberal-democracy [for] . . . clearly non-liberal systems which prevail in the Soviet countries and the somewhat different non-liberal systems of most of the underdeveloped countries of Asia and Africa have a genuine historical claim to the title democracies.[8]

In fact, it seems inarguable that liberal values in Canada are being diluted gradually by at least partial acceptance of such socialist principles as economic equality, social and economic planning, and increased intervention of government in our everyday lives.[9] More importantly, there is a school of thought (which we will describe below) which posits that the Canadian value system differs significantly from the American on just this point of commitment to liberal ideals, and that the differences spring from long-standing historical causes. However, the conflict between liberalism and socialism as sets of political values is a very central aspect of political life, not only in Canada but in other Western democracies as well. To tie the fundamental principles of democracy, such as popular sovereignty, political equality, and majoritarianism to either liberal or non-liberal values is endangering the value consensus on which democracy rests. The commitment to democracy is far more important than the commitment to liberalism or to some non-liberal ideology such as socialism, for democracy can be made compatible with either.

We have already referred to liberalism as a "semi-ideology," largely because its principles, although widely held, are seldom made explicit by those who hold them and are often held virtually unconsciously. Values such as individualism, competition, private property, and a laissez-faire relationship of the state to the individual *pervasively* and *persistently* dominate the collective mind-set of Canadians. The *pervasiveness* can be seen in the extent to which liberal values are mouthed by our politicians, crusaded for by our media and staunchly believed in by average Canadians. Even the "left" in Canada while attempting to explicitly reject liberalism never seems quite to succeed because bits and pieces of liberal values remain as part of

[8] C. B. Macpherson, *The Real World of Democracy* (The Canadian Broadcasting Corporation, Toronto, 1965), pp. 3-4.
[9] George Grant, *Technology and Empire* (Anansi, Toronto, 1968), pp. 43-44.

their unconscious intellectual baggage. For example Marxist intellectuals in Canada reject individualism but embrace the fight for individual rights, and the Socialist political parties in Canada speak of controlling capitalism but not of replacing it with a different social and political order. The irony is that the political and intellectual Marxists in Canada brand working-class commitment to liberal values as false consciousness while at the same time they are themselves precluded from being "compleat Marxists" by a deep-seated and unspoken commitment to individualism, competition, and private property.

But the pervasiveness of liberalism in the Canadian political culture is only part of the mystery. The still more puzzling phenomenon of liberalism is the dogged persistence of liberal values, even in the face of factual evidence which contradicts them. Many of our cherished liberal values are in fact but myths or ideals which bear little relationship to modern realities; yet even when confronted with evidence of the inappropriateness of these values we tend to explain away the contradictions and cling to the myths. For example, the notion of equal opportunity in the economic system—every individual has the potential to become a millionaire—is factually negated daily. There are almost no Horatio Algers (or Roy Thompsons) today, and nobody seriously believes that he or she will ever actually get rich, but we still cling to the myth, to the liberal value of equal opportunity.

The persistence of this sort of false-consciousness can in part be explained through the "gentleness" of the economic inequities in liberal societies. Even though there are wide disparities in the distribution of income, the better-off individuals in society are willing to inoculate themselves against radical change in the economic structure by providing generous welfare benefits, health care, etc. The lot of the "have-nots" in Canadian society is kept at a level far below that of the middle class but well above the level where disgruntlement might be translated into working class unrest or class revolution.

The persistence of liberal values is also made easier because of the fact that liberalism is not codified as "OUR IDEOLOGY" but rather remains as a set of vague principles. As Elia Zureik has said: "What makes the process of legitimation so successful is the absence of an explicit, articulated set of abstract political principles which could be assessed and critically examined."[10] In this sense liberalism persists because it is too vague to be a clear target for criticism.

The overall point to be made here is that while liberalism is difficult to deal with as a true ideology, there is a set of political values we call

---

[10] Zureik, *Socialization and Values*, p. 49.

liberal, and those values are so deep-rooted in our political culture that they colour the thinking even of explicitly anti-liberal critics of our system. We are presuming, then, that ours is basically a liberal society whose liberal values have been diluted (or polluted) by principles such as toryism, socialism, and corporatism and in the next section of this chapter we intend to analyze the influence of those non-liberal political values on the structure and content of Canadian liberalism. (Fortunately for us in this endeavour, the writers of textbooks are able to stand totally outside of their own liberal biases!)

The Dilution of Canadian Liberalism[11]

While all of the Anglo-Saxon democratic world has in common a commitment to the values of popular sovereignty, political equality, and majoritarianism, it is the purity of their commitment to liberalism that ultimately distinguishes their political cultures one from the other. Hence it can be generally concluded that the political culture of the United States of America is the most purely liberal, and that the political culture of the United Kingdom is the most diluted by strains of toryism. Canada it seems stands somewhere in the middle.

One of the best known of the various approaches to identifying idiosyncratically Canadian patterns of political culture is the comparative historical approach known as the "fragment theory" which was introduced by Louis Hartz and modified and elaborated by K. D. McRae and Gad Horowitz. While McRae and Horowitz differ substantially on several points[12] concerning the differences between Canadian and American value systems, they essentially agree that the English Canadian political culture is more conservative or "tory" than the U.S. They both conclude that the values of collectivism, corporatism, and an organic view of the state dilute Canadian liberalism far more than American liberalism:

[11] In the writing of this section we are highly indebted to Professor David Falcone of Duke University who synthesized much of the material in his Ph.D. Dissertation. See *Legislative Change and Output Change: A Time Series Analysis of the Canadian System* (unpublished Ph.D. Dissertation, Duke University, 1974). See also Louis Hartz (ed.), *The Founding of New Societies,* ch. 4, for Hartz's analysis and ch. 7 for McRae's and Horowitz's, "Conservatism, Liberalism and Socialism in Canada: an Interpretation," *CJPS,* 32, May 1966, 144-171, and Bell and Tepperman, *The Roots of Disunity.*

[12] For more recent material on the difference between Horowitz and McRae see: Horowitz, "Notes on 'Conservatism, Liberalism, and Socialism in Canada,' " *CJPS,* June 1978, p. 383; McRae, "Le Concept de la Société Fragmentaire de Louis Hartz: son application à l'exemple Canadien," *Canadian Journal of Political and Social Theory,* Fall 1979, p. 69.

Canadian political society has thus stressed order, loyalty, and deference to govern-ment more than popular assent. Rather than "life, liberty, and the pursuit of happi-ness," the need has been peace, order, and good government. Social equality is desired but with less fervour than in America. Hierarchy in all spheres of life is taken for granted. [13]

Paradoxically, it is pointed out by some authors, most notably Gad Horowitz[14] that it is the tory streak in the Canadian political culture which supports collectivist tendencies. Because the tory tradition is rooted in feudalism which is ultimately a system featuring an organic or collectivist relationship of the individual to the state, the Canadian political system has been far more willing to engage in egalitarian health and welfare programs than has that of the U.S. In the same sense that the feudal landlord feels responsible for the well-being of his tenants or serfs and their families, the Canadian tory feels a "noblesse oblige" toward the less fortunate members of society. The liberal assumes all people are *born* equal and that therefore all the state must provide is *equal opportunity* and justice will be served. The tory on the other hand assumes that all people *are not equal* and never will be so that the state must look after the genetically inferior members of society by providing redistributive social programs. This phenomenon, referred to as "red toryism" has meant that conserva-tive politicians have often been willing to initiate economically egali-tarian policies which one might expect to be more exclusively cham-pioned by socialists. Moreover, as Horowitz has argued, this red tory streak in our political culture has made possible the emergence and survival of "an influential and legitimate socialist movement in Eng-lish Canada as contrasted with the illegitimacy and early death of American socialism."[15]

Thus English Canadian liberal values have been diluted to the extent that Canada is inegalitarian socially and yet amenable to some of the norms of economic egalitarianism and to the use of state power to implement those norms. By contrast, the U.S. is committed to so-cial equality but opposed to limits on the laissez-faire operation of the economy which would be necessary to achieve even modest steps in the direction of economic egalitarianism. This contrast is underscored

[13] Erwin Hargrove, "Popular Leadership in Anglo-American Democracies," in Lewis Edinger (ed.), *Popular Leadership in Industrial Societies* (John Wiley and Sons, New York, 1966), p. 147.

[14] "Conservatism, Liberalism and Socialism in Canada: An Interpretation," *CJEPS* 32:2, May 1966.

[15] Horowitz, *Canadian Labour in Politics* (University of Toronto Press, Toronto, 1968), p. 9.

by Seymour Martin Lipset who uses a broader framework which includes Australia, Britain, Canada, and the U.S., to make political cultural comparisons. Lipset uses census data to show that Canadians generally evince more of a collective orientation than do Americans, albeit less than the British. Lipset also concludes on the basis of his data that Canadians are both more elitist and more ascriptive in their attitudes than Americans, but, again, less so than the British.

The points that Lipset makes are corroborated by many Canadian historical scholars on the basis of more impressionistic material.[16] Moreover Lipset and those same Canadian historians are also in agreement that another reason for Canadian-American differences revolves around the relatively tame style of Canada's westward expansion, the relative dominance of Anglican and Roman Catholic rather than Calvinist and fundamentalist religious traditions in Canada, and the non-revolutionary nature of Canada's achievement of nationhood.

Where liberal values do not form the dominant ideological dimension of the Canadian political culture is in Quebec. Here, as Ken McRae has pointed out in his adaptation of the Hartzian model to Canada, we have a "feudal fragment" which bears a stark contrast to the liberalism of English Canadian society. Canada, according to McRae, is a "dual fragment" and although he tends to understate the tory dilution of English Canadian liberalism emphasized by Horowitz, he is most astute in his description of the non-liberal value system of French Canada, which he sees as a legacy of the "ancien regime" in La Nouvelle France. While we have already spoken of the ideological idiosyncrasies of Quebec in the previous chapter, our emphasis has been upon the coincidence of cultural, ideological, and economic cleavages that characterize French-English relations in Canada. Here we wish to reverse our perspective and look at a potential area of ideological congruence between the Anglophone and Francophone segments of the Canadian political culture, corporatism. The question here is, does a common acceptance of corporatist values provide any ground for consensus between French and English Canada?

---

[16] E.g., W. L. Morton, *The Canadian Identity* (University of Wisconsin Press, Madison, 1961), pp. 84-87; Chester P. Martin, *The Foundation of Canadian Nationhood* (University of Toronto Press, Toronto, 1955); A. R. M. Lower, *Colony to Nation: A History of Canada* (Longmans Green, Toronto, 1946); J. Porter, *The Vertical Mosaic*; Erwin C. Hargrove, "Notes on American and Canadian Political Culture," *CJEPS*, 33, February 1967, pp. 21-29; and George Grant, *Lament for a Nation* (Van Nostrand, Princeton, N.J., 1967).

Corporatism in Canada

A recent scholarly application of the term corporatism to the English Canadian scene was by Robert Presthus. In his *Elite Accommodation in Canadian Politics*, Presthus provides a definition:

Corporatism is essentially a conception of society in which government delegates many of its functions to private groups which in turn provide guidance regarding the social and economic legislation required in the modern national state. Corporatism rests upon an organic view of society in which collective aspirations are seen as prior to those of any discrete individual or group, including the state. In English Canada, corporatism has been widely celebrated by both the church and many leading intellectuals. [17]

Thus, the corporatist component of our political culture conceives of society as a collection of interest groups and hence it has an anti-individualistic bias. This means that unless an individual puts forward his claims on government as part of the claims of a large group, his behaviour may be viewed as inappropriate, and political decision makers may define him as a "crank" or otherwise ignore him. Hence the corporate ideal may have major consequences for the way in which the Canadian political system operates. In fact Presthus goes on to conclude:

These components of Canadian political culture culminate, in turn, in a national political process that may be called one of elite accommodation. Essentially, . . . this is a system in which the major decisions regarding national socio-economic policy are worked out through interactions between governmental (i.e. legislative and bureacratic) elites and interest group elites. [18]

However, all would not agree with Presthus' understanding of corporatism. Leo Panitch argues that Presthus' definition "is cast at such a general level as to be virtually indistinguishable from pluralism and the long tradition of interest group theory that is intertwined with it." [19] The real difference between corporatism and pluralism is that the former tolerates fewer functional groups, features a more rigidly structured set of relationships both among the groups and between each of the groups and the state, and insists that all individuals "belong" to one of the groups. By contrast with this essentially organic view of society, interest group pluralism is rooted in liberal individ-

[17] Presthus, *Elite Accomodation in Canadian Politics*, pp. 25-26.
[18] Ibid., pp. 20-21.
[19] Panitch, "Corporatism in Canada," *Studies in Political Economy*, Spring, 1979, p. 46. See also: Panitch, "The Development of Corporatism in Liberal Democracies," *Comparative Political Studies*, April 1977, p. 61.

ualism. There are large numbers of groups competing with each other, and their relationships to each other and to the state are left to float according to the vagaries of group leadership, social and economic conditions, and widely disparate bargaining power. Individuals belong to groups as they choose and multiple overlapping memberships tend to be the rule rather than the exception. Thus, in modifying the concept of corporatism Presthus has been able to make it fit the Canadian experience, but in doing so he has likely distorted the concept so much that it doesn't particularly help us in distinguishing the Canadian political process from that of other systems.

But while it may be difficult to analyze Canadian policy and political economy as corporatist, there is a clear corporatist streak in our political culture. Hartz, Horowitz, and McRae agree that corporatism was imported into Canada in part by the earliest French settlers, who brought with them a feudal conception of society not unlike modern corporatism, and in part as a component of the conservatism which the loyalist element brought from the thirteen colonies after the American Revolution.[20] Even Leo Panitch who prefers to define corporatism as a "political form"[21] and not as an ideology admits that there is an "ideological basis for corporatism in Canada."[22] He argues that while corporatist values were inherited from the Loyalist tory streak in English Canada, and from the pre-French revolutionary feudal streak in French Canada, and while these values have reappeared in the responses of Canadian Liberalism, French Canadian Catholicism, and agrarian populism, that the values have never given birth to corporatist political forms.[23]

One of the first proponents of corporatism in Canada, although he didn't use the word, was Mackenzie King. In his *Industry and Humanity*, published first in 1918, King advocated that labour, capital, and government participate equally in the political decision-making processes, a scheme often touted today as "tripartism." As J. T. McLeod has put it, "King was not an orthodox liberal, not an advocate of individualistic, competitive laissez-faire. . . . His solution (to the

---

[20] Hartz (ed.), *The Founding of New Societies*, ch. 4; K. D. McRae, in *The Founding of New Societies*, ch. 7; and G. Horowitz, "Conservatism, Liberalism, and Socialism." It might be worthwhile to suggest a reinterpretation of their views of French-Canadian society as a "feudal fragment" to take account of the prevailing view of French-Canadian sociologists and historians that the earliest French society in North America had a predominantly mercantile value system, and that it was only after the conquest that the mercantile elements of that value system disappeared leaving the corporatist feudal fragment.

[21] Panitch, "Corporatism in Canada," p. 44.

[22] Ibid., p. 50.

[23] Ibid., p. 51.

problem of industrial conflict and class strife) was an advocacy of community interests as paramount over individual interests."[24] The fact that King's scheme was never acted upon, even though he was Prime Minister for most of thirty years of our history is a compelling testimony to the persistence and resilience of Canadian liberal values!

In Quebec, as well, the corporatist strain has appeared from time to time, most prominently in the 1930s and 1940s when it was championed by the *L'Action Nationale* and reflected in the policies of the Catholic Church and of the Union Nationale governments.[25] As Jack McLeod has pointed out:

In retrospect it seems fair to suggest that Quebec's strong corporatist strain, far from being an aberration in Canadian political thought, was well in tune with other theory and practice in Canada, emphasizing the primacy of community, but merely as a narrower linguistic community than liberals or English Canadians could contemplate. There can be no doubt, however, of the corporatist theme being indigenous to Quebec experience. Possibly this once prevalent Québécois view of the political economy of Canada is less atypical, or closer to the mainstream, than is generally acknowledged.[26]

However, advocacy of corporatism in Quebec was never coupled with implementation of the political forms. As Quebec entered its Quiet Revolution in the late fifties and sixties, the corporatist values were relegated to a minor place in the political culture of the province. In some ways the Quiet Revolution can be seen as a period when liberal values began to replace the pre-liberal thinking of the "feudal fragment" in the Canadian political culture. Finally corporatist ideas can be seen in the political philosophy of the Progressive movement in Canada during the 1920s. Both the United Farmers of Alberta and the United Farmers of Ontario advocated "group government" and "functional representation" although once in power there was virtually no attempt to actually implement these ideas. It would appear that again the indomitable values of liberalism prevailed over any effective experimentation with non-liberal (or pre-liberal) policies.

[24] J. T. McLeod, "The Free Enterprise Dodo is no Phoenix," *Canadian Forum*, August 1976, p. 12.

[25] It is interesting to note that a young intellectual by the name of Trudeau launched a scathing critique of corporatism in his *The Asbestos Strike* (James Lewis and Samuel, Toronto, 1974), pp. 25-26 (translation): "Our thinkers saw corporatism . . . as a means to tame the democratic thrust of the trade union movement. . . . Our brand of corporatism was actually devised for an elite who saw it as a means to discipline popular movements. . . ."

[26] McLeod, "The Free Enterprise Dodo," p. 12.

To return to the question posed at the end of the last section, it would seem that English and French Canada do share a streak of corporatist ideology but it is only a small part of their respective political cultures. If shared political values are to form the basis for ideological consensus between the "two solitudes," corporatism is too weak a strain at the present time to become such a vehicle.

Thus the corporatist strain is there in our political culture; it appears and reappears in party platforms, government programs, and individual proposals for reform of the decision-making apparatus of the political system; but it very seldom is manifested by positive action. Only in Quebec, where liberal values are less compelling, have corporatist ideas been significant for policy outputs and even there the persistence of such policies has been weak. Generally, as with conservatism and socialism, corporatism has been permitted only to tinge our political culture, to slightly qualify and to dilute the dominant liberal value system, but never to replace it.

CANADIAN POLITICAL ATTITUDES

Less fundamental than the basic values discussed in the preceding section are the attitudes or patterns of thought toward specific objects in the political world. Because they are more specific, our political attitudes may not be as universally accepted within the political community as our political values. On the other hand, because they are related directly to real-world objects, political attitudes are likely more important as immediate determinants of behaviour. Thus, for example, not only are individual attitudes to a particular political party likely to vary widely, but they are more likely to stimulate political action than a basic value such as popular sovereignty. The latter is so widely accepted in Canada that most Canadians neither think about it nor have to act upon it.

The Subjective Dimension

Political attitudes can be classified according to two main sets of criteria or dimensions: a subjective one and an objective one.[27] Using the subjective criteria we may classify an attitude as "cognitive," "affective," or "evaluative," according to its psychological significance for the individual who holds it. Objective criteria classify attitudes according to the phenomena on which they are based. They will be discussed in the next section.

---

[27] For an elaboration of this framework see the introductory article of Pammett and Whittington, *The Foundations of Political Culture.*

Cognitive attitudes involve simple knowledge of, or empirical beliefs about, real-world phenomena. If the manner in which we acquire cognitive attitudes is empirical or objective we can communicate them by using "is" or "is not" statements. Affective attitudes on the other hand consist of the feelings and aesthetic preferences we have for things in the real world. While it is accepted that knowledge or awareness of a political object must logically precede any feelings toward it, in many cases we acquire positive or negative feelings simultaneously with simple awareness. Affective attitudes are a reflection of our likes and dislikes and the mood in which we acquire them tends to be more emotional and aesthetic than empirical. Finally, evaluative attitudes are moral and ethical, and involve the conscious application of preexisting values or standards to real-world phenomena. Evaluative attitudes are moral judgments about the goodness or badness of a political object and are expressed as "should" or "ought" statements. These three subjective dimensions are summarized in Figure 4-1.[28]

Figure 4-1
THE SUBJECTIVE DIMENSION OF POLITICAL ATTITUDES

Type	Form	Mood	Mode of Expression
Cognitive	knowledge, beliefs, information	empirical, objective	is/is not statements
Affective	feelings, preferences	emotional, aesthetic	like/love (not) statements
Evaluative	values, judgments	moral, ethical	should/ought (not) statements

While it is helpful to make the analytical distinction among cognitive, affective, and evaluative attitudes, the distinction blurs somewhat in reality. Our values and emotions will colour our perceptions of political objects, our feelings toward them will depend upon how we perceive them, and our political evaluations will often tend to be rationalizations of our aesthetic or emotional preferences. Moreover, the intensity with which an attitude is held will have an important influence upon the extent to which it can affect our behaviour. Thus, the certainty with which we hold our beliefs, the strength of our likes

[28] Ibid.

and dislikes, and the firmness of our value commitments may be as significant as the substance of those attitudes.

The Objective Dimension

Using "objective criteria" we may classify political attitudes according to the phenomena upon which they are focused. Naturally, the primary objects of political attitudes are those related to the political system. However, attitudes toward political participation or abstention, for instance, involve perceptions of a "self to system" relationship. The attitudes to that relationship are, in the first instance, affected by the individual's perceptions of the system, but can also be affected by one's perception of oneself. Thus, "self" as a political object must be considered when evaluating complex and behaviourally significant attitudes such as efficacy and civic competence. For example, one's self-esteem can be an important factor in the level and intensity of political participation.

However, despite the fact that our political attitudes involve perceptions of self, the basic foci for our political attitudes are still objects in the political system. We can therefore categorize political attitudes as being related to the political community, the regime, or the authorities. By adding a second dimension, which views all political objects as "structural," "symbolic," or "conceptual" in form, we can classify the range of political objects in a still more detailed framework. Figure 4-2 is a nine-celled table showing the resulting objective dimensions of political attitudes with examples from the Canadian political culture.

Figure 4-2 is fairly complex and some of the categories require a bit of elaboration. Our attitudes to authorities for instance, are based mainly on indirect contact; few of us know personally the people who "rule" us. What we know of them is based rather on our view of the roles they occupy, classified in Figure 4-2 as "structural objects"; stereotypes with which we can categorize them, such as their party affiliations or the images of them which are imparted to us through the media, classified as "symbolic objects"; and finally our view of how they handle the specific issues of the day, classified as "conceptual objects." Furthermore, political values can themselves become political objects. To the extent that our political values are conceptualized or articulated as ideology it is possible for us to acquire attitudes toward them; thus, for example, Canadians learn cognitive, affective, and evaluative attitudes towards regime-related conceptual objects such as liberalism, capitalism, and welfare.

Political Negativism Obviously the ultimate utility of the two-dimensional grid we have developed here depends upon massive attitudinal surveys that would give us the data in order to fill up the

Figure 4-2

THE OBJECTIVE DIMENSION OF POLITICAL ATTITUDES

Level of System	Structural	Objective Types Symbolic	Conceptual
POLITICAL COMMUNITY (Canada)	Territorial factors: the geography of Canada, etc.	Beavers, flags, maple leaves; also personalized symbols, such as national heroes	Nationhood or nationality—the Canadian way of life or the Canadian identity
REGIME (the framework of government)	The BNA Act, parliament, the federal system, the public service, etc.	The Parliament Buildings, the Crown, etc.; also personalized symbols such as the Queen	Ideology: the principles of democracy, liberalism, socialism, conservatism, etc.
AUTHORITIES (the government of the day; the political system)	Specific political roles and (rarely) the incumbents themselves	Images of political leaders, parties, politicians	Issues

Adapted from Pammett and Whittington, *The Foundations of Political Culture.*

boxes with information about actual Canadian political attitudes. Then and only then could we have a comprehensive overview of the Canadian political culture. The only study which has tried explicitly to begin this process was undertaken by Clarke, Jenson, Leduc, and Pammett,[29] who, in a large sample survey of the 1974 electorate, uncovered important facts about the overall orientations of Canadians to the various categories of political objects. As can be seen from Table 4-1, the general conclusion is that Canadians are extremely negative in their feelings toward system objects.[30]

As can be seen from Table 4-1, Canadians have mixed feelings about political community-related objects, but their attitudes toward the regime objects are decidedly and emphatically negative in tone. This is explained by the authors of *Political Choice in Canada* as "simply a feeling that 'government' as a vague, amorphous entity is remote from the people, spending too much money, and not providing

[29] H. Clarke et al., *Political Choice in Canada* (McGraw-Hill Ryerson, Toronto, 1980).
[30] Ibid., p. 29.

Table 4-1

AFFECTIVE NATURE OF ATTITUDES TOWARD OBJECTS IN THE
CANADIAN POLITICAL SYSTEM (row percentages)

Objects of Attitudes	Positive	Neutral	Negative	N
Community structural	17%	46%	37%	1764
Community symbolic	—	—	—	—
Community conceptual	42	18	41	566
Regime structural	18	23	59	580
Regime symbolic	—	100	—	44
Regime conceptual	33	17	50	987
Authorities structural	15	11	74	442
Authorities symbolic	23	40	37	585
Authorities conceptual	9	26	65	1660
Total	20%	30%	50%	6628

adequate services."[31] Moreover, even where there is some positive response to "regime conceptual" objects, it is almost exclusively manifested in general feelings toward democracy and to the principles of the democratic process.[32] Finally, the most negative effect for political objects in Canada is at the level of the authorities. Canadians it seems are very cynical about their politicians and political parties.

While it is difficult to make accurate comparisons across time, it seems fair to say that this negativism described by Clarke et al., is a new phenomenon in Canadian politics. It is a phenomenon of the seventies and can likely be explained in part in terms of the events, issues, and personalities of that period in Canadian history. In the first place, the decade of the seventies was one dominated by major social and economic problems for which our political leaders were not able to provide solutions. Inflation ran at 8 to 10 percent per annum, unemployment rates steadily climbed, and resources were recognized as not only finite but also as virtually depleted. On this latter point, according to the 1973 figures the projected reserves of crude oil were to last us until the end of the twenty-first century, but in January 1980 a cryptic news item told us reassuringly that we would have enough fuel oil to get us through the current winter! We certainly must have been extravagant to use up a century's worth of oil in seven years. It is no wonder that Canadians have begun to be a little cynical about politics, given the apparent failure of the system to solve the major problems facing it.

A second possible cause for this negativism might be related to a

---

[31] Ibid., p. 30.
[32] Ibid.

perceived general structural breakdown in our political system. The increased acrimony in federal-provincial debate, and the apparent failure of the federal government to "take charge" in the face of economic challenges in the decade might have generated a lack of confidence in government generally. Moreover, during the seventies the point was driven home to Canadians that we are not a very important power in international affairs and may never be more than a minor actor on the global stage in the future. Rather than face this fact and deal with a reduced role in world affairs with dignity, some of our political leaders have persisted in making a pretence of having influence on the super powers.

Linked closely to the above is the third probable cause of negativism among the Canadian public, and that is the general failure of our national leaders to live up to our expectations. The dominant figure in the decade was clearly Pierre Trudeau who came in on a wave of support not parallelled since the Diefenbaker landslide of 1958. Trudeau was the new breed of leader, the man for the future, combining personal charisma and "style" with intelligence and imagination. But while two of his three children were born on Christmas Day, he could neither walk on water nor turn it into wine. Our expectations of this man were so high that it would have been impossible for him to live up to them even in the absence of the economic malaise that descended upon the country during the decade. As it turned out, Trudeau could not solve our most serious problems, and we began to see a less attractive irascibility and arrogance in his forceful personality. He "failed" us—although no one could have succeeded—and the opposition parties could offer us nothing that looked significantly better. The result of these forces was that Canadians entered the decade of the eighties with a cynical and negative set of attitudes to system-related political objects. Given the lack of available solutions to many of our problems and given the prevailing cynicism with which all governments are viewed throughout the Western world in the 1980s, the negativism identified by the authors of *Political Choice in Canada* is likely to be with us well into the next decade.[33]

PUBLIC OPINION AND OPINION FORMATION

An individual's political behaviour is determined partly by one's environment, which includes the institutional channels of participation provided by the system itself, and partly by one's political attitudes.

---

[33] We were assisted in the preparation of this section by Jon Pammett, a colleague at Carleton and a coauthor of *Political Choice in Canada*.

However, for this behaviour to be meaningful, it must be related to the specific political issues of the day. In other words the individual must formulate a personal opinion about the various issues. The collectivity of private opinions about political issues is often called *public opinion*. It is of course possible to have opinions about public affairs (such as sports or the sex lives of movie stars) which are certainly not political, but the term is to be used here in its explicitly political sense. [34]

It might logically be expected that public opinion would provide concrete guidance for the political system. However, considerable work by the Survey Research Center of the University of Michigan has shown that in the United States there is often relatively little correlation between public opinion and public policy. In some well established areas of controversy there is a reasonably close correlation between constituency opinions and the representative's stand in the legislature, but in an area such as foreign policy, there is frequently none at all. [35]

In Canada there is less empirical evidence, but at least one source suggests that there is little significant correlation between the attitudes of legislative policy makers and the opinions of their constituents. [36] On some issues, such as capital punishment, there has been an easily visible gulf between public opinion (which favours capital punishment) and legislative decision. In general, we might expect even less correspondence between the views of Canadian MPs and their constituents than between American Members of Congress and theirs; after all, MPs are restricted in their voting by a more rigid party discipline.

As far as political stability is concerned, the important question is whether the opinions of cabinet ministers, senior bureaucrats, and interest group leaders approximate public opinion. Here we are in territory where there is very little research available in Canada or anywhere else. We do know that many social values are shared by elite and mass, but as to opinion on specific issues we have little information.

---

[34] The most convenient reference in this area is the excellent booklet by R. C. Lane and D. O. Sears, *Public Opinion* (Prentice-Hall, Englewood Cliffs, 1964). On pages 117 and 118 there is an extensive bibliographical note. In addition, the student should be aware of V. O. Key Jr., *Public Opinion and American Democracy* (Knopf, New York, 1961). An excellent collection of articles on the subject can be found in Norman R. Luttbeg (ed.), *Public Opinion and Public Policy*. Each of the sources cited in this footnote is American, but the nature of the generic concept, Public Opinion, does not vary greatly from one Western democracy to another.

[35] Lane and Sears, *Public Opinion*, pp. 3-4.

[36] See A. Kornberg, Wm. Mishler, and Joel Smith, paper presented to the International Political Science Association, Montreal, August, 1973.

For the individual, holding opinions about politics may fulfil certain psychic needs. These include the need to find meaningful contact with the world, or more simply, just to have something to talk about to other people. The opinions of most individuals about political matters are not usually sophisticated or complex, and they are often inconsistent with other views held by the same individual. [37] For the individual, the inconsistency is irrelevant but simplicity is important. To most people political questions are both difficult and of relatively low significance, and unless they can be simplified the individual may tend to ignore them. Therefore, the political opinions which most people hold simplify complex issues to the point where the individual, however mistaken he may be, can take a stand and at least feel that he is participating in politics. This sense of participation, in addition to its importance for the individual (who may have been filled to his ears with public school democratic ethics and his supposed obligations thereto) is vital to the system, for it is one of the bases of political legitimacy.

Opinion Formation and Change

The formation of opinions is clearly affected by the political socialization process. The agents of opinion formation are the same as the agents of socialization in general, but in transmitting and helping to define opinions about issues and about the authorities who champion the issues, personal and group influences play perhaps the most significant role.

Group impact on opinions may occur through personal influence within the group, through mass persuasion by the group, or by the group's providing reference points for the individual. Direct personal influence within a group will depend on the nature of the group itself. The likelihood of such influence is increased if the group is a primary one—that is, one where relationships are close and "face to face." Influence is further enhanced if the group persists over long periods, if it meets frequently and if it is relatively homogeneous. If the individual has participated in decision making in the group, and if the norms have not been externally imposed, the group's influence is heightened still further. The influence of the group will also depend on the salience of current issues for the group and for the individual members. Of secondary importance is the setting in which the group finds itself—the status of the group in the larger society, the presence or absence of external opposition, and the availability of alternative groups.

[37] R. Lane, *Political Ideology* (The Free Press, New York, 1962).

Between 50 and 60 percent of Canadians belong to some form of secondary group, an organization such as a business association or trade union. Such organizations can be important in shaping an individual's opinions of public affairs.[38] Many of these organizations are used to represent their members' interests in politics, and as part of their technique they may try to shape their members' opinions in the "right" direction to support group aims.

Tertiary or categoric groups are another type, and everyone is a member of a number of these. A person does not join such a group; one is in it because of one's socioeconomic class, one's religion, one's nationality, or skin colour, or for any number of other reasons. Thus French Canadians form a categoric or tertiary group as do Blacks or Roman Catholics. The influence of a categoric group in defining a Canadian's opinions may be very great or it may be negligible, depending on whether the group has taken a stand on a particular issue, and whether or not one actually identifies with the group in which one is categorized. For example, various segments of the Roman Catholic Church took a negative stance toward the 1969 Criminal Code amendments which legalized abortion and homosexuality. Whether an individual Catholic would agree with the Church's stance would depend, among other things, on whether for the purposes of the issue one identified oneself as a Catholic rather than as something else, such as a union member or a homosexual. Nevertheless, later on we will show that membership in particular tertiary groups is correlated with a person's political participation. Indeed, in practice there is virtually no difference between the limits of these categoric groups and some of the cleavages discussed in Chapters 2 and 3. It should hardly be surprising, then, that being a member of such a group influences one's political opinions.

We have not yet examined, except incidentally, the direct influence of one individual over another in the formation of political opinions. Under what circumstances will an individual—a close friend or a political leader—be able to influence another individual, and under what circumstances will the influence not occur? To examine this question we may use the theory of cognitive dissonance.[39]

---

[38] In a 1965 survey of 2,100 Canadians, 55.5 percent belonged to some secondary organization. This particular definition excludes church membership since almost all Canadians are at least nominally affiliated with some church. We have described churches as tertiary organizations.

[39] For a fuller treatment see Lane and Sears, *Public Opinion*, ch. 5. The most authoritative treatment is in Leon Festinger, *A Theory of Cognitive Dissonance* (Stanford University Press, Stanford, 1957).

In any situation where a person is being influenced one will have three sets of "cognitions":

1. one's evaluation of the source seeking to exercise influence
2. one's judgment of what the source's position is
3. one's own opinion of the issue

Cognitive dissonance results if the three sets of cognitions are not consistent. It places a strain on the individual, the intensity of which will depend on the issue's salience. One will try to resolve the strain by rationalizing the conflicting positions. The dissonance can be resolved in many ways, but generally it will be the weakest of the three cognitions which will be changed. For example, if the person being influenced has great respect for the leader and if one perceives the leader's position to be widely different from one's own and if one does not hold the opinion strongly, then one will change one's own opinion. From this it follows that a wide difference will exist between a present opinion and that to which it may change only when the opinion is the weakest link. Should the esteem for the leader be the weakest of these three links, the change will occur in the individual's evaluation of the leader. Change may also occur in the perception of the leader's position, for the distortion of perception to relieve dissonance is also a well-known phenomenon.[40] To take a concrete example, suppose that Prime Minister Trudeau found it necessary to go on nationwide television to attempt to justify a large increase in income tax. People who were not strongly against higher taxes and who were "Trudeau fans" would be convinced of the rightness of his point of view, whereas people who were great fans of the Prime Minister and strongly against higher taxes might well misinterpret what he had said to fit with their own policy predilections.

A change of opinion will be impeded if the opinion has been tested and found to fit reality, if it is anchored somehow in group membership, if it serves some social or economic function or some psychic function for its holder, or if the holder has some public stake in it.

Public Opinion—Informed and Uninformed

Opinion may be expressed spontaneously or with little prompting, and directed to relevant authorities by knowledgeable groups or individuals. The vast majority of people do not express opinions in this

---

[40] S. E. Asch, "Effects of Group Pressure upon the Modification and Distortion of Judgements," in D. Cartwright and Alvin Zander (eds.), *Group Dynamics* (Peterson, Evanston, Ill., 1953), also Lane and Sears, *Public Opinion*, pp. 34-39.

way but, few though they may be, such informed opinions are important inputs into the policy-making process.

There is also a second type of opinion which is drawn from people by opinion-sampling techniques or by less sophisticated methods. Such opinion is likely to be, at best, poorly informed. For example, three months after a general election in Canada, 25 percent of the population typically cannot identify their Member of Parliament and 15 percent cannot name the party to which the member belongs; only about 60 percent claim ever to have heard or read anything about their MP. Yet 95 percent of the people interviewed after the 1965 election expressed an opinion about how good a job MPs from the major parties were doing, and only about 3.5 percent did not have opinions on the major issues of that campaign. Opinions are thus often held and expressed by large numbers of people in the virtual absence of information. In fact, opinions are often formed before information is gained and then information is selected to fit the opinion already held. The French-Canadian separatist may simply not notice opinions that separatism would be detrimental to the Quebec economy, while the hater of all things French will not notice media reports of brilliant work by French-Canadian doctors.

The nature of public opinion also depends upon the type of issue involved. In their historic work on the influences behind electoral choice, Berelson, Lazarsfeld and McPhee divide issues into style issues and position issues.[41] Position issues involve such questions as "should taxes be raised or lowered" or "should the anti-combines legislation be extended." They are more likely than style issues to evince a rational response, because they may be objectively rather than psychically important to the individual. Style issues such as linguistic rights issues or liquor laws typically concern matters of taste, or "style of life," and may serve the ends of self-expression. Style issues, therefore, often evoke an irrational response and engage the attention of large numbers of people. The information content of such opinions is typically very low, and information is used mainly to buttress preexistent opinions.

The Measurement of Public Opinion

There are some problems with the way in which much of what we take to be public opinion is measured. Public opinion, as expressed in the many polls we see, is usually measured in terms of its direction; that is, its position with respect to a particular policy or personality.

[41] Bernard Berelson, P. F. Lazarsfeld, W. N. McPhee, *Voting* (University of Chicago Press, Chicago, 1966), p. 184.

This is, however, incomplete information, for in order to evaluate it properly, we must also know something of the intensity with which an opinion is held. For instance, when 86 percent of Quebec's eligible voters went to the polls for the referendum on sovereignty-association, the results were as follows:[42]

Response	Number	Percentage
Oui	1,485,761	40.4
Non	2,187,991	59.6

However, those who followed the campaign know that the results are in reality very ambiguous. Some "Oui" voters may have voted that way in order to give their Quebec government a strong bargaining position vis-à-vis Ottawa and the other provinces. For others "Oui" might have been an assertion of pride in being a Québécois, something which many "Oui" voters saw as consistent with remaining Canadians too. Similarly, some "Non" voters may have been satisfied with the status quo, some may have been demonstrating favour for the Quebec Liberal party's constitutional change proposal, some may have been supporting Trudeau or Claude Ryan and some may simply have disliked the Parti Québécois.[43] While this issue was a particularly large and important one, almost any simple measure of public opinion will similarly hide a rich variety of shades of meaning.

To make matters even more difficult, while the referendum was based on a full vote, many of the public opinion polls which we see publicized are based on woefully inappropriate sampling procedures. For example, one Ottawa area MP mailed out some 50,000 questionnaires to his constituents in 1971 in an attempt to determine their opinion on several issues. He received 7,000 replies, and the results were reported locally as being highly significant because of the large number of replies received. After all, Gallup polls, which *are* reliable, have only 1,200 respondents and they are usually accurate to within plus or minus 2 or 3 percent. But the 7,000 replies in this case represented only 14 percent of the original "sample" of 50,000, whereas Gallup polls regularly get 60 to 70 percent response rates. What is

---

[42] Feldman, E. J. (ed.), *The Quebec Referendum: What Happened and What Next?* (Harvard, 1980) p. 7.
[43] In fact a recent article prepared for a conference at Duke University did indicate that the best single predictor of referendum voting was attitudes having to do with the support or lack of support for the political community. See: J. Pammett et al., *Political Support and Voting Behaviour in the Quebec Referendum* (unpublished as yet).

worse, the 7,000 respondents were self-selected, i.e., not chosen at random, so they were bound to overrepresent heavily the fringes of the population which hold strong enough opinions to bother to write back. This type of survey has almost no scientific utility unless we want to overrepresent that group which will select itself, and its results can in no way be taken as representative of public opinion at large. Large numbers of responses do not guarantee by themselves that the results will be valid. Thus, as guides to policy formulation, public opinion polls are very tricky devices indeed. One, well done, can be very valuable, but one which is poorly done—and many are—is worse than useless, for it may mislead policy makers as to the real nature of opinion.

There is little point in discussing the content of contemporary Canadian public opinion on specific issues.[44] Given the ephemeral nature of opinions and of many of the issues themselves, by the time a book can be set in type and published, the issues and the opinions are likely to have changed. What is more important for our concerns is the nature of the behaviour or political activity which results from the interaction of an individual's political values, attitudes, and opinions. And before we can discuss that we must also examine the way in which political attitudes and values are acquired—the process of political socialization. We will turn to both those questions in the next chapter.

---

[44] The most valuable source of opinion on particular issues is the periodic soundings of the Gallup poll conducted by the Canadian Institute of Public Opinion. Many universities maintain files of the raw data on which the newspaper reports are based, and there are also some valuable secondary analyses of the data. See in particular Mildred Schwartz, *Public Opinion and Canadian Identity* (University of California Press, Berkeley, 1967), and F. C. Engelmann and M. Schwartz, *Political Parties and The Canadian Social Structure* (Prentice-Hall, Toronto, 1967), ch. 10, "The Shaping of Public Opinion," pp. 204-221.

5

Canadian Political Culture: Socialization and Participation

POLITICAL SOCIALIZATION: THE LEARNING OF POLITICAL ATTITUDES, VALUES, AND OPINIONS[1]

Stated most generally, political socialization is the process whereby we acquire our political values, attitudes, and opinions. At root it is simply political learning and is the vehicle through which a political culture is transmitted from generation to generation. Political socialization is but one dimension of the total process of socialization. As political scientists we may tend to assume that "the political" is as central to the day-to-day concerns of the average Canadian as it is to us; in fact, however, politics may be a minor and intermittent concern in an individual's life.[2]

Political socialization and the more general process of socialization are in no way discrete processes. Political learning and non-political learning are profoundly related. Our manifestly political attitudes and values can be affected by our general attitudes and by aspects of our overall personalities, and it is possible, too, that political attitudes have an impact on personality development in general.

In this section we will first discuss political socialization, or how we learn about politics as an ongoing process. We will then examine the agents which teach us about politics and finally we will develop a profile of the early values, attitudes, and opinions of children as we discuss "who learns what, and when."

---

[1] Some of the ideas for this section are reflected in M.S. Whittington, "The Concept of Political Socialization and the Canadian Political System," *Quarterly of Canadian Studies*, 2, no. 5, 1973, pp. 207-215. See also major U.S. works on the subject: F. Greenstein, *Children and Politics* (Yale University Press, New Haven, 1965), *passim;* Kenneth P. Langton, *Political Socialization* (Oxford University Press, New York, 1969); Richard E. Dawson and Kenneth Prewitt, *Political Socialization* (Little, Brown, Boston, 1969); Roberta S. Sigel (ed.), *Learning About Politics* (Random House, New York, 1970); Robert Weissberg, *Political Learning, Political Choice and Democratic Citizenship* (Prentice-Hall, Englewood Cliffs, 1974); Dean Jaros, *Socialization to Politics* (Praeger, New York, 1973).

[2] See: Weissberg, *Political Learning*, pp. 20-23; also Pammett and Whittington, *The Foundations of Political Culture: Political Socialization in Canada* (Macmillan, Toronto, 1976).

Political Socialization as a Continuing Process

Political socialization is a lifelong process. While it is likely that the attitudes we acquire as children will have an important impact on our adult political attitudes, there is always the possibility that we can change our minds as we mature. We continue to learn new facts about politics, and such new information may either reinforce existing attitudes or cause us to revise our attitudes to various political objects.

That socialization is cumulative or developmental seems beyond dispute. Few would disagree that as we mature the amount of political information that we possess increases. (Table 5-1 illustrates this fact.)[3] Similarly, it is to be expected that the intensity with which we hold certain political facts to be true will vary as new information either reinforces or contradicts our existing belief.

Table 5-1

PERCENTAGE OF STUDENTS SCORING 50% OR BETTER ON TWELVE COGNITIVE QUESTIONS, BY GRADE

| | Grade in School | | | | | |
Score	4	5	6	7	8	9
50% or better (6/12)	20.7%	35.2%	56.1%	63.6%	81.5%	90.1%
Total number of respondents	816	869	884	845	896	172

However, cognitive development is but one aspect of the cumulative nature of the political socialization process; in the same way as our cognitive awareness of political objects increases over time, the sophistication of our political attitudes can also be expected to increase. While our earliest attitudes to politics may be vague per-

---

[3] Tables 5-1 to 5-16 are taken from data collected in a cross-regional survey of children's political attitudes in Canada. The study was administered with the assistance of school boards and teachers through a questionnaire filled out by the children themselves. There were two versions of the questionnaire. One was filled out by children in grades 2 and 3 as the teacher read out the questions. The second version of the questionnaire was more elaborate and was filled out by the students in grades 4 to 8 and was also administered to a small group of 9th graders. The completed study included almost 6,000 children in Halifax, Trois Rivières, Ottawa, Peterborough, St. Boniface, Lethbridge, and Port Alberni. The principals in the survey were T. G. Carroll, of Brock University, D. J. Higgins, of St. Mary's University, and M. S. Whittington of Carleton. The research was furthered through grants from the Canada Council and Carleton University and through the goodwill of the school boards and officials involved.

ceptions of political symbols and personalities and possibly diffuse affection or dislike for the objects of which we are aware, with some degree of political sophistication we become more capable of evaluating political objects with respect to our individual political value systems. Thus, while cognitive and affective attitudes dominate our political make-up in the earliest years, as we grow older, evaluative attitudes will come to take an ever larger place.

Tables 5-2 and 5-3 illustrate the development of sophistication in Canadian children's perceptions of political authority figures. In the early grades it appears that their affection for and objective assessment of the power of three "head of state" roles are closely interdependent. As they grow older, the children develop the ability to evaluate the power of an authority role in a more objective fashion. Thus, while relative affection for the Prime Minister declines slightly from grades 4 to 8, the likelihood that he will be judged the "most powerful" increases markedly; conversely, while affection for the Queen remains quite high, the likelihood that she will be judged "most powerful" declines significantly.

Table 5-2

CHILDREN'S "FAVOURITE" AMONG HEAD OF STATE ROLES (QUEEN, GOVERNOR GENERAL, PRIME MINISTER)

| Role "Liked" Best | Grade | | | | |
	4	5	6	7	8
Queen	74.0%	73.3%	69.3%	65.9%	59.4%
Governor General	9.2	12.8	16.3	20.4	29.3
Prime Minister	16.8	13.9	14.4	13.7	11.3
	100.0%	100.0%	100.0%	100.0%	100.0%
Total number of respondents	596	619	655	583	505

Table 5-3

CHILDREN'S EVALUATIONS OF MOST POWERFUL HEAD OF STATE ROLES (QUEEN, GOVERNOR GENERAL, PRIME MINISTER)

| Role Perceived as "Most Powerful" | Grade | | | | |
	4	5	6	7	8
Queen	60.5%	55.6%	46.6%	42.9%	35.3%
Governor General	10.6	12.2	11.8	11.7	11.4
Prime Minister	29.0	32.2	41.7	45.4	53.2
	100.1%	100.0%	100.1%	100.0%	99.9%
Total number of respondents	559	590	629	557	481

A further feature of the process of political socialization is that the earliest awareness of political objects occurs in the absence of any behavioural requirements. Children, while they may acquire knowledge of and feelings about political objects, are seldom, if ever, called upon to act upon those feelings. Thus their perception of themselves as actors in the political process must be anticipatory or vicarious; their political attitudes are acquired in the anticipation that at some future time personal involvement will be permitted or even expected. An example of this anticipatory socialization is the development of partisan preferences in children, which follows a pattern similar to that of the acquisition of political knowledge. While there are significant regional variations and while the intensity of the preference for a party may be weak, children do begin to make such choices at an early stage in their personal development. Table 5-4 indicates that even in grade 4 a large minority of school children can express a partisan preference and that by grade 8 a majority have such preferences.

Table 5-4

CHILDREN HAVING A PARTY PREFERENCE, BY GRADE, IN EIGHT CANADIAN COMMUNITIES

	Percentage with Party Preference in Grade					Total Number of Respondents
School	4	5	6	7	8	
Ottawa-Carleton	34.0%	40.9%	58.6%	59.0%	59.6%	1163
Ottawa	49.1	42.2	42.9	42.9	53.7	289
Peterborough, Ont. Public	18.4	23.4	34.5	38.2	48.9	395
Peterborough, Ont. Separate	34.3	12.5	16.0	36.4	54.8	126
Lethbridge, Alta.	15.4	25.0	29.9	33.3	33.7	520
Trois Rivières, Que.	40.3	51.7	54.8	48.0	*	232
St. Boniface, Man.	28.1	32.5	44.7	39.8	57.5	419
Port Alberni, B.C.	18.1	30.7	44.6	40.8	*	274
Halifax, N.S.	47.9	56.8	67.8	77.3	80.9	512

* Grades not present in schools studied.

Sources: Table from Pammett and Whittington (eds.), *The Foundations of Political Culture: Political Socialization in Canada* (Macmillan, Toronto, 1975). Data from Carroll, Higgins, and Whittington, Survey of Canadian Children's Attitudes.

The implications of the non-behavioural context of early socialization is that the pattern of socialization may be altered when an individual does become active in politics. One's perception of the voter's role or one's party preference, for instance, may be altered after some years of experience in the role. This *post-incumbency socialization* becomes particularly politically important with respect to highly political roles. The expectations that one might have of the role of MP for instance, will likely alter considerably after a few years of experience in the job. In sum, not only do our attitudes shape our political behaviour, but our experiences resulting from our behaviour shape our attitudes.

The Agents of Political Socialization

The acquisition of attitudes to objects in the world of politics is usually thought of as taking place through intermediary agents or media, which transmit and interpret the "real world" to us. While it is clear that some of our information about political objects can be acquired directly through observation of a sitting of the House of Commons, attendance at an election meeting, or even a stroll around Parliament Hill, a far greater percentage of such information is transmitted to us through our parents, peers, schools, and the mass media. These four agents of socialization not only function as lines of communication connecting us to a reality with which we cannot have direct personal contact, but they also interpret, consciously or unconsciously, the information for us. Because in our younger years almost all of our contact with political objects occurs through such agents or interpreters, particularly our parents, the agents of socialization can have a deep-seated impact on the substance and intensity of our political attitudes.

The family, since it gets to the child first, is virtually the only important socializing agency during the first few years. Tables 5-5 and 5-6 show the impact of parents' talking about politics on the cognitive awareness and partisanship of elementary school children in Canada. Like many learning processes, political socialization within the family does not usually proceed by direct parental teaching but rather by the child's picking up what is "in the air" in the family environment. If no discussion of politics occurs in the child's home, then very early in life the child may decide that political stimuli are not worth attention, and the child may never again pay much attention to politics. On the other hand, the child, if brought up in a home where politics are constantly under discussion, will begin to look for political information outside the home as well, so that he or she will be able to participate more actively in home life.

The importance of the family in arousing political interest has results which can readily be observed. Of those children whose parents talked little about politics, only 8.5 percent scored in the highest range on the test for cognitive awareness. Of those whose

Table 5-5

PARENTS "TALKING ABOUT POLITICS" AND COGNITIVE
AWARENESS

Cognitive Score	Little or No "Talking"	Lots of "Talking"
75% or better	8.5%	13.6%
50 to 74%	40.4	49.9
Less than 50%	51.2	36.5
	100.1%	100.0%
Total number of respondents	1568	2448

Table 5-6

PARENTS "TALKING ABOUT POLITICS" AND PARTY
IDENTIFICATION

Party Identification	Little or No "Talking"	Lots of "Talking"
No party identification	60.1%	42.5%
Some party identification	39.9	57.5
	100.0%	100.0%

parents talked about politics a lot, 13.6 percent scored in the highest range.

Time and again politicians reminisce about how politics was a constant topic of discussion in their childhood homes, or about how politically active their parents were.[4] This process, of course, repeats itself, and leads to certain family names appearing over and over again in politics. This may, in effect, reduce the size of the population from which politicians are drawn.

The school is another agent of political socialization. The child can pick up political information through the curriculum, particularly through formal instruction about government in "civics" type courses. Several studies have indicated that there are wide variations in the interpretations of history, political events, and the functioning of political institutions. Of particular interest are the differences between French- and English-language history texts which show radically different explanations for the events in Canadian his-

---

[4] See for example: C. G. Power, *A Party Politician* (Macmillan, Toronto, 1966), pp. 3-14.

tory.[5] Most of these studies, while they show that interpretive differences do exist in curricular materials, do not show the actual impact of these differences on Canadian children's political attitudes.[6] However, data from a national survey of Canadian elementary school children's attitudes shown in Table 5-7, indicates that, while there is a relationship between formal instruction and cognitive awareness, it is fairly weak.

Table 5-7

FORMAL "CIVICS" INSTRUCTION IN SCHOOL AND COGNITIVE AWARENESS

Cognitive Score	None	Some
75% or better	9.0%	14.4%
50 to 74%	44.3	45.7
Less than 50%	46.8	39.9
	100.1%	100.0%
Total number of respondents	4286	1110

Perhaps more important than the impact of the school curriculum on the child's perception of politics is the structure of the school itself. While on the one hand it may pass on general attitudes toward authority which are necessary to the stability of the political system, an overly authoritarian school may serve to discourage the mass participation which is likely an important component of a healthy democratic system. A school environment which is overly permissive may have equally unhappy results. Also within the context of the school, children may be confronted with "significant others," authority figures to whom they can look for advice and for a personalized model on which to pattern their own political lives. Not only the teachers, but also informal leaders among peers and cohorts may emerge as important agents in molding a child's attitudes to both authority in general and specific political objects.

The mass media can also be expected to have an impact during the period of transition from close adherence to the political views of

[5] Pratt, D., "The Social Role of School Textbooks in Canada," in Zureik and Pike, op.cit., p. 100; see: A. B. Hodgetts, *What Culture? What Heritage?* (Toronto, OISE, 1968).

[6] Trudel, M., and Jain, G., *Canadian History Text Books: A Comparative Study* (Ottawa, Queen's Printer, 1970).

parents to those of peer group opinion leaders, teachers, etc. Tables 5-8 and 5-9 illustrate the impact of reading the newspaper on political cognitive awareness and partisanship. Only 3.7 percent of those children who seldom read newspapers achieve a high cognitive score, as opposed to 16.7 percent of those who read newspapers a lot. Of those who read newspapers seldom, almost 65 percent had not developed a party identification; the corresponding percentage of those reading newspapers a lot runs considerably lower, at 43.7 percent.

Table 5-8

READING THE NEWSPAPER AND COGNITIVE AWARENESS

Cognitive Score	A Lot	Reading Some	Seldom/Never
75% or better	16.7%	8.8%	3.7%
50 to 74%	50.0	42.9	32.2
Less than 50%	33.3	48.3	64.1
	100.0%	100.0%	100.0%
Total number of respondents	1343	1784	1143

Table 5-9

READING THE NEWSPAPER AND PARTISAN IDENTIFICATION

Partisanship	A Lot	Reading Some	Seldom/Never
No party identification	43.7%	56.5%	64.9%
Party identification	56.3	43.5	35.1
	100.0%	100.0%	100.0%
Total number of respondents	1296	1305	1089

Perhaps surprisingly, no strong relationship appears to exist between exposure to TV and political awareness. This finding, illustrated in Table 5-10, possibly reflects the tendency of the child to select programs which have little or no political content. However, while children who watch a lot of TV are marginally more aware of politics than are those who watch little, the difference is so small that it may call into question the long-held assumption that there is a direct causal connection between television and political attitudes. These findings may also serve to reinforce the suggestion that the relationship between the mass media and attitudes is a two- or multi-step process, involving not only the media as the primary source of the information but other secondary agents who interpret or translate the political data for us.[7]

Table 5-10

HOURS OF TV WATCHING PER DAY AND COGNITIVE AWARENESS

Cognitive Score	2 Hours or Less	More than 2 Hours
75% or better	12.21%	12.19%
50 to 74%	44.04	46.81
Less than 50%	43.76	41.00
	100.01%	100.00%
Total number of respondents	1065	3339

Political information appears to be picked out of the media by a fairly small portion of the population whom we could call *political opinion leaders*. The majority of people pick relatively little political information directly out of the media. Instead they receive it second-hand from opinion leaders who can be found in almost every formal or informal group. The information is further processed by the recipient in accordance with preexistent beliefs and possibly even passed on to another group—perhaps the family—in which the individual functions as an opinion leader. One thing is certain: the role of the media as agents of socialization is a complex one.[8]

While most works on the subject of political socialization limit their discussion of agents to "family," "peers," "school," and "mass media," there are other socializing agents. Significantly, in a society that has come to be referred to as "organizational,"[9] and in which most adults spend many of their waking hours occupying an organizationally defined role, the organizations or institutions themselves must have a significant impact on the substance and intensity of our attitudes. To a large extent, people who operate within the context of organizations by necessity have to identify their personal best interests with those of the organization of which they are a part—"what's good for General Motors may in fact be good for me," if I happen to work for that organization. Hence some of the values of the organization either consciously or unconsciously will become internalized over time.

---

[7] E. Katz, and P. Lazarsfeld, *Personal Influence* (The Free Press, Glencoe, 1955), *passim*.
[8] See also Pammett and Proudfoot, in Pammett and Whittington, *The Foundations of Political Culture*.
[9] Presthus, Robert, *The Organizational Society* (Knopf, New York, 1962).

Voluntary associations, too, can come to influence our political attitudes through the use of "in-house" publications, by publicizing an organizational aim, and by providing an institutional vehicle through which opinion leaders can more efficiently reach a "ready-to-be-convinced" audience. Even children may feel the impact of such institutional socialization not only through the school system, as mentioned above, but also through organizations such as the Boy Scouts, which foster and disseminate the values of worship, loyalty to Queen and country, and good citizenship.

Finally, institutional or organizational agents of socialization come to play a very significant role in the process of post-incumbency socialization. As discussed above, our political elites are socialized in part through the process of incumbency. Membership in the House of Commons, cabinet, judicial system or bureaucracy cannot help but have an impact not only on the incumbent's perception of the institution of which he or she is a member, but on the importance of all related institutions. Because post-incumbency socialization affects only the elites and not the masses, and because it is the socialization of our political elites which in the long run will have an effect on the kinds of policies that our system produces, future studies of political socialization should address themselves more seriously to this aspect of the process.

Who Learns What, and When?

While it is not likely that politics has any great significance for very young children, we do know that they begin to learn about political objects at a fairly tender age. The first objects about which Canadian children become aware are ones which are primarily symbolic in content. The Canadian flag for instance is recognized by almost 90 percent of children in grades 2 and 3, and even the American flag was recognized by over 70 percent of the same sample of Canadian children. Next to symbolic objects, it would appear that the more highly personalized roles in the political system, such as that of the Prime Minister, are the most likely to be identified by children.

Thus it seems safe to conclude that the level of knowledge about political objects depends at least in part upon the nature of the object itself. Generally it is the symbolic objects which are learned about first, with awareness of the more personalized structural objects coming next, and with an awareness of the conceptual objects coming quite a bit later. But there are variables other than the nature of the political object which can also have an impact on the level of cognition. Studies consistently indicate that male children acquire more political information than do female children; in a similar fashion partisanship is higher and acquired sooner in boys than in girls. As might be expected, the socioeconomic status of parents,[10] the region of the country in which the child is living,[11] and even religion[12] are independent variables which correlate with the level and intensity of cognition and partisanship in Canadian children. Tables 5-11 to 5-14 provide several examples of the relationship between these variables and partisanship and cognition.

Table 5-11

SEX DIFFERENCES IN PARTISANSHIP

Party Identification	Male	Female
No party identification	46.3%	62.9%
Liberals	28.3	20.9
Progressive Conservatives	9.3	6.5
New Democratic Party	6.9	4.3
Others	9.2	5.4
	100.0%	100.0%
Total number of respondents	2023	2065

Table 5-12

SEX DIFFERENCES IN COGNITIVE SCORES

Cognitive score	Male	Female
75% or better	13.5%	8.3%
50 to 74%	47.2	43.4
Less than 50%	39.3	48.3
	100.0%	100.0%
Total number of respondents	2931	2882

While it is clear that some awareness of political objects occurs early in the child's life, it was also found in the 1960s that one's earliest attitudes toward the political system reflect positive affect. Young Canadian children—like their American counterparts—had a basically benevolent view of politics. Since it was suggested that one of the primary functions of political socialization is the inculcation of

[10] See: Richert, "Political Socialization in Quebec," *CJPS*, June 1973, p. 310.
[11] See: Pammett and Whittington, *The Foundations of Political Culture.*
[12] Ibid.

Table 5-13

FATHER'S OCCUPATION AND PARTY IDENTIFICATION

Party Identification	Professional	Executive, Managerial	Clerical, White Collar, Skilled Labour	Manual Labour
No party identification	47.2%	45.7%	50.5%	61.4%
Liberals	33.5	30.9	30.3	16.4
Progressive Conservatives	8.1	10.1	9.7	7.4
New Democratic Party	2.2	4.9	2.8	6.8
Others	9.0	8.4	6.7	8.0
	100.0%	100.0%	100.0%	100.0%
Total number of respondents	534	405	390	1224

Table 5-14

FATHER'S OCCUPATION AND COGNITIVE SCORE

Cognitive Score	Professional	Executive, Managerial	Clerical, White Collar, Skilled Labour	Manual Labour
75% or better	14.9%	14.1%	12.4%	7.6%
50 to 74%	47.5	51.9	44.4	37.1
Less than 50%	37.6	34.0	43.2	55.3
	100.0%	100.0%	100.0%	100.0%
Total number of respondents	550	418	403	1277

attitudes of support for the political system, this is obviously a vital point. Looking at some actual figures, it was discovered in Kingston in 1966 that among grade 4 children 52 percent thought the Prime Minister was doing a "very good" or "fairly good" job and only 5.7 percent thought he was "not very good" or "bad." By grade 8 about 60 percent of school children evaluated the Prime Minister's work positively, while only 9.5 percent made a basically negative evaluation.[13]

[13] Pammett, op. cit. See also Greenstein, *Children and Politics* (New Haven, 1965).

This benevolent view of political life may be related to the subordinate and dependent position of the child in a multitude of life situations. With age and experience, the child becomes less dependent and less dominated and thus more prone to cynicism about those in positions of authority. While it would be nice to think that such optimism and faith in our system is stimulated by inherent qualities of the Canadian system, the fact that other political systems enjoy similar loyalty from their children would indicate that the phenomenon is a function of the nature of childhood and not of the nature of the political system. Canadian children are also generally conservative, a fact that, again, is probably related to the subordination and dependency of most childhood situations.[14]

The benevolence of school children of the sixties, moreover, carries over from political personalities to issue areas. When children in both Colborne[15] and Kingston[16] were asked, in open-ended questions, about what they would do to change the world, the overwhelming majority of them mentioned things one would consider "benevolent." Helping out the poor or hungry was frequently cited, and a substantial majority said in one way or another that they would end war.

More recent studies, however, particularly in the United States, have indicated that the children of the seventies were likely to be more cynical about politics. Politicians in the age of the Vietnam war and Watergate did not look as trustworthy and as "parental" as they did in the previous decade. It would appear that American children have lost some of their idealism about politics[17] and the same seems to be the case in Canada. Stephen Ullman[18] writes about the low levels of support for the Canadian political community among the Micmac subculture in Cape Breton; Grace Skogstad describes patterns of alienation in Alberta adolescents;[19] Donald Forbes points to significant and growing pro-separatist attitudes among French-Canadian high school students; and J. -P. Richert talks of the "non-idealistic conception of government" among both English- and

---

[14] Taken from: Whittington, "Political Socialization and the Canadian Political System," p. 214.
[15] Hill, John, "Political Socialization of Children in a Rural Environment" (unpublished thesis, Queen's University, 1969).
[16] Pammett and Whittington, The Foundations of Political Culture.
[17] See particularly: H. Tolley, Children and War (Teachers College Press, N.Y., 1973); Jaros, Hirsch, and Fleron, "The Malevolent Leader: Political Socialization in an American Subculture," APSR, 1968, p. 564.
[18] See articles by Ullman and Forbes in Pammett and Whittington, op. cit.
[19] G. Skogstad, "Adolescent Political Alienation", in Zureik and Pike, op. cit., p. 185.

French-speaking elementary school children.[20] Simple observation tells us that the young of today are less benevolent and much more critical of and cynical about the political system than were their parents. The "negativism"[21] of adults in the seventies that we have described above may well be a direct reflection of the declining benevolence of the youth of the sixties. The implications for our future political culture could be significant.

One idiosyncrasy of children's political attitudes in Canada is the fact that American political objects seem to play a significant role in their world. Table 5-15 indicates the relative awareness of Canadian children for selected Canadian and American political objects. They indicate that some Canadian children were more likely to recognize the U.S. flag than the Canadian after grade 4 and that their recognition of the U.S. President was nearly as high as that of the Prime Minister. There are any number of ways to interpret a table such as this, but one should probably avoid the temptation of inferring that Canadian children know *more* about the U.S. than they do about Canada. The differences in recognition of flags are very small and do not apply before grade 4. In these data, the Prime Minister is consistently better known than the President.[22] By grade 8, nearly 25 percent of these Canadian school children could identify all four Canadian items in Table 5-15 whereas only 3.8 percent could identify all the U.S. items.

Table 5-16, which is taken from the same study as Table 5-15, indicates another facet of Canadian relations with the United States as seen through the eyes of school children. The term "affect" is used in that study to mean a positive feeling toward someone. Thus in the "affect" column of the table, we see that 78.8 percent of the children in this study chose the Queen over the President when asked, "Who is your favourite?" "Confidence" is used in the study to indicate who the respondent feels is more likely to be right if the leaders named disagreed. Thus in the "confidence" column of the table we see that 53.9 percent of these children felt that the Prime Minister was more likely to be right in a disagreement with the President. These are data

---

[20] J.-P. Richert, "Political Socialization in Quebec," *CJPS*, VI, no. 2 June 1973, p. 310.

[21] See: Clarke et al., op. cit., p. 26.

[22] These results disagree to some extent with a survey of some 200 students in ten schools in Kingston, Ontario, in December 1966. In it, 17 percent of grade 8 students could give a reasonably accurate description of the Prime Minister and 72 percent could name him while over 26 percent could describe the role of the U.S. President and 94 percent could name him. Jon Pammett, "Political Orientations in Public and Separate School Children," (unpublished M.A. thesis, Queen's University, 1967), pp. 41-2.

gathered before the Watergate scandal of 1973, which severely dam-
aged the credibility of the American President then in office, but they
likely reflect the "normal" situation.

Table 5-15

RECOGNITION OF CANADIAN AND AMERICAN POLITICAL OBJECTS,
BY GRADE[23]

Political Object	Percent of Correct Identification in Grade						
	2	3	4	5	6	7	8
Canadian flag	86.4%	91.8%	92.4%	92.0%	95.7%	95.5%	97.4%
American flag	71.7	87.7	95.8	96.7	98.2	97.1	98.8
Prime Minister	68.3	74.1	79.8	88.2	95.7	98.4	99.4
Governor General	14.3	27.8	29.3	44.0	61.7	71.1	84.8
U.S. President	25.7	42.8	57.9	69.8	89.2	89.3	93.3
Canadian cabinet	NA*	NA	14.1	21.9	28.6	38.5	51.1
American cabinet	NA	NA	4.1	3.2	6.2	6.0	10.1
Canadian MPs	NA	NA	9.5	13.6	18.0	22.9	32.0
U.S. Congressmen	NA	NA	3.3	5.2	5.2	6.0	6.8

* NA—question not asked of children in grades two and three.

Table 5-16

AMERICAN POLITICAL ROLES VERSUS CANADIAN POLITICAL
ROLES

Political Role	Affect	Confidence
Queen	78.8	70.1
President of the United States	15.8	22.0
Don't know	5.4	7.9
President of the United States	28.8	34.3
Prime Minister of Canada	64.7	53.9
Don't know	6.5	11.8
President of the United States	22.4	37.8
Governor General of Canada	70.6	50.7
Don't know	6.9	11.5

[23] The figures in Tables 5-15 and 5-16 are from Donald Higgins, "The Political Americanization of Canadian Children" in Pammett and Whittington, The Foundations of
Political Culture, p. 251.

Again, the interpretation of Table 5-16 is to some extent up to the reader, but the consistently higher levels of affect for Canadian political leaders and the somewhat lower but still considerable edge that Canadian leaders hold in confidence seem to suggest that, while significant, American cultural influence has not by any means obliterated the positive feelings Canadian children have for objects related to their political system. On the other hand it is perhaps alarming that such a sizable percentage (ranging from 15.8 percent to 37.8 percent) of Canadian children do have higher regard for the American President than they do for significant Canadian authorities.

This concludes our discussion of political socialization. Although much of the data cited is by now almost ten years old there has not been very much quantitative research in Canada with which to update the material. However, it seems likely that the same basic generalizations still apply, even where the substantive political objects might be different. Having dealt with the basic values and attitudes that characterize the Canadian political culture and having discussed the process whereby values, attitudes, and opinions are transmitted from individual to individual and from generation to generation, we must turn to an analysis of political participation and see how the attitudinal make-up of individuals affects their political behaviour.

POLITICAL PARTICIPATION IN CANADA: FROM ATTITUDE TO ACTION

Political opinions are significant for the political system only if they are translated into some kind of action by the opinion holder. The action may be voting, writing to an MP, or just talking to people at the factory; if the action is concerned with politics, we call it political participation. Obviously the participation of Canadians is a vital link—indeed it is *the* link between the environment of politics and the political system. As such it is a key part of the political process.[24] In addition, the ways in which Canadians participate in politics and the attitudes with which they do so provide a valuable additional indicator of the nature of the political culture.

We will be dealing with voting behaviour, and with the behaviour of Canadians within the contexts of political parties and interest

---

[24] As pointed out earlier, political participation can occur at the input side and at the output side of the political system. In this section, when we speak of political participation we will be referring specifically to input participation. Output-side participation will be dealt with in the context of policy making.

groups later on in the book, but for the time being we wish to make some generalizations about categories of political participation and to outline a few of the social and attitudinal correlates of such behaviour.

The Categories of Political Participation

The most elementary categorization of political participation is a differentiation between electoral and non-electoral behaviour. The former, which has received the most attention in political science, we will deal with first. Electoral behaviour or participation in the electoral process includes a wide range of activities, from actually running for elected office to simply voting for a candidate. Figure 5-1 posits three broad levels of political activity dividing participants into *gladiatorial, transitional,* and *spectator* roles in the political process. People who participate at any particular level of activity will likely participate in all or most of the activities below that level in a *hierarchy of participation*. Thus, virtually every person who holds a political office has also engaged in a variety of other political activities, including voting, campaigning either on one's own behalf or for someone else, and participating in political strategy meetings. Similarly, a person who participates in strategy meetings will certainly vote and be an active party member as well. The hierarchy of political participation, as it applies to the electoral process in Canada, is summarized in Figure 5-1.

Figure 5-1

A HIERARCHY OF ELECTORAL PARTICIPATION

Gladiatorial Level	Holding a public office
	Being a political candidate
	Holding an office within a party
	Soliciting party funds
	Attending a strategy meeting or planning a campaign
Transitional Level	Contributing money to a political party
	Being an active party member
	Contributing time in a campaign
	Attending a meeting or rally
	Contacting a public official or politician
	Attempting to convince people how to vote
Spectator Level	Initiating a political discussion
	Being interested in politics
	Exposing oneself to political stimuli
	Voting

Source: Adapted from Lester Milbrath, *Political Participation* (Rand McNally, Chicago, 1965), p. 18.

The higher up the hierarchy, the fewer participants there are. At the most, 5 percent of the Canadian people participate at the "gladiatorial" level while up to 40 percent claim to participate in "transitional" level activities.[25] The commonest of the transitional activities according to the respondents of the 1974 election study are attending a political rally or "all candidates" type meeting, and attempting to convince friends and co-workers how to vote. The latter category however is getting fairly close to the spectator form of participation. For in simply discussing politics casually with friends, one inevitably expresses a point of view and tries to sway the opinion of others, even if that isn't the main purpose of the exercise. Such discussion seems to be motivated more by *interest* than by deep commitment.

Finally, at the spectator level of activity, participation rates are generally quite a bit higher. Fewer than 5 percent of the respondents in the 1974 survey reported *never* having voted in a federal election, and between 80 and 90 percent of the respondents indicated that they had followed the campaign to some extent through the media and in discussing the election informally with friends. However we have spoken so far only of participation rates at the federal level. Table 5-17 gives a breakdown of types of political participation comparing the federal and provincial arenas. As can be seen from this table, while both provincial and federal vote frequencies are high, Canadians are more likely to exercise their federal franchise than their provincial one. The only other type of political participation which is characterized by wide federal-provincial difference is attending political meetings, where federal meetings would seem to be better attended than provincial meetings. For the most part, however, the levels of political participation in provincial elections as reported in the 1974 survey do not appear to be very different from the levels of participation in federal elections.[26]

We will discuss the overall functions of elections in Chapter 12, but it is important to recognize here that the electoral process is neither the only nor necessarily the most important forum within which to participate meaningfully in the political process. The hierarchical classification of participation in Figure 5-1 deals exclusively with *electoral* participation, and we must now turn to a consideration of non-electoral political participation.

---

[25] Wm. Mishler, *Political Participation in Canada* (Macmillan, Toronto 1979), p. 43; see also Kornberg, Smith, and Clarke, *Citizen Politicians—Canada* (Carolina Press, Durham, N.C., 1979), pp. 58-61.

[26] See also: M. Burke, H. Clarke, and L. Leduc, "Federal and Provincial Political Participation in Canada," *Canadian Review of Sociology and Anthropology*, Feb., 1978, p. 61.

Table 5-17

FREQUENCY OF DIFFERENT MODES OF POLITICAL PARTICIPATION
IN FEDERAL AND PROVINCIAL ELECTIONS[27]

		Row Percentages[a]			
		Often	Sometimes	Seldom	Never
Vote frequency[b]	Federal	60%	28%	8%	5%
	Provincial	53	28	10	10
Read newspapers	Federal	41	29	18	13
	Provincial	42	29	16	13
Discuss politics	Federal	24	37	22	17
	Provincial	26	37	20	17
Convince friends	Federal	8	13	10	69
	Provincial	9	14	9	68
Work in community	Federal	5	15	12	67
	Provincial	6	15	11	68
Attend meetings	Federal	10	15	12	69
	Provincial	5	15	11	69
Contact officials	Federal	3	11	14	72
	Provincial	3	12	11	74
Sign, sticker	Federal	5	9	4	82
	Provincial	5	9	4	82
Campaign activity	Federal	4	7	6	83
	Provincial	4	7	6	84

[a] N = 1184

[b] For vote frequency only, the categories are: "voted in all elections," "most," "some," "none."

Non-electoral participation in the Canadian political process is more difficult to substantiate than the political activity related to voting. We can glean hard data as to the actual turnout of the electorate simply through the reports of the electoral office, and for the most part survey research in Canada has tended to focus far more on the activities related to elections than on other dimensions of political participation. Nevertheless, there have been a few studies which have made a start in attempting to uncover the nature and the extent of citizen involvement in non-electoral political activities[28] and these have focussed largely upon membership and activity in interest groups. In fact 50 to 60 percent of Canadians report that they belong to at least one voluntary association, which makes us a "country of joiners" when compared to almost any other country in the world ex-

[27] From Clarke et al., op. cit., p. 86.
[28] See Presthus, *Elite Accommodation in Canadian Politics* (Toronto, 1973), pp. 22-63, and Curtis, J., "Voluntary Association Joining: A Cross National Comparative Note," *American Sociological Review*, Oct., 1971, p. 872.

cept the U.S. It would be nice to be able to conclude from this that therefore Canada is a very "participant" political culture in terms of non-electoral political activities, but unfortunately there is no necessary relationship between *belonging* to a group and being *active* in the political efforts of the group. In fact the *intensity* of the involvement of most members of voluntary associations is likely extremely low. Very few of us will ever become the group "gladiators" and actually serve as elected officers of the organization, and even such involvement within an organization may not be in any way related to its political or interest group functions. Bill Mishler concludes that: "only a small number of citizens—probably fewer than 25%—can be classified as political activists on the basis of the level and content of their participation in voluntary organizations and interest groups."[29]

Another indicator of the extent of non-electoral participation in Canada has been the response to survey questions asking about individuals' attempts to contact MPs and government officials. In the 1974 study, 16 percent of the respondents indicated that they had in fact contacted public officials and 24 percent said they had written or otherwise contacted their Members of Parliament. Such activities are clearly a form of political participation but even here there are qualifications that must be entered. On the one hand, surveys of MPs themselves indicate that a great many of the letters from constituents do not even address themselves to problems that can be classed as political. Personal problems, requests for jobs, or assistance in dealing with administrative agencies of government are far more frequent than genuine policy-related demands.[30] Hence if fewer than one-quarter of our citizens choose to avail themselves of even this low-intensity form of involvement in the political process, and if a large percentage of those who do are not concerned with political issues at all, we must conclude that such involvement is not a significant reflection of political participation in Canada.

Finally in considering the various categories of political participation we must move away from the traditional and legitimate forms to the more recent and less legitimate political activities—political protest, violence, and terrorism. While we have long thought of Canada as "the peaceable kingdom" committed to "peace, order, and good government" and opposed to any change which is not evolutionary, events in the sixties and seventies may cause us to reassess. The fact is that there have been periodic outbreaks of political protest and violence throughout Canadian history and while we are less violent

---

[29] Mishler, *Political Participation in Canada*, p. 51.
[30] Kornberg and Mishler, *Influence in Parliament: Canada* (Durham, N.C., 1976).

than, for instance, the U.S. and the U.K., such non-legitimate forms of political activity do form an aspect of our political process.[31]

In the fifties the majority of the reported acts of political violence were committed by members of the Sons of Freedom Doukhobors in Western Canada, and in the sixties it was the French-Canadian Nationalist groups such as the FLQ which claimed credit for the more violent of the acts of protest. However during the sixties we witnessed an upsurge in the number and intensity of semi-legitimate protest activities. Well into the decade of the seventies, Canada has seen an increase in the number of political strikes, riots, and demonstrations both quiet and disruptive. While it is alarming to discover that our peaceable kingdom is not as orderly as our national myths would have it, we are still significantly more peaceable than the U.K. and the U.S., countries with which Canadians most frequently seek to compare themselves. Moreover, as a factor in the overall patterns of political participation in this system, very few individual Canadians ever actually participate in riots, demonstrations, political strikes, and other more violent forms of political protest. As Bill Mishler has put it, "Despite the frequency of political protest in Canada, it is reasonable to estimate that the number of Canadians participating in the most extreme forms of political protest has never exceeded ten percent and probably has averaged less than one percent."[32]

The Determinants of Political Participation

It can be suggested that there are three basic determinants of a person's participation in politics. The first of these is the sum of the individual's socioeconomic resources: the amount of time and money one can "invest" in political activity. How much one invests will depend upon one's occupation and income, other activities which compete for one's resources, and, of course, upon the nature of the political system itself. A second and vital determinant is the individual's personality resources. Political participation at most higher levels of the hierarchy is a sociable activity and consequently has social costs and requires social resources. People who have more social aplomb and who find interaction with other people to be easy are therefore more likely to participate in politics. The third determinant is the political resources available to the citizen who wishes to participate in politics.

[31] T. Mitchell, *Violence and Politics in Canada*, paper delivered at ACSUS conference, Washington, D.C., 1979. See also Kelly, M. and Mitchell T., "Post Referendum Quebec—The Potential for Conflict," *Conflict Quarterly*, Summer 1980, pp. 15-19.
[32] Mishler, *Political Participation in Canada*, p. 35.

If there are many institutions in which one can participate, or if the existing institutions such as political parties encourage participation, then one is more likely to become involved in politics. This last point can be examined further in two ways. First, we can look at Canadian institutions such as parties to see whether they do, in fact, encourage participation. This we will do in Chapters 10 and 11. Second, we can determine whether or not Canadians feel that the political system responds to their efforts to influence it, and then determine whether or not their feelings in this respect correlate with participation. The feeling that one has a meaningful role in politics and one's confidence that the system will respond to the individual are termed a sense of *political efficacy*. Its role in Canada is summarized later in this chapter.

The next step, then, will be to outline who participates in the Canadian electoral process by examining first the socioeconomic correlates of participation and secondly the psychological determinants of participation.

Socioeconomic Factors and Political Participation   One of the most consistent correlates of political participation not only in Canada but throughout the Western democracies is the socioeconomic status of the individual. Whether we utilize subjective criteria of class (self-classification through direct questions such as, "What class do you think of yourself belonging to?"), or objective criteria such as family, personal income, occupation, or education, it is clear that lower SES correlates positively with lower levels of political participation. This finding was borne out by the data from the 1965 election survey cited in previous editions of this volume and remains a significant finding in more recent studies.[33] The exceptions or qualifications that must be entered here are all with respect to the individual objective indicators of a social class. The 1974 election study, as cited by Mishler, indicates that while high income is a good predictor of participation at the gladiatorial level in elections, and in non-electoral activities such as approaching government officials and MPs, wealthier people are "not appreciably more likely to vote or participate in political campaigns than even the poorest citizens."[34] Similarly, while occupation is a good predictor of gladiatorial participation, with members of the professions occupying a disproportionate percentage of elected offices in Canada, professional people are likely to be less concerned with participation in transitional activities such as campaigns, and are not sig-

---

[33] See: Mishler, op. cit., pp. 88-95, esp. 91.
[34] Ibid., p. 96.

nificantly more likely to vote than members of lower-status occupations groups. This may be a reflection of the fact that higher-status groups perceive their opportunities to influence the political process to be greater if they deal directly with the elected officials of government or if they actually become one themselves than if they simply exercise their franchise and/or work in somebody's campaign.

If we look at the SES of participants in political protests however, we get rather different impressions. While "hard data" on this is scarce, we can fairly safely say that much of the protest activity of the sixties and seventies was dominated by the university-age offspring of fairly high-status families, on the one hand, and by disaffected and alienated lower-status workers on the other.[35] The influence of education reflects a pattern similar to that of occupation. Levels of participation increase with education up to the high school level, but university educated people are not more likely to vote than high school graduates. Similarly, people with a university education are more likely to attempt to influence the political process through direct involvement as gladiators or in approaches to government officials individually or as active members of interest groups. The fact that the distribution of participants is similar to that demonstrated by higher-status occupations is hardly startling given that there is a direct connection between higher levels of education and the professional occupations. Again because of the importance of the university in the sixties as a fertile milieu for political protest, there is a relationship between university level education and participation in political protest.

Language, ethnicity, and religion are all fairly closely related variables, and as a combination of coincident cleavages they can affect both the opportunities for and the propensity toward political participation. However, if we expect a dramatic difference between ethnic groups, the findings of the 1965 survey as reported in the last edition of this book and the findings demonstrated by Table 5-18 will be somewhat of a disappointment. What the data do indicate is that French Canadians are less likely than English Canadians to become involved in the non-electoral activities such as contacting an MP, or being a member in a community association. Moreover, the French respondents were more likely to become involved in transitional activities, such as working in the campaign, but slightly less likely to vote in federal elections. Part of this discrepancy might be explained in terms of a more authoritarian or passive "subject" orientation to

---

[35] Stein, Michael, *The Dynamics of Right Wing Protest* (University of Toronto Press, Toronto, 1973) pp. 173-175.

the system as a whole, coupled with the expectation that the way to get a share of the patronage "goodies" handed out after elections is to be involved as a volunteer during the election campaign. However, when we look to French Canadians' participation in provincial politics we find that the discrepancy virtually disappears. Essentially it seems French Canadians view themselves as relatively more efficacious at the provincial level than at the federal level than do English Canadians, and so are more likely to vote in provincial elections, and more likely to approach provincial government officials than federal ones.[36]

Table 5-18

THE EXTENT OF POLITICAL PARTICIPATION BY ETHNIC ORIGIN[37]

Activity	British	French	Other European	Asian, Native, Other
Voting	88%	82%	85%	81%
Campaigning	38	43	43	41
Contacting MPs	26	19	26	25
Community activity	26	15	17	24
N* =	536	267	186	142

*Voting percentages are based on a total sample of 2,445. All other activities are based on a half-sample of 1,203. Ns are for the half-sample and vary slightly between activities because of differences in missing data.

As is also indicated by Table 5-18 the non-English/non-French respondents are much closer to the former than to the latter in the overall pattern of their participation in federal politics. The most significant difference is that the two "charter groups," the French and English, are disproportionally represented at the gladiatorial levels of the hierarchy of participation. The non-charter groups are only beginning to make inroads to elected office or even to candidacy in Canada, a point which will be explored more fully below in the chapter on the *authorities* of the system.

It is difficult to generalize about the ethnic/religious/linguistic composition of protest movements in Canada, partly because of the lack of hard information and partly because the pattern is only a very vague one. As Mishler has pointed out:

[36] Mishler, *Political Participation in Canada*, p.99; Van Loon and Whittington, (1976), p. 113; Clarke et. al., op. cit., p. 89.
[37] From Mishler, op. cit., p. 100.

Political protest, is most prevalent among the least assimilated groups in society as is evident from the record of French-Canadian protest during the 1960s, from the activities of radical segments of groups such as the Dukhobors in B.C. and from the ethnic composition of labour protests over the first half of this century. [38]

This has to be viewed however in the context of and qualified by history, where we find for instance that English Canadians were a dominant force in the Rebellion of 1837 in Upper Canada, and where in the 1960s the children of middle class "WASPs" were well represented in campus unrest, anti-nuclear protest, and anti-Vietnam war demonstrations.

Much has been written in Canada about the influence of geography on patterns of political behaviour. While there are clear differences in partisan choice from one region to the next, attempts to demonstrate regional variations in the level and intensity of political participation have not been particularly successful. It is difficult to find consistent regional variations in the patterns of electoral participation that hold over time. Overall differences in levels of participation by province are more likely affected by particular local political conditions than by regional cleavages. Any consistent differences which can be found are quite readily attributable to differing levels of education or income, with poorer and less well-educated regions showing lower levels of most types of participation. The level of activity in a province, however, may be temporarily increased by a heightened level of political party competition in the province, by a particularly exciting political leader, or by the emergence of a new political movement. [39] We will consider the significance of regionalism on the patterns of political *attitudes* in the next section of this chapter, but for now we feel fairly safe in dismissing regional variations in the patterns of political participation as idiosyncratic and usually temporary. [40]

Urban/rural differences in political participation in Canada are fairly significant, although the patterns of variation are unlike those characteristic of the other socioeconomic and demographic determinants of participation. According to the 1974 election survey results, the relationship between urbanization and political participation is

---

[38] Mishler, op. cit., p. 101.
[39] S. M. Lipset, *Agrarian Socialism* (University of California Press, Berkeley, 1950), discusses in detail the effect of a new movement (the CCF) on patterns of participation in Saskatchewan.
[40] See also: Mishler, op. cit., p. 58, who makes this point: "Although citizens of different provinces and regions develop distinctive political attitudes and perspectives, it appears that political participation is influenced less by regional or provincial factors than by characteristics of the individual or sub-group."

curvilinear.[41] The frequency of voting is highest in the large urban areas and in the rural or farm communities and lowest in the medium-sized cities and towns. The same curvilinear pattern applies with respect to non-electoral participation such as contacting MPs, etc., but participation in local or community activities increases linearly with the smaller size of community. Likely these differential patterns of political participation by community size can be explained two ways. The higher levels of participation in the cities will generally be a reflection of higher SES, income and education, coupled with the fact that cities are "where it's at" politically and therefore the opportunities for participation are likely higher. On the other side, the high participation in rural communities might be explained by the fact that involvement in the community affairs is a result of a circumstance of more genuine community than prevails in larger urban centres. The involvement in local matters, of which politics is one aspect, is generally higher because people know each other, deal with each other on a regular basis, and thus are more interested in being an active part of community affairs.

There are some sex and age differences in the Canadian population with respect to participation. In middle-class English Canada there is not much difference in levels of participation between men and women, but in French Canada and among people with less than a high school level of education, men are much more likely to participate than women. The pattern in Canada in this respect is similar to that in other Western democracies. In underdeveloped areas of a country, where educational levels are low, there are large differences between the sexes. Where educational levels are higher, sexual equality extends to political participation as well as to some other fields. An age profile of participation shows a peak in the middle years with a trailing off at either end. Very old or very young voters appear particularly unlikely to be active participants in the electoral process, and this pattern prevails in Canada regardless of regional, cultural, or class differences.

Any of the above facts can be explained without too much difficulty by keeping in mind what was said earlier about the individual's resources. The explanation can be further sharpened to apply to particular types of campaign activity if it is suggested that all activities have specific requirements which will call more or less directly on specific resources.[42] For example, reading about a political campaign

---

[41] Ibid., p. 105.
[42] L. Milbrath in *Political Participation* calls these requirements "dimensions"; see pp. 22 ff.

obviously requires the ability to read relatively easily. If reading about the campaign is correlated with level of education, it will be seen that as the level of education declines so does reading about politics. On the other hand, belonging to a party or working for one takes time and requires social interaction. Thus, people with more time (retired people, housewives whose children are grown up), or with flexible time requirements for their jobs (lawyers, professors, or other professional people), could be expected to and do participate in this way, more frequently than others.

Nonetheless, even a cursory glance is enough to indicate that socioeconomic factors alone are not sufficient to explain why people participate in politics. There are still many people who have all the necessary resources but pay no attention to politics. In some cases our predictions can be fairly clear. If the person in question is an older, poorly educated, rural French-Canadian woman we can assert with a considerable degree of confidence that voting is likely to be her only political act. But much of the Canadian voting-age public is middle class or working class with enough education to give it many of the necessary resources to participate; whether or not a member of this group will in fact participate must depend upon some other factors as well. We will turn now to a consideration of the psychological or attitudinal determinants of political participation.

Psychological Correlates of Participation   There are a number of psychological and attitudinal factors which might be supposed to underlie political participation. In other countries it has been found that such things as an absence of anxiety or an absence of authoritarian outlook on life are correlated with political participation. These findings have been replicated in enough different settings that we can probably expect that they are true for Canada as well, though unfortunately there has been little specific research in Canada. The 1974 election survey does permit us to look at a few of these variables.

Interest in politics, as might be expected, is an important attitudinal trait distinguishing participants and non-participants in Canada. As Mishler has pointed out, there is a strong relationship between interest in politics and the level and intensity of political participation. This bears out the findings we reported in our second edition based on the 1965 election survey. What is important to note is that while there is a high correlation between interest and activity in politics, in both the 1965 and 1974 studies, respondents in 1974 were generally less interested in politics overall. [43] In other words there appears to be

---

[43] Mishler, op. cit., p. 67.

a trend in Canada away from deep psychological involvement in the political process.

Closely related to interest is *knowledge* about the political system. The people who are the most interested also tend to know more about political objects, and as might be expected, people who score high on political information tests also tend to participate more frequently and at higher levels of the hierarchy of electoral participation. However, what is disturbing here is the apparently low level of cognitive sophistication among the Canadian electorate. The 1974 study showed that almost half of the respondents could not score 50 percent on a series of fairly straightforward questions about the powers of the federal and provincial governments. With knowledge about the system however, unlike the findings about interest, respondents in 1974 seem to have higher levels of cognitive awareness than respondents in a similar survey conducted in 1968. Hence we would appear to have a situation in Canada where the levels of cognitive political sophistication are increasing, while levels of interest in politics are declining. Perhaps political sophistication breeds boredom with politics but we will have to discuss this later in the context of the other psychological variables such as efficacy, ideological commitment, and partisanship.

Partisan loyalty, or the psychological phenomenon of identifying with a political party is a good predictor of higher levels and intensity of political participation. The findings of the 1965 election study cited in our previous edition showed a strong relationship, and the results of the 1974 election study mirror this finding. Clark et al. point out that not only is there a strong relationship between partisanship and participation, but that the *intensity* of loyalty correlates positively with the intensity of political participation.[44] But while party loyalty generally correlates with higher levels of participation in politics, there are not significant differences among the supporters of different political parties in the Canadian scene. The exception here is that supporters of the NDP seem to be more likely to become involved at the gladiatorial and transitional levels than do supporters of the two traditional parties. This however may be only a reflection of the intensity of NDP partisanship relative to PC or Liberal partisanship, or it could be a reflection of the extent to which the choice of party is based on ideological commitment. The literature in the United States indicates that very few citizens are genuinely ideological and there have been no studies which might indicate that Canadians are any different. How-

---

[44] Clarke et. al, op. cit., p. 306; see also, Mishler, op. cit., pp. 72-74.

ever as Mishler has pointed out: "Little Canadian evidence exists on the subject, but what there is suggests that ideology encourages both voting and campaign participation provided that at least one of the political parties—even a minor one—shares the citizens' preferences."[45] Hence ideological commitment likely is related to the intensity of partisanship and also to the level and frequency of political participation, but "ideologues" do not comprise a very large percentage of the Canadian citizenry.

It might be added here, that although there are not sufficient data to be certain, it seems likely that ideological commitment is a good independent predictor of participation in the non-legitimate and less legitimate forms of political participation such as demonstrations and violence. Further, it seems likely that ideologues with a strong partisan preference are less likely to seek political demonstrations and protest as a medium of expression than ideologically oriented people who cannot find a party whose stated principles conform to their own. In this sense extremist political parties may serve the purpose of moderating the incidence of non-legitimate political behaviour by co-opting potential radicals into the conventional machinery of government such as elections. As an example it seems reasonable to hypothesize that the Parti Québécois has offered a legitimate political medium for the expression of radical political views, and in so doing has reduced the attractiveness of the FLQ and its non-legitimate political tactics.

Political efficacy is the feeling or perception of one's ability to have an impact on the political process. While one of the determinants of participation in politics is the objective *opportunities* that the institutions of the system, socioeconomic factors and attitudinal resources provide to the individual, the second set of determinants are those relating to our *motivation* to participate. Such motivation to be involved depends to a large extent on how much impact we believe we are capable of having or our feelings of efficacy. Generally it can be stated that the levels of political efficacy in Canada are lower than those present in the other Anglo-American democracies.[46] Moreover, from 1965 until 1974 the levels of efficacy have generally declined in Canada, as have the general levels of *trust* in the authorities of the political system.[47]

Political efficacy is a good predictor of the levels and intensity of political participation. Although the relationship is not strong with

---

[45] Mishler, op, cit., p. 72.
[46] Mishler, op. cit., p. 75.
[47] See section above where we noted the phenomenon of "political negativism."

respect to voting, for other levels of the hierarchy of electoral participation and for non-electoral categories of political participation, the propensity to participate declines with the level of political efficacy. A possible explanation of the fact that a relatively large percentage of respondents who believe that voting is important, despite general feelings of political inefficacy, *do* habitually exercise their franchise, is that the act of voting is seen as an important symbolic affirmation of the democratic process. People, in other words, may vote out of a sense of civic duty rather than out of any faith that they can actually have an impact on policy outputs.[48] People may also become involved at the transitional levels of the political process such as in election campaigns because such activities are of social value to them. In other words it is possible that the gregariousness of an individual generally, or the extent to which one is "outgoing" in his or her personality, may be an important correlate of political participation in group type activities. Consistent with this is the finding cited in the last edition of this volume that the non-political aspects of personality can have some impact on the motivation to become involved in politics.

Finally we must conclude this very brief discussion of the relationship between efficacy and participation in Canadian politics with a cautionary note. While we have been able to cite a strong correlation between the two sets of variables, we have not been able to determine the *direction* of the causal links. It is normally assumed that efficacy determines the level of participation, that the attitudes determine the behaviour. We would like to suggest that the reverse be considered as a possible explanation of the empirical findings in this area; i.e., that people believe voting to be important because they have done it a lot and it has proven to be an easy, interesting, and psychologically satisfying experience; and, that people who do not get involved at higher levels of the hierarchy of participation give as an *excuse*, their "conviction" that such involvement is not worth their while, that it will not produce any positive results, and therefore is a waste of their valuable time. In other words, it is possible that while a sense of "civic duty" motivates people to engage in activities such as voting which do not take much time or effort, out of laziness, complacency, ignorance, or even "false consciousness," they are unwilling to invest the significantly greater time and effort required to participate in higher order political activities. As a result, a sense of "civic guilt" may cause people to rationalize their non-participation in terms of cynicism, negativism, and inefficacious statements about the higher orders of political behaviour.

---

[48] See Clarke et. al., op. cit., p. 33, and Mishler, op. cit., p. 74.

Political Participation and Political Culture

While it is difficult to generalize about any aspect of the Canadian political culture because of the socioeconomic, demographic, and attitudinal complexities of our political community, we feel that it is necessary to do so. We feel it is important to at least make the attempt to find some common patterns that generally hold despite the wide regional, economic, ethno-linguistic, and ideological variations that qualify and elaborate our macro-level conclusions. In this spirit, we hypothesize that at the highest level of generalization the patterns of political participation in Canada can be described as *"spectator-participant."*[49] This seemingly self-contradictory phrase is used for a number of reasons. First, relative to most democratic countries, Canadians do have a very high level of political participation: only the United States shows one consistently higher.[50] It must therefore be described as a *participant* political culture. Not all Canadians, however, are participants. In particular it was seen that lower socioeconomic groups do not participate except in the fairly infrequent cases where people have picked up a high level of interest in politics. Indeed, those 40 percent or so of Canadians who are below or near the poverty line[51] are almost totally excluded from the input side of the political process and consequently have to accept the outputs of the system with very little control over them. They are truly the silent poor, although it might be a mistake to assume they will remain so. With increasing levels of education they may slowly become mobilized politically, and if they do not participate within the context of the "legitimate" political system in ways which have become traditional in Canadians politics, they may learn to participate in "illegitimate" ways.

The term "spectator" in the phrase spectator-participant is used to describe the predominant motivational factors of people who do participate. To some extent and for certain categories of political participation they may be motivated by efficacy—a feeling that their efforts will be rewarded by the political system—but for the most part they appear to be motivated by a sort of spectator interest in what is going on in politics. It was seen that they perceive little ideological difference between the parties, feeling simultaneously that it matters which leaders are in power. They will apparently participate in poli-

---

[49] Robert Presthus uses a similar term, *quasi-participative*, to describe the Canadian political culture. See: *Elite Accommodation in Canadian Politics*, pp. 38 ff.

[50] Comparative data can be found in L. Milbrath, *Political Participation*, R. Lane, *Political Life*, and G. Almond and S. Verba, *The Civil Culture* (Princeton University Press, Princeton, 1963).

[51] See Chapter 2.

tics if they find the differences between these groups of people to be "interesting." Otherwise, aside from voting, they are unlikely to participate at all. Graphic illustration of this was provided during the 1968 election campaign when electoral participation was higher than it had been since the 1958 halcyon days of John Diefenbaker, largely because of the emergence of a new and interesting personality, Pierre Elliott Trudeau.

Canadians appear to approach politics much as they would a hockey game. If the game is good they will come out and cheer. On election day they may "go to the game" by voting and watching the returns on television, and if they are really interested they may participate at higher levels in the hierarchy. If their party wins they will be happy, and if it loses they may be sad, but not for long. Their involvement with "the event" has been motivated by interest and psychological identification with the principals, but not based on well-defined objective concern or deep ideological commitment.

All of this has significant implications for the political system and, in particular, for its decision makers. One famous Canadian historian has described cabinet government as a system where the citizen "gives full power of attorney to a small committee each four years or so, well knowing that virtually nothing he can do in the interval will have much effect on the groups to whom he has given his blank cheque."[52] This means that under normal circumstances, politics in Canada can be, if the authorities choose, about nothing. The system will appear to be retaining its legitimacy because the level of participation by which we measure such things, voting in elections, can remain high as long as politics are interesting. The level of interest can be kept high as long as colourful personalities are presented. Occasional infusions of new and interesting personalities or of "style issues" will serve to retain minimum democratic involvement in the system.

A further consequence of the spectator-participant nature of Canadian politics is a reinforcement of tendencies favouring the status quo. The people who most actively participate in the process are disproportionately drawn from the middle and upper-middle classes. They have reason to be satisfied with the status quo and they are organized into the types of group structure which allow them to promote their own interests in consonance with government elites. Thus:

---

[52] A. R M. Lower, *Canadians in the Making* (Longman's, Toronto, 1958), p. 281.

Government, to some extent, is pushed into the anomalous position of defending the strong against the weak. While the governmental elite plays an equilibrating role in welfare areas, much of its energy is also spent in reinforcing the security and growth of interests that already enjoy the largest shares of net social product. [53]

The spectator-participant orientation of the Canadian political culture may both allow and force political elites to behave in this way if they are to retain the legitimacy they require.

The term *apolitical* is used by political scientists to denote a politics which is not concerned with genuine ideological or policy differences, but which is highly supportive of the status quo. It would occur, for example, if all the members of the political elite—this is, all the major actors inside the political system—were basically in agreement about policies and political objectives. The real difference between the actions of one group and those of another would be slight, and the real significance of elections or other changes of power would be small. Apolitical politics may or may not be dangerous; readers can make their own judgments on this point. The main point here is that in such a system the decisions of those in authority might not and probably would not represent the real cleavages in the environment, yet popular support for the decision makers could still be made to appear adequate. [54]

This apparent legitimacy can be disadvantageous for a political system. The system will remain stable as long as the outputs are at least marginally effective in satisfying active members of the political community, and the marginal level may be considerably depressed by the distraction of people's attention from issues to personalities. However, if there is an infusion into the system of people who were formerly politically inactive, as may occur when educational levels of the lower socioeconomic classes have been raised or when significant new issues arise, the system may become unstable unless its institution can be adapted to accommodate the effective participation of many newly aroused citizens.

All of this may read like a denunciation of the Canadian political system. However, all that has been said so far is that the Canadian political culture is such that it may permit apolitical politics. It is too early in this book for us to finalize such an assessment. It must first be determined whether Canadian political institutions and the author-

---

[53] R. Presthus, *Elite Accommodation in Canadian Politics*, p. 347.
[54] Ulf Himmelstrand, "A Theoretical and Empirical Approach to Depolitization and Political Involvement," *Acta Sociologica*, vol. 6, pp. 83-111, fasc. 1-2, 1962, provides a similar analysis in the Swedish setting and arrives at similar conclusions.

ities occupying them do in fact behave in such a way as to make politics issue-less. Not only is it too early in this book; it may be too early in the history of Canadian political science. We are still only beginning to collect the quantitative data necessary to fully examine the hypotheses suggested here. While there have been many high quality studies done in Canada since 1965, one must ask different types of questions of different people at many different times in order to verify what has been said here.

SUMMARY: THE CANADIAN POLITICAL CULTURE

Some people would challenge the assumption that it is possible to make generalizations about political culture at the level of the entire political community of Canada. The past decade has seen a spate of articles attempting to define regional, provincial, or linguistic political cultures[55] and while we do not dispute the fact that region, province, or mother tongue are often good predictors of attitudinal variations, it is our contention that there is a need in Canada to try to look at the Canadian political culture as a single entity—albeit a single entity with many facets and attitudinal variations. The concept of political culture is an aggregate concept to begin with, for by definition one is talking about the *sum* of the attitudes and values of the individuals who comprise the selected unit of analysis. After all it is not that much easier to generalize, for instance, about the political culture of Ontario, or to speak of the political culture of French Canada, than it is to simply generalize about a Canadian political culture. The problem is simply one of deciding arbitrarily the level of aggregation that is desired with the realization that the more inclusive and the more sociologically complex the unit of analysis the more general and more qualified will be the conclusions. Given that the focus of this volume is the Canadian political system, and given that much of its content describes the factors that politically differentiate Canadians of different regions, classes, and ethnic groups, it is our intention to reiterate in general terms what we have discovered about the Canadian political culture.

---

[55] See: Ullman, "Regional Political Culture in Canada: Part I. A Theoretical and Conceptual Introduction," *American Review of Canadian Studies*, Autumn, 1977, pp. 1-22, and Ullman, "Regional Political Cultures in Canada: Part II"; *ARCS* Autumn, 1978, pp. 70-101, Bell and Tepperman, op. cit., Ch. 6, Simeon, R., and D. Elkins, "Regional Political Cultures" and Wilson, J., "The Canadian Political Cultures," both in *CJPS.*, Sept. 1974, pp. 397-484; Gregg, A., and Whittington, "Regional Variation in Children's Political Attitudes" in Bellamy et al., *The Provincial Political Systems* (Methuen, Toronto 1976), p. 76.

However, before we proceed it is important to look briefly at the two most influential pieces among the "multiple political cultures" school and assess what they discovered. John Wilson's article takes off from the starting assumption that provinces are in fact separate political systems, with independent powers to make decisions for their citizens in fairly wide areas of jurisdiction:

Each province is capable through the rules made by its government of giving expression to the particular goals which the society entertains without any external interference. It would be difficult to describe such a condition as anything other than political independence. [56]

Because he presumes that there must be one political culture for every independent political system, he concludes that therefore there are ten political cultures in Canada. The beauty of this distinction, although arbitrary in its own way, is that it precludes reducing the unit of analysis to the point where political scientists in Canada could be, for instance, writing articles on the political culture of "middle-aged, lower-income, Eastern European, female Jews in North Winnipeg," etc. Wilson then proceeds to look at the ten provinces in terms of their respective levels of political development, as measured by the type of political party system that has evolved in each. On the basis of a very useful three-fold classification of party systems, the author concludes that the four Atlantic provinces have *underdeveloped* political cultures, Quebec, Ontario, Manitoba, and B.C. have *transitional* political cultures, and Alberta and Saskatchewan have *developed* political cultures.

The second of these influential articles, by Richard Simeon and David Elkins, selects nine provinces (minus P.E.I.) plus English-speaking Quebeckers as the ten units of analysis. They look at variations in two attitudinal categories, efficacy and trust, and at one set of mainly behavioural indicators dubbed "political involvement." Their conclusions in many ways contradict the findings of Wilson, in that they classify B.C., Manitoba, Ontario, and English Quebec as *"citizen societies,"* Saskatchewan and Alberta as transitional, and Newfoundland, New Brunswick, and Nova Scotia, as *"disaffected societies."* Thus, while both articles confirm that there are wide provincial/ regional variations in political culture, they do not agree at all on which provinces and regions should be classified as what.

The fact that the conclusions of these two articles do not coincide

---

[56] Wilson, op. cit., p. 440-441.

could be due to a number of factors. In the first place they attempt to operationally simplify the concept of political culture by reducing it to a few indicator variables. Political culture, however, includes *all* of the values and attitudes of Canadians toward politics and specific political objects. In using fairly *exclusive* indicators for a very inclusive phenomenon, they may have simply selected inappropriate indicators. Wilson for instance uses the level of development of the party system of a province as the indicator of its political culture or, in other words, uses structural and (partly) behavioural variables as proxy measures for a set of attitudinal variables. In this way not only is the researcher forced to make the assumption that a *few* variables will reflect many, but also to assume that specific kinds of attitudinal variables underlie behavioural and structural ones. Moreover, with the specific selection of the nature of a provincial party system as an indicator one is forgetting that political structures like party systems are often more reflective of the historical circumstances that prevailed at the time of their formation, than they are of current realities. Reg Whitaker has made this point very convincingly in his *The Government Party:*

To understand the basis of party support it is not enough to understand contemporary issues and contemporary social structure. Parties in a sense represent frozen elements of earlier alignments. It is becoming increasingly obvious that only a longer historical perspective can begin to make sense of party systems [which] within a static framework raise more questions than answers.[57]

Thus for instance, the party systems of Alberta and Saskatchewan might be more a reflection of the events and circumstances of the thirties than they are of the political culture of today.

Simeon and Elkins, too, labour under the difficulty of having to select a very few variables as indicators of many, but their research introduces a more serious question about the variations in political culture *over time*. The results of the 1974 election study find that in direct contradiction to findings in the 1965 and 1968 data, Nova Scotian respondents virtually moved from the lower section of the participation and efficacy scales to the top. We might argue therefore either that Nova Scotia has moved from a "dissaffected society" to a "citizen society" in nine years, or, perhaps more realistically, that the sets of attitudes we are using as indicators are simply too fickle to be used as proxies for political culture. This points to the question of "how permanent does an attitude have to be for it to be sanctioned as part of

[57] Whitaker, *The Government Party* (University of Toronto Press, Toronto, 1977), pp. xiv-xv.

the political culture?" Obviously the moods and the opinions of Canadians with respect to specific issues and political personalities would not be long lasting enough to be called political culture, but what about the attitudinal categories such as trust and efficacy? In less than ten years the levels of efficacy and trust have varied widely in Canada, a fact which casts some doubt on the utility of such variables as indicators of political culture. Perhaps we should forget about the "hard" attitudinal data and the behavioural indicators and go back to old-fashioned analysis of history and institutions as the best indicators of what our political culture (or cultures) are all about—at least until our indicators and proxy measures get better than they would appear to be today.

To summarize what we have said about these two pioneering articles on regional political culture, it is important to make clear that our aim has not been to criticize them for failing to "prove" the existence of regional political cultures in Canada but to take from them a lesson. First of all it should be clear that it is almost as difficult to generalize about a province or region of Canada as it is to generalize about Canada itself. Second, political culture is an aggregate category and empirical research can only proceed by selecting a few proxy indicators of the multiple values and attitudes that make up the aggregate. And, thirdly, because political culture is seen as having some permanence over time, one-shot surveys do not give the researcher a very strong basis for generalizations. Survey research can only produce conclusive findings about political culture if such research is conducted longitudinally and replicated over long time periods.

With all of this qualification entered and noted, what *can* we say about the Canadian political culture by way of summary? First, from the evidence of history and from the study of Canadian political institutions we can safely say that the Canadian political culture includes a commitment to democratic values such as popular sovereignty, majoritarianism, and the political rights and freedoms associated with representative government. Secondly, again it is the evidence of history and of our political, economic, and legal institutions that tells us we have a political culture dominated by the persuasive and persistent "semi-ideology" of liberalism. While we have seen that our liberal values are qualified by streaks or strains of toryism, socialism, and corporatism, the fact remains that for all regions, ethnic groups, and social classes in Canada, liberal values dominate. Thirdly, when we come to look at Canadians' attitudes and orientations toward specific political objects, we do not have enough information to generalize effectively. On the basis of the few surveys there are, we do know that such attitudes vary quite widely with different regions, ethnic groups, and social classes and that the only general impression is one of a growing cynicism or negativism toward politics in the late sixties and early seventies. This might prove to be the beginning of what will become a dominant strain in our political culture or it might be a passing malady that will disappear as mysteriously as it appeared. Finally, on the basis of attitudinal, behavioural, institutional, and impressionistic information (not to mention a shot of introspection!), we can hypothesize that the patterns of political participation in Canada reflect *spectator, quasi-participative,* or *apolitical* attitudes toward direct personal involvement in the political process.

This concludes our discussion of the socio-cultural context of the Canadian political system. Every facet of the environment can be considered to influence the political system in some way, either actually or potentially, and one should always be alert for such influences when examining the system itself. In any finite amount of space only some of the relevant facets of the environment can be examined, but the student should watch for others which may have been neglected and should apply them to analysis wherever necessary.

PART 2

The Constitutional and Legal Environment

6

The Constitutional Context

From the point of view of a political scientist, the constitution of a political system is significant for two major reasons. First, the constitution can be viewed as a device which modifies human behaviour, for a constitution is one of the *independent variables* which influences the political process. Secondly, the constitution can be viewed as a reflection of the political culture; in this sense it is a *dependent variable* which is itself but a product of societal forces. In studying the constitution therefore, we not only discover the formal institutional parameters within which the policy process takes place but we will also find out more about the fundamental values of our political community.

THE FUNCTIONS OF THE CANADIAN CONSTITUTION

Paradoxically, all institutions of a political system must be both rigid and flexible.[1] On the one hand, rigidity is necessary if the regime is to acquire legitimacy; for, in order that the citizen may learn either positive or negative attitudes towards a political system, that system must to some extent be stable. The process of political socialization takes time, and it would be impossible to learn about the nature of our political system and its implicit values and norms if all of its institutions were constantly in a state of violent flux. On the other hand, because environmental conditions are continually changing, there is a necessity for considerable flexibility in the regime. If the system is to persist, it must be able to adapt relatively quickly to meet new problems and to relieve related stresses.

In the Canadian political system, flexibility is provided partly by political parties and pressure groups and partly by institutions such as the cabinet and the bureaucracy. All of these institutions have at least some ability to react directly and immediately to rapid environmental changes. The constitution, because it cannot be changed as easily, provides the political system with some of its necessary rigid-

[1] Talcott Parsons refers to these requisites as "pattern maintenance" and "adaptation," each of which must be achieved if the system is to persist.

ity. Thus, in the widest sense, the function of a constitution is to provide the system with a "backbone"—to give it the rigidity which is necessary if it is to persist over time. But constitutions have more immediate and more specific functions to perform, which are often unique to the individual political system, and to the particular form of government in operation. These we consider next.

The Rule of Law

The manifest function of any constitution is to define the relationship between the citizen and the state, and to the extent that the relationship can be defined at all, every country can be said to have some form of constitution. However this is too general an assertion to be of much value in the Canadian setting. What is implicit in the notion of constitutionalism, at least in the Western democracies, is the basic principle of the *rule of law*. To put it simply, for Canada and other Western nations, a constitution is one of the means of achieving the goal of a system where law is supreme.

The principle of rule of law in the British and Canadian tradition asserts that any interference with the freedom of any individual must be performed only according to the legal process and carried out by legitimate authorities. No one is exempt from the law, and no one can affect the rights of any individual except through the legal process.

But if we grant that the constitution of Canada is a means to the end of the rule of law, we must then ask why the rule of law is a norm of our political system in the first place; and, eventually we must ask whether and how this value is really honoured in Canada. The function of the rule of law is, briefly, to protect us from the arbitrary interference of government, or of government officials, in our everyday lives. The law is knowable: in principle, one can become aware, through the law, of standards of behaviour which are expected of everyone. The relationship of the individual to the political system becomes, to some extent, fixed and impartial. Aristotle pointed out that even the rule of a benevolent dictator could conceivably deteriorate to rule by whim and caprice, for even the most benevolent of dictators gets out of bed on the wrong side once in a while. The law, on the other hand, is presumed to be coldly impersonal, predictable, and rational rather than emotional.

Defining the Regime

The rule of law is thus desirable in a society that values the principle of an impartial and predictable relationship between the citizen and the authorities of the political system. The principle of the rule of law, however, is not sufficient to secure in perpetuity such a set of values, for its inherent weakness is the fact that the law is made by people and applied and interpreted by them—and people are not always impersonal, predictable, and rational. Thus, in order to prevent unjust laws from being passed and to guard against the unjust or inequitable application of laws, a constitution must go beyond the mere recognition of the rule of law; it must also define the form of regime. The Canadian constitution defines the operational structure of the political system, and it also defines the relationships among parts of the system. In Professor Corry's words, "The constitution is the frame or chassis in which the working engine of government is set."[2]

Further, the Canadian constitution defines many of the "rules of the game" of politics. It broadly defines the tactics and the means that are acceptable within the Canadian political process, and describes formal procedures that must be followed in order to secure an allocative output. The Canadian constitution, in other words, sets formal parameters beyond which the authorities may not go in performing the basic function of the allocation of resources. It does not matter what the ends are, nor how popular the ends may be; the constitution sets limits on the means that can be legitimately employed to achieve them. An example of these "rules of the game" of politics in Canada, is the principle that there should be ample time provided in the House of Commons for the opposition to criticize government policy. No matter how urgent the government policy may seem at the time, the opposition is always guaranteed at least some opportunity to debate the issue. Although the constitution does not specify exactly how much time, even in the cases where government has the power to limit debate, the opposition must still be given a substantial opportunity to make its views known in parliament.

Defining the Legitimate Role of Government

Not only does the Canadian constitution place limits on the means that can be employed in the political process, it also sets limits on the kinds of laws that can be made. Our constitution defines very broadly the area of legitimate lawmaking by giving us an "unwritten" body of fundamental principles to which all laws must conform. These principles are the norms of the regime, and they are a part of the constitution inasmuch as the constitution is an embodiment of the basic values of Canadian society. For example, a law which made it a crime to go to church would not be acceptable in Canada, because religious tolerance has long been one of the basic values of Canadian society. If

---

[2] J. A. Corry and J. E. Hodgetts, *Democratic Government and Politics* (University of Toronto Press, Toronto, 1959), p. 85.

the political attitudes in Canadian society were to change, and if religious intolerance were perceived as desirable in our system, the fundamental law would change accordingly.

Symbolic Functions

Finally, a constitution is, or should be, a source of pride and a unifying influence within a political community. Generally this is the case, and certainly it applies to the constitution of the U.S. and to the "unwritten" constitution of the U.K. In each of these systems the constitution, for widely differing reasons, has become a symbol of the society's particular brand of democracy and, indeed, an object of national pride. In Canada, however, our constitution has been much maligned, and rooted as it is in English law, it may even be a disintegrative symbol for non-British Canadians. One of the arguments for rewriting the Canadian constitution, therefore (perhaps the only compelling one), is that if agreement can be reached on such a "made in Canada" document it might become a unifying device in the struggle to maintain a united Canada.

COMPONENT PARTS OF THE CANADIAN CONSTITUTION

The British North America Act of 1867 (BNA Act), as amended, forms the core of the Canadian constitution. Legally the Act is a statute of the British parliament, the contents of which are based on the resolutions drawn up at the Quebec and London conferences by the representatives of the original four provinces. The legal-historical significance of the Act is that it created the federal union out of Upper and Lower Canada and the Maritime provinces of New Brunswick and Nova Scotia. Because at the time of Confederation the Canadas were united, the BNA Act also created the provinces of Ontario and Quebec. The scope of the BNA Act is somewhat limited; it deals with certain broad topics like the federal distribution of powers, the general form of the central government, and the bilingual dimension of Canada. The farthest the BNA Act goes in defining the principles of government in Canada is in the preamble where it states that Canada shall have a form of government "similar in principle to that of the United Kingdom." In other words, as a constitution, the BNA Act is rather restricted. It does not pretend to be the omnicompetent document that the constitution of the United States is, or was intended to be, and in fact much of what is described as the constitution of Canada is not found even implicitly in the BNA Act.

A few British statutes other than the BNA Act and some British orders in council are usually considered to be part of the Canadian constitution. The most noteworthy of these are the Statute of Westminster, the Colonial Laws Validity Act, and the order in council ceding Rupert's Land to the Dominion. These British enactments all have to do with the gradual process of withdrawal of British authority over the Dominion and its present territories, and were more significant at the time of their passage than they are now.

Some statutes passed by the Canadian parliament, such as the Alberta and Saskatchewan Acts of 1905, which created the provinces of Alberta and Saskatchewan out of the Northwest Territories can also be included in the group of constitutional components. These particular Canadian Acts are unique, in that they are not amendable by the federal parliament. Since the Alberta and Saskatchewan Acts form the constitutions of the respective provinces, once passed, they can be amended only by the provincial legislature.

Other federal statutes that can be included in any inventory of the Canadian constitution, are classed by R. M. Dawson as "organic laws."[3] These laws, although legally amendable by a simple act of parliament, involve fundamental principles of a constitutional nature. The best example of such an organic law is the Supreme Court Act, although the Canadian Bill of Rights also may be taking on such a status. While parliament may from time to time change some of the provisions of such legislation, the fundamental principles remain, for practical purposes, entrenched.

Section 92(1) of the BNA Act gives the provinces the power to make laws in relation to "The Amendment from Time to Time notwithstanding anything in this Act, of the Constitution of the Province, except as regards the Office of the Lieutenant Governor." This means essentially that the provincial legislatures have the power unilaterally to amend the constitutions of their respective domains by an ordinary statute. Any provincial statutes which amend the provincial constitutions, therefore, must, like the British or Canadian federal statutes which originally set them up, be considered a part of the Canadian constitution.

It must be noted at this juncture that not all political scientists and constitutional experts would agree that provincial or state constitutions should be considered integral parts of the constitution of a particular federal political system. Perhaps there is some justification for separating the United States constitution from the constitutions of the

---

[3] R. MacGregor Dawson, *The Government of Canada*, fifth edition, revised by Norman Ward (University of Toronto Press, Toronto, 1970), p. 63.

various states, but in Canada such a separation would distort the realities of the Canadian political system. The provinces are given the power to legislate with regard to matters that directly affect the rights and freedoms of the individual in terms of the individual's relationship with the state. An example of this would be Section 92(13) of the BNA Act which gives the provinces the legislative competence to deal with "Property and Civil Rights in the Province." If the provinces possess the power to affect the property and civil rights of Canadian citizens, then surely the provincial constitutions which regulate the exercise of this power within the provinces must be considered a part of the Canadian constitution.

It has been asserted that constitutions are basically formal rather than informal, and therefore, basically static. But constitutions consist in part of law or of collections of laws, which means that they are general prescriptions which in practice must be applied to specific cases. The application of constitutional principles to specific cases involves the interpretation of the constitution, which, in our system, is performed by the judiciary.[4] As the courts apply the constitutional principles to many different cases, a body of judicial decisions is built up which elaborates and fills out the constitution. The judicial decisions which interpret the constitution are an integral part of that constitution. In the case of Canada, because our legal system is based on the English common law tradition, and because the BNA Act states in the preamble that we are to have a form of government similar in principle to that of the U.K., precedents established in British common law make up a part of our constitution. As well, the interpretation of the BNA Act itself by the Judicial Committee of the Privy Council, which was the final court of appeal for Canada until 1949, built a large body of decisions which elaborate and clarify the act. These judicial decisions plus those of the Supreme Court of Canada since 1949 are a most important component of the constitution of Canada, especially as they have helped to clarify the federal dimension of our constitution.

In addition, the Canadian constitution includes a number of clearly defined principles such as the conventions of cabinet government and the firm, though unwritten, rule that the government must hold the support of a majority in the House of Commons or resign. These conventions are not found in the BNA Act, nor in any constitutional document, yet they are as much a part of the Canadian constitution as the BNA Act itself. Because they have no documentary manifestation,

[4] This subject is covered more extensively in Chapter 7.

however, the exact definition of them and their legal enforceability defies analysis. The only sanction that effectively enforces the principle of responsible government is the weight of public opinion that places value on it. A few of the customary and conventional parts of our constitution have been written down in some form and therefore have acquired the support of legal or quasi-legal sanction. For instance, the rules and privileges of parliament are implicitly if not explicitly entrenched in the Standing Orders and the Rules of Procedure. Generally, however, while conventions and customs involve some of the most important principles of the Canadian constitution, they exist in an unwritten form rather than as documentary and legally enforceable instruments.

Finally, a constitution can be considered to contain a number of principles or values which form the normative basis of the regime. These are difficult to pin down, for they exist largely as tacit assumptions in the minds of the members of the political community and they are passed on in very subtle ways through the process of political socialization. In Canada, they involve the whole complex of democratic political values. There is some argument whether such principles should be considered a part of the constitution itself or principles which underlie it. In this book they will be regarded as a part of the constitution.

Written and Unwritten Constitutions

It has become a tradition of political science, when making comparisons between the political system of the United Kingdom and that of the United States, to state that the former has an unwritten constitution and the latter a written constitution. This distinction is a relative rather than a categoric one, which places constitutions, for the purposes of comparison, on a continuum ranging from the hypothetical extreme of "purely written" to that of "purely unwritten." Upon examination, it rapidly becomes apparent that the constitutions of the two largest English-speaking democracies are neither purely written nor purely unwritten. Nor could any constitution be completely written if we choose to define the political value structure of a society as part of the constitution. The American constitution, while starting with the impressive document of 1789, has been filled out by conventions, judicial decisions, and statutes which express "fundamental" principles. Similarly, the constitution of the U.K., while consisting largely of principles embodied in the common law, has at its core written documents such as the Magna Carta and the Petition of Right. The Canadian constitution, consisting of a hodgepodge of written documents and unwritten conventions, falls on the continuum somewhere between the constitutions of the U.K. and the U.S.

A difficulty with the "written/unwritten" classification is that it is not clear what the criterion of evaluation is. Surely the exercise involves more than judging what proportion of a constitution is documentary and what proportion is customary. The relevant criterion seems to be whether or not an attempt has been made, at some point in history, to codify or list all the fundamental principles of a political system in a single document. This is the sense in which the constitution of the U.S. can be described as "written."

Perhaps the best method of clarifying the "written/unwritten" distinction is according to the formulae for changing the constitution.[5] The major difference between the documentary components of the British constitution and the U.S. constitution is that the former can be amended by a simple act of parliament, whereas the amendment of the U.S. constitution can only be achieved by a complicated, formal process that requires the participation of other institutions in addition to the federal Congress. The point of the distinction thus becomes not whether a constitutional principle is written or unwritten, but whether or not constitutional documents are entrenched behind a special amending formula. This gives the "written/unwritten" classification more meaning when making a comparison between the U.S. and British constitutions. Because of the confused and hybrid status of constitutional amendment in Canada, the classification can only complicate the issue here.

Finally, whatever the nature of this system of classification, it must be asked whether such a distinction has any inherent significance for the analysis of the Canadian constitution or, for that matter, any constitution. The ultimate strength or stability of a constitution does not depend on whether it is by any definition written or unwritten, but whether or not the principles it embodies are congruent with the values of the political community. If a constitution does not reflect the values of the society, it does not matter whether it is written or unwritten, it cannot last or be effective.

With that said, there may be some justification for discussing the relative merits of written and unwritten constitutions with respect to the function of political integration. Perhaps a written constitution may be more effective in creating a sense of national pride, but on the other hand, such a sense of national pride is not absent in the U.K., where the constitution, by any criterion, is basically unwritten. Also, a written constitution may be more effective in inculcating the norms of the regime to children and newcomers, for through a written constitution the values of the society are given visible manifestation.

[5] See Chapter 7.

In summary, the Canadian constitution is a conglomeration of British, Canadian, and provincial statutes, the British common law, Canadian judicial decisions, and a number of real but invisible conventions, customs, values and assumptions, all clustering rather loosely and haphazardly around the central kernel of the BNA Act. It is clearly not a written constitution, but it is not an unwritten one either—and for us the distinction is probably not very important.

THE OPERATIVE PRINCIPLES OF THE CANADIAN CONSTITUTION

It has already been established that all forms of constitutional government are rooted in the principle of the rule of law. But, if law is to "rule" us, it is going to need a lot of help from the people who occupy positions of authority in the political system. Laws must be made by somebody and they must be carried into effect by somebody. As a result, the substance of a constitution is fundamentally concerned with three political problems corresponding to the three functional classifications of allocative outputs of the political system: legislative outputs, executive outputs, and adjudicative outputs. In most political systems it is possible to make at least some functional distinction among these three types of outputs, and usually it is possible to distinguish between the organs or branches of the political system to which the constitution delegates the performance of each function.[6] However, the constitutional relationship among these branches can vary a great deal from one political system to another.

Finally it must be recognized that the three output functions of government are performed not by one but by several sovereign governments. The legislative, executive, and, to a certain extent, the adjudicative functions of government are performed by both federal and provincial governments in Canada. This operative principle of the constitution is *divided sovereignty* which adds greatly to the complexity of the political process in Canada.

The Supremacy of Parliament and the Rule of Law: The Legislative Function in Canada

The constitution of the U.S. explicitly states not only that there is to be a functional distinction among the three branches of government,

---

[6] Later, when discussing the policy process, it will be seen that it is very difficult to make realistic distinctions between different institutions such as parliament, the civil service, etc. on the basis of these particular types of functions.

but also that each of these functions should be vested in separate persons or groups of people. This principle, which is known as the *separation of power*, originated with the writings of Montesquieu, and it means in the American case that no individual is permitted to hold office in more than one branch of government at the same time. Hence for example, the President cannot be a member of the Senate or the House of Representatives during the term of office, nor can a Member of Congress be a judge at the same time as being in the House of Representatives. The logic behind the separation of powers is that the concentration of too much power in one person, or, for that matter, in one institution, is a corruptive influence. In an attempt to ensure a "good" and "just" form of government, the drafters of the United State's constitution tried to ensure that no person would be tempted by the possession of too much governmental power. Just to make sure, the principle of the separation of powers was given an added twist in the United State's constitution. It was decided that, in order to prevent the abuse of any of the three powers by occupants of the respective branches, an elaborate system of *checks and balances* would be woven into the relationship among branches. Thus, for instance, the President can veto any legislation passed by Congress, the Supreme Court can declare acts of Congress unconstitutional, the President appoints all members of the Supreme Court with the consent of two-thirds of the Senate, and the Congress can impeach the President and can override the President's veto by a two-thirds majority.

Starkly contrasting with this constitutional commitment to the principle of the separation of powers is the basic principle of the British constitution, *the supremacy of parliament*. In the British parliamentary system, not only is there no real separation of powers, but the legislative branch directly controls the executive branch, and is itself beyond interference by either the executive or the judiciary. No act of the British parliament can be declared unconstitutional by the courts, and the executive branch (to all intents and purposes, the cabinet) is not only made up of Members of Parliament but also must resign if a majority in the House of Commons fails to endorse its policies. Furthermore, no parliament may bind a future parliament by stating in a piece of legislation that that legislation is unamendable. In such a case, the later parliament, which is supreme in its own time, merely passes another law which takes precedence over the earlier one. Therefore, the principle of the supremacy of parliament vests awesome formal power in the legislative branch.

But we have already described the political system of the U.K. as being a constitutional form of government, and it has been pointed out that at the roots of the principle of constitutionalism is the principle of the rule of law. How then can there be rule of law and parliamentary supremacy without contradiction? Is parliament bound by the principle of the rule of law, or is the rule of law subject to the supremacy of parliament? The only answer here is that the concept of the rule of law must have two meanings. In the first sense, the rule of law means that any authoritative output of the political system can only be achieved by law. If this is all that the concept of the rule of law means, then a contradiction does not exist between it and the supremacy of parliament, for any act of parliament is a law or has the effect of law.

However, there is a second sense of the concept of the rule of law which implies such things as the right to have access to the courts and the right not to be imprisoned without a trial, etc. If this definition is accepted, the rule of law and the supremacy of parliament are mutually exclusive principles. Parliament in the U.K. can, by "act of parliament," abolish such revered rights as *habeas corpus*, which would mean that parliament could, in effect, "abolish" the rule of law[7] in the second sense of the term. There is no way of settling this confusion in the terminology. It would be pointless to say that "henceforth the term shall mean such and such," for the term is so widely used in both senses that the confusion would remain. It must be kept in mind that when speaking of constitutionalism generally, the first sense of the rule of law is usually what is intended, and when speaking specifically of the British constitution it is the broader sense that is intended. The significance of this distinction is that the narrower usage of the term is the purer form of the concept and the broader usage is the peculiarly British version of it.

As noted before, the preamble of the British North America Act (1867) states that Canada is to have "a Constitution similar in principle to that of the United Kingdom." This means, *prima facie*, that the supremacy of parliament is a substantive principle of the Canadian constitution. The BNA Act, however, goes beyond this broad statement of intent of the preamble, and the extent to which the Canadian parliament is really supreme must be examined in the light of the provisions of the Act which limit the power of parliament in Canada.

First of all, certain key sections of the BNA Act are not amendable by the Canadian parliament, but can be changed only by an act of the parliament of the U.K. An amendment to the Act secured in 1949

---

[7] See Corry and Hodgetts, *Democratic Government and Politics*, p. 96. Note also that we are speaking here only in strict legal terms, for in practice, because of the nature of the British political culture, there is a practical limitation on the extent to which parliament can restrict the rule of law even in the narrower sense.

states that the Canadian parliament can, from time to time, amend the constitution of Canada except as regards matters assigned exclusively to the provinces, guarantees of minority education and language rights, the provision that parliament must meet at least once a year, and the provision that no parliament shall continue for more than five years.[8] Hence, the supremacy of the Canadian parliament is legally limited by the fact that these sections of the BNA Act can be changed only by the action of the parliament of the U.K., although as will be seen later, the *de jure* limitation in this regard may not be very significant.[9]

The second and perhaps the most important limitation on the supremacy of the Canadian parliament is found in the federal distribution of legislative powers set out mainly in Sections 91-95 of the BNA Act. Because of these sections of the Act, the courts in Canada, unlike the courts in the U.K., have the power to declare acts of the federal parliament unconstitutional because they are beyond the legislative jurisdiction assigned to the federal level by the BNA Act. Many pieces of legislation passed by the Canadian parliament have been declared invalid on these grounds, and in fact, the interpretation of the federal legislative competence by the judiciary has played a significant role in remodeling Canadian federalism since 1867.[10] The important point here is that the judicial branch in Canada has the power to declare laws passed by either the federal parliament or by the legislatures of the provinces to be *ultra vires* and therefore invalid. In sum, legislative authority in Canada is divided among three separate types of legislative bodies: the parliament of the U.K., the parliament of Canada, and the legislatures of the ten provinces, with the judiciary deciding any jurisdictional disputes.

The final question concerning the extent to which the doctrine of the supremacy of parliament obtains in Canada is whether or not the combination of these three types of legislatures possesses legislative supremacy. In other words, is the legislative authority of ten provincial parliaments, one federal parliament and one imperial parliament *exhaustive*? In the United States, there are matters which are beyond the legislative competence of all levels and branches of government. These are principles which are considered to be so fundamental that no government should be able to interfere with them, and which are therefore entrenched in the constitution. Are any matters so entrenched in the Canadian constitution? Judicial opinion in this area

[8] BNA Act, 1949 (2).
[9] See Chapter 7 for a more detailed discussion of this situation.
[10] See Chapter 8.

has generally supported the doctrine of exhaustiveness, giving to the provinces and the federal parliament virtually complete authority.[11] While in a strictly legal sense this is not the case, practically speaking, the encroachment on the collective legislative authority of all eleven Canadian legislatures by the U.K. parliament's amending role is virtually nil. An entrenched Charter of Rights and Freedoms would change all of this by placing certain fundamental matters outside of the jurisdiction of either federal or provincial legislatures.

There are some minor and technical restrictions on the doctrine of amendment. One of these restrictions has come through a series of narrow judicial interpretations of the ability of the provinces and the federal parliament to delegate legislative authority to each other. The *Nova Scotia Interdelegation* case of 1951 is a landmark in this regard, the Supreme Court of Canada having found that interdelegation is incompatible with federalism.[12] While this imposes a *de jure* limitation on the doctrine of the supremacy of parliament in Canada, in practical terms it would be possible for the federal government to secure an amendment to the BNA Act specifically permitting interdelegation. Finally, there are a few laws still in effect that were passed by the united legislature of Upper and Lower Canada before Confederation. Legislation such as this cannot be repealed or legally amended because it was the product of a legislative body that no longer exists. Practically, however, it is possible for the legislatures of the Provinces of Ontario and Quebec to pass complementary laws which would change the effect of a pre-Confederation statute without actually altering it in law. Certainly, limitations such as these on the legislative competence of Canadian legislatures are of minimal importance in the total picture.

To conclude, then, the principle of the supremacy of parliament is definitely an integral part of the constitution of Canada, and while the form it takes is not as unambiguous as it is in the U.K., the implications remain as significant here as there. Unlike the constitution of the U.S., which puts some matters beyond the grasp of all legislative bodies, the constitution of the Canadian political system historically has vested total legislative authority for all practical purposes in the collectivity of federal and provincial legislatures.

---

[11] See *Bank of Toronto v. Lambe* (1887), *Olmsted*, vol. 1; *Attorney-General for Ontario v. Attorney-General for Canada* ("Labour Convention Case") (1937), *Olmsted*, vol. 3.

[12] *Attorney-General for Nova Scotia v. Attorney-General for Canada*, [1951] *SCR*, 31. See also: R. I. Cheffins and R. N. Tucker, *The Constitutional Process in Canada*, pp. 33-34 for an excellent analysis of the legal implications of this decision and its potential effect on the doctrine of the supremacy of parliament.

The Crown and Cabinet Government:
The Executive Function

The legislative function of a political system is to make laws. In Canada that function is performed, according to the constitution, by parliament. The executive function of a political system is to put the laws into effect, to carry out or to "execute" acts of parliament. In Canada, the executive power is defined by Section 9 of the BNA Act: "the Executive Government and Authority of and over Canada is hereby declared to continue and be vested in the Queen." Formally, therefore, the executive function in Canada is performed by the Queen, and we can be said to have a monarchial form of government. The most significant implication of this fact is the consequent transferral of all prerogative rights of the Crown in the U.K. to the Crown in respect of Canada. This statement, however, requires some explanation, particularly the terms *the Crown* and *prerogative rights*.

The Crown[13] is a term used to describe the collectivity of executive powers which, in a monarchy, are exercised by or in the name of the sovereign. There is nothing mystical about this term. It does not imply the existence of an authority greater than that possessed constitutionally by the reigning monarch. These executive powers vested in the Queen flow from the historic common law rights and privileges of the Crown in England which are referred to as the *royal prerogative*. Prerogative rights exist primarily because they always have, and not because they have been created at some point in time by statute. The prerogative rights and privileges of the Queen are the residue of authority left over from an age when the power of the reigning monarch was absolute. This absolute power has been whittled away bit by bit until today there are only a few remnants of it that are left to the Queen. It is important to emphasize here that prerogative rights cannot be created by statute. If a statute formally increases the power of the Crown, the effect is to delegate some of the authority of parliament to the executive, but not to vest any new prerogative rights in the person of the monarch.

On the other hand, the prerogative can be limited by statute. An example of this is in the Crown Liability Act (1952), which takes away the prerogative right of the Crown not to be held liable in tort for damages resulting from acts done by public servants or for acts done by the monarch personally. This prerogative can never be returned as a prerogative right, although a future parliament could return it as a

---

[13] See: F. MacKinnon, *The Crown in Canada* (Glenbow-Alberta Institute, McClelland and Stewart, Calgary, 1976), for an excellent analysis of a subject which has been to a large extent neglected in Canadian political science.

statutory right. Hence, the royal prerogative is slowly shrinking, and in Canada it is being replaced by statutory provisions that define the real limits of executive power.

While the royal prerogative is not what it used to be, there are still some significant executive powers that are based on it. Among these are the right of the monarch to all ownerless property (Crown land); the right to priority as a creditor in the settlement of bankruptcies, etc., and the right to summon, prorogue, and dissolve parliament. Because of the convention that these powers are all exercised "on the advice" of the Ministers of the Crown, in fact they are almost all possessed in reality by the Prime Minister and the government of the day.

In the U.K. the formal functions of the monarch are performed personally by the Queen. In Canada, while the Queen can still be called "Queen of Canada," most of the monarchial functions are peformed in her name by the Governor General at the national level and the Lieutenant-Governors at the provincial level. The appointment of the Governor General was originally the responsibility of the Queen acting on the advice of the government of the U.K. This made the Governor General effectively independent of the Canadian cabinet. Since the Imperial Conferences of 1926 and 1930, however, the Governor General has been independent of the imperial government and is now removable by the Queen only on the advice of the government of Canada. While the appointment of the Governor General is, formally, a function of the Queen, in fact it is always made today with the advice of the Canadian cabinet. Also, while the normal term of office of the Canadian Governor General is five years, this can be shortened or stretched according to the wishes of the government of the day.

While the BNA Act defines many of the powers of the Governor General, the office itself is a creature of letters patent from the monarch. By the Letters Patent of 1947, the Governor General is empowered to exercise "all powers and authorities" that belong to the Queen in right of Canada. This means that the exercise of the royal prerogative in Canada is a function of the Governor General, to be carried out by the Governor General, at personal discretion, with the advice of the Queen's Privy Council for Canada.[14] Among the powers specified by the Letters Patent of 1947 are the use of the Great Seal of Canada, the appointment of judges, commissioners, diplomats, Ministers of the Crown, etc., along with the power to dismiss or suspend them, and the power to summon, prorogue, and dissolve parliament.

---

[14] See Chapter 15 for a discussion of the Privy Council Office.

In addition to the prerogative powers that are bestowed upon the Governor General by the Letters Patent of 1947, there are certain other powers that are ceded to the Governor General by the BNA Act. Among these are the authority to appoint Senators and the Speaker of the Senate; the exclusive right to recommend legislation involving the spending of public money or the imposition of a tax; and the right, formally, to prevent a bill from becoming law by withholding assent, or by reserving the bill "for the signification of the Queen's pleasure."[15] The Governor General has the power, by Section 56 of the BNA Act, to "disallow" any provincial legislation of which he or she disapproves. The real significance of the disallowance power is that it gives to the federal government a potential veto power over all provincial acts. While it has not been used since 1943, the legal power to use it still remains as a reminder to the provinces that the Fathers of Confederation viewed the provincial legislatures as "second-class citizens."

The office of Lieutenant-Governor was created by Section 58 of the BNA Act. The holder of the office is appointed by the Governor General in Council, and the salary is set by the Canadian parliament. Furthermore, the Lieutenant-Governor is removable "for cause" by the Governor General in Council. This means that in some respects the Lieutenant-Governor is an officer of the federal government who is responsible to the Governor General. On the other hand, the courts have decided that, in fact, the Lieutenant-Governor is a representative of the Queen directly, despite the fact that the appointment and salary are controlled by the government of Canada. In an important constitutional case in 1892, the Judicial Committee of the Privy Council held that the Lieutenant-Governor was a representative of the Queen in right of the province directly and therefore could exercise all the prerogative powers that the monarch could.[16] The significance of this is that the Lieutenant-Governor, while in some respects the subordinate of the Governor General, is in other respects an equal and enjoys the same power in right of the province that the Governor General enjoys in the right of Canada. In turn, this has the effect of making the provincial governments, who are personified in the Lieutenant-Governors, more important than they would otherwise be. The BNA Act provides that the Lieutenant-Governor of the province has the power to assent to or to refuse assent to acts of the provincial legislature, and furthermore, by the BNA Act, is given the

---

[15] BNA Act, s. 55.
[16] *The Liquidators of the Maritime Bank v. the Receiver General of New Brunswick* (1892), *Olmsted*, vol. 1.

power to reserve a bill for the signification of the Governor General's pleasure. In sum, the Lieutenant-Governor in the province has powers that are analogous to and commensurate with the powers of the Governor General at the level of the federal government.

Up until now we have been speaking in rather formal and legalistic terms about the powers of the Governor General and the Lieutenant-Governors. The intention has been to clarify the strict constitutional nature of the executive function in Canada. Now, however, it is necessary to bring the discussion of the executive function down from this rarefied atmosphere and to deal with the constitutional realities of the executive function in Canada.

The BNA Act provides for a body of advisors to assist the Governor General in performing the onerous burden of executive responsibilities which come from the same Act and the Letters Patent of 1947. Section 11 of the BNA Act states that:

There shall be a Council to aid and advise in the Government of Canada, to be styled the Queen's Privy Council for Canada; and the Persons who are to be Members of that Council shall be from time to time chosen and summoned by the Governor General and sworn in as Privy Councillors, and Members thereof may be from time to time removed by the Governor General.

The BNA Act states quite specifically that the Governor General does not have to listen to advisors, but in fact even at the time of Confederation there was a well-established convention that the Governor of the colony would, in almost all cases, act purely on the advice of the government of the day. The Queen's Privy Council for Canada includes a great number of people such as ex-cabinet ministers who never function as advisors. The *cabinet,* which is not mentioned at all in the BNA Act, is really a committee of Privy Councillors, chosen by the leader of the majority party in the House of Commons from among supporters in parliament. Formally, all executive acts are performed by the Governor General in Council, but in reality, executive decisions are made by the Prime Minister and cabinet, and are "rubber-stamped" by the Governor General.

There is still a body of opinion among prominent experts which argues that one should not dismiss the Governor General as merely a "rubber stamp" for the Prime Minister and cabinet, for the simple reason that the Governor General still does possess a great deal of executive authority by virtue of the BNA Act and the prerogatives. The argument is that if the government of the day attempted to violate a basic principle of our political culture, for instance by abolishing free speech, the Governor General could step in and refuse assent to the bill, thus thwarting the culprits. In doing so, however, the Governor General would be violating a fundamental norm of our system of government, by claiming to represent the public interest better than the public's elected representatives. To say that a Governor General would never dare to oppose the will of the Prime Minister is pure speculation, but the fact remains that the norm of popular sovereignty which is at the core of the Canadian constitution imposes severe political limitations on the actual powers of the Queen's representative. The last time a Governor General went against the wishes of the Prime Minister was in 1926, when Lord Byng refused Prime Minister King a dissolution of parliament. The result was a general outcry led by Mackenzie King against the unilateral action of the Governor General, and a subsequent electoral disaster for the man who had immediately benefitted from Byng's decision, Arthur Meighen. [17]

The relationship between the Lieutenant-Governor of a province and the provincial Premier is almost identical to that between the Prime Minister of Canada and the Governor General, and the BNA Act provides that the Lieutenant-Governor may act with the advice of the executive council of the province. The executive council is, in fact, the provincial cabinet, which is chosen by the Premier. All executive decisions are made by the Premier and cabinet, and the Lieutenant-Governor, like the federal counterpart, more or less "rubber-stamps" them. As with the Governor General, the one time when a Lieutenant-Governor might be called upon to exercise some discretionary authority is in the case of the death in office of the leader of the government, where the successor is not obvious. Clearly the Lieutenant-Governor must seek the advice of the cabinet ministers, but in some cases their advice might not be unanimous. In such a situation, the Lieutenant-Governor must decide whose advice to take, on the basis of personal discretion and political acumen, for above all else the Lieutenant-Governor must ensure that there is a government. Such a situation appeared to develop at the death of Premier Maurice Duplessis of Quebec in 1959. Initially, the cabinet was by no means solidly united behind one candidate to succeed Duplessis. Apparently the cabinet managed eventually to achieve a consensus by itself, but the incident makes it clear that there is a potentially important political role to be played by the formal executive in such rare, but conceivable, circumstances. [18]

---

[17] See E. A. Forsey, *The Royal Power of Dissolution of Parliament in the British Commonwealth* (Oxford University Press, Toronto, 1968), ch. 5.

[18] For a discussion of the role the Lieutenant-Governor plays in finding a successor to a Premier who dies in office, see J. R. Mallory, "The Royal Prerogative in Canada: The Selection of Successors to Mr. Duplessis and Mr. Sauvé," *The Canadian Journal of Economics and Political Science*, vol. 26, no. 2, pp. 314-319, May 1960. See also G. F. G. Stanley, "A 'Constitutional Crisis' in British Columbia," *The Canadian Journal of Economics and Political Science*, vol. 21, no. 3, pp. 281-292, August 1955.

To conclude, the formal executive power in Canada is vested in the Crown and, in a very formal sense, we can be said to have a monarchial form of government. The Governor General exercises all of the prerogative rights and privileges of the Queen in right of Canada, according to the BNA Act and the Letters Patent that define the office. The constitutional doctrine of popular sovereignty has, however, reduced the *de facto* role of the Governor General to that of a figurehead. The real power is exercised by the Prime Minister and cabinet who obtain their legitimacy from the fact that they possess a popular mandate.

The Judicial Function

The judicial function is the hardest to distinguish of the three basic output functions of the political system.[19] In fact, it can be argued that there are only two basic output functions: making law and applying it—and both the judiciary and the executive can be perceived as applying the law to specific cases, each doing it in a slightly different fashion. There are two reasons, however, for shying away in this text from that two-fold method of classification. First, the core document of our constitution, the BNA Act, makes very definite distinctions among the Executive Power, the Legislative Power, and the Judicature.[20] Secondly, even if a functional distinction is difficult, the judicial branch in Canada can be clearly distinguished through the principle of *judicial independence,* which insulates the judiciary from any direct responsibility to either of the other two branches. The independence of the judiciary is one of the essential principles of our system of government, and as such, it merits a longer look.

The constitutional source of judicial independence flows from Sections 96 to 101 of the BNA Act. Section 99 states that Superior Court judges shall hold office during "good behaviour" up to the age of seventy-five, implying that a judge cannot be dismissed for incompetence or laziness but only for a criminal offence. Section 99 also provides that a judge is removable only by the Governor General on a joint resolution by the Senate and the House of Commons. This means that the executive can remove a judge only at the request of both Houses of the Canadian parliament, and the practice has evolved that even this is undertaken only after a judicial inquiry into the person's wrongdoings. The salary of a judge is set by statute, so that it is not possible for the judge to become involved in bargaining

---

[19] W. R. Lederman, "The Independence of the Judiciary," *Canadian Bar Review,* 1956, p. 769 ff.
[20] BNA Act, part III, IV, VII.

with the executive for salary increments, nor is it possible for the executive to "pressure" a judge through controlling the judge's livelihood. In sum, every effort is made to ensure that the judge is protected from influences that might affect objectivity in the position. As R. M. Dawson has said,

The judge is placed in a position where he has nothing to lose by doing what is right, and little to gain by doing what is wrong, and there is, therefore, every reason to hope that his best efforts will be devoted to the conscientious performance of his duty. [21]

Further to the guarantees of the personal independence of the judge is the guarantee of jurisdictional integrity that is given to the Superior Courts in Canada. A common assumption is that any governmental official will attempt to widen the scope of jurisdiction, a practice often referred to as "empire building." Limits must be placed on this sort of activity, usually by the intervention of other officials. However, the independence of the judiciary is perceived as such an important value of our system that the danger of judicial empire building is ignored. Instead, a remarkable faith in the honesty and levelheadedness of our judges is indicated by allowing Superior Courts to decide not only their own jurisdiction, but the jurisdiction of other governmental offices as well. [22] In effect, this means that the legislative branch cannot vest Superior Court jurisdiction in other than a Superior Court without first securing amendments to the BNA Act (Section 96 to 101). [23] Granted, there is nothing in law to prevent parliament from amending Section 96 to 101 or the Supreme Court Act, the latter being a federal statute to begin with, but the principle of judicial independence is a norm of our system with which even parliament cannot tamper lightly. [24]

Judicial review has been cited already as a possible limitation on the supremacy of parliament in Canada. Now it is necessary to consider to what extent the principle of judicial review is itself a part of our constitution. Judicial review is essentially the power of superior courts to "review" the decision or actions of governmental officials,

---

[21] R. McGregor Dawson, *The Government of Canada,* p. 409.
[22] See Lederman, "The Independence of the Judiciary," p. 1175.
[23] Ss. 96-101 of the BNA Act can apparently be amended (per section 91(1) of the Act). See E. Forsey, "Independence of the Judiciary," *Canadian Bar Review,* 1957, p. 240. He rejects Lederman's contention that 96-101 cannot be amended unilaterally by the federal government. See also B. L. Strayer, *Judicial Review of Legislation in Canada* (University of Toronto Press, Toronto, 1968), p. 37.
[24] See: Chapter 7 for a discussion of the implication of some constitutional reform proposals on the principle of judicial independence.

administrative boards or tribunals, other courts[25] and even parliament itself. Its significance in *administrative law* is that no official of government, administrative agency, or executive body is above or outside the law of the land.[26]

Its significance in *constitutional law* is that the courts can declare acts of Parliament or of provincial legislatures unconstitutional or *ultra vires*, and therefore void. In a broader sense, judicial review includes, as well, the ability of the courts to slow up or "brake" the legislative branch by rigid interpretation of the law.[27] It is in this broader sense that constitutional judicial review might be said to exist even in political systems such as the U.K., where strictly speaking, no act of a *supreme* parliament can ever be *ultra vires*. Hence when we speak of judicial review of legislation we must keep in mind that there are two forms or levels at which the process operates.

Professor J. E. McWhinney describes these two levels of judicial review as direct and indirect forms of judicial authority.[28] Direct judicial review is the kind exercised by, for example, the U.S. Supreme Court. The U.S. court has the power[29] to declare acts of Congress and acts of the state legislatures unconstitutional and therefore void. This judicial power exists in Canada to the extent that the judiciary here has the authority to interpret the federal distribution of powers as laid out by the BNA Act.

The constitutional status of direct judicial review in Canada, however, is confusing. The right to declare acts of parliament *ultra vires* certainly does not flow from the English common law, which recognizes the principle of parliamentary supremacy. On the other hand, this judicial right is not specifically vested in the courts by the BNA Act, either. The historical origins of the practice of direct judicial review can likely be traced to the fact that the Privy Council traditionally had that power with respect to the colonial legislatures which were subordinate to the imperial parliament. McWhinney argues that, although the Canadian parliament has long since ceased to be

[25] Note that judicial review is to be distinguished from *appeal*. The former is the broader definition and includes the latter. Review is a right of superior courts by virtue of the definition of a superior court as *independent* to determine its own jurisdiction. The right to hear appeals must be created by statute—it must be specifically vested in a court by legislation. Appeal is today virtually the only means whereby a court reviews the decision of lower courts in the same hierarchy.

[26] This will be discussed as one of the mechanisms of bureaucratic control in Chapter 18.

[27] See Edward McWhinney, *Judicial Review* (University of Toronto Press, Toronto, 1969), p. 13.

[28] Ibid.

[29] The predominant view, as set forth in *Marbury v. Madison* (1803), is that the power to review acts of Congress is "implicit" in the constitution.

subordinate, the practice of judicial review has "ripened," through continued use, into a binding convention of our constitution.[30] Probably, too, the roots of direct judicial review in Canada can be traced to pragmatic considerations flowing implicitly from the principle of federalism which is one of the critical dimensions entrenched in the BNA Act. To back up this hypothesis, it can be noted that direct judicial review of legislation in Canada has occurred almost exclusively with respect to the distribution of powers between the federal parliament and the provincial legislatures, and never has it functioned to place matters beyond the legislative competence of government generally.

Indirect judicial review, as described by McWhinney, ... is where a court, either not having the power to annul or override enactments of the legislature as "unconstitutional" or else simply choosing not to exert that power in the instant case, says in effect in the process of interpretation of a statute, that the legislature may or may not have the claimed legislative power, but it has not in the language it has used in the enactment now in question employed that power.[31]

This form of judicial review will naturally be more significant in countries like the U.K., where the constitution is extremely flexible and without clear boundaries, but such "judicial braking" will be used occasionally in countries like the U.S. and Canada, where direct judicial review is also an appropriate judicial alternative. The reason for a court's choosing indirect rather than direct review might be that the facts of the case are not clear enough to justify setting a precedent that may preclude legislative enactments in that area in the future. Or it may be the more practical reason that the court does not wish to become embroiled in the political hassle that could ensue if popular legislation were to be rendered void by a judicial decision.

Indirect judical review is achieved by a set of *presumptions* which the courts will make in the interpretation of a piece of legislation. For example, they will assume, unless the legislation states specifically to the contrary, that parliament does not intend laws to have retroactive effect; and they will not interpret any statute in such a way as to take away the citizen's right to a fair hearing. The effect is to slow up, or to "brake" the legislative branch when the judiciary feels it has overstepped the bounds of constitutional propriety, though perhaps keeping within the limits of *de jure* constitutionality.

The constitutional basis for the exercise of indirect judicial review in Canada is the English common law.[32] The limitation on this type of

---

[30] McWhinney, *Judicial Review*, p. 14.
[31] Ibid., p. 13.
[32] Ibid., p. 15 *passim*.

judicial review is that it is merely a "stalling" technique. Parliament can always, in theory, rework the legislation so that there is no ambiguity and in this way bypass even the most rigorous and stringent application of the judiciary's power of indirect judicial review. However, as Professor McWhinney points out, "at best this is likely to involve time-consuming delays and at worst, the corrective legislation may bog down completely.[33]

A further limitation on the power of judicial review may be imposed by the principle of *stare decisis*.[34] *Stare decisis* means that the judiciary is bound by previous decisions in deciding current cases. While precedents established by earlier courts are usually adhered to by the Canadian judiciary, this is done by choice and not by constitutional prescription. Lower courts are bound by the decisions of higher courts, but this aspect of the principle of *stare decisis* does not affect the constitutional implications of judicial review. More will be said about the roles of judicial review in the evolution of Canadian federalism in Chapter 8 below.

Divided Sovereignty: The Federal Principle

Divided sovereignty means basically that the legislative powers of government in Canada are divided between the federal parliament and the legislatures of the ten provinces. While we often refer to the federal and provincial "levels" of government, within their specified spheres of jurisdiction there exists no superior-subordinate relationship. The legislature of the provinces and the parliament of Canada have constitutionally distinct functions and neither can trench upon the constitutionally granted authority of the other. The term "orders" of government has increasingly come into use to express that fact.

The operative principle of divided sovereignty is ensconced in the British North America Act, and represents an intention on the part of the drafters of that act to establish a federal system of government in Canada. There have been many definitions of federalism and many approaches to its study, and while the evolution of the Canadian federal system will be discussed in subsequent chapters, a few words here on the concept itself will help to clarify the use of the term. The most important modern contribution to the study of federalism has been that of K. C. Wheare. Since the 1946 publication of Wheare's classic, *Federal Government*, theoretical writings on the concept of federalism have added relatively little except qualifications and interesting changes in emphasis.

---

[33] Ibid.
[34] See also Chapter 7.

Wheare's analysis is institutional in the sense that he views federalism as a *form of government* which embodies the "federal principle":

By the federal principle I mean the method of dividing powers so that the general and regional governments are each, within a sphere, coordinate and independent. [35]

He then draws a distinction between federal governments and federal constitutions stating that:

It is not enough that the federal principle should be embodied predominantly in the written constitution of a country. . . . What determines the issue is the working of the system. [36]

The prerequisites of a federal system are two according to Wheare:

To begin with, the communities or states concerned must desire to be under a single independent government for some purposes. . . . They must desire at the same time to retain or establish independent regional governments in some matters at least. [37]

Thus in functional terms a federal system reconciles a desire for overall *unity* with a desire for local or regional *autonomy*. In structural terms, a federal system is seen as having independent national and regional governments, each operating in a hypothetically distinct jurisdictional compartment. The federal process, or in Wheare's terms, "How Federal Government Works," will vary from federation to federation, but so long as the federal function is being performed and as long as the basic structural characteristics of federalism are present, the system can be called federal.

The major source of criticism of Wheare has come from people studying newer nations, many of which claim to be federal, and few of which conform perfectly to Wheare's definition. The reaction to this discontinuity between the term and the real world has been to redefine the term. The crux of most of these attacks on Wheare has been that his concept of federal government is "institutional," and his analysis is "legalistic." The most prominent of his detractors has been W. S. Livingstone, who argues that a legalistic definition of federalism is too narrow, and counters with a sociological one: "The essence of federalism lies not in the institutional or constitutional structure, but in society itself."[38] Livingstone goes on to state that a federal society is one whose diversity is reflected territorially, and that a federal

---

[35] K. C. Wheare, *Federal Government* (Oxford University Press, 1961), p. 11.
[36] Ibid., p. 33.
[37] Ibid., pp. 35-36.
[38] W. S. Livingstone, "A Note on the Nature of Federalism," in J. Peter Meekison (ed.), *Canadian Federalism: Myth or Reality* (Methuen, Toronto, 1971), p. 22.

government is merely a "device by which the federal qualities of the society are articulated and protected."[39]

The great weakness of Livingstone's concept of federalism is that it is so inclusive that it is virtually useless for analyzing and categorizing real political systems. He defines a federal government as one that presides over a federal society, and he defines a federal society as one that has regional or territorial diversity. With such possible exceptions as Lichtenstein, Monaco, or San Marino, all modern states have varying degrees of regional diversity and therefore all modern governments could be classed as federal. Thus, where K. C. Wheare is too restrictive in his concept of federalism, Livingstone is far too broad in his conception of the term.

Riker improves on Wheare without going as far as Livingstone. He describes federalism functionally as "the main alternative to empire as a technique of aggregating large areas under one government,"[40] and structurally as a system with a constitution having three basic characteristics; namely,

. . . 1) *two levels of government rule the same land and people, 2) each level has at least one area of action in which it is autonomous, and 3) there is some guarantee (even though merely a statement in the constitution) of the autonomy of each government in its own sphere.* [41]

Then Riker goes on to deal with the federal process as a continuous *bargaining relationship* that is carried on among the various leaders of the regional and national governments. Here, by viewing the origins and the operations of federal systems in terms of elite accommodation Riker has added significantly to Wheare's rather mechanistic and admittedly legalistic analysis of federalism.

There are many tomes written on the subject of federalism, and most of them address themselves at some stage to the problem of definition. Riker, Livingstone, and Wheare represent the general range of approaches, and likely form the foundations for most other authors' conceptions of federal government.[42] The basic characteristics common to all federal systems can be derived from these authors. First, the origins and persistence of federal forms of government depend upon continuing general agreement among the various na-

[39] Ibid.
[40] W. H. Riker, *Federalism: Origin; Operation; Significance* (Little, Brown, Boston, 1964), p. 5.
[41] Ibid., p. 11.
[42] The other significant source of inspiration for the development of the federal concept has been international relations theory and the theories dealing with international political integration. For example, see: K. W. Deutsch et al., *Political Community and the North Atlantic Area* (Princeton, 1957); Plischke, E., *Systems of Integrating the Inter-*

tional and regional leaders that some form of union is desirable and that, because of difference in priorities among the member states or provinces, there should be at least some degree of independence guaranteed to them. (R. L. Watts speaks of this in terms of social integration, in terms of an equilibrium between integrating and disintegrating pressures within society.)[43] Secondly, in structural terms, federal systems are composed of two levels of government each of which is permitted to function independently of the other in specified although probably changing areas of jurisdiction, and neither can destroy the other.[44]

The conceptual and definitional problems have arisen, moreover, only where political systems calling themselves federal have lacked these basic characteristics. In fact, most real governments can be very quickly and easily classified as either federal or non-federal, and only a few stand on the effective borderline between the federal and the non-federal and, hence, challenge the governmental taxonomists' categories. Canada, although regionally diverse, has survived for more than one hundred and ten years, and thus has the first basic federal characteristic. Also, the Canadian system does feature two levels of government, each of which is independent of the other in constitutionally specified jurisdictional bailiwicks, and for that reason too must be classified as federal. In sum, neither the Canadian political system nor the Canadian constitution is a borderline case and both can easily be classified as federal. The evolution of the Canadian federal system, and the idiosyncrasies of our particular brand of federalism will be discussed in later chapters. The fact that three separate chapters are to be devoted to federal aspects of the Canadian political system indicates the importance that must be attached to federalism as an operative principle of the constitution. However, to discuss it further at this point would serve to repeat information which is better understood within an historical context in Chapters 7 and 8 and within the context of the policy process in Chapter 16.

This concludes our discussion of the substance of the Canadian constitution. But this is only a snapshot at one point in time. In order to complete the picture we must now proceed to an analysis of the dynamic element of the Canadian constitution; its propensities and techniques for change.

---

national Community (Van Nostrand, 1964); Haas, E. B., *The Uniting of Europe* (Stanford, 1958).

[43] R. L. Watts, *New Federations* (Oxford University Press, 1966), p. 111.

[44] G. Stevenson, *Unfulfilled Union* (Macmillan, 1979). This is an important book on Canadian federalism for while it is fairly comprehensive it also takes a unique tack— first it is written from a *political economy* perspective and secondly it is unabashedly *centralist* in its prescriptions.

7

The Dynamics of Law and the Constitution in Canada

Having looked at the component parts and substantive principles of the Canadian constitution, it is now necessary to put that information within a more dynamic setting. This chapter looks at the Canadian legal system and constitution from the perspectives of three different processes. The first section takes the broadest approach possible and looks at the process of constitutional change. This section analyzes the relationship between individual and state as reciprocal, for constitutional change not only reflects changes in the political culture, but also induces change in the individual behaviour patterns that characterize the political culture. The second section looks at the nature of the positive law and the judicial system in Canada. Here the analytical focus is narrower and the emphasis is on a process whereby the specific rules of behaviour set down in statutes are applied to individuals in society—the means by which the society protects itself from individual excesses. The final section of this chapter analyzes the process whereby civil liberties are protected in Canada; here the analytical focus is on the means by which the individual is protected from the potential excesses of the state.

THE PROCESS OF CONSTITUTIONAL CHANGE

In the long run, the constitution of a political system must reflect the values of society if that political system is to persist. Hence, while it is true that the constitution provides the regime with necessary rigidity, the constitution must also have the capacity for change; it must not be so rigid that it cannot be adjusted to meet new needs and priorities in the environment of the political system. There are several ways in which the Canadian constitution can be changed. We will deal in some detail with the process of judicial review in our consideration of the history of Canadian federalism in Chapter 8. Now we wish to present an overview of the complete range of possibilities for constitutional change in Canada.

Revolution and Political Violence

The likelihood of a revolution[1] in Canada has always been fairly slim for the simple reason that the social and political issues which divide us are usually moderated by a deep-seated consensus about basic values. In this sense the perceived urgency of constitutional change has seldom been so great that people would feel the need to resort to violence to speed up the process. Even in instances where our political differences have become so severe that the *substantive consensus* about basic values has started to break down, there has remained a *procedural consensus*—an agreement as to the "rules of the game" of political and constitutional change which effectively exclude most forms of political violence or revolution. Moreover, throughout most of our history, needed changes in the Canadian constitution have been attainable through legitimate, non-violent and non-revolutionary means.

But even if compared to other countries in the world the Canadian political culture is relatively non-violent[2] it must be recognized that violence as a tactic of political change is always a possibility. It takes but one deviant individual to assassinate a political leader or place an explosive device in a public place, so that, while the dominant values of a political system may be basically non-violent, isolated violent events may periodically occur. While generally speaking, the evidence of our history has backed up the contention of our "peaceable Kingdom," isolated events, most significantly the FLQ terrorists' activities of October 1970, lend some credence to the idea that perhaps even in Canada there is a tiny but growing minority which is willing to engage in non-legitimate tactics to induce political change.[3]

---

[1] The concept of revolution has two dimensions; one emphasizes the *means* of change which are extra-legal and normally violent, and the second emphasizes the *extent* of the changes that occur. Thus, on the one hand, extremely violent "revolutionary" upheavals may produce relatively minor changes in the regime or the political community; examples of this are *coups d'état* which occur frequently in some military dictatorships. On the other hand, change of "revolutionary" dimensions may occur in the regime or political community of a system through perfectly legal and non-violent means; an example of this might be the Indian Independence Act which created the modern states of India and Pakistan out of what was previously British India.

[2] See also Chapter 4 for a further reference to violence and the Canadian political culture.

[3] See R. J. Jackson and M. Stein, *Issues in Comparative Politics* (Macmillan, Toronto, 1971), ch. 5 for a definition of revolution which combines both means and ends. Note here that violence may be considered a legitimate tactic of political change in some political cultures. Our referent in this text is the Western democracies and specifically Canada. Legitimacy, in other words, must be viewed in terms of the values of the existing regime.

The decade of the seventies did not witness an escalation of the kind of political violence that marred its first year, possibly because of effective (and sometimes questionable) countermeasures by the police and the National Security Service, but more likely because of the success of legitimate tactics of political change. The formation and rapid accession to power of the separatist Parti Québécois in the 1970s gave real hope for the possibility of achieving Quebec independence legitimately and non-violently. It seems even the most extremist factions of the independence movement were willing to draw in their claws and wait to see if the PQ could succeed.

Thus, for the time being, political violence in Quebec has again virtually disappeared, but it may be but a temporary respite. Ironically, the "NON" vote in the referendum, while in some ways an affirmation of national unity could trigger a new wave of violence in Quebec. Frustrated and impatient with the legitimate political process as a means of realizing their nationalist aspirations, the more extreme Quebec independentistes may well abandon the moderate approach of René Lévesque and revert to the terrorist tactics of 1970.

However, despite such gloomy prognostications, we feel that it is still valid to conclude that violence has not been and is not likely to become a significant means of achieving constitutional change in Canada. The likelihood of political violence here would only increase significantly if the basic attitudes of Canadians towards the legitimacy of such tactics should change. In other words widespread political violence could only occur in Canada if there were a radical alteration in the fabric of our political culture.

At the present time in Canada, a more likely form of non-legitimate constitutional change would appear to be that of a non-violent but extra-legal nature. A non-Canadian example of this form of constitutional change is the unilateral declaration of independence by the Smith regime in Rhodesia, where in an extra-legal but non-violent way, a colony broke with the mother country. In a similar vein if attempts to achieve some form of "sovereignty association" or separatism for the Province of Quebec through a formal amendment to the BNA Act or through the device of a new Canadian constitution should fail, the unilateral secession of that province is a distinct possibility. While such an action would be, strictly speaking, illegal or *ultra vires* the provincial government, it could almost certainly be achieved non-violently. The strict legality of such a move is, of course, irrelevant in the long run, for if such a change is brought about by the people of Quebec to provide a desired alteration in the regime and/or the political community, then the new regime is by its very nature legitimate to its own citizens. Furthermore, the mere fact that the breakaway province would have gained its independence "illegally" might well be rapidly forgotten, or at least ignored by Canadians, in the need to establish friendly diplomatic and economic relations with a neighbour. The distinction, therefore, between legal and illegal (or extra-legal) revolutionary constitutional change is in this context not particulary important. The more important question concerns the internal legitimacy of the change, and the measures, such as referenda or public opinion polls which the rest of Canada would accept as indicators of its acceptance and support by the people of Quebec.

Customary and Conventional Change

As pointed out in Chapter 6, conventions and customs[4] are important components of our constitution. These are rules and principles which while important are not written down anywhere. They are "binding" on governors and governed alike but only insofar as people choose to adhere to them. If a convention or a custom ceases to be congruent with the basic values of the political culture, eventually the convention will be abrogated or ignored, and ultimately forgotten. In a sense we can say simply that the customs and conventions of our constitution can be changed in the same way they originated; but where do they come from in the first place?

The origins of the customary and conventional components of the Canadian constitution lie in the misty labyrinths of English constitutional history, imported into our system as part of the ideological baggage of the earliest British settlers, and given a partial statutory sanction in the form of the preamble to the BNA Act which grants us a "constitution similar in principle to that of the U.K." This means that if there is a dispute as to what the "rule" is in Canada, and if there is no act of either the Canadian or U.K. parliaments that makes the rule explicit here, we must turn to the *practice*[5] in the U.K. as a precedent. Similarly there are uniquely Canadian conventions whose existence and applicability can only be clarified by the citation of precedents here. The problem with constitutional principles that are manifested only in their "practice" (either here or in the U.K.) is that disputes fre-

---

[4] Dawson, *The Government of Canada*, p. 65n: "No attempt has been made to distinguish between custom, usage and convention. A common distinction is to treat custom and usage as synonymous terms, and convention as a usage which has acquired obligatory force." See also D. V. Smiley, *Constitutional Adaptation and Federalism Since 1945*, Royal Commission on Bilingualism and Biculturalism Study No. 4 (Queen's Printer, Ottawa, 1970).

[5] In fact in some cases the convention in the U.K. has been given clarification or elaboration in the form of statutes such as the Magna Carta, the Bill of Rights, the Act of Settlement, and the Habeas Corpus laws. This makes the convention easier to "find" in the U.K. and to apply in Canada.

quently arise over *which* "practice" applies to the specific case, to what *extent* does it apply and how *binding* is it in the current circumstance.

The arbiter of such disputes is sometimes the courts but more often, particularly when the dispute is over conventions such as those establishing the relationship of the House of Commons to the government of the day, the effective arbiter may be a "constitutional expert" who, while learned, may be totally outside the governmental process. It is not uncommon in disputes over what the convention is in a given circumstance for the parties to the dispute to quote Bagehot's or Jennings' writings on the English constitution, and in Canada, it might be said that our unwritten constitution is effectively what Eugene Forsey says it is! However it must be reiterated that the interpretations of the accepted practice in the past, the citing of precedents and the wisdom of the constitutional experts are still more *persuasive* than legally binding. If we wish a constitutional convention to change, all it takes ultimately is the will to change it, and in most cases, the tacit acceptance or explicit (in the form of legislation) approval of the sovereign legislature(s).

As an example of constitutional change by altering a convention, one need look no further than an incident in 1968 that saw a piece of federal financial legislation defeated on third reading. On this occasion the Liberal government of Lester Pearson was a minority government, which meant that on any division in the House of Commons the government had to scrape up some support from other parties in the House to gain a majority. Owing to a miscalculation by the party whip and the acting Prime Minister, the Liberals allowed a vote on third reading at a time when there were not sufficient government supporters in the House, and the bill was defeated. Some constitutional experts (particularly in the Conservative party) cried "resign" for, they said, it was a firm convention of the constitution that if a government were defeated on a piece of financial legislation, it had to resign. The Liberals disagreed and instead referred it to the House of Commons in the form of a vote of confidence. As it turned out the government was sustained easily, because while no opposition party was very enthusiastic about the particular piece of legislation that had been defeated, the Créditistes at least, did not want an election at that time.[6]

In retrospect we can see that this incident could have been taken in

---

[6] Note that although the government was sustained in office, the defeated legislation could not be reintroduced. A basic rule of parliament is that the same bill cannot be introduced more than once in a single session.

a number of different ways. It could have been viewed, by a majority of members of the House, as a betrayal of a basic convention of our system, in which (unlikely) case, the government would have fallen on the confidence motion and the convention that the government must fall if defeated on a money bill would have been further ensconced. At the other extreme, the affirmation of the government's decision not to resign and to refer the matter to parliament for a "second opinion" could have been viewed as a precedent. In this case a new convention would have emerged whereby a particular piece of legislation could be defeated in the House without necessarily forcing the government's resignation. If this were to happen, the opposition in a minority situation would no longer have been handicapped by having to "throw the baby out with the bath water" if they don't like a piece of legislation, unless of course the government were to expressly choose to consider the matter an issue of confidence. This might have significantly enhanced the power of the opposition in minority government situations, for they would have acquired a real power to pick and choose among the government's policies without the threat of dissolution and subsequent election constantly hanging over their heads.

However the outcome in this particular case seems to have fallen somewhere between the two extremes. Subsequent minority parliaments have not operated very differently than they always have in Canada, and the 1968 incident, far from emerging as a key constitutional precedent, has faded into the category of "exceptions" and aberrations that don't quite fit the standing interpretations of the rule.

As mentioned, conventional change can also be brought about by the disuse of a given constitutional provision. The best example of this is the disallowance power of the federal government, which has not been used since 1943 and appears now to be a dead letter. The reason it has ceased to be a viable constitutional device is related to the reality of power distribution in Canada today, which is in turn related to the "coming of age" of the provinces. However, it is also possible that if the federal government had continued to make a habit of disallowing provincial acts, the provinces might never have come of age. Desuetude, therefore, may indeed play a part in determining the fate of various constitutional devices in this country.

Customary and conventional change is occurring constantly, and fundamentally, through the use and desuetude of various constitutional practices. It is a difficult form of constitutional change to pinpoint and that is why throughout this section we have used phrases such as "appears to have changed," but it does comprise a significant measure of the total of constitutional change in Canada.

Judicial Change

Judicial decisions fill out the bare bones of the constitution by interpreting it and by applying it to specific cases. In Chapter 8 we will consider such things as, for example, the way in which the federal power to regulate trade and commerce was interpreted by the Judicial Committee of the Privy Council. We will see that the Judicial Committee chose to interpret Section 91(2) to mean the regulation of *interprovincial and international* trade and commerce, but not the regulation of purely intraprovincial trade. In other words, the judiciary effectively changed the meaning of one of the provisions of the BNA Act in the process of interpreting it.

Constitutional change through judicial review has certain built-in limitations, particularly because the courts do not review all legislation automatically. It is important to recognize that the courts can only interpret a law when its interpretation becomes central to deciding a case. In other words, the courts have to wait until, in the normal course of litigation, some citizen brings a case before them and questions the validity of a given statute, before they can rule on its constitutionality. The only exception to this rule is an unusual device available to Canadian governments known as a *constitutional reference*. A reference case occurs when the federal government submits a piece of legislation to the Supreme Court of Canada for a judgment regarding its constitutionality. This device was created by a section of the Supreme Court Act, and has the effect of allowing the federal government to test the constitutionality of a law in the highest court of the land before attempting to implement it. The provinces also have the right to submit reference cases to the highest court in the province and, ultimately, the decision on such a reference can be appealed to the Supreme Court of Canada. The problem with the constitutional reference as a method of judicial change is that the judges are forced to judge the legislation not merely within the context of the facts of a single case, but within all conceivable contexts in which it can be employed. Because we will discuss a number of specific constitutional references in the next chapter, at this time we merely wish to reiterate that the reference case is one way in which the judiciary can have the opportunity to change or shape the constitution through the interpretation of federal and provincial laws.

Legislative Change

The forms of constitutional change that have been discussed thus far are all rather haphazard and incidental methods of producing change. Their end product is very difficult to plan for or to predict. This is not the case with *legislative* constitutional change, for its essence is that it is contrived, with existing regime mechanisms being employed to produce it. There are two broad types of legislative change in the Canadian political system, not including formal amendment, which will be discussed separately.

The first type of legislative constitutional change that is employed in Canada involves the alteration of *organic laws* through acts of parliament and orders in council.[7] An example of this kind of constitutional change would be the amendment from time to time of the Supreme Court Act; while the subject matter is constitutional, the method of altering it is by a simple act of parliament. In some cases, such as under the War Measures Act, the Governor General in Council is given the power to alter fundamental legislation by executive fiat. Some of the changes that were introduced by order in council during World War II significantly changed laws which could be considered constitutional. Although the achievement of change through this method is arbitrary, and not to be considered "normal" for Canada, the fact remains that it has happened in the past and may happen again in the future.

The second type of legislative change is the kind of amendment of the BNA Act which was authorized originally by the Act itself. Examples are provided by a whole class of clauses of the Act which are prefaced by "until the Parliament of Canada otherwise provides."[8] These provisions of the Act were intended to provide interim measures at the time of Confederation until parliament could get around to setting up more permanent ones. Most of these clauses are now defunct, having been replaced by statutes soon after Confederation.

Formal Amendment of the BNA Act: Joint Address

Perhaps the most significant form of constitutional change in Canada is formal *amendment* of the BNA Act. The BNA Act had no general provision for its amendment when it was passed in 1867. Since it was a statute of the parliament of the U.K., it seemed obvious at the time that it could and would be amended by ordinary British legislation. At Confederation, Canada was subordinate to the supreme British parliament, and her evolution to the independent status that she enjoys today was not foreseen by the British parliament or even by the Fathers of Confederation. The inability of the Dominion of Canada to amend the BNA Act soon became a problem for a young

---

[7] Until we discuss parliament and the policy process in Chapter 19, we will speak of parliament's performing the functions which are formally its responsibility.
[8] See, for instance, ss. 35, 40, 41 and 47 (BNA Act, 1867).

country growing rapidly both in political autonomy and in population, and faced with a growing number of responsibilities due to the
increasing involvement of government generally in matters such as
education, welfare, and public works. In response to these demands
for formal change of the BNA Act, a method, involving various conventional procedures for amendment, was gradually developed.

Canada and the U.K.   At the core of this procedure for amendment
of the BNA Act are three conventions or practices which define respectively the roles of the provinces, the federal parliament, and the
parliament of the U.K. The earliest of these to evolve was that the
parliament of the U.K. would not amend the BNA Act without an express request by Canada.[9] This convention, recognized before the
turn of the century, was affirmed by the Statute of Westminster in
1931:

4. *No act of Parliament of the United Kingdom passed after the commencement of this
act shall extend or be deemed to extend, to a Dominion as part of the law of that
Dominion, unless it is expressly declared in that act that the Dominion has requested,
and consented to, the enactment thereof.*

The standard means for requesting British legislative action has
emerged as either a petition from the Canadian government or a
"joint address" of the House of Commons and the Senate, which is
presented to the Queen, requesting an amendment to the BNA Act.
Executive petition by the government of the day was used in 1875 and
1895 to secure amendments to the BNA Act, and in these cases, the
petition was approved by the federal parliament either explicitly or
tacitly. In all other instances of amendment, however, the request has
been made by a joint address (i.e., a joint resolution) of both houses
of the Canadian parliament—and it has become a firm convention of
the constitution that amendment today must be requested by the
Canadian parliament and not unilaterally by the government of the
day.

The second convention is the positive aspect of the first: that is, the
parliament of the U.K. *will always act to* amend the BNA Act if
requested to do so by a joint address of the Canadian parliament.
While this convention has never been given statutory expression,
there has never been an occasion in Canadian constitutional history
when the parliament of the U.K. has refused to meet the request of
the "Dominion" with regard to amendment of the BNA Act, and
there is virtually no chance of this ever happening in the future.

Canada and the Provinces   The third convention or set of conven-

---

[9] In fact even the original BNA Act of 1867 was, with a few exceptions, entirely drafted
on this side of the Atlantic. While it is *formally* an act of the U.K. parliament, in reality
it is and always has been a "made in Canada" document.

tions is far more complicated than either of the first two, for it involves the extent to which the consultation and consent of the provinces should be sought by the federal government prior to petitioning the U.K. by a joint address. The rule here is complicated because the practice of amendment by joint address of the federal parliament is itself based only on constitutional convention. It is, of course, the particular procedure or practice that has been followed in the past which more or less defines the nature and limitations of this particular convention, but the situation is complicated not only by the fact that formal amendments of the BNA Act in areas logically requiring federal and provincial compliance have been rare but also by the shift of *de facto* power to the provinces which has occurred over the last two decades of "province building."

The situation is further complicated by the frequent, if unproductive, debate over proposed amending formulae among Canadian governments. In all, this is an area into which the political scientist steps with some trepidation for where the conventions regarding the powers of Canada and the U.K. are fairly clear and well established, the conventions determining the relative roles of the provinces and the federal government are not. It is the political context in which these are set which determines the circumstances under which the Canadian parliament dares to make a joint address requesting an amendment from Westminster. There are however, some facts which will guide us to a better understanding of the practice in this area.

First, the parliament of the U.K. has never amended the BNA Act on the request of a province or of any number of the provinces, unless the provinces' wishes are expressed in a joint address by both Houses of the Canadian parliament nor is there any likelihood that it would do so. Secondly, the U.K. parliament has never turned down a request for amendment by the federal government because the amendment was opposed by the provinces or any particular province.[10] It is possible that the 1907 amendment that secured an adjustment of the provincial subsidies, which was opposed formally by British Columbia, was altered slightly in its wording as a result of the objections of that province, but it is not likely today that objections by a province would precipitate changes in even the wording of an amendment requested by the Canadian parliament. Hence, in practice, the convention that has emerged is that, as far as the U.K. is concerned, it will provide any amendment that is requested by the Canadian parliament, regardless of whether it might affect the rights of the prov-

[10] For details on past practice see *The Canadian Constitution and Constitutional Amendment* (Government of Canada, Federal-Provincial Relations Office, 1978), p. 13. This paper comprises a useful survey of practice in four other federations, an historical summary and a proposal for alternatives.

inces, and regardless of whether the provinces have consented. This is merely a recognition of the fact that Canada has come of age politically and should be given the power and responsibility to make the decisions and take the political consequences that might flow from an unpopular constitutional amendment.

If the U.K. will not step in to protect the provinces when the federal government secures an amendment by joint address, the entire question of the extent to which the provinces have to be consulted on amendments involves only the provinces and the federal government. In order to understand the current practice of provincial involvement in amendments to the BNA Act, it is necessary to consider the provincial stand with respect to consultation and consent of the provinces at some stage before the actual joint address. The original argument for the participation of the provinces in the amendment of the BNA Act stems from a theory of Confederation that has become known as the *compact theory*. The compact theory of the Canadian federal system states that the Act of 1867 was in effect a treaty or a *compact* between equal participants and that, therefore, any changes made in the original agreement must be made only with consent of all of the participants. This would mean that for Canada to secure an amendment of the BNA Act, it would be necessary to canvass the views of the provinces, then prepare a draft amendment which took into account all of the provincial views and objections, and secure the unanimous consent of the provinces, before securing a joint address of the Canadian parliament. Not only would this procedure be time-consuming but it could also mean that any one province might veto an amendment that was agreed to by the rest of the provinces. To be sure, this state of affairs would protect provincial autonomy, but only at great cost in terms of other principles of our constitution such as majority rule and representation by population. The compact theory, however, has seldom been taken very seriously even by those who favour a great deal of protection for the autonomy of the provinces. Aside from the fact that such a system of constitutional amendment might prove extremely costly in terms of time, as R. M. Dawson points out, "The theory, while plausible, is constructed on sheer invention. It has no legal foundation; it has no historical foundation, and the precedents to support it are few."[11] Thus, not only is the compact theory impractical, it is also not based on either historical or legal fact.

---

[11] Dawson, *The Government of Canada*, p. 124. See also N. M. Rogers, "The Compact Theory of Confederation," *Proceedings of the Canadian Political Science Association*, 1931, pp. 205-230, and G. F. G. Stanley, "Act or Pact? Another Look at Confederation," C.H.A. *Annual Report* (Ottawa, 1956).

Another version of the compact theory of Confederation has been fairly widely espoused recently within the Province of Quebec. This version claims that the original Confederation agreement was a compact between the two founding "races" or language groups. The argument here is that no amendment of the BNA Act can be carried out without the consent of both the English-speaking and the French-speaking partners in Confederation with the latter represented by the Province of Quebec. The basic premise of this version of the compact theory would appear to have some historical justification, in that the Confederation agreement did, in some respects, recognize cultural duality in Canada. The BNA Act itself contains provisions such as the language and religion guarantees which are obviously intended to protect the rights of the French-Canadian minority. However, the argument that this should place any legal restrictions on the ability of the federal parliament to request amendments from the U.K. is unfounded in law. Thus, as a legal argument for the inclusion of the provinces in the amendment process of the BNA Act, the compact theory in either of its forms is not very persuasive.

It is also worth noting that the form of sovereignty-association espoused by the Parti Québécois is in some respects consistent with the compact theory tradition.[12] According to the white paper on sovereignty-association, a pact would be negotiated between a sovereign Quebec and "the rest of Canada" covering areas of joint jurisdiction such as tariffs and monetary policy with either party to the agreement retaining an effective veto power. The compact in this case would be between two new sovereign founding entities.

Despite the fact that the compact theory has little validity in law the custom of consulting the provinces whenever an amendment under contemplation involves their rights has in fact developed slowly over the years. The reason for this custom of course, lies in the nature of the political process in this country, for if a federal government were to unilaterally abrogate the autonomy of the provinces, it might suffer badly in the next federal election. Furthermore, our federal system works today because the provinces and the federal government have evolved a set of procedures and practices which function effectively only through cooperative arrangements. It could not operate if the federal government attempted to force BNA Act amendments down the throats of the provinces by taking unilateral action. Thus, where historical and legal argument fails, the exigencies of our political process and the ethos of cooperative federalism have justified in very

---

[12] See Gouvernement du Québec, Conseil Exécutif, *Quebec-Canada: A New Deal* (Service des Publications officielles, Quebec, 1979).

practical terms the principle of participation by the provinces in decisions to amend the BNA Act.

Formal Amendment of the BNA Act: Section 91(1)

In 1949, by a joint address of the Canadian parliament, an amendment to the BNA Act was secured which gave the federal parliament the power to amend, by simple act of parliament, the constitution of Canada with the exception of provisions that deal with the guarantees of minority language and education rights, the rights of the provinces, the provision regarding the five-year limit on the life of a parliament, and the requirement that the federal parliament meet at least once a year. This amendment itself was secured without consultation with or consent of the provinces, and although there were some objections to the unilateral action of the federal government, it all came to nothing in the end.

Ironically, it is possible that in creating this amending power in Section 91(1) of the BNA Act, the federal government may have unintentionally limited its ability to amend federal "organic laws" such as the Supreme Court Act because such legislation can be viewed as part of "the constitution of Canada" and because such federal laws guarantee certain provincial rights. While we must assume that the intention of the 1949 "amendment" was to in effect "patriate" a large portion of the BNA Act, because section 91(1) refers to the "constitution of Canada" and not to the BNA Act specifically, the courts in the future may see fit to extend the provincial rights and minority rights exclusions cited in 91(1) to all of the component parts of the constitution and not simply to the Act itself. Thus, whether the courts will interpret 91(1) to apply to all of "the constitution of Canada" or whether they will choose to interpret its scope as limited to the BNA Act only, remains to be seen, but in any event it appears that the wording of this amending power places an added moral onus on the federal government not to interfere with the rights of the provinces without their substantial consent. The 1978 proposals for constitutional amendment which included among other things, proposed changes to the Supreme Court were to be at the very least widely discussed with provinces before the federal government proceeded and the federal suggestion that provincial consent was not formally required was widely criticized.[13]

---

[13] In a 1979 reference case, the Supreme Court ruled that the federal parliament did not have the right unilaterally to change the structure of the Senate since this was an area which did affect provincial rights. While this indicated a willingness on the part of the court to interpret the scope of 91(1) fairly narrowly, in this case the Supreme Court did not deal with the question of whether the Supreme Court Act is a part of the "Constitution of Canada."

The effect of the 1949 amendment, therefore, aside from transferring the amending power for much of the BNA Act from the U.K. parliament to the parliament of Canada, is to explicitly preclude the federal government from directly tampering with minority rights and provincial rights without the consent of the provinces. When combined with the political limits on the federal use of "joint address" as an amending strategy, this means that a large part of the constitution of Canada is in practical terms unamendable. The resolution of this stalemate must therefore lie in securing federal-provincial agreement on a formal amending formula or in a unilateral resolution by the parliament of Canada to Westminster.

In Search of an Amending Formula

The question of how we should deal with the amendment of those "entrenched" parts of the constitution of Canada which are explicitly excluded from 91(1) and morally and politically precluded from change by joint address has been the subject of much debate in Canada and therefore deserves more detailed attention. Since 1927, there have been several federal-provincial conferences which were devoted almost entirely to discussions of ways in which the procedure for the amendment of the BNA Act could be completely "Canadianized"; that is, changed so that the Canadian parliament would no longer have to petition the U.K. parliament in order to get the Act amended. The parliament of the U.K. does not particularly cherish the function that it is called upon from time to time to perform on our behalf, and in fact, at the time of passage of the Statute of Westminster, Britain attempted to give the parliament of Canada the unilateral power to amend the BNA Act in its entirety. Canada refused because of pressures from the provinces.

Hence, it has certainly not been the parliament of the U.K. which stood in the way of handing over to authorities on this side of the Atlantic the power to amend the BNA Act. The problem in finding a satisfactory "all Canadian" amending scheme is that we in Canada cannot agree which authorities should have the power to amend the parts of the BNA Act which are excepted from the federal amendment power in Section 91(1). Several schemes have been proposed, the most promising of which have involved a detailed breakdown of the various clauses of the BNA Act into categories or "pigeon-holes," according to the extent of federal and provincial participation. [14] Thus, some clauses of the Act would be amendable by the federal parlia-

---

[14] See D. C. Rowat, "The 1949 Amendment and the Pigeon-Hole Method," in Paul Fox (ed.) *Politics: Canada*, 1st ed. (McGraw-Hill, Toronto, 1962), pp. 82-87.

ment and the provinces directly concerned (e.g. interprovincial boundary adjustments), and some clauses would be amendable by some combination such as by the legislatures of two-thirds of the provinces representing at least 50 percent of the population of Canada. These sorts of provisions are to ensure that a certain class of amendment which is not so fundamental as to require unanimity, could still not be passed without the support of either Ontario or Quebec or a certain percentage of the provinces in each of the major regions of Canada. Finally, some provisions may be viewed as so fundamental as to require the unanimous consent of all governments.

At the 1964 federal-provincial conference, an agreement was actually reached on a formula: all of the provinces indicated that they were content with what clauses had been included in which pigeon-holes.[15] However, almost immediately after the conference, Jean Lesage, Premier of the Province of Quebec, changed his mind and refused to give the proposal the support of his government. Quebec's sudden turnabout was probably in objection to the requirement for provincial unanimity for the amendment of matters such as language rights. If the government of the Province of Quebec were to accept this part of the amending formula, it would have meant, for example, that she could no longer bargain bilaterally with the federal government for concessions in areas such as French language rights in provinces other than Quebec. In order to pry out concessions in such areas it would have been necessary to gain the unanimous consent of the other provinces as well as that of the federal parliament. The Quebec government seems to have felt, at that time, that there was no immediate threat to its constitutional position that would require the protection of the unanimity provision and that it stood to gain considerable advantage by continuing the bilateral Quebec-Canada bargaining relationship. The Province of Quebec, it seemed, had come full circle from the defensive and inward-looking nationalism of Duplessis to the aggressive and outward-looking nationalism of Jean Lesage, at precisely that period in Canadian constitutional history when we were attempting to write a defensive and rigid amending procedure into the constitution. Those who favour a relatively flexible constitution might well be grateful that it had.

The successor to the Fulton-Favreau formula was the Victoria

---

[15] This version came to be known as the Fulton-Favreau formula after the two federal Justice Ministers who held office while it was being drafted. It required the consent of parliament and all the provincial legislatures for amendments affecting the distribution of power and the consent of parliament and two-thirds of provincial legislatures in other areas of mutual concern.

Charter of June 1971. This document, agreed to by all federal and pro-vincial representatives at a constitutional conference in Victoria, B.C., proposed that all amendments to the Canadian constitution which affected significant provisions such as the distribution of powers required "a national consensus" expressed by the consent of parlia-ment and a majority of the provincial legislatures. The concurring provinces were to include: 1) every province which at any time has ever contained 25 percent of the population of Canada (the function of this provision is to give either Ontario or Quebec a veto power, in perpetuity, although given current trends in population growth, B.C. could also enter this elite circle in the foreseeable future); 2) at least two Atlantic provinces (this gives some recognition of the fact that there are distinct regional interests in Canada that must be given a veto power over decisions as fundamental as constitutional amend-ment); 3) at least two Western provinces, provided the two have a combined population equal to 50 percent of the total population of the West.

All in all, the Victoria Charter proposes an amendment formula which is less rigid than the Fulton-Favreau, for it does not require the unanimous consent of the provinces for any matters at all. At the same time it provides protection for all major regional and ethnic in-terests in Canada. Unfortunately the Charter, as agreed to by the pro-vincial representatives in Victoria, was never given the necessary rati-fication by the legislatures of the ten provinces and the federal parliament. As was the case with the Fulton-Favreau agreement, the legislature of Quebec was the major dissenter.

In June 1978, in response to the election of the Parti Québécois and other evidence that Canadians were not satisfied with the constitu-tional *status quo*, the federal government published two white papers—*A Time for Action* which set out general principles for "consti-tutional renewal" and *The Canadian Constitution and Constitutional Amendment*, which suggested alternative formal means for constitu-tional amendment but did not choose among them. The tabling in the House of Commons of a constitutional amendment bill completed a general statement of the federal position. On that occasion the federal government proposed to proceed in two phases, first to amend the constitution, including the Supreme Court Act, with regard to exclu-sively federal concerns as specified in 91(1) of the BNA Act; and sec-ond to reach agreement with the provinces on areas of joint concern including particularly the establishment of the formal amending process.

Concrete proposals were made only for the first of these phases. The Senate was to be abolished and replaced by a *House of the Federa-tion* with significantly increased powers, increased Western and

Atlantic provinces' representation and members chosen half by the federal government and half by the provinces. Representation among parties was to be determined on the basis of popular vote in the most recent election in each jurisdiction. The Supreme Court was to be expanded from 9 to 11 and Quebec representation thereon was to rise from 3 to 4. Provinces were to be consulted before judges were appointed and appointments were to be approved by the House of the Federation. There was to be a constitutional requirement for an annual first ministers' meeting, consultation between the federal and provincial governments before appointment of Lieutenant-Governors, constitutional commitment for some federal transfer payments to provinces, and an obligation for the federal government to consult with the provinces before using its "delcaratory" power (92(10)) to bring a work or project under federal jurisdiction. Finally, a Charter of Rights and Freedoms was to be entrenched in the constitution.

As to the process of formal constitutional amendment with respect to provisions which touched upon the concerns of all or most provinces and the federal government, it was suggested that there were two possibilities in addition to the Fulton-Favreau and Victoria provisions. One was a combination of the Victoria formula with an appeal to the people via referendum. Examples proposed were that a referendum could be held in a region if the provincial governments in that region vetoed a proposal agreed to by the federal government and all other regions or that a national referendum could be held if parliament disagreed with a proposal agreed to by all four regions. The second possibility was simply the automatic use of national referenda for significant amendment proposals.

It was also pointed out that there were several possible ways of proposing amendments and that this too should be codified as part of a formal amending process. Suggestions included popular petition, a two-thirds vote of the new House of the Federation, a resolution of parliament, resolutions from any four provincial legislatures, or, four legislatures (or more), including one from each region. Again no preference was expressed.

Like their predecessors, the constitutional talks of the late seventies did not come to fruition; indeed the discussions never got far beyond early skirmishing over the Phase I proposals for changes to federal institutions. There was considerable disagreement, for example, about whether the federal government had any right to make unilateral changes to the Senate and Supreme Court, and whether these were not already joint institutions exempted from the provisions of 91(1) and therefore not changeable without provincial consent. Several provinces were suspicious that the more effective representation of regional interests in Ottawa would greatly strengthen the federal government at their expense and were therefore highly inclined to block any federal action. The federal Liberal government of Pierre Trudeau was widely believed to be nearing the end of its days and its perceived imminent disappearance did nothing to make the seven provincial Conservative governments eager to cooperate. The Parti Québécois government of Quebec, still riding high on its initial wave of popularity was hardly eager to cooperate in showing how federalism could be made more effective. The time was, once again, hardly ripe for constitutional reform even though there were many reasons to consider it urgent. The short-lived Conservative government of 1979-80 was not inclined toward formal constitutional amendment and instead of making any concrete proposals, attempted to make the existing BNA Act work more smoothly. And so was dissipated another round in the continuing search for formal constitutional reform and amendment.

The future of constitutional reform at the present is no clearer than it has been before, but the Liberal government elected in 1980 stands committed to produce a new constitution in the near future. The unrest in Quebec, the dissatisfaction of the West generally, and the fact that the current government could elect only two MPs west of Ontario, makes some positive action with respect to constitutional reform inevitable.

In view of the continuing failure of Canadians to agree upon an amending formula, it seems appropriate to ask whether any formal and rigid amending formula is necessary for our constitution. In considering this question a number of points should be made. First, the U.K. always has amended, and probably always will amend, the BNA Act when requested to do so by the parliament of Canada. However, it is still relevant to ask "what if?" at some future date, the U.K. should refuse to amend the BNA Act as we requested, or "what if?" the U.K. ceased to exist, for instance through entering a European political union. Despite the common myth that there will "always be an England," there is always some possibility that the old song is dead wrong. "How could we amend our constitution then?", the critics of the *status quo* ask. This is a valid point, but perhaps it can be answered by pointing to the ever-present possibility of extra-legal change of our constitution. If the U.K. ceased to exist, or if for some unimaginable reason she refused to heed a joint address by both houses of the Canadian parliament, Canada could still take matters into its own hands and unilaterally make the changes needed. Rhodesia did it successfully under circumstances of unfavourable world opinion that we would not, presumably, be facing in Canada. To all intents and purposes we would merely be taking what was rightfully ours *de facto,* if not in the strict letter of the British constitution.

The second, and more significant, factor is that the federal parliament today cannot, in reality, ask the U.K. for an amendment that affects provincial or minority rights without the "substantial compliance" of the provinces. The restraint on the federal parliament in this regard may or may not be a legal one, but it is certainly a binding political one. One of the things most Canadians are thought to hold dear (besides motherhood, beer, and Laura Secord) is provincial autonomy. As long as this is so, no federal government that wishes to be re-elected can afford the risk of political damage it would do itself by tampering unilaterally with the rights of the provinces. If, however, the value structure of Canadian society changed so that it became politically acceptable for the federal parliament to abrogate the autonomy of the provinces, then the fact that the provinces lack legal protection under the present amending system might assume more importance than it has today.

But let us consider this hypothetical situation for a moment. If the federal parliament had enough political support unilaterally to abrogate the rights of the provinces, then perhaps it is fair to say that it *should* be able to do so. All recent versions of the amending formula have respected the will of a "qualified majority." In fact it could even be suggested that if parliament possessed the political support to change the Canadian constitution in the area of provincial rights, then under a formula such as the Victoria Charter, or the 1978 alternatives, there would likely be sufficient support to secure the change anyway. The point here is that while an amending formula could be devised which would appear to defend established interests, it would not protect them if the bulk of public opinion turned against those interests. Like any value of the political system, provincial autonomy is only as safe as Canadians want it to be, and a constitutional amending formula would not and should not change the fact.

The conclusion, therefore (albeit a tentative one), is that the adoption of an amending scheme such as the Victoria Charter or one of its descendants would formalize the procedure for constitutional amendment in Canada without substantively changing the present situation. In the long run, the real justification for "patriating" the constitution lies in the fulfillment of psychic needs which would be satisfied by giving Canadians the right to amend their own constitution. If this is important to Canadians in their search for an identity and in the ongoing problem of cementing national unity, then that in itself is sufficient reason to keep trying to devise a mutually agreeable formula for constitutional amendment. It is likely, too that people need certainty in their dealings with government, and if our amending formula is codified and formalized, or if our constitution is rewritten in its entirety, greater constitutional certainty will, for better or for worse, be one of the effects. On the other side of the picture, however, one must consider that the Canadian constitution has worked about as well as any other constitution mankind has devised for more than one hundred and ten years, and constitutional change has been achieved through various means. Perhaps the real beauty of such an amorphous constitution is that it is not rigid. It can be changed without having to resort to formalized legal procedures, and changes that do not pan out can be revoked in the same informal and *ad hoc* manner. To expect to do better with a nation whose cleavages run as deeply as do Canada's may be a dangerous conceit.

THE ADMINISTRATION OF JUSTICE

In Chapter 6 the concept of the rule of law was introduced as a basic tenet of the Canadian constitution, but little was said there about the nature of law in general or about the origins and characteristics of the Canadian judicial system. In this section it is our intention to describe the structure of the Canadian judiciary and those aspects of the judicial process relevant to the political process as a whole. Because it is law which is the subject-matter of judicial decision making, and because, formally, it is law which constitutes, regulates, or authorizes all allocative outputs of the system, a brief discussion of the law, its nature and origins is an appropriate introduction to this section.[16]

The Nature of Law in Canada
The function of law is to regulate human behaviour. In its broadest context, the law can be viewed as including all rules of human behaviour, whether customary, moral, ethical, or religious, which have application in a given society. However, when one speaks of the law in a modern society, what is usually implied is the positive embodiment of the customary, ethical, moral, and religious values of a society in the form of statutes and judicial decisions. Law in this more formal and positive sense is concrete and explicit in a way that a code of behaviour, implicit in customs or moral standards, can never be. Furthermore, as Professor J. A. Corry points out, law in the more positive sense can be distinguished from custom and morality by the existence of explicit sanctions and positive means for enforcement: "What

---

[16] See Chapter 6 for a discussion of the principle of judicial independence and Chapter 8 for a discussion of the role of the courts in interpreting the BNA Act.

distinguishes law from customs and morality is the additional sanction of sheriffs, bailiffs, police, jails and armed forces to be called into operation if needed to coerce the stubborn."[17] For the purposes of this analysis, a narrow rather than broad definition of law has been chosen.

To perform effectively the function of providing guidelines for human behaviour in a society, the law must be *knowable*; people must be able to discover the standards of behaviour their society is imposing on them in order to be able to comply with those standards. The law must also be applied in a way which is *predictable* for the citizen. If we are to be capable of adjusting our behaviour so that it conforms to the requirements of the law, not only must we be aware of the broad principles embodied in the law, but we must also be able to predict the way in which the law will apply to us personally.[18]

The law in Canada can be said to consist primarily of statutes and judicial decisions. The former are enactments of the lawmaking institutions of the political system. They are the products of legislatures— in the strictest sense of that word. But while there is a large annual output of legislation today, legislatures do no more than add to or make alterations in a vast body of law which is already in existence and which is derived largely from other sources.[19] The bulk of the law is to be found not primarily in legislation, but in myriad judicial decisions which reflect a society's moral, ethical, religious, and customary foundations far better than the specific enactments of any legislature. In this sense, the law is incremental. It is a body of principles that have been accumulated over time and modified as the values of the society have changed—modified subtly through minute judicial reinterpretations, and from time to time modified more explicitly by legislation.

While the law is a growing thing, its growth is controlled rather than random. The element of control in Canada is injected through the *rule of precedent*, the principle of *stare decisis*. The basic principle of the rule of precedent is that judges, when making a decision today, take into account the decisions of previous courts in similar cases in the past. Precedents can be of two types: *binding* or *persuasive*. Professor Lederman points out that the former type of precedent exists where: "within any particular system of judicature the lower courts in the hierarchy are bound to follow the rules previously used to decide sufficiently similar cases in the higher court or courts of the hierar-

---

[17] Corry and Hodgetts, *Democratic Government and Politics*, p. 424.
[18] See Chapter 6 for discussion of the principle of the rule of law.
[19] Corry and Hodgetts, op. cit., p. 423.

chy."[20] Thus, in the Canadian system, decisions by higher courts are binding on lower courts in the same judicial hierarchy. However, the question as to whether a court is bound by its own precedents is dependent mainly on the court itself; a court can choose to consider itself bound by its own precedents or it can choose not to be so bound. The Supreme Court of Canada and, before 1949, the Judicial Committee of the Privy Council have chosen not to be strictly bound by their own precedents. The practice of both these courts of final appeal, however, indicates that a previous decision has a great deal of persuasive force in helping them to decide current cases, and it is seldom indeed that the Supreme Court of Canada reverses the stand it, or the JCPC, took in a previous case: "Even though a court regards its own previous decisions as persuasive only, they turn out to be so highly persuasive that the distinction from a binding precedent becomes rather dim."[21]

The Canadian legal system stems from two quite distinct legal traditions and is consequently a unique reflection of the duality of Canadian political culture. One tradition is rooted in the Roman law and the other in the English common law. Roman law is codified in the form of general rules and principles which must be applied to each case individually. It is Roman law which was adopted in varying forms throughout Western Europe at the time of the Renaissance. The settlers of New France naturally brought with them the laws of their mother country, so it is in the Province of Quebec that the Roman legal tradition is still to some extent reflected. The English common law is based on "the common custom of the realm"[22] as interpreted by judges and is derived from judicial prededents that build on earlier precedents, and so on. It is not codified; rather it is a set of principles merely implicit in the judicial decisions of England.[23] The common law came to Canada via the early English settlers and was even partially introduced into Quebec through the Conquest. Today in Quebec, *private law* (or *civil law*) is based on the *Code Civil du Québec* which is derived from the French *Code Napoléon*, whereas in the other Canadian provinces private law is based on the English common law. Criminal law in Canada is uniform across the country, being based on the Canadian Criminal Code which in turn is derived almost exclusively from the principles of English criminal jurisprudence.

---

[20] W. R. Lederman, "The Common Law System in Canada," in E. McWhinney (ed.), *Canadian Jurisprudence: The Civil Law and Common Law in Canada* (Carswell, Toronto, 1958), p. 36.

[21] Lederman, "The Common Law System in Canada," p. 37.

[22] Corry and Hodgetts, op. cit., p. 428.

[23] Note that parts of the common law are codified from time to time in various statutes such as the Criminal Code, the Landlord and Tenant Act, etc.

The Judicial System[24]

Because Canada is a federal political system, it is only natural that the Canadian judicial system should reflect federalism in its basic structure. By contrast to the U.S., however, where the federal and state courts exist separately from each other in vertically parallel hierarchies each with its distinct jurisdiction, the Canadian system of courts divides provincial and federal court jurisdiction horizontally.[25] The course of litigation in the United States may begin in either a federal or a state court and can normally be appealed only to the top of the particular hierarchy. For example, in the United States criminal law is primarily a state matter, and most criminal cases are tried only in state courts.[26] For such cases the final court of appeal is normally the supreme court of the state. There is no appeal from the supreme court of the state to the Supreme Court of the U.S. in state criminal matters, except where the issue can be couched in constitutional terms. In Canada, by contrast, while there are separate provincial and federal courts, the eventual course of litigation may move from provincial courts to a final appeal at the level of the Supreme Court of Canada. However, this statement cannot be made without qualification, for certain matters are not considered important enough to be appealable to the Supreme Court of Canada as of right. The appellate jurisdiction of the Supreme Court of Canada will be discussed in more detail below.

Not only are the various provincial and federal courts integrated in terms of jurisdiction but they are also integrated to some extent through the process of appointment set down in the BNA Act. Sections 96 to 100 provide for the appointment, removal, and salaries of all superior, county and district court judges in the provinces. The judges of these provincial courts are all appointed and paid by the federal government. Federal court judges, naturally, are also appointed by the federal government, and it is only the lesser provincial court judges who are appointed and remunerated by the provincial governments. In describing the jurisdiction and functions of the various provincial courts, the discussion will focus primarily on the Province of Ontario. While other provinces differ from Ontario in various ways, the judicial systems of all the Canadian provinces are similar and there is not sufficient room to discuss each individually. Figure 7-1 provides an overall view of the system.

---

[24] Our research in this area has been made simpler by the kind assistance of Professors Dick Abbott, Don Fraser, and King McShane, of the Department of Law at Carleton University. All errors and omissions are the responsibility of the authors alone.

[25] See ss. 92(14), 96-101 of the BNA Act, 1867.

[26] There are as well in the U.S. "federal crimes," which are tried in federal courts.

Figure 7-1

THE CANADIAN JUDICIAL SYSTEM   (in Ontario)

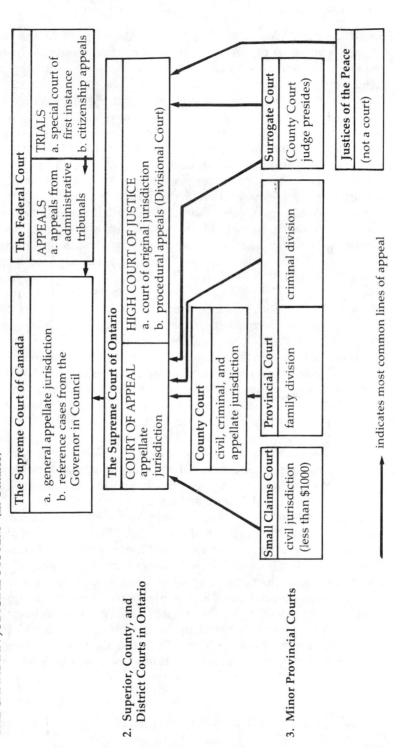

The Provincial Judicial System[27]   The lowest level of the judicial hierarchy in most provinces is the *Justice of the Peace*. A Justice of the Peace is appointed by the province or territory—formally by the Lieutenant-Governor in Council or Commissioner—and holds office "at pleasure." There are virtually no specific qualifications for the office not even legal training. The jurisdiction of a Justice of the Peace is usually territorially limited to the municipality or judicial district where the appointment takes place. Within that territory, a Justice of the Peace is permitted to administer oaths, take affirmations and declarations, and try prosecutions under municipal by-laws. Under the direction of a Provincial or Territorial Judge, a Justice of the Peace may also try summary conviction criminal offences. Other powers of a Justice of the Peace include the performing of civil marriages, the quelling of riots, and various procedural powers such as issuing warrants. Appeal from a decision of a Justice of the Peace usually goes to a Justice of the Supreme Court of the province or territory, sitting alone. Justices of the Peace in most provinces are currently being phased out and probably all of their functions will ultimately come to be performed by the more highly qualified Provincial Judges or Magistrates who possess all the powers of Justices of the Peace, *ex officio*.

It is interesting that the major exception to the decline in the role of JPs in Canada has been in the northern territories. The NWT Commissioner has recently appointed over 100 new Justices of the Peace in an attempt to bring justice "closer to the people." Most of these appointees are local people in the remotest settlements of the NWT and most of them are in fact of native origins, so that, it is hoped, minor offenses can be dealt with by judicial officials who, while lacking in formal legal training, will have a sensitivity to local problems and to the cultural idiosyncrasies of the specific settlement. By contrast, in Ontario the JP has disappeared entirely.

In Ontario, *Provincial Judges* have taken over the functions previously performed by Justices of the Peace, Magistrates, and Juvenile and Family Court Judges. In fact most Magistrates and Juvenile and Family Court Judges and many Justices of the Peace became Provincial Judges as a matter of course at the passage of the Provincial Courts and Judges Act in 1968.[28] While there are no specific qualifications for appointment as a Provincial Judge, in order to exercise the criminal jurisdiction conferred upon Magistrates by Part XVI of the Canadian Criminal Code, a Provincial Judge must be a member of the bar of one of the provinces, and must have been acting as a Provincial

---

[27] See Figure 7-1.
[28] Provincial Courts Act, Revised Statutes of Ontario 1970, c. 269.

Judge for at least five years, or must have been acting as a full-time Magistrate or a Judge of the Juvenile and Family Court before the 1968 legislation was passed.

The Provincial Judges in Ontario are appointed by the Lieutenant-Governor in Council, although provision is made for consultation with the Judicial Council for Provincial Judges. The Judicial Council was established by the 1968 legislation and is usually composed of representatives of the bench and of the bar. Its functions include consideration of the proposed appointment of Provincial Judges, advising the government, and conducting inquiries respecting complaints brought against judges in respect to their judicial capacity. A judge holds office during good behaviour until age 65, with possible reappointment to age 75, and can be removed by the Lieutenant-Governor in Council, but only for misbehaviour or for inability to perform duties, and then only after a judicial inquiry. The jurisdiction of Provincial Judges includes presiding over either the criminal[29] or the family[30] divisions of the Provincial Courts, and is, for practical purposes, limited geographically.

The criminal jurisdiction of Provincial Judges includes summary conviction trials under certain Ontario statutes and under certain federal statutes such as the Criminal Code and the Narcotics Control Act, as well as trial of indictable offences where the accused specifically selects trial by Provincial Judge. Provincial Judges may also conduct preliminary hearings for indictable offences in which the accused has chosen a jury trial or trial by Superior Court Judge. Appeal from decisions of the Provincial Judge is to a County Court Judge or a single judge of the Supreme Court of the province. Juvenile and family court jurisdiction of Provincial Judges extends to both civil and criminal matters where families and/or juveniles are involved. Appeal is as for a Provincial Court (criminal division) in criminal matters, and to a County Court Judge or to the Court of Appeal in civil matters.

Small Claims Courts, formerly known as Division Courts,[31] have been established under the Small Claims Court Act[32] in various counties and districts in the province. The judges of these courts are frequently County Court Judges who act in an additional capacity, but in other cases they are judges appointed by the Lieutenant-Governor in Council specifically as Small Claims Court Judges. The jurisdiction of Small Claims Court Judges is territorially limited to the county or the

[29] Has replaced Magistrates' Courts.
[30] Has replaced Juvenile and Family Courts.
[31] R.S.O. 1970, c. 107.
[32] R.S.O. 1970, c. 439; S.O. 1972, c. 107.

division for which they were appointed, and is limited in subject matter to civil claims of less than $1,000. Procedure in these courts is intended to be speedy, inexpensive, and informal, and specifically excludes certain tort actions such as libel, slander, breach of promise, and actions concerning estates of deceased persons. Appeal from a decision of a Small Claims Court lies with a single judge of the Court of Appeal, but only if the matter involves a sum of money greater than $200.

There is also a *Surrogate Court*[33] for each county and district of the Province of Ontario, whose jurisdiction includes most testamentary matters, determination of minor financial claims against an estate, the appointment of guardians for the children of the deceased and, generally, all such probate matters except interpretation of wills, administration of estates, and determination of actions for legacies. In all cases in Ontario the judge acting as *Surrogate Court Judge* is the County or District Court Judge, although the Lieutenant-Governor in Council is not legally restricted in this regard. Appeal from the Surrogate Court lies to the Court of Appeal, or to a single judge of the High Court of Justice,[34] depending upon the amount of money at stake.

County Court Judges[35] are appointed by the Governor General in Council, as provided for by Section 96 of the BNA Act. The courts on which these judges sit, however, are set up by the provinces who are empowered constitutionally to do so through Section 92(14) of the BNA Act which states that the provincial legislature can pass laws regarding:

The administration of justice in the province, including the constitution, maintenance and organization of provincial courts both of civil and criminal jurisdiction and including procedure in civil matters in those courts.

Thus, while the *County Courts* are provincially administered, the judges themselves are federally appointed and paid. The qualification of a County Court Judge is that he or she must be a barrister of at least ten years' standing, and tenure is during good behaviour until age 75. A County Court Judge is removable by the Governor General in Council for various statutory reasons, but only after a commission of inquiry.

The jurisdiction of the County Court Judge includes presiding over the County Court[36] in civil matters, with or without a jury. Basically,

---

[33] See Surrogate Courts Act, R.S.O. 1970, c. 451.
[34] Ibid.
[35] County Court Judges Act, R.S.O. 1970, c. 95.
[36] County Courts Act, R.S.O. 1970, c. 94; S.O. 1971, v. 2, c. 60.

the jurisdiction of the County Court includes contract actions and most tort actions when the claim does not exceed $7,500, actions regarding land if the value of the land does not exceed $7,500, partnership actions if the partnership capital does not exceed $50,000, certain actions for legacies and equitable actions if the subject matter involved does not exceed $7,500. It is important to recognize here, however, that the jurisdiction of the County Court is held concurrently with the *Supreme Court of Ontario,* and as a result actions may be commenced above the level of the County Court.

The County Court Judge also sits with a jury in the *Court of General Sessions of the Peace.* This court sits twice yearly in the county seat to hear most indictable criminal offences. *The County Court Judge's Criminal Court*[37] is composed of the County Court Judge sitting alone, and hears cases involving indictable offences where the accused has chosen trial by judge, or "speedy trial." This court also hears appeals from summary convictions by Provincial Judges. Appeals from decisions of the County Court Judge lie generally to the Ontario Court of Appeal with the exception of procedural appeals which can be heard by a single judge of the Supreme Court of the province.

The Supreme Court of Ontario has two divisions, the *High Court of Justice of Ontario,* which includes the Chief Justice of the High Court and over thirty puisne justices,[38] and the *Court of Appeal for Ontario* which includes the Chief Justice of Ontario and nine other justices of appeal. The appointment of all judges of the Supreme Court of Ontario is by the federal government, and while appointment is explicitly to either the High Court or to the Appeals Division, judges may serve in the other division if required. Appointment, as with all Superior Court Judges, is during good behaviour until age 75, and removal is only possible by order in council after a joint address of the House of Commons and the Senate. Salaries are set by federal statute and paid by the federal government, although the courts themselves are established and administered by the province.

The High Court of Justice of Ontario functions with judges sitting singly, with or without jury, and has general jurisdiction unlimited as to monetary value in all civil matters. The criminal jurisdiction of the High Court includes concurrent jurisdiction with lower courts for most indictable offences, and in the case of the most serious indictable offences, such as murder, the High Court has exclusive jurisdiction. The High Court of Justice has a separate division called the *Divisional Court* which performs the appellate functions not vested in the

[37] County Court Judge's Criminal Courts Act, R.S.O. 1970, c. 93.
[38] Judicature Act, R.S.O. 1970, c. 228.

Court of Appeal. Appeal from the High Court of Justice is to the Court of Appeal and, rarely, directly to the Supreme Court of Canada.[39]

The Court of Appeal of Ontario has a quorum of at least three judges. It functions as a general court of appeal for the province, hearing appeals from the lower courts and from certain provincial administrative tribunals, and delivering opinions on references by the Lieutenant-Governor in Council. Appeal from the Ontario Court of Appeal lies with the Supreme Court of Canada.

Federal Courts[40]   Federal courts in Canada include the Supreme Court, the Federal Court, Citizenship Courts, the Court Martial Appeal Court, and the Superior Courts in the Northwest Territories and the Yukon. The latter three types of courts are very specialized either in subject matter or geographically, but the Federal Court and the Supreme Court of Canada have more general jurisdiction and bear further discussion. *The Supreme Court of Canada* is a superior court of common law and equity in and for Canada, which was established by the Supreme Court Act in 1875.[41] The court is composed of a Chief Justice and eight puisne judges, all appointed by the Governor General in Council. An appointee must be a judge of a provincial superior court or a barrister of at least ten years' experience, and must take up residence within five miles of Ottawa. Justices of the Supreme Court of Canada hold office during good behaviour until age 75, and are removable by the Governor General in Council on joint address of the Senate and House of Commons. An additional requirement set down explicitly in the Supreme Court Act is that three of the nine judges must be appointed from the Quebec bench or bar.

The Supreme Court sits only in Ottawa and has three sessions per annum. Five judges normally constitute a quorum, except that on applications for leave to appeal, three is a quorum in civil matters. On appeal from the Province of Quebec it is mandatory that at least two of the sitting judges be from that province. Generally, the function of the Supreme Court of Canada is to be a general court of appeal, but normally the Supreme Court hears criminal appeals in the case of a capital offence only. There is an appeal as of right from the highest provincial court in civil matters where the amount exceeds $10,000 and from the highest provincial court on a constitutional reference where provincial law permits it. Appeal by leave of the highest provincial court from decisions of that court in most civil matters is per-

---

[39] This is known as an "appeal *per saltum*."
[40] See Figure 7-1.
[41] Revised Statutes of Canada 1970, c. 259, as amended.

mitted, and appeal by leave of the Supreme Court itself is permitted from final judgments of the highest court of the province, except in criminal matters.[42] The Supreme Court of Canada is also required to give opinions on matters referred to it by the Governor General in Council. In sum, the Supreme Court of Canada has all the powers of a superior court and also, since the abolition of appeals to the Judicial Committee of the Privy Council in 1949, it functions as the final court of appeal for Canada.

The Federal Court, which has replaced the Exchequer Court, was set up by the Federal Court Act, 1970.[43] The Federal Court consists of a court of original jurisdiction, known as the *Trial Division,* and a court of appeal known as the *Appeals Division.* The court is composed of a Chief Justice who functions as the president of the Appeals Division, an Associate Chief Justice who functions as the president of the Trial Division, and up to ten puisne judges. At least three of the ten must be appeal judges and the rest trial judges, and there is an additional requirement that at least four of the Federal Court Judges must be appointed from among members of the bar or bench of the Province of Quebec.

The basic requirements for appointment to the Federal Court are the same as for the Supreme Court of Canada, and tenure is during good behaviour until age 70. While appointments are specifically to either the Trial or the Appeal Division, all judges are *ex officio* members of the division to which they were not appointed.

The original jurisdiction of the Federal Court includes matters involving claims against the Crown, intergovernmental actions involving interprovincial or federal-provincial disputes, citizenship appeals, and specific jurisdiction vested in the old Exchequer Court by federal statutes such as the Excise Act, Customs Act, Income Tax Act, National Defence Act, Patent Act, and Shipping Act.

The jurisdiction of the Federal Court of Appeal includes hearing appeals from the Trial Division of the Federal Court, and review of decisions of federal boards, commissions, and tribunals. This latter appellate jurisdiction of the Federal Court is limited, by section 28 of the Federal Court Act, to cases where administrative decisions are required by law to be judicial or quasi-judicial, or where the federal board or tribunal has failed to observe the principles of natural justice, has gone beyond its jurisdiction, has made an error in law, or has based its decision on erroneous findings of fact. Furthermore, the Act provides that there will be no such appeal if other legislation already

[42] Ibid.
[43] R.S.C. 1970, c. 10.

provides for a statutory appeal to the Treasury Board, the Governor General in Council, or the Supreme Court of Canada; nor are decisions of the Governor in Council or the Treasury Board reviewable by the Federal Court. These particular limitations on the appellate jurisdiction of the Federal Court were originally subjected to some criticism from the legal profession as being regressive and contrary to the generally liberalizing effect of the legislation as a whole. Despite these so-called "privative clauses" in the Act, however, the court has actually played a useful role in overseeing federal administrative boards and tribunals.

In fact it can be argued that the Appeals Division of the Court has actually expanded its jurisdiction since its creation in 1971. The irony here is that the bulk of its expanded jurisdiction has been at the expense of the Trial Division of the same court. The trial side was originally given, by section 18 of the Act, supervisory jurisdiction to issue the traditional prerogative writs and remedies such as *mandamus, certiorari,* prohibition, etc. (but not *habeas corpus*) against federal administrative authorities. However instead of seeking these fairly simple remedies for abuses of administrative power, the tendency has been for litigants to seek redress of their legal grievances through the Appeals Division via the provisions of section 28. Thus the jurisdiction and hence the workload of the appeals side of the federal court has expanded and the trial side jurisdiction has effectively been reduced in administrative law matters. This has stimulated demands for change in the Act to resolve this internal problem, but the overall verdict on the Federal Court has to be that it has proven successful.

Decisions of the Federal Court of Appeal are appealable to the Supreme Court of Canada as of right where the matter in controversy exceeds $10,000. Other than this general provision, an appeal to the Supreme Court of Canada lies by leave of the Supreme Court itself, or by the leave of the Federal Court of Appeal. Finally, an appeal lies automatically to the Supreme Court where the dispute is interprovincial or federal-provincial in nature.

Reform of the Supreme Court of Canada   The Supreme Court of Canada has been subjected to much criticism since its creation in 1875, and has narrowly escaped abolition at several points in its history. However, since the abolition of appeals to the Judicial Committee of the Privy Council in 1949, when the Supreme Court of Canada became the final court of appeal for Canada, its position in the Canadian political system has been secure. The question now is not whether Canada needs a Supreme Court, but rather how the existing one can be improved. Much of the criticism of the Supreme Court (which applies equally to the higher provincial courts) has been levelled at the method of appointment of the judges, which is based, quite frankly, on partisan considerations and done exclusively by the federal government. This does not usually mean that a Liberal government, for example, will appoint a bad lawyer to the bench just because he or she is a Liberal, but rather that the government will find a good lawyer who is also a Liberal and give that person the appointment.

Basically, the argument against appointments to the bench which take into account party affiliation is that such a method of appointment goes contrary to the principle of an independent judiciary which is so crucial to our legal system.[44] A few exploratory studies of judicial behaviour indicate that judges usually take characteristic and predictable stands when particular issues are involved,[45] and further, that no judge is ever really independent in an absolute way, for the judge, influenced in making decisions by all sorts of personal biases, tends to interpret the law in such a way that the decision made is congruent with personal values. However, none of these studies have indicated that there is a positive correlation in Canada between the stand a judge takes on issues and the tenets of the political party which appointed the judge to the bench.

Suggestions for reform of the method of appointment of judges are twofold. In the first place, with respect to the Supreme Court, most legal experts feel that judges should be selected with some participation on the part of the existing bench, the Canadian Bar Association, the provinces, or all three. The arguments in favour of participation by the existing bench or the Canadian Bar Association contend that in order to get the best judges, the selection should be made not so much by a non-partisan body, as by or with the advice of a body of experts which has some knowledge about the requirements and qualifications of a good judge.[46] Such reform could be achieved informally, by simply co-opting the Canadian Bar Association into the selection process while continuing to make the formal appointment as provided in Sections 96 to 101 of the BNA Act. The utility of provincial participation in the process of appointing Justices to a court which so significantly affects their interests was recognized by the federal government in its 1978 Constitutional Amendment Bill. In it it

---

[44] See Chapter 6.

[45] D. E. Fouts, "Policy Making in the Supreme Court of Canada, 1950-60," and S. R. Peck, "A Scalogram Analysis of the Supreme Court of Canada, 1958-67," in G. Schubert and D. J. Danelski (eds.), Comparative Judicial Behaviour (Oxford University Press, Toronto, 1969), pp. 257-334.

[46] Note that the Judicial Council in Ontario to some extent performs this function with respect to the appointment of Provincial Judges.

was proposed to raise the size of the court to eleven and the principle of regional representation of Justices was made explicit. When a Justice was to be named from a province, the Attorney General of that province was to be informed and to agree to the appointment. If agreement proved impossible, a nominating council was to be formed consisting, at the province's option, of the federal and all provincial Attorneys General or their nominees, or of the specific federal and provincial Attorneys General concerned and a neutral chairman. A Justice was to be chosen from among three names submitted by the federal government. For reasons discussed earlier in this chapter, the Bill was never passed but it could be claimed to constitute significant recognition by the federal government of the provincial right to participate in the appointment process and some such procedure may eventually be adopted. Secondly, with respect to provincial courts, it is argued that vacancies in provincial Superior, District, and County Courts should be filled by the province and not by the federal government. In order to implement this type of reform, however, an amendment to Sections 96 to 100 of the BNA Act would be required. Amendment to the BNA Act, as we have seen, is a difficult business at best, and before altering these critical sections of the Act, it would be wise to consider more carefully how switching the locus of such appointments from the federal level to the provincial would affect the principle of judicial independence.

As outlined above, recent constitutional reform proposals have suggested changes in the structure of the Supreme Court of Canada. The key to the judicial reforms is a system of appointment to the Supreme Court which would require that the justices be selected proportionally from the various regions of Canada. What is implicit in this proposal is the principle that the regions of Canada should be *represented* on the highest court of the land, if that court is to have the final authority in settling constitutional disputes. The flaw in these proposals is that they effectively scuttle the constitutional principle of judicial independence for there is no way that a representative judiciary can function independently—the justices will be expected, quite naturally, to reflect the interests of the region from which they were appointed.

It can be countered that the Supreme Court of Canada is already representative in that three of the nine must be appointed from the bar or bench of the Province of Quebec. However, the principle here is to ensure that *expertise* in the codified civil law system of that province *(Code Civil)* is present on the court along with judges trained in the English common law system of other provinces—the aim of the Supreme Court Act is not to represent *Quebec* in constitutional cases but to ensure that there are judges sitting on the highest court of the land who have the legal training to be able to effectively cope with civil appeals from Quebec courts.

Now it is possible to make a case for a representative Supreme Court. In some democratic regimes judges are even popularly elected. However we must recognize that the constitutional implications of a change from an independent to a representative judiciary are significant—through what on the surface is mere institutional "fiddling" with the Supreme Court, we could end up with a radically different judicial process. In some ways the proposed reforms in the appointment procedures for Supreme Court justices would supplant judicial review with binding arbitration, replace the highest court of appeal with what is, in effect, an arbitration tribunal, and replace impartiality with advocacy as the *modus operandi* of judicial decision making.

Other than the appointment procedure, the major criticism of the Canadian judicial system has focussed on the jurisdiction of the Supreme Court of Canada. Particularly in the Province of Quebec it is felt that appeals from the highest court in the province to the Supreme Court in matters involving the *Code Civil du Québec* are unjust. The Supreme Court of Canada, although it includes three civil code judges, functions predominantly as a common law court, and as such it is felt that it should not have the power to overturn decisions of the highest court of Quebec in civil matters. The proposed constitutional amendment bill of 1978 proposed to answer this criticism by appointing a fourth Justice from Quebec and stipulating that *Code Civil* cases were to be heard only by those Justices.

Finally, it is sometimes argued that the Supreme Court of Canada should not have both general appeal jurisdiction and jurisdiction to settle constitutional matters. The feeling is that the Supreme Court of Canada should become a final Court of Appeal only in constitutional matters, and that either another court should be vested with final appeal jurisdiction in non-constitutional matters or the final appeal in such matters should rest with the provinces. The argument against this latter suggestion is that if there is to be uniformity of law throughout Canada there should be a system whereby provincial supreme courts are all subjected to a common source of precedent flowing from a single higher court.

In conclusion, for our concerns the most significant of the issues surrounding the Supreme Court are those which deal with its role in constitutional matters. As will become clear when we discuss the dynamics of federalism, no judicial arrangement can supplant effective political compromise and conciliation in ensuring the smooth functioning of the political system. However, the role of the Supreme Court is an essential one and the increasing attention given to issues surrounding that body during recent constitutional discussions attests to increasing recognition of the important role some such body must play in acting as the arbiter of a federal system.

CIVIL LIBERTIES IN CANADA

Canada does not have an "entrenched" Bill of Rights as part of the written constitution. The primary constitutional guarantee of Canadian civil liberties is the preamble to the BNA Act which states that we are to have a constitution similar in principle to that of the U.K. Consequently, because the U.K. has no entrenched Bill of Rights, the actual extent of the rights and freedoms of Canadians is at present enshrined only in the many centuries of British legal tradition—a fact which, while not a restriction on our liberties, makes them difficult to define precisely. Before proceeding to attempt to describe the basic rights and freedoms of Canadians, it is necessary to add a note to explain the terms involved.

Rights, Freedoms, and Liberties[47]
For the purposes of this discussion it will be assumed that the terms *liberties* and *freedoms* are synonymous. However, it is not as easy to dismiss distinctions between the terms *right* and *liberty*. In their broadest sense, *civil rights* and *civil liberties* can be viewed as meaning basically the same thing, the former term being more common in the U.S. and the latter being more popular in the U.K. and Canada. In Canada, however, the term "civil rights," as used in Section 92(13) of the BNA Act and throughout extensive judicial interpretation, is closely connected not only with individuals' rights, but also with rights that accrue through property and through contract. It is better therefore to avoid the term "civil rights" when referring to fundamental political freedoms.

In 1953, while delivering a judgment on a case involving the principle of religious freedom, Mr. Justice Ivan C. Rand attempted to clarify the distinction between civil rights and civil liberties. He assumed that every person, simply by virtue of being a person, has a total area of freedom, the limits of which are defined only by one's physical strength, mental capacity, etc. However, by virtue of being a member of a community which makes rules to which one must adhere, a person gives up a certain percentage of one's absolute, or original, freedom. Each piece of positive law, therefore, limits the individual's

---

[47] See W. S. Tarnopolsky, *The Canadian Bill of Rights* (McClelland and Stewart, Toronto, 1975), pp. 1-3.

freedom by creating some sort of obligation to obey that law. For example, a law prohibiting patricide creates an obligation in all sons not to kill their fathers, thus restricting the absolute freedom of sons. Conversely, however, such a law creates a right in all fathers not to be killed by their sons. The positive law therefore creates rights and obligations out of the existing area of absolute freedom.[48]

To return to our definitions, civil rights, in the purest sense of the term, are created through the enactment of positive laws, while civil liberties are the residual area of freedom left to an individual after the totality of the positive law is subtracted from it. However, as Professor Tarnopolsky has pointed out, most fundamental freedoms are in fact "beefed up" by the positive law.[49] By way of example, he cites religious freedom:

In those terms, then, we speak of "freedom of worship," but only as defined by law, and not including such practices as human sacrifice, for example. Such a freedom can also be protected by law, for instance, by forbidding unlawful interference with the conduct of a religious service.[50]

Another more current example of the evolution or development of a positive right out of an area of residual freedom might be occurring in the area of *privacy*. The foundation of a "right to privacy" likely lies in tradition and in the common law ("a man's home is his castle"). Violations of privacy on the part of private individuals are viewed as trespassing, and encroachments even by governmental officials such as the police require significant justification and some level of judicial involvement such as a warrant. However, most of the original tenets of a common law right to privacy involve only the physical or *territorial* dimension of privacy, which is related to the law of property.

Modern electronic technology has created a situation where *information* concerning an individual can be gathered, collated, and retrieved with frightening efficiency. It has been recognized that the common law protections of the right to territorial privacy have to be backed up by legislation to protect the informational privacy of individuals from unscrupulous business enterprises and governmental agencies as well. The positive law response to this new threat to indi-

---

[48] See *Saumur v. City of Quebec*, [1953] 2 Supreme Court Reports, p. 329.

[49] Note here that an entrenched and comprehensive Bill of Rights might be conceived of as replacing all residual freedoms with positive rights. Whatever the semantic difficulties with such a formulation of the terms, the effect would still be essentially to entrench certain freedoms once and for all behind a set of positive law barriers. In fact the effect is to create a "right to a set of freedoms," whereby the existing residue of individual freedoms is protected from any further encroachment by the positive law.

[50] W. S. Tarnopolsky, *The Canadian Bill of Rights*, p. 2.

vidual freedom has been legislation limiting the operation of consumer credit "ratings," and imposing strict limits on the use of electronic surveillance devices, by both public and private organizations. The result is that a previously unrecognized and unnecessary "right to privacy" is being defined incrementally, through a series of positive law enactments.

The 1977 Canadian Human Rights Act provides for one of the members of the Human Rights Commission to act as a "Privacy Commissioner." The function of this official is to investigate complaints arising out of Part IV of the Human Rights Act. This part of the act requires the federal government to publicize the existence of the various information banks within the bureaucracy, to provide some access to this information on the part of the individual concerned, and to limit the use to which the information can be put. In the latter case for instance, the federal government is restricted in the extent to which information gathered for one purpose and by one agency can be used by other agencies of the government or by other governments. While this legislation is a start in the right direction it will be necessary likely for a future government to introduce separate and comprehensive legislation dealing with privacy and structured in a way that its operation is complementary to expected legislation on freedom of information, for full guarantees of individual privacy vis-à-vis federal institutions to be realized. Ultimately, as well, similar legislation will have to be introduced in each of the provinces so that comprehensive protection of the right to privacy can be attained for all Canadians in dealings with all major information-gathering institutions.[51]

Finally, the point should be made here that an empirical distinction can be made between civil rights and civil liberties. The former tend to be concerned primarily with individual-to-individual relationships, whereas the latter tend to be concerned with individual-to-state relationships. Civil liberties are thus more frequently viewed as freedom from interference or restriction by the political system, and civil rights are viewed as protecting an individual from being discriminated against by another individual (as in the Civil Rights Bill in the U.S.).

Civil Liberties: What Are They?

There are several implications which derive from the fact that the BNA Act gives Canada a constitution similar in principle to that of the

---

[51] For a detailed discussion of the protection of privacy in Canada see: G. B. Sharma, "The Protection of Personal Information by the Canadian Human Rights Act" in Rowat, D. C. (ed.), *The Right to Know* (Carleton University, Ottawa, 1980) p. 83.

U.K. Because the constitution of the U.K. reflects, or did reflect in 1867, primarily liberal democratic values, Canada also has a constitution which is democratic and predominantly liberal. Fundamental freedoms or civil liberties in Canada, therefore, can be related to either liberal values or democratic freedoms.[52]

Democratic Freedoms   These include both substantive freedoms and procedural rights, and are implicit in and necessary to a democratic system of government. The democratic freedoms are instrumental in realizing the basic democratic value of political equality, and they function by setting limits on governmental interference with the individual. The substantive democratic freedoms in Canada include freedom of association, freedom of assembly, freedom of expression, freedom of conscience, and freedom of the press.

The procedural rights include freedom from arbitrary arrest, right to a fair hearing, right to counsel, and the right of *habeas corpus*. Moreover, they have come to include the rules of evidence which, in judicial proceedings, determine the admissability of evidence and the determination of privileged information. As a "right to privacy" becomes more clearly articulated, the procedural right will likely be expanded to include further protection from invasions of informational privacy through electronic eavesdropping, etc. These procedural rights institutionalize the rule of law, ensure "equality before the law" for all individuals, and prevent arbitrariness and discrimination on the part of governmental officials.

Liberal Freedoms   These are implicit in the values of liberalism, but not necessarily in the values of democracy. Where the democratic freedoms are negative, being freedom *from* government interference or hindrance, the liberal freedoms are positive, giving individuals freedom *to* do many things. In large part these liberal freedoms deal with the individual's rights in regard to property and contract, including the right to own property, the right not to be deprived thereof except through due process of law, and the freedom of contract. While it is difficult to separate liberal freedoms from democratic freedoms in a country whose values are "liberal-democratic," a possible distinction is that the former are very closely tied up with the economic system of capitalism. The liberal freedoms are therefore more important in achieving the liberal goal of a free economy than they are in achieving the democratic goals of popular sovereignty and political equality.

---

[52] Note here that the constitution of the U.K. is also parliamentary in form. The implications of this in terms of the supremacy of parliament were discussed in Chapter 6.

Egalitarian Rights These are the so-called "human rights" which are instrumental in achieving the goals of social and economic equality. Stated in the extreme, liberal and egalitarian values tend to conflict with each other, although in fact in Canada, there is gradual acceptance of limitations on the liberal freedoms to promote human rights. While the egalitarian freedoms would certainly limit governmental discrimination against classes of individuals, they also involve individual-to-individual relationships, and include freedom from discrimination in employment, accommodation, transportation, etc., by reason of race, religion, ethnic origin, or nationality.

To an extent that has never been clearly defined, some basic economic egalitarian rights also exist in Canada. These are defined in the Universal Declaration of Human Rights of the United Nations:

Every one has the right to rest and leisure, including reasonable limitation of working hours and periodic holidays with pay. . . . Everyone has the right to a standard of living adequate for the health and wellbeing of himself and of his family, including food, clothing, housing and medical care, and necessary social services and the right to security in the event of unemployment, sickness, disability, widowhood, old age, or other lack of livelihood in circumstances beyond his control. Motherhood and childhood are entitled to special care and assistance. All children, whether born in or out of wedlock, shall enjoy the same social protection. . . . Everyone has the right to education. [53]

Most Canadians would agree that these are indeed basic human rights, and egalitarianism and non-discrimination are becoming more and more important values in Canadian society. By now all of the provinces and the federal government have Human Rights Acts which guarantee protection from discrimination by government agencies and private corporations alike. The Canadian Human Rights Commission, created in 1977, has as its mandate the investigation and resolution of claims of discrimination made against federal government agencies and federally incorporated companies. The Commission has been very active since its creation and in fact has probably come a long way in discouraging would-be cases of discrimination. However, in the long run the only effective way to eliminate discrimination is to eliminate the personal prejudices which underly all acts of discrimination. In other words legislation can only affect *acts* of discrimination, whereas it is the predisposition to discriminate or the discriminatory attitudes of Canadians that must ultimately be conquered if we are to eliminate the problem.

---

[53] *The Universal Declaration of Human Rights,* Articles 24, 25, 26.

Civil Liberties: How Are They Protected?

Before speaking of the specific legal guarantees of civil liberties in Canada, it is necessary to point out that such enactments may provide merely illusory protection. If the values reflected in the statutory and common law statements defining our civil liberties are not congruent with the prevalent modes of thought and attitudes in the society at large, such laws will have little real effect on our substantive freedom. The best guarantee of fundamental freedom in society, therefore, is a consensus in the society as to what it is.

Distribution of Legislative Jurisdiction over Civil Liberties The principle of the supremacy of parliament, which was discussed in some detail in Chapter 6, means that nothing is beyond the legislative competence of parliament. A majority of the members of parliament can abrogate or abolish any civil liberties they wish to, at least in strictly legal terms. Naturally, the normative limitations on this sort of legislative behaviour are very real, and because Canada is a federal system,[54] there are further limitations as well. The BNA Act ostensibly divides up all legislative power between the federal and provincial levels. The power to alter or to clarify the substance or extent of civil liberties is therefore also divided between the federal parliament and the provincial legislatures.

Section 92(13) gives the provincial legislature the power to legislate upon matters dealing with "property and civil rights in the province," but because the exact scope of civil rights and liberties in this country is not clear to begin with, the exact parameters of this "civil rights power" have had to be defined in piecemeal fashion as various civil liberties cases arose. Some of the earliest of these involved the discriminatory treatment of orientals by certain laws in the province of British Columbia. In *Union Colliery Company of B.C. v. Bryden* (1899),[55] provincial legislation which prohibited orientals from working in underground mines was declared invalid, not on the grounds that it was discriminatory, but because it interfered with the federal government's exclusive power to pass laws regarding "naturalization and aliens."[56] Four years later, British Columbia legislation denying naturalized Canadians of Japanese extraction the right to vote in provincial elections was upheld. The Judicial Committee of the Privy Council decided that it was quite within the rights of the B.C. legislature, through Section 92(1) "amendment of the provincial constitu-

---

[54] See also Chapter 8.
[55] R. A. Olmsted (ed.), *Judicial Committee Decisions Relating to the British North America Act, 1867*, vol. 1 (Queen's Printer, Ottawa, 1954), p. 443.
[56] BNA Act, Section 91(25).

tion," to pass laws, even discriminatory ones, relating to the provincial franchise: "The policy or impolicy of such an enactment as that which excludes a particular race from the franchise is not a topic which their lordships are entitled to consider."[57] Thus, early decisions relating to civil liberties were viewed entirely in terms of deciding *which* level of government had the power to interfere with them and never whether *any* government should in fact have such power. This passive or literal approach to judicial interpretation has haunted Canadian constitutional development throughout our history,[58] and it has been particularly restrictive in the area of civil liberties.

An initial breakthrough in this area was made by Chief Justice Duff in the *Alberta Press Bill* case (1938). The "Press Bill" was declared to be *ultra vires* the province because it was dependent upon the Alberta Social Credit Act which had already been invalidated by Duff. However, the bold lawmaking that emerged from this case was the by-product of a judicial "aside" (*obiter dictum*) which was not central to deciding the case and so could not become established as binding precedent until reinforced by further decisions. The substance of the "Duff Doctrine" established in this aside is based on the preamble to the BNA Act, which states that Canada shall have a system similar in principle to that of Great Britain. This in turn implies parliamentary democracy which "contemplates a parliament working under the influence of public opinion, and public discussion,"[59] and in effect accepts as axiomatic that "the right of free public discussion of public affairs, notwithstanding its incidental mischiefs, is the breath of life for parliamentary institutions."[60] Consequently, Chief Justice Duff held that:

The parliament of Canada possesses authority to legislate for the protection of this right. . . . That authority rests upon the principle that the powers requisite for the protection of the constitution itself are by necessity implications from the BNA Act as a whole (Fort Frances Case, [1923] A.C.695) *and since the subject matter in relation to which the power is exercised is not exclusively a provincial matter, it is necessarily vested in Parliament.*[61]

Thus, while Duff did not say that such interference with a fundamental democratic freedom was beyond the competence of all legisla-

---

[57] *Cunningham v. Tomey Homma* (1903), Olmsted, op. cit., vol. 1, p. 484. See also *Quong Wing v. King* (1916), 49 S.C.R. 440.
[58] See Chapter 8.
[59] *Reference Re Alberta Statutes*, [1939] S.C.R. 100 at p. 133.
[60] Ibid.
[61] Ibid., p. 134.

tures, in stating that it was beyond the power of the province he definitely left the door open for future judges to view such matters as beyond the competence of the federal parliament as well. Perhaps more important, Duff stated once and for all that any limitation on the democratic freedoms should not be applied unequally in different provinces.

The federal-provincial distribution of the legislative power to limit the extent of civil liberties was further developed in two important cases in the fifties. In the earlier of these, *Saumur v. City of Quebec*,[62] the validity of a city by-law which prohibited the distribution of religious pamphlets on the streets without a special permit was challenged. The legislation was declared to be valid in lower courts and in the Supreme Court of the province, but the decision was finally overturned by a narrow 5 to 4 margin on appeal to the Supreme Court of Canada. In the judgment, four of the justices of the Supreme Court held that the Quebec by-law dealt merely with regulation and control of city streets, and therefore was valid. One judge, who had the deciding vote as it turned out, held that the city by-law conflicted with existing provincial legislation (the Freedom of Worship Act) and was therefore invalid. He went on to declare, however, that the power to restrict freedom of religion was quite within the jurisdiction of the provincial government. The remaining four justices, among them Mr. Justice Ivan C. Rand, held that the city by-law was invalid because it interfered with the freedom of religious expression. Utilizing the preamble of the BNA Act and the "Duff Doctrine" to varying degrees in their judgments, these four judges went on to declare that legislation interfering with a freedom as fundamental as freedom of religion was beyond the competence of a provincial legislature.

In the second important civil liberties case in the fifties, *Switzman v. Elbling* (the *Padlock* case),[63] legislation of the Province of Quebec which banned the propagation of "Communism and Bolshevism" by closing up and padlocking any premises used for those purposes, was declared invalid. While the province claimed that it was legislation dealing with "property and civil rights in the province" and therefore within its jurisdiction by Section 92(13) of the BNA Act, the majority of the Supreme Court of Canada declared that the subject matter of the impugned legislation involved primarily criminal law which is an exclusive federal area [Section 91(27)]. However, in a minority but concurring judgment, Rand, Abbott, and Kellock, three of our more "liberal" judges, held the act to be invalid because the prov-

---

[62] [1953] 2 S.C.R. 299.
[63] [1957] S.C.R. 356.

inces were not empowered to restrict the basic democratic freedom, freedom of opinion, which is implicit in the preamble to the BNA Act and in the "Duff Doctrine." They argued that such legislation could only be enacted by the federal parliament. Mr. Justice Abbott even went further than this in an *obiter dictum*, stating that such fundamental freedoms were possibly even beyond encroachment by the federal parliament, although there is little indication that subsequent courts have had any intention of following his lead.[64]

Thus, through a number of cases dealing with restrictive provincial laws, the courts have begun to sort out the federal-provincial distribution of legislative power with regard to civil liberties. Through the federal power in the area of naturalization and aliens,[65] the criminal law power,[66] and the preamble to the BNA Act, the federal parliament has been declared to have jurisdiction over many aspects of civil liberties. However, in the *Tomey Homma* case, the provinces were declared to have the power to discriminate against people on the basis of their racial origins, with respect to the right to vote; and in the *Saumur* case, a majority of the Supreme Court of Canada admitted that the provinces have the right to restrict freedom of religion. Thus, today the protection of these civil liberties lies almost entirely with the individual provinces. British Columbia has long since abolished its discriminatory practices and has guaranteed fundamental freedoms,[67] and while there is by no means uniformity from province to province, there seems to be a general agreement in all provinces that certain rights and freedoms are too fundamental to be tampered with by any government.

Because of this vague consensus, legislative abrogation of substantive democratic freedoms by the provinces has been rare in recent years. However, the record in terms of procedural rights and freedoms has not been as clean. There have been many specific cases, particularly in the Province of Quebec, of violation of basic procedural rights such as *habeas corpus* and freedom from arbitrary arrest,[68] and many provincial laws exist which provide for rather arbitrary search

---

[64] Note, however, that Mr. Justice Abbott reiterated his stand in a dissenting judgment in *Oil, Chemical and Atomic Workers International Ltd. v. Imperial Oil Ltd. and A-G for B.C.*, [1963] S.C.R. 584.

[65] See also *Winner v. SMT*, [1951] S.C.R. 887.

[66] See also *Birks and Sons v. City of Montreal*, [1955] S.C.R. 799.

[67] For a list of federal and provincial legislation protecting human rights, see P. E. Trudeau, *A Canadian Charter of Human Rights* (Queen's Printer, Ottawa, 1968), Appendix IX.

[68] Ontario, Royal Commission Inquiry into Civil Rights, *Report*, vol. 1 (Queen's Printer, Toronto, 1968), *passim*.

and seizure at the discretion of the police.[69] Nevertheless, with the press and the public ever more aware of their rights and freedoms, it seems likely that such abuses will occur less and less frequently, except when governments can manage to convince their citizens that special circumstances prevail. The sanction against repressive laws is a public opinion which is opposed to them. The danger lies either in the public's ceasing to pay much attention to the government, thus letting repressive legislation slip by unnoticed, or in the majority's coming to approve of laws which suppress the democratic freedoms of minorities.

The Canadian Bill of Rights

The focus of the discussion up until now has been on the distribution of legislative jurisdiction in the area of civil liberties, and on the civil liberties record of the provinces. Now it is time to consider a specific federal statute which purports to protect many of our fundamental freedoms, the Canadian Bill of Rights, passed in 1960.

The Canadian Bill of Rights is divided into two parts. Part I begins with a list of "the human rights and fundamental freedoms" that exist in Canada, "without discrimination by reason of race, national origin, colour, religion, or sex," and includes such things as property rights, equality before the law, freedom of religion, freedom of speech, freedom of assembly and association, and freedom of the press. The second section of Part I provides that "no law shall be construed or applied so as to" infringe certain basic procedural rights such as freedom from arbitrary arrest, freedom from cruel punishment, right to a fair trial, right to an interpreter, the right to be presumed innocent until proven guilty in criminal proceedings, the right to *habeas corpus* and to counsel, and the right to choose not to testify against oneself. The third section of Part I provides that the Minister of Justice must certify that each piece of draft legislation is consistent with the provisions of the Bill of Rights before it is introduced in the House of Commons.

Part II of the Bill states some limitations on the effect of the provisions in Part I. First, nothing in Part I can be interpreted so as to limit a right or freedom that existed before the Bill of Rights was passed. Secondly, Part I of the Bill is to apply to federal legislation only. It has no effect on legislation passed by the provinces which is within the competence of their legislatures according to the BNA Act. Thirdly, Part II provides explicitly that:

---

[69] See for instance, *Chaput v. Romain*, [1955] S.C.R. 834; *Lamb v. Benoit*, [1959] S.C.R. 321.

Any act or thing done or authorized or any order or regulation made under the author-
ity of [the War Measures Act] shall be deemed not to be an abrogation, abridgement, or
infringement of any right or freedom recognized by the Canadian Bill of Rights.

The effect of this last is that the "human rights and fundamental freedoms" enumerated in the Bill of Rights become inoperative when the
federal government decides that a state of national emergency exists
and invokes the War Measures Act.

Whether such emergency procedures can ever be justified in a
democratic political system is a question that can only be answered on
a trial and error basis. Great injustices were done to Canadians of Japanese origin during World War II simply because Canada was at war
with Japan.[70] In retrospect, this seems a shameful blot on the civil
liberties record of Canada, although at the time the government's
action under the War Measures Act was probably condoned by nearly
everyone except the Japanese Canadians themselves.[71] A similar interpretation appears to have developed with respect to the proclamation of the War Measures Act in the fall of 1970 because of unusual
circumstances in the Province of Quebec. While there was by no
means unanimous agreement that the Quebec situation required such
drastic measures, it would appear that a sizeable proportion of the
Canadian population was at the time in agreement with the government's move. However, now that the "crisis" has faded, many Canadians, including many who at the time supported the actions of the
federal and Quebec authorities, look back on the FLQ emergency
with something of the same sense of sheepishness with which we regard the treatment of the Japanese Canadians in 1942.

The only conclusion to which one can come in this regard is that if a
comprehensive emergency power is to be vested in the government
and if that emergency power is to be exercised unilaterally at the discretion of the government, the public must be aware of the anti-
democratic potential in such procedures.

The more fundamental question here, however, is whether a political system can permit legislation such as the War Measures Act and
remain "democratic." If it is possible to conceive of circumstances
when fundamental freedoms may be abrogated, then perhaps those
freedoms are not so fundamental after all. Possibly, even in so-called
democratic systems, the stability and survival of the system becomes
a more fundamental value than the substantive values implicit in the
specific regime. Democratic systems are thus caught in a dilemma: on

---

[70] See [1946] S.C.R. 248 (the *Japanese Canadians* case).
[71] While many Canadians, particularly the CCF party, consistently opposed the treatment of the Japanese Canadians they were definitely in the minority.

the one hand, if they do not take severe and arbitrary measures under certain circumstances they might be taken over and replaced by an undemocratic regime, on the other hand, by taking such measures they will be *ipso facto* less democratic themselves. There is no easy answer to this problem, but it is critical to an appraisal of the protection of civil liberties in Canada to ask the question.

Another restriction on the effectiveness of the Bill of Rights is the implication in Section 2 that the Bill can be bypassed if parliament states explicitly that a law "shall operate notwithstanding the Bill of Rights." While it is likely that parliament will seldom, if ever, actually use this power, the fact that it is written into the Bill of Rights significantly weakens its total impact.

Finally, perhaps the greatest weakness of the Bill of Rights has been the inconsistency of the Supreme Court's interpretation of it. Up until 1970, that Court has taken the general stand that legislation which existed prior to the Bill of Rights and which might on the surface appear to conflict with it must have been intended by parliament to operate notwithstanding the Bill, or the offending legislation would have been repealed. In 1963, Mr. Justice Ritchie, in delivering the majority opinion of the Supreme Court, stated that the Bill of Rights "is not concerned with 'human rights and fundamental freedoms' in any abstract sense, but rather with such 'rights and freedoms' as they existed in Canada immediately before the statute was enacted."[72] Furthermore, because the Bill of Rights is in form but another statute of the federal parliament, and because it is stated in very general terms, it is easy for the courts to interpret it in such a way that other more specific statutes are not repugnant to it.[73]

A single case in 1969 might have altered this conservative trend in interpretation to some extent. In *The Queen v. Drybones*,[74] the Supreme Court of Canada declared a section of the Indian Act invalid because it denied Indians the "equality before the law" which is guaranteed to all Canadians by the Bill of Rights. The rather timid interpretation of the Bill of Rights that the majority of the court subscribed to in *Robertson and Rossetani* was qualified, and the court agreed to view the Bill of Rights as having application to laws that existed before 1960. Mr. Justice Ritchie, in delivering the majority judgment, modified his very conservative position in the earlier case and argued that:

---

[72] *Robertson and Rossetani v. The Queen*, [1963] S.C.R. 651, at p. 654. Note that Mr. Justice Cartwright dissented in this case and argued that all legislation of the parliament of Canada was meant to conform to the Bill of Rights.

[73] See: Tarnopolsky, *The Canadian Bill of Rights*, ch. 24.

[74] *The Queen v. Drybones*, [1970] S.C.R. 282.

If a law of Canada cannot be sensibly construed and applied, so that it does not abrogate, abridge or infringe one of the rights and freedoms, recognized and declared by the Bill, then such law is inoperative *"unless it is expressly declared by an Act of the Parliament of Canada that it shall operate notwithstanding the Canadian Bill of Rights."* (p. 294)

The impugned section of the Indian Act was therefore declared to be inoperative because it created an offence which applied only to Indians and not to other classes of Canadian citizens.

However, some of the optimism about the applicability of the Bill of Rights which was generated by the *Drybones* decision has been tempered by a more recent decision of the Supreme Court. In *A-G Canada v. Lavell,* the issue involved a section of the Indian Act which provides that an Indian woman who marries a white loses her status as an Indian, whereas an Indian male can marry a white woman and not only is his status unaffected but his wife acquires Indian status. Counsel for the respondent in the appeal held that the relevant sections of the Indian Act were invalid because they constituted discrimination by virtue of sex.

A majority of the Court held that the particular section of the Indian Act was indeed valid because it involved only "the internal regulation of the lives of Indians *on* reserves." The Indian Act in this case does not discriminate between Indians and whites or between men and women, but between Indian men and Indian women, and therefore does not infringe upon the Bill of Rights.[75]

In sum, it would appear that the Supreme Court is ambivalent about the extent to which the Bill of Rights should be interpreted as rendering invalid existing federal legislation. The dilemma faced by the court would seem to be a product of the various judges' perceptions of the legitimate role of the court rather than their perceptions of the Bill of Rights itself. As Mr. Justice Abbott stated in a dissenting opinion, the Bill must have been intended as more than "rhetorical window dressing":

The Canadian Bill of Rights has substantially affected the doctrine of the supremacy of Parliament. Like any other statute it can of course be repealed or amended, or a particular law declared to be applicable notwithstanding the provision of the Bill. In form the supremacy of Parliament is maintained but in practice I think that it has been substantially curtailed. In my opinion that result is undesirable, but that is a matter for consideration by Parliament, not the courts. . . . Of one thing I am certain, the Bill will continue to supply ample grist to the judicial mills for some time to come.[76]

---

[75] For those interested in the detailed arguments presented in this case, both the majority judgment delivered by Mr. Justice Ritchie and a lengthy dissent delivered by Mr. Justice Laskin bear careful reading. The full implications of this case will only be discernible in the way it is applied to future decisions.

[76] *Lavell* case, [1974] S.C.R.

Thus in the years to come, the impact of the Bill of Rights on existing federal statutes will depend as much upon the conservative/activist balance of the judges on the court as upon the construction and interpretation of the statutes themselves. Whatever the outcome of this ongoing debate, the overall effect of the Bill of Rights and corresponding provincial enactments has been beneficial in that such fundamental statements of our political values serve as symbolic objects of political socialization. Their function is as much to educate as it is to provide binding *de jure* protection of our civil liberties. Finally, the provision in the Bill of Rights that all federal legislation must be screened by the Minister of Justice before being introduced in parliament is a sort of "pre-audit" that may deter the passage of new laws which are contrary to the basic values of the Canadian political culture.

The Charter of Rights and Freedoms

In recognition of the ambiguity which exists as to the status of the Bill of Rights, the federal government proposed in its abortive constitutional amendment Bill of 1978 that a new constitution should include a "Charter of Rights and Freedoms" which would be binding on the federal and provincial governments when they chose to "opt in" to coverage by its provisions. The Charter proposed rights such as freedom of movement within Canada, freedom of opinion and expression, rights to use and enjoyment of property, and protection and equality before the law. Language rights in education and before the courts were also to be guaranteed. The hope was that eventually further joint action by all the federal and provincial governments would result in the entrenchment of the Charter and the placing of its provisions in the position of a true constitutional guarantee but until the time that such entrenchment takes place, it is difficult to believe that the Charter's impact could be much different than that of the Bill of Rights.

The proposed Charter dropped from sight at least temporarily with the defeat of the Trudeau Liberal government in 1979, for the succeeding Conservative government represented more the prevailing English-Canadian point of view that the best guarantee of rights and freedoms lies in the political culture rather than in written guarantees. The re-election of the Trudeau Liberals in 1980 has again shifted the emphasis to the need for an entrenched body of law to guarantee rights and freedoms. The major problem with the entrenchment of a charter of human rights and freedoms in the constitution is that it becomes an explicit rejection of the notion of the supremacy of parliament. In a sense entrenchment is anti-democratic and elitist, in that it betrays a fundamental mistrust of the elected representatives of the people of Canada since it limits their power by placing a body of law beyond their reach. While the motives of the "constitution writers" of the 1970s are above reproach—who would dare to differ with the notion of guaranteeing our basic freedoms "forever"?—their well-meaning zeal must be tempered with a clear perspective on how such change will affect other significant principles of our constitution such as the supremacy of parliament and majoritarianism.

As a conclusion to this discussion of the protection of civil liberties in Canada it is necessary to qualify all that we have said about the formal and institutionalized devices for protecting the rights and freedoms of Canadians. While such institutional guarantees are important in that they may deter those who would try to abuse our freedoms, their more important role is as symbolic and educative devices. Legislation such as the Bill of Rights and the Canadian Human Rights Act is significant because it teaches Canadians about the value of civil liberties and about the importance of non-discrimination. In the final analysis it is the values and attitudes of Canadians that determine the kind of society we are going to live in, and the symbolic role that formal statements and guarantees of civil liberties play in the process of political socialization may be more important than the positive law remedies that are set down in such enactments.

Finally, it must also be emphasized that it is the values and attitudes of governmental officials, and particularly the police and national security investigators, which are the most important in determining the extent of our freedoms and the quality of life in Canada. It is essential that we begin to pay more attention to the recruitment and training of police and security officials to ensure that people with deep prejudices, closed minds, or simply lacking in tolerance are not given the sorts of wide discretionary powers that we have traditionally vested in members of the law enforcement community. If it is *desirable* to reduce prejudice and intolerance in *all* Canadians, it is absolutely *imperative* that it be eliminated from the ranks of our law enforcement officers, national security investigators, and government officials dealing with the public directly. This may mean paying our police officers and public officials a lot more than we now do in order to attract and hold good quality people in these occupations; but in the long run it will be well worth it, for the noblest sentiments expressed in civil liberties legislation come to naught if the public officials implementing and enforcing our laws don't share those sentiments.

PART 3

The Historical Environment of Canadian Federalism

8

Constitutional Development and Canadian Federalism

The Dominion of Canada came into existence with the passage of the British North America Act in 1867. Although this historic document is an Act of the parliament of the United Kingdom, it was passed at the request of the British North American colonies themselves. The details of the legislation were largely based on resolutions that had been put forward jointly by the colonies and which had been worked out over a number of years of bargaining and compromise at several colonial conferences.[1] Originally, the deliberations had included all of the British North American colonies, but Newfoundland and Prince Edward Island had soon lost their enthusiasm, and it was left to the remaining colonies, Upper and Lower Canada, New Brunswick and Nova Scotia, to come to an agreement on the terms of the union. Once the agreement had been thrashed out, it was a relatively simple matter for the U.K. parliament to put it into the form of a statute, which came into effect on July 1, 1867.

THE HISTORICAL ROOTS OF BRITISH NORTH AMERICAN UNION

In the mid-nineteenth century, as today, the most significant factor in the environment of the Canadian political system was the proximity of the United States. In the 1860s, the awareness of this fact was heightened by a number of events which gave people in the British North American colonies cause to fear direct military invasion from the south. At the conclusion of the American Civil War, the Union Army was the most powerful and advanced fighting machine in the world.[2] Furthermore, incidents during the war such as the St. Alban's raid in 1864 and the activities of the British-built Confederate

[1] For an account of these see G. P. Browne (ed.), *Documents on the Confederation of British North America* (Carleton Library, McClelland and Stewart, Toronto, 1969), p. 40.
[2] D. Creighton, *John A. Macdonald*, vol. 1, *The Young Politician* (Macmillan, Toronto, 1952), pp. 409-410.

cruiser, the *Alabama*, had incurred the displeasure of the United States.[3] The American press was advocating the invasion of Canada at the conclusion of the war, and there was a great fear in Canada that the newspapers would arouse sufficient public pressure to convince Congress and the President that invasion was, indeed, a good idea.[4]

The sense of danger was heightened by the militant activities of an American-based Irish nationalist organization, called the Fenian Brotherhood. The Fenians attracted large numbers of Irish veterans of the Civil War who were happy to re-enlist in this unofficial army in order to free Ireland from "English tyranny."[5] One of the ways in which they hoped to achieve this was by conquering Canada as a base. Their sundry pronouncements and the publicity that they gained were received with trepidation in Canada. The subsequent "invasions" of British North America by the Fenians were, in retro-spect, more comic-opera than threatening and all were repulsed by the Canadians without serious difficulty. But while the menace that the Fenians presented to Canada was exaggerated, when it was added to the existing evidence of an American predisposition to con-tinental imperialism it did reinforce Canadian perceptions of a mili-tary threat from the south.[6]

While Canadians grew increasingly alarmed at the sabre-rattling in the United States, the British, who had the responsibility for defend-ing their North American colonies, began to give every indication that they were no longer willing to go very far in that enterprise. Politi-cians in the U.K. began to speak of the necessity of shifting the responsibility for colonial defence to the colonies, and the U.K. cabi-net was not overly generous in its budgeting for such things as the fortifications of Quebec. Thus, while the Canadians were looking apprehensively at the military might of the U.S., "there was remark-ably little evidence of a sense of acute peril, of desperate urgency, in Great Britain."[7]

Economic factors also helped in setting the stage for Confederation. Again, the United States played a starring role. The immediate eco-

---

[3] See Creighton, op. cit., pp. 385-430, *passim*; Creighton, *The Road to Confederation* (Macmillan, Toronto, 1964), pp. 194-195; and W. L. Morton, *The Critical Years* (McClelland and Stewart, Toronto, 1964), p. 185.

[4] Creighton, *John A. Macdonald*, vol. 1, *passim*; and Dawson, *The Government of Canada*, p. 21.

[5] Creighton, *John A. Macdonald*, vol. 1, pp. 405-406.

[6] The best source of information on this period in Canadian history is an article by C. P. Storey, "Fenianism and the Rise of National Feeling in Canada at the Time of Confed-eration," *Canadian Historical Review*, vol. 12, pp. 238-261, September, 1931, and Morton, *The Critical Years*, pp. 195-196.

[7] Creighton, *John A. Macdonald*, vol. 1, pp. 405-406.

nomic problems of the British North American colonies actually dated back to 1846 when the Navigation Laws that gave preferential treatment to colonial trade were repealed by the U.K. However, the negative effects of this had been offset somewhat at the time by a reciprocity agreement with the U.S. which allowed Canadian primary products duty-free access to the U.S. markets. In the 1860s, partly because of generally bad Anglo-American relations and partly because of economic pressures at home, the United States served notice of its intention to terminate the reciprocity agreement. Reciprocity finally was terminated in 1866, at a time when the U.K. seemed more committed than ever to a policy of free trade. Thus, excluded from the American market and forced to compete with more advanced economies in the open British market, the British North American colonies looked at last to each other:

If preferences in Britain and the United States were not to be had, the colonies could at least give preference to each other. Commercial union of the British American provinces would weld them into a single vast trading area within which products might be freely exchanged. If the markets of all the provinces could be opened to the industries of each, an economic system would be created, which, by lessening dependence on external markets, would offer greater stability than the economies of the separate provinces could hope for, and which, because of the diversity and complementarity of its resources, would have a potential for growth. [8]

Technological changes probably also helped to accelerate the movement toward Confederation, because the colonial economies were strained by the costs of taking full advantage of this technology. The shift from sail to steam and from canals to railways, for instance, forced the colonies, especially the Maritimes, to incur large provincial debts:

By incurring debts to build the railways which they so earnestly desired, the Maritime provinces had, as it were, given hostages to fortune. By increasing the burden of fixed charges on their revenues, they had curtailed their ability to withstand adversity. [9]

Thus, union offered Nova Scotia and New Brunswick not merely the hope of new markets in the Canadas, but also the promise of a share of national revenues that would ease the burden of their debts. To ensure that the Maritimes did, in fact, gain markets in central Can-

[8] W. T. Easterbrook and H. G. J. Aitken, *Canadian Economic History* (Macmillan, Toronto, 1965), p. 251; D. Creighton, *British North America at Confederation* (Queen's Printer, Ottawa, 1963).

[9] Easterbrook and Aitken, *Canadian Economic History,* p. 250.

ada, a very specific provision for the construction of the Intercolonial Railway was written into the BNA Act itself:

It shall be the duty of the Parliament of Canada to provide for the commencement within six months after the Union, of a railway connecting the River St. Lawrence with the city of Halifax in Nova Scotia and for the construction thereof without intermission, and the completion thereof with all practicable speed. [10]

While the promise of the Intercolonial Railway looks very much like a simple "bribe" to entice the Maritimes into the Union, it can be argued that the Canadas also could anticipate certain advantages from the railway. As well as facilitating interprovincial trade, the Intercolonial Railway would provide exporters in Ontario and Quebec with an ice-free port in the winter months when Quebec City and Montreal were normally closed. [11] This was an important consideration, for Canadian businessmen feared that the abrogation of the reciprocity agreement by the U.S. might close the winter ports on the U.S. eastern seaboard to Canadian exporters. The Maritimers themselves certainly welcomed the opportunity to handle the transshipment of Canadian goods in the winter months through the ports of Halifax and Saint John.

Political factors also pushed the colonies toward Confederation. The union of 1841, which had tied Upper and Lower Canada in an uneasy political marriage, was no longer tolerable. The Act of Union had guaranteed equal representation in the colonial legislature to Canada East and Canada West, and by the 1860s, the population of Canada West (now Ontario) which was originally smaller than the population of Canada East (now Quebec) had greatly increased by an influx of immigrants. Once the people of Canada West realized that the guarantee of equal representation was working against them, they began to agitate for "rep. by pop." The French Canadians of Canada East countered with demands for guarantees of their rights as a linguistic, religious, and ethnic minority. The colonial government was left in a virtually permanent stalemate. Impetus to the Confederation idea was added by the deadlock in the legislature of the United Canadas; for Confederation, whatever its faults, offered a viable solution by providing for the separation of the Canadas into two provinces within the larger union.

When we view the history of the Confederation period in Canada, it becomes clear that the section of North America that was to become

---

[10] BNA Act, 1867, part X, section 145. This section was deleted from the Act in 1893.
[11] Easterbrook and Aitken, *Canadian Economic History*, p. 249.

the Province of Ontario had more to gain from union than any other. In fact, as Professor D. V. Smiley points out:

The complicated compromise which was finally embodied in the British North America Act reflected in large part the aspirations and interests of that populous, prosperous and dynamic region, with such concessions to Lower Canada and the Maritimes as were necessary to gain the support of their leaders for union. [12]

The Maritimes saw certain economic advantages in Confederation, but a large proportion of the people living in New Brunswick and Nova Scotia were fervently opposed to any agreement that tied them to Canada. It can even be argued that the Maritimes were never really in favour of Confederation, and were "railroaded" in by complicated political manoeuvering, the silver tongue of Sir John A. Macdonald, and the promise of a railway. French-Canadian politicians saw Confederation as a way of safeguarding their language and religious rights and, on the whole, as a lesser evil than the Union of 1841.

Generally, it can be concluded that there were no common purposes, no visions of greatness, and no noble causes which united Canada initially. Perhaps, as Professor Smiley points out: "The underlying agreement among colonial politicians which made Confederation possible was that the continuance of monarchial and parliamentary institutions and of the British connection was infinitely preferable to absorption into the U.S."[13]

But this is a very negative motivation for national unity, and it must be asked whether fear of invasion can ever produce any lasting unity among people. P. B. Waite makes this point with reference to the Fenian raids:

Fenianism could not itself create a British American national identity. . . . The effects of the Fenian invasion were direct and immediate, but like all negative effects, once removed, the elements in North America tended to revert to their original state. [14]

Thus, to return to the original query as to what motivated the British colonies in North America to seek a union of some kind, one finds a generally negative and unstable set of attitudes toward Confederation in 1867. Apparently abandoned by the mother country and left prey to the military and economic might of the war-torn but brawny U.S., the British North American colonies turned in desperation to each other.

---

[12] D. V. Smiley, *The Canadian Political Nationality* (Methuen, Toronto, 1967), pp. 13-14.
[13] Ibid., p. 2.
[14] P. B. Waite, *The Life and Times of Confederation* (University of Toronto Press, Toronto, 1962), p. 281.

THE GENESIS OF FEDERAL UNION

Having described the hesitant and uncertain way in which the colonies finally reached an agreement that some form of union was desirable for British North America, let us deal with the forces and events that influenced the decision that the union should be federal in form. The social, economic, and ethnic diversity of the colonies made a unitary form of government, or legislative union as it was then called, completely unacceptable to the Maritimes and Quebec, although evidence indicates that Macdonald and many of his Upper Canadian colleagues preferred this alternative.[15] Quebec wished to preserve its unique linguistic and religious and cultural character, and the Maritimes wished to ensure that the peculiar economic needs of their region be provided for. All provinces wished to retain control over matters that would allow them to preserve their local character and institutions. Provincial autonomy, therefore, had to be protected within any form of British North American union before the Maritimes and Quebec would agree to it.

Given the obvious differences that existed among the founding provinces, the Fathers of Confederation realized that a legislative union was not a viable alternative for British North America. Furthermore, it was hoped that Prince Edward Island, British Columbia, Newfoundland, and the Northwest could subsequently be lured into the union of 1867, in which case the regional and economic diversity of Canada would increase rather than diminish. Even Sir John A. Macdonald recognized that there could be no union *a mare usque ad marem* unless the provinces were left some degree of local autonomy. It was therefore incumbent upon the Fathers of Confederation to work out a distribution of powers between the provinces and the federal government.

The alternative of an economic and military *alliance* of the British North American colonies was initially considered as a form of union which would go a long way toward solving the immediate problems of the 1860s. At both the Charlottetown and Quebec Conferences, a British North American customs union, or *Zollverein*, was suggested—an innocuous form of union which would leave the sovereignty of the members intact. Neither a customs union nor a military alliance, however, would have provided a permanent central decision-making body or a central enforcement mechanism. In other words, since there would be no derogation of the sovereignty of the signatories of the treaty or alliance, the alliance itself would be power-

---

[15] D. Creighton, *John A. Macdonald*, vol. 1, chs. 13, 14, and 15 *passim*.

less to enforce its own provisions. Furthermore, such a weak form of union would have been ineffectual in financing the joint defence and/or economic programs of the union. A project such as the Intercolonial Railway, for instance, would have been out of the question. Sir John A. Macdonald recognized the inadvisability of a customs union, and suggested that because of the potential economic conflicts between the colonies it would not be congenial to all its members: "It is impossible to have a *Zollverein*. We must continue to have hostile tariffs unless we have a political union."[16]

A second major disadvantage of any form of union less than political union is that it would lack permanence. Members would have the right to withdraw from it at any time if they felt that its terms were no longer advantageous. It was obvious that if the economic and military problems of British North America were to be solved, they would have to be dealt with continuously over a long period of time. It was not possible to find immediate cures for the ills of the colonies, and therefore a form of union that was not "for keeps" would not be acceptable.

The third drawback of a simple alliance of the British North American colonies was that an alliance is *functionally specific*. In other words, the terms of reference or functions of the alliance are set very specifically at the outset in such a way that new needs of the members of the alliance cannot be dealt with without renegotiating the original agreement. In a rapidly changing world, a form of union that could adapt itself quickly to the performance of new functions was viewed as imperative.

There were other objections to a non-political union, such as the fact that a mere alliance would not satisfy the need for Canada East and Canada West to be separated, and the legalistic point that colonies within the British Empire were not sovereign and therefore could not enter into alliances unilaterally, even with sister colonies. These objections were secondary, however, and could have been overcome had the notion of an economic and military alliance been otherwise acceptable.

A *confederal* union was also an alternative for the British North American colonies, but when this form of union was subjected to scrutiny it was recognized that a confederation[17] would provide only

---

[16] G. P. Browne, *Documents on the Confederation of British North America*, p. 96.

[17] The term "Confederation" when applied to the Canadian union of 1867 is a misnomer, for the form of government set up by the BNA Act is definitely not confederal. " 'Confederation,' a word normally associated with the absence of a strong federal government, was deliberately misused by those who, in fact, intended to create one in an effort to confuse those who might find such a project alarming," (G. Stevenson, *Unfulfilled Union*, p. 9).

a slightly higher level of political integration than an alliance. A confederation is a union of sovereign states which features a permanent central decision-making body, or congress, to which the members of the confederation send delegates. In terms of the functions with which it deals, a confederation is considerably broader than an alliance, for the central congress is empowered to make decisions concerning a very wide range of subjects. The weakness of a confederation is that, as with an alliance, there is no transfer of sovereignty from the member states to the central congress. While empowered to make decisions, the congress is given no power to enforce them, and the members of the confederation can, if they choose, refuse to comply with any decision with which they disagree. The parties to a confederal agreement also have the right to secede from the union if they feel that its terms of reference no longer provide sufficient benefits. Thus, while the confederal form of union is functionally more diffuse than an alliance, it suffers from many of the same faults. Furthermore, the example of the United States under the Articles of Confederation in the 1780s, with the chaotic condition of government during that period, gave the Fathers of Confederation ample cause for avoiding that particular form of union.

A *federal* form of union was ultimately decided upon by the Fathers of Confederation because, unlike either an alliance or a confederal union, it vested real powers in the hands of a central decision-making body, the federal parliament. In a federal system, sovereignty is divided between the provinces and the federal parliament, and the exercise of legislative and executive powers of each is limited to subject matters allotted to them by the constitution. A federal system is also permanent in the sense that the member states or provinces do not have the constitutional right to withdraw unilaterally from the union. This prohibition might, of course, be swept aside very quickly if the people of a member state or province were determined to secede from the union. In law, however, a federal union is indivisible.

The constitution of the federal system distributes the power and the responsibility for the authoritative allocation of resources between the provinces and the federal government, and that constitutional distribution of powers is exhaustive (with the possible exception of certain basic rights and freedoms which may be entrenched in the constitution).[18] In a confederal union, on the other hand, it is simply assumed that the state or provincial governments have the responsibility for everything except a few matters that are specifically the

---

[18] See Chapter 7.

responsibility of the confederation. In other words, in the case of a confederation, the *residual power* is always left with the states and constitutes a very large area of jurisdiction, whereas in the case of a federal system, the residual power can be left with either the provinces or the federal government and the residual area of jurisdiction is, in fact, very small. The advantage of such a comprehensive definition of the powers and responsibilities of government is that the element of uncertainty is eliminated. The federal government and the provincial or state governments are each in possession of exclusive and sovereign powers which cannot be encroached upon by the other level of government. Unlike the central congress in a confederal union, the national government in a federal union has the authority to make some decisions which are binding on the citizens of the member states, and furthermore, it is granted the power to enforce them.

Finally, a federal form of government was adopted by the Fathers of Confederation because they hoped to create a union that would eventually become more than a marriage of economic expedience and military convenience. People like Sir John A. Macdonald wished to create a new political community in North America, and it is largely to their credit that Canada has evolved as more than merely a temporary association of friendly but independent neighbours.

That Canada exists today is probably the result of the effort and determination of Sir John A. Macdonald more than any other man. . . . It was he who provided the most determined leadership and who went on after the political framework of federation was accomplished to endow Canada with . . . nationhood. [19]

Thus, the fact that the form of union ultimately selected by the Fathers of Confederation was federal and not confederal was to a large part due to the political genius, vision, and ambition of Macdonald. The actual shape of our federal system and the idiosyncrasies that make Canadian federalism a genre apart also bear the stamp of Macdonald's personality and his view of the ideal relationship that should exist between the provinces and the national government in a federal system.

Having in mind the then recent and tragic experiences of the Civil War in the United States, Macdonald wanted to see as centralized a federal system as the provinces would accept: "We should concentrate the power in the federal government and not adopt the decentralization of the United States." [20] In fact, there is some evidence that

[19] Paul Martin, *Hansard*, Wednesday, January 11, 1967, p. 11651.
[20] G. P. Browne, *Documents on the Confederation of British North America*, p. 124.

Macdonald viewed federalism as a temporary arrangement to secure initial unity, and that he fully expected provincial governments to wither away from lack of exercise, leaving a basically unitary system in Canada. Some aspects of the BNA Act, 1867, do indeed indicate that the intention of the drafters of the Act was to leave the preponderance of legislative power with Ottawa. But in spite of these biases, the British North America Act does vest some significant legislative power in the provinces. One eminent political scientist has asserted: "The provinces are of equal constitutional power and status, and they operate without any serious interference from the Dominion. . . . Provincial powers are as full and complete as those of the Dominion within the areas allotted by the BNA Act."[21]

It is now necessary to turn our attention to a consideration of the federal distribution of powers in 1867 as a base point for a subsequent analysis of the evolution of the Canadian federal system.

THE DISTRIBUTION OF POWERS: CANADIAN FEDERALISM IN 1867

The legislative powers of the federal parliament are, for the most part, defined in Section 91 of the BNA Act, 1867. Section 91 is in two parts. The first part of the section is a broad and general grant of power, giving parliament the authority to make laws for "the Peace, Order, and Good Government of Canada in relation to all Matters not coming within the Classes of Subjects by this Act assigned exclusively to the Legislatures of the Provinces." The second part of the section included 29 (now 31) enumerated matters such as "the Public Debt and Property," "the Regulation of Trade and Commerce," "the Raising of Money by any Mode or System of Taxation," etc. which were intended "for greater Certainty, but not so as to restrict the Generality of the foregoing Terms of this Section."

The legislative powers of the provinces are for the most part set out in Section 92 of the Act, which has the appearance of being a far less complicated section than is 91. Section 92 does not begin with any comprehensive grant of power to the provinces, but simply states that, "In each Province, the Legislature may exclusively make Laws in relation to Matters coming within the Classes of Subjects next herein-after enumerated," and then proceeds to list sixteen matters such as "Direct Taxation within the Province in order to the raising of a Revenue for Provincial Purposes," "the Solemnization of Marriage

[21] R. M. Dawson, *The Government of Canada,* p. 78.

in the Province," "Property and Civil Rights in the Province," and "Generally all Matters of a merely local or private Nature in the Province." Thus, when Sections 91 and 92 are read together it is clear that the intention is to give the federal government a comprehensive power to make law and then to except from this general grant certain carefully specified powers which are to be retained by provincial legislatures.[22]

Section 95 established concurrent federal-provincial powers in matters of agriculture and immigration, and amendments to the Act in 1951 and 1964 added a third concurrent power in the area of pensions. While establishing the right of both levels of government to make laws with regards to the specified subjects, the section establishes federal *paramountcy* in the case of conflicting legislation dealing with agriculture and immigration:

Any Law of the Legislature of a Province relative to Agriculture or to Immigration shall have effect in and for the Province as long and as far only as it is not repugnant to any Act of the Parliament of Canada.

However, in the area of pensions, while the federal government is given the power to

. . . make laws in relation to old age pensions and supplementary benefits including survivor's and disability benefits irrespective of age . . . (Section 94A, BNA Act 1964, 12-13 Eliz. II, C. 73 (U.K.)),

in this case provincial legislation is to be paramount.

The subject of education is normally considered to rest within the exclusive jurisdiction of the provincial legislatures by Section 93 of the Act. However, Section 93 places certain limitations and conditions on the exercise of this power by the provinces. First, it states that no provincial law shall "prejudicially affect any right or privilege with respect to denominational schools" that existed at the time of union. Secondly, it states that the rights of separate schools in Upper Canada shall continue after the union and shall apply equally to Protestant separate schools in Lower Canada. The third clause of Section 93 establishes a right of appeal to the Governor General in Council if the education rights of a Protestant or Catholic minority are abrogated by a provincial legislature. Finally, in the event that the province does not respond positively to an appeal which is allowed by the Governor General in Council, provision is made for the parliament of Canada to "make remedial Laws for the due Execution of the Provisions of this

---

[22] The manner in which the Judicial Committee of the Privy Council interpreted these sections will be discussed in the next part of this chapter.

Section."[23] The significance of this section of the BNA Act is that it makes the federal government a "policeman" with the power and the responsibility to protect the education rights of religious minorities from encroachment by the provinces. This has proved an awkward burden for the federal government to bear, from time to time, for in protecting the rights of a minority, the federal government is forced to interfere with the autonomy of the provinces. If the federal government doesn't act it is damned by the minority concerned, and if it does, it is damned by the province concerned. We have already seen that one such dilemma, commonly referred to as the "Manitoba Schools Question," played a significant role in the downfall of the Conservative government in the election of 1896.[24] More recently Bill 101 (1977), Quebec legislation restricting the access of non-French-speaking residents of Quebec to English language education, posed a somewhat similar dilemma for the federal government. However, by now the tradition of federal non-intervention in areas of provincial jurisdiction is so well established that federal action was never contemplated. In any event, the constitutional protection is for *religious* education rights rather than the *linguistic* rights most directly involved in the Bill 101 case.

Finally, by Section 109 the provinces are granted full title to "all Lands, Mines, Minerals, and Royalties" within their boundaries, a concession that was not viewed as very important in the pre-petroleum era. When the Western provinces came into the federation the title to Crown lands was retained by the federal Crown until provincial pressures forced Ottawa to give them up in 1930. This control over Crown land and therefore over non-renewable natural resources has proven to be one of the major foundations of "province building" in the twentieth century, and has been the major source of provincial power since World War II.

A specific grant of federal legislative competence is specified by Section 132, which states that the Parliament of Canada

> . . . *shall have all Powers necessary or proper for performing the Obligations of Canada or any Province thereof as Part of the British Empire towards Foreign Countries arising under Treaties between the Empire and such Foreign Countries.*

This particular clause and the manner in which the courts have interpreted it will be discussed at greater length below.

Finally, to round out this "snapshot" of Canadian federalism at the time of Confederation, the federal government's power over the

---

[23] BNA Act, S. 93(4).
[24] See Chapter 3.

legislatures of the provinces contained in the *reservation* and *disallowance* provisions of the BNA Act must be mentioned. The power formally vested in the central government by these provisions amounts to a federal veto that may be applied to any act of the provincial legislatures. Through the Lieutenant-Governor of the province, who was to function relative to the Governor General as the pre-Confederation colonial governor functioned relative to the British government, it was intended that the federal government would be enabled to keep a tight reign on all provincial legislation. The Lieutenant-Governor has the power to reserve a bill "for the pleasure of the Governor General in Council" after which, if no positive action is taken by the federal official, the bill is dead. In the case of the disallowance power, the federal government can unilaterally invalidate any provincial law within a year of its passage. These powers, the reservation and disallowance, were used extensively before the turn of the century and then intermittently until the forties when the last disallowance was recorded. Today, they have become vestigial appendages in a federal system that has evolved past the stage where such heavy-handed devices are politically feasible.

Thus, the Canadian federal system at Confederation gave the lion's share of the legislative power to the federal government, established the principle of federal paramountcy in areas of concurrent jurisdiction, set up the federal government as a policeman in the area of the educational rights of religious minorities, and, just to make sure nothing had been forgotten, gave the federal government a veto power over all provincial enactments.

Had the spirit of the BNA Act of 1867 been upheld in subsequent judicial decisions, our federal system would look very different than it does today. However, that spirit was not upheld. To see the results, let us trace the development of Canadian federalism from its beginning as a highly centralized form of union to the form it takes today.

THE EVOLUTION OF CANADIAN FEDERALISM

The literature of Canadian constitutional law is replete with articles on the interpretation of Sections 91 and 92 of the BNA Act by the Judicial Committee of the Privy Council. Some commentators approve and others strongly disapprove,[25] but virtually all are agreed

---

[25] See, for instance, Kennedy, "Interpretation of the BNA Act," *Cambridge Law Journal*, vol. 8, p. 146, 1963; Macdonald, "The Constitution in a Changing World," *Canadian Bar Review*, vol. 26, p. 21, 1948; O'Connor, *Report to the Senate of Canada on the BNA Act*, annex 1, p. 25, 1939; Bora Laskin, "Peace, Order, and Good Government Reex-

that, in the process of interpreting the Act, the Judicial Committee significantly altered its effect. From the highly centralist document of 1867, the British North America Act was transformed by the incremental process of judicial review into a more truly federal constitution which vests extensive legislative authority in the hands of the provinces. All of this was accomplished by a succession of British "law lords" who took upon themselves the task of defending provincial autonomy at some cost to the English language, which had to be tortured until it met their requirements. In order to "beef up" the legislative competence of the provinces, the Judicial Committee developed certain principles of interpretation which explain the often puzzling construction placed on the crucial Sections 91 and 92.

The Erosion of the Federal Power

The thin edge of the wedge that opened the way for a provincial rights interpretation of Sections 91 and 92 was the series of Privy Council opinions which separated the peace, order, and good government clause of Section 91 from the twenty-nine enumerated subheadings of that section. This principle was initially conceived by Sir Montague Smith in the *Parsons* case in 1881,[26] and re-emphasized by Lord Watson in the *Local Prohibition* case (1896).[27] Lord Watson went a step further, placing the general part of Section 91 in a position secondary and subordinate to the enumerated subheads of both Sections 91 and 92:

The exercise of legislative power by the parliament of Canada, in regard to all matters not enumerated in s. 91, ought to be strictly confined to such matters as are unquestionably of Canadian interest and importance, and ought not to trench upon provincial legislation with respect to any of the classes of subjects enumerated in s. 92. To attach any other construction to the general power which in supplement of its enumerated powers is conferred upon the parliament of Canada by s. 91 would, in their Lordships' opinion, not only be contrary to the intendment of the act but would practically destroy the autonomy of the provinces. If it were once conceded that the parliament of Canada has authority to make laws applicable to the whole Dominion in relation to matters which in each province are substantially of local or private interest, upon the assumption that these matters also concern the peace, order and good government of the Dominion, there is hardly a subject enumerated in s. 92 upon which it might not legislate to the exclusion of the provincial legislatures.[28]

---

amined," in Lederman, *The Courts and the Canadian Constitution* (Carleton Library, McClelland and Stewart, Toronto, 1964), p. 66n. The best single article on the subject for political scientists is Alan Cairns's "The Judicial Committee and Its Critics," *Canadian Journal of Political Science*, IV. Sept. 1971. pp. 301-345.

[26] *Citizens Insurance Company of Canada v. Parsons*, 7 Appeal Cases (A.C.) 96.

[27] *Attorney-General for Ontario v. Attorney-General of Canada* [1896] A.C. 348.

[28] Ibid., p. 360.

Thus, by 1896 Section 91 had been interpreted by the Judicial Committee of the Privy Council in such a way that the once proud peace, order, and good government clause gave no exclusive jurisdiction to the federal parliament, but rather only a residual power that permitted federal legislation with regard to a few matters that could be found neither in the enumerated subheads of Section 91 nor in Section 92. The federal parliament now enjoyed exclusive jurisdiction only with regard to matters that came under the enumerated subheads of Section 91, despite the fact that the drafters of the BNA Act had anticipated that the general grant of authority at the beginning of Section 91 would put the largest part of the responsibilities of government in the hands of the central parliament.[29]

This narrow construction of the peace, order, and good government clause evolved in spite of the fact that there were earlier decisions which upheld the more generous view of this clause. In the *Russell v. the Queen* decision in 1882, federal legislation that provided for local prohibition subject to local option was upheld by the Judicial Committee on the grounds that liquor control was a subject matter not enumerated in Section 92 and therefore the federal parliament had jurisdiction through the peace, order, and good government clause. Had the principles of interpretation that were employed in this case been followed in subsequent cases, the federal power to pass laws for the peace, order, and good government of Canada might have developed along the lines anticipated by the Fathers of Confederation. However, this was not to be.

In 1883, in a decision that involved the power of the provinces to regulate the liquor trade, their lordships invented another canon of interpretation which has come to be known as the *aspect doctrine*.[30] In the case in point, the appellant was fined for an offence under an Ontario Act which regulated liquor traffic in the province. He argued that the conviction was invalid because the regulation of the traffic of liquor was a federal matter that concerned the peace, order, and good government of Canada, and he cited the *Russell* case as a precedent. In delivering the judgment of the Judicial Committee, Lord Fitzgerald held that the Ontario act was *intra vires* because it involved matters

---

[29] The argument here is very complicated and it hinges on the way in which one construes the closing words of Section 91: "and any matter coming within any of the classes of subjects enumerated in this section shall not be deemed to come within the class of matters of a local or private matter comprised in the enumeration of the classes of subjects by this act assigned exclusively to the legislatures of the Provinces." The best discussion can be found in Bora Laskin, *Canadian Constitutional Law*, second edition (Carswell, Toronto, 1960), pp. 65-75.

[30] *Hodge v. the Queen* (1883), 9 A.C. 117.

which are clearly enumerated in Section 92. He went on to state that the *Russell* case did not apply because the federal legislation that was validated in that decision involved another aspect of the regulation of the liquor traffic: "Subjects which in one aspect and for one purpose fall within section 92, may in another aspect and for another purpose fall within section 91."[31] In this way, with the birth of the aspect doctrine, the tide was turned, and the decision in the *Russell* case never did gain the respectability as a precedent that would have ensured expansion of the federal power through the peace, order, and good government clause.

The Judicial Committee of the Privy Council continued to whittle away at the introductory words of Section 91 and to reduce further the significance of the *Russell* decision. In a 1916 case, Viscount Haldane, who was to become renowned for his championing of provincial rights, and for his imaginative interpretation of Section 91, attempted to summarize the relevance of the peace, order, and good government clause at that time:

It must be taken to be now settled that the general authority to make laws for the peace, order and good government of Canada, which the initial part of Section 91 of the BNA Act confers, does not, unless the subject matter of legislation falls within some one of the enumerated heads which follow, enable the Dominion Parliament to trench on the subject matters entrusted to the provincial legislatures by the enumeration in s. 92. There is only one case outside the heads enumerated in s. 91 which the Dominion Parliament can legislate effectively as regards a province and that is where the subject matter lies outside all of the subject matters enumeratively entrusted to the province under s. 92. Russell v. the Queen is an instance of such a case.[32]

Not yet satisfied that peace, order, and good government and the *Russell* case were dead issues, Viscount Haldane continued to attack them in a series of cases in the 1920s. In the *Board of Commerce* case in 1922, he admitted that the peace, order, and good government clause might be used as a justification for federal encroachments on matters enumerated in Section 92, but only in extreme circumstances such as war or famine: "Circumstances are conceivable, such as those of war or famine, when the peace, order and good government of the Dominion might be imperilled."[33]

A year later, Haldane reinterpreted the peace, order, and good government clause as purely an emergency power, to be used in

---

[31] Ibid. See also Laskin, *Canadian Constitutional Law*, second edition, p. 79.

[32] *Attorney-General for Canada v. Attorney-General for Alberta*, [1916] I.A.C. 588; 26 D.L.R. 288.

[33] In *Re the Board of Commerce Act and the Combines and Fair Prices Act, 1919*, [1922] D.L.R. 513.

times of national crisis: "In a sufficiently great emergency such as that arising out of war, there is implied the power to deal adequately with that emergency for the safety of the Dominion as a whole."[34]

Utilizing this fully developed interpretation of the peace, order, and good government clause as an emergency power, Viscount Haldane went on to dispatch the decision of the *Russell* case once and for all, in what is perhaps the most unusual judicial dictum in the history of Canadian constitutional law:

Their Lordships think that the decision in Russell v. the Queen *can only be supported today . . . on the assumption of the Board, apparently made at the time of deciding the case of* Russell v. the Queen, *that the evil of intemperance at that time amounted to one so great and so general that at least for the period, it was a menace to the national life of Canada, so serious and pressing that the Parliament of Canada was called upon to intervene to protect the nation from disaster. An epidemic of pestilence might conceivably have been regarded as analogous.*[35]

To summarize, having virtually emasculated the peace, order, and good government clause in cases before the 1920s, the Judicial Committee then reinterpreted it as an emergency power. According to three decisions in the 1920s, the *Board of Commerce* case, the *Fort Frances* case, and the *Snider* case, the federal government could make laws for the peace, order, and good government of Canada with regard to matters that would come *prima facie* within the powers of the provincial legislatures, but only if a national emergency required it.

In the *Fort Frances* case,[36] the Judicial Committee of the Privy Council allowed that the federal government should be given the full benefit of the doubt in determining when a national emergency existed and when the state of emergency had ceased to exist. This power was extended to the federal government during both world wars when parliament vested significant powers in the federal executive through the War Measures Act. The Privy Council was not so generous, however, when the federal parliament attempted to implement a series of welfare measures, usually referred to as the Bennett "New Deal." In

---

[34]*Fort Frances Pulp and Power Co. Ltd. v. Manitoba Free Press Co. Ltd.*, [1923] 3 D.L.R. 629.

[35] *Toronto Electric Commissioners v. Snider*, [1925] 2 D.L.R. 5; also in Laskin, *Canadian Constitutional Law*, second edition, p. 241. In defense of Haldane it is possible that Canadian consumption of firewater in the 1870s was alarmingly high; O. J. Firestone, *Canadian Economic Development 1867-1953* (Bowes and Bowes London, 1958) cites the per capita consumption of spirits as 1.58 gals. in 1871 and only .59 gal. in abstemious 1951. See also, Robinson J. "Lord Haldane and the BNA Act," *U. of T. Law Journal*, XX, 1970, pp. 55-69; XXI 1971, pp. 175-251.

[36] [1923] 3 D.L.R. 1629.

the reference case that tested the validity of these measures, their Lordships refused to agree that the economic hardships of the Depression constituted a national emergency, largely because the federal government, for political reasons, had not formally declared in the legislation that one existed, and the entire legislative package was declared *ultra vires* the federal parliament.[37] Thus, after approximately fifty years of interpretation by the Judicial Committee of the Privy Council, the opening words of Section 91 had been transformed from a general and comprehensive grant of legislative competence to the federal parliament, to a grant of temporary federal power in times of national emergency. Furthermore, in fifty years of judicial review their Lordships had construed only two events as national emergencies—World War I and an "epidemic of intemperance" in the 1870s.

At a very early point in the evolution of Canadian federalism, it became clear that the Judicial Committee of the Privy Council was willing to admit exclusive federal powers with regard only to subject matters *enumerated* in Section 91. Accepting this setback, the federal authorities proceeded to try to find justification for federal legislation within the various subheads of that section. The one which seemed most comprehensive and which the federal authorities hoped would replace the legislative competence lost with the narrowing of the peace, order, and good government clause, was 91(2), "the Regulation of Trade and Commerce." In two early judgments in the Supreme Court of Canada,[38] Section 91(2) was interpreted not only as a very broad but also as an exclusive power of the Dominion. The Canadian judges, at least at the outset, seemed willing to view the regulation of trade and commerce as a comprehensive grant of power that might extend even to the regulation of trade that was carried on within the boundaries of one province. In *Citizen's Insurance Co. v. Parsons*, however, both the Supreme Court of Canada and the Judicial Committee of the Privy Council placed a far more limited construction on the federal trade and commerce power.

The words "regulation of trade and commerce" in their unlimited sense are sufficiently wide, if uncontrolled by the context and other parts of the act, to include every regulation of trade ranging from political arrangements in regard to trade with foreign governments, requiring the sanction of Parliament, down to minute rules for regulating particular trades. But a consideration of the act shows that the words were not used in this unlimited sense. In the first place the collocation of No. 2 with classes of

---

[37] *Attorney-General for Canada v. Attorney-General for Ontario (Reference Re Unemployment and Social Insurance Act)*, [1937] A.C. 355; [1937] 1 D.L.R. 684; Olmsted, vol. 3, p. 207.

[38] *Severn v. The Queen*, [1878] S.C.R. 70; *Fredericton v. The Queen*, [1880] 3 S.C.R. 505.

subjects of national and general concern affords an indication that regulations relating to general trade and commerce were in the mind of the legislature when conferring this power on the Dominion Parliament. If the words had been intended to have the full scope of which in their literal meaning they are susceptible, the specific mention of several of the other classes of subjects enumerated in Section 91 would have been unnecessary; as, 15, banking; 17, weights and measures; 18, bills of exchange and promissory notes; 19, interest; and even 21, bankruptcy and insolvency. [39]

Briefly, therefore, the federal trade and commerce power was construed so as not to interfere with the provinces' power to "regulate contracts of a particular business or trade such as the business of fire insurance in a single province." [40]

In *Montreal v. Montreal Street Railway* (1912), Lord Atkinson argued against broader interpretation of the federal trade and commerce power on the grounds that "taken in their widest sense, these words would authorize legislation by the Parliament of Canada in respect of several of the matters specifically enumerated in s. 92 and would seriously encroach upon the autonomy of the province." [41] This is notable partly because it is the same argument used by Lord Watson to justify his restrictive interpretation of the peace, order, and good government clause in the *Local Prohibition* case. While both the "collocation argument" and the "provincial autonomy argument" produced inflexibility in determining the scope of the federal trade and commerce power, [42] it took the imagination of Viscount Haldane in the *Board of Commerce* case and the *Snider* case to defuse completely the federal power. In the former decision, Haldane queried:

Must not it be taken that since the 1896 case, at all events, perhaps earlier, subs. 2 of s. 91 must be taken as containing merely ancillary powers? A power that can be exercised so as to interfere with a provincial right only if there is some paramount Dominion purpose as to which they are applicable. [43]

and in the latter, he summed up the position of the trade and commerce power, concluding that:

It must now be taken that the authority to legislate for the regulation of trade and commerce does not extend to the regulation for instance, by a licensing system, of a particular trade in which Canadians would otherwise be free to engage in the provinces. It

---

[39] Bora Laskin, *Canadian Constitutional Law*, third edition (Carswell, Toronto, 1969), p. 303.

[40] Laskin, *Canadian Constitutional Law*, second edition, p. 302.

[41] *Montreal v. Montreal Street Railway*, [1912] 1 D.L.R. 681, at p. 687. See also Laskin, *Canadian Constitutional Law*, second edition, p. 306.

[42] Laskin, *Canadian Constitutional Law*, second edition, p. 314.

[43] Quoted in Laskin, *Canadian Constitutional Law*, second edition, pp. 312-313 ([1922] 1 A.C. 191).

is, in their Lordships' opinion, now clear that, excepting so far as the power can be invoked in aid of capacity conferred independently under other words in s. 91, the power to regulate trade and commerce cannot be relied on as enabling the Dominion Parliament to regulate civil rights in the province. [44]

In this fashion, Viscount Haldane reduced the federal trade and commerce power to a "merely ancillary" power that was only relevant "in aid of" some other subhead of Section 91. Furthermore, it seems that the only aspect of trade and commerce that could be regulated by the federal government was international and/or interprovincial trade. As with the federal peace, order, and good government power, the trade and commerce power had, courtesy of Viscount Haldane, been reduced to a mere shadow of what the Fathers of Confederation had intended it to be.

In the decade after the *Snider* case, there was a partial retreat from the restrictive Haldane view of both these parts of Section 91. *In Proprietary Articles Trade Association v. Attorney-General for Canada* (the *P.A.T.A.* case), Lord Atkin gave back some respectability to the trade and commerce clause by disassociating their Lordships from the decision in the *Board of Commerce* case:

Their Lordships merely propose to disassociate themselves from the construction suggested in argument from a passage in the Judgement of the Board of Commerce case, [1922] 1 A.C. 191, 198, under which it was contended that the power to regulate trade and commerce could be invoked only in furtherance of a general power which Parliament possessed independently of it. No such restriction is properly to be inferred from that judgement. [45]

In a similar fashion, when called upon by the appellant in a 1946 case to find that the *Russell* case had been wrongly decided, Viscount Simon held that the decision in the *Russell* case should stand, and he was furthermore severely critical of the emergency power interpretation of the peace, order, and good government clause in the *Board of Commerce*, *Fort Frances* and *Snider* cases. [46] Despite these decisions, however, the damage had already been done and while, as we shall see later, other cases, particularly since the abolition of appeals to the Judicial Committee of the Privy Council in 1949, [47] may indicate the possibility of a slightly less restrictive interpretation of the federal

---

[44] Laskin, *Canadian Constitutional Law*, second edition, pp. 313-314.
[45] Laskin, *Canadian Constitutional Law*, second edition. p. 314 ([1931] 2 D.L.R. 1).
[46] *Attorney-General for Ontario v. Canada Temperance Federation*, [1946] 2 D.L.R. 1.
[47] *Attorney-General for Ontario v. Attorney-General for Canada (Reference Re Abolition of Appeals to the JCPC)*, [1947] A.C. 127.

power in the future,[48] the constitutional ground rules of Canadian federalism were likely fairly firmly established by 1925. If, therefore, much of the power that the Fathers of Confederation conceived as federal was taken away from the federal parliament, it is time to consider where that power was transferred.

Section 92(13) reads, "Property and Civil Rights in the Province" and it was intended as merely one of the sixteen subheads of Section 92. The Judicial Committee of the Privy Council, however, chose to interpret the words of this subhead in their widest connotation. They were deemed to include such things as contracts, contractual rights, and civil rights in its broadest interpretation, that is, including almost every aspect of all subject matters that are not specifically interprovincial and/or international in their scope. By construing Section 92(13) in its widest sense and by strictly limiting the interpretation of the more general sections of Section 91, the Judicial Committee transformed the property and civil rights clause into the *de facto* residual clause of the BNA Act.[49] Thus the general grant of power in the opening words of Section 91 was transferred from the federal parliament to the provincial legislatures, with the result that, fifty years after Confederation, the face of Canadian federalism would have been unrecognizable to the men who created it.

One enumerated federal power that was permitted to encroach upon subject matters that are *prima facie* covered by this wide interpretation of Section 92(13) is Section 91(27), the Dominion *criminal law power*. The competence of the federal parliament to encroach upon the area of "Property and Civil Rights in the Province" when legislating with regard to criminal law was at first questioned, particularly by Viscount Haldane, who argued that the Dominion could not create a crime where the subject matter did not by its very nature belong to "the domain of criminal jurisprudence."[50] In the *P.A.T.A.* case, mentioned above, the Judicial Committee of the Privy Council disassociated itself from the restrictive Haldane interpretation and admitted that the federal government could, in fact, declare an act to be criminal even if it has not in the past been considered so.[51] The only limitation on this federal power to declare a certain act or category of acts criminal is "the condition that parliament shall not in the guise of enacting criminal legislation in truth and in substance encroach on

---

[48] E.g., *Pronto Uranium Mine v. O.L.R.B.* et al. (1956), 5 D.L.R. (2d) 342.
[49] Royal Commission on Dominion-Provincial Relations, *Report (Rowell-Sirois Report)* (Queen's Printer, Ottawa, 1954), Book 1, p. 247.
[50] The *"Board of Commerce* case," in Laskin, *Canadian Constitutional Law*, p. 282.
[51] *Proprietary Articles Trade Association v. Attorney-General for Canada*, [1931] 2 D.L.R. 1; A.C. 310.

any of the classes of subjects enumerated in section 92."[52] Thus, the criminal law power of the federal parliament, while not to be used merely to secure entry into a field of legislation that is in pith and substance provincial, can properly encroach upon the powers of the provincial legislatures if such an encroachment is truly incidental to the achievement of a genuine federal purpose.

Before concluding this section of the chapter, mention should be made of one section of the BNA Act which affects the federal–provincial distribution of powers and which became a bone of contention in the 1930s. Section 132 defines the federal treaty-making power. Essentially, this section means that in the implementation of British Empire treaties to which Canada is a signatory, the distribution of powers in Sections 91 and 92 is inoperative, and the federal parliament possesses exclusive authority over all subject matters. In the *Aeronautics* case of 1932,[53] the JCPC held that federal legislation dealing with the regulation and control of aeronautics was *intra vires* because it had been passed to implement the provisions of a treaty that Canada had signed as a member of the British Empire. (While Lord Sankey went on to say that the legislation affected matters that "attained such dimensions as to affect the body politic of the nation," and that it therefore would have been *intra vires* the federal parliament through the peace, order, and good government clause even if it had not been passed to implement a treaty, this part of the decision was an *obiter dictum*.)

The interpretation of this federal power did not come into question until Canada gained the right to enter into treaties with foreign countries, not as a member of the Empire but as an independent signatory. The federal authorities felt that the evolution of Canada's independent role in foreign relations could not have been foreseen by the Fathers of Confederation, and that, as a result, the full power that the federal parliament had possessed with regard to the implementation of Empire treaties should continue with regard to the implementation of treaties signed by Canada in her new international role.

The first real test of this came with the *Radio Reference* of 1932. Here the decision of the Judical Committee of the Privy Council as delivered by Viscount Dunedin basically supported the view of the federal government; namely, that although federal legislation to regulate and control radio communication was passed to implement a treaty that Canada had signed as an *independent* Dominion and not as a member

---

[52] *Attorney-General for British Columbia v. Attorney-General for Canada*, [1937] 1 D.L.R. 688, as quoted in Laskin, *Canadian Constitutional Law*, second edition. p. 284.
[53] *Re Aerial Navigation*, [1932] A.C. 54.

of the Empire, it amounted to the same thing: "In fine though agreeing that the convention was not a treaty as is defined in s. 132, their lordships think that it comes to the same thing," ([1932] A.C. 304, at p. 313). The reasoning of the JCPC in this instance was that because the matter of Empire treaty implementation was dealt with as a separate subject and not included in either Section 91 or 92, and that the notion of Canada functioning as an independent Dominion was not conceivable in 1867, therefore the federal parliament should have the jurisdiction over Dominion treaty implementation through the general power for the peace, order, and good government of Canada. In other words the peace, order, and good government clause was operative as a "residuary" clause in the case of treaty implementation.

However, while the decisions of the *Radio* and *Aeronautics* cases seemed to auger well for a broad interpretation of the federal power in treaty implementation and even gave a glimmer of hope for a restoration to respectability of the general power in Section 91, such was not to be the case. In a 1937 case dealing with federal legislation purporting to implement Labour Conventions passed by the International Labour Organization of which Canada was a member, Lord Atkin effectively reversed the judgment of Dunedin in the *Radio* case. That the federal executive possessed the full power to *make* treaties with foreign countries was never seriously questioned. However, their Lordships held that the power to sign such treaties does not give the federal parliament the unfettered right to pass laws implementing them in Canada:

There is no existing constitutional ground for stretching the competence of the Dominion Parliament so that it becomes enlarged to keep pace with enlarged functions of the Dominion executive. . . . The Dominion cannot, merely by making promises to foreign countries, clothe itself with legislative authority inconsistent with the constitution which gave it birth.[54]

The Judicial Committee went on to point out that "in totality of legislative powers," the provincial legislatures and the federal parliament can, together, pass laws implementing any treaty signed by the federal executive. The fact, however, that the legislation happens to be necessary to implement a treaty does not alter the constitutional distribution of powers in Sections 91 and 92: "While the ship of state now sails on larger ventures and into foreign waters she still retains the watertight compartments which are an essential part of her original structure."[55]

---

[54] "*Labour Conventions* case," 1937, as quoted in Laskin. *Canadian Constitutional Law*, second edition, p. 286.
[55] Ibid.

It can be seen from what has been said in the past several pages that the interpretation of the BNA Act, specifically the interpretation of Sections 91 and 92 had achieved a major alteration in the relationship of the provinces to the federal parliament, up to the time when appeals to the Judicial Committee were abolished in 1949. The clear intention of the Fathers of Confederation had been to leave the provinces as relatively insignificant entities, in the possession of relatively modest legislative powers. The Judicial Committee of the Privy Council, however, according to the tradition of the British legal system, took a passive attitude to the interpretation of the BNA Act. In short, they sought to construe the terms of the Act literally, with little regard for either the intentions of the men who had drafted it, or current political opinion. Based on this principle of a literal construction of the BNA Act, if a specific matter of a particular piece of legislation came *prima facie* under one of the subheads of Section 91, then without question it was within the exclusive jurisdiction of the Dominion parliament. Secondly, if the subject matter came under one of the subheads of Section 92, the federal parliament was still the paramount authority as long as the subject was also covered by one of the enumerated subheads in Section 91. Moreover, if the jurisdiction was *shared* either could legislate in the area with the provision that if both levels of government occupied the *same* jurisdictional space, the federal laws would be unquestionably *paramount*. Thirdly, the provincial authority to make laws with respect to property and civil rights in the province,[56] was construed very broadly while the federal enumerated powers were, for the most part, construed narrowly, with the result that in the case of any doubt as to the proper location of a particular subject matter, it was, more often than not, given to the provinces. The only exception to this rule was deemed to exist in times of national emergency, when the federal power to make laws for the peace, order, and good government of Canada might permit federal encroachments on normally provincial matters. Finally, if a subject matter could not be located either among the enumerated subheads of Section 91 or within Section 92, then it came within the jurisdiction of the federal parliament through the peace, order, and good government clause as a *residuary power*.[57]

---

[56] BNA Act, S. 92(13).

[57] Cases such as this have been few and far between. The only example that comes to mind is the *Radio Reference* case in 1932. It is necessary to note, however, that even in this case there were other reasons cited for the decision. See *Reference Re Regulation and Control of Radio Communications*, [1932] 2 D.L.R. 81; Laskin, *Canadian Constitutional Law*, second edition, pp. 267-269. In fact one of the reasons for upholding federal jurisdiction was that radio communication devices could be viewed as analogous to "telegraphs" which are defined as "works or undertakings" *excluded* from provincial jurisdiction by Section 92, 10(a).

It is tempting, at this point in our analysis of the evolution of the federal-provincial distribution of powers, to pass judgment on the manner in which the Judicial Committee of the Privy Council "rewrote our constitution." However, in order to come to any verdict as to the culpability of their Lordships, it would be necessary to assume that the BNA Act as drafted in 1867 was itself beyond criticism. Clearly this is not the case, for Sections 91 and 92 contain especially ambiguous phrases which lend themselves to various and often conflicting constructions. Questions which come to mind are: if the Fathers of Confederation saw the peace, order, and good government clause as a truly comprehensive grant of power, why did they confuse the issue by adding twenty-nine "examples"?; if they viewed the trade and commerce power as a broad grant of authority to the federal parliament, why did they proceed to "collocate" other subheads which related to trade and commerce?; and if they wanted the provinces to have a modest role in the government of Canada why did they give them the ambiguous power over property and civil rights in the province? Certainly, one can maintain that many of Viscount Haldane's judgments are puzzling, but it also must be admitted that the Act itself is not exactly airtight. The purpose of this analysis is not to praise or blame the Judicial Committee of the Privy Council for altering the intention of the BNA Act, but to describe the shape into which our federal system has been moulded.

The Supreme Court of Canada and the BNA Act, 1949-1980

Two things must be remembered in looking at the interpretation of the BNA Act since the abolition of appeals to the Judicial Committee of the Privy Council. First, it is often held mistakenly that the Judicial Committee's decisions normally overturned the decisions of the Supreme Court of Canada; while that did happen, in many cases the decision of the former, in fact, merely confirmed that of the latter. Secondly, it must be recognized that it is more difficult to be a creative jurist in an area of law that has been picked over and poked at by judges for something approaching eighty years. There are a lot of "givens," a lot of deeply entrenched canons of interpretation that severely hinder the "lawmaking space" of our more recent Supreme Court judges. Thus if anyone had expected the Supreme Court of Canada to immediately begin the dismantling of the "house that Watson, Haldane, et al. built" they would have been doomed to disappointment. While there have been some changes since 1949 and these bear elaboration, we could in no way have expected radical reversals of the basic interpretive doctrines that are the heritage of the Judicial Committee of the Privy Council.

In a 1952 decision, the Supreme Court of Canada essentially reaffirmed the decision in the *Aeronautics Reference* of thirty years earlier. In this instance, the issue was whether, in the course of zoning, a municipality might make regulations affecting airports.[58] The court decided that the subject matter involved was aeronautics and aerial navigation, and that the federal government has exclusive jurisdiction over such matters because they go beyond merely local or provincial concerns. As a precedent, a majority of the Supreme Court looked to Lord Sankey's *obiter dictum* in the *Aeronautics Reference,* that the subject of aeronautics and aerial navigation was of "national importance" and therefore within the exclusive domain of the federal parliament to make laws for the peace, order, and good government of Canada, even if such legislation incidentally interfered with areas of provincial jurisdiction such as civil rights and municipal institutions.

The same "national dimension" or "national concern" interpretation of the peace, order, and good government clause of Section 91 was used again in 1956 to give the federal parliament exclusive jurisdiction to make laws with respect to labour relations in the uranium industry.[59] The Ontario Supreme Court was unanimous in affirming that the uranium industry is a matter which by its very nature went beyond matters of merely local concern and therefore was within the exclusive domain of parliament.

While the centralist "cause" was the victor in these cases of the fifties there was little net gain in terms of federal jurisdiction nor was there any indication that the opening words of Section 91 were to be given a more liberal interpretation than they had received at the hands of the Judicial Committee. The "national dimension" test really goes back to Lord Watson in the *Local Prohibition* case of 1896 and was being applied in the *Johannesson* and *Pronto* cases in a fairly conservative manner. However some hope for a more liberal interpretation of the peace, order, and good government clause as an effective *residuary* power may have been kindled by a couple of more recent decisions.

In *Munro v. National Capital Commission,*[60] in 1966, the right of the federally established NCC to expropriate land in the Ottawa area in order to create a "Green Belt" around the national capital, was challenged on the grounds that the federal parliament did not have the legislative jurisdiction to grant the NCC the power to expropriate.

[58] *Johannesson v. West St. Paul,* [1952] 1 S.C.R. 292.
[59] *Pronto Uranium Mines v. OLRB* (1956), 5 D.L.R. (2d) 342.
[60] [1966] S.C.R. 663.

The Supreme Court mentioned that the matter of a national capital region was in fact a matter that went beyond local or provincial concerns but instead of relying on the national dimension aspect of the general power to give the federal parliament the jurisdiction, the court went on to state that the matter of a national capital was not enumerated within either Section 91 or 92 and that therefore the subject came within the *residuary* power of the federal parliament to make laws for the peace, order, and good government of Canada.

Similarly, in a 1974 case, involving the validity of the Official Languages Act,[61] the Supreme Court held that all aspects of the subject of official languages *not* covered by Sections 91(1) and 133 were within the federal parliament's jurisdiction because of the residuary power implied by the opening words of Section 91. However, again while the federal government clearly "won" these cases the gains in net legislative authority and also in freeing the peace, order, and good government clause from the canons of interpretation of the JCPC were still modest. The door had been opened slightly to a more liberal interpretation of the general words of Section 91, but it was going to take a positive and radical stroke of jurisprudence to actually break out.

The opportunity to finally break out of the Watson–Haldane approach came in 1976. In what one author has called "probably the Court's most heralded decision since it became Canada's final court of appeal,"[62] the federal government's controversial Anti-Inflation Act was held to be *intra vires*.[63] According to Peter Russell, the *AIB* case was

> . . . the first clear test of whether the Supreme Court would "liberate" the Federal Parliament's general power to make laws for the "peace, order and good government of Canada" from the shackles placed upon it by the Privy Council's jurisprudence and thereby provide the constitutional underpinnings for a revolutionary readjustment of the balance of power in Canadian federalism.[64]

Sadly, the court's verdict was, all in all, pretty tame. While the federal Anti-Inflation Act was upheld by a 7-2 decision in the Supreme Court, the *rationale* of the case was the Haldane "emergency doctrine" and the jurisdiction of the federal parliament was seen as temporary—to last only as long as the "economic crisis" of inflation continued to plague us. While a minority of the court felt that the

---

[61] *Jones v. A.G. Canada* (1974), 45 D.L.R. (3d) 583.
[62] P. Russell, "The Anti-Inflation Case: The Anatomy of a Constitutional Decision," *CPA*, Winter, 1977, p. 632.
[63] Russell, op. cit.
[64] *Reference Re Anti-Inflation Act* (1976), 68 D.L.R. (3d) 452.

legislation could be upheld permanently by utilizing the national dimension interpretation of the peace, order, and good government clause, a majority of the court either rejected this view or declined to comment on the point at all.

The only substantive gain for the centralist perspective in the *AIB* case therefore, was the admission of the court that the federal parliament does not have to *proclaim* the existence of a national emergency in order to justify legislation under the emergency doctrine. According to this test, the Bennett "New Deal" legislation of the 1930s that was rejected by the courts at that time might now be *intra vires* the federal parliament! As Peter Russell has put it:

Temporary federal legislation may be upheld on emergency grounds if federal lawyers can persuade the Court that there is not enough evidence to conclude that it would have been unreasonable for parliament to have regarded a matter as an urgent national crisis at the time it passed the legislation. Given the probable deference of most Supreme Court Justices to the judgement of Parliament, this is at least a small gain for federal authority. [65]

Thus while we can conclude that the Supreme Court of Canada has generally been willing to uphold federal legislation since 1949, the justices themselves have not been willing to radically expand the scope of the general authority granted to the federal parliament by the opening words of Section 91, beyond its broad dimensions as established by the Judicial Committee.

The generally conservative approach of the courts with respect to the peace, order, and good government clause has been maintained with respect to the federal trade and commerce power as well. The Judicial Committee had made the distinction between matters of interprovincial and international trade on the one hand and matters of intraprovincial trade on the other. In the fifties, the Supreme Court of Canada clarified the distinction without significantly altering the balance of power between the federal government and the provinces. In *Reference Re Farm Products Marketing Act (Ont.)*, [66] for instance, the court reiterated the necessity for federal-provincial cooperation in marketing schemes because of the extent to which interprovincial and intraprovincial trade are intertwined. In this case the court recognized that even though a transaction is entirely intraprovincial its regulation and control is not necessarily an exclusively provincial matter.

In *Murphy v. CPR* [67] the Canadian Wheat Board Act was declared to

---

[65] Ibid, 662.
[66] [1957] S.C.R. 198.
[67] [1958] S.C.R. 626.

be *intra vires* the federal parliament because it concerned international and interprovincial trade and in *R. v. Klassen*,[68] the Court of Appeal of Manitoba took the next step and affirmed the right of the Wheat Board to regulate intraprovincial transactions, as well, as being "necessarily incidental" to the regulation of the interprovincial and international aspects of marketing grain. However, these decisions have the effect of clarifying rather than expanding the federal power over trade and commerce and they in no way have expanded the scope of Section 91(2) beyond the limits set by the Judicial Committee of the Privy Council. In fact, in a 1968 case,[69] Quebec legislation aimed at regulating intraprovincial trade which affected interprovincial transactions was declared to be *intra vires* the province because the intention of the legislation was clearly intraprovincial and the interprovincial encroachments were only incidental. Thus because the *intent* was to do something within the province's jurisdiction, unless the law came into direct conflict with federal legislation, the Quebec law could stand.

The intent of the legislation or the aims of the legislators again became the critical variable in determining the scope of federal and provincial authority over marketing in *A.G. Manitoba v. Manitoba Egg and Poultry Association* (the so-called "Chicken and Egg case"),[70] and *Burns Foods Ltd. v. A.G. Manitoba*.[71] Here provincial legislation was declared *ultra vires* because purportedly local marketing schemes had as their primary object the restriction of imports from other provinces.

Finally, in a 1976 case, *Macdonald v. Vapour Canada*,[72] the Supreme Court found a section of the federal Trade Marks Act *ultra vires* because it was intended to regulate the conduct of local trades and to establish standards of fair competition in local business ventures. In deciding the case the Supreme Court went right back to the *dicta* of the Privy Council in the *Parsons* case of 1881 to reaffirm the point that 91(2) does not extend to the regulation of individual trades entirely within a single province.

To summarize, the scope of the federal power to regulate trade and commerce has not been expanded at all by the Canadian courts since 1949 and in fact the canons of interpretation that apply to this section of the BNA Act remain virtually as they were at the time of the *P.A.T.A.* case in 1931.[73]

---

[68] (1959), 20 D.L.R. (2d) 406.
[69] *Carnation Co. Ltd. v. Quebec Agricultural Marketing Board*, [1968] S.C.R. 238.
[70] [1971] S.C.R. 689.
[71] (1974), 40 D.L.R. (3d) 731.
[72] (1976), 66 D.L.R. (3d) 1.
[73] See page 253.

The scope of the criminal law power of the federal government, Section 91(27), has not altered significantly either since 1949. In a case in 1949,[74] Mr. Justice Rand attempted to establish a test for the legitimate scope of criminal law:

A crime is an act which the law, with appropriate penal sanctions, forbids; but as prohibitions are not enacted in a vacuum, we can properly look for some evil of injurious or undesirable effect upon the public against which the law is directed. That effect may be in relation to social, economic or political interests; and the legislature has in mind to suppress the evil or to safeguard the interest threatened.[75]

Then looking at a piece of legislation that prohibited the manufacture and sale of margarine and other butter substitutes and which the federal government was trying to justify as being within the scope of its criminal law power, Rand applied his test:

Is the prohibition then enacted with a view to a public purpose which can support it as being in relation to criminal law? Public peace, order, security, health, morality: these are the ordinary though not exclusive ends served by that (criminal) law but they do not appear to be the object of the parliamentary action here. That object, as I must find it, is economic.[76]

Mr. Justice Rand concluded that the federal legislation under the guise of creating a new crime was in fact merely trying to protect the dairy producers from competition from the butter substitute producers and the Supreme Court of Canada found the federal legislation to be *ultra vires*.

The *Birks* case[77] in 1955 and the *Padlock* case[78] in 1957 saw provincial legislation dealing with religious observance and freedom of expression respectively declared *ultra vires* on the grounds that these were matters relating to the criminal law and therefore within the exclusive purview of the federal parliament by virtue of Section 91(27). The irony of provincial encroachments on fundamental freedoms being overturned only because they were deemed to be within the exclusive domain of the federal government in criminal matters is worth noting, but the net effect has not been to enhance the federal power significantly. The effect of litigation since then has been simply to reaffirm the federal criminal law power as it has been since the early

---

[74] *Reference Re Validity of Section 5(a) of the Dairy Industry Act,* [1949] S.C.R. 1 (the *Margarine* case).

[75] Ibid., p. 49.

[76] Ibid., p. 50.

[77] *Birks v. Montreal and A.G. Quebec,* [1955] S.C.R. 799. See also the section on the protection of civil liberties in Canada in Chapter 7.

[78] *Switzman v. Elbling,* [1957] S.C.R. 285. See also the section on civil liberties in Canada in Chapter 7.

1950s. In sum, the Supreme Court has not expanded the criminal law power since 1949, even if Rand's "test" might have helped to clarify its scope.[79]

Conclusion: The Supreme Court and Canadian Federalism in the 1980s

As Peter Russell said in his analysis of the *AIB* case, the Supreme Court of Canada has not put Viscount Haldane "away in mothballs,"[80] but rather since it became the final court of appeal for Canada, the Supreme Court has maintained a very legalistic and conservative adherence to the precedents of the Judical Committee. Moreover while the court in the *AIB* case agreed on the *admissability* of non-legal "social science" evidence, a fact that might be construed as a willingness to take into account the social, political, and economic realities of the times as well as the legal precedents, there was little indication in the *judgment* of that case that the court paid very much attention to the extrinsic materials. But perhaps the court has been conservative, legalistic, and cautious simply because the constitutional questions being asked have been asked so many times before; there simply is not a very great opportunity for the judges to be particularly creative as long as the issues are the scope of the peace, order, and good government clause, Sections 91(2) and (27) and Section 92 (13). Perhaps the constitutional issues of the 1980s will force the Supreme Court of Canada to play a more significant role in the political process.

Perhaps the most visible issues are those that surround the current crisis in French-English relations. Already the Supreme Court has been called upon to declare *ultra vires* some portions of the controversial Quebec language legislation,[81] and the number of constitutional questions that might arise in the process of negotiating a renewed federalism, creating sovereignty-association, or writing a completely new constitution, could force our "shy" jurists to answer some tough legal questions that Viscount Haldane never even dreamed of. Moreover if the BNA Act is ever actually replaced with a new constitution, the Canadian courts will have the opportunity to "start from scratch" in developing a completely unique body of jurisprudence.

Another area where we might expect some difficult questions of jurisdiction to be handed to the Supreme Court is that of the ownership and control of offshore minerals. When that issue was first dealt

---

[79] See also, *A.G. B.C. v. Smith*, [1967] S.C.R. 702; and *Morgantaler v. The Queen*, [1976] 1 S.C.R. 616.
[80] Russell, op. cit.
[81] *Quebec Language* case (Bill 101).

with by the judiciary in Canada[82] it was decided that the ownership of the land off B.C.'s coast would depend upon whether B.C. controlled it at the time of Confederation. Because B.C. "at no time . . . either as a colony or a province, had property in these lands," the court determined that the Crown in right of *Canada* owned the land off B.C.'s coast under the residual power of Section 91. This however may have been a costly victory for the federal government because with the discovery of gas and oil deposits off the coast of Atlantic Canada, the issue will likely be raised with respect to the Maritimes and Newfoundland—the decision in this case, particularly with respect to the latter, which entered Confederation in 1949, may prove a difficult one for the court, and possibly a serious blow for the federal government.

Finally, the courts may well be called upon to determine the nature and extent of aboriginal rights in Canada, particularly in the NWT and the Yukon. While there is not an extensive jurisprudence in this area of the law, a 1973 case involving the Nishga tribe of British Columbia[83] raised many of the relevant legal questions. Although the majority of that court decided against the natives on the basis of what is essentially a technicality, and while there was a clear decision not to declare the existence of aboriginal rights, the court did not reject the principle of aboriginal title either. In fact a dissenting judgment of a minority of the court actually made a strong and persuasive case for native claims and if the composition of the Supreme Court should change over the next few years similar judgments could well favour the natives. While the legal situation is more complex within the provinces, in the NWT and the Yukon the land claims of the native peoples are based on very solid footing indeed. It is the hope of the federal government to achieve a negotiated, political settlement of native land claims, but if such efforts should fail the court may be forced to make decisions that could have extremely far-reaching implications for the powers of the federal government in the future.

In sum, therefore, while we have seen that the Supreme Court of Canada has made it a "policy"[84] not to employ social and economic considerations in the reasoning of their constitutional decisions, they may well be faced with constitutional questions in the eighties whose answers largely lie outside of the wisdom of *stare decisis*. The vagaries of Canadian political life may well force our heretofore passive judiciary to become an active (if reluctant) participant in the policy process.

[82] *Reference Re Ownership of Offshore Mineral Rights,* [1967] S.C.R. 792.
[83] *Calder v. A.G. B.C.,* [1973] S.C.R. 313.
[84] Russell, op. cit.

9

Federal-Provincial Fiscal Relations: 1867-1981

Few subjects are as crucial to an understanding of the Canadian political system as the study of federal-provincial financial or fiscal relations. Unfortunately, however, few subjects are so poorly understood! Far from being uninteresting, it is an area capable of producing high drama as Ministers of Finance, Premiers, and Prime Ministers confront each other in federal-provincial conferences while their advisors shunt hurriedly back and forth behind the walls of the main Conference Chambers at the Conference Centre in Ottawa, seeking to find compromises which will permit the continuation of the financial arrangements which underpin Confederation. Will the First Ministers be able to forge a compromise from the seemingly irreconcilable interests of eleven different governments? Will they be able to do it in time to avoid the unilateral imposition of a solution by the federal government and a stormy exit by some of the provincial premiers? The press converges on the Conference Centre. The First Ministers emerge to face a battery of cameras and microphones. Although some dissent is expressed, an agreement has been reached. The financial foundations of Confederation have once again been shored up—and just in time.

Whatever are they doing? Why is this exercise so important? Why must we be concerned with the arcane world of financial dealings among governments?

We need not look far for the answer to that last question. At the core of most of the activities of government is the raising and spending of money. For the key decision makers in any political system, the essence of popularity and hence of survival is to be able to spend money delivering popular programs without getting caught in the nasty business of raising it. This is a situation with significant implications for the real distribution of power among governments in Canada; for it means that a political decision maker wins if he or she can deliver a program while passing the costs of raising the money for the program onto another level of government. Winning in this case means not only augmenting one's own popularity, it also means increasing the general regard with which your level of government is viewed by the public and hence increasing the real power of your level of government vis-à-vis the other. Thus, within a federation, the real distribution of power among governments is in significant measure, determined by the complex processes of fiscal relations among governments.

The parameters of the "game" of federal-provincial fiscal arrangements are established by three sets of factors. The first is the broad environment within which government is set: the demands imposed on the system by society, the demands which actors in the system succeed in creating in the society, and the economic and social context within which the system is set. The second is the set of rules about jurisdictions and hence about the matters upon which government may spend money; these are imposed upon the system by its formal constitution. The third is the set of rules which determine the revenue sources available to governments, rules also imposed by the constitution. It is the interplay of these two sets of rules in the environment which determines the nature of the whole area of federal-provincial fiscal relations.

In Canada, as we shall see in greater detail below, there is a considerable discrepancy between federal and provincial levels of government with respect to the ability to raise money and the ability to spend it. By accident and by evolution the pre-eminent ability to raise money resides with the federal government while the pre-eminent obligation to spend money, particularly on the delivery of costly services such as hospitals, social services, and education, resides with provincial governments. The dynamics of Canada's federal system have to a significant degree been created by the attempts of Canada's political decision makers to deal with the imbalance created by this discrepancy.

Recent attempts to deal with this imbalance have been spurred by two major crises. The first was the fiscal crisis created first by the Depression and subsequently by World War II. The solution to that crisis was a significant centralization of the ability to control expenditures and an even further centralization of the ability to raise money. The second crisis, at the time of writing less serious than the first, is the fiscal crisis of the early 1980s. We will see that the centralizing response to the first crisis contained within it the seeds of the second. Paradoxically, the excessive centralization of the period up to 1968 crested like a wave and then collapsed, creating, together with other economic and social factors, a very rapid decentralization and, coincidentally, a fiscal crisis for Canada and particularly for the federal government. The results of this situation may be as serious as any specific secessionist threat and its resolution is likely to constitute the major issue of fiscal federalism for the 1980s.

Admittedly, fiscal federalism comprises a complex set of issues. However the case for understanding it, if one wishes to comprehend the essence of Canadian politics, is undeniable. The details which follow are indispensable to that understanding.

THE CONFEDERATION SETTLEMENT AND THE NINETEENTH CENTURY

The nature and content of any system of public finance depends largely upon the role government is expected to play in the lives of its citizens. In 1867, the role of government was perceived in terms of "rugged individualism" and the best government was judged to be that which governed least. That meant that government should confine itself mainly to the provision of national security, including defence, to the administration of justice, and to promoting national economic development through a few essential public works.

At Confederation, these most important and costly of governmental functions were placed in the hands of the federal parliament, along with the burden of the provincial debts existing at that time. The provinces in turn, were given the responsibility for matters of a local or provincial nature. Among these were education, public welfare, and transportation within the province, all of which involved relatively modest expenditures when contrasted with the federal share in 1867. Expenditures for education and welfare, for example, amounted to a paltry 14 percent of total governmental outlay in 1866.[1]

The largest revenue sources at Confederation were customs and excise duties, which accounted for approximately 80 percent of the revenues of the colonies of Nova Scotia and New Brunswick, and 66 percent of the revenue of Canada.[2] Provincial revenue at Confederation came from real property taxes, various types of fees and permits, and provincial licensing systems. Because the BNA Act vested the responsibility for the "great functions of government" in the federal parliament, and because the Dominion was to assume responsibility for the existing debts, the major sources of revenue at that time were given to the Dominion. The federal tax power, as specified in Section 91(3) thus gives the parliament of Canada the authority over "the Raising of Money by any Mode or System of Taxation." The provinces, on the other hand, were limited by Section 92(2) to direct taxation within the province for their source of revenue.

It was felt by the Fathers of Confederation that the provinces' con-

---

[1] *Report of the Royal Commission on Dominion-Provincial Relations* (King's Printer, Ottawa, 1940), hereafter referred to as *The Rowell-Sirois Report*, Book I, p. 39.
[2] Ibid., p. 41.

trol over the public domain, with its incidental revenues and the power to impose systems of licensing, would provide adequate provincial revenues to meet what were expected to be modest needs.[3] Provincial deficits which might occur from time to time were to be met by the modest federal subsidies described below. The area of direct taxation was viewed as a sort of residual source of provincial revenue, which was not intended to be used extensively: "Direct taxes were extremely unpopular: they had never been levied by the provinces and . . . the nature of the economy made the administration of direct taxation, except by the municipalities, very difficult."[4]

The terms *direct* and *indirect* taxation require some clarification. Sections 91 and 92 do not make any clear distinction between these two terms, and it was not until a decision of the Judicial Committee in 1887 that a working definition was set down. The distinction made then has withstood the test of time, and remains even today the basic rule for determining the validity of provincial tax measures. The Judicial Committee took a definition from the writing of John Stuart Mill and stated:

Taxes are either direct or indirect. A direct tax is one that is demanded from the very persons who it is intended or desired should pay it. Indirect taxes are those that are demanded from one person in the expectation and intention that he shall indemnify himself at the expense of another. Such are the excise or customs. . . . He shall recover the amount by means of an advance in price.[5]

Thus, direct taxes include such things as personal income tax, corporate income tax, real property tax, and succession duty, and indirect taxes include such levies as customs duties and excise taxes.

The courts have tended to emphasize the intention of a provincial tax measure as the crucial determinant of its validity, and have not too seriously limited the power of the provincial legislature to tax, merely because one of the effects of a measure may be indirect. In the case of corporation income taxes, for instance, it is quite likely that corporations do attempt to indemnify themselves at the expense of the consumer, but the courts have judged such a provincial tax valid because the intention is that it shall be paid directly by the corporation. In the case of retail sales tax, the provinces have been enabled to collect from the retailer a tax which is levied on the customer because the retailer is assumed to be the "agent" of the government for the purposes of administering this tax. When the store clerk punches up

---

[3] BNA Act, S. 109. See also: *Rowell-Sirois Report*, Book I, p. 44.
[4] Ibid.
[5] *Bank of Toronto v. Lambe* (1887), as cited in Olmsted, vol. 1, p. 222. See also *Rowell-Sirois Report*, Book I, p. 59.

the cost of one's purchase, he or she is functioning on behalf of the store. When the sales tax is calculated and added to the total, the clerk is functioning as an agent of the province. By naming each retailer a sort of "tax collector," and by requiring that the tax be calculated separately, the province ensures that the sales tax can pass as direct. If the sales tax were included in the price of retail goods, and collected from the store, it would be indirect, because the retailer would be "indemnifying himself at the expense of the customer" by a rise in the retail price of the goods.

While the province is given the power to levy direct taxes, and the interpretation of the scope of "direct taxation within the province" has been very broad, this tax power has not been deemed to be exclusive. It has been felt by the courts that the terms of 91(3) are general and that they therefore give the federal parliament the power to impose both indirect and direct tax measures. Conversely, Section 92(2) is very specific and it therefore must be construed only to limit the provincial legislatures to the raising of revenues by direct taxation, and not to reserve the direct tax fields to the exclusive use of the province. In other words, the constitutional authority to levy indirect taxes rests exclusively with the parliament of Canada, and the authority to levy direct taxes is shared by the provinces and the federal government.

In retrospect, the way in which sources of revenue were distributed between the provinces and the federal government could be considered short-sighted. The drafters of the BNA Act assumed that there would be no change in the distribution of the costs of government that each would bear. Furthermore they assumed that the major revenue sources would remain the same after 1867. Both of these assumptions were to be proven incorrect.

It would be unfair, however, to criticize the Fathers of Confederation for such a lack of foresight. The changes in the environment of the Canadian political system and the demands placed upon it which have taken place since 1867 could not have been foreseen except through the gift of clairvoyance. One of the effects of these environmental changes was the enormous expansion of the revenue needs of the provinces. The federal share of the costs of government fell from more than two-thirds of the total in 1867 to less than one-half of the total seventy years later.[6] Another effect was a major change in the tax base. Customs duties, for instance, which accounted for 63 percent of the total federal revenue in 1867-68, accounted for a mere 9

---

[6] *Rowell-Sirois Report*, Book I, p. 63.

percent of the total in 1967-68.[7] Thus the balance between revenue-raising rules and expenditure rules which had been struck by the Fathers of Confederation and enshrined in the BNA Act in 1867 eventually became a serious imbalance.

THE EARLY TWENTIETH CENTURY

By the turn of the century, the federal-provincial financial structure had begun a startling metamorphosis. Following a period of economic stagnation when provincial expenditures did not increase markedly, the "wheat boom" stimulated an immense growth of overall government expenditures. The prosperity of the period generated the extra revenues and all sectors of government, federal, provincial and municipal, began to spend large sums of money on urban development, public works, and economic expansion, and from 1896 to 1913 total expenditures by all governments quadrupled.[8] Initially, at least, the costs of this rapid expansion of the role and responsibilities of government had been matched by corresponding increases in federal revenue as customs and excise receipts which at this time accounted for over 90 percent of federal revenues produced large budgeting surpluses during most of the years between 1900 and World War I.[9] Similarly provincial revenues from standard tax sources also increased, but provincial expenditures grew still more rapidly, so that the traditional tax bases of the provinces began to be squeezed dry. The inelasticity of federal subsidies and the inability of existing provincial revenue sources to cope with the rising costs of government services forced the provinces to venture into the field of direct taxation, despite the unpopularity of such measures.[10]

From 1914 to 1920, the federal government was forced to impose special taxes in order to meet the uniquely high costs of the war effort. During this period, under the provisions of the War Measures Act, the federal government virtually took over the control of the economy, and the question of federal-provincial financial relations was left in a state of suspended animation until the end of the war. During the immediate postwar period and through most of the 1920s, "in its whole fiscal policy, the Dominion was labouring for a return to prewar 'normalcy' ".[11] In pursuit of this goal, the federal government

---

[7] Canadian Tax Foundation, *The National Finances 1967-68*, (Toronto, 1969) p. 51.
[8] *Rowell-Sirois Report*, Book I, p. 80.
[9] Ibid., p. 81.
[10] Ibid., p. 87.
[11] Ibid., p. 127.

tried to reduce or withdraw the special taxes that had been imposed at the time of the war, but the economy had changed so much that it was difficult—or indeed impossible—to go back. Prewar normalcy and postwar normalcy were completely different economic species.

Between 1921 and 1930, welfare expenditures increased by 130 percent, and three-quarters of this burden fell upon the provincial governments and the municipalities.[12] Federal outlays in tnis period were limited largely to grants to the provinces through the first of Canada's major shared-cost social programs in support of provincial old-age pension schemes and unemployment relief. Meanwhile, the costs of the traditional provincial and municipal responsibilities for roads and highways grew rapidly. The coming of the automobile increased the need not only for interurban highways but for better roads and road systems within the cities and in the suburban areas.[13] Fortunately, during the 1920s, while the cost of roads and relief soared, provincial revenues increased rapidly as well. The automobile, for instance, brought in large additional revenues through taxes on gasoline and motor vehicle licences. Indeed, provincial revenues doubled from 1921 to 1930, and two-thirds of this increase was due to additional tax yields in the three fields of motor vehicle licences, gasoline taxes, and liquor control. Thus, the growing responsibilities of the provinces and the fiscal instability of the provincial financial structure were disguised to some extent by a growing economy which brought a high yield from direct taxation.

Revenues from the public domain, which had been expected to meet a large part of the costs of provincial programs, dropped to a mere 10 percent of the total provincial revenues in 1930. Succession duties and corporation taxes increased as sources of revenue during this period, but in 1930, of the total provincial revenue from these sources, 87 percent was collected in the provinces of Ontario and Quebec, which together accounted for only 60 percent of the population of Canada. The reason for this disparity was the growing number of national companies with head offices in Toronto or Montreal. The imposition of provincial corporation taxes occurs at the head office of a corporation, with the result that profits which the corporation makes elsewhere in Canada are taxed by the governments of Ontario or Quebec. This was to prove an important factor in producing serious regional disparities in per capita revenues, as corporation taxes and succession duties came to play a larger and larger role in provincial finance during the 1930s.[14]

---

[12] Ibid., p. 128.
[13] Ibid., p. 129.
[14] Ibid., p. 131.

The Canadian federal system thus entered the hard years of the Depression with a seriously unbalanced revenue structure which was already strained to the limit and too inflexible to be able to meet any major new demands for expenditure, particularly in areas of provincial responsibility. The provinces relied heavily on revenue from tax fields such as liquor control and automobile licences, which tend to be very sensitive to economic fluctuations of a general nature. Similarly, the municipalities relied entirely on real property tax revenues which declined when the value of real estate dropped during the Depression. Moreover, in relatively small provinces with homogeneous single commodity economic bases, any major decline in that base could so diminish provincial revenues as to call the financial viability of the government into question. Without the spreading of risk inherent in the diversified economic base of larger units, single industry provinces, such as the Prairie provinces, were thus extremely vulnerable, a situation which led to fiscal insolvency in the 1930s.

In addition, constitutional and practical considerations prevented the provinces from diversifying their tax base. Indirect tax measures were constitutionally beyond the competence of the provincial legislatures, and given the low per capita income of the Depression direct tax measures such as personal income tax would have produced a very low yield except perhaps in Ontario. Moreover, the federal government had already occupied the field of personal income tax, and any extra tax on the already hard-pressed individual income would have produced both further economic problems, and political unrest.

Total government expenditures on relief grew nearly tenfold from 18.4 million dollars in 1930 to 172.9 million dollars in 1935, and since responsibility for such matters lies with the provinces, the federal government transferred large portions of its revenue to the provinces to help pay for them. Provincial and regional disparities were enhanced by the incidence of the Depression, for the larger the decline in the income and the larger the consequent rise in government expenditures in the most unfavourably situated provinces, the more rapidly did local revenues and credit become hopelessly inadequate and the larger was the support which had to be obtained from the Dominion.[15]

Thus, by the mid-thirties Canadian federalism was faced with a financial crisis which was the product of several factors. First, traditional functions of government had grown far beyond the expectations of the Fathers of Confederation, and the bulk of this growth

---

[15] Ibid., p. 160. Reproduced with the permission of the Government of Canada.

involved great increases in provincial expenditures. Second, new responsibilities of government had emerged which had not even been conceived of in 1867, and the interpretation of the BNA Act by the Judicial Committee of the Privy Council had vested only the provincial legislatures with the constitutional power to deal with them. Third, the revenue structure of the Canadian federal system provided the provincial governments with inadequate tax fields to meet both the new responsibilities and the inflated traditional responsibilities. Fourth, the homogeneity and product specialization of many provincial economies meant that the decline of a single industry such as agriculture could virtually destroy the provincial financial base. Finally, the incidence of a world-wide Depression exaggerated all these factors, making worse the already serious disparities in wealth between the various regions of Canada, producing startling inequalities in the standard of governmental service from one province to the next, and creating a demand for still further expenditures in areas of provincial jurisdiction which could not be covered from existing provincial revenue sources.

The Dominion government's immediate response to this crisis was to engage in extensive new programs of intergovernmental and interregional transfers of revenue in the form of both conditional and unconditional grants to the provinces. Before discussing the specific response to the fiscal crisis of the 1930s, however, let us look briefly at the evolution of the system of federal transfer payments to the provinces from Confederation to the 1930s and at the general principles involved in the various forms these transfers could take.

FEDERAL TRANSFERS TO THE PROVINCES: EARLY YEARS AND GENERAL PRINCIPLES

The Statutory Subsidies

It was clear even to the Fathers of Confederation that the provincial revenue sources provided in 1867 were not going to meet the expenditures of the provincial legislatures, at least for a transitional period. In recognition of this, provisions for federal subsidies to the provinces were written directly into the BNA Act. Section 118, which was subsequently repealed and replaced, gave the provinces three broad types of federal grants: 1) annual grants to support provincial governments and legislatures; 2) per capita grants; and 3) payments on debt allowances. The first of these was a subsidy based on the population of the province at the 1861 census, which was to be paid to the province to assist in the initial setting up and operation of the government and legislature in the first few years. This grant was to be given to the provinces annually and in perpetuity, and was not to be adjusted with population increase. When a general revision of the federal subsidies to the provinces took place in 1907, however, this grant was raised for all the provinces. Despite this, by comparison with total federal subsidies, the grants to support the provincial governments and legislatures amounted to a mere pittance, (ranging from $100,000 for Prince Edward Island to $240,000 for Ontario).

The second subsidy, the per capita grant, was intended to be the major assistance that the federal government would render to the provinces. Based on the 1861 census, the provinces were to be given 80 cents per capita per annum in perpetuity, although the per capita grants to New Brunswick and Nova Scotia were to increase with population up to 400,000 people. The per capita grant was manipulated from time to time through the device of estimating the population of the province generously in order to entice new provinces into the federation and meet the special needs of one province or another. For instance, when British Columbia came into Confederation in 1871, her population was estimated at 60,000 when in fact it was only 34,000; and Manitoba was given the fictitious population of 17,000 when it had only 12,200.[16] While these grants were to be fixed at the figure established at the time of Confederation, the 1907 revisions of the subsidies saw the 80 cents per capita grant permitted to increase up to 2½ million people and 60 cents a head was provided for any number over that figure.

Finally, while the federal government had accepted the responsibility for all of the debts of the provinces at Confederation, it was felt that the provinces which had smaller debts should be rewarded in order to equalize the benefits that each would reap from the union. Each province was allowed a certain debt based on approximately $25 a head according to the 1861 census.[17] If the actual debt of a province amounted to less than this figure, that province was to receive 5 percent of the difference as a grant from the federal government, annually and in perpetuity. According to this scheme, while New Brunswick and Nova Scotia either broke even or gained a little from the Dominion, Ontario and Quebec had debts that were far in excess of the debt allowance. It was arranged that these provinces would pay the federal government a figure equal to 5 percent of the difference between their actual debt and the amount allowed by the Confederation agreement. This arrangement was never implemented, partly because of the difficulty of assessing how much each of Ontario and Quebec should pay on a debt that they incurred jointly

---

[16] R. M. Dawson, *The Government of Canada*, p. 102.
[17] Ibid., p. 100.

as the colony of Canada. To get around this difficulty, and to further appease the Province of Nova Scotia, the debt allowance was raised so that Ontario and Quebec broke even and New Brunswick and Nova Scotia got an even larger payment from the Dominion. As the other provinces came into the federation they also were given generous debt allowances. Even the Provinces of Alberta and Saskatchewan, which had been federal territories before their coming of age and so obviously had no debt, received an annual payment based on the difference between their debt allowance and their nonexistent debt.

In addition to these three basic kinds of subsidies, ever since Confederation there have been a number of special federal grants to various provinces and regions in order to meet special needs. New Brunswick, for example, received a grant for ten years after Confederation, and the Province of Newfoundland received a healthy subsidy on entering Confederation in 1949. Special grants were given to the Prairie provinces on entering Confederation in 1905, as compensation for the Dominion's retaining its rights to their natural resources. Even after the Dominion gave the natural resources of the Prairies back to Saskatchewan and Alberta, the compensation grant for those resources was continued. Thus, while it was assumed that the arrangements concluded at Confederation would be permanent and unalterable, in fact the federal subsidies to the provinces have undergone almost constant revision. Despite these constant adjustments the statutory subsidies today form a very tiny part of transfer payments to the provincial governments. Total federal cash transfers to the provinces in 1978-79 amounted to 10.03 billion dollars and of that only 33.9 million dollars was accounted for by statutory subsidies.[18]

Conditional Grants

The statutory subsidies discussed above have "no strings attached." When a province receives such a grant from the federal government, it may spend the money in any way that it deems suitable. Such grants to the provinces are usually referred to as *unconditional grants*, a category which also includes the equalization payments to be discussed below. From 1913 to 1970 federal transfer payments to the provinces increasingly took the form of *conditional grants*, or *grants-in-aid*. The conditional grant is offered to the province only so long as it is spent for the purposes specified by the federal government. The

---

[18] Federal-Provincial Relations Office, *Federal-Provincial Programs & Activities* (Ottawa, June 1979), pp. iv, 68.

first conditional grants were for agricultural instruction and were offered for a ten-year period. A province received the money on the condition that it be spent for agricultural instruction which met certain standards. Most conditional grants work this way, and furthermore, most require that the province itself contribute some proportion of the costs of the program.

In the early period, shared-cost or conditional grant programs were viewed as either "experimental or . . . given under extraordinary circumstances,"[19] and as such they were usually intended to terminate after a specified time period. By the close of World War I, federal grants-in-aid were provided for such things as assistance for highways, technical education, the control of venereal disease, and the maintenance of employment offices.[20] It was at that time that two schools of thought regarding the utility and the advisability of conditional grants first evolved. One group felt that the conditional grant was a handy device for pursuing vigorous policies of federal leadership in spite of the strait jacket of the BNA Act. The opponents of this particular form of subsidy agreed that it permitted the federal government to take vigorous initiatives, but they considered that it was not the federal government's job to take initiatives in areas of provincial jurisdiction.

Conditional grants do in fact permit the federal government to set spending priorities even in fields that are constitutionally beyond its legislative competence. The basic source of this federal influence is the so-called "spending power," by which the central government is free to spend its tax dollars in any way it sees fit. By offering to pay one-half of the cost of a particular program, for example in the largely provincial jurisdictions of medical or welfare services, Ottawa can usually "bribe" the province to implement programs which, constitutionally, the federal government could not undertake itself. The province will usually be forced by economic expediency to commit its limited resources to programs partially funded by the federal government, for the cost of such programs to the provincial treasury is only half that of programs which the province must fund itself. Thus by allowing the federal government to prejudice provincial priorities in predominantly provincial fields, shared-cost grants place the autonomy of the provinces in some jeopardy.[21]

---

[19] *Rowell-Sirois Report*, Book I, p. 131.
[20] Ibid.
[21] Ibid. See also: Dawson, *The Government of Canada*, p. 105; D. Smiley, "Conditional Grants and Canadian Federalism: The Issues," in Meekison, *Canadian Federalism* (first edition), pp. 256-268.

Whether this is good or bad from a provincial perspective depends on where you stand in the provincial government. Provincial program managers in areas which have conditional grants tend to love them, especially in the few years after their inception, for it puts them in a favoured bargaining position at budget time: they can go to their provincial treasurer and make the point that a dollar given to their program (perhaps to build a hospital) will call forth a matching dollar from the federal government, whereas a dollar spent on a rival program (perhaps highway construction) will not call forth any matching grant. The federal shared-cost programs are thus beloved by those parts of provincial government which benefit by them and detested by those which do not. They are probably least appreciated by the provincial treasurers and Premiers whose priorities are skewed by them. They would prefer more taxing power or unconditional grants.

The second criticism of conditional grants is based on the old maxim of the English constitution that the government which spends public funds should be accountable for them.[22] Even with sharply prescribed conditional grants, once the money has been transferred to a province, there is no absolutely sure procedure by which the federal authorities can ensure that all of the funds transferred have been spent for the purposes specified. Accountability of a government to parliament for expenditures is therefore diminished. There are auditing procedures attached to all conditional grant programs but as time goes on and the rather high level of agreement as to the aims of a shared-cost program which accompanies the inception of a program begins to deteriorate, there is an increasing tendency for provinces to attempt to maximize receipt of funds while minimizing compliance with the terms of the agreement. For example a provincial government may forward an inordinate number of claims to the federal government, knowing that "the feds" will be unable to check them all and hence will have to pay most of them. The only recourse for the federal government would be to refuse to support the province in future joint projects, a tactic which might prove politically unwise, since the people of the provinces also vote in federal elections. Hence, it is likely that the provinces, from time to time, will obtain a bit of conditional grant money for programs other than the federally sanctioned ones.

There are thus some perverse incentives built into shared-cost programs. Because the responsibility for spending and for raising money

[22] *Rowell-Sirois Report*, Book I, p. 131.

is fragmented there is less direct incentive to keep costs at the lowest level consistent with delivery of adequate programs. Indeed if the federal share rises well above 50 percent of costs as it does in some such programs, there may be an incentive for a province to *maximize* expenditures no matter how wasteful they may be because the spill-over effect of all those federal dollars may create more than enough additional tax revenue for a province to recoup all of its costs.

There is also an incentive for provincial governments to spend money in ways which will ensure federal cost-sharing even if this is not the most efficient way to deliver the program. For example early federal cost-sharing programs for hospital insurance provided support for treatment in expensive acute-care hospital beds but not for many of the services necessary to support the types of home-care treatment which later proved to be both more effective and much cheaper. Provinces were thus encouraged to go on providing more acute-care beds than would have been the case had either level of government alone been funding and operating the entire program.

For the federal government, there is a further problem inherent in the basic shared-cost mechanism. Typically under its terms the federal treasury agrees to match, according to whatever proportion is specified in the agreement, the actual program costs incurred by provincial governments. This means that the size of federal disbursements is actually under provincial control, a situation fraught with terror for a federal Finance Minister or Treasury Board President and their officials. The unpredictability of the federal expenditure budget caused by this situation is by now more apparent than real since the federal officials who operate these programs are very good at predicting actual costs. However disasters have happened ranging from an additional 50 million dollar obligation resulting from an accounting error by British Columbia in 1974, to hospital insurance cost increases which approached 20 percent per year in 1974 and 1975.

Block Funding

The increasing recognition of the problems inherent in conditional grant programs meant that no major new conditional grant programs were implemented after the Medicare Act of 1968 provided for federal sharing in the costs of medical (primarily physicians) services. It led as well to the development of a number of *block funding* programs in areas such as health insurance and the support of provincial second language education. Block funding programs usually involve the transfer of a per capita grant to provinces from the federal treasury pursuant only to the province complying with very broadly defined program parameters.

We will discuss the details of the most significant of Canada's block funding arrangements later in this chapter but the system is assumed to have three major advantages. It makes expenditures knowable in advance to all involved, a feature particularly appealing to the federal treasury. It assures a level of funding for provinces while getting the federal government out of areas of provincial jurisdiction. Finally, it is administratively quite simple, avoiding the complex auditing and reporting procedures inherent in the more specific conditions attached to conditional grants.

Block grant programs do significantly reduce federal interference in an area of provincial jurisdiction but they naturally thereby allow a proliferation of program designs. Thus the nature of access to what Canadians by now consider to be essential services may vary considerably across Canada. Moreover because the programs retain the rhetoric of conditionality (the transfers are, after all, made in order to assist the delivery of certain kinds of services) while largely eliminating the terms which could permit the federal government to affirm that the conditions are being met, they seem to promise an accountability they cannot deliver. The very nature of block grants means that accountability of the federal government to parliament and the taxpayers for the expenditure of federal tax dollars is virtually impossible.

There is thus a conflict which has not been resolved by either the conditional grant or the block funding mode of payment. The conflict is between the need for accountability for expenditure within the federal government (in both the strict accounting sense of assuring that the dollars are spent where they are intended to be spent and in the broad policy sense of assuring that the desired outcomes are effected) and the problems created by federal interference in an area of provincial jurisdiction. Starkly stated, one cannot have accountability without interference. Neither can one have national program standards without interference. Yet interference negates the provincial jurisdiction in areas which are, in the words of the BNA Act, Section 92, matters of "local or private nature within the province."

The situation is made all the more difficult by another set of conflicting factors. Political accountability at least could be assured by the complete transfer of sufficient taxing power to the provinces to allow them to raise all the money necessary to finance all the programs in their jurisdiction. In this way the government levying the taxes would be spending the money. However, these programs comprise the bulk of total government expenditures in Canada so that the federal government would lose its lion's share of the revenue-raising clout it now possesses. Given that it is generally agreed in Canada that a pre-eminent role of the federal government must be management of the economy and given that one of the two major tools available to it in accomplishing this task is the ability to tax and to spend the proceeds, such large-scale transfers of tax powers would emasculate the national government. Thus not only are the concepts of accountability and federal interference, and the concepts of a national standard and provincial autonomy in conflict, but so are the concepts of provincial fiscal accountability and national economic management. None of the mechanisms for intergovernmental transfers so far developed seem to solve the problems inherent in these conflicts.

THE FINANCIAL STRUCTURE IN CRISIS

The combination of the asymetrical distribution of tax powers and legislative jurisdiction and the economic crisis of the Depression conspired to challenge the Canadian federal system with a number of apparently insoluble problems. In particular, the federal financial structure of the early 1930s was totally inappropriate for an era which called for massive expenditures on unemployment relief; but the provincial governments were saddled not only with the responsibility for relief but with providing highways and education as well. The federal government, on the other hand, had been denied any role at all in the performance of these costly functions because of the construction placed on the terms of Sections 91 and 92 by the courts. Denied the legislative competence to deal with the problems of the thirties, the Dominion, however, possessed the revenues which were needed to pay for programs such as relief and education. The result was an enormous increase in transfer payments, in the form of both conditional and unconditional grants to the provinces. But the result, with the federal government increasingly collecting the taxes and the provinces increasingly spending them, was hardly a happy situation for federal politicians.

Besides increasing the financial difficulties of the provinces vis-à-vis the Dominion, the Depression accentuated the problem of regional disparities. Some provinces suffered more than others from the hardships of the Depression. Regional economic disparities, always significant in Canada, became an even more important force in Canadian politics, with the result that the standard of services offered to Canadians in some parts of the country was vastly poorer than the standard of services in others and it soon became obvious to the government of the day that action had to be taken to remedy the situation before it led to serious political disharmony within the federation. One major response to the financial crisis of the thirties was to appoint in 1937, a Royal Commission on Dominion-Provincial

Relations charged with undertaking "a reexamination of the economic and financial basis of Confederation and of the distribution of legislative powers in the light of the social and economic developments of the last seventy years."[23] The research by the Commission was extensive, as the commissioners travelled from one end of the country to the other several times, hearing the recommendations of provincial governments, various pressure groups, and interested individuals. The findings and recommendations were finally reported in May of 1940.

The focus of what has come to be called the *Rowell-Sirois Report* was on the two basic problems of federal-provincial finance in Canada: 1) the distribution of responsibilities and revenues between the provinces and the Dominion; and 2) the economic disparities existing among the various provinces and regions of Canada. As a solution for the former, the Commission recommended an extensive shift of both governmental functions and tax powers, and as a solution for the latter, the Commission recommended unconditional "equalization payments" from the federal treasury to the needy provinces.[24]

Specifically, the *Report* stated in its recommendations that the Dominion should take over the debts of all of the provinces, take over the responsibility for unemployment relief, and pay a National Adjustment Grant to the less fortunate regions of Canada in order to bring the standard of services there up to the national average. In return for this, however, the *Report* recommended that the provinces give up all claim to the fields of income tax, corporation taxes, corporate income taxes, and succession duties, and that the original statutory subsidies be abolished.

The recommendations of the *Rowell-Sirois Report* were discussed in federal-provincial conferences in 1940-41, and were not met with any great enthusiasm by the provinces. The "have" provinces, especially, were not willing to give up their taxing powers in return for an "allowance" from the federal government, and even the "have-not" provinces were not very happy with being raised merely to the "national average" by the national adjustment grants. By 1940, too, Canada was involved in World War II, and the focus of the national attention had shifted to matters other than federal-provincial relations. Besides, prosperity had returned and it was easy for the provinces and the Dominion to postpone any serious consideration of the Rowell-Sirois recommendations until after the war.

[23] Ibid., p. 9.
[24] R. M. Dawson, *The Government of Canada,* pp. 107-108.

THE POSTWAR PERIOD

The outbreak of war had given the federal authorities the moral justification and the legal authority (under the "emergency power" in Section 91) to usurp all of the remaining governmental spending and taxing initiatives from the provinces. The Dominion occupied, among other things, much of the field of direct taxation to the exclusion of the provinces, and paid the provinces a *rent* in lieu of the revenue that was lost to them with the result that the federal government controlled the entire revenue structure of the federation and the provinces were reduced to the state of receiving an "allowance" from the Dominion. In terms of the expectations and perceptions of the public, the federal government had become *the* government; the provinces were of secondary importance. Governmental initiative appeared to rest solely in the hands of the Dominion, and the provinces, particularly the "have-not" provinces, humbled as they were by the financial catastrophe of the Depression, seemed willing to accept the leadership of the Dominion.

Despite this apparent acceptance of the postwar leadership of the federal government, neither the "have" nor the "have-not" provinces were eager to adopt the terms of the *Rowell-Sirois Report* which would have permanently centralized both public finance and the responsibility for all major policy initiatives. The federal government countered with a new set of proposals for federal-provincial relations, which were produced in the so-called "Green Book" of 1945. These proposals, in accord with the *Rowell-Sirois Report*, would have handed over to the federal government the exclusive power to levy income taxes, corporate income taxes, and succession duties. Unlike the Commission's report, the Green Book did not provide for unconditional equalization payments to the poor provinces. Instead, the federal government proposed to subsidize the provinces through a series of shared-cost programs funded jointly by provincial revenues and federal conditional grants.[25] This alternative had been specifically singled out by the Royal Commission as undesirable:

The conditional grant as it works under Canadian conditions is an inherently unsatisfactory device. . . . We believe it to be more costly than if the service in question were financed by a single government. It unquestionably leads to delay and to periodic friction between Dominion and provincial governments.[26]

---

[25] D. V. Smiley, "Public Administration and Canadian Federalism," *Canadian Public Administration*, Vol VII, No. 3, September 1964, pp. 371-388.
[26] *Rowell-Sirois Report*, Book I, p. 259. Reproduced with permission of the Government of Canada.

Because the Green Book proposals were presented as a package deal and because the provinces would not give up their share of the key direct taxes, the Dominion-Provincial Conference of 1945 was unsuccessful in its attempts to secure a permanent arrangement. But, as Professor Smiley points out, "Almost from the day the conference was finished, federal authorities began to seek limited and piecemeal agreements with the provinces in particular matters."[27]

It seems that although provincial politicians were not willing to sell their birthright, some at least were willing to lease it and to allow the federal government to continue setting the major policy priorities. The political pressure to equalize the standards of services in the various economic regions of Canada played a large part in securing this cooperation between the provinces and the federal government; and a faint blush of nationalism, the result of a common cause and shared hardships during the war, abetted the situation. Although there was some residual bitterness in Quebec as a result of the conscription issue, for a while at least, Canadians of all regions and walks of life became accustomed to thinking in national terms, rather than provincially or regionally. The goal of raising the standard of living of the less fortunate regions of Canada was politically popular in all provinces, and the natural vehicle for programs which would achieve this goal was the federal government.

This was indeed the high tide of centralization in Canada and once again the fiscal arrangements both reflected and reinforced this fact. The keystone of postwar federal-provincial relations was formed by a series of federal-provincial fiscal agreements and by three particularly important shared-cost programs. To these we must now address ourselves.

Federal-Provincial Fiscal Arrangements, 1945-1982

Through the Wartime Tax Agreements of 1941, the provinces had ceased to levy personal income taxes, corporation income taxes, and all other corporation taxes. While these fiscal arrangements are euphemistically referred to as "agreements," the fact was that in 1941, because of the emergency conditions of wartime, the federal government possessed the constitutional power unilaterally to exclude the provinces from the field of direct taxation and, for that matter, to interfere with any of the matters reserved exclusively to the provinces by Section 92 of the BNA Act.[28] Under the circumstances,

---

[27] D. V. Smiley, "Public Administration and Canadian Federalism," p. 277.
[28] See *Fort Frances Pulp and Paper Company v. Winnipeg Free Press*, [1923] 3 D.L.R. 629; *Cooperative Committee on Japanese-Canadians v. Attorney General for Canada*, [1947] 1 D.L.R. 577; *Reference Re Validity of Wartime Leasehold Regulations*, [1950] 2 D.L.R. 1.

all the provinces entered into tax agreements with the federal government for the period 1941-1946. In return for the revenue that would be lost to them by giving up these fields of taxation to the Dominion, the provinces were to be paid a rent or a *tax rental payment* based either on the revenue yields in the vacated fields in the year 1941, or on the total cost of servicing the provincial debt. The choice between these alternative formulae of compensation for lost revenue was left to the provinces themselves, and as it turned out, Quebec, Ontario, Manitoba, and British Columbia opted for the former and the rest of the provinces opted for the latter.

In order to discourage the provinces from increasing their succession duties, provincial succession duty collections were subtracted from the federal rental payment to those provinces which elected the formula based on the cost of servicing the provincial debt (i.e., New Brunswick, Nova Scotia, Prince Edward Island, Alberta, and Saskatchewan). Another provision that was unique to these wartime agreements was that which guaranteed the existing level of provincial revenue from liquor and gasoline taxes, regardless of the rental payment formula selected by the province.[29]

1947-1957 By the time the 1941 tax rental agreement had expired, the war was over, and it was no longer possible for the Dominion to compel the provinces to enter into fiscal agreements. A second tax rental agreement which covered the period 1947-1952 was signed by most provinces, but the federal government could not convince Quebec and Ontario that it would be to their advantage to participate. These provinces, therefore, did not enter the tax rental agreements of 1947-1952, although the rest did. Upon entering Confederation in 1949, Newfoundland also agreed to the existing tax rental arrangements, which meant that eight provinces participated for most of the 1947-1952 period. During this period, the eight provinces agreed not to levy income taxes, corporation taxes, and succession duties; and in return, the federal government paid them a rent based on either a per capita payment, or on the revenue yield from the vacated tax fields in the province—except in the case of Prince Edward Island which was given a specified lump sum. The 1947-1952 tax agreement also permitted the participating provinces to levy their own 5 percent tax on corporation income in the province.

The real benefit that the provinces gained by entering the tax rental agreements of this period was that the federal government, which had set up the machinery for collection of direct taxation on a

---

[29] This was in part to compensate the provinces for revenue lost as a result of wartime rationing.

national basis during the war years, could collect the taxes more cheaply than the provinces. Most of the provinces could not afford to duplicate the federal machinery, and those which could afford it could see that the extensive administrative machinery required for the collection of personal income tax would render separate federal and provincial systems extremely inefficient. Moreover, since appearing to be the tax collector is something the vast majority of politicians seek to avoid, the offer by the federal government to act as the tax collector was not one which most provincial governments wanted to turn down. Partly for these reasons, Ontario reconsidered its position during the negotiations for the next tax rental agreements and Quebec alone refused to enter the federal-provincial tax agreements for the period 1952-1957.

The 1952-1957 agreements were generally similar to the preceding ones. The participating provinces refrained from imposing personal income taxes, corporation taxes, and succession duties. The exception was Ontario which continued to levy its own succession duties. The most significant difference in the later arrangements was that the payments to the provinces were guaranteed at a certain minimum for each province, and the actual rent paid to each province was adjusted upwards according to a formula which related per capita GNP and provincial population.[30] In other words, the "have" provinces received larger payments than the "have-not" provinces, but at the same time, the less fortunate provinces were guaranteed a certain amount regardless of the actual revenue yield of the vacated tax fields of that province. This particular provision of the 1952-1957 tax rental agreements is crucial for it contained the germ of the principle of the unconditional equalization payments to the "have-not" provinces which today form so significant a part of the federal-provincial fiscal arrangements.

1957-1962   The Tax Sharing Arrangements Act of 1956 set out the terms of the federal-provincial tax agreements for the period of 1957-1962. According to this act, the participating provinces agreed to vacate the *standard tax* fields of personal income tax, corporation taxes, and succession duties as before. The federal government, in return, agreed to pay the provinces a rent based on the revenue yield in the vacated fields. The basic federal payment to the provinces according to this agreement amounted to 10 percent of federal personal income tax collections in the province, 9 percent of corporation profits in the province, and 50 percent of the revenues of federal suc-

[30] Canadian Tax Foundation, *The National Finances, 1965-66* (Toronto, 1966), p. 126.

cession duties in the province, based on a three-year average of collections.

The 1957-1962 arrangements, however, also provided the first unconditional *equalization payment* to the poorer provinces. The federal government agreed to pay those provinces an amount sufficient to bring the per capita yield of each province in the three standard taxes up to the average per capita yield from those three years in the two wealthiest provinces. Finally, the Tax Sharing Arrangements Act also provided for a *stabilization grant* which was calculated to raise the total yield for a province up to a set minimum. That minimum was based on either the previous financial arrangements extended into current years; or the last payments under the previous arrangements but adjusted for population growth; or, 95 percent of the average payments for the previous two years under the 1957-1962 arrangements.[31] The aim of the stabilization payment was to prevent the revenue yield of the various provinces from fluctuating a great deal from one year to the next.

All of the provinces entered into these agreements to some extent. However, Quebec opted to accept only the unconditional equalization payment, and Ontario chose not to vacate the fields of corporation tax and succession duties. For those provinces which did not fully participate, a *tax abatement* was granted to provide tax room for the province. The federal government, in order to prevent the taxpayer from being doubly taxed, agreed to withdraw partially from any of the fields of income tax, corporation tax, or succession duties if a province continued to levy its own taxes. Thus, as the Province of Ontario did not vacate corporation income tax fields, the federal government abated its own corporation income tax by 9 percent of the corporation profits (an amount equal to what the province would have received as a rental payment had it chosen to rent that particular tax field). The Province of Quebec was granted, in lieu of rental payments, a tax abatement in each of the three standard tax fields which was equal to the amount the province would have been paid by the federal government had it entered the agreement (10 percent of federal personal income tax, 9 percent of the federal corporation tax, and 50 percent of the federal estate taxes).

In 1958 in response to demands by the provinces, the federal government raised the provincial share of personal income tax to 13 percent of the federal revenues collected, and provided an equivalent raise in the abatement in that tax field for the Province of Quebec. In

---

[31] Ibid., p. 127.

1960, a new twist was added to the already confusing structure of federal-provincial relations, by permitting any province which wished to do so, to "opt out" of the federal program of conditional per capita grants to the provinces in aid of university education. If a province chose to opt out of this program it would receive, in lieu of the conditional grant, 1 percent more of corporation profits in the province. It was provided that if the revenue from 1 percent of corporation profits was less than the province would have received in the form of per capita conditional grants, the federal government would make good the difference. Conversely, if the 1 percent happened to be greater than the per capita grant would have been, the province had to refund some revenue to the federal government. Only the Province of Quebec opted out of the university grants program, but the significance of this provision is that it set a precedent which led to a proliferation of "opting-out" formulae in federal-provincial programs.

Other provisions were included in the 1957-1962 agreements to meet the specific needs of the Atlantic provinces. Special Atlantic Provinces Adjustment Grants were added to the agreement in 1958, in order to meet specific economic problems which that region of Canada faced at that time. These grants were unconditional, and they amounted to an extension of the principle of equalization to secure added assistance for a region which could not make ends meet with the standard equalized federal payments. The Province of Newfoundland was also given additional annual grants by special legislation that was passed in 1959. The year 1957 also saw the inception of the first of the huge postwar federal conditional grant programs in the form of the Hospital Insurance and Diagnostic Services Act (HIDS).[32] Paradoxically, given the drawbacks of conditional grant programs from the provincial point of view, HIDS was negotiated primarily at the behest of several provincial governments including Ontario. Several provinces led by Saskatchewan already had hospital insurance and most that did not were eager to implement it but could only afford to do so with federal assistance. That assistance was negotiated at a series of federal-provincial meetings in 1956-1957 and the new federal government of 1957 went ahead and implemented the program negotiated by its predecessor.

1962-1967 Until 1962, the federal-provincial tax agreements had been based on the principle that the federal government should levy

---

[32] For details on HIDS as well as medicare see Malcolm Taylor, *Health Insurance and Canadian Public Policy* (McGill-Queen's Press, Montreal 1978). Taylor's work combines a thorough policy analysis with an excellent set of examples of the real workings of fiscal federalism.

the taxes and collect the revenue, and then pass over a percentage of the "take" to the provinces participating in the agreement. The attitude of the federal government was that the ability to tax is crucial to the federal power and that if the federal government could convince the provinces to give up at least some of this authority, it would enhance its own role in the management of the economy. However, the unfortunate consequence of this situation, from Ottawa's point of view, was that the federal government was getting a "black eye" from the public which perceived it as the government which collected all the taxes while the provinces were getting credit as the governments which delivered the most popular programs, thus making the provinces almost automatic winners in the game of fiscal federalism. If the provinces were to receive the praise from the public for spending money on popular social welfare programs, roads, etc., the federal authorities felt that the provinces should also take some of the blame for high taxes. Therefore, the Federal-Provincial Fiscal Arrangements Act (1961), which was to apply to the period of 1962-1967, set out a tax-sharing plan which was different in form from anything which had existed before. According to this Act, the federal government would undertake to withdraw partially from the taxes which it had previously shared with the provinces, in much the same way that the federal government had agreed to grant tax abatements to nonparticipating provinces in the previous agreements. Thus, the federal government would actually withdraw from the corporation income tax field to the extent of 9 percent of corporate profits and from the personal income tax field by 16 percent of the federal tax. The percentage withdrawal or abatement of the personal income tax field was to increase from 16 percent in 1962 at a rate of 1 percent per annum, until it reached 20 percent by 1966. This arrangement was subsequently altered as a result of demands from the provinces so that the total withdrawal from the field of personal income tax was 24 percent in 1966. In the field of succession duties, the federal government agreed either to pay the province 50 percent of revenues from the federal tax or to grant an abatement to the extent of 50 percent of the federal tax in the provinces that wished to levy their own succession duties. In 1963, the federal payment/abatement of succession duties was increased to 75 percent of the federal tax.

Under the 1962-1967 arrangements, the equalization payment was based on the per capita revenues from the three standard taxes as before, but the equalization base was modified to include, as well, 50 percent of the three-year average yield from taxes on natural resources in the province. This provision was added because some provinces, particularly Alberta with its vast revenues from oil and gas taxes, were receiving healthy equalization payments under the old formula, and did not really need them. What Alberta lacked in income and corporation tax revenue, she could easily make up with resource tax revenue, whereas provinces like New Brunswick suffered from low revenue yields in all tax fields. A further change in the equalization formula was to base the calculation on the national average yield in the standard taxes rather than the average yield in the two wealthiest provinces. However, in 1963, this was changed so that the equalization payment was calculated on the three standard taxes only and based on the average per capita yield in the two wealthiest provinces, as it had been in 1957-1962. While natural resources revenues thus, for the moment, did not figure in the equalization formula, it was provided that any province whose revenues from this field of taxation exceeded the national average would be faced with a deduction from its equalization grant. [33]

While the intention of the federal government in undertaking to withdraw from the shared tax fields was to distribute the political responsibility for taxes among the governments that were spending the revenues, it did not wish to penalize the provinces financially. Hence, under the Fiscal Arrangements Act, the federal government offered to continue to collect the provincial share of income tax and corporation income tax, free of charge, provided the province utilized the same tax base. As a result of this, the provinces all began levying their own income taxes and corporation income taxes in 1962, and all except the Province of Quebec, which had previously set up its own collection machinery, signed collection agreements with the federal government. In the field of corporation income tax, Ontario, like Quebec, chose to look after its own collections. During the 1962-1967 period, six of the provinces set their tax rates at the same level as the federal government's with Saskatchewan and Manitoba adopting higher rates, Quebec continuing the rates which were already in existence in that province, and Ontario raising the corporation income tax rate.

The stabilization grants continued during 1962-1967 much as they had in the previous period, with the federal government guaranteeing the provinces' yield from the standard taxes and equalization payments at a level equal to 95 percent of the average yield for the preceding two years. The Atlantic Provinces Adjustment Grants and the special grants to Newfoundland were continued for the 1962-1967 period with only slight changes. The 1 percent abatement of corpora-

---

[33] For a further explanation of this arrangement, see Canadian Tax Foundation, *The National Finances, 1965-66*, p. 128.

tion income tax in lieu of grants in aid of universities was continued as before, and the Province of Quebec alone continued to exercise this option.

In 1965, the federal government passed the Established Programs (Interim Arrangements) Act by which provinces so desiring were permitted to opt out of certain federal-provincial shared-cost programs without any financial penalty. For each program that the province chose to opt out of, the federal government allowed either an additional abatement in the field of personal income tax, or a direct cash payment in lieu of the federal share of the cost of the program. Provinces wishing to take advantage of the opting-out provisions were compelled by the federal legislation to continue the program along the same lines as the federal program for a certain specified interim period, during which they had to agree to a sort of audit by the federal authorities to ensure provincial compliance with the terms. It was furthermore provided in the Act that the additional percentage points of income tax given up by the federal government would be equalized:

An equalization payment was made to bring the per capita yield from the abatement points specified for each program up to the average per capita yield of the same number of points in the top two provinces. If the equalized abatement provided more than what the federal contribution to the program would have been, had the province not opted out, a recovery was made; conversely, if the equalized abatement fell short, an additional payment from the federal government was forthcoming. [34]

The programs to which the Established Programs (Interim Arrangements) Act applied were separated into two categories: those for which the province opting out would receive a certain number of equalized abatement points in personal income tax, and those for which the opting-out province would receive a straight cash compensation. The provinces were given until October, 1965 to decide whether or not they wanted to exercise the option set down in this legislation. When the time limit expired, only the Province of Quebec had accepted the opting-out formula, and that provincial government exercised the privilege in all of the Category I programs, and in the forestry program of Category II. The effect was to give the Province of Quebec an additional 20 percent of the personal income tax. When this is added to the 24 percent abatement of personal income tax which applied to all of the provinces by 1966, Quebec got a total abatement of 44 percent of personal income tax, 10 percent of the

[34] Canadian Tax Foundation, *The National Finances, 1967-68*, p. 132.

profits of corporations in the province, and 75 percent of succession duties. The choice made by Quebec at this time was probably determined by the high level of nationalist feeling within the province, and by the desire of the provincial authorities to focus the loyalties of the Québécois on Quebec rather than on Canada. The rest of the provinces decided to stay in the joint programs for reasons of economic efficiency: it was cheaper for them to continue to use the machinery and procedures which existed at the time rather than try to create completely new provincial ones.

The largest of the programs to which the opting-out formula was applied is the Canada Assistance Plan (CAP), based on federal legislation passed in 1964. The Canada Assistance Plan provides for 50 percent federal sharing in provincial social assistance payments and in many of the personal social services such as counselling, family services, and day care delivered by provincial and local governments. By 1980-81 payments to provinces under CAP had grown to over 1.9 billion dollars. The CAP thus became the second of the large postwar social programs to be covered by shared-cost arrangements.

1967-1977   By 1966 the renegotiation of the terms which would appear in the Federal-Provincial Fiscal Arrangements Act was well on the way to becoming an established five-yearly ritual of Canadian politics. These negotiations resemble nothing so much as an elaborate pantomime working its way up through various levels of the governmental hierarchy. Initial posturing requires that the provincial governments, usually in the person of the provincial Treasurer, should anguish about their ability to pay for the vastly expensive programs into which they have been (allegedly) "coerced" or seduced via the mechanism of shared-cost programs, or to bemoan their ability to provide for the services necessary to put their citizens on an equal footing with other Canadians. Federal authorities counter with concern over Ottawa's ability to manage the economy. Initial proposals, normally by the federal government, emerge from this posturing about one year before the dreaded deadline imposed by the expiry of the legislation. Provincial governments attack the federal proposal as hopelessly inadequate. All dissolves in apparent disarray following a "final" meeting of Finance Ministers and Treasurers just a few months before the critical deadline. In this Canadian political version of *The Perils of Pauline*, the stage is then set for the Prime Minister and Premiers to meet and, at the last possible instant and after a certain amount of additional posturing both inside and outside the Conference Centre, to snatch an agreement from the jaws of fate, saving Canada from yet another crisis.

The Federal-Provincial Fiscal Arrangements Act which emerged from this process in 1966 defined the tax agreements and the various unconditional intergovernmental transfers for the period 1967-1972.

Under it, the federal government increased its basic abatement of personal income tax from 24 percent to 28 percent of the federal tax payable in the provinces. The corporate income tax abatement, which had been 9 percent of corporate profits in the provinces other than Quebec, was raised to 10 percent in all provinces for the 1967 tax year. The abatement of succession duties remained substantially the same as it had been under the previous arrangement: i.e., the abatement for provinces that levied their own estate taxes or the federal payment for provinces that did not levy their own tax was 75 percent of the federal tax due in the provinces.

The formula for calculating equalization payments was altered radically by the 1967 arrangement. Instead of being calculated on the per capita yield of the three standard taxes, the payment was figured on the revenue yield of sixteen different provincial revenue sources. Except for the fact that by 1977 the sixteen revenue sources had risen to twenty-nine, the formula remained basically unchanged from 1967 to the end of the 1977-1982 arrangements. Although the actual mathematical calculations are rather intricate, the principle is that a national average per capita provincial revenue is calculated for each of the agreed upon number of revenue sources, and the per capita yield in each is figured for a particular province. Where the province's per capita yield is lower than the national average for a given revenue source, the province is given a *positive entitlement* and where the province's per capita yield is more than the national average for that field, the province is given a *negative entitlement*. If the total of all the entitlements for all of the revenue sources comes to a positive figure, the province receives that much in the form of a per capita equalization payment. If, on the other hand, the total of all the entitlements of any province comes to a minus figure, the province does not get any equalization payment. This equalization formula was felt to be more equitable than older formulae in the long run because, being based on a "representative" tax system consisting of all major provincial revenue sources, it gave a more accurate reflection of provincial need.[35]

In order to prevent hardship being suffered by the provinces which were to receive smaller equalization payments under the new formula, the federal government agreed to make special interim equalization payments to such provinces. Saskatchewan was the only province that would have suffered under the new formula, so the federal government granted that province a five-year transitional equalization payment based on the province's entitlement during the

---

[35] For a detailed description see Federal Provincial Relations Office, *Federal-Provincial Programs & Activities* (1978) (FPRO, Ottawa, June 1979), pp. 69-70. Virtually all intergovernmental transfers are described in this source and it is updated periodically.

last year of the 1962-1967 arrangements. An additional equalization payment was also granted to the Atlantic provinces to compensate them for revenue lost through the termination of the Atlantic Provinces Additional Grants. The amount of this additional equalization payment was exactly the same amount that they had been paid under the Additional Grants Act, so that the change here was only in the title given the specific unconditional transfer payment.

The stabilization grants were continued for the 1967-1972 period and the formula used to calculate the actual payment was based on the same principle as the equalization formula; that is, the base was the per capita yield from the sixteen provincial revenue sources in the previous year. If the revenues of a province for the current year fell below 95 percent of the yield from the previous year, the province would get a stabilization grant. Partly because of growing provincial revenues, and partly because of the generosity of the federal government to Saskatchewan and the Atlantic provinces, no payments were ever made.

The 1972 Federal-Provincial Fiscal Arrangements Act established the basic tax agreements for the five-year period 1972-1977. Under this agreement the equalization formula remained basically the same as for the previous five years, although the revenue sources on which the payment was calculated were expanded from sixteen to nineteen. Stabilization grants were also provided for in the new Act but no province actually received any payments. The federal government had withdrawn completely from the estate and gift tax fields as a result of the 1971 federal income tax reforms, and in many cases the provinces stepped in to occupy the vacated fields. The basic collection agreements which applied in the previous five years applied again as well. Other minor changes were incorporated in the legislation but the system remained virtually identical in principal to its predecessor.

The opting-out provisions were increased to provide an additional abatement of up to 24 percent of federal income tax. The percentage of the total income tax field left to the provinces varied from province to province under an arrangement whereby the revenues of the provinces were guaranteed not to fall below their 1971 level if they adopted income tax acts modelled on the federal legislation.

This "fiscal decade" also saw the establishment of the last of the major federal shared-cost social programs, namely, medicare. The Medical Care Act, passed by the federal government[36] provided for

---

[36] For a complete description see Malcolm Taylor, op. cit. Richard Simion, *Federal Provincial Diplomacy* (University of Toronto Press, 1972) also contains a description of the negotiations surrounding medicare.

50 percent federal funding of the overall national costs of public health insurance designed to cover the cost of physicians' services. The formula also provided for partial equalization among provinces. The program has proven immensely popular with the public but, paradoxically, the provincial government most directly responsible for federal participation in Hospital Insurance in 1957, Ontario, was by 1967 vehemently opposed to any new federal shared-cost programs. Its opposition plus the resentment of Quebec at this federal intrusion into an area of provincial jurisdiction combined to ensure that medicare was the last of the major federal-provincial shared-cost programs. This continued opposition plus federal concern over the rapid increases in health care costs in the early 1970s combined to lead to the next major change in federal-provincial fiscal relations, the Established Program Financing arrangements described below.

1977-82   The 1977 version of the Fiscal Arrangements Act was given a new name and to some extent a new purpose. Virtually all the features of the 1972 Fiscal Arrangements Act were kept in place. The number of revenue sources taken into account in the equalization formula rose to twenty-nine but the method of calculation remained basically the same as did the basic outlines of the tax collection agreements and the opting-out formulae. The major change in the 1977 arrangements was the addition of a provision called *Established Programs Financing* (EPF) and the result was a set of arrangements enshrined in legislation with the formidable title of *The Federal-Provincial Fiscal Arrangements and Established Programs Financing Act (1977)*. The EPF arrangements were intended to replace the older cost-sharing arrangements for Medical and Hospital Insurance programs with a combination of an abatement of tax points and a block funding formula. As well, EPF provided for a continuing tax abatement for the financing of post-secondary education. The formula is complex but, since the amounts involved (nearly 11 billion dollars in 1981-82) are by far the largest of the intergovernmental transfers, they merit some attention.

Those with a love for complex formulae are referred to the legislation itself but in essence there are four parts to the EPF arrangement. First there is a per capita block grant amounting to about one-half of the former federal contribution for health insurance, based on 1975-76 payments and escalated annually according to population and GNP increases. This block grant is payable only if provinces continue to meet the appropriate program conditions. Since it amounts to about one-quarter of the full program costs and since the programs are very popular, the federal government felt that provinces would continue to meet those conditions. Second, the federal government agreed to vacate or abate 13.5 percentage points of personal and 1 percentage point of corporate income tax and to equalize the yield from these sources in the same way as other income tax points. Third, a $20 per capita annual payment was to be provided, escalated annually in the same way as the basic block payment, and intended to provide funding "in respect of extended health care services" such as home nursing or ambulatory services. These, presumably lower-cost alternatives, were not covered by earlier cost-sharing legislation.

Finally there was a "transitional adjustment payment" intended to ensure that provinces did not suffer financially as a result of the changes. The transitional adjustment payment was intended to guarantee that provinces would receive adequate funding even if something should happen to make the rate of increase in the revenue yield of tax points decline to less than the yield of the block fund. In that case the federal government undertook to make up the difference but the federal government officials never expected such payments to become very significant and what impact this guarantee had was expected to be truly transitory. It was not to be so.

The result has been a boon to provincial treasuries and a difficult problem for the federal government. Several factors have conspired to produce this result. Because of a 1975 federal decision to index the value of personal exemptions to the rate of inflation, the yield of tax points has not risen as quickly as "nominal GNP" (the value of inflation plus real GNP increases) and the result is that the federal government has had to make good on its "transitional" guarantee, to the tune of 1 billion dollars in 1979-80. This has been an unexpected turn of events for the federal government and its impact has been exacerbated by the fact that the "transitional" nature of these payments looks very permanent indeed.

A further twist is added by the fact that provinces receive the cash grants pursuant only to rather vaguely defined program conditions such as *portability* from province to province and *access* to services which was to be unimpeded by significant financial barriers. These rather vague wordings provide provinces with an opportunity to reduce program costs in order to free up the money guaranteed by federal payments for other things such as keeping a lid on provincial taxes and deficits. In the extreme, some provinces will reduce health care costs as far as they possibly can without either forcing the federal government to suspend payment or inciting the wrath of their voters to the point where they might be turfed out of office. The result has been that by 1980 the federal government was providing enough funding to cover over 60 percent of programs in respect of which it would have been liable for only 50 percent if it had continued the old arrangements. Moreover, in 1978 when the federal government wanted to reduce the rate of expenditure growth to the rate of GNP growth minus 2 percent, it found itself locked into an 8 billion dollar expenditure for which the provincial governments received the credit and which could not be touched without unanimous provincial agreement until 1982. Given the benefits of the EPF arrangement for provincial treasuries, that agreement, needless to say, was not forthcoming. Finally, to add insult to federal injury, provincial cost saving began to be associated with the passing on to the public of some of the hitherto insured costs of health care as doctors opted out and hospitals introduced various forms of user charges. Not only was the federal government paying more, but the health care system appeared to be deteriorating.

The complications of fiscal federalism are such, however, that there are two sides to every story. Provincial authorities attest that the EPF payments are having exactly the effect intended and described in our earlier discussion of block funding versus cost-shared programs; they are resulting in lowered program costs and in the economic circumstances of the early 1980s that is just what the voter wants. If the federal government is in a fiscal bind, provincial governments say, "too bad." That merely permits the appropriate decentralization of Canada by giving more money to the provinces and in any event, the tax system changes of 1972 have consistently cost the provinces money and this is only a partial reimbursement.

By early 1981 the astute student will have recognized in media reports a familiar pattern—the claim and counterclaim rituals of the early stages of federal-provincial bargaining over the next fiscal arrangements, due in 1982. There is no doubt that EPF has created problems from the federal perspective but there is also justice in provincial claims. Since we lack a crystal ball, no outcome of the post-1982 arrangements can be predicted but students can watch another chapter in the ongoing saga of fiscal federalism unfold before them over the next few years.[37]

That saga is likely to be made doubly complex and exciting by the distortions introduced into the fiscal arrangements by the very large oil revenues accruing to the Alberta government. In one particularly ironical twist, the size of revenues flowing to Alberta from some aspects of Crown land oil leases would have made Ontario eligible for equalization payments during 1979-80 even though per capita income in that province was greater than Alberta's. Ontario did agree to a formula amendment to avoid this but, unless there is wide acceptance of

---

[37] The EPF arrangements do not automatically expire with the expiry of the rest of the Fiscal Arrangements Act. However, at the time of this writing, federal ministers and officials were vowing to make major changes after 1982 and, since they *can* do so unilaterally, some changes are more than likely. Since such changes are rarely actually made unilaterally (another of the rules of the game of fiscal federalism) students should watch for a complex bargaining process.

Alberta's argument that its revenue comes from a rapidly depleting resource and that it must have all the money it can possibly get right away to save up against that imminent rainy day when the oil wells run dry, some resolution will have to be found for the discrepancy between that province's revenues and those of every other province.

CONCLUSIONS

Table 9-1 summarizes the current situation with respect to inter-governmental transfer payments in Canada. In 1980-81, total federal expenditures were 57.9 billion dollars so the 12.3 billion dollars in total cash transfers to the provinces accounted for over 21 percent of total federal expenditures in that year. If the abated tax points in respect of EPF are included as an expenditure in the form of foregone income, such transfers account for some 27 percent of federal expenditures. The great bulk of these are provided through relatively inflexible agreements which provide important guarantees to the provinces in order to ensure consistent levels of financing for the programs and services they deliver. However we have seen that these same guarantees have the effect of tying the hands of the federal government with respect to economic management, for the money has to be raised and that makes any lowering of federal tax rates extremely difficult—particularly when combined with large federal deficits. Moreover, because a very large proportion of federal expenditures is committed to programs which are very difficult for the federal government to reduce, any reallocation of expenditures by the federal government is made more difficult.

Paradoxically this situation arose because the massive centralization of taxing powers in the hands of the federal government—a centralization made possible by the terms of the BNA Act and given impetus by World Wars I and II and the Depression of the 1930s—contained within it the seeds of its own reversal. The federal government in the 1950s and 1960s used its spending power in a sense too well, to coerce or cajole provinces into massive new social programs—or, in some cases to buy its way into popular programs which provinces would have delivered in any event. Then, faced in the 1970s with increasing cries of federal interference from provinces, grown stronger in part because of these very programs, the federal government provided the revenue guarantees which have had such deleterious effects for federal authority. That the federal government did so under the allegedly centralist Trudeau regime of the 1970s makes the situation all the more ironic.

In sum, then, a peculiar combination of 1) federal generosity with respect to equalization formulae and the provision of stabilized levels of funding for former shared-cost programs and 2) federal

Table 9-1

ESTIMATED FEDERAL TRANSFERS TO THE PROVINCES, TERRITORIES, AND MUNICIPALITIES
FISCAL YEAR 1980-81
($ MILLIONS)

Program	Nfld.	P.E.I.	N.S.	N.B.	Que.	Ont.	Man.	Sask.	Alta.	B.C.	N.W.T.	Yukon	Total
Statutory Subsidies	9.7	.7	2.2	1.8	4.4	5.5	2.2	2.1	3.4	2.1	—	—	34.1
Fiscal Equalization	377.6	85.5	447.6	387.6	1,653.6	—	299.3	62.5	—	—	—	—	3,313.7
1971 Undistributed Income on Hand	.3	*	.8	1.4	13.1	18.8	1.8	1.0	3.1	4.7	—	—	45.0
Reciprocal Taxation	6.4	2.9	14.8	9.4	35.3	38.5	—	—	—	—	—	—	107.3
Public Utilities Income Tax Transfer	4.5	1.0	—	—	1.3	20.0	2.0	*	34.0	1.5	.3	.4	65.0
Youth Allowance Recovery	—	—	—	—	-161.6	—	—	—	—	—	—	—	-161.6
Prior Year Adjustments**	—	—	—	—	—	—	—	—	—	—	—	—	150.0
Total Fiscal Transfer Cash Payments	398.5	90.1	465.4	400.2	1,546.1	82.8	305.3	65.6	40.5	8.3	0.3	.4	3,553.5
Hospital Insurance	72.0	15.4	106.1	88.1	544.9	996.1	128.2	120.3	220.8	290.2	5.1	2.2	2,589.4
Medicare	24.7	5.3	36.4	30.3	187.1	342.0	44.0	41.3	75.8	99.7	1.7	.8	889.1
Post-Secondary Education	45.2	9.7	66.6	55.3	342.1	625.3	80.5	75.5	138.6	182.2	3.1	1.4	1,625.5
Extended Health Care	15.5	3.3	22.9	19.0	169.4	230.2	27.7	26.0	55.5	69.9	1.2	.6	641.2
Prior Year Adjustments**													38.0
Established Programs Financing Cash Payments	157.4	33.7	232.0	192.7	1,243.5	2,193.6	280.4	263.1	490.7	642.0	11.1	5.0	5,783.2
Canada Assistance Plan	50.8	11.8	62.5	78.6	541.4	508.1	67.8	66.1	150.0	254.9	1.6	8.7	1,802.3
Health Resources Fund	—	1.1	8.0	—	4.2	.2	.6	.7	.3	2.2	—	—	17.3
Other Health and Welfare	.9	.5	2.1	4.6	34.6	33.2	6.4	5.7	9.5	4.3	1.2	.4	103.4
Bilingualism in Education	1.3	.8	2.9	12.6	106.5	41.0	3.9	1.7	3.5	4.2	.1	.1	178.6
Economic Development	43.7	27.9	37.6	38.4	123.5	20.1	24.7	18.5	8.0	19.7	3.8	2.0	367.9
Crop Insurance	*	.6	.1	.1	2.6	8.8	8.1	33.2	20.7	1.8	—	—	76.0
Territorial Financial Agreements	—	—	—	—	—	—	—	—	—	—	215.5	52.3	267.8
Municipal Grants	1.7	.6	8.3	5.1	34.7	66.6	8.5	3.8	9.7	14.7	1.3	1.0	156.0
Total Other Cash Payments	98.4	43.3	121.5	139.4	847.5	678.0	120.0	129.7	201.7	301.8	223.5	64.5	2,969.3

Total Cash Transfers	654.3	167.1	818.9	732.3	3,637.1	2,954.4	705.7	458.4	732.9	952.1	234.9	69.9	12,306.0
Established Programs Financing Tax Transfer													
13.5 Personal Income Tax Points	44.5	9.6	84.3	63.2	832.4	1,351.5	118.9	110.4	339.1	431.7	6.5	4.5	3,396.5
1.0 Corporate Income Tax Points	2.8	.6	5.2	3.6	59.3	109.3	10.2	9.4	52.0	36.5	.9	.3	290.2
Contracting-Out Tax Transfer													
8.5 Personal Income Tax Points for EPF	—	—	—	—	476.2	—	—	—	—	—	—	—	476.2
5.0 Personal Income Tax Points for CAP	—	—	—	—	268.0	—	—	—	—	—	—	—	268.0
3.0 Personal Income Tax Points for Youth Allowances	—	—	—	—	161.6	—	—	—	—	—	—	—	161.6
Total Tax Transfers	47.3	10.2	89.5	66.8	1,797.5	1,460.8	129.1	119.8	391.1	468.2	7.4	4.8	4,592.5
Total Cash Plus Tax Transfers	701.6	177.3	908.4	799.1	5,434.6	4,415.2	834.8	578.2	1,124.0	1,420.3	242.3	74.7	16,898.5
Fiscal Equalization—Dollars per capita	651	691	526	548	262	—	292	65	—	—	—	—	—

* Amount too small to be expressed
** Distribution not available.
Source: Treasury Board Canada, Estimates Fact Sheet #3 (80/19), 22 April 1980.

high-handedness in starting or buying into the programs in the first place left the federal government in a vulnerable fiscal position. Combined with the general decentralization underway in all large federations in the 1970s and the peculiarly Canadian condition of relatively few but large and powerful provincial governments and the additional difficulties imposed by the Quebec situation and Western alienation, the result has been an extreme form of decentralization and a federal government whose decision makers increasingly feel themselves without the real power or flexibility to manage national affairs. When these factors are added to the assumed general public reluctance to pay tax money to governments, and seasoned with the added difficulties imposed by the federal role as tax collector for the nation, the prognosis appears at first examination to be a fairly gloomy one.

However, these situations do appear to be broadly cyclical. Canada has swung through other peaks of decentralization in the 1890s and the 1920s and through peaks of centralization coinciding with World Wars I and II and the height of postwar prosperity. Given the well-known inability of social scientists to spot a trend much before it reverses itself, it may well be that this chapter is written at a high tide of decentralization which will soon be reversed.

In the meantime the current system of fiscal arrangements has many beneficial features to leaven what many feel to be its excessive decentralization. It has, for example, done much to make possible the reduction of regional disparities in the standards of services provided across Canada. The fact that Quebec is not a province *comme les autres* has been recognized *de facto* in the opting-out arrangements for various joint programs, while at the same time, the basic equality of all the provinces has been asserted by extending the privilege of opting out without financial penalty to any province that wishes to take advantage of the provision. The basis on which equalization payments are calculated has been elaborated and made more equitable among regions. Certainly many if not most of the tools required to establish a better balanced system are either in place or available. Moreover the provision for adjustment of the system every five years provides a very valuable mechanism to allow Canadian governments to move toward such a balance. Watching this arcane game is thus perhaps not so uninteresting as most Canadians think, for it is at the very core of the Canadian political process and probably better defines the fabric of Canadian federal union than any other set of institutions.

PART 4

System-Environment Linkages

10
Political Parties in the Canadian System

For many Canadians, to think of politics is to think of political parties. Media reports on politics concentrate on party reactions to issues of the day. Millions of Canadians simplify the complexities of political issues by viewing them almost exclusively through the focus of "their" party, and, to politically interested Canadians, one of the most obvious parts of political life is the activities of these large, distinctive, and highly entertaining social organizations. Yet this very visibility makes it all too easy to view the functions of parties in an inappropriate light for because of it we may attribute to parties a false importance in the policy process while failing to recognize their vital importance in the electoral process. This chapter is intended to begin a clarification of the role of political parties in Canada. Following this initial consideration of the functions and structures of parties and the more detailed consideration of the operations of Canadian parties in the next chapter we will be in a position to make a more complete assessment of the present day importance of parties in the Canadian political system.

THE ROLE OF CANADIAN POLITICAL PARTIES

Perhaps the simplest way to begin the examination of Canadian political parties is to look at their primary objective. That is, quite simply, to get people elected and preferably enough of them so that the party can formally control the government. That is not to deny that many party activists have other objectives. They may be eager to institute certain policies and they may even aim at a fundamental restructuring of Canadian society. But whatever their ultimate purpose, they have chosen the political party as the organizational device with which to gain the power to realize their ultimate goals; the immediate or operational goal of the party is to gain and hold power, and in Canada that means the use of the electoral system.[1]

---

[1] We refrain from giving a lengthy definition of a political party in this introduction, if only to avoid time-consuming and not very productive debates about whether organizations like the Créditistes are "really" political parties. We prefer to adopt the

As a by-product of their effort to achieve this electoral goal, political parties perform for the Canadian political system a number of other important functions which are discussed below.[2] All these are vital to the survival of the system and all of them are typically listed in the general literature on political parties as vital functions of parties or party systems; but all can be performed more or less efficiently by other institutions as well. Indeed in Canada and in other Western democracies most are carried out simultaneously in various parts of the political system, so that if parties fail to perform a function thought to be within their realm, the system need not necessarily suffer; another institution such as the bureaucracy or an interest group may be performing it adequately. These functions include the recruitment and training of political decision makers, the organization of the decision-making process itself, the education or political socialization of the mass public, the articulation of specific interests, the aggregation of interests, the management of the flow of information both into and out of the system, and the generation of support for the political system of which they are a part. Each of these functions of political parties now must be considered in greater detail.

Party Functions

The "Staffing" Function   Political parties are the major recruitment agencies which ensure a steady flow of personnel to fill the political offices of Prime Minister, the cabinet, the House of Commons and the Senate. This process of recruitment involves not only the selection of local candidates for elected office through constituency nominating meetings, but also the selection of party leaders through National Conventions. Similarly it is through the political party that our leaders and our potential leaders learn the business of politics. For the most part, although there are exceptions, the training for a career in politics is provided largely through party organizations at the national, provincial, and local levels. People gain valuable political experience working within a political party and then apply this experience if and when they are fortunate or competent enough to actually attain elected office in the political system.

A secondary staffing function of political parties in Canada and one

same loose definition used by Leon D. Epstein in *Political Parties in Western Democracies* (Praeger, New York, 1967), pp. 9-10, who suggests, "almost everything that is called a party in any Western democracy can be so regarded for the present purpose. This means any group, however loosely organized, seeking to elect governmental office holders under a given label."

[2] J. R. Mallory, "The Structure of Canadian Politics," in H. G. Thorburn, *Party Politics in Canada*, First Edition (Prentice-Hall, Toronto, 1967), p. 22ff.

which may be declining, is the selection and recruitment of people to fill *appointed* positions in the government. Although such patronage functions are usually described as dysfunctional in terms of efficiency and contrary to the principle of merit in appointments to public office, Canadian parties, rightly or wrongly, do continue to administer the process of recruitment for a large number of so-called patronage positions in the political system.

The "Organizing" Function   Not only do parties recruit the political decision makers in Canada but they also organize them in such a way that the parliamentary system will work. Political parties ensure that however diverse the backgrounds of cabinet ministers and Members of Parliament they at least share one thing—a pragmatic if not ideological loyalty to the machine that got them elected in the first place. Equally important, in a parliamentary system where the cabinet can lose its right to govern if defeated on a major issue in the House of Commons, parties provide a framework within which legislative support is made predictable. Provided that a cabinet does not through arrogance or complacency abuse the loyalty of its own party supporters, it can count on a secure enough tenure to be able to plan for the future. Such predictability is essential if our priority setters are to be permitted to plan their legislative programs ahead of time and to ensure themselves a secure enough tenure to be able to finish what they have begun.

Political Education and Socialization   Not only do political parties help to train men and women for the responsibilities of elected office, they also play a more general role in teaching the public about politics and about the basic political values of our system. Because they are organizations themselves, parties must recruit people to fill positions in the various constituency, provincial, and national associations. In this fashion, and by, for example, establishing campus political clubs, the party keeps itself well supplied with volunteer workers to help out in election campaigns and to run the organizations between elections. The incidental impact of this is that many Canadians get a closer look at their political system, learn about how it operates and may thus be "turned on" to politics sufficiently that they will seek to advance up the hierarchy of political participation.

But even if a person does not participate actively in politics, political parties may be important in one's political socialization. At election time (and to a lesser extent between elections), political parties provide stimuli to which people can respond. They provide publicity for the issues around which political attitudes can be shaped, and symbols with which people can identify. It would be extremely difficult for the average citizen to make voting decisions on the basis of personal knowledge of all issues. Because people are often only dimly aware of the issues and because their views are often highly inconsistent over time, they can use parties as permanent symbols to which they can attach their allegiance and with which they can simplify the realities of politics.[3]

Aggregation and Political Integration   Political parties in Canada have often been called the "broker-mediators" of society; in doing this they mediate conflict among society's competing interests. "Canadian politics, it is emphasized, are politics of moderation, or brokerage politics, which minimize differences, restrain fissiparous tendencies and thus, over time, help knit together the diverse interests of a polity weak in integration.[4] The argument is that, in order to get elected nationally, a party must appeal to a broad cross section of Canadians with all sorts of different opinions on all sorts of different issues. The party must *aggregate* a wide spectrum of interests into a voting coalition, and in so doing, it performs an integrative function for the political system as a whole.

To a large extent, of course, the performance of this mediating role

---

[3] See Philip Converse, "The Nature of Belief Systems in Mass Publics," in D. Apter (ed.), *Ideology and Discontent* (The Free Press, New York, 1964), pp. 206-262. Converse found that the reproducibility of opinions over time was often less than would have been expected had people merely guessed at their previous opinions. See also Chapter 4 above.

[4] A. Cairns describing the prevalent mode of analysis in "The Electoral System and the Party System in Canada 1921-1965," *Canadian Journal of Political Science*, vol. 1, no. 1, p. 63, March 1968. See also F. Englemann and M. Schwartz, *Political Parties and the Canadian Social Structure* (Prentice-Hall, Toronto, 1975), pp. 222-239. The general interpretation of party politics in Canada in C. Winn and J. McNemery, *Political Parties in Canada* (McGraw-Hill Ryerson, Toronto, 1976) could also be called a brokerage interpretation as could H. G. Thorburn's summary and interpretation in "Interpretations of the Canadian Party System," in H. G. Thorburn (ed.) *Party Politics in Canada* (Prentice-Hall, Scarborough, 1979). The original expressions of this "broker-mediator" function are found in H. Clokie, *Canadian Government and Politics* (Longmans Green, Toronto, 1944), pp. 81-83; J. T. McLeod, "Party Structure and Party Reform" in A. Rotstein (ed), *The Prospect of Change* (McGraw-Hill, Toronto, 1965) pp. 4-5, 9, 15; Alexander Brady, *Democracy in the Dominions*; R. M. Dawson and N. Ward, *The Government of Canada*, 4th ed. (University of Toronto Press, Toronto, 1963), pp. 468-470; J. A. Corry and J. E. Hodgetts, *Democratic Government and Politics*, 3rd ed. (University of Toronto Press, Toronto, 1963), chs. 8-9; F. H. Underhill, *Canadian Political Parties*, Canadian Historical Association pamphlet (Ottawa, 1957), pp. 4-5. For critiques of this theory, see Cairns, "The Electoral System and the Party System in Canada 1921-1965" and John Porter, *The Vertical Mosaic* (University of Toronto Press, Toronto, 1965), pp. 373-377. Cairns points out that "the necessity for inter-group collaboration in any on-going political system makes it possible to claim of any party system compatible with the survival of the polity that it acts as a nationalizing agency." (p. 63) By that interpretation, the brokerage theory of Canadian politics has very limited utility since it is really tautological. We would not agree since different political systems have different amounts of cleavage to reconcile and can use different institutions to do so. In Canada, political parties may have been more important in this reconciliation than in other systems.

depends on the nature of the particular party. It would hardly be appropriate for instance, to call the Marxist-Leninist Party a broker or a mediator, for its aim is to remake Canadian society, and to overthrow in the process, most of the interests among whom the other parties mediate. Similarly, the early CCF could hardly have been called a broker-mediator for it, too, considered capitalists to be the fount of all evil. The two major parties in Canada, on the other hand, have epitomized the brokerage pattern of politics, and the traditional analysis of Canadian political parties has tended to revolve around this fact.

At the provincial level, such aggregative behaviour may not be as necessary as at the national. In some cases there is sufficient consensus within a province to allow a party with a single overriding principle to attain power. For example, C. B. Macpherson has argued that Alberta in the 1920s and 1930s was a homogeneous single-class society with a dominant interest in relieving burdens of its "quasi-colonial" status vis-à-vis Eastern Canada. It was therefore possible for dogmatic parties which were not broker-mediators to succeed in provincial elections. Both the United Farmers of Alberta and the Social Credit Party in that province were a far cry from the older national parties with their "omnibus nature."[5]

In general, the larger and more diversified the province, the more difficult it becomes for a "party of principle" rather than a broker-mediator type of party to get into power. In Ontario, for example, only once did a party of principle gain power: The United Farmers of Ontario won office in 1919, and they were defeated at the next election and shortly disappeared from the political scene. In Quebec the early Union Nationale could be considered to have been a party of principle but the price of its survival was the adoption of brokerage behaviour very soon after its accession to power.

At the national level, the Progressives of the 1920s were a party of principle.[6] They won 65 seats in the 1921 federal election, but soon fell prey to internal dissension and were ultimately absorbed by the brokerage-oriented Liberals. The CCF was, of course, the most persistent of the non-brokerage parties at the national level. But while the CCF competed electorally for some 29 years, except for a brief period in 1944 and 1945 when its Gallup poll popularity equalled that

---

[5] C. B. Macpherson, *Democracy in Alberta* (University of Toronto Press, Toronto, 1953). See also S. M. Lipset, *Agrarian Socialism* (University of California Press, Berkeley, 1950) for an analysis of the rise of the CCF in Saskatchewan. A more detailed analysis of all of these parties is found in the next chapter.

[6] W. L. Morton, *The Progressive Party in Canada* (University of Toronto Press, Toronto, 1950).

of the two older parties, it never seriously threatened the pre-eminence of the Liberals and Conservatives. Since the formation of the NDP in 1961 from elements of the old CCF, a conscious attempt on the part of most of its leaders has led that party in the direction of creating a more broadly based coalition with what they hope to be correspondingly greater chances for electoral success. [7]

Interest Articulation   In addition to the function of aggregation, Canadian political parties perform the function of interest *articulation*. Once again, this function derives from the electoral goal of parties in Canada. Since a party wants power, it must maximize electoral support, and the simplest way of doing this, as has been suggested above, is to attempt to aggregate the interest of groups in society. Earlier, however, it was seen that there are millions of Canadians who are eligible to participate in the electoral process but do not do so: by virtue of their apathy and lack of political resources, these people are functionally disenfranchised. If a party could mobilize them it could possibly gain power even if it paid less attention to the interests of more highly politicized groups.

Canadian parties, therefore, make *some* attempts to articulate the needs and opinions of the politically weak in order to gain their support. They frame appeals in the form of policy proposals to gain the support of the poor, recent immigrants, and other voters who might not otherwise be heard. But their success is at best mixed. The voters they hope to reach are often so unaware of politics that they do not listen, and the political parties themselves are largely dominated by the middle and upper classes. Evidently it is still simpler and safer to gain power by the "tried and true" technique of articulating and aggregating the interests of the politically conscious groups—certainly that is so as long as no other party succeeds in more radical tactics of political mobilization.

Communication Functions   Canadian parties, like their counterparts throughout the world, act as communication agencies, transmitting messages from political decision makers (and their opponents) to the environment and vice versa. Between elections the transmission of information to the environment is largely carried out by elected members of the party, supported on the government side by bales of information produced by the bureaucracy and on the opposition side by opposition research offices and the small establishment that goes

---

[7] W. Baker and T. Price, "The New Democratic Party and Canadian Politics," in Thorburn, *Party Politics in Canada*, 2nd ed., pp. 168-179. A more complete analysis of the difficulty the NDP has faced in creating a broader coalition is found in Desmond Morton, *NDP: Dream of Power* (Hakkert, Toronto, 1974).

with opposition leaders' offices. Since issues are what politicians must ostensibly concentrate upon in their struggle to present themselves in the best possible light, a good deal of information is provided as a crucial by-product of the struggle for partisan advantage.

The actual transmission of the information is now done very largely through the media although in the nineteenth and early part of the twentieth century a much more direct relationship between politician and public often prevailed. However as Chapter 5 pointed out, people see the world through a perceptual screen which colours information according to their pre-existing set of attitudes. Thus, if a person has a party identification (and approximately 90 percent of Canadians claim some such identification) he or she will pick up information which tends to conform to and reinforce a partisan preference.[8] Hence the fact that parties take positions on political issues, combined with the fact that people pick up information associated with the position of "their" party, gives parties a continuing and vital role in communicating political information to society.

Closely connected with the communication of political information to society is the feedback of information to decision makers regarding the effectiveness of their policy decisions and regarding the general political climate. A party in power must have accurate information in order to assess public attitudes to its "record." Similarly, the opposition parties must know the weaknesses of the party in power in order to launch a credible attack at the time of the next election. Like most of the functions described so far, this feedback function is not performed either exclusively or particularly well by Canada's parties. The low level of activity in Canadian parties between elections, together with a number of other features of the party structure (to be discussed below) create difficulties for the parties in this respect.

Support Functions   Parties also have a series of interconnected functions which could probably best be described as *support functions*. *Specific support,* derived from satisfaction with specific policy decisions is often channelled through a political party—most frequently the party in power. But if the interpretation which sees either of the major parties as simply different sides of the same coin is correct, specific support could also be expressed through support of whichever major party is in opposition. At the lowest level this expression of support can take the form of voting and at higher levels it could be expressed

---

[8] In 1974, 89 percent of Canadians identified with or leaned toward a party and 28 percent claimed a strong identification. Sixty-four percent of those who identified with a party claim to have maintained that identity for life. H. D. Clarke et al., *Political Choice in Canada* (McGraw-Hill Ryerson, Toronto, 1979), p. 137.

either by working for a party or by donating funds to it. However support for some parties is, in effect, an expression of lack of specific support for one or another element of the political system for there are, of course, parties in Canada which have sought to overthrow the regime or the political community. Thus support for the Communist Party, is hardly support for the liberal democratic regime, and support for the Parti Québécois, which seeks to break up the existing political community, can be interpreted as a lack of support for the Canadian political system. However, the difficulty of any unambiguous interpretation of what kind of support is intended by a voter is highlighted by the fact that only a minority of Parti Québécois supporters in the key 1976 election actually supported the separatist option. Since the PQ was the only effective opposition to a discredited Liberal government, the only way to express a lack of support for the old regime was to vote PQ regardless of the separatist option. This appears to have been the intent of the majority of PQ voters,[9] and has been borne out by the *"non"* vote in the 1980 Quebec referendum.

However, even dissident parties such as the Communists or the Parti Québécois may be functional for the existing system in that they provide a legitimate channel for the expression of dissent. Were this dissent expressed entirely through rioting, bombing, and kidnapping, the total effect would be exceedingly disruptive and harmful to society. Furthermore, by providing focal points for dissent, parties like the Parti Québécois make the system's authorities aware of the fact that certain segments of society have serious grievances with which the political system must deal. Thus, oddly enough, even parties whose major goal is the overthrow of the existing regime or community may unintentionally perform useful support functions for the system to which they are opposed.

It was suggested in Chapter 5 that people participate in electoral politics primarily because they find it an interesting social activity. It is parties that provide much of the campaign pyrotechnics which, around election time, attract attention to politics. The party attempts to create support for its candidates by selling people on its policies, its leaders and, perhaps, its ideology. By creating specific support for itself, the party also incidentally creates diffuse support for the regime of which it is a part. This *diffuse support*, derived from general confi-

[9] N. Pinard and R. Hamilton, "The Parti Québécois Comes to Power: an Analysis of the 1976 Quebec Election," *Canadian Journal of Political Science*, XI, 4, December 1978, p. 739. See also the more extensive discussion of Parti Québécois support in Chapter 3.

dence and faith in the system, is important for the stability of the regime. In addition to being built by the kind of general participation pointed to above, it may be created partially through the continued satisfaction of specific needs by appropriate policy outputs. Thus, as political parties channel and create specific support, they are also helping to add to the residual capital of diffuse support which may assist the system to survive in difficult times.

Finally, diffuse support can be created directly through the process of political education, socialization, and what is often referred to as propaganda. People can be convinced that the system is good and deserving of their support through symbolic outputs as well as through allocative ones. In the attempt to get their candidates elected, parties try to identify themselves with such values of the regime as justice, freedom, equality, and democracy and an important incidental effect of this process is to make people aware of the values of the Canadian political system and to create in them a basically supportive orientation toward the regime embodying those values.

While political parties in Canada, like those in other Anglo-Saxon democracies, confine themselves almost entirely to electoral functions, in many other Western democracies—Israel, Austria, and Sweden are examples—parties perform an array of tasks for their members, including the provision of cooperative buying services, leisure-time activities, special educational programs, and even burial societies.[10] Since nations where at least some political parties perform these functions outnumber those where they do not, Canada must be considered a sort of anomaly with respect to the rather limited social services performed by its parties.

Parties and Party Systems

So far we have considered the functions performed for the system by the individual party. But the aggregate of those individual organizations, the *party system*, also has important effects. The fact that in the Canadian party system several parties are competing for political office at election time means that the voter is presented with a choice. It matters little whether that choice is made according to perceived differences in the parties' leadership, policies, or campaign "style"; as long as the voter has some real choice, one basic requirement for the persistence of a democratic system is fulfilled.[11] A second result of

---

[10] Leon D. Epstein, *Political Parties in Western Democracies* (Praeger, New York, 1969), pp. 119-120.

[11] How "real" are the alternatives with which we are presented at election time is a matter for discussion. The fact remains, though, that the Canadian's choice is still greater than the simple "yes" or "no" offered to the citizen of a one-party state.

party competition is that political leaders can be kept accountable. We can vote to "throw the rascals out" because we can draw a line between "rascals" and "non-rascals"; the party labels and party discipline provide us with this line. As we shall see when we discuss the policy process, this accountability is of a very general nature only; yet it remains important to the workings of the Canadian system that the voter have this vehicle for expressing any disaffection, secure in the knowledge that another team is waiting to take over political leadership.

Finally in a recent article by Jane Jenson and Janine Brodie, the point is made that a critical function of the party system is to provide the electorate with a definition of what politics is all about. The party system sets the agenda for political debate; the parties in the aggregate, "shape the interpretation of what aspects of politics should be considered political, how politics should be conducted, what the boundaries of political discussion most properly may be and what kinds of conflicts can be resolved through the political process." The authors go on to argue that it is through this process of defining "the political" that the Canadian party system has given us agenda for political decision making that focus on regionalism and ethnicity rather than on class.[12]

Up to this point we have painted an essentially rosy picture of the potential activities of political parties and the party system in Canada. However, it will be suggested in what follows that Canadian parties do not necessarily perform even their electoral activities very well. The combination of the structural features of our parties and the nature of the electoral process may produce significant problems for the political system or they may result in many of the functions which we have here attributed to political parties being performed elsewhere in the political system. This is a consideration to which we will return at length later.

CANADIAN PARTY STRUCTURES

Typologies of Party Structures
The most durable typology of party structures is that first suggested by the French political scientist, Maurice Duverger. He suggested that political parties could be broadly typified as being *mass parties, cadre*

---

[12] J. Brodie and J. Jenson, *Crisis, Challenge and Change: Class and Party in Canada* (Methuen, Toronto, 1980).

parties, or militia parties.[13] *Mass parties* are characterized by extra-parliamentary origins and by the fact that the mass party organization has control over the legislative branch of the party in policy making. The British Labour Party, continental Social Democratic parties and, perhaps, the NDP or Parti Québécois could be adduced as examples of mass parties. The early CCF and, particularly, the Social Credit movement in Alberta are other Canadian examples. However, an important qualification must be entered. Roberto Michels, writing early in the twentieth century, noticed that the Social Democratic parties in Europe showed a discouraging tendency to be controlled by small cliques within either the legislature or the party executive.[14] His "iron law of oligarchy," which posits that large organizations—no matter how democratic their origins and ideology—will be controlled by a relatively small group of people at the top, limits the extent to which any political party can be controlled by its mass membership. At a certain point the requirements of efficiency appear to override the requirements of democracy.

Militia parties are parties which have a tightly organized central core with highly dedicated supporters. In mass and cadre parties, the party is a relatively minor part of the life of most members, but in a militia party the party is virtually everything. The militia party is essentially an organizational weapon to be used to overthrow an existing political system or to maintain a totalitarian one. The Canadian Communist Party would like to be a militia party but is too weak to be properly categorized as such. The *Front de Libération du Québec* is the closest recent Canadian example. The Communist Party of the Soviet Union and the Chinese Communist Party are the classic examples of militia parties.

---

[13] M. Duverger, *Political Parties* (John Wiley and Son, New York, 1963), first published in 1951. Englemann and Schwartz have modified this typology to fit Canada. See *Political Parties and the Canadian Social Structure.* Other authorities posit different classifications. For example, Leon D. Epstein (*Political Parties in Western Democracies*) suggests a four-fold classification as follows:
Rural—with a bare skeletal organization
Urban—patronage based
Urban—middle class mass-membership
Urban—socialist working class
This classification seems to mix incentive and structural bases of classifications. Moreover, it is difficult to envisage just how to classify accurately Canadian parties in it. They are not patronage-based in the U.S. sense, yet it would be difficult to categorize the older parties as middle class mass-membership and they are certainly not urban socialist or rural. Some other recent studies of political parties have made no real attempt to classify party structures: C. Winn and J. McNemeny have not used any classification in *Political Parties in Canada* nor did Jean Blondel in *Political Parties* (Wideworld House, London, 1978). We have returned to the standard Duverger typology with an elaboration of the cadre classification as suggested below.
[14] Roberto Michels, *Political Parties* (Free Press, Glencoe, Ill., 1949).

Cadre parties are characterized by the fact that a relatively small group of leaders overtly holds power in the party. The small, well-organized elite which controls the party itself is usually to be found in the legislature. With the possible exception of the NDP, traditional Canadian parties are of this type. Here it will be argued that even the NDP should be considered basically a cadre party.

Structural Types

Within cadre parties, however, a further structural differentiation can be suggested. A cadre party may take the form of a hierarchy, a stratarchy, an alliance of sub-coalitions, or an open accordion.[15] A *hierarchical* party structure is pyramidal with a single leader at the top and direct and clear lines of authority running through successive levels to the bottom. A traditionally organized bureaucracy is typical of this organizational form. However, neither Canadian political parties, nor most other large Western political parties, operate with this structure, for the lines of communication from top to bottom within a political party are generally very weak. Party members often do not know what the leaders are doing, and even when they do, they will not necessarily follow. The leaders of Canadian political parties have very limited coercive powers over party members, and followers may consequently make statements and act in ways which are not at all what party leaders might like.

In recognition of this, it has been suggested that most large political parties, especially in North America, more closely approximate a *stratarchy*.[16] A stratarchy is basically a hierarchical structure in which the lines of communication and authority between and within levels are rather weak. In Canada, constituency association executives often have only the faintest idea of what the "higher" level is doing, and even when they do know they may take actions or suggest policies which actually run counter to national party policy. More important, the provincial organizations of Canadian parties can in no way be viewed as subordinate to the national organization as we might expect in a classical hierarchical structure.

Parties may take on a structural form which could be described as an *alliance of sub-coalitions*.[17] In this type of structure, the party consists of a miscellany of groups, each fairly cohesive in itself and bound loosely to others in the party. Party members are there by virtue of

---

[15] This classification was first suggested by S. Eldersveld, *Political Parties* (Rand McNally, Chicago, 1964), pp. 47-178.

[16] Ibid., pp. 98-117.

[17] Ibid., pp. 73-97.

their attachment to the sub-coalitions rather than to the party itself. For example, this type of structure could occur if several religious groups, unions, trade associations, and community organizations came together in an attempt to gain power. Within Canadian parties this kind of structure occasionally occurs at the local level. In some local organizations of the NDP, for instance, union locals and labour councils may be allied with community associations. In Canada, however, an alliance of sub-coalitions is rare. Canadians usually join and work for political parties *per se* rather than joining them as a result of belonging to some other organization.

Finally, a party structure may be described as an *open accordion*.[18] This term means that the party structure is extremely loose and flexible with respect to membership, expanding and contracting according to the party's needs. Moreover, the "open accordion" concept implies that the party can be used by its members as an avenue of upward mobility. No Canadian political party is likely to deny membership to anyone except the most notorious criminal—and sometimes not even then. And, in a survey of delegates to the 1968 Liberal party leadership convention and the 1967 Conservative convention, some 13 percent of respondents asserted that they had found membership in the party to be helpful to them financially, and 36 percent felt that membership had been helpful in their social lives.[19]

Canadian Party Structure: Generalizations[20]

Figure 10-1 shows, in very general form, an organizational chart for Canadian political parties. Arrowheads have purposely been left off the connecting lines because in a stratarchial structure it is not always possible to say in what direction influence flows. For example, although it is normal on party organization charts to show the national executive as subordinate to the national convention, in practice the relationship may be reversed. At levels below national or provincial offices, the party structures virtually cease to exist between elections. The local strategists and workers retire to their Kiwanis Clubs, neighbourhood committees, or union halls and the local voters return to whatever they were doing before they made their trip to the

---

[18] Ibid., pp. 47-72.

[19] The data are derived from a mail survey of the delegates to the 1968 Liberal party convention. For this data we are grateful to Professor H. G. Thorburn, G. Perlin, and J. Lele of Queen's University. See also: A. Kornberg et al., *Citizen Politicians— CANADA* (Carolina Press, Durham, N.C., 1979).

[20] Detailed information on a specific party organizations is also provided in Chapter 11.

polls and watched the returns on television. Except for the local MP, small national and constituency offices, and a few hyperactive local strategists, the party disappears.

This disappearance has many ramifications for Canadian politics. It means, first, that between elections, it is difficult to communicate with parties through channels other than the federal or provincial

Figure 10-1

CANADIAN POLITICAL PARTIES: GENERAL PICTURE

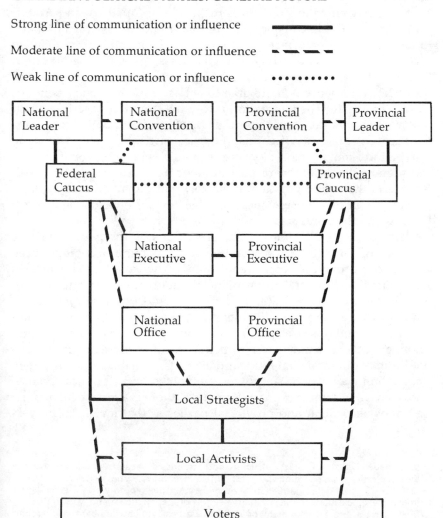

executive, or the Member of Parliament or the legislature. It is the well-organized representatives of middle-class or business Canada who are most able to do that. Although since 1973, MPs have been provided with a small budget to maintain local offices, and although virtually all of them try to be in their ridings frequently, the local machinery is not appropriate to effectively articulate the interests of the poverty-stricken, the poorly educated, and the unemployed. Because these people are, generally, loath to approach an organization as "bourgeois" as a Canadian political party, the party must approach them. However, except at election time, it does not have enough activists to do so.

As we have mentioned, in this respect both Canadian and American parties stand in conspicuous contrast to political parties in many other Western democracies.[21] In Britain, Israel, the Scandinavian nations, Austria, and, to a somewhat lesser extent, other Western nations, the political party is much more a continuing living presence in society and hence is more able to act as an intermediary between citizen and state. The temptation is to draw from this assertion about party structures the conclusion that the Canadian political system is deficient in some way. This may be true, particularly with respect to the political mobilization of poorer Canadians but no proper conclusion can be drawn in this respect until we have examined other institutions of the political system. It is likely that Canadian parties play a minor role in this process because other institutions such as interest groups and the bureaucracy do it more effectively.

Perhaps one of the most curious features of the general picture shown in Figure 10-1 is the general lack of communication between federal and provincial party organizations down at least to the level of local strategists. Federal and provincial leaders frequently disagree or simply fail to communicate. The national and provincial executives and offices are often formally unconnected, and the national and provincial conventions, except for their having some members in common, are quite separate and independent. Since there are only a limited number of local strategists and activists available, and since their motivation may well be simply to be involved in the political "game" or to scrounge some patronage "goodies" there is a great deal of overlap between federal and provincial parties at that level. At the very

---

[21] A more detailed account of the structure and activities of Western political parties between elections can be found in Leon D. Epstein, *Political Parties in Western Democracies*, pp. 98-166. Political parties in developing countries typically play a much larger role between elections. For a summary see Joseph Lapalombara and Myron Weiner, "The Origin and Development of Political Parties" in Lapalombara and Weiner (eds.), *Political Parties and Political Development* (Princeton University Press, Princeton, N.J., 1966).

bottom of the hierarchy of participation, however, there may again be considerable differentiation between federal and provincial parties for Canadian voters frequently vote for different parties at the federal and provincial levels and about one-third of Canadian voters show different long-term partisan loyalties at the federal and provincial levels of government.[22]

Lest we conclude that the structural differentiation between federal and provincial parties is a dysfunctional aspect of Canadian politics, we should note that it leaves provincial and federal governments free to agree or disagree regardless of the party labels of the party in power. This feature may be particularly appropriate in a federal regime where intergovernmental bargaining is a critical dimension of policy making. This long-standing feature of the Canadian party system has stubbornly resisted sporadic efforts by federal-level parties to change it. Attempts to impose federal control over provincial parties inevitably cause a furor in the provinces, with the result that the federal party must either retreat or watch the provincial party sever its ties with the national party.[23] Thus while the Canadian political system can be described as federal, its political parties are at best only confederal.

The most extreme example of the independence of a provincial party is the Liberal party in Quebec. Here, the federal and provincial organizations are formally completely separate, and informally, very nearly so. There is frequent disagreement on fundamental issues between the federal and provincial Liberals, and yet the Liberal party is consistently successful in Quebec at both levels. The fact that parties with strong policy disagreements can share equal success with a common electorate probably bears out the contention that parties in Canada tend to play a small role in policy making. Getting elected is their major concern and by this measure the federal and provincial Liberal Parties in Quebec would seem to be very effective organizations indeed.[24]

While the national and provincial executives and party head offices continue to exist between elections, the lines of communication between them and the parliamentary parties are often weak. The

---

[22] H. D. Clarke et al., *Political Choice in Canada*, p. 141 indicate that only 44 percent of Canadians studied in 1974 showed consistant patterns of identification (in both direction and intensity) across the two levels of government.

[23] For an example of this type of battle, see E. R. Black, "Federal Strains within a Canadian Party," *Dalhousie Review*, Vol. 45, No. 3, 1965.

[24] Paul André Comeau, "La Transformation du parti libéral québécois," *Canadian Journal of Economics and Political Science*, Vol. 31, No. 3, pp. 358-368, Aug. 1965. See also V. Lemieux, "Heaven is Blue, Hell is Red," in M. Robin (ed.), *Canadian Provincial Politics* (Prentice-Hall, Scarborough, 1978), pp. 248-282.

national executive committees meet at least annually, and MPs are often also members of the executive; but the feeling persists, especially in the caucus, that the executive exists to administer the party electoral machinery, and the caucus to determine party policy. Since members of legislatures are the most visible part of the party between elections, what they say or do is what the press reports and what the public picks up about the party. The extraparliamentary executives are thus automatically relegated to second place in policy making.

Attached to the executive of most provincial and national parties is a permanent party office under the direction of a National or Provincial Director. The staff of this office is never very large. Until very recently, a typical national party office might contain—between elections—a chief party organizer, an executive secretary for the party, two or three party researchers or administrative assistants, a public relations person, and a typist or two. Over the last decade there has been some expansion, but this has been slow, largely because between elections party organizations tend to be chronically short of money. This problem no doubt accounts in part for the fact that Canadian party offices have not grown into large, well-organized institutions such as exist in Britain or most European nations.[25]

Another location in Figure 10-1 where lines of communication are weak where they might be expected to be strong, is between the national and provincial offices, and their local strategists and workers. The problem again derives partly from the lack of work to do in a party organization between elections, and partly from the lack of finances for the permanent party organization. More surprising, however, is the fact that these lines of communication do not always become strong even during election campaigns. The torrent of directives, literature and information which issues from provincial or national headquarters at election time is sometimes ignored by the local organizations which feel that the local issues, on which they are better informed than the party bureaucrats in the capital, are likely to determine the outcome in their riding.

The parliamentary structure of virtually all Canadian parties revolves around the *caucus*. The parliamentary caucus is really just a regular meeting of the elected legislators of the party. While the legislature is in session, caucus meets at least once a week in plenary session. As well, there may be meetings of regional caucuses consisting of all the members from a particular region. In an opposition party, caucus meetings can often be quite lively; since very few members are unequivocally recognized as party leaders, almost all MPs feel free to

---

[25] The structure of each party's national headquarters is discussed in greater detail in Chapter 11.

have their say, and consequently policy debates can become heated. In the caucus of a governing party, the situation may be different. There are clearly recognized party leaders—the Prime Minister and the cabinet. The government backbenchers have the clearly defined role of supporting the policies put forward by the leaders. The cabinet has access to considerable expertise from the public service and from its political technocrats in the PMO, and it is more likely to listen to these experts than to its own non-expert backbenchers on matters of policy. By the time caucus sees the policies, they have often been approved by cabinet and may even be in their final legislative form. However this is not to assert that the government caucus has no influence on priority determination or policy formulation. Backbench government MPs take their representational roles seriously and while they virtually always will support their leaders in public they may well disagree with them in private particularly on issues which deeply affect their region. They may, in particular be able to influence the priority ordering which cabinet assigns to issues and in that way have a significant effect on the shape of policy.

However, generally in the end the cabinet will proceed along a course determined elsewhere than in caucus. In reactions to this relegation to a relatively minor role in government policy making, periodic "backbench revolts" occur in caucus, during which the backbenchers demand more policy influence. The upshot of these minor revolts, which seem to occur once in the life of every government has typically been a few minor concessions by the cabinet, which disappear gradually over a few years until another backbench revolt occurs.[26]

The general picture of Canadian political parties shown in Figure 10-1 places the *convention* near the top of the party structure, but in reality it is rather difficult to fit into the picture. Until recently conventions were not a regular feature of Canadian politics. In the two older parties they were held whenever there was a need to elect a new leader and only sporadically at other times.[27] Currently the Liberals,

---

[26] More detailed material on caucus is presented in Chapter 19.

[27] While there is considerable material available on leadership conventions in Canada, there is very little on regular policy conventions. For a more detailed discussion of the nature and role of leadership conventions see D. V. Smiley, "The National Party Leadership Convention in Canada: A Preliminary Analysis," *Canadian Journal of Political Science*, Vol. 1, No. 4, pp. 373-397, Dec., 1968. See also J. Wearing, "Party Leadership and the 1966 Conventions," *Journal of Canadian Studies*, Vol. 2, No. 1, Feb., 1967; "A Convention for Professionals: The PCs in Toronto," *Journal of Canadian Studies*, Vol. 2, No. 4, Nov., 1967; "The Liberal Choice," *Journal of Canadian Studies*, Vol. 3, No. 2, May 1968; and John Courtney, *The Selection of National Party Leaders in Canada* (Prentice-Hall, Toronto, 1974).

Conservatives and New Democrats are all committed to holding a mass gathering of the party faithful every two years.

For all three parties the convention performs similar functions, related more to improving levels of participation, maintaining group solidarity and garnering free publicity via press and television coverage than to the establishment of party policy. The national NDP convention may have slightly more influence over party policy than the Liberal and Conservative conventions but, because the NDP has never been in power, and does not have to "deliver" its convention agreements, that might be expected. The November 1969 NDP conference in Winnipeg, however, was more or less typical of all Canadian conventions, the only major difference being that the back-benchers' policy proposals "talked out" by the party leaders were somewhat more radical than those regularly handled with more or less disdain by the leaders of the older parties. That particular convention was preceded by a great build-up of publicity surrounding the nationalist "Waffle Manifesto" drafted by a left-wing group of the extra-parliamentary party. The parliamentary wing of the party countered with a much less radical policy statement, which, supported by the rhetoric of the parliamentary party and the conservatism of the labour unions, was easily pushed through the convention. To no one's surprise the party leader, Tommy Douglas, was given an overwhelming vote of confidence—something the voters had denied him at the last election. Meanwhile other potential leadership candidates, hoping desperately that Douglas would step down before too long, vowed undying support for their leader. The convention adjourned, the faithful went home, and the party carried on with little change in stated policy. Some NDP MPs even remained in Ottawa throughout the convention because, after all, parliament was sitting.

A similar fate awaits many of the policy resolutions put forward at Liberal and Conservative conventions. Should the policy proposal accord with what the parliamentary leaders want, its chance of acceptance is good. Should it be contrary to the leaders' thinking, then even if the convention accepts the policy it will not appear in any legislative program proposed by the parliamentary wing until the leaders are convinced its time has come. Medicare, for example, was adopted by a Liberal convention in 1919 but not enacted by the parliamentary party until almost half a century later.[28] According to Joseph

---

[28] After the 1966 convention Prime Minister Pearson said in the House of Commons that convention resolutions would be "taken very seriously as a guide to policy," but that they "did not establish policy." Even this was perhaps too generous an assessment of their significance. Joseph Wearing, "Party Leadership and the 1966 Convention," *Journal of Canadian Studies*, Vol. 2, No. 1, p. 24.

Wearing, the convention exerts a strong "moral force on the leadership"[29] of the party, and despite the formal accountability of the party to the convention on policy matters, a moral obligation is all that is really incurred.

The convention functions to create group solidarity. By bringing party members together, it renews acquaintances and rekindles identity with the cause; in so doing, it improves party morale and the chances of success in the next election. A convention may conceivably also make MPs and leaders aware of changes in the environment which they might otherwise miss in their preoccupation with parliament. While policy changes may not be immediate, they may eventually result from the seeds sown at such conventions.

Even a leadership convention, held to elect a new party leader, is not entirely different.[30] It is bigger, noisier and more exciting than a policy convention and it gets the party vast amounts of free publicity which helps in its attempts to get elected. And since leadership may be more important than principles in determining party policy, the installation of a new leader engenders more interest than any policy resolutions. However even the shifts in direction produced by a change in leadership have usually been small. The election of Pierre Trudeau as Liberal leader in 1968 while generating vast changes in style, made little long-term difference to the direction of the Liberal Party, and the same can be said for the election of Ed Broadbent as leader of the NDP, and of Joe Clark as Conservative leader.

For the party activists and the public alike, leadership races within parties may be very much like elections. They focus attention on the party just as elections focus attention on the political system, and they provide a game which activists can play and the public can watch—not unlike a spectator sport. While everyone would like to see the leader of his or her choice win, the contest has "fun-value" in itself. Although there is little published data on the attitudes accompanying activity in leadership races, there is no reason to suppose that attitudes toward politics within parties should be any different from those toward the struggle between parties. There are occasional "sore losers" at conventions, but they are the rare exception rather than the rule.

Another type of party activity which came into increasing use in the late 1960s was the "thinkers' conference." These were usually small conferences in out-of-the-way locations or at out-of-season vacation resorts, attended by those MPs and MLAs who liked to see them-

---

[29] Ibid., p. 25.
[30] See John Courtney, *The Selection of National Party Leaders in Canada*.

selves as policy "thinkers"; those party members who could afford to pay for their own transportation, accommodation, and registration fees; and a fair number of "resource people" or academics who lent or rented themselves out for such occasions. The purpose of these meetings was to keep the party in touch with current trends in the intellectual community and to provide policy initiatives. Conferences such as those at Niagara Falls (Conservatives) and Harrison Hot Springs (Liberals) in the autumn of 1969 may indeed have had some influence over party policy. Earlier thinkers' conferences—such as that of the Liberals at Kingston in 1960 and that of the Conservatives at Montmorency Falls in August 1967—did produce discernible changes in party policy. The conference at Kingston helped push the Liberal party some distance to the left in the early and mid-1960s, and laid the groundwork for the rapid growth in government spending in the late 1960s; while that at Montmorency Falls produced the Conservative party's not overly successful flirtation with the *deux nations* theory.[31] The Niagara Falls Conference in 1969 kept the Progressive Conservatives from moving fully in support of a guaranteed annual income, even though the leader espoused the concept. In spite of one policy meeting of Liberal "thinkers" during that party's brief vacation from power in 1979, such conferences seem to have fallen out of favour in the 1970s, perhaps reflecting a desire on the part of the parliamentary wing of the parties to maintain closer control over party policies and to avoid the tongue lashings which were sometimes issued by "resource people" brought to the meeting.

The party structures discussed up to this point have been primarily at the national or the provincial level. In 1969 parties entered municipal politics in Toronto and it is conceivable, if not particularly probable, that the next few years will see further efforts by political parties in large urban areas.[32] The success of national parties in Toronto was relatively limited. Both the Liberals and the NDP, after a fairly intensive effort in 1970, agreed to keep a low profile in 1972 and have abstained from conducting city-wide campaigns since then.[33] Even the specifically municipal "Civac" party which had considerable success in Toronto in 1970 disintegrated in 1972 as three of its leaders all decided to run for mayor. In Montreal, Mayor Jean Drapeau leads a

---

[31] Dalton Camp, "Reflections on the Montmorency Conference," *Queen's Quarterly*, Vol. 76, No. 2, pp. 185-199, Summer, 1969.

[32] James Lightbody, "Party Politics and Local Elections," *Journal of Canadian Studies*, Vol. 6, No. 1, pp. 39-44, February, 1971.

[33] Stephen Clarkson, "Barriers to the Entry of Parties in Toronto Area Politics," in L. Axworthy and James M. Gillies (eds.), *The City: Canada's Prospects, Canada's Problems* (Butterworth, Toronto, 1973).

political party of sorts but it is really a personal machine rather than a real political party and is unlikely to survive his disappearance from the scene.

In summary, there is very little real activity by municipal political parties in Canada, whether they be off-shoots of the national parties or purely local phenomena. Perhaps the question is of little overall significance; the national party allegiance of most local politicians is well known anyhow, and there is nothing to suggest that they would behave much differently in office if they were elected under national labels than if they were not.

In the next chapter we will turn to a discussion of the specific features of Canada's political parties. When that has been done we will be in a position to draw some further conclusions about the way in which parties and the party system actually do function within the Canadian political system.

11

The Parties: An Historical Perspective

Having discussed the overall role of political parties and the party system in the Canadian political system, we turn in this chapter to a more detailed examination. First we will consider the early history of Canada's party system, examining the two older parties in some detail, and then we will discuss the more recent arrivals on the Canadian party scene.

THE RISE AND FALL OF THE TWO-PARTY SYSTEM, 1840-1917

Like any social structures which have managed to survive, the Liberals and Conservatives have undergone a continuous process of adaptation in response to changes in their environment. The origins of the present day party system in Canada can be traced back to the legislature of the United Provinces of Upper and Lower Canada following the Act of Union of 1840.[1] The early years of the Union government were characterized by a series of coalitions among various factions in the assembly. The factions, formed around various strong leaders, were quite stable. The coalitions of factions which constituted the "parties" at first were quite unstable but tended to become more constant as time went on until Macdonald and Cartier managed to develop a "Liberal-Conservative" coalition which was sufficiently stable to create Confederation.

The gradual evolution of firmer party lines which had begun in the pre-Confederation era continued after 1867. Between 1867 and 1873 the Canadian government still consisted of a loose collection of many of the Liberal and Conservative elements which had initially favoured Confederation. Their unity, such as it was, arose out of a common desire to build a nation and to keep it together. Macdonald may have been the leader, but each of his ministers had his own personal fol-

---

[1] E. M. Reid, "The Rise of National Parties in Canada," *Papers and Proceedings of the Canadian Political Science Association*, Vol. 4, 1932. See also G. M. Hougham, "The Background and Development of National Parties," in H. G. Thorburn, *Party Politics in Canada* (3rd Edition) (Prentice-Hall, Scarborough, 1972), pp. 2-14, and H. G. Thorburn, "The Development of Political Parties in Canada" in *Party Politics in Canada* (4th edition), 1979, pp. 2-12.

lowing in both the House of Commons and the country. Building a government consisted of keeping enough of these factions together to form a voting bloc in parliament.

Within the first House of Commons there were "Tory" and "Grit" factions, but there were, as well, other kinds of groupings. On the government side sat cabinet members, their personal supporters, and assorted "loose fish" or "ministerialists" who had been elected by their constituents for the express purpose of supporting the government in hopes of gaining patronage prizes. The existence of ministerialists was made possible by a system of non-simultaneous elections whereby the party in power could call an election in safe seats first and then gradually work out to less favourable ridings. In addition to giving the party in power a great advantage, by allowing it to create its own bandwagon, this system also removed any uncertainty on the part of ridings which wanted to ensure their share of patronage by electing a loose fish, for it indicated to the local candidate which way he was to lean.

However, even by 1867 there were beginning to emerge some consistent patterns to the Liberal-Conservative governing coalition and to their Liberal opponents. The former comprised Cartier's "Bleus", consisting of the French-Canadian majority blessed by the Church establishment, Macdonald's Ontario Tories, big business interests from Montreal arranged around Alexander Galt and various supporters of the Grand Trunk Railway. Their orientation was firmly protectionist, expansionist, and pro-business. The Liberal opposition consisted of Ontario Clear Grits—agrarian reformers loosely tied to George Brown and the Globe—plus the parti Rouge—radical reformers from Quebec. The Liberals' orientation was anti-railroad, anti-protectionist, and pro-agrarian. Maritime members, with the exception of a group of Nova Scotia MPs associated with Joseph Howe and initially opposed to Confederation, made what alliances they could to ensure patronage for their area. For another ten years, individual MPs would move back and forth from one element of the coalition to another or even from government to the opposition, but the positions of the elements and the leaders were relatively stable.

In 1872, the group in power made the mistake of getting caught accepting rather large kickbacks (under the guise of "election fund contributions") from the promoters of the Canadian Pacific Railway, and although they won the election of 1872, they were forced to resign shortly thereafter when the dimensions of the "Pacific Scandal" became known.[2] The Liberals who replaced them from 1873 to

---

[2] The "Pacific Scandal," as it was called, is covered thoroughly in Pierre Berton, *The National Dream* (McClelland and Stewart, Toronto 1970), ch. 3, pp. 90-134.

1878 under Alexander Mackenzie had little to offer in the way of policy and lacked any cohesive party organization. Indeed in 1873 it was not even absolutely certain who their leader was; Mackenzie had to fight a continual battle with Edward Blake, who was apparently unable to decide whether he really wanted to lead the party, but who nonetheless retained great personal popularity. After five years in power, the Liberals had developed virtually none of the organizational attributes necessary to retain office and in 1878 they were defeated by the much better organized Conservatives.

The first ten years of Confederation, then, were characterized by growing party cohesion in the dominant coalition with much slower development in the opposition. The lack of simultaneous elections and of the secret ballot made party organization in the years before 1878 a rather different problem than it is today. Further, the process of functional differentiation of institutions—which accompanies industrialization and modernization in any society—takes time, and in political parties no less than in other Canadian institutions, the process was just beginning in the last third of the nineteenth century.

By 1878 there were simultaneous elections by secret ballot in Eastern Canada, so that it was necessary for candidates to choose party lines before, not during, an election. This fact alone produced much firmer party lines in Canada. From 1878 to 1891 there was a consolidation of Conservative party lines under Macdonald and under his "National Policy" of railway construction, westward expansion, and protective tariffs. The Liberal party was characterized by a period of aimlessness and lack of organization in what was a fairly stable coalition, followed by a reformulation and regrouping under Laurier.

The West was the particular home of non-partisan and ministerialist politics. Its primary concern was to ensure that the railway went through and Westerners would have supported any ministry that would build the railroad. In practice, that meant Macdonald's Conservatives—and the "kindly" Conservative government made it easy for Westerners to support the government party by delaying the introduction of simultaneous elections in the West. This may account for the fact that strong two-party traditions never developed there. Provincial governments in Manitoba and British Columbia, and later in Saskatchewan and Alberta, sometimes went under standard party labels, but the lack of strong bipartisan competition led to an administrative form of government which later lent itself to easy capture by third-party movements.

The years from 1896 to 1917 could perhaps be characterized as "the golden age" of two-party politics in Canada. The Conservative and Liberal parties, led by Robert Borden and Wilfrid Laurier respectively

both had well-organized electoral machines and well-disciplined parliamentary parties. No other party movements of any significance
existed. Sectional discontent had not yet made a strong impression
on the Canadian scene, ethnic cleavage was dormant for the time
being, and the rural-urban cleavage which was to spawn the Progressive movement of the 1920s had not yet become important. Economic
prosperity minimized dissent, and those who were discontented
could move west to start again; the two-party system was able to successfully accommodate interests because the job was, for once, not
particularly difficult.

Although Laurier was defeated in 1911, the equilibrium of the two-
party system persisted until 1917. World War I, the "Conscription
Crisis" of 1917, and the formation of the Union Government ended
those days. Some three years after the outbreak of World War I, it
became necessary, in Prime Minister Borden's view, to institute conscription in order to keep up the size of Canada's forces in Europe.
We have seen in Chapter 3 that French Canadians felt that the war
had little relevance to their lives, and this attitude, combined with
evidence of inhospitable treatment received by any French Canadians
who did join the armed forces, ensured the opposition of French Canada to conscription. In an effort to unite Canadian opinion, Borden
formed a Union Government with most English-speaking Liberals
supporting him; but practically all French-speaking Liberals opposing
him. The election which followed all but isolated French Canada, and
temporarily destroyed the Liberal coalition which Laurier had so carefully constructed. In addition, it spelled the end of any strong support
for the Conservative party in Quebec. The end of the war found the
Canadian two-party system in a state of disarray from which it has
never recovered.

Although the immediate cause of the collapse of the two-party
system was the conscription crisis and the formation of the Union
Government, a number of more fundamental causes lay in the background. The Conservative party structure had become overcentralized in Eastern Canada, particularly in Ontario, while the Liberals
had become too strongly identified with their French-Canadian
leader and with French Canada. The lack of any strong party tradition
in the West was shortly to result in the election there of many Progressive MPs. Moreover, the parties had stopped trying to win elections by creating a consensus and had turned to the tactic of playing
on ethnic cleavages while virtually ignoring rural-urban problems
and the East-West cleavage. An excessive emphasis on ethnic cleavage was dangerous, as was an excessive concentration on fulfilling
the demands of war. By failing to take account of other demands,
both older parties moved out of touch with their environment and

lost the broadly based support needed to maintain a two-party system. Finally, both parties were entering periods of instability in leadership. The Liberals recovered quickly and were able once again to build enough of a national coalition to win elections; the Conservatives have been in a more or less perpetual leadership crisis since 1921.

The period from 1921 to 1980 has seen tremendous changes in the environment of Canadian politics, but relatively few changes in the structure of the two older parties. The point is made by Reginald Whitaker:

As S. M. Lipset and Stein Rokkan have noted, (in most western democracies), the party alternatives and, in remarkably many cases, the party organizations, are older than the majorities of the national electorates, reflecting the cleavage structures of the 1920s. In the Canadian case it is the 1930s which would seem to be the decisive period for the freezing of party alternatives. . . . All this suggests that to understand the basis of party support, it is not enough to understand contemporary issues and contemporary social structure. Parties in a sense represent frozen elements of earlier alignments. [3]

One of the consequences of the, perhaps inevitable, failure of the major Canadian political parties to adapt adequately to the social changes of the 1920s and 1930s was the rapid rise of a host of minor parties. The next part of this chapter will look first at the two older parties from 1921 to the present, and then at the many smaller parties that sprang up in the same period.

MODERN PARTY POLITICS: THE MAJOR PARTIES, 1921-1980

The Liberals

In 1921 the Liberal party of Canada elected as its leader a most unlikely man, W. L. Mackenzie King. Historians have not treated King kindly, and his biographers—even his official biographer—have made of him a less than heroic figure. [4] Yet in some ways King can be

---

[3] Reginald Whitaker, *The Government Party* (University of Toronto Press, Toronto, 1977) pp. XIV, XV.

[4] There are a number of biographies of King. The best is undoubtedly the series of volumes begun by R. MacGregor Dawson and continued by Blair Neatby, *William Lyon Mackenzie King: A Political Biography* (University of Toronto Press, Toronto, 1958 and 1963). See also J. W. Pickersgill, *The Mackenzie King Record*, Vol. 1, 1939-1944, and Vol. 2, 1944-1948 (University of Toronto Press, Toronto, 1960 and 1970). Many of King's diaries became available in 1975, and they provide fascinating pictures of the man and his view of Canadian politics in his era. The Diaries are in the National Archives, Ottawa.

viewed as a hero even if an unprepossessing one. He took over a party decimated by the events of the previous five years and rebuilt it into an organization which, for more than half a century has dominated Canadian electoral politics at the federal level. That he did so by equivocation, occasional deceit, large doses of compromise, and with the help of a medium, his departed mother, a dead dog, and the position of the hands on a clock is perhaps as much a measure of policy making in Canada as of the man himself.

The party that King and his helpers constructed is a cadre party in many of the senses described by Duverger but it has features of at least two of the other structural variants discussed earlier. First, it was and remains a stratarchy. There are nominal lines of authority and communication between the leader and the provincial and constituency levels, but in practice these lines of authority remain weak. In contrast to the highly centralized nature of the Conservative party under Bennett, the Liberals showed considerable decentralization both in financial structure—which King claimed not even to know about—and in policy matters.[5]

Second, the national Liberal party since 1921 has been an "open accordion." It has had to be in order to swallow up, first, most of the agrarian discontent of the West in the 1920s, and later, a portion of the unrest which characterized Quebec in the 1960s. King and his party accommodated much of the Western agrarian protest because they were primarily oriented towards electoral success and, unlike the somewhat more dogmatic Conservatives under Meighen and Bennett, they were willing to make room in their party leadership and on their platform for this discontent. Later the party under Pearson was also able to accommodate at least some of the Quebec unrest by allowing the Quebec provincial Liberal party to become an almost completely separate entity and by recruiting prominent leaders of reform in Quebec such as Pierre Trudeau.

The structure of the Liberal party has changed surprisingly little and, even then, very slowly since the days of King. The parliamentary organization and the cabinet are undoubtedly the centre of power in the federal party, yet their control over provincial organizations is minimal. In British Columbia, Alberta, and Manitoba, the provincial liberals are a negligible political force. The Ontario Liberal party has fairly close organizational ties with the federal party, but the relative electoral successes of the two parties would seem to indi-

---

[5] Reginald Whitaker, *The Government Party* is the definitive study of the Liberal party during much of its period of dominance. There are valuable organizational diagrams of the parties in C. Winn and J. McMenemy, *Political Parties in Canada*, 168-173.

cate that in the voter's mind there is little connection, and Whitaker suggests that in some respects the federal Liberals, in power, prefer to deal with the Ontario Tories. Certainly "saw-offs" are not uncommon. By long-standing arrangement the Liberals back off from provincial elections in Northern Ontario while the Conservatives run only a nominal campaign in federal elections. The Quebec Liberal party is essentially a separate entity, yet at the level of campaign workers and local strategists, many of the same people work for both the federal and the provincial organizations. In the Maritimes, on the other hand, the ties between federal and provincial parties appear to be closer than in the rest of Canada.

There is some problem here in separating organizational myth from political reality. Except in Quebec, there is no separation in the Liberal party constitution, between the federal and the provincial parties; one provincial organization is supposed to subsume both federal and provincial constituency organizations. However, the concentration of real power within the federal and provincial cabinets or legislative caucuses, which are totally separate organizations, ensures that there is a considerable split between the effective federal party and the effective provincial parties.

The national office of the Liberal party has a National Director acting as the full-time head of the party structure. Under the National Director are a number of divisions concerned with such functions as Communications, Policy and Research, Administration, Organization, Finance, Youth, and Printing. The largest of these divisions is Communications, which includes information officers, the editor of the national Liberal party magazine, and a speakers' bureau. The full-time staff between elections numbers about 25. This is large by past standards of Canadian parties, but during the 1970s when almost every office in the public service was expanding, the national office did not grow much. This might suggest something either about the importance of its role or about the financial state of the Liberal party, but compared with the large and elaborate research establishments of British political parties, the office is small indeed.

Both the older parties have experienced innumerable problems keeping the extra-parliamentary wing of the party—which does much of the work in election campaigns—in touch with the elected politicians. This has been more of a problem for the Liberals than for the Conservatives, perhaps because the Liberals have been in power more often. The cabinet ministers, who are at the centre of power both in government and in the party, are notoriously busy and getting them to hold still long enough to communicate even with their own power base in the party has been difficult. More to the point, however, they may not wish to stay in active communication. A cadre party, after all, is built upon domination by the parliamentary wing.

In recent years the extra-parliamentary wing of the Liberal party has extracted from the elected members several structures to build better contact between the MPs and the executive of the party. The most important of these when the party has been in power has been the *political cabinet*. It consists of the real cabinet, the regional caucus chairman and the President and the National Director of the Liberal Party of Canada. It has met (with varying degrees of regularity—depending partly on the nearness of an election) at intervals of about one month. Its agenda, set by the party executive rather than by the Prime Minister, is designed to keep the executive in touch with cabinet thinking and, to a lesser extent, to keep the cabinet in touch with party executive thinking. The party also has had provincial advisory groups of varying degrees of vigour consisting of the provincial president, one cabinet minister from the province, and one caucus member from the province. Nominally, they report directly to the party leader.

During election campaigns the Liberal party's extra-parliamentary structures expand, as the skeleton of full-time workers is fleshed out with hundreds of volunteers. The key national structure during a campaign is the National Campaign Committee, which has traditionally consisted of the National Campaign Chairman, the National Organizer, the National Treasurer (all appointed by the party leader), and representatives of each of the 10 provincial campaign committees, chosen in consultation with the provincial Liberal associations. For the 1974 campaign the Liberals had two co-chairmen. Senator Keith Davey, formerly the National Director of the party, and Transport Minister Jean Marchand. In 1979 and 1980 Marchand was replaced as co-chairman by Marc Lalonde.

The National Campaign Committee plans and directs the general strategy of the campaign. It consults with advertising experts and pollsters and draws up the national advertising campaign. In recent elections, instead of hiring one advertising agency, the Liberals have drawn together advertising experts from several agencies to form a "communications group" attached to the National Campaign Committee. This group not only advises the national committee on its advertising program, but also deals directly with each provincial campaign executive to help adapt the national advertising campaign to that province's needs. Finally for the 1980 campaign, the Liberals created a *Platform Committee* composed of twenty members elected from the caucus, and twenty extra-parliamentary party members backed by the expertise of the party leader's staff. The committee looked at the 1979 campaign with a view to discovering what went wrong and came up with a strategy to overcome the mistakes of the 1979 campaign with a better platform in 1980. It apparently worked.

The National Treasurer heads the Standing Finance Committee of the party. This informal committee swings into action early in the campaign to provide the wherewithal for all of the other activities. In addition to the funding provided from the public purse under the Election Expenses Act of 1974, the party's sources are mainly large corporations and wealthy individuals, and the fund-raising structure reflects this fact. Many of these donors hedge their bets by giving money to both of the older parties, 60 percent to the one in power, 40 percent to the one in opposition, or if the race appears close, 50 percent to each. In 1979, for example, both the Royal Bank and the Canadian Imperial Bank of Commerce gave $25,000 to each party as did Canadian Pacific.[6] The "bag-men," as the fund raisers have come to be known, are generally well-to-do business people or lawyers who have good connections with corporation heads. The "first string bag-men"—to whom the many other collectors report—are located in the major cities of Canada, where business interests are concentrated. In 1974 the party's chief bag-man was Senator John Godfrey, a Toronto Rosedale lawyer, while in 1980 another Toronto lawyer, Rob Brydon, took over the Liberal's top financial job.

It has been traditional for Liberal party leaders to disclaim all knowledge of the sources of their party's campaign funds and hence to deny any temptation to reward the benevolent for their generosity.[7] To suspicious minds such ignorance has always seemed unlikely and pursuant to the 1974 election expenses legislation, the names of all donors who have given more than $100 must be disclosed.

Even while the funds are being raised, the campaign is underway. Indeed, payments for campaign costs are usually made on the instalment plan as donations are received. The National Campaign Committee arranges for national advertising, which includes radio and TV production, plans the leader's tour and big special events, and arranges for the extra staff needed at national headquarters. The provincial committees take charge of the leader's tour in their province, supplement the national advertising if necessary and, if funds are available, distribute nationally gathered dollars for use at the constituency level. They also provide advice and information to candidates. In most provinces, the national party simply takes over the provincial party office for the duration of the campaign. The Quebec Campaign Committee of the federal wing of the party has exercised considerable autonomy in both planning and fund-raising and has run its own campaign virtually coordinate with the national committee. The

---

[6] *Globe and Mail,* July 4, 1979, p. 1.
[7] K. Z. Paltiel, *Financing Political Parties in Canada* (McGraw-Hill, Toronto, 1970) is the best single account of the process of election finance in Canada.

appointment of Jean Marchand, at that time the federal leader in Quebec, as co-chairman of the National Campaign Committee in 1974 indicated that this pattern had been formalized and the arrangement was repeated in 1979 and 1980 with the appointment of Marc Lalonde. Locally, the party's structures and activities vary greatly from one constituency to another and often reflect the local candidate's own idiosyncrasies. Chapter 12, which deals with elections in Canada, gives a general description of campaign activity at this level.

No picture of a political party would be complete without some view of its supporters.[8] The Liberal base of support is paradoxically both broad and narrow. It is broad in the sense that no other Canadian party can claim to draw support from such a broad social spectrum; yet it is narrow in some of its regional aspects such as in its electoral dependency on the French-Canadian vote and its appalling weakness in the West in 1979 and 1980. However, Liberal support in Quebec is not only from French Canadians, for within Quebec, English Quebeckers also heavily support the Liberal party. Moreover, there is also some evidence that much of the Liberal-French connection in Quebec and Liberal weakness in the West is actually a reflection of voter support or aversion for Trudeau.[9] There is also strong support for the Liberals from French minorities outside of Quebec. Franco-Ontarians and Acadians support the federal (and provincial) Liberals in overwhelming proportions and there was no evidence in 1979 and 1980 that this support is evaporating at all.

High-socioeconomic-status voters have tended to support the Liberal party more than have others, and Western farmers have tended to avoid it like the plague. Yet Eastern farmers have traditionally given a larger portion of their vote to the Liberals than to other parties. The general lack of enthusiasm of Western voters for the Liberal party is well known and is reflected in figures which show that rural, small town, and farmer support for the Liberals is somewhat lower than the proportion of those groups in the population. In 1979 and 1980 this trend was still more pronounced.

In spite of strong efforts by all other parties, the Liberals have con-

---

[8] We have not footnoted in detail this or subsequent sections on the basis of party support. They rely particularly on three sources: John Meisel, *Working Papers on Canadian Politics* (McGill-Queen's Press, Montreal, 1972), pp. 34-51; Mildred Schwartz, "Canadian Voting Behaviour," prepared for R. Rose (ed.), *Electorial Behaviour, A Comparative Handbook* (New York, Free Press, 1973); and H. D. Clarke et al., *Political Choice in Canada* (McGraw-Hill Ryerson, 1979).

[9] J. Meisel, op. cit. p. 35. See also, Pammett et al., "Change in the Garden: The 1979 Federal Election," paper presented to the C.P.S.A. conference 1980, pp. 7-17.

sistently had greater appeal to minority groups ranging from the large English and French minorities in Quebec and Ontario respectively to "new Canadians"—immigrants who have arrived since 1945. The party also has been better supported by younger voters than older ones. Liberal voters also have tended to be more satisfied with their economic situation, and more optimistic than Conservative, NDP, or Créditiste supporters. Professor John Meisel has summed up this picture by asserting that:

The Liberal party can be thought of as being most progressive or "modern," in the sense of appealing most to those elements in society which feel at home in the so-called "advanced" urbanized and highly technological world usually associated with urban North America. This is not to say, of course, that the supporters of the other parties were all, or even predominantly, antique rustics dwelling in some sort of retarded psychological middle age but rather that the Liberals, on the whole, contained a larger proportion of "modern" electors . . . than the others. [10]

As Reginald Whitaker has suggested in his major study of the Liberals, the essence of the structure and support of the party and the explanation of its long period of dominance over Canadian federal politics is that people have come to identify the Liberal party as the "government party." [11] In this situation, virtually all real power within the party inheres in the leader and the cabinet and the party depends upon a compounding of the control over government to perpetuate its electoral advantage. Whereas European and British parties in the mid-twentieth century have build up extensive organizations outside the legislative wing of the party, for most purposes, the Liberals have utilized the apparatus of the federal government itself as their proxy extra-parliamentary organization.

Under this system, individual cabinet ministers are essentially clients of the Prime Minister. They hold their positions of prestige and authority at his behest and in return they provide loyalty and they use their departmental organizations not just to operate the functions of the modern state but also to provide the rewards necessary to motivate party workers and to ensure electoral support. The most powerful of them also operate as power brokers in order to consolidate support in the regions and in turn to represent those regional interests at the centre. The locus of power within the party, then, lies very obviously with the Prime Minister and the cabinet.

One thing this system does not provide is the money to run elec-

---

[10] Meisel, op. cit., p. 38.
[11] The remainder of this discussion of the Liberal party relies directly on Reginald Whitaker, *The Government Party*, particularly p. 401ff.

tion campaigns or, more properly since the 1974 Election Expenses Act, the money to allow your party to spend more than others at election time. For that the Liberals remain dependent on the corporate elite, and the major function of the extra-parliamentary wing is the raising of money. This also means that for the "government party" life becomes a matter of balancing the mass of voters necessary for electoral victory against the elite who finance that victory and who operate the economy. Whitaker points out that over the last sixty years under successive leaders, the Liberals have become very adroit at calling in one side or the other of this equation to redress any imbalance.

In general, this is a satisfactory situation as long as the party holds office. However, as Whitaker points out, the organizational structure of a cadre party operating in a federal system without firm class support and with heavy reliance on the public service as its organizational base is particularly vulnerable once it has lost office. In part the problems result from the fact that the party's provincial bases are not really bases at all, but rather problematic elements in the overall structure of the national party, with different electorates, different concerns, and even different sources of party funding. This means that a federal cadre party out of office cannot fall back on the provincial parties as a firm base of support for the national party in its hour of organizational need.

Because of its lack of an organizational base outside the government structure *per se*, when the party loses office it is faced with the problem of rapidly creating, out of almost nothing, an extra-parliamentary organization which it can ride back into power—and which it will tend to jettison as soon as it attains power. The Liberals had no opportunity to do this between 1957 when they narrowly lost an election and 1958 when John Diefenbaker called a second election: the result was, for them, electoral disaster. Only the self-destructive tendencies of the federal Conservative party saved them from a similar fate in the elections of 1979-1980.

Even in office the maintenance of power for the dominant party in this system is a highly delicate exercise. The ministerialist, regional power-broker system requires that cabinet ministers stay in close touch with their regions and the interests of their voters and clientele. Yet the problems with which they grapple in office are highly complex and the solutions are worked out and put into operation through giant bureaucracies. Because they solve most major policy problems through the mobilization of the expertise of bureaucracies, the major power mediators in the government are in some danger of losing touch with their voters. Traditional patron-client relationships tend to be replaced with bureaucratic clientelism—farmers are represented by the Department of Agriculture, industry by Industry, Trade and Commerce, ex-service-men by the Department of Veterans Affairs, etc. Thus ministerialism becomes administrative government, politics becomes bureaucracy, and the Liberals become The Government Party.

These problems are increased by the difficulty a party may have in recruiting and holding talent under this system. Because effective control over policy resides in public sector bureaucracies controlled by ministers, it is difficult to motivate people interested in policy change to become involved in the extra-parliamentary party. Rather the dominant reward the party can offer its top honchos is recruitment into the federal public service, bypassing the party structure altogether. Thus faithful supporters of the government of the day may be recruited to the public service after having served as acolytes of various ministers or the Prime Minister for a couple of years. However, once in the public service the supporter is to some extent neutralized, being proscribed by law and tradition from direct partisan participation. This situation becomes most acute at election time when many of the party's previous supporters, now ensconced in non-partisan offices, back off from the party. It becomes all the more acute if there appears any possibility that the party might lose. The strict neutrality of erstwhile government supporters in the bureaucracy in Ottawa as the 1979 campaign wore on and a change of government appeared more and more possible was evidence of this problem. Thus paradoxically, by attempting to perpetuate its hold on power through planting its supporters in the tenured ranks of the public service, the party has also placed its supporters above the necessity for continued partisan loyalty.

What conclusion we can draw from this is perhaps best left stated by the foremost student of the Liberal party. Although he was speaking of the 1940s and 1950s, Reginald Whitaker's words ring true as a conclusion equally applicable in the 1980s.

Perhaps this may be a final, paradoxical, conclusion to be drawn from this study. The curious lack of definition of Canadian parties, which has troubled so many observers of our politics, is only reinforced as the evidence concerning their structures is marshalled. The Liberal party was an organization seeking not so much to consolidate its distinct partisan identity as to embed itself within the institutional structures of government. Its fulfilment was not so much organizational survival as it was institutionalization as an aspect of government: control over recruitment channels to senior levels of office. The deadening of political controversey, the silence, the greyness which clothed political life at the national level in the 1950s, were reflections of a Liberal ideal of an apolitical public life. In place of politics there was bureaucracy and technology. This in no sense meant that Canada stood still. Profound changes were taking place in the nation's political economy. But these changes tended to take place outside the realm of traditional political debate. Instead, it was between the great bureaucracies, whether public (federal and provincial) or private (Canadian and American), that debate and policy refinement took place. The Liberal party had truly become the Government party—an instrument for the depoliticization and bureaucratization of Canadian public life. The vision of Mackenzie King in his almost forgotten Industry and Humanity had begun to take shape: "whether political and industrial government will merge into one, or tend to remain separate and distinct" was King's question for the future in 1918. He concluded that "the probabilities are that for years to come they will exist side by side, mostly distinguishable, but, in much, so merged that separateness will be possible in theory only." [12]

The Conservatives

While Mackenzie King set the tone of party structure for the Liberals from 1921 on, it may be a proper description of the Progressive Conservatives to suggest that no leader has succeeded in putting any very permanent stamp on the party. Since 1917 instability has been its most prominent characteristic. Arthur Meighen, Borden's successor as party leader, seemed unable to develop the "common touch" and this, combined with total lack of support in Quebec (in 1921 he won only 18 percent of the vote there, and no seats), ensured that he was a failure as a leader in that most vital of tasks—getting elected. [13] R. B. Bennett, who succeeded him, did win an election, and from 1930 to 1935 definitely did set the tone of the party. This was made all the easier for Bennett since he also "owned" the party in that he was its largest financial backer. He thus completely dominated the party organization, "a benefit which his party scarcely survived." [14] The Conservative party's misfortune in getting elected for a period which spanned most of the worst years of the depression ensured that it would fail electorally in 1935. It seems doubtful that any government or party could have successfully resolved the deep cleavages and crises caused by the Depression, but the Conservatives had developed an overcentralized structure that was singularly inappropriate for even attempting the task.

Bennett's departure from the leadership was followed by another of those periods in Conservative party history which could most charitably be called a prolonged interregnum. One leader after another failed to lead the party out of the electoral wilderness. Between 1940 and 1956, the Conservative party went through four leaders, and even supported an abortive comeback attempt by Arthur

---

[12] R. Whitaker, op. cit., p. 408.
[13] Roger Graham, *Arthur Meighen* (Clarke, Irwin & Co., Toronto, 1960). If the literature on the Liberals is thin, that on the Progressive Conservatives is almost non-existent. The material presented here is pieced together largely from news reports during election campaigns.
[14] K. Z. Paltiel, *Political Party Financing in Canada*, p. 17.

Meighen.[15] Finally, in 1957 and 1958 the perpetual leadership crisis seemed to be resolved when John Diefenbaker led the party to electoral victory. However, Diefenbaker's leadership ended with deep acrimony and a badly divided party in 1967 and his successor, Robert Stanfield never did succeed in reuniting the party during the eight years that he was leader. His successor, Joe Clark, did finally succeed in getting the various warring factions within the party to work sufficiently in harness to enable the party to win a minority victory in the 1979 general election; but whether his leadership will survive the party's defeat in the 1980 general election is a moot point, particularly given that one-third of delegates to the 1981 party convention voted for a leadership review.

The basic structure of the Conservative party in the last half-century has been, like that of the Liberals essentially of the stratarchical-cadre genre. But unlike the Liberal structure, there have been few aspects of the open accordion about the Conservative party. Only very recently has any very concerted effort been made by Conservatives to woo the Quebec voter or to understand French Canada, and it is by no means certain that the party is unanimously committed to this effort. Certainly what efforts the party has made have not borne fruit. The proportion of Francophones supporting the Conservatives declined from 17 percent in 1968 to 14 percent in 1974 and to 13.4 percent in 1978. After the party's 1979 victory in the federal election it found itself with just one Francophone MP and only 13 percent of the popular vote in Quebec; efforts to entice other prominent French Canadians into the cabinet failed completely.

The Conservatives have occasionally tried to increase their support by recruiting other groups. In the 1940s they attempted to gain Progressive support from the West by choosing as their leader the former Progressive Premier of Manitoba, John Bracken, and adding the name "Progressive" to their party masthead. Unfortunately for the Conservatives, Mackenzie King had co-opted most Western Progressive support some twenty years previously. Under Diefenbaker, the Conservatives tried to become the party of the "other" ethnic groups of Canada, but in attempting this they alienated as many New Canadians as they attracted by an overemphasis on the "differences" in their cultural backgrounds. At any rate they were not successful in attracting much permanent support from such groups since only about 15 percent of recent immigrants supported the Conservatives in

[15] See J. Granatstein, *The Politics of Survival 1939-1945* (University of Toronto Press, Toronto, 1967).

1968 as opposed to the 72 percent who supported the Liberals.[16] Even among longer established immigrant groups the Conservatives have tended to do less well than the Liberals. In 1974, 36 percent of Canadians of Northern and Western European extraction supported the Conservatives and 48 percent the Liberals. For Eastern Europeans the figures are 58 percent Liberal and 27 percent Conservative.[17]

The formal structure of the Conservative party is rather similar to that of the Liberals and there are also many similarities in the two parties' informal structure.[18] Like the Liberals, the Conservatives have a permanent staff at a national party headquarters, and several regional offices with permanent staff. Like the Liberals, a vital component of Conservative party structure is the voluntary part which appears, magically, just before each election.

The permanent party organization consists of a national organizer and his staff (which is also part of the election campaign staff) and sundry public relations and clerical help in the Ottawa headquarters. The Progressive Conservative National Headquarters has traditionally been slightly smaller than the Liberal party headquarters, typically totalling about 20 people. During the Conservatives' years in opposition the staff of the office of the Leader of the Official Opposition also played a crucial role in the party structure. The executive and special assistants and advisors in the opposition leader's office, while formally on the House of Commons staff and payroll, were actually engaged in the overall direction and development of strategy for the party. For example, the national campaign director for 1979 and 1980, Lowell Murray, was employed in this office. In this sense the opposition leader's staff are performing functions which are analagous to those performed in the Prime Minister's office for the party in power. In fact after the Conservative election victory of 1979 virtually all of the key staffers moved with the new Prime Minister into the Prime Minster's office and conversely, as the Liberals moved over to become the official opposition several of their key political staffers (those who were not already in the public service or the Senate) moved into positions in the opposition leader's office.

In 1969 parliament voted funds for the establishment of small parliamentary research offices for the caucuses of the opposition parties,

---

[16] M. Schwartz, "Political Behaviour and Ethnic Origin," in J. Meisel (ed.), *Papers on the 1962 Election,* pp. 253-272; John Meisel, *Working Papers on Canadian Politics,* pp. 37-38.

[17] Harold Clarke et al., *Political Choice in Canada,* p. 104.

[18] See the Organizational Chart in C. Winn and J. McMenemy, *Political Parties in Canada,* pp. 170-1.

and in 1970 similar funds were provided for the government caucus. The amount provided for each party is proportional to its strength in the House of Commons. The money is formally used to provide research services for MPs and most of the duties of the eight or nine researchers and the Director and his assistant in the major parties' offices do involve the provision of research material for MPs. However, the research offices also provide broader policy research for the party as a whole, help out during annual meetings and conventions, and provide some auxiliary headquarters' support during campaigns.

At election time the National President and National Secretary of the party, both of whom hold part-time positions, are augmented by a National Campaign Chairman and a group of fund raisers who start about the job of collecting money. The regional and provincial organizers (some of whom may be permanent employees of the party), suddenly spring to life and constituency organizations, generally consisting of a Campaign Chairman and many helpers, together with poll captains who work at the individual poll level, appear where nothing was before. Candidates are nominated and the contest begins.

It takes little imagination to recognize that the Conservative party is no less centralized and controlled by its parliamentary wing than is the Liberal; both are clear examples of cadre party structure. In power the lines of control available to a PC prime minister are identical to those of a Liberal prime minister. In opposition the PC leader controls all the key appointments including all members of the staff of the leader of the opposition, the membership of the treasury (money spending) and finance (money raising) committees, the shadow cabinet and the membership of various caucus committees. The sole exception, and this is as true for the Liberals as the Conservatives, is the National President. He or she is elected by the convention and the convention does not always select the candidate favoured by the leader. Of course in a cadre party any resulting tension redounds as much or more to the disadvantage of the extra-parliamentary party as to the parliamentary wing.

With regard to popular support, "it is generally safe to assume that for practically every statement made about the Liberal party the reverse holds for the Conservative voters."[19] Thus in 1974, 53 percent of Liberal support came from Catholics versus 20 percent of Conservative support. While only 6 percent of Liberal voters in 1968 were farmers, 15 percent of Conservatives were. Fifty-three percent of

[19] J. Meisel, *Working Papers on Canadian Politics,* p. 41-43.

those with 13 or more years of education voted Liberal in 1974 whereas 30 percent voted Conservative. Seventy-two percent of those of French origin voted Liberal whereas only 12 percent of them voted Conservative. Among those of British origin the result was much more closely balanced with 42 percent supporting the Liberals and 41 percent the Conservatives in 1974.

Conservative voters also were more likely than Liberals to be middle-aged or older, and to come from small towns or rural areas. Only in the Atlantic provinces were these tendencies reversed—there the PCs drew more heavily than the Liberals from upper-class urban voters. This pattern is perhaps attributable to the residual personal appeal of the former leader Robert Stanfield in his home-base Atlantic region, and the heavy rural and Western appeal of the ex-leader John Diefenbaker on his home ground as well as to the Western origins of the current leader. Such patterns of personal appeal can be remarkably stable in Canadian politics, often persisting for decades; the suggestion has sometimes been made that this pattern is the Canadian counterpart of the more strongly persistent party identification of United States voters.[20]

Perhaps the most important overall point which emerges from an examination of Conservative party support is its relative lack of homogeneity. Liberal support was, with the partial exception of the West, more evenly distributed across the country and, as John Meisel has noted in all of his election studies since the late 1950s, shows less regional variation in the way supporters look at the party and the leader. This may produce problems and strains in the Conservative party when it attempts to develop policies which will appeal to its supporters and also broaden the base of party support. If the supporters themselves are a highly "mixed bag" with highly divergent views of the world, reconciliation becomes difficult. Indeed, this divergent support is reflected among party activists as well. As Meisel notes,

The task of reconciling the demands of the most active members from the Atlantic and Prairie regions and from Ontario (or, to put it slightly differently, those of the vestigial Drew men, the Stanfield admirers and the Diefenbakerites), imposes extremely awkward tensions on the leadership which, as a consequence, makes it difficult for the national party to appear forceful and consistent both inside and outside the House of Commons.[21]

[20] The instability of party identification is explored further in Peter Regenstreif, *The Diefenbaker Interlude* (Longmans, Toronto, 1965). These figures are derived from Harold Clarke et al., *Political Choice in Canada*, pp. 93-132.
[21] J. Meisel, *Working Papers*, p. 46.

This situation, combined with the electoral victory by the Progressive Conservatives in 1979 confronted the party with a real organizational dilemma equal in magnitude if opposite in direction to that faced by the outgoing Liberals. For the Liberals the problem was to develop a real extra-parliamentary structure outside the government, in English Canada, which they could use to return to power. For the Conservatives the problem was to learn to use the levers of government to perpetuate their hold on government.

In order to do so the party had to overcome what George Perlin has referred to as their minority party syndrome; a series of attributes which made it extremely difficult for the party to seize and, particularly, to retain power.[22] This difficulty in seizing power, hypothesizes Perlin, is caused by the fact that being out of government allows MPs and activists to express all kinds of divergent views and therefore makes them interact on a basis which makes conflict resolution difficult. This in turn produces an appearance of factionalism, a perception that the party is not fit to govern and ends inevitably in electoral defeat. Even out of power, Liberals have managed to keep their disagreements largely hidden and, even in power, the Conservatives, due to their "opposition party mentality" have not. Moreover, since the party is viewed as an opposition party, it attracts those more interested in opposing than in governing.

By 1979 there were some signs that this syndrome might be weakening. The looming possibility of a Conservative victory led to recruitment of a rather different type of candidate—people with significant administrative as well as political experience. The party had, for only the second time in 35 years chosen a federal rather than a provincial politician as its leader.[23] Joe Clark, as leader, had succeeded in papering over many of the cracks in the party structure so the appearance of factionalism was diminished if not eliminated.

However the transition from a party in opposition to a "government party," along the lines of the federal Liberals during their lengthy periods in office, requires massive organizational changes both within the party and in government itself. Perlin predicted that the party would not succeed. He argued that the Progressive Conservatives would win the occasional election,

---

[22] George Perlin, "The Progressive Conservative Party," in H. G. Thorburn, *Party Politics in Canada,* pp. 165ff and *The Tory Syndrome* (McGill-Queen's Press, Montreal, 1980).

[23] It is almost certainly not a coincidence that the PCs have only won elections under federally trained leaders. No former provincial premier has ever become Prime Minister of Canada.

. . . when there is serious social, economic or political strain or when the Liberal party falls victim to what John Meisel has argued is its disposition (as a result of its habituation to office) to become too arrogant in its exercise of power. However both the historical evidence and the theory proposed to explain it suggests that even when the party wins it is likely to be subject to instability. In the long run, therefore, unless there is some dramatic change in the context of federal politics, the Conservative party may be expected to suffer from internal divisiveness and unstable leadership and to hold office only for brief intervals between extended periods of Liberal rule. [24]

George Perlin wrote and published these words well before the Progressive Conservatives' brief period in office in 1979. Given the party's behaviour during that period and particularly its display of an uncanny instinct for self-destruction, Perlin's analysis will mark him forever as one of the great pundits of Canadian political analysis.

MODERN PARTY POLITICS: THE MINOR PARTIES, 1921-1980

Major studies of the two older parties are still rather scarce. With respect to the minor parties, however, the situation is far different. Canada's minor parties have existed over limited time spans, they have usually been small, and they have been "different" enough to stimulate the scholar's interest. They have, in short, formed ideal material for academic studies. A great deal is known for example about the rise and fall of the Progressive movement. Indeed it may not be an exaggeration to suggest that more is known about it than about the Liberal Party of Canada, although Reg Whitaker's massive *The Government Party* has gone a long way to redressing this problem. Similarly, many political scientists have been supporters of the CCF and NDP and have, naturally enough wanted to write about "their" party and their experience. It must be remembered, however, that except in certain provinces, the newer parties have been less important than the older ones in any overall picture of party politics and one can only welcome the fact that students of Canadian political parties such as Perlin and Whitaker have begun to pay more attention to our major parties.

The Progressive Movement

In November of 1919 there was a provincial election in Ontario and, when the smoke had cleared, the largest single group in the legislature and the backbone of the new coalition government was the

[24] G. Perlin, op. cit., p. 167.

United Farmers' Party of Ontario—the Ontario version of a movement whose political arm came to be known nationally as the Progressive Party.[25] The movement grew in strength in the ensuing years, and in the 1921 federal election, any notion that Canada still had a two-party system was shattered when 65 Progressive MPs were elected, making them the second largest group in the House of Commons with 15 more seats than the Conservative party.[26] Where did they come from, and what was the structure of this newly emergent force in Canadian politics?

Compared to other Canadian parties, the Progressives relied upon relatively homogeneous electoral support. Aside from a few small business interests from Manitoba, the group's support was almost entirely rural. They gained 28 percent of the vote in the federal election in Ontario in 1921 and won 24 seats, with virtually all their support coming from farming areas. In Manitoba they captured 44 percent of the vote and 12 seats, in Saskatchewan 61 percent and 15 seats, and in Alberta 56 percent and 11 seats. In general, the more agricultural the economy of a province, the more likely it was to return Progressives. Even New Brunswick which virtually never breaks with older party lines returned a Progressive MP from a rural constituency in 1921 and Nova Scotia gave the Progressives 15 percent of the vote although the group won no seats there.

What can explain this sudden outpouring of support of a new rural political movement? The first part of the answer to this question is that the rise of agrarian political consciousness was not quite as sudden as it appears. Party lines were always weak in the West. In Ontario there had been previous sporadic bursts of support for agrarian movements with, for instance, the Patrons of Industry, an agrarian protest party, winning 17 seats in the Ontario provincial election of 1894.

However, only in the period immediately following World War I did a number of factors coalesce to increase the support of the farmers' movement. The government in Ottawa really was dominated by Eastern urban and big-business interests, and these interests did use the traditional political parties as their means of control.

---

[25] The other party in the coalition was the small Independent Labour Party.

[26] The words "movement" and "party" are both used in political science literature to describe the Progressives. There are a number of excellent studies of the group. Two are: W. L. Morton, *The Progressive Party in Canada* (University of Toronto Press, Toronto, 1950), and P. F. Sharp, *The Agrarian Revolt in Western Canada* (University of Minnesota Press, Minneapolis, 1948, reprinted by Octagon Press, New York, 1971). On the Alberta wing of the party, see. C. B. Macpherson, *Democracy in Alberta* (University of Toronto Press, Toronto, 1954), pp. 62-92.

Rural Ontario was being rapidly depopulated, as farm families moved to the city, and the insecurity of farm life combined with the feeling that the farmer was a dying species led to cooperative action. Tariff structures had been hurting the farmers for years by keeping produce prices down and farm equipment prices up. The problem was brought to a head by an over-supply of agricultural produce after World War I and by a recession following the war. The conscription of farmers' sons in 1917 after the government had specifically promised to exempt them, and the Union Government's ignoring of farmers' protest marches helped to convince farmers that the older parties were not responsive to their needs.

To a significant degree, the farmers were right! Both their view of economic structures and their view of the parliamentary political system which supported these structures had considerable basis in fact. However, the attribution of pure malevolence or greed as the cause was more dubious: it may have been that national economic development at the turn of the century really was best accomplished by a mercantile system and it may have been that calls for a shift Westward in influence in Canada were premature.

Be that as it may, it has been seen above that there are reasons why the older parties were not then, and are not now, structurally adequate to articulate genuine protest movements or to accommodate them when they arise. Instead they responded in 1921 much as they do now: only after the agrarian interests became politically mobilized and formed new social and political structures did the older parties adjust and attempt to assimilate them.

The farmers concentrated much of their criticism on the caucus-dominated structure of older parties because, as they pointed out, the agrarian-dominated Western regional caucuses were inevitably out-voted by the parties' Eastern interests. They therefore surmised that the only way to make themselves heard in parliament was to get outside of caucus altogether and form a new movement; where conflict resolution within the older parties failed, they attempted to achieve their ends through the process of interparty competition.

The problem with their theories was that they had to be applied within a parliamentary system and since the farmers had rejected the idea of a legislative caucus, there were no structural mechanisms for achieving integration among the progressive MPs. Within four years, the movement had lost much of its impetus as the lack of internal cohesion produced a series of warring factions. The militant Alberta faction and the highly ideological "Ginger Group" could not work with the more moderate parts of the Ontario and Manitoba wings. Without cohesion they were not a credible alternative government and the best they could hope for were the results they had already

attained in 1921. Consequently it became relatively easy for Mackenzie King to absorb some of the leaders and most of the followers into
the Liberal party.

Structurally, the Progressive party was an alliance of sub-
coalitions. Each of the sub-coalitions was a regionally based collection
of farm organizations. The only well-acknowledged national leader
was T. A. Crerar, a dissident Liberal, but he broke with the movement and resigned as leader in 1922, subsequently returning to the
Liberal fold. What overall national cohesion existed was provided by
adherence to a few common principles expressed in "The Farmers
Platform." The most important of these ideas was simply opposition
to the old party system and to Eastern business interests. There was
considerable emphasis among Progressives on grass-roots democracy, but the means of achieving it varied from one regional sub-
coalition to another. Thus, the Manitoba farmers' government experimented with legislation to provide for the recall of MPs to face their
constituents in a by-election if a specified proportion of the voters in a
riding requested it, and other wings of the Progressive party toyed
with various forms of the referendum.

In the Progressive party, conventions were considerably more
important in policy making than they had been in the older parties,
although by 1923 yet another split was developing within the movement between elected representatives, who were beginning to resent
excessive interference in "their" affairs by conventions, and the mass
membership of the movement, which wanted to maintain its influential position. Most of the structural decentralization of the movement
and its emphasis on constituency control derived from its anti-party
ideology for within the party, this ideology was extended into a form
of syndicalism or corporatism, with a call for representation by occupational group rather than geographic constituency. This was combined with a call for cabinets which would not be overthrown if they
lost a vote in parliament. The concept of occupational group representation was, however, quite antithetical to the Canadian parliamentary tradition of representation based on territorial constituencies. The notion that a government need not resign unless defeated
on an explicit vote of confidence went against the then emerging
trend toward consolidation and centralization of control within parliamentary parties although, as will be seen when we come to discuss
current ideas in parliamentary reform, that idea reemerges each time
there is a minority government. But in the context of the times the
Progressives' ideology was unworkable without rather significant
revolutionary action and the farmers were much too conservative—
and too weak politically—to espouse real revolution.

The Progressive movement perished of its own structural deficiencies. By the mid-1920s the Progressive party had ceased to be an institution in Canadian national politics, although it continued to be important in provincial governments in the West, remaining in power in Alberta until the Social Credit sweep in 1935, and in Manitoba in one form or another for some 30 years.

The Social Credit

Strictly speaking, Social Credit is a financial theory developed by Major C. H. Douglas, a retired British army engineer, although it contains elements of a broader view of society as well. The root of the theory is the "A plus B theorem" where A is the flow of purchasing power to the people (i.e., wages, salaries, and dividends) and B is bank charges, overhead costs, taxes, and the cost of raw materials. The discrepancy between purchasing power (A) and the costs of production (A plus B) was thought to be a permanent feature of modern capitalism and would always result in the people getting less than their share of the economic pie. The resulting deficiency in demand was assumed to be at the root of the Depression of the 1930s. The solution offered by Social Credit theory was to give people more purchasing power in the form of a bonus.

A functional financial system should be concerned with the issue of credit to the consumer up to the productive capacity of the producers so that the consumers' real demands may be satisfied and the productive capacity of the industrial system may be capitalized and developed to the fullest extent.[27]

As with the Progressive movement, Social Credit also featured a critique of parliamentary democracy, pointing out that control over Members of Parliament had escaped the little person and now rested with large financial interests.

At first glance, the Social Credit is a highly complex phenomenon. It has held power in two provinces and it has had a significant presence in the House of Commons. Yet the federal and provincial segments of the party were frequently scarcely on speaking terms and the ties among the various branches of the party have never been strong. The Quebec-based wing of the party, the Raillement des Créditistes was basically provincial in orientation but its real presence was felt only in federal politics. In fact the Social Credit was not a single party at all but rather a set of at least three separate parties operating largely independently of each other in quite different venues.

[27] J. A. Irving, *The Social Credit Movement in Alberta*, p. 6.

While there are common threads, it is probably best to treat the three major segments, in Alberta, Quebec, and B.C. somewhat separately. **Alberta**   By the end of the third decade of this century, the Progressive movement no longer acted as an effective vehicle for protest in the West. Yet the Depression and the prolonged drought on the Prairies in the early 1930s served, if anything, to emphasize still further the differences between Eastern and Western Canada. As a result, by 1935 a new protest movement had established itself in Alberta provincial politics. On August 22, 1935, Alberta voters eliminated all members of the government formed by the United Farmers of Alberta (the Alberta wing of the Progressives) and filled 56 of the 63 seats in their legislature with followers of Social Credit.[28]

In Alberta the sudden ascendancy of Social Credit was due primarily to the coincidence of the Depression of the 1930s with the organizational and histrionic abilities of William Aberhart. The peculiar ideology of Social Credit was certainly useful but other factors were more important.

Aberhart began his working life as a school teacher and preacher. After moving to Alberta as a young man, he founded the Prophetic Bible Institute. Given his skill and the limited range of alternative Sunday afternoon activities in Alberta in the early 1930s, Aberhart's religious radio broadcasts soon enjoyed tremendous popularity. John Irving describes him as combining:

. . . the functions of the prophet with the executive capacities of the great planner and organizer. . . . Aberhart's imposing physical presence, his performances as organizer and orator, his resolute and inflexible will, his infinite resourcefulness, his ability to hypnotize people by his voice, his contagious belief in himself—all these characteristics combined to produce in many people the attitude that here is the Leader.[29]

He began to use radio to present the ideas of Social Credit in 1932, and these broadcasts together with an excellent grass roots political organization, swept him into power in 1935. After a few attempts to apply Social Credit principles through legislation, the Alberta Social Credit movement, thwarted by the realities of the constitution and the economic system, became a political party of more or less standard form. The prosperity of the province following the oil boom

---

[28] There are three major accounts of the Social Credit Movement in Alberta. These are C. B. Macpherson, *Democracy in Alberta*; J. A. Irving, *The Social Credit Movement in Alberta* (University of Toronto Press, Toronto, 1959); and J. R. Mallory, *Social Credit and the Federal Power in Canada* (University of Toronto Press, Toronto, 1954). On the politics of Alberta in general see J. A. Long and F. Q. Quo, "Alberta: The Politics of Consensus," M. Robin (ed.), *Canadian Provincial Politics*.

[29] J. A. Irving, *The Social Credit Movement in Alberta*, p. 337.

ensured the re-election of Social Credit governments in the province for 36 years until 1971, when resurgent Alberta Conservatives captured the province.

In Alberta, Social Credit was "essentially a people's movement which sought to reform, but not to revolutionize the existing social order by changing the patterns of certain institutions."[30] It was born of the amalgamation of the social disruption of the Depression, the alienation of Westerners from Eastern institutions, the conservative entrepreneural ethic of Alberta, and the particular genius of William Aberhart. It survived under his successor E. C. Manning's ability to run a successful administration and under the prosperity ushered in by the discovery of oil in 1948. It perished, essentially of old age and the voters' desire for change, in 1971 soon after Manning's retirement. It has since largely faded from the scene in Alberta gaining only 8 percent of the vote and four seats in 1975 and 20 percent, again with four seats, in 1979.

Quebec Most similar to the Alberta party has been the Raillement des Créditistes, the Quebec-based wing of the party.[31] It is characterized by the same pragmatism and leadership orientation allowing it to exploit regional cultural characteristics and it has shown a similar vulnerability to decline once the strong leader disappears.[32] The Créditistes, too, started life as a protest movement, and they have been successful in Quebec largely because rural Quebeckers did not find the federal Conservative party a credible alternative to the Liberals, and because the Liberals had in the view of many voters, ceased to look after their interests. It has been suggested that in situations where one party is dominant for long periods of time as have been the Liberals in Quebec, the regular opposition party will lose its credibility and be replaced by a third party.[33] The same situation may well account in part for the rise of Social Credit in Alberta.

The void left by the failure of the Conservatives in Quebec was filled by Réal Caouette who exploited the new medium of television

---

[30] Ibid., p. 334.

[31] The Raillement des Créditistes has also been extensively studied. See particularly Maurice Pinard, *The Rise of A Third Party* (Prentice-Hall, Englewood Cliffs, 1971), and Michael Stein, *The Dynamics of Right Wing Protest: A Political Analysis of Social Credit in Quebec* (Toronto, 1973), Graham White, "One Party Dominance and Third Parties," André Blais, "Third Parties in Canadian Provincial Politics," and Maurice Pinard, "Third Parties in Canada Re-Visited," all in *Canadian Journal of Political Science*, September 1973. Although the major success of the Raillement has been in federal elections it is realistic to treat them as a Quebec party in accord with their electoral base.

[32] C. Winn and J. McMenemy, *Canadian Political Parties*, pp. 37-38.

[33] M. Pinard, *The Rise of A Third Party*. This is one basic theme of Pinard's book.

as effectively as Aberhart had exploited radio. In the 1962 federal election, the Créditistes won 26 seats in rural Quebec and captured 26 percent of the Quebec vote. Up to 1974 they held over 18 percent of the federal vote in Quebec and won never fewer than 9 seats. For a time after the 1962 election they were, outside of Montreal, the dominant federal electoral force in the province.[34]

Early in 1970 the Créditiste party also entered provincial politics. They entered hurriedly and were forced into action before they were ready, when the Union Nationale government called a snap election. Nonetheless, they did achieve considerable success. The region of Quebec which voted Créditiste in federal elections showed itself willing to support the party provincially, and the result was 13 seats in the National Assembly. These seats were taken largely from the Union Nationale and were important in the overthrow of that government. However the Créditistes were unable to build their provincial strength into a permanent power base. In the 1973 provincial election the party's support declined and they were able to capture only 2 seats. They were crushed in the Parti Québécois victory in 1976.

The fortunes of the Raillement des Créditistes have declined precipitously since 1974 and particularly since the death of Réal Caouette in 1976. Between then and the 1979 election the party went through four leaders including one from Manitoba, chosen in an ill-starred attempt to give the party a national identification outside Quebec. The leader for the 1979 election—chosen just six weeks before election day—was Fabien Roy. Roy was a popular populist deputy in the Quebec National Assembly with separatiste leanings. He was supported in his federal campaign by the Parti Québécois leadership but his impact was in no way comparable to Caouette's and the separatiste identification probably cost the party votes among its traditionally conservative electorate. In that election the party gained only five seats and it was completely eliminated in the 1980 election. With Caouette's death, the Raillement des Créditistes appears to have lost not only its founder and its leader, but its organizational base as well.

British Columbia   In British Columbia, the Social Credit party won a minority victory in the provincial election of 1952. Here again the roots of the movement had some things in common with the roots in Quebec and Alberta.[35] Economic conditions in B.C. were not nearly

---

[34] M. Stein, "Quebec's Créditistes" in H. G. Thorburn, *Party Politics in Canada* (4th edition), p. 255.

[35] Martin Robin, "British Columbia, The Company Province," in M. Robin (ed.), *Canadian Provincial Politics* (Prentice-Hall, Scarborough, 1978), and E. R. Black, "British Columbia, The Politics of Exploitation," in H. G. Thorburn, *Party Politics in Canada*.

as bad as they were in Alberta in 1935 or in rural Quebec in 1962, but the B.C. government in 1952 was a tired coalition of Conservatives and Liberals in the process of disintegration. Neither of the older parties had much in the way of provincial organization, the CCF was too militant and too small to gain broad support, and the only credible alternative that emerged was the Social Credit party.

The 1952 socred campaign was run with considerable help from Alberta, but without a leader, for W. A. C. Bennett, a dissident former Conservative, did not become leader until after the election. Social Credit was helped in the election by the two older parties who enacted an "alternative vote" electoral scheme intended to shut out the socialist hordes of the CCF—a scheme which aided significantly in their own demise and left the CCF essentially as before.[36] Bennett, surmising that a proportional representation system rarely works to the advantage of parties in power, promptly eliminated it after the election.

The party was and is virtually non-ideological, although Bennett once defined Social Credit simply as "the opposite of socialism." In British Columbia, Social Credit fell rather than charged into power, but a prosperous economy and an ebullient, if not overly polished, party image kept it there for some twenty years until its defeat by the NDP in 1972. During that time, the various antics and policy peregrinations of "Wacky" Bennett served to create the image of B.C. politics as a sort of low-comedy form of entertainment; but it would be hard to dispute his electoral success.

Unlike its namesakes in Quebec and Alberta, Social Credit was able to rejuvenate after its electoral defeat. Initially the accession to the leadership by W. A. C. Bennett's son, Bill Bennett, was taken as further proof of the low-comedy aspect of B.C. politics. However the Social Credit under Bennett the younger did defeat the provincial NDP in 1975 and retained power in 1979. Under Bill Bennett, B.C.'s Social Credit party has become relatively moderate, effectively retaining a base of middle-class and small entrepreneur support. Any remnant of Social Credit theory has long since disappeared from its repertoire.

In two of the three cases, then, Social Credit caught on because a charismatic leader, skilled in using a new medium, arrived at a time when there were no other effective vehicles of protest. In all three cases effective political alternatives were lacking because the politics of the area were dominated by one party. The ideology of Social Credit, while not itself at the foundation of the party's power, had its

[36] E. R. Black, op. cit., p. 292.

uses because it was easy to understand and because it blamed troubles on those convenient bugbears, the absentee financial interests. Finally, like many Canadian protest or minor parties, Social Credit has generally done well in provincial politics and poorly in federal politics, with the Créditiste wing being the exception to the rule.

There is a good explanation for the relative success of Social Credit provincially: it is one we will see again with the CCF-NDP. The impossibility of gaining national power with a regionally based protest group has made all protest movements conscious that their only real chance to gain power is in provincial elections. This has led to a concentration of the best party leaders and workers at the provincial level; the Alberta Social Credit party has taken only sporadic interest in federal politics, and the British Columbia wing of the party little more. The federal orientation of the Créditistes can best be explained through Pinard's theory of one-party dominance and the consequent rise of a third party. That the third party used the Social Credit rhetoric was probably in large measure a coincidence; any other moderately conservative and relatively simple rhetoric would have served equally well. In fact, then, Social Credit is not a single phenomenon at all but rather three very loosely related regional parties and, with the exception of B.C., of increasingly historical rather than current significance.

The CCF-NDP: Socialism in Canada

We aim to replace the present capitalistic system, with its inherent injustice and inhumanity, by social order from which the domination and exploitation of one class by another will be eliminated, in which economic planning will supersede unregulated private enterprise and competition and in which genuine democratic self-government based upon economic equality will be possible.

These words are from the "Regina Manifesto," the declaration of principles passed at the first annual convention of the Cooperative Commonwealth Federation, in Regina in 1933. Since 1921, J. S. Woodsworth had led a tiny group of Socialist MPs in the federal parliament, and by 1932, the Depression, Woodsworth's own leadership, and the intense interest of many Canadian farm and labour leaders and academics led to the formation of a formal party structure oriented toward the principles outlined in the Regina Manifesto.

The CCF held to its militantly socialist party platform for the first twenty years of its life, but by 1956 it had begun to change its ideological face.[37] While it continued to call for an egalitarian and classless

---

[37] Leo Zakuta, *A Protest Movement Becalmed: A Study of Change in the CCF* (University of Toronto Press, Toronto, 1964), pp. 169-173.

society, the party began to shift toward the ideological centre in Canadian politics in response to the fact that its national electoral support appeared to have peaked in 1944-45 without moving the party into national power. No longer did the CCF consider it necessary to nationalize all industry, and no longer did it call for the eradication of capitalism. Its new ideology was expressed in the Winnipeg declaration of 1956 calling for

. . . the application of social planning. Investment of available funds must be channelled into socially desirable projects; financial and credit resources must be used to help maintain full employment and to control inflation and deflation.

This was a set of principles which either the Liberals or Progressive Conservatives could have happily endorsed. Support for the party, however, continued to run at only 14 to 16 percent of the popular vote.

Meanwhile, organized labour in Canada—particularly the Canadian Labour Congress—began to take an interest in openly supporting a political party, and the logical choice was, of course, the CCF. A change of name, however, seemed desirable, in order to expunge the Western rural image that went with the old title. The result was a dissolution of the old Cooperative Commonwealth Federation and the formation of the New Democratic Party in 1961.[38] For the most part NDP activists consisted of the same people as had the CCF, but by now sufficiently chastened to be willing to modify their principles somewhat in order to gain power. The years of watching policy making and trying to woo recalcitrant voters had left some marks. These changes, plus the influx of labour influences into the party machinery have added a dash of pragmatism to the NDP and the party leadership is now predominantly social democratic in the tradition of English rather than Marxian socialism.[39] And like most social democratic parties, it has drifted to the right even as the structure of capitalist society has drifted to the left.

What has been said about ideological drift in the CCF-NDP, however, should not be interpreted to mean that the party is identical to

[38] The best study of the CCF is W. D. Young, *The Anatomy of a Party: The National CCF 1932-61* (University of Toronto Press, Toronto, 1969). For the post-1961 period, see: Desmond Morton, *NDP: The Dream of Power* (Hakkert, Toronto, 1974), and N. H. Chi and George Perlin, "The NDP: A Party in Transition," in H. G. Thorburn (ed.), *Party Politics in Canada* (4th edition), pp. 177-187. See also Brodie and Jenson. op. cit.

[39] Robert Hackett in "The Waffle Conflict in the NDP," in H. G. Thorburn (ed.), *Party Politics in Canada* differentiates between the democratic socialism position and the social democrat position. The former is much more militantly left wing favouring broader government control and more public ownership than the latter. The latter is the establishment position in the party.

the older parties. For example, the CCF-NDP has been more pacifist and is less likely to support the Canadian military establishment and defence expenditures than are those parties. The party itself has never been as extremely pacifist as its first leader, J. S. Woodsworth, who voted against Canada's entry into World War II, but it stood some distance from the older parties in this regard—particularly in the past, when the military aspect of foreign policy received much more attention than it does today. As well, the CCF-NDP remains more committed to economic equality than the older parties. The Liberals and Progressive Conservatives will both express their allegiance to the concept of "equality of opportunity," but the NDP has tended to be more favourable to the concept of equality of outcome in the here and now. While vast amounts of public ownership are no longer part of its platform it is a somewhat stronger advocate than the Liberals and far to the left of the Conservatives on this score.

The NDP has also tended to be more nationalistic—or perhaps isolationist—than either of the major parties.[40] Thus it has, since 1969, opposed Canadian participation in military alliances. It has been suggested that its position on questions of Canadian nationalism is really much closer to that of the Conservatives than to that of Liberals, and that in particular there are close parallels between the Conservative position under John Diefenbaker and the NDP position.[41]

The various ideological tendencies in the party have led to some severe organizational stresses and strains. The most recent of these was caused by the strongly nationalistic and left-wing "Waffle" group which sought a return to the guiding socialist principles of the party and far greater Canadian control of Canadian industry. In lines reminiscent of the Regina Manifesto the Waffle declared, "Capitalism must be replaced by socialism, by national planning of investment and by public ownership of the means of production in the interests of the Canadian people as a whole." The group became sufficiently strong that in the 1971 leadership convention, their candidate ran a fairly close second to the winner, David Lewis. However, the conservative trade union wing of the party and the almost equally conservative (for a socialist party) parliamentary caucus were able to force the expulsion of the group as an entity from the Ontario party in 1973. The group's direct influence has vanished since then although the

---

[40] Garth Stevenson, "Foreign Policy," in C. Winn and J. McMenemy, *Political Parties in Canada*.

[41] See George Grant, *Lament for a Nation: The Defeat of Canadian Nationalism* (McClelland and Stewart, Toronto, 1965), for a provocative evaluation of the Diefenbaker position on Canadian-U.S. relationships. Grant sees many similarities between NDP and Conservative positions.

Waffle did succeed in moving the rhetoric of the party to the left and might claim some indirect credit for the creation of PetroCan—a concession gained from the minority Liberal government by the NDP in 1973.[42] The current national leader, Ed Broadbent, was associated with the original drafting of the Waffle manifesto although his political rhetoric since then has been in line with the much more conservative mainstream of the party.

It has often been suggested that the CCF and NDP have been the parties of innovation in Canadian politics. The Liberals, especially, have often been accused of (or praised for) continually moving to adopt ideas which have been developed and popularized by the NDP or the CCF and gaining the credit for putting them into play. This phenomenon, which is observed in some European party systems, is called "contagion from the left." William Chandler has found some empirical evidence for this in provinces where the NDP is a major factor in provincial politics.[43] The impact seems to be greatest with respect to health and social welfare—that is in those social policy areas where the CCF and NDP have traditionally been most active. However the effects are not always very large and the relationship not always clear or simple. For example in 1975 the Ontario Progressive Conservative reaction to a minority government situation in which the NDP was the leading opposition party was a sharp turn to the right and severe restraint for health and social service programs.

Structurally, the NDP is not so different from the older parties as its origins and ideology might lead one to expect. Its leader, like the leader of the two older parties, is elected at a convention and is subjected to a vote of confidence at biennial party conventions. An NDP convention is somewhat different in style to a convention of the Liberals or PCs, being more serious and more policy oriented and the presence of a large bloc of trade union representatives from affiliated unions would be alien to either of the older parties. But outcomes of conventions are not so different. No CCF or NDP leader once elected has ever been seriously challenged by the convention and the NDP caucus is likely to consider convention resolutions as advisory—not as compulsory positions to which they must hold.

The party is not formally a federation. However like its older party counterparts it is in reality very nearly federal in structure with its

---

42 N. H. Chi and G. Perlin, "The NDP: A Party in Transition," p. 184.
43 William M. Chandler, "Canadian Socialism and Policy Impact: Contagion from the Left?" *Canadian Journal of Political Science*, X:4, December 1977, pp. 755-780, and G. Caplan, *The Dilemma of Canadian Socialism: The CCF in Ontario* (Toronto, McClelland and Stewart, 1973).

provincial party organizations being fully autonomous but represented both at the national convention and on the National Council. The latter body is formally responsible for the operation of the party between elections and meets at least twice yearly at the call of the party executive. However the Council has more than 100 members and such large groups generally rule more in form than in substance. The real operation of the party machinery is directed by the twenty-eight executive members of the council and by the party caucus. The NDP leader's office is a smaller establishment than those of the two older parties, but this is partially compensated for by the somewhat higher level of activity of constituency and provincial associations between elections. In sum, however, the locus of control for most matters in the NDP is not much different from the older parties, residing primarily in the leader and parliamentary caucus, the national executive and the permanent officers of the party.[44]

The relationship between the NDP and organized labour in Canada has not been a consistent one. The party includes a bloc of union delegates from affiliated unions in its conventions and the unions for years provided the bulk of financial support for the party. However NDP governments have not been overly sympathetic to unions: in B.C. an NDP government allowed more union competition and ended a strike by legislation as did the NDP government of Saskatchewan. When he was NDP premier of Manitoba, Ed Schreyer was a consistent advocate of wage and price controls, a policy which is anathema to union leaders.[45] In federal politics the Canadian Labour Congress has vacillated between vociferous support for the NDP and an emphasis on direct involvement in policy making in concert with whatever party is in power.

In 1979 the CLC made its biggest push to provide union support for the party with direct participation by union activists in most aspects of the federal campaign of that year. The result was a spectacular failure with the NDP share of the vote actually declining in the Toronto and Southern Ontario region where Canadian Labour Congress efforts were concentrated and the CLC was conspicuous by its silence in the 1980 federal election. There was, as well, a steady decline in the NDP share of the union vote from 28 percent in 1968 to 22 percent in 1974, all of which has prompted Desmond Morton to conclude that

---

[44] There is an extensive description of the NDP party structure in C. Winn and J. McMenemy, *Political Parties in Canada*, pp. 167-190.

[45] Desmond Morton "Labour's New Political Direction," in G. H. Thorburn, *Party Politics in Canada*, pp. 206-213. See also David Kwavnick, *Organized Labour and Pressure Politics* (McGill-Queen's Press, Montreal, 1972), and Gad Horowitz, *Canadian Labour in Politics* (Toronto, University of Toronto Press, 1968).

"Big Labour is a lot smaller in Canada than either its friends or its enemies like to pretend."[46] In part the problem is simply Canadian union members' tendency to relate unions only to their jobs, leaving politics to the specific agencies of the traditional parties. In part the problem lies with the Canadian Labour Congress itself which is simply too weak vis-à-vis its affiliates to get them to do much of anything out of line with the standard "bread and butter" North American unionism which concentrates on wages and working conditions.

There are some substantial differences between the base of support of the NDP and those of the older parties. The religious distribution of NDP votes is broadly similar to that of the Conservatives, lacking the very heavy Roman Catholic bias of the Liberals. This, however is largely a reflection of the party's lack of support in Quebec. Some 45 percent of NDP votes in 1974 came from either skilled or unskilled labour versus 40 percent of the Liberals and 33 for the PCs. Fifty-five percent of NDP votes come from subjectively perceived "lower" classes compared to just 45 percent for the Liberals, and the NDP have a higher proportion of "other" ethnic voters than either older party. NDP votes are more heavily concentrated in metropolitan areas than those of the older parties (in spite of the signal weakness in Montreal) and the age distribution of its voters is skewed toward youth. The NDP draws disproportionately from union voters; in 1968, 31 percent of them voted NDP compared to 16 percent of the population as a whole.[47]

The profile of NDP supporters suggests that while Canadian politics in general is not class based, support for the NDP to some extent is. Thus we have the phenomenon of a somewhat class-based party in what is not a class-voting system.[48] There is also a strong regional bias to NDP support. The CCF was born in Saskatchewan, had its first substantial victory there, and both the CCF and its successor, the NDP, have been strong there ever since in both federal and provincial

[46] Desmond Morton, "Labour's New Political Direction," p. 213.
[47] N. H. Chi and G. Perlin, "The NDP: A Party in Transition," p. 179.
[48] Donald Blake, "The Measurement of Regionalism in Canadian Voting Patterns," *Canadian Journal of Political Science*, 5, (1972), 55-81 suggests on the basis of the result of several federal elections that the class basis of overall Canadian voting patterns has not increased significantly, while the impact of ethnic, regional, and religious factors has remained strong. Again it should be emphasized that this does not mean that there is no class basis to NDP voting but rather that the impact of class voting on the whole system is not strong. H. Clarke et al. found in examining the 1965, 1968, and 1974 elections that social class was a statistically significant correlate of NDP support only in 1974. More generally, "Several measures of social class all failed to yield strong correlations with voting behaviour in any of those national surveys." *Political Choice in Canada*, p. 116.

elections. Another area of consistent support has been Winnipeg, and more recently support spread out across the province, producing NDP victories in the 1969 and 1973 Manitoba provincial elections, a proportion of the popular vote in federal elections which has risen from 24 percent in 1965 to 32 percent in 1979 and 5 of the 12 seats in that election. There is also sufficient support centred in the powerful West coast trade union movement to have enabled the party to capture British Columbia's provincial government from 1968 to 1975. However, the NDP remains largely without support in Quebec, most of the Atlantic region, and large sections of Ontario outside the metropolitan areas. It is conceivable that these holes may eventually be filled in and although the NDP made gains in the Atlantic provinces in 1979 and 1980, current movement in this direction is very slow. Until the NDP can increase its appeal east of Ontario, it is highly improbable that it will be a serious contender for national office.

As a socialist movement which has had some electoral successes, the CCF-NDP is unique on this side of the Atlantic. Why has this been possible in Canada and not in the United States? Gad Horowitz, developing the ideas of Louis Hartz, suggests one important reason.[49] Using a dialectical analysis, he posits that socialism, as an acceptable ideology in a society, can only grow out of confrontation of Toryism with nineteenth-century Liberalism.[50] If either of the two ingredients is missing, the essential dialogue cannot take place and socialism cannot develop. The United States can be looked at, ideologically, as a fragment thrown off from Europe—particularly from Britain—at a time when Liberalism was ascendant. The Tory streak is missing in the United States however because most Tories who were in the United States at the time of the American Revolution left and came to Canada. Ideological dialogue is therefore less likely in the U.S. than in Canada and nineteenth-century Liberalism remains basically unchallenged in the U.S. because other ideologies are simply not tolerated by American society. In Canada there is a predominance

---

[49] These ideas are expressed in Gad Horowitz, "Conservatism, Liberalism and Socialism in Canada: An Interpretation," in *Canadian Journal of Economics and Political Science*, Vol. 32, No. 2, May, 1966. Hartz' ideas are expounded in several places, most notably Louis Hartz, *The Liberal Tradition in America* (Harcourt, Brace and World, New York, 1955) and *The Founding of New Societies* (Harcourt, Brace and World, New York, 1964). See also K. D. McRae, "The Structure of Canadian History," in Hartz, *The Founding of New Societies*. See also Chapter 4.

[50] Horowitz' ideas have also engendered considerable controversy. Horowitz himself summarizes the arguments and replies to his critics in "Notes on Conservatism, Liberalism, and Socialism in Canada," *Canadian Journal of Political Science*, XI, 2 (June 1978), pp. 383-399.

of the same Liberal tradition, but it is tempered with a "Tory touch" which has allowed Canadians both to see the state as something greater than the sum of its parts and to tolerate the socialist ideology which is the dialectical synthesis of the two older ideologies.[51]

Interpretations of Third-Party Movements in Canada

By now it may very well be obvious to the reader that there is much in common among various third-party movements in Canadian politics, even when they have such widely disparate ideological stances as the Social Credit and the NDP. Virtually all of them originate either in Quebec or in Western Canada; with the exception of the United Farmers of Ontario, no important third party has ever originated elsewhere. Virtually all of them have expressed discontent with Canada's central political institutions. None of them has yet grown to be a major party, yet with the exception of the Progressives, all have persevered in political action, resisting absorption by the older parties and continuing to exist today.

These common features have led several political scientists to suggest reasons why third parties have been such a persistent feature of the Canadian party system. The most frequently used and probably the most convincing explanation revolves around the parliamentary system itself and the demands it makes on political parties. Professor Hugh Thorburn sums up this point of view when he writes:

Canadian parties, although vague in their policies, are disciplined parliamentary groups requiring of their members a high degree of conformity. The leader has great authority and there is little room for dissidence. Protest, then, must occur outside the old parties, and if it is to be effective must itself assume the form of a political party.[52]

Because of the necessity of maintaining cohesive parliamentary voting blocs, party discipline must be high. In the United States, very loose party discipline allows protest to occur within parties, so the

---

[51] We have ended this section of the chapter without discussing those political parties which operate exclusively on the Quebec stage, the Union Nationale and the Parti Québécois. It is our feeling that we cannot do justice to the details of the party system within any province, particularly Quebec, without going into more detail than we have space for here. As well there is some discussion of the Quebec situation in Chapter 3. In effect, each of the ten separate party systems deserves several pages of treatment and since this text is not intended to cover provincial politics in detail we have not provided it here. The interested reader is referred to M. Robin (ed.), *Canadian Provincial Politics* (Prentice-Hall, Scarborough, 1978).

[52] *Party Politics in Canada*, (4th edition), p. 169.

formation of third-party groups is seldom necessary. In Canada, by contrast, if radical dissent is to be heard at all, it must be heard outside the confines of the older parties.

The Canadian federal system may also have provided some incentive to the formation of third parties, for even if a minor party cannot win a national election, it does have a fair chance of winning power in a province. Every province west of New Brunswick has, at some time, had a third-party government.

At first glance, a similar potential for third-party power might appear to exist in the American states, but there are important differences between the Canadian and U.S. situations. First, state elections in the United States are held in conjunction with national elections. The ability of the national parties to dominate the media makes it very difficult for a smaller party to compete. Secondly, winning power in an American state is not necessarily as desirable as winning power in a Canadian province. Since American federalism is far more centralized than the Canadian variant, an American state is not nearly so attractive to an aspiring political party as a Canadian province.

The coincidence of social cleavage with some provincial or sectional boundaries, and the relative homogeneity of the provinces have also been important in fostering third-party movements. It would be difficult to imagine much success for the Union Nationale or the Parti Québécois in a Quebec which was 50 percent English. C. B. MacPherson attributes much of the early success of third-party movements in Alberta to the relative social homogeneity of that province. The CCF may have succeeded in Saskatchewan partially because of a similar homogeneity.[53]

Another theory to account for the rise of third parties in Canada has been suggested by Professor Maurice Pinard.[54] Canadian electoral politics is characterized by long periods of one-party dominance. Looking specifically at the rise of the Créditistes in Quebec, Pinard hypothesized that the long period of Liberal party dominance in federal politics in rural Quebec led to a perception on the part of Quebeckers that the Conservative party was not a legitimate alternative. They voted Progressive Conservative in 1958 so as not to be cut off politically from the party in power, but they shortly discovered that the Conservatives under Diefenbaker did not pay any attention to them. If they were still not satisfied (and rural Quebec has had a great deal to be dissatisfied about), their only legitimate outlet for protest

[53] C. B. Macpherson, *Democracy in Alberta,* and S. M. Lipset, *Agrarian Socialism,* passim.
[54] Maurice Pinard, "The Rise of a Third Party." See also the discussion of this theory in the *Canadian Journal of Political Science,* Vol. VI, No. 3, September, 1973.

was through a third party, and the Raillement des Créditistes provided this. A similar situation prevailed in Alberta in 1935—there was
no effective opposition to the United Farmers government, and hence
no place for voters to express their discontent, until Social Credit
came along. One could apply this type of analysis fruitfully to others
of Canada's third-party movements.

There were other reasons for the particular success of third parties
in the West. C. B. MacPherson has suggested that the Prairies constituted a quasi-colonial economy with respect to the East, that they had
effectively only one class of citizens, and that the result of this was a
"quasi-party" system[55] with one party or movement dominating for a
long period only to be replaced almost completely by another. Thus
the one-crop economy and lack of social cleavage on the prairies may
well have made possible the type of mass party political action represented by the CCF in Saskatchewan and the Social Credit and United
Farmers in Alberta.

Finally, a suggestion about the genesis of the CCF victory in
Saskatchewan in 1944 has been made by S. M. Lipset.[56] Given the
one-crop economy of that province and the antipathy which Western
farmers felt for Eastern grain-marketing organizations, the Saskatchewan farmers early organized a series of wheat pools and cooperatives. These organizations produced many active citizens who later
used the wheat pool cooperative structure to organize party opposition to the Liberal government then in power. Such a social infrastructure was not available in other provinces, and it did much to aid
the organization of the CCF in Saskatchewan as a strong political
force. The mass membership nature of the NDP in Saskatchewan has
persisted. In 1971 the average constituency membership for the NDP
in Saskatchewan was 2059. In Manitoba and B.C. it was just over 500
and in Ontario, 281.[57]

Undoubtedly all of these explanations have some validity. It is in
the coincidence of two or more such factors that one finds the most
fertile ground for third-party activity. Whatever the explanation,
however, third-party politics have done much to give the Canadian
political system its distinctive complexion.

CONCLUSION: PARTIES AND THE PARTY SYSTEM

One of the favourite exercises of political scientists has been the
attempt to characterize the party systems of various nations. The

---

[55] Macpherson, op cit. See especially pp. 215-250.
[56] Lipset, op cit. This is a general theme running through this book.
[57] N. H. Chi and George Perlin, "The New Democratic Party," in H. G. Thorburn,
Party Politics in Canada, p. 187.

most widely accepted descriptive parameter has been the number of parties. Thus the United States is usually characterized as a "two-party" system, as are Britain and Germany. Scandinavian nations are usually described as "multi-party" as are France and Israel.

There are obvious difficulties with this classification scheme; lumping the party systems of France, Israel and Norway together does relatively little to help us to understand the political systems of those countries. The classical two-party system—Britain—found itself with a minority government in 1974 and the "third-party" contender for the presidency of the U.S. in 1968 gathered 13.9 percent of the popular vote.

The numerical typing of party systems is rather difficult to apply to Canada. Does Canada have a "one-party dominant" system because the Liberals held power in Ottawa for 47 of 59 years up to 1979? Do we have a two-party system because the Conservatives have proven capable of defeating the Liberals? Do we have a three-party system because the CCF-NDP has received consistent support and has, in every federal election for forty years, won at least a few seats? Or is it a multi-party system? After all, the Créditistes and Social Credit have shown considerable staying power, and most provinces have had other than Liberal or Conservative governments.[58]

If a simple numerical typology is inadequate, H. G. Thorburn has recently identified a number of alternative ways of analyzing the Canadian party system.[59] Several analysts prefer to disregard the impact of third parties (which were indeed insignificant until the last sixty years) preferring to view the party system simply as two alternative groups trying to exert a broad enough appeal to get elected but devoid of ideological or policy differences. In these interpretations, much is made of the flexibility in ideology and policy orientations of the alternative parties. Thus: "No man in Canada has been more inconsistent than the man who has followed either political party for a generation."[60] And according to Lord Bryce: "In Canada ideas are

[58] There is an extended discussion of the complications and difficulties of applying a numerical typology to party systems in Giovanni Sartori, *Parties and Party Systems* (Vol. 1) (Cambridge University Press, Cambridge 1976), pp. 119-129. "By now there is a nearly unanimous agreement that the distinction among one-party, two-party, and multiparty systems is highly inadequate. And we are even told that a judgement as to the number of major parties obscures more than it illuminates. . . . By now classifications of party systems are a plethora and confusion and profusion seems to be the rule." [p. 119]

[59] H. G. Thorburn, "Interpretations of the Canadian Party System," in *Party Politics in Canada*, pp. 34-52.

[60] Sir John Williston, cited in Alexander Brady, *Democracy in the Dominions* (Toronto, University of Toronto Press, 1947), p. 94 and in Thorburn op cit., p. 36.

not needed to make parties for they can live by heredity and, like the Guelfs and Ghibellines of medieval Italy, by memories of past combats."[61] A more modern variant of this theory is J. R. Mallory's "national mood" interpretation which sees differences of mood and style between the two major parties as the significant determinants of success. A party remains in power as long as it is in tune with "the national mood," until that mood changes and leaves it high and dry. Devotees of this approach would thus claim that in 1979 the Progressive Conservatives under Joe Clark were more in tune with the national mood than the Liberals under Pierre Trudeau. Presumably, however, either the national mood or the Liberal party changed rapidly in 1979 for by early 1980 the Liberals were back in power.

One of the most recent statements of a similar point of view is found in C. Winn and J. McMenemy's, *Political Parties in Canada*. Their general theme is that while there are differences in style and electoral support these "have a negligible effect on policy. Thus implemented programs exhibit few systematic differences from one party government to another."[62] Again they see the Canadian party struggle essentially as one between two groups whose real policy orientations are not much different from each other.

Still another variant of this interpretation is to paint the two major parties as tools of the dominant corporate elites. Thus Frank Underhill asserts:

The real function of the two-party system since the Laurier era has been to provide a screen behind which the controlling business interests pull the strings to manipulate Punch and Judy who engage in mock combat before the public. Both parties take for granted that their first duty in office is to assist the triumphant progress of big business in the exploitation of the country's resources.[63]

This interpretation remains a prevalent one particularly in the neo-Marxian view of Canadian politics.[64]

A second broad mode of analysis sees the party system as a one-party dominant one. This theme relies on the fact that both federally and in the provinces one party tends to remain in power for a long

[61] Brady, op. cit., p. 103.
[62] C. Winn and J. McMenemy, *Political Parties in Canada*, p. 1.
[63] Frank Underhill, *In Search of Canadian Liberalism* (Toronto, MacMillan, 1961), p. 168.
[64] F. Engelmann and M. Schwartz, *Canadian Political Parties* (2nd ed.) (Prentice-Hall, Scarborough, 1975). See also K. Z. Partiel, "Canadian Election Expense Legislation," in H. G. Thorburn, op. cit., pp. 100-110, and *Financing Political Parties in Canada* (McGraw-Hill, Toronto, 1970). The Marxian and neo-Marxian interpretations are expressed in various articles in Leo Panitch, *The Canadian State* (Toronto, University of Toronto Press, 1977).

period once it takes office. C. B. MacPherson's quasi-party theory of Alberta politics, described earlier, is one variant of this theme while another is Maurice Pinard's one-party dominance theory of the rise of third parties. At the federal level the very title of Reginald Whitaker's *The Government Party* suggests the same view. Reinforcing this interpretation, George Perlin has posited that the Progressive Conservatives are a permanent opposition with a mind-set which will cause them to self-destruct once in power.[65]

H. G. Thorburn's synthesis of these various interpretations forms an appropriate conclusion. He suggests that at the federal level Canada has a persistent government party (the Liberals), a persistent opposition party (the PCs) and a persistent third party (the NDP). Recruitment patterns reinforce these positions with those attracted to power opting for the Liberals and those inclined to opposition roles to the PCs. The NDP attracts opposition types who are prepared to go slightly beyond ideological conformity, providing a natural safety valve. The Conservatives are close enough to the Liberals that should the latter become incompetent or lose touch with the nation a safe alternative is readily available. As well, because they are more responsive than the Liberals to peripheral regions, the Conservatives help sustain the system. The NDP maintains an innovative role with respect to social policy as well as a "tribune" function permitting the vocal expression of varying degrees of dissent. Overall, "The Canadian party system and therefore the political system for which it supplies the direction is both narrowly controlled by a fairly closed elite of office holders and their associates and susceptible to influence from a broad spectrum of opinions."[66] In this interpretation, whatever major social policy innovations do get implemented are viewed as a price which must be paid in order to maintain the stability of the system and keep the dominant groups in power.

That interpretation says little about the tendency of the Canadian party system to turn up minority governments and an addendum could be made on that score. The internal structures of Canada's major political parties have been rather slow to change over the last half-century. The locus of power, and the backgrounds of the leaders are remarkably similar to what they were even before World War I. Yet society has changed greatly in that period, and if the parties as individual structures have not changed much, it may be that the party *system* has. If the Liberal and Conservative parties themselves have

---

[65] George Perlin, "The Progressive Conservative Party," in H. G. Thorburn, op. cit., pp. 161-168 and *The Tory Syndrome, passim*.

[66] H. G. Thorburn, "Interpretations of the Canadian Party System," p. 48.

ceased to be omnibus vehicles for aggregating the country's vast array of political interests, it may be that the party system as a whole articulates and aggregates interests. Thus, the frequently recurring minority governments may well be the vehicle whereby the party system aggregates the interest that was once aggregated within the older parties themselves.[67]

Overall, when we consider the functions of political parties pointed to earlier and then consider to what extent these may in fact be performed by other institutions, the overall significance of parties is cast in a clearer, and not necessarily more flattering light. It will be recalled that these functions included:

1) The mobilization and structuring of the vote
2) The recruitment and training of political leaders and decision makers
3) Mobilization of support for leaders and for the system, political socialization, and political integration among the public
4) Aggregation of interests by the performance of a mediation and brokerage function in society
5) Communication in both directions between political leaders and the public
6) The organization of a government
7) The articulation of specific interests in policy proposals

John Meisel has suggested that parties are at a relative disadvantage in performing most or all of these tasks and that there has been a substantial downgrading of the role of political parties over the last generation.[68] In particular he would agree with the contention that very many of these functions have been lost to the bureaucracy. In particular, with respect to the potential policy role of parties Meisel contends:

There is little doubt that a great many decisions about what is placed on the public agenda are forced upon political parties by events, non-political decision makers and very often the preferences of powerful civil servants whose responsibility to the politicians is increasingly more formal than real. Even the organization of the govern-

---

[67] This point is elaborated and examined from several angles in John Meisel, *Working Papers on Canadian Politics*, pp. 51-60. The election of majority governments such as happened in July 1974 seems now to be the exception rather than the rule.
[68] The case is made in many of Meisel's writings cited in the footnotes. A similar case is increasingly made about parties in other political systems. For example Frank Sorauf writes in the introduction to *Party Politics in America* (3rd edition) (Little Brown, Boston, 1976), "In this book a strong case will be made for the proposition that the political parties have lost their pre-eminent position as political organizations and that competing organizations now perform many of the activities that have traditionally been regarded as the parties' exclusive prerogatives." [p. 5]

ment—the way in which legislation is drafted and considered by the Cabinet and its committees, the extent to which outside interests are consulted, the manner in which policies are administered—is more likely to reflect the wills of a small number of senior civil servants than the decisions of senior party officials, including the ministers. It is indeed questionable whether the government party leader—the prime minister—continues to function as a party person after accession to power or whether the party role and influence are maintained as a successful administration becomes accustomed to power and develops close relationships with senior civil servants. [69]

A number of reasons for the decline in the influence of parties can be suggested. The increasing complexity of issues and the rise of the bureaucratic state are interconnected phenomena but regardless of which came first, increasing technical complexity does tend to make issues extremely difficult for legislators to handle. The increasing role of many interest groups and the increasing relations between them and client-oriented senior bureaucrats who speak the same technical language they do has also been significant in diminishing ministerial, parliamentary, and pa.·ty influence. Another unfortunate effect of the increasing specialization and compartmentalization of government concerns is that "the *general* interest as aggregated by political parties tends to receive scant attention and parties are left with little choice but to approve what has already been decided by others." [70] The increasing number of issues which are dealt with in meetings between federal and provincial officials and ministers also tends to diminish the policy role of parties and of parliament for, increasingly, prior commitments made between the two orders of government preclude the making of significant changes by politicians who are not directly a part of that process.

The rise of the electronic media has stolen much of the political communication role from parties although it may have created a new role for them—the recruitment of media stars and the provision of "spectaculars" (leadership conventions) to launch those stars. In a related vein the rise of investigative journalism may have usurped some of the party's opposition role and its job of uncovering government improprieties—but it should be remembered that there has been investigative journalism of one form or another ever since there has been journalism at all.

The increasing use of public opinion polling by cabinet and by government departments has short-circuited another part of political parties' communication function. No longer do leaders have to rely on

---

[69] J. Meisel "The Decline of Party in Canada," in H. G. Thorburn, *Political Parties in Canada*, pp. 120-121.

[70] J. Meisel "The Decline of Party in Canada," p. 123.

the time consuming and potentially inaccurate practice of canvassing members of their party to find out where the public stands on an issue. The polls have replaced the "pols" as sources of information about public opinion. The only limitation of this technique has been the cost of public opinion polling, a significant limitation to parties in opposition but not to the bureaucracy or to the party in power.

The apparent decline of parties in Canada is matched in other Western democracies and so would appear to be part of a general trend.[71] In view of this Frank Sorauf has suggested that in Western democracies we have so far seen three phases in the evolution of parties and party systems. In the first phase parties began as loose organizations of limited access and narrow appeal. They were largely restricted to electioneering activities and could perform these functions without highly complex organizations because of the limited franchise. In the second phase, parties expanded along with the electorate. North American parties, with the exception of Canadian third parties, expanded less rapidly than their European counterparts but on both continents the aggregation and mobilization of the new electorate was the primary concern and parties dominated the political loyalties of the relatively unsophisticated citizenry. In the third and current phase, political interests become more complex and heterogeneous with an increasing differentiation of politics. Political loyalties of the by now more sophisticated citizenry are given to other organizations such as special interest groups as well as to parties. Parties lose their monopoly over many of their traditional functions and become, at best, first among equals among mass political organizations.

That description would appear to fit well with the evolution of Canadian political parties. Because of their crucial electoral functions they will certainly not disappear but we should not be surprised to see their relative importance in performing other functions decline still further.

---

[71] F. J. Sorauf, *Party Politics in America,* particularly p. 439 and Anthony King, "Political Parties in Western Democracies," *Polity,* Vol. 2, 1969, pp. 111-141.

12

The Electoral Process*

Federal general elections are the grand spectator events of Canadian politics. They are to the majority of Canadians, the most visible and the most intrinsically interesting aspects of the political process. Moreover, voting is the commonest and in some ways the easiest form of political participation. Between 70 and 80 percent of the eligible population will in fact show up at the polls on the day of a federal election, and the campaign leading to that election, of all political phenomena in Canada, is the most widely covered by the media and the most closely watched by the public.

THE FUNCTIONS OF THE ELECTORAL PROCESS

The primary function of the electoral system in Canada is to provide for an orderly and democratic succession from one set of political authorities to another. It permits the citizens of Canada to periodically review the performance of their political leaders and to pass judgment as to whether they should be permitted to continue or be replaced by a new set of authorities. While this may seem to be fairly obvious and unremarkable within the liberal democratic context of our system, in fact, we must keep in mind that many political systems do not provide such procedures for democratic review and peaceful change of the political leadership. Moreover, even in some systems that do provide an electoral system we find that it is adhered to in form but not in spirit; people are called upon to vote from time to time but informal restrictions on candidacy and rather unsubtle discouragement of those who would dare to oppose the existing regime ensure that there is never a real choice between alternative candidates on the ballot. In Canada however, elections are real contests and the electors are faced with at least some choice when they go to the polls.

Because of this, perhaps the most important function of the electoral process is the generation of support for the political system. It is

* We would like to acknowledge the assistance we received from our colleagues at Carleton, K. Z. Paltiel, Jon. H. Pammett, and Jane Jenson in the preparation of this chapter.

obvious that elections elicit support for a group of candidates: the winners of the election! And because the successful electoral candidates take over the authority roles of the system the election is in a way a vote of confidence for the actual people who will lead us for a while. This electoral result becomes the *mandate* to govern and gives the government of the day the legitimacy to effectively lead the country. However, elections also generate support for the system as a whole—for the regime and for the political community.

Support for the regime results from the fact that the election forces people to become interested and even directly involved in the democratic process. They learn about the rules of the game of politics and are faced with a very practical demonstration of the nature and extent of the power of the mass public in a democratic election. Because elections do produce change in the occupants of the elected offices of our political system, the periodic occurrence of such phenomena serves to remind even the most cynical citizen that while democracy works in strange ways, it still works.

Support for the political community is also a significant side benefit of the electoral process. For the eight weeks of a campaign all those Canadians who pay any attention to public affairs are focussed on one event. Over a half million Canadians are working toward one particular day. For a brief period national issues supersede most local issues. Thus elections are among the rarest of events in Canada for they focus the attention of the entire political community on a national phenomenon and unite them in a single goal—that of selecting the men and women who will represent us in the House of Commons, and indirectly selecting the people who will lead us in the government of the day. In this manner, elections function as agents of national integration, reaffirming, at least for a day, that East and West, French and English, we are ultimately, "all in the same boat."

Taken at the most superficial level, elections are simply devices for choosing the men and women who will occupy the seats in the House of Commons. This happens in two stages, first *recruiting* the candidates to carry the political parties' colours into the campaign through the nomination process, and then *selecting* from among the party candidates on election day. In sum, to the uninitiated, a Canadian federal election is simply a complicated system of democratic "staffing" whereby certain positions in our political system are filled. However, elections may also perform an input or *policy initiation* function for the political system. During a campaign, parties search high and low for votes, and this search may lead them to articulate the interests of groups in the population which might otherwise remain in the background, for if enough non-voters can be motivated to cast a ballot, the outcome of a close election might possibly be altered. Since approximately half a million Canadians are working for the political parties during a national election campaign, if a relevant issue exists, it will likely be discovered by someone.

These imputed input functions have a nice ring to them, for they suggest a picture of political parties, ever vigilant for the vote, forming a vital link between the citizen and the policy-making apparatus of the modern state. There are, however, a number of flaws. The most important is that most political decisions in Canada are made with little input from the party organization. Thus, even if the articulation of policy needs does occur, it is to some extent ineffectual; once in power, parties seem to pay little attention to their election platforms. Politics in New Brunswick are not entirely typical of Canadian politics, but the following words will ring true to most people who have carefully observed parties in office:

It is not unusual to find an item (expressed in different words) appearing on four election platforms of the same party in a row. The fact that the party was in power throughout the entire period and might presumably have enacted the required legislation during this time does not seem to occur to those who draw up the platform. [1]

Moreover, party platforms and the policies that parties suggest during elections are, for the most part, highly nebulous: they usually contain a little bit for everyone but almost no detail which could facilitate their conversion to specific policy outputs. For example, the Liberal program for the 1963 election contained such items as:

PROSPERITY FOR CANADIANS
Fundamentals for a Sound Economy
Cure unemployment . . .
Manage the nation's finances well . . .
Expand Canada's foreign trade . . .
A new Liberal government will act positively. It will have a constructive plan for free trade with Britain, the United States, and the European Common Market, as a step towards the establishment of an Atlantic Community. Commonwealth nations, Japan, and other interested countries will be invited to join in progressively reducing the barriers to world trade.
Planning and Finance
Make monetary policy an instrument for steady economic growth. A new Liberal government will take clear responsibility for the money supply, credit policies, and the exchange rate of the Canadian dollar.

---

[1] H. G. Thorburn, *Politics in New Brunswick* (University of Toronto Press, Toronto, 1961), p. 107.

It will improve the country's financial machinery, to make more Canadian capital available for industry and to safeguard the consumer against credit abuses.

It would be difficult to find people anywhere in Canada who would not espouse these policies in 1963 or 1981. They have appeared in virtually every Liberal and Conservative party platform since at least 1945.

It is also increasingly difficult to say just what the party platform is. In recent elections national parties have avoided going into an election with something called "the platform." Rather, a series of promises is unveiled by the leader during the campaign itself, an art developed to a high degree by the Liberals in the 1979 election which they managed to fight almost wholly without reference to specific issues or policies.

This is not to deny that Canadian parties frequently work out programs in considerable detail before they take office. The background papers for party annual meetings or biennial conventions attest to this. However, once a party takes power in Ottawa, this type of discussion paper usually recedes in importance and is superseded in the cabinet's eyes by inputs from the public service. This can be a source of considerable tension between party workers and a newly elected government and between a cabinet and the public service. For example when the Progressive Conservatives took office in Ottawa in May of 1979, they found that public servants had an array of reasons why almost all of the new government's campaign pledges could not be kept. Many ministers felt badly trapped between a party structure eager to put a "Conservative stamp" on government and the bureaucracy which could amply demonstrate why this would be very difficult to do.

In spite of all this, elections are important in spurring parties toward the aggregation and articulation of interests in Canadian politics; the threat of future elections forces cabinet ministers to ensure at least some minimal level of performance by their departments and it also forces them to hold new policies up to the litmus of broad public acceptability. While that may not always be the most propitious measure of a policy's advisability it is better than many other tests which could be applied.

There are three other latent or incidental functions of the electoral process in Canada which have particular importance. First, elections have a "sociability function." Party workers work hard for little or no monetary reward, so many participants in the electoral process must be there because it is fun. Indeed, for many a middle-aged Canadian, the election may be the high point of social and organizational life for a four-year period.

Secondly, elections provide "spectator interest." Whatever effect election campaigns have on the final outcome, they do make a fine national show with leaders dashing to and fro trying to establish their images, followed by retinues of weary and beery reporters who daily fill television screens with carefully staged two-minute clips of leaders in action, and newspapers with all manner of fact, fancy, and comment on the race. Then there is the thrill of the race itself, with Gallup polls and assorted pundits giving us a week-by-week picture of the positions of the various parties. At the local level, coffee parties and all-candidates' meetings abound and for eight weeks at a stretch local television producers are spared any anxiety about how to fill up television time and local publishers any anxiety about what to use to fill the space between advertisements.

Third, in some parts of Canada elections are still a minor means of redistributing income or services. Middle-class metropolitan ridings see relatively little of this and it is, perhaps, a dying tradition even in much of the countryside, but votes can still be bought and public works can still be built, in regions which might otherwise lack them. The votes of local opinion leaders—not necessarily the upper class of a community—are particularly valuable. Although many party workers are volunteers, some are paid something for their efforts and these are usually the less well-to-do. In Quebec the "good old days" are now disappearing, but there, until recently, a provincial election in a marginal riding was always good for at least one road paving and a considerable number of farm electric installations, usually carried out by a local contractor who, incidentally, supported the governing party. Even today, in Newfoundland, each election sees some extension of the pavement in small towns and outports. Electoral patronage was not necessarily the most efficient redistribution system on earth, but then neither are the bureaucratic redistribution systems we have today. Indeed, Hubert Guindon has pointed out that:

The possibly unanticipated effect of the crackdown on patronage funds (by the Lesage government in Quebec), in actual fact, was to halt or substantially reduce the flow of provincial funds to the lower social strata. Holding up the new "bureaucratic" public morality was a hidden net reorienting of public expenditures to the other social classes.[2]

THE ELECTORAL SYSTEM IN CANADA

While elections are held at all levels of government in Canada as well as in the selection of school boards, hospital boards, and other minor

[2] Hubert Guindon, "Social Unrest, Social Class and Quebec's Bureaucratic Revolution," *Queen's Quarterly*, vol. 71, no. 2, 1964 and in Thorburn, *Party Politics in Canada*, p. 188.

bodies with specific local responsibilities, the focus of this section will be primarily upon the federal level. The most important electoral event at the federal level is, of course, the general election where all seats in the House of Commons are up for grabs. *By-elections* are held in specific constituencies to fill vacancies that may occur between general elections due to the death or resignation of the incumbent, and the rules that apply in elections for the most part apply equally, but on a smaller scale for all by-elections. Because they are such complex events, elections cannot be understood if viewed as a single process. Therefore we will look at the Canadian electoral system as a number of separate but interrelated sub-processes with a wide variety of participants or actors. Before proceeding to an examination of these sub-processes it is necessary to provide a brief sketch of the players, or the *dramatis personae* who participate in the spectacle of a federal general election in Canada.

Dramatis Personae

The Voters The most numerous, and in some ways perhaps, the most important players in an election are the voters themselves. It is this large body of Canadians who ultimately must cast the ballots that determine the winners and the losers in an election. Who votes and who does not, is determined partly by the psychological and motivational characteristics of the Canadian electorate, and partly by the formal rules that set down the qualifications for voting, or the *franchise*. The former are simply the complex determinants of political participation, which have been discussed at length in Chapter 5 and need not be reexamined here. It suffices to say that some people who have the *right* to vote and who are on the voters' list will not exercise their right for reasons of personal choice.

The franchise is defined by the Canada Elections Act. The basic rule today is that any Canadian citizen[3] of eighteen years or older has the right to vote in a general election, or in a by-election being held in the constituency in which the voter resides. Voters may cast but one ballot, may vote only for a candidate whose name appears on the ballot (there are no "write in" votes in the Canadian system), and must vote in the constituency in which his or her name appears on the voters' list.[4] The Elections Act, however, goes on to exclude certain classes of individuals specifically. Those disqualified from voting are the Chief

---

[3] The requirement here used to be "British subject" and not citizenship.
[4] Special provisions are made for members of the armed forces, Canadians residing outside the country, etc., to vote in their "home" constituency even though they may not, at the time of the election, physically live there.

Electoral Officer and assistant, the Returning Officers in each constituency (except that the RO has the deciding vote in the case of a tie), federally appointed judges (except Citizenship Court judges), inmates of penal institutions and mental institutions, and persons convicted of offences under the Elections Act.

Thus we can state fairly safely that the Canadian electoral system today features universal adult suffrage. However what seems to be an obvious criterion for a liberal democratic regime, has not always been accepted so fully in Canada. For a large part of the period between 1867 and 1920 when the Dominion Elections Act was passed, the federal franchise was determined by the provincial elections acts. This meant that the qualifications and disqualifications of voters in federal elections varied with the whim and prejudice of provincial governments and, incidentally, meant that a citizen's right to vote was not consistent across the country. Many provinces originally had a property qualification for voting, a reflection of a basically elitist attitude to the responsibilities of choosing a government. The feeling was that people who owned property had a stake in the community and would be more responsible (and more conservative) in casting a ballot. Women were generally excluded from voting until World War I, and in Quebec women were actually disfranchised in provincial elections until 1940. Still more unusual and undemocratic were the provisions in the B.C. Elections Act up to 1945 that disqualified even Canadian citizens who were of Oriental or Hindu descent. Because provincial rules determined the federal franchise until World War I Orientals were also thus disqualified from voting in federal elections as well. Some provinces also have had literacy requirements for voting, and while such provisions would not disfranchise a significant number of Canadians today, when they were in effect, the literacy rate was significantly less than universal. Nevertheless, despite the rather tarnished history of provincial franchises, all such disqualifications by now have been removed, and today the provincial elections acts define a voter in a manner close to identical to the Canada Elections Act.[5]

The federal franchise has not always been as universal as it is today either. The most glaring exceptions have been in the treatment of native peoples. The Inuit ("Esquimeau person" in the 1934 Dominion Franchise Act) were explicitly excluded until 1950, and because there were no federal electoral districts in the territorial regions of Keewatin

[5] See: Qualter, T. H., *The Election Process in Canada* (McGraw-Hill Ryerson, Toronto, 1970). See also: Anstett, A., and T. Qualter, "Election Systems," in Bellamy, Pammett, and Rowat, *The Provincial Political System* (Methuen, Toronto, 1976), pp. 147-176.

and Franklin where most Inuit reside, it was not until the creation of the NWT constituency after the 1961 census that most Inuit were able to vote for the first time. Indians living on reserves were also explicitly excluded from the franchise until 1960 when such discriminatory provisions were removed from the Elections Act.

The only significant restriction on the principle of universal adult suffrage today in Canada results from the nature of voters' lists. Unlike many electoral systems, the federal one features temporary voters' lists which are prepared anew at the time of each election. All of the provinces (except for B.C. which has a permanent voters' list) use this system of pre-election *enumeration* in order to prepare a list of eligible voters. While such a system has benefits in that the voter does not have to "register," but rather, is automatically placed on a list, its major flaw is that, in the process of enumeration, many potential voters are missed and hence do not get on the preliminary list. This means that the onus shifts to the individuals who must specifically apply to have their names added to the list. A lot of people simply never bother to check to see if they are on the preliminary lists and thus end up being disfranchised administratively. They have all the qualifications to be electors, but because of the nature of the enumeration process they end up losing their vote for that particular election. All in all, however, while we might consider a move to a permanent voters' list or to a system of self-registration, probably far fewer potential voters are lost in the existing enumeration process than are lost through idosyncratic factors such as apathy, alienation, illness and the weather on election day.

In sum therefore, the federal franchise in Canada is extended to all adult citizens and while some will be disfranchised through administrative errors associated with our temporary voters' lists, by far the best predictors of non-voting in our system are the psychological and the motivational ones. These have been dealt with at length in our section on political participation in Chapter 5, and will be dealt with briefly in the section of this chapter entitled "THE DYNAMICS OF CANADIAN ELECTORAL BEHAVIOUR."

The Candidates The qualifications and disqualifications for candidacy in a federal election are set down in the Canada Elections Act. The basic rule is that candidates must be electors—they must be eligible to vote in a Canadian election. Disqualifications include persons found guilty of corrupt election practices, persons involved in contractual relationships with the Crown, persons employed by the Crown (except public servants on leave of absence and cabinet ministers), and members of a provincial legislature or a territorial council. Candidates must be nominated by twenty-five electors from within the constituency and they must make a deposit of $200.

While in the past candidates in federal elections were required to own a certain amount of property, this stipulation was abolished soon after Confederation. Residence qualifications to be a candidate in a federal election are that the individual must reside in Canada: this means that there is no legal requirement that candidates be residents of the constituencies in which they are running, although candidates who are "parachuted" into a riding by the party leadership are sometimes spurned at the polls by the local party faithful. In provincial elections acts, residence in the province is a requirement of being a candidate, although as with the federal act, there is no requirement that the candidate be a resident of the constituency.

Because we now have "registered" political parties in Canada, if candidates wish to have a party affiliation listed beside their names on the ballot, their candidacies must be sanctioned by the party leader, and this in turn means that candidates must have been nominated at a party nomination meeting according to the rules established by the party constitution. More will be said about the informal partisan aspects of the nomination procedure later in this chapter.

The Political Parties   We will discuss the party campaign machinery at a later point in this chapter, but it is necessary at this juncture to deal briefly with the formal aspects of the political parties' role in the election system. Section 13 of the Canada Elections Act sets out the conditions and procedures for registration of a political party. Essentially it is the responsibility of the Chief Electoral Officer to maintain a "registry of political parties" and to determine which applications for registration meet the stipulations set down in the act. In order to be registered the party must field at least fifty candidates in an upcoming election, and to maintain continuous registration the party must have twelve seats in the House of Commons at dissolution. The only restriction on registration besides the number of candidates and sundry formal requirements having to do with information about the party's address, the names of the party executive, chief party agent, and the party auditor, is that the name of the party must not be the same or even too similar to the name of an already registered party. This latter requirement is to prevent a marginal group from calling itself, for instance, the Conservative Progressive party, or the NPD and picking up gratuitous support from the "careless minority" who thought they were voting for a major political party. Despite these provisions, in the thirty-first general election in 1979 there were nine parties which had the party name on the ballot paper, one of which called itself the Libertarian Party. Although this label might have been deemed rather close to another, more prominent party in Canadian politics, the results of the election indicate that very few Liberal voters were fooled by the similarity in name. How many Libertarians voted Liberal by mistake is impossible to estimate!

Election Officials   There are a number of offices created and defined by the Canada Elections Act but the most important of these is that of the *Chief Electoral Officer* (CEO), who is appointed "during good behaviour" or until "age sixty five" by the Governor General in Council and has the effective rank of deputy minister. The CEO, whose salary is set by statute, has independence from the government of the day in the same way that a superior court judge has. The responsibilities of this office are to "exercise general direction and supervision over the administrative conduct of elections," and generally to enforce all of the provisions of the Elections Act. The CEO is also granted very broad discretionary powers to adapt the election process in the event of "unusual or unforeseen" circumstances. This power was in fact exercised in the 1980 election to permit the voters' lists for the 1979 election of less than a year earlier to suffice as the preliminary lists for 1980. This reduced the cost and administrative fuss of the second election by foregoing the enumeration process.

The office of the *Representation Commissioner* which was originally established in 1964 was intended to coordinate the process of electoral boundaries adjustments (redistribution). In effect the federal Representation Commissioner was a member of each of the eleven Electoral Boundaries Commissions which make the recommendations to the House of Commons concerning federal constituency boundary adjustments in the provinces and the territories. However in August 1979 the office of the Representation Commissioner was abolished and most of the responsibilities were transferred to the CEO.

For each electoral district in Canada, the Governor General in Council appoints a *Returning Officer* (RO). The Returning Officer is appointed permanently or until age sixty-five and the requirements of tenure are that the RO remain a resident of the constituency for which the appointment is made, maintain a non-partisan stance in the performance of duties, and in general do the job defined by the Elections Act. The RO's responsibilities are to manage the election process in the electoral district, to appoint enumerators, to appoint an *Election Clerk* for the constituency, and to appoint a *Deputy Returning Officer* (DRO) for each of the polls within the constituency. The Returning Officer must maintain an office in the constituency from the time the election writs are issued and either the RO or the Election Clerk must be on duty in the office during the hours the polls are open throughout the election period.

Deputy Returning Officers hold office at the pleasure of the RO in the electoral district and can be removed by the RO at any time. The role of the DRO is to administer the election process at the level of the individual polling station, and to oversee the balloting and "unofficial count" in the poll. To assist in these duties, the DRO is required by the Act to appoint a *Poll Clerk*.

As mentioned above, the Returning Officer of each constituency must appoint enumerators who are charged with the responsibility for preparing the preliminary voters' lists in each polling division. Two enumerators are appointed for each urban poll, and the Canada Elections Act requires that the RO select them "so that they represent two different and opposed political interests." The procedure for achieving such bipartisan representation in each pair of urban enumerators is also set down in the Act. Essentially the RO asks the successful candidate and the candidate who placed second to each nominate "a fit and proper person." "Fit and proper" in this instance means an honest but faithful partisan! While the enumerators are supposed to travel in pairs to ensure that there is no "padding" of the voters' list and no deliberate deletion of selected individuals, it is often the case that the enumerators split the work load between them and work individually just to save time. While no system is perfect, there are relatively few deliberate abuses of this system[6] and accidental omissions from the list can be caught on revision before the final lists are prepared.

A very definite benefit of this system from a partisan standpoint is that the local candidates of the two most successful parties in the previous election are able to dole out some minor patronage in return for a little volunteer work later on in the campaign. Rural enumerators work singly rather than in pairs and their appointment is by the RO. Because the appointment of ROs is open to partisan favouritism in the first place, it is not remarkable that rural enumerators tend to be supporters of the political party that was in office at the time that the RO was appointed.

The Election Expenses Act originally provided that the Chief Electoral Officer must appoint an official to serve as the *Commissioner of Election Expenses*. His job was to deal with complaints arising under the Election Expenses Act and the original appointee was simply the Assistant Chief Electoral Officer, who was the second in command to the CEO. However, it soon became clear that the burdens of this office were such that it would be better performed by an entirely separate individual who could concentrate on the job full time. Since then the parliament of Canada passed legislation extending the jurisdiction of the Commissioner to all provisions of the Canada Elections Act as well. The new role is to function as a sort of "elections ombudsman" to deal with all manner of complaints having to do with

---

[6] One incident of this type was reported in the 1979 report of the CEO.

the conduct of elections and including, of course, campaign financing. The official title of this office was changed to *The Commissioner of Canada Elections* to reflect the expanded mandate, and as well the Commissioner was given the power to prosecute offenders under the Canada Elections Act. This latter provision was intended to take the responsibility for such prosecutions away from the influence of the Attorney General for Canada who being a member of the government, could be accused of partisanship.

There are other minor officials and functionaries who are "bit players" in the complex theatre that is a Canadian general election, such as the scrutineers, or "party agents" who are present in each polling station, the party auditors who are required under the Election Expenses Act, and the staff of the CEO. However, they do not play a significant enough role in the election itself to bear closer scrutiny at this point. Their roles will become apparent as we move to a discussion of the election process itself.

The Election Process

Redistribution The machinery of redistribution comes to life after each decennial census is reported. Its purpose is simply to ensure that the structure of our constituencies is such that Canadians are more or less equally represented in the House of Commons. The general rule is that the number of people represented by one Member of Parliament should be roughly equal from constituency to constituency. In the past, with some ridings in suburban regions growing very rapidly and others in rural areas, particularly in the Atlantic provinces, shrinking in population we have seen pronounced disparities between the relative significance of people's votes in different regions.

However, even the principle of equal representation has to be adjusted a bit in a country with the vastness and diversity of Canada. Thus for instance it has generally been agreed that because a rural constituency is larger in physical size, it could be based on a smaller population size than a geographically compact but densely populated urban district. Furthermore it has long been recognized that because of our federal system, the House of Commons should be minimally reflective of all regions of the country. Hence it is generally accepted that PEI's four seats, while comprising far smaller constituencies than for example the Metro Toronto ridings, are a deviation from the norm of equal representation that can be tolerated.[7]

---

[7] In fact P.E.I. and N.B. are pegged at four and ten seats respectively by the BNA Act which stipulated that no province should have fewer members of the House than Senators.

Nevertheless, it is accepted as well that the boundaries of the constituencies must from time to time be changed according to shifts in population, and the problem is how to achieve such boundary changes with a minimum of partisan strife and a minimum of unfair partisan advantage. At one time the changes in electoral boundaries were the prerogative of the House of Commons. This meant that the government of the day was always in a position of being able to adjust the ridings in such a way as to maximize its own electoral success. However, since 1964 Canada has had a system of electoral boundaries' adjustments which is premised on the all-party acceptance of the need for impartiality.

The current system of redistribution in Canada is based on eleven impartial electoral boundaries commissions, one for each province and one for the Yukon and the NWT. These are made up of a judge from the province, who is appointed by the Chief Justice of the Provincial Supreme Court, and two other members who are appointed by the Speaker of the House of Commons, one of whom is usually the speaker of the provincial legislature. While the original legislation provided that the Representation Commissioner should be a member of each provincial commission, with the abolition of that office in 1979 and the transfer of those responsibilities to the Chief Electoral Officer, this provision has been deleted from the Act. The base from which these Electoral Boundaries Commissions begin is the number of seats assigned by the BNA Act to their province. This base is established through a complicated formula which allocates seats to the provinces according to the size of their population relative to that of Quebec. Quebec is assigned a set number of seats (75 currently, but to be adjusted upwards by four after each decennial census). The formula also categorizes provinces as "small," "intermediate," and "large" and tends to slightly favour the smaller and intermediate provinces over the large ones. It is the responsibility of the Chief Electoral Officer to calculate each province's entitlement of seats by applying the formula in the BNA Act to the census data as soon as the Chief Statistician of Canada gives the CEO the required information. Having made these calculations, the CEO then instructs the Electoral Boundaries Commissions to get to work and allocate the available seats within their provinces.

The various Commissions start by establishing a provincial "electoral quotient" which is the figure arrived at by dividing its population (according to the most recent decennial census) by the number of seats allocated to the province. From here it is the responsibility of the Commission to draw constituency boundaries in such a way that constituency populations come as close as possible to the "electoral quotient" for the province. They are permitted to deviate from this equal representation rule under certain circumstances specified by the Electoral Boundaries Readjustment Act as follows:

. . . (i) special geographic considerations, including in particular the sparsity or density of population of various regions of the province, the accessibility of such regions or the size or shape thereof, appear to the commission to render such a departure necessary or desirable, or
(ii) any special community or diversity of interests of the inhabitants of various regions of the province appears to the commission to render such a departure necessary or desirable, . . .

The Act goes on however to specify that in no case should the electoral districts in a province deviate from the quotient by more than 25 percent, plus or minus.

The preliminary reports of the Commissions are then open to public scrutiny and comment within the province and after any changes brought about at this stage are completed, the completed report of the Commission is sent on to the CEO. The Speaker then tables all of the reports of the Electoral Boundaries Commissions in the House of Commons. The House has thirty days to examine the reports and objections signed by ten members can be filed with the Speaker. These are then debated and the results of the debate along with the appropriate copies of Hansard are sent back to the relevant Commission for reconsideration. The ultimate step in the process of redistribution is the approval of the reports of the Electoral Boundaries Commissions by order in council.[8]

Timing of Elections   Barring the defeat of a government in the Commons, the timing of an election in Canada is wholly the prerogative of the Prime Minister, who decides, with more or less advice from the cabinet and personal advisors, on the exact date. This has not always been so clearly the case. From 1876 to 1926 it seemed generally conceded that it was the right of the Prime Minister to decide the occurrence and the timing of elections; at least he always did so. However, in 1926, Lord Byng refused Mackenzie King a dissolution and asked Arthur Meighen to attempt to form a government in the existing House. Meighen did so but was almost immediately himself defeated on a vote of confidence. King campaigned in the ensuing election largely on this issue and won a clear majority of seats. In spite of some subsequent debate, King's victory established the principle that not only does the Prime Minister alone have the right to control the timing of elections under normal circumstances, but also that even

[8] The formal electoral machinery is described in greater detail in T. Qualter, *The Election Process in Canada*.

after a defeat in the House of Commons on a vote of want of confidence, the Prime Minister has the right to advise and very largely to control whether there should be a dissolution and election or whether the opposition leader should be called upon to try to form a government.

The issue could have arisen again after the 1972 federal election, when the Liberals were returned with only two more seats than the Conservatives, the NDP holding the balance of power with 31 seats. If the Liberals had been defeated in a vote of confidence when they met parliament, would it have been Prime Minister Trudeau's right to ask for another election, or would he have been obliged by constitutional convention merely to resign and let the Governor General call upon the leader of the opposition to form a government? If the principle enunciated above stands, the Governor General would have had to do whatever the Prime Minister suggested, but some constitutional experts did assert that even if the Prime Minister had requested dissolution, the Governor General could have denied him that privilege and called instead on Mr. Stanfield.

As it turned out, the issue blew over leaving nothing more than residual deposits in the bank accounts of sundry academic constitutional experts who appeared on radio and television in the days following the election, and it is likely that if Mr. Trudeau had done anything, he would simply have resigned, leaving the options open for the Governor General. The constitutional experts did seem to agree that once the Liberals had won one or two votes of confidence in the House and had their Throne Speech accepted, the normal rules would then apply; dissolution would be a Prime Ministerial prerogative or else would follow automatically from a major government defeat. One and one-half years later the government was in fact defeated and dissolution did follow, virtually automatically, as it did again in somewhat similar circumstances in November of 1979.

Customarily, if the government in power is in a majority, elections will occur at about four-year intervals, although the maximum allowable term under the BNA Act is five years. A government will not wait out the full five years unless it is in trouble, and then the results are not likely to be propitious—a fact discovered to their regret by Robert Bourassa in 1976 and Pierre Trudeau in 1979. A Prime Minister will usually make a decision about precise election timing on the basis of information from the party about its state of preparedness, from the cabinet about how any policy initiatives undertaken by the party are progressing, and particularly from information obtained from public opinion polls and interpreted by personal advisors about the party standing across the country. Depending on his temperament, the Prime Minister may also feel moved to look at horoscopes or tea leaves, or to consult his long-dead mother, for the timing of an election can be a tricky business.

Once a decision on timing has been made, the Prime Minister visits the Governor General, who has the formal power to dissolve parliament and call an election. In the provinces the Premier visits the Lieutenant-Governor, who has a similar formal power with regard to provincial elections. The Governor General then issues the writs in the name of Her Majesty declaring the election, the Chief Electoral Office transmits the writs to his 282 Returning Officers and the electoral machinery goes into motion:

The whole town and country is a hive of politics, and people who have only witnessed gatherings such as the House of Commons at Westminster and the Senate at Washington and never seen a Conservative convention at Tecumseh Corners or a Liberal Rally at the Concession Schoolhouse, don't know what politics means.

So you may imagine the excitement in Mariposa when it became known that King George had dissolved the Parliament of Canada and had sent out a writ or command for Missinaba County to elect for him some other person than John Henry Bagshaw because he no longer had confidence in him. [9]

Enumeration   By the time electoral writs are issued, the official electoral machinery under the direction of the Chief Electoral Officer is ready to begin moving. Indeed, the apparatus is ready a considerable time before the usual four years have passed, since there is always the possibility of a "snap election" called by a Prime Minister at a moment which he thinks will best serve his party and in a time of minority government there is always the possibility of a government defeat in the House of Commons. Neither the rapid succession of federal elections beginning in 1962 nor the unexpected fall of the Progressive Conservatives in 1979 caught the Electoral Office totally unprepared, although, in the latter case, the huge job of preparing for an election so soon after the previous one subjected it to considerable strain.

As soon as the Governor General or Lieutenant-Governor has signed the electoral writs, instructions go out to the Returning Officers and enumerators begin to knock on doors to list the eligible voters. As mentioned above the job of enumerator is a minor patronage position which, in urban areas, goes to supporters of the two parties which led the polls in the previous election. The enumeration process must start on the 49th day before polling day and it must finish by the 44th day. Since some time is required to get out the writs

---

[9] From *Sunshine Sketches of a Little Town* by Stephen Leacock, reprinted by permission of The Canadian Publishers, McClelland and Stewart Limited, Toronto.

calling for the whole process to begin, this means that an election cannot usually take place in less than 60 days.[10] A preliminary list of voters is compiled and posted on neighbourhood telephone poles so that people may see if their names are on the list (and can determine the occupations of their neighbours!). Copies of the preliminary list are also sent to the Chief Electoral Office. Potential voters whose names do not appear on the list then have five to eight days in which to challenge their omission before *revising officers*—a simple procedure which normally requires only a declaration on the voter's part. Final lists are then prepared and the polls set up.

Polling the Electors   Elections are generally held on Mondays, and the specific Monday selected is at the discretion of the Prime Minister. Polling stations are often located in the houses of the supporters of the "right party" and the owners of the house being used are paid for the use of their premises. While this used to be a fairly significant bit of patronage, today in the more affluent areas, the remuneration is hardly worth the inconvenience of a stampede through one's house and so churches and schools tend to be used more and more as polling stations.

The polling station has to be set up in such a manner that there are tables or desks for the use of the poll clerk and the party scrutineers and with one or two polling booths where the voters can mark their ballots in privacy. The principle of the *secret ballot* is a long standing requirement of truly free elections, and the Canada Elections Act very carefully specifies the procedures for protecting this right. There are also provisions in the Act for *"proxy voting"* on behalf of an elector who is unable to get to the poll personally for the reasons of illness etc. *Advance polls* are established for those who must be out of town on voting day and these are run on the ninth and seventh days before the election. The votes from advance polls are not counted until after the close of regular polls. Ironically, while there is a provision in the Canada Elections Act that requires all drinking establishments and liquor outlets to be closed during the time that the polls are open on election day this provision does not apply for advance polls. Perhaps the increased use of advance polls by electors that has been noted in the last couple of elections is reflective of the Canadian voter "needing a drink" before making a decision. At any rate the Chief Electoral Officer's report on the 1979 election suggests that the pre-Confederation philosophy that "booze and politics don't mix" is no longer

---

[10] T. Qualter, *The Election Process in Canada,* pp. 163-4. His diary of a federal election, pp. 162-166, provides a valuable summary of the whole process.

applicable and that the parliament of Canada should soberly consider the deletion of such provisions from the Elections Act.[11]

Counting the Vote After the regular polls close on voting day the Deputy Returning Officers in charge of each poll count the ballots under the watchful eyes of the party agents or *scrutineers*. This is an entirely unofficial count although it is usually accurate and it is the results of this unofficial count, tabulated in newsrooms and party headquarters, that produce the excitement on election night. The ballot boxes are delivered to the Returning Officer after the unofficial count, and the RO then has the responsibility of keeping them until the official count which may not be sooner than seven days after the election. By this time, of course, the excitement is over in all but ridings which were very close and where the armed service vote, which is added at this time, may be decisive.

In the case of close elections, or if irregularities are alleged in the conduct of the election, either the Returning Officer or one of the candidates may apply for a recount. The recount is performed by a judge in the presence of the candidates or their agents. In the case of a tie even after a recount, the Returning Officer must cast the deciding vote in the constituency. When all of this is over with, the Returning Officer then returns the election writ declaring the candidate with the most votes the winner to the Chief Electoral Officer.

The Partisan Campaign

National Campaign Headquarters So far, in discussing preparation for elections, parties have been mentioned only in passing, but parallel to the official activity during an election campaign, there is a great deal of unofficial activity. Indeed, by the time the Prime Minister visits the Governor General to ask for a dissolution, political parties will already have undergone the long process of waking up from their deep sleep of the previous few years, oiling and polishing their local machines, nominating candidates, reactivating their national organizations, and generally acting like the textbook pictures we have always had of parties. The actual setting of the election date is rather like the firing of the starter's gun. Unfortunately, as we will see, sometimes the runners trip over the starting blocks.

At national campaign headquarters a number of things will be happening. Schedules for speaking tours by the leaders will be set up for the whole campaign. An avalanche of party literature, speaker's

---

[11] Canada, Chief Electoral Officer, *Statutory Report 1979* (Supply and Service Canada, Ottawa, 1979), pp. 25-26.

handbooks, etc. will descend on the local constituency associations. Party "bag-men" will redouble their efforts, and budgetary priorities will be set by a small, sometimes informal, campaign committee under the National Chairman. New staff and volunteers will be taken on, and press releases and speeches ground out by the yard. National polls will be commissioned in order to divine the "major issues"— which are invariably inflation, unemployment, and the economy.

The Constituency Organizations   At the local level, events will be much more variable. Some local election machines are highly efficient, and some are comedies of errors. Nominations of candidates will usually have taken place some time before the campaign begins, but in some ridings the announcement of the election date will find one or more parties so ill-prepared that no candidate is available; and in others, parties may have delayed nomination meetings in order to take advantage of the publicity they generate. Nomination procedures vary from party to party and from riding to riding. At the one extreme are completely open conventions where anyone who has paid nominal party membership dues may vote, while at the other extreme are carefully controlled nominating conventions where all the delegates are handpicked by the party executive to avoid any unfortunate "errors." In practice most nominating conventions lie somewhere between the two extremes, with the delegates representing poll organizations or other small units in the riding. In truth, parties are as often embarrassed by a lack of potential nominees as by an excess, and at every election some constituency executives face the unpleasant task of searching frantically for someone to run as the party candidate. If all else fails, a member of the party executive will accept a "draft" and carry the party's colours into the local campaign.

Ideally, the earliest stages of an election campaign will see the establishment of a careful schedule of activities peaking on election day. Local workers will be recruited and fund raising will be attempted in earnest. Poll captains will be appointed to coordinate party efforts in a given neighbourhood. Some tentative door-to-door canvassing will begin, rising in intensity as the great day approaches, and mail and telephone campaigns will be conducted to reach as many voters as the party workers can find. On voting day the poll captain will arrange for the transportation of any known supporters who could not otherwise make it to the polls, and scrutineers will sit in the polling station to ensure that irregularities do not occur, and, equally important, to chat with friends and neighbours.

In practice it may be difficult to find willing party workers and parties can always use more people. Canvassing itself is often a hit-and-miss affair, with large sections of the city, especially in lower class areas, left untouched, and phone campaigns are also usually rather spotty. In most homes the candidates' literature is "filed" in the garbage can. Meanwhile, communication is flowing back and forth between the constituencies and local, provincial, and national headquarters and, as befits a stratarchical structure, much of it gets lost or is grossly misinterpreted along the way. Yet the whole structure does lumber ahead toward election day. Leaders crisscross the country, leaving enthusiasm—or sometimes black despair—in their wakes. Money flows into close ridings and out of safe or hopeless ones. The media give millions of dollars of free publicity to the parties and the parties spend millions of dollars sponsoring events for the electorate to watch and the media to report.

Financing the Election   All this activity costs money, and the spending is often regarded with a jaundiced eye by the public. It is true that the total amounts spent are high. Professor Norman Ward has estimated that the total real costs of running the electoral machinery in 1972 amounted to about $47,000,000 per year, an estimate made as "a trial run at the job by a political scientist who, it must be conceded, is not convinced that it can be done."[12] Inflation affects this area not less than others and by 1980 the real cost was probably close to $100 million. Lest this amount be regarded as excessive, Professor Ward goes on to conclude of his 1972 figures:

A sum rounded upward to $47,000,000 for the annual costs of democracy . . . may seem enormous, but it is barely $2.40 a head. . . . Even taking the most extravagant view of the costs of the electoral and parliamentary process and the supporting activities, it would be difficult to argue that the democratic parts of Canada's governmental machinery are an expensive indulgence.

Another leading authority, Professor K. Z. Paltiel, has estimated that the total expenditure by parties in the 1972 election campaign was at least 31 million dollars, up at least 30 percent from 1968.[13] Expenditures by individual candidates ranged from $92,100 declared

---

[12] Norman Ward, "Money and Politics," *Canadian Journal of Political Science*, Vol. 5, No. 3, Sept. 1972, pp. 335-347. This article also gives a brief description of efforts at reform in the area of electoral finance.

[13] The following descriptive material on election expenses is from K. Z. Paltiel, "Some Aspects of Campaign Finance in Canada," paper presented to the International Political Science Association, Montreal, August 1973. For historical material see K. Z. Paltiel, *Political Party Financing in Canada* and the Committee on Election Expenses, *Studies in Canadian Party Finance* (Queen's Printer, Ottawa, 1966). See for general overview, K. Z. Paltiel, "Public Financing Abroad: Controls and Effects," in Malbin, M. (ed), *Parties Interest Groups and Campaign Finance Laws* Washington, 1979, p. 354; *Party Candidate and Election Finance*, Royal Commission on Corporate Concentration, Study No. 22, Ottawa, 1976.

by mining magnate Stephen Roman (who was defeated) down to nothing but $200, the required deposit from all candidates. The average reported expenditure per candidate was $18,700 for the Liberals, $16,500 for the PC, $5,400 for the NDP, and $1,885 for the Social Credit. Since 1974 the expenditures by candidates have been limited by election expense legislation described below.

At the national level alone the Liberals, in 1972, raised over 6.5 million dollars and spent at least 5.9 million dollars, with the largest amounts being disbursed by provincial party organizations either for their own expenses or as partial reimbursement to candidates for local expenses. The national office itself spent nearly 1.3 million dollars, mainly on the leader's tours, the media, and printing. The money was raised largely in Ontario and Quebec with at least 50 bag-men prowling Ontario, ever watchful for corporate or individual donors. The National Campaign chairman himself canvassed the ninety largest firms in the province. It is important, in view of what we said earlier about the small size of the national headquarters between elections, that $600,000 of the money raised in 1972 had to be allocated to paying off the accumulated deficit of the national office, whose approximately $350,000 annual operating costs were not easily covered by the party in non-election years.

By comparison with the Liberals, the PCs raised almost 4 million dollars at the national level in 1972 and managed to spend nearly $200,000 more than they raised. Their donors are also concentrated in Ontario and to a much lesser extent in Quebec, but they also received substantial amounts of money from Alberta. Like the Liberals, they receive the bulk of their money from large (over $1,000) donors and—even more than the Liberals—they tend to spend it in areas where their support is greatest, or in marginal areas rather than on lost causes in safe Liberal or NDP seats.

By contrast with the older parties, the NDP in 1972 raised and spent on the national level only $370,000, but the straight comparison of this figure with the Liberals' 6.5 million dollars is misleading. The NDP provincial organizations provide support for the national headquarters whereas the situation is reversed in the older parties, so the appropriate comparison should be between the NDP's $370,000 and the Liberal headquarters' expenditure on the national campaign of 1.3 million dollars. Even so, the contrast is obvious. The NDP headquarters costs about $250,000 to operate between elections but because of the constancy of the NDP's union support, it does not operate at a deficit between elections as do the older parties.

The financing of the electoral activities of Canadian parties has depended heavily on donations from corporations or, in the case of the NDP, large labour unions. Party bag-men have lists of corporations which have given in the past and can be expected to do so again, and the calling of an election will see them knocking discreetly on the doors of company presidents or treasurers. It has already been noted that many corporations follow a 60-40 policy, dividing their donations 60 percent to the party in power and 40 percent to the major opposi tion party as an "insurance" gesture.[14] In situations where a change of government seems probable, corporations may reverse the propor- tions of donations going to government and opposition or more often may follow a 50-50 rule. In many cases, corporate giving is regular- ized and counted as a regular budgetary expenditure, although in other cases company donations may be highly personalized. In one such case a rookie bag-man was sent by the Ontario Provincial Liberal Association to a medium-sized southern Ontario firm and was firmly rebuffed by the president, who insisted that his company had never given money to the Liberal party. A veteran bag-man was then called back into action and sent around to jog the president's memory. The happy ending for the Liberal party was that the appearance of a famil- iar face was enough to revive the president's memory, and the party coffers were enriched by a tidy sum.

In non-election years, party operations are also financed by indi- vidual and corporate donations; the election expenses we have been discussing so far are additional to normal operating expenditures and are garnered by special financial campaigns. In 1978, total income used to finance the day-to-day operations of the party was 5.4 million dollars for the Conservatives and just over 5 million dollars for the Liberals.

In addition to money, corporations often make substantial gifts of services. This is particularly true of public relations and advertising agencies, which may donate the services of large staffs together with supporting supplies. Corporations that give money may often do so for relatively non-immediate reasons having to do with the preserva- tion of "the system" or "a good business climate." Advertising agen- cies, however, hope to benefit immediately from large governmental contracts for tourist advertising, the publicizing of new programs, and other governmental work, and if they have picked the winning party they are often suitably rewarded.

In addition to these sources of funds, there are assorted semi- institutionalized sources which come under the general heading of

---

[14] It might be argued that the "insurance" is against an NDP victory. Corporations likely do not care much whether there is a Tory or Liberal government in power, but they normally prefer to keep the more "threatening" socialists in the political wilder- ness.

"kickbacks" or "rake-offs." For example, it is rumoured that in some provinces distilleries are assessed a regular percentage of gross sales which goes to the coffers of the party in power as an informal "tax" for listing their brands in liquor outlets. In another province, rumour has it that there are specialized lawyers who are very good at getting liquor licences. Their fees are high, but they don't get to keep quite all of them. A certain percentage goes to make the gears of the administrative machinery run more smoothly and, incidentally, tends to help the fortunes of the party in power.

These methods of party finance are obviously open to the grossest abuse, and the whole question of campaign finance in Canada has been a constant target for reformers. Early in 1974, parliament passed a series of sweeping reforms which have done much to change the face of campaign financing in Canada.[15] The legislation requires disclosure of the names and amounts given by any donor who provides over $100 to a party while also allowing tax credits to the donors on a sliding scale depending on the amount given. It requires that the public purse pay half the cost of television time for parties and provides for the allocation among parties of a total of 6½ hours of time on all TV stations according to a complex formula related to seats in the Commons and to popular vote. It limits total spending by national parties to 30 cents per voter for the total number of voters registered in constituencies where the party has candidates. Since there were just over 15 million registered voters in Canada in 1979, the parties with candidates in every riding were allowed total expenditures of just over 4.5 million dollars for their national campaigns—about the same amount spent in the two previous elections in 1972 and 1974. It also limited the amounts which can be spent by individual candidates to $1 for each of the first 15,000 voters on the list, 50 cents for each of the next 10,000 voters, and 25 cents for any voters over 25,000. Any candidate who gets 15 percent of the vote will be reimbursed for part of his or her expenses—about one-third of them in an average riding. Parties and candidates, through their official agents, must provide full accounting of all money spent and received and the gifts of services mentioned above must be declared as part of overall expenditures.

While the legislation goes a long way in reducing abuses of the electoral system, there are still some problems. The expenditure limits seemed high in 1974 and were considered acceptable by the

---

[15] A detailed account is available in K. Z. Paltiel, "Some Aspects of Campaign Finance in Canada," and a more general account is available in the *Globe and Mail*, January 4, 1974, p. 1.

parties in 1979 and 1980, but they are not indexed for inflation and will likely require a fairly frequent revision. The proportion of costs paid out of the public purse is still quite low; generally about one-sixth of overall costs, so parties still must engage in substantial internal money-raising activities. A tax credit system has made it more attractive for individual donors to give money while disclosure rules have made some corporations more reticent. The result has been an evening out of the amounts available to parties, with the NDP being the biggest relative winners.

The legislation is rigourously enforced by the Chief Electoral Officer, backed by the Commissioner of Canada Elections and, with the exception of slowness in reporting on the part of some local candidates, non-reporting by some fringe candidates, and some difficulty in defining provisions with respect to the gratuitous provision of services to candidates, it is fairly well observed. One of the major enforcement problems seems to be in the area of individuals and corporations doing their own unsolicited advertising on behalf of candidates or political parties. In 1979 the CEO reported twenty-one complaints arising out of persons other than the gladiators themselves who were disseminating information that effectively supported or opposed policies clearly identifiable with one of the political parties. The Elections Expenses Act does not restrict the right of individuals to publicise their opinions about public policy during the election period as long as they do it "in good faith" and as long as there is no "collusion" between the parties or candidates and the individuals. Because either collusion or bad faith are difficult if not impossible to prove, this loophole in the legislation will be difficult to close and in fact there were no prosecutions resulting from the twenty-one complaints in the 1979 election.

The other area of difficulty in enforcement has come with respect to the provisions of the Elections Expenses Act which prohibit campaign advertising on the day of the election and on the day immediately preceding polling day. However, the legislation does not prevent the media from dealing with public affairs, from reporting the activities of the party leaders and even from interviewing the candidates during the blackout period. Forty-five such cases were brought to the attention of the Commissioner of Canada Elections regarding the 1979 campaign but no prosecutions resulted. The CEO in his *Report* points out the difficulty in interpreting the meaning of the act in this respect and suggests the terms of the act and its intentions be clarified in the future. Ultimately it would seem, again, that the only real control possible here is the good faith and the cooperation of the media, the parties, and the individual candidates in ensuring that the spirit of the legislation is maintained. Overall, the legislation does constitute a potential major reform in the electoral system in Canada. Together with such legislation as the Electoral Boundaries Readjustment Act, and a political culture which demands comparatively high standards of electoral morality, Canada is better served than most countries by the standards of behaviour in the electoral process.

The Single Member Plurality System

In spite of all the positive attributes of the Canadian electoral system, it has been widely argued that its basic structural feature, the single member plurality system of electing MPs, is highly dysfunctional when viewed in the overall context of the political system.

One of the traditional defences of the present electoral system in Canada was that it provides the Canadian political system with electoral majorities and consequently with government stability. However, the occurrence of five minority governments in Canada between 1957 and 1979 set some scholars wondering about the validity of this assertion. In the first place, minority government in Canada has been relatively effective when assessed in terms of policy outputs, which may reduce the need for a system that is geared to provide parliamentary majorities. But secondly, many scholars, most notably Alan Cairns, have identified a number of anomalies and pointed out some potentially negative features of the electoral system.[16]

Aside from the elections of 1940 and 1958, when a majority of voters actually supported one party, the present system has consistently given the party gaining a plurality of votes more seats than its share of votes.[17] However, it has transformed a minority of votes into a stable majority of seats on only nine of seventeen occasions and it has occasionally reduced an opposition with a fair amount of public support to numerical ineffectiveness in the Commons. In thirteen of the last twenty-one elections, the electoral system has either not produced a majority government or has left the opposition ineffectually small. Moreover, the system encourages minor parties, such as the

---

[16] A. C. Cairns, "The Electoral and the Party System in Canada, 1921-65," *Canadian Journal of Political Science*, vol. 1, no. 1, March 1968. See also the critique of Cairns' ideas in J. A. A. Lovink, "On Analyzing the Impact of the Party System in Canada," *Canadian Journal of Political Science*, vol. 3, no. 4, pp. 497-516, and Cairns' reply, pp. 517-521. More generally see Douglas Rae, *The Political Consequences of Electoral Laws* (Yale Press, New Haven, 1977), Edward Tufte, "The Relationship Between Seats and Votes in Two-Party Systems," *American Political Science Review*, v. 67, 1973, pp. 540-54, and Duff Spafford, "The Electoral System of Canada," *American Political Science Review*, v. 64, 1970, pp. 168-176.

[17] The 1972 election constitutes a minor exception to this rule since it provided a better balance than usual between popular vote and seats won. We have updated some of the numbers in this section to take account of elections which took place after Cairns published his article. Those elections seem to have confirmed his theories.

Social Credit or the Créditistes, with sectional bases of support while damaging minor parties such as the NDP, with a geographically broader base of support. For example, in 1935 the Reconstruction Party got 9 percent of the vote and exactly one seat, while Social Credit with less than half as many votes got seventeen seats. In 1963, 13 percent of the vote garnered seventeen seats for the NDP, while 12 percent of the vote gained twenty-four seats for Social Credit and the Créditistes.

The results of the 1979 election again constituted a striking demonstration of the potential for imbalance in representation. The Liberals, with 40 percent of the vote did get 40 percent of the seats, but the PCs with only 35.9 percent of the vote got 48 percent of the seats and the NDP with 17.8 percent of the vote just 9 percent of the seats. Thus the NDP with half the number of supporters of the Conservatives got just one-fifth the number of seats and the government of the day was supported by just over one-third of the voters. Although the Liberals won in 1980, the regional imbalance between seats and votes was exaggerated still more, particularly in the West and in Quebec.

Cairns goes on to point out that, within a given party, representation in the House of Commons by region has seldom been proportional to the party's votes by region. For example, in 1945 the CCF gained 260,000 votes in Ontario (32 percent of its total) yet won no seats, while the 167,000 votes the party received in Saskatchewan (21 percent of its total) resulted in 64 percent of its federal seats.[18] From 1921 to 1965 the Liberals had 752 electoral victories in Quebec, to the Conservatives' 135. Cairns continues, "The ratio of 5.6 Liberals to each Conservative in the House of Commons contrasts sharply with the 1.9 to 1 ratio of Liberals and Conseratives at the level of voters."[19]

As these results indicate, the peculiar arithmetic of the single member constituency system works differently for large than for small parties. A large party will gain the maximum number of seats if its support is widely dispersed while a small party will obtain the maximum number of seats if its support is concentrated in a few areas.[20] The popular wisdom that the Liberals "waste" support in Quebec and the Conservatives "waste" support on the prairies has some basis in fact.

All of this, Cairns and many other analysts ranging from academics to the Pépin-Robarts Task Force on National Unity suggest, exagger-

---

[18] Cairns, "The Electoral and the Party System in Canada, 1921-65," p. 61.
[19] Ibid., p. 62.
[20] Richard Johnston and Janet Ballantyne "Geography and the Electoral System," *Canadian Journal of Political Science*, v. 10, December 1977, p. 855.

ates the already deep sectional cleavages in Canadian society by ensuring that any partisan discrepancy among regions will be magnified significantly by the electoral process. Such a system has made adequate representation from Quebec impossible in the Progressive Conservative party, and has ensured that whenever that party does get into power it will lack inputs from Quebec. Thus, although the Progressive Conservatives won 13.4 percent of the popular vote in Quebec in 1979, the new Prime Minister was faced with forming a cabinet with only two elected Ministers from the 75 constituencies in that province. The mirror image of that problem exists for the Liberals who had to create a 1980 cabinet with just two MPs elected from west of Ontario and none from west of Manitoba.

There are still more disadvantages to this electoral system. We have already mentioned that the present electoral system, or at least the two major parties, are often posited as being unifying or nationalizing agencies. Cairns suggests a rather different interpretation:

Sectionalism has been rendered highly visible because the electoral system makes it a fruitful basis on which to organize electoral support. Divisions cutting through sections, particularly those based on the class system, have been much less salient because the possibility of pay-offs in terms of representation has been minimal.[21]

There are several instances in Canadian history where parties have emphasized regional and, more particularly, ethnic differences in order to get elected. In Quebec in the 1920s and 1930s, Liberal campaigns were often directed toward stirring up the fears and animosities of French Canada in order to maximize electoral support in specific sections and thus maximize the number of seats held. The "Gordon Churchill strategy" in 1957 was another example of the effects of sectionalism. Over the years it had become clear to the Conservatives that money spent in Quebec was money lost, even though a substantial minority of Quebec voters might support them, for they would get very few seats. The decision was consequently made in 1957 to forget about Quebec and concentrate on the rest of the country. The result was a handsome pay-off in terms of seats. Perhaps, however, this analysis should not be pushed too far. Until 1957 and since 1965 the Conservatives consistently did spend a large proportion of their campaign funds in Quebec, and all regions of the country have shown a propensity to swing their votes one way or another together.[22] Indeed, given the different relationship between seats and votes, for major and for minor parties, the proper seat maximizing strategy for a major party is to attempt to disperse its votes

[21] Ibid., p. 64.
[22] Beck, *Pendulum of Power*, pp. 422-423.

while the proper strategy for a minor party is to concentrate them. The persistent efforts by the Conservatives since 1963 to gain more votes in Quebec and the persistent and equally frustrating effort by the Liberals to do the same in the West attest to the parties' recognition of this. Cairns concludes that on balance, the electoral system in Canada has a detrimental effect on national unity: "This is essentially because sectional politics has an inherent tendency to call into question the very nature of the political system and its legitimacy. Classes, unlike sections, cannot secede from the political system and are consequently more prone to accent its legitimacy."[23]

We need not agree entirely with this analysis, but it does force us to ask a very important two-part question. Are Canadian party politics primarily brokerage politics, impeded only slightly by the counterforces from the electoral system, as Dawson, Corry, and most of the political scientists of the forties, fifties and early sixties have suggested? Or, does Canadian unity suffer from the divisive effects of an electoral system that makes visible our regional cleavages? Such conflict is exacerbated by the federal structure and only slightly counterbalanced by the brokerage activities of some of its national political actors; and while we should not rush into the adoption of panaceas such as proportional representation electoral reform should remain on the agenda for constitutional change in the 1980s.

There are additional problems of the party electoral system, less directly connected with the single member plurality system. There are frequent delays and inaction in the priority stage of the policy process because of partisan manoeuvring for electoral advantage by cabinets and opposition parties. There may be an inefficient national distribution of program funds because of attempts to hold power in certain constituencies. There may be deliberate distortions and confusion in political communication, and the uncertainty of a political career is a major deterrent to many excellent people who might seek office under conditions of greater certainty. Whether those can be overcome is more doubtful, but no other political system can legitimately claim a much better record than Canada in this respect.

THE DYNAMICS OF CANADIAN ELECTORAL BEHAVIOUR

The target of all this electoral activity is the Canadian voter. What effect does it all have on him or her? Is all of the campaign activity worthwhile or do Canadian voters merely troop to the polls to cast

---

[23] Cairns, op. cit., p. 75. Cairns has failed here to note that classes may question the legitimacy of the regime without questioning the political community.

their ballots on the basis of factors such as ethnic origin, religion, or their parents' party loyalties, factors which cannot be changed by the parties no matter what they do in the campaign?

The answer, according to the most thorough study of why Canadians vote the way they do, is that there is indeed a significant effect, although that effect may be manifested in behavioural shifts that occur too slowly to be reflected in a single election campaign. As Table 12-1, taken from *Political Choice in Canada* by Harold Clarke, Jane Jenson, Lawrence Leduc, and Jon Pammett indicates, only 38 percent of Canadian voters in 1974 could be categorized as "durable" partisans; voters who show consistent, stable, and strong patterns of support for a particular party.[24] The other 62 percent of Canadian voters are "flexible" partisans. These are people who are "either unstable in their partisanship over time, inconsistent between the federal and provincial levels of the Canadian political system, or weak in their intensity of partisanship", who do not hold an identity at the federal level or who define themselves as independents. The authors of *Political Choice in Canada* added the level of political interest to their table because the addition of the variable does much to differentiate among voters influenced by various factors: people with high levels of interest cast their ballots affected by different factors than those with low levels of interest.

Given the results shown in Table 12-1, it would appear that the aggregate electoral results, displayed in Table 12-2, present an image of considerably more stability than in fact exists in Canada. In aggregate terms the electorate is fairly stable but the volatility of the individual voter does occasionally make possible the kind of large electoral swing which allowed the Progressive Conservatives to go from a small opposition party in 1956 to a sweeping majority in 1958 and the Liberals to climb over 7 percent in popular support between the May

[24] The discussion in this section is based largely on Clarke et al., *Political Choice in Canada* (McGraw-Hill Ryerson, Toronto, 1979). The typology of partisanship is found on pp. 303 ff. and Table 12-1 is from p. 308. In summarizing a great deal of material in the little space available in a textbook a good deal of richness is inevitably lost, particularly when the original source already summarizes a great deal of material. The interested reader is therefore urged to consult the original. There is considerable literature on this controversy. See, for example, Adam Przeworski, "Institutionalization of Voting Patterns, or, Mobilization the Source of Decay," *American Political Science Review*, 1975, pp. 49-67; P. M. Sniderman, H. D. Forbes and Ian Melzer, "Party Loyalty and Electoral Volatility: a study of the Canadian Party System," *Canadian Journal of Political Science*, 1974, pp. 266-288; Donald E. Blake, "1896 and all that: Critical Elections in Canada," *CJPS*, June 1979, pp. 259-279; Jane Jenson, "Party Loyalty in Canada: The Question of Party Identification," *CJPS*, 1975, pp. 543-553; David Elkins, "Party Identification, A Conceptual Analysis," *CJPS*, 1978, pp. 419-446; and Jane Jenson's, "Comment: The Filling of Wine Bottles is Not Easy," in the same issue. The last three of these articles deal with the volatility of the electorate, the first three with volatility of electoral results.

Table 12-1

A TYPOLOGY OF THE 1974 CANADIAN ELECTORATE, BASED ON PARTISANSHIP, POLITICAL INTEREST, AND VOTE HISTORY[a]

Political Interest	The "Permanent" Electorate[b] (100%)[d] Partisanship		The "Transient" Electorate[c] (25%) Partisanship		The New Voters (81%) Partisanship	
	Durable	Flexible	Durable	Flexible	Durable	Flexible
High	10.3%	15.3%	1.1%	1.9%	0.4%	1.2%
Moderate	8.1	13.2	1.7	2.6	0.7	0.3
Low	10.8	19.3	3.6	6.1	1.4	2.0
	29.2%	47.8%	6.4%	10.6%	2.5%	3.5%

[a]Total N for all types = 2238.
[b]Persons who "always" or "usually" vote in federal elections and who voted both in 1972 and 1974.
[c]Persons who "do not always" vote in federal elections, or who did not vote in one of the 1972 or 1974 elections.
[d]Percent of group voting in 1974.

Source: Harold Clarke, Jane Jensen, Lawrence Leduc and Jan Pammett, *Political Choice in Canada* (McGraw-Hill Ryerson, Toronto, 1979) p. 308.

Table 12-2

DISTRIBUTION OF THE VOTE IN ELEVEN FEDERAL ELECTIONS, 1945-1974 (PERCENTAGES)

	1945	1949	1953	1957	1958	1962	1963	1965	1968	1972	1974	1979	1980
Liberal	41%	49%	49%	41%	34%	37%	41%	40%	46%	39%	43%	40.0%	44.0%
PC	27	30	31	39	43	37	33	32	31	35	35	36	33
NDP/CCF	16	13	11	11	9	14	14	18	17	18	15	18	20
Social Credit	4	4	5	7	2	12	12	8	4	8	5	5	1.6
Other	12	4	4	2	1	x	x	2	2	1	1	1.5	1.7
% Turnout	76	74	67	74	79	79	79	75	76	77	71	76	76

x Less than 1%

Source: Clarke et al., op. cit., p. 358, and Chief Electoral Office Canada.

1979 and February 1980 elections. It also makes possible the kind of situation described earlier in which an apparently perpetual provincial dynasty can fall from pre-eminence to almost instant oblivion. Thus although there is considerable controversy about the stability of the Canadian electorate, relative to that of other countries, the resolution of the controversy probably lies in the direction pointed to by Clarke et al.: the electorate as an aggregate is relatively stable, the individual voter is likely to be flexible or volatile and hence the possibility always exists of major electoral reversals in Canada. Let us look further at the factors which influence this volatility.

Earlier in discussions of the individual parties we indicated something of the socioeconomic and demographic composition of party voting. However, while the aggregate impact of these variables does add up to some seemingly consistent patterns of inter-party differences, the ability of these variables to predict the voting behaviour of individual Canadians is relatively limited. What appear at first to be consistent patterns, and what struck pioneering political scientists in the field of election studies as constituting rather good explanations of the voting behaviour of individual Canadians, turn out on closer examination to constitute convenient descriptions of overall bases of party support at a given moment; but they do not tell us much about how individual Canadians make their voting decisions or about the circumstances under which they change their minds. The large numbers of people involved in socioeconomic categories give an appearance of consistent bases of support which evaporate as we look more closely at how Canadians decide their vote.

For that portion of the electorate which shows stable, long-term partisan attachments, region, religion, father's party identification, and socioeconomic class accounted in 1974 for about 37 percent of the variation in support for the older parties and 17 percent for the NDP. But these voters constitute only 38 percent of the electorate. For the flexible voters the amount of variance explained by these standard variables drops to 5 percent for the Liberals and 11 percent for the Conservatives. Given that 31 percent of the electorate changed their vote or entered (or re-entered) the electorate in the short 2-year period between the 1972 and 1974 elections it is obvious that we will have to look further than simple socioeconomic and demographic variables to get a proper picture of how Canadians make up their minds how to vote. The authors of *Political Choice in Canada* found the most appropriate explanation in the interaction between the typology of voters proposed in Table 12-1 and the short-term orientation of voters to parties, issues, leaders, and local candidates.

For the durable low interest partisans, the long-term component accounts for 77 percent of the variance in Liberal voting and the several short-term variables for an addi-

tional 7 percent. In the analysis of Liberal voting among flexible high interest partisans, however, past vote explains only 22 percent of the variance and short-term forces (issues, leaders and local candidates) account for fully 41 percent. [25]

In 1974, then, short-term factors (leadership, issues, local candidates, and short-run feelings about political parties) were crucial determinants for 62 percent of the voters. The impact of those factors deserves more consideration here.

It is a truism of Canadian political analysis that Canadians are highly leadership-oriented when they come to make their voting decision. Survey results indicate that orientations toward the leader do make a considerable difference but that short-term favourable or unfavourable attitudes toward parties are of greater significance. For example, Table 12-3 indicates that the percentage voting Liberal varied much more markedly in 1974 according to whether evaluation of the party was positive, neutral, or negative than according to whether the attitude toward the leader was positive, neutral, or negative. [26] Similar results are seen for all parties and for both the 1968 and 1974 elections. It is important that the pattern, if not the intensity, is consistent between the 1968 election when "Trudeaumania" was afoot, and in 1974 when leadership was not a crucial issue since that suggests that even in highly leadership-oriented contests, independent perceptions of parties do exist and are important determinants of voting choice. Contrary to popular wisdom, then, in Canada the party and the leader are not synonymous even in the short run.

Leadership has its greatest impact among that 25 percent of the electorate characterized as "flexible, low-interest partisans," but it is important to note that for no party and at no level of interest does leadership orientation ever exceed long-term party identification in explanatory power. However, this hardly means that the parties are wrong to place as much emphasis as they do on leadership. Aside from attention to the party structure which recruits workers and leaders and which mobilizes the vote—and maybe not even aside from that—leadership is the variable over which parties can exercise an influence that has the greatest net impact on voting. We will see below that the net impact of issues and of local candidates most often washes out because of the large variety of issues and of local candidates. There is, of course, no such variety with respect to leadership. Thus, if the tide is moving in the right direction on the leadership issue, large net gains are possible, something which the federal Liber-

---

[25] *Political Choice in Canada*, p. 344.
[26] Ibid., p. 328.

als realized to their delight in 1968 and to their chagrin in 1979, and which the Conservatives regretted mightily in 1980.

If the impact of leadership is concentrated on flexible, low-interest voters, the impact of issues is concentrated mainly among flexible, highly interested voters. For this group, constituting more than 15 percent of Canadian voters, the importance of issues for voting choice

Table 12-3

VOTE BY RELATIVE AFFECT FOR LEADERS AND PARTIES, 1974 AND 1968 (PERCENT VOTING FOR PARTY)

Panel A: Liberal Voting				
	1974		Attitude Toward Liberal Leader	
		Positive	Neutral	Negative
Attitude Toward	Positive	94	77	63
Liberal	Neutral	68	52	33
Party	Negative	25	17	5
	1968		Attitude Toward Liberal Leader	
		Positive	Neutral	Negative
Attitude Toward	Positive	94	79	52
Liberal	Neutral	79	46	29
Party	Negative	45	16	5

Panel B: PC Voting				
	1974		Attitude Toward PC Leader	
		Positive	Neutral	Negative
Attitude Toward	Positive	94	95	81
PC	Neutral	86	58	46
Party	Negative	44	23	6
	1968		Attitude Toward PC Leader	
		Positive	Neutral	Negative
Attitude Toward	Positive	93	89	75
PC	Neutral	75	46	28
Party	Negative	33	23	6

Panel C: NDP Voting				
	1974		Attitude Toward NDP Leader	
		Positive	Neutral	Negative
Attitude Toward	Positive	86	80	54
NDP	Neutral	26	25	22
Party	Negative	19	4	1
	1968		Attitude Toward NDP Leader	
		Positive	Neutral	Negative
Attitude Toward	Positive	88	60	39
NDP	Neutral	51	31	18
Party	Negative	8	4	1

Source: Clarke et al., op. cit., p. 328.

exceeds that of the local candidate and tends to approximate that of leadership. As was the case with leadership, the impact of either issues or the local candidate is considerably lower among the durable partisans no matter what their level of interest in politics.

The problem with respect both to issues and local candidates is that for them to have a significant net effect on electoral results, there must be a significant skewness—that is one party must be perceived much more favourably than another with respect to some key issue or the overall national impact of the perception of local candidates must be to favour one party. Given the almost random effect of local candidate selection procedures the latter is extremely unlikely and as would be expected the overall effect of local candidates in 1974 was such as to favour one major party (the PCs) over the other by only 1.7 percent.

Similarly, because there are so many possible issues, their overall effect tends to wash out in aggregate electoral results. At times of course, this is not true; one issue tends to dominate and then if one or another party can establish a positive image with respect to that issue, it may gain considerable mileage. For a short period after the election of the Parti Québécois, national unity was just such an issue for the federal Liberals. However, for the most part in recent years, inflation has been the major issue and no party has been able to establish a very positive image in dealing with it. In 1974 for example, 33 percent of the national sample identified inflation as an important issue whereas no other single issue was mentioned by more than 10 percent of the electorate. Presumably similar results would pertain for the 1979 and 1980 elections. However, among those identifying inflation as most important in 1974, 15.1 percent switched to the Liberals because of it and 12.5 percent claimed to have switched to the Conservatives. These results—a bit surprising in view of the fact that the Liberals were already in power and might therefore have been held culpable for inflation—indicate that no party gained much net benefit from the inflation issue. With rare exceptions such as the national unity issue in 1979, this type of situation may always pertain since once one party identifies an issue as important, the others are forced to as well and all of them may then simply provide convenient rationalizations for voters who would have supported them on other grounds.[27] Nonetheless, because 15 percent of Canadian voters appear to pay a lot of attention to issues, because that 15 percent is highly flexible in its voting behaviour, and because leaders and parties must use issues as the medium through which they present

[27] Ibid., pp. 337-338.

themselves, they do remain an important component of political choice in Canada.

CONCLUSION

Throughout most of the last sixty years, the Liberal party has been the "government party" in Ottawa. Provincial party systems often produce an almost equally predominant government party. The regional basis of party representation in parliament appears to be highly resistant to change except for a few "swing" regions. Yet the picture which is emerging from recent research into Canadian voting behaviour is of an electorate in which the individual voters are highly flexible in their behaviour even if the system appears not to be. The relative stability of the Canadian electorate and the Canadian party scene is perhaps then more apparent than real. Indeed the authors of *Political Choice in Canada* conclude: "All of the evidence previously examined—the flexibility of partisanship, the relative weakness of long term forces, the short term nature of party images and the importance of leaders and issues—suggest the high potential for change in the electorate from one election to another."[28] In contradiction to some of the prevailing wisdom about the voting behaviour of Canadians they further conclude:

The importance of short term factors . . . is enhanced by the inability of social or demographic divisions in the population to manifest themselves at election time. Divisions between the sexes, age groups, rural and urban areas or social classes have only very limited electoral significance in federal politics. Even religion and ethnicity . . . are not strongly related to voting behaviour. In a sense then, many Canadians approach electoral choice relatively free of those societal forces which might tend to "predetermine" their votes. . . . While there are certainly regional variations in aggregate electoral outcomes, there is no evidence that region or province of residence per se has a major impact on the way individual voters make up their minds.[29]

What has tended to be constant in Canada over the last half-century is the structure and behaviour of the organizations whose main function it is to deal with that electorate and to reflect its views in order to gain electoral success. But even given the "government party" nature of the federal Liberals and of several provincial parties and the opposition mentality of the federal Conservatives and NDP, the net result of the combination of party structure and electoral behaviour is that either at the federal or the provincial level there is always some prospect for electoral change. Perhaps the federal elections of 1979 and 1980 are the best possible indication of this long-range stability and short-range capacity for change.

[28] Ibid., p. 383.
[29] Ibid., p. 392.

13

Interest Groups in Canada

Interest groups are active everywhere in Canadian politics. The industry-financed Canadian Tax Foundation criticizes and examines the whole financial structure of government in Canada. The Canadian Bar Association often works closely with the federal Department of Justice and various provincial attorneys general. Ethnic associations are vital to the operation of the Canada Employment and Immigration Commission and to the delivery of all government services among immigrant groups. The commercial banks work hand in hand with the Bank of Canada. At times, the Canadian Federation of Agriculture appears to be almost an extension of various Departments of Agriculture. Federal and provincial Departments of Labour work very closely with labour unions. Provincial medical associations and provincial governments bargain over the fees to be paid doctors by government medical plans. The list could be multiplied endlessly. Wherever government turns its hand, there it will find some kind of organized group operating—and wherever groups operate they find that government activities overlap their own.

SOME THEORETICAL CONSIDERATIONS

Gabriel Almond has suggested something of the importance of interest groups in modern society:

Interest groups articulate political demands in the society, seek support for these demands among other groups by advocacy and bargaining and attempt to transform these demands into authoritative public policy by influencing the choice of political personnel and the various processes of public policy making and enforcement. [1]

Another perspective on the role of interest groups is provided by Harry Eckstein, who suggests:

In democratic systems parties must perform simultaneously two functions which are on the evidence, irreconcilable: to furnish effective decision makers and to represent, accurately, opinions. The best way to reconcile these functions in practice is to supplement the parties with an alternative set of representative organizations which can affect decisions without affecting the position of the decision makers. This is the pre-

---

[1] Gabriel Almond, "Interest Groups and the Political Process," in R. C. Macridis and B. E. Brown, *Comparative Politics* (Dorsey Press, Homewood, Ill., 1964), pp. 132-3.

eminent function of pressure groups in effective democratic systems, as the competi-
tion for power is the pre-eminent function of parties. [2]

Eckstein, then, differentiates the major function of political parties—furnishing decision makers—from the major political function of interest groups—influencing political decisions.

Interest groups also perform other functions in Canadian society. The vast majority of Canadian groups make their demands through legitimate channels and by legitimate means. They thus tend to buttress the political system in its present form and to provide, at least implicitly, support for that system. Moreover since they constitute a principal channel through which various major interests in the country can participate in the making of public policy, they help to legitimize not only specific policy outputs but also the system which produces those policies. Governments will often actively solicit the participation of major interests for just that reason. [3]

A related way in which the interest-group structure of Canadian society provides support for the political system is by providing an integrative force in society which can "connect" the individual to the political system. As the sociologist Emile Durkheim put it:

Collective activity is always too complex to be able to be expressed through the single and unique organ of the state. Moreover, the state is too remote from individuals, its relations with them too external and intermittent to penetrate deeply within individual consciences and socialize them within. When the state is the only environment in which men can live communal lives, they inevitably lose contact, become detached and society disintegrates. A nation can be maintained only if, between the state and the individual, there is intercalated a whole series of secondary groups near enough to the individuals to attract them strongly to their sphere of action and drag them, in this way, into the general torrent of social life. [4]

---

[2] Harry Eckstein, *Pressure Group Politics* (George Allen and Unwin, London, 1960; published in the United States by Stanford University Press), p. 163. There is no agreement in the literature on whether the term *pressure group* is more appropriate than *interest group*. We have chosen the term interest group since we wish to emphasize the multiple functions of these groups, of which the application of political pressure is only one. In general, however, the two terms can be read interchangeably. Both of the preceeding quotations are also cited in Englemann and Schwartz, *Political Parties and the Canadian Social Structure*, pp. 92-114. Their chapter on interest groups provides a good coverage of the subject.

[3] Paul Pross, "Pressure Groups: Adapative Instruments of Political Communication" in Paul Pross (ed.), *Pressure Group Behaviour in Canadian Politics* (McGraw-Hill Ryerson, Toronto, 1975), p. 6.

[4] Emile Durkheim, *The Division of Labour* (The Free Press, Glencoe, 1947), cited in R. Presthus, *Elite Accommodation in Canadian Politics* (Macmillan, Toronto, 1973). While we have alluded to Presthus at some length in this chapter, his work has not found universal acceptance among Canadian scholars. See, for example, R. E. B. Simeon's review (in *Canadian Journal of Political Science*, Sept. 1974, pp. 567-71) and that by John Meisel (in *Canadian Forum*, May-June 1974, p. 44). Critics such as Simeon have more to criticize in Presthus' research and presentation than in the conclusions which we have quoted in this text.

On the output side, interest groups aid the system in the implementation of policy for groups often act as the agents of the state in the application of rules to individuals and in the dissemination of information about new policies.

We will consider both these input and output functions in more detail shortly, but clearly, interest groups are ubiquitous in the politics of Western democracies. This ubiquity has led some political scientists—most notably, Arthur Bentley—to adopt a *group approach* to the entire study of politics. In his book *The Process of Government*, Bentley wrote: "When the groups are stated, everything is stated. When I say everything I mean everything. . . . The whole of social life in all its phases can be stated in . . . groups of active man."[5] Bentley was writing in 1908, when hyperbole was more popular in academic writing than it is today, but there are some modern disciples of the Bentley approach, among them David Truman, author of *The Governmental Process*. Eckstein has summarized the modern group approach (typified by Truman) as asserting that:

Politics is the process by which social values are authoritatively allocated; this is done by decisions; the decisions are produced by activities; each activity is not separate from every other, but masses of activity have common tendencies in regard to decisions; these masses of activities are groups; so the struggle between groups (or interests) determines what decisions are taken.[6]

This, as Eckstein states, is a truism and has very limited analytical value. What is more, the critics of this approach continue, as a tool of analysis it puts an impossible load on the researcher because it insists that he delineate the entire galaxy of interests which could affect any decision he wants to investigate in even the most indirect and remote fashion. Moreover, it denies the individuality of decision makers, thus discouraging investigators from even considering the impact of powerful individuals in the process.[7] It leads political science into a sort of fatalism which eulogizes the effects of organized interests because they are there, and leads political scientists (and the decision

---

[5] Quoted in Harry Eckstein, "Group Theory and the Comparative Study of Pressure Groups," in H. Eckstein and D. Apter (eds.), *Comparative Politics* (The Free Press, Glencoe, 1963), p. 390.

[6] Eckstein, "Group Theory and the Comparative Study of Pressure Groups," p. 391.

[7] Roy Macridis, "Groups and Group Theory," in Macridis and Brown, *Comparative Politics*, p. 140. Another cogent criticism of group theory is found in Stanley Rothman, "Systematic Political Theory: Observations on the Group Approach," *American Political Science Review*, XLIV, No. 1, March 1960, pp. 15-33.

makers whose activities the groups legitimate) to ignore all those who are not organized into interest groups.[8]

There are other functions that interest groups perform for the political system which are ascribed to them by the pluralist theories of political life. Pluralism has been one of the most prominent analytical postures in American political science since the fifties and Canadian scholars such as J. A. Corry[9] have attempted to apply the pluralist paradigm to Canada as well. Pluralist theory begins with the recognition that: "There are many sources of power other than the state. In our differentiated society there will be many basic interests represented by organizations able and willing to use power."[10] There are three basic implications of this diffusion of power within society for the nature of the political process, each of which must be considered briefly.

First, unlike the early capitalist thinkers who viewed the state as the source of *all* power and control, the pluralists see the state as only *one of many* power centres in the society. Therefore the pluralists do not see state intervention in the economy as being as great a threat to the capitalist system as do the more conservative capitalist thinkers. The pluralists thus can remain loyal to capitalism and at the same time accept the growth of government with equanimity. In this way the expansion of the role of government in the economy can be reconciled with the commitment to a free-enterprise economy, because the government is simply another actor among many in the market system.

Secondly, the notion of many competing groups in society, each of which has some real political power, also challenges the Marxist assumption that society is comprised of but two significant groups, those who own the means of production and those who work for the owners. While the pluralists do not go so far as to reject the notion of class conflict, they see such conflict rather as but one of the many intergroup conflicts that characterize the pluralist process of *bargaining* for political and economic advantage in the society. Thus, interest groups function to divide our attention, diverting us from what Marxists see as the *only* important political cleavage—class—and prevent-

---

[8] The central theme of T. Lowi, *The End of Liberalism* (W. W. Norton and Co., second edition, 1979, New York) is that this eulogization of groups pervades both politics and political science in the United States and leads to an abdication of their proper responsibilities on the part of political leaders. We return to Lowi's ideas at the end of this chapter.

[9] J. A. Corry and J. E. Hodgetts, *Democratic Government and Politics* (University of Toronto Press, Toronto, 1959), pp. 299-307.

[10] T. J. Lowi, *The End of Liberalism*, p. 42.

ing or forestalling a revolutionary change in the social order. This function of interest groups can be good or bad depending upon how satisfied one is with the existing social order.

Finally, pluralist theory also serves as a rationalization of the presence of elitism in liberal democracies. The existence of elites and their dominance in all societies is generally accepted by most theories of political life. The dilemma of democratic societies is that it is difficult to reconcile democratic values such as popular sovereignty with a political process where the most important decisions in the society are made by a tiny elite. Pluralist theory attempts to make that reconciliation. The pluralist or "interest group liberalism" argument is that although citizens do not participate directly in the policy process, they belong to groups and participate indirectly by selecting the leaders or elites of those groups. The elites in turn engage in a process of bargaining, accommodation, and compromise on behalf of and, allegedly, in the interest of the members of the group they are leading. Pluralism therefore, "is the belief that democratic values can be preserved in a system of multiple competing elites who determine public policy through a process of bargaining and compromise in which voters exercise meaningful choices in elections and (in which) new elites can gain access to power."[11]

There are however some serious flaws in the pluralists' claims which stem from the fact that political reality does not conform very faithfully to the theory. Robert Presthus, for instance, points out that the groups which form the base of pluralist democracy usually become oligarchic and internally undemocratic.[12] Moreover, he goes on to state in one of his later works which deals specifically with Canada, that the process of bargaining among the groups becomes one of *elite accommodation* where the leaders of the groups serve their mutual interests more than they serve the interests of the group they are supposed to represent.[13] To back up this contention of elite accommodation Canadian authors such as Porter,[14] Clement,[15] and Olson[16] demonstrate that the elites have so much more in common with each other than they have with their mass constituency, that it is inevitable that the intergroup bargaining process will end up primarily serving the narrow interests of the elites.

---

[11] Dye and Zeigler, *The Irony of Democracy* (Duxbury Press, Belmont, 1975), p. 10.
[12] Presthus, *Men at the Top* (Oxford Press, New York, 1964), ch. 1.
[13] Presthus, *Elite Accommodation in Canadian Politics*, ch. 1.
[14] J. Porter, *The Vertical Mosaic, passim.*
[15] W. Clement, *The Canadian Corporate Elite, passim.*
[16] D. Olson, *The State Elite* (McClelland and Stewart, Toronto, 1980).

Thus while it is likely accurate to state that interest groups do function to diffuse power more widely throughout the society and to take at least a portion of the raw decision-making power of our society away from the formal organs of the state, some of the more grandiose claims of the American pluralists have to be taken more critically, especially in the Canadian context. We must look closely at whether the diffusion of power to groups that is identified by proponents of interest group liberalism serves to accommodate democratic values with the fact of elitism, or whether it merely marginally increases the size of the ruling class in Canada. Finally we must also assess the extent to which the dominant socioeconomic and ethnic elites in Canadian society have managed to capture and control the key decision-making roles of the Canadian political system. This question will be assessed in detail in the following chapter on the authorities of the system.

We have merely touched here on a very deep and important argument in the study of politics. In true Canadian fashion however, we can reconcile it, however uncomfortably, by coming down firmly astride the fence. Very few Canadian political scientists fit neatly under the heading of group theorists or pluralists and, if the relative paucity of information on interest groups in Canada is any indication, Canadian political scientists seem to lean too far the other way.[17] Without going as far as Bentley or Truman or the American pluralists, we can certainly acknowledge the key role that organized interests play in the Canadian—or any—political system and simply turn our minds to an attempt to further elucidate that role.

A TYPOLOGY OF GROUPS

To make sense out of the activities of the great number of interest groups in Canada, it may be useful to classify them in some way. One can then anticipate that groups which fall in the same classification or category will tend to behave in similar ways. There are a number of bases on which such a typology could be constructed: the structure of groups, their origin, their activity, or their goals.

One typology divides interest groups into economic and non-economic groups. The economic groups are, in turn, subdivided into

---

[17] An exception is Robert Presthus whose two major works on interest groups in Canada, *Elite Accommodation in Canadian Politics* and *Elites in the Policy Process* (Macmillan, Toronto, 1974) expound a view much closer to that of Truman and Bentley than many Canadian political scientists are comfortable with.

agriculture, labour, and business groups; and the non-economic into nine sub-types.[18] Such a scheme however, tells us relatively little about the activities of a group or about its orientation toward government.

Another, more useful, taxonomy involves classifying groups according to a number of paired opposite categories. The paired opposites suggested by Robert Presthus are:

Compulsory	vs.	Voluntary
Temporary	vs.	Permanent
Economic	vs.	Instrumental
Mass	vs.	Selective
Producer	vs.	Consumer
Local-Provincial	vs.	Federal
Federated	vs.	Unitary
Oligarchical	vs.	Participative
Private	vs.	Public[19]

While these categories are useful, and while we hesitate to add yet another classificatory scheme to a field which already has too many, we prefer to categorize interest groups in Canada along four more-or-less independent continua, one referring to orientation, one to structure, a third to origin, and a final one to degree of mobilization. Any particular interest group can be located toward one side or the other of each of these continua.

The first continuum refers to *orientation*. It can be suggested that the activities of interest groups can tend toward either the *self-interested* or the *promotional*.[20] Self-interested groups tend to be economic in their orientation, whereas promotional groups are usually interested in doing things for some reason related to the good of the community. For example, the Canadian Manufacturers' Association is usually concerned with securing an economic, political, and social environment which will be advantageous to its own members. It is thus a self-interested group, as is the Canadian Federation of Agriculture which, when it approaches government, is concerned basically with securing outputs advantageous to the interests of Canadian farmers. On the other hand, members of the John Howard Society, which is interested in penal reform and prisoner rehabilitation, do not them-

[18] Engelmann and Schwartz, *Political Parties and the Canadian Social Structure*, pp. 95-96.
[19] *Elite Accommodation in Canadian Politics*, p. 67.
[20] S. E. Finer, *Anonymous Empire* (Pall Mall, London, 1958), p. 3.

selves expect ever to become prisoners. Thus, the John Howard Society is a promotional interest group.

A second continuum, perhaps the most useful one for predicting the methods of operation of a group, is that between *issue-oriented* and *institutionalized* groups.[21] In essence this continuum refers to structure. An institutionalized group is relatively well structured and of long standing. It will possess continuity and cohesion and a stable membership willing to support the organization's leaders. It will have extensive knowledge of those sectors of government which affect its activities and good access to important decision makers. While such groups have concrete operational objectives, generally the maintenance of the organization itself and of its privileged access to decision makers is more important than any single issue. Such groups are therefore reluctant to use really heavy-handed tactics.

Issue-oriented groups, as the name implies, are ephemeral and concerned only with one or two issues. Their structural characteristics are almost completely opposite to those of institutionalized groups. Intermediate points on the continuum would see groups defined as "fledgling" or "mature" as they move from more purely issue-oriented to more purely institutionalized.

A third continuum is between groups which have been primarily responsible for their own creation and maintenance, and groups which have been either created or strongly encouraged by government itself. The former type we call *autonomous* pressure groups, while the latter are *reverse* groups. Reverse pressure groups may be created because political decision makers are anxious to have all the inputs they can get before they set out to make policy, because they wish to create generalized support for their approach or specific support for some important policies, or because they wish to counter some other organized interest running against the decision maker's own policy predilections. In addition to this function of creating or mobilizing a clientele, they may also be used for communication with an otherwise poorly organized portion of the public or even to administer some aspects of an agency's programs. If there is no existing organized interest to which they can turn, policy makers will often try to create a completely new interest group which they can then use in this process. Alternatively, they may attempt to reinforce existing groups. At one time or another at least half of all federal government departments have created such groups.[22]

---

[21] Paul Pross, op. cit., pp. 8-18 provides an elaboration of this typology.
[22] R. Presthus, *Elite Accommodation in Canadian Politics*, p. 79.

As would be expected, it is not always simple to decide where a particular interest group fits. For example, although the John Howard Society was not created by the government, the Departments of Justice and the Solicitor General provide support for the organization—speakers for meetings, information and other services, and personnel, since many members of the society are employees of those departments. The Consumers' Association of Canada has been given government grants to continue expressing the viewpoint of the consumer and might have difficulty surviving without its ties to government, although it would not likely admit to such dependence. The Canadian Council on Social Development receives a substantial portion of its funds from National Health and Welfare, and the National Welfare Council which, as an advisory committee to the federal Minister of Health and Welfare probably comes as close as possible to the pure reverse interest group type, occupies space in the federal department's headquarters building and is funded entirely by the department.[23]

Finally, groups may be placed on a continuum defined by their degree of mobilization, according to whether they are *active* or *categoric* groups. This continuum assumes that there are latent interest groups in society which may become active only if a pressing issue presents itself. For example, practising Christians can hardly be viewed as a single cohesive interest group, yet if the political system were to threaten to outlaw religious practices, this categoric group would soon become active. A categoric group, then, is one to which people belong by virtue of some classification into which they fall and one which could conceivably coalesce if the right issue presented itself. An active group, on the other hand, is just that: one which has ongoing activities.[24]

NON-POLITICAL FUNCTIONS OF INTEREST GROUPS

Throughout this chapter we will be focussing on the governmental role of interest groups. This, however, is not necessarily their primary

---

[23] Helen Jones Dawson, "The Consumers' Association of Canada," *Canadian Public Administration*, Vol. 4, No. 1, March 1963, p. 96, W. T. Stanbury, *Business Interest and the Reform of Canadian competition Policy* (Methuen, Toronto, 1977), and J. Goldstein, "Public Interest Groups and Public Policy: The Case of the Consumers' Institute of Canada," *Canadian Journal of Political Science*, 12 March, 1979, pp. 137-156.

[24] See D. Truman, *The Governmental Process* (Alfred A. Knopf, New York, 1965), pp. 23-26. A distinction similar to our own is made here between *categoric* and *institutionalized groups*.

activity. In fact, many interest groups' "political activity—activity carried on within the political system—is a minor and unwelcome addition to more general concerns."[25] These more general concerns comprise a number of other functions necessary to their own members and to society.[26] Thus, for example, the primary activity of the Canadian Construction Association—one of the most active interests in Ottawa—is the dissemination of information and the maintenance of communication among the various members of the Association; and the most important activities of the Alcoholism and Drug Addiction Research Foundation—in some ways a reverse interest group—relate less to the activities of government than to research and publicity about drug problems.

One of the major preoccupations of any organization is, of course, self-maintenance. Many institutionalized groups are bureaucracies, and the bureaucrats in them are quite naturally interested in maintaining a job to do and an organization within which to do it.[27] There is often a delicate exchange relationship between political and non-political activities within an interest group. The leadership of the group requires resources to carry out its activities. It may get those resources in return for success in political lobbying and in turn be able to build further political successes and further organizational strength on the resources so gained. In effect for the interest group insiders, political success and access becomes the equivalent of profit in the more purely private sector.

The organizational maintenance imperative also occasionally leads to the situation where the greatest enemy of an interest group is another interest group pursuing the same goal, for both are competing for the same clientele and for the recognition of the same governmental agencies.[28] For example, the Consumers' Association of Canada and the Canadian Home Economics Association do not always get along well and may compete with each other even though their goals are the same.[29] The Canadian Federation of Agriculture and the

---

[25] Paul Pross, op. cit., p. 3.

[26] Lowi, *The End of Liberalism*, pp. 36-38. On page 38, Lowi points out that "all such interest groups possess political power but only occasionally are they politicized. The rest of the time they administer."

[27] For a series of examples, see David Kwavnick, "Pressure Group Demands and the Struggle for Organizational Status: The Case of Organized Labour in Canada," *Canadian Journal of Political Science*, Vol. 3, No. 1, pp. 56-72, March 1970.

[28] D. Kwavnick, "Pressure Group Demands and the Struggle for Organizational Status," p. 58.

[29] H. Dawson, "The Consumers' Association of Canada," p. 113. Elsewhere, however, the author points out that one of the most successful tactics of the CAC is harnessing other interest groups to pressure government. See pp. 111-112.

National Farmers Union often find themselves implacably opposed, even though one would expect their goals to be similar. The classic cases of this type of behaviour are to be found in the annals of labour union relations. For example, David Kwavnick has hypothesized that one of the major incidents of labour unrest in Quebec in the 1970s— the Lapalme mail truck drivers' strike—was exacerbated because it became the focal point for strife between the Quebec-based Confederation of National Trade Unions and the nationally based Canadian Labour Congress. Kwavnick goes on to contend that "the CNTU leadership risked, and ultimately sacrificed, the most vital interests of the Lapalme drivers in a dispute which ultimately concerned only those leaders' ambitions for organizational aggrandizement."[30] Thus, for interest groups, no less than for other large organizations, the welfare of the organization may become the primary goal even to the detriment of the membership.

THE INPUT ACTIVITIES OF INTEREST GROUPS

The input activities of interest groups involve the initiation of policy, attempts to influence the process of priority determination, and efforts to shape the details of policy development to their own ends or to block policy changes which groups feel might be detrimental. With respect to these activities three basic questions can be asked. First where must the group apply pressure in order to have its demands recognized? Second, what methods are employed by the group? Third, what are the determinants of success of a group?

The Focus of Activity

The location at which pressure is applied and the channels of communication on which a group concentrates are related to the structure of the government and its decision-making processes, and to the structure of the pressure group itself.

The Structure of Government[31]   Interest groups in Canada face two

---

[30] Kwavnick, "Pressure Group Demands and Organizational Objectives: The CNTU, the Lapalme Affairs and National Bargaining Units," *Canadian Journal of Political Science* VI, No. 4, December, 1973, p. 583. See also Kwavnick, *Organized Labour and Pressure Group Politics: The Canadian Labour Congress: 1956-1968* (McGill-Queen's University Press, Montreal, 1972).

[31] The reader is referred, for general information, to the articles by Paul Pross, Gabriel Almond and Harry Eckstein cited above, to Eckstein's *Pressure Group Politics* to Pross' *Pressure Group Behaviour in Canadian Politics,* and to Robert Presthus' *Elites in the Policy Process.* Specifically Canadian examples are also drawn from articles by Helen Jones Dawson (in addition to those cited above, see "Relations Between Farm Orga-

essential facts about Canadian government: its federal structure and its parliamentary nature. The former means that the system's effective power is widely dispersed geographically. The latter means that within each of the regional power centres real decision-making authority is found in the executive part of government—the cabinet and the bureaucracy.

Divided jurisdiction in the Canadian federal system frequently makes it necessary for a group to exert influence at both federal and provincial levels of government. For example, when the insurance companies were trying to block government-sponsored medical care insurance, they were forced to operate at both governmental levels. At the federal level they attempted to block enabling legislation which permitted the federal government to enter into cost-sharing arrangements with the provinces; and at the provincial level they attempted to prevent the actual implementation of the plan. On the other hand, when insurance companies have tried to block compulsory, government-sponsored auto insurance, they have had to operate exclusively at the provincial level where the jurisdiction in such matters lies. Under the existing system of federalism, decisions are often taken at both levels of governments simultaneously. Thus, if a group wants to achieve some end in Canada it may find that it is necessary to ensure that both levels of government pass parallel pieces of legislation and that can involve it in dealing with eleven separate legislative or regulatory items.

The federal system of government thus poses the problems of additional costs, of the need to call forth additional legislation, and of "where shall we concentrate our efforts?" for Canadian interest groups. However, it also presents opportunities for groups to exercise influence on one level of government by using the other level to make its case. As part of a highly successful fight against tax reform proposals, mining companies found it an effective tactic first to convince provincial governments in provinces where their major opera-

nizations and the Civil Services in Canada and Great Britain," *Canadian Public Administration*, Vol. 10, No. 4, p. 460 Dec. 1967); from M. G. Taylor "The Role of the Medical Profession in the Formulation and Execution of Public Policy," *Canadian Public Administration*, Vol. 3, 1960, pp. 223-225 and *Health Insurance & Canadian Public Policy* (McGill-Queens, Montreal, 1978); from Ronald W. Lang, *The Politics of Drugs* (Lexington, Mass., Saxon House, Lexington Books, 1974); from Englemann and Schwartz, *Political Parties and the Canadian Social Structure*; from some valuable journalistic accounts in "Pressure Groups in Canada," *Parliamentarian*, Jan. 1970, prepared by the Research Branch of the Library of Parliament in Ottawa; from Hugh Winsor, "Lobbying: A Comprehensive Report on the Art and its Practitioners," *The Globe Magazine*, Feb. 27, 1971, pp. 2-7; and Clive Baxter, "Familiars in the Corridors of Power," *Financial Post*, July 12, 1975 p. 6.

tions were located of the alleged detrimental impact of the reforms on investment and employment in that province. Provincial Treasurers then made the mining companies' point in discussions with Ottawa over the reform proposals.[32] David Kwavnick has found that labour unions will act so as to reinforce the strength of one level of government vis-a-vis the other in order to carry their demands and according to their assessment of where they have the best access.[33]

Since modern government in Canada concentrates the bulk of power in the cabinet and the bureaucracy, parliament is not the primary focus for interest group activity. As one experienced lobbyist said, "When I see Members of Parliament being lobbied, it's a sure sign to me that the lobby lost its fight in the civil service and the cabinet."[34] He might have added that while the group lobbying MPs may occasionally win some temporary victory, its chances of success in the longer run are slight unless they can convince some cabinet ministers as well. Most interest groups and their agents in Ottawa acknowledge this fact, a point made clear when Robert Presthus asked interest group leaders about their primary focus of attention. As Table 13-1 indicates, Canadian group leaders are far more likely than their American counterparts to concentrate on cabinet and the bureaucracy.

Table 13-1

TARGET OF INTEREST GROUP ACTIVITY IN THE UNITED STATES AND CANADA (FIGURES ARE PERCENTAGES OF GROUPS USING EACH LOCATION AS A PRIMARY TARGET)

Location	United States	Canada
Bureaucracy	21	40
Legislators	41	10
Legislative Committees	19	7
Cabinet	4	19
Executive Assistants	3	5
Judiciary	3	3
Others	9	6

Yet is is surprising how much effort occasionally goes into a pressure campaign when legislation is before parliament. One of the most

---

[32] M. W. Bucovetsky, "The Mining Industry & the Great Tax Reform Debate," in Paul Pross, op. cit.

[33] David Kwavnick, "Interest Group Demands & the Federal Political System: Two Canadian Case Studies" in Paul Pross, op. cit.

[34] Quoted in Englemann and Schwartz, *Political Parties and the Canadian Social Structure*, p. 105.

spectacular examples of a group's failure to recognize the disadvantage of struggling once a bill has reached parliament was provided by the Pharmaceutical Manufacturers Association of Canada (PMAC) and its president Dr. William Wigle.[35] The PMAC began to exert pressure in December of 1967 when the government introduced Bill C-190 which would allow the importation of drugs with the consequent lowering of drug prices in Canada. The PMAC organized many witnesses to go before the parliamentary committee studying the bill, besieged reporters with propaganda, attempted to get suppliers of the pharmaceutical industry to write MPs, urged drug company presidents to contact the 100 top industrialists in Canada and request them to write cabinet ministers and the Prime Minister; in general, they applied pressure wherever they could. The PMAC won an apparent victory, for the bill died on the order papers before the Liberal leadership convention. But the victory was short-lived. In the following session, the bill was re-introduced and, notwithstanding the PMAC's earlier efforts, it passed in March 1969. No doubt the PMAC was successful in delaying the legislation somewhat, but if a government is really committed to a piece of legislation, it will be a rare pressure campaign that will stop its passage. In fact, Dr. Wigle and the PMAC had lost the fight long before the bill was approved in parliament; once the cabinet had approved the establishment of a bureaucratic interdepartmental committee to investigate drug prices, it had already signalled an intention to do something about high drug prices. Had the PMAC learned of this committee in time, then contacted and worked with the appropriate officials, and had it reached the cabinet ministers before the cabinet ever decided to present legislation, its chances of success might have been much greater.

There are, of course, exceptions to the rule that the parliamentary arena is a bad one for interest groups to play in. In a minority government situation, the cabinet has tended to pay a great deal more attention to parliament than during majority parliaments. From 1972 to 1974 any group which could enlist NDP members to its cause was in a very powerful position since the government of the day was completely dependent upon the NDP for its survival. Too, in a minority situation, parliamentary committees do not have a majority of government members so the possibility of achieving significant amendments in committee is increased. Since minority governments have been increasingly common in Canada, since 1962, this factor may be

[35] Described in "Pressure Groups in Canada," *Parliamentarian* Jan. 1970, pp. 15, 16. Dr. Wigle also headed the Canadian Medical Association's fight against medicare so he has been more conspicuous by his presence than his success.

increasing the significance of parliament in the lives of interest groups.

Sometimes simply delaying a piece of legislation is worthwhile to a group and some important pieces of legislation have been much delayed, blocked, or radically altered after introduction to parliament. Notable cases have been the Combines Investigation Act, several aspects of the tax reform proposals of 1973, and legislation respecting beef marketing boards. The exceptions may well be evidence of limited government commitment or of successful behind-the-scenes lobbying directed at the cabinet. Certainly in all the cases cited a very considerable effort was directed at the cabinet and the bureaucracy.

The cabinet is a particularly fruitful pressure point and the relationship between individual ministers and interest groups may be quite close. For instance, when they entered the cabinet during the Pearson years, both C.M. Drury and Mitchell Sharp were members of the Canadian Manufacturers' Association. James Gardiner, Minister of Agriculture for many years under Mackenzie King, developed a close personal relationship with the Canadian Federation of Agriculture dating, oddly enough, from the time in 1941 when the delegates to a London convention of that association held him a virtual prisoner for several hours until he agreed to some concessions. C.D. Howe, of all people, seems to have gotten along particularly well with the Consumers' Association of Canada.

Meetings between cabinet ministers and interest group leaders go on constantly and it would be a rare week indeed when a minister's schedule did not provide for several meetings with such representatives. Ministers often welcome such representations as a counterpoise to the advice of their officials and certainly if a group can succeed in convincing a strong minister of the rightness of its case, its chances of success are greatly enhanced.

Here, too, a group faces difficulties in keeping up with new structures and procedures since many of the key priority decisions and most of the key choices among policy alternatives are made within cabinet committees. A key problem for any interest group in Ottawa is to determine the membership of the committee in order to attempt to discuss matters with its members and their advisors. Under Liberal governments in particular, that has tended to pose a significant problem in that the names of committee members are kept confidential.

One technique of dealing with cabinet which is well publicized but which is not very effective in any specific sense is the "annual briefing." Each year several large national groups, such as the Canadian Labour Congress, the Canadian Chamber of Commerce, and the Canadian Manufacturers' Association, present an annual brief to the whole cabinet, with much attendant fanfare. Such briefs are generally filled with pious generalizations; they do let the cabinet know something about the "mood of the country" but they are not usually useful in any specific policy issues. They also provide us with an opportunity to see ministers at their most human: being forced to sit in the midst of a busy day and listen to platitudes or badly researched policy proposals often brings out the testier side of the ministerial character.

Clearly then, groups are not blind to the pivotal role of the cabinet in the policy process. But neither are they blind to the fact that while individual ministers come and go, the bureaucracy is forever. Thus, if they wish to maintain that ongoing influence which is vital to them, it is relationships with the public service which must be their primary concern. The close ties between the Canadian Federation of Agriculture and officials in the Department of Agriculture, between veterans' groups and the Department of Veterans Affairs, between consumers' groups and several departments, between the medical associations and the various departments of health, have already been noted. To these one could add the close relationships of industry and trade associations with various branches of Industry, Trade and Commerce and Supply and Services, of financial institutions with federal and provincial finance ministries, of mining associations with resource and mining ministries or of the oil industry with the governments of the producing provinces. The list can be multiplied endlessly.

In dealing with the bureaucracy, probably the major problem for an interest group operating in Ottawa or in one of the larger provincial capitals is to determine who to attempt to influence. Policy structures, the details of the policy process and the influence of individuals in the policy process all shift rapidly in modern governments. To an insider the shifts can be dizzying—to an outsider they are nearly unfathomable. For example, the changes in cabinet committee structure from the Pearson to the Trudeau and the Trudeau to the Clark governments and the creation of new agencies supporting those committees have changed the location of appropriate pressure points. Where, before, an industry association might be content that it had done its work well if it had good dealings with the branches of the federal department of Industry, Trade and Commerce and with a few regulatory agencies, now to maximize its influence it may have to deal with central agencies such as the Treasury Board or Privy Council Office and it would do well to try to cultivate good relations with the Ministry of State for Economic Development and all or most of the departments headed by some seventeen "economic development ministers." Recent structural and procedural changes are covered in detail in Chapter 15; here the point is that for interest groups, keeping track of where to exert influence is a constant problem.

For the sake of completeness, the role that political parties play in this process should be mentioned although in Canada it is generally not directly important. Much has been made of the interrelationship between parties and interest groups in other political systems. In Britain most labour unions are directly affiliated with the Labour party. In the United States it has sometimes been suggested that the Democratic party is little more than a coalition of interest groups. However, in both Britain and the United States, the groups which have been most successful—at least with respect to their political activities— tend to shy away from formal party affiliations. After all, the party might lose the election and even if it wins, as many British unions have found to their chagrin, it may be easier to affect policy from outside the party hierarchy than from within. Except for the direct affiliation of some union locals with the NDP, and the close ties between that party and the Canadian Labour Congress, Canadian interest groups have generally avoided formal connections with political parties. At election time, the parties themselves will attempt to incorporate the most important demands of the main groups in their platforms; but these platforms mean very little and the more active members of interest groups know it. At other times, the interest group which wishes to approach a political party faces exactly the same problems as anyone else—it is nearly impossible to find a Canadian political party between elections. Even if a group succeeds in that enterprise, the party structures are of practically no value in directly influencing an output of the political system.

Even in the matter of campaign finance, the role of interest groups is not particularly significant. True, some groups and many corporations form the financial backbone of the major parties but, as we indicated when discussing party finance, they do not typically attempt to use donations to buy specific influence. The publication of the names of donors would now make this difficult and even before the most recent series of election expense reforms, party leaders attempted to isolate themselves from knowledge of major donors.

Interest Group Structure   Most large Canadian interest groups are federations, and the provincial bodies which make up these federations are often, in turn, coalitions of local groups. Frequently the local and provincial organizations are more powerful than the national structure.[36]

The Canadian Hospital Association is typical. It has a national

---

[36] Helen Jones Dawson, "National Pressure Groups & the Federal Government," in Paul Pross, op. cit., p. 30.

headquarters staff of about 25 and rents modest quarters in an office building in Ottawa, whereas the Ontario Hospital Association has a far larger staff and owns a large office complex which it shares with Blue Cross in Toronto. In such organizations it is often difficult to arrive at any consistent national viewpoint for that requires the finding of common ground among provincial organizations with widely disparate interests. The national director or president is liable to find him or herself contradicted by some provincial group whenever a point is being made and this dilutes their strength in dealing with government. Moreover, very often there are no direct dues paying members of the national organization. National headquarters thus exists on funds provided more or less reluctantly by the provincial associations and since what they give to headquarters they lose for themselves, the central office is almost certain to find itself underfunded. Other groups such as the National Farmers Union, have no effective central structure at all.

All of these factors will have some influence on the way in which groups make contact with governments. While the Canadian Hospital Association does work with the federal government, its provincial affiliates are often relatively much more influential in their own provinces. The National Farmers Union has almost no influence on national policy, but in the Prairie provinces it is a most important group. Similarly, the Canadian Chamber of Commerce has a general role in Ottawa as spokesman for a segment of the business community but it is at the local level that the Chamber's power is greatest. When the Alberta government was amending the Alberta Labour Act, both the provincial Chamber and some local Chambers were frequently consulted. The Calgary Chamber of Commerce presented its views in Edmonton, and when the legislation was drafted the ministers of Labour and Industry and Development arrived in Calgary to discuss the draft legislation with the local chamber.[37] That the national organization does not usually yield such direct power in Ottawa is partly a reflection of the decentralized structure of the group.

There are some exceptions: a few interest groups, whether or not they are formal federations, have become, in fact, highly centralized. The Consumers' Association of Canada does most of its governmental work from Ottawa, as does the Canadian Manufacturers' Association. In such cases, of course, contact between the federal government and the national organization is much stronger than that between the provincial government and provincial organizations.

[37] Engelmann and Schwartz, *Canadian Political Parties*, p. 104.

The Methods of Influence

The methods of influence used by interest groups approaching government may be broken down into several categories. Direct and continuous contact is probably the most effective technique, but the presentation of briefs and other sporadic contact may also be useful. The numerous advisory committees of the Canadian government may provide a convenient channel of access and interlocking memberships between political structures and the interest groups may be even more effective. Influencing public opinion in order to get through to the government is sometimes used and its use may be increasing although this is not a favourite technique in Canada.

Direct Contact and Briefing   One analyst—perhaps slightly biased, for he had served on the ill-fated Housing Task Force of 1969—has suggested that:

The Ottawa based lobby and the pressure group organizations which had an interest in urban matters such as the Canada Welfare Council and the Federation of Mayors and Municipalities were closely linked to CMHC and the ruling structure of the federal government. So in effect there was a closed system of policy making populated by a small number of men who, over the years, had become well acquainted with each other and each other's views. [38]

Whether for good or evil, the same situation prevails in many vital areas of government policy. Indeed it is the most important way in which groups can exercise influence. In the field of agricultural policy making, the executives of the Canadian Federation of Agriculture tend to retain their positions over long periods and thus build up close and continuing contacts with the Minister of Agriculture and departmental officials. Over the years the relationship has become very close and rather informal and has led to the situation, also common in other interest group-government relationships, where the group will never publicly name or criticize a departmental official. [39] The Consumers' Association of Canada has spent much time and effort establishing a liaison with senior civil servants in many departments and has succeeded to the extent that it is now often consulted informally before action is taken. For example, Statistics Canada informally consults the Association before revising its consumer price index. [40] As for the Canadian Manufacturers' Association: "The over-

---

[38] Lloyd Axworthy, "The Housing Tax Force—A New Policy Instrument," unpublished paper read at the Canadian Political Science Association, Winnipeg, June 4, 1970.

[39] H. Dawson, "Relations Between Farm Organizations and Civil Service in Canada and Great Britain," p. 452. The federation may complain in private to the minister about an official with whom they are having trouble.

[40] H. Dawson, "The Consumers' Association of Canada," p. 109.

whelming bulk of CMA input is and will continue to be in the form of unpublicized, informal discussions with constant interchange of visits between government officials and CMA staff and committee personnel." This process of consultation has virtually eliminated the need for formal submissions except for those cases in which it is appropriate to provide rather full documentation of research in support of a particular policy proposal.[41]

The most successful groups in using these techniques have permanent Ottawa offices and cultivate a wide range of contacts within the bureaucracy. For the most part they too create an image of reliability about the information they provide and about guarding confidences passed on to them by their contacts. They are able to keep their own members from excesses such as intemperate statements to the press or strident public speeches. They shy away from dealing (publicly at least) with the opposition; their work is with the government. The representatives often hold office for long periods for it is essential that they know their own sector and the major actors in it very well. In all ways they seek accommodation, not confrontation—at least so long as their vital interests are met.[42] Continuing contacts may also be made at the cabinet level. Canadian groups attempt to influence both the ministers who deal primarily with their subject area and, if the interest group has a well-defined locus of activity, the minister responsible for representing their region. Generally the technique is simple. The group leaders request a meeting. If the group is important enough in the minister's sector, they get it. A succinct briefing is then the best way to attempt to convince the minister of a point. Often the same officials with whom the group deals on a more day-to-day basis will be present and the minister will discuss the points made later with them—another reason why the effective group keeps up its bureaucratic contacts.

Another form of direct contact is the presentation of briefs to the standing and special committees of the House of Commons. This tactic has, in the past seldom proven very effective by itself. Indeed, it could not be expected to be very effective since the committee stage follows second reading of a bill, which constitutes approval in principle of its major measures. Instead, ministers and their officials tend to seize upon briefs favourable to their position as tangible evidence of wide support for their policies, and to ignore briefs which are against

---

[41] "Improve Business-Government Ties," *The Financial Post*, October 7, 1972, p. 39 quoted in W. T. Stanbury, op. cit., pp. 2, 3.

[42] See "The Lobbyists," a three-part series in the *Globe & Mail*, Toronto, October 25, 27, 28, 1980.

them. Again there are exceptions such as the fight against anti-combines legislation but even in the exceptional cases where a bill is withdrawn or altered significantly during committee stage, the briefing of committees is but one part of a well-orchestrated campaign.

Direct contact between groups and government may also be of a more sporadic nature. Sporadic contact at the executive level will occur when a group which normally is not politically active becomes so because of a particular issue. For example, before 1970, detergent manufacturers had not been noted for political activity and were quite unknown at the Department of Energy, Mines and Resources, but the formation of policy to limit the phosphate content of detergents brought them to the door of the minister. Contact between groups and political decision makers may also involve write-in campaigns, or deluges of telegrams may be organized and groups of delegates may attempt to see MPs or cabinet ministers.

The contact people in Ottawa, whose job it is to provide continuing representation of interests before government, range from local lawyers and relatively unheralded officers of small trade associations up to the "super-stars" of the lobbying game. Some of the latter, such as Ross Tolmie of the Ottawa law firm bearing his name, have acted as representatives of just one company (in Tolmie's case, Trans-Canada Pipelines). Others such as Mel Jack and David Golden (of the Brewers Association and the Air Industries Association, respectively), have represented large industrial groups. Still others such as Bill Lee work for different clients at different times.

The best lobbyists have in common excellent connections with politicians and senior bureaucrats and many of them have been in and out of top political and bureaucratic jobs. Mel Jack was formerly executive assistant to George Hees and a moving force behind Mr. Hees' success as Minister of Transport and, later, Trade and Commerce. Bill Lee was executive assistant to Paul Hellyer in the latter's sojourn as Minister of National Defence, and managed the 1968 Liberal election campaign for Mr. Trudeau. Lee's partner for a time was William Neville who began as an executive assistant to a Liberal cabinet minister, later ran as a Conservative candidate, and subsequently landed as Principal Secretary to Prime Minister Clark. David Golden was Deputy Minister of Defence Production, then became head of the Air Industries Association, and then helped set up the Department of Industry before returning to private industry, from whence he emerged as president of the government's communications satellite corporation, Telesat.

The lesser lights of the direct contact business are certainly more numerous. Over 400 national associations have Ottawa offices, a figure which has doubled over the last decade. It is not always necessary to retain a big-name lobbyist for an organization to have an input to the policy process. Bureaucrats often welcome contact with interest groups as alternative sources of information and for alternative perspectives on the policy-related or administrative issues with which they may be concerned. Moreover, the backing of a strong interest group can assist the bureaucrats in convincing the Treasury Board or the cabinet that one of their programs should be given a bigger slice of the budgetary pie.

In summary, the most effective presentations of interest-group views are the kind that the public never hears about: they involve direct and informal contact between the bureaucracy and interest groups during the process of policy formulation and, occasionally, between group leaders and cabinet ministers. A formal brief is relatively rare in these circumstances, although the fortunate or diligent group that learns from friendly insiders that policy related to its interests is being drafted, and then manages to get a brief to the officials and ministers concerned may be in a good position to influence the formulation process. This is more likely to occur if informal and continuing contacts are religiously maintained.

The Advisory Committee   Advisory committees are committees of outside experts, or representatives of various interest groups concerned with a particular issue area. They are formed to advise ministers or officials on policies, and virtually every federal department can boast several. Organizations like the Canadian Tax Foundation and the Canadian Bar Association act in many ways as advisory committees to the departments concerned with their areas of expertise. The Canadian Federation of Agriculture is asked to appoint representatives to advisory boards in the field of agricultural policy, and the head of the Alberta Wheat Pool holds a seat on the Canadian Wheat Board. At one time or another, the Canadian Manufacturers' Association has held positions on at least thirty-five different advisory boards and committees and the Canadian Labour Congress must sometimes feel that its major raison d'être is to provide members for advisory committees.[43]

The importance of such committees in the policy process varies from department to department and from time to time. Helen Jones Dawson concludes that in the field of agricultural policy making, such groups are more important in Britain than in Canada.[44] On the other hand, Malcolm Taylor once concluded that in the field of Canadian

---

[43] "Pressure Groups in Canada," *Parliamentarian*, Jan., 1970, p. 19.
[44] Dawson, "An Interest Group: The Canadian Federation of Agriculture," p. 147.

medical policy making they are extremely powerful.[45] Taylor, however, wrote that article before the fight over government-sponsored health insurance came to a head in the mid-1960s. The members of the Canadian Medical Association lost this fight even though they put all their resources into it and their representatives on advisory committees consistently spoke out against the plan. Their representatives on such committees are currently less listened to by senior Health and Welfare officials than they once were.

Not all interest groups are anxious to serve on advisory committees. For one thing, they may realize that such committees are often set up by government not to consult but rather to explain policies on which the government has already settled, and to co-opt potential opponents. Interest groups may also feel that if they are consulted about a policy they then lose their right to criticize it, or at least their credibility when they do so is compromised. Thus, while advisory committees have become a ubiquitous feature of the Canadian bureaucracy it is safe to assert only that the amount of influence that interest groups exert through them varies widely.

Interlocking Memberships One of the most effective routes of access to decision makers is the very direct one provided by the fact that political decision makers themselves are often members of the interest groups which seek to influence decisions. The membership of some cabinet ministers in the Canadian Manufacturers' Association has already been mentioned, and a search through the biographies in the *Parliamentary Guide* will provide many similar examples.

A fairly powerful example, though not an isolated one, is that of Anthony Abbott who was minister of Consumer and Corporate Affairs and, later, Minister of State for Small Business in the Trudeau cabinets of 1976-79. Mr. Abbott was

. . . appointed President of the Retail Council of Canada in 1971. A few years later he became an M.P. and in September 1976 he was appointed minister. Having participated in preparing the council's brief in respect of the competition act, four years later Mr. Abbott, as an M.P., was able to examine the representatives of the council when they appeared before the House of Commons committee examining the Stage I amendments. It is fair to say that Mr. Abbott, on becoming the minister, was familiar with business views on competition policy legislation.[46]

In addition, many of the Senators in Ottawa double as lobbyists and particularly as industry representatives. In 1973, Senator J. J.

[45] Taylor, "The Role of the Medical Profession in the Formulation and Execution of Public Policy," pp. 245ff.

[46] W. T. Stanbury, *Business Interests & the Reform of Canadian Competition Policy 1971-5*, p. 209.

Connolly represented both IBM and Gulf Canada in Ottawa and Gulf's president noted that the Senator "occasionally opens doors for us and provides the proper atmosphere" for discussions with officials. The fourteen members of the Senate Committee on Banking, Trade and Commerce held 116 corporate positions and directorships in 1975. The committee deals with such legislation as anti-combines law and the Bank Act. The easy access which people such as these could have to government policy makers makes them important "mouthpieces" for organized interests. Many of the doctors who have been health ministers or senior officials in federal and provincial Departments of Health have also been medical association members. The suggestion that the Canadian Medical Association is consulted whenever medical personnel are appointed to government advisory committees or similar positions is an exaggeration but they are frequently consulted as are other professional associations in appropriate circumstances.[47] Many of Ottawa's higher-level bureaucrats or their spouses are members of the Consumers' Association of Canada—a fact which can hardly hurt that organization's political activities.

A peculiar, but conceivably significant form of interlocking membership is that of part-time trade association representatives in the parliamentary Press Gallery. Membership in the Gallery does constitute an excellent entrée to ministers' offices and as ex-Gallery President Charles Lynch put it, it is "a continuing problem. It's always been assumed over the years that the Gallery is used in this way by certain people, but it is very difficult to police."[48]

On occasion, an interest group will succeed in getting one of its members on a Royal Commission in which it is interested. The Hall Royal Commission on Health Services included two members nominated by the Canadian Medical Association.[49] In this case, however, it is interesting to note that the Commissioners were true to their task rather than to the Medical Association, and were instrumental in the preparation of a report which the medical association itself roundly condemned.

An even more important type of influence on political decisions occurs as people move from the private sector into a government department concerned with regulating the industry from which they come. The situation is further complicated when the same individual

[47] Engelmann and Schwartz, *Political Parties and the Canadian Social Structure*, p. 100.
[48] *The Ottawa Citizen*, March 4, 1976, p. 33, cited in W. T. Stanbury, op. cit., p. 37.
[49] Ibid., p. 100. See also Malcolm Taylor, *Health Insurance & Canadian Public Policy*, passim.

later moves back again to the private sector. When the Department of Industry, Trade and Commerce is recruiting employees to regulate the iron and steel industry, it naturally looks to people from that industry for, after all, their experience is relevant. Later these same people may move back to a more-or-less grateful corporation. Such influence is not necessarily harmful but the close web of contact and friendship which can be woven between those who regulate and those who are regulated, and between groups demanding certain policies and those who have the power to make the policies does bear continuing scrutiny.

Public Relations Because of the importance of Congress in the decision-making process in the United States, groups in that country frequently attempt to bolster their position by conducting large-scale public relations campaigns which will they hope, add general public support for their cause to that of their own members. This, they hope, will in turn convince influential congressmen of the wisdom of supporting their cause. By contrast, because of the relatively minor policy role played by backbench Members of Parliament, Canadian groups depend more on their access to bureaucratic decision makers and on the expertise they possess than on demonstrated public support. Public relations campaigns are thus less important in Canada as an everyday aspect of influence on government. Nevertheless, because public support, or the appearance of it, can never be ignored by political decision makers, groups will from time to time launch large-scale public relations offensives to supplement their other sources of influence.

Often it is groups which have been unsuccessful in establishing good lines of access to the decision makers, or groups which do not control a certain area of expertise, which are forced to utilize the public relations campaigns as a tactic of political influence and other times it will be a group which stands to lose a good deal by a decision which it has been unsuccessful at blocking at an earlier stage in the policy process. The Canadian Mining Association, which stood to be directly affected by the changes outlined in the 1969 White Paper on Taxation, turned to a series of radio commercials and newspaper advertisements to gain support for its position and it reinforced this by garnering editorial support for its line of reasoning. The Ontario Farmers' Union, which has had difficulty in developing good channels of access to the decision makers, has organized several marches and tractor parades in an attempt to gain public sympathy for the plight of the farmer. Such instances, however, are not as common in Canada as they are in the U.S. The lengthy series of newspaper advertisements for American fighter aircraft in the years before a final decision on what fighter aircraft to choose for Canada has been rather an anomaly in Canadian politics, however effective it may have been. Indeed, such campaigns are looked upon in Canada with some disdain—not only by the authorities in the system, but by other interest groups as well—for the recourse to these tactics is often taken to be indicative of weakness or of failure in more traditional tactics. However given the success of such public relations campaigns as that operated by the various manufacturing interests against anti-combines legislation or by the Canadian Mining Association one might be tempted to attribute a little more efficacy than is usually attributed to such tactics. [50]

Occasionally a public relations campaign will backfire badly. In 1978, as part of its continuing struggle to gain higher fees within medicare, the Ontario Medical Association began to publicize the fact that many physicians were leaving Ontario to practise in the U.S. where incomes were considerably higher. Presumably the intention was to create public pressure on the government to raise fee schedules and hence to "keep our doctors at home." The result was rather different. The Ministry of Health had become convinced that a significant component of their difficulties in controlling health care costs was created by too many physicians generating demand for extra services. The Ministry estimated that every extra doctor in the province generated about $250,000 per year in extra demand for services. With no statistical indication that anyone's health was much improved by extra physicians and with Ontario already having a population to physician ratio better than that recommended by any world authority, the Health Ministry was not particularly sorry to see doctors leaving. Moreover the public reaction when a physician whose average earnings were over $55,000 wanted to leave to get more money in the United States was something less than sympathetic, the more so as the average industrial wage in the province was approximately $15,000 at the time. The Medical Association did not do particularly well in fee negotiations that year and quickly dropped that campaign in favour of encouraging doctors to opt out of the medical plan in order to put upward pressure on fees.

In any event, successful groups seldom employ only one tactic at a time. A full-scale campaign will involve several techniques used simultaneously to back up continuing close contact with decision

---

[50] One point of view which dissents from the conventional wisdom is that of S. D. Clarke. Writing in 1938, Clarke suggested "the major changes in government policy have been brought about through the mobilization of public opinion rather than through the application of technical counsel." In "The Canadian Manufacturers' Association." *CJEPS*, 4, 1938, p. 522.

makers. For example, when the Consumers' Association of Canada began its campaign against trading stamps, it requested that all its members write to MPs and ministers, it made submissions to local authorities and to federal and provincial attorneys general, it made submissions to the Prime Minister and Minister of Justice, it obtained the full support of many other groups including the Retail Merchants Federation, the Canadian Federation of Agriculture, the Canadian Labour Congress, and various women's groups, and simultaneously it provided material for the media so that they too could become involved in the issue. In spite of this impressive effort, the Association was not totally successful. Speculation as to why leads directly to the next consideration of this chapter: namely, what determines the effectiveness of interest groups influencing the policy process?

The Determinants of Success

Some groups are much more successful in influencing governmental processes than are others. Yet even the highly successful groups occasionally suffer significant reversals in their attempts to influence policy. Our look at the determinants of the success or failure of a group will examine the group's own structure and that of government, the existing policy orientations of the government and the extent of conformity of the group's interest to the needs of the environment.[51]

The Structure and Resources of the Group   Plainly enough, one of the most important resources any group can have is money, and most interest groups, even those we might usually consider well-to-do, are chronically short of it. The Canadian Federation of Agriculture is probably fairly typical; it receives widely varying amounts of money from year to year, as farm fortunes rise and fall. Many industry associations suffer the same problem for they are vulnerable to cutbacks whenever their industry hits a cyclical downturn. Promotional interest groups seem to suffer even more difficulty in finding money than self-interest groups like the CFA and groups lying toward the issue-oriented side of the institutionalized continuum, particularly when they are also promotional in nature, are the most vulnerable of all.

Not all interest groups are perpetually short of funds; indeed some of the most powerful are very well financed. The Canadian Manufacturers' Association had an annual budget of nearly 1 million dollars in the late 1960s. By 1973 its annual salary bill alone for its full time staff was greater than 1 million dollars and presumably current dollar fig-

---

[51] For a similar formulation, see Eckstein, *Pressure Group Politics*, pp. 15-39.

ures would be at least double that figure. Overall the CMA budget is equal to that of our national political parties.[52] It also carries a contingency fund which, even in the early 1970s, was over half a million dollars. Its main source of funds is membership dues from over 9,000 firms representing more than 80 percent of Canada's manufacturing capacity. For its money, the CMA is able to buy, among other things, a permanent staff of well over 100, with at least 70 experts in various fields related to the promotion of interests of Canadian industry. Thus CMA briefs to governments are invariably well prepared and often influential in the formulation of regulations or the creation of new legislation.

With its budget, the CMA is able to carry on a wide array of activities.[53] In addition to briefing the bureaucracy and the cabinet, it sends an annual "delegation" to Ottawa to interview most of the cabinet ministers and many deputy ministers. However, its most effective activities are almost certainly related to its efforts to influence the implementation of legislation. The CMA studies all regulations made under the Customs Act, the Excise Tax Act, the Income Tax Act, and the various Sales Tax Acts, and makes representations to the bureaucracy in those areas where the departments have wide discretionary power. It is very concerned with the formulation and application of all regulations dealing with restrictive trade practices, monopolies, combines and mergers. It cooperates with provincial Departments of Education and with federal Manpower authorities to provide information about what employee skills are required and what training programs would be useful. Such pervasive contacts with government are made possible by the large financial resources available to the CMA. With its impressive organization, solid financing, and concentrated interest in the outcome of the policy process for its members, it is hardly surprising that the Association is so successful.

The number of members an interest group can boast is a less important determinant of success than one might expect. Decision makers know that a person's membership in a group does not guarantee agreement with the group's views on a particular issue. If sheer numbers were the determining factor, labour organizations would be Canada's most important interest groups. In fact, a more important attribute of a group may be its organizational cohesiveness. If an organization's executive really does speak for its members and if the members might be mobilized en masse in support of the group's

---

[52] "Pressure Groups in Canada," *Parliamentarian*, January, 1970, pp. 13-14, and W. T. Stanbury, op. cit., p. 208ff.
[53] "Pressure Groups in Canada," p. 18.

ideas, any threats which the group makes or implies will have considerable credibility.

The prestige of a group is important. Decision makers may be impressed by the group's ideas in direct proportion to how impressed they are by its members as individuals. Almost everyone will at least listen to the medical associations, but the Amalgamated Association of Apprentice Septic-Tank Pumpers or the Canadian Institute of Motorcycle Buffs might have more difficulty getting a hearing. Monopoly over a certain area of expertise is a potent factor in determining the prestige of a group. The Canadian Bar Association, for instance, is always listened to with respect by authorities both because it is the only national spokesman for the legal profession in Canada and because it has established a reputation for reason in its recommendations. The power of knowledge was recognized early on by John Bulloch in his struggle to make the Canadian Federation of Independent Businessmen into a significant political force. Said Bulloch:

I began to see how the system is stacked in favour of those who own all the lawyers. I found out that the big corporations, without being conspiratorial, control the knowledge factory in the country, all the positions that government takes are the product of conversation, the chinwags, that go on between the experts who are owned by the major corporations and the trade unions and the experts who work for government. It's a mandarin to mandarin process. [54]

Prestige may also depend on how much the government needs the expert resources of the group, on the past record of the group in its relationship with the government, and on the socioeconomic status of group members.

Given all these factors it is not surprising that many of the promotional and issue-oriented interest groups have great difficulty playing in the same arena with their institutionalized and self-interested counterparts. They lack funds. Their leaders come and go and serve largely on a voluntary basis. The leaders can never be sure that members will follow them. The techniques used by the groups are often distasteful to elite policy makers and the groups are seldom able to keep up their activities long enough to seriously disrupt the policy process and seldom able to ensure that members will turn out for demonstrations. Those few which can (some native peoples' organizations are examples) have considerable success in gathering concessions. Issue-oriented and promotional groups also suffer from diffi-

---

[54] Quoted in Alexander Ross, "How to Join the March to New Politics," *Quest*, February 1977, p. 47, cited in W. T. Stanbury, op. cit., p. 212.

culties in defining their own priorities since no clear economic self-interest defines it for them. The job of influencing policy is thus quite different and much more difficult for most of the issue-oriented and promotional groups than it is for members of well-institutionalized and well-connected groups.

The Structure of Government   There is a great deal of disagreement among those who write about interest groups concerning just what influence the structure of government has on group effectiveness. It is often suggested that interest groups are more successful in the U.S. than in Canada because the congressional system with its many centres of decision making is much more open to group activity than the parliamentary system. In the U.S., if a group is not successful at the Presidential level it may still influence Congress or the bureaucracy, each of which is a separate centre of power. In Canada, if a group fails with the bureaucracy and cabinet, which are closely tied together, it is in considerable trouble.

Such suggestions oversimplify the situation. Britain, with a system more centralized than Canada's, has a very high level of interest group activity, so a parliamentary form of government need not mitigate against such activity. Moreover, because Canadian groups tend to deal with the bureaucracy, much of their activity is hidden from public view. These quiet dealings with anonymous bureaucrats certainly create an *appearance* of lesser activity than prevails in the United States, but perhaps the actual level of influence may be as great or even greater in Canada.[55] There has as yet been very little investigation of interest group activity in the provinces and that too may lead to a consistent underestimation of the strength of interest group activity in Canada.

It is difficult to determine whether Canada's federal system aids or hinders interest group activity. On the one hand we have suggested that it does provide more sites at which change undesirable to a group can be blocked. On the other hand, it imposes on groups, most of which are perpetually short of money, the necessity to cover several capital cities simultaneously if they are to be truly effective and it often forces a federalized structure upon the groups which is no less onerous for the groups than for the nation. Thus most groups, unlike the Canadian Manufacturers' Association, are forced to concentrate on only a few issues which affect them and on immediate goals.

There is probably a mutually reinforcing effect between the distribution of power within the federal system and the activities of interest groups. The distribution of power influences the structure, cohe-

[55] See particularly Robert Presthus' *Elites in the Policy Process*.

sion, and even the existence of groups while the groups in turn will attempt to influence the distribution of powers so as to enhance the strength of the governments with which they are most closely affiliated.[56] Thus for example, national student organizations in Canada, the National Federation of Canadian University Students (NFCUS) and its successor the Canadian Union of Students (CUS), waxed and waned in strength directly in proportion to the level of involvement of the federal government in university education. The Canadian Labour Congress tends to make demands (such as a stronger federal involvement in health insurance plans) which will result in a strengthening of the federal role, and the Confederation of National Trade Unions tends to make demands which will reinforce the strength of "their" government in Quebec. "Strong governments give rise to strong interest groups which can realistically make demands when satisfaction would necessitate an expansion of the role of the government upon which the demands are made."[57]

But whatever the overall impact of federalism, it does provide a larger number of points of access than the interest group would have in a unitary system. Given that the ultimate minimum requirement for the political success of any interest group is *access*, we can conclude that groups in Canada have a wide range of opportunities for political influence. On the other hand, rapid changes within federal and provincial government structures and constant shifts in the balance of power between the various levels of government conspire to impose upon interest groups a requirement for nimbleness and constant attention to the question of "who is doing what" in areas of interest to the group.

Overall Government Policy   Sometimes external factors, such as the state of the economy, may force the government into a position where interest groups' demands can have very little effect. In other instances a group may find its demands receiving sympathetic attention no matter what it does. For example, in 1969-70, the federal government decided that to ease inflation it would be necessary to cut back government expenditures. A major expenditure in the past had been a 50 million dollar annual loan fund for municipal sewage treatment plants. In 1970 the demand for such loans increased greatly, and The Canadian Federation of Mayors and Municipalities, together with many promotional groups interested in pollution control, asked for a large increase in the size of the fund. Their request was viewed sympathetically by most government officials, yet the fund was raised to only 75 million dollars when at least 150 million dollars could

---

[56] David Kwavnick, "Interest Group Demands & the Federal Political System."
[57] Paul Pross, *Pressure Group Behaviour in Canadian Politics*, p. 83.

have been profitably spent. What had happened was a simple clash of priorities, which had to be resolved by cabinet which, in the prevailing fiscal climate, could not possibly have agreed to the entire appropriation demanded by interest groups and bureaucrats in the Department of the Environment. Welfare groups, whose demands usually involve an increase in government expenditures, also fare badly in times of austerity, while in times of government expansion even the most poorly organized group can succeed. The government restraint climate of 1969-70 was more than matched in the late 1970s with the consequence that virtually all new expenditure proposals came under scrutiny and few interest group demands calling for higher expenditures could be met.

The Nature of the Environment   An interest group will succeed best if its overall aims are in keeping with the prevailing values of the society in which it operates. In Canada the activities of interest groups are generally perceived, at least by government decision makers and other elites, to be legitimate and worthwhile: the environment is supportive of their activities. For instance 93 percent of the MPs interviewed in the early 1970s agreed that "most legislators do not regard the activities of lobbyists as a form of improper pressure," and 85 percent agreed that "interest groups are necessary to make government aware of the needs of all the people."[58] Former federal Minister of Finance, Donald MacDonald is quoted by columnist Donald MacGillivry as saying:

What is of greatest value is for the minister to be apprised of the impact of the legislation from the particular viewpoint of the group concerned. Legislation must of necessity speak generally but there may be special cases which persons in a particular industry or group might recognize more easily than can someone in government surveying industry or the community generally.[59]

The supportive nature of the environment for interest groups activity in Canada appears to apply more to business-oriented than to consumer-oriented groups. W. T. Stanbury sums the situation up by pointing out that "the socially approved pursuit of a living profit together with large-scale intervention by government in the nation's economic life has resulted in a combination of economic affairs unequally suited to ensure the dominance of producer interests over consumer interests."[60]

[58] Robert Presthus, "Interest Groups & the Canadian Parliament," p. 455.
[59] Cited in J. E. Anderson, "Pressure Groups & the Canadian Bureaucracy," in W. D. Kernaghan, *Bureaucracy in Canadian Government*, p. 102.
[60] W. Stanbury, *Business Interests & the Reform of Canadian Competition Policy 1971-5*, p. 45.

Summary: Group Impact on Government Policy

Access to the decision makers of government is the *sine qua non* of interest group influence on public policy, but in a way, that is all it is. Access is a necessary but not a sufficient condition for political influence in Canada for, having convinced decision makers to listen to the group's "case," the group must still be convincing about the merits of its argument. Or to put this in the context of our policy model, access guarantees that the group will be able to *initiate* policies—to get the information into the system—but in order to influence the process of *priority determination*, the group must be able to convince the political executive that its particular demands are more deserving of attention than competing demands. Because a minister must ultimately seek re-election, he or she will not always meet the demands of big business at the cost of broader if less articulate or less organized interests; the group must make its case on both technical grounds and on the grounds of some wider appeal to public interest and public support. Similarly, because the bureaucrat must ultimately sell a policy idea to the minister, he or she must not automatically accede to the demands of a close friend or client unless those demands have at least some broad support in Canadian society.

By way of illustration, we can return to the example of the Canadian Medical Association at the height of its power in the late 1950s and early 1960s. Having analyzed that group's activities, one writer attributed its relatively high degree of success not only to its privileged access to the focal point of decision making in its field, but also to:

a) The Association's prestige
b) The identification of the medical profession with the public interest
c) The cohesiveness of membership
d) The lack of articulation of an opposing point of view
e) General agreement among key policy makers on the group's high level of responsibility and public interest[61]

When a group has this much going for it *as well* as ready access, the probability of success is certainly very high.

THE OUTPUT ACTIVITIES OF INTEREST GROUPS

Some organizations are deeply involved in the administration of government policy. For example, even though they might shudder to

---

[61] M. Taylor, "The Role of the Medical Profession in the Formulation and Execution of Public Policy," p. 254.

think so, doctors are acting as public employees when they make out birth and death certificates, hospital admissions, or health insurance claims. When they sit on hospital boards or workmen's compensation boards and when they administer public health programs, they are acting as agents for important executive outputs of the political system and many argue that, in practising under medicare, they are really employees of the state, something which is anathema to many of them. Indeed "no other group is as deeply involved in public administration . . . despite the fundamental antipathy between the healing arts and bureaucracy."[62] Similarly, the Canadian Legion is vital in the administration of veterans' pensions through close cooperation with the Department of Veterans Affairs.

More broadly, when a regulation is promulgated, the government publishes the regulation in the Canada (or provincial) Gazette, but no one seriously expects everyone who is affected to read about it there. The expectation is that the various associations which are concerned with the regulation will, through their agents or headquarters in Ottawa, disseminate the appropriate information to those concerned.

The output activities of interest groups can be divided into those of an administrative nature, where the group or its members are a direct part of the output process, and those of an informational nature, where the group is acting as an indirect agent of the political system.

Administrative Functions

One of the most important administrative functions of many groups—and certainly the most cherished by the group—itself is self-regulation. For example, society makes the assumption that it would be undesirable to have a large number of unqualified people claiming to be doctors or dentists or lawyers or perhaps even teachers. Accordingly, governments delegate self-policing powers to medical associations, bar associations, and some teachers' groups, which allow them to define who is qualified to practise their profession. This self-regulatory mechanism extends far in Canadian society, for not only are professions controlled in this way, but so also are trades and crafts. The function extends beyond the mere definition of who is qualified to practise, to include a definition of ethical or fair practices and appropriate fee structures. In this form it extends beyond professional association and trade unions and into the business community through Better Business Bureaus and other business associations. Were it not for the self-regulatory functions of many interest groups

---

[62] Ibid., p. 108.

in society, the governmental structure in Canada would have to be considerably larger than it is now. The self-regulatory function is particularly valuable to groups because of the monopoly position it gives group members in the provision of services—and of course in receiving the rewards therefrom. The right to restrict numbers of practitioners of a trade is crucial in maintaining the incomes of the members of the trade and so is guarded jealously by the association holding that right.[63]

The actual administration of government programs is also an important function of many groups. The administrative tasks which many doctors carry out under government medical insurance programs have already been mentioned. Elevator cooperatives and farmers' associations administer many aspects of government farm price support programs. Groups interested in fighting pollution provide inspection services and warn government agencies of sources of pollution. Universities administer some aspects of student aid programs subject to advice, in some cases, by faculty associations and by government. These activities cannot be viewed as anything but an integral part of government activity; the interest groups in such cases become an extension of the output side of the political system.

Information Dissemination

Probably the most important of output activities of interest groups, however, is the dissemination of information about government policies. People cannot obey the law unless they know what it is, and they cannot take advantage of government programs unless they know about them. Interest groups often provide the required information and the required notification of what is the law. Here endless examples can be provided. Virtually every trade association, union, or promotional group at least publishes a newsletter, and much of the work of the head offices of interest groups consists of determining which government activities are pertinent to the group's interests and by then informing members about those activities.

The factors which affect the usefulness of interest groups as output institutions for the political system are broadly similar to those which affect their value as input devices. Of particular importance are group cohesiveness or dedication to a single set of aims and the possession of good internal communications. Obviously, the strength of the offices in the capital cities is important—especially the effectiveness of

---

[63] Carolyn Touhy, "Private Government, Property & Professionalism," *CJPS*, IX:4, Dec. 1976, p. 668.

their communication with the governmental structures with which they are concerned.

Scholars who have studied interest groups have tended to concentrate almost exclusively on the input side of their activities. While this aspect is vital, the failure to look seriously at the output activities of groups can result in a substantial underestimation of their importance in modern government. The political system in Canada and in other developed countries has become highly dependent on these activities and wise group leadership will try to take advantage of this fact when making demands upon political decision makers.

CONCLUSIONS

One of the greatest difficulties in writing about interest groups in Canada—indeed in any industrialized Western society—is the problem of determining where to place them in any conceptual scheme of the political system. They are traditionally placed on the input side of the process and at the boundary of the political system; but, in this chapter, we have seen examples of their participation not only at the policy initiation stage of the process but as well at the very core of the policy process, in priority determination and policy formulation and in policy implementation as well. In short, interest groups pervade the whole of the policy process in Canada, so much so that at least one analyst has been led to characterize the Canadian political process as a process of elite accommodation between interest group and governmental elites,[64] and a whole school of analysis—consociationalism—has been erected on a very similar foundation and applied widely in Canadian political science.[65] Although we have continually indicated the difficulty of assessing the relative strength of groups in various nations, Canada is not unique in respect to the significance of its organized interests. The group approach to politics was one early recognition of this significance and a latter-day recognition of the all-pervasive role of interest groups in the United States is found in Theodore Lowi's description of the American system as one of "interest-group liberalism."

Interest groups provide undoubted benefits in Canadian society. Since there are far more Canadians who participate in interest group activities than in political parties we might be tempted to define such groups as the pre-eminent representative structures in Canadian society. There is no doubt that if one wishes to influence the political

[64] Robert Presthus, *Elite Accommodation in Canadian Politics.*
[65] Consociationalism is described in detail in Chapter 3.

system in the periods between elections, the channels afforded by interest groups are more effective than those provided by parties. We have seen, too, that groups provide information to government and to their own members, that they are prominent in the administration of government policy, and that they create a support structure for the political system upon which much of its legitimacy depends.

However one must be careful not to go too far in eulogizing the interest group system and, as Lowi is at great pains to point out with respect to the U.S., one must recognize the dangers inherent in too heavy a reliance upon them as the real and only representative structures of society. We pointed out in an earlier chapter that about 40 percent of Canadians are not integrated in any way into the interest group structure of Canada, and that this 40 percent is generally within the lower strata of society. Thus, if the influence of interest groups is as significant as we have suggested, such groups may act to reinforce the disparity of power and if political leaders react only to organized interests and disregard the needs of the relatively inarticulate members of our society then the consequences for unorganized Canadians will continue to be disastrous.[66]

There are of course, limits to the power of interest groups.[67] The cabinet has a collective policy role which may effectively counter pressure on individual ministers, and the requirements of party unity in the parliamentary system limit the legislature as an arena for lobbyists. The public service is by no means always sympathetic to interest group demands and does on occasion act as an effective counterpoise and as a representative of less articulate interests; for even the largest and wealthiest interest group can in no way approach the research resources available to even smaller federal departments. One should not underestimate the tenacity of the public servant in pursuing either the public good as he or she sees it or the aggrandizement of his or her own power, and both of these may be inimical to interest group desires. For example W. T. Stanbury suggests that the survival of any vestige of anti-combines legislation in Canada in spite of the massive attack by business

. . . is not the result of the counter-pressure of consumer interest groups such as the Consumers' Association of Canada but rather of the efforts of a handful of senior officials in the Bureau of Competition policy in the Department of Consumer and Corporate Affairs. They kept the flame burning. It is hard to overestimate their impor-

[66] This line of reasoning is carried much further in Lowi's classic, The End of Liberalism (Norton, Chicago, 1979).
[67] Similar limitations have been described for Britain by R. M. Punnett, British Government and Politics, 2nd. ed. (W. W. Norton, New York, 1971), pp. 152-156.

tance to the maintenance of any form of competition policy in this country. Both within the bureaucracy and in the wider policy arena they operate in an environment almost unflaggingly hostile to the virtues of competition and the consumer interest.

This is hardly a unique case and it would have potentially disastrous consequences for many millions of Canadians and perhaps even for the political system as a whole if the round of government and bureaucrat-bashing so prevalent in Western democracies in the late 1970s were to obliterate even this counterpoise to organized interests. Such interests are a legitimate and vital component of the Canadian political system, but if no effective counterpoise is provided to them, they will naturally dominate the system to such an extent that any pretence to any equality of opportunity or to any form of a just society will scarcely even merit the description of empty rhetoric.

PART 5

Inside the System

14

Authorities and Elites in the Canadian Political System

Not everyone shares equally in the making of political decisions; time after time we are confronted with the fact that effective political power rests in the hands of relatively few people in Canadian society. These people are the political decision makers, the authorities, or the political elite. This chapter looks at some of them in more detail.

PROBLEMS OF DEFINITION[1]

There are nearly as many definitions of the term political elite as there are people who have studied the subject. Part of the confusion stems from the highly value-laden nature of the concept of elitism. The elites can be the "good guys" as they are in Plato's *Republic*. Philosopher kings, whose mandate stems from the fact that they are an aristocracy of knowledge and wisdom, are the ones most suited to rule and it is therefore tautological to Plato that their hegemony cannot legitimately be challenged. On the opposite end of the spectrum, the political elites are seen by, for instance, neo-Marxists as the "bad guys"—as a ruling class which governs in its own selfish interest and which acts in the interest of the people only to legitimise itself and to maintain its hegemony. Between these extremes there are interpretations of both the morality and instrumentality of political elites ranging along the entire continuum.

In our own definition of political elites we would like to attempt to avoid the normative senses of the term and to define the Canadian political elite functionally and structurally. Functionally we define the political elite as a relatively small group of people who share a relatively large amount of the power to influence policy decisions in Canada. The problem presented by this functional definition however is how to actually identify the members of the elite and distinguish

---

[1] For a broader consideration of the general questions of definition and approach as applied to Canada, see Dennis Forcese, "Elites and Power in Canada," in John Redekop (ed.), *Approaches to Canadian Politics* (Prentice Hall, Toronto, 1978) and the more complete treatment in Dennis Forcese, *The Canadian Class Structure*, 2nd Edition (McGraw-Hill Ryerson, Toronto, 1980).

them from non-elites. In order to solve this very practical problem, therefore, we also define the Canadian political elite in structural or *positional* terms.[2] That is, we define the political elite as those men and women who occupy roles, offices, or positions in the political system that vest formal decision-making power in their incumbents. Thus while we will define *elite* as the people who influence policy decisions, we will operationalise that definition as the people who occupy certain powerful positions in the government.[3]

In these terms, the Canadian political elite is comprised of upper-level bureaucrats, Members of Parliament, cabinet ministers and the leaders of some of the largest and most important interest groups with whom they routinely interact, and superior court judges.[4] This positional definition includes by no means all of the positions that are significant in the making of authoritative decisions for our society. However, it does provide a manageable number of actors with whom to deal. Furthermore, as will become evident during the description of the policy-making process throughout the rest of the book, these positions do bestow on their holders a disproportionate amount of political power. Finally, most Canadian analysts of the political elites have used a similar definition and so it is possible to find the data that will help us explain the current situation.

The reader is cautioned that this might be considered too restrictive a definition. Every government has advisors who are important in the decision-making process and who are not covered in this sort of definition. Sometimes it might be the wife of the premier, sometimes a trusted friend of top cabinet members or bureaucrats, or some anonymous middle-level technocrat whose influence may stem from his expertise in a narrow but important policy field. We cannot include all such people in our definition nor can we hope to describe them, for the members of an elite who are not there by right of a formal position may move in and out faster than those who are, and in any event they

---

[2] John Porter, in *The Vertical Mosaic*, adopts this approach. He attempts to differentiate between the political and the bureaucratic elite, but we suggest that in terms of the actual making of decisions, such a differentiation is not necessarily appropriate. Porter's work has recently been extended and updated by Wallace Clement in *The Canadian Corporate Elite* (Carleton Library, McClelland and Stewart, Toronto, 1975), and by Dennis Olsen, *The State Elite* (McClelland and Stewart, Toronto, 1980).

[3] Suzanne Keller, *Beyond the Ruling Class* (Random House, New York, 1963), p. 4 describes elites in general as "a minority of individuals designated to serve a collectivity in a socially valued way. . . . Socially significant elites are ultimately responsible for the realization of major social goals and for the continuity of the social order."

[4] The description of the elite which follows refers almost exclusively to the federal level of government. Our positional definition would not change for provincial elites, but the socioeconomic composition of the elite could be expected to vary slightly from province to province.

are, by their very nature, difficult to trace. The influence of such people may be great, but in ideological and socioeconomic background, they are not likely to differ much from the positional elite through whom they must communicate their ideas. In spite of the credence often accorded the proverbial Toronto cab driver, very few of the upper-middle-class professional men and women who make up most of the Canadian political elite would choose people much different from themselves for their confidants.

ELITE STUDIES AND APPROACHES

In truth virtually any realistic approach to the study of politics is an elite approach for in no political system are the critical decisions of state actually taken by the masses. The most critical of the elite theorists assert that the political and economic systems of modern capitalist societies are controlled by a coherent industrial-military-political ruling class which attempts to ensure that in policy making its own interests supersede those of the masses.[5] The pluralists on the other hand, as we have pointed out earlier, hold that there are multiple competing elites rather than a single cohesive ruling class, and that the competition among these elites ensures that mass interests are reflected in policy decisions.[6] In the middle of these two approaches to the role of elites in modern societies stand authors such as Dye and Zeigler. While critical of the pluralist assumptions about the distribution of power in the modern industrialized nations, these authors go on to argue that the "irony of democracy" is that it is *only the elites* who are committed to democratic values. Speaking of the U.S., they state that:

[5] The writer most usually cited as the ultimate proponent of this view is C. Wright Mills, *The Power Elite* (Oxford University Press, New York, 1959). There are many others who use this perspective—for example, most of the community power studies of the 1950s do so. It is also a common component of popular or semipopular writings on politics. In general, the pure elite model has been more the province of sociologists than political scientists. There is relatively little pure elite theory in Canadian political science although the Marxian mode of analysis can be construed as being in this vein. See for example, Leo Panitch (ed), *The Canadian State* (University of Toronto Press, 1978). Our consideration of the nature of Canadian political culture deals with closely related issues. See Chapter 5.

[6] See for example the classic examples of this approach in Robert Dahl, *Who Governs?* (Yale University Press, New Haven, 1961); Edward Banfield, *Political Influence* (University of Chicago Press, Chicago, 1961); or Nelson Polsby, *Community Power Studies* (Yale University Press, 1964). The pluralist approach is more often utilized by political scientists than by sociologists and probably was the most commonly accepted approach in Canadian political science in the fifties and sixties.

Democratic values have survived because elites not masses govern. Elites in America—leaders in government, industry, education, and civic affairs; the well educated, prestigiously employed, and politically active—give greater support to basic democratic values and "rules of the game" than do the masses. . . . In short, it is the common man not the elite who is most likely to be swayed by anti-democratic ideology; and it is the elite and not the common man who is the chief guardian of democratic values. [7]

This is likely equally true in the Canadian case.

While they do not go so far as to ascribe to elites the custodianship of our democratic values, people such as Porter and Presthus who have addressed themselves specifically to the Canadian scene assert that while there may indeed be some competition among elites and some differentiation of elites depending upon the issue involved, most of them have been drawn disproportionately from a fairly narrow portion of society, mainly the upper-middle class. Having shared the same basic socialization, our elites thus tend to bring a common set of biases to bear upon their decisions. [8]

Our assumptions in this text are also on the middle ground. As we have already indicated we do not assume that there is a single cohesive ruling class which controls the Canadian political system, either nationally or in any of the larger provincial jurisdictions. But at the same time we do assume that there is a good deal of ideological congruence among the various elites. Like Robert Presthus, "We assume that these three elites (interest group leaders, M.P.s and high level bureaucrats) play the major role in shaping and carrying out public policy, through a sustained process of mutual accommodation encouraged by a battery of compatible social, experiential and ideological ties." [9]

This does not imply that there is complete harmony among the elites. In fact evidence of serious schisms appears in the newspapers every day. We are accustomed to often acrimonious partisan conflict among members of the political elite, profound differences between, for instance, the primary and secondary sectors of the economic elite and competition among regional elites for the relative benefits of national policy. However some form of accommodation based on a shared view of the state and their role in it is usually worked out. The small size of the Canadian national elite compared to what might be

---

[7] Dye and Zeigler, op. cit., pp. 14-15. See also P. Backrach, *The Theory of Democratic Elitism* (Boston, 1967).

[8] Robert Presthus, *Elite Accommodation in Canadian Politics* and *Elites in the Policy Process;* John Porter, *The Vertical Mosaic.* D. Olsen, *The State Elite.* Most academic analysts stand on the middle ground in this controversy.

[9] *Elite Accommodation in Canadian Politics*, p. 268.

found in the United States or Britain, has made possible a situation where considerable interaction is probable, and where a high degree of self-consciousness of elite status could be expected to develop.[10]

Interaction between the governmental elite and the one-quarter of interest groups who are most active politically, the shared socio-economic properties, their strategic political roles and . . . the pervasive cohesion among them on selected ideological and cognitive dimensions all tend to provide behavioural and effective commonalities that enable them to interact effectively.[11]

It is this fact which leads Presthus to characterize Canadian politics primarily in terms of a system of elite accommodation. The position of Porter and his "disciples" Clement and Olsen, while based more on the sociological determinants of elite behaviour than on their role in the policy process, is not much different in its conclusion. While Canadian political scientists may use different terms, most of them show a broadly similar interpretation[12] to either that of Porter or Presthus, or both.

Clearly, then, it is important for an understanding of how the Canadian political system works that we understand the nature and composition of these elites. In the remainder of this chapter we will look at the socioeconomic backgrounds of these decision makers and the manner in which they will approach the allocation of resources in Canada.[13] We can then attempt to determine whether there is a common set of attitudes among these elites and what this might mean to an interpretation of Canadian politics.[14] Given that we have already considered interest group leaders and their political connections in the previous chapter we will concentrate in this chapter primarily upon elites *within* the political system. However the links and common attitudes among elites within the political system and those in the linkage institutions at the boundary of the system are important determinants of political decision making.

---

[10] Ibid., p. 274.
[11] Ibid., p. 332.
[12] Neither is the position of Presthus' major critics Richard Simeon and John Meisel. They take issue more with the details of Presthus' analysis and with his data manipulations more than with his ideological stance.
[13] Interest group leaders and behaviour are dealt with primarily in Chapter 13, as is the pluralist interpretation of democratic politics.
[14] Canadians, no less than other people, have an ongoing fascination about their elite which gives rise to an array of popular literature on the subject. See as examples Peter Newman, *The Canadian Establishment* (McClelland and Stewart, Toronto, 1975) or *The Bronfmann Dynasty* (McClelland and Stewart, Toronto, 1978) or Peter Foster, *The Blue-Eyed Sheiks* (Collins, Toronto, 1979). Such accounts provide interesting detail to complement broad brush or primarily statistical academic approaches.

THE CABINET IN CANADA

In describing the people who make up the cabinet in Canada, there are two possible approaches. One can examine the process through which a Prime Minister constructs a cabinet, in order to see what constraints exist, and what groups the Prime Minister seeks to represent in the structure of the cabinet. Alternatively, one can examine the *results* of cabinet formation—the types of people who end up in the cabinet when the selection process has been completed. This section will concentrate on the latter method, but it would be artificial to discuss the results of "cabinet making" without saying something in passing about the actual process of selecting a cabinet.

One can look at the people who have become Canadian ministers from a number of perspectives: their geographical distribution, their ethnic and social backgrounds, and their career patterns can all be examined. When that is done, one can take a fresh look at the well-worn question of how Canada's various social cleavages are represented in the cabinet for, as will be seen, this highest level of decision making in Canada is consciously designed to be representative of some of the country's major cleavages.

The Provincial and Ethnic Distribution of Cabinet Ministers

"I think I may defy them to show that the cabinet can be formed on any other principle than that of a representation of the several provinces in that cabinet. Your federal problem will have to be worked out around the table of the Executive Council."[15] This prediction was made in 1865 by Christopher Dunkin, one of the most perceptive critics of the original Confederation settlement. From the very first days of Confederation, it was obvious that the Senate, which was intended to represent regions and/or provinces in Ottawa, would not suffice as an arbiter of the regional cleavages of the federation. The Senate itself had little real power and the basis of its representation was only very imperfectly based on federal principles. Yet four distinctive colonies had been brought together and each was anxious to retain some substantial degree of control over federal political decision making. In the first cabinet, Cartier would accept no fewer than four positions for Quebec, of which three were to be held by French Canadians. Ontario, which was larger than Quebec, had to demand one more seat, and if Nova Scotia and New Brunswick were to have any say in

---

[15] Christopher Dunkin, *Confederation Debates* (Queen's Printer, Ottawa, 1951), pp. 497, 513.

the councils of Confederation, they should have two posts apiece. The federal principle of cabinet composition was thus immediately established as the most important determinant of cabinet structure and there has been no substantial change since.

In 1966 Lester Pearson's cabinet had at least one minister from each province in which the Liberals could muster a seat. The Prime Minister would no doubt have been happy to represent Saskatchewan and Alberta in his cabinet as well, but those provinces were not kind enough to give him the chance. The one prairie Liberal who was elected was immediately put in the cabinet and given the Veteran's Affairs portfolio.

Table 14-1 compares the 1966 Pearson cabinet with the early 1974 Trudeau model, and the short-lived 1979 Clark model. While we have not added the figures on the 1980 Trudeau cabinet, it differs relatively little from earlier Trudeau cabinets and thus the same basic trends obtain. With respect to the 1974 Trudeau cabinet, with the temporary exception of New Brunswick, each province had at least one minister, although once again the Prairie provinces made the Prime Minister's task of selection very simple by returning so few Liberals, a favour which they again bestowed upon him in 1980.[16] The first edition of the Trudeau cabinet, in 1968, was the only one in history to have more Quebeckers than Ontarians, but subsequently the distribution of portfolios within the Trudeau cabinet returned to normal, with more Ontario than Quebec ministers.

The Clark cabinet of 1979 retained the same principles of provincial representation but again with some distortions introduced by the whims of the electorate. Clark could muster only two Quebec MPs and although he appointed both to the cabinet, he was left with the problem of finding more Quebec ministers to avoid too great an underrepresentation of that province. He appointed two Senators from Quebec to cabinet but even so was left with a considerable imbalance between his four Quebeckers and his twelve Ontarians. Significant efforts to recruit other Quebeckers had not met with success by the time his government fell after six and one-half somewhat harried months in office.

Clark also appointed an *inner cabinet*, as described in more detail in

---

[16] The omission of New Brunswick was rectified immediately after the 1974 election. Alberta again failed to give the Prime Minister a chance to represent it in the cabinet but a Senator from Alberta was appointed to the ministry, in a partial attempt to compensate for Alberta's unrepentant Conservatism. When Jack Horner crossed the floor in 1977 he was immediately welcomed into the cabinet as Alberta representative, a move he regretted at the next election. In 1980 Trudeau was forced to go to the Senate for cabinet representation in Saskatchewan, Alberta, and B.C.

Table 14-1

PROVINCIAL REPRESENTATION IN THE CABINET UNDER PEARSON, TRUDEAU, AND CLARK

Province	Pearson (Dec. 1966)		Trudeau (Feb. 1974)		Clark (Nov. 1979)	
	Cabinet	Liberal MPs Elected	Cabinet	Liberal MPs Elected	Cabinet	PC MPs Elected
Newfoundland	1	7	1	3	2	2
Prince Edward Island	0	0	1	1	1	4
Nova Scotia	2	2	1	1	1	8
New Brunswick	3	6	0	5	1	4
Quebec	7	56	11	56	4	2
Ontario	10	51	12	36	12	58
Manitoba	1	1	1	2	1	7
Saskatchewan	0	0	1	0	1	10
Alberta	0	0	0	0	3	21
British Columbia	2	7	2	4	3	19
Yukon	—	—	—	—	1	1

Chapter 15 and there was considerable grumbling in provinces such as Nova Scotia, Saskatchewan, and New Brunswick which were not represented in it. The grumblings from British Columbia were sufficiently loud that a minister from that province was added to the inner cabinet. Pierre Trudeau did not feel the need to take explicit account of regional representation in his cabinet *Committee on Priorities and Planning* (his version of an inner cabinet) so the issue of whether or not regional representation is required in inner-cabinet-type structures remains for the moment unsettled.

Historically, the same pattern of regional representation in cabinet has been evident. Table 14-2 is intended to summarize the historical data up to 1965. The reader should concentrate on the corrected percent column rather than the simple percent column. For comparative purposes the provincial distribution of population by provinces for 1971 is also shown in the table. It can be seen readily that the distribution of cabinet ministers and of population by province was roughly parallel up to 1965 and Table 14-1 confirms that this rough parallelism has persisted. However, the provinces of Saskatchewan and Alberta appear to have had rather fewer than their share of ministers, and the Maritimes rather more than their share. Perhaps some explanation of this can be found in the fact that during the long postwar period of Liberal dominance, the Western provinces have often returned only MPs from minor parties or from the Progressive Conservative party, who could not be considered for the cabinet, whereas the Maritimes have consistently returned MPs primarily from the two major parties and have supplied a constant flow of Liberals.

Table 14-2

THE DISTRIBUTION OF CABINET MINISTERS BY PROVINCE, 1867-1965

Province	Percent of Ministers	Corrected Percent*	Percent of National Population, 1971
Newfoundland	0.9	4.6	2.4
Prince Edward Island	2.4	2.4	0.5
Nova Scotia	8.9	8.4	3.7
New Brunswick	8.0	7.6	3.0
Quebec	32.0	30.4	27.9
Ontario	30.8	29.2	35.7
Manitoba	5.3	5.2	4.6
Saskatchewan	2.4	3.7	4.3
Alberta	2.7	4.2	7.5
British Columbia	4.4	4.3	10.1

* To take account of the different lengths of time various provinces have been in Confederation, the figures in the first column have been multiplied by the numbers of years between when a province joined Confederation and 1965. The figures so derived were totalled and new percentage distribution within that total was calculated.

The number of ministers shown from Quebec may be somewhat misleading, for, relative to English Canadians, French Canadians have tended to stay in the cabinet for shorter periods. When the distribution is examined by "person-years," the parallel with provincial populations in every period since Confederation is almost exact, although the shorter period of service of French Canadians in the cabinet may have acted to diminish their real power. Alternately such a rapid turnover may be a reflection of a more profound disgruntlement with their role in federal decision making.

The ethnic distribution of cabinet ministers shows similar patterns. In 1966, the Pearson cabinet contained nine French-Canadian ministers and eighteen English-Canadian ministers, including the Prime Minister, in a cabinet of thirty members. The 1974 composition of 30 percent French ministers is very close to the average since Confederation and, once again, the proportion of French-Canadian ministers very closely paralleled the proportion of French Canadians in the population. We have already described the difficulties Joe Clark faced in striking a proper ethnic balance in his 1979 cabinet, for he had but one Francophone MP. The important point is that he considered this an extremely serious problem as would any Prime Minister anxious to strike a proper linguistic balance among his ministers.

As with provincial representation, the attempt to provide proportional representation by ethnic group, at least between the French and English segments of the population, has been intentional. On the other hand, "other" Canadians have not been as well represented in the cabinet. Occasionally someone such as J. T. Thorson, a man of Icelandic descent who was minister of National War Services in 1941 and 1942, does enter the cabinet; and Trudeau's short-lived appointment of Stanley Haidasz as Minister of State in charge of "multiculturalism" and the tenure of Barney Danson as Minister of Defence could certainly have been construed as an attempt at representing "other" ethnic groups. Clark's cabinet contained more ministers with non-charter ethnic group backgrounds including Ray Hnatyshyn, Steve Paproski, and Don Mazankowski. However, with the exception of Paproski, who was Minister of Multiculturalism, it is doubtful that there was any conscious attempt to represent ethnic diversity; Hnatyshyn and Mazankowski were probably appointed on the basis of regional representation and merit. There has, in short, been no clear pattern set in this respect.

In the nineteenth and early twentieth centuries there was also an attempt to provide balanced representation of sub-groups within the portion of the cabinet having its roots in the British Isles. Thus, under Macdonald or Laurier, the well-balanced cabinet would have perhaps one-quarter of its members of English descent, one-quarter Scottish and about 20 percent Irish. Each of these nationalities formed a powerful and cohesive voting group in Canada, and a Prime Minister could offend them only at his peril.

Another interesting pattern becomes evident if we look at the distribution of ministers in recent cabinets by the rural or urban location of their riding. In the Pearson cabinet, twelve of twenty-six cabinet ministers came from the three metropolitan areas of Toronto, Montreal, and Vancouver, which, together, had only about 26 percent of the Canadian population at that time. There were nine ministers from smaller urban centres and five from ridings where there was no town with more than 25,000 residents. In the 1970 cabinet, fourteen of the twenty-eight ministers came from metropolitan areas and only four from rural ridings. This is partly a reflection of the fact that there are very few Liberals elected from rural ridings, the more-or-less exclusive property of the Conservatives, a fact confirmed by the Clark cabinet of 1979-80. That ministry had only five ministers from metropolitan areas and ten of the twenty-seven elected ministers came from rural ridings. Just as Liberal cabinets had over-represented urban and metropolitan Canada, the Conservative cabinet over-represented rural areas.

It should be clear by now that although the cabinet is not representative of rural-urban cleavages, it is intended to be an ethnically and provincially representative institution. At one time there was also a type of hidden under-representation in the French-English distribution in the cabinet, which becomes apparent when one examines the distribution of portfolios by ethnic groups. Until 1968, no French Canadian had ever led the department of Industry, Trade and Commerce (or its organizational ancestors) and up to 1978, none had been Minister of Finance. This situation pertained no less under Canada's first two French-Canadian Prime Ministers than under their English counterparts, but it was corrected by Pierre Trudeau as part of his policy of ensuring French-Canadian representation at the highest levels in Ottawa. Under Trudeau, virtually all of the heaviest portfolios, including Finance, were held by Francophones at one time or another.

There may be some reasons for the historical under-representation of Francophones in the most important financial portfolios of the cabinet. The great majority of cabinet ministers from Quebec have been lawyers; most of them have known relatively little about business or finance and were unknown to Bay or St. James Streets. Consequently, French-Canadian ministers were usually not considered for the portfolios mentioned above. But whatever the reason, the tendency, until recently, to assign French Canadians to portfolios such as Public Works, Postmaster General, or Veterans Affairs, with the hope that at cabinet meetings they would not speak unless spoken to, did lead to an under-representation of French Canadians in the most significant positions in the decision-making process.

One caveat must be entered to the general assumption that it is possible to equate portfolio with power. Sometimes portfolios which have very little departmental responsibility can be very powerful depending upon the person who occupies the portfolio. Occasionally, "light" or less visible portfolios are given to vital ministers in order to free them to consider broader questions of national policy. Thus some of the less visible portfolios such as Treasury Board (occupied in 1974 by C. M. Drury and subsequently by Jean Chrétien) or Communications (once occupied by Gérard Pelletier) or Minister of State for Federal-Provincial Relations (occupied in 1977 and 1978 by Marc Lalonde) may be held by ministers with a considerable amount of personal influence in cabinet decision making.

The Socioeconomic Background of Cabinet Ministers

The cabinet is clearly intended to be representative of provincial and ethnic cleavages in Canada, but is it representative in other ways? If so, one would expect to find in it a social cross section of Canadians. A reader who has even a passing knowledge of Canadian politics will realize that this is simply not the case. The poor are not represented in the cabinet by any of their number, nor are Canadian Indians or Inuit, nor are unskilled labourers. Women are vastly under-represented. But how far does the discrepancy go? How socially unrepresentative is the cabinet?

Both by education and by occupation, cabinet ministers have been distinctly unrepresentative of the general population. Between 1867 and 1965, fully 52 percent of Canada's cabinet ministers were lawyers, whereas the proportion of lawyers in the population is far less than 1 percent. Lately the preponderance of lawyers has perhaps grown slightly less. Table 14-3 indicates that in the 1966 Pearson cabinet only nine of twenty-seven members were lawyers, but in the Trudeau cabinet of 1974 the proportion was up again to fifteen out of thirty and exactly the same number and proportion of lawyers were present in Joe Clark's 1979 cabinet. Some 22 percent of ministers since Confederation have been from the business world, 6.5 percent have been farmers, and 4 percent have come from the public service. Only six ministers since Confederation have had a labour background or a close connection with labour.

A similar bias pertains if one looks at the educational background of Canada's ministers. Only 2 of the more than 400 since Confederation have had no formal education, and only 17 percent stopped at elementary school. Only one minister since World War II has not had at

Table 14-3

OCCUPATIONS OF CABINET MINISTERS

Occupation before Entering Politics	Pearson Cabinet (1966)	Trudeau Cabinet (1974)	Clark Cabinet (1979)
Law	9	15	15
Other professions	7	6	6
Civil service	5	2	0
Business	5	4	5
Farm	0	2	1
Labourer	0	0	0
Politician (no other experience)	0	0	3
Other	1	1	0

least high-school education. In the fairly typical 1970 cabinet, there were two members with only high-school education, one who had attended technical college, seven who stopped after one university degree, ten lawyers, and nine members with a postgraduate degree or some postgraduate studies. In terms of education then the cabinet has been far from a microcosm of the Canadian social structure.

The family backgrounds of the members of the political elite have been examined both by John Porter in 1960 and by Dennis Olsen, a student of Porter's who replicated a portion of his mentor's study for a period up to 1973. Both conclude that the socioeconomic origins of cabinet ministers are basically middle class with Olsen noting that the only change from Porter's findings was that *both* the upper-class and the working-class segments of Canadian society lost ground to the middle-class. Fully 69 percent of Olsen's 1961-1973 population of cabinet ministers have middle-class origins, and there is no indication that the trends have been altering during the 1970s.[17]

Religion and the Cabinet

One more aspect of the "representative" nature of the Canadian cabinet should be mentioned, and that is its religious composition. In the 1970 cabinet there were fourteen Roman Catholics, four members from the United Church and the Anglican Church, one Baptist, two Presbyterians, and three "others." Between Confederation and 1965, there were almost equal numbers of Anglican, Presbyterians and United Church or Methodist cabinet ministers while about 35 percent of cabinet ministers were Catholics. In an age when religious differences no longer stir people's deepest passions in Canada, the reli-

[17] See: Olsen, op. cit., pp. 29-32.

gious affiliation of cabinet ministers is of no great consequence. Indeed since 1970 it has become quite difficult to trace the religious background of cabinet ministers since they are very often not reported in the biographical sketches distributed at the time of their appointment. Yet, as Chapter 3 demonstrated, there was a time when religious differences in Canada were taken more seriously, and in that era a proper balance of religions within the cabinet was vital.

The evidence thus suggests that religion has not been a great factor in the selection of cabinet ministers in Canada over the last fifty years and it is more probable that the distribution of cabinet posts on the basis of religion is, in fact, a by-product of other factors. Thus, the appointment of Jewish ministers by Trudeau both in 1974 and in 1980 is more a reflection of the high quality of people involved than it is of an attempt to represent their faith. Moreover, the geographical and ethnic bases of cabinet distribution dictate that a reasonably constant Catholic/Protestant ratio will prevail anyway. Other fluctuations in the religious distribution of cabinet members probably reflect the random fluctuations characteristic of any small population. It seems ludicrous to think of a modern Prime Minister saying, as Alexander Mackenzie once did: "I may, with feelings of pride, refer to the standing of the members of the Cabinet. . . . In the matter of religious faith there are five Catholics, three members of the Church of England, three Presbyterians, two Methodists, one Congregationalist and one Baptist."[18] It is possible that if a Prime Minister discovered that he had appointed twenty-seven Roman Catholics he might feel a bit embarrassed, but much beyond that the question of religious distribution does not go.[19]

Aside from geographical and ethnic cleavages then, the cabinet is anything but representative. In part, this is a reflection of what cleavages are the most important in Canadian politics, but it is also a reflection of other factors. The vast preponderance of male lawyers, especially in our earlier cabinets, was partly due to the fact that a law career was considered the appropriate one for a young man to follow if he wanted to go into politics, and, of course, it was well understood that no right-thinking young lady would consider a political career at all. The elite nature of present cabinets thus may result to some extent

[18] William Buckingham and George W. Ross, *The Honourable Alexander Mackenzie: His Life and Times* (reissued by Greenwood, New York, 1969), p. 354.
[19] But see Paul Fox, "The Representative Nature of the Canadian Cabinet," in Fox, *Politics: Canada*, 3rd edition (McGraw-Hill Ryerson, Toronto 1970), especially p. 341. Later in his career, even Mackenzie asserted "I have no sympathy personally with the feeling that appears to be growing . . . that every available place should be filled in accordance with the religious views of certain portions of our population." Mackenzie, *Papers*, Vol. I. p. 121.

from the facts that middle and upper-middle-class socialization patterns are more likely to give a person the skills and attitudes essential to the performance of political roles, and that upper-middle-class occupations are more likely to provide the flexibility of hours and careers necessary to politicians.

The Career Patterns of Cabinet Ministers

What do people do in order to point their careers toward a cabinet post? There is a wide variety of possible ways into the cabinet but some career paths are more common than others. Many ministers, particularly in Liberal cabinets since World War II have been welcomed into the cabinet more or less directly from outside parliament, especially from the public service. The most prominent example was Lester Pearson, but others such as Marc Lalonde, "Bud" Drury, and Mitchell Sharp have also been taken directly into the cabinet from government posts or very shortly after leaving such positions. A similar attempt was made in 1975 with Pierre Juneau who was appointed Minister of Communications, after serving as head of the Canadian Radio-Television Commission. He was, however, defeated in his attempt to get elected in Hochelaga, resigned from the cabinet and reappeared in the bureaucracy. It is not uncommon to arrange beforehand that a political candidate will join the cabinet if both the candidate and the party are successful in a general election. [20]

In the early years of Confederation, it was usual for ministers to serve a fairly long apprenticeship in parliament before being appointed to the cabinet. The relative importance of parliament in a minister's activities has decreased steadily over the years, while the importance of administrative, departmental, federal-provincial, and general priority-setting duties has steadily increased. For this reason it has become increasingly the norm to choose ministers not on the basis of parliamentary experience but rather on the basis of policy-making skills, administrative capabilities or, occasionally, tactical skills in electioneering. This has occasionally led to the spectacle of a cabinet which was administratively quite competent but which could not defend its activities before parliament. [21] Cabinets have also been

---

[20] The Clark cabinet of 1979 contained no ministers with civil service backgrounds. In part this is related to the "government party" syndrome of the Liberals described in Chapter 11 and in part to the evident mistrust with which the Progressive Conservative party viewed the public service before it took office.

[21] This point requires some qualification. The Pearson cabinets of 1963-1968 seemed particularly prone to parliamentary pratfalls caused by legislative inexperience. However, by the late 1970s many members of those early Pearson cabinets were still in office, well-experienced in the parliamentary game, and hence, less liable to make

tending to get younger in the post-World War II era. Prior to 1945, the average age of a man on entering the cabinet was 50 years. Pearson's 1965 cabinet had an average age of 47.7 years at appointment, nearly the same as that of the Clark conservatives, while Trudeau's 1970 cabinet ministers averaged only 44.4 years of age at the time of their appointment.

It has occasionally been suggested that in Canadian politics there is no place in public life for a person to go after leaving the cabinet. Thus a defeated minister must go back to private industry in order to earn a living. The result of this, it is alleged, is that ministers are never free of the necessity to look over their shoulder to be certain that they are not offending industry, with the result that they are psychologically (if not ideologically) limited as creative spokesmen for other interests in society.[22] Evidence does not really support this suggestion. Only 26 percent of the cabinet ministers who left their portfolios for any reason from 1867 to 1965 returned to private life. Olsen cites a slight increase in the number of cabinet ministers who exited directly to business in the 1961-1977 period, from 9 percent to 19 percent.[23] But there are far more jobs in politics or public life for former cabinet members than is popularly supposed and Olsen's data show that more than one-third of the ministers who left the cabinet in 1961-1973 took "patronage" opportunities in the Senate, the judiciary, and other order-in-council positions. Another 25 percent stayed active in politics after they left the cabinet.[24]

The Senate, which has little direct role in the policy process has at least one vital indirect role; since Confederation, it has provided a good "pasture" for over 20 percent of retired cabinet ministers. Provided that the party does not go out of power before he or she leaves office, a minister can be fairly well assured of appointment to the Senate. The importance of this role of the Senate must not be underestimated, for it means that ministers need not depend on the goodwill of the private sector for employment when they retire from office. An increase in pensions would not necessarily be a functional alterna-

the spectacular goofs which characterized Liberal cabinets in the 1960s. Most of the holders of major portfolios in the Clark cabinet had previous parliamentary experience and therefore faced little difficulty in defending most of their policies in the House. Their collective tragic flaw was that none of them had any experience in government. In attempting to apply the lessons they had learned in opposition to the problems of being the government, they soon ended up back in opposition.

[22] Porter, *The Vertical Mosaic*, ch. 12, especially pp. 405-411. See also Chapter 16, below.

[23] Olsen, op. cit., pp. 38-39.

[24] Ibid.

tive to the Senate in this respect, since many ex-ministers wish to remain active.

As pointed out above, a lot of ex-ministers simply return to being ordinary MPs before eventually retiring. This happens most commonly when a government is defeated, but Pierre Trudeau did demote several of his former cabinet ministers to the backbenches in 1974, perhaps establishing for Canada a precedent often followed in Great Britain. Another 12 percent went into the judiciary, 10 percent became Lieutenant-Governors, and 10 percent went into some form of public service, usually on a board or commission. Thus, contrary to some analyses, the ex-cabinet minister does have available places in public life when the days in power are over.

The Business Connections of Cabinet Ministers[25]

There have frequently been close connections between cabinet ministers and the Canadian business community. The politics of the immediate post-Confederation era were largely concerned with railways, and cabinet ministers were deeply involved. Thus, six of the original directors of the Grand Trunk Railway were cabinet ministers and in 1885, while he was a cabinet minister, Sir Charles Tupper had no qualms about accepting $100,000 of CPR stock—a gift given in grateful appreciation of his help in selling CPR bonds. Earlier, while acting as Secretary of State, Sir Charles had simultaneously held three paid directorships; yet none of these activities precluded his serving as Prime Minister for a brief stretch in 1896, nor were they held against him at any time.

Laurier continued to be a director of Mutual Life Assurance during his term as Prime Minister,[26] and one of his ministers, Allen Bristol Aylesworth, carried on a private law practice at the same time as he held the Justice portfolio. Sir Robert Borden refused to permit his ministers to maintain outside business connections but Mackenzie King had no such compunctions. His Minister of Justice—Lomer Gouin—was simultaneously a director of the Bank of Montreal, the Cockshutt Plough Co., Montreal City and District Savings Bank, Royal Trust, and the Mount Royal and Mutual Life Assurance Companies.

In 1922 King stated, "In the long run we will gain more in virility in our public life by leaving some matters to conscience and honour

---

[25] See also William A. Matheson, *The Canadian Cabinet and the Prime Minister: A Structural Study,* unpublished Ph.D dissertation, Carleton University, April, 1973, pp. 249-258.

[26] Ibid., p. 252.

rather than by seeking to enforce prohibitions that may be too severe and too drastic."[27] One of the major sources of strength in King's and St. Laurent's cabinets was C. D. Howe who had been, prior to his appointment in 1935, a highly successful construction engineer. The C. D. Howe Co. of which he "disposed" before taking office, continued to receive government business and to employ Howe's son and son-in-law. Mr. St. Laurent's cabinets also contained two ministers who retained private business practices after entering the cabinet; George Prudham was one, and the other was J. J. McCann, who retained a directorship in Guaranty Trust even though his department, National Revenue, often engaged in negotiation with that company. Mr. St. Laurent may have been embarrassed, but the ministers remained unrepentant even under an opposition barrage. In more recent years, however, convention has required ministers to divest themselves of directorships and holdings before taking office, a practice followed for example, by Eric Kierans and Robert Winters in recent Liberal cabinets and by most ministers with such connections in more recent cabinets.

In 1973 the question of conflict of interest in cabinet ministers was broached directly by the Prime Minister in the House of Commons, but no legislation was introduced. Instead, Mr. Trudeau said:

Guidelines are preferable to additional legislation. . . . An element of discretion, to be exercised by a minister on the basis of discussion with the Prime Minister of the day, seems the best solution. . . . A minister will be expected in the future, as is the policy today, to resign any directorships in commercial or other profit-making corporations that he may hold before becoming a minister.[28]

Cabinet ministers are also covered by the provisions of the "Independence of Parliament Act," which would require disclosure of any pecuniary interest or benefit which the member might have in any matter upon which he wished to speak in parliament.[29]

Under the Trudeau administrations ministers were required to place their assets in a trust which would either maintain them exactly as they were at the time the minister was appointed or administer them on a "blind" basis so that the minister could not know what transactions were taking place. Prime Minister Clark issued similar but more stringent guidelines applying not just to ministers but to their immediate families.[30] Assets could be placed only in blind

---

[27] Ibid., p. 253.
[28] Statement on Conflict of Interest, House of Commons, July 18, 1973.
[29] *Members of Parliament and Conflict of Interest*, Information Canada, July, 1973, p. 34.
[30] Conflict of Interest Guidelines for Ministers of the Crown, Privy Council Office, Ottawa, August 1, 1979, mimeo.

trusts. Activities after the minister left cabinet were sharply curtailed. For a period of two years ex-ministers could not serve on Boards of Directors of corporations with which they dealt as ministers, nor could they act on behalf of any such people or corporations or act as a lobbyist. For a period of one year they could not accept jobs with companies with which they formerly dealt or act as consultant to them. The past-employment guidelines were significant innovations since several ex-Trudeau ministers, most notably John Turner and Donald Macdonald, both ex-ministers of Finance, had gone almost directly from cabinet onto the Boards of various corporations and had immediately taken up legal practices, some aspects of which might have contravened the Clark guidelines.

Overall, there may be some dangers inherent in the heavily middle-class professional male bias of this highest decision-making body in the country. It is difficult to make equitable and sympathetic decisions affecting welfare, poverty, abortion, or discrimination if few of the decision makers have ever been welfare cases, or been poor, or pregnant, or suffered discrimination. However, it must also be pointed out that it is not necessary for a person to be the mirror image of the people he represents to be a good representative. It is at least possible that ministers can represent people quite unlike themselves, because "being a good representative" is a learned skill which, in theory at least, may be unconnected with social background. We will return to this issue after we have discussed the representative nature of the bureaucracy.

THE BUREAUCRACY IN CANADA

We have made the point frequently in this book that the Canadian public service is a vital cog in the policy-making machinery of government. Together with the cabinet and the various constellations of interest groups which revolve around any given issue, Canada's senior bureaucrats must be viewed as largely responsible for the shape of public policy in Canada. Who are these people and where do they come from? What are their career patterns and their socio-economic backgrounds?

The Ethnic Distribution of Bureaucrats

No one will disagree, I am sure, with the notion that the execution of public policy in Canada deserves the best minds and the highest executive, administrative and professional skills available in the land. The Civil Service Act recognizes this requirement and makes provision for its fulfillment. However it is an unfortunate fact that the Public Service of Canada has, up to now, been unable to attract and retain its fair share of competent persons reflecting the two cultures of Canada. We have not succeeded in recruiting, particularly for intermediate and senior positions, a sufficient number of well qualified citizens from French Canada, and it is the Commission's view that this vacuum is detrimental to the public interest. [31]

This statement, made by the chairman of the Public Service Commission is a reflection of the concern which federal leaders felt, and feel, at the small number of French Canadians in senior positions in the federal bureaucracy. The situation has undergone some rather sharp fluctuations in the past. For example, the proportion of French Canadians in highly responsible positions in the public service declined steadily from some 25 percent in 1918 to 8.1 percent in 1949. [32] Paradoxically, the cause of the decline during this period, and hence of many subsequent problems, was a rationalization of recruiting methods and the introduction of a merit system of recruitment and promotion in 1918. Under the old patronage system, French-Canadian cabinet ministers and Members of Parliament were allowed to appoint their ethnic *confrères* to civil-service positions. Under the "merit" system largely English-speaking boards tended to equate merit with facility in the English language, and French representation in the federal bureaucracy fell drastically. Nathan Keyfitz has pointed out:

There is a tendency for the English to judge the French not by the breadth of their vision, nor by their ability to communicate, but by their mastery of the intricacies of English usage and vocabulary and even by their pronunciation of English. Since the French, in judging one another attach very little weight to speaking English at all and none whatsoever to whether it is spoken with a good accent, they will, as far as this element is concerned, arrange one another in a different order of merit from that in which English speakers make the choices. (The English) not only choose too few French but they also do not choose the right ones. [33]

The general response of the federal government has been to redefine the concept of merit somewhat to make ability in both of Canada's official languages a component of merit in a way it has not been in the past. Thus many of the lower- and middle-rank jobs in the

---

[31] J. J. Carson, "The New Role of the Civil Service Commission," an outline of remarks to the Federal Institute of Management, Ottawa, Feb., 1966. Quoted in V. S. Wilson, *Staffing in the Canadian Federal Bureaucracy,* unpublished Ph.D. dissertation, Queen's University, 1970.

[32] Chambre de commerce du District de Montréal, *Mémoire soumis à la commission royal d'enquête sur le service civil fédéral,* avril, 1946.

[33] Nathan Keyfitz, "Canadians and Canadiens," *Queen's Quarterly,* vol. 77, 1963, no. 2, p. 174. The presence of Francophones on the selection boards has improved the situation somewhat since 1963, but there is still some tendency for the English to rate the French by the ability of the latter to speak English.

public service, and all of the upper-rank jobs have been classified as requiring some level of capability in both official languages. The level of capability varies according to the job itself but no one can be brought in or moved to fill any of the 2000 or so top jobs unless he or she is either already bilingual or willing to undergo continuous training to become so.

The problem of ensuring adequate high-level Francophone participation, then, has proven quite difficult. In part it stems from the fact that Ottawa is still an English-speaking milieu, hardly calculated to make a Francophone feel at home. In part it stems from the attachment which many, if not most, young, highly-educated Francophone Quebeckers have felt for the *séparatiste* cause or for working for "their" government in Quebec. In part it is simply a reflection of salary differences since public service salaries in Quebec at the executive level are considerably higher than elsewhere in Canada.

Despite all, however it is significant that the distribution by ethnic origin of members of the Canadian bureaucratic elite is not as bad as it has been.[34] In 1953 John Porter found that fully 84 percent of federal senior bureaucrats were British and 13 percent were French. By contrast, in 1973 Olsen discovered that the percentage of British origins had declined to 65 percent and the percentage of French had risen to 24 percent. While French Canadians make up 28 percent of the population (as of 1971) so that their representation in the senior bureaucracy is slightly less than proportional, the fact remains that in thirty years this situation has improved vastly. Unfortunately the non-charter groups, while better represented than before, are still only 11 percent of the senior bureaucracy and 27 percent of the population.

The Socioeconomic Background of Bureaucrats

While there have been few cabinet ministers with less than middle-class background, a significant proportion of the middle levels of the federal bureaucracy has either a farming or a working-class background. Indeed, the public service appears to be an important path of upward mobility in Canada—provided that somewhere along the way our potential Horatio Alger manages to obtain a university degree. However, Olsen's data indicate that the bureaucratic elite of 1980 is more middle class than was the comparable elite studied by

---

[34] See: Olsen, op. cit., p. 79. See also: C. Beattie, J. Désy and S. Longstaff, "Bureaucratic Careers: Anglophones and Francophones in the Canadian Public Service," Internal Report for the Royal Commission on Bilingualism and Biculturalism, p. 211.

John Porter in 1953.[35] Today, nearly 75 percent of that elite can be characterized as having middle-class origins.

As mentioned above, a university education is extremely important in climbing to higher decision-making levels in the federal service. In 1967, some 81 percent of the people at "Senior Officer" levels (director, director-general, and assistant deputy minister) had obtained at least one degree,[36] and Olsen shows that in 1973 fully 92 percent of officers in these positions were in this category.[37] Many of them in 1967 had more than one degree and the proportion with a postgraduate degree has been increasing since. Olsen reports an increase from 43.6 percent in 1953 to 61.2 percent in 1973.[38] The particular university one has attended is not of much significance. Some 18 percent of top-level public servants attended the University of Toronto, 8 percent McGill, and 7 percent Queen's University; these figures are close to the proportional size of these universities in the 1940s and 1950s when such people were students.

There has been a great deal of discussion about whether the Canadian public service, like the cabinet, should mirror fairly accurately the regional cleavages in Canada. Whatever the theoretical merits of representative bureaucracy, the fact is that the federal bureaucracy has traditionally exhibited a strong bias, in its middle levels, towards those who were born in Ontario, particularly those born in Ottawa. Some 36 percent of Canadians lived in Ontario in 1971; yet 48.3 percent of the middle- and upper-rank civil servants in 1965 were born in Ontario, and 23 percent grew up in the Ottawa-Hull region which had only 2 percent of the nation's population.[39] Among French-Canadian, middle-rank civil servants, fully 43 percent grew up in Ottawa-Hull. This bias is explicable. People tend to stay where they are brought up. Moreover, in the Ottawa-Hull area, a civil service job is looked upon as a legitimate form of work, whereas this is not always true in other areas of the country. Nonetheless, this heavy centralist bias is regrettable and may in fact lead to a lack of sympathy toward "peripheral" Canadians when decisions are being made. It is perhaps difficult to create policies appropriate for the West or the Maritimes if the policy maker knows these regions only from an airplane window.

---

[35] Olsen, op. cit., p. 79.
[36] P. J. Chartrand and K. L. Pond, "A Study of Executive Career Paths in the Public Service of Canada," Public Personnel Association, Chicago, 1970.
[37] Olsen, op. cit., p. 79.
[38] Ibid.
[39] More recent data is not available in published sources although the public service commission does keep a record of such information.

One of the most important biases in the makeup of the senior levels of the public service is the underrepresentation of women. Table 14-4 indicates that the proportion of women diminishes drastically as one moves up the salary (and responsibility) scale in the federal public service. Thus, while women make up over 80 percent of the lowest-paid workers in the public service, they make up only 5.8 percent of the two highest categories. Since the educational level of women in the public service is not vastly different from that of men, one would have to infer a significant bias against the recruitment of women into the most important bureaucratic positions. The suspicion is increased when one notes that in 1980, among the most senior positions in the federal bureaucracy (at the deputy-ministerial level), there is just one woman.

The Career Patterns of Bureaucrats

There is a great deal of switching between private and public careers among top-level bureaucrats. Among public servants at the deputy-minister level, a full 80 percent followed a private-public career pattern, working first outside the public service.[40]

The overall picture which emerges of the typical senior executive in the federal government is one of a thoroughly upper-middle-class male. In 1980 his salary was likely about $46,000. He was 50 years old and had at least a B.A., most likely in a social or management science. He was bilingual—at least by the standards of the federal government, which is to say that if he was Anglophone he likely read French very well, understood most of what was said in French and could, at the cost of some offense to his listeners' ears and French syntax, make himself understood. There was about one chance in four that he was Francophone and this chance decreased the higher his rank. He was more likely to have come from Central Canada than from the periphery.

What motivates a person to go into a civil service career? At the middle levels, such a career can be very attractive. Salaries are competitive with salaries in industry. The work is varied, and there are many opportunities for advancement in many different types of work. At the top level, however, motivations may well be different. Salaries, while hardly at starvation level, are far lower than those of

---

[40] V. S. Wilson, "Staffing in the Canadian Federal Bureaucracy," ch. 8 of Professor Wilson's thesis has been very helpful in writing this section. See also P. J. Chartrand and K. L. Pond, op. cit., pp. 47-75. Data has been updated by referring to the annual report of the Public Service Commission, produced annually by the PSC, Ottawa.

Table 14-4
SEX AND LINGUISTIC DISTRIBUTIONS OF FEDERAL PUBLIC SERVICE POSITIONS BY SALARY, 1978

Salary in 1978	Men	Women	Francophones	Percentage Who Are Women	Percentage Who Are Francophones*
Under 9,500	1,240	6,038	1,368	83.0	28.7
9,500-13,999	42,237	43,708	22,760	50.9	29.00
14,000-18,999	68,610	23,237	22,972	25.3	26.5
19,000-23,999	23,376	4,446	6,514	16.0	24.9
24,000-28,999	12,148	1,445	2,954	10.6	23.0
29,000-33,999	8,174	423	1,385	4.9	17.0
34,000-38,999	4,437	107	561	2.4	13.4
39,000-49,999	2,053	80	257	3.8	13.2
50,000 and over	48	1	8	2.0	20.0
Totals	162,323	79,485	58,779	32.9	26.3

* Does not include the 29,730 employees whose first official language was not specified.

Source: Public Service Commission of Canada, Annual Report, 1978, Ottawa, 1979.

top executives in the private sector.[41] The responsibilities are often huge and the work load crushing. At such levels, other compensations—such as the opportunity to actually do something for the public welfare, the chance to work on huge programs of nation-wide importance, and love of the power that derives from this opportunity may well be the primary motivations.

Even at that, the motivation is sometimes difficult to comprehend. The ability to exert much control over policy is constrained by the large number of actors involved, and even the ability to manage one's own department is severely constrained by the impositions of central agencies and of public sector unions and hiring and firing procedures. Given all of these factors, together with the relatively low esteem in which the public service is held by the public, it often requires a strong sense of public duty to ignore opportunities elsewhere.[42]

The term "mandarin" no longer fits the senior civil servant so well as it once did. Through the 1960s and 1970s there has been a growing heterogeneity in the ethnic origins and early career patterns of Canada's senior bureaucrats. The situation has changed then, since 1953, when Porter found senior civil servants to be a rather collegial group with enough in common that each one knew all the others and shared a value system so completely that decisions could be transmitted by a sort of osmosis, or "group think"!

There are no comprehensive data on provincial public servants.[43] In the larger provinces, public-service posts are well paid, and the higher-level civil servants in Quebec, Ontario, and perhaps B.C. and Alberta may be no less important as factors in national decision making than their federal counterparts. On the other hand, holding a deputy-minister post in a Maritime province may give relatively little real power to the incumbent, when viewed in national perspective, and the financial rewards may be commensurately smaller. Provincial civil services differ quite markedly from one another in their makeup, and as yet research has not gone much farther than to point out that

---

[41] It may seem strange to rate the salaries of deputy ministers, who in 1981 could earn up to $84,000 per year as relatively low. However, when compared with corporation presidents, who usually head organizations which are smaller than government departments but who frequently earn six-figure salaries, they are indeed low. The comparison with the salaries paid professional athletes is even more discrepant.

[42] An alternative interpretation is that for the calibre of person attracted to these positions under current circumstances, alternative possibilities are not available elsewhere. To the extent that is true, that is most unfortunate for Canadians, given the importance of the public sector in Canada.

[43] For data which include a sample of provincial bureaucrats see Olsen, op. cit. However his data do not isolate provincial elites for specific analysis.

these differences exist.[44] It is unlikely that their socioeconomic makeup differs very greatly from that of the federal bureaucracy.[45]

Just as it was appropriate to raise the question of the extent to which a cabinet which is not truly socially representative can be responsive to social needs, so too it is appropriate to raise that question with respect to the bureaucracy. There is a large body of literature on the issue.[46] Its conclusions are tentative and sometimes even contradictory. Indeed there are two quite constant but opposed themes which run through the literature on representative bureaucracy. One suggests that bureaucracies are far from capable of acting representatively and major administrative controls are therefore essential while the other suggests that bureaucracies can indeed be responsive to the needs of their clientele and that the "administrative culture" is in fact a quite faithful reproduction of the broader political culture.[47] In Canada, the evidence suggests that the socioeconomic backgrounds of the most senior bureaucrats would make this latter interpretation unlikely to apply but there is also more concrete evidence based upon attitude and behaviour. Lee Sigelman and William Vanderbok suggest: "(Our) findings provide precious little empirical support for the notion that careerist civil servants in Canada are more broadly responsive than legislators. . . . Almost invariably it was the legislators, not the bureaucrats who were more favourably disposed to the needs of the less favoured and advantaged."[48] Sigelman and Vanderbok also find that the senior bureaucracy is less representative of the Canadian social fabric than are the legislators so it is possible that their lesser responsiveness is caused in part by this factor.

MEMBERS OF PARLIAMENT

Among the most visible of Canada's political elites are the Members of Parliament. While their role in deciding what policies the govern-

---

[44] Porter, *The Vertical Mosaic*, ch. 14, pp. 417-457. See also Robert Presthus, op. cit.

[45] There is some information on backgrounds to be gleamed from the pages of D. Bellamy, J. H. Pammett, and D. C. Rowat, *The Provincial Political Systems* (Methuen, Toronto, 1976). On provincial MPs see H. D. Clarke, Richard Price, and Robert Krause, "Backbenchers" in op. cit., pp. 214-236.

[46] For Canadian literature see Lee Singleman and W. G. Vanderbok, "Legislators, Bureaucrats, and Canadian Democracy," *CJPS*, x:3, September 1977, pp. 615-623 and Kenneth Kernaghan, "Representative Bureaucracy," *CPA*, 21:4, winter 1978, p. 489 ff. Singleman and Vanderbok also provide a valuable succinct review of the literature.

[47] The first point of view derives from Herman Finer, "Administrative Responsibility in Democratic Government," *Public Administration Review*, 1, 1940-41, 335-350. The second derives from Carl Friedrich, "Public Policy and the Nature of Administrative Responsibility," in Friedrich and E. G. Mason (eds.), *Public Policy* (Cambridge, Harvard Press, 1940), 3-24.

[48] Singleman and Vanderbok, op. cit., pp. 621, 619.

ment will promulgate is sometimes marginal, they are nonetheless the most visible link between the public and the rest of Canada's political elites. Because they have important symbolic significance in addition to whatever policy role they may play, it is important to ask ourselves what they "look like" with respect to ethnicity, socio-economic status, career patterns, and the like.

The Socioeconomic Background of MPs[49]

Since Canadian MPs are elected from geographically based consti-tuencies which are apportioned among the provinces roughly in accordance with population, there is no point in describing the pro-vincial distribution of MPs. Nor is there as much point now as there once was in discussing the rural-urban distribution of federal MPs, since decennial redistributions of seats by impartial electoral bound-aries commissions has at least partially rectified the huge rural over-representation of MPs which persisted until the late 1950s.

The ethnic distribution of MPs shows a heavy bias towards the two charter ethnic groups. Thus 94 percent of all MPs since 1940 have been of either British or French descent while only 78 percent of the general population is either British or French. The distribution between the English and French groups has been quite equitable since French MPs normally represent French ridings. It is unfortunate that in the past there have not been included within the ranks of MPs more "other" Canadians. In a body which is as symbolically impor-tant as the House of Commons, that sort of representation might be quite valuable. The elections of the 1970s however have shown some increase in the number of non-charter group candidates, MPs, and even cabinet ministers. The religious distribution of MPs parallels fairly closely that of the general public. Thus, from 1940 to 1972 some 56 percent of MPs were Protestant, 41 percent Catholic, and 3 percent "other." The corresponding population percentages were 50, 45, and 5.

It is when we turn to the class backgrounds of MPs that we find the greatest discrepancies between the public and their representatives. Table 14-5 indicates that the occupational status of MPs, though not

---

[49] We have drawn heavily in this section on D. J. Falcone, unpublished Ph.D. disserta-tion, Duke University, 1974. See also D. Hoffman and N. Ward, *Bilingualism and Biculturalism in the Canadian House of Commons*, Royal Commission on Bilingualism and Biculturalism, Document No. 3 (Queen's Printer, Ottawa, 1970), especially ch. 2; Dennis Forcese and John DeVries, "Occupational and Electoral Success in Canada; the 1974 Election," *CRSA*, 14(3) 1977, 331-340; and Dennis Forcese, *The Canadian Class Structure*.

as high as that of cabinet ministers, is nonetheless quite high. Only about 14 percent of the general public hold occupations which could be classified "high-status" but 65 percent of MPs and 81 percent of cabinet ministers did so before entering politics. Although lawyers make up much less than 1 percent of the Canadian population, 41 percent of all new MPs elected between World War II and the 1965 election were lawyers. Since Confederation the proportion of lawyers in the House of Commons has risen steadily from 19 percent before 1895 to 25 percent between 1895 and 1945, and to nearly 40 percent, since then.[50] Lawyers appear especially likely to be election winners—the proportion of winners who are lawyers normally exceeds the proportion of candidates who are lawyers. The proportion of lawyers among winners in the 1974 election dropped to under 25 percent but it is too soon to determine if this presages a trend.[51]

Table 14-5

OCCUPATIONAL STATUS OF CABINET MINISTERS, MPs, AND THE PUBLIC, SHOWING THE PERCENTAGE OF EACH GROUP IN "HIGH STATUS" OCCUPATIONS PRIOR TO ENTERING POLITICS

Period	Cabinet Ministers	MPs	Public
1867-1904	80.4%	71.8%	8.6%
1905-1939	83.0	73.8	11.0
1940-1979	81.0	65.0	15.0

Source: 1867-1968, D. J. Falcone, Ph.D. dissertation, Duke University, 1974; 1968-1979 Dennis Forcese and J. Devries, Occupational & Electoral Success in Canada," and *Parliamentary Guides.*

As one might expect, the educational level of MPs is correspondingly much higher than that of the public at large. Since 1940 some 70 percent of MPs have been to university, compared with a general population figure of less than 10 percent.[52] Moreover, MPs have tended to come disproportionately from homes with a relatively high socioeconomic status. Some 16 percent of MPs elected in 1962 had fathers who were professionals, whereas in 1921 (when most of these

[50] Norman Ward, *The Canadian House of Commons: Representation* (University of Toronto Press, Toronto, 1950), p. 132. A. Kornberg, *Canadian Legislative Behaviour* (Holt, Rinehart and Winston, New York, 1967), p. 43, and data supplied by Professor R. R. March.
[51] Kornberg, *Canadian Legislative Behaviour*, p. 44. For 1974 figures see Forcese and DeVries, op. cit.
[52] D. J. Falcone, op. cit.

fathers would have been working), only 6 percent of the labour force could have been classified as professional. Thus, Canadian MPs, like their legislative counterparts elsewhere in the Western world, are territorially but not socially representative. Table 14-6 summarizes the occupational and educational backgrounds of MPs in 1978 and compares them to American Senators and candidates for the British House of Commons.

Table 14-6

OCCUPATION AND LEVEL OF EDUCATION OF CANADIAN MPs, AMERICAN SENATORS, AND CANDIDATES FOR THE BRITISH HOUSE OF COMMONS

Occupation and Education	Canadian MPs	American Senators	Candidates for British Commons
Professional	60%	70%	55%
Proprietor-Manager	26	26	28
Farmer	7	4	6
Blue collar or clerical	7	—	12
College or University	72	85	63
Less than College	28	15	37

Source: Canada: *Parliamentary Guide* 1978; U.S.: *Congressional Quarterly*, 96th Congress, v. 37 No. 3, p. 81; Britain; Colin Mellors, *The British M.P.* (Saxon House, London, 1978), pp. 43-4, 65.

The Career Patterns of MPs

Aside from what has already been said about the occupational backgrounds of MPs, what can one assert about their political careers? Are most of them rank amateurs in politics or do they have significant amounts of political experience before coming to the House of Commons?

Both Kornberg and Ward have found that a larger proportion of MPs did have considerable political experience before they were elected to the House of Commons. In the period between 1921 and 1954, 31 percent had been members of various provincial legislative assemblies, and 5 percent had been in a provincial cabinet. However, since Confederation the proportion of MPs with prior experience in provincial or municipal politics has been steadily declining. In the parliament elected in 1887, which was fairly typical of other parliaments of that time, only 34 percent of MPs had no prior experience in provincial or municipal politics. By 1945, the proportion of MPs without prior experience had risen to 60 percent, and by 1978 it had become the relatively rare exception for MPs to have experience in other legislative bodies.[53] Fewer than 30 percent of MPs in the 28th Parliament had been candidates for public office and fewer than one-tenth of current MPs have ever sat in provincial legislatures.[54] The federal House of Commons no longer seems to be considered the summit of a political career. Indeed at least since the turn of the century the concept of a hierarchy of political careers in Canada with the House of Commons at the top has not pertained. A lack of experience in other legislative bodies cannot necessarily be equated with a complete lack of political experience. Many Canadian MPs have served a political apprenticeship in their own party organizations but this does not provide the same type of experience as formal elected office.[55]

Not least among the disincentives of political life in Canada is the difficulty many MPs find in returning to private life.[56] A few MPs trickle into the Senate, the judiciary or to the various commissions and boards of the public service. For the most part, however, defeated MPs return to private life or retire. Unless professional qualifications are held it may be quite difficult for an ex-MP to find private sector employment since it is difficult to suggest for what private sector jobs a parliamentary career provides pertinent experience. Stories of MPs requiring two years to find employment are not uncommon and this problem suggests another reason for the heavy concentration of professionals in parliament and presumably in the U.S. and British legislatures as well.

In spite of this problem, members of the 25th Parliament were found to have a relatively high level of satisfaction with their jobs:

75 percent said there were no other public offices in which they were interested; 9 percent were interested in judgeships or appointments to the Senate; 7 per cent wanted to return to provincial politics; 6 percent said they would like to be the mayors of cities in which they resided and an additional 3 per cent said they were interested in other public offices but they would not reveal what these were.[57]

Allen Kornberg attributes this satisfaction to a number of factors, but it is possible that the major one was that he was interviewing just

---

[53] Ward, *The Canadian House of Commons: Representation*, p. 123. Current data is from *Parliamentary Guides*.

[54] D. J. Falcone, op. cit.

[55] Kornberg, *Canadian Legislative Behaviour*, pp. 54-55.

[56] Ward, *The Canadian House of Commons: Representation*, p. 145, has a tabulation of the careers of ex-MPs up to 1935. His data, however, must be interpreted carefully for he has apparently not separated ex-ministers from other MPs. The ex-ministers, of course, get a disproportionate share of the "plums."

[57] Kornberg, *Canadian Legislative Behaviour*, p. 35; used by permission of Holt, Rinehart and Winston, Inc.

after an election. Whether legislators would feel the same way half-way through a parliament or with an election approaching is more problematical. Backbench MPs are frequently quoted as expressing considerable dissatisfaction with their jobs and in particular with the amount of influence they can exert over the making of policy.[58]

It is perhaps paradoxical, in view of the highly public nature of their jobs and the need to gain support from a broad spectrum of voters, that MPs can be so unlike the people they represent. They are representative of the French and English divisions in Canadian society and they are quite representative with respect to religion and geography, but there the resemblance ends. MPs are not at all representative of whatever class differences exist in Canadian society. Some writers have suggested that this may be caused by the deferential nature of Canadian society compared to, for example, the United States or Australia.[59] However, the "deferential" British regularly elect approximately 15 percent union leaders and working-class people to their parliament, while, as Table 14-6 indicates, our allegedly non-deferential southern neighbours elect congressmen almost exclusively from upper socioeconomic groups. Perhaps the easiest explanation of the non-representative nature of our parliamentary elite is simply the lack of a working-class party in Canada comparable in size to the British or Australian Labour parties.

THE JUDICIAL ELITE IN CANADA

Judges are naturally an elite group because of the relatively few judgeships that are available in Canada, and because of the special qualifications one must have to become a judge. Moreover because of the principle of judicial independence which dominates our entire legal process, the mode of appointment of judges and the operation of the judicial process may serve to exacerbate the elitist nature of our courts.

The qualifications of a judge in Canada (and here we are restricting our discussion to the superior and county court judges who are appointed by the Governor General in Council according to Section 96 of the BNA Act) are basically that he or she must have been a member of the bar of one of the provinces for at least ten years. This means automatically that the person appointed must have had at

---

[58] See M. Atkinson, unpublished Ph.D. dissertation, Carleton University, 1976, and R. Jackson and M. Atkinson, *The Canadian Legislative System* (Macmillan, Toronto, 1975).

[59] R. Alford, *Party and Society, passim.*

least some undergraduate training in a university, likely a bachelor's degree, and a law degree. Furthermore to be a member of the bar of a province an individual must have a law degree from a recognized institution, must have undergone a period of articling, must have taken the provincial "Bar Admission Course" which is usually approximately six months' duration, and must have passed the bar admission examinations which are set, administered, and marked by the provincial law society. In other words in the same manner that the senior bureaucrats are an elite by virtue of educational level, so the judiciary in Canada is an elite by virtue of the fact that explicit educational requirements are a prerequisite for even being considered for a sanctioned place in the professional pool from which judges are exclusively selected.

When we move a step further to consider the sorts of people who get to law school in the first place, as one might expect, the recruitment for these institutions is disproportionately from the upper and middle classes of Canadian society. As Dennis Olsen points out, "Lawyers in Canada are certainly not drawn from a representative cross section of the population. . . . The class and ethnic biases that will ultimately find their expression in the composition of the high courts have their beginning in the selection for law school."[60] Although there has been a tendency on the part of many law schools in recent years to attempt to include people from non-charter ethnic groups, people from working class or farm backgrounds, and persons other than the sons and daughters of lawyers, Olsen goes on to point out that the subsequent career patterns of lawyers still reflect ethnic and socioeconomic biases. He finds that the "plum" legal positions such as partnerships in corporations and specialization in the more lucrative subdisciplines of the profession tend to be dominated by charter group and upper-middle-class Canadians. The only significant exceptions to these generalizations would seem to be women and Jews who are making definite inroads into the legal profession in Canada.[61]

Reinforcing the heavily selective process of recruitment to the legal profession in Canada is the even more selective process which fills the approximately 600 federally appointed judgeships. Because of the principle of judicial independence judges are appointed until age seventy-five, are given a fixed salary by parliament, and are placed in a position where they are expected literally to be "above" the temptations that face mere mortals. For the most part judges cannot be fired,

[60] Olsen, op. cit., p. 44.
[61] Ibid.

except for gross crimes or misdemeanors. Even blatantly biased judgments or incompetence are not sufficient cause for dismissal, although our system of appeals does provide a litigant (with sufficient cash) the opportunity of overturning biased or incompetent judgments in a higher court. Because judges are going to hold office "for the duration," therefore, the process of appointing them in the first place is very important and the responsibility for such appointments lies *de facto* with the federal cabinet particularly the Prime Minister and the Minister of Justice.[62]

Considering the fact that it is members of the political elite who select the members of the judicial elite, it seems likely that even the best intentioned Minister of Justice is going to automatically and unconsciously lean toward a personal view of what constitutes a "good judge." This means in the long run that the appointments to the bench will tend to reflect the same class and ethnic biases as the political elite. As Olsen states, "the political elites are looking for someone very much like themselves,"[63] when they select judges.

Where the largest amount of criticism has been levelled at the judicial appointment process is in the area of the political affiliation of the appointees. Historically, certainly the members of the bench have been selected unabashedly from the ranks of the party faithful. Certainly there has been a consistent attempt to select good legal minds for the judgeships, but all things being equal, a Liberal government will select a "good Liberal lawyer" over a "good Conservative lawyer" most of the time. While there is some indication that the patronage dimension of judicial selection and appointment is declining— Porter found in 1960 that 57 percent of appointments[64] had a previous party affiliation and Olsen found that figure had slipped to 42 percent in 1973[65]—a judgeship is still a handy reward to be doled out by grateful Prime Ministers to defeated or "worn out" cabinet ministers or to deserving supporters. Since the late 1960s the practice has been for the federal Justice Minister to submit potential appointees to a committee of the Canadian Bar Association. The aim of this practice was to ensure that legal qualifications rather than political ones would be the critical determinants of who might become a judge in the Canadian courts. This procedure has likely worked fairly well, for in fact there have been an increasing number of non-partisan or even "wrong party" appointments to the bench since that time. The critics

[62] See Chapter 7.
[63] Olsen, op. cit.
[64] Porter, op. cit., p. 415.
[65] Olsen, op. cit., p. 45.

of the procedure however argue that the political elites and the elite of the legal profession which dominates the CBA are virtually identical in terms of their class and ethnic origins, and the end result of the procedure is simply that "some degree of control over judicial appointments has now shifted from politicians to the legal profession; that is, in reality, from lawyers wearing political garb to lawyers wearing legal garb."[66] Without judging the overall impact of the involvement of the profession in the appointment of judges, however, it is clear that such a procedure has reduced and may well prove to reduce quite drastically in the future the extent to which the power of judicial appointment is to be used simply as a partisan patronage power.

Beyond the claims of partisanship in the appointment process, all the critics of the elitism of the Canadian judiciary can say is that the class and ethnic origins of the judges is reflective of the biases in the legal profession itself; the judiciary in Canada is, indeed, dominated by ethnic charter group and middle-class Canadians. Moreover the gains that have been made by women in the legal profession generally in the past few years are not reflected in the appointments to the bench; judgeships in Canada, except for very rare exceptions, are a male preserve.

Finally, while the focus of this chapter is more on *who* the elites in Canada are than how the Canadian system helps them to maintain their hegemony, we must say a few words about the elitist nature of the legal process itself. The problem here is, in part, that it costs money to use our court systems. Lawyers' fees alone are beyond the means of many Canadians, and the legal process, especially in higher level courts, is dominated exclusively by members of the legal profession. This means that the lower-class Canadians and the non-charter ethnic group Canadians tend to dominate the docket in the lower courts and middle-class Canadians tend to dominate the business of the higher courts.

This stratification is in part because the jurisdiction in civil matters is determined by the amount of money involved.[67] It is therefore natural in some respects for the middle-class Canadians to be before the higher courts simply because they, by definition, have more money. Similarly, there are definite correlations between minor criminal offences which are dealt with by lower courts, and non-charter ethnicity (particularly native people), lower socioeconomic status and "urban core" place of residence. Thus while we could see the legal

[66] Ibid., p. 47.
[67] See Chapter 7.

system as *reflective* of serious social, economic, and ethnic inequities in Canadian society, it is difficult to lay the blame for these problems at the feet of the judiciary.

On the other hand when we turn to *appeal* cases, we find that such use of the courts, except in serious criminal offences, is almost exclusively restricted to more privileged Canadians. Here the legal system can be blamed, for the access to the avenues of appeal in our system are virtually closed to all but the middle-class Canadian by reasons of cost. Even "legal aid" programs which are in operation in all provinces, and which are aimed at providing free access to legal advice to those who cannot afford it, only begin to solve the problem. As studies cited by Dennis Olsen show, many potential users of the legal aid system don't even know of its existence[68] and those that have discovered the program often find that they end up being represented by a very "green" (if earnest and well meaning) recent graduate of the Bar Admissions Course. Legal aid therefore is a step in the right direction but it is only a step. Ultimately we have to develop better devices for ensuring that all Canadians of all ethnic and socioeconomic groups have equivalent access to the courts.

The verdict on the elite nature of our judicial system is very difficult to arrive at. The involvement of the legal profession in the appointment of "Section 96" judges has helped to reduce the amount of partisan bias in the selection process, and any further evolution in this direction can only improve the credibility if not the operational effectiveness of the courts. However, it is also argued that the judiciary in Canada is an educational elite; this point is incontrovertible. On the other hand to have a non-elite judiciary in a system built on the premise of judicial independence is likely impossible. Most Canadians would agree that it is better to be judged by a well-trained professional who is paid to be an *objective* arbiter of disputes and not an advocate of any particular point of view. This means that judgeships will continue to be limited to members of the legal profession, and that any significant improvement in the ethnic and class representativeness of the Canadian judiciary will depend upon democratizing the law schools and the legal profession in general, and not in structural changes to the legal system.

CONCLUSIONS

There is no such thing as a "politically irrelevant" elite, for elites are normally defined as those who have a disproportionate share of

[68] Olsen, op. cit.

power in society, and such people will naturally be involved in the authoritative allocation of a society's resources. John Porter has suggested that many of Canada's elites are interconnected; many are members of more than one sub-elite and they cannot help but carry ideas from one to another. Thus, for example, the late Robert Winters, who finished a fairly close second to Pierre Trudeau in the Liberal party leadership race of 1968 moved back and forth freely between the political world and the business world, where he was president of such corporations as Rio Algom and Brascan. In a different vein, Jean Marchand moved from being president of the Confederation of National Trade Unions, Quebec's largest grouping of labour unions, to being a powerful member of the federal cabinet. Pierre Trudeau provides an excellent example of inter-elite connections. His father was a millionaire, which by most reckoning puts him in the economic elite; he edited the small but influential periodical, *Cité Libre*, which puts him in the communications elite; he lectured at the University of Montreal law school, edited a seminal book entitled *La Grève de l'amiante*, and wrote many articles, which qualify him as part of the intellectual elite; and he has certainly managed to get into the political elite.

In *The Vertical Mosaic*, Professor Porter identified not only political and bureaucratic elites, which were approximately the same ones as those discussed here, but also labour, communications, and religious elites. Porter was able to show that the political and economic elites, and to a lesser extent the religious and communications elites, shared common backgrounds such as those described in this chapter. Wallace Clement in the *Canadian Corporate Elite*, has more recently found that the social background of elites in the mid-1970s was not greatly different than what Porter found in the 1960s although the proportion of United States citizens in what he defined as the Canadian corporate elite had increased greatly. This material did not show, although it implied, that those common backgrounds led to common attitudes and values which would lead to similar policy predilections. Thus Porter was not able to show directly whether or not the elites at the top of each segment of Canadian society were likely to agree among themselves because they were elite, or were likely to disagree because they "represented" different segments of Canadian society which might easily have differing interests.

The evidence suggests at least the possibility of a shared overall attitude toward issues among elites combined with a certain amount of inter-elite conflict over specific issues. Robert Presthus has demonstrated in *Elite Accommodation in Canadian Politics*, that the common factors in the social backgrounds of various elites have led at least the political, bureaucratic, and industrial elites to have many attitudes in common.[69] The members of Presthus' elites were hardly intensely ideological creatures; their most cherished common ethic was perhaps best characterized as "managerial" or pragmatic. The process of accommodation among them was lubricated primarily by agreement on this managerial ethic.[70] But commitment to the managerial ethic—that the problem is not to provide sweeping social changes but rather to maintain and operate more efficiently the system we already have—is certainly enough to provide a basis for interaction and above all provides a decision-making atmosphere that will most often favour the status quo over radical social change. When that interaction is further facilitated by common backgrounds and overlapping membership in clubs, on boards of directors, boards of governors, or whatever, we find in Canada no less than in any other developed nation the framework for the politics which Presthus characterizes as "elite accommodation," which others have described as consociational, what the neo-Marxists call "class injustice," and which we earlier suggested might be identified as having strong corporatist threads.

There are elements of both heterogeneity and homogeneity among Canada's politically relevant elites. Regional, French-English, and religious cleavages are, on the whole, quite faithfully reflected in the composition of elites; occupational, educational, and general class differences are not. The upper socioeconomic class bias is most marked in the family backgrounds of cabinet ministers and perhaps least marked among bureaucrats, although even there the educational requirements eliminate the vast majority of Canadians from contention and ensure that whatever the background, the senior bureaucracy is thoroughly upper middle class by the time it takes office.

The temptation is to conclude from this analysis that the political process in Canada is bound to favour middle- and upper-class Canadians. When one adds the evidence presented earlier concerning political participation and political socialization and the information on interest group activity and when one looks at the distributional impact of most Canadian public policy, that evidence begins to appear overwhelming. A very large body of Canadians may be placed by the combination of these circumstances and the nature of the political system in a "subject" orientation toward the outputs they receive. Cut off by their lack of education, money, membership in interest groups, or representation among decision makers, they have little

---

[69] Presthus, *Elite Accommodation*, ch. 11.
[70] Ibid., p. 344.

real control at all over what emerges from "their" political system and less possibility of achieving the lion's share of benefits from it.

On the other hand there are some small cracks in the elite monolith, which the tough-minded critics of the system such as Olsen dismiss as "exceptions," as conscious attempts on the part of the dominant class to renew itself, or as cynical gestures to legitimize the status quo.[71] If we choose to be more optimistic we can point to the fact that a few non-charter group Canadians are "making the team" of the state elite—Haidasz, Hnatyshyn, Mazankowski, Paproski, Danson, Gray, and Kaplan have made it to the cabinet; Reisman, two Ostrys, Shoyama and Rasminsky among others have made it to the mandarinate; the Chief Justice of the Supreme Court of Canada is a Jew; the Governor General is of German descent; Barrett and Schreyer were non-charter group provincial premiers; and we now have both Inuit and Indian MPs and Senators. In terms of the class composition of our state elite the fact is that 15 percent of the top bureaucrats, at least one supreme court judge, Emmett Hall, and a number of cabinet ministers have family backgrounds *outside* the upper and middle strata of society. It is to be hoped that these cases indicate a growing accessibility of the elite ranks in our political system and perhaps the next decade will see still more significant lower-class and non-charter-ethnic encroachments on the Canadian state elite.

Perhaps too, the real significance of these "success stories" is symbolic; they may function to encourage non-elite Canadians to actually pursue avenues of upward mobility such as higher education. In fact when we consider that education is the elite characteristic which has actually been reinforced since Porter's 1953 study, it is not difficult to conclude that the problem with Canadian democracy is not that the ranks of the state elite are inaccessible but that our institutions of higher learning and particularly the law schools are too exclusively the preserves of the "well born." The solutions to elite dominance in the Canadian system may therefore be to democratize the educational system so that more of the children of working-class Canadians can acquire the qualifications that open the doors to careers in politics, the bureaucracy, and the judicial system.

[71] Olsen, op. cit., p. 22.

15

Priority Determination: Cabinet and Executive Support Agencies

A complex society such as ours generates an almost infinite array of social and economic problems that lend themselves to governmental consideration. Hence the range of policy options open to governmental decision makers is as broad and as complex as the society itself. Unfortunately while the demands being made on government are virtually infinite, the resources required for meeting those demands are finite. Moreover the demands of one group of individuals often will conflict directly with the needs of others; to satisfy one interest will frequently mean thwarting or actively prejudicing others. Thus given both multiple and conflicting demands, and scarce resources, it is not surprising that the central concern of modern political decision makers is often less with solving societal problems than it is with determining which problems deserve most to be solved. The process of deciding which problems a government should face, and which it should face first, we refer to as *priority determination*.

Before the process of priority determination can get underway, it is first necessary to decide which level of government, the federal or provincial, is the most appropriate for dealing with the problem at hand. Where there is no dispute as to the federal/provincial jurisdictional boundaries, this part of the priority determination process is virtually automatic. However, as we have seen, the constitutional division of powers is not very precise and in fact most major policy issues today will involve both levels of government. Thus a closely related set of problems must be faced where a policy issue is not indisputably in the jurisdictional bailiwick of a single level of government; first, where there is a head-on dispute with each side claiming jurisdiction, the dispute must be resolved either by compromise and bargaining or by judicial review, and secondly, where both sides recognise the fact of divided jurisdiction and see the necessity for mutual cooperation, the mechanisms of interjurisdictional policy coordination must be fired up and put to work. It is the responsibility of these coordinative mechanisms to sort out the conflicting priorities of all of the governments involved and to resolve any conflicts as to priorities among them. This federal-provincial aspect of the priority determination phase of policy making in Canada will be addressed in greater detail in the next chapter. Suffice it to say at this juncture that the settlement of interjurisdictional disputes and the coordination of federal provincial priorities is in fact a critical part of the priority determination process.

While no one part of the political system possesses a monopoly over the determination of priorities, where new policies are concerned the cabinet is by far the most important institution involved. But the determination of policy priorities in fact begins in the environment of the political system during the initiation stage. There the various agencies of policy initiation such as political parties and interest groups reduce and combine policy demands in such a way as to maximize both the substantive benefits to their members and the likelihood of success. Thus, by determining which policy options to ask for and when, the policy initiators themselves help to define the framework within which cabinet-level priority decisions ultimately are made.

The main support for the cabinet in its determination of priorities is provided by the executive support agencies of the government, most notably the Prime Minister's Office (PMO), the Privy Council Office (PCO), the Department of Finance, the Treasury Board Secretariat, and other Ministries of State attached to cabinet committees. Indeed these agencies often begin the process of priority determination well before their political masters are forced to take action. They do so because a major problem in establishing policy priorities is the provision of adequate information, a task which may mean finding or generating new data or, at least equally often, filtering and selecting from what would be for already overburdened cabinet ministers an overload of undigested information. The executive support agencies act as information "gatekeepers" to filter and organize the deluge of information which would otherwise inundate and possibly paralyze the ministers. This so-called "briefing function" (for much of the work is done by preparing briefing notes and in verbal "briefing sessions") is at the heart of the power of the executive support agencies.

It has been a characteristic of the late 1970s that the federal government and several provincial governments have experimented with a rapid series of realignments and reorientations among the types of formal executive support agencies described here; such changes have been all the more dizzying by changes in the structures of cabinets themselves.[1] In part this is a reflection of the growing realization that

---

[1] In fact a similar process can be seen to have occurred in many other industrialized countries.

moving programs around like blocks among operating departments will not in itself achieve the end of a reasonably consistent and integrated set of policies in any given area. Instead, current conventional wisdom has it that some increases in *central coordination and control* within government is necessary to achieve this end. In part it is a reflection of the growing difficulties political executives have in producing reasonably consistent—or at least not blatantly self-contradictory—policies in complex societies where the role of government has increased greatly. In part it is a reaction to the fiscal constraint which has afflicted all governments and of the recognition that under straitened financial circumstances, policy initiatives cannot grow like topsy but rather must be balanced by other policy reductions. The complex trade-offs involved require a more sophisticated set of support mechanisms than was needed when the only real question about a policy proposal was "How will it sell in Moose Jaw?"

Whatever the reasons, this rapid creation or realignment of such agencies means problems for the intrepid textbook writer whose writings face the danger of instant obsolesence. Moreover, the impermanence of these structures means there is a dearth of published material providing sober reflection on their impact on Canadian politics.[2] The reader is therefore urged to be alert to changes in the cabinet and central agencies for it is a reasonable prediction that change will continue to take place.[3]

The following sections of this chapter will comprise a more detailed consideration of the priority-determining activities of the Canadian cabinet, with particular attention to the institutional mechanisms which have evolved to cope with the complexity of the modern policy process. Here we will not only describe the structure of the cabinet itself, but also look at key political and financial advisory bodies operating in the federal executive arena.

---

[2] There are exceptions. Aided by the fact that structural changes among executive support agencies may appear greater than the real changes in the process and by the fact that there are certain verities introduced into these activities by virtue of the nature and socialization processes of the people who are recruited into the agencies, several authors have produced work that retains its value in spite of the changes. See, for example, G. B. Doern & Peter Aucoin, *Public Policy in Canada* (Macmillan, Toronto, 1979); articles by Doern, Aucoin, J. J. Rice, H. Kroeker, V. S. Wilson, J. Langford, and M. Prince; Colin Campbell & George Szablowski, *The Superbureaucrats* (Macmillan, Toronto, 1979); R. M. Punnett, *The Prime Minister in Canadian Government & Politics* (Macmillan, Toronto, 1977); R. W. Phidd & G. B. Doern, *The Politics & Management of Canadian Economic Policy* (Macmillan, Toronto, 1978), particulary chapters 1-5; and Thomas Hockin, *Apex of Power*, 2nd ed. (Prentice-Hall, Toronto, 1978).

[3] Probably the best source for immediate updates on changes among these agencies is *The Financial Post*. Most of the authors listed in footnote 2, above, have retained their interest in central agencies and their more recent publications will likely deal with changes.

THE CABINET: STRUCTURE AND PROCESS

Cabinet ministers are busy people requiring considerable administrative and advisory support. In addition to the departmental staff, these functions are performed by the many young gentlemen in dark suits and striped ties, or young ladies in beige skirts who stalk the corridors and antechambers adjacent to ministerial lairs, politely fending off most would-be visitors, quietly ushering in those deemed worthy of audience, and controlling the flow of paper to their minister. Simply by determining who is important enough to get a personal hearing with the minister, and which memoranda and briefing notes he or she needs to see, these gatekeepers can have an impact on what policy options ultimately get to the cabinet level.

In a similar way, correspondence secretaries must filter the tons of incoming mail, bringing the most important correspondence (as they see it) to the ministers' attention, and ensuring that appropriate replies are drafted for all letters. Press secretaries also must help to interpret the opinions expressed by daily newspapers all across Canada, and inform the decision makers of trends in public opinion as reflected by the press. Thus, while there is no doubt that priority decisions must ultimately be made by the political executive, the nature and number of the policy options from which they choose and the information upon which they base their choices are to a large extent defined by the gatekeepers who choreograph the political tattoo of information, ministerial appointments, correspondence, and daily media exposure.

However, the ultimate priority-determining function is performed—in our political system—not by individual ministers, but by the cabinet as a whole. Certainly as an individual, and particularly as the formal administrative head of a department, the cabinet member will have an input in the determination of policy alternatives, in the formulation of specific policies, and in the decision as to the best options for implementation; but when it comes to governmental policy priorities, the responsibility for the decision lies with the cabinet as a collective unit. One of Canada's senior public servants has summarized the situation:

Who is it that develops and decides upon government programs—the individual minister or the cabinet as a whole? To most of us the answer will be self-evident; it is the individual minister and his officials who develop program alternatives but it is the cabinet as a whole which chooses the programs. [4]

---

[4] A. W. Johnson, "Management Theory and Cabinet Government," p. 75.

It is to a further look at the behaviour of that body as a whole and of the agencies designed to support it that we now turn.

The Standing Committee Structure of Cabinet

The cabinet is formally a committee of the Queen's Privy Council for Canada, but since that august body has met only twice since 1867, it has no consequence beyond providing its members with the prefix "the Honourable." The cabinet, which is the *de facto* executive instrument in Canada, in turn delegates the responsibility for priority determination among a number of committees of its own.

The Evolution of the Cabinet Committee System   The creation of a committee structure for cabinet was begun under Lester Pearson in the mid-1960s. Prior to that, most issues were dealt with by cabinet as a whole with the formation of occasional sub-committees to deal with particular problems. The structure was slowly elaborated and the procedures slowly formalized during the pre-1979 Trudeau government. The cabinet under Pierre Trudeau's first government had nine standing committees including the Cabinet Committee on Planning and Priorities, which was chaired by the Prime Minister and was occasionally likened to a sort of "inner cabinet." Its smaller size, the eminence of its chairman, and the fact that the most powerful cabinet ministers were its members made it a better forum for important discussions than a full-scale cabinet meeting where twenty-five to thirty ministers might be present. Relative to the Committee on Planning and Priorities, the mandate of the Cabinet Committee on Social Policy, for example, was considerably more restricted, dealing only with matters arising from the policy concerns of departments falling within its own subject area.

In 1979 the newly instated Clark government reduced the size of the Committee on Priorities and Planning, renamed it the *Inner Cabinet* and reduced the total number of standing committees to seven. The 1980 Trudeau government has kept the reduced number of committees but gone back to calling the Inner Cabinet the Priorities and Planning Committee.

The Committee Systems in Operation   Each of the committees meets regularly, usually once a week. Ministers normally are members of two or three committees, and all the committees have a small permanent secretariat which is provided by the PCO. In addition to performing the duties described below, these secretariats assist the ministers with committee paperwork, help to set committee agenda, brief the chairmen, write the committee decisions, and generally facilitate the flow of information from the line departments of government to the cabinet.

Items to be dealt with by cabinet normally are dealt with first by standing committees. However, there are also special committees of the cabinet established from time to time to deal with specific policy problems. For example, there is a semi-permanent Labour Relations Committee, which deals with particularly serious national strikes, and there have been special committees on Western grain and on tax reform—the latter working on the White Paper on Taxation and its implementation in 1969 and the early 1970s.

Under the Trudeau cabinet in the late 1970s the normal flow of cabinet business was from the sponsoring minister to the PCO secretariat to be placed on the agenda of the appropriate cabinet committee. Discussion there produced a "Committee Recommendation." The item then went to Treasury Board for consideration of its financial and personnel implications. The Treasury Board recommendation together with the committee recommendation then went to Plenary Cabinet where decisions were usually confirmed, although major discussions could take place there and decisions could be overturned, particularly when Treasury Board and the subject committee differed.

As mentioned above, the structure and operations of cabinet were changed considerably after the election of the Progressive Conservative government in May of 1979. The major structural innovations were the creation of an Inner Cabinet and of two Ministries of State, for Social and for Economic Development,[5] while the major innovation in process was the creation of what came to be called the "envelope" system of financial and policy management. The Ministries of State and the envelope system will be described in more detail below. However, the normal formal flow of cabinet business under this system is from the sponsoring ministry to a committee of all the deputy ministers in a particular policy sector. Following discussion there, the item might be aborted but more likely will be forwarded to the appropriate cabinet committee by the sponsoring minister and via the PCO. Following cabinet committee discussion a decision, called a "Committee Recommendation" is prepared and forwarded to Inner Cabinet. These "C.R.s" are nearly always approved by Inner Cabinet for part of the essence of the system is the delegation of real decision-

[5] The Ministry of State for Social Development never actually came into formal existence under the 1979 government since the order in council creating it required debate in the House of Commons and the House self-destructed before getting to that task. The Ministry did exist de facto under a deputy minister styled as a "Special Advisor to the Prime Minister" and staffed itself by secondment from departments. No Minister of State for Social Development could be formally appointed but the chairman of the Cabinet Committee on Social and Native Affairs, David MacDonald acted as the de facto Minister. Jean Chrétien was appointed as the designated Minister of State for Social Development when the Liberal government was returned in 1980.

Figure 15-1

THE COMMITTEE STRUCTURE OF THE CABINET
(1979 Trudeau Version)

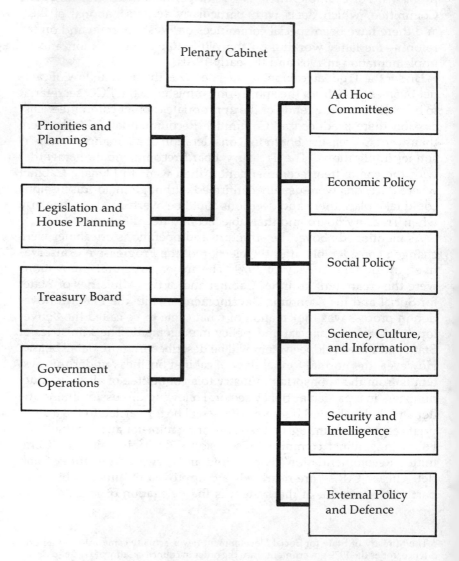

making authority to the committees of cabinet. The full cabinet very seldom met and at the time of the Clark government's defeat seemed to be well on the way to disappearance.

Figure 15-2

THE COMMITTEE STRUCTURE OF THE CABINET
(1979 Clark Version)

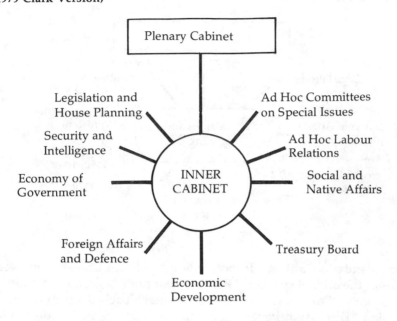

As outlined in Figure 15-3, we can see that the reincarnated Trudeau government of 1980 has maintained the basic outlines of this process, substituting the Priorities and Planning Committee of Cabinet for the Inner Cabinet. The only significant difference besides nomenclature, is that the full cabinet has regained some of the ultimate authority it possessed before the Clark innovations.

The Inner Cabinet had a membership of 12 ministers comprising, in addition to the Prime Minister who chaired it, the chairmen of the standing committees, the Minister of Finance and some other ministers personally close to the Prime Minister. The Priorities and Planning Committee of 1980 has a virtually identical structure and as with its predecessor, the Inner Cabinet, it performs four major roles. First it allocates budgets to the standing committees. These are in effect the cheques or spending targets in the "envelopes" of the envelope system. Second, it reviews all committee decisions. Third, it deals directly with particularly big or particularly important issues or those which cut across the lines of responsibility of other committees. And fourth, it has some program responsibilities of its own such as equalization payments to the provinces and general responsibilities for fiscal transfer payments.

Figure 15-3

THE COMMITTEE STRUCTURE OF THE CABINET
(1980 Trudeau Version)

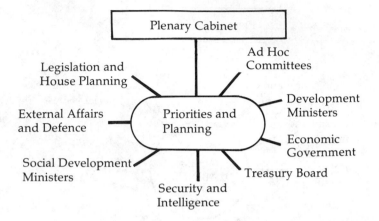

Memoranda to Cabinet   In both the Liberal and Conservative versions of the cabinet structure, the normal input to a cabinet committee has been a "Memorandum to the Cabinet" backed up by a more detailed "Discussion Paper." The memoranda are not made public but the discussion papers, which contain all of the information of the memoranda, often amplified with considerable technical detail but without the "political considerations," are sometimes publicly available.[6] By far the largest number of these documents are written within the bureaucracy. They may express demands arising within the bureaucracy (for example, when officials ask for change in departmental terms of reference or programs); they may result from demand inputs which have been communicated through bureaucratic channels; or they may represent departmental responses to ministerial requests generated by political communication channels such as caucus, the party organization, PMO, or the minister's own contacts. Items appearing before cabinet committees may also be written by individual ministers, by the Privy Council Office or by the Ministries of State, but documents from these sources are relatively rare. Memoranda produced personally by a minister may appear when ministers want to deal with politically extremely sensitive topics. Those pro-

---

[6] The discussion papers were to become available under the much delayed Freedom of Information Act.

duced by the Ministries of State may appear when officials feel that they have seen policy needs that Departments have missed because of the fragmented nature of their responsibilities; when the subject is a major policy change cutting across the interests of several departments or perhaps significantly changing a department mandate; when a major statement of priorities is required; or when financial issues dealing with a whole sector require cabinet consideration. All memoranda to cabinet bear the signature of a minister or a group of ministers, who then become responsible for piloting the document through cabinet with the aid of their departmental officials.

The Cabinet Committee System in the 1980s   The creation of an Inner Cabinet, of the "envelope" system and the delegation of much effective final decision-making power to committees together with the virtual elimination of full cabinet as a decision-making body under the Progressive Conservative government which took office in 1979 marked a quantum jump in the elaboration of cabinet structure; a jump which has been to a large extent retained under the subsequent Liberal government.

However, it is likely too soon to assess the implications of these changes over the long run. At first glance they appear to decentralize power within the cabinet while removing power from individual departments. The impression that power has been removed from individual departments will be increased when we come to discuss the expenditure management process, for the departments now have less control than they did over the internal reallocation of funds and fewer opportunities to take policy initiatives which do not fit the overall mandate of "their" cabinet committee. As to decentralization within cabinet, the picture is less clear. True, committees have gained the bulk of final authority for decisions on most of the issues in their field. However, this real freedom is sharply constrained by the limitations on their expenditures in the form of expenditure envelopes. Moreover, there is considerable interaction among the chairmen of the cabinet committees in Planning and Priorities Committee and there is parallel interaction among the most senior of Ottawa's deputy ministers—those who head the Department of Finance, the Treasury Board Secretariat, and the Ministries of Social and Economic Development in a small committee chaired by the Prime Minister's highest official, the Secretary to the Cabinet, and Clerk of the Privy Council. Overall, then, a very considerable centralization of control appears to have been occurring in Ottawa along with the evolution of the cabinet structure. We will examine this situation further as we look at the behaviour of cabinet and at the structure and relationships among the agencies which support cabinet in its priority determinations.

It must be noted here that the complexity of cabinet structures varies from province to province. In some of the larger ones, cabinet committee structure and procedures rival or surpass those of the federal government in complexity, while in the smaller provinces there may be considerably fewer ministers and not much need for a complex cabinet structure. [7] While we do not intend to deal with the structure of provincial cabinets in any detail, some additional considerations will be raised in the next chapter.

Inside the Cabinet: Prime Ministerial Power and Collective Responsibility

To this point our emphasis has been upon the role of the cabinet acting as a collective unit. However, before considering the executive support agencies which assist the cabinet in the collective determination of governmental priorities, it is necessary to say something about behavioural patterns and the distribution of power within that collectivity.

In Canadian politics, the Prime Minister is much more than "first among equals." Aided by the doctrine that all members of the cabinet are jointly responsible for any cabinet decision and must resign if they are unable to support or at least acquiesce in a policy, he sets the tone and style of the government and can establish the broad outlines of its most important policies. A Diefenbaker, a Pearson, or a Trudeau stamps his era of Canadian politics unmistakably with his style and ideas. However, there are also many checks on what a Prime Minister can do to influence priority determination. [8]

Undoubtedly the most important of these checks is simply the domestic and international environment of the political system. By this we mean no more—and no less—than that the Prime Minister is subject to the same limitations as other politicians. For example, no matter how much he might personally want to do so, there is no way that a Prime Minister could institute a real guaranteed annual income of $20,000 per capita. The environment of the political system is simply not productive enough to provide the goods and services involved. A related environmental constraint derives from the vast

---

[7] The Ontario structure for example is at least as complex as that of the federal government. See G. B. Doern, "Horizontal and Vertical Portfolios in Government," in G. B. Doern and V. S. Wilson, *Issues in Canadian Public Policy* (Macmillan, Toronto, 1974), and Kenneth Bryden "Cabinets," in D. Bellamy, J. Pammett & D. Rowat, *The Provincial Political Systems* (Methuen, Toronto, 1976).

[8] See also the discussion in R. M. Punnett, *The Prime Minister in Canadian Government & Politics* and in Thomas Hockin, "The Prime Minister and Political Leadership: An Introduction to Some Restraints and Imperatives," in Hockin (ed.), *Apex of Power*, pp. 1-22, and "Two Canadian Prime Ministers Discuss the Office," ibid., pp. 184-199

number of inputs which would face a modern Prime Minister were there any attempt to exercise absolute power in the executive policy process. Even with expanded central agencies there is, realistically, no way in which a Prime Minister or any one person could even hope to deal personally with more than a tiny fraction of the issues facing government.

Cabinet colleagues also place restraints on the Prime Minister's power to set priorities. While as their leader, the Prime Minister can likely force them to accept any single policy initiative he chooses, he will choose not to force the point on most issues. The reason is that, like any person, the Prime Minister only has so much power; and, in many ways, that power may be very much like currency—it can be spent, but it should be spent judiciously. Invested judiciously it multiplies; spent too widely, on too many separate items and against the interests of too many colleagues, it diminishes and may vanish. Thus, except for a few concerns to which there is a personal, vital attachment, the Prime Minister is always somewhat amenable to being "convinced" by colleagues. No one would resign from the cabinet in a huff if the Prime Minister pushed a few small items down its collective throat; but a cabinet must, in the parliamentary system, at least appear to work as a team, and too many such incidents could be damaging to the image of cabinet solidarity. A Prime Minister must walk a narrow line between allowing ministers too much leeway—creating consequent disarray, disunity, and bickering on the team, and allowing them too little—thus bringing himself to ruin through defections. The problems of the Pearson cabinets are amply illustrative of the former fault, while the breakup of the Diefenbaker cabinet in 1963 illustrates the latter. [9]

---

[9] The results of too much personal exercise of power during the last days of the Diefenbaker cabinet are particularly well covered in Patrick Nicholson, *Vision and Indecision* (Longmans, Canada, Toronto, 1968), particularly pp. 227-266. On the assorted fiascos of the Pearson era, see Peter C. Newman, *The Distemper of Our Times* (McClelland and Stewart, Toronto, 1969), and Judy LaMarsh, *Memoirs of a Bird in a Gilded Cage* (McClelland and Stewart, Toronto, 1969), as well as the last two volumes of Pearson's *Memoirs* (University of Toronto Press, 1973 & 1975). Peter C. Newman, *Renegade in Power, The Diefenbaker Years* (McClelland and Stewart, Toronto, 1963) is also highly instructive and useful. See also the volumes of the Mackenzie King biography, *William Lyon Mackenzie King*, by R. M. Dawson and Blair Neatby. For many examples of Prime Ministerial management style combined with a more objective assessment, see R. M. Punnett, *The Prime Minister in Canadian Politics*. The first four books mentioned are examples of "inside" books about politics in Ottawa. These books do provide valuable insight into the working of politics in Ottawa. However, when dealing with them the reader should try to maintain a broader perspective. Politics is not simply the activities of a few people in Ottawa or provincial capitals. It is an extremely complex process set in an extremely complex environment. Its actors in capital cities are only transient figures who shape some events, and are, in turn, shaped by them.

In addition, the cabinet has some control over the Prime Minister by virtue of its numbers, the personal strength of its members, the access and contact which ministers have to information and sources in the bureaucracy, and the personal followings which some ministers have managed to establish either in caucus or in the country at large. On the other hand, the Prime Minister has power over their jobs. He can reorganize the cabinet at any time and remove troublesome ministers to lower-status portfolios, to the backbenches, to the Senate, or to the judiciary.

It is sometimes suggested that one of the major ways in which a cabinet and Prime Minister can control parliament is through the threat of dissolution. The same thing could be considered applicable to a particularly recalcitrant cabinet, but one should not overemphasize this point because a dissolution carries risks for the Prime Minister as well as for the cabinet. Moreover, the thought of fighting an election with a cabinet in disarray, as Diefenbaker had to in 1963, can hardly be appealing to a Prime Minister. And finally, it should be remembered that three of the last five prime ministers have had a distinct lack of fondness for elections.

Perhaps the greatest source of control that a Prime Minister has over the cabinet is simply personal popularity. Highly popular or freshly elected Prime Ministers, or those who have established a solid tradition of getting themselves and their parties re-elected have rarely had much trouble with their cabinets. This Prime Ministerial asset will, of course, vary a great deal from leader to leader, as well as from cabinet to cabinet, and from time to time. The Pierre Elliott Trudeau of March 1980, fresh from a major electoral victory, was more powerful vis-à-vis his cabinet colleagues than was the personally unpopular and about to be defeated Pierre Elliott Trudeau of March 1979.

The Limits to Cabinet Supremacy in Priority Determination

If there are constraints acting on the Prime Minister when dealing with the cabinet, there are equal constraints on the cabinet and Prime Minister when they are acting together to determine priorities. In the first place, there are the environmental constraints which one should by now expect. Another significant restriction on the actions of both federal and provincial governments derives from the division of powers under the British North America Act. It will do the federal government little good to establish elementary education as a high priority area unless the provinces can somehow be induced to go along. Nor will it be very useful for the provinces to establish the revision of the criminal code as a high priority area unless the federal government cooperates and leads in the venture. The role of the federal-provincial process in the determination of priorities as well as in the more detailed formulation of policies is so vital that we devote the whole of the next chapter to it. For the moment, it is necessary only to keep in mind that it forms the greatest of the formal constraints on priority determination in Canada.

Paradoxically, the line bureaucracy—by far the largest source of information for the cabinet—can also be viewed as one of its greatest constraints. The bureaucracy's near monopoly over many types of information ensures that the cabinet is highly dependent upon it when most priority decisions are made. Despite attempts, chronicled in the rest of this chapter, to alleviate this dependency somewhat—via task forces (themselves usually composed of bureaucrats), Royal Commissions and the expansion of the PMO, the PCO, the Ministries of State and ministers' personal staffs—Canadian cabinets are still perhaps more dependent on their bureaucracies than are most other Western governments. We have already seen that interest groups, which in other polities sometimes form a counterbalance to the power of the bureaucracy, often work through and with it in Canada. Canadian party structures are not really adequate as alternative information sources—unlike their counterparts in places like Britain and the Scandinavian countries. Nor do Canadian legislatures form an effective counterweight to bureaucratic power. The image of the well-intentioned but slightly naive cabinet minister on his or her own against a sea of plotting, scheming, power-grabbing bureaucrats often portrayed in the press is a far overstated caricature of reality. But reality still is that bureaucracies are, among other things, large information-gathering networks and will, if counterweights are not provided, dominate priority determination no less than they do other stages of the political process.

EXECUTIVE SUPPORT AGENCIES: THE CABINET'S ADVISORS

Figure 15-4 presents a taxonomy of the various agencies which provide support to cabinet in its priority determination role classified according to their function. The agencies are classified by the primary and formal roles but in practice all of them are concerned to a greater or lesser degree with all of the functions.

In particular, political considerations colour all of the deliberations of these agencies; since their function is to provide support for political leaders, it could hardly be otherwise. It is important, however, to differentiate between partisan considerations and political considerations. The Prime Minister's Office, ministerial staff, the party structure and caucus provide support to ministers because those ministers

Figure 15-4

EXECUTIVE SUPPORT AGENCIES FOR PRIORITY DETERMINATION

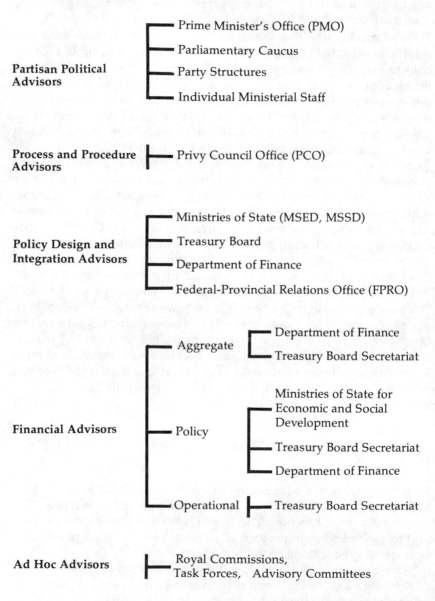

are of a particular partisan stripe. If the government changes, these people lose their jobs. Indeed even if the incumbent of a position changes without a change of government, they are likely to be jobless. Their support is thus for a very particular set of people. By contrast, all of the other support agencies provide support for the elected government of the day regardless of its partisan stripe for as long as it is in office. When it is defeated they provide support for the next government. They are employed on a permanent basis by the government and not by a particular party. They, being human, have their preferences as to parties and incumbents but they will generally serve regardless of their personal feelings for they are career public servants.

The distinctions are not always easy to make in practice but they do hold with considerable regularity. Aside from the partisan advisors, very few holders of positions in executive support agencies change with a change in government. The change from a sixteen-year-old Liberal government to a Progressive Conservative one was accompanied by a change of the head of the Privy Council Office—however, his successor came from within the ranks—by the "resignation" of one other top PCO official who was in any event near retirement age, and by the removal of the Deputy Minister of Finance. The return of the Liberals saw the reinstatement of the former head of the PCO, the transfer of that position's temporary incumbent to another public service job, and the "resignation" of the Tory-appointed Deputy Minister of Finance. All other changes which occurred were nothing more than would have happened in any event. Any impression that these agencies are hives of partisanship is quite unfounded—not necessarily because ministers would not like to make them so but because they are staffed by officials recruited under the "merit" system which makes the use of overt partisan appointments difficult and because the successful heads of these agencies jealously guard their partisan neutrality.[10]

Partisan Political Advisors

The PMO   Since the Prime Minister bears the pre-eminent responsibility for the political fortunes of the government, it is the Prime Minister's Office which bears the largest responsibility among support agencies for the provision of partisan political advice.[11] The PMO is

---

[10] For a complete description of the types of incumbents of these agencies see Colin Campbell & George Szablowski, *The Superbureaucrats*.

[11] See the description of the PMO in Marc Lalonde, "The Changing Role of the Prime Minister's Office," *Canadian Public Administration*, Vol. 14, no. 4, Winter 1971, pp. 487-537. For a much more controversial point of view see Denis Smith, "President and Parliament: The Transformation of Parliamentary Government in Canada," and the different point of view expressed by Joseph Wearing in "President or Prime Minister," both in Thomas Hockin (ed.), *Apex of Power*. More recently, see Thomas D'Acquino, "The Prime Minister's Office: Catalyst or Cabal," and Denis Smith, "Comments on the Prime Minister's Office: Catalyst or Cabal," both in *Canadian Public Administration*, Vol. 17, no. 1, Spring 1974.

always staffed at the senior levels by close partisan advisors and people whose advice is valued by the Prime Minister. The office staff itself has grown rapidly over the last twelve years and currently has over a hundred members. By contrast R. B. Bennett had a staff of about twelve during the 1930s while King, St. Laurent, and Diefenbaker had about thirty staff members and Pearson about forty.[12] However, it is not so evident that the number of top policy advisors has increased. About half the staff of the PMO is there to handle the vastly increased volume of Prime Ministerial mail.

The uses a Prime Minister will make of the PMO will vary from leader to leader and even from time to time. In the early Trudeau years the PMO was avowedly a source of many major policy initiatives. Later, as an election approached and then a minority government and another election followed, the PMO became much more a political machine devoted to electoral politics, providing a kind of political technocracy to advise the Prime Minister on the political pros and cons of various policy options. While it has tended to remain that way since, with most policy initiatives coming from other agencies, the few exceptions have been important ones. In August 1978, for example, the PMO and the Prime Minister almost alone produced a major series of restraint proposals and established the first national refundable tax credit program.[13] Indeed it has been argued that the creation of major policy changes in Canada requires a sudden centralization of authority of the sort which can only occur in the federal government when the Prime Minister and the PMO suddenly take power into their own hands, acting before the web of opposition which can form rapidly in Ottawa has had time to mobilize.

Partisan political advice is also provided by parliamentary caucus and individual MPs. The caucuses of all major parties meet at least weekly and there are a series of regional caucus and caucus committee meetings as well. Ministers are members of caucus and generally try to attend meetings so there is considerable exposure on their part to the ideas of their fellow members. Individual MPs will also try to get ideas to ministers either by buttonholing them or through office appointments. Ministers, although not always enthusiastic about it, are generally willing to see them. Since ministers and backbenchers share at least a common interest in being re-elected and since that can depend on highly visible priority decisions, there is some tendency to listen to parliamentary advice. We will say more about the role of

[12] R. M. Punnett, *The Prime Minister in Canadian Government and Politics*, p. 77.
[13] R. Van Loon, "Reforming Welfare in Canada," *Public Policy*, Fall, 1979.

caucus committees and the government backbenchers in the chapter on parliament.

The Extra-Parliamentary Party   We have already discussed at length the structures and lines of communication (or, more often the lack of them) which link the party outside parliament with the government. Although a few highly influential party functionaries may have a considerable impact on policy, the weakness of these links makes that a relatively rare phenomenon. Indeed those party functionaries who are powerful will usually exert their influence from a formal position somewhere else in the political system; perhaps the PMO or the Senate.

Beyond this, the role of the extra-parliamentary party, for instance through the annual policy convention, is more persuasive than binding in any way. The major limitation on the power of the party organization is ultimately the fact that the PMO has better information upon which to base its political advice.

The Ministers' Staff   Finally, the personal staffs of the ministers, the executive assistants, and the special assistants who work directly for the minister, can be influential in partisan political decisions. While they have no formal responsibility for such advice, the fact that such people often are seasoned veterans of the political wars, who over many years of experience have gained a good measure of political savvy, makes them good critics when the ministry wants to bounce new policy ideas around. Moreover, the very physical closeness of a minister's personal staff to the minister means that such people become the first audience before which the political popularity of new policy ideas gets tested. However, the political advisory function of a minister's personal staff is not at all systematic, and as with other informal sources of political advice, their influence is severely limited by their inability to compete with the more professional and better organized resource people in the PMO.

Process Advisors: The Privy Council Office

The Structure of the PCO   The PMO and its non-partisan first cousin, the Privy Council Office share office space in the immediate vicinity of Parliament Hill, space which symbolizes both their role of serving the cabinet committees which meet there and their proximity to power. Since the late 1960s the role of the PCO has evolved from that of an agency almost entirely concerned with flowing paper to cabinet, through a somewhat abortive attempt to coordinate all aspects of government policy, to a position as architect of much of the machinery and process of government in Ottawa; a task which is now combined with the function of providing major logistical and decision-making support for the cabinet.

The current organizational structure of the PCO is largely dictated by the cabinet committee structure itself.[14] There are secretariats for each cabinet committee, normally with four to eight officers and an assistant secretary to the cabinet and these secretariats are grouped under two or three deputy secretaries. There are also secretariats or directorates responsible for the machinery of government, government communications, legislation and planning of the parliamentary end of government business, and senior personnel. The whole structure is headed by Canada's highest ranking public servant, the Secretary to the Cabinet. Paradoxically the President of the Privy Council has no direct responsibility for the Privy Council Office. That post is at present used to give a position in the cabinet to the government House Leader and to ensure that there are no particular departmental responsibilities to impede the President's efforts in manoeuvering the government's program through the House of Commons.

The PCO and the Senior Bureaucracy Since 1968 there have been continual changes in the structure and functions of the Privy Council Office and in its relations with other central agencies, all reflecting an attempt to make the rather fundamental changes in the locus of power within the federal government to which we have already alluded. To understand this evolution we will have to go back to the years prior to 1968 when (with the possible exception of the Diefenbaker era) not only did the bureaucratic establishment dominate the process of policy formulation, but the senior bureaucratic "mandarins" played a major role in the process of priority determination as well.[15]

The pre-eminent position that senior bureaucrats occupied for a number of years in Ottawa is humorously illustrated in the story of the ambitious young man who wrote the Prime Minister asking that he be given a position in the cabinet. The Prime Minister replied to the effect that he did not feel that the member had the depth of experience, the breadth of knowledge, and the intellectual vigour required for such an exalted position. Undaunted, the young M.P. wrote back: "My dear Prime Minister, I believe you misunderstood the nature of my request: high as my ambition can aspire, I do not expect to become a Deputy Minister; I merely want to be a Minister."[16]

---

[14] For details concerning the organization of the structures described in this chapter, see *The Organization of the Government of Canada* published biennially by Macmillan, Toronto.

[15] See F. Schindeler, "The Prime Minister and Cabinet: History and Development," pp. 27-8, and Maurice Lamontagne, "The Influence of the Politician," *Canadian Public Administration*, Vol. XL, no. 3, Fall 1968, p. 265, as well as R. M. Punnett, *The Prime Minister in Canadian Government and Politics.*

[16] By kind permission of Professor Thomas Hockin, Senator Maurice Lamontagne, and Mr. Fred Schindeler, from "The Prime Minister and Cabinet: History and Development" in Thomas Hockin (ed.), *Apex of Power* (Prentice-Hall, Toronto, 1971).

The influence of the mandarins over the determination of priorities was based on a number of factors, some related to structural features of the system and others to the personal characteristics of the individuals involved. The most important of the structural factors was the Deputy Ministers' control over the flow of information upwards from the departmental technocracy and downwards from the cabinet. A large vestige of this particular source of policy influence still resides with the senior bureaucrats.

The most important personal factor contributing to the hegemony of the mandarin was the combination of expertise in a substantive field and long experience as a participant in the policy process. Because the mandarin's experience extended over a number of years and frequently, through a series of different ministries, the senior bureaucrat often possessed a perspective that was much broader than that of his political boss. The result was that the deputy minister could have a profound influence on the minister not only because the deputy possessed a higher level of technical competence in the field, but often because over the years a "feel" for the political marketplace had been acquired; the deputy had a political acumen which had significance both in the roles of political and technical advisor. While the influence of the mandarins would naturally also be related to the willingness of the individual ministers and the government of the day to take their advice, for the most part they either became "trusted" and therefore influential, or they simply ceased to be "mandarins." It was apparently the intention of the 1968 Trudeau government to temper this influence through the obvious solution of providing alternative sources of policy advice.

During the Diefenbaker era, alternative information had been derived from the Conservative party, from the personal acquaintances of the Prime Minister and the cabinet, from the press, and from the mind of the leader himself. The somewhat strained relations between the leader and the bureaucracy during the Diefenbaker years ensured that there was less chance of priorities being determined by the bureaucracy, and that more than "normal" attention was paid to these alternate sources. Similar alternatives had been available during the Liberal years prior to 1957, but Liberal Prime Ministers had shown little propensity to use them. Prime Minister Trudeau and his advisors, on the other hand, appear to have recognized that the most effective counter for one bureaucratic institution is another bureaucratic institution with parallel responsibilities. The political advisory power of the mandarins was to be attenuated through the increase in size and influence of the PMO and their technical advice was to be placed in competition with that coming from a revamped PCO.

The PCO in the Eighties The Privy Council Office never did quite succeed in fulfilling the hopes (or fears) expressed for it in the 1970s. While composed of regular public service personnel, the PCO was nonetheless viewed by many old-style senior bureaucrats as an organization of "upstarts" and "outsiders." This was probably inevitable; any new agency will be viewed in that light and it is a problem which is overcome by time. The larger problems were internal. The initial head of the PCO under this new system declined to add much in the way of technical expertise to the organization and its ability to conduct independent analyses and critiques of policy proposals emanating from departments remained very limited.[17] His successor, Michael Pitfield, followed a somewhat similar course, and although he strengthened the agency considerably by the quality of his senior appointments, it once again did not achieve the critical mass necessary to perform major independent policy analyses.

The causes of the problem may well have lain in good intentions. The other central agencies of the early 1970s, the Treasury Board Secretariat and the Department of Finance, did conduct independent appraisals of most major policy proposals. The dictates of efficiency would seem to have argued against duplicating their work in another agency and producing thereby a degree of central agency warfare. However, the other agencies did primarily financial and economic impact analyses with the result that no one did much in the way of social impact analysis. Equally important, no one, in spite of desultory efforts from time to time on the part of all the agencies involved, ever succeeded in getting an established set of priorities from the cabinet and examining the diverse proposals emanating from departments in the light of these priorities. The result was a predictable dispersion of government activities and a lack of coherent strategies in fields such as industrial development or social or cultural policy. In retrospect it seems unlikely that the PCO could have forced such coherence since it had no means of effecting control over government expenditures. The agencies which did have such control (Treasury Board and Finance) had no way of determining priorities and no way of forcing ministers to make trade-offs. We will look at more recent attempts to solve these problems in the next section.

In the meantime, it must be pointed out that the procedural and organizational mandate that the PCO continues to possess gives it very considerable power within the federal government; a power which is also retained by cabinet secretariats in most provincial gov-

---

[17] See Gordon Robertson, "The Changing Role of the Privy Council Office," *Canadian Public Administration*, v. 14, 4, Winter 1971, for a description of changes by the first head of the revamped agency.

ernments. Since cabinet committees are the key decision points for priority decisions, control over the agendas of committees and over the wording of their decisions is a significant source of power. In the case of the two major spending committees, these powers are shared with the Ministries of State for Economic and Social Development but the ultimate control over agendas still resides in the PCO secretariats. The writing of "Committee Recommendations" to full cabinet, which are usually simply ratified by that body, is done by PCO officials after cabinet committee discussions. A decision is circulated in draft format before it is finalized but there is always some latitude to shade nuances and while a PCO officer cannot produce a "C.R." which flies in the face of all discussion, there is always the possibility of a bit of shaping to be done.

Further influence accrues to the PCO because of its overall responsibility for the organization of the whole federal bureaucracy and because of its power to tender advice to the Prime Minister via the Secretary to the Cabinet on all senior personnel matters; but the final, and perhaps most significant, source of PCO influence is the briefing of the Prime Minister. These briefings are a joint PCO and PMO function with the PCO having primary responsibility for all but the political aspects of the briefing notes. The source of material for PCO notes is most often within operating departments but it will also be gleaned from other central agencies and outside sources and the responsible officer will often have had sufficient years of experience with the subject matter to add considerable shape to the material. As we have seen, these briefing notes are far from the only source of Prime Ministerial information but they are seen by the leader and they are significant.

Policy Design and Integration Advisors

We have seen that among the problems faced by the PCO in the 1970s in its attempts to help rationalize and integrate government policy was the lack of statements of government priorities operationalized by reference to accompanying financial statements, and the lack of ability to do much in the way of detailed analysis of ongoing programs and of possible changes in them. To this should be added lack of any mechanism other than full cabinet meetings to permit, or force, ministers to trade off one program or policy against another and thus to make their priorities manifest in output terms.

Ministries of State   One early attempt to solve the problem of lack of analysis and knowledge and the lack of priorities was the creation in the early 1970s of Ministries of State for the relatively confined subject areas of science and technology and urban affairs. These ministries had no direct control over departmental budgets, no large budgets of their own and no dedicated cabinet committee through which to report. They were to collect and if necessary conduct research into their subject areas and they were to use the power of superior knowledge and persuasion to provide program integration. However, contrary to the old adage, in this case it turned out that knowledge is not power—at least not sufficient power to move a large department or a minister set on having his or her way. At the time of this writing one such ministry—that for science and technology remains alive; a vestige of an unsuccessful experiment in coordination.

A later but similar attempt to deal with this problem was made on the economic policy and particularly the economic development front.[18] By 1978 it was obvious that if Canada was to compete successfully in international trade, some coherent industrial strategy was required. Consequently a "Board of Economic Development Ministers" was created under the chairmanship of Robert Andras, one of the most powerful of the cabinet ministers. The board met regularly for several months but faced persistent problems because, while it discussed policy and while its deliberations were informed by a strong deputy minister and secretariat, there was no way to force the integration of policies and no way to force trade-offs of one expenditure versus another. The solution was a relatively simple one—give the Board (soon to be reconstituted as the Cabinet Committee on Economic Development) responsibility for control of the entire economic development budget. The arrival on the scene of an Inner Cabinet was originally unrelated to this evolution but with its arrival the final piece was in place for it constituted a source which could assign authoritatively the economic development budget and, by assigning also social development, foreign and defence, and operational envelopes, denote the relative priority each area was to receive. These budgetary envelopes had to be administered and, more important, cabinet committees had to be given support in the making of trade-offs necessary to stay within the limits of the budget envelopes and in ensuring the integration of policy. This job would be most difficult on the economic development and social policy scenes. Thus two new central agencies in the form of Ministries of State for Social and Economic Development were to be created. We have already seen that the return of a Liberal government in March 1980 did not change the trend of this evolution except that the allocation of envelope figures was to be carried out by the reincarnated Cabinet Committee on Priorities and Planning rather than by the now defunct Inner Cabinet.

---

[18] See R. W. Phidd and G. B. Doern, *The Politics and Management of Canadian Economic Policies* for a much more detailed description of the early steps of this evolution.

These ministries of state are relatively small, containing approximately a hundred staff members. The formal internal structures will vary from time to time according to the predilections of the inhabitants; however, they have common functions and common modes of operation. Each engages in long-range planning activities for its sector. Each administers the forecast expenditures of the programs within its envelope with the current year finances being managed by the Treasury Board. Each attempts to ensure policy coordination throughout its sector. Each gains its primary power by acting as a gatekeeper in the policy and financial management systems: before proposals go to the appropriate cabinet committee they are normally widely discussed with Ministry officials and considered by a committee of deputy ministers chaired by the Deputy Minister of State. The cabinet committee is provided with written advice on the basis of these deliberations and in addition the ministry may, and frequently will, separately brief the chairman of the cabinet committee, particularly if it has objections to the proposal. Coordination and integration within the sector is to be achieved through the overview functions of these agencies and because of the fact that proposals will not normally proceed to cabinet committees before a thorough examination by the ministries themselves. In addition the ministries may actually initiate their own proposals and may retain responsibility for coordinating "events" such as national sector conferences or federal-provincial negotiations in their sector.

FPRO   Overall policy integration with respect to federal-provincial concerns was, in the late 1970s to be the responsibility of the Federal-Provincial Relations Office (FPRO) and its Minister of State. The geneology of the FPRO can be traced to the original reorganization of the cabinet committee system by the newly elected Trudeau government of 1968. The plan at that time was for a committee of cabinet on Federal-Provincial Relations to coordinate the federal side in all dealings with the provinces and the staff support for this committee was to be a branch of the PCO under a deputy secretary to the cabinet. The coordinative role of the cabinet committee however never really blossomed for the simple reason that relations with the provinces were either so all-encompassing in their scope that the Prime Minister himself and the Committee on Priorities and Planning would carry the ball, or so narrow and "portfolio specific" that the individual federal departments would organise things through their own federal provincial relations branches. The end result was that while the committee remained officially in existence until the defeat of the Liberals in 1979, it seldom met after 1974, and completely ceased to function when the Ministry of State for federal-provincial relations was established in 1977.

In the meantime, the federal-provincial relations secretariat in the PCO had evolved into the FPRO by 1975 when it was given a separate existence under a full Secretary to the Cabinet (Gordon Robertson, who had been *the* Secretary to the Cabinet until Michael Pitfield was given that job in 1975). The FPRO went through a growth spurt aided by the fact that the Canadian Unity Information Office was domiciled within it, and remained a separate bureaucratic agency presided over by a full Secretary to the Cabinet under both the Clark and 1980 Trudeau administrations. The only change in the status of the FPRO is that under the 1980 Trudeau government the position of Minister of State for Federal-Provincial Relations has disappeared and the FPRO now reports directly to the Prime Minister.

While the FPRO seems to have some potential for growth under its current leadership and given its role in the business of constitutional reform, it has never been able to gain the broad coordinative clout of the other central agencies. Unlike its sisters, the FPRO does not control a budgetary envelope, and thus it is not in a position to play a "financial gatekeeper" role in the bureaucracy. Thus the other departments of government have no incentive to submit themselves to the coordinative efforts of the FPRO because it has no real power over them. Under its original leadership it did have a significant role in briefing the PM on the federal-provincial aspects of issues, but the line departments and the other central agencies have simply found it too easy to ignore or overlook in their day-to-day affairs.

Today the FPRO has as its major responsibility, besides the specialised role it plays in the current chapter of the ongoing saga of Canadian constitutional reform, a monitoring and surveillance function vis-à-vis departmental policy or budgetary proposals that might have an impact in the intergovernmental arena. In effect the FPRO is called upon to vet the line departments in order to ensure that they not forget the federal-provincial aspects of their policy decisions. Whether it can ever evolve into a coordinator of federal activities in the intergovernmental arena is an unknown; but current attitudes both in other central agencies and in the key line departments who have to deal with the provinces would indicate that such a role would be opposed fairly vigorously.

Finance and TBS The Department of Finance and the Treasury Board Secretariat also have policy integration roles. More and more the Treasury Board is coming to function as the Board of Management for the government.[19] It retains responsibility for current year bud-

---

[19] The concept is most fully outlined in the *Report of the Royal Commission on Financial Accountability* (the "Lambert" Commission) (Ottawa, Queen's Printer, 1979).

gets and, along with the Department of Finance, is charged with advising cabinet on the size of future year allocations to various "envelopes." More important in this context, the Treasury Board is in a unique position to effect control and coordination through its responsibilities for labour relations, for many aspects of personnel policy, for administrative and financial policy and effectiveness evaluation (functions handled formally by the Comptroller-General who reports through the President of the Treasury Board), for most aspects of administrative procedures, and for personnel allocations.

The Department of Finance retains primary responsibility for advising the government on overall aspects of economic policy, for the bulk of transfer payments to the provinces, and for the effect of government policies on the economy. It is Inner Cabinet's primary advisor at the time when future year expenditure allocations are made. Finally it is responsible for all aspects of the raising of revenues and hence all aspects of the taxation system including those devices intended to provide financial inducements to people and corporations to behave in certain ways—the so-called "tax expenditures." If any policy proposal is to be carried out through the tax system or if it will have a significant effect on the economy or government revenues, the role of the Department of Finance becomes paramount. Since many policies fall into these categories, its role in policy integration is a far-reaching one.

Interdepartmental Committees   One major device for establishing priorities among the various departments and agencies of the Canadian government which are not a part of the central agency "mafia," is the interdepartmental coordinating committee. Typically, an interdepartmental committee will be created wherever more than one department is responsible for a single subject area. For example, because many departments within the federal government have responsibility for programs which bear upon Northern development there is an Advisory Committee on Northern Development (ACND), on which the Departments of Transport, Environment, National Health and Welfare, Energy, Mines and Resources, as well as Indian Affairs and Northern Development are each represented. Similarly, there have been interdepartmental committees within the federal government on water and resources, on pesticides, and on many other subjects. Frequently the formal membership of one of these committees will consist of deputy ministers or assistant deputies, but the meetings are generally attended by the middle-ranking delegates of the formal members. This is perhaps fortunate since the bulk of professional expertise is concentrated at these middle levels, and if any detailed policy work is to be done, these delegates are perhaps the most appropriate people to do it.

The manifest function of interdepartmental committees is to ensure the coordination of policies in some issue area. However, their effectiveness is often negated by a latent function—the pursuit of departmental interests. Interdepartmental "coordination" often becomes a competitive process through which departments bargain for aggrandizement or defence of their own spheres of authority. This is a necessary reflection of the fact that the members of these committees spend most of their time taking care of their own departmental responsibilities and only a relatively small part of their time in interdepartmental coordination. Moreover, it may be inevitable, given the segregated hierarchical structures of the Canadian bureaucracy. People naturally tend to view matters in the light of the interests of the department in which they spend so much of their working day, and on whose growth and prosperity their own careers may depend.

This defensive posture of committee members may have severe repercussions for the policy-making process, as it tends to preclude a truly problem-oriented approach to issues. For example, if both the Department of Environment and the Department of Energy, Mines and Resources are eager to expand their influence over the uses of energy resources, it means that each may view the other's quite legitimate actions as a "power grab" and act either to block them, or to provide a counter-offensive of its own. The institutional forums of interdepartmental coordination often become the arena for these battles, and the result may be committee deadlock, or much bureaucratic redundancy with no clear policy decision. The problem is compounded by the fact that the cabinet may often choose to delay its own decisions if there is lack of consensus among its bureaucratic advisors. In cases like this, the cabinet may simply wait until one group or the other has gained ascendancy and a clear-cut policy alternative has been articulated.

There are partial solutions to such blockages. First, the Prime Minister can move to break up such deadlocks by a pre-emptive reallocation of departmental responsibility. Second and more important, perhaps, is the fact that the interdepartmental priority-setting process is not purely a conflict situation: in fact, not all departments are "imperialistic" and indeed most individual bureaucrats are genuinely interested in solving substantive problems even if they sometimes get in one another's way. Because many of the middle-level specialists in a given subject area get to know each other personally, there are many channels of informal communication which can help to ease the process of interdepartmental coordination. Furthermore, department heads are not always anxious to expand their own departmental work-loads and are often willing to share the burden.

This tendency may be reinforced because, where senior bureaucrats have difficulty delegating authority, they quickly find themselves in a position where they cannot imagine their organization undertaking greater responsibilities, even when there may be considerable spare capacity lower down in the department.

A third partial solution is to be found in another aspect of the activities of the central agencies. The major central agencies are represented on virtually all of the formal interdepartmental coordinating committees, sub-committees, working groups and so on. They are there not because they have programs in these particular areas but rather because of their coordinative and supervisory responsibilities. Thus, attached to these agencies are people whose job it is to stay on top of interdepartmental coordination mainly by attending an endless round of meetings. These people then report back to the appropriate division of their own agency, producing a check on all facets of interdepartmental activity.

The overall verdict on interdepartmental committees however must be that they do not achieve many great coordinative successes. In fact some participants have dubbed the interdepartmental committee system "institutionalized discord"—the coordinate mechanism, in other words, has simply become in several respects one of the battlegrounds where interdepartmental combat occurs.

The failure of the interdepartmental committees to effectively coordinate and to resolve conflict may stem from the fact that interdepartmental conflicts are not resolvable. In fact most interdepartmental disputes are zero-sum games, where if one side wins, the other loses. Hence there is no incentive to resolve the conflict or to facilitate coordination and indeed there is an incentive to minimize risk by retaining the ambiguous situation. But, on the positive side the committees themselves have become an important formal communications link within the bureaucracy. Most lateral communication in the federal bureaucracy is either informal or conducted at the very top of the hierarchy, and the provision of formal, lateral lines of communication is likely a positive step. Finally, one of the latent but positive results of the interdepartmental committee system is that it forces interpersonal contact among the bureaucratic adversaries. If knowing each other produces a better environment for cooperation this might prove to be beneficial—on the other hand, "familiarity breeds contempt." In sum, we should not expect any radical breakthroughs in coordination through the committee system, but the existence of these institutions certainly cannot hurt.

The Neo-Mandarinate By now the astute reader may be moved to ask—with so many agencies having a role in the coordination and integration of policy, who coordinates the coordinators? In part this is achieved through the Planning and Priorities Committee of Cabinet where all of the ministerial heads of the integrating agencies sit and where the financial envelopes are established. In part it is achieved through one formal and one less formal committee of deputy ministers. The formal committee is the Committee on Senior Officers (COSO). COSO was originally formed to advise the Clerk of the Privy Council and Cabinet Secretary, Michael Pitfield, on the evaluation and appointment of deputy ministers and assistant deputy ministers. It has performed this service but Pitfield also used COSO to try out new policy ideas and to attempt to achieve better integration of approaches. COSO still exists and is still used for both purposes. It has more recently been supplemented by regular, if fairly informal, meetings among the Deputy Ministers of Finance, Economic Development, Social Development, and the Secretary of the Treasury Board, chaired by the Cabinet Secretary. This group discusses both policy and management issues of major concern to the government and since it consists of the deputy heads of all the major integrating and coordination agencies it could itself be viewed, along with Cabinet Committee on Planning and Priorities, as the major centre of policy coordination in the government of Canada.

What seems to be emerging, then, parallel with the formal structures depicted here, is a "neo-mandarinate" consisting of the deputy heads of central agencies. It is unlikely they will achieve the pre-eminence or policy dominance of the old mandarins but whether they will succeed in better integrating and coordinating the disparate activities of modern government departments remains an open question.

Financial Advisors

Figure 15-4 indicated that four agencies played the pre-eminent roles in advising cabinet on financial issues. We have already seen some indication of the interrelationships among them. The Department of Finance is responsible for overall economic management, for the raising of revenues, and for the economic forecasts and fiscal framework on which expenditure allocations are based. The Treasury Board with its Secretariat is responsible for the management of current year expenditures, for the allocation of resources to programs, for the provision of advice on the allocation of funds between one broad area and another, and for general management of the public service. The Ministries of State for Economic Development and Social Development are responsible for supporting the cabinet committees for the two major expenditure areas as they make policy priority choices within their expenditure envelopes, for helping to develop policy initiatives within the envelopes, for ensuring the development and maintenance of long range expenditure projections, and for assuring coordination within the envelope.

To see the relationship between these bodies and their role in the policy process we can consider that process from two perspectives; first from that of a policy proposal taking shape and coming forward and second from that of the complex budgetary process.

Financial Priorities and New Policies   If the federal cabinet were considering making a major priority decision (to go ahead or to hold back) on a program of income supplementation for the "working poor" in Canada, a number of stages would be gone through. First there is the essential initiation stage described earlier, the most important part of which for our present concerns is the assessment of the amount of demand for such a program. Since some of these types of proposals are essentially generated from within the bureaucracy, it may be more proper to suggest that it is an assessment of the amount of support for the policy which is called for at this stage. Indeed as pointed out earlier, the matter would not normally come to the cabinet's attention at all unless there were some spontaneous public pressure or unless the bureaucracy had succeeded in creating some. Since the inputs would normally have been channelled at least partially through relevant departments (particularly, in this example, National Health and Welfare), those departments themselves would be pushing for a priority decision. And since most major policy areas, including the one in this example, are in areas of divided jurisdiction, discussions with provincial governments at both the ministerial and bureaucratic levels would also be going forward simultaneously. However, some of the most important questions in approaching a priority decision on a matter such as income supplementation concern the financial feasibility and the macro-economic effects of such a step, the place of such a costly proposition within the government's overall scheme of priorities, and the fit between this policy and other government income-support policies delivered by an array of departments.

The Department of Finance has as one of its duties the responsibility for preparing economic forecasts and projections for the whole economy and for government revenues. This information will become a vital part of the data required to make a priority decision on all substantive policy issues. If the Department of Finance is forecasting declining government revenues, then the cabinet will be extremely reluctant to take on a big new program however desirable it may otherwise be. Similarly, if the Department of Finance opines that an income supplementation program will create critical economic problems in the country, the cabinet may well be reluctant to assign a high priority to such an item. This, together with advice on the allocation of resources among the broad sectors of government, is what is meant in Figure 15-4 by the provision of aggregate financial advice. Since cabinet ministers are not normally economists and since they are too busy to be able to engage in extensive searches for alternative information, they are rather at the mercy of the Department of Finance at this stage in the process.

Closely connected to the foregoing questions are the problems of how such a program could be fitted in with current government activity in other fields and whether the federal budget could stand the strain. The Ministry of State for Social Development, working within the social policy budgetary envelope for the next several fiscal years must determine whether the potential increase in expenditure can be covered or whether the adoption of a new policy will necessitate the deletion of some current programs, an increase in the deficit, or a tax increase. If either of the latter two financing mechanisms are required, the Department of Finance and the cabinet Planning and Priorities Committee will re-enter the fray. The relevant Ministry of State must also consider the fit of the proposed program with on-going programs in its policy area and advise ministers on the fit of the proposal with overall governmental priorities. The ministries can also originate program proposals themselves in order to meet priorities or to replace older programs. This policy initiation function may become more important as the ministries develop since many of the program changes required may cut across the boundaries of several departments. This is what is meant in Figure 15-4 by the provision of policy advice by financial advisors.

Unlike the Department of Finance and the Ministries of State which are structurally the same as any other department, the Treasury Board is a statutory committee of the Privy Council. The Board itself is composed of five cabinet members whose portfolios affect the financial affairs of the government of Canada, the Minister of Finance, *ex officio*, and the President of the Treasury Board who is its chairman and is also the minister in charge of the Secretariat. We have seen that the Treasury Board has two broad sets of responsibilities. The first of these relates to the "management" of the public service. In this regard it attempts to improve the public service as an administrative system, offers advice to the line managers of government as to how they might improve their individual operations, acts as the "Employer" for purposes of collective bargaining, and issues "guidelines" for administrative and financial procedures, guidelines which have the effect of law. In part these functions are carried out within the Secretariat but many of the financial management issues are handled in the office of the Comptroller-General, a quasi-independent secretariat which also reports to the Treasury Board. This management function is a vital one but is more properly dealt with when we consider bureaucratic processes.

Its second set of responsibilities relates to the budgetary process. The Financial Administration Act which is the legislation governing the expenditure process, delegates to Treasury Board responsibility as the overseer of the budgetary process. In this role, Treasury Board Secretariat keeps track of current and projected expenditures within envelopes according to a common set of rules and it also approves current expenditures and allocates personnel resources. Thus the determination of whether and how a new program proposal such as our example can be afforded is dealt with not only by Ministries of State and Finance but also by Treasury Board. Since the latter also determines the allocation of person years to new programs, it is in the position of being able to decide whether a new program will even be effectively implemented.

What we have done here so far is to use a hypothetical example of a new policy proposal in order to demonstrate the respective roles of the financial advisory agencies of the government of Canada in the process of determining substantive policy priorities. Now, however, we must shift gears and move to a consideration of the role of these agencies in the ongoing process of establishing expenditure priorities among the current operational programs of the government.

Financial Priorities and the Budgetary Process   It should be clear by now that there is a very direct relationship between budgetary processes and the determination of priorities. It seems obvious that this should be so but until the late 1970s, the budgetary process looked only eighteen months ahead and was used much more as an administrative tool than as an instrument to bring financial considerations into priority determination.[20] The result was a stop-start system of priority determination; if revenues were rising almost any policy proposed would be accepted by cabinet but when "restraint" hit, no new policies would be accepted and no adjustments made. In an attempt to smooth out this cycle and to allow adjustments to be made at any time, the trend in the late 1970s and early 1980s has been to attempt to

---

[20] For a description of the older budgetary system see A. W. Johnson, "The Treasury Board of Canada and the Machinery of Government in the 1970s," *Canadian Journal of Political Science*, Vol. IV, No. 3, September 1971, pp. 354-356. When Mr. Johnson wrote that article he was Secretary of the Treasury Board. For a more extensive critique of the older system see Douglas Hartle, *The Expenditure Budget Process in the Government of Canada* (Canadian Tax Foundation, Toronto, 1978). Some comments on the evolutionary process described here are provided in D. Hartle, "The Report of the Royal Commission on Financial Management and Accountability: a Review," *Canadian Public Policy*, Summer 1979, pp. 366-382.

stretch out the budgetary cycle to a multi-year process and to make priority determination fit within this cycle while still leaving sufficient flexibility to deal with emergency situations as they arise. This change did not happen suddenly and there have been earlier attempts to introduce priority or goal setting into the budgetary cycle, most notably the influential but somewhat abortive Planning Programming Budgeting System (PPBS) of the early 1970s.[21] It is not likely that the system described herein will be the "final answer" either so the reader will have to remain alert to changes. However, the direction of the evolution is clearly towards longer time horizons, closer ties between the expenditure budget and priority determination, and expanded power for the constellation of agencies supporting cabinet in these endeavours.

The cycle begins with the preparation, by the Department of Finance, of four-year projections of economic conditions and hence of government revenues, and the parallel preparation of expenditure forecasts by the Treasury Board Secretariat in consultation with the Ministries of State. Immediately, of course, the budgetary system is at risk because the making of economic projections one month ahead is difficult and the making of four-year projections is somewhere between a black art, and blind luck—sanctified, of course by computer print-outs. Expenditure projections, which themselves depend on economic assumptions such as rate of inflation and unemployment, not to mention oil prices, are equally difficult to make with any accuracy. Nonetheless, if the basic objective is to determine relative priorities and to make them more explicit by assigning dollar values to them, the exercise can still be effective as long as common assumptions are adhered to throughout the system. On the basis of these

---

[21] Much has been written about PPBS. On the general system, see F. J. Lyden and E. G. Miller (eds.). *Planning, Programming, Budgeting: A Systems Approach to Management* (Markham, Chicago, 1965), or David Novich, *Program Budgeting* (Harvard University Press, Cambridge, 1965), or J. Burkehead, *Government Budgeting* (John Wiley and Son, New York, 1966), or H. A. Hovey, *The Planning-Programming-Budgeting Approach to Government Decision-Making* (Praeger, New York, 1968). On Canadian applications, see Canada, Treasury Board, *Planning, Programming, Budgeting Guide* (Queen's Printer, Ottawa, 1968), Canada, Treasury Board, *Statement to the Senate Committee on Science Policy*, by S. S. Reisman, Feb. 2, 1969; G. Guruprasad, "Planning for Tax Administration in Canada: The PPB System in National Revenue and Taxation," *Canadian Public Administration*, Vol. 16, no. 3, Autumn 1973, pp. 399-421; A. W. Johnson, "The Treasury Board and the Machinery of Government in the 1970s," Michael Hicks, "The Treasury Board of Canada and its Clients, Five Years of Administrative Reform 1966-1971," *Canadian Public Administration*, Vol. 16, no. 2, Summer 1973; and Douglas Hartle, *The Expenditure Budget Process in the Government of Canada*. The second edition of this text also contains an extensive section on PPBS, see pp. 357-359.

projections of the overall "pie" available, the Planning and Priorities Committee of Cabinet allocates revenues to the various broad sectors of government over the four years following the current fiscal year. These allocations are the expenditure "envelopes" which form the budgetary bases within which the various policy sectors must then distribute funds internally among the multitude of competing programs that make up the sector.

Within the Ministries of State and the Treasury Board Secretariat, the allocations are then compared to projected expenditures in order to determine how much financial elbow room the sector has for new programs over the next four years or alternately, how much is required in the way of reductions in current programs in order to provide any such room. Since the federal government, under either party, has been committed to rates of expenditure growth lower than the rate of GNP increases, and at times even lower than the rate of inflation, the exercise of matching expenditures to envelope allocations has tended to require considerable cutting of older programs.

Given the restraints introduced by the envelope management systems and the commitment to rates of government expenditure growth lower than GNP increases, if the government is to implement any new programs, it must create a policy reserve. This reserve then constitutes the money available for assignment to new priorities. The bulk of expenditures—normally over 90 percent—remain part of the "A-Budget" or "A-Base." Perhaps the greatest problem facing this or any other attempt to allow governments to change their priorities is the sanctity of the A-Base. Once a program is created it is extremely difficult to eliminate it, for every program has both a clientele and a bureaucratic agency to deliver it each of which will lose significant benefits if the program vanishes. By contrast the benefits in eliminating the program are usually so widely distributed among taxpayers as to be virtually negligible to any one of them. Those who benefit from the program will have an incentive to fight hard to keep it; those who benefit from its elimination have no such strong incentive and hence are relatively indifferent. For the political priority setter, concerned with avoiding the kind of conflict which can result in electoral defeat, the A-Base which finances existing programs therefore takes on the kind of sanctity which requires extraordinary courage, extraordinary stubbornness, or extraordinary tendencies to self-destruction to overturn. The result in a time of rising revenues need not necessarily be a major problem but in a time of declining revenues it can produce virtual paralysis.

However, if we assume that some policy reserves can be created— as indeed they were in both the Social and Economic policy envelopes during the first year of application of the envelope system by a combination of fairly major program changes and the cutting of some small programs and some administrative overhead—then the problem becomes one of choosing new priorities for the expenditure proposals. At this point all of the advisory functions described to this point come into play.

The four-year expenditure cycle contains within it a much more sharply focussed eighteen to twenty-four-month cycle. Approximately twelve months before the start of a fiscal year, the Secretary of the Treasury Board sends a "call letter" to all departments and agencies asking them to prepare concrete "program forecasts" accompanied by "strategic overviews" for the forthcoming fiscal year. The strategic overview ideally specifies all the forces likely to impinge on departmental expenditures in the twelve to twenty-four-month period for which the program forecast is to be valid. The forecast itself suggests what expenditures departments think will be necessary to cover their ongoing activities (their A-Base) during the next fiscal year. A process of bargaining and negotiation ensues among Treasury Board, interested in keeping overall expenditures down, the Ministries of State interested in keeping expenditures within envelope limits while providing some extra funds for policy reallocations, and operating departments, interested in keeping up expenditure levels for all their activities. The bargaining goes through numerous iterations, the result of which is the completion, by the end of December preceding the April 1 start of the next fiscal year, of the Main Estimates. These, in the form of a metropolitan telephone-book-sized "Blue Book" are tabled in the House of Commons early in the new calendar year, are considered in parliamentary committees and passed, usually unchanged, in the form of expenditure "votes." These constitute authority for the Receiver General to disburse the funds to departments for expenditure.

In practice this is a very complex process and it is accompanied by procedures for supplementary estimates and for the audit and evaluation of expenditures, the details of which are considered in Chapter 16. It is made further complicated by the fact that the whole system is properly described as a rolling cycle. As the Main Estimates are being tabled, the four-year revenue and expenditure projections are being rolled forward one more year, the intermediate years updated, new program forecasts are being prepared, new policy reserves created, and new priority determinations made. What is important for our concerns is that the priority determinations and the new policy expenditures are usually made in the early stages of the program forecast or program review exercise and the possibility of making adjustments becomes more and more difficult as the time for the tabling of Main Estimates approaches. In order partially to deal with this rigidity, cabinet has a reserve fund which can be allocated in emergencies and there is in addition a Treasury Board operating reserve which can be used to cover unanticipated cost increases.

The image which emerges from this is one of considerable complexity and of a priority management system in a state of considerable flux as governments attempt to grapple with the problem of maintaining enough flexibility to permit the choice of new priorities in an era when social and financial pressures appear to preclude any substantial increase in revenues and expenditures. The objectives of Canadian government and indeed of governments throughout the Western world have been quite consistent in this regard since at least the early 1970s and the historical threads can be traced back to the 1920s. For example, the Treasury Board manual on PPBS from 1974 defines the then new expenditure and priority management system as involving the following concepts:

a) *The setting of specific objectives*
b) *Systematic analysis to clarify objectives and to assess alternative ways of meeting them*
c) *The framing of budgetary proposals in terms of programs directed toward the achievement of the objectives*
d) *The projection of the costs of these programs a number of years in the future*
e) *The formulation of plans of achievement year by year for each program, and*
f) *An information system for each program to supply data for the monitoring of achievement of program objectives and the appropriateness of the program itself*

The manual goes on to emphasize that this is a process for determining priorities through resource allocation by asserting:

The elements of the Canadian government PPB system have been developed . . . within the context of total resource allocation. By the latter phrase is meant that there is an explicit recognition that the total resources are limited in terms of the individual and collective demands of departments and there has to be a setting of priorities by the government itself in light of which departments can plan and budget. . . . Program budgeting is primarily concerned with resource allocation within the department. [22]

With the important exception of an emphasis upon sector-wide rather than departmental reallocation, the same concepts underlie expenditure management in the 1980s. [23]

---

[22] Canada, Treasury Board, *Planning, Programming, Budgeting Guide,* p. 4. Reproduced by permission of Information Canada.

[23] The system is similar in many respects to attempts to introduce a long-term planning cycle in Britain. There, the system has run into several of the problems outlined above, exacerbated by chronic inflation much higher than in Canada. See M. Wright, "Public Expenditure in Britain: The Crisis of Control," *Public Administration,* V. 55, Summer 1977.

Ad Hoc Executive Support Agencies: Royal Commissions and Task Forces

Frequently, areas of special concern to the cabinet are dealt with by special task forces or Royal Commissions set up by cabinet decree. The use of task forces and to a lesser extent, Royal Commissions, has in recent years become increasingly popular at both federal and provincial levels of government as a way of combining external and governmental expertise in a particular area.[24] Royal Commissions of Inquiry have a long history in Canadian politics.[25] At first they were usually set up to investigate particularly sensitive areas where some wrongdoing in the governmental structure was suspected, and they were usually headed by a Justice. They had little real importance in the policy-making process. By the mid 1960s, however, they were used increasingly to investigate areas of policy concern, such as taxation, health services, and bilingualism and biculturalism. Today's typical Royal Commission is small—with one, two, or three commissioners and a staff of some ten or twelve; but the Carter Commission on Taxation and the Hall Commission on Health Services both had considerably larger staffs of experts, while the Royal Commission on Bilingualism and Biculturalism featured nine commissioners with a staff of hundreds and managed, for a few brief years, to eliminate almost completely unemployment among Canadian social scientists. A government is not formally bound by a Royal Commission Report, but by the very act of appointing the commission, it indicates substantial concern about a problem. Since most commissions publish most of their findings, and since there has, presumably, been considerable public interest in the issue under study, governments usually move to implement at least a part of what the commissions suggest.

It has often been suggested that governments will appoint a Royal Commission when they want to defuse an issue or to bury it in studies. No doubt this is the intention behind the appointment of many commissions but in following this route a government must be aware that it is creating a ticking time bomb. Eventually the commission will report. The Report will be made public and will be widely read. Since the commission is quite independent, the government cannot easily control its output and since it is viewed by the public as being independent and impartial, there may be very considerable

---

[24] M. Lamontagne, "The Influence of the Politician," pp. 271-366, especially p. 266ff.
[25] John C. Courtney, "In Defense of Royal Commissions," *Canadian Public Administration*, Vol. 12, no. 2, pp. 198-212, Summer, 1969. See also H. R. Hanson, "Inside Royal Commissions," *Canadian Public Administration*, Vol. 2, no. 3, pp. 356-364, Fall, 1969, and C. E. S. Walls, "Royal Commissions: Their Influence on Public Policy," *Canadian Public Administration*, Vol. 12, no. 3, pp. 365-371, Fall, 1969.

pressure to implement its proposals. The Hall Commission almost certainly sped up the provision of public health insurance in Canada The Carter Commission helped create a demand for tax reform even if the reform was considerably different than what the commission proposed.

Perhaps for these reasons governments frequently make use of task forces rather than Royal Commissions to provide input and advice on priorities. The task force is a structure much less formal than the Royal Commission, but it is coming into increasing use at both federal and provincial levels. Task forces vary widely in formality, size, and structure, but frequently have one overall director and a small staff of professionals, and typically, they farm out much of their research responsibilities in the form of contracts. Many of them, including the ones that are most important at the priority-setting stage of the policy process, report directly to a cabinet committee through some responsible minister, but the term "task force" is also increasingly used to describe lower-level working groups set up to investigate some area of concern within a department. As far as governments are concerned, the great advantage of the task force is that its work can usually be kept secret. Consequently, if a government does not like what it is told, it simply fails to publish the task force's report and makes its priority determination in favour of the status quo.

CONCLUSIONS

As can be seen, the ways in which priorities are established within the federal government are highly complex. Moreover, if the provincial and municipal levels are added to the process, something we will do in the next chapter, it becomes extremely complicated indeed. How, then, can any overall sense be made of this part of the policy process?

There is, perhaps, one framework which is more useful than others: the whole priority process might be viewed as a set of bargaining relationships. Since resources are scarce they must be rationed, and as soon as people begin to feel any sort of shortage they will begin to bargain to maximize their satisfactions.[26] Thus, when deci-

---

[26] See, for example, Thomas C. Schelling, "An Essay on Bargaining," *The American Economic Review*, Vol. 66, no. 3, pp. 281-306, June, 1956. The classic statement of this approach, developed in the United States, but we suggest also very applicable to Canada, is Aaron Wildavsky, *The Politics of the Budgetary Process*, 2nd ed. (Little, Brown, Boston, 1974). See also Ira Shaskansky, *The Politics of Taxing and Spending* (Bobbs Merrill, Indianapolis, 1969), and H. Heclo and A. Wildavsky, *The Private Government of Public Money* (University of California Press, Berkeley, 1974), and G. T. Allison, *Essence of Decision* (Little Brown, Boston, 1970), particularly "model 3."

sion makers discover that not all of the demands they consider important can be satisfied, they will begin to trade off one project against another in an attempt to ensure that those which they consider to be most important can be satisfied. Officials who are well down the line are concerned with only one or two programs or parts of programs that directly affect them, and it is usually up to them to administer these projects, not bargain for them in the first instance. The higher officials in departments and agencies bargain within their own departments to ensure that their own spheres of influence survive and expand. In the game of interdepartmental politics, departments themselves are engaged in a continuous process of bargaining and building coalitions to maximize their own departmental power and to "optimize" their own "program mix."

At the cabinet and intergovernmental levels, this bargaining process is particularly evident. Cabinet ministers must frequently trade their support on one issue for the support of a colleague on another, and federal-provincial conferences at the first ministers' level—or more particularly the back rooms and dinner parties at those conferences—tend to be the arenas for a great deal of intergovernmental bargaining. Thus, while the structures for priority determination tend to look somewhat different at various levels within the political system, and at different times within each level, there do tend to be underlying similarities of process which shape the nature of priority determination.

Before we leave the subject of priority determination, there are two particularly important points which need to be emphasized, especially since they draw attention to dangers and problems in the Canadian political system. The less important of these is the problem of blockages caused by breakdown in the bargaining process among bureaucratic agencies. These blockages are caused by the normal desire of departments or agencies to expand, and the necessity—in view of the scarcity of resources—of doing so partially at the expense of other departments and agencies. Blockages developed in this way introduce major inefficiencies into priority determination.

There is, however, a larger problem revolving around the establishment of new priorities for Canada. In the end, such priorities are normally set by political people. No matter how important the bureaucracy may be in priority determination, the final gatekeepers are still the cabinet ministers. Their motivation is, at least partially, to get votes for what is being done. Thus, the determination of new priorities may be largely induced by immediate demands, for only if a politician is acting directly in response to a demand is he or she likely to get much immediate recognition for those actions. No one gets much political credit for planning ahead and thus solving a problem if the problem has not yet become serious enough to be perceived by the public. Hence, political systems often tend to respond to crises rather than to anticipate them. Those who must formulate new policies are often thrust into the middle of a problem with no time ever to attempt to develop long-range strategy, rational goals, or activities and processes which will get them to those goals.

This point cannot be taken too far, however, for politicians have to do two things to keep themselves in power. They must, of course, win elections, but at an even more fundamental level, they must maintain support for the system of government within which they work. A regime which is constantly faced with crises may eventually lose public support and collapse. Therefore, in addition to responding to demand inputs, a cabinet must plan ahead to some extent in order to avoid critical crises, and to avoid giving the appearance of merely stumbling from one crisis to another.

We should leave this chapter as we began it by warning the reader that although there are underlying commonalities in the process, the relationships among agencies, the occupants of positions, and many of the surface rules of the game can change very quickly. What remains constant is the necessity to select priorities, the need to do it at least partially in the context of restricted resources, and the consequent requirement that bargaining and trade-offs lie at the root of the whole process.

16

Federalism and the Policy Process: Intergovernmental Priorities

We have seen in Chapters 8 and 9 that the responsibility for policy making in Canada is distributed among the various provinces and the federal government, each of which is sovereign in its own jurisdictional sphere and each of which possesses at least some of the financial resources necessary for carrying into effect its own policies. It is the intention of this chapter to attempt an overview of intergovernmental relations in Canada and to attempt some generalizations about the impact of divided jurisdiction on the policy process.[1]

THE PROBLEM: INTERJURISDICTIONAL POLICY COORDINATION

That there is a need for intergovernmental coordination in Canada is not difficult to establish. The very existence of a federal system is predicated on the existence of regional diversity. The cultural and economic variance among the regions of our federation produces wide differences in policy priorities not only among the provinces, but between the provinces and the federation as a whole. If all policy issues docilely conformed to the rigid jurisdictional boundaries established by the BNA Act and its judicial interpreters, the conflicting priorities of the various governments in Canada would not be a serious problem. However, there are, in fact, very few subject areas of public policy today which do not in some way fall into the jurisdic-

[1] The influence of the writings of Donald Smiley on our basic approach to Canadian federalism will quickly become obvious to the reader. However, since his influence has been so broad it is easier to acknowledge our debt in a single comprehensive footnote. Of the many works by Professor Smiley, see especially: *Canada in Question: Federalism in the Eighties* (McGraw-Hill Ryerson, Toronto, 1980); *Conditional Grants and Canadian Federalism* (Canadian Tax Foundation, Toronto, 1963); *The Canadian Political Nationality* (Methuen, Toronto, 1967); "The Two Themes of Canadian Federalism," *Canadian Journal of Economics and Political Science*, Vol. 31, no. 1, 1965; "Federalism and the Public Policy Process," and "Cooperative Federalism: An Evaluation," in J. P. Meekison (ed.), *Canadian Federalism: Myth or Reality* (Methuen, Toronto, 1971); and "Public Administration and Canadian Federalism," *Canadian Public Administration*, Vol. VII, no. 3, 1964, pp. 371-388.

tional bailiwicks of more than one government. Thus, if government in Canada is to meet the problems of a modern society with policies which are both appropriate and effective, there must be coordination of the efforts of eleven governments. Such coordination of federal and provincial policies can be achieved only if there is agreement on basic social goals, and a willingness to seek, through compromise, some mutually acceptable policy priorities which will maximize the achievement of those goals. The agreement on basic goals is reflected in our political culture—such a value consensus is either already present, or there is nothing that can be done about it. The necessary compromises on governmental priorities however, can be achieved only through a process of intergovernmental bargaining.

In the previous chapter we discussed the process of interdepartmental competition and coordination in terms of bargaining; similarly the process of intergovernmental competition and coordination is also one of bargaining. However, intergovernmental bargaining is substantially different from interdepartmental bargaining for the simple reason that the latter occurs among legally *subordinate* agencies. While the *de facto* decision-making power usually rests within the complex maze of interdepartmental coordination, any "logjams" that might crop up in the negotiations can ultimately be settled by cabinet-level or central agency intervention. This not only encourages the bureaucrats to compromise in the interest of avoiding an imposed settlement which might please nobody, but it also means that stalemates will generally not be permitted to stand in the way of needed action to solve pressing problems. While we cannot underestimate the primacy of the bureaucratic-level bargaining process, in the final analysis, hierarchical processes of control do exist and these can be utilized where interdepartmental bargaining has broken down.

By contrast to interdepartmental bargaining within a single government, intergovernmental bargaining occurs between legally equal and sovereign entities. There is no superior authority which is empowered to intervene and force a settlement when the negotiations have broken down. The judicial system can to some extent play the role of arbitrator in intergovernmental disputes, but only if the stalemate involves jurisdictional issues, and then only if the courts are asked to do so. As was seen in Chapter 7, the Canadian judiciary cannot initiate litigation; it can act only when legal action is initiated by parties to a real dispute, or when a government "refers" a piece of legislation for judicial opinion. Thus in the arena of federal-provincial relations, the basic socio-political medium of control known as hierarchy is absent. The federal-provincial dimension of policy making is therefore a "purer" form of bargaining than either the process of interdepartmental bargaining which occurs within a single government, or the process of intergroup and group-system bargaining which was discussed in Chapter 15.

The implications of the fact that federal-provincial relations in Canada involve a process of bargaining among constitutionally "equal" parties is that intergovernmental conflict can only be resolved if the active process of self-interested "horse trading" is tempered with some fundamental consensus. There must be some mutual feelings of good will, a basic agreement on very fundamental values, and most importantly, the shared acceptance of Canada as a legitimate political community; these attitudes form the pedestal upon which the machinery of intergovernmental conflict resolution is mounted.

Such attitudes do appear to be generally encouraged by the matrix of public opinion. The empirical evidence on the national unity question shows us that while provinces are an important focus for Canadians, in fact people tend on the average to "feel more warmly" toward Canada than they do toward their province. However the authors of *Political Choice in Canada*[2] also discovered that affection for Canada relative to the province is weaker in the peripheral provinces than it is in the central provinces. Newfoundlanders, likely because their province was the last into Confederation, actually feel more warmly about their province, and P.E.I. and Alberta respondents, in 1974, rated the country and the province about equally "in their hearts."

The feeling of "warmth" toward Canada is balanced by the fact that when respondents in the same national survey were asked which *government* they "feel closest" to, in every province except Ontario (and to a lesser degree Quebec) they picked the provinces. As one might expect, the farther the respondent lives from Ottawa, the stronger the attachment to the provincial government. Finally, when asked which level of government is more important in their lives, "Canadians give equal weight to each, a judgement which matches that of most impartial observers."[3]

The conclusion to be taken from this attitudinal data is that "the two levels of government are perceived by the population as jointly important and having positive characteristics."[4] While this does not provide us with a complete explanation for the legitimacy or persistence of the Canadian political community, it does indicate that the existence of a governmental system featuring divided jurisdiction, with the provinces and the federal government resolving conflict

---

[2] Clarke et al., op. cit., ch. 3.
[3] Ibid., p. 81.
[4] Ibid.

through a process of bargaining, political conciliation, and compromise, is accepted by the populace. As Clarke et al. put it, intergovernmental conflict resolution

. . . *works best in a situation where the population is not polarized into opposing camps, as federalists or provincial rightists, but rather where for some purposes they look to the federal actors and for others they turn to their provincial governments.*

Our examination of attitudes toward the federal system and behaviour within it has led to the conclusion that such a polarization has not taken place in Canada.[5]

Thus while it is difficult to find a unifying philosophy, dominant myth, or glowing symbol of our Canadianness, it may be that the processes that we have evolved for settling disputes unite us. In this way, like boxers who have "gone the distance" in the ring as opponents, in the end, find a common bond that unites them, so Canadians are united by their political differences. Thus, somewhat ironically, perhaps we can be defined by our *conflicts* and by the uniquely Canadian way of resolving them. Certainly at the elite level this would seem to be the case. Olsen argues that while the public performances of politicians at federal-provincial conferences show us a picture of constant bickering and profound disagreement,

. . . *more candid views show Canadians a smiling group of chattering politicians and bureaucrats enjoying each others' company while basking in the afterglow of their common public performance. Thus the conflicts between and among members of the state elite are real, while at the same time they are simply an expectation associated with their role . . . a hard driving negotiator fighting for a jurisdictional interest . . . as well as . . . a convivial colleague.*[6]

We will say more about the extent and significance of the almost constant interaction among officials and technocrats of both levels of government which comprises a large part of the process of intergovernmental relations.

Our conclusion about the legitimacy of the Canadian political community is thus that Canadian unity is *sui generis*. The national unifying myths, economic interdependencies, and cultural homogeneity which form the basis of political community in other countries are not present—or else are weak—in Canada. In fact most Canadians see ethnic and regional conflict as a constant; what makes us unique and what provides the basis of political community is that we never doubt that the conflicts will be resolved. Thus by contrast to countries such

[5] Op. cit., p. 90.
[6] Denis Olsen, op. cit., pp. 18-19.

as the U.S. and the U.K. where the existence of political community was a prerequisite for a political system, in Canada we did it backwards. We started with a set of political institutions and processes and it is our common faith in these institutions and processes which now forms the basis of political community, and is thus the glue that holds the pieces of the Canadian mosaic together.

THE EVOLUTION OF INTERJURISDICTIONAL COORDINATION

In the earliest days of the federation, the dominant medium of federal-provincial coordination was the political and bureaucratic hegemony of the Dominion rather than any true process of bargaining. Despite the anti-federal sentiments in the Maritimes, the leadership of the federal government in matters of public policy was virtually unchallenged by the then confused and demoralized provinces. This is likely a partial reflection of the ultimate "capture" by the Dominion of the most prominent political figures of the colonial era, in the 1860s and 1870s. Canadian politicians expected that the major functions of government would be performed by the Dominion, and for a brief time the provincial politicians were either convinced as well, or too timid and insecure to complain.

While this "quasi-hierarchical" process of coordination never became firmly established, an analagous situation does occur even today when the War Measures Act is proclaimed; during such times, the federal distribution of powers is effectively suspended and the federal government can achieve the necessary policy coordination by fiat. Needless to say, this is rare and has only passing relevance for the problem of intergovernmental coordination.

It did not take long for the provinces to begin to assert their sovereign right to establish their own priorities in public policy. They quickly matured during the 1870s and 1880s and became capable of recruiting committed and capable politicians and public servants. The provinces very rapidly acquired the confidence and the political legitimacy to challenge the policy priorities of the federal government when those touched upon matters within the legislative jurisdiction of the provinces. The dominant mechanism of interjurisdictional coordination during this period of classical federalism was the arbitration of jurisdictional disputes by the judiciary. In fact, it can be argued that this period was characterized by an almost total lack of interest in coordination. Both the federal government and the provinces seemed willing to presume that all matters of concern to policy makers could be parcelled out "once and for all' to one or other of the various governments in Canada, and that any apparent overlap in jurisdiction was simply a cue to ask the courts to refine their interpretations with a new pronouncement.

That this combative attitude to federal-provincial relations continued well into the twentieth century was due to the essentially uncomplicated nature of the issues facing the policy makers of the day and to the competing goals of nation building and province building.[7] That the sovereign governments in Canada had different policy priorities was beyond question, but the kinds of policy alternatives being considered were usually straightforward enough that they lent themselves more readily to being introduced and administered unilaterally, by either the federal government or one of the provinces.

While the settlement of jurisdictional disputes through judicial arbitration occurs today,[8] it is used somewhat less now than it was in the first fifty years of the federation. The decline of this mode of conflict resolution in Canada was precipitated in large part by social and economic forces. In the first place, where power to make policy had once depended primarily upon the constitutional jurisdiction to do so, the expanding scope and the complexity of the problems facing government in the twenties and thirties dictated that the costs of implementing the programs would become an even more serious constraint. Often it was the case that the provinces, while possessing the full jurisdiction to initiate policies, lacked the money to finish the job. The federal government, on the other hand, seemed to possess the necessary resources, but all too often it lacked the jurisdiction.

The second factor precipitating the decline of the combative style of federal-provincial relations was the untidiness of contemporary problems. Policy makers began to recognize that most issues facing them were interrelated, and that it was impossible for a single level of government to produce a policy which would deal comprehensively with major social problems which crossed jurisdictional boundaries. It was a combination of the growing financial crisis facing the provinces and the realization that one government acting alone lacked the full jurisdiction to deal adequately with most contemporary policy matters which led to the adoption of a coordinative mechanism based on true interjurisdictional bargaining.

Through the thirties, the mood of federal-provincial relations remained basically combative; however, the desperate circumstances

[7] The best discussion of the process of "province building" and of its significance for the structure of Canadian federalism is found in Garth Stevenson's, *Unfulfilled Union* (Macmillan, 1979), ch. 5. See also J. Richards, and L. Pratt, *Prairie Capitalism: Power and Influence in the New West* (McClelland and Stewart, Toronto, 1979).

[8] See Chapter 8. See also, P. Russell, "The Anti-Inflation Case: The Anatomy of a Constitutional Decision," *CPA*, Winter 1977, 632-665.

of the period forced genuine federal-provincial coordination. Differences in priorities among the various governments were resolved through the negotiation of piecemeal agreements to meet specific problems. The emphasis was on specific problem solving and not on the consummation of a new style of federalism. The attitude was that federal-provincial cooperation and the coordination of federal and provincial programs were only necessary evils, and the most common policy manifestations of these bargains were shared-cost programs or federal conditional grants to the nearly bankrupt provinces. While not a highly integrated system of conflict resolution, the piecemeal coordinative efforts of the thirties flowed from a genuine bargaining situation; the bargaining "capital" (or "currency") used in the negotiations was jurisdiction and tax revenues. The provinces, for the most part, could promise to implement necessary social legislation which met federally established standards, in return for which the federal government would pay all or a percentage of the operating costs of the programs. While naturally some provinces were financially better off than others and hence could afford to "hold out" for better offers from the "feds," by and large, because the provinces possessed equal jurisdictional clout, all nine could take an active part in periodic negotiations.

But the process of Canadian federalism changed somewhat during the war years. At the termination of hostilities the provinces were resigned to the fact that for a while at least the federal government would be in the driver's seat; having provided both substantive and psychic leadership during the war, the federal government would continue to assume that role in the public eye for the period of postwar economic reconstruction. The federal government maintained this initiative in policymaking into the fifties, setting many of the priorities for the provinces through the traditional instrument of conditional grants and subsidies which the provinces could not politically afford to reject. The provincial role in the meantime was to act as a brake on the activities of Ottawa.

However, as the war became merely tragic history, and as the Canadian economy continued to grow despite minor setbacks, the federal government began to fade in the eyes of the public as the government that necessarily could and should set our political goals. The initiative began to shift again to the provinces, who could now afford to get back to the business of "province building." Moreover the public focus and public expectations turned to social programs and highway construction, both of which lie in provincial spheres of jurisdiction. Also, toward the end of this period, Quebec was involved in what has loosely been referred to as the "Quiet Revolution," with the result that the erstwhile passive and defensive nationalism that had characterized the province's posture towards federalism became aggressive and assertive. The government of the Province of Quebec began to demand a sufficient share of the tax dollar to be economically *maître chez lui* and to run its own programs, instead of merely sharing the cost and administrative responsibility for those which were federally sponsored. Taking the lead from Quebec, the other provinces also began to assert themselves, reflecting the new confidence inspired by an economic and administrative "coming of age" and a patent dissatisfaction with "the inherent paternalism of the grant-in-aid device."

But the rejuvenated political muscles of the provinces did not precipitate a return to the federalism of the thirties. Not only had the mood of federal-provincial relations become more "cooperative" and less combative, but the interjurisdictional bargaining ceased to be purely piecemeal and problem-oriented. There was by now a tendency to seek more completely integrated programs such as the comprehensive tax-sharing system.[9] Moreover, the provinces were growing very important with respect to their contributions to the effects on the Canadian economy as a whole, and it was becoming clear that any meaningful control over economic fluctuations would have to be exercised through joint federal and provincial action. An example of this is the effort to stem the tide of inflation in Canada through a policy of fiscal restraint. In order to regulate the Canadian economy, it is no longer sufficient for the federal government to undertake an austerity program or to grant tax incentives to certain industries. Unilateral action by the federal government will only make a "dent" in the economic status quo; the provinces themselves control directly, or through their municipalities, well over half the public sector expenditures and are therefore in a position to strongly affect the working of the economy through fiscal measures that are constitutionally within their exclusive jurisdiction. The regulation of the Canadian economy, which has traditionally been considered one of the prerogatives of the central government, must now be achieved through federal-provincial cooperation. Thus, where cooperative federalism was characterized at one time by the federal government's sharing the responsibility for provincial matters with the provinces, the tables have been turned, and cooperative federalism today includes the additional sharing of federal matters with the provinces.

As intergovernmental policy coordination became more holistic in its focus, the bargaining process became a regular, indeed a constant,

---

[9] See Chapter 9.

activity for the eleven governments. It is obvious that this would tax the resources of the smaller provinces more than those of the big ones, but the introduction of unconditional federal subsidies for the poorer provinces in the form of equalization grants helped to cover some of the administrative costs of maintaining constant intergovernmental liaison. Despite the new administrative burdens of cooperative federalism, therefore, possession of the basic bargaining capital of jurisdiction over social programs permitted all of the provinces to participate actively in the negotiations. Coordination was ultimately achieved where it was necessary to integrate federal and provincial programs, and mutual compromise in the interest of solving Canada's problems was made easier by the basic mood of cooperation. However, before moving to a consideration of the current trends in federalism in Canada, it is necessary to describe the institutional devices which have evolved to facilitate the almost constant process of interjurisdictional bargaining.

THE STRUCTURES OF INTERJURISDICTIONAL COORDINATION

In the early years of federal-provincial relations, meetings of federal and provincial officials occurred in an *ad hoc* manner, and at fairly senior levels in the governmental hierarchies. Meetings of the Premiers and the Prime Minister would be called at irregular intervals, usually at the initiative of the federal government, to discuss specific problems of concern to all jurisdictions. In recent times however, these conferences have become institutionalized to the extent that they now meet on a fairly regular basis and include bureaucratic as well as political decision makers. While *ad hoc* meetings still occur, the necessity for such informal talks is reduced by the existence of many formal bodies which meet at least annually if not more often.

In an article published in 1965, Edgar Gallant (then a Deputy Secretary to the Cabinet) remarked that "the number of [federal-provincial] conferences and committees doubled over eight years."[10] In absolute terms the number of such committees had risen from 64 in 1957 to 125 in 1965, which by most standards is indeed a remarkable rate of growth. However, based on information sifted from an *Inventory of Federal Provincial Committees* (2 vols.), compiled by the PCO in 1972, the number of interjurisdictional institutions in existence at the time

[10] E. Gallant, "The Machinery of Federal Provincial Relations," *C.P.A.*, December, 1965, p. 515.

could be established at more than 400.[11] While growth of such institutions seems to have stabilized since the mid-1970s, it is still safe to conclude even from the imperfect data available to us that more is happening in the federal-provincial arena every day. What is more interesting than numbers, however, is the distribution of these institutions among various policy areas and governmental decision-making levels, and their internal structure.

The Distribution of Interjurisdictional Bodies by Policy Area

Because the inventory which is the source of these data was compiled from submissions by federal departments listing their own interjurisdictional affiliations, it is possible to make some rough generalizations as to the distribution of these bodies among broad policy areas. All federal-provincial committees can likely be categorized in this manner with the exception of the First Ministers' Conference which concerns itself with macro-priority determination in all policy areas of concern to both the federal government and the provinces and with such weighty matters as constitutional reform and energy pricing agreements.

The largest number of committees has traditionally been in the policy areas of the environment and health and welfare. The reasons for this concentration of federal-provincial institutions in these two broad areas is related in part to the political relevance of such issues in contemporary Canadian society, and in part to the degree of jurisdictional "untidiness," or overlap which characterizes the fields. Indeed in a paradoxical way, the former point is borne out by the fact that as the federal government has moved out of a number of shared cost programs in the health and welfare field,[12] and as the political importance of environmental issues has been overshadowed by energy

---

[11] The inventory listed about 400 committees, but there is considerable duplication in the list owing to the fact that committees attended by more than one federal department were sometimes listed twice. On the other hand, there are many subcommittees which went completely unlisted, so that while no exact figures can be stated, the general trends indicated by this inventory can still be very helpful in making some generalizations about the nature of such committees in Canada. A more recent study uses a different set of classifications and arrives at a lower total figure of 158 "méchanismes de liaison intergovernmentale." The lower figure is a result of a data base which does not include the many bilateral operational committees which exist for instance under The Canada Water Act. See: G. Veilleux "L'évolution de Méchanismes de liaison intergovernmentale," in Simeon, R. (ed.), *Confrontation and Collaboration* (IPAC, Toronto, 1979), p. 35.

[12] See Chapter 9.

problems,[13] the amount of intergovernmental activity in these fields has declined sharply.

The corollary of the latter point, that where the jurisdiction is clear and settled there will be less intergovernmental contact, is, however, only partly true. In fact, where the matter is clearly within the legislative jurisdiction of the federal government such as Veterans Affairs, or National Defence, it holds true that there is little federal-provincial interaction. On the other hand, in areas such as housing, highways, education, and urban affairs, which are fairly clearly provincial matters, it is not unusual to see a number of interjurisdictional bodies in existence to coordinate the activities of the several governments involved. Thus, it would seem plausible to hypothesize that the federal government's "spending power"[14] combined with its relative wealth and the need for national coordination of policies in areas of provincial jurisdiction such as education or highways gives it a potential bargaining lever even in policy areas totally within the jurisdiction of the provinces. Unfortunately for those of a centralist bent, however, the federal spending power is far more significant when dealing with the "have not" provinces than it is when dealing with the wealthier provinces. The bargaining process which is at the root of cooperative federalism is thus not only more one-sided in favour of the federal level than it might appear at first glance, but it is also extremely asymmetrical in its effect on the various provinces.

The Distribution of Interjurisdictional Bodies by Decision-Making Level

Another important dimension in the analysis of interjurisdictional institutions is the decision-making level of government at which they operate. The level is determined first by whether the personnel on the committee are political or bureaucratic, and second, if they are bureaucrats, by their organizational "rank" or position in a governmental hierarchy. For clarity and ease of discussion we have defined four decision-making levels at which interjurisdictional committees operate in Canada: the *political,* the *senior bureaucratic* (including deputy ministers and assistant deputy ministers), the *technical* or professional, and the *operational.* It must be noted that operational and technical committees (while functionally quite distinct) may in fact

---

[13] See M. Whittington, "The Department of the Environment" in Doern, G. B., (ed.), *Spending Tax Dollars* (Ottawa, 1980).

[14] Simply, the power of the federal government to spend money on any matter it chooses, provided it does not pass legislation which is *ultra vires.*

include personnel at approximately the same level or rank. The former tend to be involved directly in the implementation of joint federal-provincial programs, while the latter tend to act more as policy-analysis and research groups. Finally, in attempting to distinguish between operational and technical committees, we will discover, in fact, that implementation and policy advice frequently flow from the same committee.

The actual distribution of committees among these four decision-making levels in Canada is uneven. For the most part, there will be but one political-level committee in each policy area, composed of appropriate federal and provincial cabinet ministers. On the other hand, more than two-thirds of the total committees in any given policy area will be at the technical and operational levels. One can thus conclude that the most common form of federal-provincial interaction occurs below the ministerial level meetings which we read about in the papers, and in fact most are even *below* the senior bureaucratic level.

The problem with analyzing federal-provincial committees in the context of their numerical distribution by decision-making level is that this does not take into account comparative measures of their impact on policy outputs. For instance, perhaps the most important interjurisdictional committee in operation in Canada today (with the possible exception of the First Ministers' Conference) is the Continuing Committee on Fiscal and Economic Matters. This is a senior bureaucratic-level committee composed mainly of the Deputy Ministers of Finance or the Deputy Provincial Treasurers. Its responsibility is to provide technical support for the Conference of the Ministers of Finance and, to a large extent, for the Conference of the First Ministers. The fact that this body meets more frequently than its political-level "parent" committees, the fact that it is composed of highly skilled professionals in key administrative roles, and the fact that the committee membership is more constant than that of the political-level bodies, mean that this committee is in a position of great potential influence over the country's broad fiscal priorities, and over the coordination of measures designed to cope with the economic difficulties that we can expect to continue at least through the first years of the eighties.

The Distribution of Interjurisdictional Committees by Inclusiveness

Federal-provincial committees can also be classified according to the number of governments included. Because of the amount of attention paid to the political-level conferences by the media, one might get the impression that interjurisdictional committees are for the most part omnilateral, or composed of representatives of all eleven governments. This is far from the case, for in fact, far more than half of the bodies listed in the 1972 PCO inventory are bilateral, composed of representatives of the federal government and one province only. Less exclusive than the bilateral committees, and yet more inclusive than the omnilateral committees, are the multilateral committees composed of the federal government and some but not all of the provinces. In most policy areas, multilateral committees are more numerous than the omnilateral ones and less numerous than the bilateral ones. A major exception to the general rule about the predominance of bilateral committees is in the areas of finance, fiscal relations and constitutional reform where almost all of the active committees are omnilateral. Regional Economic Expansion offers the opposite extreme where for instance almost all of the committees are bilateral.

The overall distribution of interjurisdictional committees by decision-making level and by inclusiveness is illustrated graphically with examples in Figure 16-1. As illustrated by this chart, the political-level committees tend to be omnilateral almost exclusively. The reason for this is three-fold: first the ministers are less likely than their bureaucratic and technical staff to be able to deal with the "nitty gritty" type of bargaining that often occurs at the bilateral level; second, it is at the political level that the final agreement on priorities affecting the federation as a whole must be agreed upon—while often the political-level meetings only confirm agreements hacked out by lower-level officials, formal agreements must ultimately come at the ministerial level; and finally, the ministers at the federal level tend to be too busy to devote the time needed to haggle individually with the provinces. They prefer to meet only after some general agreement has been worked out at lower levels through bilateral and multilateral talks.

By contrast, almost all of the technical and operational level committees are either bilateral or multilateral. Some of the technical level committees in the area of finance, in fact, involve representatives of all of the provinces and the federal government, but for the most part the role of the technical people is more specific—not only in terms of subject matter but in terms of geography as well.

Structural Variations

Up until now we have spoken only of federal-provincial committees. While such committees make up by far the largest percentage of interjurisdictional bodies in Canada, it must be pointed out that there are other organizational forms. The interprovincial committees are bodies

Figure 16-1

INCLUSIVENESS OF COMMITTEES

Decision-Making Level of Committees	Omnilateral	Multilateral	Bilateral
Technical and Operational	Few—e.g., some technical level financial committees	Some—e.g., Prairie Provinces Water Board, Atlantic Tidal Power Programming Board	Most—e.g., Coordinating Committee on Northern Ontario Water Resources
Senior Bureaucratic	Most—e.g., Continuing Committee on Fiscal and Economic Matters	Some—e.g., Federal-Provincial Atlantic Fisheries Conference	Some—e.g., Joint Planning Committees of DREE, Consultative Committees under Canada Water Act, Manpower Needs Committees
Political	Most—e.g., Plenary Conference of First Ministers, Conference of Ministers of Finance	Very few—e.g., Forestry Ministers' Conference, (because P.E.I. has very little forestry)	None—Ministers are too busy for the most part —some *ad hoc* meetings such as between Alberta and Ottawa over oil pricing

which exclude the federal government, although in many cases the "feds" are permitted to send an observer.

As with the federal-provincial bodies, the interprovincial ones can be classified as omnilateral, (including all provinces), multilateral, or bilateral (including two provinces). They also vary as to the decision-making level in the same way that the federal-provincial committees do, and for the most part the generalizations about the distribution of such bodies by level and inclusiveness apply to the interprovincial arena as well. While it has been suggested that some political-level, multilateral, interprovincial committees—such as the Council of the Maritime Premiers and the Prairie Provinces Economic Council—are "proto-coalitions" which will ultimately strengthen the federal-provincial bargaining power of individual regions, there has been little hard evidence that this trend is developing. For the most part, the provinces will squabble among themselves as much as or more than they currently do with the federal government, and moreover, informal and *ad hoc* collusion among groups of provinces tends to be a better way of maximizing the provincial bargaining position on any particular issue.

A third structural variation in intergovernmental bodies is the "Tri-Level Conference." This type of committee features representatives not only of the federal government and the provinces, but of municipalities as well. While the federal government has very little constitutional authority in the area of urban affairs, its vast financial resources and its access to the multitude of experts in federal agencies ensure that there will inevitably be a federal presence in policy decisions affecting the cities. The provinces are very jealous of their primacy in the urban area but they have agreed to permit the federal government to invest its money in urban projects which have the joint approval of the provinces and the municipalities concerned. Such federal contributions to municipal development are negotiated in conferences where all three governments are represented, but where the municipal officials attend formally as part of the provincial delegation.[15] While it is still difficult to assess the impact of tri-level conferences on intergovernmental relations in Canada, it seems fairly certain, given the growing importance of urban problems as a policy concern, that this institutional form will become more common.

Another organizational form often included in compilations of intergovernmental institutions, is the *federal advisory council*. While

---

[15] The province of Manitoba is an exception in this regard for during the 1970s the City of Winnipeg was permitted to attend tri-level conferences as a *de facto* independent party to the negotiations.

organizations of this sort are formally unilateral, being established under federal statute to advise a federal minister, and usually located within the organizational labyrinth of a federal department, they often feature representatives from provincial governments. Edgar Gallant points out that "their composition, with representation from all provincial governments, is such that they do, in effect, function as federal-provincial committees to a large extent."[16] Gallant, however, goes on to cite examples of these advisory committees, most of which seem to have disappeared since his article was first published in 1965. On the basis of this admittedly flimsy evidence of the attrition of such federal advisory councils, and with the knowledge that "true" federal-provincial committees have proliferated in the same period of time, it seems reasonable to hypothesize that the unilateral advisory council is declining in relative importance in federal-provincial relations.

While up until now our focus has been upon interjurisdictional coordinative bodies which are purely governmental in composition, we must note that there are some committees which operate in the intergovernmental arena but which have non-governmental members as well. Perhaps the best examples of this genre of inter-jurisdictional body are the subcommittees of the Atlantic Fisheries Committee, dealing with sport fish and composed of relevant governmental representatives as well as local anglers' associations and commercial fishermen. While this "mixed composition" type of committee is not yet common, it could become more conventional with increasing emphasis on direct public involvement in decision making and with the growing incidence of joint government/private-sector enterprises such as Syncrude. There are advantages to such organizational forms. On the one hand, intergovernmental bargaining must occur with representatives of the private sector looking on, thus "keeping government honest." On the other hand, by including members of public-interest groups in the early stages of policy development, policy ideas can be "presold" or legitimized before they enter the political arena through co-opting of non-governmental organizations.

Support Staff: Intergovernmental Bureaucracy
While we have indicated that interjurisdictional coordination has become institutionalized and less *ad hoc* than it once was, the same is not true of the support staff for the committees. Generally the provi-

---

[16] Gallant, op cit., p. 515.

sion of secretariat services to intergovernmental committees even today is still primarily *ad hoc,* worked out informally by the members of the committee. The most common arrangement seems to be for the necessary support staff to be provided by the government whose representative chairs the particular committee. This has meant in the past that federal departments often provided support services for federal-provincial committees for the simple reason that the "feds" had the financial and manpower resources to be able to afford it. This trend, however, has been reversed to some extent by the fact that a number of the provinces also have the resources to provide support staff, and in fact they are increasingly suspicious of support services domiciled in the federal bureaucracy. In the case of interprovincial committees, the secretariat is normally part-time, composed of temporarily seconded officials of the government which chairs the meetings. As chairmanship of interprovincial committees often rotates, this means that the secretariat to the committee is located in a different provincial capital in each year.

While permanent support staff is the exception rather than the rule for interjurisdictional committees in Canada, there are significant exceptions, and the current trend is if anything away from *ad hoc* or rotating secretariats. The commonest form of permanent secretariat is a staff paid by and located in Ottawa. This is the case with the important Continuing Committee on Fiscal and Economic Matters whose secretariat is a division of the Department of Finance, and with the Canadian Intergovernmental Conference Secretariat which provides the logistical support and documentation for a range of senior intergovernmental committees. The latter is nominally supported by the federal and provincial governments but few of the provincial governments have actually paid their share of the bills.

The strengths of permanent secretariats are that they provide continuity and a level of expert advice which the committee could not achieve with rotating secondments from year to year. However, the great potential weakness of this organizational form is obviously that one government will come to dominate the setting of committee agenda, the briefing of conferees, and to an extent, the conduct of the meetings themselves. While the provincial members have the opportunity to bring their own advisors to meetings, some smaller provinces can either ill afford the expense or do not have expert advisors in the same numbers and quality as the "feds." In addition to the fairly obvious advantage to the federal government of having the committee "on its payroll," the legitimacy of the secretariat may be doubted by provincial officials who, quite rightly, come to feel that the support staff is "in Ottawa's pocket."

An experiment aimed at overcoming the weakness of the federally domiciled style of permanent secretariat in intergovernmental affairs was tried with the Canadian Council of Resource and Environment Ministers (CCREM). This interjurisdictional body has the status of a private corporation, although its members and its Board of Directors consist of federal and provincial cabinet ministers. The presidency of the Council rotates annually among the member governments, and the secretariat is permanent, composed of staff who are employees of the corporation but not of any of the member governments. The effectiveness of the CCREM in the ten years from 1963 to 1973 was related largely to its secretariat which operated as a clearing house for information, as a direct non-governmental link with the public through its publications, and as the administrative and support component of a number of major omnilateral conferences at political, senior bureaucratic, and technical levels. Perhaps the greatest strength of this secretariat was that it never carried the brand of any government; its explicit mandate was to serve all eleven governments equally. The obvious problem of such a body is the difficulty in exercising political control over it. The fact that it is permanent and independent of any single government gives it the potential to become an "intergovernmental bureaucracy" within the federation, analogous, perhaps, to the permanent staff of international organizations. The fear of "losing control" of the secretariat caused some of the CCREM's member governments to become increasingly suspicious of it. Some of the provincial ministers on the council came to view the CCREM and particularly its permanent secretariat as dangerous competitors in the process of wooing public support for environmental policy reforms. Consequently since 1973 we have seen a drastically reduced role for the Council itself and a reduction of the secretariat to a very small "caretaker" operation. Whatever its ultimate fate, the secretariat of the CCREM is an organizational form which could still be used as a prototype for future forays into interjurisdictional coordination.

Finally, in the seventies there was a rapid evolution of very specialized bureaucratic structures designed to deal with intergovernmental matters. The Quebec Department of Federal-Provincial Relations was the prototype of this kind of agency, and was set up originally in 1961 by the Lesage government (since 1967 it has been reconstituted as Intergovernmental Affairs). In the 1970s the wealthier provinces, Ontario, Alberta, and Saskatchewan, and the federal government[17]

---

[17] We have already discussed the role of the FPRO in our section on central agencies in the previous chapter.

have followed Quebec's example, and it seems likely that any province which can afford it will follow suit in the current decade.

While this trend is significant as an indication of the growing importance of the intergovernmental arena to all governments in Canada, it also has implications for bureaucratic politics. What has happened is that a new breed of specialized official, analogous to the foreign service officers who represent Canada in international dealings, has emerged. These public servants are not directly involved with specific programs, but rather have influence over a wide range of policy areas that have an intergovernmental component. These intergovernmental diplomats may evolve as important "power brokers" within both federal and provincial bureaucracies as the intensity of intergovernmental relations grows during the 1980s, and can perhaps be seen as a part of the emergent "neo-mandarinate" discussed in Chapter 15 above.

TRENDS IN CANADIAN FEDERALISM

Executive Federalism

As the need for continual federal-provincial consultation and cooperation increases in response to the growing interdependence of all social and economic problems, the institutions of interjurisdictional cooperation which have been described above will continue to grow in terms of their political significance. These bodies will increasingly be entrusted with the responsibility for making policy decisions which affect the allocation of resources in Canada. The critical political decisions will more and more frequently be referred to the federal and provincial representatives who meet at federal-provincial conferences, and there is little to indicate that existing institutions are capable of countering the trend.

There is a startling lack of attention paid to federal-provincial relations in either parliament or the provincial legislatures. There is virtually no contact between legislators of the eleven senior governments and there are no federal-provincial committees composed of legislators other than cabinet ministers. Certainly members of the opposition parties in the legislature are completely locked out of the process.[18] While there is no question that the phenomenon of *execu-*

---

[18] See John Meisel, "The Decline of Party in Canada," in H. G. Thorburn, (ed.), *Party Politics in Canada* (Prentice-Hall, Toronto, 1979), pp. 119-136. Note that the offer by Prime Minister Trudeau in 1980 to permit the opposition parties to participate in constitutional reform negotiations is an exception.

tive federalism [19] has contributed to the continued shrinking of the role of parliament and the provincial legislatures in the policy process, the causal links are likely in the reverse direction; that is, the evolution of executive federalism is a symptom of the general impotence of legislative institutions vis-à-vis the executive branch. As Garth Stevenson has pointed out: "Executive federalism may be as much a consequence as a cause of the weakness of legislatures in a system of responsible government where a single, disciplined party normally holds a majority of the seats."[20] While it could be suggested that the representatives at intergovernmental conferences continue to feel a responsibility to their home governments, that responsibility is not direct. The legislature "back home" does not exercise day-to-day control on its delegates; rather, it functions as an "electoral college" which goes no further than making the initial choice of who will represent the government in the particular interjurisdictional arena.

Similarly the party system does not appear to play a very significant role in the resolution of intergovernmental conflict. Even where the governments at the provincial and federal levels share the same party label, there does not appear to be a significantly greater propensity to "get along." While some authors such as Stevenson suggest that there is still a residual role for the party system in this regard— "The importance of party ties in resolving or avoiding federal-provincial conflict can not yet be completely dismissed, particularly in the Atlantic provinces where the federal and provincial parties remain fairly integrated"[21]—unless there are some fairly radical changes in either the party system or the process of intergovernmental relations, we must conclude with Donald Smiley that "political parties are thus of decreasing importance in the Canadian federal system. Partisan politics have relatively limited capacities for effecting the resolution of federal-provincial conflicts either through intra-party relations or general elections."[22]

The irony of the trend towards "executive federalism" is that while it fosters decentralization and exaggerates the centrifugal forces in the federation it is manifested in a heavy concentration of decision-making power in the hands of a very tiny political elite. Certainly, where the key priority decisions are made by "committees of eleven" at federal-provincial conferences, democratic control is more difficult than in a system where such decisions are approved by a parliament

---

[19] See Smiley, *Canada in Question*, ch. 4.
[20] *Unfulfilled Union*, p. 203.
[21] Stevenson, op. cit., p. 191.
[22] Smiley, op. cit., p. 146.

of 282 men and women from all parts of Canada and by provincial legislatures comprising hundreds more. Thus while the dominance of any one government is being reduced as power is dispersed among several, the power of the state in general, is becoming more and more concentrated, through the phenomenon of executive federalism.

Bureaucratic Federalism

As we have seen, executive federalism may have helped to precipitate a new trend toward a concentration of power in the Canadian system. However, in earlier chapters, we have spoken of the general tendency for policy making to depend more and more upon technical inputs from various non-elected officers of government residing in the federal and provincial bureaucracies. When these two trends are viewed together with the fact of the increased number of interjurisdictional committees operating at the senior bureaucratic, technical, and operational levels of government, one cannot avoid the suspicion that perhaps it is bureaucratic and not political executives who dominate "executive federalism."

Undoubtedly, the bureaucratic executives play an increasingly dominant role in interjurisdictional coordination at the stages of policy formulation and implementation. However, it is more difficult to maintain that bureaucratic committees dominate interjurisdictional priority determination, for the policies under consideration must ultimately be justified to eleven electorates by the ministers concerned. Nevertheless, given that there is more constant interaction among the non-elected officials, and given that politically successful programs will often be contingent upon technical feasibility, it is likely that ideas will often be generated by senior bureaucratic and technical committees and adopted with only formal consideration as priority items by the ministerial committees. While it is impossible to conclusively show that this tendency is a fact, we do know from even the most casual observation that little real bargaining goes on in the public portions of ministerial meetings; to the extent that intergovernmental priorities are determined by the politicians, therefore, the process is *in camera* and not "in front of camera."

We can come to the cautious conclusion, then, that *bureaucratic federalism* exists to the extent that the macro-level bargaining positions of the political officials at conferences are often worked out by their bureaucratic advisors, and that any interjurisdictional deals involving the formulation or implementation of joint policies are worked out mainly in bureaucratic, technical, or operational bodies considered by cabinets "back home" and then stamped with approval (or, more rarely, rejection) at ministerial conferences.

The overall significance of bureaucratic federalism is that inter-governmental coordination is probably improved. In the first place, as the frequency of interaction has increased at the non-elected levels of government, the people involved in the bargaining process actually come to know each other. They often supplement formal exchanges at committee meetings with informal contact through telephone calls and correspondence.[23] Secondly, because the personnel involved are not constrained directly by a critical and partisan public back home, the non-elected committees can bargain more honestly. Bureaucrats may be able to assume a problem-orientation partly because they do not have to be as concerned as the politician with faithfully advocating the interests of a particular region; there is greater freedom for compromise. But a problem-orientation is also more likely because of shared *professional* concerns of the bureaucrats; for instance, if forestry officials are meeting to set up a program for combatting a spruce budworm epidemic, they are usually more concerned with solving the real world problem in forestry than they are with defending provincial priorities. The combination of shared professional interests, personal ties such as friendships which grow through long-standing formal and informal contact, and a non-partisan milieu, thus tends to facilitate coordination at the bureaucratic level. As advisors to the ministers, the bureaucrats can in turn help to ease the more public and political dimension of federal-provincial bargaining, and contribute to an overall environment within which macro-level interjurisdictional compromise and cooperation is possible.

One must be careful, however, not to take these speculations too far. Anything more than the most trivial detail must eventually be at least tacitly ratified at the ministerial level, and most ministers are far from being only automatons manipulated by their bureaucratic establishments. Sometimes the right to ministerial control is honoured more in the breach than the observance, but it would be a foolish bureaucrat who ignored the minister's wishes—expressed or implied—on a major policy question.

---

[23] Note that the basic evidence for that hypothesis was uncovered in a series of thirty-four interviews with members of federal-provincial committees from all ten provinces and the federal government which were conducted in the summer of 1972. While most of the interviewed were in the resources field, it does not seem unlikely that they were fairly typical of the sorts of people involved in interjurisdictional coordinative activities, and in fact, they represented a good mix of senior bureaucrats and technical personnel. Subsequent discussions with federal and provincial officials indicate that the trend is still intact in 1980.

Bilateral Federalism: "Divide and Conquer"

Coupled with the related trends of bureaucratization and executive federalism is the apparent tendency for intergovernmental relations in Canada to be carried on in bilateral rather than multilateral or omnilateral committees. This tendency toward bilateral committees can be explained in part by the need for federal-provincial coordination in the implementation of many joint programs; a large percentage of the bilateral committees are in fact at the operational level, and are exclusive in their composition simply because the particular program being administered involves only two governments.

However, this tendency toward bilateral rather than multi- or omnilateral interaction may reflect more complex trends in the nature of federal-provincial bargaining. The multilateral meetings, particularly at the ministerial level, do not appear to be particularly effective as forums for intergovernmental bargaining; at the First Ministers' Conference, for instance, it is not uncommon for eleven separate sets of policy priorities to be presented as bargaining "positions." The number of combinations of positions possible as compromise solutions in an eleven-person situation is so great that negotiation becomes very difficult. The individuals doing the bargaining have difficulty recognizing all options open to them, let alone choosing the one that maximizes the benefits to their government. The result is that the provincial representatives are often hesitant about making a deal in a multilateral or omnilateral situation for fear of "missing something"; they instead do what is safest, and simply state and restate the position that they started with.

Given the difficulty of bargaining in a highly complex omnilateral conference, and given the evidence of much bilateral interaction in operational and technical committees, one might hypothesize that there is, in fact, a lot of bilateral interaction at the more senior levels as well. This will not be manifested by the existence of many formal or permanent bilateral committees; the ministers and senior bureaucrats are simply too busy to be involved in regular meetings. However, it seems reasonable that informal bilateral meetings between a federal minister and the provincial counterpart may occur frequently to discuss specific policy questions. In such a meeting, with only two governments present, and only two sets of priorities to deal with, bargaining is a much simpler process. Moreover, as such meetings are informal and *ad hoc*, they will not be publicized to any great extent although the meetings between Alberta and Ottawa on the question of oil pricing have tended to go against this rule. However, the more important point is that the bilateral meetings themselves are held behind closed doors so that the "horse trading" can go on in a fairly honest manner, with little need for the governmental representatives to engage in symbolic combat or to posture for television cameras.

But not only is compromise facilitated through informal bilateral bargaining; it may also be that the federal government can use this type of negotiation to control the bargaining process at omnilateral meetings. On a one-to-one basis, the federal government can often dominate a bargaining situation, where on a one-to-ten basis the provinces hold sway. By consummating deals in several bilateral situations before going to the multilateral conferences, the federal government may be able to "divide and conquer." The only counter to this trend may result from an increased amount of bilateral interaction among the provinces. By making deals among themselves, the provinces can establish united bargaining positions before facing the "feds" in a bilateral situation; such temporary coalitions may offset the potential domination by the national government, but to be truly effective, the tactic will have to be used more frequently than it is at present.

Finally, the wealthier provinces and those which are influential in the intergovernmental arena have actually reached a level of sophistication where they do not fear the bilateral bargaining process. Provinces such as Alberta which has real clout because of its oil reserves, prefer to bargain with the "feds" one-to-one, for the simple reason that in an omnilateral meeting Ottawa will have strong allies in the ranks of the energy-consuming provinces such as Ontario. "Divide and conquer" it seems can work both ways!

Rationalist Federalism

In the first part of this chapter we determined that federal-provincial coordination was essentially a process of bargaining. In the trends discussed thus far, we have simply presumed that the traditional "capital" goods used for bargaining in the Canadian system have remained unchanged; that the provinces, for the most part, will bargain from their position of jurisdictional strength in key policy areas such as welfare and education, and that the federal government will bargain with its large revenues and spending power. It may be however, that the bargaining levers of the federal partners have changed.

A general trend in policy making which we have noted before is the increasing use of policy planning. No longer is it considered adequate for policy makers to make decisions about what we should do in future on the basis of what we are doing now. In rejecting this erstwhile acceptable "incremental" mode of setting new policies, the advocates of planning argue that decisions today should be more than linear extensions of past ones. Instead, policy decision should be made on the basis of full knowledge of present public demands, projections identifying future needs, a full awareness of all present policy options, and a careful analysis of the relative costs and benefits of each policy option. The determination of the policies which should be implemented must then be made with a view to maximizing long-range benefits, and minimizing political and financial costs. This approach is normally referred to as *rationalist* (as opposed to *incrementalist*), and rests on two "pillars of analysis"—systems analysis and cost benefit analysis. The former pillar assumes the interrelationship of all policies and posits the necessity to consider all options before coming to a decision; the latter pillar assumes that relative costs and benefits of policy options can be measured quantitatively, and that choices among alternatives should be based on such information. While the success of such techniques in real decision-making situations may be limited, the principles of policy planning have been adopted to some extent by almost all governments in Canada. The impact of this new emphasis on policy planning, and that of rationalist policy analysis on interjurisdictional relations are still not clear. However, one apparent change is that the ability to bargain effectively in the intergovernmental arena is linked to whether a government's policy priorities are articulated in rationalist terms. The ability to bargain in this fashion is in turn linked to the number and quality of manpower resources available to the particular government. That the federal government and the wealthier provinces can afford to buy the commitment of high-priced policy planners is beyond question. However, the poorer provinces are less able to pay for sufficient high-priced help and may be reduced to accepting on faith the kinds of policy alternatives articulated by the "have" provinces and the federal government. In this sense, a new lever or "capital" with which to bargain successfully in the interjurisdictional sphere is the possession of expert manpower resources; governments lacking this resource may be functionally disfranchised from taking a full part in federal-provincial relations.

One possible way to offset the tendency in interjurisdictional relations toward a virtually permanent oligarchy of the "have" provinces and the federal government is for the federal government to increase unconditional grants to the poor provinces in absolute rather than per capita terms. Although it is unlikely that the larger provinces would ever accept this measure, it would, if adopted, perhaps increase the financial ability of the "have-not" provinces to hire the necessary manpower. A perhaps more feasible solution (although one which has never been tried) is to establish an intergovernmental secretariat patterned after the secretariat of the CCREM but composed of planners and policy analysts. This would provide the provinces with access to a bank of experts responsible to all governments equally, and while it would only partially offset the advantage of the bigger governments, it might be a step in the right direction. However in the absence of a remedy, the implication of rationalist federalism is that intergovernmental relations will continue to be asymetrical, with a select few provinces and the federal government dominating centre stage and determining the major policy priorities in the 1980s.

This concludes the discussion of possible trends in modern federal-provincial relations in Canada, and also concludes our chapter on federalism and public policy. Much of what has been said in this final section has been speculative. All that can be said in conclusion is that, whatever constitutional settlements may come, Canadian federalism is today, and always has been, in a state of flux; it has evolved from what it was in 1867 to what it is today through constant adaptation to new environmental circumstances. It is today a very tightly inte-grated network of federal-provincial consultative bodies at various governmental levels. There is a constantly changing relationship among the actors in the federal system, as each of the provinces and the federal government attempt to maximize their bargaining advan-tages vis-à-vis the others. However, for the most part, there remains under this coverlet of constant conflict, a willingness to seek agree-ment, to compromise, and to continue to bargain. In this combination of flexibility with commitment to an ongoing process lies its strength.

17

The Canadian Bureaucracy: Functions and Structures

Before proceeding further with our analysis of the policy process and the role of the bureaucracy in it, it is necessary—even though we have already used the term often—to say a few words of clarification about *bureaucracy*. Long used as a term of contempt by the media, its adjectival form, bureaucratic, has come to be associated by the public, with qualities such as inefficiency, "red tape," depersonalization, and slowness of execution. There is, however, a purer use of the term which is derived from the literature of organization theory and which has implications relating only to the objective structural characteristics of a certain type of organization. In this sense, bureaucracy is a purely descriptive rather than a pejorative term. We are here applying the latter connotation of the term, and do not mean to imply inefficiency, red tape, or depersonalization, all of which result, in fact, from perversions of bureaucratic structures.

The classic description of the pure bureaucracy derives from the work of Max Weber, but R. K. Merton has provided us with what is perhaps the most complete brief description:

There is integrated a series of offices, of hierarchized statuses, in which inhere a number of obligations and privileges closely defined by limited and specific rules. Each of these offices contains an area of imputed competence and responsibility. Authority, the power of control which derives from an acknowledged status, inheres in the office and not in the particular person who performs the official role. Official action ordinarily occurs within the framework of preexisting rules of the organization. The system of prescribed relations between the various offices involves a considerable degree of formality and clearly defined social distance between the occupants of these positions. Formality is manifested by means of a more or less complicated social ritual which symbolizes and supports the "pecking order" of the various offices. Such formality, which is integrated with the distribution of authority within the system, serves to minimize friction by largely restricting (official) contact to modes which are previously defined by the rules of the organization. Ready calculability of others' behaviour and a stable set of mutual expectations is thus built up. Moreover, formality facilitates the interaction of the occupants of offices despite their (possibly hostile) private attitudes toward one another. In this way, the subordinate is protected from the arbitrary action of his superior, since the actions of both are constrained by a mutually recognized set of rules. Specific procedural devices foster objectivity and restrain the "quick passage of impulse into action." [1]

---

[1] R. K. Merton, "Bureaucratic Structure and Personality," *Social Forces,* 18(1940), 561-568. Weber's classic statement is in H. H. Gerth and C. Wright Mills (eds.), From *Max Weber: Essays in Sociology* (Oxford University Press, New York, 1946), pp. 196-244.

Thus, a bureaucracy is simply a form of organization, with precise structural characteristics. While bureaucracy can be used to apply to governmental and non-governmental organizations alike, in common usage in the discipline of political science the term refers specifically to the *public service* or to the *administrative branch* of government. The focus of this chapter is on the role of the non-elective officials of government, the bureaucrats, who work within the Canadian public service, the public services of the various provinces, municipalities and territorial governments, and within the multitude of government agencies and corporations which are not formally a part of the public service.

We will see that Canadian bureaucratic structures, like their counterparts elsewhere in the world, do not perfectly mirror the ideal type as set out in the statements of Weber and Merton. There is considerably more flexibility in bureaucratic structures than is implied in the classical descriptions of bureaucracy. This is a desirable attribute of real-world bureaucracies since it enables them to react more effectively to the multifaceted strains imposed on them by the modern world. However, the ideal type presented here provides us with a bench mark against which to measure real bureaucracies and is, as a first approximation, still a reliable guide to much of the internal form of administrative structures in Canada. We will return to a more detailed classification and description of bureaucratic structures after we have examined the functions of the Canadian bureaucracy.

THE FUNCTIONS OF THE CANADIAN BUREAUCRACY

The Policy Function

That the public service[2] in Canada has a significant and positive role in the policy process is now accepted as fact. As we have indicated this role is based largely on the concentration of expertise within the public service, making the bureaucracy the major source of information concerning the technical and financial feasibility of policy alternatives faced by the politicians. As the complexity of our society increases, the reliance of political decision makers on bureaucratic specialists tends to increase commensurately.

It has already been mentioned that the bureaucracy performs important functions as an initiator of policy and a channel of policy

---

[2] The term "public service" will be generally used here to refer to the entire bureaucracy, including Crown agencies as well as the "public service," as defined in the Public Service Employment Act.

initiation to be used by other institutions in the political system. Beyond this first-stage policy role, the bureaucracy becomes more and more deeply involved in the business of policy making. When priorities are being established, bureaucratic institutions such as the Treasury Board Secretariat and the Department of Finance have a great deal of control over policy planning because of their expertise in the area of public finance. It is in this particular area that the increasing application of rationalist principles to the budgetary process tends to regularize and perhaps even to further aggrandize the position of the bureaucrat in the Canadian policy process.

Federal-provincial committees at the bureaucratic level also play an important role in the setting of policy priorities in Canada. Specifically, these intergovernmental bodies are usually concerned with coordination of federal-provincial programs; but, for example in the process of researching the problems of fiscal relations, the Coordinating Committee on Fiscal and Economic Matters has great influence on the spending priorities of both levels of government. The same is true of the Continuing Committee of Federal and Provincial Deputy Ministers of Welfare which, since 1973, has formed a focal point for continuing review and has major implications for government expenditures for years to come. However, while intergovernmental bureaucratic committees can and do affect the setting of governmental priorities in Canada, their greatest impact is felt at the *formulation* stage of policy making.

As was pointed out in Chapter 1, the bureaucracy is the core institution at the formulation stage of policy making in Canada. Although it is often interdepartmental committees or the cabinet that decide which department will be responsible for policy formulation in a certain area, and although several departments (under the aegis of the interdepartmental committee) look at most major policy decisions, the actual detailed formulation of specific policies is normally accomplished by the individual departments of the public service. Through briefing notes, discussion papers, reports and, most important, through "cabinet documents," the departments set out the few policy alternatives which are most feasible in technical, administrative, financial, and even political terms and the realistic options for government action are most frequently defined thereby.[3]

While policy formulation has been described here as a stage in the policy process which follows priority determination, it is, in fact,

[3] See M. J. Prince, "Policy Advisory Groups in Government Departments," in Doern and Aucoin (eds.), *Public Policy in Canada* (Macmillan, Toronto, 1979), pp. 275-300.

often the case that the bureaucracy's formulation activity has begun long before any clear priority has been established. Indeed, the cabinet often finds it impossible to make a clear priority decision in the absence of a good deal of detailed advice on policy formulation. The bureaucratic institutions are ever alert to indicators of future government priorities and the officials within the various government departments attempt to anticipate cabinet-level decisions and begin working on policy areas which are likely to be given priority or which they feel should be pushed forward to cabinet. One reason for this anticipatory activity by the institutions of the Canadian bureaucracy is that a department which has already prepared some proposals is more likely to be given the responsibility for policy formulation and ultimate implementation than one which is unprepared. Another reason is that the department may have already been asked to comment on the feasibility of the proposal at the earliest priority stage. And, of course, the department may have played a role in the initiation of the policy in the first place. Thus, bureaucratic involvement at the initiation and priority-determination stages of the process may not only determine which department gets the jobs of formulation and implementation, but may also result in many of the formulation decisions having been made early in the process. We will deal with the policy role of the bureaucracy in greater detail in Chapter 18, when we discuss the bureaucratic process.

The Output Functions

Rule Making While the policy role of the Canadian bureaucracy may seem to place significant power in the hands of the bureaucrats and technocrats, this power is merely advisory and subject to the ultimate approval of the elected officials of our government. However, in many areas, even the formal power to directly convert policy to legislative output has been delegated to various administrative agencies of the government of Canada.

The delegation of legislative power to the executive is not a particularly new phenomenon in Canada; for instance, in time of national emergency, Canadian legislation has, for many years, granted very broad powers to the executive to make law by order in council. While this delegation of legislative power achieves a "short-circuiting" of the normal procedures of lawmaking by the sovereign parliament, the concerned citizen might take some solace in the fact that the *de facto* executive in this country is the cabinet, which is ultimately responsible to the public. However, two factors must be taken into account when assessing the total affect of such legislation on the democratic process. First, since the cabinet is not an expert body, it often must *redelegate* the power to make law by order in council to non-elected officials from government departments, in police forces, and in a multitude of regulatory agencies. Moreover, as legislation becomes more technical and more complex, this function of executive lawmaking will tend to rest increasingly with non-elected officials. Second, legislation today requires such detail that the elected actors in the policy process do not have time to go much beyond debating the broad principles of the policy either before or after the non-elected officials have made their decisions. Hence, the legislation setting up the Canadian Transportation Commission for instance, sets down certain broad objectives, creates the commission, and then delegates to it the power to make detailed regulations as to air traffic, etc. To take another example, the post office makes regulations regarding postal rates, contents of packages, the use of mails, etc., which directly affect our postal privileges and the quality of service we receive. In each case, elected officials may discuss broad policy issues, but they seldom discuss the details of regulations made by bureaucrats pursuant to the legislation. The point is that the power actually to make regulations which have the effect of law and which must directly affect the citizen frequently rests with bureaucrats, and not with the constitutionally supreme lawmaker, parliament, or with even the political executive, the cabinet. A most important bureaucratic function, therefore, is the power to make decisions which themselves constitute legislative outputs of the political system.[4]

Another important rule-making function of the bureaucracy is the internalized making of regulations regarding the administrative process itself. For instance, an agency such as the Public Service Commission is concerned directly and constantly with problems of staffing. The Public Service Commission was created in the first place precisely to take matters of promotion, recruitment, and discipline out of the hands of the politicians. It was felt that public service appointments should be based not on patronage but rather on the merits of the individual job applicant and the requirements of the

---

[4] See E. A. Driedger, "Subordinate Legislation," *Canadian Bar Review*, Vol. 38, no. 1, pp. 1-34, March, 1980. See also: "Delegated Legislation in Canada" in Kernaghan and Willms, *Public Administration in Canada: Selected Readings* (Methuen, Toronto, 1971), p. 406. There is also a burgeoning literature dealing with regulation as one of the broad functions of government generally, and then focusing on the specific structures and processes of regulation, most of which are bureaucratic. See especially the work of G. B. Doern; *The Regulatory Process in Canada* (Toronto, 1978); "Regulatory Process and Regulatory Agencies," in Doern and Aucoin (eds.), op. cit., pp. 158-189; "Rationalizing the Regulatory Decision Making Process; The Prospects for Reform," E.C.C., Working Paper #2, OTTAWA, 1979. See also: D. C. Hartle, *Public Policy Decision Making and Regulations* (IRPP, Toronto, 1979).

position to be filled; the logical way of doing this was to create a central agency that was independent of political control and to give it the power to make regulations necessary for bringing into effect a career public service based on the *merit principle*. Similarly, each department or agency must produce sets of rules outlining internal procedures and practices. The decisions as to what these rules should be are all made directly by administrative officials and are subject to little practical control by politicans. Although it is perhaps difficult to characterize these rules as outputs of the political system, such administrative regulations are very important through their potential effect on the administration side of the administrator-to-public relationship.

Rule Application It has been seen that the Canadian constitution distinguishes between executive and judicial functions. However, under closer scrutiny, one finds that the executive function and the judicial function are broadly similar in that they both require the application of general rules to specific cases. Viewed in this way, the rule-application function of the bureaucracy includes both executive and judicial decision making, and with respect to time, resources and immediate impact on the public, it constitutes the central function of the Canadian bureaucracy.

In the process of administering the law, it is necessary to employ a great deal of discretion. Laws are stated very generally, and inevitably they do not take into account the infinite number of circumstances in which they might apply. Hence, to use an example from Corry and Hodgetts' *Democratic Government and Politics*, the administration of the Pure Food and Drug Act requires inspectors to make discretionary decisions as to whether permits should be issued or revoked.[5] Obviously, such a decision is not only administrative, but judicial and legislative as well. Indeed, so great is the discretionary power granted to the bureaucrat entrusted with administering the act that the distinction between legislative, executive, and judicial functions becomes illusory. Part of this blurring of the distinctions between the three functions of government occurs because the role of government generally has become positive. Thus, as government moved from a "thou-shalt-not" or punitive orientation to a more positive or preventative orientation, much of the responsibility for applying the law has moved from the judiciary to the administrative branch of government.

---

[5] Corry and Hodgetts, *Democratic Government and Politics*, p. 528. In this and similar cases, the law usually states that the ultimate decision rests with the responsible minister, but in fact the vast majority of cases never reach his notice, so the real power resides in the inspector.

Rule application by the bureaucracy, however, involves more than taking purely preventive measures as cited in the example above. Rather, the bureaucracy today is vested with judicial or quasijudicial functions as well, requiring bureaucratic officials to make decisions which have punitive and compensatory effects on individuals. In other words, there are administrative agencies in Canada which function in much the same way as a court except that the members of such administrative tribunals are not judges but bureaucrats. The Canadian Pension Commission and the Canada Labour Relations Board are examples of quasijudicial bodies functioning within the framework of the bureaucracy. These administrative boards are empowered to make decisions which for example, could grant a pension to one person and not to another, or certify one bargaining agent and not another. In making such decisions, which are administrative in form, a board determines rights and privileges of individuals in the same way a court does; and, by establishing procedures for dealing with various types of cases, the same board makes law. An administrative body can thus exercise administrative, judicial, and legislative functions in the course of administrative decision making.

A sort of hybrid function of some bureaucratic agencies in Canada combines the role of policy advisor and adjudicator. This is the *investigative function* which is distinguishable from the policy advisory function because the focus of the investigation is a specific case or situation, and which can be differentiated from the adjudicative function because the findings of the board or commission are only recommendatory to the minister. For example, many regulatory agencies in Canada such as the Canadian Transportation Commission (CTC) the Atomic Energy Control Board (AECB) and the National Energy Board (NEB) are required by law to investigate accidents which occur in the industries they are regulating and to report the findings to the minister. In the case of the CTC and the National Energy Board, the regulatory agency is vested with the powers of a superior court of record when conducting hearings which implies the right to subpoena witnesses to require the presentation of documents and to convict people for contempt of court.

Symbolic Outputs   There is a class of governmental outputs which cannot be called legislative, executive, or judicial.[6] More frequently today one can see the political system producing outputs which take the form of information, and the basic agencies for the dissemination of information from the political system are found predominantly

[6] See Chapter 1 re "symbolic outputs."

within the bureaucracy.[7] For example, it is necessary to inform the public of changes in the law. Some years ago, amendments to the Criminal Code made it an offence to drive while one's blood alcohol is in excess of .08 percent. In order to ensure that the public is aware of this new legislation, the Department of Justice publicized the changes widely on radio, TV, and in the newspapers. All new legislation is in fact published in the *Canada Gazette,* and the onus in law is on the individual citizen to find out what the law is and to obey it. However, it is also recognized by the government that a piece of legislation such as the "breathalizer" law is designed to act as a deterrent and will only be effective if everyone is aware of it. Furthermore, laws such as this affect so many people that it pays the government politically to widely publicize the fact that they are in effect.

Information outputs—such as the campaign to inform the public about the "breathalizer" law—are produced by the bureaucracy, possibly at the urging and certainly with the acquiescence of the cabinet. Outputs of such information are purely informative; what they say is, in effect: "Here is a new law. You must, as with all laws, obey it." However, other outputs of information are not so neutral as this one. Consider, for example, campaigns by the Department of Manpower and Immigration to increase the number of summer jobs for students. Here a bureaucratic agency is not stating that there is any law in existence; instead, it is actively campaigning to convince businesspeople to hire a certain class of worker. What is implicit in this piece of government advertising is the proposition that students should be hired instead of other classes of workers in the society. Perhaps this is not purely the brainchild of a group of public servants in a government department, but rather of some political advisor to the cabinet who feels that university and college students and/or their parents are politically a more important force than are other types of unemployed. That is not really important to our discussion; the point is that somebody has decided that an output of information should be made which appears to be completely neutral and yet which is very definitely favourable to one class of person and not another.

Whether, in the examples cited above, the decision to disseminate information was bureaucratic or political does not matter as much as the fact that the bureaucracy *can* do this almost unilaterally, subject to only the most cursory ministerial supervision. Most government departments publish information in the form of brochures, pam-

---

[7] See also Chapter 13. There it is pointed out that interest groups also may play an important part in the dissemination of information.

phlets, and even quarterly magazines, all aimed at simply informing a segment of the public; and yet most of these publications impart sets of values and points of view. This is not necessarily a result of public servants consciously attempting to propagandize, but rather it is often simply a function of the nature of information. It is impossible to publish information without some editing; and in the process of editing, the values of the editor are served, either consciously or unconsciously.

Most departments have information services branches[8] and some agencies, such as Statistics Canada, are concerned primarily with the collection, compilation, and publication of information. While the people in these bureaucratic roles likely try very hard to be impartial, they are only human, with biases, prejudices, and misconceptions of reality. Thus, what is virtually unavoidable is that the bureaucrats who are charged with the responsibility for producing information packages will inevitably colour the outputs with their own values. It can be hoped that the values that are pushed will be congruent with those of the society at large; but more important, if one recognizes that the potential for bias, intentional or not, is very real, one will be able to evaluate all outputs in a critical light.

The rationalization of the educative function of the Canadian bureaucracy was attempted in the creation of a semi-independent administrative agency known as Information Canada. The role of this agency was to provide information about the policies of the government, and its goal was to create a more informed public which would be subsequently more capable of participating in the policy process. Whether or not it is even possible to inform the public to that extent is another question, but what concerns us here is the nature of Information Canada, *per se*. Most critical comment originally zeroed in on the potential for political propaganda from such an agency. While fear was expressed that the government in power would be enabled to promote its own particular programs at the expense of the Canadian taxpayer, this did not seem to happen to a significantly greater extent than it did in the pre-Info-Can days. The fairly rapid demise of Information Canada likely came about because the departmental information offices resisted the centralization of the "information-out" function which Info-Can implied. The departmental officials resented and denounced as ineffective the attempt to centralize functions which they felt should remain decentralized and this made it a ready target during one of the federal government's periodic bouts of austerity.

---

[8] See Royal Commission on Government Organization, *Report, vol.* 3, (Queen's Printer, Ottawa, 1962), pp. 63-72.

Despite the failure of the Info-Can experiment, the symbolic educative or informative function of the Canadian bureaucracy is a rapidly expanding and important one. While this type of output is not itself an "allocation," it is, nonetheless, a vital ancillary to the allocation process, for it ensures that citizens know what rules have been made, and it supplies active citizens with information through which they can interact with the political system. The constant output of information from within the bureaucracy will be a beneficial development if the public can avoid being brainwashed by seemingly neutral (but in reality coloured) facts emanating from "impartial" bureaucratic editors. Since most of the public will pay no attention whatever to these outputs, and since those who do will be among the better-educated or more actively concerned citizens, it seems at least plausible to hope that such "brainwashing" will be minimized.

Finally the movement to a more "open" bureaucracy with a Freedom of Information Act will go some of the way to ensuring that the public can get information directly, instead of waiting to see what the public servants are willing to give up. While at this writing the Freedom of Information legislation is still awaiting parliamentary approval, it is safe to speculate that the overall effect will be positive. The only negative result will be the increased person-years required to provide assistance to the members of the public who seek information—the immediate beneficiaries may well turn out to be the information services branches of departments and agencies whose share of the budgetary pie can be expected to grow handsomely!

Systemic Functions Beyond the operational functions described above, the Canadian bureaucracy also performs a number of ancillary or latent functions for the political system as a whole. First, what is in some ways but an extension of its role in the generation of symbolic outputs, the bureaucracy likely plays a part in the fundamental process of creating diffuse support for the political system. The accomplishments of Canadian government agencies in world affairs, in scientific research and in the effective delivery of services to Canadian citizens can have a legitimizing effect for the system. When a career diplomat gains worldwide recognition and praise for efforts in a faraway embassy, or when a foreign government decides to buy one of our Canadian developed CANDU reactors it may help to generate a pride in Canadians about Canadian accomplishments and in so doing help to create support for our political community. Similarly when it is publicized that, for instance, Air Canada has maintained an excellent air-safety record, or when a film produced by the National Film Board receives wide acclaim it may help to legitimize the role of government in those sorts of enterprises and foster support for the regime. Thus while there may be a lot of public cynicism and disgruntlement with the evils and inefficiencies of "bureaucracy" the fact remains that bureaucracy is so pervasive in our society that without a certain amount of praise for and faith in our more successful public enterprises, the system would likely fail very rapidly.

Another systemic role played by bureaucracy, and here we need not even be specific to Canada in our generalization, is that of maintaining stability and continuity over time. For those who are committed to radical and rapid social change, this may well be viewed as a dysfunction of bureaucracy, but any system must have a static or conservative element which enables it to persist over time. The constitution, a stable party system, or a stable economy may perform this function to varying degrees in different political systems, but because, as we have seen, bureaucracies are by definition predictable and, by empirical observation, almost pathologically inert, they provide continuity and stability even in a regime where other stabilizing institutions are failing.

Finally, it may be that the bureaucracy in Canada is performing a representative function in policy making. Ironically the normal line of argument regarding the role of the technocrats in the formulation of public policy is that, because the elected representatives of the people in parliament have little say in technical decisions, democracy is being slain by technocracy. The counter to this is that if in fact the technocrats are becoming more influential than parliament in the policy process we must look to the composition of the technocracy before we judge the trend to be undemocratic. In Chapter 14 we considered this issue and concluded, unfortunately, that the evidence is inconclusive. The bureaucracy overrepresents males, central Canada, and high-status Canadians in a manner much like parliament, cabinet and other elite institutions so there may be little to choose among our various political institutions, including the bureaucracy, on this score.

At another and more important level however, it may be that the bureaucracy is an important representative institution in Canada; not because bureaucrats and technocrats reflect a broad cross section of our society, but because of structural factors. In Canada most departments of government can identify a clientele group in the political community at large. The function of the department, in the administrative process, is to implement programs designed to benefit that clientele and, in the policy process, to represent the interests of that clientele in policy initiation and priority determination. Thus, policy advisory units within clientele-oriented departments press their political masters to adopt new policies or new programs which will serve the interests of their clients. We cannot pretend that the department fosters the interests of its clients for purely altruistic motives; rather the motivation is that if the department can invent and sell fancy new programs to the cabinet, the department's share of the budgetary pie and the size of its manpower establishment will grow accordingly. Thus, serving the interests of a clientele is merely "good business"—a device for building or expanding a departmental empire. But whatever the motives, the fact remains that the clientele-oriented departments of government may well represent the larger interests in Canadian society better and more consistently than the MPs and perhaps even better than interest groups.

To conclude what is as yet a fairly speculative set of comments about the representative functions of the Canadian bureaucracy, we must enter an important qualification. While structural factors may encourage bureaucrats to act as representatives of their clientele, officials are still an elite by virtue of the level of education required in their jobs. This means that in the long run, the technocratic elites will only be as representative as the educational and other institutions that incubate, hatch, and mature their career aspirations.

Far from being the passive instrument of the era of the negative state, then, the modern bureaucracy has a very active role to play in government. Bureaucratic agencies not only implement law, but they make law; they adjudicate; they make policy; and they control the outflow of masses of information to the general public. Moreover, because bureaucracy is such a pervasive force in the operation of the political system, it may well be performing broader systemic functions which heretofore have been considered the exclusive domain of other state institutions. Now, however, it is necessary to proceed to a discussion of the structures and the organizational forms which have evolved to perform these functions.

THE STRUCTURE OF THE CANADIAN BUREAUCRACY

It has already been explained that the term bureaucracy refers to a kind of organization with certain structural characteristics. We asserted that prime among its characteristics is its large size; most of the other factors of bureaucratic structure have evolved to accommodate the preeminent problem of "bigness." Bureaucratic structures feature a well-developed division of labour whereby the officials occupying roles within the organization perform clearly defined functions. Ideally there is no duplication of effort and no overlapping of roles within a bureaucracy, although this is more difficult to achieve in practice than in the abstract.

Furthermore, it was noted that a bureaucratic role is defined by the office itself and not by the incumbent of the office. This is essential if bureaucratic behaviour is to be predictable in the short run, and if there is to be continuity over time in the performance of the duties of that office. Continuity over time is also facilitated by the keeping of detailed written records of all actions taken by the bureaucratic officers. In this way every decision can be backed up by precedents established in the past, and in turn, itself becomes part of the body of precedents for future decisions. There is no legal rule of precedent in bureaucratic decision making, but the fact is that if someone else has made a certain decision in the past and has "gotten away with it," the chances are that a similar decision today can be justified by the officer responsible. Also contributing to the continuity of bureaucratic decision making is the fact that the holding of a bureaucratic office is a full-time occupation. In recent years, bureaucratic officers have been tenured, rather than holding office merely at the pleasure of the employer. Finally, although it is not unique to bureaucratic organizations, the basic mechanism of control within a bureaucracy is hierarchical. This means that authority flows downward through the organization with each level of the organization being responsible to the level above.

Before proceeding to describe the bureaucratic structures in the Canadian government, we can look briefly at the reasons for adopting a bureaucratic type of organization; given all of its real or imagined malfunctions, what is good about the bureaucratic form? First of all, because equality is a value of our system of government, it is necessary, when applying the law to specific cases, to treat similar cases in a similar fashion. Bureaucratic organization permits a maximum of impartiality in dealing with the public by *routinizing* the decision-making process. Second, the application of the law must be predictable to be fair, and a bureaucratic system can be made highly predictable. The problem here is that in applying the law equally and impartially, the person with the "special case," who requires an equitable decision instead of an impartial one, is frequently penalized. How many times have we all met with the standard bureaucratic answer that "If we do that for you we will have to do it for everyone else as well"; or, "We are sorry but our regulations do not permit any exceptions." Thus, while bureaucratic procedures are valid for, perhaps, 90 percent of the cases, for the 10 percent that may be exceptional, the system imposes difficulties. The justification for such a system is that it is the only way we have of dealing fairly and at reasonable cost with the majority of the vast number of cases that come up.

Modern bureaucracies have, of course, developed some mechanisms for dealing with special cases. Many large programs dealing directly with the public have some form of appeal procedure, and individual bureaucrats at the operating levels do have some discretion in dealing with special cases. We will note too, in our discussions of the functions of parliament that one of the most important parts of the MP's role is helping constituents who have not been adequately dealt with by the bureaucracy. More and more Canadian governments are utilizing ombudsmen to ensure that special cases are fairly dealt with. Nonetheless, in conclusion we must return to the rather unsatisfactory comment that bureaucratic organization is the best-known way of dealing with bigness in government and that some problems inevitably arise.

The basic organizational form found in the Canadian bureaucracy is the *department*, accounting for almost two-thirds of the employees of the federal government. Most of the non-departmental agencies are classed as *Crown corporations*, although there are a number of federal government agencies—such as the Bank of Canada, the Canada Council, the Canadian Wheat Board, and the National Arts Centre—which operate in a manner similar to Crown corporations but which are not formally classified as such. Moreover, since the 1970s we have seen a rapid increase in the use of "mixed" public-private agencies and "joint" federal-provincial or Canadian-American corporations. Finally, there are the central control agencies such as the Treasury Board Secretariat, the Privy Council Office, and the Public Service Commission which are dealt with elsewhere in the text.

The Government Department[9]

Several characteristics distinguish the departmental form of organization from other types within the Canadian bureaucracy. First, a government department is answerable directly to a cabinet minister who functions as its formal head and who, conversely, is responsible for the actions of both the department and the departmental officials. The practical effectiveness of the minister in heading a department will depend to a large extent upon his or her competence and personality, but while there is a lot of room for the minister to provide encouragement and to generate excitement within the department, generally the administrative decisions will be left to the permanent officials. There is even a theory that the best minister is one who has ideas and influential stature in the cabinet, but who knows very little about the line functions of the department itself. The minister can then represent the broad interests of the department in cabinet meetings, but is not motivated to meddle in the internal affairs of the

[9] See A. M. Willms, "Crown Agencies," in W. D. K. Kernaghan (ed.), *Bureaucracy in Canadian Government* (Methuen, Toronto, 1969), pp. 23-25.

department. Perhaps this theory is just the wishful thinking of public servants who would prefer to keep the political head of the department involved in "political" priority decisions and out of their hair. On the other hand, this situation may occur in reality simply because the minister is too busy with other things to become very involved in the administrative process.

The second distinguishing characteristic of the government department is the fact that it is subject to the *estimates system* of budgeting, which means simply that the money appropriated to the department by parliament must be spent in the manner directed by parliament. The coming of the system of Planning Programming Budgeting (PPB) and the adoption of the more centralized *envelope* system of budgetary apportionment have not changed this basic fact of departmental finance, although such systems permit planning of departmental programs over longer than one-year periods, subject to the approval of the Treasury Board and relevant cabinet committees.

The third characteristic of the government department is that it recruits departmental officials under the supervision of the Public Service Commission. With the exception of deputy ministers and some temporary and part-time help, all of the personnel of government departments are public servants under the Public Service Employment Act and are recruited according to the principle of merit.

The Deputy Minister The administrative head of the department is a deputy minister. This appointment is a prerogative not of the minister of a department but of the Prime Minister, usually advised by a senior "mandarin," normally the Secretary to the Cabinet. This process of appointment gives the Prime Minister some measure of control over individual departments even if a minister becomes recalcitrant or remiss, but since the deputy minister usually works in very close contact with the minister and at arms length from the Prime Minister, this power is more formal than real. The deputy minister (DM), unlike a public servant, holds office "at the pleasure" of the government.

Perhaps the major function of the deputy minister is a *managerial* one; i.e., he or she must function as the manager of an organization called a department and must therefore plan, direct, and control the department. Like all managers in large organizations, the deputy minister must set intradepartmental policy, participate in the selection of officers for senior positions within the department (subject to the merit principle), and coordinate departmental activities through executive leadership. The function of coordination is usually facilitated through the delegation of some managerial functions to subordinates, and in many departments through a *central management com-*

mittee or *executive committee,* which consists of the deputy minister as chairman and all of the assistant deputies as members. The management committee sets the broad objectives and priorities of the department and examines any new proposals which may emerge from the bowels of the organization, and deals as well with such "vital" management questions as the date of the departmental picnic. However, properly operated, the committee can do much, together with the budget process, to rationalize intradepartmental priorities, and can be used effectively by the deputy minister as a tool of internal planning and liaison. The deputy minister does not have permanent tenure, and it is considered quite proper for a new government to occasionally ask that the DMs in certain key departments resign. Similarly, the DM, in a department such as Finance, may offer to resign without being asked if a different political party takes over after an election. It is essential that the minister have confidence in the permanent head of the department (and vice versa) if he or she is to be able to function effectively as its political head; if there are suspicions that the existing DM is still friendly to the old government, it is best that there be a replacement. While DMs are not tenured, it must be emphasized that, in most cases, a change in government does not necessitate their removal. Usually the incoming government is glad to have the help of such senior bureaucrats in "learning the ropes," and the DMs are willing to adapt to the needs and programs of their new political masters.

The deputy minister is responsible for the maintenance of liaison with people in other departments as well. This is necessary partially because each department must depend to some extent on other departments whose function is to provide services for the rest. The most important example of such a service department is the Department of Supply and Services which was created by a 1969 governmental reorganization. This type of liaison is not usually difficult and does not normally require much of the deputy's personal time, but in addition, liaison must be maintained with other departments which have similar or overlapping line responsibilities. All of this is achieved through a semi-institutionalized process of protocol and interdepartmental "diplomacy" which has evolved to meet at least some of the needs of interdepartmental coordination and overall public service efficiency. DMs also act as intergovernmental "diplomats," a function which has already been discussed when we looked at federal-provincial relations.

In terms of the policy process in Canada, the most important function of the deputy minister is to act as the senior departmental advisor to the government. His is the key role in the transmission of policy information from administrative underlings with many types of

Figure 17-1

FUNCTIONS OF THE DEPUTY MINISTER

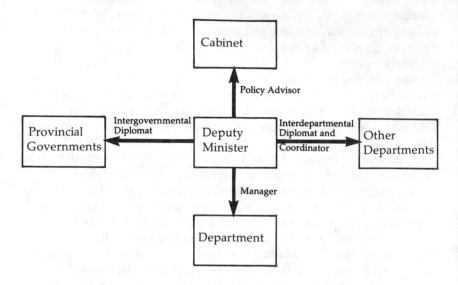

expertise to the minister and through the minister, to the cabinet. Because of their positions in the departments themselves, and in most cases because of their many years of administrative experience, deputy ministers must go beyond merely transmitting neutral information to their superiors. They are expected to interpret and explain the advice flowing from the departments; and where political decisions are required by the minister and the cabinet, they must, to the best of their abilities tender political or quasipolitical advice when asked. While the DM is but one person and incapable of total understanding of the specialist decisions made by his administrative underlings, as a professional manager the DM is in a good position to decide which of several departmental technical advisors the government should put its faith in. It has been mentioned before that one of the important aspects of cabinet decisions at the policy-formulation stage of the policy process is deciding which policy advice to convert into formal outputs. It is in this respect that the advice of the deputy minister as a manager of expertise is invaluable to the government. Because the DM knows the advisors, and not only because of an understanding of the substance of their advice, the DM can decide which advice is likely to be better.

In summary, the deputy minister of a Canadian government department basically plays the role of a manager of a very large organization. However, as we will see in the next chapter, the nature of government organization with its emphasis on political account-ability and control places unique powers and restrictions on the man-agement function, and the extent to which the DM can exercise those unique powers and cope with those unique restrictions ultimately rests on personal ability. Deputy ministers, both in Ottawa and the provinces, hold some of the most difficult and important jobs in Can-ada, and play a very central role in the entire working of the Canadian political system.

The Internal Structure of Departments   The internal functions of an organization can broadly be classed as *line* or *staff*. In Canada this dis-tinction is based on the type of relationship between various intra-departmental administrative structures and the goals of the depart-ment as a whole. To use the example of a specific department, the goal of the Department of National Revenue, simply stated, is tax col-lection. Those branches of the department involved directly in collect-ing tax revenues are said to be performing line functions. On the other hand, there are branches and/or divisions of the same depart-ment involved in matters such as personnel, administration, finance, and legal advice, none of which directly involves the performance of the line function. These branches of the department are said to per-form a staff function, and they exist to assist the line managers in an advisory capacity or through the performance of a service.[10]

The basic structure of a government department is hierarchical with the deputy minister at the top of the pyramid. Under the DM there are a number of subordinate levels. Each of these is itself hierarchical in structure, and each is directly accountable to the level above. The staff role carries no direct authority over the line officers, and the branches of the department involved in the performance of staff func-tions are often organized more simply than those of the line.

When we come to look at some departments, (such as Finance) which have a constant and very direct connection with policy, and departments (such as Manpower and Immigration or Energy, Mines and Resources) which are deeply involved in the contemporary policy process because of current public interest and political priorities in the areas of immigration, employment and unemployment or energy pol-icy, the line and staff distinction becomes somewhat confused. If there is a policy and planning branch in a government department, the officers in that branch will have a purely advisory relationship

---

[10] Professor Willms makes a distinction between three kinds of functions: line, staff, and service. We have retained the more traditional classification here because, for purposes of explaining the workings of a government department, the important point is to set the line function off from the rest. Service functions are very close con-ceptually to staff functions, and hence the distinction is more important for public administration than it is for an introductory text in Canadian politics.

with the officers in the various operations or line branches. In other words, the relationship of the policy branch to the line branches of the organization will be a staff relationship. On the other hand, one of the major goals of many modern government departments such as the Ministries of State is to formulate policy for the cabinet. Thus, policy formulation becomes itself a line function of that department. A manager in the policy and planning branch will therefore have a staff relationship with the managers in the operations branches, and a line relationship with other officers in his own branch and with his deputy minister. This same line and staff confusion occurs when we look at, for instance, information services in a department. As has already been seen, an important function of a modern bureaucracy is to disseminate information; this is, within one context, a line function. However, the information services division of a department also performs a service and therefore has a staff relationship with the other branches and divisions.

Thus, while it is important to recognize the distinction between line and staff functions within a department, the attempt to classify on the basis of this distinction must fail if carried too far. Modern bureaucratic organizations are far too complicated structurally to permit anything but the broadest of generalizations. The aim of this section is to set out some of the principles and terms that can be employed when looking at any specific department. If one is really to understand the structure of the Canadian bureaucracy today, however, one must analyze each government department separately, for they are all different, displaying their own organizational quirks and idiosyncrasies. A department-by-department analysis is beyond the scope of this text, so we must be satisfied with the few generalizations and specific examples above.

Non-Departmental Agencies

The *Crown corporation* is a non-departmental bureaucratic institution with a corporate form created by the government to perform a public function. Such institutions aim at combining the need for some degree of public accountability with the freedom of initiative usually associated (rightly or wrongly) with private enterprise. While Crown corporations must report through a minister to parliament, particularly in budgetary matters, they are not subject to either the estimates system of budgeting or to the direct control of a minister in the same way that a government department is.[11] Personnel administration in

[11] C. A. Ashley and R. G. H. Smails, *Canadian Crown Corporations* (Macmillan, Toronto, 1965), pp. 99-160.

Crown corporations, furthermore, differs from that within a government department in the extent to which the Public Service Commission regulates recruitment, promotion, and transfer procedures. In
the case of the departmental corporation, the employees are public
servants. In the other types, however, employees generally are not
affected by the terms of the Public Service Employment Act, for personnel matters are dealt with internally and independently. Similarly, most Crown corporations are not subject to the Public Service
Staff Relations Act with respect to collective bargaining, and in fact
proprietary corporations are governed by the Industrial Relations
Disputes Investigation Act as are private companies.

Basically, Crown corporations differ from government departments
in the degree of political control exercised over them. As we noted
above, the minister is the formal head of a department, and a deputy
minister is the administrative head. However, because the Crown
corporation is designed to give a measure of freedom of action, it is
usually headed by an independent board which is appointed by the
government for a set period of time. The members of this board
usually include a full-time chairman or president who functions as
the administrative head and chief executive of the corporation, and
part-time members who meet as a board only a few times each year.
In the case of some Crown corporations, members of the board
include public servants from other governmental agencies. The relationship of the chief executive of the corporation to the board itself
will differ depending on the nature of the corporation and the personalities involved.

The activities of Crown corporations, unlike those of government
departments, are not supervised directly by a cabinet minister.
Indeed, independence from direct ministerial control is one of the
major reasons for creating a Crown corporation. Despite this, mainly
because it is felt that public enterprises financed by public money
should be subjected to at least some parliamentary control, each
Crown corporation is assigned to a minister of the Crown through
which it must report to parliament. The minister, however, does not
in any way direct the activities of the corporation, and conversely, is
in no way personally responsible for the activities of the corporation.
Rather, the minister acts as a communication link between the corporation, which is engaged in public enterprise and which, in most
cases, is spending public money, and parliament. The bulk of the
work on behalf of a Crown corporation for which the minister reports
will entail piloting the corporation's estimates through the House of
Commons. Naturally it is possible for a minister to influence corporation policy informally but this is difficult to document. All that can be
said is that informal ministerial control over a Crown corporation will

depend largely on the personalities involved and the political circumstances of the times.

The greatest restriction on the activities of a Crown corporation occurs through its financial relationship with the government of Canada, particularly in the case of corporations whose activities are totally financed out of the Consolidated Revenue Fund by parliamentary appropriations. While the estimates for most Crown corporations are voted in far less detailed form than departmental estimates, the fact remains that most of their expenditures do have to be annually and publicly justified. Furthermore, with the exception of a few specified Crown corporations, the accounts of Canadian Crown corporations are subject to audit by the Auditor General. While this is a post-audit control, somewhat analogous to closing the barn door after the horse has run off, the executive of a Crown corporation must still be aware that careless expenditure of public money "this time" may result in a less generous appropriation "next time."

Finally, Crown corporations are controlled by the legislation which creates them. The terms of reference of a Crown corporation are set down in a statute which is subject to amendment or repeal by act of parliament. While this does not in any way approach the directness of control exercised over a government department, it does define jurisdictional limits beyond which the corporation is not competent to act. The Financial Administration Act defines three basic types of Crown corporations: departmental corporations, agency corporations, and proprietary corporations. We will deal with each of these in turn and then move to a consideration of other non-departmental forms of organization.

Departmental Corporations A departmental corporation is an agency of the government of Canada which is engaged in "administrative, supervisory, or regulatory services" in much the same way as a department. Schedule B of the Financial Administration Act lists the following as departmental corporations:

Agricultural Stabilization Board
Atomic Energy Control Board
Director of Soldier Settlement
The Director, The Veterans' Land Act
Economic Council of Canada
Fisheries Prices Support Board
Medical Research Council
National Museums of Canada
National Research Council
Science Council of Canada
Canada Employment and Immigration Commission

For purposes of the Financial Administration Act, these corporations are exactly the same as regular government departments. For instance, a departmental corporation does not buy, sell, or own any assets in its own name but always in the name of the Crown in right of Canada. Similarly, all of the financial affairs of this type of corporation are carried out through the Consolidated Revenue Fund and are subject to the control of the Treasury Board, Auditor General, etc. However, while the money spent by a departmental corporation must be appropriated by parliament and encumbered from the Consolidated Revenue Fund as with a government department, there is a much greater degree of independence in how the funds appropriated are actually spent. The estimates for a departmental corporation are usually put through parliament in the form of one vote in the estimates of the department through whose minister the corporation must report to parliament. Hence, the National Museums of Canada, which is a departmental corporation reporting to parliament through the Secretary of State, gets its money for any given budgetary year in the form of one item in the main estimates of the Department of Secretary of State. Where the government department must be able to justify through the minister every item of expenditure for the upcoming year to a skeptical parliament, the entire budget for a Crown corporation is debated (if at all) as one item. The limitation on this independence is the fact that the Treasury Board must examine and approve the estimates for a departmental corporation before they are included in the departmental estimates. Hence, independence from parliamentary control may not mean very much when one considers that the Treasury Board, which exercises much of the real financial control over government expenditure, has as close a look at a "Schedule B" corporation's financial needs as it has at a department's.

The boards of departmental corporations and their chairmen are generally appointed by the Governor General in Council. The tenure of these positions varies from set ten-year periods to "the pleasure of Her Majesty in right of Canada," as with other boards. The employees of departmental corporations are often appointed by the Public Service Commission and hold office during good behaviour. Thus, most of the employees of the National Museums of Canada are public servants as are the employees of the Director of Soldier Settlement or the Director of the Veterans' Land Act. On the other hand, the employees of some departmental corporations are not public servants, their remuneration and terms of employment being set by the board itself. This is the case with corporations such as the Agricultural Stabilization Board.[12] Other departmental corporations come

---

[12] Ashley and Smails, op. cit., p. 107.

somewhere between these two extremes in their employment practices.

Finally, all of the departmental corporations must submit to the minister responsible an annual report which must be tabled in the House of Commons within fifteen days. This report is provided for in most of the legislation setting up the various departmental corporations, and its function is essentially to provide publicity for the activities of the organization, acting, perhaps, as a sort of deterrent to abuses of power or squandering of public funds. The effectiveness of the annual reports as a control measure is very difficult to assess, and likely varies with the political sensitivity of the subject matter dealt with by the particular Crown corporation.

Agency Corporations An agency corporation is defined in the Financial Administration Act as "a Crown corporation that is an agent of Her Majesty in right of Canada and is responsible for the management of trading or service operations on a quasi-commercial basis, or for the management of procurement, construction, or disposal activities on behalf of Her Majesty in right of Canada."

Schedule C of the Financial Administration Act lists the following as agency corporations:

Atomic Energy of Canada Limited
Canadian Arsenals Limited
Canadian Commercial Corporation
Canadian Dairy Commission
Canadian Film Development Corporation
Canadian Livestock Feed Board
Canadian National (West Indies) Steamships Limited
Canadian Patents and Development Limited
Canadian Saltfish Corporation
Crown Assets Disposal Corporation
Defence Construction (1951) Limited
Loto Canada
National Battlefields Commission
National Capital Commission
National Harbours Board
Northern Canada Power Commission
Royal Canadian Mint
Uranium Canada Limited

Unlike departmental corporations, agency corporations are subject to the sections of the Financial Administration Act that apply specifically to Crown corporations. However, the act itself goes on to state that where there is a conflict between its provisions and those of another act, the latter will prevail. The agency corporations which have "Limited" after their name were set up under the Companies Act and the rest were set up by separate acts. The boards of directors of the "Limited" corporations are formally appointed by the shareholders; but, because the shares are held in trust for the Crown, in fact the Governor General in Council makes the appointments.[13] Most of the other corporations are headed by a board of directors which is appointed for a set term by the Governor General in Council.

The employees of the agency corporations are all appointed by the management of the corporation itself, and the salaries and conditions of work are also determined in a manner similar to private industry. While the National Harbours Board is an exception, agency corporations are empowered to maintain accounts in their own names in any bank which is formally approved by the Minister of Finance. The operating budget of the corporation is scrutinized by the minister through which the corporation reports to parliament, but the actual estimates for operating costs are placed before parliament in the form of one item in departmental estimates. Capital budgets of agency corporations are subject to more detailed scrutiny by parliament, and as with departmental corporations, an annual report including financial statements must be presented to the minister responsible at the end of the financial year. These reports are then tabled in parliament. All of the financial statements of the agency Crown corporations are subject to the scrutiny of the Auditor General.

The agency corporations display a great diversity in terms of their real financial status; for while some, such, as Canadian Patents and Development Ltd., operate at a profit, others, like the National Battlefields Commission, operate entirely on parliamentary appropriations. Similarly, while some of these corporations, like the Northern Canada Power Commission, hold large capital assets, others, like Canadian Arsenals Ltd., hold very little in the way of capital assets. Many of these agencies are also subsidized in part through the provision of office facilities and furniture by the Department of Public Works in the same way that a government department is.

The legal position of agency corporations is much the same as any corporation under the Corporations Act. All agency corporations (with the exception of the National Harbours Board and the National Battlefields Commission) can be sued in any court just as if they were not agents of the Crown. This is important in that it places them in much the same legal position vis-à-vis their clientele as any firm operating in the private sphere. By making them legally directly responsible for their activities, the government can also afford to

[13] Ibid., p. 112.

grant them a great deal of independence from financial and political control.

Proprietary Corporations   A proprietary corporation is defined as a Crown corporation which is responsible either for the management of lending or financial operations, or for the management of commercial or industrial operations involving the producing of or dealing in goods and the supplying of services to the public. These corporations are furthermore expected to function without the aid of parliamentary appropriations. The following are listed as proprietary corporations in Schedule D of the Financial Administration Act:

> Air Canada
> Canada Deposit Insurance Corporation
> Canadian Broadcasting Corporation
> Cape Breton Development Corporation
> Central Mortgage and Housing Corporation
> Eldorado Aviation Limited
> Eldorado Nuclear Limited
> Export Development Corporation
> Farm Credit Corporation
> Federal Business Development Bank
> Freshwater Fish Marketing Corporation
> National Railways, as defined in the Canadian National-
>   Canadian Pacific Act (RSC 1952, c. 39)
> Northern Transportation Company Limited
> Petro Canada
> Pilotage Authorities:
>   Atlantic Pilotage Authority
>   Great Lakes Pilotage Authority
>   Laurentian Pilotage Authority
>   Pacific Pilotage Authority
> St. Lawrence Seaway Authority
> Seaway International Bridge Corporation Limited
>   (formerly Cornwall International Bridge Company Limited)
> Teleglobe Canada

Many of the proprietary corporations in Canada not only have a direct commercial relationship with the public, but also are in competition with private corporations performing the same functions or providing the same services. The best examples of this kind of competitive Crown corporation are Air Canada and the CBC, each of which must compete with other firms in the private sphere. Because these proprietary corporations must compete with private industry, they have been guaranteed a great deal of protection from both parliamentary and public scrutiny. The principle has been established, for instance, that information regarding salaries of individuals will not be released to parliament and the annual reports of the proprietary corporations, unlike those of the agency corporations, are only required to include the sort of information required from a private firm under the Companies Act. Like agency corporations, proprietary corporations are subject to the Financial Administration Act except where the terms of that act conflict with another—in which case the latter legislation applies. Similarly, proprietary corporations are legally liable in the same way that any non-government corporation is.

The directors of the corporations are appointed in much the same way as the directors of agency corporations, by the Governor General in Council. Exceptions here are the Canada Mortgage and Housing Corporation, the Export Development Corporation, and the Farm Credit Corporation whose boards of directors are in part composed of senior departmental officials. Ashley and Smails point out that these corporations should likely not be included in Schedule D of the Financial Administration Act for they have far less freedom in the determination of corporate policy than do the other proprietary corporations. While the membership of the boards of these three corporations includes people from several different departments, "the policies of these corporations cannot but be, as they are meant to be, a reflection of government policy."[14] The employees of the proprietary corporations, on the other hand, are all appointed by the management of the particular corporation and not through the Public Service Commission.

Financial control over the activities of proprietary Crown corporations is similar to the control exercised through the Financial Administration Act over agency corporations. Each one is required to submit a capital budget to the minister through whom it reports to parliament. This capital budget is subsequently approved by the cabinet and submitted to parliament by the minister. Some of these corporations, such as Air Canada, are required by their individual legislation to also submit an operating budget, although this is not the case with the corporations set up under the provisions of the Companies Act. A form of financial control is also exercised over the activities of these Crown corporations through the power of parliament to vote special financial assistance to make up deficits. While it is stated in the Finan-

---

[14] Ashley and Smails, op. cit., pp. 128-129. See also Royal Commission on Government Organization (Glassco Commission), *Report*, Vol. 5, p. 63; see: Langford, J. W., "Crown Corporations as Instruments of Policy" in Doern and Aucoin, op. cit., p. 239 for a general discussion of Crown corporations and the policy process.

cial Administration Act that proprietary corporations are normally expected to operate without appropriations, in fact most of them from time to time (and some of them all the time) require help from parliament to balance their operation-cost budgets. None of the proprietary corporations gets free accommodation or furniture from the Department of Public Works and, like private firms, they have to pay corporation income taxes. Many of the proprietary corporations are subject to the scrutiny of the Auditor General, although others such as Air Canada are not. This fact has frequently been a bone of contention introduced in parliamentary debates, although recent developments in the government's attitude to the office of the Auditor General indicate there will likely not be any change in this regard.

"Para"-Crown Corporations   There are many corporations wholly owned and operated by the government of Canada which are not listed in Schedules B to D of the Financial Administration Act. While these are not classed as departmental, agency, or proprietary corporations, they perform mostly the same kinds of functions as those corporations listed in the Financial Administration Act, and therefore should be considered briefly at this point.

Most of these unclassified Crown corporations are set up by separate federal legislation to perform functions which require a degree of independence of action; but, for often unstated reasons, they have not been included in the Financial Administration Act. The best examples of this sort of bureaucratic agency are the Bank of Canada, the Canadian Wheat Board, and the Social Sciences and Humanities Research Council, each of which has been set up by its own special legislation. These corporations display as many varieties of internal organization and procedures for control as there are acts. Because of their structural diversity, that is all that can be said about them here. It should also be mentioned, at this point, that there are many government corporations at the provincial level which function in approximately the same way that their federal counterparts do. Naturally, because of their organizational diversity and great numbers we can do no more in this study than mention the fact of their existence.

Finally it must be pointed out that there are a number of intradepartmental agencies which have a position of relative independence within the department, but which are not strictly Crown corporations. These independent boards and commissions are usually set up by special legislation to perform functions which require a degree of independence from direct political or ministerial control and which come within the organizational boundaries of one of the departments. Basically, these independent boards and commissions function in the same way as departmental corporations. Examples of this type of bureaucratic agency are the National Energy Board, Canadian Pension Commission, the Fisheries Research Board, the Board of Grain Commissioners, and the Canada Labour Relations Board. There are many more such organizations and there are also other important agencies of the government of Canada which function in much the same way as departmental corporations but which have varying relationships with the cabinet, parliament, and the departments. Again unfortunately the scope of this text does not permit a more detailed analysis of these structurally diverse and multifunctional bureaucratic agencies.

Joint Corporations   There are a number of government corporations and commissions in existence which are unique not because of their line functions but because their structure, composition, and legislative mandates are intergovernmental. Examples of these are the federal-provincial agencies such as the interprovincial and territorial boundary commissions, the only active ones today being the Manitoba-Saskatchewan Boundary Commission and the Alberta-British Columbia Boundary Commission each consisting of a commissioner from the provinces concerned and the Surveyor-General of Canada as the federal representative. Another example of joint federal-provincial enterprise is provided by Syncrude where federal and provincial governments as well as the private sector are joint participants.

In the international sphere, there are also joint Canadian-U.S. corporations and commissions in existence. Some of these such as the International Joint Commission and the International Boundary Commission have been in existence for a long time and are concerned more with the settlement of international disputes than with the management of some genuinely joint enterprise. However a more current trend is for such joint bodies to have operational responsibilities, for managing or developing a shared resource. Perhaps the earliest such body is the Columbia River Permanent Engineering Board which was set up in 1964 and more recent examples include the Roosevelt Campobello International Park Commission, where a Canada/U.S. board actually administers an international park jointly. While such bodies are still the exception it seems likely particularly in the areas of conservation and recreation that there will be greater need for them in the future both in the federal-provincial and international context.

Mixed Corporations   A prominent phenomenon of the late 1960s and 70s is the mixed public-private enterprise, and by 1980 the federal government was the majority shareholder in about fifteen of such corporations. One of these mixed corporations, the Canada Development Corporation (CDC) has over seventy subsidiaries located not only in Canada but around the world as well. Because these mixed enterprise corporations have a major responsibility to their private sector partners and shareholders, a major corporate goal is to make money. However, because these are at least partly "public enterprises" there are policy-related goals as well which likely complicate and qualify the single-minded search for profits.

Some of the larger of these mixed corporations besides CDC are Telesat Canada and Panarctic Oils Ltd., which differ from Crown corporations and other wholly owned government enterprises in that they are not subject to any of the provisions of the Financial Administration Act, their corporate budgets are in no way subject to the approval of the government, and for the most part the role of the government is reduced to that defined for a shareholder under company law. Needless to say one of the major problems that will face governments in the 1980s is to find ways of accommodating the unique requirements of mixed enterprise with the traditional imperatives of political accountability that characterizes all government activity in a liberal democracy.

This concludes our analysis of the various institutional forms found within the Canadian bureaucracy. Although it has been sketchy, it has pointed to a few of the tentative generalizations that can be made about the structures which dominate the formulation stage of the policy process in Canada. We must now turn to a discussion of the bureaucratic process—to attempt to explain how these bureaucratic institutions actually fit into the political process.

18

The Bureaucratic Process: Management, Policy Making, and Control

This chapter is concerned with how the bureaucracy goes about attaining its goals. As with any organization the essence of that process is *management*, defined simply as *the coordination of individual effort to accomplish group or organizational goals*. While management essentially involves coordination of individual effort, that coordination, in either the public or the private sector, can be broken down into a number of sub-processes or activities, including planning, organizing, staffing, directing, and controlling. Each of these activities will be discussed separately, but before we do so it is important to elaborate the characteristics which differentiate management in the private sector from management in the public sector—if only because so many analysts fail to note the differences and hence prescribe "cures" for various presumed ills of public sector management which have no hope whatever of success.

The first and major difference is simply that private management is analytically less complex. That is so because the basic organizational goals in the private sector can for the most part be reduced to one—making a profit.[1] This means that secondary criteria of evaluating management systems such as efficiency and economy can be employed in their literal sense. The organization that survives and which makes a profit for its shareholders is obviously blessed with "good management" and one which goes bankrupt or fails to make money is not. By contrast, for public management the criteria for being successful are not so clear. How, for instance, can one reduce the administration of a welfare program, the enforcement of the law, or the funding of medical research to profit? The goals of government are regulatory, distributive, redistributive, and punitive but seldom

---

[1] Note that while profitability is the fundamental goal of private sector organizations, many organizations do not behave in such a way as to maximize profits. See Charles Perrow, *Complex Organizations* (Scott Foresman, Glenview, 1972). Most organization theorists treat such behaviour as dysfunctional thus maintaining the proposition that such organizations should be profit maximizing; i.e., that profit maximization is the highest private-sector goal.

accumulative as they are for most private sector organizations. The ultimate measure of the worth of government is how effectively it has contributed to the happiness of most of its citizenry and not how frugally it has managed to run its operation, nor how much wealth it has been able to accumulate for its "owners." Thus, public management is different in part because the ultimate goals of the organization are so diffuse and so very difficult to define in concrete and measurable terms.

A second problem faced by the public manager that a counterpart in a private corporation is able to avoid, is that the goals of government are sometimes mutually exclusive. Redistributive policies, for instance, take money from those who have more and give it to those who have less, and the latter will inevitably find this arrangement more pleasing than the former and demand compensating outputs— which they often get! Thus, it is almost axiomatic that all government policies will please some people and displease others. In the overall attempt to satisfy as many Canadians as possible, managers in one part of the bureaucracy may be pursuing goals which directly conflict with the goals of those in another part of the government: with obvious consequences for interagency or interdepartmental coordination.

Thirdly, management in the public sector is distinguished by the extent to which one of the sub-processes, *control,* is emphasized. The need for accountability of bureaucrats to the elected branches of the government is a given in a democratic political system, and the consequence of this for the bureaucratic process is that the systems of financial administration and personnel administration are oriented more toward controlling the line managers than they are toward the facilitation of the managerial role. Indeed this emphasis on control in public management is so pronounced that we will discuss control in a completely separate section of the chapter.

Finally, the bureaucratic process in the government of Canada, as we have seen, is distinguished by the extent to which public servants are called upon to tender policy advice to the political arm of the government when it is determining priorities and choosing modes of policy implementation. Much has been said about this function in previous sections of the book. But because it is a major thesis of this text that the bureaucracy is a central actor in this most central activity of the political process it is necessary now to look specifically at how the bureaucrats and technocrats actually go about the business of generating and disseminating the information on which their political masters depend in their work.

In order to elaborate on the bureaucratic process in the public sector in Canada we will break down the rest of this chapter into three parts, addressed to each of the three broad sets of activities in which the bureaucracy is involved: management, policy making, and control.

MANAGEMENT IN THE CANADIAN BUREAUCRACY

We have already remarked that the core processes of management involve planning, organizing, staffing, directing, and controlling. In this section we consider the first four of these, leaving the issue of control to a separate section because of its particular complications in the Canadian public sector.

Planning

Planning is at the core of any system of management whether in the private or public sector. Essentially all this means is that it is necessary to decide what to do and how best to do it before actually launching into the task. In other words it is necessary to define operational goals and to develop the means of accomplishing those goals before actually trying to do anything. In the private sector, because the goals are fairly well agreed upon, the manager's task is to plan the most effective and efficient means of getting there. In government, however, the task is not so simple. Not only are the goals less clearly defined and less agreed upon, but the means of accomplishing them must fit within the particular norms of a liberal democratic polity and must comply with the particular rationale of a set of decision makers in cabinet whose main and quite legitimate motivation is to get themselves re-elected. These constraints on the process of goal determination and on the choice of means have two important implications for the planning process in the public sector, each of which deserves further discussion.

The Bifurcation of Planning   First of all because one of the requirements of a democratic system is that the goals of government must reflect the will of the public, those goals are inevitably set by the politically accountable cabinet. It is, as we have seen, the cabinet and its executive support agencies which take the major role not only in the determining of policy priorities but as well in approving the means to be employed by the bureaucracy in implementing those priorities. Hence, there is a *bifurcation of planning* in government. The permanent officials of the government, those entrusted with the task of managing policy implementation do not have a veto on goal determination. If the politicians, as they sometimes are prone to do, set goals which are not implementable and which are perhaps adopted contrary to the advice of the bureaucrats, the public service managers are nevertheless faced with trying to do their best in accomplishing them. In this sense the ultimate responsibility for setting goals is separated from the ultimate responsibility for accomplishing them, a situation which all senior managers in the public service have found extremely frustrating at, at least, some time in their careers.

Similarly, the public managers often do not have a free hand in working out the techniques and procedures for accomplishing the goals that have been set for them. Rather the public manager, while perhaps highly influential in determining the means of policy implementation, must still develop procedures which meet the requirements of the political arm of the government. Thus politically significant but administratively difficult procedures may be forced upon the manager in the public service.

Thus, the bifurcation of the planning function in government reduces the ability of the public service manager to plan in the same way as a counterpart in the private sector. Basically the infusion of politics into the planning process means that there is not only a "derationalization" of the process of goal determination, but that there is, as well, a situation where because means are as significant as ends in a democratic system; efficiency becomes a "negotiable" criterion of managerial effectiveness.

Planning as Evaluation   The second implication of a governmental context for the planning function is that there is an almost paranoid concern with keeping the bureaucracy *accountable* to the political branches of government. This has meant that managerial tools such as the expenditure budget, which in the private sector are employed as planning mechanisms, in the public service have been geared almost single-mindedly to maintaining the accountability of the department to parliament and the cabinet. Even budgetary devices such as Planning Programming Budgeting System (PPBS), which is distinguishable from other budgetary systems precisely because of its emphasis on planning, failed in the Canadian public service in large part because it was converted from a tool to help managers to a system of central control *over* the managers. As some public managers have commented whimsically, "they took away the first 'P,' (planning) and left only a little 'p' and some 'BS.' "

Thus, with the bifurcation of the planning function and the extreme concern with control and accountability in the public service of Canada, what was left to managers was the ability to assess their performance over time, given the constraints imposed by their public sector context. While the managers in the public sector cannot plan very systematically, they can at least set baseline targets for themselves which take into account the "givens" imposed on them by the politicians and try to improve their own procedures over time. They are thus left in the position of trying to measure the extent to which they have made the most of a bad situation.

The result of this attitude among responsible managers in the federal bureaucracy has been an attempt to emphasize the evaluative dimension of the planning process. Many systems of evaluation of managerial performance have been tried such as Cost Benefit Analysis and Operational Performance Measurement System (OPMS). These tools of evaluation were developed to permit managers to set realistic performance targets that take into account the ultimate goals their programs are expected to achieve, the relationship of their programs to complementary ones in other agencies, and the constraints imposed on them by the political environment within which they must operate. In this way the manager is permitted to see how well he or she has done in reaching a predetermined goal, to evaluate the branch's effectiveness in "hitting" the target, and to permit experimentation with new procedures that might prove more efficient.

One major problem with many of these systems of performance evaluation, however, has been that once in place, despite the best intentions of their creators, they inevitably become highly centralized in the manner in which they are enforced. The pervasive concern with control means that instead of the system of evaluation being regarded by the manager as a tool for assessing the performance of his unit, the system comes to be viewed as a mechanism of centralized surveillance and control and ultimately as a threat to the manager's personal security. Whether this conversion of systems of evaluation from tools of line management to contrivances of central control is a deliberate "plot" of the central agencies is a moot point; the fact remains that it happens consistently in the federal bureaucracy. It remains to be seen whether the still evolving Office of the Comptroller General, which is charged with developing procedures for evaluation, can escape this role of "central agency villain" in the eyes of the line managers. When to this particular problem is added equally vexing problems of ill-defined methodology for evaluation and the general diffuseness of goals referred to above, the prognosis is not very encouraging.

Overall, then, the planning function of public sector management is very seriously constrained by the "givens" of a democratic political system. Because of the bifurcation of the planning function and because of the dominance of the mechanisms of control, the only aspect of the planning process which thrives in the federal government is performance evaluation; and, as we have seen, even that dimension of the planning process tends to face problems of over-centralization, inadequate methodology, and unstated or unmeasurable goals.

As we move, now, to a discussion of the managerial activities of organizing, staffing, and directing we must keep in mind the operational primacy of planning in all decision-making activity. Even within the other analytically discrete sub-processes that make up the process of management, it must be remembered that planning must occur as well. Hence, while the public service manager may be denied a central role in the setting of policy goals and in determining the overall means of goal attainment in the federal bureaucracy, there remains a responsibility, on a smaller scale, for the manager to "plan" strategies for organizing, staffing, and directing the department. Hence as we discuss organizing, staffing, and directing keep in mind that planning must be seen as part of each activity as well as a sub-function in its own right.

Organizing

In order for individuals to work effectively toward the attainment of organizational goals, a contrived structure of roles (an organization) must be designed and maintained. The student must recognize however that bureaucracies have both formal and informal organizational structures. The latter reflect unplanned patterns of personal and psychological interaction that develop within any group of people. Informal leaders will inevitably emerge in any working place and these people sometimes rival the authority of the formal leaders or the "bosses" by virtue of their personal charisma, job competence, or long-time experience in the particular work place. While the phenomenon of informal organization, which occurs in all formal social structures, has implications for the managerial function of "directing," we want to concentrate here upon the formal and not the informal aspects of bureaucracy. We must keep in mind, however, that parallel to the contrived formal structure of government there is an invisible informal network which can have an impact on the effectiveness of the organization.

The rest of this section will focus on the managers' role in defining the intradepartmental *span of control* and unified chain of command within government agencies, and in outlining the principles which determine the interdepartmental distribution of responsibilities in the federal bureaucracy.

Span of Control and Chain of Command   The span of control in a hierarchical organization is defined by the number of individuals at any level who must report directly to a supervisor, senior manager, or "boss." Thus, if a government department has six assistant deputy ministers (ADMs) who report directly to the deputy minister (DM), the latter's span of control is six. Different textbooks on management have tried to define the optimum span of control but without success because the appropriate span of control will vary with the nature of the organization, the personalities of the people involved, and the significance of informal organizational structures in either facilitating or short-circuiting the vertical communication links. Generally, however, a span of control exceeding eight is thought to be too "wide"— one is incapable of effectively directing the operation if one has to ride herd on more than eight immediate subordinates.

Where span of control defines the breadth of an organizational hierarchy, the concept of *chain of command* has to do with the "length" of the hierarchy. The length of the chain of command is the number of levels from top to bottom in the organization. Obviously, if the span of control is to remain less than, for example, eight, as organizations become larger, the chain of command lengthens. While it is not possible to state that there is any universal optimum length of chain of command, generally as the chain of command lengthens, the senior manager will be called upon increasingly to delegate responsibilities to subordinates. Thus, an important part of the managerial activity of organizing is to structure the formal organization in such a way that the span of control and the chain of command permit effective delegation of responsibilities without losing control over the "extremities" of the operation.

Finally, closely related to the concept of chain of command is the concept of *unity of command*. What this means is that in a hierarchical organization there should be only one boss at the top. According to this principle, subordinate managers in a government department, for instance, must not have more than one superior; the chain of command must lead directly from top to bottom in the organization and it must be clear to managers at every level to whom they are responsible. It is impossible for a middle-level manager to function effectively if there is more than one boss giving orders.

To apply these concepts to the process of management in the federal public service in Canada, we can begin by stating that in some ways the activity of organizing is the one least affected by the fact that the manager is in the public sector. The questions of length of chain of command and span of control tend to be left pretty well to the line managers and there is a minimum of meddling by the political branches of the government. Because of the rapid growth of most government departments in Canada in the last twenty years, the senior managers, in attempting to delegate responsibility while at the same time maintaining control, have generally opted to lengthen the chain of command and narrow the span of control at the top of the organization. Thus, a typical organization chart of a federal department in 1956 might have had six or seven *directors* reporting directly to the DM, where a typical department in 1980 might have as many as three or four levels of management between the DM and the directors and a span of control of four or five. The increase in the senior management positions in the federal public service has been remarkable in the past two decades; where DMs and directors were the first and second line managers in government organizations twenty years ago, today we can see a proliferation of associate deputy ministers, ADMs, senior ADMs and directors-general, all inserted *between* the DM and director levels of the department.

Limits to the Unity of Command   It is hard to evaluate the effectiveness of this trend in maintaining the unity of command in the federal bureaucracy because the workability of the various organizational forms depends upon the actual people involved and upon the idiosyncrasies of the informal organizational features of the department. In the latter case one of the factors which can affect the unity of command in the organization is the extent to which the minister and personal staff can bypass the DM (and personal staff) in influencing directly the activities at lower levels of the department. It is by now commonplace for ministers who fear they will be kept in the dark by their DMs and who wish to remain informed about the actual operation of the department to have bright young men and women from within the bowels of their department seconded to them as "special assistants." Besides functioning as technical advisors to the minister, such people are also often called upon to maintain informal communication links with their friends and colleagues in the department, thus giving the minister a kind of "spy network" which serves to keep the deputy minister honest in any dealings with his superior. However, while such informal communications systems might be used by a minister to actually subvert the chain of command or to permit direct ministerial influence on the operational activities of the department, for the most part the use to which they have been put by the political executive has been passive and defensive rather than manipulative.

The other way in which the chain of command can be subverted in the federal government is through the activities of the central agencies, particularly the Treasury Board Secretariat. While formally mandated only with providing assistance and advice for the line managers in the departments, the advisory branches of TBS have been able to do some arm twisting in getting senior managers to adopt "recommended" procedures. However, here the problem is one of inter-agency conflict and does not often subvert the internal chain of command within the department.

Where the TBS does sometimes subvert the chain of command

within a department is in its role in scrutinizing the departmental estimates and in the program review stage of the budgetary cycle, for in this process the TBS does have the authority unilaterally to alter the department's priorities. However the staff officers in the financial branch of the department will usually have established prior informal contact with the personnel in the TBS who will ultimately be dealing with the department's forecasts. This informal communication network between departmental program officers or financial administrators and TBS people helps to ease the way for departmental spending proposals by working out the deals and bargains before the formal package of departmental estimates is submitted to the Board. In this way the informal communications system facilitates the budgetary process and likely improves upon the formal machinery of the estimates. On the negative side however such informal processes can subvert the chain of command within the department. Because it is the friendly folks in the Financial Administration Branch of the department who maintain the links with the TBS and not the senior managers, the latter can become "small-time" power brokers within the department. Their influence with a key central agency makes them informal leaders who can nibble away at the formal authority defined by the departmental chain of command. Thus while it is not the intention of the TBS to subvert the formal power structure of the department the Secretariat can sometimes have that effect by becoming part of the informal interagency bargaining networks that play a growing role in the preparation of the estimates.

Informal organization is therefore one of the variables that affects the effectiveness of the formal command and control mechanisms of the federal bureaucracy. However, depending upon the skill of the senior manager of the government in "directing" and staffing the department, the informal organizational structures can become benign implements to be used to improve the overall effectiveness of the formal organization that the manager has helped to design and maintain.

The Principles of Departmentalization Where formal organization is virtually imposed on the senior managers of the government of Canada is in the interdepartmental structure of the bureaucracy. The interdepartmental distribution of responsibilities and jurisdiction is based on the closely related principles of *function* and *clientele*. The Department of Labour and the Department of Agriculture, for instance, exist to perform administrative and policy-making functions in certain specific areas relating to labour and farmers respectively. Basically, the name of a department will give some indication of the function it is intended to perform and the clientele to which it is expected to cater. However, while the distribution of functions between the various departments is intended to eliminate inter-departmental confusion and conflict over who is to do what, there is much overlapping of departmental jurisdiction. The result of this jurisdictional conflict is a process whereby bureaucratic agencies compete with each other for jurisdiction in areas of potential overlap. Thus, the Departments of Energy, Mines and Resources, Indian Affairs and Northern Development, Environment, Transport, National Health and Welfare, and Agriculture all have some responsibility for water-pollution control. Which of these departments ultimately emerges supreme in the various aspects of this policy area will depend on a process of interdepartmental bargaining, cabinet decisions, and the political influence of each department's clientele.

As time passes and conditions change, new departments spring up and other departments disappear. Sometimes the functions of one department are absorbed into another, and at other times two departments will be amalgamated administratively even though the functions are not very closely related. Often it is apparent that the demands of a certain clientele perpetuate the existence of archaic departments long after their functions should have been absorbed into newer departments. For instance, the Department of Veteran's Affairs, continues to exist even though it is difficult for an administrator to see why such matters are not merely placed under the jurisdiction of the Department of Health and Welfare. The politician knows better—there are still several hundred thousand veterans and their dependants in age categories where voter turnout is high.

Some government departments like Secretary of State have a sort of "catch-all" jurisdiction; any matters that are not important enough or large enough to be placed in a separate department are administratively lumped together here. Still other departments such as Supply and Services and Public Works perform a number of services for all of the other departments. The Post Office is somewhat unique in that it carries on dealings with the general public on a quasi-commercial basis and in fact will soon become a Crown corporation. On the other hand, some of the more traditional departments of government such as National Defence and External Affairs have responsibilities which are only secondarily concerned with any specific clientele in Canada.

Hence, the rationale for the interdepartmental distribution of responsibilities in Canada is very difficult to state in any succinct fashion. Departments exist for a number of reasons, and most of them justify their existence through some specific function that they perform or some clientele that they serve. Because government reorganizations are usually reflective of political trends in the world at large more so than of considerations of administrative efficiency, the role of the public manager in this process is usually small.

Staffing

The managerial activity referred to as staffing essentially involves manning the organization—by recruiting candidates for positions in the organization, by selecting the best people from those recruited, by training the ones selected so that they can do the job required of them, and by facilitating the development of their careers in the organization. In the private sector, the senior manager has control over virtually all aspects of the process of staffing and usually is assisted in this process by a fairly sizeable personnel branch. However, ultimate decisions as to hiring and firing of employees, and decisions as to promotion, transfer, and discipline rest with senior management within the organization. In the public service, however, the authority of the senior manager is not as comprehensive. In the federal bureaucracy, the senior manager must share the staffing function with central agencies such as the Treasury Board and particularly the Public Service Commission.

Legislation passed in 1967 has as one of its major aims the implementation of the Glassco Commission's admonition to "let the managers manage." As a result, the legislation purported to give the deputy minister and his delegates a great deal of flexibility in dealing with the management of human resources within the department and at the same time to ensure uniform standards and procedures across the public service through the Treasury Board and the Public Service Commission. For practical purposes however, the DM is forced to operate within very tightly defined procedures and guidelines set by the central agencies, and his independent authority over the staffing process within his department is very restricted.

According to the Financial Administration Act, the Treasury Board as the central management agency of the government, has the responsibility for the management of all personnel functions in the public service. Most significant among the Treasury Board's personnel administration functions is the responsibility to act as the "employer" in all collective negotiations with the employee unions. This is a very serious limit to the deputy's authority, for if there is a dispute within the department between management and employee, the DM does not have the power to act as management independently of the Treasury Board.

The Public Service Commission   The creation of the first Civil Service Commission in Canada in 1908 was precipitated by changes that occurred in the functions of the bureaucracy and in the attitudes of Canadians concerning the nature of the public service. At one time there had been a general acceptance of the state of affairs where appointment to bureaucratic office was based not on the qualifications of the applicant and the requirements of the job but on partisan considerations. Liberal governments rewarded the party faithful by granting them jobs in the public service and Conservative governments did the same.[2] The short-run effect of this practice was to aid the political parties in building strong party organizations in most of the country's constituencies. As the parties built up bases of support, however, they no longer needed the promise of patronage appointments to entice people into working for the party, and the administrative problem of distributing the patronage had become a great headache to the party leader.

People, furthermore, began to consider such tactics morally and ethically improper, and movements sprang up to reform the civil service. Finally, as the role of government expanded, the jobs to be done in the public service began to require a degree of expertise that was often sadly lacking in a person who was appointed for reasons of political preference. The upshot of all of these changes was that the recruitment practices of the public service were changed from the principle of patronage to the principle of *merit*. In other words, applicants for public service positions were now to be chosen on the basis of their qualifications and the requirements of the position, and if more than one person fit the same position, the choice between them was to be made on the basis of a competitive examination. The original Civil Service Commission was set up to supervise the implementation of the *merit system* of recruitment in the public service.

Today, the Public Service Commission is made up of three commissioners—all of whom are appointed for a set term by the Governor in Council, with salaries set by parliament—and a large permanent staff. The functions of the Public Service Commission include the overseeing of the merit system and other responsibilities related to staffing the public service of Canada, as well as certain types of appeals concerned with staffing. In short, because of its large measure of control over the people who get into the Canadian public service, the Public Service Commission is an important independent agency in the staffing process. In practice however, while the PSC controls the rules within which the process of staffing must be carried on, the central agencies have delegated the responsibility for staffing the department with the exception of the most senior levels of the bureaucracy, to the department.

Training and Development The staffing function however, does not cease with recruitment. As with any organization, it is necessary

---

[2] Political biographies give many of the details of the development of patronage in Canada. See especially Donald Creighton, *John A. Macdonald*, Vol. 2: *The Old Chieftain*, *passim*.

to train the people who are part of it, not only with respect to the technical skills of the specific occupation, but also with respect to the goals of the organization. The employee who has been thoroughly socialized into a bureaucratic organization will likely function more enthusiastically and even more efficiently than the person who looks on his occupation as "just a living." Hence there is an almost constant process of training and development[3] within the Canadian bureaucracy which, by molding the attitudes of public servants, very subtly affects bureaucratic decision making. The formal responsibility for training and development is shared by the senior managers in the departments and the Treasury Board. However the latter has for the most part delegated its responsibility in this area to the Public Service Commission. Thus training and development programs within the federal bureaucracy are run by the managers in the departments, by the Public Service Commission and often through the cooperation of both.

Thus it is that the DM does not have nearly as much control over staffing activity as his counterpart in the private sector. Because as was pointed out elsewhere, the kinds of decisions being made in an organization and the type of managerial system which is to prevail will depend largely on the kinds of people within the organization, the restrictions placed on the role of management in matters of staffing reduce the overall impact of the senior bureaucrats.

The Obligations of Public Employment Having discussed the nature of the recruitment selection and training process in the public service, this is perhaps an appropriate juncture to say something of the nature of employment in the federal bureaucracy and to outline some of the rights, obligations, and restrictions attached to the role of public servant.

Public servants have traditionally been viewed as different from employees in the private sector. In part this is because they are "servants of the public" and should therefore take a highly responsible attitude to their jobs; but by far the greatest justification for treating public servants differently from their counterparts in private industry is simply their proximity to politics. Because they have access to information that the general public does not, and because they are involved in the process of policy formulation, public servants could potentially do a great deal of damage to the government of the day.

---

[3] The Glassco Commission distinguishes between *training*, which teaches people specific skills and techniques, and *development*, which provides periodic exposure to broad courses on subjects related only tangentially to the job itself. Each can be important in the process of socializing an employee to the organizational norms.

By leaking information to the opposition parties or by "sabotaging" government projects, the public servant could potentially bring down the government. Thus, the tradition has evolved that while the public servant must be cognizant of personal responsibility to the public, if this conflicts with the interests of the government, the public servant must look to the latter first since it is the government—not the bureaucrat—which must ultimately face the public. For instance, when a senior actuary in the public service felt that it was his responsibility to the public to tell them through the media that the government's proposed Canada Pension Plan was unwise and actuarily unsound, he was immediately dismissed.

In order to protect the government from this kind of "betrayal," there are clauses in the Official Secrets Act providing for severe penalties for public servants who make unauthorized statements based on official information. Furthermore, public servants must take an oath of office upon entering the federal public service in which each swears not to "disclose or make known any matter that comes to my knowledge by reason of such employment." Violation of this principle can mean immediate dismissal, as it did to a senior executive in the Central Mortgage and Housing Corporation who "leaked" a secret cabinet document to some Indian groups.

There are also restrictions on the extent to which a public servant can become involved in politics. He or she can vote, contribute money to parties, and attend meetings while a public servant, but cannot actively campaign on behalf of a candidate or run for elected office. Since the passage of the most recent Public Service Employment Act, public servants have been permitted to request a leave of absence without pay from their jobs to seek election at the federal, provincial, or municipal levels. The restrictions on the political activities of provincial public servants are generally similar to those at the federal level.

Directing

The key to the managerial activity of directing is the motivation of human resources within an organization so that the individuals will be willing to put the goals of the group before their individual goals at least while on the job. For the most part this can be achieved if the goals of the organization happen to be congruent with those of the individual or if the organization can offer inducements which benefit the individual in some material fashion. The former rarely occurs except in voluntary associations, but in the case of bureaucratic organizations the inducement to employees is almost always a monetary reward in the form of a salary or wages.

In the private sector, the manager has a great deal of control over the relative financial rewards (and penalties) to be allotted to his personnel. By influencing the processes of promotion, by parcelling out the opportunities for advancement through training programs, and by having the power to impose disciplinary sanctions, the manager in the private sector has the tools, the material sanctions and inducements, to motivate human resources. By stark contrast, the manager in the federal bureaucracy has very little direct control over the salary, benefits, and career development opportunities of employees. Because, as we will see later, it is the Treasury Board and not the deputy minister which functions as the employer in collective bargaining, the latter is severely limited in the extent to which the managerial prerogatives, which are used as motivators in the private sector, can be exercised. Thus while the ability to manipulate sanctions and inducements as motivaters in the process of directing exists, it must be shared by the DM and the central officers in the PSC and the TBS.

Lacking in personal control over the material factors of motivation, the public service manager must therefore resort to the more ethereal "leadership skills" in attempting to get the most out of subordinates. It is the qualities of the individual manager *per se* such as charisma, professional expertise, and overall job competence and not what the manager can "do for" the employee which must be employed as motivators. If the manager is "liked" and "respected" by the employees, or if they believe in the kinds of goals he is trying to accomplish, they will work harder and more enthusiastically at their jobs; on the other hand if they hold him in low regard and spend a lot of time figuring out how to avoid work, the manager has only limited options with which to discipline them.

The other problem is that lacking in the formal authority to reward and punish subordinates, a manager in the public service may find it difficult to compete with informal leaders in the organization. The one edge that the manager in the private sector has when dealing with informal organization is possession of full authority within the formal organization. In the government however, the ability of the manager to motivate underlings may hinge on his ability to become part of or at least to figure out how to use the informal authority patterns in the organization. Thus managerial leadership in government is not "command" as it tends to be in most hierarchical organizations, but a complex of personality resources, social and political skills, and a full awareness of the informal alliances, friendships, and personal animosities among the people employed. Directing in this sort of an organizational environment resembles more an art form than a professional skill.

This concludes our discussion of the process of management in the

Canadian bureaucracy. While the overall conclusion has to be that the manager in the public sector generally works within extremely severe constraints imposed by the overall environment of government, by the central agencies, and by the requirements for political accountability, the Canadian bureaucracy does get managed somehow. It is easy to be critical of management in the bureaucracy, but before attempting any overall verdict, it is necessary first to look at the role of the bureaucracy and of senior managers in the policy process. Here the manager must function as a facilitator and coordinator of expert knowledge, a role which is virtually non-existent in the private sector, and which involves a set of managerial skills which are unique to government.

THE MANAGEMENT OF POLICY MAKING

We have already touched upon the role of the Canadian bureaucracy in the policy process elsewhere in the text. We have analyzed its place in the process of priority determination within the context of our discussion of the cabinet and the central agencies but we have not said very much at all about policy formulation or policy initiation as sets of activities within the federal departments. It is the aim of this section of the chapter to describe these activities and to explain the responsibilities of the senior bureaucrats as managers of policy-relevant information.

Policy Initiation
At the policy initiation stage we see the bureaucracy acting both as a channel of input and *gatekeeper* in filtering demands from the environment, and as an *advocate* for the interests of a specific clientele. In the advocacy role the government department enters into a sort of symbiotic relationship with the relevant interest groups in jointly attempting to convince the priority setters in the cabinet and the central agencies to meet the policy demands of their shared clientele. The interest group–department relationship is symbiotic because a successful campaign which influences the priority setters to embrace the desired policy or program, benefits both the department and the interest group. The latter benefits directly in that the clientele group it represents gets an immediate payoff from the new program. The former benefits through the increased budget and human resources it gets to implement the new policy.

To act as an effective channel of input, the departmental manager is required simply to maintain open lines of communication and to establish a close working relationship with the key interest groups in the appropriate policy sector. This means that the department is functioning as a representative institution, often directly in competition with other institutions such as parliament, the political parties, and the electoral system. However, the most effective bureaucratic agencies in the process of channeling policy ideas into the system are those which take more than simply a passive role in the process. It is not uncommon for government officials today to become involved as social animators. It is not necessary to simply wait for demands to emerge if the department has anticipated needs of a clientele group before the group itself has felt those needs. Hence the departmental policy managers in the 1970s have become increasingly involved in the process of education of their clients and in assisting the groups whose interests they serve to better organize and to more effectively articulate their demands to government. In effect, modern clientele-oriented agencies of government, at both federal and provincial levels, not only help to articulate the policy demands of their clients, they also may help to create and organize the interest groups with which they must deal.

In sum, government departments, in functioning as channels of input for demands from interest groups, often go far beyond the passive gatekeeper role and become active advocates of client interests. Moreover, in some cases the department will actually enter into a sort of "collusion" with the interest groups in the environment in attempting to generate and articulate policy demands to the priority setters in the cabinet and in the central agencies.

Policy Innovation   Thus, in its role as a channel for input from the environment, the bureaucracy functions not only as a "facilitator" but also as an active "manipulator" of the flow of information from the environment to the system. However, a further mode of bureaucratic involvement in the process of policy initiation is still more active and direct. Here the government agency actually creates its own policy demands internally, and triggers the mechanisms of priority determination through a process referred to in the argot of systems analysis as *"withinput."* In effect withinput activity in the bureaucracy is manifested by a process of policy innovation which is essentially internal.

The basic problem for the senior bureaucratic manager in organizing the department to act as an agency of innovation stems from the very nature of bureaucratic organization. The raison d'être of bureaucracy is to make administrative behaviour predictable and this is accomplished largely through the *routinization* of decision making. In an organization geared to predictability and routinization, creativity and innovativeness become negative or dysfunctional traits. Hence the challenge of the public service manager is to find organizational devices which will permit innovative activity and at the same time not compromise the basic organizational goal of routinization— to integrate creativity and predictability.

Ghettoization of Innovation   Two managerial devices have been employed in an attempt to resolve the inherent contradiction between the goals of innovation and routinization in federal bureaucratic structures. The first device is the "ghettoization" of innovation. This is achieved through organizing the department so that the "policy branch" or "policy planning branch" is encapsulated and insulated from the line operators. The aim here is to foster creative thinking and experimentation within the "ghetto" and at the same time to prevent the mood in the policy branch from infecting the line administration and hampering the normal routine.

One problem with the ghettoization of innovation is that after a period of time, even these very carefully designed policy structures tend to routinize their operations. If this is allowed to develop to its logical extreme we end up with the somewhat paradoxical situation where the creativity and imagination within these units becomes routinized. "Routinized innovation" is of course not very innovative at all, and to offset this tendency a second managerial device has been developed in the government of Canada, which might be dubbed "personnel transfusion." The aim of these personnel transfusions is to ensure a constant supply of "new blood" to the "policy ghetto" which works against the relentless forces of routinization. Thus it is rare for an individual to serve more than a few years in one of the policy branches of government. People simply get rotated out and either find a transfer to another government agency or back to the line operations of the same department.

The operational results of these managerial tactics for facilitating innovation within the federal bureaucracy while not cataclysmic, are worth note. The most prominent result has been a high output of *procedural* innovations. A large number of improvements in the managerial process itself have been spawned as a direct product of the "brain storming" that goes on in these policy units. Much of the experimentation with new systems of performance evaluation, operational planning, and different organizational modes which has been witnessed in the past decade in the federal public service has been at least partly the result of the activities of the planning and policy branches in the various departments. Unfortunately, little of it has been overwhelmingly successful.

In the process of substantive policy development the success rate has been somewhat better. The focus here has been in thinking up "neat new things" the department might do for its clients, and in developing novel strategies for trying to sell the ideas to the sombre superbureaucrats in the central agencies, and to the cabinet. While the "batting average" for getting such new policy ideas adopted is not high, where the policy innovators can define a new clientele and help to mobilize them in support of a new program, there is usually a possibility of at least partial success.

Innovation and Crisis Management   Finally, the innovative ghettos have had some impact in the business of "crisis management." We have already spoken of the evolution of "crisis government" within the context of the process of priority determination. This mode of decision making may have become a discrete style of governance in the 1970s. However, here we wish to say something about the role of crisis management in the policy initiation stage of policy making.

In essence a "crisis approach" to policy initiation involves the departmental policy branches in a process of "anticipatory innovation" or of policy "contingency planning." Here the policy innovator uses a combination of "vigilance," achieved through maintaining good lines of communication with clientele groups, and "intelligence" operations designed to uncover, through research, public needs, or clientele demands before they become manifest. Often this means anticipating what the clientele will need in the near future, before the clientele or its representative interest group become aware of the fact themselves.

Obviously, as we have stated it above, the process of crisis management must be seen as simply an important implement of good government. However, it is the ends to which such innovative activities are put that determine their ultimate outcome. In its purest form, crisis management is a rationalist device which utilizes the ideas of bureaucratic innovators to prevent crises by foretelling them and nipping them in the bud. The commonest adulteration of rationalist crisis management in the Canadian system is characterized by a Machiavellian use of the imminent crisis for political gain. Here the policy innovators anticipate the crisis and set up the contingency responses but then wait for the crisis to develop before reacting. In this way the government will gain political kudos for having risen to the occasion and saved the day! The extreme perversion of crisis management, however, is where the policy innovators, possibly in cahoots with the political leadership, actively precipitate crises so that they will have a justification for implementing policy responses that might be otherwise unacceptable to the public. This sort of Orwellian manipulation of the public by the government, while clearly a potential tactic, is likely not used very much in Canada. Such deliberate and cynical manipulation of the public will for political (or bureaucratic) gain is simply unacceptable to people socialized to the values of our political culture. Besides, they might get caught!

Innovation and Incrementalism Despite attempts to make the bureaucratic dimensions of the policy process innovative and to permit the effective management of crises, there remain severe limitations on the effectiveness of these devices. In fact most new policies that come to the surface at the priority determination phase of the policy process are simply linear extensions of existing policies—logical outgrowths of current practice rather than genuinely new policy initiatives. But why, then, does innovation in government meet with only limited success, and why does the process of new policy development remain so relentlessly "incremental?"

Incrementalism prevails because it is safe. In a decision-making environment characterised by *uncertainty*—the inability to predict the future accurately—it is always easier for the policy makers either to decide to do nothing, or to opt for small adjustments to the status quo. In a situation of incomplete information it is risky to attempt "great leaps" forward with radical policy options, for the "great leap" may precipitate unforeseen consequences which are more serious than the problem the policy is designed to solve in the first place.[4] Finally the persistence of incrementalism in the policy process may be reflective of the fact that the kinds of real-world changes the policy makers are faced with are themselves incremental—simply, perhaps less is unexpected than in the past. Although we are faced with serious problems such as an economic malaise, energy shortfalls, and ethnic conflict, these are "chronic" and not "acute" ills. Developments in these problems are neither sudden nor totally unexpected, and it may be that the most appropriate policy responses are in the manner of constant but incremental adjustments as new information becomes available.

Policy Formulation

As we have explained elsewhere, policy formulation involves developing a policy idea into a detailed set of proposals for implementation. While this part of the process occurs analytically after a priority has been established, in fact the proposals for implementation are being developed at the initiation and priority stages. What distinguishes the formulation stage is that the process is more exclusively internal to the department. Where the focus at the stage of policy initiation is upon generating new policy ideas which can be "sold" to the priority setters, once a priority has been established the problem for the department is to concern itself with developing the means of achieving the desired goals.

---

[4] On this point, the classic statements remain Herbert Simon's *Administrative Behaviour* and James March and Herbert Simon, *Organisations*.

The "stuff" of policy formulation is ultimately specialized information and technical data which must be brought to bear on the problems of how to achieve policy goals defined by the priority setters. The activity of policy formulation is basically problem solving and the role of the manager in this process is to coordinate the efforts of the technical staff of the department. As with the process of policy initiation, it is the policy branch of the department that often plays the central role in formulation. Here, however, the goal is not so much to define policy problems and to attempt to convince the cabinet and central agencies that they are deserving of a policy response, but rather to develop the most practical and effective procedures for achieving agreed upon goals. Because "implementability" is a concern at this stage there is a much greater need to integrate the efforts of the technocrats in the "innovation ghettos" with the operational expertise that resides in the line managers who, ultimately, will actually have to get the job done. This is a major challenge to the senior managers in the department, and it can prove to be a difficult task.

The problem of integrating policy considerations and operational considerations is made difficult by the isolation of the policy branch from the line functions in the department. While, as we have seen, the isolation or "ghettoization" of the policy advisors is essential if innovativeness is to be reconciled with routinization, even the most brilliant policy ideas must be ultimately reformulated in such a way that they can be put into effect. Beyond the problems of blending the creative juices of the policy advisory branch with the more pedestrian concerns of the line administrators, the senior manager must also ensure that the policy proposal, once formulated, is acceptable to the central agencies and to the cabinet. This means that the central agencies must be "in on" the process almost from the start to ensure that the means being developed are financially feasible and practically acceptable.

While in terms of time and of the number of people directly involved, policy formulation is not the largest role played by the Canadian bureaucracy, it is certainly the largest *policy* role. And because policy formulation involves greater utilization of technical expertise than do other stages of policy making, it is this function of the bureaucracy which is the most difficult to control. Usually the department will offer alternate proposals for accomplishing the policy goals defined by the priority setters. Superficially this means that the cabinet and its advisors must make the choice among the options developed by the department. However, in most cases the choice will be an illusion, for inevitably one alternative, the one preferred by the department, will be painted with far more attractive colours than its competition. Furthermore, by the time a large team of highly specialized economists has spent seven hours a day for eighteen months putting together material such as might be found in a white paper on taxation, it is unlikely that their political "masters" in the cabinet will be able to mount an effective criticism of the detailed substance of their recommendations.

Sometimes, to weaken any potential criticism in central agencies, cabinet, or parliament in advance, it is a completely feasible tactic for the team of experts to cook up and include a few "throwaway" items in their proposals. Obviously "red herrings" can be carefully integrated into the policy paper to draw the fire of the opposition, whether it be the media, interest groups, or potential dissenters in cabinet. Then, after a period of debate, the technical advisors can graciously accede to the wishes of their political critics and excise the troublesome proposals. In this way, it is possible to retain intact the basic structure of a policy option (as recommended by the technical people) while giving the critics a feeling of efficacy. While the actual use of this tactic is difficult to document and while it is clearly devious on the part of the technical advisors, its use is sometimes apparent in the formulation process. Perhaps the greatest impediment to this type of behaviour, particularly when bureaucrats attempt to use it in dealing with the cabinet, is that the technical experts themselves, in various departments, are rarely sufficiently agreed to mount this sort of "attack" on the cabinet's supremacy.

In fact it may be an "irony of technocracy" that the degree of specialization of technical policy advisors is both their source of strength and their greatest weakness as well. In this sense the specialized policy advisor can become so expert in a narrow field that the substance of the advice given is virtually unassailable by the non-expert cabinet and difficult to challenge even for the "generalist-manager" type of senior bureaucrat to whom the advisor reports. However, on the other side of the coin, the technocrats become so specialized that they lack perspective on the overall policy implications of their advice and end up being erudite but irrelevant. At the broadest level of speculation we can hypothesize that this phenomenon may be symptomatic of a fundamental weakness in the policy formulation process in many modern industrialized systems. If the experts are too specialized to see or understand the significance of their knowledge in relationship to the input of their equally specialized peers in different areas of expertise, and if the senior bureaucratic generalists in the government in whom we vest the responsibility for integrating and coordinating the process of policy formulation cannot deal meaningfully with the substance of the highly technical information being generated from within their policy advisory groups, is there anybody with the "Philosopher-King-like" combination of skills to actually pilot the ship of state?

This situation (which is admittedly painted in the extreme here to make the point) goes a long way to explain the apparent failure (or limited success) of many of the rationalist experiments such as PPBS and Management by Objectives (MBO). A partial remedy to the problem may lie in fostering a different view or ethos of management in both federal and provincial bureaucracies. Where the function of management in traditional bureaucratic structures is viewed as the coordination of personnel and materials toward the attainment of organizational goals, in bureaucratic agencies mandated to produce policy advice, the function of the manager is to organize expertise in such a way that it can be directed not only to the attainment of predetermined goals, but to the determination of the goals as well. While there are clear indications in the government of Canada that there is a new breed of senior bureaucrats who possess these policy skills as well as the perspective to use them effectively in the process of "managing" the technical information generated from within their departments, there is still too wide a variation from agency to agency in the performance of this critical policy formulation function.

Finally, to return to our discussion of the bureaucracy and the policy process, astute, "policy wise" managers will also be looking even further down the road than cabinet approval, to the parliamentary stage of the process. In recognition of the fact that getting legislation through the House quickly and with a minimum of fuss requires some "trade offs" between government and the opposition, it is sometimes prudent to include some expendable proposals even after the conclusion of the formulation stage. By judiciously retaining a few "red herring" clauses in the draft legislation the formulators can "draw the fire" of the ever-vigilant opposition. In this way the government has some items upon which to yield to opposition pressure (after an appropriate struggle) in return for a speedy passage of the remainder of the package through the House of Commons.

This concludes what is admittedly a fairly cursory look at the process of bureaucratic policy making. We have not said much about the policy-related process of interdepartmental coordination because that was dealt with in Chapter 15. Similarly we have not dealt with the role of the line departments in the budgetary process for that will be discussed within the context of processes of control in the next section.

THE PROCESS OF CONTROL

The concern in this section is with the modes of control or of the constraints placed on bureaucratic decision making by other governmental institutions. Here we will look at political control of the bureaucracy in terms of the relationship between the cabinet and the line managers, at the financial control established by the budgetary system, at judicial review of administrative decisions and finally at one of the most significant constraints on the public sector manager today, the system of collective bargaining.

Control by Cabinet

As has already been stated, bureaucratic power flows from the concentration of various kinds of expertise within the bureaucracy and from the degree of control over the flow of information to the cabinet. The bureaucracy influences priority determination and largely dominates policy formulation because it is expected to advise the cabinet on the basis of the information it possesses. However, while the bureaucracy occupies a position of great importance in the policy process, ultimate political power still rests with the cabinet and the Prime Minister. Whether on whim or political exigency, whether wisely or unwisely, the cabinet and the Prime Minister can and do periodically choose to disregard bureaucratic advice, even when that advice was requested by the government in the first place.

The actual exercise of this ultimate control by the cabinet is usually limited to situations where the action demanded by political expediency is not congruent with the course of action indicated by technical or administrative considerations. When this happens, the political advisors to the cabinet (such as those in the Prime Minister's Office), the party structure, the Privy Council Office, and the cabinet ministers and Prime Minister themselves, tend to be in a position of competition vis-à-vis the bureaucracy proper. If the cabinet as a whole or the Prime Minister should become convinced that the political considerations are more important than the technical, financial, or administrative ones, the regular bureaucrats will, at least for the moment, lose out. This situation of competing advice from the political advisors and the bureaucratic advisors can exist at all stages of the decision-making process, although in many cases it is likely that political and other considerations will in fact coincide. The point that must be emphasized in this regard is simply that the political advisors, particularly in the Privy Council and Prime Minister's Offices, or the cabinet ministers themselves may function as an alternate source of information which can—in some instances—place major restrictions on the power of the bureaucracy.

When it comes to the process of management in the public service the presence of political control is more difficult to demonstrate. Naturally, in the case of policy decisions relating to organization and reorganization of the departmental structure of the bureaucracy, the planning apparatus that includes the cabinet and the central agencies will supersede the line managers, and political considerations will tend to hold more weight than administrative ones. Nevertheless the mechanisms of control here tend to be dominated by central agency types rather than the politicians themselves, so for the most part what appears to be "political" control over the bureaucracy is in fact central agency control over the line managers in the departments.

Financial Control: The Budgetary Process[5]

Further mechanisms of control over the policy-making role of the Canadian bureaucracy and over the line managers are to be found in the budgetary process.[6] With gradual implementation of a system of Planning, Programming, and Budgeting, the role of the Treasury Board in the determination of spending priorities was greatly enhanced. To the extent that the Treasury Board Secretariat bears much of the responsibility for controlling government spending, PPBS can be viewed as an aggrandizement of bureaucratic power, for the Secretariat is, after all, a part of the bureaucracy. On the other hand, if one views the Treasury Board in terms of its formal composition as a committee of the Privy Council, PPBS can be viewed as placing new restrictions on the priority-setting role of the bureaucracy. Certainly, the power of the individual department and the line manager in some ways has been decreased through the placing of new power in the hands of the more centralized Treasury Board Secretariat and if the recommendations of the Lambert Commission are acted upon, the TBS will become a still more powerful *Board of Management*. On the other hand, one might argue that departmental power has been increased somewhat by permitting program planning over a multi-year rather than a one-year period although even here the introduction of the envelope system would seem to put the departmental officials in a position where they must constantly bow to the wisdom of the central planning agencies.

The "Public Purse"   Additional control over the bureaucracy is exercised through the traditional processes of public finance. According to Norman Ward, there are two basic principles of public finance in Canada: first, that the executive should have no money which is not granted to it or otherwise sanctioned by parliament; and, second, that the executive should make no expenditures except those authorized

---

[5] H. R. Balls, "Financial Administration in Canada," in Kernaghan, *Bureaucracy in Canadian Government*, pp. 57-64.

[6] See also Chapter 15 for a discussion of the budgetary process and priority determination.

specifically by parliament.[7] In brief, therefore, the executive branch and its operational arm, the bureaucracy, can only get funds through parliamentary appropriation, and it can only spend those funds for purposes specified by parliament. The implementation of these two basic principles is facilitated by a complicated set of practices and procedures. In the first place, there must be a budget which is a clear enunciation of the present financial needs of the government, the plans for the upcoming year and a general statement of the financial "state of the nation." This is normally provided at least annually, and it is the responsibility of the government of the day to prepare it and justify its contents to parliament. More will be said about the budget and the budget debate in the following chapter.

The basic premise of the entire system of public finance in Canada is that the public purse strings are held by parliament. While there are *de facto* limitations on the power of parliament to control public spending, these will be dealt with in a subsequent discussion of parliament and the legislative process. Here it is necessary to describe only the formal process of appropriating public money through the system of *estimates*. Basically, this is a system of appropriation of funds by parliament in advance to meet the estimated costs of the various governmental programs in the next year.

Since the program-review[8] stage of preparing the departmental estimates has been mentioned at several points in our analysis already, the discussion here commences when the program review has been completed and the Treasury Board has set *spending targets* based on expenditure *guidelines* issued by the cabinet. At this time— usually in late summer—a letter is issued asking the departments to prepare their estimates for the upcoming year. In fact, the various branches and divisions of the department have already been preparing estimates since the spring in anticipation of the Treasury Board's letter, and by late September the deputy minister (and in some cases the departmental policy committee) reviews the total estimates of the department. In late fall the minister himself reviews the departmental estimates and gives them formal approval, usually without making many significant changes. It must be noted that in discussing this process as a series of distinct stages, we distort the true picture; for in fact, the minister and the deputy minister, the various branch directors and division chiefs, and officials in the Treasury Board staff are in

[7] N. Ward, *The Public Purse* (University of Toronto Press, Toronto, 1955), *passim*.
[8] See P. L. Little and C. L. Mitchell, "The Program Budget: Planning and Control for the Public Sector," in Kernaghan and Willms, *Public Administration in Canada: Selected Readings*, pp. 188-195.

continuous contact. Often this is informal contact, characterized by a phone call from one person to another, but its effect is to keep the people involved in the preparation of the estimates aware of what to expect from the next stage of the process.

Once the estimates have been approved by the minister, they are sent to the TBS which goes over them in great detail, with an eye to cutting down on expenses. The Treasury Board's concern at this point is with economy and frugality—not with the overall advisability of the various departmental programs which have already been approved in principle.

Having passed the meticulous and penny-pinching staff of the Treasury Board Secretariat, the estimates are then handed to the Treasury Board itself whose responsibility it is to put all of the estimates of all of the departments in some kind of a perspective. If the spending priorities set at the program-review stage have been reasonably accurate and if, in preparing the estimates, the departments have adhered to the original targets and programs, there should be no significant changes at this stage. However, because the PPB system is in disfavour now and has never been fully made operational in Canada, there are often major changes made even at this stage in the preparation of the estimates. Such changes inevitably produce hurt feelings and bitterness on the part of the bureaucrats whose estimates have been reduced or eliminated. However, because of the almost constant informal contact among senior bureaucrats in the TBS, Department of Finance, and the various other government departments, these changes are never completely unanticipated.

Having survived the scrutiny of the Treasury Board, the formal approval of the cabinet as a whole is not usually difficult, or of any interest. It is possible at this stage for a minister whose department has been seriously affected by Treasury Board's frugality to die in flames before his colleagues, although it is unlikely that they should be very impressed unless they have been equally hard done by.

After cabinet approval, the *main estimates* are printed up in a form usually referred to as the *Blue Book,* and tabled in the House of Commons. The *Blue Book* not only lists the actual "votes" which ultimately will be passed in parliament but it also includes supporting details that give an even more specific breakdown of the department's estimated expenses for the coming year. The main estimates themselves ultimately become the Appropriation Act, whereas the supporting details are stated merely for the information of the members of parliament and the general public, and as more detailed guidelines for the spending of funds by the department.

The estimates for the various departments are then given to an appropriate standing committee of the House of Commons to be considered in detail. These committees go over the estimates item by item, calling upon officials of the department whose estimates are being discussed to defend its programs and estimated expenditures. The committees then report back to the House of Commons and the estimates of all the departments are passed through parliament as one bill like any other piece of legislation. When this *Supply Bill* has passed through parliament and has been assented to by the Governor General, it becomes the Appropriation Act, part of the law of the land. [9]

Spending the Appropriations   Once the money has been appropriated by parliament, it can be spent only by the executive. Parliament does not spend money, it merely appropriates it. The actual spending of money requires an *encumbrance* of funds from the revenue pool of the government of Canada, the *Consolidated Revenue Fund*. The money is encumbered by the Treasury Board to the departments as they need it for specific purposes. The Deputy Minister of Services and Deputy Receiver General for Canada, acts as a "gatekeeper" for the Consolidated Revenue Fund, ensuring that the expenditure for which the money is being encumbered is within the terms of the Appropriation Act, that there are sufficient funds in the Fund to meet the cost, and that appropriate vouchers for the goods and services purchased are forthcoming. The function of the Deputy Minister of Services is, in effect, a pre-audit function. He is assisted by officers located throughout the public service who are responsible not only for operational audit of the financial affairs of the department to which they are attached but also for the preparation of the accounts of the departments. While to an increasing extent (because of the recommendations of the Glassco Commission) the internal-audit or operational-audit function is being performed not by treasury officers seconded to the department but by departmental officials themselves, in the case of the smaller departments and agencies of the government of Canada, the Department of Supply and Services still supplies these financial officers on request to perform operational-audit functions. Finally the Office of the Comptroller General is responsible for developing and overseeing the implementation of sound accounting and operational audit procedures.

When it comes time for the department to spend the money encumbered to it, it must spend it for the exact purposes stated in the Appropriation Act; although, with the approval of the Treasury Board, the department is permitted to deviate somewhat from the more detailed presentation of the estimates in the *Blue Book*. Nor-

[9] See Chapter 19.

mally, however, it is expected that the department will closely adhere even to the supporting details of the *Blue Book* as well as to the votes of the Appropriation Act itself. Of course, all departments are bound by the Appropriation Act and are not permitted to use funds appropriated for one purpose for something else. Furthermore, money voted for a certain purpose is voted for one year only. If the money is not spent by the end of the fiscal first year it reverts or "lapses" to the Consolidated Revenue Fund.

Additional Supply   The discussion up until now has centred on the preparation of the main estimates and the main supply bill, which indeed involves the most important and the most substantial appropriation of public funds. However, there are a few additional kinds of supply which must be mentioned briefly here.

The *supplementary estimates,* which are intended to meet contingencies unforeseen at the time of the preparation of the main estimates, are voted late in the parliamentary session. It is expected that these will not be large, although they seem to increase in amount annually. *Further supplementary estimates* are introduced just before the close of the fiscal year to look after any additional items not covered by the main or supplementary estimates. These are sometimes voted near the end of the parliamentary session, and as a result they are passed without too much fuss by MPs who want to get on with the summer recess.

Interim supply is passed after the current fiscal year, but before the main estimates are approved. A vote of interim supply merely assumes that the main supply bill will pass successfully, and approves expenditures in amounts such as one-twelfth or one-sixth of the main estimates. This permits the departments to continue to carry out their programs even while parliament is considering whether or not to give them the money to do so. An interesting problem would arise if a main supply bill were actually defeated; for, with the longer parliamentary sessions that are frequent today, it is not unusual for the departments to have been voted a significant percentage of the main estimates by the time the main supply bill is actually passed. Such a defeat, however, is highly unlikely and supply is granted virtually automatically by June 30.

Finally, when parliament is not in session the government can spend money through the use of *Governor General's warrants.* These are expected to be used only for emergencies, and are subsequently approved by parliament in the formal way as part of the next supplementary estimates.

Post Audit   The Auditor General also performs a significant control function. He is an officer of parliament, not of the government, and he is responsible only to parliament. His salary is set by statute and he can be removed from office only through a joint address by the House of Commons and the Senate. The office was created in 1878 and its functions today are defined in the Financial Administration Act. Basically, the role of the Auditor General is to check up on all expenditures in the public service to ensure that money has been spent efficiently and according to law, and to bring any matter involving the financial affairs of the government which he deems to be relevant to the attention of parliament. In short, he performs the function of post-audit of the public accounts. The basic strength of the Auditor General flows from his power of access to all of the government's financial "books", and his ability to make public any indiscretions found therein. The *Report of the Auditor General* comes out annually, and is tabled in the House of Commons. The normal procedure at this stage is for the Auditor's report to be handed over immediately to the House of Commons Public Accounts Committee for more detailed study, a procedure which will be dealt with in greater detail in the next chapter. The basic weakness inherent in the office of the Auditor General is that his staff consists of public servants, and not parliamentary officials like himself. This means that the "establishment" of the office of the Auditor General depends on recommendations of cabinet and TBS. There is nothing in law to prevent the government of the day from cutting back on the staff of the Auditor General and in this way weakening his effectiveness as a "financial watchdog" for parliament. In fact, however, no government can politically afford to go too far in this regard, for the Auditor General to some extent symbolizes the financial authority of parliament. Any attempt to limit his independence from the government of the day, although quite legal, might do political damage to the party that so dared.

Judicial Safeguards

Judicial control over the Canadian bureaucracy is exercised not with respect to policy decisions or advice from public servants, but rather with respect to administrative decisions. In the case of most administrative functions, public officials are granted fairly wide discretionary powers with which to carry out their responsibilities. Within the area of discretion granted them by law, public servants enjoy a significant degree of independence from judicial control. However, the courts will review the administrative decisions of public officials to determine whether or not these decisions were within the jurisdiction granted to the official by law. In other words, if the public official has made a discretionary decision which is lacking in good judgment but is within the jurisdiction granted by law, the courts will take no action. However, if an official makes a decision or takes administrative action which is beyond his competence, or *ultra vires* his discretionary powers, the courts will step in to quash the decision. Note that this can occur only with respect to administrative decisions— actual outputs of the political system that originate in the bureaucracy. In the case of policy decisions or advice, the bureaucratic official is formally only making a recommendation to the political decision makers in the process. A policy recommendation has no immediate or necessary impact on citizens, for it does not become a system output except at a much later stage.

If administrative decisions are judicial or quasi-judicial in nature, the courts will act to control the bureaucracy in another way. Here the courts question not only the jurisdiction of the administrative official or board, but the procedures followed in coming to the decision. Basically, a judicial control over bureaucratic decisions exists if an individual is affected by that decision and if the administrative official or board in making the decision has not adhered to the principles of *Natural Justice*. The principles of Natural Justice define the standards for fair procedures in coming to decisions that affect the rights and privileges of individuals. The first principle is that no one should be a judge in his own cause. In other words, the administrative officials on the board or tribunal which is making the decision must be impartial and not directly affected themselves by the outcome of the hearing. The second principle is that the individual affected by the decision has a right to be heard. His side must be aired and considered by the board before a decision is made. If either of these principles has been ignored by a bureaucratic agency or by an individual bureaucrat in coming to a judicial or quasi-judicial decision, the court will order that the decision be quashed.[10]

It is important to emphasize the nature of judicial remedies as mechanisms of control over the bureaucracy. In the case of many decisions by bureaucratic agencies or officers the decisions are not appealable. However they are *reviewable* which means that the court, while not empowered to reconsider the case on its substantive merits, is empowered to look at the procedures of the bureaucratic decision. If the court decides that the board, tribunal, or administrative officer either acted *ultra vires* or acted *intra vires* but improperly, the result is that the original decision is nullified or quashed. The problem, particularly where the court quashes a decision because it was taken improperly, is that the tribunal of first instance can go back, implement the correct procedures, and bring down exactly the same decision. Thus, judicial review, while ensuring fairness in administrative deci-

[10] See Chapter 7 for a discussion of the Federal Court.

sions, does not permit the court actually to *replace* the administrative decision with its own in the manner of appeal.

Dissatisfaction with the effectiveness of judicial remedies in curbing abuses of bureaucratic power is growing. Not only are the courts unable to deal with misuse of discretionary power unless the administrative act is also *ultra vires*, but even in cases where judicial action is appropriate, the backlog of cases means that litigants must often wait years for satisfaction. One solution at the federal level has been to create an explicitly administrative court, the *Federal Court*, which has jurisdiction to hear appeals from federal boards and tribunals. A partial solution in some of the provinces has been to appoint an *ombudsman*[11] whose function is to investigate complaints by individuals who feel they have been wronged by some bureaucratic decision. As an independent official of the legislature whose salary is set by statute, the ombudsman has broad powers of access to most public files and a modest staff to aid in investigations. Unlike the courts, the ombudsman, can investigate cases where the bureaucratic decision has been *intra vires*, but, in terms of equity, a bad decision. However, the ombudsman has the power only to investigate, to publicize abuses of bureaucratic power, and in some cases to initiate legal action much as a private citizen would. The ombudsman cannot alone order a decision to be quashed. In the final analysis, the ombudsman can only be an effective check on bureaucratic excesses if the bureaucrats themselves respect or fear the office. Much of the work has to be done by phone call to the official about whom there has been a complaint. The official might agree to reconsider the decision, to change it somewhat or to rehear the case, and will, at least, offer reasons for the decision. The ombudsman idea is being considered at present in a number of other provinces, and there is ultimately some possibility that the federal government will adopt the practice for the federal bureaucracy.

Collective Bargaining

Some amount of control over the decisions of bureaucrats is exercised by agencies and procedures that are themselves a part of the bureaucratic process. This is, of course, a different kind of control from that exercised by the courts, which are institutions outside the bureaucracy itself. Perhaps the subtlest form of this "control from within" is imposed through recruitment and training, which we have discussed earlier with respect to the process of management. However, one of the newest and potentially more important mechanisms of intra-bureaucratic control is the system of collective bargaining that is developing in the federal public service.

[11] See Donald Rowat, *The Ombudsman* (University of Toronto Press, Toronto, 1965).

The Evolution of Collective Bargaining in the Public Service   Until 1966, the public servant, as an employee, had very little in the way of true bargaining rights vis-à-vis the government-as-employer. The attitude was that the government, being a sovereign employer, could not constitutionally or morally be coerced in any way by the public service unions, or "staff associations" as they have been euphemistically called. This meant essentially that the public servants could organize in much the same way that any union in the private sector could, but that their relationship with the government employer was a "consultative" one and in no way a bargaining one. In a bargaining relationship, after all, the parties involved each have certain inducements and sanctions with which to threaten or entice the other side into meeting their demands. In private industry, the employer holds the power to raise wages and/or alter working conditions, and, in the last resort, to "lock out" the employees. The employees on the other hand, have the threat of strike action as an ultimate bargaining weapon. In such a situation each side holds certain powers that enable it to bargain with the other side. Up until 1966, therefore, while there were joint councils which facilitated the consultation of the government-as-employer with the staff associations and while the relationship was filled with good intentions, there was no collective bargaining relationship because the staff side had no bargaining power.

Because of the unique situation of staff relations in the public service before the current collective bargaining legislation, a very special kind of quasi-collective bargaining relationship emerged. Given the fact that they had no economic sanctions to bring to bear against the "sovereign employer," the staff associations very slowly began to realize that politically—in terms of the number of votes that they represented in certain constituencies—they did have a real bargaining power. It was not the direct economic sanction of the labour union, but the subtler political sanction of the pressure group. The demand of the public service "union" was not "meet our demands or we will strike," but "meet our demands or our members will vote against you in the next election." While this sort of a bargaining relationship is hardly overwhelming and while it did not in any way give the staff associations the power of labour unions in the private sector, it did permit them to speak with greater authority when making wage demands on the government. Members of Parliament in constituencies with large numbers of public servants, particularly in the Ottawa area, were forced to become spokesmen for the staff associations; and a failure to adequately support their demands could very well spell a defeat at the polls.

The Current System   With the collective bargaining legislation, the public service staff associations were given a genuine system of collective bargaining. In 1967 the Public Service Staff Relations Act (PSSRA) established a system of collective bargaining for federal public servants which includes the right to strike. The act also sets up a Public Service Staff Relations Board (PSSRB) which is responsible for certification of the bargaining agents on the staff side. Excluded from the collective bargaining system are employees in managerial positions, those acting in confidential, policy-related capacities, and part-time and casual workers. Any disputes over exclusionary decisions are settled by the PSSRB and its decisions are final and binding.

There are at present almost ninety certified bargaining units in the federal public service and most of them are affiliated with either the Public Service Alliance of Canada (PSAC) or the Professional Institute of the Public Service (PIPS). As we have pointed out earlier in this chapter, the Treasury Board is the bargaining agent for the government in all of its negotiations with the employee associations, although in some cases, most notably the Post Office, the senior managers in the department are given a major role in the bargaining process.

While generally "terms and conditions of employment and related matters" can be the subject of a collective agreement, there are several matters explicitly excluded from the process by the PSSRA. For instance, because the PSSRA cannot be interpreted so as to interfere with the supremacy of parliament, any matter that requires legislative implementation is not bargainable, nor are matters dealt with in legislation such as the Public Service Employment Act, the Superannuation Act, the Government Vessels Discipline Act, etc. Perhaps the most objectionable exclusions to the unions are the matters of the "merit system" under the jurisdiction of the Public Service Commission, and matters having to do with the Organization of the Government. The former include such things as recruitment, promotions, transfers, discharge for incompetence, layoffs and pension benefits, and the latter include subjects such as job evaluation and classification, all of which are normally bargainable in the private sector.

As with any collective bargaining system there is a provision for settlement of disputes. In the case of disputes that arise in the negotiation of a collective agreement, or *"interest disputes"* the PSSRA provides for two distinct methods of settlement: *compulsory arbitration* and *conciliation* (with the right to strike). The bargaining agent has the right to decide which route to take, but the decision must be made before bargaining begins and the union is bound to stick to the method chosen until the settlement is reached.

In the first years of the PSSRA the tendency was for bargaining agents to opt for the arbitration method of settlement. By this system either a single arbitrator or a three-person arbitration tribunal is set up by the PSSRB. Both sides present their cases and the arbitrator reaches a decision which is binding on both sides. In recent years however, the trend has been for more and more of the bargaining units to opt for the conciliation route. Here the PSSRB names a conciliation board or a single conciliator who attempts to assist the parties to come to an agreement that is mutually acceptable. The recommendations of a conciliation board are not binding, however, and if the union is not satisfied its next step is to strike. It is perhaps a weakness of the system that the bargaining unit is not permitted to switch to compulsory arbitration if conciliation fails. Instead the employee side must either accept the unsatisfactory conciliation board finding or go out on strike.

Besides "interest disputes," the PSSRA provides for the settlement of grievances as well. Unlike the private sector, the right to grieve under the PSSRA is extended not only to employees who are excluded by the act, but it is also extended to many matters that do not come within the collective agreement. There are two methods of grievance settlement each of which applies in a different set of circumstances. In the case of grievances arising out of the interpretation of a collective agreement or out of disciplinary actions which involve severe penalties such as dismissal or financial penalty, the procedure involves four internal hearings up to the deputy minister level and thence if no settlement is reached, to adjudication. Adjudicators are appointed from within the PSSRB and their decisions are final and binding. The second type of grievance is that involving the job evaluation system. This is one of the matters generally excluded from the collective bargaining system and is generally viewed as a prerogative of the employer in the Federal Public Service. As a result the grievance is heard by *classification officers* only and their decisions are not adjudicable.

The *National Joint Council* which was the major institution of staff relations before the PSSRA, exists today and has become a useful forum for discussion of matters which are not formally bargainable. The NJC is also useful for consultations between the employer and the employee organizations where a "service-wide" approach is more useful than piecemeal bargaining.

We must now return to our first assumption: that the collective bargaining relationship in the public service is a form of intrabureaucratic control. This control exists to the extent that the government employer (the management side) and the government employee (the staff side) have power over each other. Each limits the other's freedom of action because each holds inducements and sanctions with which to convince the other to at least partially meet its demands. The employer in the modern public service collective-bargaining relationship is the Treasury Board. In other words, the Treasury Board is the agency which actually does the "horse trading" with the staff associations that ends in a compromise collective agreement. The effect of this rather new power relationship is certainly to reduce the power of the line managers. It hinders their ability to motivate their subordinates because the employer authority is vested in the Treasury Board. Let it suffice to say here that the staff associations, which include among their members people who, in the aggregate, are involved in policy making, which still retain the residual political power of a pressure group, and which now possess the right to strike, have the potential for considerable political power in the Canadian system.

Management and Control: A Conclusion

Thus we have seen that the most effective mechanisms of control over the bureaucracy as a whole are those related to the budget and financial accountability. Moreover the 1979 *Report of the Royal Commission on Financial Management and Accountability (The Lambert Report)* advocates reforms which would tighten still more the control of the central agencies over the line bureaucracy. While the goal of making the bureaucracy accountable to the political arm of government is noble and an ideal to be sought after with fervour, too much attention to accountability can severely tie the hands of the senior managers and hamper their ability to get the job done. Thus, reforms in this area must proceed on the middle ground. It is necessary to try to develop controls which make the bureaucracy as a whole accountable to the cabinet, and which at the same time recognize the need to let the managers do their jobs without excessive meddling on the part of the central agencies. To make line bureaucrats more accountable to central agency bureaucrats would not make the bureaucracy "writ large" more accountable and it certainly handcuffs the managers in the departments.

Control over the policy role of the bureaucracy is more problematical. With the exception of certain broad powers exercised by the cabinet (which may decide to disregard its advisors) or by a vigilant press (which may criticize policy formulation on those rare occasions when it can penetrate the veil of secrecy) there are very few direct checks over the policy advice provided by bureaucrats. The press, academics, interest groups, the parliamentary opposition, and even the provincial governments are to a large extent prevented from evaluating the policies formulated by federal bureaucrats by the strong control over information and technical expertise possessed by the large numbers of federal policy advisors; moreover, outsiders can only rarely find out what that advice has been. The situation is exacerbated by strong Canadian traditions of administrative secrecy and by the

Official Secrets Act described above. It is clear that the Canadian public is not always well served by this situation; one of the most important reforms which is being considered by the Canadian government is a Freedom of Information Act which guarantees freer access for the public to the information necessary to criticize the bureaucratic policy makers.

Finally, given the role of the senior bureaucrats as managers of the information generating and disseminating machinery which produces policy advice in Canada, it is possible that one medium of control over the technocrats is a skilled corps of "policy managers" possessing the standard managerial skills that the public sector shares with industry, understanding the ins and outs of the adversarial process of bureaucratic politics, and finally and most importantly trained to manage technical information.

We would like to conclude with a note on the general quality of management in the Canadian public service. While public service managers in both federal and provincial bureaucracies perform all of the same functions as private sector managers, they must do so within the awkward constraints placed upon them by an organization whose raison d'être is difficult to define and whose dominant concern turns out to be accountability and control. On top of this, public managers must also function as coordinators of expertise in the process of initiation and formulation of public policy—roles completely alien to their counterparts in the private sector.

It is all too easy to decry the lack of efficiency in the public service and to lay the blame at the feet of senior management. Similarly, the media, and management wizards from industry repeatedly offer as solutions, the adoption, holus bolus, of the managerial techniques and philosophy of the private sector. We demur! Given the situational constraints, the quality of management in public life in Canada is pretty damn good and the facile application of private sector nostrums is no more likely to improve it than would the application of public sector precepts improve the performance of private sector managers.

This concludes our discussion of the Canadian bureaucracy. The reader will have to look further into other sources listed in the bibliography for more detailed information about the structures and processes of this country's bureaucracy. We have attempted to give a perspective on the bureaucracy in the political process and to demonstrate that, while the bureaucracy is crucial to the process of policy formulation, it is also an important actor in every other aspect of the political process in Canada.

19

Parliament: The Policy Refinery

Parliament, the legislative branch of government in Canada, is legally the supreme authority for all matters falling within federal jurisdiction. The legal implications of the constitutional principle of parliamentary supremacy have already been discussed at great length and there is no need to reiterate them here. In this chapter our concern is with parliament's role in the policy process. It will be seen that, while parliament is legally supreme, it is functionally subordinate to the cabinet and the bureaucracy in the making of public policy. Today, parliamentary supremacy is largely a mythical expression of the belief that in our system of government ultimate political power *should* reside in the elected representatives of the people. But it is also a reflection of the continued commitment of Canadians to the basic value of popular sovereignty, and despite the very real functional limitations on parliament's ability to be truly "supreme," the myth remains significant not only as a symbol but as an operative principle of our form of democratic polity. Moreover, to the extent that the roles of cabinet ministers making policy decisions in the cabinet chamber are intertwined with their roles as Members of Parliament, there is a day-to-day linkage between the myth and the reality of the policy process.

The structure of the Canadian legislature is *bicameral*: that is, parliament consists of two separate legislative bodies, the House of Commons and the Senate. The House of Commons is the elected branch of parliament and is therefore more important than the Senate which is an appointed body. The bulk of our analysis of the role of parliament in the policy process will therefore focus on the House of Commons.

THE FUNCTIONS OF PARLIAMENT

The Policy Function[1]
Chapter 1 sets up a linear descriptive model of the policy process in Canada which posits policy making as a four-stage process. Generally speaking, parliament dominates only at the fourth (refinement

---

[1] For the best overview description of this see: R. J. Jackson and M. M. Atkinson, *The Canadian Legislative System* (Macmillan, Toronto, 1980).

and legitimation) stage of that process. However, it can and does have some impact at all stages of policy making, and we must comment briefly on that before proceeding to the more detailed discussion of parliament as a core institution at the policy-refining and formal output stage.

As an initiator of policy ideas, parliament still has ample opportunity to influence policy decisions. As was pointed out in Chapter 1, the basic problem of policy initiation is one of communication. It is necessary to communicate one's policy idea to the cabinet which functions as the main priority-setting institution in Canadian government. Parliament functions as a communication link between the public at large and the cabinet. When people make demands on the political system, they often make such inputs by writing letters or speaking to a Member of Parliament. This particular input channel was especially important at an early period in Canadian political history when other channels of access to the political decision-makers were not as well developed as they are now. As an input channel today, however, parliament is in competition with many other institutions such as interest groups, parties, the media, and the bureaucracy, and most of these other institutions can communicate policy ideas to the cabinet as well as, if not better than, parliament. Furthermore, some of the modern techniques such as survey research, and institutions such as large departmental field organizations have permitted the cabinet and the bureaucracy to go out into the environment of the system and actively seek out new policy ideas. Hence, parliament's role as a communicator of new policy ideas to the system's priority setters has been much diluted. Parliament can still convey demands to the cabinet, but there are many other institutions and many other techniques which achieve the same end and can possibly achieve it more effectively.

The MP can also function as policy initiator in a very immediate way by communicating a personal idea directly to the cabinet. One example of policy initiation by an individual MP was the abolition of capital punishment. The idea was introduced in parliament originally as a private member's bill and was subsequently picked up by the cabinet and re-introduced as government policy. Perhaps the classic example is the inception of an old-age security scheme in Canada, for the introduction of that idea was largely the work of W. S. Woodsworth. Indeed, in an earlier era, Woodsworth used parliament as an effective platform to prompt Liberal governments into much of the social welfare legislation that we have today. Occurrences such as these are no longer frequent, however, in spite of a cabinet decision in 1973 to have all private member's bills examined by the bureaucracy with a view to allowing some which are in line with government priorities to pass.

An MP's influence on the cabinet will depend in part on the prestige, knowledge, and background of the individual involved. Where a course of action being considered by the cabinet is likely to affect a particular geographic region of Canada, there is some chance that concerted opposition or support by that region's members will influence the cabinet in setting its priorities. However, the cabinet will probably have independent sources of information about the attitudes of the people in the affected region, and if the independent information contradicts the position of the MPs, the cabinet is just as likely to heed the former. Thus, the role of parliament at the priority-setting stage of policy making depends on the willingness of the cabinet to be influenced by the MPs, and on the availability and substance of competing advice.

Policy formulation is the business of the bureaucracy subject to the control of the cabinet. Parliament's role at this stage is virtually non-existent, because of the generally technical and complex nature of the problem of formulating policy alternatives. In terms of expertise and available time, the MP is ill-equipped to contribute much at this stage of policy making.

However, parliament is the core institution at the refinement stage of the policy process. While it is the legislative drafting branch of the Department of Justice which converts the raw policy as formulated by the cabinet and bureaucracy into a bill, and while the cabinet committee on Legislation and House Planning conducts a clause-by-clause review of pending legislation, it is parliament which "cleans up" and polishes the draft so that it is a workable piece of legislation without unintended and perverse consequences. In the House of Commons, and more specifically in the standing committees, the MPs go over government policy proposals, tightening up the wording, criticizing the weaknesses, suggesting amendments, and, through public debate, publicizing the inherent advantages and disadvantages of the bill. In subsequent discussion of parliament, we will focus mainly on this aspect of its policy function.

Finally, parliament is one of the institutions involved in the ultimate conversion of government policy to system output. While the formal votes in the House of Commons and the Senate may appear to be merely pro forma steps akin to executive proclamation[2] and the

---

[2] The power to proclaim a law or not to do so is potentially an important one controlled by the Prime Minister. Before a law can be implemented it must be proclaimed and this is an executive prerogative. If the Prime Minister does not like a law or part of a law passed by parliament, he can exercise an effective veto by simply not having it proclaimed or by delaying proclamation. Whether this will be necessary will depend upon factors such as the prevalence of minority parliaments and the consistency of party discipline. An unproclaimed law can also be banked as a threat by a government in dealing with a potentially recalcitrant segment of society.

Governor General's assent, this final ratification or rejection of government policy proposals may, in fact, be the most significant function of parliament. It is true that the number of government proposals actually defeated in parliament is very small, but this is partially the result of parliamentary watchfulness which may have discouraged governments from introducing intemperate legislation in the first place, and of the fact that many a controversial piece of legislation is simply allowed to die on the order paper without any government attempt to bring it forward for second or subsequent readings. So it is the ultimate power to reject a government's legislative proposals in a formal vote which is significant as a deterrent even though its formal exercise has been extremely rare.

Functional Limitations on Parliamentary Supremacy

The functional subordination of parliament to the cabinet in policy making has been mentioned previously, but we have yet to say why this is the case. To examine this point, it is necessary to look first at the control exercised by the cabinet over its own backbenchers, and then consider the cabinet control exercised over the opposition MPs, particularly in the minority government situation.

Party Discipline: Government Control over Government Backbenchers   The control by the Prime Minister and cabinet over the government backbenchers is one aspect of what is usually known as party discipline. It is maintained by threat of the various sanctions and by the various inducements cited below, although it is seldom indeed that the government is forced overtly to impose a sanction or withhold a promise in order to enforce discipline. Usually these powers of the parliamentary leadership are tacitly recognized and accepted by the government MPs so that party discipline is maintained without resort to specific sanctions.

Perhaps the most important single factor facilitating the cabinet's control over its own backbenchers in the House of Commons is the simple fact that the cabinet ministers are the parliamentary leaders of the party. There is a natural tendency and willingness in each MP to accept the control of a Prime Minister who has been selected as party leader at a convention and who is responsible to a large extent, in this era of "leadership politics," for the party's success at the polls. Besides this, the very fact that backbenchers and cabinet ministers are members of the same political party provides at least limited grounds for a consensus. This point should not be overemphasized, for as has been pointed out in an earlier chapter, the major Canadian political parties tend not to be heavily ideological and are "omnibus" or "brokerage" parties which attempt to aggregate large numbers of interests, and a fairly wide range of political views. However, while Canadian parties are often fraught with internal disagreements, the obvious fact remains that the government of the day will more likely be able to find agreement among its own backbenchers than among the opposition members. And, where a majority of MPs are from the government party, the ability to control the government side of the House is, naturally, all that is needed to control parliament.

The power of dissolution is the basic constitutional control the Prime Minister possesses over the backbench MP. According to this constitutional convention, the Prime Minister has the sole power to advise the Governor General to dissolve parliament and call an election. In a general election MPs must put their jobs on the line, and for most members, this means a tough struggle. Not very many MPs have seats so "safe" that they can afford to campaign without great energy and large outlays of money, and the "typical" Canadian federal election will see some 30-40 percent of them losing their jobs. Thus, although parliament has never been dissolved in order to force dissident government backbenchers into line, the fact that most MPs do not enjoy fighting for their jobs probably has some effect on their attitudes to the government's policies. While it would be unwise for a government to call an election to whip its own backbenchers into line—it would show the public that there was a split in the party's ranks and members of the cabinet have even more to lose than backbenchers—the threat of dissolution can be very important in controlling the House of Commons in a minority government situation.[3]

A subtler but very real power of the government to control its own members flows from the control over the party purse strings. Fighting elections today, in the era of TV campaigns and "Madison Avenue" techniques, is an expensive proposition, and an individual candidate who is not supported by one of the political parties will usually be unable to afford the kind of campaign that will ensure a high probability of success. Thus, the Prime Minister and cabinet, and to a certain extent the leaders of the opposition parties, can control maverick backbenchers through either explicit or implicit threat of withdrawal of party financial assistance in the next election campaign.

There are non-financial elements of party support in an election which can be almost as important to the MP as assistance from the party treasurer. MPs who have been "good" and supported the government in parliament will be assured of a visit to their constituencies by one of the party's notables to assist them in their campaigns. In an election campaign, for instance the visit to a constituency of the party leader might well enhance the prestige of the local candidate and

---

[3] We will provide more detailed description of minority government below.

hence have an effect on the outcome of that riding's contest. Furthermore, while the party leaders must beware of overtly meddling with the autonomy of the constituency nominating process, if it is known that a sitting member is unlikely to get support from the national level of the party or if it is made clear that the candidate is not in the "good graces" of the party leader, the local people might be influenced to "ditch" the member. Finally, if all else fails, the Canada Elections Act gives to the leader of a political party the right to refuse a candidate the privilege of having the name of the party appear beside his or her name on the ballot. While a constituency association could still choose to nominate such an individual, they would clearly be dissuaded from doing so if their candidate had to be listed as an "independent" on the ballot. This technique was employed by Robert Stanfield, the leader of the Progressive Conservative Party in the 1974 election when he refused to sanction the candidacy of Leonard Jones in Moncton. The local party organization, although split on the issue, selected a new candidate, and Jones, a popular ex-Mayor of the city ran as an independent. In that case the sanction was not wholly effective since Jones still won the seat but, deprived of caucus membership, his power in Ottawa was virtually non-existent and he did not run in the subsequent election.

Expulsion from the party caucus is another technique of control that can be exercised by the leadership of a parliamentary party if a maverick MP gives trouble. The case of Ralph Cowan, a Liberal member from Toronto during the 1960s, is a good example. By constantly levelling bitter criticisms at the Liberal government, Cowan became such an embarrassment to the party that he was finally expelled from the caucus. This meant that he was not informed of the party's plans and policies, and thus had to sit as a virtual independent in the House of Commons. When the next election was called, Cowan tried to get the Liberal nomination in his constituency again and failed. (Mr. Cowan ran instead as an independent and was defeated.) However, while it is possible to use the rather drastic measure of expulsion from caucus in the case of a single MP, this technique cannot be used to control the opposition of large numbers of government MPs, for the simple reason that it publicizes the party's internal disunity and could, if party standings are close in the House, result in the government's defeat.

The major inducement available to a government to control its backbenchers is the promise that the well-behaved and efficient member may be promoted to the cabinet, or at least to a temporary sojourn as parliamentary assistant to a minister. Since these positions bestow both income and prestige, potential dissidents may consider them sufficiently desirable incentives for toeing the line. The con-

verse of this, however, is that the offer of a cabinet post or othe.
favours controlled by the party leader can sometimes induce a disgruntled backbencher to switch parties. Not surprisingly, members
who have been induced into crossing the floor of the House, are
usually rejected by their constituents in the next general election.

Party discipline is similarly applied in the relationship of the opposition leaders to their backbenchers. The situation varies from party to
party, but with the exception of the power of dissolution, the sanctions and inducements available to the government to control its
backbenchers are also available to the leaders of opposition parties.
For instance the hope for a cabinet post if and when the opposition
party comes to power can keep dissident opposition backbenchers in
line. But while party discipline is a factor in the relationship of the
leaders of the opposition parties to their backbenchers, it is not as
important here as it is for the government party. The leaders of the
opposition party can afford to tolerate a higher degree of dissension
and disagreement among their MPs because the fate of a government
does not hang in the balance; if a few opposition backbenchers split
with the leaders of the party "on division" (formal vote in the House
of Commons) the result will be little more than embarrassment for the
opposition leader. Furthermore, when criticizing the government, an
opposition MP can "oppose" in a number of ways. As long as the MP
is against the policy of the government, the leaders of the opposition
will generally permit some deviation from the party line.

The primary focus of the analysis thus far has been on the relationship of the government to the government backbenchers, for in a
majority government situation, the basic problem of maintaining control over the House of Commons is co-extensive with the problem of
government party discipline. If the cabinet in a majority government
situation can control its own backbenchers, it can stay in power. In
fact, there has never been a case of a majority government's defeat in
Canada by a vote in the House of Commons, and the likelihood of
that eventuality in the future is virtually nil. As a Liberal backbencher
from Toronto was quoted as saying, "We're on call sometimes 14 or
16 hours a day just to support legislation that usually we didn't have
any part in framing and sometimes don't even particularly like."

Government Control over the Parliamentary Opposition In a
majority government situation, the basic strengths and weaknesses of
the opposition parties in parliament are determined primarily by the
procedures of the House of Commons. Since they are never going to
be able to outvote the government on any policy proposal, the opposition parties must content themselves with using subtler techniques
to attempt to influence policy.

The basic power of the opposition in the House of Commons stems
from its ability to control time through debate. The House rules of

procedure are founded on a balance between two conflicting principles of parliamentary democracy. The first is that the government should be able to get on with the business of governing in an efficient and expeditious fashion, and the second is that the opposition should have ample time to criticize the government's proposals. In other words, the opposition should be able to "oppose," but not to the extreme of obstructionism, and the government should be able to get its programs through the House of Commons efficiently, but not without permitting thorough and often tiresome debate.

Until recently, the bias of House of Commons procedures was toward the needs of the opposition parties at the expense of government. If every opposition member were to speak as long as the rules permitted on every stage of the debate, most legislation would be debated almost endlessly. Given this situation, the opposition, although unable to vote down the government's legislation, could achieve the same end by the technique of filibuster, or endless debate. However, in order to prevent filibustering, the procedures of the House of Commons have always provided for closure, which is a counter-technique whereby the government party, with the aid of the Speaker, can unilaterally terminate a debate. While these techniques have long been a part of the rules of debate in the House, they have not often been used; it is bad politically for the opposition to filibuster and be branded "obstructionist," or for the government to apply closure and be branded dictatorial or "heavy-handed." In practice, the government will usually make deals with the opposition regarding the specifics of the legislation being debated. In return for a minor change in the legislation, the opposition parties will often agree to limit their criticism to a few spokesmen for the party, and thus speed up the passage of the bill in question. The government will seldom agree to a change in the substance of legislation in return for this kind of agreement, and this fact is generally respected by the opposition parties.

In the spring of 1969, a fundamental change in the Standing Orders of the House of Commons was passed after long debate and, ultimately, only after the government was forced to invoke closure. The point of contention at that time was Standing Order (S.O.)75(c) which provides for unilateral limitation of debate at each stage of the passage of a bill through the house. If the government cannot achieve the agreement of all parties or at least of a majority of the parties in setting time limits for debate, it is permitted unilaterally to impose the desired time limits. Initially it was feared that this would take away the fundamental source of opposition influence in the House of Commons, the control of time. However, the extensive use of S.O. 75(c) by a government would be a very unpopular tactic with the public, for its effect is to "gag" the opposition almost as effectively as closure.

It is still far better for both the government and the opposition to seek some sort of mutually acceptable agreement on the limitation of debate. Hence, while procedurally the balance may have shifted from the opposition to the government, actual practice indicates that the government-opposition relationship has not substantially altered as a result of the passage of S.O. 75(c).

The great flaw in the argument that the opposition can influence policy through control over parliamentary time is that this power is a negative one. It is indeed possible to stall the government, and it is possible even to influence the government to make minor changes in its legislation, but if the government is committed to it, the substance of the legislation is non-negotiable. Furthermore, the government can usually stand firm even on the minor demands of the opposition if it chooses, and the opposition can merely balk temporarily.

The other technique of government which can be employed to enhance its bargaining power vis-à-vis control of time in the House, is the legislative "red herring." Here the government puts contentious legislation to which it is only mildly committed on the order paper along with less contentious legislation to which it is committed, so that the government house leader has something to "give away" to the opposition. The theory is that the contentious legislation "draws the fire" of the opposition parties, and the government can agree to withdraw it in return for a promise of easy passage for other government proposals, which while less contentious, are more important to the Prime Minister and the cabinet. This tactic can also be used at later stages of the legislative process where clever drafting can see to it that there are "attackable" but also non-essential "red herring" clauses deliberately written into government bills. This allows the opposition to feel it is having an impact without compromising the overall integrity of a piece of legislation. The only limit to this sort of tactic is the "savvy" of the opposition house leaders who should be aware that their opposite numbers are not above such puckish pranks.

Other than its control over the time to be used in the passage of government legislation, the opposition has only one fundamental strength in attempting to influence the government. This is the traditional power to criticize publicly the government's policy proposals. In debates in the House of Commons, and increasingly in the lobby of parliament before the TV cameras,[4] the opposition MPs do their very

---

[4] Although the debates in the House are now televised in their entirety, very few TV stations are willing to "bump" their own programming to pick up the Commons broadcast. In fact a few stations broadcast taped versions of the oral question period, and special events such as the budget speech, but for the most part very few Canadians actually "watch" parliament on TV. While of interest to political scientists and

best to make the government's policies appear foolhardy, irresponsible, dangerous, opportunistic, or just plain silly. The arguments they present to back this up are designed to convince the voting public that a new government should be put in power at the earliest opportunity. Unfortunately, the great weakness of the opposition parties in endeavouring to convince the public that the government policy is bad is— once again—their lack of information and expertise. By the time the opposition parties are involved in the policy process, the legislation they are considering has usually been the object of intensive research by innumerable experts in task forces, royal commissions, interdepartmental committees, government departments, the central agencies—all of which have probably taken into account the recommendations of interest groups and other private institutions. If and when the Freedom of Information Act is passed, there may be some increase in the amount of technical information available to opposition MPs. However, it is unlikely that the government will give its enemies in the House much information directly relevant to specific policy proposals. Moreover, the demands on an MP's time, as it is, make it very unlikely that he or she will be able effectively to analyze a large increase in the amount of technical information. Thus, the likelihood is slim that a handful of MPs, with little time to spare for even cursory research, will ever be able to add much substantial criticism of such heavily studied proposals.

Finally, in the context of what has been said in Chapter 16 above, about executive federalism, the MP is effectively excluded from one of the key arenas of policy making in Canada, the federal-provincial one. So many of the critical priority decisions in our system are taken behind closed doors by senior cabinet ministers and their top hired hands from the bureaucracy that the MP is almost completely shut out of this level of the process. As Robert Stanfield has said: "The frustrations of Members of Parliament are increased by federal-provincial deals, agreements and resulting legislation which confront Parliament as *faits accomplis*. There may be no way to avoid this in contemporary Canada, but federal-provincial arrangements have significantly reduced the role of Parliament."[5]

Thus, while the opposition can criticize government policy both publicly and in the House, the impact of this criticism is not likely to

the relatives or friends of the MPs, for the most part the goings on of the Canadian House of Commons cannot match the ratings of "Hockey Night in Canada," or "Charlie's Angels."

[5] Stanfield, R., "The Legislative Process: Myths and Realities," in W. A. W. Neilson and J. C. MacPherson (eds.), *The Legislative Process in Canada: The Need for Reform* (IRPP, Butterworths, Toronto, 1978), pp. 44-45.

be great. Empowered and expected to criticize the government, the opposition in the House of Commons is functionally disqualified from doing so through its lack of information and expertise and through its exclusion from the strategic forums of policy decision making in the cabinet and in the intergovernmental committees. The really significant arguments will have been made and met already by competing experts in the various institutions vested with the responsibility for advising the government, and these arguments may never see the light of day.

Minority Government   The relationship of the cabinet to parliament is significantly altered when there is a minority government situation in the House of Commons. Minority government occurs when the government party does not have a majority of the seats in the House of Commons; in order to stay in power, it must at all times be able to secure the support of some members of other parties. The government in this case is usually formed by whichever of the major parties holds a plurality of seats, although it is conceivable that a party standing second in number of seats could form the government. The third party or parties hold the balance of power in the House, and can choose either to defeat the government by voting against it, or to maintain the government by siding with it. As was pointed out earlier, the government can often be sustained at length in this situation.

The Liberals have been particularly successful in maintaining minority governments, most notably in the period of 1963-68 when they managed to stay in power with little difficulty. Throughout this time, the minority Liberal government needed only a few opposition votes to retain control of the House of Commons, and with thirty to fifty seats in the hands of the NDP, Ralliement Créditiste and Social Credit, it was usually a simple matter to find them. The real strength of the Liberal government during this period was that it stood pretty much "in the middle" on most issues, with the NDP and Créditistes taking positions to the left and right of the government respectively. Virtually all of the government's policy proposals were opposed by the Conservative official opposition "on principle," and by either the Créditistes or the NDP. However, the two minor parties were never able to vote on the same side because of their radically different points of view, and because through much of that period, the third-party MPs feared an election as much as the Liberals did. Again, in the period from 1972 to 1974, the Liberals formed a minority government and successfully stayed in power by consistently acquiring support from the NDP. They were eventually defeated in a vote of no confidence when the NDP finally abandoned them, but in the subsequent election the Liberals were swept to power with a majority, and the ranks of the NDP were seriously depleted, confirming a fear of third-party MPs that the forcing of elections in such circumstances could well cost them their seats.

The lesson of these two examples is not only that the problem of controlling the House of Commons in a minority government situation is much more complicated and difficult than it is in the majority situation, but that it is still quite possible to govern if some adjustments are made. In the 1972-74 period, for example, it was common practice for cabinet ministers to consult opposition spokesmen before bringing bills forward, and ministers could be certain that they would have great difficulty in getting their bills on the order paper at all if they could not convince their cabinet colleagues and the Prime Minister that sufficient discussions had taken place with the opposition to assure passage of the legislation. Meetings between government and opposition House Leaders, weekly events in any case, became much more frequent and the views of the opposition House Leaders were given much more weight both in House scheduling and in cabinet deliberations. With such efforts, a minority government can be made to work very successfully.

If the 1972-74 parliament provides us with an example of a successful minority government, the 1979-80 one demonstrates how fragile a minority can be if not properly managed. Prime Minister Clark took the approach that he would govern "as though he had a majority," likely in the belief that if defeated his party would be returned with a majority, and likely in the belief that the Liberals, preoccupied with the initial labour pains of a leadership convention to replace Pierre Trudeau, would not permit the Tory government to fall. The result was that the Tories introduced a stringent budget, refused to accede to any of the demands of the other parties, and were defeated on an NDP non-confidence motion. Trudeau "rose from the ashes," withdrew his resignation as leader of the party, and received a majority government from the same electorate that had turfed him out less than a year previously. The lesson of the Clark interlude is that minority government can work *only* if the Prime Minister is willing to seek compromise with the opposition parties. Moreover, with the demise of the Ralliement Créditiste in the 1980 election another problem has been added for the plurality party in the minority situation for we have returned to a basic three-party system, which means that the opportunities for government-opposition "deals" to hold off defeat in the House are somewhat reduced for minority governments in the future.

In the spring of 1968 a constitutional issue arose and was settled in a manner which has at least the potential of altering the status of minority governments. The Liberal government was defeated, quite by accident, because of a very high rate of absenteeism on the part of the government backbenchers. The vote had been on the third reading of an important piece of financial legislation, and such a defeat of an important government bill would normally have meant the resignation of the government and an immediate election. At this time the Liberals were embroiled in a leadership campaign, and the opposition parties were not prepared to fight an election either. The solution was for the government to introduce a motion of confidence in itself at the next sitting of the House, essentially asking the House of Commons if it "really" wanted an immediate election. The government was given a vote of confidence by a majority of the House and was permitted to stay in power. The significance of this is that whereas previously a minority government could force unpalatable legislation on the opposition by threat of election, now, it is at least possible to argue that the legislation can be defeated without forcing the resignation of the government. However the experience of the 1972-74 and 1979-80 minority periods does not give any indication that this potential device will ever be employed except as it was in 1968, to patch up a mistake.

To conclude this section, it can be re-emphasized that while there is a potential for greater policy-making power in the hands of the opposition in the situation of minority government, there still remain severe limitations on the ability of the opposition to exercise this power. Firstly, the fact remains that the opposition does not have the access to expert advice as does the cabinet, and cannot therefore deal as meaningfully with policy issues. Secondly, procedure in the House of Commons is such that any control that is exercised by the opposition is largely negative in nature. Thirdly, as has been pointed out above, the existing alignment of political parties in Canada militates against concerted opposition effort. The opposition parties are often too divided among themselves to unite to defeat the government in a minority situation. Finally, majority government has become a sort of norm of our system of government, and, in spite of its prevalence, a minority situation is always viewed as atypical and merely temporary. In fact the 1965 election which was called by the Liberal minority government was fought in part on the issue of a return to majority government, although in that case the electorate was not convinced.

Government Party Caucus   It has been seen that party discipline prevents the government MP from either voting against the government on division, or from actively criticizing government policy in debates in the House of Commons. The government MP is alleged to have a say in the policies of the government in the caucus, where, it is traditionally held, the MP can influence policy through concerted criticism and articulate dissent. Caucus consists of all of the supporters of a political party in the House of Commons and is intended to establish a communication link between the party leaders and the rank and file. While all parties have a caucus, the one which is most potentially significant in the policy process is that of the government. The meetings of government caucus occur weekly while the House is sitting; they are attended by the cabinet ministers and they are held in camera. The tradition of caucus procedure is that decisions are not made by a formal vote, but rather that a consensus is achieved through dialogue and a willingness to seek mutually satisfactory agreement. Because the meetings are held in camera, the MPs can speak their minds freely, with no fear of endangering the image of party unity.

When there is backbench solidarity in caucus it is possible for the members to stall or even completely arrest legislative proposals put forward by the cabinet, but this happens very seldom. The odds that a group as diverse in its interests as the caucus will ever be unanimous in opposition to the cabinet are very slight. For the most part, the cabinet can bank on divergencies of opinion among the backbenchers in caucus being at least as wide as the gulf between the cabinet and the rank and file. The basic weakness of the caucus, however, stems from its relative lack of information. The minister who is proposing and defending a given policy in caucus has a fund of facts and figures from which to draw, while the MP with limited research facilities and limited personal expertise, cannot compete with the vast array of expert advice that the minister has close at hand.

A secondary argument about the caucus' utility as a policy organ of the party posits the role of the MP as a representative of interests. The argument is that the cabinet can "test" its legislative proposals by submitting them for the consideration of a representative body. In most cases today, however, the MP is not as well equipped as the Prime Minister and the political advisors to speak authoritatively about the wishes of Canadians and the feasibility, in political terms, of any particular policy proposal. Again, the problem is not so much that the articulation of interests has been avowedly taken away from parliament or, more specifically, from the caucus, but that other institutions such as the bureaucracy and the centralized political advisory bodies are competing with the MP in the performance of this function.

After a great deal of criticism from Liberal backbenchers, a new set of ground rules for caucus procedure and a major reorganization of the federal Liberal caucus itself was approved by the cabinet and introduced in the fall of 1969. Basically, the new rules bind the ministers to introduce all legislative proposals in caucus before introducing them in the House. Previously, it had been a fairly common practice to discuss the policy proposals in caucus after the legislation had actually been introduced and the government had already been publicly committed to it. While there has been little to suggest that the new rules have made the caucus any more effective as an organ for changing the government's mind about policy proposals, at least the Liberal backbenchers are now "the first to know" when the cabinet is about to introduce a policy.[6]

In an attempt to permit a degree of specialization in caucus deliberations, the same 1969 reorganization also divided the Liberal caucus into functional sub-committees roughly paralleling the Standing Committees of the House itself. A similar system was subsequently adopted by the other parties although in the case of the NDP, because of smaller numbers, the procedure does not have to be as formalized. Each of these sub-committees of the caucus is given some research assistance to enable it to develop a measure of expertise in a particular area of concern. While this is generally a good idea, the fact remains that one or two graduate students working on a given policy area will not enable a caucus sub-committee to compete with a minister who has an entire government department to provide research assistance. While these changes will make the discussion in caucus marginally more meaningful, they do not alter fundamentally the relationship between the caucus and the cabinet in the policy process.

Basically, then, the caucus is neither sufficiently united nor equipped with expertise and research personnel to effectively initiate substantive changes in government policy proposals. New freedom of information legislation might be expected to result in a somewhat stronger policy role for caucus, for backbench MPs are hampered by the same problems as the public in access to relevant data. However, even the most liberal of freedom of information provisions will not ensure that caucus or the public gets information as early as does the cabinet. Since the timeliness of data has as much to do with its utility in the policy process as its quality and quantity, the relative power of caucus and cabinet is unlikely to be changed by any freedom of information stipulations. More and more then, the function of the caucus is to assist the government in scheduling the parliamentary speeches of its members, and to inform them what to expect in the upcoming parliamentary week.

The General Audit Function[7]

Perhaps, because of the functional limitations on the role of the parliament in the policy process, the most important function of parlia-

---

[6] Jackson and Atkinson cite two examples. See op. cit., p. 70.
[7] Jackson and Atkinson refer to this as the "surveillance" function of parliament (op. cit., pp. 25-26).

ment today is what we might call the general audit function. This is not a financial audit, although, through the Public Accounts Committee parliament does, in a sense, audit the financial affairs of the government. Rather, the general audit function of the Canadian parliament involves broadly based public criticism of the total record of the government. This process goes on almost constantly, and brings to the attention of the press and the public many of the shortcomings and potential shortcomings of the government of the day. Because of party discipline and loyalty, the general audit of the overall record of the government is performed primarily by the opposition parties and not by the government backbenchers. Furthermore, the focus of this kind of criticism is not specific policy proposals but the "state of the nation" in broad terms. While the general audit of the government's record goes on at all stages of government legislation, the bulk of such criticism comes out through various procedural devices and special debates which occur intermittently during each parliamentary session. Each of these deserves more detailed mention.

The Throne Speech Debate   The Standing Orders of the House of Commons provide for a debate on the Address in Reply to His Excellency's Speech.[8] The Speech from the Throne is prepared by the closest advisors to the Prime Minister and read by the Governor General to a joint sitting of the House of Commons and the Senate. In this speech, which is delivered at the opening of parliament, there is a review of the "state of the nation" and a statement of the legislative program of the government in the coming session. Eight days are set aside for opposition criticism and comment on the record of the government, and on these days the normal rules of "relevance" that apply in debates in the House are suspended. Backbench members have the opportunity to speak their minds on anything that has been bothering them or any matter which is of special concern to their constituents, while government frontbenchers may use the occasion to defend aspects of government policy. The tendency is for the backbenchers to make special pleas for local needs and interests and for the opposition frontbenchers to use the debate to introduce motions of non-confidence in the government. The April 1980 debate was used by the government to put its case against the Quebec sovereignty-association referendum. The subject matter of the Throne Speech Debate, while varied, does not usually involve specific policy proposals of the government but tends, rather, to be devoted to broad criticisms and defences of the record. To the extent that the speeches of the various MPs are reported in their home

---

[8] Standing Order 38(1).

newspapers, this debate is helpful in showing the voters back home that their MP in Ottawa is working on their behalf. Similarly, to the extent that the frontbench speeches of the opposition parties are reported in the news media, the Throne Speech Debate functions to publicize the real and imagined shortcomings of the government as seen through opposition eyes.

The Business of Supply and Ways and Means   A total of twenty-five days spread over three separate supply periods is allotted to the opposition for debating the business of supply. On these allotted days, or opposition days, opposition motions take precedence over government business, and debates on the motions are limited to twenty minutes per speaker with the exception of the mover and seconder. The function of these allotted days is to permit the opposition an ample opportunity to criticize the government's spending policy. The debates on these days constitute an important part of the general audit function of parliament in that they force the government to defend publicly its spending policy against tough opposition criticism. In fact, normally six of these opposition days end in votes on non-confidence motions.

The Budget Debate   This is the second "free-for-all" debate that occurs during the parliamentary year—the first being the Throne Speech Debate. During the Budget Debate the backbenchers are permitted to put on the record their own comments on the government's overall financial policy for the benefit of their constituents and the nation. The Budget Debate begins after the Minister of Finance has brought down the budget in the House of Commons, and it lasts for six days. As with the Throne Speech Debate, the relevancy rule for speeches is relaxed and MPs can wander fairly far afield in seeking to embarrass the government or to make themselves look good, although one is encouraged to speak to the ways and means proposals set down in the budget.

"S.O. 26 and 43" Debates   Standing Order 26 of the House of Commons provides for a motion to adjourn the House "for the purpose of discussing a specific and important matter requiring urgent consideration." If a matter has arisen suddenly which is not likely to be brought before the House of Commons in any other way, and which is not a purely administrative matter, this Standing Order permits a special debate to consider it immediately. The Speaker is given final say as to whether or not the matter is urgent and whether it is a matter for consideration under S.O. 26. If the Speaker decides that the matter is deserving of further consideration, the motion to adjourn is held over until the evening sitting of the House, at which time the matter is debated. There is no formal time limit on this form of debate, although the Speaker can declare the motion to adjourn "carried" when he or she "is satisfied that the debate has been concluded" and forthwith adjourn the House until the next day.

A time limit of twenty minutes is placed on speeches in a S.O. 26 debate. While such debates are not granted frequently, we are seeing more and more of them since the 1969 rules revisions. Basically these debates function to permit the opposition to raise issues with which the government is not dealing in the House, and to make public their opinion that the government should be doing something. While a S.O. 26 debate will not be granted to discuss something the government has already done but with which the opposition disagrees, it is an important means for pointing out something the government should be doing but is not. Moreover, it is not necessary that the Speaker grant the request for a debate in order for S.O. 26 to serve its purpose. Simply by requesting a debate, the opposition can suggest that something is amiss and requires attention.

A procedure which is akin to S.O. 26 and which is being used more and more frequently is defined by Standing Order 43. This is a procedure whereby a member can ask for leave of the House to present a motion without the standard "notice." The obvious intention of S.O. 43 is to permit the House to set aside regular business in order to deal with genuine unforeseen circumstances, and its use requires unanimous consent. This procedure has been seized upon by the opposition backbenchers as an opportunity to raise an issue even though there is little hope that they will achieve the necessary unanimity to permit an actual debate. As Jackson and Atkinson have pointed out, this probably is not a good tactic for the opposition to employ because a "43" precedes Question Period and possibly detracts from the "keynote" first question of the leader of the opposition which sets the theme for that first hour of the daily business: "The abuse of this rule restricts the time parliament has at its disposal and, because they directly precede the oral question period, such motions detract attention from the main questions of the day."[9]

The Question Period The question period provides the most interesting and lively interchange between ministers and opposition members in the daily routine of the House of Commons. It is the question period which is covered most closely by the press gallery, and in the public eye it is likely that the question period is viewed as the most important opportunity for the opposition to attack the government. Any backbencher, including those on the government side of the House, can ask a question of a minister, but because of party discipline, because the government backbencher can usually get the

---

[9] Jackson and Atkinson, op. cit., p. 93 (First edition).

information wanted without a formal question, and because the Speaker traditionally recognizes opposition members more often than government members, the question period has become a time almost exclusively for opposition questions.

Questions simply seeking information from a minister of the Crown are normally written down and placed on the Order Paper. The answers to such written questions are in turn handed to the Clerk of the House and subsequently printed in Hansard. The function of this form of question is to assist MPs in gathering information relevant to their interests and those of their constituents. However, in some cases the opposition will ask questions simply in order to get "on the record" information that might be embarrassing to the government in the future. Sometimes, if the answer is potentially embarrassing, an opposition member will ask for an oral answer. Oral answers are requested by placing an asterisk beside the written question. No member may have more than three "starred" questions in the Order Paper at the same time.

More important, however, than either the written question or the starred questions, are those asked during the daily forty-minute Oral Question Period. Its purpose is to permit a member to ask a minister "questions on matters of urgency,"[10] or questions that should be answered immediately rather than placed on the Order Paper. The Speaker is formally empowered to direct that an oral question is not urgent and therefore should be placed on the Order Paper, although in practice, this stipulation is seldom invoked. Generally the Oral Question Period, particularly since it is that part of the parliamentary day which is usually seen on our television sets and reported in the press, is an opportunity for the opposition to ask questions which could potentially embarrass the government. The question must be very carefully phrased in order to force the minister to answer it on the opposition's terms, for there is no debate permitted during the question period. Sometimes a member will receive the permission of the Speaker to ask a "supplementary" question if the minister has evaded the point of the main question, although even then it is difficult to pin down the minister if that minister is determined to be evasive. One of the interesting features of the Oral Question Period is the seemingly random banter that is carried on by members who have not been recognized by the Speaker. Such heckling and wisecracking, which is often reported verbatim in Hansard, provides some opportunity for backbenchers on both sides of the House to put a few comments on the record on behalf of their side. What usually ensues is a

---

[10] S.O. 39(5).

verbal fencing match with opposition members sparring with the ministers, attempting to bait them into saying something that is an embarrassment to the government. The minister must "keep cool" and not be goaded into saying anything more than is necessary to provide factual information or, as is often the case, to gracefully evade the question.

A member who is not satisfied with the answer to a question may serve notice of an intention to raise the matter "on the adjournment" of the House. This procedure provides for a thirty-minute debate at the termination of the daily sitting wherein the member raising the question is given seven minutes to speak, and other members must limit their comments to three minutes each. Questions asked on the adjournment are more important in the U.K. than in Canada, but they provide an opportunity to debate a question which would not be debatable in the Oral Question Period. Generally, adjournment debates are simply another opportunity for the opposition members to attempt to embarrass the government, and for all members to raise questions involving the interests of their particular constituencies or regions.

Questions in the House thus perform two functions. First, they can provide the MP with information. Second, they can give the opposition MPs an opportunity to expose the shortcomings of the government. However, the limitations on questions as a device for parliamentary criticism of the government are many. In the first place, the minister may refuse to answer the question on the grounds that a government policy statement is forthcoming, or that to answer would be a breach of national security. Secondly, in the case of questions on the Order Paper, the minister can take a long time to answer the question or may even choose not to answer at all. At the end of each session of parliament there is always a long list of questions on the Order Paper which have not been answered and which probably never will be. Finally, the minister can simply refuse to answer the question, even in the Oral Question Period. There is nothing which compels a minister to answer parliamentary questions, although for political reasons a minister cannot afford to treat parliament with indifference or disdain. Furthermore, unanswered questions get asked over and over again until either an answer is obtained or the public is made aware of the fact that a minister is "covering up," withholding information from the Canadian people.

Perhaps the most important limitation of the question period as a tool that facilitates the general audit function of parliament is the simple fact that most of the exchanges that occur between opposition members and ministers deteriorate to a mere banter. Often this is a relatively friendly session of wisecracks and "in jokes" which does not become elevated to the discussion of any matters of substance. The questions asked are "loaded" and the answers given are usually evasive and designed to "defuse" the question rather than to answer it. Once in a while the question period provides truly bitter exchanges between members, with much name-calling by the principals and jeering by the rest. Sometimes such an exchange causes a minister to blurt out information which the government would have preferred to keep quiet. The best example of this was the exchange between members of the opposition and Justice Minister Cardin which ultimately precipitated the so-called Munsinger Scandal in 1966.

Thus, while at times the question period does not accomplish anything of substance, it functions to keep the government alert. Corruption in high places is sometimes uncovered through the opposition's use of the question period and the threat of such public exposure perhaps serves as a conscience for the government. Despite its limitations, therefore, the question period remains one of parliament's most important procedural devices for criticizing the cabinet and for auditing the record of the government.

Opportunity for broad criticism of government policy comes up during the proceedings on public bills and at almost all stages of parliamentary debate, but on these occasions the debate is usually restricted to the specific legislation being considered. In other words, the Speaker will enforce the relevancy requirement for all speeches at all stages in the normal process of passing public bills. Thus, the best opportunity for broadly criticizing the cabinet and publicly auditing the government's record occurs in the various special debates and in the question period. The effectiveness of the opposition in parliament as an auditor of the record of the government is lessened by that lack of information and expertise which is the fundamental weakness of the MP in the policy process. Nevertheless, there is still an important function to be performed here, and it is hoped that with the addition of research assistants in the research offices of the various parties, through other means such as the "parliamentary internship" program whereby young university graduates serve for one year as assistants to individual MPs, and with the much broadened forum provided by the televising of parliament, the MP can remain an effective political auditor even though he or she can no longer be an effective policy maker.

The Representative Function: The MP and the Constituency

It has been seen that parliament as an institution and individual MPs as actors in that institution are functionally disqualified from having a substantive impact on government policy decisions. The primary policy role of parliament is to refine and polish government policy and not to set priorities or formulate policy outputs. Because of this limitation on parliament's policy role, we hypothesize that the most important aspects of the MP's representative role must be limited to non-policy matters. The MP today is acting more and more as a channel through which the individual constituent can register and seek redress for grievances. The types of problems being dealt with by MPs do not require large-scale policy decisions in order to effect a remedy; they involve inequities in the application of existing policies to individual cases, which can be remedied by specific administrative action. The redress of many individual grievances can be achieved through simple means such as a telephone call to the minister or public official involved, or, if that should fail, through a question in the House of Commons which has the effect of publicizing an injustice or inequity being perpetrated by the administration. This function of the MP is like that of an ombudsman. Because the MP has some official status in Ottawa and because of the power to publicly assert the case in parliament, the MP is in a good position to act as an ombudsman for individual constituents, or at least for those constituents who have the initiative to request assistance. The ombudsman function of the MP is carried out in a non-partisan context. MPs, in other words represent all of their constituents and not just those who voted for them or for their parties.

This same concern with the inequities and injustices inevitably committed by large government administrations probably also affects the individual MP's role in the policy-refining stage of the policy process, where parliament can and does take a positive and active role. At this stage, administrative consequences missed by the cabinet and the bureaucracy are sometimes seen by parliament. Because of a familiarity with the sorts of problems created by carelessly drafted legislation, the MP can attempt to minimize the number of grievances likely to arise from the administration of an act while it is at the refining stage of the policy process. Thus, the MP represents the interests of individual constituents not only in seeking to redress grievances, but also in attempting to prevent their occurrence.

The ombudsman function of the MP is important to the system, for it creates support for the system among people who might otherwise feel that they have no access to the authorities. While many MPs still feel that their most important role is to represent the interests of their constituencies, their regions, or the country as a whole in the policy process, it is unlikely that backbench MPs will ever again be able to take a very positive policy role. However, as long as the MP remains alert to the injustices and inadequacies in the implementation of pub-lic policy, particularly as they affect individual Canadians, such unfortunate concomitants of "big government" can perhaps be min-imized.

Summary and Conclusions: The Functions of Parliament

The functions of parliament include the positive functions of refining policy and converting it into legislative outputs of the system. How-ever, in relation to the political system as a whole, parliament's more "negative" ratification/rejection and general audit functions are of much greater importance. In the extreme case, if it is clear that the Prime Minister is losing his marbles—if he should grow a little mous-tache, comb his hair down over one eye, and start wearing a uniform to work—it is still open to parliament to say, "party discipline be damned," and to reject his proposals. More routinely, it is through day-by-day criticism and comment by the opposition parties in the House of Commons and the publicizing of that criticism through the press and the televising of debates that the government is kept on its toes. Cabinet ministers are constantly called upon publicly to justify the government's record through procedural devices such as the question period and a number of special debates. Finally, what may be a very important aspect of the role of the individual MP, but one which has not been extensively studied, is the ombudsman function. The MP in this regard is both an elected "watchdog" and a communi-cation link between the anonymous bureaucrat and the individual cit-izen.

More could be said here about secondary functions of parliament in the Canadian political system. For instance, parliament is a symbol of some of the things we believe in, like representative democracy and responsible government. It could be argued that this symbolic func-tion of parliament is as important as the policy, audit, and ombuds-man functions discussed above, if not more so; after all, parliament and the provincial legislature are the symbols around which most Canadians centre their perceptions of politics. On the other hand, a more cynical argument suggests that parliament is no longer of any significance in the Canadian political process and that it functions purely as an "electoral college" through which we indirectly elect a Prime Minister on the pattern of a U.S. presidential election. This, however, is a textbook and not a polemic. There are many points of view about the function and importance of parliament in our political system today; we have tried to state some of them and to take a mid-dle ground in describing them. The reader must decide, personally, just how important parliament is in the process.

THE ORGANIZATION OF PARLIAMENT

The House of Commons

Officers of the House   The most important office of the House of Commons is the Speakership.[11] The office of Speaker of the House was created by the BNA Act, Section 44, which states that:

The House of Commons on its first assembling after a General Election shall proceed with all practicable speed to elect one of its members to be speaker.

The main function of the Speaker, to preside over the debates in the House of Commons, is also defined by the BNA Act, although the elaboration of the duties of this role are left to the Standing Orders. Constitutionally it is clear that the Speaker is an officer of the House who is selected by the House itself and not by the cabinet. In practice, however, because of the functional supremacy of the cabinet in the parliamentary process, the Speaker is nominated by the Prime Minister and is usually elected without opposition. Almost invariably, the Speaker is a member from the government side of the House, although it is expected that he or she will function in a non-partisan and impartial manner. More recently, the tradition of impartiality has become more firmly established. Since 1963, the Speaker has been nominated by the Prime Minister with the leader of the opposition as the seconder. In 1968 the Conservatives went one step further by indicating that they were willing to permit Mr. Lamoureux to continue as the Speaker even if they won the election, despite the fact that he had originally been elected as a Liberal. To facilitate this, the Speaker ran as an independent and the Conservatives did not run a candidate against him in his own riding. This paved the way for procedural changes that have streamlined debate in the House by making most procedural rulings by the Speaker not subject to appeal to the House. The response of the first Speaker to possess this grant of final authority in procedural matters was to take an extremely fair and impartial stand, often in opposition to the wishes of the government. Although Lamoureux did not contest the 1974 election, his replacement was James Jerome, a Liberal backbencher who proved to be so impartial and fair in his dealings with all parties in the House that the Conservatives agreed to leave him in that post when they came to

---

[11] See W. F. Dawson, *Procedure in the Canadian House of Commons* (University of Toronto Press, Toronto, 1962), ch. 2, for a detailed description of the office of the Speaker of the Canadian House of Commons. See also D. S. Macdonald, "Changes in the House of Commons—New Rules," *Canadian Public Administration* Vol. 12, Spring 1970.

power in 1979. Jerome, in turn, did not run in 1980 and has been replaced by Jeanne Sauvé, an ex-Liberal cabinet minister and the first woman ever to occupy the Speaker's chair. The Speaker does not participate in debates except where necessary to defend the internal estimates of the House of Commons. Furthermore, Standing Orders are explicit that the Speaker cannot vote except to break a tie.

Thus far all that has been discussed is the Speaker's function as a presiding officer of the House. A secondary function of the office is to act as the administrative head of the House of Commons. The Speaker is responsible for the internal economy of the House, for the staffing of the House with permanent employees such as secretaries, and for preparing the estimates of internal costs and piloting them through the House of Commons. Thus, in some ways, the Speaker is like a minister of a small department who is responsible in a formal way for the administrative policies of that department.

The *Deputy Speaker* of the House is elected at the same time as the Speaker.[12] The functions of this position are to take the place of the Speaker when the latter is not able to be present and to act as the Chairman of Committees of the Whole. Like the Speaker, the Deputy Speaker is elected for the duration of a parliament and is expected to be proficient in whichever of the official languages is not the language of the Speaker. The general practice is that the Deputy Speaker is selected from among the members of the government party although, with the office of the Speaker becoming less partisan than in the past, there is some possibility that the office of the Deputy Speaker will be affected as well.

In the absence of the Deputy Speaker, Standing Orders provide for the temporary appointment by the Speaker of any member to chair the Committee of the Whole.[13] However, it is more common today, for a *Deputy Chairman of Committees* (appointed for the duration of the session) to function as the Chairman of the Committee of the Whole in the absence of the Deputy Speaker. This person also can take over as Speaker in the unlikely case that both the Speaker and the Deputy Speaker are absent.[14] This appointment is made by the House and is invariably a member of the government party.

The *Clerk of the House*[15] is the permanent head of the House of Commons staff. The function of this position is to supervise all permanent officers and staff of the House of Commons, to ensure that the Order

[12] See S.O. 53(1).
[13] See S.O. 53(4).
[14] See S.O. 53(5).
[15] See S.O. 80-83.

Paper for the day is prepared and delivered to the Speaker, to print up certain documents for the distribution to all members of the House, and to ensure that two copies of every bill presented in the House are forwarded to the Minister of Justice.[16] In short, the Clerk of the House is a "deputy minister" of the House of Commons. His "department" is the permanent staff of the House, and the "minister" is the Speaker. The Clerk of the House is the most important permanent officer of the House of Commons.

It is interesting to note here that the House of Commons staff of approximately 3,000 persons including the Library of Parliament, are not public servants according to the Public Service Employment Act but are the employees of parliament directly. They have a separate pension system, a separate system of employee-employer relations, and they are not subject to the regulations of the Public Service Commission. While this situation is merely a reflection of the need for parliament to be independent from the whims of the government of the day in managing its own internal affairs, there is growing discontent among many of the employees themselves who would like to have the benefits and the collective bargaining rights of public servants. The coming two years will likely see a settlement of this problem, although the nature of the agreement is impossible to speculate upon.

In this discussion of the officers of the House of Commons we must also say a word about the *party whips*.[17] While they are not strictly officers of the House, but rather officers of the various political parties represented there, they must be included in this section because of the important role they play in the organization of the business of the House. They are appointed by the parties to represent their respective interests in the *Striking Committee* (which assigns individual MPs to committees), and to maintain party discipline. They ensure that the members are all present when there is to be a recorded vote in the House, and they check to see that the members vote the "right" way on division. Finally, arrangements between parties, for instance concerning the limitation of debate and the agenda for the sitting day, are sometimes worked out through the whips. Thus, while the whips are

---

[16] This latter provision is to comply with the provision of the Canadian Bill of Rights. (See chapter 7.)

[17] A. Herbert Morrison, *Government and Parliament: A Survey From the Inside* (Oxford University Press, New York, 1964); Robert J. Jackson, *Rebels and Whips: An Analysis of Discipline and Cohesion in British Political Parties* (St. Martin's Press, New York, 1968). The best recent work on procedural aspects of the House of Commons is J. Stewart, *The Canadian House of Commons: Procedure and Reform* (McGill-Queens, Montreal, 1977).

in no way official House of Commons officers, they do have an integral part to play in the day-to-day workings of the House, and particularly, in enforcing party discipline.

The *House Leaders* of the various parties are responsible for the overall in-House conduct of their own MPs, and consequently for the overall flow of business through the House. The government House Leader is a member of the cabinet, and is responsible for seeing that the business of the government gets through the House as quickly as possible. Each opposition House Leader acts as formal spokesman of his or her caucus to negotiate with the government House Leader the apportioning of the scarce time of the House. The high prestige of House Leaders and the fact that they are really chosen by the party leaders to take much of the legislative load off their own backs ensure that they can usually direct the caucus to do what they think is necessary to expedite the legislative process.

The Committee of the Whole   Standing Order 75(3) states that "any Bill based on a supply or ways and means motion after second reading thereof shall stand referred to Committee of the Whole." The Committee of the Whole is composed of all the members of the House sitting as a committee with the Speaker out of the chair and the Deputy Speaker presiding. Standing Orders generally apply when the House is sitting as a Committee of the Whole, with the exception that speeches have a shorter time limit, relevancy criteria are more strictly enforced, and debate is less formalized. Today, the function of the Committee of the Whole is primarily symbolic with the exception of Ways and Means (Taxation) Bills which are still given detailed clause by clause consideration in Committee of the Whole after second reading. Traditionally, all legislation was considered clause by clause in the Committee of the Whole after second reading or approval in principle. Now, however, the clause-by-clause consideration of non-money bills is given in the appropriate Standing Committee, thus making the Committee-of-the-Whole stage unnecessary. Similarly, special Committees of the Whole—the Committee of Supply and the Committee of Ways and Means—were once required to give clause-by-clause consideration to all financial legislation. The Committee of Supply was responsible for the detailed consideration of the estimates before a supply bill could be introduced, a task now left to the Standing Committees.[18] The Committee of Ways and Means was required to deal separately with taxation proposals before introducing the actual bills in the House; but now this is achieved through a blan-

---

[18] Macdonald, "Changes in the House of Commons—New Rules," p. 33.

ket motion by the Minister of Finance that "the House approve in general the budgetary policy of the Government." In 1969, the Committee of Supply and the Committee of Ways and Means were abolished. Thus, the function of the Committee of the Whole is today mostly symbolic, as its main substantive functions have been taken over by the Standing Committees.

Division   Debates in the House of Commons which have been commenced by a specific motion inevitably end in a vote. The basic rule in a parliamentary system is that a majority of those present in the House decide the outcome of a motion. When debate on a question has been concluded, the Speaker "puts the question" to the House by reading the main motion and any amendments. Those in agreement say "aye" and those against say "nay," and the Speaker announces which side has won—according to personal interpretation. If at least five members rise to demand a recorded vote or a "division," the "division bells" are rung, to inform members not sitting in the House at the time that a division is about to occur. Sometimes the division bells are rung for more than twenty minutes in order to allow the party whips to round up as many votes as they can, although, in most cases, ten minutes is sufficient to summon members from offices and other places within the parliament buildings. When the whips of the various parties are content that they have as many as possible of their members present, the doors of the House are closed and the vote is taken. Members register their votes by standing in their places in the House of Commons to be counted by the Clerk of the House. When the vote is counted and recorded, the Speaker announces the outcome.

Recorded votes in the House are very time-consuming, but fortunately many votes in the House are settled without a formal division; in most circumstances it is obvious to all members that the government has a majority of the members in the House, so that there is never any real question that the government will be able to carry any motion. In recognition of this, the opposition parties force a recorded vote only on non-confidence motions, second reading of important bills, etc. For the most part, the question is decided by a voice vote with the Speaker declaring the government side to have carried the motion.

A member who is going to be absent from the House for a time will often arrange to "pair" with a member of the opposition party. This means that both members agree not to vote on division if one is absent from the House. This practice, while based only on gentleman's agreement, means that even if many members are absent from the House, there is no danger that the government will fall by mistake. The practice of pairing is obviously more important in the situation of a minority government than when the government has a healthy majority. Frequently after a division, a member who abstained from voting will rise in his place and state the way he would have voted had he not been paired. The supervision of pairing in the House is usually left to the whips, who organize pairs for members and who ensure that their own members who are paired do not vote on division. It is interesting to note that on one occasion in 1926 the government was defeated in the House by one vote because of a "broken pair" and although everyone was embarrassed, the vote stood and the government was forced to resign.[19]

Rules of Debate   Some discussion has already been devoted to the basic functions of the Canadian parliament. However, what has been left unsaid until now is the fact that the general method or technique whereby parliament performs all of these functions is debate. Above all else, the House of Commons would appear to an uninitiated observer primarily as a forum of debate, for it is debate which occupies the bulk of time in the parliamentary day. The rules of debate are consequently an important aspect of the parliamentary process.

The rules of debate, as already pointed out, are enforced by the Speaker, Deputy Speaker, or Deputy Chairman of Committees. The chair does not exercise control over debate in an arbitrary fashion; there are definite rules and procedures which the Speaker is called upon to apply from time to time in the course of debate. It is a basic principle that every member who wishes to speak to a question should be permitted to do so. The problem faced by the Speaker is, therefore, not *who* should be permitted to speak, but who should be permitted to speak first. The procedure for being recognized by the Speaker, or for catching the Speaker's eye, is for the member wishing to speak to rise in his or her place[20] in the House. The Speaker attempts to switch attention from the government side of the House to the opposition side, to permit a fair alternation of speakers by party. The Speaker's job has been greatly simplified through the practice of the party whips supplying the Speaker with a daily list of members who wish to speak on that day. In the question period, it is traditional that the Speaker first recognizes the official opposition leader and then turns to the leader of one of the minor opposition parties.[21] In debates, however, the basic rule is that the parties have themselves worked out which of their members they wish to have heard and in which order, and the Speaker merely rotates from one

---

[19] See W. F. Dawson, op. cit., ch. 10.
[20] S.O. 28-29.
[21] See Dawson, op. cit., pp. 103-104.

party to another. If the whips have done their job, there will be only one person from a given party rising to address the House at any given time.

Speeches in the House have a time limit of forty minutes when the Speaker is in the chair,[22] and no member may speak more than once on any question. The exceptions to this rule are the Prime Minister, the leader of the official opposition, any minister moving a Government Order, and any member making a motion of non-confidence in the government, all of whom may speak more than once, and for longer than forty minutes.[23] A twenty-minute time limit applies to speeches during Private Members' Hour and during various extraordinary types of debates such as those under Standing Order 26.

It is a convention of parliamentary debate that members should not read their speeches but should deliver them *extemporaneously*.[24] This is not a written rule, however, and cannot be enforced by the Speaker. The result is that any member who so desires will read the speech, with some kidding and heckling from other members who observe the practice. The stock reply by a member who is chided for reading a speech is that he or she is merely following extensive notes very closely. There is a similar rule that the member may not repeat a point in a speech and that arguments made previously by other members may not be repeated.[25] The former is applied infrequently by the Speaker, and the latter never; it defies enforcement. There are also rules requiring relevance[26] in debate, which are similarly difficult to apply. The major impetus for relevance in speeches comes from the party whips, who try to ensure that time is not wasted during important debates. As already seen, there are certain debates, such as the Throne Speech Debate and the Budget Debate, to which the requirement of relevance does not apply at all.

In addition to the more explicit rules of debate, there is a general rule that members should not use what is euphemistically called "unparliamentary language." What this means is that the members should treat each other with politeness and should not revert to name-calling or *ad hominem* arguments in debate. Generally the members do abide by this rule, and it is seldom that the Speaker is called upon to rebuke a member for the use of unparliamentary language.[27] Unparliamentary comments by members other than the

---

[22] S.O. 31(1).
[23] S.O. 31(2).
[24] Dawson, op. cit., p. 104.
[25] Ibid., p. 108.
[26] Ibid., p. 109.
[27] Ibid., p. 110-114.

member who has the floor usually go unrecognized formally, and appear in Hansard as "Some Hon. Members: Oh, Oh!" The phrase "Oh, Oh!" is a cryptic euphemism for earthy comments ranging from those which cast aspersions on the Honourable Member's ancestry to harmless but quaint colloquialisms such as "yer mother wears army boots," or "fuddle-duddle."

Privilege   Parliamentary privilege is the sum of the rights and privileges of both Houses of the Canadian parliament which function to place parliament in a position above all other institutions and individuals in the land. These rights are held by parliament as a whole and by each individual MP. They include such rights as freedom from arrest arising out of civil action while the House is in session, exemption from jury duty or from subpoena as a witness, the protection from libel actions for the content of speeches in the House and publications of the House. Another part of parliamentary privilege in Canada is the right of parliamentary committees to hear witnesses under oath. Breaches of privilege are considered to be analogous to contempt of court, and are punishable by imprisonment, fine, or simply censure by the House itself. For matters of privilege, the House can act as court, calling witnesses "before the Bar of the House of Commons."

The real importance of parliamentary privilege has waned. Its significance today is primarily as a symbolic reminder of the principles of freedom of speech and freedom from arrest which were at one time not so widely accepted as they are today. Occasionally today, a member will rise in the House on a question of privilege to complain about statements made about him or her in the press, or to complain about the conduct of another member, but in most cases the question raised has very little to do with privilege as such, and sometimes is merely a stalling technique. As Professor W. F. Dawson has pointed out:

At the root of the problem is the ignorance of the Canadian House of the true meaning of privilege, which is essentially the defensive weapon of a legislature which has been used to protect itself against interference. The Canadian House has never had to fear such trouble and has never bothered to develop a defence. [28]

Sporadic attempts to raise questions of privilege in the Canadian House of Commons have been motivated by purely partisan needs and not by genuine threats to the security and freedom of the House. Parliamentary privilege, therefore, while important for its historical

[28] Ibid., p. 54.

meaning, is not an important aspect of the modern parliamentary process in Canada.[29]

Committees in the House of Commons

One of the first responsibilities of the House of Commons at the beginning of the first session of each parliament is to appoint a Committee of Selection, or as it is usually known, a Striking Committee. The Striking Committee is made up of seven MPs, usually including the chief whips of the opposition parties, a representative of the ministry, and the Chief Government Whip who acts as the chairman. The function of the Striking Committee is to select the members of the Standing Committees of the House within ten days of the commencement of the session, and to ensure that all committees have a full complement of members throughout the session.

At the present time, there are eighteen Standing Committees of the Canadian House of Commons, thirteen of which are the Specialist Committees in various substantive areas of government policy. The thirteen are as follows, membership in brackets:

Agriculture (30)
Communications and Culture (20)
External Affairs and National Defence (30)
Finance, Trade and Economic Affairs (20)
Fisheries and Forestry (20)
Health, Welfare and Social Affairs (20)
Indian Affairs and Northern Development (20)
National Resources and Public Works (20)
Justice and Legal Affairs (20)
Labour, Manpower and Immigration (20)
Regional Development (20)
Transport (20)
Veterans Affairs (20)

In addition to these Specialist Committees, there are seven Standing Committees of the House responsible for various matters outside the realm of government legislation *per se*. These are as follows:

Miscellaneous Estimates (20)
Miscellaneous Private Bills and Standing Orders (20)
Privileges and Elections (20)

[29] See Dawson, op. cit., ch. 3, for a general discussion of privilege in Canada.

    Public Accounts (20)
    Procedure and Organization (12)
    On Management and Members Services (12)
    Northern Pipelines[30] (15)

The Striking Committee is also responsible for appointing the House members of the three *Joint Standing Committees* of the Senate and House of Commons, which are as follows, with *House* representation in brackets.

    Printing (23)
    The Library of Parliament (21)
    Regulations and other Statutory Instruments (12)

Special Committees, such as the Committee on Egg Marketing, and *Special Joint Committees*, such as the Committee on Employer-Employee Relations in the Public Services, or the Committee on the Constitution are set up from time to time to deal with specific problems in specific policy areas. The Striking Committee is also responsible for assigning members to these.

Membership on the Standing Committees is usually limited to a maximum of twenty, but the Committee on Agriculture and the Committee on External Affairs and National Defence have as many as thirty members, while others such as Procedure and Organization Committees are limited to only twelve. Standing Order 65(5) specifies that Special Committees should consist of not more than fifteen members. The guiding principle for selection of committee members by the Striking Committee is that the parties should have representation proportional to their membership in the House itself. Thus, in a twenty-member committee, a typical distribution by party in 1980 might be: Liberals, eleven; Conservatives, six or seven; and NDP two or three. In the case of the Liberals and Conservatives, party whips assign their party's allotment of members to the various committees according to the membership on the Party Caucus Committees which correspond roughly to the Specialist Committees of the House. Thus, a Conservative MP who is a member of the Caucus Committee on Agriculture is likely also to be a member of the House Committee on Agriculture. The NDP usually determines its members in a less formal way, depending largely upon which committees the MP wishes

---

[30] Standing Orders specify that this committee ceases to exist when the Northern Pipeline Agency does. Hence, while it is a committee, it is a Special Committee, seen as being permanent only as long as the N.P.A. exists.

to sit on, and seniority in the party caucus. It is generally accepted that the Striking Committee bases its selection of committee membership entirely on the recommendation of the party whips, and does not interfere with a party's wishes except with regard to the number of members allocated to each party for each committee.

Membership on committees is subject to change simply through notification of the Clerk of the House by the Chief Government Whip. Such changes are granted to the opposition parties as a matter of course, on request. Cabinet ministers are never selected as members of the Standing Committees, but Parliamentary Secretaries are often temporarily appointed to committees dealing with the policy areas that concern their ministers. Although a minister may testify before a committee, the Parliamentary Secretary is generally expected to speak on the minister's behalf when a piece of legislation which the minister has introduced in the House is being considered by the relevant Specialist Committee. Conversely, the Parliamentary Secretary is expected to keep the minister posted on developments in the committee hearings.

The Chairman and Vice Chairman of Standing Committees are elected by the committees themselves, and because the government has a majority of the members of the committees, these officers are normally government MPs. The single exception to this rule is the Public Accounts Committee which in recent years, has been chaired by a member of the opposition. From time to time, an opposition committee person with unique interest or expertise in the area of the committee's responsibility will be elected Vice Chairman, but such occurrences are, as yet, relatively rare in Canada. The function of the chair in Canadian committees is primarily to preside over the hearings of the committee and not to assume the aggressive and dominant role of the chairmen of U.S. Congressional committees. While this is a general rule, the practice of committees in this regard varies widely from committee to committee and from chairman to chairman.

Procedure in the Standing Committees of the Canadian House of Commons is basically the same as that for the House itself, with the exception that Standing Orders restricting the length of speeches and the number of times of speaking do not apply, in order to ensure a less formal discussion of the issues. The committees hear witnesses, mainly from the public service but frequently from the private sector and the academic community, and they report back to the House of Commons. All committee hearings are public in Canada, although neither the press nor the general public seems to give very much attention to the proceedings of most committees.

Committees of the House are all staffed by clerks who are permanent employees of the House of Commons. While there is a potential

for these people to acquire some degree of power vis-à-vis their committees, simply by virtue of their continuance in the same roles for a
number of parliaments, they tend to be rather junior people with
purely clerical responsibilities.

The Functions of the House Committees[31]

The Standing Committees of the House of Commons have at least
four major functions to perform in the legislative process. First, they
are expected to take the major role in the detailed consideration and
refinement of public bills; secondly, they are delegated the responsibility for detailed scrutiny of the estimates before the supply bills are
introduced formally and given first reading; thirdly, both Standing
Committees and Special Committees are sometimes requested to conduct pre-legislative investigation of policy proposals much in the
same way that a Royal Commission or task force would; and fourthly,
the Public Accounts Committee is responsible for performing a parliamentary "post audit" of the public accounts and the report of the
Auditor General. Beyond these four major functions, the committees
of the House also undertake a number of sundry tasks assigned to
them specifically or to joint House of Commons–Senate committees.
These all must be considered in detail.

Refining Government Policy: The Legislative Function The most
important function of Committees of the House of Commons as
regards the policy process is the detailed scrutiny and polishing of
government bills. After a bill has been given second reading, it is normally referred to the appropriate Standing Committee. The committee studies the legislative proposal, hears witnesses from the public
service and experts from other sectors, and proposes changes that it
feels would have the effect of improving the quality of the final legislative output. The committees can perform this function much more
effectively than the House itself because their pattern of debate is
more open and procedurally less restrictive. It is possible for the committee members simply to discuss the issues involved, rather than
debate them, as is the case in the House.

Furthermore, the principle of the legislation has already been
accepted by the House at second reading, and consequently, the

---

[31] For more detailed discussion of the committee system and of possible reforms see
the following: C. E. S. Franks, "The Reform of Parliament," *Queen's Quarterly*,
Spring 1969, pp. 113-117; "The Dilemma of The Standing Committees of the Canadian House of Commons," *CJPS*, Dec. 1971, pp. 461-476; and "Procedural Reform in
the Legislative Process," in W. A. W. Neilson and J. C. MacPherson (eds.), *The
Legislative Process in Canada: The Need for Reform*, p. 256. See also: J. Stewart, op. cit.

focus of the committee's deliberations is genuinely on improving the end product, although the opposition parties may still try to sneak substantive changes into an act under the guise of improving the wording. Whereas in the House debate on second reading the opposition parties perform the negative role of opposition, in committee they can concentrate on more positive criticism of the form of the legislation and they often propose useful amendments to the bills before them. The argument that committees are to a lesser extent partisan forums for debate than the House of Commons must be qualified by the fact that the matters they discuss (the details) are less likely to lend themselves to partisan divisions. However, it must be remembered that partisanship runs deep in the House of Commons. Most disagreements, even in committees, tend to go along party lines and party discipline is enforced by the government much in the same way that it is in House debates. If an opposition member proposes in committee an amendment with which the government does not agree, the amendment will be defeated on division in the committee. Nevertheless, it is not uncommon for an opposition proposal in committee to be accepted by the government if it is agreed that the suggestion would genuinely improve the bill.

There are some limitations and weaknesses in the committee system which must be considered to clarify its role in the policy process. The first and most obvious is that a committee considering a government bill reports back to the House of Commons; all decisions made in committee are merely decisions to recommend something to the House, and have no final or binding effect by themselves. At the report stage, a recommendation of the committee can be simply reversed by a vote of the whole House. Paradoxically, a further limitation on the effectiveness of committees is the fact that, although they are intended to be specialist bodies which develop some expertise in certain subject matters of legislation, there is, in practice, a very high turnover both in the membership of committees and in the membership of the House itself; consequently, the average committee person does not have time to become very much of an expert. Members of parliament tend to be generalists and not specialists; they often become interested in a specific issue which perhaps concerns their constituency or region, but their interests rarely extend to the entire subject area of any one committee's specialization.[32] While the majority of MPs will remain on a committee for a full session, quite a number will move from one committee to another, according to

---

[32] Not only is turnover very high but attendance is extremely sporadic. See Jackson and Atkinson, op. cit., ch. 6.

which committee is studying which bill and where the party wishes to concentrate its best committee people.

The basic tasks of committees in dealing with government bills, then, are to refine the legislation, to attempt to foresee difficulties that might arise in the administration of the legislation, and to make such amendments as are necessary to achieve the desired improvements. Committees dealing with bills that have already passed second reading are precluded by the rules of procedure from making substantive changes in the legislation, and are precluded by party discipline and the recommendatory nature of their decisions from making even small changes with which the government does not agree.

Detailed Scrutiny of Estimates: The Business of Supply   Before the procedural changes of 1969 abolished the Committee of Supply, it was that committee's responsibility to go over the departmental estimates in detail. Now the estimates for a particular department go instead to the appropriate Standing Committee for detailed consideration. Thus, for instance, the estimates of the Department of National Health and Welfare are reviewed by the Committee of Health, Welfare and Social Affairs, the Department of National Defence estimates are reviewed by the Committee on External Affairs and National Defence, and so forth. This has meant a large saving of time for the House of Commons, but it has increased commensurately the amount of time each member must spend in committee. Currently, by far the largest part of the time spent in committees is devoted to a consideration of the departmental estimates.[33]

The ability of a Standing Committee to effectively criticize the spending plans of a given department is limited once again by the lack of independent expertise in the committee. The witnesses called to back up the estimates of the department are themselves departmental officials and furthermore, by the time the estimates reach parliament, they have already run the gauntlet of criticism from the cabinet, cabinet committees, Ministries of State, Treasury Board, Treasury Board Secretariat, and the departmental financial experts themselves. It is unlikely that the Standing Committee will be able to improve substantially or reduce the estimates; of course, the fact that the minister of each department must publicly justify estimated expenditures in committees probably prevents carelessness in the preparation of the estimates in the first place.

Finally, it must be mentioned that the opposition parties can, to

---

[33] In fact, there is never enough time to consider the estimates thoroughly in committee and S.O. 58(14) states that they "shall be deemed to have been reported" by May 31 whether the committee is through with them or not.

some extent, use the consideration of the estimates in committee as an additional forum for criticism of the government's programs and policy priorities. In this sense, the committee stage of the estimates is at least as important for the general audit function of parliament as it is for improving the detailed estimates.

Pre-Legislative Functions: Policy Committees   It is becoming more common in Canada for House committees to be used as investigatory bodies to examine policy proposals before the legislative stage. In this way, the committees can play a role at both the priority-setting and formulation stages of the policy process. In the priority-setting stage, the House committee may travel across the country hearing briefs submitted by interested parties in order, apparently, to gather information that ultimately can be used by the cabinet in setting priorities. The recommendations that the committee comes up with are not as important as the data it gathers about the attitudes of the public toward the particular problem. At the policy-formulation stage, the committees again act as information gatherers but usually with respect to a specific set of policy alternatives such as those set down in a government white or "coloured" paper. In this case the priority has already been set and the problem faced by the committee is to discover public attitudes to the various alternatives.

There are Standing Committees capable of taking on investigatory duties in most policy areas, although it is in this area of committee work that one most frequently sees the creation of Special Committees. The contribution that committees of the House of Commons can bring to the policy process at the pre-legislative stages is the ability to conduct hearings and listen sympathetically to the submissions of the public. Here the committees can augment the government-sponsored task forces and Royal Commissions, and the bureaucratic political advisory bodies in sounding public attitudes before any concrete policy commitments have been made.

Investigatory committees, although they report back to the House of Commons, can afford to be less partisan than committees involved in the refining of government legislation. At the pre-legislative phase the government is not firmly committed to any policy, and if the findings of the committee differ from the government's attitudes to the problem being studied, the government can still back down without losing face. Furthermore, whereas a Standing Committee's report on a government bill is subject to debate in the House at the report stage, the reports of committee investigations need not be debated at all.

An obvious latent function of the pre-legislative use of House committees is the stimulation of wider participation in the policy process and the creation of feelings of efficacy among the public and the MPs. The extent to which investigatory committees will actually affect policy will depend entirely on the quality of the information gathered and the consistency of that information with that gathered through other agencies. In short, there is a definite potential for additional input to the policy process through the use of parliamentary committees at the earlier stages of the process. The development of that potential will depend on the willingness of the government to utilize it fully and on the recognition by the public and the committees themselves that such non-expert inputs can seldom be accepted without the additional input of expert advice. There must be a realistic understanding that simple committee recommendation of a policy alternative does not necessarily ensure its implementation, particularly if there exists a mass of technical advice which contradicts the committee findings.

The Public Accounts Committee: The Post Audit Function The Canadian Public Accounts Committee is perhaps the most specialized of the Standing Committees of the House of Commons, and it is in some ways the most effective. It consists of twenty members, and, like other committees, is controlled numerically by the government party. However, unlike the other Standing Committees, Public Accounts has had, since 1957, an opposition member as its chairman. Furthermore, the Auditor General, who is an independent officer of parliament, makes the job of the committee easier by providing it with expert assistance in scrutinizing the accounts of the government's expenditures. The functions of the Public Accounts Committee are to investigate the financial shortcomings of the government— as pointed out by the Auditor General, and as discovered through independent examination of the Public Accounts by the committee members themselves—and to make recommendations to the government as to how it should improve its spending practices.

The basic weakness of this procedure as a meaningful exercise of control over the financial affairs of the government is that the government usually chooses not to heed the recommendations. Each year the Auditor General lists a number of recommendations, made over the past years by the Public Accounts Committee, which have never been implemented by the government. Furthermore, the government frequently releases the Public Accounts to the committee only very late in the session and this has the effect of making the recommendations of the committee seem out of date by the time they are presented. This situation could be improved by making automatic the referral of the Public Accounts to the committee instead of waiting for a specific referral by the government. As it stands today, it is not uncommon for the committee to fail to make any inquiries at all before the prorogation of parliament.

To summarize, the Public Accounts Committee has considerable potential for investigating and publicizing the financial bungling and sleight-of-hand of the government and government officials, but as yet it has not been very successful. The committee reports directly to the House, as do all Standing Committees, but the report does not produce any debate; it is simply received by the House and forgotten or ignored by the government. This committee could be made more effective by instituting certain procedural reforms, and by creating a public consciousness of the importance of its role and the relevance to the citizen of its recommendations.

Miscellaneous Committee Functions Finally, mention must be made of the fact that there are a number of Standing Committees whose functions are basically outside the realm of government policy. The Commons Committee on Miscellaneous Private Bills, for instance, exists primarily to look at private bills already approved by the Senate. The bulk of the work here has usually been performed by the Senate and the Senate committees, and the Commons committee merely gives its approval to the legislation.

The Committees on Privileges and Elections and on Procedure and Organization are concerned primarily with the internal affairs of the House of Commons. They are relatively inactive most of the time, becoming active only when specific circumstances necessitate. The Joint Committees are mainly concerned with mundane business such as running the parliamentary restaurant, the library of parliament, and the printing services; while these committees are actually quite active, their role is not critical to the working of the Canadian political system and hence does not deserve more than this cursory mention.

The exception to this rule is the Joint Standing Committee on Regulations and other Statutory Instruments which was set up in 1972 pursuant to the Statutory Instruments Act of 1971. The function of this committee is to scrutinize all *subordinate legislation*[34] in much the same way that the "Scrutiny Committee" in the U.K. does. Given the amount of subordinate legislation and the general extent of delegation of legislative functions to executive and bureaucratic officers, such a committee could come to perform an invaluable control function vis-à-vis the bureaucracy. Moreover, it could in some ways aggrandize the general audit function of parliament and give to the Senate a new and genuine responsibility. The success or failure of this committee, however, will depend on the way in which its man-

---

[34] This is legislation which is passed by executive or administrative officials, pursuant to "enabling legislation" which is passed by parliament, and which vests wide discretionary authority to make subordinate regulations which have the effect of law, in officials and agencies *other than* the supreme lawmaking agency, parliament.

date is carried out, and not on the principles stated in its charter. No final   assessment of the role of the Committee on Regulations and Statutory Instruments can be made until it has had a few more years of operation. So far, however, it has not lived up to the potential indicated above.

This concludes the discussion of the functions of parliamentary committees. The verdict, briefly, is that they are necessary to streamline the parliamentary process, and that they are central actors in the refining of government legislation. They have some positive role to play in assessing government policy proposals through the investigation of the public's attitudes via public hearings, etc. However, for most of the same reasons that parliament as a whole has a restricted role in the policy process, the committees of the House of Commons do not occupy a very important place at the most critical stages of policy making.

THE SENATE

The Canadian parliament is bicameral in structure, consisting of the House of Commons and the Senate. The House of Commons (or "lower house") functions virtually exclusively as the effective legislative branch of the Canadian political system, while the Senate (or "upper house") plays a relatively insignificant role in the legislative process. While it is likely that the Senate was always intended to be a minor partner in the business of passing legislation, its legislative role was once seen as more significant than it has become today. The Senate was originally viewed as the representative of various regions of the federation, with the Maritimes, Quebec, Ontario, and the West alloted twenty-four Senators each. The entry of Newfoundland in 1949 added six more Senators and two more seats were added in 1975 to give representation to the NWT and the Yukon. This makes up today's total of 104. The importance of the Senate today as a regional and provincial representative is not significant because other institutions such as the cabinet and the federal-provincial conferences, which are more deeply involved in the policy process, are much better equipped to perform this function. The 1979 and 1980 House of Commons elections have underrepresented the government parties in certain regions of the country, and one response to this has been to appoint Senators to the cabinet in order to give Quebec, in the case of the short-lived Clark government, and the West in the case of the 1980 Trudeau government some representation. Although this has considerably enlivened the daily question period in the Senate, it remains to be seen whether it will enhance the role of the Senate in the policy process or whether it will simply reduce the credibility of the governments forced to employ Senators as policy-related ministers.

The second function of the Senate as perceived by the Fathers of Confederation was to act as a conservative restraint on the young, the impressionable, and the impulsive in the House of Commons. In order to secure this more sober voice in the legislative process, Senators are required to be at least thirty years of age and to own property valued at a minimum of $4,000 in the province they represent. Unlike the members of the lower house who are elected, Senators are appointed by the Governor General in Council and enjoy permanent tenure until age seventy-five.[35]

Most of the factors which function to restrict the role of the House of Commons in the policy process apply also to the Senate. Specifically, the Senate cannot compete with the cabinet as a priority setter, and it lacks the expertise to become deeply involved in policy formulation. There are, however, even more handicaps placed on the policy role of the Senate than on that of the House of Commons. First of all, a Senator is not elected to office as is an MP, but is appointed by the government at the time when a vacancy occurs. This has meant traditionally that the party in power appoints people who have shown themselves to be faithful: Liberal governments have appointed Liberals, and Conservative governments have appointed Conservatives, much to the annoyance of the NDP which is virtually unrepresented in the upper house. The effect of this partisan pattern of Senate appointments has been to deny the Senate both the legitimacy enjoyed by the House by virtue of popular election and the respect which would accrue to a body which is independent of partisanship. In recent times there has been less reluctance to appoint Senators from non-government parties and from among people who have been basically non-partisan in their politics, but this has not been done often enough to give us a standard for evaluating its effect on the role or effectiveness of the upper chamber.

Another weakness of the Senate has been the tendency to offer Senate posts largely to people whose useful political lives have terminated. As a reward for many years of faithful service to the party, an old politician is "retired" by being put in the Senate. Because of this tendency, the image of the Senate is that of an "old folks' home" for tired and retired party faithfuls, an image which severely restricts the prestige of the upper house. Again the more recent

---

[35] Until 1965, tensure was for life. Senators appointed before that date have the option today of staying on or retiring at age 75. Any Senator appointed since 1965 must retire at age 75.

trends may somewhat counter this opinion. First, the appointment to the Senate of people such as Eugene Forsey, whose useful lives are hardly at an end, has greatly enhanced the prestige of the upper house in the eyes of the public and in the eyes of public officials.[36] Second, the Senate has been used several times in recent years to provide a home base in Ottawa, an office on Parliament Hill and a secure, if modest, income for important party backroom people. Senators Keith Davey and Lowell Murray, the leading political strategists for the Liberal and Conservative parties, are the foremost examples. Another way in which a younger group was being introduced into the Senate will likely not take hold in Canada. This was the appointment to the Senate of "frontbench losers," potential cabinet ministers who could not get elected to the House of Commons, as a device for getting them into the cabinet. Although it has the effect of bringing younger people into the Senate, this ploy has been seen as impugning the electoral process and as spurning the will of the public, by appointing people to high political office when they have been rejected explicitly in a democratic election.

The Senate is not permitted constitutionally to introduce money bills, and in practice it cannot amend or defeat money bills either. (There is still some question as to the constitutionality of Senate amendments of money bills, but in practical terms the Senate does not even attempt to amend them today.) Because of the lack of government ministers in the Senate, virtually all government bills are by convention introduced in the House of Commons. It is increasingly rare for the Senate even to attempt to amend a government bill that has been passed by the lower house, let alone to defeat it. While the Senate is legally empowered to make substantive amendments to or even to defeat government legislation passed by the House of Commons, and although Senators occasionally brandish this threat as a way to get ministerial attention or minor amendments, the legitimacy of any significant interference by the Senate in the policy process is questionable in a system that values popular sovereignty. The important exception to this is the device of having Senate committees study the subject matter of all government bills (including money bills) before they are introduced in the Senate, and while they are being considered in the House. Through this procedure the Senate can suggest amendments to the government which, if accepted, can then be presented to the House of Commons for approval before the bill actually reaches the Senate. In this way the wisdom to be found among

---

[36] The irony here is that Forsey was forced to give up his seat at age 75 because of the 1965 amendment, even though he was one of the most active Senators at the time of his retirement.

the Senators can be brought to bear profitably on government proposals without raising the spectre of an appointed body amending the wishes of the elected representatives of the people who sit in the lower house.

Despite the fact that the Senate is not a very active institution in the Canadian policy process today, there are a few items on the positive side of the ledger. Most important, the Senate does most of the parliamentary work involved in private bills, giving the overworked House of Commons more time for dealing with government legislation. Secondly, committees of the Senate are becoming more and more involved in investigations of political problems that might otherwise be left to Royal Commissions. An example of the use of a Senate committee in a pre-legislative investigatory role is the 1970-71 study done on the mass media in Canada. Because the Senate is less involved in the politics of the day, it can conduct such studies without the danger of sensationalism and "grandstanding" on the part of the committee people which might occur if the same investigation were undertaken by the more "political" House of Commons. Also, of course, the House of Commons simply would not have the time to conduct hearings in the leisurely fashion typical of the Senate. Thus, through Senate committees, the Canadian upper house can contribute some meaningful inputs to the policy process and simultaneously relieve some of the pressure on the time of the House of Commons.

The Senate also performs an important function for the Canadian party system, in that it permits the party in power to retire party faithfuls without too seriously alienating them, or imposing on them financial disaster. The Senate is, in this sense, a convenient place for stacking "over-age pols" who might cause political embarrassment if permitted to continue in the House of Commons, or who might be forced back into the private sector at a rather advanced age. The importance of this function of the Senate should not be minimized, for it provides some slight job security for the politician. A politician, particularly a cabinet minister, who manages to retire while his or her party is in office is likely to get either a Senate seat or some other patronage position. As a consequence, the politician need not constantly pander to private interests in the hope that they might be future employers when his or her days in politics are done.

By way of conclusion to these brief remarks about the Senate, it should be mentioned that reform or abolition of the upper house, has been considered continually since 1867. Some reforms have been tried, such as compulsory retirement at age 75, but functionally, the Senate has not changed significantly since Confederation. Basically, however, there is little that can be done in the way of incremental structural or procedural reform which will improve the Senate. If it is made elective, the House of Commons will be duplicated. We have an elected House already, and although the American system has a bicameral elective legislature, there is no reason to assume that one is needed here. If the Senate were abolished, there are functions that it performs today which would have to be taken over by the already overworked House of Commons.

We have seen earlier that there are also a number of current proposals for reform of the upper house which see it being converted to a "House of the Federation" or a "House of the Provinces." By giving all or part of the power to appoint the members of the upper chamber to the provincial governments themselves it is felt that the Senate can be made more representative of regional interests within the central government, thus revitalizing both the moribund upper house and the ailing federal system in one fell swoop! The problem however is that a more powerful Senate would have to take power away from either the elected House of Commons or the unseen labyrinth of interjurisdictional institutions. While some diminution of the influence of the latter might be desirable, the transfer of power from the House of Commons—which is, after all, representative of all parts of Canada even if the government of the day is not—to a less directly elected body is a proposition which would require very careful scrutiny. On the other hand, if a House of the Provinces were to remain just a minor legislative partner in the federal parliament, the provinces would "catch on" to the fact that they were simply being given more extensive representation in a relatively powerless institution and under these circumstances their participation would be lukewarm at best.

Aside from such a radical restructuring the major hope for improvement, therefore, seems to rest in functional changes. If, instead of proliferating commissions and bureaucratic task forces to undertake investigations that should be non-partisan in focus and visible to the public, the government would delegate still more investigatory powers to the Senate and appoint more Senators who are capable of taking a vigorous role in this respect, the upper house might be given a more meaningful role in the policy process.[37]

THE LEGISLATIVE PROCESS: PARLIAMENT AND GOVERNMENT POLICY

Before discussing the steps a bill must pass in order to become law, some terminological clarification is necessary. Once a policy has been

[37] For further enlightenment on the role of the Senate, see F. A. Kunz, *The Modern Senate of Canada 1925-1963* (University of Toronto Press, Toronto, 1965); R. A. MacKay, *The Unreformed Senate of Canada* (Carleton Library, McClelland and Stewart, Toronto, 1963); R. M. Dawson, *The Government of Canada*, ch. 15.; and C. Campbell, *The Canadian Senate: A Lobby from Within* (Macmillan, Toronto, 1978).

formulated and a draft of the proposed legislation has been completed by the Department of Justice, it is then introduced in the House of Commons by the minister responsible for that particular subject area of policy. At this stage the policy proposal takes the form of a *bill*. When a bill has been passed by parliament it becomes an *act*, and after formal assent by the Governor General and proclamation, an act becomes *law*. Thus, although parliament may have some impact at any of several stages of the policy process, the *formal* involvement of parliament in the policy process is limited to converting bills introduced by the government into acts. This process naturally includes the refining of government policies and their ultimate conversion to formal outputs of the political system.

All bills introduced in parliament can be classed as either *public* or *private*, depending on whether their effect is intended to be general or specific. Private bills are aimed at altering the law only insofar as it affects an individual or a corporate individual. Examples of this kind of legislation are laws altering the charters of companies or incorporating companies. Most such private bills are introduced in the Senate where they are discussed and revised in detail by committees. Passage by the House of Commons is usually more or less perfunctory, with first, second and third reading virtually simultaneous. Private bills that have been passed by the Senate are frequently passed by the House of Commons in packages rather than individually, a practice which speeds up the process considerably.

Public bills, on the other hand, are intended to have a general effect and to alter the law as it affects all Canadians. Public bills take up by far the largest amount of parliamentary time, for it is by such measures that government policies are converted to outputs of the system. Most of the legislation passed by parliament can be classed as public, examples being the Canada Water Act, the Canada Pension Act, the Canadian Grain Act, etc. Public bills, because they generally involve the implementation of government policy, are introduced in the House of Commons by the minister concerned. In contrast with private bills, public bills provide the focal points for heated partisan debate in the House of Commons.

As noted above, most public bills originate with the government and hence are referred to as *government bills*. There are, however, provisions in the rules and procedures of the House of Commons for the introduction of public bills by individual MPs. This type of public bill is a *private member's bill*, signifying that it is the creation of an individual MP and has nothing to do with the government or government policy. [Note here that "private members' " bills are completely different from "private" bills, the former term signifying the originators of the legislative proposals and the latter signifying their intended applications.] Private members' bills, although procedurally a part of the parliamentary process, seldom go very far in the House of Commons, in fact, it is rare indeed for a private member's bill to go beyond first reading, unless the government likes the idea and adopts it as its own policy. This does not happen often, and it is possible to say with confidence that consideration of private members' bills does not constitute an important part of the policy role of parliament.

The high mortality rate of private members' bills results from the fact that only four hours per week (one hour each day except Wednesday) are devoted to private members' business.[38] There is usually a long list of private members who wish to introduce their "pet bills," and they all must take turns in spending the allotted one-hour units of private members' time debating their proposals. Once a member has used a private members' hour to introduce a bill, the member's name drops to the bottom of the long list and he or she doesn't get another chance until everyone else has had a turn. The result is that most private members' bills are introduced, debated for one hour, and never dealt with again. Bills accorded this treatment are said to have been "talked out." At the end of the parliamentary session, any government or private members' bills which are not completely passed by parliament lapse and must be reintroduced at the next session.

It would be misleading, however, to limit our assessment of private members' bills to their function in the policy process. The more important function of the private member's bill is that it permits the MP to state publicly the policy proposals he or she considers important and feels the government is ignoring. Such bills are often passed down the line for consideration by bureaucrats, who may eventually incorporate the ideas in government bills. The MP can, in other words, put on the record a point of view on a certain policy area. Furthermore, by introducing a bill which favours the constituency's interests, the MP can publicize problems which exist there and are, perhaps, unique. In this way, the MP can use the private member's bill as a device to assist in the performance of the representative, or ombudsman, function that was discussed earlier. In the past, opposition members have often utilized the private members' hours to perform the general audit function of parliament. By raising contentious issues through the introduction of a private member's bill, an opposition member can attempt to embarrass the government without committing the opposition as a whole to a firm stand on the issue. Thus it can be concluded that, although the private member's bill is not important as a category of legislative proposals to be considered by

[38] S.O. 15(4).

parliament, it is a useful device for criticizing the government's policy priorities and for publicizing special problems and needs within certain regions and constituencies of the country.[39]

Government bills occupy the lion's share of the time available in the Canadian House of Commons, and it is the passage of these bills which must be considered at greater length as part of the policy process. The procedures for dealing with government bills differ slightly depending on whether or not the legislation in question involves the spending or raising of public money. Money bills, such as the Main Supply Bill or tax amendments, cannot constitutionally be introduced in the Senate, and while there is no similar restriction on *non-money bills,* virtually all government bills are introduced in the House of Commons simply because most of the cabinet members sit there. With these few points by way of introduction, let us now follow the passage of a government bill through parliament.

Government bills are introduced by a minister in the House of Commons upon a *motion for leave* which specifies the title of the bill and which may include a brief explanation of the provisions of the proposed legislation. After forty-eight hours the bill may then be given *first reading;* this occurs in a non-debatable and non-amendable motion, "That this bill be read a first time and be printed."[40] First reading is very much a pro-forma stage in the process and simply serves to get the legislation before the House. The bill is then printed in both languages and made available to the members of the House.

Second reading of the bill takes place on a motion by the Minister that it be granted second reading and referred to the appropriate Standing Committee. The motion is debatable but not amendable, and the focus of second reading is upon the *principle* of the legislation. When the debate is concluded the motion is voted on and the bill stands as referred to a Standing Committee. The only exception here is that Ways and Means and Supply bills are referred to the Committees of the Whole after second reading.

The committee stage involves a clause by clause consideration of the legislation. The committee takes the main role in refining the legislation, and when its deliberations are concluded, the bill as amended, is reported back to the House of Commons. The *report stage* provides the members with the opportunity to move amendments to the bill. After twenty-four hours notice of the intentions to move an

---

[39] For an excellent discussion of the significance of Private Members' bills, see Stewart Hyson, "The Role of the Backbencher—an Analysis of Private Members' Bills in the Canadian House of Commons," *Parliamentary Affairs,* vol. XXVII, no. 3, Summer 1974, pp. 262-272.

[40] S.O. 74(5).

amendment, any MP may "amend, delete, insert or restore any clause"[41] of the bill. These amendments are debatable, each member having the opportunity to speak once for twenty minutes, except that the Prime Minister, leader of the opposition, the sponsoring minister of the bill, and the member moving the amendment may speak for forty minutes.

The report stage gives the greatest opportunity to stall for time in an attempt to pressure the government to make changes. If there are a lot of amendments and if all opposition MPs were to speak their allotted twenty minutes on the amendment, the House could be tied up for a long period of time indeed. The only defense against this sort of "filibuster" is for the government to invoke "closure" or to secure time limits on the debate by the use of Standing Order 75(c), both being procedures which are so heavy-handed that the government is loath to use them. The Speaker has the power to combine amendments that are similar in intent in an effort to streamline the procedures at the report stage but even this does not very effectively restrict the power of the opposition to use up valuable time in an effort to force concessions on the government.

When the report stage is concluded, the minister moves "that the bill as amended be concurred in."[42] This motion is not amendable or debatable. Third reading is moved, usually at the next sitting of the House and while the motion to read the bill for a third time is debatable and while general amendments are allowed, this stage of the process is normally pretty perfunctory.

After third reading the bill then goes to the Senate where it is also given three readings and committee hearings. If the Senate amends the legislation it must come back to the House for approval or rejection of the Senate changes, although if there were a stalemate between the Senate and the House, the legislation would end up dying on the order paper. When the Senate is finished with the bill it is presented to the Governor General for Royal Assent. Depending upon what is provided for in the bill itself, the legislation may stand *proclaimed* immediately or it may take effect at a later date.

This concludes our discussion of the role of parliament in the Canadian political system. Parliament performs an important function in refining and legitimizing legislation which was usually "dreamt up" elsewhere and given priority by the cabinet. As we have seen the role of parliament at other stages of the policy process is a sharply circumscribed one. Parliament is important as an ombudsman, as an elec-

[41] S.O. 74(12).
[42] S.O. 74(12).

toral college, and as an auditor of the government's record. Its symbolic position as the focus—around which revolve the more active parts of the policy-making process—is vital to the way Canadians relate to their political system, but one must be careful not to base the evaluation of parliament as an institution on a misapprehension about its role in the policy process. Parliament plays a central role in Canadian politics, but it is not the role usually ascribed to it at service club luncheons.

APPENDIX I

A Consolidation of the British North America Acts 1867 to 1975*

FOREWORD

The law embodied in the *British North America Act, 1867* has been altered many times otherwise than by direct amendment, not only by the Parliament of the United Kingdom, but also by the Parliament of Canada and the legislatures of the provinces in those cases where provisions of the British North America Act are expressed to be subject to alteration by Parliament or the legislatures, as the case may be. A consolidation of the British North America Acts with only such subsequent enactments as directly alter the text of the Act would therefore not produce a true statement of the law.

In preparing this consolidation an attempt has been made to reflect accurately the substance of the law contained in the series of enactments known as the British North America Acts and other enactments modifying the provisions of the original *British North America Act, 1867.*

The various classes of enactments modifying the original text of the *British North America Act, 1867,* have been dealt with as follows:

I. DIRECT AMENDMENTS

1. *Repeals*

Repealed provisions (e.g. section 2) have been deleted from the text and quoted in a footnote.

2. *Amendments*

Amended provisions (e.g. section 4) are reproduced in the text in their amended form and the original provisions are quoted in a footnote.

3. *Additions*

Added provisions (e.g. section 51A) are included in the text.

4. *Substitutions*

Substituted provisions (e.g. section 18) are included in the text, and the former provision is quoted in a footnote.

II. INDIRECT AMENDMENTS

1. *Alterations by United Kingdom Parliament*

Provisions altered by the United Kingdom Parliament otherwise than by direct amendment (e.g. section 21) are included in the text in their altered form, and the original provision is quoted in a footnote.

2. *Additions by United Kingdom Parliament*

Constitutional provisions added otherwise than by the insertion of additional provisions in the British North America Act (e.g. provisions of the *British North America, 1871* authorizing Parliament to legislate for any territory not included in a province) are not incorporated in the text, but the additional provisions are quoted in an appropriate footnote.

3. *Alterations by Parliament of Canada*

Provisions subject to alteration by the Parliament of Canada (e.g. section 37) have been included in the text in their altered form, wherever possible, but where this was not feasible (e.g. section 40) the original section has been retained in the text and a footnote reference made to the Act of the Parliament of Canada effecting the alteration.

4. *Alterations by the Legislatures*

Provisions subject to alteration by legislatures of the provinces, either by virtue of specific authority (e.g. sections 83, 84) or by virtue of head 1 of section 92 (e.g. sections 70, 72), have been included in the text in their original form, but the footnotes refer to the provincial enactments effecting the alteration. Amendments to provincial enactments are not referred to; these may be readily found by consulting the indexes to provincial statutes. The enactments of the original provinces only are referred to; there are corresponding enactments by the provinces created at a later date.

III. SPENT PROVISIONS

Footnote references are made to those sections that are spent or are probably spent. For example, section 119 became spent by lapse of time and the footnote reference so indicates; on the other hand, section 140 is probably spent, but short of examining all statutes passed before Confederation there would be no way of ascertaining definitely whether or not the section is spent; the footnote reference therefore indicates the section as being probably spent.

The enactments of the United Kingdom Parliament or the Parliament of Canada, and Orders in Council admitting territories, referred to in the footnotes, may be found in Appendix II to the Revised Statutes of Canada, 1970, and in the subsequent sessional volumes of the statutes of Canada.

The reader will notice inconsistencies in the capitalization of nouns. It was originally the practice to capitalize the first letter of all nouns in British Statutes and the *British North America Act, 1867,* was so written, but this practice was discontinued and was never followed in Canadian statutes. In the original provisions included in this consolidation nouns are written as they were enacted.

THE BRITISH NORTH AMERICA ACT, 1867

30 & 31 Victoria, c. 3.

(Consolidated with amendments)

An Act for the Union of Canada, Nova Scotia, and New Brunswick, and the Government thereof; and for Purposes connected therewith.

(29th March, 1867.)

WHEREAS the Provinces of Canada, Nova Scotia and New Brunswick have expressed their Desire to be federally united into One Dominion under the Crown of the United Kingdom of Great Britain and Ireland, with a Constitution similar in Principle to that of the United Kingdom:

And whereas such a Union would conduce to the Welfare of the Provinces and promote the Interests of the British Empire:

And whereas on the Establishment of the Union by Authority of Parliament it is expedient, not only that the Constitution of the Legislative Authority in the Dominion be provided for, but also that the Nature of the Executive Government therein be declared:

And whereas it is expedient that Provision be made for the eventual Admission into the Union of other Parts of British North America: (1)

I.—PRELIMINARY.

1. This Act may be cited as The British North America Act, 1867. Short title.

2. Repealed. (2)

---

(1) The enacting clause was repealed by the *Statute Law Revision Act. 1893*, 56-57 Vict., c 14 (U.K). It read as follows:

> Be it therefore enacted and declared by the Queen's Most Excellent Majesty, by and with the Advice and Consent of the Lords Spiritual and Temporal, and Commons, in this present Parliament assembled, and by the Authority of the same, as follows:

(2) Section 2, repealed by the *Statute Law Revision Act, 1893*, 56-57 Vict., c. 14 (U.K.), read as follows:

> **2.** The Provisions of this Act referring to Her Majesty the Queen extend also to the Heirs and Successors of Her Mamesty, Kings and Queens of the United Kingdom of Great Britain and Ireland.

II.—UNION.

Declaration of
Union.

3. It shall be lawful for the Queen, by and with the Advice of Her Majesty's Most Honourable Privy Council, to declare by Proclamation that, on and after a Day therein appointed, not being more than Six Months after the passing of this Act, the Provinces of Canada, Nova Scotia, and New Brunswick shall form and be One Dominion under the Name of Canada; and on and after that Day those Three Provinces shall form and be One Dominion under that Name accordingly. (3)

Construction of
subsequent
Provisions of
Act.

4. Unless it is otherwise expressed or implied, the Name Canada shall be taken to mean Canada as constituted under this Act. (4)

Four Provinces.

5. Canada shall be divided into Four Provinces, named Ontario, Quebec, Nova Scotia, and New Brunswick. (5)

---

(3) The first day of July, 1867, was fixed by proclamation dated May 22, 1867.

(4) Partially repealed by the *Statute Law Revision Act, 1893*, 56-57 Vict., c. 14 (U.K.). As originally enacted the section read as follows:

> **4.** The subsequent Provisions of this Act, shall, unless it is otherwise expressed or implied, commence and have effect on and after the Union, that is to say, on and after the Day appointed for the Union taking effect in the Queen's Proclamation; and in the same Provisions, unless it is otherwise expressed or implied, the Name Canada shall be taken to mean Canada as constituted under this Act.

(5) Canada now consists of ten provinces (Ontario, Quebec, Nova Scotia, New Brunswick, Manitoba, British Columbia, Prince Edward Island, Alberta, Saskatchewan and Newfoundland) and two territories (the Yukon Territory and the Northwest Territories).

The first territories added to the Union were Rupert's Land and the North-Western Territory, (subsequently designated the Northwest Territories), which were admitted pursuant to section 146 of the *British North America Act, 1867* and the *Rupert's Land Act, 1868*, 31-32 Vict., c. 105 (U.K.), by Order in Council of June 23, 1870, effective July 15, 1870. Prior to the admission of these territories the Parliament of Canada enacted the *Act for the temporary Government of Rupert's Land and the North-Western Territory when united with Canada* (32-33 Vict., c. 3), and the *Manitoba Act* (33 Vict., c. 3), which provided for the formation of the Province of Manitoba.

British Columbia was admitted into the Union pursuant to section 146 of the *British North America Act, 1867*, by Order in Council of May 16, 1871, effective July 20, 1871.

Prince Edward Island was admitted pursuant to section 146 of the *British North America Act, 1867*, by Order in Council of June 26, 1873, effective July 1, 1873.

On June 29, 1871, the United Kingdom Parliament enacted the *British North America Act, 1871* (34-35 Vict., c. 28) authorizing the creation of additional provinces out of territories not included in any province. Pursuant to this statute, the Parliament of Canada enacted *The Alberta Act*, (July 20, 1905, 4-5 Edw. VII, c. 3) and *The Saskatchewan Act*, (July 20, 1905, 4-5 Edw. VII, c. 42), providing for the creation of the provinces of Alberta and Saskatchewan respectively. Both these Acts came into force on Sept. 1, 1905.

Meanwhile, all remaining British possessions and territories in North America and the islands adjacent thereto, except the colony of Newfoundland and its dependencies, were admitted into the Canadian Confederation by Order in Council dated July 31, 1880.

The Parliament of Canada added portions of the Northwest Territories to the adjoining provinces in 1912 by *The Ontario Boundaries Extension Act*, 2 Geo. V, c. 40, *The Quebec Boundaries Extension Act, 1912*, 2 Geo. V, c. 45 and *The Manitoba Boundaries Extension Act, 1912*, 2 Geo. V, c. 32, and further additions were made to Manitoba by *The Manitoba Boundaries Extension Act, 1930*, 20-21 Geo. V, c. 28.

The Yukon Territory was created out of the Northwest Territories in 1898 by *The Yukon Territory Act*, 61 Vict., c. 6, (Canada).

Newfoundland was added on March 31, 1949, by the *British North America Act, 1949*, (U.K.), 12-13 Geo. VI, c. 22, which ratified the Terms of Union between Canada and Newfoundland.

6. The Parts of the Province of Canada (as it exists at the passing of this Act) which formerly constituted respectively the Provinces of Upper Canada and Lower Canada shall be deemed to be severed, and shall form Two separate Provinces. The Part which formerly constituted the Province of Upper Canada shall constitute the Province of Ontario; and the Part which formerly constituted the Province of Lower Canada shall constitute the Province of Quebec. *Provinces of Ontario and Quebec.*

7. The Provinces of Nova Scotia and New Brunswick shall have the same Limits as at the passing of this Act. *Provinces of Nova Scotia and New Brunswick.*

8. In the general Census of the Population of Canada which is hereby required to be taken in the Year One thousand eight hundred and seventy-one, and in every Tenth Year thereafter, the respective Populations of the Four Provinces shall be distinguished. *Decennial Census.*

III.—EXECUTIVE POWER.

9. The Executive Government and Authority of and over Canada is hereby declared to continue and be vested in the Queen. *Declaration of Executive Power in the Queen.*

10. The Provisions of this Act referring to the Governor General extend and apply to the Governor General for the Time being of Canada, or other the Chief Executive Officer or Administrator for the Time being carrying on the Government of Canada on behalf and in the Name of the Queen, by whatever Title he is designated. *Application of Provisions referring to Governor General.*

11. There shall be a Council to aid and advise in the Government of Canada, to be styled the Queen's Privy Council for Canada; and the Persons who are to be Members of that Council shall be from Time to Time chosen and summoned by the Governor General and sworn in as Privy Councillors, and Members thereof may be from Time to Time removed by the Governor General. *Constitution of Privy Council for Canada.*

12. All Powers, Authorities, and Functions which under any Act of the Parliament of Great Britain, or of the Parliament of the United Kingdom of Great Britain and Ireland, or of the Legislature of Upper Canada, Lower Canada, Canada, Nova Scotia, or New Brunswick, are at the Union vested in or exerciseable by the respective Governors or Lieutenant Governors of those Provinces, with the Advice, or with the Advice and Consent, of the respective Executive Councils thereof, or in conjunction with those Councils, or with any Number of Members thereof, or by those Governors or Lieutenant Governors individually, shall, as far as the same continue in existence and capable of being exercised after the Union in relation to the Government of Canada, be vested in and exerciseable by the Governor General, with the Advice or with the Advice and Consent of or in conjunction with the *All Powers under Acts to be exercised by Governor General with Advice of Privy Council, or alone.*

Queen's Privy Council for Canada, or any Member thereof, or by the Governor General individually, as the Case requires, subject nevertheless (except with respect to such as exist under Acts of the Parliament of Great Britain or of the Parliament of the United Kingdom of Great Britain and Ireland) to be abolished or altered by the Parliament of Canada. (6)

Application of Provisions referring to Governor General in Council.

13. The Provisions of this Act referring to the Governor General in Council shall be construed as referring to the Governor General acting by and with the Advice of the Queen's Privy Council for Canada.

Power to Her Majesty to authorize Governor General to appoint Deputies.

14. It shall be lawful for the Queen, if Her Majesty thinks fit, to authorize the Governor General from Time to Time to appoint any Person or any Persons jointly or severally to be his Deputy or Deputies within any Part or Parts of Canada, and in that Capacity to exercise during the Pleasure of the Governor General such of the Powers, Authorities, and Functions of the Governor General as the Governor General deems it necessary or expedient to assign to him or them, subject to any Limitations or Directions expressed or given by the Queen; but the Appointment of such a Deputy or Deputies shall not affect the Exercise by the Governor General himself of any Power, Authority or Function.

Command of armed Forces to continue to be vested in the Queen.

15. The Command-in-Chief of the Land and Naval Militia, and of all Naval and Military Forces, of and in Canada, is hereby declared to continue and be vested in the Queen.

Seat of Government of Canada.

16. Until the Queen otherwise directs, the Seat of Government of Canada shall be Ottawa.

IV.—LEGISLATIVE POWER.

Constitution of Parliament of Canada.

17. There shall be One Parliament for Canada, consisting of the Queen, an Upper House styled the Senate, and the House of Commons.

Privileges, etc., of Houses.

18. The privileges, immunities, and powers to be held, enjoyed, and exercised by the Senate and by the House of Commons, and by the Members thereof respectively, shall be such as are from time to time defined by Act of the Parliament of Canada, but so that any Act of the Parliament of Canada defining such privileges, immunities, and powers shall not confer any privileges, immunities, or powers exceeding those at the passing of such Act held, enjoyed, and exercised by the Commons House of Parliament of the

(6) See the notes to section 129, *infra*.

United Kingdom of Great Britain and Ireland, and by the Members thereof. (7)

19. The Parliament of Canada shall be called together not later than Six Months after the Union. (8)

20. There shall be a Session of the Parliament of Canada once at least in every Year, so that Twelve Months shall not intervene between the last Sitting of the Parliament in one Session and its first Sitting in the next Session. (9)

The Senate.

21. The Senate shall, subject to the Provisions of this Act, consist of One Hundred and four Members, who shall be styled Senators. (10)

22. In relation to the Constitution of the Senate Canada shall be deemed to consist of Four Divisions:—

1. Ontario;
2. Quebec;
3. The Maritime Provinces, Nova Scotia and New Brunswick, and Prince Edward Island;
4. The Western Provinces of Manitoba, British Columbia, Saskatchewan, and Alberta;

which Four Divisions shall (subject to the Provisions of this Act) be equally represented in the Senate as follows: Ontario by twenty-four senators; Quebec by twenty-four senators; the Maritime Provinces and Prince Edward Island by twenty-four senators, ten thereof representing Nova Scotia, ten thereof representing New Brunswick, and four thereof representing Prince Edward Island; the Western Provinces by

---

(7) Repealed and re-enacted by the *Parliament of Canada Act, 1875*, 38-39 Vict., c. 38 (U.K.). The original section read as follows:

> **18.** The Privileges Immunities, and Powers to be held, enjoyed, and exercised by the Senate and by the House of Commons and by the Members thereof respectively shall be such as are from Time to Time defined by Act of the Parliament of Canada, but so that the same shall never exceed those at the passing of this Act held, enjoyed, and exercised by the Commons House of Parliament of the United Kingdom of Great Britain and Ireland and by the Members thereof.

(8) Spent. The first session of the first Parliament began on November 6, 1867.

(9) The term of the twelfth Parliament was extended by the *British North America Act, 1916*, 6-7 Geo. V, c. 19 (U.K.), which Act was repealed by the *Statute Law Revision Act, 1927*, 17-18 Geo. V, c. 42 (U.K.).

(10) As amended by the *British North America Act, 1915*, 5-6 Geo. V, c. 45 (U.K.), and modified by the *British North America Act, 1949*, 12-13 Geo. VI, c. 22 (U.K.), and the *British North America Act, (No. 2) 1975*, S.C. 1974-75-76, c. 53.

The original section read as follows:

> **21.** The Senate shall, subject to the Provisions of this Act, consist of Seventy-two Members, who shall be styled Senators.

The *Manitoba Act* added two for Manitoba; the Order in Council admitting British Columbia added three; upon admission of Prince Edward Island four more were provided by section 147 of the *British North America Act, 1867*; *The Alberta Act* and *The Saskatchewan Act* each added four. The Senate was reconstituted at 96 by the *British North America Act, 1915*, six more Senators were added upon union with Newfoundland, and one Senator each was added for the Yukon Territory and the Northwest Territories by the *British North America Act, (No. 2) 1975*.

twenty-four senators, six thereof representing Manitoba, six thereof representing British Columbia, six thereof representing Saskatchewan, and six thereof representing Alberta; Newfoundland shall be entitled to be represented in the Senate by six members; the Yukon Territory and the Northwest Territories shall be entitled to be represented in the Senate by one member each.

In the Case of Quebec each of the Twenty-four Senators representing that Province shall be appointed for One of the Twenty-four Electoral Divisions of Lower Canada specified in Schedule A. to Chapter One of the Consolidated statutes of Canada. (11)

Qualifications of Senator.

23. The Qualification of a Senator shall be as follows:

(1) He shall be of the full age of Thirty Years:

(2) He shall be either a natural-born Subject of the Queen, or a Subject of the Queen naturalized by an Act of the Parliament of Great Britain, or of the Parliament of the United Kingdom of Great Britain and Ireland, or of the Legislature of One of the Provinces of Upper Canada, Lower Canada, Canada, Nova Scotia, or New Brunswick, before the Union, or of the Parliament of Canada, after the Union:

(3) He shall be legally or equitably seised as of Freehold for his own Use and Benefit of Lands or Tenements held in Free and Common Socage, or seised or possessed for his own Use and Benefit of Lands or Tenements held in Franc-alleu or in Roture, within the Province for which he is appointed, of the Value of Four thousand Dollars, over and above all Rents, Dues, Debts, Charges, Mortgages, and Incumbrances due or payable out of or charged on or affecting the same:

(4) His Real and Personal Property shall be together worth Four thousand Dollars over and above his Debts and Liabilities:

---

(11) As amended by the *British North America Act, 1915,* the *British North America Act, 1949,* 12-13 Geo. VI, c. 22 (U.K.), and the *British North America Act, (No. 2) 1975,* S.C. 1974-75-76, c. 53. The original section read as follows:

22. In relation to the Constitution of the Senate, Canada shall be deemed to consist of Three Divisions:

1. Ontario;

2. Quebec;

3. The Maritime Provinces, Nova Scotia and New Brunswick; which Three Divisions shall (subject to the Provisions of this Act) be equally represented in the Senate as follows: Ontario by Twenty-four Senators; Quebec by Twenty-four Senators; and the Maritime Provinces by Twenty-four Senators, Twelve thereof representing Nova Scotia, and Twelve thereof representing New Brunswick.

In the case of Quebec each of the Twenty-four Senators representing that Province shall be appointed for One of the Twenty-four Electoral Divisions of Lower Canada specified in Schedule A. to Chapter One of the Consolidated Statutes of Canada.

(5) He shall be resident in the Province for which he is appointed:

(6) In the Case of Quebec he shall have his Real Property Qualification in the Electoral Division for which he is appointed, or shall be resident in that Division. (11A)

24. The Governor General shall from Time to Time, in the Queen's Name, by Instrument under the Great Seal of Canada, summon qualified Persons to the Senate; and, subject to the Provisions of this Act, every Person so summoned shall become and be a Member of the Senate and a Senator.

Summons of Senator.

25. Repealed. (12)

26. If at any Time on the Recommendation of the Governor General the Queen thinks fit to direct that Four or Eight Members be added to the Senate, the Governor General may by Summons to Four or Eight qualified Persons (as the Case may be), representing equally the Four Divisions of Canada, add to the Senate accordingly. (13)

Addition of Senators in certain cases.

27. In case of such Addition being at any Time made, the Governor General shall not summon any Person to the Senate, except upon a further like Direction by the Queen on the like Recommendation, to represent one of the Four Divisions until such Division is represented by Twenty-four Senators and no more. (14)

Reduction of Senate to normal Number.

(11A) Section 2 of the *British North America Act, (No. 2) 1975,* S.C. 1974-75-76, c. 53 provided that for the purposes of that Act (which added one Senator each for the Yukon Territory and the Northwest Territories) the term "Province" in section 23 of the *British North America Act, 1867,* has the same meaning as is assigned to the term "province" by section 28 of the *Interpretation Act,* R.S.C. 1970, c. I-23, which provides that the term "province" means "a province of Canada, and includes the Yukon Territory and the Northwest Territories."

(12) Repealed by the *Statute Law Revision Act, 1893,* 56-57 Vict., 14 (U.K.). The section read as follows:

> **25.** Such Persons shall be first summoned to the Senate as the Queen by Warrant under Her Majesty's Royal Sign Manual thinks fit to approve, and their Names shall be inserted in the Queen's Proclamation of Union.

(13) As amended by the *British North America Act, 1915,* 5-6 Geo. V, c. 45 (U.K.). The original section read as follows:

> **26.** If at any Time on the Recommendation of the Governor General the Queen thinks fit to direct that Three or Six Members be added to the Senate, the Governor General may by Summons to Three or Six qualified Persons (as the Case may be), representing equally the Three Divisions of Canada, add to the Senate accordingly.

(14) As amended by the *British North America Act, 1915,* 5-6 Geo. V, c. 45 (U.K.). The original section read as follows:

> **27.** In case of such Addition being at any Time made the Governor General shall not summon any Person to the Senate, except on a further like Direction by the Queen on the like Recommendation, until each of the Three Divisions of Canada is represented by Twenty-four Senators and no more.

Maximum Number of Senators.

28. The Number of Senators shall not at any Time exceed One Hundred and twelve. (15)

Tenure of Place in Senate.

29. (1) Subject to subsection (2), a Senator shall, subject to the provisions of this Act, hold his place in the Senate for life.

Retirement upon attaining age of seventy-five years.

(2) A Senator who is summoned to the Senate after the coming into force of this subsection shall, subject to this Act, hold his place in the Senate until he attains the age of seventy-five years. (15A)

Resignation of Place in Senate.

30. A Senator may by Writing under his Hand addressed to the Governor General resign his Place in the Senate, and thereupon the same shall be vacant.

Disqualification of Senators.

31. The Place of a Senator shall become vacant in any of the following Cases:

(1) If for Two consecutive Sessions of the Parliament he fails to give his Attendance in the Senate:

(2) If he takes an Oath or makes a Declaration or Acknowledgment of Allegiance, Obedience, or Adherence to a Foreign Power, or does an Act whereby he becomes a Subject or Citizen, or entitled to the Rights or Privileges of a Subject or Citizen, of a Foreign Power:

(3) If he is adjudged Bankrupt or Insolvent, or applies for the Benefit of any Law relating to Insolvent Debtors, or becomes a public Defaulter:

(4) If he is attainted of Treason or convicted of Felony or of any infamous Crime:

(5) If he ceases to be qualified in respect of Property or of Residence; provided, that a Senator shall not be deemed to have ceased to be qualified in respect of Residence by reason only of his residing at the Seat of the Government of Canada while holding an Office under that Government requiring his Presence there.

Summons on Vacancy in Senate.

32. When a Vacancy happens in the Senate by Resignation, Death, or otherwise, the Governor General shall by Summons to a fit and qualified Person fill the Vacancy.

---

(15) As amended by the *British North America Act, 1915*, 5-6 Geo. V, c. 45 (U.K.), and the *British North America Act, (No. 2) 1975*, S.C. 1974-75-76, c. 53. The original section read as follows:

28. The Number of Senators shall not at any Time exceed Seventy-eight.

(15A) As enacted by the *British North America Act, 1965*, Statutes of Canada, 1965, c. 4 which came into force on the 1st of June 1965. The original section read as follows:

29. A Senator shall, subject to the Provisions of this Act, hold his Place in the Senate for Life.

33. If any Question arises respecting the Qualification of a Senator or a Vacancy in the Senate the same shall be heard and determined by the Senate.

34. The Governor General may from Time to Time, by Instrument under the Great Seal of Canada, appoint a Senator to be Speaker of the Senate, and may remove him and appoint another in his Stead. (16)

35. Until the Parliament of Canada otherwise provides, the Presence of at least Fifteen Senators, including the Speaker, shall be necessary to constitute a Meeting of the Senate for the Exercise of its Powers.

36. Questions arising in the Senate shall be decided by a Majority of Voices, and the Speaker shall in all Cases have a Vote, and when the Voices are equal the Decision shall be deemed to be in the Negative.

The House of Commons.

37. The House of Commons shall, subject to the Provisions of this Act, consist of two hundred and eighty-two members of whom ninety-five shall be elected for Ontario, seventy-five for Quebec, eleven for Nova Scotia, ten for New Brunswick, fourteen for Manitoba, twenty-eight for British Columbia, four for Prince Edward Island, twenty-one for Alberta, fourteen for Saskatchewan, seven for Newfoundland, one for the Yukon Territory and two for the Northwest Territories. (17)

38. The Governor General shall from Time to Time, in the Queen's Name, by Instrument under the Great Seal of Canada, summon and call together the House of Commons.

39. A Senator shall not be capable of being elected or of sitting or voting as a Member of the House of Commons.

---

(16) Provision for exercising the functions of Speaker during his absence is made by the *Speaker of the Senate Act*, R.S.C. 1970, c. S-14. Doubts as to the power of Parliament to enact such an Act were removed by the *Canadian Speaker (Appointment of Deputy) Act, 1895*, 59 Vict., c. 3, (U.K.).

(17) The figures given here would result from the application of section 51, as enacted by the *British North America Act, 1974*, S.C. 1974-75-76, c. 13 and amended by the *British North America Act, 1975*, S.C. 1974-75-76, c. 28. At press time effect had not yet been given to this readjustment as contemplated by the *Electoral Boundaries Readjustment Act*, R.S.C. 1970, c. E-2. Section 6 of the *Representation Act, 1974* provides that the number of members of the House of Commons and the representation of the provinces therein on the thirtieth day of December, 1974, remain unchanged until adjusted pursuant to section 51(1). As of that date the number of members was 264, as follows: 88 for Ontario, 74 for Quebec, 11 for Nova Scotia, 10 for New Brunswick, 13 for Manitoba, 23 for British Columbia, 4 for Prince Edward Island, 19 for Alberta, 13 for Saskatchewan, 7 for Newfoundland, 1 for the Yukon Territory, and 1 for the Northwest Territories. The original section (which was altered from time to time as the result of the addition of new provinces and changes in population) read as follows:

> 37. The House of Commons shall, subject to the Provisions of this Act, consist of one hundred and eighty-one members, of whom Eighty-two shall be elected for Ontario, Sixty-five for Quebec, Nineteen for Nova Scotia, and Fifteen for New Brunswick.

Electoral
districts of the
Four Provinces.

40. Until the Parliament of Canada otherwise provides, Ontario, Quebec, Nova Scotia, and New Brunswick shall, for the Purposes of the Election of Members to serve in the House of Commons, be divided into Electoral Districts as follows:

1.—ONTARIO.

Ontario shall be divided into the Counties, Ridings of Counties, Cities, Parts of Cities, and Towns enumerated in the First Schedule to this Act, each whereof shall be an Electoral District, each such District as numbered in that Schedule being entitled to return One Member.

2.—QUEBEC.

Quebec shall be divided into Sixty-five Electoral Districts, composed of the Sixty-five Electoral Divisions into which Lower Canada is at the passing of this Act divided under Chapter Two of the Consolidated Statutes of Canada, Chapter Seventy-five of the Consolidated Statutes for Lower Canada, and the Act of the Province of Canada of the Twenty-third Year of the Queen, Chapter One, or any other Act amending the same in force at the Union, so that each such Electoral Division shall be for the Purposes of this Act an Electoral District entitled to return One Member.

3.—NOVA SCOTIA.

Each of the Eighteen Counties of Nova Scotia shall be an Electoral District. The County of Halifax shall be entitled to return Two Members, and each of the other Counties One Member.

4.—NEW BRUNSWICK.

Each of the Fourteen Counties into which New Brunswick is divided, including the City and County of St. John, shall be an Electoral District. The City of St. John shall also be a separate Electoral District. Each of those Fifteen Electoral Districts shall be entitled to return One Member. (18)

Continuance of
existing
Election Laws
until Parlia-
ment of Canada
otherwise
provides.

41. Until the Parliament of Canada otherwise provides, all Laws in force in the several Provinces at the Union relative to the following Matters or any of them, namely,— the Qualifications and Disqualifications of Persons to be elected or to sit or vote as Members of the House of Assembly or Legislative Assembly in the several Provinces, the Voters at Elections of such Members, the Oaths to be taken by Voters, the Returning Officers, their Powers and Duties, the Proceedings at Elections, the Periods during

---

(18) Spent. The electoral districts are now established by Proclamations issued from time to time under the *Electoral Boundaries Readjustment Act*, R.S.C., c. 1970, E-2, as amended for particular districts by Acts of Parliament, for which see the most recent Table of Public Statutes.

which Elections may be continued, the Trial of controverted Elections, and Proceedings incident thereto, the vacating of Seats of Members, and the Execution of new Writs in case of Seats vacated otherwise than by Dissolution,—shall respectively apply to Elections of Members to serve in the House of Commons for the same several Provinces.

Provided that, until the Parliament of Canada otherwise provides, at any Election for a Member of the House of Commons for the District of Algoma, in addition to Persons qualified by the Law of the Province of Canada to vote, every Male British Subject, aged Twenty-one Years or upwards, being a Householder, shall have a Vote.(19)

42. Repealed. (20)

43. Repealed. (21)

44. The House of Commons on its first assembling after a General Election shall proceed with all practicable Speed to elect One of its Members to be Speaker.

As to Election of Speaker of House of Commons.

45. In case of a Vacancy happening in the Office of Speaker by Death, Resignation, or otherwise, the House of Commons shall with all practicable Speed proceed to elect another of its Members to be Speaker.

As to filling up Vacancy in Office of Speaker.

46. The Speaker shall preside at all Meetings of the House of Commons.

Speaker to preside.

47. Until the Parliament of Canada otherwise provides, in case of the Absence for any Reason of the Speaker from the Chair of the House of Commons for a Period of Forty-eight

Provision in case of Absence of Speaker.

---

(19) Spent. Elections are now provided for by the *Canada Elections Act*, R.S.C. 1970 (1st Supp.), c. 14; controverted elections by the *Dominion Controverted Elections Act*, R.S.C. 1970, c. C-28; qualifications and disqualifications of members by the *House of Commons Act*, R.S.C. 1970, c. H-9 and the *Senate and House of Commons Act*, R.S.C. 1970, c. S-8.

(20) Repealed by the *Statute Law Revision Act, 1893*, 56-57 Vict., c. 14 (U.K.). The section read as follows:

> **42.** For the First Election of Members to serve in the House of Commons the Governor General shall cause Writs to be issued by such Person, in such Form, and addressed to such Returning Officers as he thinks fit.
>
> The Person issuing Writs under this Section shall have the like Powers as are possessed at the Union by the Officers charged with the issuing of Writs for the Election of Members to serve in the respective House of Assembly or Legislative Assembly of the Province of Canada, Nova Scotia, or New Brunswick; and the Returning Officers to whom Writs are directed under this Section shall have the like Powers as are possessed at the Union by the Officers charged with the returning of Writs for the Election of Members to serve in the same respective House of Assembly or Legislative Assembly.

(21) Repealed by the *Statute Law Revision Act, 1893*, 56-57 Vict., c. 14 (U.K.) The section read as follows:

> **43.** In case a Vacancy in the Representation in the House of Commons of any Electoral District happens before the Meeting of the Parliament, or after the Meeting of the Parliament before Provision is made by the Parliament in this Behalf, the Provisions of the last foregoing Section of this Act shall extend and apply to the issuing and returning of a Writ in respect of such vacant District.

consecutive Hours, the House may elect another of its Members to act as Speaker, and the Member so elected shall during the Continuance of such Absence of the Speaker have and execute all the Powers, Privileges, and Duties of Speaker. (22)

Quorum of House of Commons.

48. The Presence of at least Twenty Members of the House of Commons shall be necessary to constitute a Meeting of the House for the Exercise of its Powers, and for that Purpose the Speaker shall be reckoned as a Member.

Voting in House of Commons.

49. Questions arising in the House of Commons shall be decided by a Majority of Voices other than that of the Speaker, and when the Voices are equal, but not otherwise, the Speaker shall have a Vote.

Duration of House of Commons.

50. Every House of Commons shall continue for Five Years from the Day of the Return of the Writs for choosing the House (subject to be sooner dissolved by the Governor General), and no longer.

Readjustment of representation in Commons.

51. (1) The number of members of the House of Commons and the representation of the provinces therein shall upon the coming into force of this subsection and thereafter on the completion of each decennial census be readjusted by such authority, in such manner, and from such time as the Parliament of Canada from time to time provides, subject and according to the following Rules:

Rules.

1. There shall be assigned to Quebec seventy-five members in the readjustment following the completion of the decennial census taken in the year 1971, and thereafter four additional members in each subsequent readjustment.

2. Subject to Rules 5(2) and (3), there shall be assigned to a large province a number of members equal to the number obtained by dividing the population of the large province by the electoral quotient of Quebec.

3. Subject to Rules 5(2) and (3), there shall be assigned to a small province a number of members equal to the number obtained by dividing
(*a*) the sum of the populations, determined according to the results of the penultimate decennial census, of the provinces (other than Quebec) having populations of less than one and a half million, determined according to the results of that census, by the sum of the numbers of members assigned to those provinces in the readjustment following the completion of that census; and

---

(22) Provision for exercising the functions of Speaker during his absence is now made by the *Speaker of the House of Commons Act*, R.S.C. 1970, c. S-13.

(*b*) the population of the small province by the quotient obtained under paragraph (*a*).

4. Subject to Rules 5(1)(*a*), (2) and (3), there shall be assigned to an intermediate province a number of members equal to the number obtained

(*a*) by dividing the sum of the populations of the provinces (other than Quebec) having populations of less than one and a half million by the sum of the number of members assigned to those provinces under any of Rules 3, 5(1)*b*), (2) and (3);

(*b*) by dividing the population of the intermediate province by the quotient obtained under paragraph (*a*); and

(*c*) by adding to the number of members assigned to the intermediate province in the readjustment following the completion of the penultimate decennial census one-half of the difference resulting from the subtraction of that number from the quotient obtained under paragraph (*b*).

5. (1) On any readjustment,

(*a*) if no province (other than Quebec) has a population of less than one and a half million, Rule 4 shall not be applied and, subject to Rules 5(2) and (3), there shall be assigned to an intermediate province a number of members equal to the number obtained by dividing

(i) the sum of the populations, determined according to the results of the penultimate decennial census, of the provinces (other than Quebec) having populations of not less than one and a half million and not more than two and a half million, determined according to the results of that census, by the sum of the numbers of members assigned to those provinces in the readjustment following the completion of that census, and

(ii) the population of the intermediate province by the quotient obtained under subparagraph (i);

(*b*) if a province (other than Quebec) having a population of

(i) less than one and a half million, or

(ii) not less than one and a half million and not more than two and a half million

does not have a population greater than its population determined according to the results of the penultimate decennial census, it shall, subject to Rules 5(2) and (3), be assigned the number of members assigned to it in the readjustment following the completion of that census.

(2) On any readjustment,

(*a*) if, under any of Rules 2 to 5(1), the number of members to be assigned to a province (in this paragraph referred to as "the first province") is smaller than the number of members to be assigned to any other province not having a population greater than that of the first province, those Rules shall not be applied to the first province and it shall be assigned a number of members equal to the largest number of members to be assigned to any other province not having a population greater than that of the first province;

(*b*) if, under any of Rules 2 to 5(1)(*a*), the number of members to be assigned to a province is smaller than the number of members assigned to it in the readjustment following the completion of the penultimate decennial census, those Rules shall not be applied to it and it shall be assigned the latter number of members;

(*c*) if both paragraphs (*a*) and (*b*) apply to a province, it shall be assigned a number of members equal to the greater of the numbers produced under those paragraphs.

(3) On any readjustment,

(*a*) if the electoral quotient of a province (in this paragraph referred to as "the first province") obtained by dividing its population by the number of members to be assigned to it under any of Rules 2 to 5(2) is greater than the electoral quotient of Quebec, those Rules shall not be applied to the first province and it shall be assigned a number of members equal to the number obtained by dividing its population by the electoral quotient of Quebec;

(*b*) if, as a result of the application of Rule 6(2)(*a*), the number of members assigned to a province under paragraph (*a*) equals the number of members to be assigned to it under any of Rules 2 to 5(2), it shall be assigned that number of members and paragraph (*a*) shall cease to apply to that province.

6. (1) In these Rules,

"electoral quotient" means, in respect of a province, the quotient obtained by dividing its population, determined according to the results of the then most recent decennial census, by the number of members to be assigned to it under any of Rules 1 to 5(3) in the readjustment following the completion of that census;

"intermediate province" means a province (other than Quebec) having a population greater than its population determined according to the results of the penultimate decennial census but not more than two and a half million and not less than one and a half million;

"large province" means a province (other than Quebec) having a population greater than two and a half million;

"penultimate decennial census" means the decennial census that preceded the then most recent decennial census;

"population" means, except where otherwise specified, the population determined according to the results of the then most recent decennial census;

"small province" means a province (other than Quebec) having a population greater than its population determined according to the results of the penultimate decennial census and less than one and a half million.

(2) For the purposes of these Rules,

(*a*) if any fraction less than one remains upon completion of the final calculation that produces the number of members to be assigned to a province, that number of members shall equal the number so produced disregarding the fraction;

(*b*) if more than one readjustment follows the completion of a decennial census, the most recent of those readjustments shall, upon taking effect, be deemed to be the only readjustment following the completion of that census;

(*c*) a readjustment shall not take effect until the termination of the then existing Parliament. (23)

---

(23) As enacted by the *British North America Act 1974*, S.C. 1974-75-76, c. 13, which came into force on December 31, 1974. The section, as originally enacted, read as follows:

> **51.** On the Completion of the Census in the Year One Thousand eight hundred and seventy-one, and of each subsequent decennial Census, the Representation of the Four Provinces shall be readjusted by such Authority, in such Manner, and from such Time, as the Parliament of Canada from Time to Time provides, subject and according to the following Rules:
>
> (1) Quebec shall have the fixed Number of Sixty-five Members:
>
> (2) There shall be assigned to each of the other Provinces such a Number of Members as will bear the same Proportion to the Number of its Population (ascertained at such Census) as the Number Sixty-five bears to the Number of the Population of Quebec (so ascertained):
>
> (3) In the Computation of the Number of Members for a Province a fractional Part not exceeding One Half of the whole Number requisite for entitling the Province to a Member shall be disregarded; but a fractional Part exceeding One Half of that Number shall be equivalent to the whole Number:
>
> (4) On any such Re-adjustment the Number of Members for a Province shall not be reduced unless the Proportion which the Number of the Population of the Province bore to the Number of the aggregate Population of Canada at the then last preceding Re-adjustment of the Number of Members for the Province is ascertained at the then latest Census to be diminished by One Twentieth Part or upwards:
>
> (5) Such Re-adjustment shall not take effect until the Termination of the then existing Parliament.

The section was amended by the *Statute Law Revision Act, 1893*, 56-57 Vict., c. 14 (U.K.) by repealing the words from "of the census" to "seventy-one and" and the word "subsequent".

By the *British North America Act, 1943*, 6-7 Geo VI, c. 30 (U.K.) redistribution of seats following the 1941 census was postponed until the first session of Parliament after the war. The section was re-enacted by the *British North America Act, 1946*, 9-10 Geo. VI, c. 63 (U.K.) to read as follows:

> **51.** (1) The number of members of the House of Commons shall be two hundred and fifty-five and the representation of the provinces therein shall forthwith upon the coming into force of this section and thereafter on the completion of each decennial

census be readjusted by such authority, in such manner, and from such time as the Parliament of Canada from time to time provides, subject and according to the following rules:—

(1) Subject as hereinafter provided, there shall be assigned to each of the provinces a number of members computed by dividing the total population of the provinces by two hundred and fifty-four and by dividing the population of each province by the quotient so obtained, disregarding, except as hereinafter in this section provided, the remainder, if any, after the said process of division.

(2) If the total number of members assigned to all the provinces pursuant to rule one is less than two hundred and fifty-four, additional members shall be assigned to the provinces (one to a province) having remainders in the computation under rule one commencing with the province having the largest remainder and continuing with the other provinces in the order of the magnitude of their respective remainders until the total number of members assigned is two hundred and fifty-four.

(3) Notwithstanding anything in this section, if upon completion of a computation under rules one and two, the number of members to be assigned to a province is less than the number of senators representing the said province, rules one and two shall cease to apply in respect of the said province, and there shall be assigned to the said province a number of members equal to the said number of senators.

(4) In the event that rules one and two cease to apply in respect of a province then, for the purpose of computing the number of members to be assigned to the provinces in respect of which rules one and two continue to apply, the total population of the provinces shall be reduced by the number of the population of the province in respect of which rules one and two have ceased to apply and the number two hundred and fifty-four shall be reduced by the number of members assigned to such province pursuant to rule three.

(5) Such readjustment shall not take effect until the termination of the then existing Parliament.

(2) The Yukon Territory as constituted by Chapter forty-one of the Statutes of Canada, 1901, together with any Part of Canada not comprised within a province which may from time to time be included therein by the Parliament of Canada for the purposes of representation in Parliament, shall be entitled to one member.

The section was re-enacted by the *British North America Act, 1952*, S.C. 1952, c. 15 as follows:

51. (1) Subject as hereinafter provided, the number of members of the House of Commons shall be two hundred and sixty-three and the representation of the provinces therein shall forthwith upon the coming into force of this section and thereafter on the completion of each decennial census be readjusted by such authority, in such manner, and from such time as the Parliament of Canada from time to time provides, subject and according to the following rules:

1. There shall be assigned to each of the provinces a number of members computed by dividing the total population of the provinces by two hundred and sixty-one and by dividing the population of each province by the quotient so obtained, disregarding, except as hereinafter in this section provided, the remainder, if any, after the said process of division.

2. If the total number of members assigned to all the provinces pursuant to rule one is less than two hundred and sixty-one, additional members shall be assigned to the provinces (one to a province) having remainders in the computation under rule one commencing with the province having the largest remainder and continuing with the other provinces in the order of the magnitude of their respective remainders until the total number of members assigned is two hundred and sixty-one.

3. Notwithstanding anything in this section, if upon completion of a computation under rules one and two the number of members to be assigned to a province is less than the number of senators representing the said province, rules one and two shall cease to apply in respect of the said province, and there shall be assigned to the said province a number of members equal to the said number of senators.

4. In the event that rules one and two cease to apply in respect of a province then, for the purposes of computing the number of members to be assigned to the provinces in respect of which rules one and two continue to apply, the total population of the provinces shall be reduced by the number of the population of the province in respect of which rules one and two have ceased to apply and the number two hundred and sixty-one shall be reduced by the number of members assigned to such province pursuant to rule three.

5. On any such readjustment the number of members for any province shall not be reduced by more than fifteen per cent below the representation to which such province was entitled under rules one to four of this subsection at the last preceding readjustment of the representation of that province, and

(2) The Yukon Territory as bounded and described in the schedule to chapter Y-2 of the Revised Statutes of Canada, 1970, shall be entitled to one member, and the Northwest Territories as bounded and described in section 2 of chapter N-22 of the Revised Statutes of Canada, 1970, shall be entitled to two members. (24)

Yukon Territory and Northwest Territories.

51A. Notwithstanding anything in this Act a province shall always be entitled to a number of members in the House of Commons not less than the number of senators representing such province. (25)

Constitution of House of Commons.

52. The Number of Members of the House of Commons may be from Time to Time increased by the Parliament of Canada, provided the proportionate Representation of the Provinces prescribed by this Act is not thereby disturbed.

Increase of Number of House of Commons.

Money Votes; Royal Assent.

53. Bills for appropriating any Part of the Public Revenue, or for imposing any Tax or Impost, shall originate in the House of Commons.

Appropriation and Tax Bills.

54. It shall not be lawful for the House of Commons to adopt or pass any Vote, Resolution, Address, or Bill for the Appropriation of any Part of the Public Revenue, or of any Tax or Impost, to any Purpose that has not been first recommended to that House by Message of the Governor General in the Session in which such Vote, Resolution, Address, or Bill is proposed.

Recommendation of Money Votes.

55. Where a Bill passed by the Houses of the Parliament is presented to the Governor General for the Queen's Assent, he shall declare, according to his Discretion, but subject to the Provisions of this Act and to Her Majesty's Instructions, either that he assents thereto in the Queen's Name, or that he withholds the Queen's Assent, or that he reserves the Bill for the Signification of the Queen's Pleasure.

Royal Assent to Bills, etc.

---

there shall be no reduction in the representation of any province as a result of which that province would have a smaller number of members than any other province that according to the results of the then last decennial census did not have a larger population; but for the purposes of any subsequent readjustment of representation under this section any increase in the number of members of the House of Commons resulting from the application of this rule shall not be included in the divisor mentioned in rules one to four of this subsection.

6. Such readjustment shall not take effect until the termination of the then existing Parliament.

(2) The Yukon Territory as constituted by chapter forty-one of the statutes of Canada, 1901, shall be entitled to one member, and such other part of Canada not comprised within a province as may from time to time be defined by the Parliament of Canada shall be entitled to one member.

(24) As enacted by the *British North America Act, 1975*, S.C. 1974-75-76, c. 28.

(25) As enacted by the *British North America Act, 1915*, 5-6 Geo. V, c. 45 (U.K.).

Disallowance by Order in Council of Act assented to by Governor General.

56. Where the Governor General assents to a Bill in the Queen's Name, he shall by the first convenient Opportunity send an authentic Copy of the Act to one of Her Majesty's Principal Secretaries of State, and if the Queen in Council within Two Years after Receipt thereof by the Secretary of State thinks fit to disallow the Act, such Disallowance (with a Certificate of the Secretary of State of the Day on which the Act was received by him) being signified by the Governor General, by Speech or Message to each of the Houses of the Parliament or by Proclamation, shall annul the Act from and after the Day of such Signification.

Signification of Queen's Pleasure on Bill reserved.

57. A Bill reserved for the Signification of the Queen's Pleasure shall not have any Force unless and until, within Two Years from the Day on which it was presented to the Governor General for the Queen's Assent, the Governor General signifies, by Speech or Message to each of the Houses of the Parliament or by Proclamation, that it has received the Assent of the Queen in Council.

An Entry of every such Speech, Message, or Proclamation shall be made in the Journal of each House, and a Duplicate thereof duly attested shall be delivered to the proper Officer to be kept among the Records of Canada.

V.—PROVINCIAL CONSTITUTIONS.

Executive Power.

Appointment of Lieutenant Governors of Provinces.

58. For each Province there shall be an Officer, styled the Lieutenant Governor, appointed by the Governor General in Council by Instrument under the Great Seal of Canada.

Tenure of Office of Lieutenant Governor.

59. A Lieutenant Governor shall hold Office during the Pleasure of the Governor General; but any Lieutenant Governor appointed after the Commencement of the First Session of the Parliament of Canada shall not be removeable within Five Years from his Appointment, except for Cause assigned, which shall be communicated to him in Writing within One Month after the Order for his Removal is made, and shall be communicated by Message to the Senate and to the House of Commons within One Week thereafter if the Parliament is then sitting, and if not then within One Week after the Commencement of the next Session of the Parliament.

Salaries of Lieutenant Governors.

60. The Salaries of the Lieutenant Governors shall be fixed and provided by the Parliament of Canada. (26)

Oaths, etc., of Lieutenant Governor.

61. Every Lieutenant Governor shall, before assuming the Duties of his Office, make and subscribe before the Governor

---

(26) Provided for by the *Salaries Act*, R.S.C. 1970, c. S-2.

General or some Person authorized by him Oaths of Allegiance and Office similar to those taken by the Governor General.

62. The Provisions of this Act referring to the Lieutenant Governor extend and apply to the Lieutenant Governor for the Time being of each Province, or other the Chief Executive Officer or Administrator for the Time being carrying on the Government of the Province, by whatever Title he is designated.

Application of provisions referring to Lieutenant Governor.

63. The Executive Council of Ontario and of Quebec shall be composed of such Persons as the Lieutenant Governor from Time to Time thinks fit, and in the first instance of the following Officers, namely,—the Attorney General, the Secretary and Registrar of the Province, the Treasurer of the Province, the Commissioner of Crown Lands, and the Commissioner of Agriculture and Public Works, with in Quebec the Speaker of the Legislative Council and the Solicitor General. (27)

Appointment of Executive Officers for Ontario and Quebec.

64. The Constitution of the Executive Authority in each of the Provinces of Nova Scotia and New Brunswick shall, subject to the Provisions of this Act, continue as it exists at the Union until altered under the Authority of this Act. (28)

Executive Government of Nova Scotia and New Brunswick.

65. All Powers, Authorities, and Functions which under any Act of the Parliament of Great Britain, or of the Parliament of the United Kingdom of Great Britain and Ireland, or of the Legislature of Upper Canada, Lower Canada, or Canada, were or are before or at the Union vested in or exerciseable by the respective Governors or Lieutenant Governors of those Provinces, with the Advice or with the Advice and Consent of the respective Executive Councils thereof, or in conjunction with those Councils, or with any Number of Members thereof, or by those Governors or Lieutenant Governors individually, shall, as far as the same are capable of being exercised after the Union in relation to the Government of Ontario and Quebec respectively, be vested in and shall or may be exercised by the Lieutenant Governor of Ontario and Quebec respectively, with the Advice or with the Advice and Consent of or in conjunction with the respective Executive Councils, or any Members thereof, or by the Lieutenant Governor individually, as the Case requires, subject nevertheless (except with respect to such as exist under Acts of the Parliament of Great Britain, or of the Parliament of the

Powers to be exercised by Lieutenant Governor of Ontario or Quebec with Advice, or alone.

---

(27) Now provided for in Ontario by the *Executive Council Act,* R.S.O. 1970, c. 153, and in Quebec by the *Executive Power Act,* R.S.Q. 1964, c. 9.

(28) A similar provision was included in each of the instruments admitting British Columbia, Prince Edward Island, and Newfoundland. The Executive Authorities for Manitoba, Alberta and Saskatchewan were established by the statutes creating those provinces. See the footnotes to section 5, *supra.*

United Kingdom of Great Britain and Ireland,) to be abolished or altered by the respective Legislatures of Ontario and Quebec. (29)

Application of Provisions referring to Lieutenant Governor in Council.

66. The Provisions of this Act referring to the Lieutenant Governor in Council shall be construed as referring to the Lieutenant Governor of the Province acting by and with the Advice of the Executive Council thereof.

Administration in Absence, etc., of Lieutenant Governor.

67. The Governor General in Council may from Time to Time appoint an Administrator to execute the Office and Functions of Lieutenant Governor during his Absence, Illness, or other Inability.

Seats of Provincial Governments.

68. Unless and until the Executive Government of any Province otherwise directs with respect to that Province, the Seats of Government of the Provinces shall be as follows, namely,—of Ontario, the City of Toronto; of Quebec, the City of Quebec; of Nova Scotia, the City of Halifax; and of New Brunswick, the City of Fredericton.

Legislative Power.

1.—ONTARIO.

Legislature for Ontario.

69. There shall be a Legislature for Ontario consisting of the Lieutenant Governor and of One House, styled the Legislative Assembly of Ontario.

Electoral districts.

70. The Legislative Assembly of Ontario shall be composed of Eighty-two Members, to be elected to represent the Eighty-two Electoral Districts set forth in the First Schedule to this Act. (30)

2.—QUEBEC.

Legislature for Quebec.

71. There shall be a Legislature for Quebec consisting of the Lieutenant Governor and of Two Houses, styled the Legislative Council of Quebec and the Legislative Assembly of Quebec. (31)

Constitution of Legislative Council.

72. The Legislative Council of Quebec shall be composed of Twenty-four Members, to be appointed by the Lieutenant Governor, in the Queen's Name, by Instrument under the Great Seal of Quebec, One being appointed to represent each of the Twenty-four Electoral Divisions of Lower Canada in this Act referred to, and each holding Office for the Term of his Life, unless the Legislature of Quebec otherwise provides under the Provisions of this Act.

---

(29) See the notes to section 129, *infra.*

(30) Spent. Now covered by the *Representation Act,* R.S.O. 1970, c. 413.

(31) The Act respecting the Legislative Council of Quebec, S.Q. 1968, c. 9, provided that the Legislature for Quebec shall consist of the Lieutenant Governor and the National Assembly of Quebec, and repealed the provisions of the *Legislature Act,* R.S.Q. 1964, c. 6, relating to the Legislative Council of Quebec. Sections 72 to 79 following are therefore completely spent.

73. The Qualifications of the Legislative Councillors of Quebec shall be the same as those of the Senators for Quebec.

74. The Place of a Legislative Councillor of Quebec shall become vacant in the Cases, *mutatis mutandis*, in which the Place of Senator becomes vacant.

75. When a Vacancy happens in the Legislative Council of Quebec by Resignation, Death, or otherwise, the Lieutenant Governor, in the Queen's Name, by Instrument under the Great Seal of Quebec, shall appoint a fit and qualified Person to fill the Vacancy.

76. If any Question arises respecting the Qualification of a Legislative Councillor of Quebec, or a Vacancy in the Legislative Council of Quebec, the same shall be heard and determined by the Legislative Council.

77. The Lieutenant Governor may from Time to Time, by Instrument under the Great Seal of Quebec, appoint a Member of the Legislative Council of Quebec to be Speaker thereof, and may remove him and appoint another in his Stead.

78. Until the Legislature of Quebec otherwise provides, the Presence of at least Ten Members of the Legislative Council, including the Speaker, shall be necessary to constitute a Meeting for the Exercise of its Powers.

79. Questions arising in the Legislative Council of Quebec shall be decided by a Majority of Voices, and the Speaker shall in all Cases have a Vote, and when the Voices are equal the Decision shall be deemed to be in the Negative.

80. The Legislative Assembly of Quebec shall be composed of Sixty-five Members, to be elected to represent the Sixty-five Electoral Divisions or Districts of Lower Canada in this Act referred to, subject to Alteration thereof by the Legislature of Quebec: Provided that it shall not be lawful to present to the Lieutenant Governor of Quebec for Assent any Bill for altering the Limits of any of the Electoral Divisions or Districts mentioned in the Second Schedule to this Act, unless the Second and Third Readings of such Bill have been passed in the Legislative Assembly with the Concurrence of the Majority of the Members representing all those Electoral Divisions or Districts, and the Assent shall not be given to such Bill unless an Address has been presented by the Legislative Assembly to the Lieutenant Governor stating that it has been so passed. (32)

---

(32) The Act respecting electoral districts, S.Q. 1970, c. 7, s. 1, provides that this section no longer has effect.

3.—ONTARIO AND QUEBEC.

81. Repealed. (33)

Summoning of Legislative Assemblies.

82. The Lieutenant Governor of Ontario and of Quebec shall from Time to Time, in the Queen's Name, by Instrument under the Great Seal of the Province, summon and call together the Legislative Assembly of the Province.

Restriction on election of Holders of offices.

83. Until the Legislature of Ontario or of Quebec otherwise provides, a Person accepting or holding in Ontario or in Quebec any Office, Commission, or Employment, permanent or temporary, at the Nomination of the Lieutenant Governor, to which an annual Salary, or any Fee, Allowance, Emolument, or Profit of any Kind or Amount whatever from the Province is attached, shall not be eligible as a Member of the Legislative Assembly of the respective Province, nor shall he sit or vote as such; but nothing in this Section shall make ineligible any Person being a Member of the Executive Council of the respective Province, or holding any of the following Offices, that is to say, the Offices of Attorney General, Secretary and Registrar of the Province, Treasurer of the Province, Commissioner of Crown Lands, and Commissioner of Agriculture and Public Works, and in Quebec Solicitor General, or shall disqualify him to sit or vote in the House for which he is elected, provided he is elected while holding such Office. (34)

Continuance of existing Election Laws.

84. Until the Legislatures of Ontario and Quebec respectively otherwise provide, all Laws which at the Union are in force in those Provinces respectively, relative to the following Matters, or any of them, namely,—the Qualifications and Disqualifications of Persons to be elected or to sit or vote as Members of the Assembly of Canada, the Qualifications or Disqualifications of Voters, the Oaths to be taken by Voters, the Returning Officers, their Powers and Duties, the Proceedings at Elections, the Periods during which such Elections may be continued, and the Trial of controverted Elections and the Proceedings incident thereto, the vacating of the Seats of Members and the issuing and execution of new Writs in case of Seats vacated otherwise than by Dissolution,—shall respectively apply to Elections of Members to serve in the respective Legislative Assemblies of Ontario and Quebec.

Provided that, until the Legislature of Ontario otherwise provides, at any Election for a Member of the Legislative Assembly of Ontario for the District of Algoma, in addition

---

(33) Repealed by the *Statute Law Revision Act, 1893,* 56-57 Vict., c. 14 (U.K.). The section read as follows:

> 81. The Legislatures of Ontario and Quebec respectively shall be called together not later than Six Months after the Union.

(34) Probably spent. The subject-matter of this section is now covered in Ontario by the *Legislative Assembly Act,* R.S.O. 1970, c. 240, and in Quebec by the *Legislature Act,* R.S.Q. 1964, c. 6.

to Persons qualified by the Law of the Province of Canada to vote, every male British Subject, aged Twenty-one Years or upwards, being a Householder, shall have a vote. (35)

85. Every Legislative Assembly of Ontario and every Legislative Assembly of Quebec shall continue for Four Years from the Day of the Return of the Writs for choosing the same (subject nevertheless to either the Legislative Assembly of Ontario or the Legislative Assembly of Quebec being sooner dissolved by the Lieutenant Governor of the Province), and no longer. (36)

Duration of Legislative Assemblies.

86. There shall be a Session of the Legislature of Ontario and of that of Quebec once at least in every Year, so that Twelve Months shall not intervene between the last Sitting of the Legislature in each Province in one Session and its first Sitting in the next Session.

Yearly Session of Legislature.

87. The following Provisions of this Act respecting the House of Commons of Canada shall extend and apply to the Legislative Assemblies of Ontario and Quebec, that is to say,—the Provisions relating to the Election of a Speaker originally and on Vacancies, the Duties of the Speaker, the Absence of the Speaker, the Quorum, and the Mode of voting, as if those Provisions were here re-enacted and made applicable in Terms to each such Legislative Assembly.

Speaker, Quorum, etc.

4.—NOVA SCOTIA AND NEW BRUNSWICK.

88. The Constitution of the Legislature of each of the Provinces of Nova Scotia and New Brunswick shall, subject to the Provisions of this Act, continue as it exists at the Union until altered under the Authority of this Act. (37)

Constitutions of Legislatures of Nova Scotia and New Brunswick.

---

(35) Probably spent. The subject-matter of this section is now covered in Ontario by the *Election Act*, R.S.O. 1970, c. 142, the *Controverted Elections Act*, R.S.O. 1970, c. 84 and the *Legislative Assembly Act*, R.S.O. 1970, c. 240, in Quebec by the *Elections Act*, R.S.Q. 1964, c. 7, the *Provincial Controverted Elections Act*, R.S.Q. 1964, c. 8 and the *Legislature Act*, R.S.Q. 1964, c. 6.

(36) The maximum duration of the Legislative Assembly for Ontario and Quebec has been changed to five years by the *Legislative Assembly Act*, R.S.O. 1970, c. 240, and the *Legislature Act*, R.S.Q. 1964, c. 6 respectively.

(37) Partially repealed by the *Statute Law Revision Act, 1893*, 56-57 Vict., c. 14 (U.K.) which deleted the following concluding words of the original enactment:

> and the House of Assembly of New Brunswick existing at the passing of this Act shall, unless sooner dissolved, continue for the Period for which it was elected.

A similar provision was included in each of the instruments admitting British Columbia, Prince Edward Island, and Newfoundland. The Legislatures of Manitoba, Alberta and Saskatchewan were established by the statutes creating those provinces. See the footnotes to section 5, *supra*.

89. Repealed. (38)

6.—THE FOUR PROVINCES.

Application to Legislatures of Provisions respecting Money Votes, etc.

90. The following Provisions of this Act respecting the Parliament of Canada, namely,—the Provisions relating to Appropriation and Tax Bills, the Recommendation of Money Votes, the Assent to Bills, the Disallowance of Acts, and the Signification of Pleasure on Bills reserved,—shall extend and apply to the Legislatures of the several Provinces as if those Provisions were here re-enacted and made applicable in Terms to the respective Provinces and the Legislatures thereof, with the Substitution of the Lieutenant Governor of the Province for the Governor General, of the Governor General for the Queen and for a Secretary of State, of One Year for Two Years, and of the Province for Canada.

VI.—DISTRIBUTION OF LEGISLATIVE POWERS.

Powers of the Parliament.

Legislative Authority of Parliament of Canada.

91. It shall be lawful for the Queen, by and with the Advice and Consent of the Senate and House of Commons, to make Laws for the Peace, Order, and good Government of Canada, in relation to all Matters not coming within the Classes of Subjects by this Act assigned exclusively to the Legislatures of the Provinces; and for greater Certainty, but not so as to restrict the Generality of the foregoing Terms of this Section, it is hereby declared that (notwithstanding anything in this Act) the exclusive Legislative Authority of the Parliament of Canada extends to all Matters coming within the Classes of Subjects next herein-after enumerated; that is to say,—

1. The amendment from time to time of the Constitution of Canada, except as regards matters coming within the classes of subjects by this Act assigned exclusively to the Legislatures of the provinces, or as regards rights or privileges by this or any other Constitutional Act granted or secured to the Legislature or the Government of a province, or to any class of persons with respect to

---

(38) Repealed by the *Statute Law Revision Act, 1893*, 56-57 Vict., c. 14 (U.K.). The section read as follows:

5.—ONTARIO, QUEBEC, AND NOVA SCOTIA.

89. Each of the Lieutenant Governors of Ontario, Quebec and Nova Scotia shall cause Writs to be issued for the First Election of Members of the Legislative Assembly thereof in such Form and by such Person as he thinks fit, and at such Time and addressed to such Returning Officer as the Governor General directs, and so that the First Election of Member of Assembly for any Electoral District or any Subdivision thereof shall be held at the same Time and at the same Places as the Election for a Member to serve in the House of Commons of Canada for the Electoral District.

schools or as regards the use of the English or the French language or as regards the requirements that there shall be a session of the Parliament of Canada at least once each year, and that no House of Commons shall continue for more than five years from the day of the return of the Writs for choosing the House: provided, however, that a House of Commons may in time of real or apprehended war, invasion or insurrection be continued by the Parliament of Canada if such continuation is not opposed by the votes of more than one-third of the members of such House. (39)

1A. The Public Debt and Property. (40)
2. The Regulation of Trade and Commerce.
2A. Unemployment insurance. (41)
3. The raising of Money by any Mode or System of Taxation.
4. The borrowing of Money on the Public Credit.
5. Postal Service.
6. The Census and Statistics.
7. Militia, Military and Naval Service, and Defence.
8. The fixing of and providing for the Salaries and Allowances of Civil and other Officers of the Government of Canada.
9. Beacons, Buoys. Lighthouses, and Sable Island.
10. Navigation and Shipping.
11. Quarantine and the Establishment and Maintenance of Marine Hospitals.
12. Sea Coast and Inland Fisheries.
13. Ferries between a Province and any British or Foreign Country or between Two Provinces.
14. Currency and Coinage.
15. Banking, Incorporation of Banks, and the Issue of Paper Money.
16. Savings Banks.
17. Weights and Measures.
18. Bills of Exchange and Promissory Notes.
19. Interest.
20. Legal Tender.
21. Bankruptcy and Insolvency.
22. Patents of Invention and Discovery.
23. Copyrights.
24. Indians, and Lands reserved for the Indians.
25. Naturalization and Aliens.
26. Marriage and Divorce.

---

(39) Added by the *British North America (No. 2) Act, 1949*, 13 Geo. VI, c. 81 (U.K.).

(40) Re-numbered by the *British North America (No. 2) Act, 1949*.

(41) Added by the *British North America Act, 1940*, 3-4 Geo. VI, c. 36 (U.K.).

27. The Criminal Law, except the Constitution of Courts of Criminal Jurisdiction, but including the Procedure in Criminal Matters.

28. The Establishment, Maintenance, and Management of Penitentiaries.

29. Such Classes of Subjects as are expressly excepted in the Enumeration of the Classes of Subjects by this Act assigned exclusively to the Legislatures of the Provinces.

And any Matter coming within any of the Classes of Subjects enumerated in this Section shall not be deemed to come within the Class of Matters of a local or private Nature comprised in the Enumeration of the Classes of Subjects by this Act assigned exclusively to the Legislatures of the Provinces. (42)

---

(42) Legislative authority has been conferred on Parliament by other Acts as follows:

1. The *British North America Act, 1871,* 34-35 Vict., c. 28 (U.K.).

2. The Parliament of Canada, may from time to time establish new Provinces in any territories forming for the time being part of the Dominion of Canada, but not included in any Province thereof, and may, at the time of such establishment, make provision for the constitution and administration of any such Province, and for the passing of laws for the peace, order, and good government of such Province, and for its representation in the said Parliament.

3. The Parliament of Canada may from time to time, with the consent of the Legislature of any Province of the said Dominion, increase, diminish, or otherwise alter the limits of such Province, upon such terms and conditions as may be agreed to by the said Legislature, and may, with the like consent, make provision respecting the effect and operation of any such increase or diminution or alteration of territory in relation to any Province affected thereby.

4. The Parliament of Canada may from time to time make provision for the administration peace, order, and good government of any territory not for the time being included in any Province.

5. The following Acts passed by the said Parliament of Canada, and intituled respectively,—"An Act for the temporary government of Rupert's Land and the North Western Territory when united with Canada"; and "An Act to amend and continue the Act thirty-two and thirty-three Victoria, chapter three, and to establish and provide for the government of "the Province of Manitoba," shall be and be deemed to have been valid and effectual for all purposes whatsoever from the date at which they respectively received the assent, in the Queen's name, of the Governor General of the said Dominion of Canada.

6. Except as provided by the third section of this Act, it shall not be competent for the Parliament of Canada to alter the provisions of the last-mentioned Act of the said Parliament in so far as it relates to the Province of Manitoba, or of any other Act hereafter establishing new Provinces in the said Dominion, subject always to the right of the Legislature of the Province of Manitoba to alter from time to time the provisions of any law respecting the qualification of electors and members of the Legislative Assembly, and to make laws respecting elections in the said Province.

The *Rupert's Land Act 1868,* 31-32 Vict., c. 105 (U.K.) (repealed by the *Statute Law Revision Act, 1893,* 56-57 Vict., c. 14 (U.K.)) had previously conferred similar authority in relation to Rupert's Land and the North-Western Territory upon admission of those areas.

2. The *British North America Act, 1886,* 49-50 Vict., c. 35, (U.K.).

1. The Parliament of Canada may from time to time make provision for the representation in the Senate and House of Commons of Canada, or in either of them, of any territories which for the time being form part of the Dominion of Canada, but are not included in any province thereof.

3. The *Statute of Westminster, 1931,* 22 Geo. V, c. 4, (U.K.).

3. It is hereby declared and enacted that the Parliament of a Dominion has full power to make laws having extra-territorial operation.

Exclusive Powers of Provincial Legislatures.

92. In each Province the Legislature may exclusively make Laws in relation to Matters coming within the Classes of Subject next herein-after enumerated; that is to say,— *Subjects of exclusive Provincial Legislation.*

1. The Amendment from Time to Time, notwithstanding anything in this Act, of the Constitution of the Province, except as regards the Office of Lieutenant Governor.

2. Direct Taxation within the Province in order to the raising of a Revenue for Provincial Purposes.

3. The borrowing of Money on the sole Credit of the Province.

4. The Establishment and Tenure of Provincial Offices and the Appointment and Payment of Provincial Officers.

5. The Management and Sale of the Public Lands belonging to the Province and of the Timber and Wood thereon.

6. The Establishment, Maintenance, and Management of Public and Reformatory Prisons in and for the Province.

7. The Establishment, Maintenance, and Management of Hospitals, Asylums, Charities, and Eleemosynary Institutions in and for the Province, other than Marine Hospitals.

8. Municipal Institutions in the Province.

9. Shop, Saloon, Tavern, Auctioneer, and other Licences in order to the raising of a Revenue for Provincial, Local, or Municipal Purposes.

10. Local Works and Undertakings other than such as are of the following Classes:—

    (*a*) Lines of Steam or other Ships, Railways, Canals, Telegraphs, and other Works and Undertakings connecting the Province with any other or others of the Provinces, or extending beyond the Limits of the Province;

    (*b*) Lines of Steam Ships between the Province and any British or Foreign Country;

    (*c*) Such Works as, although wholly situate within the Province, are before or after their Execution declared by the Parliament of Canada to be for the general Advantage of Canada or for the Advantage of Two or more of the Provinces.

11. The Incorporation of Companies with Provincial Objects.

12. The Solemnization of Marriage in the Province.

13. Property and Civil Rights in the Province.

14. The Administration of Justice in the Province, including the Constitution, Maintenance, and Organization of Provincial Courts, both of Civil and of Criminal Jurisdiction, and including Procedure in Civil Matters in those Courts.

15. The Imposition of Punishment by Fine, Penalty, or Imprisonment for enforcing any Law of the Province made in relation to any Matter coming within any of the Classes of Subjects enumerated in this Section.

16. Generally all Matters of a merely local or private Nature in the Province.

Education.

Legislation respecting Education.

93. In and for each Province the Legislature may exclusively make Laws in relation to Education, subject and according to the following Provisions:—

(1) Nothing in any such Law shall prejudicially affect any Right or Privilege with respect to Denominational Schools which any Class of Persons have by Law in the Province at the Union:

(2) All the Powers, Privileges, and Duties at the Union by Law conferred and imposed in Upper Canada on the Separate Schools and School Trustees of the Queen's Roman Catholic Subjects shall be and the same are hereby extended to the Dissentient Schools of the Queen's Protestant and Roman Catholic Subjects in Quebec:

(3) Where in any Province a System of Separate or Dissentient Schools exists by Law at the Union or is thereafter established by the Legislature of the Province, an Appeal shall lie to the Governor General in Council from any Act or Decision of any Provincial Authority affecting any Right or Privilege of the Protestant or Roman Catholic Minority of the Queen's Subjects in relation to Education:

(4) In case any such Provincial Law as from Time to Time seems to the Governor General in Council requisite for the due Execution of the Provisions of this Section is not made, or in case any Decision of the Governor General in Council on any Appeal under this Section is not duly executed by the proper Provincial Authority in that Behalf, then and in every such Case, and as far only as the Circumstances of each Case require, the Parliament of Canada may make remedial Laws for the due Execution of the

Provisions of this Section and of any Decision of the
Governor General in Council under this Section. (43)

*Uniformity of Laws in Ontario, Nova Scotia and New
Brunswick.*

94. Notwithstanding anything in this Act, the Parliament
of Canada may make Provision for the Uniformity of all or
Legislation for
Uniformity of
Laws in Three
Provinces.

---

(43) Altered for Manitoba by section 22 of the *Manitoba Act*, 33 Vict., c. 3 (Canada),
(confirmed by the *British North America Act, 1871*), which reads as follows:

22. In and for the Province, the said Legislature may exclusively make Laws in
relation to Education, subject and according to the following provisions:—

(1) Nothing in any such Law shall prejudicially affect any right or privilege with
respect to Denominational Schools which any class of persons have by Law or
practice in the Province at the Union:

(2) An appeal shall lie to the Governor General in Council from any Act or
decision of the Legislature of the Province, or of any Provincial Authority, affecting
any right or privilege, of the Protestant or Roman Catholic minority of the Queen's
subjects in relation to Education:

(3) In case any such Provincial Law, as from time to time seems to the Governor
General in Council requisite for the due execution of the provisions of this section, is
not made, or in case any decision of the Governor General in Council on any appeal
under this section is not duly executed by the proper Provincial Authority in that
behalf, then, and in every such case, and as far only as the circumstances of each
case require, the Parliament of Canada may make remedial Laws for the due
execution of the provisions of this section, and of any decision of the Governor
General in Council under this section.

Altered for Alberta by section 17 of *The Alberta Act*, 4-5 Edw. VII, c. 3 which reads as follows:

17. Section 93 of The British North America Act, 1867, shall apply to the said
province, with the substitution for paragraph (1) of the said section 93 of the
following paragraph:—

(1) Nothing in any such law shall prejudicially affect any right or privilege with
respect to separate schools which any class of persons have at the date of the passing
of this Act, under the terms of chapters 29 and 30 of the Ordinances of the
Northwest Territories, passed in the year 1901, or with respect to religious instruction in any public or separate school as provided for in the said ordinances.

2. In the appropriation by the Legislature or distribution by the Government of
the province of any moneys for the support of schools organized and carried on in
accordance with the said chapter 29 or any Act passed in amendment thereof, or in
substitution therefor, there shall be no discrimination against schools of any class
described in the said chapter 29.

3. Where the expression "by law" is employed in paragraph 3 of the said section
93, it shall be held to mean the law as set out in the said chapters 29 and 30, and
where the expression "at the Union" is employed, in the said paragraph 3, it shall be
held to mean the date at which this Act comes into force.

Altered for Saskatchewan by section 17 of *The Saskatchewan* Act, 4-5 Edw. VII, c. 42, which
reads as follows:

17. Section 93 of the British North America Act, 1867, shall apply to the said
province, with the substitution for paragraph (1) of the said section 93, of the
following paragraph:—

(1) Nothing in any such law shall prejudicially affect any right or privilege with
respect to separate schools which any class of persons have at the date of the passing
of this Act, under the terms of chapters 29 and 30 of the Ordinances of the
Northwest Territories, passed in the year 1901, or with respect to religious instruction in any public or separate school as provided for in the said ordinances.

2. In the appropriation by the Legislature or distribution by the Government of
the province of any moneys for the support of schools organized and carried on in
accordance with the said chapter 29, or any Act passed in amendment thereof or in
substitution therefor, there shall be no discrimination against schools of any class
described in the said chapter 29.

3. Where the expression "by law" is employed in paragraph (3) of the said
section 93, it shall be held to mean the law as set out in the said chapters 29 and 30;
and where the expression "at the Union" is employed in the said paragraph (3), it
shall be held to mean the date at which this Act comes into force.

any of the Laws relative to Property and Civil Rights in Ontario, Nova Scotia, and New Brunswick, and of the Procedure of all or any of the Courts in Those Three Provinces, and from and after the passing of any Act in that Behalf the Power of the Parliament of Canada to make Laws in relation to any Matter comprised in any such Act shall, notwithstanding anything in this Act, be unrestricted; but any Act of the Parliament of Canada making Provision for such Uniformity shall not have effect in any Province unless and until it is adopted and enacted as Law by the Legislature thereof.

Old Age Pensions.

Legislation respecting old age pensions and supplementary benefits.

94A. The Parliament of Canada may make laws in relation to old age pensions and supplementary benefits, including survivors' and disability benefits irrespective of age, but no such law shall affect the operation of any law present or future of a provincial legislature in relation to any such matter. (44)

Agriculture and Immigration.

Concurrent Powers of Legislation respecting Agriculture, etc.

95. In each Province the Legislature may make Laws in relation to Agriculture in the Province, and to Immigration into the Province; and it is hereby declared that the Parliament of Canada may from Time to Time make Laws in relation to Agriculture in all or any of the Provinces, and to Immigration into all or any of the Provinces; and any Law of the Legislature of a Province relative to Agriculture or to Immigration shall have effect in and for the Province as long and as far only as it is not repugnant to any Act of the Parliament of Canada.

Altered by Term 17 of the Terms of Union of Newfoundland with Canada (confirmed by the *British North America Act, 1949*, 12-13 Geo. VI, c. 22 (UK.)), which reads as follows:

> **17.** In lieu of section ninety-three of the British North America Act, 1867, the following term shall apply in respect of the Province of Newfoundland:
>
> In and for the Province of Newfoundland the Legislature shall have exclusive authority to make laws in relation to education, but the Legislature will not have authority to make laws prejudicially affecting any right or privilege with respect to denominational schools, common (amalgamated) schools, or denominational colleges, that any class or classes of persons have by law in Newfoundland at the date of Union, and out of public funds of the Province of Newfoundland, provided for education,
>
> (a) all such schools shall receive their share of such funds in accordance with scales determined on a non-discriminatory basis from time to time by the Legislature for all schools then being conducted under authority of the Legislature; and
>
> (b) all such colleges shall receive their share of any grant from time to time voted for all colleges then being conducted under authority of the Legislature, such grant being distributed on a non-discriminatory basis.

(44) Added by the *British North America Act, 1964*, 12-13, Eliz. II, c. 73 (U.K.). Originally enacted by the *British North America Act, 1951*, 14-15 Geo. VI, c. 32 (U.K.), as follows:

> **94A.** It is hereby declared that the Parliament of Canada may from time to time make laws in relation to old age pensions in Canada, but no law made by the Parliament of Canada in relation to old age pensions shall affect the operation of any law present or future of a Provincial Legislature in relation to old age pensions.

VII.—JUDICATURE.

96. The Governor General shall appoint the Judges of the Superior, District, and County Courts in each Province, except those of the Courts of Probate in Nova Scotia and New Brunswick. *Appointment of Judges.*

97. Until the laws relative to Property and Civil Rights in Ontario, Nova Scotia, and New Brunswick, and the Procedure of the Courts in those Provinces, are made uniform, the Judges of the Courts of those Provinces appointed by the Governor General shall be selected from the respective Bars of those Provinces. *Selection of Judges in Ontario, etc.*

98. The Judges of the Courts of Quebec shall be selected from the Bar of that Province. *Selection of Judges in Quebec.*

99. (1) Subject to subsection two of this section, the Judges of the Superior Courts shall hold office during good behaviour, but shall be removable by the Governor General on Address of the Senate and House of Commons. *Tenure of office of Judges.*

(2) A Judge of a Superior Court, whether appointed before or after the coming into force of this section, shall cease to hold office upon attaining the age of seventy-five years, or upon the coming into force of this section if at that time he has already attained that age. (44A) *Termination at age 75.*

100. The Salaries, Allowances, and Pensions of the Judges of the Superior, District, and County Courts (except the Courts of Probate in Nova Scotia and New Brunswick), and of the Admiralty Courts in Cases where the Judges thereof are for the Time being paid by Salary, shall be fixed and provided by the Parliament of Canada. (45) *Salaries etc., of Judges.*

101. The Parliament of Canada may, notwithstanding anything in this Act, from Time to Time provide for the Constitution, Maintenance, and Organization of a General Court of Appeal for Canada, and for the Establishment of any additional Courts for the better Administration of the Laws of Canada. (46) *General Court of Appeal, etc.*

VIII.—REVENUES; DEBTS; ASSETS; TAXATION

102. All Duties and Revenues over which the respective Legislatures of Canada, Nova Scotia, and New Brunswick before and at the Union had and have Power of Appropria- *Creation of Consolidated Revenue Fund.*

(44A) Repealed and re-enacted by the *British North America Act, 1960,* 9 Eliz. II, c. 2 (U.K.), which came into force on the 1st day of March, 1961. The original section read as follows:

> **99.** The Judges of the Superior Courts shall hold Office during good Behaviour, but shall be removable by the Governor General on Address of the Senate and House of Commons.

(45) Now provided for in the *Judges Act,* R.S.C. 1970, c. J-1.

(46) See the *Supreme Court Act,* R.S.C. 1970, c. S-19, and the *Federal Court Act,* R.S.C. 1970, (2nd Supp.) c. 10.

tion, except such Portions thereof as are by this Act reserved to the respective Legislatures of the Provinces, or are raised by them in accordance with the special Powers conferred on them by this Act, shall form One Consolidated Revenue Fund, to be appropriated for the Public Service of Canada in the Manner and subject to the Charges in this Act provided.

Expenses of
Collection, etc.

103. The Consolidated Revenue Fund of Canada shall be permanently charged with the Costs, Charges, and Expenses incident to the Collection, Management, and Receipt thereof, and the same shall form the First Charge thereon, subject to be reviewed and audited in such Manner as shall be ordered by the Governor General in Council until the Parliament otherwise provides.

Interest of
Provincial
Public Debts.

104. The annual Interest of the Public Debts of the several Provinces of Canada, Nova Scotia, and New Brunswick at the Union shall form the Second Charge on the Consolidated Revenue Fund of Canada.

Salary of
Governor
General.

105. Unless altered by the Parliament of Canada, the Salary of the Governor General shall be Ten thousand Pounds Sterling Money of the United Kingdom of Great Britain and Ireland, payable out of the Consolidated Revenue Fund of Canada, and the same shall form the Third Charge thereon. (47)

Appropriation
from Time to
Time.

106. Subject to the several Payments by this Act charged on the Consolidated Revenue Fund of Canada, the same shall be appropriated by the Parliament of Canada for the Public Service.

Transfer of
Stocks, etc.

107. All Stocks, Cash, Banker's Balances, and Securities for Money belonging to each Province at the Time of the Union, except as in this Act mentioned, shall be the Property of Canada, and shall be taken in Reduction of the Amount of the respective Debts of the Provinces at the Union.

Transfer of
Property in
Schedule.

108. The Public Works and Property of each Province, enumerated in the Third Schedule to this Act, shall be the Property of Canada.

Property in
Lands, Mines,
etc.

109. All Lands, Mines, Minerals, and Royalties belonging to the several Provinces of Canada, Nova Scotia, and New Brunswick at the Union, and all Sums then due or payable for such Lands, Mines, Minerals, or Royalties, shall belong to the several Provinces of Ontario, Quebec, Nova Scotia, and New Brunswick in which the same are situate or arise, subject to any Trusts existing in respect thereof, and to any Interest other than that of the Province in the same. (48)

---

(47) Now covered by the *Governor General's Act*, R.S.C. 1970, c. G-14.

(48) The four western provinces were placed in the same position as the original provinces by the *British North America Act, 1930*, 21 Geo. V, c. 26 (U.K.).

110. All Assets connected with such Portions of the Public Debt of each Province as are assumed by that Province shall belong to that Province.

Assets connected with Provincial Debts.

111. Canada shall be liable for the Debts and Liabilities of each Province existing at the Union.

Canada to be liable for Provincial Debts.

112. Ontario and Quebec conjointly shall be liable to Canada for the Amount (if any) by which the Debt of the Province of Canada exceeds at the Union Sixty-two million five hundred thousand Dollars, and shall be charged with Interest at the Rate of Five per Centum per Annum thereon.

Debts of Ontario and Quebec.

113. The Assets enumerated in the Fourth Schedule to this Act belonging at the Union to the Province of Canada shall be the Property of Ontario and Quebec conjointly.

Assets of Ontario and Quebec.

114. Nova Scotia shall be liable to Canada for the Amount (if any) by which its Public Debt exceeds at the Union Eight million Dollars, and shall be charged with Interest at the Rate of Five per Centum per Annum thereon. (49)

Debt of Nova Scotia.

115. New Brunswick shall be liable to Canada for the Amount (if any) by which its Public Debt exceeds at the Union Seven million Dollars, and shall be charged with Interest at the Rate of Five per Centum per Annum thereon.

Debt of New Brunswick.

116. In case the Public Debts of Nova Scotia and New Brunswick do not at the Union amount to Eight million and Seven million Dollars respectively, they shall respectively receive by half-yearly Payments in advance from the Government of Canada Interest at Five per Centum per Annum on the Difference between the actual Amounts of their respective Debts and such stipulated Amounts.

Payment of interest to Nova Scotia and New Brunswick

117. The several Provinces shall retain all their respective Public Property not otherwise disposed of in this Act, subject to the Right of Canada to assume any Lands or Public Property required for Fortifications or for the Defence of the Country.

Provincial Public Property.

118. Repealed. (50)

---

(49) The obligations imposed by this section, sections 115 and 116, and similar obligations under the instruments creating or admitting other provinces, have been carried into legislation of the Parliament of Canada and are now to be found in the *Provincial Subsidies Act*, R.S.C. 1970, c. P-26.

(50) Repealed by the *Statute Law Revision Act, 1950*, 14 Geo. VI, c. 6 (U.K.). As originally enacted the section read as follows:

118. The following Sums shall be paid yearly by Canada to the several Provinces for the Support of their Governments and Legislatures:

	Dollars
Ontario	Eighty thousand.
Quebec	Seventy thousand.
Nova Scotia	Sixty thousand.
New Brunswick	Fifty thousand.

Two hundred and sixty thousand; and an annual Grant in aid of each Province shall be made, equal to Eighty Cents per Head of the Population as ascertained by the Census of One thousand eight hundred and sixty-one, and in the Case of Nova Scotia and New Brunswick, by each subsequent Decennial Census until the Population of each of those two Provinces amounts to Four hundred thousand Souls, at which Rate such Grant shall thereafter remain. Such Grants shall be in full Settlement of all future Demands on Canada, and shall be paid half-yearly in advance to each Province; but the Government of Canada shall deduct from such Grants, as against any Province, all Sums chargeable as Interest on the Public Debt of that Province in excess of the several Amounts stipulated in this Act.

The section was made obsolete by the *British North America Act, 1907*, 7 Edw. VII, c. 11 (U.K.) which provided:

1. (1) The following grants shall be made yearly by Canada to every province, which at the commencement of this Act is a province of the Dominion, for its local purposes and the support of its Government and Legislature:—

(*a*) A fixed grant—
where the population of the province is under one hundred and fifty thousand, of one hundred thousand dollars;
where the population of the province is one hundred and fifty thousand, but does not exceed two hundred thousand, of one hundred and fifty thousand dollars;
where the population of the province is two hundred thousand, but does not exceed four hundred thousand, of one hundred and eighty thousand dollars;
where the population of the province is four hundred thousand, but does not exceed eight hundred thousand, of one hundred and ninety thousand dollars;
where the population of the province is eight hundred thousand, but does not exceed one million five hundred thousand, of two hundred and twenty thousand dollars;
where the population of the province exceeds one million five hundred thousand, of two hundred and forty thousand dollars; and

(*b*) Subject to the special provisions of this Act as to the provinces of British Columbia and Prince Edward Island, a grant at the rate of eighty cents per head of the population of the province up to the number of two million five hundred thousand, and at the rate of sixty cents per head of so much of the population as exceeds that number.

(2) An additional grant of one hundred thousand dollars shall be made yearly to the province of British Columbia for a period of ten years from the commencement of this Act.

(3) The population of a province shall be ascertained from time to time in the case of the provinces of Manitoba, Saskatchewan, and Alberta respectively by the last quinquennial census or statutory estimate of population made under the Acts establishing those provinces or any other Act of the Parliament of Canada making provision for the purpose, and in the case of any other province by the last decennial census for the time being.

(4) The grants payable under this Act shall be paid half-yearly in advance to each province.

(5) The grants payable under this Act shall be substituted for the grants or subsidies (in this Act referred to as existing grants) payable for the like purposes at the commencement of this Act to the several provinces of the Dominion under the provisions of section one hundred and eighteen of the British North America Act 1867, or of any Order in Council establishing a province, or of any Act of the Parliament of Canada containing directions for the payment of any such grant or subsidy, and those provisions shall cease to have effect.

(6) The Government of Canada shall have the same power of deducting sums charged against a province on account of the interest on public debt in the case of the grant payable under this Act to the province as they have in the case of the existing grant.

(7) Nothing in this Act shall affect the obligation of the Government of Canada to pay to any province any grant which is payable to that province, other than the existing grant for which the grant under this Act is substituted.

(8) In the case of the provinces of British Columbia and Prince Edward Island, the amount paid on account of the grant payable per head of the population to the provinces under this Act shall not at any time be less than the amount of the corresponding grant payable at the commencement of this Act, and if it is found on any decennial census that the population of the province has decreased since the last decennial census, the amount paid on account of the grant shall not be decreased below the amount then payable, notwithstanding the decrease of the population.

See the *Provincial Subsidies Act*, R.S.C. 1970, c. P-26, *The Maritime Provinces Additional Subsidies Act*, 1942-43, c. 14, and the Terms of Union of Newfoundland with Canada, appended to the *British North America Act, 1949*, and also to *An Act to approve the Terms of Union of Newfoundland with Canada*, chapter 1 of the statutes of Canada, 1949.

119. New Brunswick shall receive by half-yearly Pay- Further Grant
ments in advance from Canada for the Period of Ten Years to New
Brunswick.
from the Union an additional Allowance of Sixty-three thousand Dollars per Annum; but as long as the Public Debt of
that Province remains under Seven million Dollars, a Deduction equal to the Interest at Five per Centum per Annum on
such Deficiency shall be made from that Allowance of Sixty-
three thousand Dollars. (51)

120. All Payments to be made under this Act, or in Form of
Payments.
discharge of Liabilities created under any Act of the Provinces of Canada, Nova Scotia, and New Brunswick respectively, and assumed by Canada, shall, until the Parliament of
Canada otherwise directs, be made in such Form and Manner
as may from Time to Time be ordered by the Governor
General in Council.

121. All Articles of the Growth, Produce, or Manufac- Canadian
Manufactures,
ture of any one of the Provinces shall, from and after the etc.
Union, be admitted free into each of the other Provinces.

122. The Customs and Excise Laws of each Province Continuance of
Customs and
shall, subject to the Provisions of this Act, continue in force Excise Laws.
until altered by the Parliament of Canada. (52)

123. Where Customs Duties are, at the Union, leviable Exportation
and Importa-
on any Goods, Wares, or Merchandises in any Two Provinces, tion as
those Goods, Wares, and Merchandises may, from and after between Two
Provinces.
the Union, be imported from one of those Provinces into the
other of them on Proof of Payment of the Customs Duty
leviable thereon in the Province of Exportation, and on
Payment of such further Amount (if any) of Customs Duty
as is leviable thereon in the Province of Importation. (53)

124. Nothing in this Act shall affect the Right of New Lumber Dues
in New
Brunswick to levy the Lumber Dues provided in Chapter Brunswick.
Fifteen of Title Three of the Revised Statutes of New Bruns-
wick, or in any Act amending that Act before or after the
Union, and not increasing the Amount of such Dues; but the
Lumber of any of the Provinces other than New Brunswick
shall not be subject to such Dues. (54)

125. No Lands or Property belonging to Canada or any Exemption of
Public Lands,
Province shall be liable to Taxation. etc.

---

(51) Spent.

(52) Spent. Now covered by the *Customs Act*, R.S.C. 1970, c. C-40, the *Customs Tariff*, R.S.C. 1970, c. C-41, the *Excise Act*, R.S.C. 1970, c. E-12 and the *Excise Tax Act*, R.S.C. 1970, c. E-13.

(53) Spent.

(54) These dues were repealed in 1873 by 36 Vict., c. 16 (N.B.). And see *An Act respecting the Export Duties imposed on Lumber*, etc., (1873) 36 Vict., c. 41 (Canada), and section 2 of the *Provincial Subsidies Act*, R.S.C. 1970, c. P-26.

Provincial
Consolidated
Revenue Fund.

126. Such Portions of the Duties and Revenues over which the respective Legislatures of Canada, Nova Scotia, and New Brunswick had before the Union Power of Appropriation as are by this Act reserved to the respective Governments or Legislatures of the Provinces, and all Duties and Revenues raised by them in accordance with the special Powers conferred upon them by this Act, shall in each Province form One Consolidated Revenue Fund to be appropriated for the Public Service of the Province.

IX.—MISCELLANEOUS PROVISIONS.

General.

127. Repealed. (55)

Oath of
Allegiance, etc.

128. Every Member of the Senate or House of Commons of Canada shall before taking his Seat therein take and subscribe before the Governor General or some Person authorized by him, and every Member of a Legislative Council or Legislative Assembly of any Province shall before taking his Seat therein take and subscribe before the Lieutenant Governor of the Province or some Person authorized by him, the Oath of Allegiance contained in the Fifth Schedule to this Act; and every Member of the Senate of Canada and every Member of the Legislative Council of Quebec shall also, before taking his Seat therein, take and subscribe before the Governor General, or some Person authorized by him, the Declaration of Qualification contained in the same Schedule.

Continuance of
existing Laws,
Courts,
Officers, etc.

129. Except as otherwise provided by this Act, all Laws in force in Canada, Nova Scotia, or New Brunswick at the Union, and all Courts of Civil and Criminal Jurisdiction, and all legal Commissions, Powers, and Authorities, and all Officers, Judicial, Administrative, and Ministerial, existing therein at the Union, shall continue in Ontario, Quebec, Nova Scotia, and New Brunswick respectively, as if the Union had not been made; subject nevertheless (except with respect to such as are enacted by or exist under Acts of the Parliament of Great Britain or of the Parliament of the United Kingdom of Great Britain and Ireland,) to be repealed, abolished, or altered by the Parliament of Canada, or by the Legislature of

---

(55) Repealed by the *Statute Law Revision Act, 1893*, 56-57 Vict., c. 14 (U.K.). The section read as follows:

127. If any Person being at the passing of this Act a Member of the Legislative Council of Canada, Nova Scotia, or New Brunswick to whom a Place in the Senate is offered, does not within Thirty Days thereafter, by Writing under his Hand addressed to the Governor General of the Province of Canada or to the Lieutenant Governor of Nova Scotia or New Brunswick (as the Case may be), accept the same, he shall be deemed to have declined the same; and any Person who, being at the passing of this Act a Member of the Legislative Council of Nova Scotia or New Brunswick, accepts a Place in the Senate, shall thereby vacate his Seat in such Legislative Council.

the respective Province, according to the Authority of the Parliament or of that Legislature under this Act. (56)

130. Until the Parliament of Canada otherwise provides, all Officers of the several Provinces having Duties to discharge in relation to Matters other than those coming within the Classes of Subjects by this Act assigned exclusively to the Legislatures of the Provinces shall be Officers of Canada, and shall continue to discharge the Duties of their respective Offices under the same Liabilities, Responsibilities, and Penalties as if the Union had not been made. (57)

Transfer of Officers to Canada.

131. Until the Parliament of Canada otherwise provides, the Governor General in Council may from Time to Time appoint such Officers as the Governor General in Council deems necessary or proper for the effectual Execution of this Act.

Appointment of new Officers.

132. The Parliament and Government of Canada shall have all Powers necessary or proper for performing the Obligations of Canada or of any Province thereof, as Part of the British Empire, towards Foreign Countries, arising under Treaties between the Empire and such Foreign Countries.

Treaty Obligations.

133. Either the English or the French Language may be used by any Person in the Debates of the Houses of the Parliament of Canada and of the Houses of the Legislature of Quebec; and both those Languages shall be used in the respective Records and Journals of those Houses; and either of those Languages may be used by any Person or in any Pleading or Process in or issuing from any Court of Canada established under this Act, and in or from all or any of the Courts of Quebec.

Use of English and French Languages.

The Acts of the Parliament of Canada and of the Legislature of Quebec shall be printed and published in both those Languages.

Ontario and Quebec.

134. Until the Legislature of Ontario or of Quebec otherwise provides, the Lieutenant Governors of Ontario and Quebec may each appoint under the Great Seal of the Province the following Officers, to hold Office during Pleasure, that is to say,—the Attorney General, the Secretary and Registrar of the Province, the Treasurer of the Province, the Commissioner of Crown Lands, and the Commissioner of Agriculture and Public Works, and in the Case of Quebec the

Appointment of Executive Officers for Ontario and Quebec.

---

(56) The restriction against altering or repealing laws enacted by or existing under statutes of the United Kingdom was removed by the *Statute of Westminster, 1931*, 22 Geo. V, c. 4 (U.K.)

(57) Spent.

Solicitor General, and may, by Order of the Lieutenant Governor in Council, from Time to Time prescribe the Duties of those Officers, and of the several Departments over which they shall preside or to which they shall belong, and of the Officers and Clerks thereof, and may also appoint other and additional Officers to hold Office during Pleasure, and may from Time to Time prescribe the Duties of those Officers, and of the several Departments over which they shall preside or to which they shall belong, and of the Officers and Clerks thereof. (58)

Powers, Duties, etc. of Executive Officers.

135. Until the Legislature of Ontario or Quebec otherwise provides, all Rights, Powers, Duties, Functions, Responsibilities, or Authorities at the passing of this Act vested in or imposed on the Attorney General, Solicitor General, Secretary and Registrar of the Province of Canada, Minister of Finance, Commissioner of Crown Lands, Commissioner of Public Works, and Minister of Agriculture and Receiver General, by any Law, Statute, or Ordinance of Upper Canada, Lower Canada, or Canada, and not repugnant to this Act, shall be vested in or imposed on any Officer to be appointed by the Lieutenant Governor for the Discharge of the same or any of them; and the Commissioner of Agriculture and Public Works shall perform the Duties and Functions of the Office of Minister of Agriculture at the passing of this Act imposed by the Law of the Province of Canada, as well as those of the Commissioner of Public Works. (59)

Great Seals.

136. Until altered by the Lieutenant Governor in Council, the Great Seals of Ontario and Quebec respectively shall be the same, or of the same Design, as those used in the Provinces of Upper Canada and Lower Canada respectively before their Union as the Province of Canada.

Construction of temporary Acts.

137. The words "and from thence to the End of the then next ensuing Session of the Legislature," or Words to the same Effect, used in any temporary Act of the Province of Canada not expired before the Union, shall be construed to extend and apply to the next Session of the Parliament of Canada if the Subject Matter of the Act is within the Powers of the same as defined by this Act, or to the next Sessions of the Legislatures of Ontario and Quebec respectively if the Subject Matter of the Act is within the Powers of the same as defined by this Act.

As to Errors in Names.

138. From and after the Union the Use of the Words "Upper Canada" instead of "Ontario," or "Lower Canada" instead of "Quebec," in any Deed, Writ, Process, Pleading, Document, Matter. or Thing. shall not invalidate the same.

---

(58) Spent. Now covered in Ontario by the *Executive Council Act*, R.S.O. 1970, c. 153 and in Quebec by the *Executive Power Act*, R.S.Q. 1964, c. 9.

(59) Probably spent.

139. Any Proclamation under the Great Seal of the Province of Canada issued before the Union to take effect at a Time which is subsequent to the Union, whether relating to that Province, or to Upper Canada, or to Lower Canada, and the several Matters and Things therein proclaimed, shall be and continue of like Force and Effect as if the Union had not been made. (60)

As to issue of Proclamations before Union, to commence after Union.

140. Any Proclamation which is authorized by any Act of the Legislature of the Province of Canada to be issued under the Great Seal of the Province of Canada, whether relating to that Province, or to Upper Canada, or to Lower Canada, and which is not issued before the Union, may be issued by the Lieutenant Governor of Ontario or of Quebec, as its Subject Matter requires, under the Great Seal thereof; and from and after the Issue of such Proclamation the same and the several Matters and Things therein proclaimed shall be and continue of the like Force and Effect in Ontario or Quebec as if the Union had not been made. (61)

As to issue of Proclamations after Union.

141. The Penitentiary of the Province of Canada shall, until the Parliament of Canada otherwise provides, be and continue the Penitentiary of Ontario and of Quebec. (62)

Peniteniary.

142. The Division and Adjustment of the Debts, Credits, Liabilities, Properties, and Assets of Upper Canada and Lower Canada shall be referred to the Arbitrament of Three Arbitrators, One chosen by the Government of Ontario, One by the Government of Quebec, and One by the Government of Canada; and the Selection of the Arbitrators shall not be made until the Parliament of Canada and the Legislatures of Ontario and Quebec have met; and the Arbitrator chosen by the Government of Canada shall not be a Resident either in Ontario or in Quebec. (63)

Arbitration respecting Debts, etc.

143. The Governor General in Council may from Time to Time order that such and so many of the Records, Books, and Documents of the Province of Canada as he thinks fit shall be appropriated and delivered either to Ontario or to Quebec, and the same shall thenceforth be the Property of that Province; and any Copy thereof or Extract therefrom, duly certified by the Officer having charge of the Original thereof, shall be admitted as Evidence. (64)

Division of Records.

---

(60) Probably spent.

(61) Probably spent.

(62) Spent. Penitentiaries are now provided for by the *Penitentiary Act*, R.S.C. 1970, c. P-6.

(63) Spent. See pages (xi) and (xii) of the Public Accounts, 1902-03.

(64) Probably spent. Two orders were made under this section on the 24th of January, 1868.

Constitution of
Townships in
Quebec.

144. The Lieutenant Governor of Quebec may from Time of Time, by Proclamation under the Great Seal of the Province, to take effect from a Day to be appointed therein, constitute Townships in those Parts of the Province of Quebec in which Townships are not then already constituted, and fix the Metes and Bounds thereof.

145. Repealed. (65)

XI.—ADMISSION OF OTHER COLONIES

Power to admit
Newfoundland,
etc., into the
Union.

146. It shall be lawful for the Queen, by and with the Advice of Her Majesty's Most Honourable Privy Council, on Addresses from the Houses of the Parliament of Canada, and from the Houses of the respective Legislatures of the Colonies or Provinces of Newfoundland, Prince Edward Island, and British Columbia, to admit those Colonies or Provinces, or any of them, into the Union, and on Address from the Houses of the Parliament of Canada to admit Rupert's Land and the North-western Territory, or either of them, into the Union, on such Terms and Conditions in each Case as are in the Addresses expressed and as the Queen thinks fit to approve, subject to the Provisions of this Act; and the Provisions of any Order in Council in that Behalf shall have effect as if they had been enacted by the Parliament of the United Kingdom of Great Britain and Ireland. (66)

As to Represen-
tation of
Newfoundland
and Prince
Edward Island
in Senate.

147. In case of the Admission of Newfoundland and Prince Edward Island, or either of them, each shall be entitled to a Representation in the Senate of Canada of Four Members, and (notwithstanding anything in this Act) in case of the Admission of Newfoundland the normal Number of Senators shall be Seventy-six and their maximum Number shall be Eighty-two; but Prince Edward Island when admitted

---

(65) **Repealed** by the *Statute Law Revision Act, 1893,* 56-57 Vict., c. 14, (U.K.). The section reads as follows:

X.—INTERCOLONIAL RAILWAY.

145. Inasmuch as the Provinces of Canada, Nova Scotia, and New Brunswick have joined in a Declaration that the Construction of the Intercolonial Railway is essential to the Consolidation of the Union of British North America, and to the Assent thereto of Nova Scotia and New Brunswick, and have consequently agreed that Provision should be made for its immediate Construction by the Government of Canada: Therefore, in order to give effect to that Agreement, it shall be the Duty of the Government and Parliament of Canada to provide for the Commencement, within Six Months after the Union, of a Railway connecting the River St. Lawrence with the City of Halifax in Nova Scotia, and for the Construction thereof without Intermission, and the Completion thereof with all practicable Speed.

(66) All territories mentioned in this section are now part of Canada. See the notes to section 5, *supra.*

shall be deemed to be comprised in the Third of Three Divisions into which Canada is, in relation to the Constitution of the Senate, divided by this Act, and accordingly, after the Admission of Prince Edward Island, whether Newfoundland is admitted or not, the Representation of Nova Scotia and New Brunswick in the Senate shall, as Vacancies occur, be reduced from Twelve to Ten Members respectively, and the Representation of each of those Provinces shall not be increased at any Time beyond Ten, except under the Provisions of this Act for the Appointment of Three or Six additional Senators under the Direction of the Queen. (67)

---

(67) Spent. See the notes to sections 21, 22, 26, 27 and 28, *supra*.

APPENDIX II

Text of Proposed Constitutional Resolution Filed by the Deputy Attorney General of Canada with the Supreme Court of Canada on April 24, 1981*

* Department of Justice/Ministère de la Justice

Consolidation of proposed constitutional resolution tabled by the Minister of Justice in the House of Commons on February 13, 1981 with the amendments approved by the House of Commons on April 23, 1981 and by the Senate on April 24, 1981

THAT, WHEREAS in the past certain amendments to the Constitution of Canada have been made by the Parliament of the United Kingdom at the request and with the consent of Canada;

AND WHEREAS it is in accord with the status of Canada as an independent state that Canadians be able to amend their Constitution in Canada in all respects;

AND WHEREAS it is also desirable to provide in the Constitution of Canada for the recognition of certain fundamental rights and freedoms and to make other amendments to that Constitution;

A respectful address be presented to Her Majesty the Queen in the following words:

To the Queen's Most Excellent Majesty:
Most Gracious Sovereign:

We, Your Majesty's loyal subjects, the House of Commons of Canada in Parliament assembled, respectfully approach Your Majesty, requesting that you may graciously be pleased to cause to be

714

laid before the Parliament of the United Kingdom a measure containing the recitals and clauses hereinafter set forth:

An Act to give effect to a request by the Senate and House of Commons of Canada

Whereas Canada has requested and consented to the enactment of an Act of the Parliament of the United Kingdom to give effect to the provisions hereinafter set forth and the Senate and the House of Commons of Canada in Parliament assembled have submitted an address to Her Majesty requesting that Her Majesty may graciously be pleased to cause a Bill to be laid before the Parliament of the United Kingdom for that purpose.

Be it therefore enacted by the Queen's Most Excellent Majesty, by and with the advice and consent of the Lords Spiritual and Temporal, and Commons, in this present Parliament assembled, and by the authority of the same, as follows:

Constitution Act, 1981 enacted

1. The *Constitution Act, 1981* set out in Schedule B to this Act is hereby enacted for and shall have the force of law in Canada and shall come into force as provided in that Act.

Termination of power to legislate for Canada

2. No Act of the Parliament of the United Kingdom passed after the *Constitution Act, 1981* comes into force shall extend to Canada as part of its law.

French version

3. So far as it is not contained in Schedule B, the French version of this Act is set out in Schedule A to this Act and has the same authority in Canada as the English version thereof.

Short title

4. This Act may be cited as the *Canada Act*.

SCHEDULE B

CONSTITUTION ACT, 1981

PART I

CANADIAN CHARTER OF RIGHTS AND FREEDOMS

Whereas Canada is founded upon principles that recognize the supremacy of God and the rule of law:

Guarantee of Rights and Freedoms

Rights and freedoms in Canada

1. The *Canadian Charter of Rights and Freedoms* guarantees the rights and freedoms set out in it subject only to such reasonable limits prescribed by law as can be demonstrably justified in a free and democratic society.

Fundamental Freedoms

Fundamental freedoms

2. Everyone has the following fundamental freedoms:

(*a*) freedom of conscience and religion;

(*b*) freedom of thought, belief, opinion and expression, including freedom of the press and other media of communication;

(*c*) freedom of peaceful assembly; and

(*d*) freedom of association.

Democratic Rights

Democratic rights of citizens

3. Every citizen of Canada has the right to vote in an election of members of the House of Commons or of a legislative assembly and to be qualified for membership therein.

Maximum duration of legislative bodies

4. (1) No House of Commons and no legislative assembly shall continue for longer than five years from the date fixed for the return of the writs at a general election of its members.

716

Continuation in special circumstances

(2) In time of real or apprehended war, invasion or insurrection, a House of Commons may be continued by Parliament and a legislative assembly may be continued by the legislature beyond five years if such continuation is not opposed by the votes of more than one-third of the members of the House of Commons or the legislative assembly, as the case may be.

Annual sitting of legislative bodies

5. There shall be a sitting of Parliament and of each legislature at least once every twelve months.

Mobility Rights

Mobility of citizens

6. (1) Every citizen of Canada has the right to enter, remain in and leave Canada.

Rights to move and gain livelihood

(2) Every citizen of Canada and every person who has the status of a permanent resident of Canada has the right

(*a*) to move to and take up residence in any province; and

(*b*) to pursue the gaining of a livelihood in any province.

Limitation

(3) The rights specified in subsection (2) are subject to

(*a*) any laws or practices of general application in force in a province other than those that discriminate among persons primarily on the basis of province of present or previous residence; and

(*b*) any laws providing for reasonable residency requirements as a qualification for the receipt of publicly provided social services.

Legal Rights

Life, liberty and security of person

7. Everyone has the right to life, liberty and security of the person and the right not to be deprived thereof except in accordance with the principles of fundamental justice.

Search or seizure

8. Everyone has the right to be secure against unreasonable search or seizure.

Detention or
imprisonment

9. Everyone has the right not to be arbitrarily detained or imprisoned.

Arrest or
detention

10. Everyone has the right on arrest or detention

(*a*) to be informed promptly of the reasons therefor;

(*b*) to retain and instruct counsel without delay and to be informed of that right; and

(*c*) to have the validity of the detention determined by way of *habeas corpus* and to be released if the detention is not lawful.

Proceedings in
criminal and
penal matters

11. Any person charged with an offence has the right

(*a*) to be informed without unreasonable delay of the specific offence;

(*b*) to be tried within a reasonable time;

(*c*) not to be compelled to be a witness in proceedings against that person in respect of the offence;

(*d*) to be presumed innocent until proven guilty according to law in a fair and public hearing by an independent and impartial tribunal;

(*e*) not to be denied reasonable bail without just cause;

(*f*) except in the case of an offence under military law tried before a military tribunal, to the benefit of trial by jury where the maximum punishment for the offence is imprisonment for five years or a more severe punishment;

(*g*) not to be found guilty on account of any act or omission unless, at the time of the act or omission, it constituted an offence under Canadian or international law or was criminal according to the general principles of law recognized by the community of nations;

(*h*) if finally acquitted of the offence, not to be tried for it again and, if finally found guilty and punished for the offence, not to be tried or punished for it again; and

(*i*) if found guilty of the offence and if the

punishment for the offence has been varied between the time of commission and the time of sentencing, to the benefit of the lesser punishment.

Treatment or punishment

12. Everyone has the right not to be subjected to any cruel and unusual treatment or punishment.

Self-crimination

13. A witness who testifies in any proceedings has the right not to have any incriminating evidence so given used to incriminate that witness in any other proceedings, except in a prosecution for perjury or for the giving of contradictory evidence.

Interpreter

14. A party or witness in any proceedings who does not understand or speak the language in which the proceedings are conducted or who is deaf has the right to the assistance of an interpreter.

Equality Rights

Equality before and under law and equal protection and benefit of law

15. (1) Every individual is equal before and under the law and has the right to the equal protection and equal benefit of the law without discrimination and, in particular, without discrimination based on race, national or ethnic origin, colour, religion, sex, age or mental or physical disability.

Affirmative action programs

(2) Subsection (1) does not preclude any law, program or activity that has as its object the amelioration of conditions of disadvantaged individuals or groups including those that are disadvantaged because of race, national or ethnic origin, colour, religion, sex, age or mental or physical disability.

Official Languages of Canada

Official languages of Canada

16. (1) English and French are the official languages of Canada and have equality of status and equal rights and privileges as to their use in all institutions of the Parliament and government of Canada.

Official languages of New Brunswick

(2) English and French are the official languages of New Brunswick and have equality of status and equal rights and privileges as to their use in all institutions of the legislature and government of New Brunswick.

Advancement of status and use

(3) Nothing in this Charter limits the authority of Parliament or a legislature to advance the equality of status or use of English and French.

Proceedings of Parliament

17. (1) Everyone has the right to use English or French in any debates and other proceedings of Parliament.

Proceedings of New Brunswick legislature

(2) Everyone has the right to use English or French in any debates and other proceedings of the legislature of New Brunswick.

Parliamentary statutes and records

18. (1) The statutes, records and journals of Parliament shall be printed and published in English and French and both language versions are equally authoritative.

New Brunswick statutes and records

(2) The statutes, records and journals of the legislature of New Brunswick shall be printed and published in English and French and both language versions are equally authoritative.

Proceedings in courts established by Parliament

19. (1) Either English or French may be used by any person in, or in any pleading in or process issuing from, any court established by Parliament.

Proceedings in New Brunswick courts

(2) Either English or French may be used by any person in, or in any pleading in or process issuing from, any court of New Brunswick.

Communications by public with federal institutions

20. (1) Any member of the public in Canada has the right to communicate with, and to receive available services from, any head or central office of an institution of the Parliament or government of Canada in English or French, and has the same right with respect to any other office of any such institution where

(*a*) there is a significant demand for communications with and services from that office in such language; or

(*b*) due to the nature of the office, it is reasonable that communications with and services from that office be available in both English and French.

Communications by public with New Brunswick institutions

(2) Any member of the public in New Brunswick has the right to communicate with, and to receive available services from, any office of an institution of the legislature or government of New Brunswick in English or French.

Continuation of existing constitutional provisions

21. Nothing in sections 16 to 20 abrogates or derogates from any right, privilege or obligation with respect to the English and French languages, or either of them, that exists or is continued by virtue of any other provision of the Constitution of Canada.

Rights and privileges preserved

22. Nothing in sections 16 to 20 abrogates or derogates from any legal or customary right or privilege acquired or enjoyed either before or after the coming into force of this Charter with respect to any language that is not English or French.

Minority Language Educational Rights

Language of instruction

23. (1) Citizens of Canada

(*a*) whose first language learned and still understood is that of the English or French linguistic minority population of the province in which they reside, or

(*b*) who have received their primary school instruction in Canada in English or French and reside in a province where the language in which they received that instruction is the language of the English or French linguistic minority population of the province,

have the right to have their children receive primary and secondary school instruction in that language in that province.

Continuity of language instruction

(2) Citizens of Canada of whom any child has received or is receiving primary or secondary school instruction in English or French in Canada, have the right to have all their children receive primary and secondary school instruction in the same language.

Application where numbers warrant

(3) The right of citizens of Canada under subsections (1) and (2) to have their children receive primary and secondary school instruction in the language of the English or French linguistic minority population of a province

(*a*) applies wherever in the province the number of children of citizens who have such a right is sufficient to warrant the provision to them out of public funds of minority language instruction; and

(*b*) includes, where the number of those children so warrants, the right to have them receive that instruction in minority language educational facilities provided out of public funds.

Enforcement

Enforcement of guaranteed rights and freedoms

24. (1) Anyone whose rights or freedoms, as guaranteed by this Charter, have been infringed or denied may apply to a court of competent jurisdiction to obtain such remedy as the court considers appropriate and just in the circumstances.

Exclusion of evidence bringing administration of justice into disrepute

(2) Where, in proceedings under subsection (1), a court concludes that evidence was obtained in a manner that infringed or denied any rights or freedoms guaranteed by this Charter, the evidence shall be excluded if it is established that, having regard to all the circumstances, the admission of it in the

proceedings would bring the administration of justice into disrepute.

General

Aboriginal rights and freedoms not affected by Charter

25. The guarantee in this Charter of certain rights and freedoms shall not be construed so as to abrogate or derogate from any aboriginal, treaty or other rights or freedoms that pertain to the aboriginal peoples of Canada including

(*a*) any rights or freedoms that have been recognized by the Royal Proclamation of October 7, 1763; and

(*b*) any rights or freedoms that may be acquired by the aboriginal peoples of Canada by way of land claims settlement.

Other rights and freedoms not affected by Charter

26. The guarantee in this Charter of certain rights and freedoms shall not be construed as denying the existence of any other rights or freedoms that exist in Canada.

Multicultural heritage

27. This Charter shall be interpreted in a manner consistent with the preservation and enhancement of the multicultural heritage of Canadians.

Rights guaranteed equally to both sexes

28. Notwithstanding anything in this Charter, the rights and freedoms referred to in it are guaranteed equally to male and female persons.

Rights respecting certain schools preserved

29. Nothing in this Charter abrogates or derogates from any rights or privileges guaranteed by or under the Constitution of Canada in respect of denominational, separate or dissentient schools.

Application to territories and territorial authorities

30. A reference in this Charter to a province or to the legislative assembly or legislature of a province shall be deemed to include a reference to the Yukon Territory and the Northwest Territories, or to the appropriate legislative authority thereof, as the case may be.

Legislative powers not extended

31. Nothing in this Charter extends the legislative powers of any body or authority.

Application of Charter

Application of
Charter

32. (1) This Charter applies

(*a*) to the Parliament and government of Canada and to all matters within the authority of Parliament including all matters relating to the Yukon Territory and Northwest Territories; and

(*b*) to the legislature and government of each province and to all matters within the authority of the legislature of each province.

Exception

(2) Notwithstanding subsection (1), section 15 shall not have effect until three years after this Act, except Part VI, comes into force.

Citation

Citation

33. This Part may be cited as the *Canadian Charter of Rights and Freedoms*.

PART II

RIGHTS OF THE ABORIGINAL PEOPLES OF CANADA

Recognition of
aboriginal and
treaty rights

34. (1) The aboriginal and treaty rights of the aboriginal peoples of Canada are hereby recognized and affirmed.

Definition of
"aboriginal
peoples of
Canada"

(2) In this Act, "aboriginal peoples of Canada" includes the Indian, Inuit and Métis peoples of Canada.

PART III

EQUALIZATION AND REGIONAL DISPARITIES

Commitment to
promote equal
opportunities

35. (1) Without altering the legislative authority of Parliament or of the provincial legislatures, or the rights of any of them with respect to the exercise of their legislative authority, Parliament and the legislatures, together with the government of Canada and the provincial governments, are committed to (*a*) promoting equal opportunities for the well-being of Canadians;

(*b*) furthering economic development to reduce disparity in opportunities; and

(*c*) providing essential public services of reasonable quality to all Canadians.

Commitment respecting public services

(2) Parliament and the government of Canada are committed to the principle of making equalization payments to ensure that provincial governments have sufficient revenues to provide reasonably comparable levels of public services at reasonably comparable levels of taxation.

PART IV

CONSTITUTIONAL CONFERENCES

Constitutional conferences

36. (1) Until Part VI comes into force, a constitutional conference composed of the Prime Minister of Canada and the first ministers of the provinces shall be convened by the Prime Minister of Canada at least once in every year.

Participation of aboriginal peoples

(2) A conference convened under subsection (1) shall have included in its agenda an item respecting constitutional matters that directly affect the aboriginal peoples of Canada, including the identification and definition of the rights of those peoples to be included in the Constitution of Canada, and the Prime Minister of Canada shall invite representatives of those peoples to participate in the discussions on that item.

Participation of territories

(3) The Prime Minister of Canada shall invite elected representatives of the governments of the Yukon Territory and the Northwest Territories to participate in the discussions on any item on the agenda of a conference convened under subsection (1) that, in the opinion of the Prime Minister, directly affects the Yukon Territory and the Northwest Territories.

PART V

INTERIM AMENDMENT PROCEDURE AND RULES FOR ITS REPLACEMENT

Interim procedure for amending Constitution of Canada

37. Until Part VI comes into force, an amendment to the Constitution of Canada may be made by proclamation issued by the Governor General under the Great Seal of Canada where so authorized by resolutions of the Senate and House of Commons and by the legislative assembly or government of each province.

Amendment of provisions relating to some but not all provinces

38. Until Part VI comes into force, an amendment to the Constitution of Canada in relation to any provision that applies to one or more, but not all, provinces may be made by proclamation issued by the Governor General under the Great Seal of Canada where so authorized by resolutions of the Senate and House of Commons and by the legislative assembly or government of each province to which the amendment applies.

Amendments respecting certain language rights

39. (1) Notwithstanding section 41, an amendment to the Constitution of Canada

(*a*) adding a province as a province named in subsection 16(2), 17(2), 18(2), 19(2) or 20(2), or

(*b*) otherwise providing for any or all of the rights guaranteed or obligations imposed by any of those subsections to have application in a province to the extent and under the conditions stated in the amendment,

may be made by proclamation issued by the Governor General under the Great Seal of Canada where so authorized by resolutions of the Senate and House of Commons and the legislative assembly of the province to which the amendment applies.

Initiation of amendment procedure

(2) The procedure for amendment prescribed by subsection (1) may be initiated only by the legislative assembly of the province to which the amendment applies.

Initiation of amendment procedures

40. (1) The procedures for amendment prescribed by sections 37 and 38 may be initiated either by the Senate or House of Commons or by the legislative assembly or government of a province.

Revocation of authorization

(2) A resolution made or other authorization given for the purposes of this Part may be revoked at any time before the issue of a proclamation authorized by it.

Limitation on use of interim amendment procedure

41. Sections 37 and 38 do not apply to an amendment to the Constitution of Canada where there is another provision in the Constitution for making the amendment, but the procedure prescribed by section 37 shall be used to amend the *Canadian Charter of Rights and Freedoms* and any provision for amending the Constitution, including this section.

Coming into force of Part VI

42. Part VI shall come into force

(*a*) with or without amendment, on such day as may be fixed by proclamation issued pursuant to the procedure prescribed by section 37, or

(*b*) on the day that is two years after the day this Act, except Part VI, comes into force,

whichever is the earlier day but, if a referendum is required to be held under subsection 43(3), Part VI shall come into force as provided in section 44.

Provincial alternative procedure

43. (1) The legislative assemblies of seven or more provinces that have, according to the then latest general census, combined populations of at least eighty per cent of the population of all the provinces may make a single proposal to substitute for paragraph 46(1)(*b*) such alternative as they consider appropriate.

Procedure for perfecting alternative

(2) One copy of an alternative proposed under subsection (1) may be deposited with the Chief Electoral Officer of Canada by

each proposing province within two years after this Act, except Part VI, comes into force but, prior to the expiration of that period, any province that has deposited a copy may withdraw that copy.

Referendum

(3) Where copies of an alternative have been deposited as provided by subsection (2) and, on the day that is two years after this Act, except Part VI, comes into force, at least seven copies remain deposited by provinces that have, according to the then latest general census, combined populations of at least eighty per cent of the population of all the provinces, the government of Canada shall cause a referendum to be held within two years after that day to determine whether

(*a*) paragraph 46(1)(*b*) or any alternative thereto approved by resolutions of the Senate and House of Commons and deposited with the Chief Electoral Officer at least ninety days prior to the day on which the referendum is held, or

(*b*) the alternative proposed by the provinces,

shall be adopted.

Coming into force of Part VI where referendum held

44. Where a referendum is held under subsection 43(3), a proclamation under the Great Seal of Canada shall be issued within six months after the date of the referendum bringing Part VI into force with such modifications, if any, as are necessary to incorporate the proposal approved by a majority of the persons voting at the referendum and with such other changes as are reasonably consequential on the incorporation of that proposal.

Right to vote

45. (1) Every citizen of Canada has, subject only to such reasonable limits prescribed by law as can be demonstrably justified in a free and democratic society, the right to vote in a referendum held under subsection 43(3).

Establishment of Referendum Rules Commission

(2) If a referendum is required to be held under subsection 43(3), a Referendum Rules Commission shall forthwith be established by commission issued under the Great Seal of Canada consisting of

(*a*) the Chief Electoral Officer of Canada, who shall be chairman of the Commission;

(*b*) a person appointed by the Governor General in Council; and

(*c*) a person appointed by the Governor General in Council

(i) on the recommendation of the governments of a majority of the provinces, or

(ii) if the governments of a majority of the provinces do not recommend a candidate within thirty days after the Chief Electoral Officer of Canada requests such a recommendation, on the recommendation of the Chief Justice of Canada from among persons recommended by the governments of the provinces within thirty days after the expiration of the first mentioned thirty day period or, if none are so recommended, from among such persons as the Chief Justice considers qualified.

Duty of Commission

(3) A Referendum Rules Commission shall cause rules for the holding of a referendum under subsection 43(3) approved by a majority of the Commission to be laid before Parliament within sixty days after the Commission is established or, if Parliament is not then sitting, on any of the first ten days next thereafter that Parliament is sitting.

Rules for referendum

(4) Subject to subsection (1) and taking into consideration any rules approved by a Referendum Rules Commission in accordance with subsection (3), Parliament may enact laws respecting the rules applicable to the holding of a referendum under subsection 43(3).

Proclamation

(5) If Parliament does not enact laws under subsection (4) respecting the rules applicable to the holding of a referendum within sixty days after receipt of a recommendation from a Referendum Rules Commission, the rules recommended by the Commission shall forthwith be brought into force by proclamation issued by the Governor General under the Great Seal of Canada.

Computation of period

(6) Any period when Parliament is prorogued or dissolved shall not be counted in computing the sixty day period referred to in subsection (5).

Rules to have force of law

(7) Subject to subsection (1), rules made under this section have the force of law and prevail over other laws made under the Constitution of Canada to the extent of any inconsistency.

PART VI

PROCEDURE FOR AMENDING
CONSTITUTION OF CANADA

General procedure for amending Constitution of Canada

46. (1) An amendment to the Constitution of Canada may be made by proclamation issued by the Governor General under the Great Seal of Canada where so authorized by

(*a*) resolutions of the Senate and House of Commons; and

(*b*) resolutions of the legislative assemblies of at least a majority of the provinces that includes

(i) every province that at any time before the issue of the proclamation had, according to any previous general census, a population of at least twenty-five per cent of the population of Canada,

(ii) two or more of the Atlantic provinces, and

(iii) two or more of the Western provinces.

Definitions

(2) In this section,

"Atlantic provinces"

"Atlantic provinces" means the provinces of Nova Scotia, New Brunswick, Prince Edward Island and Newfoundland;

"Western provinces"

"Western provinces" means the provinces of Manitoba, British Columbia, Saskatchewan and Alberta.

Amendment authorized by referendum

47. (1) An amendment to the Constitution of Canada may be made by proclamation issued by the Governor General under the Great Seal of Canada where so authorized by a referendum held throughout Canada under subsection (2) at which

(*a*) a majority of persons voting thereat, and

(*b*) a majority of persons voting thereat in each of the provinces, resolutions of the legislative assemblies of which would be sufficient, together with resolutions of the Senate and House of Commons, to authorize the issue of a proclamation under subsection 46(1),

have approved the making of the amendment.

Authorization of referendum

(2) A referendum referred to in subsection (1) shall be held where directed by proclamation issued by the Governor General under the Great Seal of Canada, which proclamation may be issued where

(*a*) an amendment to the Constitution of Canada has been authorized under paragraph 46(1)(*a*) by resolutions of the Senate and House of Commons;

(*b*) the requirements of paragraph 46(1)(*b*) in respect of the proposed amendment have not been satisfied within twelve months after the passage of the resolutions of the Senate and House of Commons; and

(*c*) the issue of the proclamation has been authorized by the Governor General in Council.

Time limit for referendum

(3) A proclamation issued under subsection (2) in respect of a referendum shall

provide for the referendum to be held within two years after the expiration of the twelve month period referred to in paragraph (*b*) of that subsection.

Amendment of provisions relating to some but not all provinces

48. An amendment to the Constitution of Canada in relation to any provision that applies to one or more, but not all, provinces may be made by proclamation issued by the Governor General under the Great Seal of Canada where so authorized by resolutions of the Senate and House of Commons and of the legislative assembly of each province to which the amendment applies.

Amendments respecting certain language rights

49. (1) Notwithstanding section 55, an amendment to the Constitution of Canada

(*a*) adding a province as a province named in subsection 16(2), 17(2), 18(2), 19(2) or 20(2), or

(*b*) otherwise providing for any or all of the rights guaranteed or obligations imposed by any of those subsections to have application in a province to the extent and under the conditions stated in the amendment,

may be made by proclamation issued by the Governor General under the Great Seal of Canada where so authorized by resolutions of the Senate and House of Commons and the legislative assembly of the province to which the amendment applies.

Initiation of amendment procedure

(2) The procedure for amendment prescribed by subsection (1) may be initiated only by the legislative assembly of the province to which the amendment applies.

Initiation of amendment procedures

50. (1) The procedures for amendment prescribed by subsection 46(1) and section 48 may be initiated either by the Senate or House of Commons or by the legislative assembly of a province.

Revocation of authorization

(2) A resolution made for the purposes of this Part may be revoked at any time before the issue of a proclamation authorized by it.

Right to vote

51. (1) Every citizen of Canada has, subject only to such reasonable limits prescribed by law as can be demonstrably justified in a free and democratic society, the right to vote in a referendum held under section 47.

Establishment of Referendum Rules Commission

(2) Where a referendum is to be held under section 47, a Referendum Rules Commission shall forthwith be established by commission issued under the Great Seal of Canada consisting of

(*a*) the Chief Electoral Officer of Canada, who shall be chairman of the Commission;

(*b*) a person appointed by the Governor General in Council; and

(*c*) a person appointed by the Governor General in Council

(i) on the recommendation of the governments of a majority of the provinces, or

(ii) if the governments of a majority of the provinces do not recommend a candidate within thirty days after the Chief Electoral Officer of Canada requests such a recommendation, on the recommendation of the Chief Justice of Canada from among persons recommended by the governments of the provinces within thirty days after the expiration of the first mentioned thirty day period or, if none are so recommended, from among such persons as the Chief Justice considers qualified.

Duty of Commission

(3) A Referendum Rules Commission shall cause rules for the holding of a referendum under section 47 approved by a majority of the Commission to be laid before Parliament within sixty days after the Commission is established or, if Parliament is not then sitting, on any of the first ten days next thereafter that Parliament is sitting.

Rules for referendum

(4) Subject to subsection (1) and taking into consideration any rules approved by a Referendum Rules Commission in accord-

ance with subsection (3), Parliament may enact laws respecting the rules applicable to the holding of a referendum under section 47.

Proclamation

(5) If Parliament does not enact laws under subsection (4) respecting the rules applicable to the holding of a referendum within sixty days after receipt of a recommendation from a Referendum Rules Commission, the rules recommended by the Commission shall forthwith be brought into force by proclamation issued by the Governor General under the Great Seal of Canada.

Computation of period

(6) Any period when Parliament is prorogued or dissolved shall not be counted in computing the sixty day period referred to in subsection (5).

Rules to have force of law

(7) Subject to subsection (1), rules made under this section have the force of law and prevail over other laws made under the Constitution of Canada to the extent of any inconsistency.

Limitation on use of general amendment procedure

52. (1) The procedures prescribed by section 46, 47 or 48 do not apply to an amendment to the Constitution of Canada where there is another provision in the Constitution for making the amendment, but the procedures prescribed by section 46 or 47 shall, nevertheless, be used to amend any provision for amending the Constitution, including this section.

Idem

(2) The procedures prescribed by section 46 or 47 do not apply in respect of an amendment referred to in section 48.

Amendments by Parliament

53. Subject to section 55, Parliament may exclusively make laws amending the Constitution of Canada in relation to the executive government of Canada or the Senate or House of Commons.

Amendments by provincial legislatures

54. Subject to section 55, the legislature of each province may exclusively make laws amending the constitution of the province.

Matters
requiring
amendment
under general
amendment
procedure

55. An amendment to the Constitution of Canada in relation to the following matters may be made only in accordance with a procedure prescribed by section 46 or 47:

(*a*) the office of the Queen, the Governor General and the Lieutenant Governor of a province;

(*b*) the *Canadian Charter of Rights and Freedoms;*

(*c*) the rights of the aboriginal peoples of Canada set out in Part II;

(*d*) the commitments relating to equalization and regional disparities set out in section 35;

(*e*) the powers of the Senate;

(*f*) the number of members by which a province is entitled to be represented in the Senate;

(*g*) the method of selecting Senators and the residence qualifications of Senators;

(*h*) the right of a province to a number of members in the House of Commons not less than the number of Senators representing the province; and

(*i*) the principles of proportionate representation of the provinces in the House of Commons prescribed by the Constitution of Canada.

Consequential
amendments

56. (1) Class 1 of section 91 and class 1 of section 92 of the *Constitution Act, 1867* (formerly named the *British North America Act, 1867*), the *British North America (No. 2) Act, 1949*, referred to in item 22 of Schedule I to this Act and Parts IV and V of this Act are repealed.

Idem

(2) When Parts IV and V of this Act are repealed, this section may be repealed and this Act may be renumbered, consequential upon the repeal of those Parts and this section, by proclamation issued by the Governor General under the Great Seal of Canada.

PART VII

AMENDMENT TO THE CONSTITUTION ACT,
1867

Amendment to
Constitution
Act, 1867

57. The *Constitution Act, 1867* (formerly named the *British North America Act, 1867*) is amended by adding thereto, immediately after section 92 thereof, the following heading and section:

*"Non-Renewable Natural Resources,
Forestry Resources and Electrical Energy*

Laws respecting
non-renewable
natural
resources,
forestry
resources and
electrical
energy

92A. (1) In each province, the legislature may exclusively make laws in relation to

(*a*) exploration for non-renewable natural resources in the province;

(*b*) development, conservation and management of non-renewable natural resources and forestry resources in the province, including laws in relation to the rate of primary production therefrom; and

(*c*) development, conservation and management of sites and facilities in the province for the generation and production of electrical energy.

Export from
provinces of
resources

(2) In each province, the legislature may make laws in relation to the export from the province to another part of Canada of the primary production from non-renewable natural resources and forestry resources in the province and the production from facilities in the province for the generation of electrical energy, but such laws may not authorize or provide for discrimination in prices or in supplies exported to another part of Canada.

Authority of
Parliament

(3) Nothing in subsection (2) derogates from the authority of Parliament to enact laws in relation to the matters referred to in that subsection and, where such a law of Parliament and a law of a province conflict, the law of Parliament prevails to the extent of the conflict.

Taxation of
resources

(4) In each province, the legislature may make laws in relation to the raising of money by any mode or system of taxation in respect of

(*a*) non-renewable natural resources and forestry resources in the province and the primary production therefrom, and

(*b*) sites and facilities in the province for the generation of electrical energy and the production therefrom,

whether or not such production is exported in whole or in part from the province, but such laws may not authorize or provide for taxation that differentiates between production exported to another part of Canada and production not exported from the province.

"Primary
production"

(5) The expression "primary production" has the meaning assigned by the Sixth Schedule.

Existing powers
or rights

(6) Nothing in subsections (1) to (5) derogates from any powers or rights that a legislature or government of a province had immediately before the coming into force of this section."

Idem

58. The said Act is further amended by adding thereto the following Schedule:

"THE SIXTH SCHEDULE

Primary Production from Non-Renewable Natural Resources and Forestry Resources

1. For the purposes of section 92A of this Act,

(*a*) production from a non-renewable natural resource is primary production therefrom if

(i) it is in the form in which it exists upon its recovery or severance from its natural state, or

(ii) it is a product resulting from processing or refining the resource, and is not a manufactured product or a product resulting from refining crude oil, refining upgraded heavy crude oil, refining gases or liquids derived from coal or refining a synthetic equivalent of crude oil; and

(*b*) production from a forestry resource is primary production therefrom if it consists of sawlogs, poles, lumber, wood chips, sawdust or any other primary wood product, or wood pulp, and is not a product manufactured from wood."

PART VIII

GENERAL

Primacy of Constitution of Canada

59. (1) The Constitution of Canada is the supreme law of Canada, and any law that is inconsistent with the provisions of the Constitution is, to the extent of the inconsistency, of no force or effect.

Constitution of Canada

(2) The Constitution of Canada includes

(*a*) the *Canada Act*;

(*b*) the Acts and orders referred to in Schedule I; and

(*c*) any amendment to any Act or order referred to in paragraph (*a*) or (*b*).

Amendments to Constitution of Canada

(3) Amendments to the Constitution of Canada shall be made only in accordance with the authority contained in the Constitution of Canada.

Repeals and new names

60. (1) The enactments referred to in Column I of Schedule I are hereby repealed or amended to the extent indicated in Column II thereof and, unless repealed, shall continue as law in Canada under the names set out in Column III thereof.

Consequential amendments

(2) Every enactment, except the *Canada Act*, that refers to an enactment referred to ·

in Schedule I by the name in Column I thereof is hereby amended by substituting for that name the corresponding name in Column III thereof, and any British North America Act not referred to in Schedule I may be cited as the *Constitution Act* followed by the year and number, if any, of its enactment.

French version of Constitution of Canada

61. A French version of the portions of the Constitution of Canada referred to in Schedule I shall be prepared by the Minister of Justice of Canada as expeditiously as possible and, when any portion thereof sufficient to warrant action being taken has been so prepared, it shall be put forward for enactment by proclamation issued by the Governor General under the Great Seal of Canada pursuant to the procedure then applicable to an amendment of the same provisions of the Constitution of Canada.

English and French versions of certain constitutional texts

62. Where any portion of the Constitution of Canada has been or is enacted in English and French or where a French version of any portion of the Constitution is enacted pursuant to section 61, the English and French versions of that portion of the Constitution are equally authoritative.

English and French versions of this Act

63. The English and French versions of this Act are equally authoritative.

Commencement

64. Subject to section 65, this Act shall come into force on a day to be fixed by proclamation issued by the Governor General under the Great Seal of Canada.

Exception

65. Part VI shall come into force as provided in Part V.

Short title and citations

66. This Schedule may be cited as the *Constitution Act, 1981*, and the Constitution Acts 1867 to 1975 (No. 2) and this Act may be cited together as the *Constitution Acts, 1867 to 1981*.

Bibliography

GENERAL REFERENCE WORKS

A. Frameworks for the Study of Political Systems

Almond, G. A. and G. B. Powell, Jr.: *Comparative Politics: A Developmental Approach* (Little, Brown, Boston, 1978).

Dahl, R. A.: *Modern Political Analysis* (Prentice-Hall, Englewood Cliffs, 1970).

_____ and C. E. Lindblom: *Politics, Economics and Welfare* (Harper and Row, New York, 1963).

Deutsch, K. W.: *The Nerves of Government* (The Free Press, New York, 1966).

Easton, David: *A Framework for Political Analysis* (Prentice-Hall, Englewood Cliffs, 1965).

_____: *A Systems Analysis of Political Life* (John Wiley and Sons, New York, 1965).

Lasswell, H.: *Politics: Who Gets What, When, How?* (Meridian, Cleveland, 1958).

Lemieux, V.: *Les Cheminements de l'Influence: Systèmes Stragéries et Structures du Politique* (Les Presses de l'Université Laval, Montreal, 1980).

Parsons, T. and E. A. Shills (eds.): *Toward a General Theory of Action* (Harper and Row, New York, 1962).

Young, R. (ed.): *Approaches to the Study of Politics* (Northwestern University Press, Evanston, 1958).

B. General Works on Canada

Bernard, A.: *Politics in Canada and Quebec*, 2nd ed. (University of Quebec, Montreal, 1977).

Blishen, B. R. et al. (eds.): *Canadian Society: Sociological Perspectives*, 3rd ed. (Macmillan, Toronto, 1968).

Cheal, D.: "Models of Mass Politics in Canada," *Canadian Review of Sociology and Anthropology*, vol. 15, 3, 1978, pp. 325-338.

Christian, William: "Harold Innis as Political Theorist," *Canadian Journal of Political Science*, vol. 10, 1, 1977, pp. 21-42.

Corry, J. A. and J. E. Hodgetts: *Democratic Government and Politics* (University of Toronto Press, Toronto, 1959).

Dawson, R. M.: *The Government of Canada*, revised by N. Ward (University of Toronto Press, Toronto, 1970).

Flaherty, D. H.: "Access to Historic Census Data in Canada: A Comparative Analysis," *Canadian Public Administration*, vol. 20, 3, 1977, pp. 481-498.

Fortin, P.: "La dimension économique de la crise politique canadienne," *Canadian Public Policy*, vol. 4, 3, 1978, pp. 309-324.

Fox, Paul (ed.): *Politics: Canada*, 4th ed. (McGraw-Hill Ryerson, Toronto, 1977), pp. 599-637.

Glazebrook, G. P. de T.: *A History of Canadian Political Thought* (McClelland and Stewart, Toronto, 1966).

Guinsberg, T. N. and A. L. Renber: *Perspectives on the Social Sciences in Canada* (University of Toronto Press, Toronto, 1974).

740

Higgins, D. J. H.: *Urban Canada: Its Government and Politics* (Macmillan, Toronto, 1977).

Hockin, T. A.: *Government in Canada* (McGraw-Hill Ryerson, Toronto, 1976).

Jenson, J. and B. Tomlin: *Canadian Politics: An Introduction to Systematic Analysis* (McGraw-Hill Ryerson, Toronto, 1977).

Khan, R. A., S. A. MacKown, and J. D. McNiven: *An Introduction to Political Science* (Irwin-Dorsey, Ltd., Georgetown, Ont., 1972).

Laxer, J.: *Liberal Idea of Canada* (Lorimer, Toronto, 1977).

Mann, W. E. (ed.): *Canada: A Sociological Profile*, (Copp Clark, Toronto, 1968).

Minogue, K. R.: "Humanist Democracy: The Political Thought of C. B. Macpherson," *Canadian Journal of Political Science*, vol. 9, 3, 1976, pp. 377-422.

Porter, J.: *The Vertical Mosaic* (University of Toronto Press, Toronto, 1965).

Redekop, J. H.: *Approaches to Canadian Politics* (Prentice-Hall, Toronto, 1978).

Roussopoulus, D.: "Beyond Reformism: The Ambiguity of the Urban Question," *Our Generation*, vol. 11, 2, 1977, pp. 46-58.

Rowat, D. C.: *Your Local Government*, 2nd ed. (Macmillan, Toronto, 1975).

Sabourin, M. Louis (ed.): *Le Système Politique du Canada* (Edition de l'Université d'Ottawa, Ottawa, 1969).

Schultz, R. and O. M. Kruhlak: *The Canadian Political Process*, 3rd ed. (Holt, Rinehart & Winston, Toronto, 1979).

Schwartz, M. A.: "The Social Make-up of Canada and Strains in Confederation," *Canadian Public Policy*, vol. 3, 4, 1977, pp. 458-470.

Simeon, R. E. B.: "The 'Overload Thesis' and Canadian Government," *Canadian Public Policy*, vol. 2, 4, 1976, pp. 541-552.

Smiley, D.: "Must Canadian Political Science be a Miniature Replica?" *Journal of Canadian Studies*, vol. 9, 1, 1974, pp. 31-41.

Sodurlund, N. C. et al.: "A Critique of the Hartz Theory of Political Development as Applied to Canada," *Comparative Politics*, vol. 12, 1, 1979, pp. 63-67.

Svacek, Victor: "The Elusive Marxism of C. B. Macpherson," *Canadian Journal of Political Science*, vol. 9, 3, 1976, pp. 395-422.

Taylor, Charles: *The Pattern of Politics* (McClelland and Stewart, Toronto, 1970).

Thorburn, H.: "Canadian Pluralist Democracy in Crisis," *Canadian Journal of Political Science*, vol. 11, 4, 1978, pp. 723-738.

Tindal, C. R.: *Local Government in Canada* (McGraw-Hill Ryerson, Toronto, 1979).

Urquhart, M. G. (ed.) and K. A. H. Buckley (assistant ed.): *Historical Statistics of Canada* (Macmillan, Toronto, 1965).

Vaughan, F., J. P. Kyba, and O. P. Dwivedi (eds.): *Contemporary Issues in Canadian Politics* (Prentice-Hall, Toronto, 1970).

Van Loon, R. J. and Michael S. Whittington: "Alternative Styles in the Study of Canadian Politics: A Brief Rejoinder," *Canadian Journal of Political Science*, vol. 7, 1, 1974, pp. 132-134.

Wand, Bernard: "C. B. Macpherson's Conceptual Apparatus," *Canadian Journal of Political Science*, vol. 4, 4, 1971, pp. 526-540.

Ward, Norman: "Money and Politics: The Costs of Democracy in Canada," *Canadian Journal of Political Science*, vol. 5, 1973, p. 335.

————: "Alternative Styles: A Comment," *Canadian Journal of Political Science*, vol. 7, 1, 1974, pp. 128-129.

Warkentin, John (ed.): *Canada: A Geographical Interpretation* (Methuen, Toronto, 1968).

White, W. L., R. H. Wagenberg, and R. C. Nelson: *Introduction to Canadian Politics and Government* (Holt, Rinehart and Winston, Toronto, 1972).

C. The Policy Process in Canada

Abdel-Malek, T. and A. K. Sarkar.: "An Analysis of the Effects of Phase II Guidelines of the Foreign Investment Review Act," *Canadian Public Policy*, vol. 3, 1, 1977, pp. 36-49.

Abouchar, A.: "Traffic Forecasts for the Pickering (Second Toronto International) Airport: A Critical Examination," *Canadian Public Policy*, vol. 3, 1, 1977, pp. 14-22.

Anderson, F. J.: "Price Formation in the Canadian Crude Oil Sector," *Canadian Public Policy*, vol. 2, 1, 1976, pp. 17-32.

Andrew, Caroline, André Blais, Rachel DesRosiers: "Le logement public à Hull," *Canadian Journal of Political Science* vol. 8, 1975, pp. 403-430.

Armstrong, C.: "Federalism and Government Regulation: The Case of the Canadian Insurance Industry, 1927-1934," *Canadian Public Administration*, vol. 19, 1, 1976, pp. 88-101.

Aucoin, P. and R. French: "The Ministry of State for Science and Technology," *Canadian Public Administration*, vol. 17, 3, 1974, pp. 461-481.

Baccigalupo, A.: "L'Informatique Dans Les Administrations Publique et Para-Publiques Québécoises," *Canadian Public Administration*, vol. 17, 4, 1974, pp. 542-562.

Baldwin, J. R.: "The Evolution of Transportation Policy in Canada," *Canadian Public Administration*, vol. 20, 4, 1977, pp. 600-631.

Beckman, M. Dale: "The Problem of Communicating Public Policy Effectively: Bill C-256 and Winnipeg Businessmen" *Canadian Journal of Political Science*, vol. 8, 1, 1975, pp. 138-143.

Berkes, F.: "Management of Recreational Fisheries in Northern Quebec: Policies versus Tools," *Canadian Public Policy*, vol. 4, 4, 1978, pp. 460-473.

Bregha, F.: "The Mackenzie Valley Pipeline and Canadian Natural Gas Policy," *Canadian Public Policy*, vol. 3, 1, 1977, pp. 63-75.

Brown, John C. Lloyd: "Membership in Canadian Regulatory Agencies," *Canadian Public Administration*, vol. 20, 3, 1977, pp. 513-533.

Bryden, K.: *Old Age Pensions and Policy-Making in Canada* (McGill, Queens University Press, Montreal, 1974).

Burke, D. P.: "Hellyer and Landymore: The Unification of the Canadian Armed Forces and an Admiral's Revolt," *American Review of Canadian Studies*, vol. 7, 1978, pp. 3-27.

Campbell, H. F.: "A Benefit/Cost Rule for Evaluating Public Projects in Canada," *Canadian Public Policy*, vol. 1, 1975, pp. 171-275.

Carrothers, A. W. R.: "Collective Bargaining as Public Policy: Let us not Pre-empt Disaster," *Canadian Public Administration*, vol. 18, 4, 1975, pp. 527-540.

Castonguay, C.: "An Analysis of the Canadian Bilingual Districts Policy," *American Review of Canadian Studies*, vol. 6, 2, 1976, pp. 57-73.

Chamber, E. J. et al.: "Bill C-20: An Evaluation from the Perspective of Current Transportation Policy and Regulatory Performance," *Canadian Public Policy*, vol. 4, 1, 1980, pp. 47-62.

Chapman, I. and M. Gibbons: "Innovation and the Senate: Report on Science Policy," *Journal of Canadian Studies*, vol. 13, 1, 1978, pp. 30-37.

Contandriopoulos, A. P.: "Changer l'organisation du système de santé plutôt que limiter le nombre de médecins: Un commentaire de l'article d'Evans," *Canadian Public Policy*, vol. 2, 1976, pp. 161-168.

Copes, P.: "Canada's Atlantic Coast Fisheries: Policy Development and the Impact of Extended Jurisdiction," *Canadian Public Policy*, vol. 4, 2, 1978, pp. 155-271.

Corbett, David: *Canada's Immigration Policy: A Critique* (Published under the auspices of the Canadian Institute of International Affairs, University of Toronto Press, Toronto, 1957).

Corry, J. A.: "Changes in the Functions of Government," in *The Canadian Historical Association Report of Annual Meeting 1945* (University of Toronto Press, Toronto, 1945), pp. 15-24.

Darling, H.: "What Belongs in Transportation Policy," *Canadian Public Administration*, vol. 18, 4, 1975, pp. 659-669.

Davies G. W.: "Macroeconomic Effects of Immigration: Evidence from CANDIDE, TRACE, and RDX2," *Canadian Public Policy*, vol. 3, 1977, pp. 299-306.

Denton, F. T. and B. G. Spencer: "On the Prospect of a Labour Shortage," *Canadian Public Policy*, vol. 4, 1978, pp. 101-118.

Dewees, D. N. and L. Waverman: "Energy Conservation: Policies for the Transport," *Canadian Public Policy*, vol. 3, 1977, pp. 171-185.

Dingle, J. F.: "Management Information Systems, Economic Theory and Public Policy," *Canadian Public Policy*, vol. 1, 1975, pp. 536-545.

Doern, G. Bruce: *The Role of Interdepartmental Committees in the Policy Process* (Carleton University, Unpublished M.A. Thesis, Ottawa, 1966).

———: *Political Policy-making: A Commentary on the Economic Council's Eighth Annual Review and the Ritchie Report* (The Private Planning Association of Canada, Montreal, 1972).

———: "Recent Changes in the Philosophy of Policy-making in Canada," *Canadian Journal of Political Science*, vol. 4, 2, 1976, pp. 243-264.

———: *The Regulatory Process in Canada* (Macmillan, Toronto, 1978).

——— and Peter Aucoin: *The Structures of Policy Making in Canada* (Macmillan, Toronto, 1971).

——— and R. W. Morrison (eds.): *Canadian Nuclear Policies* (Institute for Research on Public Policy, Montreal, 1980).

——— and R. W. Phidd: *The Politics and Management of Canadian Economic Policy* (Macmillan, Toronto, 1978).

Drury, C. M.: "Quantitative Analysis and Public Policy Making," *Canadian Public Policy*, vol. 1, 1975, pp. 89-96.

Evans, R. G.: "Does Canada Have Too Many Doctors?—Why Nobody Loves an Immigrant Physician," *Canadian Public Policy*, vol. 2, 1976, pp. 147-160.

Forget, C. E.: "Développement et Implantation de l'idée de Régionalisation des Services de Santé et des Services Sociaux au Québec," *Canadian Public Policy*, vol. 1, 1975, pp. 402-414.

Freeman, M. M. R. and L. M. Hackman: "Bathurst Island NWT: A Test Case of Canada's Northern Policy," *Canadian Public Policy*, vol. 1, 1975, pp. 402-414.

Friedmann, K. A.: "Controlling Bureaucracy: Attitudes in the Alberta Public Service Towards the Ombudsman," *Canadian Public Administration*, vol. 19, 1, 1976, pp. 51-87.

——— and A. G. Milne: "The Federal Ombudsman Legislation: A Critique of Bill C-43," *Canadian Public Policy*, vol. 6, 1, 1980, pp. 63-77.

744   BIBLIOGRAPHY

Globerman, S.: "Canadian Science Policy and Technological Sovereignty," *Canadian Public Policy*, vol. 4, 1978, pp. 34-35.

Globerman, S. and S. H. Book: "Formulating Cost and Output Policies in the Performing Arts," *Canadian Public Policy*, vol. 2, 1976, pp. 33-41.

Hartle, D. G.: "The Public Servant as Advisor: The Choice of Policy Evaluation Criteria," *Canadian Public Policy*, vol. 2, 1976, pp. 424-438.

———: *Public Policy Decision Making and Regulation* (Institute for Research on Public Policy, Montreal, 1979).

Hawkins, F.: "Immigration and Population: The Canadian Approach," *Canadian Public Policy*, vol. 1, 1975, pp. 285-295.

Helliwell, J.: "The National Energy Board's 1974-1975 Natural Gas Supply Hearings," *Canadian Public Policy*, vol. 1, 1975, pp. 415-425.

———: "Arctic Pipelines in the Context of Canadian Energy Requirements," *Canadian Public Policy*, vol. 3, 1977, pp. 344-354.

Hockin, Thomas A. (ed.): *Apex of Power: The Prime Minister and Political Leadership in Canada* (Prentice-Hall, Toronto, 1971).

Hodgetts, J. E.: "The Civil Service and Policy Formation," in J. E. Hodgetts and D. C. Corbett (eds.): *Canadian Public Administration* (Macmillan, Toronto, 1960).

Johnson, A. N.: "Public Policy: Creativity and Bureaucracy," *Canadian Public Administration*, vol. 21, 1, 1978, pp. 1-15.

Johnston, D. M.: "Coastal Zone Management in Canada: Purposes and Prospects," *Canadian Public Administration*, vol. 20, 1, 1977, pp. 140-151.

Jones, J. C. A.: "The Bureaucracy and Public Policy: Canadian Merger Policy and the Combines Branch, 1965-1971," *Canadian Public Administration*, vol. 18, 1, 1975, pp. 269-296.

Kernaghan, K.: "Representative Bureaucracy: The Canadian Perspective," *Canadian Public Administration*, vol. 21, 4, 1978, pp. 489-512.

Kierans, E.: "Notes on the Energy Aspects of the 1974 Budget," *Canadian Public Policy*, vol. 1, 1975, pp. 426-432.

Kirby, M. J. L. et al.: "The Impact of Public Policy-Making Structures and Processes in Canada," *Canadian Public Administration*, vol. 21, 3, 1978, pp. 407-417.

Kliman, M. L.: "The Setting of Domestic Air Fares: A Review of the 1975 Hearings," *Canadian Public Policy*, vol. 3, 1977, pp. 186-198.

Lacroix, R. et C. Montmarquette: "Inflation et Indexation: Perspective canadienne et considérations théoriques," *Canadian Public Policy*, vol. 1, 1975, pp. 185-195.

Leiss, W.: "The Social Consequences of Technological Progress: Critical Comments on Recent Theories," *Canadian Public Administration*, vol. 13, 3, 1970, pp. 246-262.

Lepore, G.: "Effluent Charges and Pollution Control: A Case Study," *Canadian Public Policy*, vol. 2, 1976, pp. 482-491.

Levitt, Kari: *Silent Surrender: The Multi-National Corporation in Canada* (Macmillan, Toronto, 1970).

Lindblom, Charles E.: *The Policy-Making Process* (Prentice-Hall, Englewood Cliffs, 1968).

———: "The Science of Muddling Through," in A. Etzioni (ed.): *Readings on Modern Organizations* (Prentice-Hall, Englewood Cliffs, 1969), pp. 154-165.

Lowi, T.: "Decision Making vs. Policy Making: Toward An Antidote For Technocracy," *Public Administration Review*, vol. 30, 1970, pp. 314-325.

———: *The End of Liberalism*, 2nd ed. (W. W. Norton, New York, 1979).

Lukasiewicz, J.: "Public Policy and Technology: Passenger Rail in Canada as an Issue in Modernization," *Canadian Public Policy,* vol. 5, 4, 1979, pp. 518-532.

Lundquist, L. J.: "Do Political Structures Matter in Environmental Politics? The Case of Air Pollution Control in Canada, Sweden, and the United States," *Canadian Public Administration,* vol. 17, 1, 1974, pp. 119-141.

Matthews, R.: "Ethical Issues in Policy Research: The Investigation of Community Resettlement in Newfoundland," *Canadian Public Policy,* vol. 1, 1975, pp. 204-216.

McFadyen, S.: "The Control of Foreign Ownership of Canadian Real Estate," *Canadian Public Policy,* vol. 2, 1976, pp. 65-77.

Meyboom, P.: "In-House vs. Contractual Research: The Federal Make or Buy Policy," *Canadian Public Administration,* vol. 17, 4, 1974, pp. 563-585.

Mills, C. W.: *The Power Elite* (Oxford University Press, New York, 1956).

Mishler, N. and D. B. Campbell: "The Health State: Legislative Responsiveness to Public Health Care Needs in Canada, 1920-1970," *Comparative Politics,* vol. 10, 4, 1978, pp. 479-498.

Mitchell, C. L.: "The 200-Mile Limit: New Issues, Old Problems for Canada's East Coast Fisheries," *Canadian Public Policy,* vol. 4, 1978, pp. 172-183.

Moffat, M. J. and T. E. Reid: "Comment on Indicators and Policy Formation," *Canadian Public Administration,* vol. 19, 4, 1976, pp. 633-637.

Muller, F. G.: "Distribution of Air Pollution in the Montreal Region," *Canadian Public Policy,* vol. 3, 1977, pp. 199-204.

Muller, R. A.: "A Simulation of the Effect of Pollution Control on the Pulp and Paper Industry," *Canadian Public Policy,* vol. 2, 1976, pp. 91-102.

Nord, D. C.: "The 'Problem' of Immigration: The Continuing Presence of the Stranger Within Our Gates," *American Review of Canadian Studies,* vol. 7, 2, 1978, pp. 116-133.

Osberg, L.: "Unemployment Insurance in Canada: A Review of the Recent Amendments," *Canadian Public Policy,* vol. 2, 2, 1979, pp. 223-235.

Paquin, M. and R. A. Hurtubise: "L'Utilisation de la Méthode des cas et des Jeux de Simulation Dans L'Enseignement de L'Administration Publique," *Canadian Public Administration,* vol. 17, 2, 1978, pp. 242-258.

Pitfield, M.: "The Shape of Government in the 1980's: Techniques and Instruments for Policy Formulation at the Federal Level," *Canadian Public Administration,* vol. 19, 1, 1976, pp. 8-20.

Raynauld, A.: "Social Indicators: The Need for a Broader Socio-Economic Framework," *Canadian Public Administration,* vol. 18, 1, 1975, pp. 91-103.

Relyea, H. C.: "The Provision of Government Information: The Federal Freedom of Information Act Experience," *Canadian Public Administration,* vol. 20, 2, 1977, pp. 317-341.

Renaud, François and Brigitte Von Schoenberg: "L'implantation des conseils régionaux de la santé et des services sociaux: analyse d'un processus politique," *Canadian Journal of Political Science,* vol. 7, 1, 1974, pp. 52-69.

Rickover, R. M.: "The 1977 Bank Act: Emerging Issues and Policy Choices," *Canadian Public Policy,* vol. 2, 1976, pp. 372-379.

Ritchie, R. S.: "Public Policies Affecting Petroleum Development in Canada," *Canadian Public Policy,* vol. 1, 1975, pp. 66-79.

Roberts, L. U.: "Some Unanticipated Consequences of Affirmative Action Policies," *Canadian Public Policy,* vol. 5, 1, 1979, pp. 90-96.

Rowan, M.: "A Conceptual Framework for Government Policy-Making," *Canadian Public Administration,* vol. 13, no. 3, 1970, pp. 277-296.

Ruppenthal, K. M. and W. T. Stanbury (eds.): *Transportation Policy: Regulation Competition and the Public Interest* (The Centre for Transportation Studies, University of British Columbia, Vancouver, 1976).

Sayeed, K. B.: "Public Policy Analysis in Washington and Ottawa," *Policy Sciences*, vol. 4, no. 1, 1973, pp. 85-101.

Sharman, G. C.: "The Police and the Implementation of Public Law," *Canadian Public Administration*, vol. 21, 2, 1977, pp. 291-304.

Sharp, M.: "Decision-Making in the Federal Cabinet," *Canadian Public Administration*, vol. 19, 1, 1976, pp. 1-7.

Skogstad, G.: "The Farm Products Marketing Agencies Act: A Case Study of Agricultural Policy," *Canadian Public Policy*, vol. 6, 1, 1980, pp. 89-100.

Smith, L. B.: *Anatomy of a Crisis: Canadian Housing Policy* (Fraser Institute, Vancouver, 1977).

Sokolsky, J. J.: "The Canada-US Alaska Highway Pipeline: A Study in Environmental Decision-Making," *American Review of Canadian Studies*, vol. 9, 2, 1979, pp. 84-112.

Spragge, G. L.: "Canadian Planners' Goals: Deep Roots and Fuzzy Thinking," *Canadian Public Administration*, vol. 18, 2, 1975, pp. 216-234.

Stanbury, W. T.: *Business Interest and Reform of Canadian Competition Policy, 1971-75* (Methuen, Toronto, 1977).

Star, S.: "In Search of a Rational Policy," *Canadian Public Policy*, vol. 1, 1975, pp. 328-342.

Steele, G. G. E.: " 'Needed—A Sense of Proportion!' Notes on the History of Expenditure Control," *Canadian Public Administration*, vol. 21, 3, 1977, pp. 433-443.

Tassé, R.: "The Role of Social Science in Crime, and Delinquency Policy," *Canadian Public Administration*, vol. 19, 2, 1976, pp. 267-278.

Taylor, M. G.: "Quebec Medicare: Policy Formulation in Conflict and Crisis," *Canadian Public Administration*, vol. 15, 2, 1972, pp. 211-250.

————: *Health Insurance and Canadian Public Policy* (McGill-Queen's University Press, Montreal, 1978).

Villanueva, A. B.: "Nuclear Power, Private Attorneys-General, and the Regulatory Process," *Canadian Public Administration*, vol. 18, 3, 1975, pp. 399-408.

Waters, W. G.: "Investment Criteria and the Expansion of Major Airports in Canada," *Canadian Public Policy*, vol. 3, 1977, pp. 23-35.

Wolfe, D. A.: "Economic Growth and Foreign Investment: A Perspective on Canadian Economic Policy, 1945-1957," *Journal of Canadian Studies*, vol. 13, 1, 1978, pp. 3-20.

Wood, J. R.: "East Indians and Canada's New Immigration Policy," *Canadian Public Policy*, vol. 4, 1978, pp. 547-567.

THE ENVIRONMENT

A. Geographical and Economic Cleavages

Alford, R. R.: "The Social Bases of Political Cleavage in 1962," in John Meisel (ed.), *Papers on the 1962 Election* (University of Toronto Press, Toronto, 1965), pp. 203-234.

Armstrong, D. E. et al.: "Income Distribution in Canada: A Reply to Needleman and Shed," *Canadian Public Policy*, vol. 5, 4, 1979, pp. 510-517.

Armstrong, Muriel: *The Canadian Economy and its Problems* (Prentice-Hall, Toronto, 1970).

Black, Errol: "One Too Many Reports on Poverty in Canada" (Review Article), *Canadian Journal of Political Science,* vol. 5, 1972, pp. 439-443.

Blackman, W. J.: "A Western Canadian Perspective on the Economy of Confederation," *Canadian Public Policy,* vol. 3, 1977, pp. 414-430.

Blake, D. E.: "LIP and Partisanship: An Analysis of the Local Initiatives Program," *Canadian Public Policy,* vol. 2, 1976, pp. 17-32.

Brewis, Thomas Newton: *Regional Economic Policies in Canada* (Macmillan, Toronto, 1969).

——— and G. Paquet: "Regional Development in Canada: An Exploratory Essay," *Canadian Public Administration,* vol. 11, 2, 1968.

———, H. E. English, Anthony Scott, and Pauline Jewett: *Canadian Economic Policy,* rev. ed. (Macmillan, Toronto, 1965).

Brym, R. J.: "Regional Social Structure and Agrarian Radicalism in Canada: Alberta, Saskatchewan and New Brunswick," *Canadian Review of Sociology and Anthropology,* vol. 15, 3, 1978, pp. 339-351.

Buckley, Helen, and Eva Tihan: *Canadian Policies for Rural Adjustment* (Queen's Printer, Ottawa, 1967).

Cameron, David, M.: "Regional Integration in the Maritime Provinces," *Canadian Journal of Political Science,* vol. 4, 1971, pp. 24-25.

Classen, H. B.: "The Chimera of the Homogeneous State," *Queen's Quarterly,* vol. 79, 4, 1972, pp. 458-469.

Coburn, David and Virginia L. Edwards: "Objective and Subjective Socioeconomic Status: Intercorrelations and Consequences," *Canadian Review of Sociology and Anthropology,* vol. 13, 1976, pp. 178-188.

Copithorne, L.: "Natural Resources and Regional Disparities: A Skeptical View," *Canadian Public Policy,* vol. 5, 2, 1979, pp. 181-194.

Cuneo, Carl J. and James E. Curtis: "Quebec Separatism: An Analysis of Determinants within Social-Class Levels," *Canadian Review of Sociology and Anthropology,* vol. 11, 1974, pp. 1-29.

Curtis, James E. and Ronald D. Lambert: "Status Dissatisfaction and Outgroup Rejections: Cross-cultural Comparisons within Canada," *Canadian Review of Sociology and Anthropology,* vol. 12, 1975, pp. 178-192.

——— and ———: "Educational Status and Reactions to Social and Political Heterogeneity," *Canadian Review of Sociology and Anthropology,* vol. 11, 1976, pp. 189-203.

Dehem, R. et al.: "Concepts of Regional Planning," *Canadian Public Administration,* vol. 9, 1966, pp. 158-176.

Easterbrook, W. T. and M. H. Watkins: *Approaches to Canadian Economic History* (McClelland and Stewart, Toronto, 1967).

Economic Council of Canada: *Living Together: A Study of Regional Disparities* (Supply and Services, Ottawa, 1977).

———: *Annual Reviews* (Supply and Services, Ottawa).

Ferguson, C. B.: "Maritime Union," *Queen's Quarterly,* vol. 77, 2, 1970, pp. 167-179.

Flanagan, Thomas: "Political Theory of the Red River Resistance: The Declaration of December 8, 1869 (Note)," *Canadian Journal of Political Science,* vol. 11, 1978, pp. 153-164.

Grayson, J. Paul and L. M. Grayson.: "The Social Base of Interwar Political Unrest in Urban Alberta," *Canadian Journal of Political Science,* vol. 7, 1974, pp. 289-313.

Guindon, Hubert: "Two Cultures: An Essay on Nationalism, Class and Ethnic Tension," in Richard H. Leach (ed.): *Contemporary Canada* (Duke University Press, Durham, 1968), pp. 33-59.

Hanson, E. J.: "The Future of Western Canada: Economic, Social, and Political," *Canadian Public Administration*, vol. 18, 1, 1975, pp. 104-120.

Howland, R. D.: *Some Regional Aspects of Canada's Economic Development* (Queen's Printer, Ottawa, 1957).

Innis, H.: *Essays in Canadian Economic History* (University of Toronto Press, Toronto, 1956).

Kalbach, W. E.: "Demographic Concerns and the Control of Immigration," *Canadian Public Policy*, vol. 1, 1975, pp. 302-310.

Krueger, R., F. Sargent, A. de Vos, and N. Pearson (eds.): *Regional and Resource Planning in Canada* (Holt, Rinehart and Winston, Toronto, 1963).

Lipset, S. M.: "Social Structure and Political Activity," in B. R. Blishen et al. (eds.): *Canadian Society: Sociological Perspectives*, 3rd ed. (Macmillan, Toronto, 1968), pp. 396-409.

MacPherson, C. Brough: *Democracy in Alberta: Social Credit and the Party System*, 2nd ed. (University of Toronto Press, Toronto, 1962).

Martin, F.: "Incidence de la crise de l'energie sur le developpement regional canadien," *Canadian Public Policy*, vol. 1, 1975, pp. 39-46.

Myers, Gustavus: *A History of Canadian Wealth* (Argosy-Antiquarian, New York, 1968).

Needleman, L.: "Income Distribution in Canada: Policy Implications," *Canadian Public Policy*, vol. 5, 3, 1979, pp. 497-505.

Nelson, J. G. and M. J. Chambers: *Process and Method in Canadian Geography*, 4 vols. (Methuen, Toronto, 1969, 1970).

Newman, Peter: *The Canadian Establishment* (McClelland and Stewart, Toronto, 1975 and 1976).

Norrie, K. H.: "Some Comments on Prairie Economic Alienation," *Canadian Public Policy*, vol. 2, 1976, pp. 211-224.

Officer, L. H. and L. B. Smith (eds.): *Canadian Economic Problems and Policies* (McGraw-Hill, Toronto, 1970).

Pesando, J. E.: "The Indexing of Private Pensions: An Economist's Perspective on the Current Debate," *Canadian Public Policy*, vol. 5, 1, 1979, pp. 80-89.

Raynauld, Andre: *The Canadian Economic System* (Macmillan, Toronto, 1967).

Rea, K. J. and J. T. McLeod (eds.): *Business and Government in Canada* (Methuen, Toronto, 1969).

Reid, T. E., (ed.): *Contemporary Canada: Readings in Economics* (Holt, Rinehart and Winston, Toronto, 1969).

Rinehart, James W. and Ishmael O. Okraku: "A Study of Class Consciousness," *Canadian Review of Sociology and Anthropology*, vol. 11, 1974, pp. 197-213.

Schartz, Mildred A.: *Politics and Territory* (McGill-Queen's University Press, Montreal, 1974).

Shedd, M. S.: "The Measurement of Income Distribution in Canada: Policy Implications," *Candian Public Policy*, vol. 5, 4, 1979, pp. 506-509.

Sinclair, P. R.: "Political Powerlessness and Sociodemographic Status in Canada," *Canadian Review of Sociology and Anthropology*, vol. 16, 2, 1979, pp. 125-135.

Stevenson, P.: "Class and Left-Wing Radicalism," *Canadian Review of Sociology and Anthropology*, vol. 14, 1977, pp. 269-284.

Tepperman, L. J.: *Social Mobility in Canada* (McGraw-Hill Ryerson, Toronto, 1975).

Usher, D.: "Some Questions About the Regional Development Incentives Act," *Canadian Public Policy,* vol. 1, 1975, pp. 557-575.

Veltman, C. J.: "Demographic Components of the Francisation of Rural Quebec: The Case of Rawdon," *American Review of Canadian Studies,* vol. 6, 2, 1976, pp. 22-41.

Warkentin, John (ed.): *Canada: A Geographical Interpretation* (Methuen, Toronto, 1968).

Weller, G. R.: "Hinterland Politics: The Case of Northwestern Ontario," *Canadian Journal of Political Science,* vol. 10, 4, 1977, pp. 727-754.

Woodward, R. S.: "The Effectiveness of DREE's New Location Subsidies," *Canadian Public Policy,* vol. 1, 1975, pp. 217-230.

B. Stratification: Cleavages and Poverty

Abella, Irving (ed.): *On Strike: Six Key Labour Struggles in Canada, 1919-1949* (James, Lewis & Samuel, Toronto, 1974).

Adams, Ian: *The Poverty Wall* (McClelland and Stewart, Toronto, 1970).

_____: *The Real Poverty Report* (McClelland and Stewart, Toronto, 1970).

Allan, Richard: *The Social Passion: Religion and Social Reform in Canada, 1914-28* (University of Toronto Press, Toronto, 1971).

Armstrong, D. E., P. H. Friesen, and D. Miller: "The Measurement of Income Distribution in Canada: Some Problems and Some Tentative Data," *Canadian Public Policy,* vol. 3, 1977, pp. 479-488.

Avery, Donald: "Continental European Immigrant Workers in Canada, 1896-1919: From 'Stalwart Peasants' to Radical Proletariat," *Canadian Review of Sociology and Anthropology,* vol. 12, 1975, pp. 53-64.

Baetz, R. C. and K. Collins: "Equity Aspects of Income Security Programs," *Canadian Public Policy,* vol. 1, 1975, pp. 487-498.

Banting, K.: "The Radical Interpretation of Social Security: A Critique," *Canadian Public Policy,* vol. 1, 1975, pp. 520-526.

Canada, Parliament, Senate Special Committee on Poverty: *Proceedings: 28th Parliament* (Ottawa, 1969).

Canada, Privy Council Office, Special Planning Secretariat: *Meeting Poverty* (Ottawa, 1965). (Hereafter referred to as "MP" issues.)

_____: "Profile of Poverty in Canada" (MP-6).

_____: "Statistical Profile and Graphic Presentation of Urban Poverty" (MP-15).

_____: "The Nature of Poverty in Canada," by D. R. Richmond (MP-26).

_____: "Social Aspects of Poverty," by Daniel Thursz (MP-30).

Chi, N. H.: "Class Voting in Canadian Politics," in O. Kruhlak, R. Schultz, and S. Pobihushchy: *The Canadian Political Process: A Reader,* rev. ed. (Holt, Rinehart and Winston, Toronto, 1973).

Cuneo, Carl J. and James E. Curtis: "Social Aspiration in the Educational and Occupational Status Attainment of Urban Canadians," *Canadian Review of Sociology and Anthropology,* vol. 12, 1975, pp. 6-24.

Curtis, James E.: *Social Stratification in Canada* (Prentice-Hall, Toronto, 1973).

Federal-Provincial Conference on Poverty and Opportunity: "Profile of Poverty in Canada" (digest of papers prepared for the Conference), *Labour Gazette,* vol. 66, May, 1966.

Finkel, A.: "The 'Beautiful People' of Winnipeg," *Canadian Dimension,* vol. 7, 4, 1970, pp. 10-18.

Frank, J. A. and Michael Kelly: "Etude Preliminarie sur la violence collective en Ontario et au Quebec, 1963-1973" (Note), *Canadian Journal of Political Science*, vol. 10, 1977, pp. 145-157.

Goffman, I. J.: "Canadian Social Welfare Policy," in Richard H. Leach (ed.): *Contemporary Canada* (Duke University Press, Durham, 1968).

Grayson, J. Paul and L. M. Grayson: "The Social Base of Interwar Political Unrest in Urban Alberta," *Canadian Journal of Political Science*, vol. 7, 2, 1974, pp. 289-313.

Guindon, Hubert: "Social Unrest, Social Class and Quebec's Bureaucratic Revolution," *Queen's Quarterly*, vol. 71, 1964, pp. 150-162.

Hull, B.: "Equity Aspects of Income Security Programs: A Comment," *Canadian Public Policy*, vol. 1, 1975, pp. 498-502.

Johnson, A. W.: "Canada's Social Security Review 1973-1975: The Central Issues," *Canadian Public Policy*, vol. 1, 1975, pp. 456-472.

Kent, Thomas Worrall: *Social Policy for Canada: Towards a Philosophy of Social Security* (Policy Press, Ottawa, 1962).

Laycock, J. E.: "New Directions for Social Welfare Policy," in A. Rotstein (ed.), *The Prospect of Change: Proposals for Canada's Future* (McGraw-Hill, Toronto, 1965), pp. 308-327.

Li, P. S.: "The Stratification of Ethnic Immigrants: The Case of Toronto," *Canadian Review of Sociology and Anthropology*, vol. 15, 1, 1978, pp. 31-40.

_____: "A Historical Approach to Ethnic Stratification: The Case of the Chinese in Canada, 1858-1930," *Canadian Review of Sociology and Anthropology*, vol. 16, 3, 1979, pp. 320-332.

Lorimer, James and Myfanwy Phillips: *Working People* (James, Lewis & Samuel, Toronto, 1971).

Mann, W. E.: *Poverty and Social Policy in Canada* (Copp Clark, Toronto, 1970).

Milling, G. B.: "Immigration and Labour—Critic or Catalyst?" *Canadian Public Policy*, vol. 1, 1975, pp. 311-316.

Paltiel, Freda L.: *Poverty: An Annotated Bibliography and References*, (Canadian Welfare Council, Ottawa, 1966). Supplement I—March, 1967. Supplement 11—October, 1967.

Pelletier, M.: "Le revenu minimum garanti: une stratégie de bien-être social ou un instrument de politique économique?" *Canadian Public Policy*, vol. 1, 1975, pp. 503-510.

Pinard, M.: "Poverty and Political Movements," in B. R. Blishen et al. (eds.): *Canadian Society: Sociological Perspectives*, 3rd ed. (Macmillan, Toronto, 1968), p. 462.

Plunkett, T. J. and W. Hooson: "Municipal Structure and Services (Graham Commission)," *Canadian Public Policy*, vol. 1, 1975, pp. 367-375.

Porter, John: "The Economic Elite and the Social Structure in Canada," in B. R. Blishen et al. (eds.): *Canadian Society: Sociological Perspectives*, 3rd ed. (Macmillan, Toronto, 1968), p. 754.

Reuber, G.: "The Impact of Government Policies on the Distribution of Income in Canada: A Review," *Canadian Public Policy*, vol. 4, 1978, pp. 505-529.

Richmond, A. H.: "Immigrant Adaptation: A Critical Review of 'Three Years in Canada,' " *Canadian Public Policy*, vol. 1, 1975, pp. 317-327.

Schlesinger, Benjamin: *Poverty in Canada and the United States: Overview and Annotated Bibliography* (University of Toronto Press, Toronto, 1966).

Smith, David C.: *Incomes Policies—Some Foreign Experiences and Their Relevance for Canada* (Queen's Printer, Ottawa, 1966). Economic Council of Canada Special Study no. 4.

Steinberg, C.: "The Welfare Rip-off and All That: A Comment," *Canadian Public Policy*, vol. 1, 1975, pp. 480-486.

Teeple, Gary (ed.): *Capitalism and the National Question in Canada* (University of Toronto Press, Toronto, 1972).

Van Ober, Hadley: "Canadian Approaches to Rural Poverty," *Journal of Farm Economics*, vol. 49, 5, 1967, pp. 1209-1224.

Wilson, J.: "Sociological Aspects of Poverty: A Conceptual Analysis," *Canadian Review of Sociology and Anthropology*, vol. 2, 4, 1965, pp. 175-189.

———: "Politics and Social Class in Canada," *Canadian Journal of Political Science*, vol. I, 1968 pp. 288-308.

C. Ethnic and Religious Cleavage and "The French-Canadian Question"

NOTE: There is a large bibliography on French Canada in vol. 1, 1968 pp. 107-118 of the *Canadian Journal of Political Science*. It constitutes the most complete material readily available for the period up to November, 1967.

Adamson, Christopher R., Peter C. Findlay, Michael K. Oliver, and Janet Solberg: "The Unpublished Research of the Royal Commission on Bilingualism and Biculturalism" (Review Article), *Canadian Journal of Political Science*, vol. 7, 4, 1974, pp. 709-720.

Allard, M.: *The Last Chance: The Canadian Constitution and French Canadians* (Editions Ferland, Quebec, 1964).

Ares, Richard: *Les positions—éthniques, linguistiques et religieuses des canadiens français à la suite du recensement de 1971* (Les Éditions Bellarmin, Montréal, 1975).

Bakvis, H.: "French Canada and the Bureaucratic Phenomenon," *Canadian Public Administration*, vol. 21, 1, 1978, pp. 103-124.

Barbeau, R.: *Le Québec, est-il une colonie?* (Éditions de l'homme, Montreal, 1962).

Bauer, Julien: "Patrons et Patronat au Québec," *Canadian Journal of Political Science*, vol. 9, 3, 1976, pp. 473-491.

Beaujot, R. P.: "A Demographic View on Canadian Language Policy," *Canadian Public Policy*, vol. 5, 1979, pp. 16-29.

Bélanger, M.: "Le Rapport Bélanger: Dix Ans Après," *Canadian Public Administration*, vol. 19, 3, 1976, pp. 457-465.

Benjamin, Jacques: "La minorité en Etat bicommunautaire: quatre études de cas," *Canadian Journal of Political Science*, vol. 4, 4, 1971, pp. 447-496.

———: "La rationalisation des choix budgétaires: les cas québécois et canadien," *Canadian Journal of Political Science*, vol. 5, 3, 1972, pp. 348-364.

Bergeron, Gérard: *Le Canada Français après deux siècles de patience* (Sévil, Paris, 1967).

———: *L'Indépendence oui, mais . . .* (Les Editions Quinze, Montréal, 1977).

———: *Ce jour-là . . . le referendum* (Les Editions Quinze, Montréal, 1978).

Bernard, André: *What Does Quebec Want?* (James Lorimer, Toronto, 1978).

Bonenfant, Jean-Charles: "Le bicaméralisme dans le Québec," *Canadian Journal of Economics and Political Science*, vol. 29, 1963, pp. 495-504.

———: "Les études de la Commission royale d'enquète sur le bilinguisme et le biculturalisme" (Note bibliographique), *Canadian Journal of Political Science*, vol. 4, 1971, pp. 406-416.

——— and J. C. Falardeau: "Cultural and Political Implications of French-Canadian Nationalism," *Canadian Historical Association Annual Report* (Ottawa, 1946).

Bourgault, P.: *Québec Quitte ou Double* (Ferron, Montréal, 1970).

Bourque, G. and N. Laurin-Frenette: "Classes sociales et idéologies nationalistes au Québec 1960-1970," in *L'Homme et la Société* (Paris, 1972).

Brachet, B.: "La crise du fédéralisme canadien et le problème québécois," *Revue du Droit publique et de la Science politique,* vol. 88, 2, 1972, pp. 303-324.

Breton, R.: "The Socio-political Dynamics of the October Events," *Canadian Review of Sociology and Anthropology,* vol. 9, 1, 1972, pp. 33-56.

Brichant, A.: *Option Canada; The Economic Implications of Separatism for the Province of Quebec* (The Canada Committee, Montreal, 1968).

Brossand, Jacques: *L'accession à la souveraineté et le cas du Québec* (Les presses de l'université de Montréal, Montréal, 1976).

Brotz, H.: "Multiculturalism in Canada: A Muddle," *Canadian Public Policy,* vol. 6, 1, 1980, pp. 41-46.

Brunet, Michel: *Québec-Canada anglais: Deux intinéraires un affrontement* (Editions H.M.H., Montréal, 1978).

Canada: *A Preliminary Report of the Royal Commission on Bilingualism and Biculturalism* (Queen's Printer, Ottawa, 1965).

Canadian Broadcasting Corporation: *Québec: Year Eight* (Glendon College Forum, Toronto, 1968).

Carson, J. J.: "Bilingualism Revisited: Or the Confessions of a Middle-Aged and Belated Francophile," *Canadian Public Administration,* vol. 21, 4, 1978, pp. 539-547.

Castonguay, C.: "Why Hide the Facts? The Federalist Approach to the Language Crisis in Canada," *Canadian Public Policy,* vol. 5, 1, 1979, pp. 4-15.

Chaput, M.: *Why I am a Separatist* (Ryerson, Toronto, 1962).

Chaput-Rolland, S.: *My Country: Canada or Québec* (Macmillan, Toronto, 1966).

Charbonneau, M.: "La Commission Des Valeurs Mobilières du Québec," *Canadian Public Administration,* vol. 20, 1, 1977, pp. 87-139.

Chodos, Robert and Nick Auf Der Maur (eds.): *Quebec—A Chronicle, 1968-1972* (James, Lewis & Samuel, Toronto, 1972).

Clark, S. D.: *Church and Sect in Canada* (University of Toronto Press, Toronto, 1948).

Cody, H.: "The Ontario Response to Québec's Separatist Challenge," *American Review of Canadian Studies,* vol. 7, 1, 1978, pp. 43-55.

Cohen, R. I.: *Quebec Votes* (Saje Publications, Montreal, 1965).

Comeau, P. A.: "Acculturation ou assimilation: technique d'analyse et tentative de mesure chez les Franco-ontariens," *Canadian Journal of Political Science,* vol. 2, 2, 1969, pp. 158-172.

Cook, Ramsay: *Canada and the French-Canadian Question* (Macmillan of Canada, Toronto, 1976).

——— (ed.): *French-Canadian Nationalism: An Anthology* (Macmillan, Toronto, 1969).

Corbett, E. M.: *Quebec Confronts Canada* (Copp Clark, Toronto, 1967).

d'Allemagne, A: *Le colonialisme au Québec* (Editions Renaud et Bray, Montréal, 1966).

Dawson, Robert MacGregor: *The Conscription Crisis of 1944* (University of Toronto Press, Toronto, 1961).

Desbarat, P.: *The State of Quebec* (McClelland and Stewart, Toronto, 1965).

Dion, G.: "Securalisation in Quebec," *Journal of Canadian Studies* vol. 3, 1, 1968, pp. 35-44.

Dion, Léon: *Le bill 60 et la société Québécoise* (Editions H.M.H., Montréal, 1967).

———: *Quebec: The Unfinished Revolution* (McGill-Queen's University Press, Montreal, 1976).

Dooley, D. J.: "Quebec and the Future of Canada," *The Review of Politics*, vol. 27, no. 1, Jan. 1965.

Drache, Daniel (ed.): *Québec—Only the Beginning: The Manifestos of the Common Front* (New Press, Toronto, 1972).

Dumont, F. and Y. Martin: *Situation de la recherche sur le Canada français* (Les Presses de l'Université Laval, Québec, 1962).

——— and Jean-Paul Montminy (eds.): *Le Pouvoir dans la société canadienne-française* (Les Presses de l'Université Laval, Québec, 1966).

Elkin, F.: "Ethnic Revolutions and Occupational Dilemmas," *The International Journal of Comparative Sociology*, vol. 13, 1, 1972, pp. 48-54.

Even, A.: "Domination et développement au Nouveau-Brunswick," *Recherches Sociographiques*, vol. 12, 3, 1971, pp. 271-318.

Forsey, E. A.: "Canada: Two Nations or One?" *Canadian Journal of Economics and Political Science*, vol. 28, 4, 1962, pp. 485-501.

———: "The British North America Act and Biculturalism," *Queen's Quarterly*, vol. 71, 2, 1964, pp. 141-149.

Fortin, P. et al.: "Quebec in the Canadian Federation: A Provisional Evaluative Framework," *Canadian Public Administration*, vol. 21, 4, 1978, pp. 558-578.

Frechette, P.: "L'économie de la Confédération: un point de vue québécois," *Canadian Public Policy*, vol. 3, 1977, pp. 431-440.

Garigue, P.: *L'opition politique du Canada français* (Editions du Levrier, Montréal, 1963).

———: *Bibliographie du Québec, 1955-1965* (Les Presses de l'Université de Montréal, Montréal, 1967).

Gélinas, A.: "Les parlementaires et l'administration publique au Québec," *Canadian Journal of Political Science*, vol. 1, 2, 1968, pp. 164-179.

Gérin-Lajoie, P.: *Pourquoi le bill 60* (Editions du Jour, Montréal, 1963).

Gow, J. I.: "Les Québécois, la guerre et la paix, 1945-60," *Canadian Journal of Political Science*, vol. 3, 1, 1970, pp. 88-122.

———: "Histoire administrative du Québec et théorie administrative," *Canadian Journal of Political Science*, vol. 4, 1, 1971, pp. 141-145.

Garnier, G.: "Les Enterprises Multi-nationales et L'Indépendence Eventuelle du Québec," *Canadian Public Policy*, vol. 5, 1, 1979, pp. 59-69.

Grant, D. (ed.): *Quebec Today* (University of Toronto Press, Toronto, 1960).

Groupe des Recherches Sociales: *Les électeurs québécois* (Montréal, 1960).

Guindon, Hubert: "Social Unrest, Social Class, and Quebec's Bureaucratic Revolution," *Queen's Quarterly*, vol. 71, 2, 1964, pp. 150-162 (plus correction vol. 71, 3, 1964, p. XIII).

———: "The Church in French-Canadian Society," *Canadian Dimension*, vol. 4, 3, Mar-Apr. 1967, pp. 29-31.

———: "Two Cultures: An Essay on Nationalism, Class and Ethnic Tension in Contemporary Canada," in O. Kruhlak, R. Schulz, and S. Pobihushchy: *The Canadian Political Process: A Reader* (Holt, Rinehart and Winston, Toronto, 1970).

———: "The Modernization of Quebec and the Legitimacy of the Canadian State," *Canadian Review of Sociology and Anthropology*, vol. 15, 2, 1978, pp. 227-245.

Hughes, Everett Cherrington: *French Canada in Transition* (University of Chicago Press, Chicago, 1943).

Jones R.: *Community in Crisis—French-Canadian Nationalism in Perspective* (McClelland and Stewart, Toronto, 1967).

Joy, R. J.: "Languages in Conflict: Canada, 1976," *American Review of Canadian Studies*, vol. 6, 2, 1976, pp. 7-21.

Jutreas, R.: *Québec libre* (Les éditions actualité, Montréal, 1965).

Keyfitz, N.: "Canadians and Canadiens," *Queen's Quarterly*, vol. 70, 2, 1963, pp. 163-182.

Kwavnick, D.: "The Roots of French-Canadian Discontent," *Canadian Journal of Economics and Political Science*, vol. 31, 4, 1965, pp. 509-523.

———— (ed.): *The Tremblay Report* (Carleton Library, McClelland and Stewart, Toronto, 1972).

Lamontagne, L.: *Le Canada français d'aujourd'hui* (University of Toronto Press, Toronto, 1970).

Lanphier, C. Michael and Raymond N. Morris: *Three Scales of Inequality: Perspectives on French-English Relations* (Longman Canada, Don Mills, 1977).

Latouche, Daniel: "Anti-séparatisme et messianisme au Québec depuis 1960," *Canadian Journal of Political Science*, vol. 3, 4, 1970, pp. 559-578.

————: "La vrai nature de . . . la révolution tranquille" (Note), *Canadian Journal of Political Science*, vol. 7, 3, 1974, pp. 525-536.

Laurendeau, Andre: *La crise de la conscription, 1942* (Les éditions du jour, Montréal, 1962).

Laurin, C.: *Ma Traversée du Québec* (Les éditions du jour, Montréal, 1970).

Lévesque, René: *Option Quebec* (Les éditions de l'homme, Montréal, 1968; English edition: McClelland and Stewart, Toronto, 1968).

————: *La Solution: Programme du Parti Québécois* (Les éditions du jour, Montréal, 1970).

————: *La Souveraineté et l'Economie* (Les éditions du jour, Montréal, 1970).

————: "For an Independent Quebec," *Foreign Affairs* (Toronto), vol. 34, July 1976, pp. 733-744.

————: *My Quebec* (Totem Books, Toronto, 1979).

Levitt, J. (ed.): *Henri Bourassa on Imperialism and Biculturalism, 1900-1918* (Copp Clark, Toronto, 1970).

Lieberson, Stanley: *Language and Ethnic Relations in Canada* (John Wiley and Sons, New York, 1970).

Lijphart, Arend: "Cultural Diversity and Theories of Political Integration," *Canadian Journal of Political Science*, vol. 4, 1, 1971, pp. 1-14.

MacRae, C. F. (ed.): *French Canada Today* (Report of the Mount Allison 1961 Summer Institute, Sackville, 1961).

Maheux, A.: "French Canadians and Democracy," *University of Toronto Quarterly*, vol. 27, 1958, pp. 341-351.

Mallory, J. E.: "The Canadian Dilemma: French and English," *Political Quarterly*, vol. 41, 3, 1970, pp. 281-297.

Marier, R.: "Les objectifs sociaux du Québec," *Canadian Public Administration*, vol. 12, 2, 1969, pp. 181-197.

McRae, K. D.: "The Structure of Canadian History," in L. Hartz: *The Founding of New Societies* (Longmans, Toronto, 1964).

————: "Bilingual Language Districts in Finland and Canada: Adventures in the Transplanting of an Institution," *Canadian Public Policy*, vol. 4, 3, 1978, pp. 331-351.

McRoberts, Kenneth and Dale Posgate: *Quebec: Social Change and Political Crisis* (McClelland and Stewart, Toronto, 1976).

_____ and _____: *Quebec: Social and Political Crisis Revised* (McClelland and Stewart, Toronto, 1980).

Meisel, J.: "Religious Affiliation and Electoral Behaviour: A Case Study," in John Courtney (ed.): *Voting in Canada* (Prentice-Hall, Toronto, 1967), pp. 144-161.

Meyers, H. B.: *The Quebec Revolution* (Harvest House, Montreal, 1964).

Milner, Henry: *Politics in the New Quebec* (McClelland and Stewart, Toronto, 1978).

_____ and Sheilagh Hodgins Milner: *The Decolonization of Quebec: An Analysis of Left-Wing Nationalism* (McClelland and Stewart, Toronto, 1973).

Murray, Vera and Don Murray: *De Bourassa à Lévesque* (Editions Quinze, Montréal, 1978).

Neatby, H. B.: "Mackenzie King and French Canada," *Journal of Canadian Studies*, vol. 11, 1, 1976, pp. 3-13.

Noel, S. J. R.: "Consociational Democracy and Canadian Federalism," *Canadian Journal of Political Science*, vol. 4, 1, 1971, pp. 15-18.

Oliver, M.: "Quebec and Canadian Democracy," *Canadian Journal of Economics and Political Science*, vol. 23, 5, 1957, pp. 504-515.

Orban, E.: *Le Conseil Legislatif du Québec* (Bellarmin, Montréal, 1967).

_____: "La fin du bicameralisme au Québec," *Canadian Journal of Political Science*, vol. 2, 3, 1969, pp. 312-326.

Paquette, Gilbert and Jean-Pierre Charbonneau: *L'Option* (Les éditions de l'homme, Montréal, 1978).

Pare, G.: *Au-delà du Séparatisme* (Collection les idées du jour, Montréal, 1966).

Parti Pris: *Les Québécois* (Maspero, Paris, 1967).

Pelletier, R.: "Le militant du R.I.N. et son parti," *Recherches Sociographiques*, vol. 13, 1, 1972, pp. 41-72.

Pinard, Maurice: "Working Class Politics: An Interpretation of the Quebec Case," *Canadian Review of Sociology and Anthropology*, vol. 7, 2, 1970, pp. 87-109.

Premier Congrès des Affaires Canadiennes: *The Canadian Experiment: Success or Failure?* (Les Presses de l'Université Laval, Québec, 1962).

Quebec: *Report of the Royal Commission of Inquiry on Constitutional Problems, Tremblay Report*, 4 vols. (Queen's Printer, Quebec, 1956).

_____: *Le Rapport de la Commission Royale D'Enquete sur L'Enseignment, le Rapport Parent*, 3 vols. (L'imprimeur de la reine, Québec, 1963-1966).

_____: *Le Rapport de la Commission Royal d'Enquete sur La Fiscalité, le Rapport Bélanger* (L'imprimeur de la reine, Québec, 1966).

Quesnel-Ouellet, Louise: "Régionalisation et urbaine conscience politique régionale; la communauté de Québec," *Canadian Journal of Political Science*, vol. 4, 2, 1971, pp. 191-205.

_____: "Situations et attitudes face au changement dans les structures municipales,"*Canadian Journal of Political Science*, vol. 6, 2, 1973, pp. 195-218.

Quinn, Herbert Furlong: *The Union Nationale: A Study in Quebec Nationalism* (University of Toronto Press, Toronto, 1963).

Raynauld, A.: "Les implications économiques de l'option Québec," *Le Devoir*, 24 avril, 1970, p. 5, col. 1.

Reid, Malcolm: *The Shouting Signpainters: A Literary and Political Account of Quebec Revolutionary Nationalism* (McClelland and Stewart, Toronto, 1972).

Rioux, Marcel: "Conscience ethnique et conscience de classe au Québec," *Recherches Sociographiques,* vol. 6, 1, 1965, pp. 23-32.

―――― (ed.): *L'église et le Quebec,* les textes du reunion de l'Institut Canadien des affaires Publiques, 1961 (Les éditions du jour, Montréal, 1961).

―――― and Y. Martin: *French-Canadian Society* (McClelland and Stewart, Toronto, 1964).

Rotstein, A. (ed.): *Power Corrupted: The October Crisis and the Repression of Quebec* (New Press, 1971).

Rutan, G. F.: "Two views of the concept of sovereignty: Canadian-Canadien," *Western Political Quarterly,* vol. 24, 3, 1971, pp. 456-466.

Ryan, C.: "Un cas pertinent: le Quebec," *Canadian Public Policy,* vol. 2, 1976, pp. 587-595.

Schwartz, M.: "Political Behaviour and Ethnic Origin," in John Meisel (ed.): *Papers on the 1962 Election* (University of Toronto Press, Toronto, 1965), pp. 253-71.

Scott, F. R. and M. Oliver (eds.): *Quebec States her Case* (Macmillan, Toronto, 1964).

Seguin, M.: "Genese et historique de l'idée séparatiste au Canada français," *Laurentie,* no. 119, 1962.

Siegfried, A.: *The Race Question in Canada* (McClelland and Stewart, Toronto, 1966).

Simeon, R.: "Quebec 1970: the dilemma of power," *Queen's Quarterly,* vol. 79, 1, 1972, pp. 100-107.

Sloane, T.: *Quebec: The Not-So-Quiet Revolution* (Ryerson, Toronto, 1965).

Smith, Denis: *Bleeding Hearts—Bleeding Country: Canada and the Quebec Crisis* (Hurtig, Edmonton, 1971).

Societe St. Jean Baptiste de Montréal: *Le fédéralisme: l'acte de l'Amérique du Nord britannique et les Canadiens français,* Mémoire au comité parlementaire de la constitution du gouvernement du Québec (Les éditions de l'agence Duvernay, Montréal, 1964).

Stein, Michael B.: *The Dynamics of Right-Wing Protest: A Political Analysis of Social Credit in Quebec* (University of Toronto Press, Toronto, 1973).

Thomson, Dale: *Quebec Society and Politics: Views from the Inside* (McClelland and Stewart, Toronto, 1973).

Troisième Congres des Affaires Canadiennes: *Les nouveaux Québécois* (les Presses de l'Universite Laval, Quebec, 1964).

Trudeau, P. E.: "Some Obstacles to Democracy in Quebec," *C.J.E.P.S.,* vol. 24, 3, 1958.

―――― : *Federalism and the French Canadians* (Macmillan, Toronto, 1968).

―――― (ed.): *The Asbestos Strike* (James, Lewis & Samuel, Toronto, 1974).

Vaillancourt, F.: "La Charte de la Langue Française du Québec: un essai d'analyse," *Canadian Public Policy,* vol. 4, 3, 1978, pp. 284-308.

―――― : "La Situation Démographique et Socio-Economique des Francophones du Québec: Une Revue," *Canadian Public Policy,* vol. 5, 4, 1979, pp. 542-558.

Vallieres, Pierre: *Negres blancs d'Amerique* (Editions Parti Pris, Montreal, 1968).

―――― : *White Niggers of America,* translated by Joan Pinkham (McClelland and Stewart, Toronto, 1971).

―――― : *Choose!* (New Press, Toronto, 1972).

Veltman, C. J.: "Ethnic Assimilation in Quebec: A Statistical Analysis," *American Review of Canadian Studies,* vol. 5, 2, 1975, pp. 104-129.

Wade, M. (ed.): *Canadian Dualism: Studies of French-English Relations* (University of Toronto Press, Toronto, 1960).
_____: *The French-Canadian Outlook: A Brief Account of the Unknown North Americans* (McClelland and Stewart, Toronto, 1964).
_____: *The French Canadians*, vol. 1, 1760-1911, vol. 2, 1912-1967 (Macmillan, Toronto, 1968).
Whitaker, Reginald: "The Competition for Power: Hobbes and the Quebec Question," *Canadian Forum*, vol. 58, February, 1979, pp. 6-10.
Wilson, V. S. and W. A. Mullins: "Representative Bureaucracy: Linguistic/Ethnic Aspects in Canadian Public Policy," *Canadian Public Administration*, vol. 21, 4, 1978, pp. 513-538.
Woolfson, P.: "The French Fact: Linguistic Challenge, Demographic Reality, Political Distortion," *American Review of Canadian Studies*, vol. 6, 2, 1976, pp. 1-6.

POLITICAL ATTITUDES

A. Political Socialization

Abramson, Paul: "The Differential Political Socialization of English Secondary School Students," *Sociology of Education*, vol. 40, 1967, pp. 246-269.
Atherton, P. J.: "Education: Radical Reform in Nova Scotia," *Canadian Public Policy*, vol. 1, 1975, pp. 384-392.
Baldus, B. and V. Tribe: "The Development of Perceptions and Evaluations of Social Inequality among Public School Children," *Canadian Review of Sociology and Anthropology*, vol. 15, 1, 1978, pp. 50-60.
Bender, Gerald J.: "Political Socialization and Political Change," *The Western Political Quarterly*, vol. 20, part I, 1967, pp. 772-727.
Briggs, J. L.: "The Creation of Value in Canadian Inuit Society," *International Social Science Journal*, vol. 31, 3, 1979, pp. 393-403.
Cameron, David R. and Laura Summers: "Non-Family Agents of Political Socialization: A Reassessment of Converse and Dupeux," *Canadian Journal of Political Science*, vol. 5, 3, 1972, pp. 418-432.
Chalmers, J. N.: "Strategy for Native Education, 1960-1970," *Journal of Canadian Studies*, vol. 11, 3, 1976, pp. 37-49.
Clausen, John A.: "Recent Developments in Socialization Theory and Research," *The Annals of the American Academy of Political and Social Science*, vol. 377, 1968, pp. 139-155.
Cuneo, Carl, J.: "The Social Basis of Political Continentalism in Canada," *Canadian Review of Sociology and Anthropology*, vol. 13, 1, 1976, pp. 50-70.
Dawson, Richard and Kenneth Prewitt: *Political Socialization* (Little, Brown, Boston, 1968).
Easton, David: "The Theoretical Relevance of Political Socialization," *Canadian Journal of Political Science*, vol. 1, 1968, pp. 125-146.
Froman, Lewis A., Jr.: "Learning Political Attitudes," *Western Political Quarterly*, vol. 15, 1962, pp. 304-313.
Greenstein, Fred I.: "The Benevolent Leader: Children's Images of Political Authority," *American Political Science Review*, vol. 54, 1960, pp. 934-943.
_____: *Children and Politics* (Yale University Press, New Haven, 1965).

758   BIBLIOGRAPHY

Hess, Robert D. and Judith V. Torney: *The Development of Political Attitudes in Children* (Aldine Publishing Co., Chicago, 1967).

Hill, John L. A.: "Political Socialization of Children in a Rural Environment," (Unpublished M.A. thesis, Queen's University, 1969).

Hodgetts, A.: *What Culture, What Heritage? A Study of Civic Education in Canada* (Ontario Institute for Studies in Education, Toronto, 1970).

Hyman, Herbert H.: *Political Socialization* (The Free Press, Glencoe, 1959).

Jabbra, J. G. and R. G. Landes: "Political Orientation among Adolescents in Nova Scotia: An Exploratory Analysis of a Regional Political Culture in Canada," *Indian Journal of Political Science*, vol. 37, 4, 1976, pp. 75-96.

Jaros, Dean: *Socialization to Politics* (Praeger, New York, 1973).

Jennings, M. Kent: "Pre-adult Orientations to Multiple Systems of Government," *Midwest Journal of Political Science*, vol. 11, 1967, pp. 291-317.

Johnstone, John C.: *Young People's Images of Canadian Society* (Queen's Printer, Ottawa, 1969).

Kendall, J.: "A Canadian Construction of Reality: Northern Images of the United States," *American Review of Canadian Studies*, vol. 4, 1, 1974, pp. 20-36.

Kornberg, Allan and Norman Thomas: "The Political Socialization of National Legislative Elites in the United States and Canada," *Journal of Politics*, vol. 27, 1965, pp. 761-775.

———— and Joel Smith: "Self-concepts of American and Canadian Party Officials," *Polity*, vol. 3, 1, 1970, pp. 70-99.

————, ————, and David Bromley: "Some Differences in the Political Socialization Patterns of Canadian and American Party Officials: A Preliminary Report," *Canadian Journal of Political Science*, vol. 2, 1, 1969, pp. 64-88.

Lane, Robert E.: *Political Life* (Free Press, Glencoe, 1959).

Langton, K. P.: *Political Socialization* (Oxford University Press, New York, 1969).

Mathews, R.: "Susanna Moodie, Pink Toryism, and Nineteenth Century Ideas of Canadian Identity," *Journal of Canadian Studies*, vol. 10, 3, 1975, pp. 3-14.

Pammett, J. H.: "The Development of Political Orientations in Canadian School Children," *Canadian Journal of Political Science*, vol. 4, 1, 1971, pp. 132-141.

———— and M. S. Whittington (eds.): *Foundations of Political Culture: Readings on Political Socialization in Canada* (Macmillan, Toronto, 1976).

Pross, A. P. and V. S. Wilson: "Graduate Education in Canadian Public Administration: Antecedents, Present Trends and Portents," *Canadian Public Administration*, vol. 19, 4, 1976, pp. 515-541.

Redekop, John H.: "Authors and Publishers: An Analysis of Textbook Selection in Canadian Departments of Political Science and Sociology" (Note) *Canadian Journal of Political Science*, vol. 9, 1, 1976, pp. 107-120.

Reilly, Wayne G.: "Political Attitudes among Law Students in Quebec," *Canadian Journal of Political Science*, vol. 4, 1, 1971, pp. 122-131.

Richert, J. P.: "English and French-Canadian Children's Perception of the October Crisis," *Journal of Social Psychology*, vol. 89, 1, 1973, pp. 3-13.

————: "Political Socialization in Quebec: Young People's Attitudes toward Government" (Note), *Canadian Journal of Political Science*, vol. 6, 2, 1973, pp. 303-313.

————: "Canadian National Identity: An Empirical Study," *American Review of Canadian Studies*, vol. 4, 1, 1974, pp. 89-98.

Schonfeld, N. R.: "Political Attitudes, Expressed Views and the Centrality of Politics: A Case Study of French Secondary School Students," *Canadian Journal of Political Science*, vol. 12, 1, 1979, pp. 21-54.

Simeon, Richard and D. J. Elkins: "Regional Political Cultures in Canada," *Canadian Journal of Political Science*, vol. 7, 1974, pp. 397-437.

Smith, J. and A. Kornberg: "Self Concepts of American and Canadian Party Officials: Their Development and Consequences," *Social Forces*, vol. 49, 2, 1970, pp. 210-226.

_____, _____, and D. Bromley: "Patterns of Early Political Socialization and Adult Party Affiliation," *Canadian Review of Sociology and Anthropology*, vol. 5, 3, 1968, pp. 123-155.

Solberg, Patricia Anne: "Attitudes of Canadian Veterans to Political Economic Issues," *Journal of Social Psychology*, vol. 38, 1953, pp. 73-86.

Trudel, Marcel and Genevieve Jain: *Canadian History Textbooks* (Queen's Printer, Ottawa, 1970).

Ullman, S. H.: "Nationalism and Regionalism in the Political Socialization of Cape Breton Whites and Indians," *American Review of Canadian Studies*, vol. 5, 1, 1975, pp. 66-97.

_____: "Regional Political Cultures in Canada: Part I: A Theoretical and Conceptual Introduction," *American Review of Canadian Studies*, vol. 7, 2, 1977, pp. 1-22.

_____: "Regional Political Cultures in Canada: Part II," *American Review of Canadian Studies*, vol. 7, 2, 1978, pp. 70-101.

Williams, T. R.: "Some Facts and Fantasies Concerning Local Autonomy in the Metropolitan Toronto School System," *Canadian Public Administration*, vol. 17, 2, 1974, pp. 274-288.

Wilson, John: "The Canadian Political Cultures: Towards a Redefinition of the Nature of the Canadian Political System," *Canadian Journal of Political Science*, vol. 7, 3, 1974, pp. 438-483.

Woolfson, P.: "Value Orientation of Anglo-Canadian and French-Canadian School Children in a Quebec Community near the Vermont Border," *American Review of Canadian Studies*, vol. 4, 1, 1974, pp. 75-88.

Zeligs, Rose: "Children's Concepts and Stereotypes of Turk, Portuguese, Roumanian, Arab, Chinese, French-Canadian, Mulatto, South American, Hawaiian and Australian," *Journal of Genetic Psychology*, vol. 83, 1953, pp. 171-178.

B. Public Opinion

Alford, R. R.: "The Social Bases of Political Cleavage in 1962," in J. Meisel (ed.): *Papers on the 1962 Election* (University of Toronto Press, Toronto, 1964).

Almond, G. and S. Verba: *The Civic Culture* (Princeton University Press, Princeton, 1963).

Armstrong, J.: "Canadians in Crisis: The Nature and Source of Support for Leadership in a National Emergency," *Canadian Review of Sociology and Anthropology*, vol. 9, 4, 1972, pp. 299-324.

Converse, Philip E.: "The Nature of Belief Systems in Mass Publics," in D. Apter (ed.): *Ideology and Discontent* (The Free Press, New York, 1964), pp. 206-262.

_____, Georges Dupeux, and John Meisel: "Continuities in Popular Political Culture: French and Anglo-Saxon Contrasts in Canada," (paper prepared for the International Conference on Comparative Electoral Behaviour, Ann Arbor, Michigan, April, 1967).

Cunningham, R. B.: "Attitudes on Pollution and Growth in Hamilton, or There's an Awful Lot of Talk These Days about Ecology," *Canadian Journal of Political Science,* vol. 5, 3, 1972, pp. 389-401.

Devall, W. B.: "Support for Civil Liberties Among English-speaking Canadian University Students," *Canadian Journal of Political Science,* vol. 3, 3, 1970, pp. 433-449.

Dion, L.: "Regimes d'opinions publiques et systemes ideologiques," *Ecrits du Canada Français,* vol. 12, 1962.

Doern, G. B. and A. M. Maslove (eds.): *The Public Evaluation of Government Spending* (Institute for Research on Public Policy, Montreal, 1978).

Friedmann, Karl, A.: "The Public and the Ombudsman: Perceptions and Attitudes in Britain and in Alberta," *Canadian Journal of Political Science,* vol. 10, 3, 1977, pp. 497-525.

Katz, D. et al. (eds.): *Public Opinion and Propaganda* (Holt, Rinehart and Winston, New York, 1960).

Key, V. O.: *Public Opinion and American Democracy* (Alfred A. Knopf, New York, 1961).

Lane, R. E. and D. O. Sears: *Public Opinion* (Prentice-Hall, Englewood Cliffs, 1964).

Lippman, W.: *Public Opinion* (Macmillan, New York, 1960).

Lipset, S. M.: *Political Man* (Anchor-Doubleday, Garden City, 1969).

_____, Paul Lazarsfeld, Allen Barton, and Juan Linz: "The Psychology of Voting," in Lindzey Gardner (ed.): *Handbook of Social Psychology, II* (Addison-Wesley, Cambridge, 1965), pp. 1124-1175.

Luttbeg, Norman R. (ed.): *Public Opinion and Public Policy: Models of Political Influence* (The Dorsey Press, Homewood, Ill., 1968).

McDonald, L.: "Attitude Organization and Voting Behaviour in Canada" (1968 federal elections), *Canadian Review of Sociology and Anthropology,* vol. 8, 3, 1971, pp. 164-184.

Ornstein, M. D. et al.: "Public Opinion and the Canadian Political Crisis," *Canadian Review of Sociology and Anthropology,* vol. 15, 2, 1978, pp. 58-205.

Qualter, T. H.: "The Manipulation of Popular Impulse: Graham Wallas Revisited," *Canadian Journal of Economics and Political Science,* vol. 25, 2, 1969, pp. 165-173.

Regenstreif, S. P.: *The Diefenbaker Interlude: Parties and Voting in Canada, an Interpretation* (Longmans, Toronto, 1965).

Reilly, W. G.: "Political Attitudes among Law Students in Quebec," *Canadian Journal of Political Science,* vol. 4, 1, 1971.

Schwartz, M.: *Public Opinion and Canadian Identity* (Fitzhenry and Whiteside, Toronto, 1967).

Usher, D.: "The English Response to the Prospect of the Separation of Quebec," *Canadian Public Policy,* vol. 4, 1, 1978, pp. 57-87.

C. The Mass Media

Babe, R. E.: "Regulation of Private Television Broadcasting by the Canadian Radio-Television Commission: A Critique of Ends and Means," *Canadian Public Administration,* vol. 19, 4, 1976, pp. 552-586.

Breed, W.: "Social Control in the Newsroom: A Functional Analysis," *Social Forces,* vol. 33, 4, 1955, pp. 326-335.

Bruce, C.: *News and the Southams* (Macmillan, Toronto, 1968).

Cabatoff, Kenneth: "Radio-Quebec: Une Institution Publique a la Recherche d'un Mission," *Canadian Public Administration*, vol. 19, 4, 1976, pp. 542-551.

Canada, Committee on Broadcasting: *Report* (Queen's Printer, Ottawa, 1965).

———, Royal Commission on Broadcasting: *Report*, 2 vols. (Queen's Printer, Ottawa 1957).

———, Royal Commission on Publications: *Report*, 2 vols., the *O'Leary Report*, (Queen's Printer, Ottawa, 1961).

———, Senate: *Report of the Senate Committee on the Mass Media*, 3 vols., esp. *The Uncertain Mirror*, vol. III (Queen's Printer, Ottawa, 1971).

Compton, Neil: "The Mass Media," in Michael Oliver (ed.): *Social Purpose for Canada* (University of Toronto Press, Toronto, 1961), pp. 50-87.

Cook, R.: *The Politics of John W. Dafoe and the Free Press* (University of Toronto Press, Toronto, 1963).

Dahrin, R.: "The Media and the Rise of P. E. Trudeau," *Canadian Dimension*, vol. 5, June-July, 1968, pp. 5-6.

Dexter, Lewis Anthony and David Manning White (eds.): *People, Society and Mass Communications* (The Free Press, New York, 1964).

Donnelly, M.: *Dafoe of the Free Press* (Macmillan, Toronto, 1968).

Eggleston, W.: "The Press in Canada," *The Royal Commission on National Development in the Arts, Letters and Sciences, Massey Report* (King's Printer, Ottawa, 1951).

Ferguson, George Victor: *Press and Party in Canada: Issues of Freedom* (Ryerson, Toronto, 1955).

Gordon, D. R.: *Language, Logic and the Mass Media* (Holt, Rinehart and Winston, Toronto, 1966).

Hamlin, D. L. B. (ed.): *The Press and the Public* (University of Toronto Press, Toronto, 1962).

Harkness, R.: *J. E. Atkinson of the Star* (University of Toronto Press, Toronto, 1963).

Hornby, Robert: *The Press in Modern Society* (Muller, London, 1965).

Irving, John Allan (ed.): *Mass Media in Canada* (Ryerson, Toronto, 1962).

Kersterton, Wulfred H.: *A History of Journalism in Canada* (McClelland and Stewart, Toronto, 1967).

Lloyd, Trevor Owen and Jack McLeod (eds.): *Agenda 1970* (University of Toronto Press, Toronto, 1968).

Morton, Desmond: "Democracy and the Mass Media," *The Canadian Forum*, vol. 49, July 1969, pp. 82-84.

Ostman, R. E.: "CBC's 'The World at Six' Looks at the U.S.: Content Analysis as an Aid to Understanding the Media," *American Review of Canadian Studies*, vol. 7, 1977, pp. 33-50.

Peers, R.: *The Politics of Canadian Broadcasting, 1920-1951* (University of Toronto Press, Toronto, 1969).

Qualter, T. H. and K. A. MacKirdy: "The Press of Ontario and the Election," in John Meisel: *Papers on the 1962 Election* (University of Toronto Press, Toronto, 1964), pp. 145-168.

Schultz, J.: "Whose News? The Struggle for Wire Distribution 1900-1920," *American Review of Canadian Studies*, vol. 10, 1980, pp. 27-62.

Seymour-Ure, Colin: "The Parliamentary Press Gallery in Ottawa," *Parliamentary Affairs*, vol. 16, 1962-63, pp. 36-41.

Singer, B. D.: "Violence, Protest, and War in Television News: The U.S. and Canada," in *Public Opinion Quarterly*, vol. 34, 1970-71, pp. 611-616.

Stewart, N. B.: "The CBC: Canadian? Regional? Popular? An Examination of Program Objectives for English Television," *Canadian Public Administration*, vol. 18, 1975, pp. 337-365.

Stursberg, Peter: *Mr. Broadcasting: The Ernie Bushnell Story* (Peter Martin Associates, Toronto, 1971). -

Wagenberg, Ronald H. and Walter C. Soderlund: "The Effects of Chain Ownership on Editorial Coverage: The Case of the 1974 Canadian Federal Election," *Canadian Journal of Political Science*, vol. 9, 1976, pp. 682-689.

Weir, E. A.: *The Struggle for National Broadcasting in Canada* (McClelland and Stewart, Toronto, 1965).

Wilson, H. H.: "Techniques of Pressure: Anti-nationalization Propaganda in Britain," *Public Opinion Quarterly*, vol. 15, Summer, 1951, pp. 225-242.

Windlesham, David J. G. H.: *Communication and Political Power* (Cape, London, 1966).

D. Political Participation

Alford, R. R.: *Party and Society* (Rand-McNally, Chicago, 1963).

Black, J. H. and N. E. McGlen: "Male-Female Political Involvement Differentials in Canada, 1969-1974," *Canadian Journal of Political Science*, vol. 12, 1979, pp. 471-498.

Burke, M. et al.: "Federal and Provincial Political Participation in Canada: Some Methodological and Substantive Considerations," *Canadian Review of Sociology and Anthropology*, vol. 15, 1978, pp. 61-75.

Campbell, Angus: "The Passive Citizen," *Acta Sociologica*, vol. 6, (fasc. 1-2), pp. 9-21.

_____ et al.: *Elections and the Political Order* (John Wiley and Sons, New York, 1966).

Clarke, H. et al.: *Political Choice in Canada* (McGraw-Hill-Ryerson, Toronto 1978).

Eulau, Heinz and Peter Schneider: "Dimensions of Political Involvement," *Public Opinion Quarterly*, vol. 20, Spring, 1956, pp. 128-142.

Eyzenck, H. J.: *The Psychology of Politics* (Routledge and Kegan Paul, London, 1954).

Frenkel-Brunswick, Else: "The Interaction of Psychological and Sociological Factors in Political Behaviour," *American Political Science Review*, vol. 46, 1952, pp. 44-65.

Katz, Elihu and Paul Lazarsfeld: *Personal Influence* (The Free Press, Glencoe, 1955).

Kim, Y. C.: "The Concept of Political Culture in Comparative Politics," *Journal of Politics*, vol. 26, 1964, pp. 313-336.

Kornberg, A. et al.: "Federalism and Fragmentation: Political Support in Canada," *Journal of Politics*, vol. 4, 1979, pp. 889-906.

_____: "Public Support for Community and Regime in the Regions of Contemporary Canada," *American Review of Canadian Studies*, vol. 10, 1980, pp. 75-93.

Lane, R. E.: *Political Life* (The Free Press, Glencoe, 1959).

_____: *Political Ideology* (The Free Press, New York, 1962)

Levin, Murrary B.: *The Alienated Voter* (Holt, Rinehart and Winston, New York, 1960).

Lipset, S. M.: *Agrarian Socialism* (University of California Press, Berkeley, 1950).

MacInnis, Grace: "Women in Politics," *The Parliamentarian*, vol. 53, 1972, pp. 8-12.

MacKinnon, Frank: *Posture and Politics: Some Observations on Participatory Democracy* (University of Toronto Press, Toronto, 1973).

Meisel, John: *The Canadian General Election of 1957* (University of Toronto Press, Toronto, 1962).

———: *Papers on the 1962 Election* (University of Toronto Press, Toronto, 1964).

———: "Citizen Demands and Government Response," *Canadian Public Policy*, vol. 2, 1976, pp. 564-572.

Milbrath, L. : *Political Participation* (Rand-McNally, Chicago, 1965).

Miller, W.: *Political Participation in Canada* (Macmillan, Toronto, 1979).

Nie, Norman H., G. Bingham Powell, Jr., and Kenneth Prewitt: "Social Structure and Political Participation: Developmental Relationship, I and II," *American Political Science Review*, vol. 63, 1969, pp. 301-378, 808-872.

Polsby, Nelson, W.: *Community Power and Political Theory* (Yale University Press, New Haven, 1963).

Presthus, Robert: *Men at the Top: A Study in Community Power* (Oxford Press, 1968).

Scarrow, Howard A.: "Patterns of Voter Turnout in Canada," *Midwest Journal of Political Science*, vol. 5, 1961, pp. 351-365.

Sewell, John: *Up Against City Hall* (James, Lewis & Samuel, Toronto, 1972).

Sproule-Jones, Mark and Kenneth D. Hart: "A Public-Choice Model of Political Participation," *Canadian Journal of Political Science*, vol. 6, 1973, pp. 175-194.

Templeton, Frederick: "Alienation and Political Participation," *Public Opinion Quarterly*, vol. 30, 1966, pp. 249-261.

Van Loon, R. J.: "Political Participation in Canada: The 1965 Election," *Canadian Journal of Political Science*, vol. 3, 1970, pp. 376-399.

Welch, Susan: "Dimensions of Political Participation in a Canadian Sample," *Canadian Journal of Political Science*, vol. 8, 1975, pp. 553-559.

E. Canadian Nationalism

Abella, Irving M.: *Nationalism, Communism and Canadian Labour: The C.I.O., the Communist Party and the Canadian Congress of Labour 1935-1956* (University of Toronto Press, Toronto, 1973).

Aubery, P.: "Nationalisme et lutte des classes au Québec," *American Review of Canadian Studies*, vol. 5, 1975, pp. 130-145.

Blishen, B. R. et al. (eds.): *Canadian Society: Sociological Perspectives*, 3rd ed. (Macmillan, Toronto, 1968),

Caldwell, G.: "English-Speaking Quebec in the Light of Its Reaction to Bill 22," *American Review of Canadian Studies*, vol. 6, 1976, pp. 42-56.

Canada, Prime Minister: *Federalism for the Future* (Queen's Printer, Ottawa, 1968).

———,———: *The Constitution and the People of Canada* (Queen's Printer, Ottawa, 1969).

———, Privy Council Office: *White Paper on a Domestic Satellite Communication System for Canada* (Queen's Printer, Ottawa, 1968).

———, Royal Commission on Bilingualism and Biculturalism: *Preliminary Report* (Queen's Printer, Ottawa, 1965).

————, Task Force on the Structure of Canadian Industry: *Foreign Ownership and the Structure of Canadian Industry, The Watkins Report* (Queen's Printer, Ottawa, 1968).

Clarkson, Stephen (ed.): *An Independent Foreign Policy for Canada?* The University League for Social Reform (McClelland and Stewart, Toronto, 1968).

Cook, R.: *French Canadian Nationalism* (Macmillan, Toronto, 1969).

————: *The Maple Leaf Forever: Essays on Nationalism and Politics in Canada* (Macmillan, Toronto, 1971).

Crispo, John H.: *International Unionism: A Study in Canadian-American Relations* (McGraw-Hill, Toronto, 1967).

Easterbrook, William Thomas and Hugh G. J. Aitkin: *Canadian Economic History* (Macmillan, Toronto, 1956).

Eayrs, James George: *The Art of the Possible: Government and Foreign Policy in Canada* (University of Toronto Press, Toronto, 1961).

Gibbins, Roger: "Models of Nationalism: A Case Study of Political Ideologies in the Canadian West," *Canadian Journal of Political Science*, vol. 10, 1977, pp. 341-373.

Gordon, Walter Lockhart: *A Choice for Canada* (McClelland and Stewart, Toronto, 1966).

Grant, G. P.: *Technology and Empire* (House of Anansi, Toronto, 1969).

————: *Lament for a Nation: The Defeat of Canadian Nationalism* (McClelland and Stewart, Toronto, 1970).

Horowitz, Gad: *Canadian Labour in Politics* (University of Toronto Press, Toronto, 1968).

Johnson, H. G.: "Problems of Canadian Nationalism," *International Journal*, vol. 16, 1961, pp. 238-249.

———— *The Canadian Quandary* (McGraw-Hill, Toronto, 1963).

———— "The Economics of the 'Brain Drain': The Canadian Case," *Minerva*, vol. 3, 1965, pp. 299-311.

————: "The Watkins Report: Towards a New National Policy," *International Journal*, vol. 23, 1968, pp. 615-622.

Kierans, Eric W.: *Challenge of Confidence: Kierans on Canada* (McClelland and Stewart, Toronto, 1967).

Laczko, L.: "English Canadian and Québécois Nationalism," *Canadian Review of Sociology and Anthropology*, vol. 5, 1978, pp. 206-217.

Levitt, Kari: *Silent Surrender: The Multi-National Corporation in Canada* (Macmillan, Toronto, 1970).

Logan, Harold Amos: *Trade Unions in Canada* (Macmillan, Toronto, 1948).

Lumsden, Ian (ed.): *Close the 49th Parallel: The Americanization of Canada* (University of Toronto Press, Toronto, 1970).

McInnis, Edgar: *Canada, a Political and Social History* (Holt, Rinehard and Winston, New York, 1959).

Morton, W. L.: *The Canadian Identity* (University of Toronto Press, Toronto, 1972).

Ontario, Legislative Assembly: *Final Report on Economic Nationalism of the Select Committee on Economic and Cultural Nationalism* (Queen's Printer, Toronto, 1975).

Pearson, L. B.: "Canada's Role as a Middle Power," in J. King Gordon (ed.): *Canada's Role as a Middle Power* (Canadian Institute of International Affairs, Toronto, 1966).

Resnick, P.: *Land of Cain: Class and Nationalism in English Canada* (New Star Books, Vancouver, 1972).

Rutan, G.: "Doctrinal Folly in the Name of Canadianism: Doctrine of the 'New' Nationalism in Canada," *American Review of Canadian Studies,* vol. 4, 1974, pp. 37-53.

Safarian, A. E.: *Foreign Ownership of Canadian Industry* (McGraw-Hill, Toronto, 1966).

Schwartz, Mildred A.: *Public Opinion and Canadian Identity* (University of California Press, Berkeley, 1967).

Smiley, Donald Victor: *The Canadian Political Nationality* (Methuen, Toronto, 1967).

Underhill, Frank Hawkins: *In Search of Canadian Liberalism* (Macmillan, Toronto, 1960).

United Nation's Educational Scientific and Cultural Organization: *Communication in the Space Age: the Use of Satellites by the Mass Media* (Paris, 1968).

Vaughan, F.: "Precedent and Nationalism in the Supreme Court of Canada," *American Review of Canadian Studies,* vol. 6, 1976, pp. 3-31.

Wyman, Ken, Robin Mathews, and G. Lermer: "The Task Force Report on Foreign Ownership," *Canadian Dimension,* vol. 5, April-May, 1968, pp. 15-20.

THE CANADIAN CONSTITUTION

A. General Materials

Cairns, A. C.: "The Living Canadian Constitution," *Queen's Quarterly,* vol. 77, 4, Winter, 1970.

Cheffins, R. I.: *The Constitutional Process in Canada,* 2nd ed. (McGraw-Hill Ryerson, Toronto, 1976).

Clokie, H. M.: "Basic Problems of the Canadian Constitution," *Canadian Journal of Economics and Political Science,* vol. 8, 1942.

Corry, J. A.: "The Prospects for the Rule of Law," *Canadian Journal of Economics and Political Science,* vol. 21, 1955, pp. 405-415.

_____ and J. E. Hodgetts: *Democratic Government and Politics* (University of Toronto Press, Toronto, 1959).

Dawson, R. M.: *The Government of Canada,* revised by N. Ward (University of Toronto Press, Toronto, 1970).

Dicey, A. V.: *Introduction to the Study of the Law of the Constitution* (Macmillan, London, 1966).

Jennings, W. I.: *The Law and the Constitution* (University of London Press, London, 1959).

_____: *The British Constitution* (Cambridge University Press, London, 1966).

Keith, A. B.: *The Governments of the British Empire* (Macmillan, London, 1935).

Kennedy, W. P. M.: *The Constitution of Canada, 1534-1937* (Oxford University Press, London, 1938).

B. Democratic Values

Clarke, S. D.: "The Frontier and Democratic Theory," in Royal Society of Canada, *Proceedings and Transactions,* June, 1954, p. 65.

Cnudde, C. F. and D. E. Neubaur (eds.): *Empirical Democratic Theory* (Markham, Chicago, 1969).

Corry, J. A. and J. E. Hodgetts: *Democratic Government and Politics* (University of Toronto Press, Toronto, 1959).

Dahl, R. A.: *A Preface to Democratic Theory* (University of Chicago Press, Chicago, 1963).

MacIver, R. M.: *The Web of Government* (The Free Press, New York, 1965).

Macpherson, C. B.: *The Real World of Democracy* (C.B.C., Toronto, 1965).

Mayo, H. B.: *An Introduction to Democratic Theory* (Oxford University Press, New York, 1960).

Sartori, G.: *Democratic Theory* (Praeger, New York, 1965).

Schumpeter, J. A.: *Capitalism, Socialism and Democracy* (Harper and Row, New York, 1950).

Underhill, F. H.: "Some Reflections on the Liberal Tradition," in F. H. Underhill: *In Search of Canadian Liberalism* (Macmillan, Toronto, 1960).

UNESCO: *Democracy in a World of Tension* (Paris, 1951).

C. Civil Liberties

Batshaw, H.: "A Landmark Decision against Discrimination in Canada," *Revue des Droits de l'Homme*, vol. 4, 1971, pp. 207-211.

Canada, Parliament: *Minutes of Proceedings and Evidence,* Special Joint Committee on Human Rights and Fundamental Freedoms (King's Printer, Ottawa, 1947), no. 1-7 and (1947-8), no. 1-11.

———: *Proceedings* (King's Printer, Ottawa, 1950), no. 1-10.

———: *Minutes of Proceedings and Evidence Concerning Bill C-79* (Queen's Printer, Ottawa, 1960).

———: *Royal Commission on Security,* Abridged (Queen's Printer, Ottawa, June, 1969), *passim.*

———: *Protection of Privacy Act, 1973.*

Canadian Bar Review, articles in vol. 37, 1959, by:

    Bowker, W. F.: "Basic Rights and Freedoms: What are They?" pp. 43-65.

    Laskin, Bora: "An Inquiry into the Diefenbaker Bill of Rights," pp. 77-134.

    Lederman, W. R.: "The Nature and Problems of a Bill of Rights," pp. 4-15.

    Pigeon, L. P.: "The Bill of Rights and the British North America Act," pp. 66-76.

    Scott, F. R.: "The Bill of Rights and Quebec Law," pp. 135-146.

Clokie, H. M.: "Basic Problems of the Canadian Constitution," *Canadian Bar Review,* vol. 20, May, 1942, pp. 395-429; Dec., 1942, pp. 817-840.

Deudney, S. J.: "The Data Bank Society," *Canadian Chartered Accountant,* vol. 98, March, 1971, pp. 175-179.

Devall, W. B.: "Support for Civil Liberties among English-speaking Canadian University Students," *Canadian Journal of Political Science,* vol. 3, 1970, pp. 433-449.

Gopalakrishna, K. C.: "The Canadian Bill of Rights," *Journal of Constitutional and Parliamentary Studies,* vol. 5, 1971, pp. 24-226.

How, W. G.: "The Case for a Canadian Bill of Rights," *Canadian Bar Review,* vol. 36, 1958, pp. 750-796.

Kinsella, N. A.: "The Canadian Model for the Protection from Discrimination," *Revue des Droits de l'Homme,* vol. 4, July, 1971, pp. 270-277.

Lawford, Hugh: "Privacy versus Freedom of Information," *Queen's Quarterly,* vol. 78, 1971, pp. 365-371.

Lowman, R.: "New Wiretap Law," *Toronto Star*, May 18, 1974, p. 4.

MacGuigan, Mark R.: "The Development of Civil Liberties in Canada," *Queen's Quarterly*, vol. 72, 1965, pp. 270-288.

Manitoba: *Personal Investigations Act*, 1971.

McWilliams, P.: "Safeguard Against False Police Records," *Toronto Globe & Mail*, May 3, 1974, p. 7.

Ontario, Royal Commission on Civil Rights: *Report Number One*, 3 vols., (Queen's Printer, 1968).

_____: *Report Number Two* (Queen's Printer, Toronto, 1968).

_____: "A Democratic Approach to Civil Liberties," *University of Toronto Law Journal*, vol. 119, 1969, pp. 109-131.

Russell, Peter H. (ed.): *Leading Constitutional Decisions* (McClelland and Stewart, Toronto, 1965).

_____: "Mr. Trudeau's Bill of Rights: Disadvantages," *The Canadian Forum*, vol. 49, March, 1969, pp. 274-276.

Ryan, S.: "Charting Our Liberties," *Queen's Quarterly*, vol. 66, 1959, pp. 389-404.

Schmeiser, Douglas, A.: *Civil Liberties in Canada* (Oxford University Press, London, 1964).

Scott, Francis Reginald: *Civil Liberties and Canadian Federalism* (University of Toronto Press, Toronto, 1959).

Sharp, J. M.: "Consumers and the Laws of Privacy," *Canadian Consumer*, vol. 3, April, 1973, pp. 17-19.

Tarnopolsky, Walter Surma: *The Canadian Bill of Rights* (Carswell, Toronto, 1963).

Trudeau, Pierre Elliott: *A Canadian Charter of Human Rights* (Queen's Printer, Ottawa, 1968).

D. Operative Principles of the Constitution

Beaudoin, G.: "Les Aspects Constitutionnels du Referendum," *Etudes Internationales*, vol. 8, 2, 1977, pp. 197-207.

Cheffins, R. I.: *Constitutional Process in Canada*, 2nd ed. (McGraw-Hill Ryerson, Toronto, 1976).

Cloutier, Edouard: "Les conceptions americaine, canadienne-anglaise et canadienne-francaise de l'idée d'égalité," *Canadian Journal of Political Science*, vol. 9, 1974, p. 581.

Cobham, Viscount: "The Governor General's Constitutional Role," *Political Science*, vol. 15, 2, Sept., 1963.

Corry, J. A.: "The Prospects for the Rule of Law," *Canadian Journal of Economics and Political Science*, vol. 21, 1955, pp. 405-415.

_____ and J. E. Hodgetts: *Democratic Government and Politics* (University of Toronto Press, Toronto, 1959).

Dawson, R. M.: *The Government of Canada*, revised by N. Ward (University of Toronto Press, Toronto, 1970).

_____ (ed.): *Constitutional Issues in Canada, 1900-1931* (Oxford University Press, London, 1933).

Dawson, W. F.: *Procedure in the Canadian House of Commons* (University of Toronto Press, Toronto, 1962).

Esberey, J. E.: "Personality and Politics; A New Look at the King-Byng Dispute," *Canadian Journal of Political Science*, vol. 6, 1973, pp. 37-55.

Evatt, H. V.: "The Discretionary Authority of Dominion Governors," *Canadian Bar Review*, vol. 28, 1940, pp. 1-9.

————: *The King of the Dominion Governors; A Study of the Reserve Powers of the Crown in Great Britain and the Dominions* (Cass, London, 1967).

Forsey, E. A.: *The Royal Power of Dissolution of Parliament in the British Commonwealth* (Oxford University Press, Toronto, 1943).

————: "Independence of the Judiciary," *Canadian Bar Review,* vol. 35, 1957, p. 240.

————: "The Extension of the Life of Legislatures," *Canadian Journal of Economics and Political Science,* vol. 26, 1960, pp. 604-616.

————: *Essays on Freedom and Order* (McClelland and Stewart, Toronto, 1973).

Franck, T.: "The Governor General and the Head of State Functions," *Canadian Bar Review,* vol. 32, 1954, pp. 1084-1099.

Graham, Roger (ed.): *The King-Byng Affair, 1926: A Question of Responsible Government* (Copp Clark, Toronto, 1967).

Hendry, J. McL.: *Memorandum on the Office of Lieutenant-Governor of a Province: Its Constitutional Character and Functions* (Department of Justice, Ottawa, 1955).

Kennedy, W. P. M.: "The Office of Governor General of Canada," *Canadian Bar Review,* vol. 3, 1953, pp. 994-999.

LaForest, G. V.: *Disallowance and Reservation of Provincial Legislation* (Department of Justice, Ottawa, 1955).

Laskin, B.: *Canadian Constitutional Law* (Carswell, Toronto, 1969).

Lederman, W. R.: "The Independence of the Judiciary," *Canadian Bar Review,* vol. 3, 4, 1956, pp. 769-809; 1139-1179.

Mallory, J. R.: "Disallowance and the National Interest: The Alberta Social Credit Legislation of 1937," *Canadian Journal of Economics and Political Science,* vol. 14, 1948, pp. 342-357.

————: "The Lieutenant-Governor as a Dominion Officer: The Reservation of the Three Alberta Bills in 1937," *Canadian Journal of Economics and Political Science,* vol. 14, 1948, pp. 502-507.

————: *Social Credit and the Federal Power in Canada* (University of Toronto Press, Toronto, 1954).

————: "Seals and Symbols: From Substance to Form in Commonwealth Equality," *Canadian Journal of Economics and Political Science,* vol. 22, 1956, pp. 281-291.

————: "The Election and the Constitution," *Queen's Quarterly,* vol. 64, 1957-58, pp. 465-483.

————: "The Appointment of the Governor-General: Responsible Government, Autonomy and the Royal Prerogative," *Canadian Journal of Economics and Political Science,* vol. 26, 1960, pp. 96-107.

————: "The Royal Prerogative in Canada: The Selection of Successors to Mr. Duplessis and Mr. Sauve," *Canadian Journal of Economics and Political Science,* vol. 26, 1960, pp. 314-325.

McGregor, D. A.: *They Gave Royal Assent: The Lieutenant-Governors of British Columbia* (Mitchell Press, Vancouver, 1967).

McWhinney, E.: *Judicial Review in the English Speaking World* (University of Toronto Press, Toronto, 1969).

————, J. R. Mallory, and E. A. Forsey: "Prerogative Powers of the Head of State (The Queen or Governor General)," *Canadian Bar Review,* vol. 35, nos. 1, 2, 3, Jan., Feb., March, 1957, pp. 92-96; 242-244; 368-369; 369-371.

Morton, W. L.: "The Meaning of Monarchy in Confederation," in Royal Society of Canada, *Transactions,* Fourth Series, vol. 1, 1963, pp. 271-282.

Russell, P. H.: "The Anti-Inflation Case: The Anatomy of a Constitutional Question," *Canadian Public Administration*, vol. 20, 1977, pp. 632-665.

Saywell, J. T.: "The Crown and the Politicians: The Canadian Succession Question, 1891-1896," *Canadian Historical Review*, vol. 37, 1956, pp. 309-337.

_____: *The Office of Lieutenant-Governor* (University of Toronto Press, Toronto, 1957).

Scott F. R.: *Essays on the Constitution* (University of Toronto Press, Toronto, 1977).

Stanley, G. F. G.: "A 'Constitutional Crisis' in British Columbia," *Canadian Journal of Economics and Political Science*, vol. 21, 1955, pp. 281-292.

Strayer, B.: *Judicial Review of Legislation in Canada* (University of Toronto Press, Toronto, 1969).

Ward, N.: *The Public Purse: A Study in Canadian Democracy* (University of Toronto Press, Toronto, 1962).

_____: *The Canadian House of Commons: Representation* (University of Toronto Press, Toronto, 1963).

Willis-O'Connor, H.: *Inside Government House* (Ryerson, Toronto, 1954).

CONSTITUTIONAL AND LEGAL PROCESSES

A. The Process of Change

Alexander, E. R.: "A Constitutional Strait Jacket for Canada," *Canadian Bar Review*, vol. 43, 1965, pp. 262-313.

Angers, F. A.: "Le Problème du Repatriement de la Constitution," *L'Action Nationale*, vol. 54, novembre, 1964, pp. 291-297.

Brady, A.: "Constitutional Amendment and the Federation," *Canadian Journal of Economics and Political Science*, vol. 29, 1963, pp. 486-494.

Canada, Prime Minister: *The Constitution and the People of Canada* (Queen's Printer, Ottawa, 1969).

Canadian Bar Review: vol. 45, no. 3, Sept., 1967 (special issue on the Constitution, "Canada 1867-1967").

Clokie, H. M.: "Basic Problems of the Canadian Constitution," *Canadian Journal of Economics and Political Science*, vol. 8, 1942, pp. 1-32.

Cook, Ramsay: *Provincial Autonomy, Minority Rights and the Compact Theory, 1867-1921*, Studies of the Royal Commission on Bilingualism, and Biculturalism, no. 4 (Queen's Printer, Ottawa, 1969).

Efrat, E. S.: "Federations in Crisis—The Failure of the Old Order," *Western Political Quarterly*, vol. 25, 1972, pp. 589-599.

Favreau, Guy: *The Amendment of the Constitution of Canada* (Department of Justice, Ottawa, 1965).

Gérin-Lajoie, P.: *Constitutional Amendment in Canada* (University of Toronto Press, Toronto, 1950).

Laskin, B.: "Amendment of the Constitution: Applying the Fulton-Favreau Formula," *McGill Law Journal*, vol. 11, 1965, pp. 2-18.

Lederman, W. R.: "The Process of Constitutional Amendment for Canada," *McGill Law Journal*, vol. 12, no. 4, 1966.

Livingstone, W. S.: "The Amending Power of the Canadian Parliament," *American Political Science Review*, vol. 34, 1951, pp. 437-439.

Lower, A. R. M.: "Two Ways of Life: The Spirit of Our Institutions," *Canadian Historical Review*, vol. 28, 1947, pp. 383-400.

MacDonald, V. C.: "The Constitution in a Changing World," *Canadian Bar Review*, vol. 26, 1948, pp. 21-45.

Morin, Jacques-Yvan: "Le repatriement de la constitution," *Cité Libre*, vol. 26, décembre, 1964, pp. 9-12.

O'Hearn, Peter J. T.: *Peace, Order and Good Government* (Macmillan, Toronto, 1964).

Rowat, D. C.: "Recent Developments in Canadian Federalism," *Canadian Journal of Economics and Political Science*, vol. 18, 1952, pp. 1-16.

Stanley, G. F. G.: "Act or Pact? Another Look at Confederation," in *Canadian Historical Association Annual Report* (Ottawa, 1956).

B. The Judicial Process

Arvay, J.: "Newfoundland's Claim to Offshore Mineral Resources: An Overview of the Legal Issues," *Canadian Public Policy*, Winter, 1979, pp. 32-44.

Bruce, C. J.: "The Calculations of Foregone Lifetime Earnings: Three Decisions of the Supreme Court of Canada," *Canadian Public Policy*, Spring, 1979, pp. 155-167.

Clark, J. A.: "Appointments to the Bench," *Canadian Bar Review*, vol. 30, 1952, pp. 28-36.

Cunningham, W. B.: "Labour Relations Boards and the Courts," *Canadian Journal of Political Science*, vol. 30, 1964, pp. 499-511.

Dahl, Robert: "The Too Limited Jurisdiction of the Supreme Court," *Canadian Bar Review*, vol. 25, 1947, pp. 573-586.

_____: "Decision Making in a Democracy: The Supreme Court as a National Policy-Maker," *Journal of Public Law*, vol. 6, 1957, pp. 279-295.

Fera, N.: "Review of Administrative Decisions under the Federal Court, October, 1970," *Canadian Public Administration*, vol. 14, 1971, pp. 580-594.

Fouts, D.: "The Supreme Court of Canada, 1950-60," in Glendon A. Schubert and David J. Danelski (eds.): *Comparative Judicial Behaviour* (Oxford University Press, New York, 1969), ch. 10.

Garant, P. et al.: "Le Contrôle Politique des Organismes Autonomes à Fonctions Régulatrices et Quasi-Judiciaires," *Candian Public Administration*, vol. 20, 1977, pp. 444-468.

Hogg, Peter: *Constitutional Law of Canada* (Carswell, Toronto, 1978).

Kinnear, H.: "The County Judge in Ontario," *Canadian Bar Review*, vol. 32, Jan./Feb., 1954.

Laskin, Bora: "The Supreme Court of Canada: a Final Court of and for Canadians," *Canadian Bar Review*, vol. 29, 1951, pp. 1038-1079.

_____: "Our Civil Liberties—the Role of the Supreme Court," *Queen's Quarterly*, vol. 61, 1954-55, pp. 455-471.

_____: *Canadian Constitutional Law, Cases, Text and Notes on Distribution of Legislative Power*, 4th ed. (Carswell, Toronto, 1973).

_____: *Canadian Constitutional Law*, 4th ed., revised by Albert S. Abel (Toronto, Carswell, 1975).

L'Ecuyer, Gilbert: *La Cour Suprême du Canada et le Partage des Compétences 1949-1978* (Gouvernement du Québec, Ministère des affaires intergouvernamentales, Québec, 1978).

Lederman, William Ralph: *The Courts and the Canadian Constitution* (McClelland and Stewart, Toronto, 1964), pp. 106-175.

_____: "Thoughts on Reform of the Supreme Court of Canada," in Ontario Advisory Committee on Confederation: *Background Papers and Reports*, vol. II (Queen's Printer of Ontario, Toronto, 1970).

_____: "Thoughts on Reform of the Supreme Court of Canada," *Alberta Law Review*, vol. 8, 1, 1970, pp. 1-17.

Logan, G. R.: "Historical Sketch of the Supreme Court of Canada," *Osgoode Hall Law Journal*, vol. 3, 1964.

Lyon, J. Noel: "A Fresh Approach to Constitutional Law: Use of a Policy-Science Model," *Canadian Bar Review*, vol. 45, 1967, pp. 554-577.

MacDonald, V. C.: "The Privy Council and the Canadian Constitution," *Canadian Bar Review*, Dec., 1951, pp. 1021-1037.

MacKinnon, F.: "The Establishment of the Supreme Court of Canada," *Canadian Historical Review*, 1946.

McWhinney, Edward: "Federal Supreme Courts and Constitutional Review," *Canadian Bar Review*, vol. 45, 1967, pp. 578-607.

Millward, P. J.: "Judicial Review of Administrative Authorities in Canada," *Canadian Bar Review*, 1961, pp. 351-395.

Morin, Jacques-Yvan: "Le Québec et l'Arbitrage Constitutionnel: De Charybde en Scylla," *Canadian Bar Review*, vol. 45, 1967, pp. 608-626.

Morley, J. T.: "The Justice Development Commission: Overcoming Bureaucratic Resistance to Innovative Policy-Making," *Canadian Public Administration*, vol. 19, 1976, pp. 121-139.

_____: "The Supreme Court of Canada, 1958-1966," *Canadian Bar Review*, vol. 45, 1967, pp. 666-725.

Peck, S. R.: "A Behavioural Approach to the Judicial Process: Scalogram Analysis," *Osgood Hall Law Journal*, vol. 1, April, 1967.

Read, H. E.: "The Judicial Process in Common Law Canada," *Canadian Bar Review* vol. 37, 1959, pp. 265-293.

Russell, Peter H.: "Constitutional Reform of the Canadian Judiciary," paper delivered at the A.C.L.T. meetings in Calgary, June, 1968.

_____: "The Jurisdiction of the Supreme Court of Canada; Present Policies and a Programme for Reform," *Osgood Hall Law Journal*, vol. 6, 1968, pp. 1-91.

_____: *Bilingualism and Biculturalism in the Supreme Court of Canada* (Queen's Printer, Ottawa, 1969).

_____: "Constitutional Reform of the Canadian Judiciary," *Alberta Law Review*, vol. 8, 1970, pp. 1-17.

_____: *Leading Constitutional Decisions: Cases on the British North America Act*, rev. ed. (McClelland and Stewart, Toronto, 1973).

Strayer, B. L.: *Judicial Review of Legislation in Canada* (University of Toronto Press, Toronto, 1968).

Tarnopolsky, W. S.: *The Canadian Bill of Rights*, 2nd ed. (McClelland and Stewart, Toronto, 1975).

Weiler, Paul: *In the Last Resort: A Critical Study of the Supreme Court of Canada* (Carswell, Toronto, 1974).

Whyte, J. D. and W. R. Lederman: *Canadian Constitutional Law*, 2nd ed. (Butterworths, Toronto, 1977).

FEDERALISM

Aitchison, J. H.: "Interprovincial Cooperation," in James Hermiston Aitchison (ed.): *The Political Process in Canada* (University of Toronto Press, Toronto, 1963), pp. 153-170.

Andrew, C.: "Le Rapport Fullerton: Perspective de la Science Politique," *Canadian Public Policy*, vol. 2, 1975, pp. 162-179.

Angus, H. F.: "Two Restrictions on Provincial Autonomy," *Canadian Journal of Economics and Political Science*, vol. 21, 1955, pp. 445-446.

Baldwin, J. R.: "Transportation Policy and Jurisdictional Issues," *Canadian Public Administration*, vol. 18, 4, 1975, pp. 630-641.

Beck, J. M.: "Canadian Federalism in Ferment," in Richard H. Leach (ed.): *Contemporary Canada* (Duke University Press, Durham, 1968), pp. 148-176.

Bell, D. and L. Tepperman: *The Roots of Disunity: A Look at Canadian Political Culture* (McClelland and Stewart, Toronto, 1979).

Bercuson, David Jay (ed.): *Canada and the Burden of Unity* (Macmillan of Canada, Toronto, 1977).

Bissonnette, B.: *Essai sur la Constitution du Canada* (Les éditions du jour, Montréal, 1963).

Black, E. R.: "Federal Strains within a Canadian Party," in H. Thornburn (ed.): *Party Politics in Canada*, 3rd ed. (Prentice-Hall, Toronto, 1972).

———— and Alan C. Cairns: "A Different Perspective on Canadian Federalism," *Canadian Public Administration*, vol. 9, 1966, pp. 27-44.

Brachet, B.: "La crise du fédéralisme canadien et le problème québécois," *Revue du Droit public et de la Science politique en France et a l'étranger*, vol. 88, 1972, pp. 303-324.

Brady, Alexander: "Quebec and Canadian Federation," *Canadian Journal of Economics and Political Science*, vol. 25, 1959, pp. 259-270.

Brossard, J.: *L'immigration: Les droits et pouvoirs du Canada et du Québec*, (Presses de l'Université de Montréal, Montréal, 1967).

Browne, G. P.: *The Judicial Committee and the BNA Act* (University of Toronto Press, Toronto, 1967).

Brun, Henri: "Le Labrador a l'heure de la contestation," (Note bibliographique), *Canadian Journal of Political Science*, vol. 6, 1973, pp. 518-520.

Brunet, J.: "La croissance de la machine gouvernementale fédérale et le développement de la région de la capitale," *Canadian Public Policy*, vol. 1, 1975, pp. 148-157.

Buck, Arthur Eugene: *Financing Canadian Government* (Public Administration Service, Chicago, 1949), chs. 10, 13, pp. 215-252, 333-348.

Burns, R. M.: "The Royal Commission on Dominion-Provincial Relations: The Report in Retrospect," in Robert Mills Clark (ed.): *Canadian Issues* (University of Toronto Press, Toronto, 1961), pp. 143-157.

————: *One Country or Two?* (McGill-Queen's University Press, Montreal, 1971).

Byers, R. B. and Robert W. Reford (eds.): *Canada Challenged: The Viability of Confederation* (Canadian Institute of International Affairs, Toronto, 1979).

Cairns, Alan, C.: *From Interstate to Intrastate Federalism in Canada*, Institute Discussion Paper (Institute of Intergovernmental Relations, Queen's University, Kingston, 1979).

Canada: *Canadian Confederation at the Crossroads: The Search for Federal-Provincial Balance* (The Fraser Institute, Vancouver, 1978).

Canada, Senate: *Report to the Honourable Mr. Speaker Relating to the Enactment of the BNA Act, 1867, O'Connor Report* (Queen's Printer, Ottawa, 1939).

Canada Committee: *Declaration by English and French-Speaking Canadians* (Montreal, 1966).

Caplan, Neil: "Some Factors Affecting the Resolution of a Federal-Provincial Conflict," *Canadian Journal of Economics and Political Science,* vol. 2, 1969, pp. 173-186.

Carson, George Barr Jr.: "The Spinning Wheel, the Stone Ax, and Sovereignty," *Canadian Journal of Political Science,* vol. 7, 1974, pp. 70-85.

Cheffins, R. I.: *The Constitutional Process in Canada* (McGraw-Hill Ryerson, Toronto, 1976).

Cole, Taylor: *The Canadian Bureaucracy and Federalism, 1947-1965* (University of Denver, Denver, Colorado, 1966).

Cook, R.: *Provincial Autonomy, Minority Rights and the Compact Theory, 1867-1921,* Royal Commission on Bilingualism and Biculturalism, Studies, no. 4 (Queen's Printer, Ottawa, 1969).

Creighton, D. G.: *The Road to Confederation: The Emergence of Canada, 1863-1867* (Macmillan, Toronto, 1964).

_____: *Canada's First Century: 1867-1967* (Macmillan of Canada, Toronto, 1970).

Crepeau, Paul André and C. B. Macpherson (eds.): *The Future of Canadian Federalism; l'Avenir du fédéralisme canadien* (University of Toronto Press, Toronto; les Presses de l'Université de Montréal, Montréal, 1965).

Dawson, Robert M. (ed.): *Constitutional Issues in Canada, 1900-1931* (Oxford University Press, London, 1933), ch. 9, Dominion-Provincial Relations, pp. 431-471.

Doern, G. B.: "Vocational Training and Manpower Policy: A Case Study in Intergovernmental Liaison," *Canadian Public Administration,* vol. 12, 1969, pp. 63-71.

Dubuc, A.: "Une interpretation économique de la constitution," *Socialisme 66, Revue du socialisme internationale et Québécois,* no. 7, janvier, 1966 pp. 3-21. In English in *Canadian Forum,* vol. 45, March 1966, pp. 272-274.

Dufour, André: "Le Statut Particulier," *Canadian Bar Review,* vol. 45, 1967, pp. 437-453.

Dyck, R.: "The Canada Assistance Plan: The ultimate in Cooperative Federalism," *Canadian Public Administration,* vol. 19, 1976, pp. 587-602.

Eggleston, Wilfred: *The Road to Nationhood: A Chronicle of Dominion-Provincial Relations* (Oxford University Press, Toronto, 1946).

_____: "Recent Trends in Federal-Provincial Relations," *The Canadian Banker,* vol. 59, 1952, pp. 66-78.

Etudes Internationales VII, Juin 1977: *Le Canada et le Québec* (Centre des relations internationales, Université Laval).

Faribault, M. and R. Fowler: *Ten to One: The Confederation Wager* (McClelland and Stewart, Toronto, 1965).

Forsey, E.: "Canada: Two Nations or One? *Canadian Journal of Economics and Political Science,* vol. 28, 1962, pp. 485-501.

Gelinas, A.: "Trois modes d'approche à la détermination de l'opportunité de la décentralisation de l'organisation politique principalement en système fédéral," *Canadian Public Administration,* vol. 9, 1966, pp. 1-26.

Gettys, Cora Luella: *The Administration of Canadian Conditional Grants: A Study in Dominion-Provincial Relationships* (Public Administration Service, Chicago, 1938).

Hall, D. J.: "The Spirit of Confederation: Ralph Heintzman, Professor Creighton, and the Bicultural Compact Theory," *Journal of Canadian Studies,* vol. 9, 1974, pp. 24-42.

Hare, F. K.: "Regionalism and Administration: North American Experiments," *Canadian Journal of Economics and Political Science,* vol. 13, 1947, pp. 563-571.

Hawkins, G. (ed.): *Concepts of Federalism,* Proceedings of 34th Couchiching Conference (Canadian Institute on Public Affairs, Toronto, 1965).

———: *The Idea of Maritime Union,* Report of a Conference sponsored by the Canadian Institute on Public Affairs and Mount Allison University (Sackville, N.B., 1965).

Johnson, A. W.: "The Dynamics of Federalism in Canada," *Canadian Journal of Political Science,* vol. 1, 1968, pp. 18-39.

Kear, A. R.: "Cooperative Federalism: A Study of the Federal-Provincial Continuing Committee on Fiscal and Economic Matters," *Canadian Public Administration,* vol. 6, 1963, pp. 43-56.

LaForest, G. V.: *Natural Resources and Public Property under the Canadian Constitution* (University of Toronto Press, Toronto, 1969).

Lamontagne, M.: *Le Federalisme Canadien* (Les presses universitaires Laval, Quebec, 1954).

Lamy, P.: "Language Planning and Language Use: Canada's National Capital Area," *American Review of Canadian Studies,* vol. 6, 1976, pp. 74-87.

La Societé St. Jean Baptiste de Montréal: *Le Federalisme, l'Acte de l'Amerique du Nord Britannique et les Canadiens Français,* Memoir au comite parlementaire de la constitution du gouvernement du Québec (Les éditions de l'agence Duvernay, Montréal, 1964).

Laundy, P.: "Report of the Task Force on Canadian Unity," *Parliamentarian,* vol. 60, 1979, pp. 133-140.

Leach, R. H.: "Interprovincial Co-operation: Neglected Aspects of Canadian Federalism," *Canadian Public Administration,* vol. 2, 1969, pp. 83-99.

———: *Perceptions of Federalism by Canadian and Australian Civil Servants* (Centre for Research on Federal Financial Relations, Australian National University, Canberra, 1976).

——— (ed.): *Contemporary Canada* (University of Toronto Press, Toronto, 1968).

Lederman, William Ralph: "The Concurrent Operation of Federal and Provincial Laws in Canada," *McGill Law Journal,* vol. 9, 1963, pp. 185-199.

———: *The Courts and the Canadian Constitution* (McClelland and Stewart, Toronto, 1964).

———: "Some Forms and Limitations of Cooperative Federalism," *Canadian Bar Review,* vol. 45, 1967, pp. 409-436.

———: "Cooperative Federalism: Constitutional Revision and Parliamentary Government in Canada," *Queen's Quarterly,* vol. 78, 1971, pp. 7-17.

Livingston, W. S.: *Federalism and Constitutional Change* (Oxford University Press, Oxford, 1963).

Lower, A. R. M., F. R. Scott et al.: *Evolving Canadian Federalism* (Duke University Press, Durham, 1958).

MacEwan, Paul: *Confederation and the Maritimes* (Lancelot Press, Windsor, Nova Scotia, 1976).

Macmahon, A. W.: Administering Federalism in a Democracy (Oxford University Press, New York, 1958).

Mallory, J. R.: The Structure of Canadian Government (Macmillan, Toronto, 1971).

Maxwell, James Ackley: *Federal Subsidies to the Provincial Government in Canada* (Harvard University Press, Cambridge, 1937).

McRae, K. D.: Switzerland: *Example of Cultural Co-existence* (Canadian Institute of International Affairs, Toronto, 1964).

_____: *The Federal Capital: Government Institutions*, Royal Commission on Bilingualism and Biculturalism Studies, no. 1 (Queen's Printer, Ottawa, 1969).

McWhinney, E.: *Comparative Federalism, States' Rights and National Power* (University of Toronto Press, Toronto, 1962).

_____: "The 'Quiet Revolution' in French Canada and its Constitutional Implications for Canadian Federalism," *Jahrbuch des Offentlichen Richts der Genewart*, vol. 19, 1970, pp. 331-353.

Meekison, J. P. (ed.): *Canadian Federalism: Myth or Reality*, 3rd ed. (Methuen, Toronto, 1977).

Miller, D. R.: "A Shapely Value Analysis of the Proposed Canadian Constitutional Amendment Scheme," *Canadian Journal of Political Science*, vol. 6, 1973, pp. 140-143.

Moore, A. M.: "Fact and Fantasy in the Unity Debate," *Canadian Public Policy*, vol. 5, 1979, pp. 206-222.

_____ and J. Harvey Perry: *Financing Canadian Federation: The Federal-Provincial Tax Agreements* (Canadian Tax Foundation, Toronto, 1953).

Morin, Claude: *Le Pouvoir Quebecois . . . en Negociation* (Boreal Express, Quebec, 1972).

_____: *Quebec versus Ottawa: The Struggle for Self-Government 1960-72* (University of Toronto Press, Toronto, 1976).

Noel, S. J. R.: "Consociational Democracy and Canadian Federalism," *Canadian Journal of Political Science*, vol. 4, 1971, pp. 15-18.

O'Hearn, P.: *Peace and Good Government* (MacMillan, Toronto, 1964).

Oliver, Michael (ed.): *Social Purpose for Canada* (University of Toronto Press, Toronto, 1961).

Olmstead, R. A.: *Decisions Relating to the BNA Act, 1867, and the Canadian Constitution, 1867-1954*, 3 vols. (Queen's Printer, Ottawa, 1954).

Pearson, L. B.: *Federalism of the Future* (Queen's Printer, Ottawa, 1968).

Pepin, G.: *Les Tribunaux Administratifs et La Constitution: Etude des articles 96 a 101 de l'A.A.N.B.* (Les presses de l'Université de Montréal, Montréal, 1969).

Perry, J. H.: "Conditional Grants," in Institute of Public Administration of Canada: *Proceedings of the Annual Conference* (Toronto, 1953), pp. 352-386.

Proceedings of the Conference on the Future of the Canadian Federation: *Options* (University of Toronto, Toronto, 1977).

Riker,W. H.: *Federalism:Origin,Operation,Significance* (Little,Brown,Boston,1964).

Rioux, Marcel: *Quebec in Question* (James, Lewis & Samuel, Toronto, 1971).

Robinson, Albert and James Cutt: *Public Finance in Canada: Selected Readings* (Methuen, Toronto, 1968).

Rowat, D. C.: "Recent Developments in Canadian Federalism," *Canadian Journal of Economics and Political Science*, vol. 18, 1952, pp. 1-16.

_____: "The Problems of Governing Federal Capitals," *Canadian Journal of Political Science*, vol. 1, 1968, pp. 345-356.

Russell, P.: *The Supreme Court of Canada as a Bilingual and Bicultural Institution*, Royal Commission on Bilingualism and Biculturalism, Documents, no. 1 (Information Canada, Ottawa, 1970).

_____: *Leading Constitutional Decisions*, rev. ed. (McClelland and Stewart, Toronto, 1973).

_____ (ed.): *Nationalism in Canada* (McGraw-Hill, Toronto, 1966).

Ryerson, S. B.: *Unequal Union: Confederation and the Roots of Conflict in the Canadas 1815-1873*, 2nd ed. (Progress, Toronto, 1973).

———— et al. (eds.): "The Two Canadas: Towards a New Confederation? A Symposium," *The Marxist Quarterly*, no. 15, Autumn, 1965, pp. 56-59.

Scarfe, B. L. and T. L. Powrie: "The Optimal Savings Question: An Alberta Perspective," *Canadian Public Policy*, vol. 6, Supplement, 1980, pp. 166-179.

Simeon, Richard (ed.): *Must Canada Fail?* (McGill-Queen's University Press, Montreal, 1977).

Smiley, Donald Victor: *Conditional Grants and Canadian Federalism* (Canadian Tax Foundation, Toronto, 1963).

————: *The Rowell-Sirois Report* (Carleton Library, McClelland and Stewart, Toronto, 1963).

————: "The Two Themes of Canadian Federalism," *Canadian Journal of Economics and Political Science*, vol. 31, 1965, pp. 80-97.

————: *The Canadian Political Nationality* (Methuen, Toronto, 1967).

————: "Rationalism or Reason: Alternative Approaches to Constitutional Review in Canada," (paper delivered at the Progressive Conservative "Priorities for Canada," Conference, Niagara Falls, Ontario, Oct. 12, 1969).

————: *Constitutional Adaption and Canadian Federalism Since 1945*, Royal Commission on Bilingualism and Biculturalism, Documents, no. 4 (Queen's Printer, Ottawa, 1970).

————: "The Structural Problem of Canadian Federalism," *Canadian Public Administration*, vol. 14, 1971, pp. 326-343.

————: *Canada in Question: Federalism in the Seventies*, 3rd ed. (McGraw-Hill Ryerson, Toronto, 1976).

————: "Territorialism and Canadian Political Institutions," *Canadian Public Policy*, vol. 3, 1977, pp. 449-457.

Smith, Denis: *Bleeding Hearts, Bleeding Country* (M. G. Hurtig, Edmonton, 1971).

Soucy, E.: "Confederation ou federalisme cooperatif?" *L'Action Nationale*, vol. 54, octobre, 1964, pp. 168-173.

Task Force on Canadian Unity, Report: *A Future Together: Observations and Recommendations* (Supply and Services, Ottawa, 1979).

Taylor, M. G.: *Health Insurance and Canadian Public Policy: The Seven Decisions That Created the Canadian Health Insurance System* (McGill-Queen's Press, Montreal, 1978).

Torrance, Judy: "The Response of Canadian Governments to Violence," *Canadian Journal of Political Science*, vol. 10, 1977, pp. 473-496.

Traves, T. D.: "Some Problems With Peacetime Price Controls: The Case of the Board of Commerce of Canada, 1919-1920," *Canadian Public Administration*, vol. 17, 1974, pp. 85-95.

Tremblay, A.: *Les Compétences Législatives au Canada et les Pouvoirs Provinciaux en Matière de Propriété et de Droits Civils* (Editions de l'Université, Ottawa, 1967).

Trudeau, Pierre Elliott: *Federalism and the French Canadians* (Macmillan, Toronto, 1968).

————: *The Constitution and the People of Canada* (Queen's Printer, Ottawa, 1969).

————: *A Time for Action: Towards the Renewal of the Canadian Federation* (Queen's Printer, Ottawa, 1978).

Underhill, F. H.: *The Image of Confederation* (CBC, Toronto, 1964).

Usher, D.: "How Should the Redistributive Power of the State Be Divided between Federal and Provincial Governments," *Canadian Public Policy*, vol. 6, 1980, pp. 16-29.

Waines, W. J.: "Dominion-Provincial Financial Arrangements: An Examination of Objectives," *Canadian Journal of Economics and Political Science*, vol. 19, 1953, pp. 304-315.

Waite, P. B.: *The Life and Times of Confederation* (University of Toronto Press, Toronto, 1967).

West, E. D. and S. L. Winer: "The Individual, Political Tension, and Canada's Quest for a New Constitution," *Canadian Public Policy*, vol. 6, 1980, pp. 3-15.

Wheare, K. C.: *Federal Government*, 4th ed. (Oxford University Press, London, 1963).

PARTIES AND ELECTIONS IN CANADA

Note: No attempt has been made to section this part of the bibliography as most studies of parties bear, at least incidentally, on many themes. For example, it is difficult to discuss minor parties in Canada without also discussing the major ones and vice versa. As well, discussing elections without also discussing parties is virtually impossible.

Abella, Irving M.: *Nationalism, Communism and Canadian Labour: The C.I.O., the Communist Party and the Canadian Congress of Labour 1935-1956* (University of Toronto Press, Toronto, 1973).

Aitchison, J. H. (ed.): *The Political Process in Canada* (University of Toronto Press, Toronto, 1963).

Alford, Robert R.: *Party and Society: The Anglo-American Democracies* (Rand McNally, Chicago, 1963).

Anderson, Grace M: "Voting Behavior and the Ethnic-Religious Variable: A Study of a Federal Election in Hamilton, Ontario," *Canadian Journal of Economics and Political Science*, vol. 32, 1966, pp. 27-37.

Aube, N. R. Hudon and V. Lemieux: "L'Étude du Patronage des Partis Provinciaux du Québec de 1944 à 1970," *Recherches Sociographiques*, vol. 13, 1972, pp. 125-138.

Beck, J. M.: "Socialist or Democratic Party?" *Dalhousie Review*, vol. 41, 1961, pp. 387-393.

_____: "The Electoral Behaviour of Nova Scotia in 1965," *Dalhousie Review*, vol. 46, 1966, pp. 27-38.

_____: *Pendulum of Power: Canada's Federal Elections* (Prentice-Hall, Toronto, 1968).

_____ and D. J. Dooley: "Labour Parties New and Old," *Dalhousie Review*, vol. 40, 1960, pp. 323-328.

Beeching, W. C. and M. Lazarus: "Le socialisme en Saskatchewan: trop ou trop peu," Socialisme 64, *Revue du Socialisme International et Québécois*, no. 2, automne, 1964, pp. 16-32.

Bergeron, G.: "Political Parties in Quebec," *University of Toronto Quarterly*, vol. 27, 1958, pp. 352-368.

Blais, André: "Third Parties in Canadian Provincial Politics," *Canadian Journal of Political Science*, vol. 6, 1973, pp. 442-438.

_____: "Politique agricole et résultats électoraux en milieu agricole au Québec," *Canadian Journal of Political Science*, vol. 11, 1978, pp. 333-381.

————, H. Cantin, and J. Crête: "Les élections comme phénomène de décision collective: les élections fédérales de 1957 a 1965 au Québec," *Canadian Journal of Political Science*, vol. 3, 1970, pp. 522-539.

————, Rachel Destrosiers, and François Renaud: "L'effet en amont de la carte électorale: le cas de la région de Québec à l'élection fédérale de 1968," *Canadian Journal of Political Science*, vol. 7, 1974, pp. 648-671.

Blake, Donald E.: "The Measurement of Regionalism in Canadian Voting Patterns, *Canadian Journal of Political Science*, vol. 5, 1972, pp. 55-81.

————: "Constituency Contexts and Canadian Elections: An Exploratory Study," *Canadian Journal of Political Science*, vol. 11, 1978, pp. 279-305.

Borden, H. (ed.): *Robert Laird Borden: His Memoirs* (Macmillan, New York, 1938).

Boudreau, J. A.: "The Medium of the Message of William Aberhart," *American Review of Canadian Studies*, vol. 7, 1978, pp. 18-30.

Brady, Alexander: *Democracy in the Dominions*, 3rd ed. (University of Toronto Press, Toronto, 1958).

Brodie, J. and J. Jensen: *Political Parties and Social Class in Canada* (Methuen, Toronto, 1980).

Cairns, Alan, C.: "The Electoral System and the Party System in Canada, 1921-1965," *Canadian Journal of Political Science*, vol. 1, 1968, pp. 55-80.

————: "The Governments and Societies of Canadian Federalism," *Canadian Journal of Political Science*, vol. 10, 1977, pp. 695-725.

————: "A Reply to J. A. A. Lovink, 'On Analysing the Impact of the Electoral System on the Party System in Canada,' " *Canadian Journal of Political Science*, vol. 3, 1970, pp. 517-521.

Canada: *Report of the Committee on Election Expenses* (Queen's Printer, Ottawa, 1966).

————: "The NDP and the Waffle," *Canadian Dimension*, Special Supplement, vol. 8, 8, April, 1971.

Caplan, Gerald L.: *The Dilemma of Canadian Socialism: The CCF in Ontario* (McClelland and Stewart, Toronto, 1973).

Careless, J. M. S.: *Brown of the Globe*, vol. 1, *The Voice of Upper Canada 1818-1859* (Macmillan, Toronto, 1959); vol II, *Statesmen of Confederation 1860-1880* (Macmillan, Toronto, 1963).

Carrigan, O.: *Canadian Party Platforms, 1867-1968* (Copp Clark, Toronto, 1968).

Casstevens, T. W. and W. A. Denham III: "Turnover and Tenure in the Canadian House of Commons, 1867-1968," *Canadian Journal of Political Science*, vol. 3, 1970, pp. 655-661.

Cherwinski, W. J. C.: "Bibliographical Note: The Left in Canadian History, 1911-1969," *Journal of Canadian Studies*, vol. 9, November, 1969, pp. 51-60.

Churchill, G.: "Recollections and Comments of Election Strategy," *Queen's Quarterly*, vol. 77, 1970, pp. 499-511.

Clark, S. D.: *Movements of Political Protest in Canada 1640-1840* (University of Toronto Press, Toronto, 1959).

Clarke, Harold D.: "Partisanship and the Parti Québécois: The Impact of the Independence Issue," *American Review of Canadian Studies*, vol. 7, 1978, pp. 28-47.

————, Richard Price, and Robert Krause: "Constituency Service among Canadian Provincial Legislators: Basic Findings and a Test of Three Hypotheses," *Canadian Journal of Political Science*, vol. 8, 1974, pp. 520-542.

Clarkson, Stephen: *City Lib.: Parties and Reform* (A.M. Hakkert, Toronto, 1972).

Comeau, Paul-Andre: "La transformation du parti liberal québécois," *Canadian Journal of Economics and Political Science*, vol. 31, 1965, pp. 358-367.

Conway, J. F.: "Populism in the United States, Russia, and Canada: Explaining the Roots of Canada's Third Parties," *Canadian Journal of Political Science*, vol. 11, 1978, pp. 99-124.

Cook, Ramsay: *The Politics of John W. Dafoe and the Free Press* (University of Toronto Press, Toronto, 1966).

———— (ed.): *Politics of Discontent* (University of Toronto Press, Toronto, 1962).

Copes, P.: "The Fisherman's Vote in Newfoundland," *Canadian Journal of Political Science*, vol. 3, 1970, pp. 577-604.

Cornell, Paul G.: *The Alignment of Political Groups in Canada, 1841-1957* (University of Toronto Press, Toronto, 1962).

Courtney, J. C.: *Voting in Canada* (Prentice-Hall, Toronto, 1967).

————: *The Selection of National Party Leaders in Canada* (Macmillan, Toronto, 1973).

————: "Prime Ministerial Character: An Examination of Mackenzie King's Political Leadership," *Canadian Journal of Political Science*, vol. 9, 1976, pp. 78-100.

Croisat, M.: "Centralisation et décentralisation au sein des partis politiques canadiens," *Revue française de Science politique*, vol. 20, 1970.

Cunningham, Robert: "The Impact of the Local Candidate in Canadian Federal Elections," *Canadian Journal of Political Science*, vol. 4, 1971, pp. 287-290.

Curtis, James E. and Ronald D. Lambert: "Voting, Election Interest, and Age: National Findings for English and French Canadians," *Canadian Journal of Political Science*, vol. 9, 1976, pp. 293-307.

Davis, Morris: "Ballot Behaviour in Halifax Revisited," *Canadian Journal of Political Science*, vol. 30, 1964, pp. 538-558; pp. 648-671.

Dawson, R. M.: *The Conscription Crisis of 1944* (University of Toronto Press, Toronto, 1961).

————: *The Government of Canada*, 5th ed. (University of Toronto Press, Toronto, 1970).

Denman, N.: *How to Organize an Election* (Les éditions du jour, Montreal, 1962).

Dion, l'Abbé G. et l'Abbé L. O'Neill: *Le chrétien et les élections* (Les éditions de l'homme, 8me éd., Montréal, 1960).

———— ————: *Le chrétien en démocratie* (Les éditions de l'homme, Montréal, 1961).

Dion, L.: "The Concept of Political Leadership: An Analysis," *Canadian Journal of Political Science*, vol. 1, 1968, pp. 2-17.

————: "A la recherche d'une méthode d'analyse des partis et des groupes d'intéret," *Canadian Journal of Political Science*, vol. 2, 1969, pp. 45-63.

————: "Politique consultative et système politique," *Canadian Journal of Political Science*, vol. 2, 1969, pp. 226-244.

Elkins, David J.: "The Perceived Structure of the Canadian Party Systems," *Canadian Journal of Political Science*, vol. 7, 1974, pp. 704-524.

————: "Party Identification: A Conceptual Analysis" (Note), *Canadian Journal of Political Science*, vol. 11, 1978, pp. 419-435.

———— and Donald E. Blake: "Voting Research in Canada: Problems and Prospects," *Canadian Journal of Political Science*, vol. 8, 1975, pp. 313-325.

Engelmann, Frederick C.: "Membership Participation in Policy-Making in the CCF," *Canadian Journal of Economics and Political Science,* vol. 22, 1956, pp. 161-173.

———— and M. A. Schwartz: *Political Parties and the Canadian Social Structure,* 2nd ed. (Prentice-Hall of Canada, Toronto, 1975).

Epstein, L. D.: "A Comparative Study of Canadian Parties," *The American Political Science Review,* vol. 58, 1964, pp. 46-59.

————: *Political Parties in Western Democracies* (Praeger, New York, 1967).

Ferguson, G. V. and F. H. Underhill: *Press and Party in Canada: Issue of Freedom* (Ryerson, Toronto, 1955).

Filley, Walter O.: "Social Structure and the Canadian Political Parties: The Quebec Case," *Western Political Quarterly,* vol. 9, 1956, pp. 900-914.

Fox, Paul: "Canada's Most Decisive Federal Election," *Parliamentary Affairs,* vol. 11, 1957-58, pp. 287-294.

————: "Early Socialism in Canada," in J. H. Aitchison (ed.): *The Political Process in Canada* (University of Toronto Press, Toronto, 1963).

Gagne, Wallace and Peter Regenstreif: "Some Aspects of New Democratic Party Urban Support in 1965," *Canadian Journal of Economics and Political Science,* vol. 33, 1967, pp. 529-550.

Gilsdorf, Robert R.: "Cognitive and Motivational Sources of Voter Susceptibility to Influence" (Note), *Canadian Journal of Political Science,* vol. 6, 1973, pp. 624-638.

Granatstein, J. E.: *The Politics of Survival: The Conservative Party of Canada, 1939-1945* (University of Toronto Press, Toronto, 1967).

Grossman, L. A.: *Les électeurs Québécois* (Groupe de Recherches Sociales, Montréal, 1960).

————: " 'Safe' Seats: The Rural Urban Pattern in Ontario," *Canadian Journal of Economics and Political Science* (Notes), vol. 29, 1963, pp. 367-371.

Gwyn, R.: *The Shape of Scandal: A Study of a Government in Crisis* (Clarke Irwin, Toronto, 1965).

Hagy, J. W.: "Le Parti Québécois in the 1970 Election," *Queen's Quarterly,* vol. 77, 1970, pp. 266-281.

Hahn, Harlan: "Voting in Canadian Communities: A Taxonomy of Referendum Issues," *Canadian Journal of Political Science,* vol. 1, 1968, pp. 462-469.

Hamelin, Jean Jacques Letarte and Marcel Hamelin: "Les élections provinciales dans le Québec," *Cahiers de Géographie de Québec,* vol. 4, 1958-60, pp. 5-207.

Hamilton, Richard and Maurice Pinard: "The Basis of Parti Québécois Support in Recent Quebec Elections," *Canadian Journal of Political Science,* vol. 9, 1976, pp. 3-26.

Harbron, J. D., "The Conservative Party and National Unity," *Queen's Quarterly,* vol. 69, no. 3, Autumn 1962.

————: "The Conservative Party and National Unity," *Queen's Quarterly* vol. 69, 1962-63, pp. 347-360.

Havel, J. E.: *Les citoyens de Sudbury et la politique* (Laurentian University Press, Sudbury, 1966).

Heasman, D. J.: "The Fragmentation of Canadian Politics," *Parliamentary Affairs,* vol. 16, and vol. 17, 1963, pp. 419-427.

————: "The Politics of Canadian Nationhood," *Parliamentary Affairs,* vol. 19, 1966, pp. 144-161.

Higginbotham, C. H.: *Off the Record: The C.C.F. in Saskatchewan* (McClelland and Stewart, Toronto, 1968).

Hoffman, David: "Intra-Party Democracy: A Case Study," *Canadian Journal of Economics and Political Science*, vol. 27, 1961, pp. 223-235.

Hogan, G.: *The Conservative in Canada* (McClelland and Stewart, Toronto, 1963).

Hooke, Alf: *Thirty Plus Five: I Know, I was There* (Institute of Applied Arts, Edmonton, 1971).

Horowitz, G.: "Tories, Socialists and the Demise of Canada," *Canadian Dimension*, vol. 2, 4, May-June, 1965.

_____: "Conservatism, Liberalism, and Socialism in Canada: An Interpretation," *Canadian Journal of Economics and Political Science*, vol. 32, 1966, pp. 143-171.

_____: *Canadian Labour in Politics* (University of Toronto Press, Toronto, 1968).

_____: "Toward the Democratic Class Struggle," in Trevor Lloyd and Jack McLeod (eds.): *Agenda 1970* (University of Toronto Press, Toronto, 1968).

_____: "Notes on Conservatism, Liberalism and Socialism in Canada" (Note), *Canadian Journal of Political Science*, vol. 11, 1978, pp. 383-399.

Hougham, G. M.: "Canada First: A Minor Party in Microcosm," *Canadian Journal of Economics and Political Science*, vol. 19, 1953, pp. 174-184.

Hunter, W. D. G.: "The New Democratic Party: Antecedents, Policies, Prospects, *Queen's Quarterly*, vol. 69, 1962-63, pp. 361-376.

Irvine, William: *Does Canada Need a New Electoral System?* (Institute of Inter-governmental Relations, Queen's University, Kingston, 1979).

Irving, J. A.: *The Social Credit Movement in Alberta* (University of Toronto Press, Toronto, 1959).

Jacek, H., J. McDonough, R. Shimizu, and P. Smith: "The Congruence of Federal-Provincial Campaign Activity in Party Organizations: The Influence of Recruitment Patterns in Three Hamilton Ridings," *Canadian Journal of Political Science*, vol. 5, 1972, pp. 190-205.

_____, _____, _____, and _____: "Social Articulation and Aggregation in Political Party Organizations in a Large Canadian City," *Canadian Journal of Political Science*, vol. 8, 1975, pp. 274-298.

Jackman, R. W.: "Political Parties, Voting and National Integration," *Comparative Politics*, vol. 4, 1972, pp. 511-536.

Jenson, J.: "Comment: The Filling of Wine Bottles is Not Easy" (Note), *Canadian Journal of Political Science*, vol. 11, 1978, pp. 437-446.

_____ and P. Regenstreif: "Some Dimensions of Partisan Choice in Quebec, 1969," *Canadian Journal of Political Science*, vol. 3, 1970, pp. 308-317.

Jewett, Pauline: "Voting in the 1960 Federal By-Elections at Peterborough and Niagara Falls: Who Voted New Party and Why?" *Canadian Journal of Economics and Political Science*, vol. 28, 1962, pp. 35-53.

Johnston, Richard and J. Ballantyne: "Geography and the Electoral System" (Note), *Canadian Journal of Political Science*, vol. 10, 1977, pp. 857-866.

Joyce, J. G. and H. A. Hosse: *Civic Parties in Canada* (Canadian Federation of Mayors and Municipalities, Toronto, 1970).

Kamin, Leon: "Ethnic and Party Affiliations of Candidates as Determinants of Voting," in S. Sidney Ulmer (ed.): *Introductory Readings in Political Behaviour* (Rand McNally, Chicago, 1961).

Kay, Barry, J.: "Voting Patterns in a Non-Partisan Legislature: A Study of Toronto City Council," *Canadian Journal of Political Science*, vol. 4, 1971, pp. 224-242.

782 BIBLIOGRAPHY

————: "An Examination of Class and Left-Right Party Images in Canadian Voting," (note), *Canadian Journal of Political Science*, vol. 10, 1972, pp. 127-143.

Keddies, V.: "Class Identification and Party Preference among Manual Workers," *Canadian Review of Sociology and Anthropology*, vol. 17, 1980, pp. 24-36.

Knowles, S.: *The New Party* (McClelland and Stewart, Toronto, 1961).

Kornberg, A. and W. Mischler: *Influence in Parliament* (Duke University Press, 1976).

————, J. Smith, and D. Bromley: "Some Differences in the Political Socialization Patterns of Canadian and American Party Officials: A Preliminary Report," *Canadian Journal of Political Science*, vol. 2, 1969, pp. 64-88.

————, ————, and H. Clarke: "Attributes of Ascribed Influence in Local Party Organization in Canada and the United States," *Canadian Journal of Political Science*, vol. 5, 1972, pp. 200-233.

————, ————, and ————: *Citizen Politicians in Canada* (Carolina Academic Press, 1979).

Lambert, R. D. and A. A. Hunter: "Social Stratification, Voting Behaviour, and the Images of Canadian Federal Political Parties," *Canadian Review of Sociology and Anthropology*, vol. 16, 3, 1979, pp. 287-304.

Land, Brian: *Eglinton: The Election Study of a Federal Constituency* (Peter Martin Associates, Toronto, 1965).

Laponce, J. A.: "Non-Voting and Non-Voters: A Typology," *Canadian Journal of Economics and Political Science*, vol. 33, 1967, pp. 75-87.

————: "Canadian Party Labels: An Essay in Semantics and Anthropology," *Canadian Journal of Political Science*, vol. 2, 1969, pp. 141-157.

————: *People vs. Politics* (University of Toronto Press, Toronto, 1969).

————: "Post-dicting Electoral Cleavages in Canadian Federal Elections, 1949-1968: Material for a Footnote," *Canadian Journal of Political Science*, vol. 5, 1972, pp. 270-286.

Laporte, Pierre: *The True Face of Duplessis* (Harvest House, Montreal, 1960).

Lavau, G.: "Partis et Systèmes Politiques: Intéractions et Fonctions," *Canadian Journal of Political Science*, vol. 2, 1969, pp. 18-44.

Laxer, J.: "The Socialist Tradition in Canada," *Canadian Dimension*, vol. 6, December January, 1960-70, pp. 27-33.

League for Social Reconstruction: *Social Planning for Canada* (Nelson, Toronto, 1935).

Lederle, John W.: "The Liberal Convention of 1919 and the Selection of Mackenzie King," *Dalhouise Review*, vol. 27, 1947-1948.

————: "The Liberal Convention of 1893," *Canadian Journal of Political Science.*, vol. 16, 1950, pp. 42-52.

Leduc, L., Jr.: "Party Decision-making: Some Empirical Observations on the Leadership Selection Process," *Canadian Journal of Political Science*, vol. 4, 1971, pp. 97-118.

———— and Walter L. White: "The Role of the Opposition in a One-Party Dominant System: The Case of Ontario," *Canadian Journal of Political Science*, vol. 7, 1974, pp. 86-100.

————, Harold Clarke, Jane Jenson, and Jon H. Pammett: "A National Sample Design," *Canadian Journal of Political Science*, vol. 7, 1974, pp. 701-708.

Lemieux, Vincent: "La Composition des Preferences Partisanes," *Canadian Journal of Political Science*, vol. 2, 1969, pp. 397-418.

_____: "Le Patronage Politique dans l'Ile d'Orléans," *L'Homme*, vol. 10, 2, April-June, 1970, pp. 22-44.

Leslie, Peter M: "The Role of Political Parties in Promoting the Interests of Ethnic Minorities," *Canadian Journal of Political Science*, vol. 2, 1969, pp. 419-433.

Levitt, J.: "Henri Bourassa and the Progressive 'Alliance' of 1926," *Journal of Canadian Studies*, vol. 9, 1974, pp. 17-23.

Lightbody, J.: "Swords and Ploughshares: The Election Prerogative in Canada," *Canadian Journal of Political Science*, vol. 5, 1972, pp. 287-291.

_____: "Electoral Reform in Local Government: The Case of Winnipeg," *Canadian Journal of Political Science*, vol. 11, 1978, pp. 307-332.

Lipset, S. M.: "Democracy in Alberta," *Canadian Forum*, vol. 34, 1954, pp. 175-177.

_____: *Political Man, The Social Bases of Politics* (Doubleday, New York, 1963).

_____: *Agrarian Socialism: The Cooperative Commonwealth Federation in Saskatchewan* (Anchor Books, Doubleday, New York, 1968).

Long, J. A.: "Maldistribution in Western Provincial Legislatures: The Case of Alberta," *Canadian Journal of Political Science*, vol. 2, 1969, pp. 345-355.

_____ and Brian Slemko: "The Recruitment of Local Decision-Makers in Five Canadian Cities: Some Preliminary Findings," *Canadian Journal of Political Science*, vol. 7, 1974, pp. 550-559.

Lorimer, James: *The Real World of City Politics* (James, Lewis and Samuel, Toronto, 1970).

_____: *A Citizen's Guide to City Politics* (James, Lewis and Samuel, Toronto, 1972).

Lovink, J. A. A.: "On Analysing the Impact of the Electoral System on the Party System in Canada," *Canadian Journal of Political Science*, vol. 3, 1970, pp. 497-516.

Lyons, W. E.: *One Man—One Vote* (McGraw-Hill, Toronto, 1970).

Macpherson, C. B.: *Democracy in Alberta: The Theory and Practice of a Quasi-Party System* (University of Toronto Press, Toronto, 1953).

MacQuarrie, Heath N.: "Robert Borden and the Election of 1911," *Canadian Journal of Economics and Political Science*, vol. 25, 1959, pp. 271-286.

_____: *The Conservative Party* (McClelland and Stewart, Toronto, 1965).

Mallory, J. R.: "Style and Fashion: A Note on Alternative Styles in Canadian Political Science," *Canadian Journal of Political Science*, vol. 7, 1974, pp. 129-132.

_____: "The Two Clerks: Parliamentary Discussion of the Role of the Privy Council Office," *Canadian Journal of Political Science*, vol. 10, 1977, pp. 3-19.

Marchak, Patricia: *Ideological Perspectives on Canada* (McGraw-Hill Ryerson, Toronto, 1975).

Massam, Bryan H.: "Forms of Local Government in the Montreal Area, 1911-71: A Discriminant Approach," *Canadian Journal of Political Science*, vol. 6, 1973, pp. 243-253.

_____ and J. D. Anderson (eds.): *Emerging Party Politics in Urban Canada* (McClelland and Stewart, Toronto, 1972).

Mayer, L.: "Federalism and Party Behaviour in Australia and Canada," *Western Political Quarterly*, vol. 23, 4, December, 1970.

McDonald, L.: "Social Class and Voting: A Study of the 1968 Canadian Federal Election in Ontario," *British Journal of Sociology*, vol. 22, 4, December, 1971.

784   BIBLIOGRAPHY

McGeer, Pat: *Politics in Paradise* (Peter Martin Associates, Toronto, 1972).
McGuigan, M. and T. Lloyd: *Liberalism and Socialism* (Exchange for Political Ideas in Canada, Toronto, 1964).
McHenry, D. E.: *The Third Force in Canada: The Cooperative Commonwealth Federation, 1932-1948* (University of California Press, Berkeley, 1950).
McNaught, Kenneth W.: "CCF: Town and Country," *Queen's Quarterly*, vol. 61, 1954-55, pp. 175-177.
————: *A Prophet in Politics* (University of Toronto Press, Toronto, 1959).
Meisel, John: "Religious Affiliation and Electoral Behaviour," *Canadian Journal of Economics and Political Science*, vol. 22, 1956.
————: "Formulation of Liberal and Conservative Programs in 1957 Canadian General Election," *Canadian Journal of Economics and Political Science*, vol. 26, 1960.
————: *The Canadian General Election of 1957* (University of Toronto Press, Toronto, 1962).
————: "The June 1962 Election; Break-up of Our Party System," *Queen's Quarterly*, vol. 69, 1962.
————: "The Stalled Omnibus: Canadian Parties in the 1960s," *Social Research*, vol. 30, 3, Sept., 1963.
————: "L'évolution des partis politiques canadiens," *Cahiers de la Société canadienne de Science politique*, no. 2, 1966.
————: "Les transformations de partis politiques canadiens," *Cahiers de la Société canadienne de Science politique*, no. 2, 1966.
————: "Canadian Parties and Politics," in R. H. Leach: *Contemporary Canada*, (University of Toronto Press, Toronto, 1968).
————: "Cleavages, Parties and Values in Canada," *IPSA*, World Congress, August, 1973.
————: *Working Papers on Canadian Politics*, rev. ed. (McGill-Queen's University Press, Montreal, 1973).
————: "Political Culture and the Politics of Culture," *Canadian Journal of Political Science*, vol. 7, 1974, pp. 601-615.
————: "Classic Dilemma," *Canadian Forum*, vol. 59, May, 1979, pp. 15 and 17.
————: "New Challenge to Parliament: Arguing over Wine Lists on the 'Titanic'?" *Journal of Canadian Studies*, vol. 14, 1979, pp. 18-25.
———— (ed.): *Papers on the 1962 Election* (University of Toronto Press, Toronto, 1964).
Meynaud, J.: *Agent et politique* (Le Centre de documentation et de recherches pontique, College Jean-de-Brebeuf, Montreal, 1966).
Morrison, K. L.: "The Businessman Voter in Thunder Bay: The Catalyst to the Federal-Provincial Voting Split?" *Canadian Journal of Political Science*, vol. 6, 1973, pp. 219-229.
Morton, D.: "The Effectiveness of Political Campaigning: The NDP in the 1967 Ontario Election," *Journal of Canadian Studies*, vol. 4, 3, August, 1969, pp. 21-33.
————: "Polling the Soldier Vote: The Overseas Campaign in the Canadian General Election of 1917," *Journal of Canadian Studies*, vol. 10, 1975, pp. 39-58.
Morton, W. L.: *The Progressive Party in Canada* (University of Toronto Press, Toronto, 1950).
Muller, Steven: "Massive Alternation in Canadian Politics," *Foreign Affairs*, vol. 36, 1958, pp. 633-644.

_____: "Federalism and the Party System in Canada," in J. P. Meekison: *Canadian Federalism: Myth or Reality?* (Methuen, Toronto, 1968), pp. 119-132.

Murrary, Vera: *Le Parti québécois: de la fondation a la prise du pouvoir* (Hurtubise HMH, Montréal 1976).

Neill, R. F.: "Social Credit and National Policy in Canada," *Journal of Canadian Studies*, vol. 3, 1, Feb., 1968, pp. 3-13.

Newman, P. C.: *Renegade in Power: The Diefenbaker Years* (McClelland and Stewart, Toronto, 1963).

_____: *The Distemper of Our Times: Canadian Politics in Transition, 1963-1968* (McClelland and Stewart, Toronto, 1968).

Nicholson, P.: *Vision and Indecision: Diefenbaker and Pearson* (Longman Canada, Toronto, 1968).

Nixon, Robert (ed.): *The Guelph Papers* (Ontario Liberal Party Conference, Toronto, 1968).

Ogmundson, R.: "Liberal Ideology and the Study of Voting Behaviour," *Canadian Review of Sociology and Anthropology*, vol. 17, 1980, pp. 45-54.

Oliver, M. (ed.): *Social Purpose for Canada* (University of Toronto Press, Toronto, 1961).

Palda, Kristian, S.: "Does Advertising Influence Votes? An Analysis of the 1966 and 1970 Quebec Elections" (Note), *Canadian Journal of Political Science*, vol. 6, 1973, pp. 638-655.

Paltiel, Khayyam Z.: *Political Party Financing in Canada* (McGraw-Hill, Toronto, 1970).

_____: "Party and Candidate Expenditures in the Canadian General Election of 1972," *Canadian Journal of Political Science*, vol. 7, 1974, pp. 341-352.

Pammett, John, Lawrence Leduc, J. Jenson, Harold D. Clarke: "The Perception and Impact of Issues in the 1974 Federal Election," *Canadian Journal of Political Science*, vol. 10, 1977, pp. 93-126.

Peacock, D.: *Journey to Power: The Story of a Canadian Election* (Ryerson, Toronto, 1968).

Penner, N.: *The Canadian Left* (Prentice-Hall, Toronto, 1977).

_____ (ed.): *Winnipeg 1919: The Strikers' Own History of the Winnipeg General Strike* (James, Lewis & Samuel, Toronto, 1973).

Perlin, G.: *The Tory Syndrome* (McGill-Queen's University Press, Montreal, 1980).

_____ and Patti Peppin: "Variations in Party Support in Federal and Provincial Elections: Some Hypotheses," *Canadian Journal of Political Science*, vol. 4, 1971, pp. 28-286.

Petryshyn, J.: "R. B. Bennett and the Communists: 1930-1935," *Journal of Canadian Studies*, vol. 9, 1974, pp. 43-54.

Pickersgill, J. W.: *The Liberal Party* (McClelland and Stewart, Toronto, 1962).

Pinard, Maurice, "One Party Dominance and Third Parties," *Canadian Journal of Economics and Political Science*, vol. 33, 1967, pp. 358-373.

_____, *The Rise of a Third Party: A Study in Crisis Politics*, (Prentice-Hall, Englewood Cliff, N.J., 1971).

_____, "Third Parties in Canada Revisited: A Rejoinder and Elaboration of the Theory of One-Party Dominance," *Canadian Journal of Political Science*, vol. 6, 1973, pp. 439-460.

_____ and Richard Hamilton: "The Independence Issue and the Polarization of the Electorate: The 1973 Quebec Election", *Canadian Journal of Political Science*, vol. 10, 1977, pp. 215-259.

———— and ————: "The Parti Quebecois Comes to Power: An Analysis of the 1976 Quebec Election", *Canadian Journal of Political Science*, vol. 11, 1978. pp. 739-775.

Punnett, R. M.: "Leadership Selection in Opposition: The Progressive Conservative Party of Canada," *Australian Journal of Politics and History*, vol. 17, 1971, pp. 188-201.

Qualter, T. H.: "Representation by Population: A Comparative Study," *Canadian Journal of Economics and Political Science*, vol. 33, 1967, pp. 246-268.

————: "Seats and Votes: An Application of the Cube Law to the Canadian Electoral System," *Canadian Journal of Political Science*, vol. 1, 1968, pp. 336-344.

————: *The Election Process in Canada* (McGraw-Hill, Toronto, 1970).

Quinn, H. F.: "Third National Convention of the Liberal Party," *Canadian Journal of Economics and Political Science*, vol. 17, 1951, pp. 228-233.

————: "The Role of the Liberal Party in Recent Canadian Politics," *Political Science Quarterly*, vol. 68, 1953, pp. 396-418.

————: *The Union Nationale: A Study in Quebec Nationalism* (University of Toronto Press, Toronto, 1963).

Rasmussen, Jorgen: "A Research Note on Canadian Systems," *C.J.E.P.S.*, vol. 33, 1967, pp. 98-106.

Rayside, David M.: "The Impact of the Linguistic Cleavage on the "Governing" Parties of Belgium and Canada", *Canadian Journal of Political Science*, vol. 11, 1, 1961.

————: "Federalism and the Party System: Provincial and Federal Liberals in the Province of Quebec," *Canadian Journal of Political Science*, vol. 11, 1978, pp. 449-528.

Regenstreif, Peter: "The Canadian General Election of 1958," *Western Political Quarterly*, vol. 13, 1960, pp. 349-373.

————: "Some Aspects of National Party Support in Canada," *C.J.E.P.S.*, vol. 29, 1963, pp. 59-74.

————: "Ideology and Leadership in the Canadian Party System," (prepared for delivery to the 1964 Annual Meeting of the American Political Science Association, Chicago, Illinois, Sept., 1964).

————: *The Diefenbaker Interlude: Parties and Voting in Canada* (Longman Canada, Toronto, 1965).

————: "Note on the 'Alternation' of French and English Leaders in the Liberal Party of Canada," *C.J.P.S.*, vol. 2, 1969, pp. 118-122.

Reid Escott, M.: "Canadian Political Parties: A Study of the Economics and Racial Basis of Conservatism and Liberalism in 1930," *Contributions to Canadian Economics*, vol. 6, 1933, pp. 7-39.

Richardson, B. T.: *Canada and Mr. Diefenbaker* (McClelland and Stewart, Toronto, 1962).

Ricketts, E. F. and H. Waltzer: "Electoral Arrangements and Party System: The Case of Canada," *Western Political Quarterly*, vol. 23, 1970, pp. 695-714.

Robin, M.: "The Social Basis of Party Politics in British Columbia," *Queen's Quarterly*, vol. 72, 1965, pp. 675-690.

————: *Radical Politics and Canadian Labour, 1880-1930* (Queen's University, Kingston, 1968).

————: *The Rush for Spoils: The Company Province 1871-1933* (McClelland and Stewart, Toronto, 1972).

————: *Pillars of Profit: The Company Province 1934-1972* (McClelland and Stewart, Toronto, 1973).

_____ (ed.): *Canadian Provincial Politics: The Party Systems of the Ten Provinces* (Prentice-Hall, Toronto, 1972).

Roboy, M.: "The Future of Montreal and the MCM," *Our Generation*, vol. 12, 4, pp. 5-18.

Rodney, W.: *Soldiers of the International: A History of the Communist Party of Canada 1919-1929* (University of Toronto Press, Toronto, 1968).

Roussopoulus, D. (ed.): *The New Left in Canada* (Our Generation Press, Montreal, 1970).

Rowat, D. C. (ed.): *Provincial Government and Politics: Comparative Essays*, 2nd ed. (Department of Political Science, Carleton University, Ottawa, 1973).

Sancton, Andrew: "The Application of the 'Senatorial Floor' Rules to the Latest Redistribution of the House of Commons: The Peculiar Case of Nova Scotia," *Canadian Journal of Political Science*, vol. 6, 1, March, 1973.

Sankoff, David and Koula Mellos: "La régionalisation électorale et l'amplification des proportions," *Canadian Journal of Political Science*, vol. 6, 1973, pp. 380-398.

Santos, C. R.: "Some Collective Characteristics of the Delegates to the 1968 Liberal Party Leadership Convention," *Canadian Journal of Political Science*, vol. 3, 1970, pp. 299-308.

Scammon, R. M.: "Election of the Canadian House of Commons, May 22, 1979," *World Affairs*, vol. 142, 1979, pp. 135-137.

Scarrow, Howard A.: "Federal-Provincial Voting Patterns in Canada," *C.J.E.P.S.*, vol. 26, 1960, pp. 289-298.

_____: "By-Elections and Public Opinion in Canada," *Public Opinion Quarterly*, vol. 25, 1961, pp. 79-91.

_____: "Patterns of Voter Turnout in Canada," *Midwest Journal of Political Science*, vol. 5, 1961, pp. 351-364.

_____: *Canada Votes: A Handbook of Federal and Provincial Election Data* (The Hauser Press, New Orleans, 1962).

_____: "Voting Patterns and the New Party," *Political Science*, vol. 14, 1962, pp. 3-15.

_____: "Distinguishing between Political Parties: The Case of Canada," *Midwest Journal of Political Science*, vol. 9, 1965, pp. 61-76.

Schindeler, F.: "One Man, One Vote: One Vote, One Value," *Journal of Canadian Studies*, vol. 3, 1, Feb., 1968, pp. 13-20.

_____ and David Hoffman: "Theological and Political Conservatism: Variations in Attitudes Among Clergymen of One Denomination, *C.J.P.S.*, vol. 2, 1968, pp. 429-441.

Schreiber, E. M.: "Class Awareness and Class Voting in Canada," *Canadian Review of Sociology and Anthropology*, vol. 17, 1980, pp. 37-44.

Schultz, H. J.: "The Social Credit Back-Benchers' Revolt, 1937," *Canadian Historical Review*, vol. 41, 1960, pp. 1-18.

_____: "Portrait of a Premier: William Aberhart," *Canadian Historical Review*, vol. 45, 1964, pp. 185-211.

Schwartz, Mildred A.: *Politics and Territory* (McGill-Queen's University Press, Montreal, 1974).

Simmons, James W.: "Voting Behaviour and Socio-economic Characteristics: The Middlesex East Federal Election, 1965," *Canadian Journal of Political Science*, vol. 33, 1967, pp. 389-400.

Smiley, Donald V.: "The Two-Party System and One-Party Dominance in the Liberal Democratic State," *C.J.E.P.S.*, vol. 24, 1958, pp. 312-322.

_____: "Consensus, Conflict and the Canadian Party System," *Canadian Forum*, vol. 40, Jan., 1961, pp. 223-224.

————: "Canada's Poujadists: A New Look at Social Credit," *Canadian Forum*, vol. 42, 1962, pp. 121-123.

————: "The National Party Leadership Convention in Canada: A Preliminary Analysis," *C.J.P.S.*, vol. 1, 1968, pp. 373-397.

————: "The Case against the Canadian Charter of Human Rights," *Canadian Journal of Political Science*, vol. 2, 1969, pp. 277-291.

————: "Canada and the Quest for a National Policy," *Canadian Journal of Political Science*, vol. 8, 1975, pp. 40-62.

Smith, David E.: "A Comparison of Prairie Political Developments in Saskatchewan and Alberta," *Journal of Canadian Studies*, vol. 40, 1, Feb., 1969, pp. 17-26.

————: *Prairie Liberalism: The Liberal Party in Saskatchewan* (University of Toronto Press, Toronto, 1975).

Sniderman, Paul M., H. D. Forbes, and Ian Melzer: "Party Loyalty and Electoral Volatility: A Study of the Canadian Party System," *Canadian Journal of Political Science*, vol. 7, 1974, pp. 268-288.

Stark, Frank: "The Prime Minister as Symbol: Unifier or Optimizer" (Note), *Canadian Journal of Political Science*, vol. 6, 1973, pp. 514-515.

Stein, Michael B.: "Le Crédit social dans la province de Québec: Somaire et développements," *Canadian Journal of Political Science*, vol. 6, 1973, pp. 563-581.

————: *The Dynamics of Right-Wing Protest: A Political Analysis of the Social Credit in Quebec* (University of Toronto Press, Toronto, 1973).

Stewart, Walter: *Divide and Con: Canadian Politics at Work* (New Press, Toronto, 1973).

Sutherland, S. L. and Eric Tanenbaum: "Rokeach's Value Survey in Use: An Evaluation with Criterion Attitude Scales and Party Identification," *Canadian Review of Sociology and Anthropology*, vol. 12, 1975, pp. 551-564.

Swamson, Donald: "Manitoba's Election: Patterns Confirmed," *Canadian Forum*, vol. 53, September, 1973, pp. 4-7.

Taylor, Charles: *The Pattern of Politics* (McClelland and Stewart, Toronto, 1970).

Taylor, K. W. and N. Wiseman: "Class and Ethnic Voting in Winnipeg: The Case of 1941," *Canadian Review of Sociology and Anthropology*, vol. 14, 1977, pp. 174-187.

Teeple, Gary (ed.): *Capitalism and the National Question in Canada* (University of Toronto Press, Toronto, 1972).

Thomas, L. G.: *The Liberal Party in Alberta: A History of Politics in the Province of Alberta, 1905-1921* (University of Toronto Press, Toronto, 1959).

Thorburn, H. G.: *Politics in New Brunswick* (University of Toronto Press, Toronto, 1961).

———— (ed.): *Party Politics in Canada*, 4th ed. (Prentice-Hall, Toronto, 1979).

Tyre, R.: *Douglas in Saskatchewan: The Story of a Socialist Experiment* (Mitchell Press, Vancouver, 1962).

Underhill, F. H.: *Canadian Political Parties*, Canadian Historical Association Booklet, no. 8, (Ottawa, 1957).

————: "The Revival of Conservatism in North America," *Transactions of the Royal Society of Canada*, vol. 52, series 3, June, 1958, pp. 1-19.

————: *In Search of Canadian Liberalism* (Macmillan, Toronto, 1960).

Vallières, P.: "Le Parti Socialiste du Québec à l'heure de la révolution tranquille," *Cité libre*, vol. 15, no. 63, janvier, 1964, pp. 22-25.

Van Loon, Rick: "Political Participation in Canada: The 1965 Election," *Canadian Journal of Political Science*, vol. 3, 1970, pp. 376-399.

Ward, N.: "A Century of Constituencies," *Canadian Public Administration*, vol. 10, 1967, pp. 105-122.

_____ and D. Spafford (eds.): *Politics in Saskatchewan* (Longman Canada, Toronto, 1968).

Wearing, J.: "How to Predict Canadian Elections," *Canadian Commentator*, vol. 7, 2, February, 1963, pp. 2-4.

_____: "Party Leadership and the 1966 Conventions," *Journal of Canadian Studies*, vol. 2, 1, Feb., 1967, pp. 23-27.

_____: "A Convention for Professionals: The PCs in Toronto," *Journal of Canadian Studies*, vol. 2, 4, Nov., 1967, pp. 3-16.

_____: "The Liberal Choice," *Journal of Canadian Studies*, vol. 3, 2, May, 1968, pp. 3-20.

_____: "The Trudeau Phenomenon," *C.J.P.S.*, vol. 2, 1969, pp. 369-372.

_____: *Liberal Party of Canada* (McGraw-Hill Ryerson, Toronto, 1980).

Westell, Anthony: *Paradox: Trudeau as Prime Minister* (Prentice-Hall, Toronto, 1972).

Whalen, H.: "Social Credit Measures in Alberta," *C.J.E.P.S.*, vol. 18, 1952, pp. 500-517.

Whitaker, R.: *Government Party: Organizing and Financing the Liberal Party of Canada, 1930-1958* (University of Toronto Press, Toronto, 1977).

White, Graham: "One-Party Dominance and Third Parties: The Pinard Theory Reconsidered," *Canadian Journal of Political Science*, vol. 6, 1973, pp. 399-421.

Williams, J. R.: *The Conservative Party in Canada, 1920-1949* (Duke University Press, Durham, 1956).

Wilson, J.: "The Decline of the Liberal Party in Manitoba Politics," *Journal of Canadian Studies*, vol. 10, 1975, pp. 24-41.

_____ and D. Hoffman: "The Liberal Party in Contemporary Ontario Politics," *Canadian Journal of Political Science*, vol. 3, 1970, pp. 177-204.

Winham, G. R. and R. B. Cunningham: "Party Leader Images in the 1968 Federal Election," *C.J.P.S.*, vol. 3, 1970, pp. 37-55.

Winn, Conrad and John McMenemy: "Political Alignment in a Polarized City: Electoral Cleavages in Kitchener, Ontario," *Canadian Journal of Political Science*, vol. 6, 1973, pp. 230-242.

_____ and _____ (eds.): *Political Parties in Canada* (McGraw-Hill Ryerson, Toronto, 1976).

Wiseman, Nelson and K. W. Taylor: "Ethnic vs. Class Voting: The Case in Winnipeg, 1945," *Canadian Journal of Political Science*, 1974, pp. 314-328.

_____ and _____: "Class and Ethnic Voting in Winnipeg during the Cold War," *Canadian Review of Sociology and Anthropology*, vol. 16, 1979, pp. 60-76.

Wrong, Denis H.: "Ontario Provincial Elections 1934-1955; A Preliminary Survey of Voting," *C.J.E.P.S.*, vol. 23, 1957, pp. 395-403.

_____: "The Pattern of Party Voting in Canada," *Public Opinion Quarterly*, vol. 21, 1957, pp. 252-264.

Young, Walter D.: "The Peterborough By-Election: The Success of a Party Image," *Dalhousie Review*, vol. 40, 1960-61, pp. 505-519.

_____ *The Anatomy of a Party: The National CCF 1932-1961* (University of Toronto Press, Toronto, 1969).

_____ *Democracy and Discontent: Progressivism, Socialism and Social Credit in the Canadian West* (Ryerson, Toronto, 1969).

Zakuta, L.: *A Protest Movement Becalmed: A Study of Change in the C.C.F.* (University of Toronto Press, Toronto 1964).

Zipp, John F.: "Left-Right Dimensions of Canadian Federal Party Identification: A Discriminant Analysis," *Canadian Journal of Political Science,* vol. 11, 1978, pp. 251-277.

POLITICAL BIOGRAPHIES

Political biographies and memoirs are a valuable source of information about political parties and elections. The following list is updated from Paul Fox, *Politics: Canada,* 4th ed. (McGraw-Hill Ryerson, Toronto, 1977), pp. 280-282.

Archer, J. and J. A. Munro: *One Canada: Memoirs of the Rt. Hon. J. G. Diefenbaker (1895-1956)* (MacMillan, Toronto, 1975).

Barrette, A.: *Mémoires,* vol. 1 (Librairie Beauchemin, Montréal, 1966).

Beal, J. R.: *The Pearson Phenomena* (Longman, Toronto, 1964).

Beck, J. M.: *Joseph Howe, Voice of Nova Scotia* (Carleton Library, McClelland and Stewart, Toronto, 1964).

Benson, N. A.: *None of It Came Easy: The Story of J. G. Gardiner* (Burns and MacEachern, Toronto, 1955).

Borden, H. (ed.): *Robert Laird Borden: His Memoirs,* 2 vols. (Macmillan, Toronto, 1938).

Borden, R. L.: *His Memoirs,* 2 vols. (Carleton Library, McClelland and Stewart, Toronto, 1969).

———— (ed. by H. Borden): *Letters to Limbo* (University of Toronto Press, Toronto, 1971).

Bothwell, R. and Wm. Kilbourn: *C. D. Howe, A Biography* (McClelland and Stewart, Toronto, 1978).

Bourassa, A., A. Bergevin, and C. Nish (eds.): *Henri Bourassa, Biography, Bibliographical Index, and Index of Public Correspondence, 1895-1924,* (Les éditions de l'Action Nationale, Montréal, 1966).

Bourassa, R.: *Bourassa/Quebec!* (Les éditions de l'homme, Montréal, 1970).

Brown, R. C.: *Robert Laird Borden: A Biography,* vol. 1, 1854-1914 (Macmillan, Toronto, 1975).

Camp, Dalton: *Players and Politicians* (McClelland and Stewart, Toronto, 1970).

————: *Points of Departure* (Deneau and Greenberg, Ottawa, 1979).

Careless, J. M. S.: *Brown of the Globe,* vol. 1, *The Voice of Upper Canada, 1818-1859* (Macmillan, Toronto, 1959); vol. II, *Statesman of Confederation, 1860-1880* (Macmillan, Toronto, 1963).

Casgrain, T.: *Une femme chez les hommes* (Les éditions du jour, Montréal, 1972).

Chalout, R.: *Memoires politiques* (McClelland and Stewart, Toronto, 1969).

Chodos, R. et al.: "David (Lewis): The Centre of His Party," *Last Post,* vol. I, 7, April-May, 1971.

Creighton, D.: *John A. Macdonald: The Young Politician* (Macmillan, Toronto, 1952); *The Old Chieftain* (Macmillan, Toronto, 1955).

Dafoe, J. W.: *Laurier: A Study in Canadian Politics* (Carleton Library, McClelland and Stewart, Toronto, 1963).

Dawson, R. M.: *William Lyon Mackenzie King: A Political Biography, 1874-1923,* vol. I (University of Toronto Press, Toronto, 1958).

Dempson, P.: *Assignment Ottawa* (General Publishing, Don Mills, 1968).

Donaldson, G.: *Fifteen Men: Canada's Prime Ministers from Macdonald to Trudeau* (Doubleday, Toronto, 1969).

Drury, E. C.: *Farmer Premier: The Memoirs of the Hon. E. C. Drury* (McClelland and Stewart, Toronto, 1966).

Ferns, H. S. and Ostry, B.: *The Age of Mackenzie King: The Rise of the Leader* (Heinemann, London, 1955).

Gordon, Walter: *A Political Memoir* (McClelland and Stewart, Toronto, 1977).

Graham, R.: *Arthur Meighen*, vol. I, *The Door of Opportunity* (Clarke, Irwin, Toronto, 1960); vol. II, *And Fortune Fled* (Clarke, Irwin, Toronto, 1963); vol. III, *No Surrender* (Clarke, Irwin, Toronto, 1965).

Gwyn, R.: *Smallwood: The Unlikely Revolutionary*, rev. ed. (McClelland and Stewart, Toronto, 1972).

_____: *Northern Magus* (McClelland and Stewart, Toronto, 1980).

Haliburton, E. D.: *My Years with Stanfield* (Lancelot, Windsor, N.S., 1972).

Heaps, L.: *The Rebel in the House: The Life and Times of A. A. Heaps, M.P.* (Niccolo, London, England, 1970).

Hutchison, B.: *The Incredible Canadian* (Longman, Green, Toronto, 1952).

_____: *Mr. Prime Minister, 1867-1964* (Longman, Toronto, 1964).

Institute canadien des affaires publiques: *Nos hommes politiques* (Les éditions du jour, Montréal, 1964).

Johnson, L. P. V. and O. MacNutt: *Aberhart of Alberta* (Institute of Applied Arts, Edmonton, 1970).

Kendle, John: *John Bracken: A Political Biography* (University of Toronto Press, Toronto, 1980).

King. W. L. M.: *Industry and Humanity* (University of Toronto Press, Toronto, 1973).

LaMarsh, Judy: *Memoirs of a Bird in a Gilded Cage* (McClelland and Stewart, Toronto, 1969).

Lapalme, G. E.: *Mémoires*, vol. 1-3, (Leméac, Montréal, 1969-73).

Laporte, P.: *The True Face of Duplessis* (Harvest House, Montreal, 1960).

LaRoque, H.: *Camilien House, le p'tit gars de Ste. Marie* (Les éditions de l'homme, Montréal, 1961).

MacInnis, G.: *J. S. Woodsworth, A Man to Remember* (Macmillan, Toronto, 1953).

Mardiros, A.: *William Levine: A Life of a Prairie Radical* (Lorimer, Toronto, 1979).

McGregor, F. A.: *The Fall and Rise of Mackenzie King: 1911-1919* (Macmillan, Toronto, 1962).

McKenty, N.: *Mitch Hepburn* (McClelland and Stewart, Toronto, 1967).

McNaught, K.: *A Prophet in Politics: A Biography of J. S. Woodsworth* (University of Toronto Press, Toronto, 1959).

Munro, J. A. and A. I. Inglish (eds.): *Mike: The Memoirs of the Right Honourable Lester B. Pearson, vol. II, 1948-1957* (University of Toronto Press, Toronto, 1973).

Nadeau, J.-M.: *Carnets politiques* (Editions Partis Pris, Montréal, 1966).

Neatby, H. B.: *William Lyon Mackenzie King, 1924-1932: The Lonely Heights*, vol. 2 (University of Toronto Press, Toronto, 1963).

_____: *Laurier and a Liberal Quebec: A Study in Political Management* (McClelland and Stewart, Toronto, 1973).

_____: *William Lyon Mackenzie King, 1932-1939: Prism of Unity*, vol. 3 (University of Toronto Press, Toronto, 1976).

Newman, P. C.: *Renegade in Power: The Diefenbaker Years* (Carleton Library, McClelland and Stewart, Toronto, 1963).

Oliver, Peter: *G. Howard Ferguson: Ontario Tory* (University of Toronto Press, Toronto, 1977).

Pearson, L. B.: *Mike: The Memoirs of the Right Honourable Lester B. Pearson*, vol. I, *1897-1948* (University of Toronto Press, Toronto, 1972); vol. II, *1948-1957* (1973); vol. III, *1957-1968* (1975).

Pickersgill, J. W.: *The Mackenzie King Record*, vol. 1, *1939-1944* (University of Toronto Press, Toronto, 1960); vol. 2, with D. Forster: *1944-1945* (1968); vol. 3, *1945-1946* (1970); vol. 4, *1947-1948* (1971).

———: *My Years with Louis St. Laurent* (University of Toronto Press, Toronto, 1975).

Provencher, J.: *René Lévesque, portrait d'un québécois* (Les éditions la presse, Montréal 1973); English edition (Gage, Toronto, 1975).

Roberts, L.: *C.D.: The Life and Time of Clarence Decatur Howe* (Clarke, Irwin, Toronto, 1957).

———: *The Chief: A political Biography of Maurice Duplessis* (Clarke, Irwin, Toronto, 1963).

Rolph, W. K.: *Henry Wise Wood of Alberta* (University of Toronto Press, Toronto, 1950).

Ryan, O.: *Tim Buck: A Conscience for Canada* (Progress Books, Toronto, 1975).

Schull, J.: *Laurier, The First Canadian* (Macmillan, Toronto, 1965).

———: *Edward Blake: The Man of the Other Way* (Macmillan, Toronto, 1975).

———: *Edward Blake: Leader and Exile* (Macmillan, Toronto, 1976).

———: *The Great Scot: A Biography of Donald Gordon* (McGill-Queens Press, Montreal, 1979).

Schultz, H. J.: "Portrait of a Premier: William Aberhart," *Canadian Historical Review*, vol. XXXV, 3, September, 1964.

Sévigny, P.: *This Game of Politics* (McClelland and Stewart, Toronto, 1965).

Shaw, B. (ed.): *The Gospel According to Saint Pierre* (Trudeau) (Richmond Hill Pocket Books, Simon and Schuster, 1969).

Sheppard, C.-A.: *Dossier Wagner* (Les éditions du jour, Montréal, 1972).

Sherman, P.: *Bennett* (W.A.C.) (McClelland and Stewart, Toronto, 1966).

Smallwood, J. R.: *I Chose Canada* (Memoirs) (Macmillan, Toronto, 1973).

Smith, D.: *Gentle Patriot—A Political Biography of Walter Gordon* (Hurtig, Edmonton, 1973).

Steeves, D. G.: *The Compassionate Rebel: Ernest E. Winch and His Times* (Evergreen Press, Vancouver, 1960).

Stevens, G.: *Stanfield* (McClelland and Stewart, Toronto, 1973).

Stewart, M. and D. French: *Ask No Quarter: A Biography of Agnes MacPhail* (Longman, Green, Toronto, 1959).

Stewart, W.: *Shrug—Trudeau in Power* (New Press, Toronto, 1972).

Stinson, L.: *Political Warriors: Recollections of a Social Democrat* (Queenston House, Winnipeg, 1975).

Stursberg, Peter: *Diefenbaker: Leadership Gained, 1956-1962* (University of Toronto Press, Toronto, 1975).

———: *Diefenbaker: Leadership Lost, 1962-67* (University of Toronto Press, Toronto, 1976).

Thomson, D. C.: *Alexander MacKenzie: Clear Grit* (Macmillan, Toronto, 1960).

———: *Louis St. Laurent: Canadian* (Macmillan, Toronto, 1967).

Thordarson, B.: *Lester Pearson, Diplomat and Politician* (Oxford University Press, Toronto, 1974).

Trudeau, P. E.: *Conversation with Canadians* (University of Toronto Press, Toronto, 1972).

Van Dusen, T.: *The Chief* (Diefenbaker) (McGraw-Hill, Toronto, 1968).

Wallace, W. S.: *The Macmillan Dictionary of Canadian Biography*, 3rd ed. (Macmillan, Toronto, 1963).

Ward, N. (ed.): *A Party Politician: The Memoirs of Chubby Power* (Macmillan, Toronto, 1966).

Watkins, E.: *R. B. Bennett* (Kingswood House, Toronto, 1963).

Westell, A.: *Paradox: Trudeau as Prime Minister* (Prentice-Hall, Toronto, 1972).

Young, W. D.: "M. J. Coldwell: The Making of a Social Democrat," *Journal of Canadian Studies*, vol. IX, 3, August, 1974.

Zink, L.: "Trudeaucracy," *Toronto Sun*, 1972.

Zolf, L.: *Dance of the Dialectic* (James, Lewis and Samuel, Toronto, 1973).

INTEREST GROUPS

Badgley, Robin F. and Samuel Wolff: *Doctors' Strike* (Macmillan, Toronto, 1967), pp. 133-153.

Beland, F.: "L'Anti-Contrès," *Recherches Sociographiques*, vol. 13, 1972, pp. 381-397.

Belanger, P. R. and L. Maheu: "Pratique politique étudiante au Québec," *Recherches Sociographiques*, vol. 13, 1972, pp. 309-342.

Bentley, A. F.: *The Process of Government*, edited by Peter Odegard (Belknap Press of Harvard University Press, Cambridge, 1967).

Berry, G. R.: "The Oil Lobby and the Energy Crisis," *Canadian Public Administration*, vol. 17, 1974, pp. 600-635.

Cameron, et al.: "A Crisis in the Organization of Health Care," in Richard Laskin (ed.): *Social Problems. A Canadian Profile* (McGraw-Hill, New York, 1964), pp. 330-360.

Clark, S. D.: *The Canadian Manufacturers' Association* (University of Toronto Press, Toronto, 1939).

_____: "Group Interests in Canadian Politics," in J. H. Aitchison, *The Political Process in Canada* (University of Toronto Press, Toronto, 1963).

Dawson, H. J.: "The Canadian Federation of Agriculture," *Canadian Public Administration*, vol. 3, 1960, pp. 134-149.

_____: "The Consumers Association of Canada," *Canadian Public Administration*, vol. 6, 1963, pp. 92-118.

_____: "Relations between Farm Organizations and the Civil Service in Canada and Great Britain," *Canadian Public Administration*, vol. 10, 1967, pp. 450-470.

Dion, Léon: *Société et politique—le Vie des Groupes: Tome 1, Fondements de la société libérale; Tome 2, Dynamique de la société libérale* (Les Presses de l'Université Laval, Québec, 1971).

Doern, G. B.: *Science and Politics in Canada* (McGill-Queen's Press, Montreal, 1971).

Eckstein, Harry: *Pressure Group Politics* (Allen and Unwin, London, 1960).

_____: "Group Theory and the Comparative Study of Pressure Groups," in H. Eckstein and D. Apter (eds.): *Comparative Politics* (The Free Press, Glencoe, 1963).

Gouldner, Janet W.: "The Doctors' Strike: Change and Resistance to Change in Saskatchewan," in Seymour Martin Lipset (ed.): *Agrarian Socialism* (Anchor Books, Doubleday, Garden City, 1968), pp. 393-404.

Horowitz, Gad: *Canadian Labour in Politics* (University of Toronto Press, Toronto, 1968).

Krueger, Cynthia: "Praise Protest: The Medicare Conflict in Saskatchewan," in Seymour Martin Lipset (ed.): *Agrarian Socialism* (Anchor Books, Doubleday, Garden City, 1968), pp. 405-434.

Kwavnick, D.: "Pressure Group Demands and the Struggle for Organizational Status: The Case of Organized Labour in Canada," *Canadian Journal of Political Science*, vol. 3, 1970, pp. 56-72.

————: *Organized Labour and Pressure Politics: The Canadian Labour Congress, 1956-1968* (McGill-Queen's University Press, Montreal and London, 1972).

————: "Pressure-Group Demands and Organizational Objectives: The CNTU, the Lapalme Affair, and National Bargaining Units," *Canadian Journal of Political Science*, vol. 6, 1973, pp. 582-601.

Litvak, Isaiah, A. and Christopher J. Maule: "Interest-Group Tactics and the Politics of Foreign Investment: The Time-Reader's Digest Case Study," *Canadian Journal of Political Science*, vol. 7, 1974, pp. 616-629.

Lowi, T. M.: *The End of Liberalism* (W. W. Norton, New York, 1969).

Macridis, Roy: "Groups and Group Theory," in R. C. Macridis and B. E. Brown: *Comparative Politics* (Dorsey Press, Homewood, Ill., 1964), pp. 139-144.

Manzer, R.: "Selective Inducements and the Development of Pressure Groups: The Case of the Canadian Teacher's Association," *C.J.P.S.* vol. 2, 1969, pp. 103-117.

Park, L. C. and F. W. Park: *Anatomy of Big Business in Canada* (James, Lewis and Samuel, Toronto, 1973).

Porter, John: *The Vertical Mosaic* (University of Toronto Press, Toronto, 1965), ch. 17, pp. 520-558.

Presthus, Robert: "Interest Groups and the Canadian Parliament: Activities, Interaction, Legitimacy and Influence," *Canadian Journal of Political Science*, vol. 4, 1971, pp. 444-460.

————: *Elite Accommodation in Canadian Politics* (Macmillan, Toronto, 1973).

Pross, A. P.: "Canadian Pressure Groups in the 1970s: Their Role and Their Relations with the Public Service," *Canadian Public Administration*, vol. 18, 1975, pp. 121-135.

————: *Pressure Group Behaviour in Canadian Politics* (McGraw-Hill Ryerson, Toronto, 1975).

Taylor, Malcolm G.: "The Role of the Medical Profession in the Formulation and Execution of Public Policy," *Canadian Public Administration*, vol. 3, 1970, pp. 233-55.

Thornburn, H. G.: "Pressure Groups in Canadian Politics," *C.J.E.P.S.*, vol. 30, 1964, pp. 157-174.

Truman, David Bicknell: *The Governmental Process* (Knopf, New York, 1951).

Zeigler, Harmon: *Interest Groups in American Society* (Prentice-Hall, Englewood Cliffs, 1964).

THE AUTHORITIES AND ELITES OF THE CANADIAN POLITICAL SYSTEM

Many of the political biographies previously listed are relevant here since they present descriptions and background information on many of Canada's more important politicians. In addition, see:

Clement, Wallace: *The Canadian Corporate Elite: An Analysis of Economic Power* (McClelland and Stewart, Toronto, 1975).

————: "Inequality of Access: Characteristics of the Canadian Corporate Elite," *Canadian Review of Sociology and Anthropology*, vol. 12, 1975, pp. 33-52.

Dion, Léon: The Concept of Political Leadership: An Analysis," *Canadian Journal of Political Science*, vol. 1, 1968, pp. 2-17.

Fox, Paul: "The Representative Nature of the Canadian Cabinet," in Paul Fox (ed.): *Politics: Canada* (McGraw-Hill, Toronto, 1970), pp. 341-345.

Gibson, F. W. (ed.): *Cabinet Formation and Bicultural Relations*, Royal Commission on Bilingualism and Biculturalism, Study No. 6, (Queen's Printer, Ottawa, 1970).

Hockin, Thomas A.: *Apex of Power: The Prime Minister and Political Leadership in Canada* (Prentice-Hall, Toronto, 1971).

House, J. D.: "The Social Organization of Multinational Corporations: Canadian Subsidiaries in the Oil Industry," *Canadian Review of Sociology and Anthropology*, vol. 14, 1977, pp. 1-14.

Irvine, William P.: *Cultural Conflict in Canada: The Erosion of Consociational Politics* (University Microfilms, Ann Arbor, Mich., 1973).

Kornberg, Alan: "The Social Basis of Leadership in a Canadian House of Commons," *Australian Journal of Politics and History*, vol. 11, 1965, pp. 324-334.

_____: *Canadian Legislative Behavior: A Study of the 25th Parliament* (Holt, Rinehart and Winston, New York, 1967).

_____: "Parliament in Canadian Society" in A. Kornberg, Lloyd A. Musolf et al.: *Legislatures in Developmental Perspective* (Duke University Press, Durham, 1970), pp. 55-128.

_____ and Norman C. Thomas: "The Political Socialization of National Legislative Elites in the United States and Canada," *Journal of Politics*, vol. 27, 1965, pp. 761-775.

_____ and _____: "Representative Democracy and Political Elites in Canada and the United States," *Parliamentary Affairs*, vol. 19, 1965-66, pp. 91-102.

_____ and H. H. Winsbrough: "The Recruitment of Canadian Members of Parliament," *American Political Science Review*, vol. 63, 1968, pp. 1242-1257.

Note: See also the extensive list of studies by Kornberg and his collaborators in the "Parliamentary Process" section of the bibliography, infra.

Laponce, J. A.: "The Religious Background of Canadian M.P.'s," *Political Studies*, vol. 1, 1958, pp. 253-258.

MacQuarrie, H. N.: "The Formation of Borden's First Cabinet," *C.J.E.P.S.*, vol. 23, 1957, pp. 90-104.

McRae, K. D. (ed.): *Consociational Democracy* (McClelland and Stewart, Toronto, 1974).

Noel, S. J. R.: "Consociational Democracy and Canadian Federalism" *C.J.P.S.*, vol. 4, 1971, pp. 15-18.

Olsen, D.: *The State Elite* (McClelland and Stewart, Toronto, 1980).

Porter, John: *The Vertical Mosaic* (University of Toronto Press, Toronto, 1965).

Pratt, L. R. and A. Tupper: "The Politics of Accountability: Executive Discretion and Democratic Control," *Canadian Public Policy*, vol. 6, Supplement, 1980, pp. 254-264.

Presthus, Robert: *Elite Accommodation in Canadian Politics* (Macmillan, Toronto, 1974).

Rempel, H. D.: "The Practice and Theory of the Fragile State: Trudeau's Conception of Authority," *Journal of Canadian Studies*, vol. 10, 1975, pp. 24-38.

Rick, H.: "From a Study of Higher Civil Servants in Ontario," *Canadian Public Administration*, vol. 17, 1974, pp. 328-334.

Royal Commission on Bilingualism and Biculturalism, Queen's Printer, Ottawa, 1970. Many of the studies and working papers prepared for the Royal Commission bear incidentally on the composition of decision-making elites in Canada.
Studies such as

Beattie, C. J. Desy, and S. Longstaff: *Bureaucratic Careers, Anglophones and Francophones in the Canadian Public Service,*
or

Chartrand, P. J. and K. L. Pond: *A Study of Executive Career Paths in the Public Service of Canada,*
or

Van Loon, R. J.: *The Structure and Membership of the Canadian Cabinet* are particularly relevant. Five copies of all internal studies have been deposited in the National Library, Ottawa and a complete listing is available there. In addition a nearly complete listing together with a short description of each report can be found in Volume 1 of the Report of the Royal Commission. Some studies have been published separately by the Queen's Printer. These are listed under the authors' names in the appropriate parts of the bibliography.

Santos, C. R.: "A Theory of Bureaucratic Authority," *Canadian Public Administration*, vol. 21, 1978, pp. 243-267.

Schindeler, F.: "The Ontario Cabinet: Definition, Size and Representative Nature," *Canadian Public Administration*, vol. 9, 1966, pp. 334-347.

Smith, David and Lorne Tepperman: "Changes in the Canadian Business and Legal Elites, 1870-1970," *Canadian Review of Sociology and Anthropology*, vol. 11, 1974, pp. 97-109.

Stevenson, Garth: "Foreign Direct Investment and the Provinces: A Study of Elite Attitudes," *Canadian Journal of Political Science*, vol. 7, 1974, pp. 630-647.

Stewart, G. T.: "Political Patronage under MacDonald and Laurier, 1878-1911," *American Review of Canadian Studies*, vol. 10, 1980, pp. 3-26.

Ward, Norman: *The Canadian House of Commons: Representation*, 2nd ed. (University of Toronto Press, Toronto, 1963).

———— and David Hoffman: *Bilingualism and Biculturalism in the Canadian House of Commons*, Royal Commission on Bilingualism and Biculturalism, Study No. 3 (Queen's Printer, Ottawa, 1970).

CABINET AND POLICY

Abel, Albert S.: "Administrative Secrecy", *Canadian Public Administration*, vol. 11, 1968, pp. 440-448.

Banks, M. A.: "Privy Council, Cabinet and Ministry in Britain and Canada: A Story of Confusion," *Canadian Journal of Economics and Political Science*, vol. 31, 1965, pp. 193-205. See also "Comments" by Eugene Forsey, ibid, vol. 31, 1965, p. 575 and Trevor Lloyd, ibid, vol. 32, 1966 pp. 88-90, and "Reply", ibid, vol. 32, 1966, pp. 90-93.

Barbe, Raoul P.: "Le contrôle parlementaire des enterprises publiques au Canada," *Canadian Public Administration*, vol. 12, 1969, pp. 463-480.

Campbell, Colin & G. Szablowski: *The Super Bureaucrats: Structure and Behaviour in Central Agencies* (Macmillan, Toronto, 1979).

Canada, Parliament, House of Commons, Special Committee on Statutory Instruments: *Third Report* (Queen's Printer, Ottawa, 1969).

_____, Royal Commission on Government Organization: *Report, Vol. 1, Management of the Public Service* (Queen's Printer, Ottawa, 1962-1963).

_____, Treasury Board: *Planning, Programming, Budgeting Guide* (Queen's Printer, Ottawa, 1969).

Doern, G. Bruce: "Mr. Trudeau, the Science Council and P.P.B.: Recent Changes in the Philosophy of Policy Making in Canada," (a paper prepared for the Annual Meeting of the Canadian Political Science Association, June 3, 1970, Winnipeg, Manitoba).

_____: "Recent Changes in the Philosophy of Policy-Making in Canada," *Canadian Journal of Political Science*, vol. 4, 1971, pp. 243-264.

_____: *Political Policy-Making: A Commentary on the Economic Council's Eighth Annual Review and the Ritchie Report* (Private Planning Association, Montreal, 1972).

_____ and Peter Aucoin: *Public Policy in Canada* (Macmillan, Toronto, 1979).

_____ and Richard Phidd: *The Politics and Management of Canadian Economic Policy* (Macmillan, Toronto, 1978).

_____ and V. S. Wilson: *Issues in Canadian Public Policy* (Macmillan, Toronto, 1974).

Driedger, Elmer A.: *The Composition of Legislation; Legislative Forms and Precedents*, 2nd ed. rev. (Supply and Services, Ottawa, 1976).

Dror, Yehenzkel: "Policy Analyst: A New Professional Role in Government Service," *Public Administration Review*, vol. 27, 1967, pp. 197-203.

_____: *Public Policy Making Reexamined* (Chandler Publishing Co., San Francisco, 1968).

Etzioni, A.: "Mixed Scanning: A 'Third' Approach to Decision-making," *Public Administration Review*, vol. 27, 1967, pp. 385-392.

Forsey, Eugene: "Mr. King and Parliamentary Government," *C.J.E.P.S.*, vol. 17, 1951, pp. 451-467.

French, Richard: *How Ottawa Decides* (Lorimer, Toronto, 1980).

Gibson, F. W. (ed.): *Cabinet Formation and Bicultural Relations: Seven Case Studies*, Royal Commission on Bilingualism and Biculturalism, no. 6 (Queen's Printer, Ottawa, 1970).

Gow, Donald John Lutton: *Canadian Federal Administration and Political Institutions: a Role Analysis* (unpublished Ph.D. dissertation, Queen's University, Kingston, 1967).

Hawkins, Freda: *Canada and Immigration: Public Policy and Public Concern* (McGill-Queen's University Press, Montreal, 1972).

Heeney, A. D. P.: "Cabinet Government in Canada and Some Recent Developments in the Machinery of the Central Executive," *C.J.E.P.S.*, vol. 12, 1964, pp. 282-301.

_____: "Mackenzie King and the Cabinet Secretariat," *Canadian Public Administration*, vol. 10, 1967, pp. 366-375.

Hockin, Thomas A. (ed.): *Apex of Power: The Prime Minister and Political Leadership in Canada* (Prentice-Hall, Toronto, 1971).

Hodgetts, J. E.: "Parliament and the Powers of the Cabinet," *Queen's Quarterly*, vol. 52, 1945, pp. 465-477.

_____: "The Civil Servant and Policy Formulation," *C.J.E.P.S.*, vol. 23, 1957, pp. 467-479.

Jackson, Robert J. and Michael M. Atkinson: *The Canadian Legislative System* (Macmillan, Toronto, 1975).

Johnson, A. W.: "The Treasury Board of Canada and the Machinery of Government of the 1970s," *Canadian Journal of Political Science*, vol. 4, 1971, pp. 346-366.

Kersell, John E.: "Parliamentary Debate of Delegated Legislation," *Canadian Public Administration*, vol. 2, 1959, pp. 132-144.

————: *Parliamentary Supervision of Delegated Legislation: the United Kingdom, Australia, New Zealand and Canada* (Stevens, London 1960).

Knight, K. W.: "Administrative Secrecy and Ministerial Responsibility," *C.J.E.P.S.* vol. 32, 1966, pp. 77-83.

Lalonde, M.: "The Changing Role of the Prime Minister's Office," *Canadian Public Administration*, vol. 14, 1971, pp. 509-537.

LaMarsh, Judy: *Memoirs of a Bird in a Gilded Cage* (McClelland and Stewart, Toronto, 1969).

Lamontagne, M.: "The Influence of the Politician," *Canadian Public Administration*, vol. 11, 1968, pp. 263-271.

Lloyd, T.: "The Reform of Parliamentary Proceedings," in Abraham Rotstein: *The Prospect of Change* (McGraw-Hill, Toronto, 1965), pp. 23-39.

MacQuarrie, H. N.: "The Formation of Borden's First Cabinet," *C.J.E.P.S.*, vol. 23, 1957, pp. 94-103.

Mallory, J. R.: "Delegated Legislation in Canada: Recent Changes in Machinery," *C.J.E.P.S.*, vol. 19, 1953, pp. 462-67.

————: "The Minister's Office Staff: An Unreformed Part of the Public Service," *Canadian Public Administration*, vol. 10, 1967, pp. 25-34.

————: "Mackenzie King and the Origins of the Cabinet Secretariat," *Canadian Public Administration*, vol. 10, 1976, pp. 254-266.

McKeough, W. Darcy: "The Relations of Ministers and Civil Servants," *Canadian Public Administration*, vol. 12, no. 1.

Morton, W. L.: "The Formation of the First Federal Cabinet," *Canadian Historical Review*, vol. 36, 1955, pp. 113-125.

Newman, Peter C.: *Renegade in Power; the Diefenbaker Years* (McClelland and Stewart, Toronto, 1963).

————: *The Distemper of Our Times; Canadian Politics in Transition, 1963-1968* (McClelland and Stewart, Toronto, 1968).

"Planning-Programming-Budgeting System: A Symposium," *Public Administration Review*, vol. 26, 1966, pp. 243-310.

Porter, John: *The Vertical Mosaic* (University of Toronto Press, Toronto, 1965), pp. 386-416.

Punnett, R. M.: *The Prime Minister in Canadian Government and Politics* (Macmillan, Toronto, 1977).

Robertson, R. G.: "The Canadian Parliament and Cabinet in the Face of Modern Demands," *Canadian Public Administration*, vol. 11, 1968, pp. 272-279.

————: "The Changing Role of the Privy Council Office," *Canadian Public Administration*, vol. 14, 1971, pp. 487-508.

Rowan, M.: "A Conceptual Framework for Government Policy-Making," *Canadian Public Administration*, vol. 13, 1970, pp. 277-296.

Rowat, D. C.: "How Much Administrative Secrecy?" *C.J.E.P.S.*, vol. 32, 1965, pp. 479-498.

————: "Administrative Secrecy and Ministerial Responsibility: a Reply," *C.J.E.P.S.*, vol. 32, 1966, pp. 84-87.

Rutherford, G. S.: "Delegation of Legislative Power to the Lieutenant-Governors in Council," *Canadian Bar Review*, vol. 26, 1948, pp. 533-544.

Schindeler, Fred: "The Prime Minister and the Cabinet: History and Development," in T. Hockin (ed.): *Apex of Power*, (Prentice-Hall, Toronto, 1971), pp. 22-47.

_____ and C. M. Lamphier: "Social Science Research and Participatory Democracy in Canada," *Canadian Public Administration*, vol. 12, 1969, pp. 481-498.

Scott, F. R.: "Administrative Law: 1923-1947," *Canadian Bar Review*, vol. 26, 1948, pp. 268-285.

Sharp, Mitchell: "The Bureaucratic Elite and Policy Formation," in W. D. K. Kernaghan (ed.): *Bureaucracy in Canadian Government* (Methuen, Toronto, 1969), pp. 82-87.

Smith, Denis: "President and Parliament: The Transformation of Parliamentary Government in Canada," in O. Kruhlak et al (eds.): *The Canadian Political Process* (Holt, Rinehart and Winston, Toronto, 1970), pp. 367-382.

Tennant, P.: "The NDP Government of British Columbia: Unaided Politicians in an Unaided Cabinet," *Canadian Public Policy*, vol. 3, 1977, pp. 489-503.

Ward, Norman: *The Public Purse* (University of Toronto Press, Toronto, 1962).

White, W. L. and J. C. Strick: *Policy, Politics and the Treasury Board in Canadian Government* (Science Research Associates, Don Mills, Ont., 1971).

Wildavsky, Aaron B.: *The Politics of the Budgetary Process* (Little, Brown, Boston, 1964).

FEDERALISM AND PUBLIC POLICY

A. Intergovernmental Institutions

Atkey, R. G.: "The Role of the Provinces in International Affairs," *International Journal*, vol. 26, 1970-71, pp. 249-273.

Belanger, G.: "Questions de Base à Toute Réforme du Financement Municipal," *Canadian Public Administration*, vol. 20, 1977, pp. 370-379.

Black, E. R. and A. C. Cairns: "A Different Perspective on Canadian Federalism," *Canadian Public Administration*, vol. 9, 1966, pp. 27-44.

Brewis, T. N. and Gilles Paquet: "Regional Development and Planning in Canada; an Exploratory Essay," *Canadian Public Administration*, vol. 11, 1968, pp. 123-162.

Canada, Constitutional Conference: *Proceedings*, Ottawa, February 5-7, 1968 (Queen's Printer, Ottawa, 1968).

_____, _____: *A Briefing Paper on Discussion within the Continuing Committee of Officials* (Secretariat, December, 1968).

_____, _____: *Report of the Continuing Committee of Officials to the Constitutional Conference* (Privy Council Office, December, 1968).

_____, _____: *Proceedings*, Ottawa, February 10-12, 1969 (Queen's Printer, Ottawa, 1969).

_____, _____: *Report of the Conclusions of the Meeting*, First Working Session, June 11-12, 1969.

_____, Federal-Provincial Relations Division: *Federal-Provincial Grants and the Spending Power of Parliament* (Queen's Printer, Ottawa, June, 1969).

_____, _____: *Taxing Power and the Constitution of Canada* (Queen's Printer, Ottawa, June, 1969).

————, Prime Minister: *Federalism for the Future; a Statement of Policy by the Government of Canada* (Queen's Printer, Ottawa, 1968).

Caplan, Neil: "Some Factors Affecting the Resolution of a Federal-Provincial Conflict," *Canadian Journal of Political Science,* vol. 2, 1969, pp. 173-186.

Cody, H.: "The Evolution of Federal-Provincial Relations in Canada: Some Reflections," *American Review of Canadian Studies,* vol. 7, 1977, pp. 55-83.

Cole, R. Taylor: "The Universities and Governments under Canadian Federalism," *Journal of Politics,* vol. 34, 1972, pp. 524-553.

Dehem, R.: *Planification économique et fédéralisme* (Laval, Quebec, 1968).

Doern, G. B.: "Canadian Intergovernmental Liaison: Tax Agreements, Fiscal Policy and Conditional Transfers," (a paper prepared in the Institute of Intergovernmental Relations, Queen's University).

Dupré, J. Stefan, Graeme McKechnie, David M. Cameron, and Theodore B. Rotenberg: *Federalism and Policy Development: The Case of Adult Occupational Training in Ontario* (University of Toronto Press, Toronto, 1973).

Gallant, Edgar: "The Secretariat of the Constitutional Conference," in W. D. K. Kernaghan (ed.): *Bureaucracy in Canadian Government* (Methuen, Toronto, 1969), pp. 47-50.

———— and R. M. Burns: "The Machinery of Federal-Provincial Relations: I and II," *Canadian Public Administration,* vol. 8, 1965, pp. 515-534.

Guindon, H.: "The Social Evolution of Quebec Reconsidered," *C.J.E.P.S.,* vol. 26, 1960, pp. 533-551.

Hodgetts, J. E.: "Regional Interests and Policy in a Federal Structure," *C.J.E.P.S.,* vol. 32, 1966, pp. 3-14.

Johnson, A. W.: "The Dynamics of Federalism in Canada," *C.J.P.S.,* vol. 1, 1968, pp. 18-39.

Jones, Richard: *Community in Crisis: French-Canadian Nationalism in Perspective* (McClelland and Stewart, Toronto, Montreal, 1967).

Koehler, N. C. Jr.: "The Impact of Canadian Energy Policy on Changing Federal-Provincial Relations: Competition Between Alberta and Ottawa," *American Review of Canadian Studies,* vol. 7, 1977, pp. 1-32.

MacDonald, V. C.: *Legislative Power and the Supreme Court in the Fifties* (Butterworths, Toronto, 1961).

Manzer, Ronald A.: "The National Organization of Canadian Education," *Canadian Public Administration,* vol. 11, 1968, pp. 492-508.

McLarty, R. A.: "Organizing for a Federal-Provincial Fiscal Policy," *Canadian Tax Journal,* vol. 15, 1967, pp. 412-420.

McWhinney, E.: "The New Pluralistic Federalism in Canada," *La Revue Juridique Thémis,* vol. 2, 1967, pp. 139-149.

Neill, R. F.: "National Policy and Regional Development: A Footnote to the Deutsch Report on Maritime Union," *Journal of Canadian Studies,* vol. 9, 1974, pp. 12-19.

Ontario Advisory Committee on Confederation: *Background Papers and Reports,* volumes I and II (title on dust jacket "The Confederation Challenge") (Queen's Printer, Toronto, 1967, 1970).

Ontario Economic Council: *Intergovernmental Relations* (Queen's Printer, Toronto, 1977).

Paltiel, K. Z.: "Federalism and Party Finance: A Preliminary Sounding," in Canada Committee on Election Expenses: *Studies in Canadian Party Finance* (Queen's Printer, Ottawa, 1966), pp. 1-22.

Porter, J.: "Post-industrialism, Post-nationalism and Post-secondary Education," *Canadian Public Administration,* vol. 14, 1971, pp. 32-50.

Quebec: *Le Québec dans le Canada de demain:* vol. 1, *Avenir constitutionnel et statut particulier;* vol. 2, *Vers un nouveau partage des pouvoirs,* (Editions du Jour, Publications 62, 63, Montréal, 1967).

Reagan, M. D.: The *Report on Maritime Union Commissioned by the Governments of Nova Scotia, New Brunswick and Prince Edward Island* (Queen's Printer, Fredericton, Halifax, Charlottetown, 1970).

_____: *New Federalism* (Oxford University Press, New York, 1972).

Rowat, D. C.: "Relations between Universities and Governments in Canada," *Journal of Constitutional and Parliamentary Studies,* vol. 5, 1971, pp. 8-21.

Russell, Peter H.: *Leading Constitutional Decisions,* rev. ed. (McClelland and Stewart, Toronto, 1973).

Rutan, G. R.: "Provincial Participation in Canadian Foreign Relations," *Journal of Inter-American Studies and World Affairs,* vol. 13, 1971, pp. 230-245.

Schultz, R.: "Intergovernmental Cooperation, Regulatory Agencies and Transportation Regulation in Canada: The Case of Part III of the National Transportation Act," *Canadian Public Administration,* vol. 19, 1978, pp. 183-207.

_____: "Federalism and the Regulatory Process," Federal-Provincial Relations Office, Ottawa, 1979, mimeo.

Sharp, M.: *Federalism and International Conferences on Education* (Queen's Printer, Ottawa, 1968).

Simeon, Richard E. B.: *Federal-Provincial Diplomacy: The Making of Public Policy in Canada* (University of Toronto Press, Toronto, 1972).

_____ (ed.): *Confrontation and Collaboration—Intergovernmental Relations in Canada Today* (Institute of Public Administration of Canada, Toronto, 1979).

Smiley, Donald Victor: *Conditional Grants and Canadian Federalism* (Canadian Tax Foundation, Toronto, 1963).

Stein, S. B.: "Symposium on Intergovernmental Relations," *Public Administration Review,* vol. 23, 1968, pp. 3-29.

_____: "Environmental Control and Different Levels of Government," *Canadian Public Administration,* vol. 14, 1971, pp. 129-144.

Torrelli, M.: "Les relations extérieures du Québec," *Annuaire français de Droit international,* vol. 16, 1970, pp. 275-303.

Weidner, E. W.: "Decision-Making in a Federal System," in Aaron B. Wildavsky (ed.): *American Federalism in Perspective* (Little, Brown, Boston, 1967), pp. 229-255.

Wilson, V. Seymour: "Federal-Provincial Relations and Federal Policy Processes," in Bruce Doern and Peter Aucoin: *Public Policy in Canada:* (Macmillan, Toronto, 1979), pp. 190-212.

B. Federal-Provincial Finance

Ballentine, J. G. and W. R. Thirsk: "The Effects of Revenue Sharing on the Distribution of Disposable Incomes," *Canadian Public Policy,* vol. 6, 1980, pp. 30-40.

Bastien, R.: "La Structure Fiscale du Fédéralisme Canadien: 1945-73," *Canadian Public Administration,* vol. 17, 1974, pp. 96-118.

Benson, E. J.: *The Taxing Powers and the Constitution of Canada* (Queen's Printer, Ottawa, 1969).

Birch, A. H.: *Federalism, Finance, and Social Legislation in Canada, Australia, and the United States* (Clarendon, Oxford, 1955).

Bird, R. M.: "The Incidence of the Property Tax: Old Wine in New Bottles," *Canadian Public Policy*, vol. 2, 1976, pp. 323-334.

Boucher, M.: "La réforme fiscale de l'impôt sur le revenu des particuliers était-elle nécessaire?" *Canadian Public Policy*, vol. 1, 1975, pp. 527-535.

Break, G. F.: *Intergovernmental Fiscal Relations in the U.S.* (Brookings Institute, Washington, 1967).

Breton, A.: "A Theory of Government Grants," *Canadian Journal of Economics and Political Science*, vol. 31, 1965, pp. 175-187. See also J. C. Weldon: "Public Goods (and Federalism)," ibid., vol. 32, 1966, pp. 230-238; reply by Breton: ibid., vol. 32, 1966, pp. 238-242; also Breton: "A Theory of the Demand for Public Goods," ibid., vol. 32, 1966, pp. 455-467; and David M. Winch: "Breton's Theory of Government Grants," ibid., vol. 33, 1967, pp. 115-117.

Broadway, R. W.: *Intergovernmental Transfers in Canada* (Canadian Tax Foundation, Toronto, 1980).

Brydon, Marion H.: *Occupancy of Tax Fields in Canada* (Canadian Tax Foundation, Toronto, 1965).

Cameron, N.: "The Taxation of Policyholders' Life Insurance Income," *Canadian Public Policy*, vol. 3, 1977, pp. 129-140.

Canada: *Report to the Royal Commission on Dominion-Provincial Relations* (Rowell-Sirois Report), Book I, *Canada: 1867-1939*, Book II, *Recommendations:* Book III, *Documentation* (King's Printer, Ottawa, 1940) (reprinted in one volume 1954); also Appendices 1-8.

————: *Dominion-Provincial Conference on Reconstruction: Submission and Plenary Conference Discussion* (King's Printer, Ottawa, 1946).

————: *Report of the Royal Commission on Taxation*, 6 vols. (Carter Commission) (Queen's Printer, Ottawa, 1966).

————, Minister of Finance: *Report of the Tax Structure Committee to the Federal-Provincial Conference of Prime Ministers and Premiers*, Ottawa, February 16-17, 1970.

Canadian Tax Foundation: *The National Finances 1965-66* (Toronto, 1969-70).

Careless, A. D.: *Initiative and Response: The Adaptation of Canadian Federalism to Regional Development* (McGill-Queen's University Press, Montreal, 1977).

Carter, G. C.: *Canadian Conditional Grants Since World War II* (Canadian Tax Foundation, Toronto, 1971).

Christofides, L. N.: "The Federal Government's Budget Constraint 1955-1975," *Canadian Public Policy*, vol. 3, 1977, pp. 291-298.

Clark, D. H.: *Fiscal Need and Revenue Equalization Grants*, Canadian Tax Papers No. 49 (Canadian Tax Foundation, Toronto, 1969).

Cohen, J. and M. Krashinsky: "Capturing the Rents on Resource Land for the Public Landowner: The Case for a Crown Corporation," *Canadian Public Policy*, vol. 2, 1976, pp. 411-423.

Collings, A. F.: "The A.H.S.T.F.: An Overview of the Issues," *Canadian Public Policy*, vol. 6, 1980, pp. 158-165.

Courchene, T. J. and J. R. Velvin: "Energy Revenues: Consequences for the Rest of Canada," *Canadian Public Policy*, vol. 6, 1980, pp. 192-212.

Crowley, R. W.: "Intergovernmental and Fiscal Aspects (Graham Commission)," *Canadian Public Policy*, vol. 1, 1975, pp. 376-383.

Crozier, R. B.: "Deficit Financing and Inflation: A Review of the Evidence," *Canadian Public Policy*, vol. 3, 1977, pp. 270-277.

Dehem, R. and J. N. Wolfe: "The Principles of Federal Finance and the Canadian Case," *C.J.E.P.S.*, vol. 21, 1955, pp. 64-72.

Doern, G. B. (ed.): *Spending Tax Dollars: Federal Expenditures 1980-81* (School of Public Administration, Carleton University, Ottawa 1980).

Dupre, J. S.: "Contracting Out: A Funny Thing Happened on the Way to the Centennial," *Report of the Proceedings of the Eighteenth Annual Tax Conference* (Canadian Tax Foundation, Toronto, 1965).

———: "Tax-Powers vs. Spending Responsibilities: An Historical Analysis of Federal-Provincial Finance," in A. Rotstein (ed.): *The Prospect of Change* (McGraw-Hill, Toronto, 1965).

Gainer, W. D. and T. L. Powrie: "Public Revenue from Canadian Crude Petroleum Production," *Canadian Public Policy*, vol. 1, 1975, pp. 1-12.

Gillespie, W. I.: "The June 1975 Budget: Stabilization and Distribution Effects," *Canadian Public Policy*, vol. 1, 1975, pp. 546-556.

Good, D. A.: *The Politics of Anticipation: Making Canadian Federal Tax Policy* (School of Public Administration, Carleton University, Ottawa 1980).

Graham, J. F., A. W. Johnson, and J. F. Andrews: *Intergovernmental Fiscal Relationships,* Canadian Tax Papers No. 40 (Canadian Tax Foundation, Toronto, Dec., 1964).

Grey, R.: "Conditional Grants in Aid," *Proceedings of the Fifth Annual Conference* (The Institute of Public Administration of Canada, Toronto, 1953).

Grubel, H. G. and S. Sydneysmith: "The Taxation of Windfall Gains on Stocks of Natural Resources," *Canadian Public Policy*, vol. 1, 1975, pp. 13-29.

Hanson, E. J.: *Fiscal Needs of the Canadian Provinces,* Canadian Tax Papers No. 23 (Canadian Tax Foundation, Toronto, Feb., 1961).

Johnson, H. G.: "Inflation, Unemployment and the Floating Rate," *Canadian Public Policy*, vol. 1, 1975, pp. 176-184.

Johnson, J. A.: "Provincial-Municipal Intergovernmental Fiscal Relations," *Canadian Public Administration*, vol. 12, 1968, pp. 166-180.

Institute of Intergovernmental Relations: *Intergovernmental Liaison on Fiscal and Economic Matters: Report* (Queen's Printer, Ottawa, 1968).

LaForest, G. V.: *The Allocation of Taxing Powers under the Canadian Constitution* (Canadian Tax Foundation, Toronto, 1967).

———: *Natural Resources and Public Property under the Canadian Constitution* (University of Toronto Press, Toronto, 1969).

Mackintosh, W. A.: "Federal Finance (Canada)" in G. Sawer (ed.): *Federalism: an Australian Jubilee Study* (F. W. Cheshire, Melbourne, 1952), pp. 80-109.

———: *The Economic Background of Dominion-Provincial Relations* (McClelland and Stewart, Toronto, 1964).

May, R.: *Federalism and Fiscal Adjustment* (Queen's Printer, Ottawa, 1968).

McDougall, I.: "Canada's Oil and Gas: An 'Eleventh Hour' Option That Must Not Be Ignored," *Canadian Public Policy*, vol. 1, 1975, pp. 47-57.

Moore, A. M.: "Income Security and Federal Finance," *Canadian Public Policy*, vol. 1, 1975, pp. 473-480.

———, J. H. Perry, and D. I. Beach: *The Financing of Canadian Federation: The First Hundred Years,* Canadian Tax Paper No. 43 (Canadian Tax Foundation, Toronto, 1966).

Musgrave, R. A.: *The Theory of Public Finance* (McGraw-Hill, New York, 1959), ch. 8.

Nowlan, D. M.: "Centrifugally Speaking: Some Economics of Canadian Federalism," in T. Lloyd and J. T. McLeod (eds.): *Agenda 1970* (University of Toronto Press, Toronto, 1968), pp. 177-196.

Officer, L. H. and L. B. Smith: *Canadian Economic Problems and Policies* (McGraw-Hill, Toronto, 1970).

Ontario: *Report of the Committee on Taxation* (Smith Committee), 3 vols. (Queen's Printer, Toronto, 1967).

————, Department of Treasury and Economics: *Intergovernmental Policy Coordination and Finance* (Staff Papers, Toronto, 1970).

Pans-Jenssen, A.: "Resource Taxation and the Supreme Court of Canada: The Cigol Case," *Canadian Public Policy*, vol. 5, 1979, pp. 45-58.

Pattison, J. C.: "Government Deficits and Inflation: The Evidence Reconsidered," *Canadian Public Policy*, vol. 3, 1977, pp. 285-290.

Perry, J. H.: *Taxes, Tariffs and Subsidies: A History of Canadian Fiscal Development*, 2 vols. (University of Toronto Press, Toronto 1955).

————: "What Price Provincial Autonomy?" *C.J.E.P.S.* vol. 21, 1955, pp. 432-446.

————: *Taxation in Canada*, 3rd ed. (University of Toronto Press, Toronto, 1961).

Plunkett, T. J.: "The Property Tax and the Municipal Case for Fiscal Reform," *Canadian Public Policy*, vol. 2, 1976, pp. 313-322.

Quebec: *Report of the Royal Commission on Taxation* (Bélanger Report) (Queen's Printer, Quebec, 1965).

Richardson, R. M.: "Deficit Financing and Inflation: A Reply to the Crozier Report and the Department of Finance," *Canadian Public Policy*, vol. 3, 1977, pp. 278-284.

Robinson, A. J. and J. Cutt (eds.): *Public Finance in Canada: Selected Readings* (Methuen, Toronto, 1968).

Salyzyn, V.: "Federal-Provincial Tax Sharing Schemes," *Canadian Public Administration*, vol. 10, 1967, pp. 161-166.

Saskatchewan: *Report of the Royal Commission on Taxation* (Queen's Printer, Regina, 1965).

Saunders, S. A. and E. Back: *The Rowell-Sirois Commission Part 1, A Summary of the Report* (Ryerson, Toronto, 1940).

Scott, Anthony (ed.): *Natural Resource Revenues: A Test of Federalism* (University of British Columbia Press, Vancouver, 1975).

Shearer, Ronald (ed.): *Exploiting our Economic Potential* (Holt, Rinehart and Winston, Toronto, 1968).

Sherbaniuk, D. J.: "Is the Property Tax a Good Tax?" *Canadian Public Policy*, vol. 2, 1976, pp. 310-312.

Simeon, R.: "Natural Resource Revenues and Canadian Federalism: A survey of the Issues," *Canadian Public Policy*, vol. 6, 1980, pp. 182-191.

Smiley, D. V.: *Conditional Grants and Canadian Federalism*, Canadian Tax Paper No. 32 (Canadian Tax Foundation, Toronto, Feb. 1962).

————: "The Rowell-Sirois Report, Provincial Autonomy, and Post-War Canadian Federalism," *C.J.E.P.S.*, vol. 28, 1962, pp. 54-69.

————: "Block Grants to the Provinces: A Realistic Alternative?" *Report of the Proceedings of the Eighteenth Annual Tax Conference* (Canadian Tax Foundation, Toronto, 1965).

————: *Constitutional Adaptation and Canadian Federalism Since 1954*, Document 4 of the Royal Commission on Bilingualism and Biculturalism (Queen's Printer, Ottawa, 1970).

———— and R. M. Burns: "Canadian Federalism and the Spending Power: Is Constitutional Restriction Necessary?" *Canadian Tax Journal*, vol. 17, 1969, pp. 468-482.

Smith, L. B.: "Myths and Realities in Mortgage Finance and the Housing Crisis," *Canadian Public Policy*, vol. 2, 1976, pp. 240-248.

Trudeau, P. E.: *Federal-Provincial Grants and the Spending Power of Parliament* (Queen's Printer, Ottawa, 1969).

_____: *Income Security and Social Services* (Queen's Printer, Ottawa, 1969).

Waverman, L.: "The Two-Price System in Energy: Subsidies Forgotten," *Canadian Public Policy*, vol. 1, 1975, pp. 76-88.

Woodside, K.: "Tax Incentives vs. Subsidies: Political Considerations in Governmental Choice," *Canadian Public Policy*, vol. 5, 1979, pp. 248-256.

C. The Provinces

Angers, B.: "Considérations sur le financement des municipalités du Québec," *Canadian Public Policy*, vol. 2, 1976, pp. 599-606.

Beck, J. M.: *The Government of Nova Scotia* (University of Toronto Press, Toronto, 1957).

Bellamy, D. et al. (eds.): *Provincial Political Systems* (Toronto, Methuen, 1976).

Benjamin, J.: "La rationalization des choix budgétaires: les cas québécois et canadien," *Revue canadienne de Science politique*, vol. 5, 1972, pp. 348-364.

Bonin, B.: "L'Immigration étrangére qu Québec," *Canadian Public Policy*, vol. 1, 1975, pp. 296-301.

Canada: *Report of the Advisory Commission on the Development of Government in the Northwest Territories* (Carrothers' Report) (Queen's Printer, Ottawa, 1966).

Chandler, M. A. and W. M. Chandler: *Public Policy and Provincial Politics* (McGraw-Hill Ryerson, Toronto, 1979).

Donnelly, M. S.: *The Government of Manitoba* (University of Toronto Press, Toronto, 1963).

Drugge, S. E. and T. S. Veeman: "Industrial Diversification in Alberta: Some Problems and Policies," *Canadian Public Policy*, vol. 6, 1980, pp. 221-235.

Duprat, J.-P.: "Les institutions québécois," *Revue juridique et économique de Sud-Ouest, Série juridique*, vol. 22, 1971, no. 1-2, pp. 3-31; no. 3-4, pp. 191-223.

Dussault, R. and R. Bernatchez: "La fonction publique canadienne et québécoise," *Canadian Public Administration*, vol. 15, 1, 1972, pp. 74-159.

_____ and _____: "La fonction publique canadienne et québécoise: suite," *Canadian Public Administration*, vol. 15, 2, 1972, pp. 259-374.

Elton, D. K. (ed.): "One Prairie Province?" *Lethbridge Herald*, Lethbridge, 1970.

Evans, R. G.: "Health Services in Nova Scotia: A View from the Graham Report," *Canadian Public Policy*, vol. 1, 1975, pp. 355-366.

Gartner, G. J.: "A Review of Cooperation among the Western Provinces," *Canadian Public Administration*, vol. 20, 1977, pp. 174-187.

Gow, J. I.: "The Modernization of the Quebec Civil Service," *International Review of Administrative Sciences*, vol. 36, 1970, pp. 234-242.

————: "Histoire administrative du Québec et théorie administrative," *C.J.P.S.*, vol. 4, 1971, pp. 141-145.

Graham, J. F.: "An Introduction to the Nova Scotia Royal Commission on Education, Public Services and Provincial-Municipal Relations," *Canadian Public Policy*, vol. 1, 1975, pp. 349-354.

Guindon, H.: "Social Unrest, Social Class and Quebec's Bureaucratic Revolution," *Queen's Quarterly*, vol. 17, 1964, 150-162.

Johnson, J. A.: "Municipal Tax Reform—Alternatives to the Real Property," *Canadian Public Policy*, vol. 2, 1976, pp. 335-346.

Krueger, R. R.: "The Provincial-Municipal Government Revolution in New Brunswick," *Canadian Public Administration*, vol. 13, 1970, pp. 51-99.

Kwavnick, David (ed.): *The Tremblay Report* (McClelland and Stewart, Toronto, 1973).

Leith, J. C.: "What is Ontario's Mineral Resource Policy?" *Canadian Public Policy*, vol. 4, 1978, pp. 352-363.

Lomas, A. A.: "The Council of Maritime Premiers: Report and Evaluation after Five Years," *Canadian Public Administration*, vol. 20, 1977, pp. 188-200.

MacKinnon, F.: *The Government of Prince Edward Island* (University of Toronto Press, Toronto, 1951).

Manitoba: *Report of the Royal Commission on Local Government and Finance* (Michener Report) (Winnipeg, 1964).

Mansbridge, S. H.: "Of Social Policy in Alberta: Its Management, Its Modification, Its Evaluation and Its Making," *Canadian Public Administration*, vol. 21, 1978, pp. 311-323.

Mathias, Philip: *Forced Growth* (James, Lewis & Samuel, Toronto, 1971).

Matthews, R.: "Perspectives on Recent Newfoundland Politics," *Journal of Canadian Studies*, vol. 9, 1974, pp. 20-34.

Mayo, H. B.: "Newfoundland's Entry into the Dominion," *C.J.E.P.S.*, vol. 15, 1949, pp. 505-522.

McMillan, M. L. and K. H. Norrie: "Province-building vs. A Renter Society," *Canadian Public Policy*, Feb., 1980, pp. 213-220.

Nelles, H. V.: *The Politics of Development: Forests, Mines and Hydro Electric Power in Ontario 1849-1941*, (Macmillan, Toronto, 1974).

"Newfoundland: Nation and Province," *Canadian Forum*, Special Issue, March, 1974.

Noel, S. J. R.: *Politics in Newfoundland* (University of Toronto Press, Toronto, 1971).

Perry, Robert L.: *Galt U.S.A.* (Maclean-Hunter, Toronto, 1971).

Price, Trevor (ed.): *Regional Government in Ontario* (Science Research Associates, Don Mills, 1971).

Schindeler, F. F.: *Responsible Government in Ontario* (University of Toronto Press, Toronto, 1969).

Swainson, Donald (ed.): *Oliver Mowat's Ontario* (Macmillan, Toronto, 1972).

Tuohy, C. J.: "Medical Politics after Medicare: The Ontario Case," *Canadian Public Policy*, vol. 2, 1976, pp. 192-210.

Tupper, A.: "Public Enterprise as Social Welfare: The Case of the Cape Breton Development Corporation," *Canadian Public Policy*, vol. 4, 1978, pp. 530-546.

Zastow, M.: "Recent Constitutional Developments in Canada's Northern Territories," *Canadian Public Administration*, vol. 10, 1967, pp. 167-180.

CANADIAN BUREAUCRACY

A. Administrative Process

"Aspects of Municipal Administration: A Symposium," *Canadian Public Administration*, vol. 11, 1968, pp. 18-96.

Baar, C.: "Patterns and Strategies of Court Administration in Canada and the United States," *Canadian Public Administration*, vol. 20, 1977, pp. 242-274.

Babe, R. E.: "Public and Private Regulation of Cable Television: A Case Study of Technological Change and Relative Power," *Canadian Public Administration*, vol. 17, 1974, pp. 187-225.

Baker, Walter: "Management by Objectives: A Philosophy and Style of Management for the Public Sector," *Canadian Public Administration*, vol. 12, 1969, pp. 427-443.

Balls, H. R.: "Improving Performance of Public Enterprise through Financial Management and Control," *Canadian Public Administration*, vol. 13, 1970, pp. 101-123.

_____: "Common Services in Government," *Canadian Public Administration*, vol. 17, 1974, pp. 226-241.

_____: "Decision-Making: The Role of the Deputy Minister," *Canadian Public Administration*, vol. 19, 1976, pp. 417-431.

Benning, J. A.: "Canadian University Service Overseas and Administrative Decentralization," *Canadian Public Administration*, vol. 12, 1969, pp. 515-550.

Bieler, J. H., R. M. Burns, and A. W. Johnson: "The Role of the Deputy Minister, I, II, and III," *Canadian Public Administration*, vol. 4, 1961, pp. 352-373.

Bolduc, R.: "Le Perfectionnement Des Cadres," *Canadian Public Administration*, vol. 17, 1974, pp. 482-494.

Bridges, The Rt. Hon. Lord: "The Relationship between Ministers and the Permanent Departmental Head," *Canadian Public Administration*, vol. 7, 1964, pp. 269-281.

Brunet, J. et al.: "La Gestion Ministérielle et Les organismes Centraux," *Canadian Public Administration*, vol. 17, 1974, pp. 321-327.

Brunet, M. et A. Vinet: "Le Pouvoir Professionnel Dans le Domaine de la Santé et Des Services Sociaux," *Canadian Public Policy*, vol. 5, 1979, pp. 168-180.

Cameron, D. M.: "Power and Responsibility in the Public Service: Summary of Discussion," *Canadian Public Administration*, vol. 21, 1978, pp. 358-372.

Carrothers, A. N. R.: "Quelques Aspects du Management du Ministère Des Affaires Exterieures du Canada," *Canadian Public Administration*, vol. 20, 1977, pp. 499-512.

Dahamni, A.: "Quelques Aspects du Management du Ministère Des Affaires Exterieures du Canada, *Canadian Public Administration*, vol. 18, 1975, pp. 171-188.

DesRoches, J. M.: "The Evolution of the Organization of Federal Government in Canada," *Canadian Public Administration*, vol. 5, 1962, pp. 408-427.

Dobell, N. M.: "Interdepartmental Management in External Affairs," *Canadian Public Administration*, vol. 21, 1978, pp. 83-102.

Doern, G. Bruce et al.: "The Structure and Behaviour of Canadian Regulatory Boards and Commissions: Multi-disciplinary Perspectives," *Canadian Public Administration*, vol. 18, 1975, pp. 189-215.

Dussault, R.: "L'Evolution du Professionalisme au Québec," *Canadian Public Administration*, vol. 20, 1977, pp. 275-290.

Forrest, D. G.: "Performance Appraisal in Government Service," *Canadian Public Administration*, vol. 12, 1969, pp. 444-453.

Fowke, D. V.: Toward a General Theory of Public Administration for Canada," *Canadian Public Administration*, vol. 19, 1976, pp. 34-40.

Gagnon, J.: "Les Communications Administratives," *Canadian Public Administration*, vol. 17, 1974, pp. 495-498.

_____: "Le Cadre Général Des Institutions Administratives et la Déconcentration Territoriale," *Canadian Public Administration*, vol. 18, 1979, pp. 253-268.

Gélinas, A.: "Les Parlementaires et l'Administration Publique au Québec," *Canadian Journal of Political Science*, vol. 1, 1968, pp. 164-179.

Gérin-Lajoie, P.: "CIDA in a Changing Government Organization," *Canadian Public Administration*, vol. 15, 1972, pp. 46-58.

Gilbert, M.: "The Glassco Commission Report," *Canadian Public Administration*, vol. 5, 1962, pp. 385-401.

_____: "L'information gouvernementale et les courriéristes parlementaires au Québec," *Canadian Journal of Political Science*, vol. 4, 1971, pp. 26-51.

Hartle, D. G.: "Techniques and Processes of Administration," *Canadian Public Administration*, vol. 19, 1976, pp. 21-33.

Heeney, Arnold D. P.: *Things that are Caesar's: Memoirs of a Canadian Public Servant* (University of Toronto Press, Toronto, 1972).

Hodgetts, J. E.: *Canadian Public Service: A Physiology of Government 1867-1970* (University of Toronto Press, Toronto, 1973).

_____: "The Public Service: Its Past and the Challenge of Its Future," *Canadian Public Administration*, vol. 17, 1974, pp. 17-25.

_____ and D. C. Corbett (eds.): *Canadian Public Administration* (Macmillan, Toronto, 1960).

Hodgson, J. S.: "The Impact of Minority Government on the Senior Civil Servant," *Canadian Public Administration*, vol. 19, 1976, pp. 227-237.

Jacques, J. and E. J. Ryan, Jr.: "Does Management by Objectives Stifle Organizational Innovation in the Public Sector?" *Canadian Public Administration*, vol. 21, 1978, pp. 16-25.

Kasurak, P. C.: American Dollar Diplomats in Canada, 1927-1941: A Study in Bureaucratic Politics," *American Review of Canadian Studies*, vol. 9, 1979, pp. 57-71.

Kernaghan, Kenneth: "An Overview of Public Administration in Canada Today," *Canadian Public Administration*, vol. 11, 1968, pp. 291-308.

_____: *Bureaucracy in Canadian Government*, 2nd ed. (Methuen, Toronto, 1973).

_____: "Codes of Ethics and Administrative Responsibility," *Canadian Public Administration*, vol. 17, 1974, pp. 527-541.

_____: "Politics, Policy and Public Servants: Political Neutrality Revisited," *Canadian Public Administration*, vol. 19, 1976, pp. 432-456.

_____: "Changing Concepts of Power and Responsibility in the Canadian Public Service," *Canadian Public Administration*, vol. 21, 1978, pp. 389-406.

_____ (ed.): *Public Administration in Canada: Selected Readings*, 3rd ed. (Methuen, Toronto, 1977).

_____ and A. M. Willms (eds.): *Public Administration in Canada: Selected Readings*, 2nd ed. (Methuen, Toronto, 1971).

Kitchen, A.M.: "Some Organizational Implications of Providing an Urban Service: The Case of Water," *Canadian Public Administration*, vol. 19, 1975, pp. 297-308.

Laframbois, H. L.: "Administrative Reform in the Federal Public Service: Signs of a Saturation Psychosis," *Canadian Public Administration*, vol. 14, 1971, pp. 303-325.

Landry, R.: "L'Imputabilité des Sociétées d'Etat," *Journal of Canadian Studies*, vol. 14, 1979, pp. 97-108.

Legault, A.: "L'organisation de la défense au Canada," *Études internationales*, vol. 3, 1972, pp. 198-220.

Lemieux, V.: "L'Information Administrative au Québec: Faits et Interpretations," *Canadian Public Administration*, vol. 18, 1975, pp. 409-427.

_____ et al.: "La Régulation des Affaires Sociales: Une Analyse Politique," *Canadian Public Administration*, vol. 19, 1974, pp. 37-54.

Lemire, Jean-Marc: "Program Design Guidelines," *Canadian Public Administration*, vol. 20, 1977, pp. 666-678.

Mallory, J. R.: "The Minister's Office Staff: An Unreformed Part of the Public Service," *Canadian Public Administration*, vol. 10, 1967, pp. 25-34.

McKeough, W. Darcy: "The Relations of Ministers and Civil Servants," *Canadian Public Administration*, vol. 12, 1969, pp. 1-8.

Rea, K. J. and J. T. McLeod (eds.): *Business and Government in Canada: Selected Readings* (Methuen, Toronto, 1969).

Ridler, N. B.: "PPB-Its Relevance to Financially Constrained Municipalities," *Canadian Public Administration*, vol. 19, 1976, pp. 238-253.

Ritchie, R. S., A. D. P. Heeney, M. W. MacKenzie, and M. G. Taylor: "The Glassco Commission Report," *Canadian Public Administration*, vol. 5, 1962, pp. 385-401.

Rowat, Donald C.: *The Ombudsman Plan: Essays on the Worldwide Spread of an Idea* (McClelland and Stewart, Toronto, 1973).

Santos, C. R.: "Public Administration as Politics," *Canadian Public Administration*, vol. 12, 1969, pp. 213-223.

School of Public Administration, Carleton University: *Approaches to the Study of Federal Administrative and Regulatory Agencies, Boards, Commissions and Tribunals* (Carleton University, Ottawa, 1974).

Shoyama, T. K.: "Advisory Committees in Administration," *Proceedings of the Ninth Annual Conference* (The Institute of Public Administration of Canada, Toronto, 1957).

Stead, G. W.: "The Treasury Board of Canada," *Proceedings of the Seventh Annual Conference* (The Institute of Public Administration of Canada, Toronto, 1955).

Steele, G. G. E.: "The Treasury Board as a Control Agency," *Canadian Public Administration*, vol. 4, 1961, pp. 197-205.

Studnicki-Gizbert, K. W.: "The Administration of Transport Policy: The Regulatory Problems," *Canadian Public Administration*, vol. 18, 1975, pp. 642-658.

Tellier, P. M.: "Pour une réforme des cabinets de ministres fédéraux," *Canadian Public Administration*, vol. 11, 1968, pp. 414-427.

Williams, R. and D. Bates: "Technical Divisions and Public Accountability," *Canadian Public Administration*, vol. 19, 1976, pp. 603-632.

Willis, J., J. E. Eades, H. F. Angus et al.: "The Administrator as Judge," *Proceedings of the Eighth Annual Conference* (The Institute of Public Administration of Canada, Toronto, 1956).

Willms, A. M.: "The Administration of Research on Administration in the Government of Canada," *Canadian Public Administration*, vol. 10, 1967, pp. 405-416.

Winham, G. R.: "Bureaucratic Politics and Canadian Trade Negotiation," *International Journal*, vol. 33, 1978, pp. 64-89.

B. The Public Service: Personnel Administration

Armstrong, R.: "Some Aspects of Policy Determination in the Development of the Collective Bargaining Legislation in the Public Service of Canada," *Canadian Public Administration*, vol. 11, 1968, pp. 485-493.

Bauer, F.: "The Public Service Staff Relations Act and Collective Bargaining 1967-1969," *Civil Service Review*, vol. 43, 2, June, 1970, pp. 54, 56, 58, 60, 62.

Blackburn, G. A.: "A Bilingual and Bicultural Public Service," *Canadian Public Administration*, vol. 12, 1969, pp. 36-44.

Callard, K. B.: *Advanced Training in the Public Service*, Governmental Studies Number 1 (The Institute of Public Administration of Canada, Toronto, 1958).

Canada, Civil Service Commission: *Personnel Administration in the Public Service* (Heeney Report) (Queen's Printer, Ottawa, 1959).

———, Preparatory Committee on Collective Bargaining in the Public Service of Canada: *Report* (Queen's Printer, Ottawa, 1965).

———, Task Force on Labour Relations, Canadian Industrial Relations: *Report* (Queen's Printer, Ottawa, 1968).

Carson, J. J.: "The Changing Scope of the Public Servant," *Canadian Public Administration*, vol. 11, 1968, pp. 407-413.

Cloutier, S.: "Le Statut de la Fonction Publique du Canada: Son histoire," *Canadian Public Administration*, vol. 10, 1967, pp. 500-513.

———: "Senior Public Service Officials in a Bicultural Society," *Canadian Public Administration*, vol. 11, 1968, pp. 395-406.

Code, Taylor: *The Canadian Bureaucracy 1939-1947* (Duke University Press, Durham, 1949).

———: *The Canadian Bureaucracy and Federalism, 1947-1965* (University of Denver, Denver, 1966).

Côté, E. A.: "The Public Services in a Bicultural Community," *Canadian Public Administration*, vol. 11, 1968, pp. 280-290.

Coulson, Herbert H.: "The Professional Worker and Collective Bargaining," *Civil Service Review*, vol. 41, 1968, pp. 40-42.

Crispo, John H. B. (ed.): *Collective Bargaining and the Professional Employee* (Centre for Industrial Relations, University of Toronto, Toronto, 1965).

Deslauriers, R. C.: "First Collective Agreements in the Public Service of Canada," *Civil Service Review*, vol. 41, 2, June, 1968, pp. 24-36.

Deutsch, J. J.: "Some Thoughts on the Public Service," *C.J.E.P.S.*, vol. 23, 1957.

———: "The Public Service in a Changing Society," *Canadian Public Administration*, vol. 11, 1968, pp. 1-8.

Dowdell, R. H.: "Personnel Administration in the Federal Public Service," in A. M. Willms and W. D. K. Kernaghan (eds.): *Public Administration in Canada: Selected Readings* (Methuen, Toronto, 1968), pp. 360-388.

Edwards, Claude: "Effects of Collective Bargaining on Staff Associations," *Civil Service Review*, vol. 41, September, 1968, pp. 24, 26, 28, 30, 32, 34, 36.

———: "Address to the Conference on Collective Bargaining in Public Employment, San Francisco", *Civil Service Review*, vol. 42, 1, March, 1969, pp. 2, 4, 6, 8, 10, 12, 14, 16.

———: "Collective Bargaining in Canada between the Federal Government and its Employees," *Civil Service Review*, vol. 43, 2, June, 1970, pp. 2, 4, 6, 8, 10, 12.

Finkelman, Jacob: "Some Aspects of Public Service Bargaining in Canada," *Civil Service Review*, vol. 43, 1, March, 1970, pp. 18, 20, 22, 24, 26, 28.

Frankel, S. J.: *A Model for Negotiation and Arbitration between the Canadian Government and its Civil Servants* (McGill University Press, Montreal, 1962).

———: *Staff Relations in the Civil Service: The Canadian Experience* (McGill University Press, Montreal, 1962).

Gosselin, E., G. Dozois, R. Boyd, and G. Lalande: "L'administration publique dans un pays bilingue et bicultural: actualités et propos," *Canadian Public Administration*, vol. 6, 1963, pp. 407-433.

Gow, Donald: "Public Administration Training: For Whom? For What?" *Optimum*, vol. 1, 3, Winter, 1970, pp. 22-33.

Heeney, Arnold: "Civil Service Reform 1958," *C.J.E.P.S.*, vol. 25, 1959, pp. 1-10.

———: *The Things That Are Caesar's: The Memoirs of a Canadian Public Servant* (University of Toronto Press, Toronto, 1972).

Hodgetts, J. E.: *Pioneer Public Service: An Administrative History of the United Canadas, 1841-1867* (University of Toronto Press, Toronto, 1955).

———: "Challenge and Response: A Retrospective View of the Public Service of Canada," *Canadian Public Administration*, vol. 7, 1964, pp. 409-421.

——— and O. P. Dwivedi: "The Growth of Government Employment in Canada," *Canadian Public Administration*, vol. 12, 1969, pp. 224-238.

———, William McCloskey, Reginald Whitaker, and V. Seymour Wilson: *The Biography of an Institution: The Civil Service Commission of Canada, 1908-1967* (McGill-Queen's University Press, Montreal, 1972).

Kwavnick, D.: "French Canadians and the Civil Service of Canada," *Canadian Public Administration*, vol. 11, 1968, pp. 97-112.

Laberge, E. P.: "Collective Bargaining in the Public Service of Canada," *International Review of Administrative Sciences*, vol. 36, 1970, pp. 234-242.

Robinson, K. R.: "Labour Unions in the Armed Forces," *Civil Service Review*, vol. 43, 3, September, 1970, pp. 2, 4, 6, 8, 10, 12, 14, and 28.

Slivinski, L. W. and B. Desbiens: "Managerial Job Dimensions and Job Profiles in The Canadian Public Service: A Pilot Study," *Studies in Personnel Psychology*, vol. 2, 2, October, 1970, pp. 36-52.

Subramaniam, V.: "Representative Bureaucracy: A Reassessment," *American Political Science Review*, vol. 61, 1967, pp. 1010-1019.

Swettenham, John and David Kelly: *Serving the State: A History of the Professional Institute of the Public Service of Canada 1920-1970* (LeDroit, Ottawa, 1970).

"Symposium on Collective Negotiations in the Public Service," *Public Administration Review*, vol. 28, 1968, pp. 111-147.

Tunnoch, G. V.: "The Bureau of Government Organization, Improvement by Order-in-Council, Committee and Anomaly," *Canadian Public Administration*, vol. 8, 1965, pp. 558-568.

Vaison, R. A.: "Collective Bargaining in the Federal Public Service: The Achievement of a Milestone in Personnel Relations," *Canadian Public Administration*, vol. 12, 1969, pp. 108-122.

Wilson, V. Seymour: *Staffing in the Canadian Federal Bureaucracy* (Queen's University, unpublished Ph.D. thesis, Kingston, 1970).

C. The Budgetary Process

Balls, H. R.: "New Techniques in Government Budgeting: Planning, Programming and Budgeting in Canada," *Public Administration*, vol. 48, 1970, pp. 289-305.

Bird, Richard M.: *The Growth of Government Spending in Canada*, Tax Papers No. 51 (Canadian Tax Foundation, Toronto, July, 1970).

Botner, S. B.: "Four Years of PPBS: An Appraisal," *Public Administration Review*, July/August, 1970, pp. 423-431.

Brownstone, M.: "The Canadian System of Government in the Face of Modern Demands," *Canadian Public Administration*, vol. 11, 1968, pp. 428-439.

Canada: *Estimates, The Blue Book for the Fiscal Year Ending March 31, 1982* (Queen's Printer, Ottawa, 1981), or any other year; they have a certain sameness.

————, Parliament, House of Commons, Standing Committee on Miscellaneous Estimates, *Minutes of Proceedings and Evidence Respecting Bill C-172—and Act to Amend the Financial Administration Act*, Nos. 10-12 (Queen's Printer, Ottawa, 1969).

————, Royal Commission on Government Organization, *Report*, vol. 1, (Queen's Printer, Ottawa, 1962-63).

————, Task Force on Government Information, *To Know and Be Known*, (Queen's Printer, Ottawa, 1969).

————, Treasury Board, Program Branch: *Program Forecast and Estimates Manual* (Ottawa, 1972, (periodically revised).

Canadian Tax Foundation: *The National Finances—An Analysis of the Revenues and Expenditures of the Government of Canada* (published annually by the Canadian Tax Foundation, Toronto).

Cutt, James: "Efficiency and Effectiveness in Public Sector Spending: The Programme Budgeting Approach," *Canadian Public Administration*, vol. 13, 1970, pp. 396-426.

Doern, G. Bruce: "Mr. Trudeau, The Science Council and P.P.B.: Recent Changes in the Philosophy of Policy Making in Canada," Paper presented to 42nd Annual Meeting of Canadian Political Science Association, June 3, 1970, Winnipeg, Manitoba.

Harper, E. L. et al.: "Implementation and Use of P.P.B. in Sixteen Federal Agencies," *Public Administration Review*, vol. 29, 1969, pp. 623-632.

Hinrichs, Harley H. and G. M. Taylor (eds.): *Program Budgeting and Cost Benefit Analysis* (Goodyear Publishing Co., Pacific Palisades, 1969).

Hodgetts, J. E.: "The Civil Servant and Policy Formation," *C.J.E.P.S.*, vol. 23, 1957, pp. 467-479.

Johnson, A. W.: "PPB and Decision Making in the Government of Canada," speech to 50th Anniversary Conference of Society of Industrial Accountants, June, 18, 1970.

————: "The Treasury Board of Canada and the Machinery of Government of the 1970's," *Canadian Journal of Political Science*, vol. 4, 1971.

Lamontagne, M.: "The Influence of the Politician," *Canadian Public Administration*, vol. 11, 1968, pp. 263-271.

Lévesque, R.: *Program Budgeting in the Canadian Government* (M.A. thesis, Carleton University, 1969).

Lyden, J.F.: *Planning, Programming, Budgeting: A Systems Approach in Management* (Markham, Chicago, 1967).

Normanton, E. L.: *The Accountability and Audit of Governments* (Manchester University Press, Manchester, Eng.; Praeger, New York, 1966).

Novick, David (ed.): *Program Budgeting* (Harvard University Press, Cambridge, 1965).

"Planning-Programming-Budgeting System: A Symposium," *Public Administration Review*, vol. 26, 1966, pp. 243-310.

Robinson, A. J. and James Cutt: *Public Finance in Canada: Selected Readings* (Methuen, Toronto, 1968).

Strick, J. C.: "Recent Development in Canadian Administration," *Public Administration Review*, vol. 48, 1970, pp. 69-85.

Ward, Norman: *The Public Purse* (University of Toronto Press, Toronto, 1962).

White, W. L. and J. C. Strick: *Policy, Politics and the Treasury Board in Canadian Government* (Science Research Associates, Don Mills, Ontario, 1970).

Wildavsky, Aaron B.: *The Politics of the Budgetary Process* (Little, Brown, Boston, 1964).

D. Crown Corporations

Ashley, C. A.: *The First Twenty-five Years: A Study of Trans-Canada Air Lines* (Macmillan, Toronto, 1965).

_____ and R. G. H. Smails: *Canadian Crown Corporations* (Macmillan, Toronto, 1965).

Barbe, R. P.: "Le contrôle parlementaire des entreprises au Canada," *Canadian Public Administration*, vol. 12, 1969, pp. 463-480.

Canada, Committee on Broadcasting: *Report* (The Fowler Report) (Queen's Printer, Ottawa, 1965).

Corbett, D.: *Politics and the Airlines* (University of Toronto Press, Toronto, 1965).

Friedman, W. (ed.): *The Public Corporation: A Comparative Symposium* (Carswell, Toronto, 1954).

Hull, W. H. N.: "The Public Control of Broadcasting: The Canadian and Australian Experiences," *C.J.E.P.S.*, vol. 28, 1962, pp. 114-126.

_____: "The Fowler Report Revisited: A Broadcasting Policy for Canada," address to the 38th Annual Meeting of the Canadian Political Science Association, Sherbrooke, Quebec, June 1966.

Kristjanson, K.: "Crown Corporations: Administrative Responsibility and Public Accountability," *Canadian Public Administration*, vol. 11, 1968, pp. 454-459.

Shea, A. A.: *Broadcasting, The Canadian Way* (Harvest House, Montreal, 1963).

Spry, G.: "The Decline and Fall of Canadian Broadcasting," *Queen's Quarterly*, vol. 68, 1961-62, pp. 213-225.

Weir, E. A.: *The Struggle for National Broadcasting in Canada* (McClelland and Stewart, Toronto, 1965).

E. Task Forces and Royal Commissions

Axworthy, L.: "The Housing Task Force—A New Policy Instrument," a paper prepared for the 42nd Annual Meeting of the Canadian Political Science Association, Winnipeg, Manitoba, June 4, 1970.

Bryden, M. and M. Gurney: "Royal Commission Costs," *Canadian Tax Journal*, vol. 14, 1966, pp. 157-159.

Courtney, J. C.: "Judges as Royal Commissioners," *Dalhousie Review*, vol. 44, 1964, pp. 413-417.

———: "In Defense of Royal Commissions," *Canadian Public Administration*, vol. 12, 1969, pp. 198-212.

Cronin, Thomas E. and Sanford D. Greenberg (eds.): *The Presidential Advisory System* (Harper and Row, New York, 1969).

Dion, Léon: "Politique consultative et système politique," *C.J.P.S.*, vol. 2, 1969, pp. 226-244.

Doern, G. Bruce: "The Role of Royal Commissions in the General Policy Process and in Federal-Provincial Relations," *Canadian Public Administration*, vol. 10, 1967, pp. 417-433.

———: "Pressure Groups and Canadian Bureaucracy: Scientists and Science Policy Machinery," in W. D. K. Kernaghan (ed.): *Bureaucracy in Canadian Government* (Methuen, Toronto, 1969), pp. 112-119.

Fowke, V. C.: "Royal Commissions and Canadian Agricultural Policy," *C.J.E.P.S.*, vol. 14, 1948, pp. 163-175.

Gillespie, W. I.: "Decision Making by Official Commission," in A. J. Robinson and James Cutt (eds.): *Public Finance in Canada: Selected Readings* (Methuen, Toronto, 1968), pp. 57-60.

Hanser, Charles J.: *Guide to Decisions: The Royal Commission* (Bedminster Press, Totawa, N.J., 1965).

Hanson, H. R.: "Inside Royal Commissions," *Canadian Public Administration*, vol. 12, 1969, pp. 356-364.

Henderson, G. F.: *Federal Royal Commissions in Canada 1867-1966: A Checklist* (University of Toronto Press, Toronto, 1967).

Hodgetts, J. E.: "The Role of Royal Commissions in Canadian Government," in Institute of Public Administration of Canada: *Proceedings of the 3rd Annual Conference* (Toronto, 1951).

———: "Should Canada be De-commissioned? A Commoner's View on Royal Commissions," *Queen's Quarterly*, vol. 70, 1963-64, pp. 475-490.

———: "Public Power and Ivory Power," in Trevor Owen Lloyd and Jack McLeod (eds.): *Agenda 1970* (University of Toronto Press, Toronto, 1968), pp. 256-280.

Lithwick, N. H.: "Housing in Search of a Crisis," *The Canadian Forum*, February, 1969, pp. 250-251.

McLeod, T. H.: "Glassco Commission Report," *Canadian Public Administration*, vol. 6, 1963, pp. 386-406.

New Brunswick: *Participation and Development: The New Brunswick Task Force Report on Social Development and Social Welfare* (Queen's Printer, Fredericton, 1971).

Saywell, John T.: "The Royal Commission on Bilingualism and Biculturalism," *International Journal*, vol. 20, 1964-65, pp. 378-382.

Schindeler, Fred and C. M. Lamphier: "Social Science Research and Participatory Democracy in Canada," *Canadian Public Administration*, vol. 12, 4, Winter, 1969, pp. 481-498.

Silcox, Peter: "To Commission—or Not To Commission," *Canadian Public Administration*, vol. 5, 1962, pp. 253-304.

———: "The Proliferation of Boards and Commission," in Trevor Lloyd and Jack McLeod (eds.): *Agenda 70* (University of Toronto Press, Toronto, 1968), pp. 115-134.

Tunnoch, G. V.: "The Glassco Commission: Did It Cost More Than It Was Worth?" *Canadian Public Administration*, vol. 7, 1964, pp. 389-397.

Walls, C. E. S.: "Royal Commissions—Their Influence on Public Policy," *Canadian Public Administration*, vol. 12, 1969, pp. 365-371.

Willms, A. M.: "The Administration of Research on Administration in the Government of Canada," *Canadian Public Administration*, vol. 10, 1967, pp. 405-416.

Wyman, Ken, Robin Mathews, and G. Lermer: "Articles Reviewing the Task Force Report on Foreign Ownership," *Canadian Dimension*, vol. 5, 4, April-May, 1968, pp. 15-20.

F. Advisory Councils

Burns, R. M.: "The Economic Council of Canada: Reflections Prompted by the Fourth Review," *Canadian Tax Journal*, vol. 16, 1968, pp. 600-605.

Canada, Parliament, Senate, Special Committee on Science Policy: *Proceedings* Phase 1, 27th Parl., 1967-68, and 28th Parl., nos. 1-30, plus subsequent proceedings (Queen's Printer, Ottawa).

Carter, L. A.: "Canadian Science Policy: Doubts Raised About Advisory Apparatus," *Science*, vol. 161, August 2, 1968, pp. 450-451.

Cook, Ramsay: "Loyalism, Technology and Canada's Fate," *Journal of Canadian Studies*, vol. 5, 3, August, 1970, pp. 50-60.

Doern, G. Bruce: "Scientists and Science Policy Machinery," in W. D. K. Kernaghan (ed.): *Bureaucracy in Canadian Government* (Methuen, Toronto, 1969).

———: "The National Research Council: The Causes of Goal Displacement," *Canadian Public Administration*, vol. 13, 1970, pp. 140-184.

———: "The Political Realities of Science Policy Making in the Federal Government," *Science Forum*, vol. 3, 3, June, 1970, pp. 21-25.

———: "The Senate Report on Science Policy: A Political Assessment," *Journal of Canadian Studies*, vol. 6, 2, May, 1971, pp. 52-51.

———: *Science and Politics in Canada* (McGill-Queen's University Press, Montreal, 1972).

Gilpin, Robert and Christopher Wright (eds.): *Scientists and National Policy Making* (Columbia University Press, New York, 1964).

——— and ———: "Technological Strategies and National Purpose," *Science*, vol. 169, July 31, 1970, pp. 441-448.

Glassco Commission: *Scientific Research and Development*, vol. 4, report 23, (Queen's Printer, Ottawa, 1962-3).

Gunning, Harry E.: "Canadian Science Policy and the OECD Report: A Critical Analysis," *Science Forum*, vol. 2, 6, December, 1969, pp. 3-6.

Heller, Walter W.: "Economic Policy Advisers," in Thomas E. Cronin and S. D. Greenberg (eds.): *The Presidential Advisory System* (Harper and Row, New York, 1969), pp. 29-39.

Jackson, R. W.: "Major Programs in R & D: Where the Means Justify the Ends," *Science Forum*, vol. 2, 2, April, 1969, pp. 10-14.

Kaliski, S. F. (ed.): *Canadian Economic Policy Since the War* (Canadian Trade Committee, Montreal, 1966).

Line, Richard J. and Arthur J. R. Smith: "Economic Planning for Canada," in M. H. Watkins and D. F. Forster (eds.): *Economics Canada* (McGraw-Hill, Toronto, 1963), pp. 35-46. See also pp. 161-167.

Organization for Economic Cooperation and Development (OECD): *Reviews of National Science Policy Canada* (OECD, Paris, 1969).

Paquet, Gilles: "The Economic Council as Phoenix," in Trevor Owen Lloyd and Jack McLeod (eds.): *Agenda 1970* (University of Toronto Press, Toronto, 1968), pp. 135-158.

Phidd, R. W.: "The Economic Council of Canada: Its Establishment, Structure, and Role in the Canadian Policy-Making System, 1963-1974," *Canadian Public Administration*, vol. 18, 1975, pp. 428-473.

Science Council of Canada: *Annual Reports* (Queen's Printer, Ottawa).

_____: *Towards a National Science Policy for Canada*, Report no. 4, (Information Canada, Ottawa, 1968).

_____, Committee on Industrial Policies: *Uncertain Prospects: Canadian Manufacturing Industry, 1971-1977* (Science Council of Canada, Ottawa, 1977).

Thistle, Mel: *The Inner Ring: The Early History of the National Research Council of Canada* (University of Toronto Press, Toronto, 1966).

Trainor, Lynn: "The Americanization of Canadian Science: How We Lose by Default," *Science Forum*, vol. 2, 2, April, 1970, pp. 3-8.

Verney, D. V.: "The Role of the Private Social Science Research Council of Canada in the Formation of Public Science Policy," *Canadian Public Policy*, vol. 1, 1975, pp. 107-117.

Watkins, M: "Technology and Nationalism," in Peter Russel (ed.): *Nationalism in Canada* (McGraw-Hill, Toronto, 1966), pp. 284-302.

PARLIAMENTARY PROCESS

Abel, A. S.: "Administrative Secrecy," *Canadian Public Administration*, vol. 11, 1968, pp. 440-448.

Abrams, Matthew J.: *The Canada-United States Parliamentary Group* (Parliamentary Centre for Foreign Affairs/Canadian Institute for International Affairs, Toronto, 1973).

Aitchison, J. H.: "The Speakership of the Canadian House of Commons," in Robert Mills Clark (ed.): *Canadian Issues* (University of Toronto Press, Toronto, 1961), pp. 23-56.

Albinski, H. S.: "The Canadian Senate: Politics and the Constitution," *American Political Science Review*, vol. 57, 1963, pp. 378-391.

Anderson, S. V.: *Canadian Ombudsman Proposals* (University of California Press, Berkeley, 1966).

Atkinson, M.: "Reform and Inertia in the Nova Scotia Assembly," *Journal of Canadian Studies*, vol. 14, 1979, pp. 133-145.

Balls, H. R.: "The Watchdog of Parliament: The Centenary of the Legislative Audit," *Canadian Public Administration*, vol. 21, 1978, pp. 584-617.

Bryden, K.: "Executive and Legislature in Ontario: A Case Study on Governmental Reform," *Canadian Public Administration*, vol. 18, 1975, pp. 235-252.

Burns, R. M.: "Second Chambers: German Experience and Canadian Needs," *Canadian Public Administration*, vol. 18, 1975, pp. 541-568.

Byers, R. B.: "Perceptions of Parliamentary Surveillance of the Executive: The Case of Canadian Defence Policy," *Canadian Journal of Political Science*, vol. 5, 1972, pp. 234-250.

Byrne, D.: "Some Attendance Patterns Exhibited by Members of Parliament during the 28th Parliament," *Canadian Journal of Political Science*, vol. 5, 1972, pp. 135-141.

Cairns, A. C.: "The Judicial Committee and Its Critics," *Canadian Journal of Political Science*, vol. 4, 1971, pp. 301-345.

Campbell, C.: *The Canadian Senate: Lobby from Within* (Macmillan, Toronto, 1978).

Casstevens, Thomas W. and William A. Denham, III: "Turnover and Tenure in the Canadian House of Commons, 1867-1969," *Canadian Journal of Political Science*, vol. 3, 1970, pp. 655-661.

Charney, Harold D. and Richard G. Price: "A Note on the Pre-Nomination Role Socialization of Freshmen Members of Parliament" (Note), *Canadian Journal of Political Science*, vol. 10, 1977, pp. 391-406.

Clarke, Harold D.: "The Ideological Self-Perceptions of Provincial Legislators" (Note), *Canadian Journal of Political Science*, vol. 11, 1973, pp. 617-633.

Clarkson, S.: "Barriers to Entry of Parties into Toronto's Civic Politics: Towards a Theory of Party Penetration," *Canadian Journal of Political Science*, vol. 4, 1971, pp. 206-223.

Connolly, J. J.: "The Senate of Canada," *The Parliamentarian*, vol. 53, 1972, pp. 95-103.

Courtney, J. C.: "Recognition of Canadian Political Parties in Parliament and in Law", *Canadian Journal of Political Science*, vol. 11, 1978, pp. 33-60.

Denham, R. A.: "The Canadian Auditors General—What Is Their Role?" *Canadian Public Administration*, vol. 17, 1974, pp. 259-273.

_____: "New Public-Sector Audit Legislation in Canada," *Canadian Public Policy*, vol. 4, 1978, pp. 474-488.

Ducasse, R.: "Les Députés et la Fonction Parlementaire: Eléments d'une Enquête à l'Assemblée Nationale du Québec," *Journal of Canadian Studies*, vol. 14, 1974, pp. 109-116.

Esberey, J. E.: "Focus on Parliament," *Queen's Quarterly*, vol. 43, 1957, pp. 475-573.

_____: "Personality and Politics: A New Look at the King-Byng Dispute," *Canadian Journal of Political Science*, vol. 6, 1973, pp. 37-55.

Forsey, Eugene: "The Extension of the Life of Legislatures," *C.J.E.P.S.*, vol. 29, 1963, pp. 604-616.

_____: "Parliament's Power to Advise," *C.J.E.P.S.*, vol. 29, 1963, pp. 203-210.

_____: "The Problem of 'Minority' Government in Canada," *C.J.E.P.S.*, vol. 30, 1964, pp. 1-11.

Franks, C. E. S.: "The Legislature and Responsible Government," in Norman Ward and Stafford Duff (eds.): *Politics in Saskatchewan* (Longmans Canada, Toronto, 1968), pp. 20-43.

_____: "The Committee Clerks of the Canadian House of Commons," *The Parliamentarian*, vol. 50, 1969, pp. 159-162.

_____: "The Dilemma of the Standing Committees of the Canadian House of Commons," *Canadian Journal of Political Science*, vol. 4, 1971, pp. 461-476.

Geller-Schwartz, L.: "Minority Government Reconsidered," *Journal of Canadian Studies*, vol. 14, 1979, pp. 67-79.

Hamel, Jacques and Yvon Thériault: "La fonction tribunitienne et la députation créditiste à l'Assemblée Nationale du Québec: 1970-3," *Canadian Journal of Political Science*, vol. 9, 1975, pp. 3-21.

Hawkins, G. (ed.): *Order and Good Government*, Proceedings, of the 33rd Couchiching Conference (Canadian Institute on Public Affairs, Toronto, 1965).

Hockin, T. A.: "The Advance of Standing Committees in Canada's House of Commons: 1965 to 1970," *Canadian Public Administration*, vol. 13, 1970, pp. 185-202.

———: *Apex of Power: The Prime Minister and Political Leadership in Canada* (Prentice-Hall, Toronto, 1971).

———: "Flexible and Structured Parliamentarianism: From 1848 to Contemporary Party Government," *Journal of Canadian Studies*, vol. 14, 1979, pp. 8-17.

Hoffman D. and N. Ward: *Bilingualism and Biculturalism in the Canadian House of Commons*, Document no. 3 of the Royal Commission on Bilingualism and Biculturalism (Queen's Printer, Ottawa, 1970).

Jackson, R. J. and M. M. Atkinson: *The Canadian Legislative System*, 2nd ed. (Macmillan, Toronto, 1974).

Jennings, Sir William Ivor: *Parliament*, 2nd ed. (Cambridge University Press, Cambridge, 1957), chs. 4-6, 10-11.

Jewett, P.: "The Reform of Parliament," *Journal of Canadian Studies*, vol. 1, 3, November, 1966, pp. 11-15.

Johnson, J. K. (ed.): *The Canadian Directory of Parliament, 1867-1967* (Public Archives of Canada, Ottawa, 1968).

Kersell, J. E.: "Statutory and Judicial Control of Administrative Behaviour," *Canadian Public Administration*, vol. 19, 1976, pp. 295-307.

Knowles, Stanley Howard: *The Role of the Opposition in Parliament* (Woodsworth Memorial Foundation, Ontario, 1957).

Kornberg, Allan: "The Rules of the Game in the Canadian House of Commons," *Journal of Politics*, vol. 26, 1964, pp. 358-80.

———: *Some Differences in Role Perceptions among Canadian Legislators* (University of Michigan Press, Ann Arbor, 1964).

———: "The Social Bases of Leadership in a Canadian House of Commons," *Australian Journal of Politics and History*, vol. 11, 1965, pp. 324-334.

———: "Caucus and Cohesion in Canadian Parliamentary Parties," *The American Political Science Review*, vol. 60, March, 1966, pp. 83-92.

———: *Canadian Legislative Behavior: A Study of the 25th Parliament* (Holt, Rinehart and Winston, New York, 1967), ch. 3, pp. 42-62.

———: "Parliament in Canadian Society," in Allan Kornberg and Lloyd D. Musolf (eds.): *Legislatures in Developmental Perspective* (Durham, Dube, 1970), ch. 3, pp. 55-128.

——— and N. Thomas: "The Purposive Roles of Canadian and American Legislators: Some Comparisons," *Political Science*, vol. 18, 2, September, 1965, pp. 36-50.

——— and ———: "Representative Democracy and Political Elites in Canada and the United States," *Parliamentary Affairs*, vol. 19, 1, Winter, 1965-66, pp. 91-102.

———, David Falcone, and William Mischler: "Socio-economic Change, Legislative Composition, and Political System Outputs in Canada, 1867-1968," in *Sage Series in Comparative Legislatures*, no. 1, November, 1972.

Kunz, E. A.: *The Modern Senate of Canada, 1925-1963: A Re-appraisal* (University of Toronto Press, Toronto, 1965).

Lambert, N.: "Reform of the Senate," (*Winnipeg Free Press*, April, 1950), pamphlet no. 30.

Lamontagne, M.: "The Influence of the Politician," *Canadian Public Administration*, vol. 11, 1968, pp. 263-271.

Laponce, Jean: "The Religious Background of Canadian MPs," *Political Science*, vol. 6, 1968, pp. 253-258.

Laundy, Philip: *The Table: Being the Journal of the Society of Clerks-at-the-Table in Commonwealth Parliaments,* vol. 34, 1965, pp. 20-30.

_____: "Procedural Reform in the Canadian House of Commons," *The Parliamentarian,* vol. 50, 1969, pp. 155-157.

_____: "The Future of the Canadian Speakership," *The Parliamentarian,* vol. 53, 1972, pp. 113-117.

Levy, Gary: "Canadian Participation in Parliamentary Associations," *Canadian Journal of Political Science,* vol. 7, 1974, pp. 352-357.

Lloyd, Trevor: "The Reform of Parliamentary Proceedings," in A. Rotstein (ed.): *The Prospect of Change: Proposals for Canada's Future* (McGraw-Hill, Toronto, 1965), pp. 23-39.

Long, John Anthony: "Maldistribution in Western Provincial Legislatures: The Case of Alberta," *Canadian Journal of Political Science,* vol. 2, 1969, pp. 345-355.

Lovink, J. A. A.: "Who Wants Parliamentary Reform?" *Queen's Quarterly,* vol. 79, 1972, pp. 505-513.

Lyon, P. V.: "A New Idea for Senate Reform," *Canadian Commentator,* vol. 6, 7-8, 1962, p. 24.

Macdonald, Donald S.: "Change in the House of Commons—New Rules," *Canadian Public Administration,* vol. 13, 1970, pp. 30-39.

MacKay, R. A.: *The Unreformed Senate of Canada,* rev. ed. (McClelland and Stewart, Toronto, 1963).

MacLeod, Alex: "The Reform of the Standing Committees of the Quebec National Assembly: A Preliminary Assessment," *Canadian Journal of Political Science,* vol. 8, 1975, pp. 22-39.

Mallory, J. R.: "Delegated Legislation in Canada: Recent Changes in Machinery," *C.J.E.P.S.,* vol. 19, 1953, pp. 462-471.

_____: "The Uses of Legislative Committees," *Canadian Public Administration,* vol. 6, 1963, pp. 1-14.

_____: "Vacation of Seats in the House of Commons: The Problem of Burnaby-Coquitlam," *C.J.E.P.S.,* vol. 30, 1964, pp. 125-130.

_____: "Parliamentary Scrutiny of Delegated Legislation in Canada: A Large Step Forward and a Small Step Back," *Public Law,* 1972, pp. 30-42.

_____: "Parliament: Every Reform Creates a New Problem," *Journal of Canadian Studies,* vol. 14, 1979, pp. 26-34.

_____ and B. A. Smith: "The Legislative Role of Parliamentary Committees in Canada: The Case of the Joint Committee on the Public Service Bills," *Canadian Public Administration,* vol. 15, 1972, pp. 1-23.

Matheson, W. A.: *Prime Minister and the Cabinet,* (Methuen, Toronto, 1976).

McDonald, D. C.: "The Alberta Ombudsman Act," *University of Toronto Law Journal,* vol. 19, 1969, pp. 257-263.

McInnes, S.: "Improving Legislative Surveillance of Provincial Public Expenditures: The Performance of the Public Accounts Committees and Auditors General," *Canadian Public Administration,* vol. 20, 1977, pp. 36-86.

McNaught, Kenneth: "Parliamentary Control of Foreign Policy?" *International Journal,* vol. 11, 1956, pp. 251-260.

Meisel, J.: "New Challenges to Parliament: Arguing over Wine Lists on the Titanic?" *Journal of Canadian Studies,* vol. 14, 1979, pp. 18-25.

Morin, J.-Y.: "Un nouveau rôle pour un Sénat moribond," *Cité libre,* vol. 15, 68, juin-juillet, 1964, pp. 3-7.

Neilson, W. A. W. and J. C. MacPherson (eds.): *The Legislative Process in Canada: The Need for Reform* (Institute for Research on Public Policy, Montreal, 1978).

Ogmundson, R.: "A Social Profile of Members of the Manitoba Legislature 1950, 1960, 1970," *Journal of Canadian Studies*, vol. 12, 1977, pp. 79-84.

Organ, E.: *Le Conseil legislatif de Québec* (Bellarmin, Montreal, 1967).

Page, D.: "Streamlining the Procedures of the Canadian House of Commons, 1963-1966," *C.J.E.P.S.*, vol. 33, 1967, pp. 27-49.

Pasis, Harvey, E.: "The Inequality of Distribution in the Canadian Provincial Assemblies" (Note), *Canadian Journal of Political Science*, 1972, pp. 433-436.

Pelletier, R.: "Le Député Un Législateur Defaillant?" *Journal of Canadian Studies*, vol. 14, 1979, pp. 48-56.

Poel, Dale H.: "The Diffusion of Legislation among the Canadian Provinces: A Statistical Analysis," *Canadian Journal of Political Science*, vol. 9, 1976, pp. 603-626.

Porter, John: *The Vertical Vosaic: An Analysis of Social Class and Power in Canada* (University of Toronto Press, Toronto, 1965), pp. 386-416.

Pothier, D.: "Parties and Free Votes in the Canadian House of Commons," *Journal of Canadian Studies*, vol. 14, 1979, pp. 80-96 (nine articles on the operation of the legislature). See also K. W. Knight: "Administration Secrecy and Ministerial Responsibility," ibid., vol. 32, 1966, pp. 77-84 and D. C. Rowat: "A Reply," ibid., vol. 32, 1966, pp. 84-87.

Premont, J.: "Publicité de documents officiens," *Canadian Public Administration*, vol. 11, 1968, pp. 449-453.

Punnett, M.: *Prime Minister in Canadian Politics* (Macmillan, Toronto, 1977).

Regenstreif, S. P.: "Some Aspects of National Party Support in Canada," *C.J.E.P.S.*, vol. 29, 1963, pp. 59-74.

Reid, Alan D.: "The New Brunswick Ombudsman Act," *University of Toronto Law Journal*, vol. 18, 4, 1968, pp. 361-371.

Robertson, R. G.: "The Canadian Parliament and Cabinet in the Face of Modern Demands," *Canadian Public Administration*, vol. 11, 1968, pp. 272-279.

Rowat, Donald Cameron: "An Ombudsman Scheme for Canada," *C.J.E.P.S.*, vol. 28, 1962, pp. 543-556.

———: "Recent Developments in Ombudsmanship," *Canadian Public Administration*, vol. 10, 1967, pp. 35-46.

——— (ed.): *The Ombudsman: Citizen's Defender*, 2nd ed. (University of Toronto Press, Toronto, 1968).

Sancton, Andrew: "The Application of the 'Senatorial Floor' Rules to the Latest Redistribution of the House of Commons: The Peculiar Case of Nova Scotia," *Canadian Journal of Political Science*, vol. 6, 1977, pp. 56-64.

Sigelman, Lee and William G. Vanderbok: "Legislators, Bureaucrats and Canadian Democracy: The Long and the Short of It" (Note), *Canadian Journal of Political Science*, vol. 10, 1977, pp. 615-623.

Smith, D.: *The Speakership of the Canadian House of Commons: Some Proposals* (paper prepared for the House of Commons' Special Committee on Procedure and Organization) (Queen's Printer, Ottawa, 1965).

Soldatos, P.: "La problématique de l'incompatabilité des fonctions ministérielles et du mandat de député en système politique étatique de type parlementaire," *Canadian Journal of Political Science*, vol. 5, 1972, pp. 251-269.

Stewart, John: *The Canadian House of Commons, Procedure and Reform* (McGill-Queen's University Press, Montreal, 1977). (The first chapter is a monumental analysis of the parliamentary aspects of the Canadian constitutional system.)

_____: "Strengthening the Commons," *Journal of Canadian Studies*, vol. 14, 1979, pp. 35-47.

Thomas, P. G.: "Theories of Parliament and Parliamentary Reform," *Journal of Canadian Studies*, vol. 14, 1979, pp. 57-66.

Thornburn, H. G.: :"Parliament and Policy-Making: The Case of the Trans-Canada Gas Pipeline," *C.J.E.P.S.*, vol. 23, 1957, pp. 516-531.

Turner, J. N.: "The Senate of Canada—Political Conundrum," in R. M. Clark (ed.): *Canadian Issues: Essays in Honour of Henry F. Angus* (University of Toronto Press, Toronto, 1961).

_____: *Politics of Purpose* (McClelland and Stewart, Toronto, 1968), ch. 2.

Walker, H. W.: "Parliamentary Procedure," *Queen's Quarterly*, vol. 58, 1951-52, pp. 228-236.

_____: "Question Time in Parliament," *Queen's Quarterly*, vol. 59, 1952-53, pp. 64-71.

Wallace, D. M.: "Budget Reform in Saskatchewan: A New Approach to Program-Based Management," *Canadian Public Administration*, vol. 17, 1974, pp. 586-599.

Ward, Norman: *The Canadian House of Commons: Representation* (University of Toronto Press, Toronto, 1950).

_____: "Called to the Bar of the House of Commons," *Canadian Bar Review*, vol. 35, 1957, pp. 529-546.

_____: "Parliamentary Bilingualism in Canada," *Parliamentary Affairs*, vol. 10, 2, Spring, 1957, pp. 155-164.

_____: *The Public Purse: a Study in Canadian Democracy*, Canadian Government Series, 11 (University of Toronto Press, Toronto, 1962).

_____: "The Committee on Estimates," *Canadian Public Administration*, vol. 6, 1963, pp. 35-42.

_____: "Responsible Government: An Introduction," *Journal of Canadian Studies*, vol. 14, 1979, pp. 3-7.

White, G.: "Teaching the Mongrel Dog New Tricks: Sources and Directions of Reform in the Ontario Legislature," *Journal of Canadian Studies*, vol. 14, 1979, pp. 117-132.

White, Walter L. and Lawrence Leduc: "The Role of Opposition in a One-Party Dominant System: The Case of Ontario," *Canadian Journal of Political Science*, vol. 7, 1974, pp. 86-100.

Winn, Conrad and James Twiss: "The Spatial Analysis of Political Cleavages and the Case of the Ontario Legislature," *Canadian Journal of Political Science*, vol. 10, 1977, pp. 287-310.

SELECTED ISSUE AREAS

A. Foreign Policy

Alper, Donald K. and Robert L. Monahan: "Bill C-58 and the American Congress: The Politics of Retaliation," *Canadian Public Policy*, vol. 4, 1978, pp. 184-192.

Barry, D.: "The United States and the Development of the Canada-European Community Contractual-Link Agreement," *American Review of Canada Studies*, vol. 10, 1, 1980, pp. 63-74.

Berry, Glyn R.: "The West Indies in Canadian External Relations: Present Trends and Future Prospects," *Canadian Public Policy*, vol. 3, 1977, pp. 50-62.

Cohn, Theodore: "Food Surpluses and Canadian Food Aid," *Canadian Public Policy*, vol. 3, 1977, pp. 141-154.

————: "Canadian Aid and Trade in Skim Milk Powder: Some Recent Issues," *Canadian Public Policy*, vol. 4, 1978, pp. 213-226.

Colthart, J. and S. Clark: "British and Canadian Responses to American Expansionism," *American Review of Canadian Studies*, vol. 2, 2, 1978, pp. 48-60.

English, E. H.: "The Role of Canada-U.S. Relations in the Pursuit of Canada's National Objectives," *American Review of Canadian Studies*, vol. 6, 1, 1976, pp. 32-55.

Finkle, P. Z. R.: "Canadian Foreign Policy for Marine Fisheries: An Alternative Perspective," *Journal of Canadian Studies*, vol. 10, 1, 1975, pp. 10-23.

Grubel, Herbert G.: "Canada's Stake in the New International Economic Order," *Canadian Public Policy*, vol. 3, 1977, pp. 324-337.

Helleiner, G. K.: "Canada and the New International Economic Order," *Canadian Public Policy*, vol. 2, 1976, pp. 451-465.

Henry, J.: "La Politique canadienne d'aide à la région soudano-sahélienne," *Canadian Public Policy*, vol. 2, 1976, pp. 455-481.

Johnson, B.: "Governing Canada's Economic Zone," *Canadian Public Administration*, vol. 20, 1, 1977, pp. 152-173.

———— and M. W. Zacher (eds.): *Canadian Foreign Policy and the Law of the Sea* (University of British Columbia, Vancouver, 1977).

Langdon, F. C.: "Canada's Struggle for Entrée to Japan," *Canadian Public Policy*, vol. 2, 1976, pp. 54-64.

Lyon, P. V.: *Canada and the Third World* (Macmillan, Toronto, 1976).

———— and B. W. Tomlin: *Canada as an International Actor* (Macmillan, Toronto, 1979).

Page, D.: "Unlocking Canada's Diplomatic Record," *International Journal*, vol. 33, 1978, pp. 251-280.

Rasmussen, E. K.: "The 1978 Great Lakes Water Quality Agreement and Prospects for U.S.-Canada Pollution Control," *Boston College International and Comparative Law Review*, vol. 2, 1979, pp. 499-520.

Redekop, John H.: "A Reinterpretation of Canadian-American Relations," *Canadian Journal of Political Science*, vol. 9, 1976, pp. 227-243.

Sarbadhikari, P. and C. A. Jecchinis: "The Nature of Canadian International Development Aid," *International Studies*, vol. 17, 1978, pp. 347-359.

Stevenson, G.: *Foremost Nation; Canadian Foreign Policy and a Changing World* (McClelland and Stewart, Toronto, 1977).

Swanson, R. F.: "Canadian Diplomatic Representation in the United States," *Canadian Public Administration*, vol. 18, 1975, pp. 366-398.

————: "Canadian Consular Representation in the United States," *Canadian Public Administration*, vol. 20, 1977, pp. 342-369.

————: "The Ford Interlude and the U.S.-Canadian Relationship," *American Review of Canadian Studies*, vol. 7, 1978, pp. 3-17.

Tomlin, B. W.: *Canada's Foreign Policy: Analysis and Trends* (Methuen, Toronto, 1978).

Tynan, F. M.: "Canadian-American Relations in the Arctic: The Effect of Environmental Influences Upon Territorial Claims," *Review of Politics*, vol. 41, 1979, pp. 402-427.

Wonnacott, R. J.: "Canada's Future in a World of Trade Blocs: A Proposal," *Canadian Public Policy*, vol. 1, 1975, pp. 118-130.

B. Economic and Social Policy Issues

Alexander, D.: "The Political Economy of Fishing in Newfoundland," *Journal of Canadian Studies*, vol. 11, 1, 1976, pp. 32-40.

Andrews, M. N.: "Attitudes in Canadian Women's History, 1945-1975," *Journal of Canadian Studies*, vol. 12, 4, 1977, pp. 69-78.

Armstrong, Hugh and Pat Armstrong: "The Segregated Participation of Women in the Canadian Labour Force, 1941-71," *Canadian Review of Sociology and Anthropology*, vol. 12, 1975, pp. 370-384.

Avery, D. and P. Neary: "Laurier, Borden and a White British Columbia," *Journal of Canadian Studies*, vol. 12, 4, 1977, pp. 24-34.

Axline, A. et al.: *Continental Community? Independence and Integration in North America* (McClelland and Stewart, Toronto, 1974).

Bairstow, F.: "Final Position Arbitration," *Canadian Public Administration*, vol. 18, 1, 1975, pp. 55-64.

Bercuson, D. J.: "Western Labour Radicalism and the One Big Union: Myths and Reality," *Journal of Canadian Studies*, vol. 9, 2, 1974, pp. 3-11.

Berkowitz, S. D. and Robert K. Logan (eds.): *Canada's Third Option* (Macmillan, Toronto, 1978).

Bernier, Bernard: "The Penetration of Capitalism in Quebec," *Canadian Review of Sociology and Anthropology*, vol. 13, 1976, pp. 422-434.

Bocking, R.C.: *Canada's Water for Sale?* (James Lewis and Samuels,Toronto,1972).

Bourque, G.: "Class Nation and the Parti Québécois," *Studies in Political Economy: A Socialist Review*, Autumn, 1979, 2, pp. 129-158.

Brown, M. C.: "Economic Dimensions of the Unemployment Problem," *Journal of Canadian Studies*, vol. 9, 1974, pp. 55-61.

Chorney, H. et al.: "The State and Political Economy," *Canadian Journal of Political and Social Theory*, vol. 1, 1977, pp. 71-86.

Clark, S. D.: "The Canadian Manufacturing Association and the Tariffs," *Canadian Journal of Economics and Political Science*, vol. 5, 1939, pp. 11-39.

Clayton, F. A.: "Real Property Tax Assessment Practices in Canada," *Canadian Public Policy*, vol. 2, 1976, pp. 347-362.

Clement, Wallace: *Continental Corporate Power; Economic Linkages Between Canada and the United States* (McClelland and Stewart, Toronto, 1977).

Coleman, N.: "The Class Bases of Language Policy in Quebec 1949-1975," *Studies in Political Economy: A Socialist Review*, Spring, 1980, vol. 13, pp. 93-118.

Conway, J. F.: "The Prairie Populist Resistance to the National Policy," *Journal of Canadian Studies*, vol. 14, 3, 1979, pp. 77-91.

Craven, P.: *An Impartial Umpire: Industrial Relations and the Canadian State* (University of Toronto Press, Toronto, 1980).

_____ and T. Traves: "The Class Politics of the National Policy, 1872-1933," *Journal of Canadian Studies*, vol. 14, 3, 1979, pp. 14-38.

Cuneo, C. J.: "Class Exploitation in Canada," *Canadian Review of Sociology and Anthropology*, vol. 15, 1978, pp. 284-300.

_____: "Class Contradictions in Canada's International Setting," *Canadian Review of Sociology and Anthropology*, vol. 16, 1979, pp. 1-20.

_____: "State Class, and Reserve Labour: The Case of the 1941 Canadian Unemployment Insurance Act," *Canadian Review of Sociology and Anthropology*, vol. 16, 1979, pp. 147-170.

_____: "State Mediation of Class Contradictions in Canadian Unemployment Insurance," *Studies in Political Economy: A Socialist Review*, Spring, 3, 1980, pp. 37-66.

824 BIBLIOGRAPHY

Dales, J. H.: "National Policy: Myths, Past and Present," *Journal of Canadian Studies*, vol. 14, 3, 1979, pp. 92-94.

Dauphin, R.: "Une Nouvelle Politique Economique Canadienne," *Journal of Canadian Studies*, vol. 14, 3, 1979, pp. 118-125.

Doern, G. Bruce: "The Political Economy of Regulating Occupational Health: The Ham and Beaudry Reports," *Canadian Public Administration*, vol. 20, 1, 1977, pp. 1-35.

——: *Government Intervention in the Canadian Industry Nuclear* (Institute for Research on Public Policy, Montreal, 1980).

Dosman, E. J.: *The National Interest: The Politics of Northern Development 1968-1975* (McClelland and Stewart, Toronto, 1975).

Eagle, J. A.: "Sir Robert Borden, Union Government and Railway Nationalization," *Journal of Canadian Studies*, vol. 14, 3, 1979, pp. 39-49.

Forcese, Dennis: *The Canadian Class Structure*, 2nd ed. (McGraw-Hill Ryerson, Toronto, 1979).

Foster, B.: "The Coming of the National Policy: Business Government and the Tariff, 1876-1975," *Journal of Canadian Studies*, vol. 14, 3, 1979, pp. 39-49.

Fournier, P.: *The Quebec Establishment: The Ruling Class, and the State* (Black Rose Books, Montreal, 1976).

——: "The New Parameters of the Quebec Bourgeoisie," *Studies in the Political Economy: A Socialist Review*, Spring, 3, 1980, pp. 67-92.

Fowke, V.: *The National Policy and the Wheat Economy* (University of Toronto Press, Toronto, 1957).

French, D. C.: *Faith, Sweat and Politics: The Early Trade Union Years in Canada* (McClelland and Stewart, Toronto, 1962).

Gillis, R. P.: "The Ottawa Lumber Barons and the Conservation Movement, 1880-1914," *Journal of Canadian Studies*, vol. 9, 1, 1974, pp. 14-30.

Gilmour, J.: "Industrialization and Technological Backwardness: The Canadian Dilemma," *Canadian Public Policy*, vol. 4, 1978, pp. 20-33.

Glenday, D. et al.: *Modernization and the Canadian State* (Macmillan, Toronto, 1978).

Gonick, Cy.: *Inflation or Depression* (Lorimer, Toronto, 1975).

Grayson, J. P. and L. M. Grayson: "Class and Ideologies of Class in the English-Canadian Novel," *Canadian Review of Sociology and Anthropology*, vol. 15, 3, 1979, pp. 265-283.

Guindon, H.: "Socialist Unrest, Social Class and Quebec's Bureaucratic Revolution," *Queen's Quarterly*, vol. 71, 1964, pp. 150-163.

Hedley, Max J.: "Independent Commodity Production and the Dynamics of Tradition," *Canadian Review of Sociology and Anthropology*, vol. 13, 1976, pp. 413-421.

Horowitz, G.: *Canadian Labour in Politics* (University of Toronto Press, Toronto, 1968).

Hunter, N. T.: "The Decline of the Tariff—But Not of Protection," *Journal of Canadian Studies*, vol. 14, 3, 1979, pp. 111-117.

Hutcheson, J.: *Dominance and Dependency* (McClelland and Stewart, Toronto, 1978).

Irwin, N. A.: "Canadian Transportation Infrastructure," *Canadian Public Administration*, vol. 18, 4, 1975, pp. 601-629.

Jenkin, M.: "The Prospects for a New National Policy," *Journal of Canadian Studies*, vol. 14, 3, 1979, pp. 126-141.

Jump, G. V. and T. A. Wilson: "Macro-economic Effects of the Energy Crisis, 1974-75," *Canadian Public Policy*, vol. 1, 1975, pp. 30-38.

Kniewasser, A. G.: "The Effect of A.H.ST.F. on Capital Markets," *Canadian Public Policy*, February, 1980, pp. 245-253.

Kresl, P. K.: "The 'New Nationalism' and Economic Rationality," *American Review of Canadian Studies*, vol. 4, 1, 1974, pp. 2-19.

_____: "Before the Deluge: Canadian and Foreign Ownership, 1920-1955," *American Review of Canadian Studies*, vol. 6, 1, 1976, pp. 88-125.

Langdon, G.: "The Emergence of the Canadian Working Class," *Journal of Canadian Studies*, May-August, 1973, pp. 22-35.

Laxer, J.: *Canada's Energy Crisis* (Lorimer, Toronto 1975).

_____: *Big, Tough, Expensive Job; Imperial Oil and the Canadian Economy* (Porcepic, Toronto, 1976).

Laxer, R. M.: *Canada's Unions* (Lorimer, Toronto, 1976).

_____: *Technological Change and the Workforce* (Ontario Institute for Studies in Education, Toronto, 1978).

_____: *Unions and the Collective Bargaining Process* (Ontario Institute for Studies in Education, Toronto, 1978).

_____: *Union Organization and Strikes* (Ontario Institute for Studies in Education, Toronto, 1978).

_____ (ed.): *The Political Economy of Dependency* (McClelland and Stewart, Toronto, 1973).

Legare, A.: "Les Classes Sociaux et le Gouvernement PQ à Québec," *Canadian Review of Sociology and Anthropology*, vol. 15, 2, 1978, pp. 218-226.

LeMay, J. A.: "Quebec and Economic Interdependence with The United States: A Focus on Hydro Quebec," *American Review of Canadian Studies*, vol. 10, 1, 1980, pp. 94-109.

Lesser, B.: "Comments on 'Regulatory Failure and Competition by G. B. Reschenthaler,' " *Canadian Public Administration*, vol. 20, 2, 1977, pp. 389-392.

Levy, T. A.: "The International Economic Interests and Activities of the Atlantic Provinces," *American Review of Canadian Studies*, vol. 5, 1975, pp. 98-113.

Lindsey, J. K.: "The Conceptualization of Social Class", *Studies in Political Economy: A Socialist Review*, Spring, 3, 1980, pp. 17-36.

Lipsig-Mummé, C.: "Quebec Unions and the State: Conflict and Dependence," *Studies in Political Economy: A Socialist Review*, Spring, 3, 1980, pp. 119-146.

Lipton, C.: *The Trade Union Movement of Canada, 1827-1959* (Canadian Social Publications, Montreal, 1967).

Macdonald, H. I.: "Economic Policy: Can We Manage the Economy Any More?" *Canadian Public Policy*, vol. 2, 1976, pp. 553-563.

MacDonald, L. R.: "Merchants against Industry: An Idea and Its Origins," *Canadian Historical Review*, vol. 53, 1975, pp. 25-39.

Macdonald, W. A.: "Government Growth and the Limits of Intervention," *Canadian Public Policy*, vol. 2, 1976, pp. 577-586.

Mahon, R.: "Regulatory Agencies: Captive Agents or Hegemonic Apparatus," *Studies in Political Economy: A Socialist Review*, Spring, 1, 1979, pp. 162-200.

Marchak, P.: "Labour in a Staples Economy," *Studies in Political Economy: A Socialist Review*, Autumn, 2, 1979, pp. 7-36.

May, J. D.: "Investment Incentives as Part of an Industrial Strategy," *Canadian Public Policy*, Winter, 1979, pp. 70-79.

McMillan, C. J.: "The Changing Competitive Environment of Canadian Business," *Journal of Canadian Studies*, vol. 13, 1, 1978, pp. 38-48.

Mealing, S. R.: "The Concept of Social Class in the Interpretation of Canadian History," *Canadian Historical Review,* vol. 46, 3, 1965, pp. 30-49.

Mills, A.: "The Canadian Left and Marxism," *Canadian Journal of Political and Social Theory,* vol. 2, 2, 1978, pp. 104-108.

Miller, F. C.: "The Macro-economic Effects of Federal Wage and Price Controls," *Canadian Public Policy,* vol. 2, 1976, pp. 607-615.

Miller, J. R.: "The Jesuit Estates Act Crisis: An Incident in a Conspiracy of Several Years Standing," *Journal of Canadian Studies,* vol. 9, 3, 1974, pp. 36-50.

Norrie, K. H.: "The National Policy and the Rate of Prairie Settlement: A Review," *Journal of Canadian Studies,* vol. 14, 3, 1979, pp. 63-76.

Offe, C.: "The Separation of Form and Content in Liberal Democratic Politics," *Studies in Political Economy: A Socialist Review,* Spring, 3, 1980, pp. 5-16.

Panitch, L.: "Corporatism in Canada," *Studies in Political Economy: A Socialist Review,* Spring, 1, 1979, pp. 43-92.

―――― (ed.): *The Canadian State: Political Economy and Political Power* (University of Toronto Press, Toronto, 1977).

Parker, I.: "Harold Innis, Karl Marx and Canadian Political Economy," *Queen's Quarterly,* vol. 84, 4, 1977, pp. 60-90.

―――――: "The National Policy, Neoclassical Economics and the Political Economy of Tariffs," *Journal of Canadian Studies,* vol. 14, 3, 1979, pp. 95-110.

Patterson, G.: "An Enduring Canadian Myth: Responsible Government and the Family Compact," *Journal of Canadian Studies,* vol. 12, 3, 1977, pp. 3-16.

Pennanen, G.: "Goldwin Smith, Wharton Barker, and Erastus Miman: Architects of Commercial Union," *Journal of Canadian Studies,* vol. 14, 3, 1979, pp. 50-62.

Pentland, H. C.: "The Western Canadian Labour Movement, 1897-1919," *Canadian Journal of Political and Social Theory,* vol. 3, 2, 1979, pp. 53-78.

Phillips, P.: "The Hinterland Perspective: The Political Economy of Vernon C. Fowke," *Canadian Journal of Political and Social Theory,* vol. 2, 2, 1974, pp. 35-46.

―――――: "Land Tenure and Economic Development: A Comparison of Upper and Lower Canada," *Journal of Canadian Studies,* vol. 9, 2, 1974, pp. 35-46.

―――――: "The National Policy Revisited," *Journal of Canadian Studies,* vol. 14,, 3, 1979, pp. 3-13.

Pratt, L.: *Tar Sands: Syncrude and the Politics of Oil* (Hurtig, Edmonton, 1976).

―――― and J. Richards: *Prairie Capitalism* (McClelland and Stewart, Toronto, 1979).

Purvis, Douglas D.: "The Exchange Rate Regime and Economic Policy in Theory and Practice," *Canadian Public Policy,* vol. 3, 1977, pp. 205-218.

Raabe, C.: "Business Images of the P.Q.: Investment and the Political Economy," *American Review of Canadian Studies,* vol. 9, 2, 1979, pp. 130-147.

Rea, K. J. and J. T. McLeod (eds.): *Business and Government in Canada* (Methuen, Toronto, 1976).

Reschenthaler, G. B.: "Regulatory Failure and Competition," *Canadian Public Administration,* vol. 19, 3, 1976, pp. 466-486.

―――――: "Regulatory Failure and Competition: A Reply," *Canadian Public Administration,* vol. 20, 2, 1977, pp. 93-394.

Rich, H.: "The Vertical Mosaic Revisited: Towards a Macro-sociology of Canada," *Journal of Canadian Studies*, vol. 11, 1, 1976, pp. 14-31.

Ridler, N. B.: "Some Economic Implications of the Projected Age Structure of Canada," *Canadian Public Administration*, Autumn, 1979, pp. 533-541.

Rosenbluth, G.: "Economists and the Growth Controversy," *Canadian Public Policy*, vol. 21, 1976, pp. 225-239.

Rothenberg, S.: "The Impact of Affluence: Restrictions of Foreign Investment in Canada," *American Review of Canadian Studies*, vol. 9, 2, 1979, pp. 72-83.

Roussopoulos, D.: "Beyond Reformism: The Ambiguity of the Urban Question," *Our Generation*, vol. 11, 2, pp. 46-58.

Ruggeri, G. C.: "On the Regressivity of Provincial Sales Taxation in Canada," *Canadian Public Policy*, vol. 4, 1978, pp. 364-372.

Ruppenthal, K. M.: "Transport in Canada: Needs, Trends and Problems," *Canadian Public Administration*, vol. 18, 4, 1975, pp. 587-600.

Ryerson, S.: "Who's Looking after Business," *This Magazine*, vol. 10, 5-6, 1976, pp. 41-46.

Schecter, S.: "Urban Politics in Capitalist Society," *Our Generation*, vol. 1, 1, pp. 28-40.

Skogstad, G.: "Agrarian Protest in Alberta," *Canadian Review of Sociology and Anthropology*, vol. 17, 1, 1980, pp. 55-73.

Strong-Boag, V.: "Canadian Feminism in the 1920s: The Case of Nellie L. McClung," *Journal of Canadian Studies*, vol. 12, 4, 1977, pp. 58-68.

Thibeault, A. and L. Wyant: "Investor Reaction to the Political Environment in Quebec," *Canadian Public Policy*, Spring, 1979, pp. 236-247.

Thirsk, Wayne R. and Robert A. Wright: "The Impact of the Crude Oil Subsidy on Economic Efficiency in Canada," *Canadian Public Policy*, vol. 3, 1977, pp. 355-364.

Trofimenkoff, S. M.: "Henri Bourassa and the Women Question," *Journal of Canadian Studies*, vol. 10, 4, 1975, pp. 3-11.

Wallace, Clement and David Drache: *A Practical Guide to Canadian Political Economy* (Lorimer, Toronto, 1978).

Watkins, G. C. and M. Walker: *Oil in the Seventies: Essays on Energy Policy* (Fraser Institute, Vancouver, 1977).

Whitaker, R.: "Scientific Management Theory as Political Ideology," *Studies in Political Economy: A Socialist Review*, Autumn, 2, 1979, pp. 75-108.

Williams, Glen: "Canada: The Case of the Wealthiest Colony," *This Magazine*, vol. 10, 1, Feb.-Mar., 1976, pp. 28-32.

Wilson, John: "Politics and Social Class in Canada: The Case of Waterloo South," *Canadian Journal of Political Science*, vol. 1, 1968, pp. 288-309.

Zerker, S.: "George Brown and the Printer's Union," *Journal of Canadian Studies*, vol. 10, 1, 1975, pp. 42-48.

INDEX